TRADEMARKS AND UNFAIR COMPETITION

TRADEMARKS AND UNFAIR COMPETITION

SEVENTH EDITION

David C. Hilliard

Joseph Nye Welch, II

Uli Widmaier

Members of the Chicago Bar
Adjunct Professors, Northwestern University School of Law
Lecturers, University of Chicago Law School

ISBN: 9781-4224-2220-5
ISSN: 1941–6598

NOTE TO USERS

To ensure that you are using the latest materials available in this area, please be sure to periodically check the LexisNexis Law School web site for downloadable updates and supplements at www.lexisnexis.com/lawschool.

Editorial Offices
744 Broad Street, Newark, NJ 07102 (973) 820-2000
201 Mission St., San Francisco, CA 94105-1831 (415) 908-3200
www.lexisnexis.com

MATTHEW⬥BENDER

(2008–Pub.725)

PREFACE

The Internet has sparked phenomenal growth in the importance and scope of trademark law. At the same time, constitutional issues – pertaining to the Commerce Clause, the Patent and Copyright Clause, the Supremacy Clause, and the First Amendment – are reshaping modern trademark law, have been outcome-determinative in many high-profile cases, and are fueling influential debates in the academic literature. There continues to be an overall sense of excitement as the law responds to new technologies and increasingly sophisticated forms of communication. Law schools now routinely provide a broad and sophisticated curriculum for the study of all aspects of intellectual property law. Law firms and corporate legal departments across the United States and abroad aggressively expand their intellectual property resources. This growth has resulted in intense intellectual ferment within academia, the courts and the practicing bar. Like patent and copyright law, trademark and unfair competition law are in a state of rapid evolution. Many hitherto unquestioned principles are now being rethought, foundational changes in the policy rationales and the doctrinal and constitutional dimensions of this ancient body of law are being considered and implemented, false leads are being weeded out (or, sometimes, newly introduced). E-commerce and technological developments have raised new questions about the relationship of trademark law to other bodies of intellectual property law. The U.S. Supreme Court's selection of cases to be heard reflects these trends, and the recent decisions of that court are featured in this edition of the textbook.

We have sought in this textbook to provide for students an organized guide to the opinions, treatises, and commentary, a delineation of the principal questions and problems to be expected, and a synthesis of the current and developing law under each of the subdivisions of our Table of Contents. The explosion in e-commerce and Internet litigation affects every chapter. Throughout the casebook, we focus on examining trademark law's place in the constitutional scheme. we pay great attention to the relationship of trademark law with the other areas of intellectual property law.

This book was initially prepared to meet the needs of teaching a law school course. It has evolved to its present state with the benefit of enlightening criticism from law students at Northwestern University and the University of Chicago, as well as from the many practicing lawyers to whom it has been exposed. Acknowledgment is most appreciatively expressed to our colleagues, Sarah Wohlford, Jake Linford, and Michelle Ybarra, for their scholarly contributions to this edition. We also express our warmest thanks and appreciation to Tammy B. McCarron for her preeminent work in readying the manuscript for publication. Finally, we dedicate this volume to Beverly W. Pattishall (1916-2002), a great colleague, scholar and friend.

D.C.H.
J.N.W.
U.W.

Synopsis

CHAPTER 6   **INFRINGEMENT OF TRADEMARK RIGHTS 199**

CHAPTER 1
PRINCIPLES OF TRADEMARK AND UNFAIR COMPETITION LAW

CONTENTS

1.01   Historical Development

Trademark law is both more important and more in flux than ever. Its inherent resilience and flexibility continue to facilitate the development of e-commerce and commercial use of the internet. The fundamental principles of commercial identification remain viable today, even though their origins trace back into antiquity. Just as today the owners of brand names, domain names, and other trade identities seek protection against imitative uses by others, so did their conceptual ancestors. Yet the rapidly shifting factual scenarios that trademark law has been called upon to resolve in recent years have raised novel questions, throwing its relationship with other species of intellectual property law—copyright, patent, right of publicity, and trade secret law—into sharp relief. Courts and scholars are increasingly examining the place of trademark law in the constitutional scheme. Issues concerning the impact on trademark law of the Commerce Clause, the Patent and Copyright Clause, the Supremacy Clause, and the First Amendment are outcome-determinative in much of modern trademark law and have been fueling heated debates in the academic literature. Beneath the constitutional, doctrinal and factual debates and innovation, the recent battles in courts and academia often have an old-fashioned tinge, focusing on ancient issues about the justifications underlying trademark law. Is it more of a property right protecting predominantly the manufacturer, or is it more of a consumer protection right protecting the public from confusion and deception? Does it find its ultimate normative rationale in the explanation favored by Law and Economics scholars, lowering consumer search costs, or in the commonsense conception of fair play, protecting tradespersons with good reputations from cheaters, as the label "unfair competition law" suggests? Whether in constitutional or high-tech garb, these are ultimately the questions that drive trademark law today.

The makers' identifying marks have been found on prehistoric implements, weapons, pottery, and other articles of commerce. During the development period of our common law in England, those who sold goods, wares and produce that were the fruit of their own labor or craftsmanship likewise identified those products, or their places of business such as shops, inns, or pubs, with their own means for trade identity. Sometimes it was their name, sometimes something more fanciful, but there soon developed problems and controversies arising out of uses by others of the same or similar names and marks for the same or similar goods or services. Because of the basic need in such controversies for writs of prohibition or injunctions, they usually were brought to the Chancellor.

The London shoemaker of the seventeenth century could not suffer such damage from another's use of a mark as would call for intervention of the law unless and until the mark he employed to identify his own wares had come to signify their source through his own use. Likewise, that shoemaker needed little from the law beyond preventing continuation of a nearby competitor's use of the same or a similar mark likely to deceive the earlier user's customers and divert his trade. Accordingly, the law grew and unconsciously developed around the fundamental use that became its basic rationale. It evolved in sophistication, case by case, as was needed to cope with the increasing complexities of commerce and the artfulness of poachers, but it remained rooted in and normatively dependent upon the proposition that the results of prior use were all that needed or deserved the law's protection. U.S. trademark law has always stayed true to these normative foundations. In 1918, the Supreme Court explained that:

> "[t]here is no such thing as property in a trademark except as a right appurtenant to an established business or trade in connection with which the mark is employed. The law of trademarks is but a part of the broader law of unfair competition; the right to a particular mark grows out of its use, not its mere adoption; its function is simply to designate the goods as the product of a particular trader and to protect his good will against the sale of another's product as his; and it is not the subject of property except in connection with an existing business. *Hanover Milling Co. v. Metcalf*, 240 U.S. 403, 412-414, 36 Sup. Ct. 357. The owner of a trademark may not, like the proprietor of a patented invention, make a negative and merely prohibitive use of it as a monopoly. *See United States v. Bell Telephone Co.*, 167 U.S. 224, 250, 17 S. Sup. Ct. 809; *Bement v. National Harrow Co.*, 186 U.S. 70, 90, 22 S. Sup. Ct. 747; *Paper Bag Patent Case*, 210 U.S. 405, 424, 28 S. Sup. Ct. 748. In truth, a trademark confers no monopoly whatever in a proper sense, but is merely a convenient means for facilitating the protection of one's good-will in trade by placing a distinguishing mark or symbol—a commercial signature—upon the merchandise or the package in which it is sold." *United Drug Co. v. Theodore Rectanus Co.*, 248 U.S. 90, 97-98 (1918)

The issues of the controversies were, of course, ones of deceit, or the likelihood of deceit, arising out of a latecomer's use of a name or mark. Eventually, a small body of law developed for coping with these problems of name and mark confusion and likelihood of confusion in trade. In some areas of commercial activity, precedent was derived from the activities of the guilds and the law merchants, but all was directed pragmatically toward the needs of fair resolution of the problems that came before them, and they were problems essentially sounding in deceit. See generally F. I. SCHECTER, THE HISTORICAL FOUNDATIONS OF TRADEMARK LAW (1925); E. S.ROGERS, GOOD WILL, TRADEMARKS AND UNFAIR TRADING (1914); Rogers, *Some Historical Matter Concerning Trademarks*, 9 MICH. L. REV. 29 (1910); *L. E. Daniels, The History of the Trademark*, 7 TRADEMARK REP. 239 (1911); *Mark P. McKenna, The Normative Foundations of Trademark Law*, 82 NOTRE DAME L. REV. 1839 (2007). It came to pass, therefore, that the common law, and later the statutory law, on the subject of trademarks and other means for identifying the source of goods and services, was structured upon the proposition of prohibiting commercial confusion as to the source of goods or services.

The recorded development of this area of the law is surprisingly recent. What was believed to be the first written reference to a trademark case had been described as "an irrelevant reminiscent dictum," F. I. SCHECTER, *supra*, at 6, appearing in a non-trademark case decision entitled *Southern v. How*, Popham 143, 79 Eng. Reprint 1243, first reported in 1656. English courts ever since have relied upon *Southern v. How* for their ancient jurisdiction to prevent trademark piracy.* The basic proposition of protecting against confusing or deceitful use of names and marks is that the prior user is entitled to be protected because presumably some recognition has been achieved by the use that can be the subject of confusion or deception by a subsequent confusingly similar use. It is plain that governmental grants of limited monopoly to encourage invention or the literary arts have nothing to do with the subject.

In *Dastar Corp. v. Twentieth Century Fox Film Corp.*, 539 U.S. 23, 37 (2003), the U.S. Supreme Court re-emphasized this foundational line of demarcation between grant-based and use-based intellectual property, holding that Congress may not use unfair competition law to create a "species of perpetual patent and copyright."

"The United States took the [trademark and unfair competition] law of England as its own." *Moseley v. V Secret Catalog, Inc.*, 537 U.S. 418 (2003), quoting from PATTISHALL, HILLIARD, and WELCH II, *Trademarks and Unfair Competition.* Indeed, even as recently as fifty years ago, some British decisions often were cited to our courts as persuasive authority in trademark cases. It is intriguing that an early reference to trademark law in America is a notation in the court records of Fairfax County, Virginia disclosing that in 1772 George Washington, a resident of the county and then only a farmer and businessman, went to the court to record a trademark for his flour which he proposed to name simply "G. Washington."

Not until the 1825 decision in *Snowden v. Noah,* Hopk. Ch. 347 (N.Y. Ch.) does there appear a reported decision in anything really resembling a trademark case, and it was hardly a step forward in our law. It was an action by the recent purchaser of a New York newspaper called *The National Advocate.* He sought to enjoin the seller from publishing in New York a paper entitled *The New York National Advocate.* The court refused on the ground that the names were sufficiently distinct to prevent deception. The first trademark statute was that of the State of New York, passed in 1845. No federal trademark statute existed until the Act of 1870, but by then eleven additional state trademark statutes had been passed. At that time, there were only 62 reported American trademark cases. Although scanty in number, many of the earlier American trademark cases are intriguing, and they uniformly disclose the basic rationale of protection against deceit respecting a prior use.

The first American treatise writer on trademark law, Francis H. Upton, states in his 1860 work, *Treatise on the Law of Trademarks*, that the peculiar phrasing of our Patent Act of 1842 may have led to the erroneous practice by some "of availing of its provisions to secure what is supposed to be an equivalent to trademark property." Upton also states quite correctly that: "The right of property in trademarks does not partake in any degree of the nature and character of a patent or copyright, to which it has sometimes been referred– nor is it safe to reason from any supposed analogies existing between them." Note the Supreme Court's continued commitment to this principle, as explained in in *Dastar Corp. v. Twentieth Century Fox Film Corp.*, 539 U.S. 23 (2003), excerpted in Chapter 9.

Originally, intent to defraud was conceived to be a legal necessity for any trademark cause of action, but it was soon recognized that the absence of intent to trade upon another's good will was neither cure nor comfort for the aggrieved party. Thus, the

---

* A trademark case, first reported in 1584, many years before *Southern v. How,* has since surfaced: *Sandforth's Case,* Cory's Entries, BL MS. Hargrave 123, fo. 168 (nearly complete portion of complaint); HLS MS. 2071, fo. 86 (abstract of case); HLS MS. 5048 fo. 118 v (abstract of case), reprinted in Baker and Milsom, *Sources of English History— Private Law to 1750,* 615–18 (1986). In that case the plaintiff clothmaker was held to have a cause of action against defendant's "deceitful mark[ing]" of its cloths with plaintiff's mark, *J.G.* and design. For a discussion of *Sandforth's* case and its rediscovery, as well as *Southern v. How,* see Stolte, *How Did Anglo-American Trademark Law Begin? An Answer to Schecter's Conundrum,* 8 FORDHAM INTELL. PROP./ MEDIA & ENT. L.J. 505 (1999) (discussing *Sandforth's Case* and its rediscovery, as well as *Southern v. How*).

prerequisite of proof of intent to defraud in trademark cases was gradually relaxed and eventually disappeared, and the simple test of likelihood of confusion or deception as to the source of goods or services of a prior user became the criterion for relief.

1.02   The Nature of Trademark and Unfair Competition Law

Unfair competition is the genus of which trademark infringement is one of the species. Under this view, all trademark cases are in fact cases of unfair competition. In 1916, the Supreme Court explained this principle in detail:

> The redress that is accorded in trademark cases is based upon the party's right to be protected in the good will of a trade or business. The primary and proper function of a trademark is to identify the origin or ownership of the article to which it is affixed. Where a party has been in the habit of labeling his goods with a distinctive mark, so that purchasers recognize goods thus marked as being of his production, others are debarred from applying the same mark to goods of the same description, because to do so would in effect represent their goods to be of his production and would tend to deprive him of the profit he might make through the sale of the goods that the purchaser intended to buy. Courts afford redress or relief upon the ground that a party has a valuable interest in the good will of his trade or business, and in the trademarks adopted to maintain and extend it. The essence of the wrong consists in the sale of the goods of one manufacturer or vendor for those of another. . . . This essential element is the same in trademark cases as in cases of unfair competition unaccompanied with trademark infringement. In fact, the common law of trademarks is but a part of the broader law of unfair competition.. . . .

Hanover Star Milling Co. v. Metcalf, 240 U.S. 403, 412–13 (1916) (emphasis added, citations and quotation marks omitted). *See also Elgin Nat'l Watch Co. v. Illinois Watch Case*, 179 U.S. 665, 674 (1901) ("[T]he manufacturer of particular goods in entitled to the reputation they have [sic] acquired, and the public is entitled to the means of distinguishing between those and other goods; and protection is accorded against unfair dealing, whether there be a technical trademark or not. The essence of the wrong consists in the sale of the goods of one manufacturer or vendor for those of another."). The principle of law has been reduced to a single sentence—no one has any right to represent his or her goods as the goods of another, and this is merely the duty to abstain from fraud. This is the foundation of the concept of trademark protection. Whether any particular contrivance is calculated to result in the sale of one person's goods as those of another is a question of fact in each case. If it can be shown as a fact that a trader's goods are known on the market and distinguished from others by any name, whether descriptive, geographical, or personal, or by any device, whatever its nature, or by color of label or style of dress, then this element, whatever it may be, represents goodwill that should be protected against use or imitation by another in any way likely to deceive the public as to the origin of the product or enable the sale of the defendant's article as and for complainant's. The extent of the restraint imposed on another's use of the particular element varies, depending on the facts in a particular case, from use coupled with such announcements as will effectually prevent mistake, to prohibition of all use in cases where no amount or attempted distinction will be effective.

The inaptness of the term "unfair competition law" has been described in 1 NIMS, THE LAW OF UNFAIR COMPETITION AND TRADEMARKS, 2–3* (4th ed. 1947):

> This action is the embodiment in law of the ancient rule of the playground — "Play fair!" For generations the law has enforced justice. In this action the basis is fairness — quite a different ethical principle. Many decisions have been approved as just that were in fact most unfair. The maxim *caveat emptor* is

---

* Copyright 1947 by Baker, Voorhis & Co., Inc. Reprinted with permission of West Group

founded on justice; the more modern rule that compels the use of truth in selling goods is founded on fairness. The rule of fairness conflicts with the rule of *caveat emptor.*

> It is unfortunate that the body of law termed unfair competition was christened with that title. It is a misnomer. It is misleading because . . . these rules also cover cases where there is no competition between the parties. To describe it with any accuracy is very difficult; for, though the common law of unfair competition may be a "limited concept," the acts to which these rules have been found to apply are ever changing in character as social and business conditions change. It applies to misappropriation as well as misrepresentation; to the selling of another's goods as one's own, to misappropriation of what equitably belongs to a competitor; to acts that lie outside the ordinary course of business and are tainted by fraud, coercion, or conduct otherwise prohibited by law. Most courts continue to confine it to acts that result in the passing off of the goods of one man for those of another, but this limitation is not universally accepted. The English term, "Passing Off," or its equivalent, "Palming Off," is hardly more satisfactory than our name "Unfair Competition."

There is a distinction, often unnoted but basic in the law of unfair competition. On the one hand, there is the group of unfair acts referred to generally as trademark and unfair competition law. On the other hand, there are a great many additional acts that are lumped together into the area of unfair competition law and classified as unfair competition but that do not generally relate to confusion as to the source of products or services.

Traditionally, trademark and unfair competition law prohibits any conduct that is likely to confuse or deceive consumers as to the source of goods or services. The tortious conduct may take the form of trademark infringement, copying of trade names, labels, commercial dress or the like. If the torts are in fact ones of confusion or deception as to source or sponsorship of goods or services, they are all to be approached with the same legal philosophy and reasoning. It should be noted, however, that even under a strong fairness conception — rather than, say, the Law and Economics conception that periodically has held sway at the Supreme Court (*see* Section 1.04,) — the requirement of confusion or deception does not imply that intent to confuse or deceive is a necessary element of a trademark claim. To that extent, trademark and unfair competition are strict liability claims.

Other types of tortious acts are also broadly referred to as unfair competition but ordinarily do not comprise deception as to source. False descriptions of goods, for example, really have nothing to do with deception as to source or sponsorship and are a different kind of tort than is unfair competition. The same is true of misrepresentation, trade disparagement, or false and deceptive advertising claims generally. Some degree of falsity in advertising claims is not uncommon, but when the claims are likely to materially deceive the public, legal remedies exist. Likewise, certain acts prohibited by the antitrust laws fall within the general category of unfair competition, as does the law of misappropriation. In fact, an almost limitless variety of competitive "dirty tricks" can be said to fall within unfair competition law.

At common law, such competitive dirty tricks usually were not actionable, because there was no injury for which there was a known remedy. As stated by Judge Learned Hand in *Ely-Norris Safe Co. v. Mosler Safe Co.,* 7 F.2d 603, 604 (2ᵈ Cir. 1925):

> The reason, as we think, why such deceits have not been regarded as actionable by a competitor, depends only upon his inability to show any injury for which there is a known remedy. In an open market it is generally impossible to prove that a customer, whom the defendant has secured by falsely describing his goods, would have bought off the plaintiff, if the defendant had been truthful. Without that, the plaintiff, though aggrieved in company with other honest traders, cannot show any ascertainable loss. He may not recover at law, and the

equitable remedy is concurrent. The law does not allow him to sue as a vicarious avenger of the defendant's customer.

Moreover, the common law principle of *caveat emptor* similarly discouraged or barred action by the consumer. As stated by Justice Holmes in *Deming v. Darling*, 20 N.E. 107 (Mass. 1889):

> [S]ome cases suggest that bad faith might make a seller liable for what are known as seller's statements, apart from any other conduct by which the buyer is fraudulently induced to forebear inquiries. *Pike v. Fay*, 101 Mass. 134. But this is a mistake. It is settled that the law does not exact good faith from a seller in those vague commendations of his wares which manifestly are open to difference of opinion, which do not imply untrue assertions concerning matters of direct observation, (*Teague v. Irwin*, 127 Mass. 217), and as to which it always has been "understood, the world over, that such statements are to be distrusted."

Gradually, there developed in the law a primarily statutory basis for business and consumer protection against such unfair trade practices. *Federal Trade Commission v. Tashman*, 318 F.3d 1273, 1277 (11th Cir. 2003) (now, "*caveat emptor* is simply not the law"). These statutory changes and more innovative private causes of action have afforded a more effective way of curbing trademark infringement and other kinds of unfair competition.

1.03 Protection of the Private Interest

As a part of the developing law of trademarks, and particularly with the advent of the registration statutes, there appeared the notion that the right in a trademark is an actual property right. In 1879, the United States Supreme Court stated that the right to adopt and use a symbol or a device to identify one's merchandise with oneself and distinguish it from that of others was a right long recognized by the common law. *Trade-Mark Cases*, 100 U.S. 82, 92 (1879). The notion that trademark rights are property rights remains strong. *See, e.g., U.S. v. Millstein*, 481 F.3d 132, 137 (2^{d} Cir. 2007) (in affirming restitution to the trademark owner for damage to its brand from defendant's counterfeits, the Second Circuit observed, "it is well settled that trademarks are a form of property"). In *College Savings Bank v. Florida Prepaid Postsecondary Education Expense Board et. al.*, 527 U.S. 666 (1999), Justice Scalia, referring to trademark rights, stated in *dicta* that "the hallmark of a protected property interest is the right to exclude others." The rise of the internet may have contributed to that belief. *See, e.g., Kremen v. Cohen*, 337 F.3d 1024 (9th Cir. 2003) (holding that domain names are property, not simply service contracts, i.e. that they are a form of intangible property capable of unlawful conversion). The "property" concept, nevertheless, has an inherent conflict with the historic deception as to source rationale for trademark and unfair competition law. *See* Widmaier, *Use, Liability, and the Structure of Trademark Law*, 33 HOFSTRA L. REV. 2 (2005) (decrying "the propertization of trademarks" and endorsing a return to traditional principles).

There has developed, however, along with mass marketing and worldwide e-commerce, an obvious and compelling commercial need to protect what Justice Frankfurter describes below as the "commercial magnetism" or "drawing power of a congenial symbol." That need has heightened the tension between the property conception and the use-based conception of trademark law, as exemplified by the two following cases.

MISHAWAKA RUBBER & WOOLEN MFG. CO. v. S. S. KRESGE CO.
United States Supreme Court
316 U.S. 203 (1942)

FRANKFURTER, JUSTICE

The petitioner, which manufactures and sells shoes and rubber heels, employs a trade-mark, registered under the Trade-Mark Act of 1905, 33 Stat. 724, 15 U.S.C. § 81 *et seq.*, consisting of a red circular plug embedded in the center of a heel. The heels were not sold separately, but were attached to shoes made by the petitioner. It has spent considerable sums of money in seeking to gain the favor of the consuming public by promoting the mark as assurance of a desirable product. The respondent sold heels not made by the petitioner but bearing a mark described by the District Court as "a circular plug of red or reddish color so closely resembling that of the plaintiff [petitioner] that it is difficult to distinguish the products sold by the defendant from the plaintiff's products." The heels sold by the respondent were inferior in quality to those made by the petitioner, and "this tended to destroy the good will created by the plaintiff in the manufacture of its superior product." Although there was no evidence that particular purchasers were actually deceived into believing that the heels sold by the respondent were manufactured by the petitioner, the District Court found that there was a "reasonable likelihood" that some purchases might have been induced by the purchaser's belief that he was obtaining the petitioner's product. "The ordinary purchaser, having become familiar with the plaintiff's trademark, would naturally be led to believe that the heels marketed by the defendant were the product of the plaintiff company."

*   *   *

The protection of trade-marks is the law's recognition of the psychological function of symbols. If it is true that we live by symbols, it is no less true that we purchase goods by them. A trade-mark is a merchandising short-cut which induces a purchaser to select what he wants, or what he has been led to believe he wants. The owner of a mark exploits this human propensity by making every effort to impregnate the atmosphere of the market with the drawing power of a congenial symbol. Whatever the means employed, the aim is the same—to convey through the mark, in the minds of potential customers, the desirability of the commodity upon which it appears. Once this is attained, the trademark owner has something of value. If another poaches upon the commercial magnetism of the symbol he has created, the owner can obtain legal redress.

*   *   *

Reversed.

COLLEGE SAVINGS BANK v. FLORIDA PREPAID POSTSECONDARY EDUCATION EXPENSE BOARD, et. al.
United States Supreme Court
527 U.S. 666 (1999)

SCALIA, JUSTICE

*   *   *

College Savings filed the instant action alleging that Florida Prepaid violated § 43(a) of the Lanham Act by making misstatements about its own tuition savings plans in its brochures and annual reports. Florida Prepaid [a state institution] moved to dismiss this action on the ground that it was barred by [state] sovereign immunity. It argued that Congress had not abrogated sovereign immunity in this case because the TRCA [Trademark Remedy Clarification Act of 1992] was enacted pursuant to Congress's powers under Article I of the Constitution and, under our decisions in *Seminole Tribe [v. Florida*, 517 U.S. 44 (1996)] and *Fitzpatrick [v. Bitzer*, 427 U.S. 445 (1976)] Congress can abrogate state sovereign immunity only when it legislates to enforce the Fourteenth Amendment. . . .

*   *   *

Section 1 of the Fourteenth Amendment provides that no State shall "deprive any person of . . . property . . . without due process of law." Section 5 provides that "[t]he Congress shall have power to enforce, by appropriate legislation, the provisions of this article." We made clear in *City of Boern v. Flores*, 521 U.S. 507, 117 S.Ct. 2157, 138 L.Ed.2d 624 (1997), that the term "enforce" is to be taken seriously that the object of valid § 5 legislation must be the carefully delimited remediation or prevention of constitutional violations. Petitioner claims that, with respect to § 43(a) of the Lanham Act, Congress enacted the TRCA to remedy and prevent state deprivations without due process of two species of "property" rights: (1) a right to be free from a business competitor's false advertising about its own product, and (2) a more generalized right to be secure in one's business interests. Neither of these qualifies as a property right protected by the Due Process Clause.

As to the first: The hallmark of a protected property interest is the right to exclude others. That is "one of the most essential sticks in the bundle of rights that are commonly characterizes as property." *Kaiser Aetna v. United States*, 444 U.S. 164, 176, 100 S.Ct. 383, 62 L.Ed.2d 332 (1979). That is why the right that we all possess to use the public lands is not the "property" right of anyone—hence the sardonic maxim, explaining what economists call the "tragedy of the commons," res publica, res nullius. The Lanham Act may well contain provisions that protect constitutionally cognizable property interests notably, its provisions dealing with infringement of trademarks, which are the "property" of the owner because he can exclude others from using them. *See, e.g., K Mart Corp. v. Cartier, Inc.*, 485 U.S. 176, 185-186, 108 S.C. 950, 99 L.Ed.2d 151 (1988) ("Trademark law, like contract law, confers private rights, which are themselves rights of exclusion. It grants the trademark owner a bundle of such rights"). The Lanham Act's false-advertising provisions, however, bear no relationship to any right to exclude; and Florida Prepaid's alleged misrepresentations concerning its own products intruded upon no interest over which petitioner had exclusive dominion.

*   *   *

Petitioner argues that the common-law tort of unfair competition "by definition" protects property interests, Brief for Petitioner 15, and thus the TRCA "by definition" is designed to remedy and prevent deprivations of such interest in the false-advertising context. Even as a logical matter, that does not follow, since not everything that protects property interests is designed to remedy or prevent deprivations of those property interests. A municipal ordinance prohibiting billboards in residential areas protects the property interests of homeowners, although erecting billboards would ordinarily not deprive them of property. To sweep within the Fourteenth Amendment the elusive property interests that are "by definition" protected by unfair- competition law would violate our frequent admonition that the Due Process Clause is not merely a "font of tort law." *Paul v. Davis*, 424 U.S. 693, 701, 96 S.Ct. 1155, 47 L.Ed.2d 405 (1976).

Petitioner's second assertion of a property interest rests upon an argument similar to the one just discussed, and suffers from the same flaw. Petitioner argues that businesses are "property" within the meaning of the Due Process Clause, and that Congress legislates under § 5 when it passes a law that prevents state interference with business (which false advertising does). Brief for Petitioner 19-20. The assets of a business (including its good will) unquestionably are property, and any state taking of those assets is unquestionably a "deprivation" under the Fourteenth Amendment. But business in the sense of the activity of doing business, or the activity of making a profit is not property in the ordinary sense and it is only that, and not any business asset, which is impinged upon by a competitors' false advertising.

* * *

Affirmed.

STEVENS, JUSTICE dissenting

* * *

The majority . . . assumes that petitioner's complaint has alleged a violation of the Lanham Act, but not one that is sufficiently serious to amount to a "deprivation" of its property. . . . I think neither of those assumptions is relevant to the principal issue raised in this case, namely, whether Congress had the constitutional power to authorize suits against States and state instrumentalities for such a violation. In my judgment the Constitution granted it ample power to do so. Section 5 of the Fourteenth Amendment authorizes Congress to enact appropriate legislation to prevent deprivations of property without due process. Unlike the majority, I am persuaded that the Trademark Remedy Clarification Act was a valid exercise of that power, even if Florida Prepaid's allegedly false advertising in this case did not violate the Constitution. My conclusion rests on two premises that the court rejects.

First, in my opinion "the activity of doing business, or the activity of making a profit," . . . is a form of property. The asset that often appears on a company's balance sheet as "good will" is the substantial equivalent of that "activity." It is the same kind of "property" that Congress described in § 7 of the Sherman Act, 26 Stat. 210 and in § 4 of the Clayton Act, 38 Stat. 731. A State's deliberate destruction of a going business is surely a deprivation of property within the meaning of the Due Process Clause.

Second, the validity of a congressional decision to abrogate sovereign immunity in a category of cases does not depend on the strength of the claim asserted in a particular case within that category. Instead, the decision depends on whether Congress had a reasonable basis for concluding that abrogation was necessary to prevent violations that would otherwise occur. Given the presumption of validity that support all federal statutes, I believe the Court must shoulder the burden of demonstrating why the judgment of the Congress of the United States should not command our respect. It has not done so. [End of dissent].

* * *

Notes on Protection of the Private Interest

One problem with applying a property concept to the trademark field is that trademarks comprised of ordinary words or names such as "Chicago," "Supreme" or "Jones" may acquire strong source-indicating significances but are difficult to characterize legally as any particular party's "property." The same sort of impediment is encountered in cases involving unfair competition claims based upon the similarity of the color or design of labeling or packaging, and this is so even though deception results. Thus, if only a property right exists, deceptive acts that do not involve a unique, fanciful or coined trademark are not readily prohibited since the existence of actual proprietary rights must first be established. Moreover, the property concept often relies in practice upon the support afforded by trademark registration certificates, a "proof of ownership" often unavailable in unfair competition cases.

As a result of the contradictions and limitations imposed by the property rationale, evolving trademark doctrine tended to merge somewhat the concept of invasion of a property right with the fundamental tort concept based upon a merchant's interest in being protected from confusion or deceptions as to source or identity.

Prior to the *College Savings v. Florida Prepaid* decision, the Supreme Court in *Hanover Star Milling Co. v. Metcalf*, 240 U.S. 403 (1916), explicated the at best highly attenuated notion of property that needs to be used when speaking of trademark rights. The Court's explanation shows the fine conceptual and linguistic line between the property conception and the use-based conception of trademark law:

> Common-law trademarks, and the right to their exclusive use, are, of course, to be classed among property rights . . .; but only in the sense that a man's right to the continued enjoyment of his trade reputation and the good will that flows from it, free from unwarranted interference by others, is a property right, for the protection of which a trademark is an instrumentality. . . . [T]he right grows out of use, not mere adoption. In the English courts it often has been said that there is no property whatever in a trademark, as such. . . . But since in the same cases the courts recognize the right of the party to the exclusive use of marks adopted to indicate goods of his manufacture, upon the ground that a man is not to sell his own goods under the pretense that they are the goods of another man; he cannot be permitted to practice such a deception, nor to use the means which contribute to that end. He cannot therefore be allowed to use names, marks, letters, or other indicia, by which he may induce purchasers to believe that the goods which he is selling are the manufacture of another person; it is plain that in denying the right of property in a trademark it was intended only to deny such property right except as appurtenant to an established business or trade in connection with which the mark is used. . . . In short, the trademark is treated as merely a protection for the good will, and not the subject of property except in connection with an existing business. The same rule prevails generally in this country.

Later the reliance upon a property theory in trademark cases was further eroded by Justice Holmes in *DuPont v. Masland*, 244 U.S. 100, 102 (1917), as follows: "The word property as applied to trade-marks and trade secrets is an unanalyzed expression of certain secondary consequences of the primary fact that the law makes some rudimentary requirements of good faith." This recognition of commercial integrity as the basis for trademark protection was also voiced in 1914 by trademark law's then-preeminent practitioner and authority, Edward S. Rogers:

> It was soon realized that trade could be stolen without resort to infringement of technical trade-marks, without violation of any then recognized property right. All manner of contrivances were employed — labels, packages and the like, were imitated, which resulted in public deception and private injury without, it was thought, subjecting the perpetrator to legal liability. The lawyers and courts at once found that their property theory was unworkable. Certainly no property could be claimed in the color of a label, or in the arrangement of the printed matter upon it, or in the shape of a bottle, or in any of the numberless things that help to identify a particular man's goods and that were being imitated for the purpose of stealing away his customers and appropriating his good will.

> It was perfectly clear that a man's trade could be taken away from him unlawfully and his customers deceived into purchasing a spurious article, in other ways than by imitation of his technical trademark, and it was a reproach to the law and courts of justice if they would sit idly by and see this go on. To meet this situation there has lately developed a considerable body of law dealing with this class of cases that, in this country, for want of a better name, are called cases of "unfair competition" or "unfair trading;" in Great Britain "passing off;" in France "concurrence deloyale;" and in Germany "unlauterer Wettbewerb."

GOOD WILL, TRADEMARKS AND UNFAIR TRADING, 126–127 (1914).

Thus, as commerce became increasingly complex and commercial pirates became more sophisticated, it was recognized that there are many aspects of trade identity that should be protected from many and perhaps unending varieties of deceptively tortious conduct.

Judge Learned Hand's famous statement in *Yale Electric Corp. v. Robertson*, 26 F.2d 972, 973–974 (2[d] Cir. 1928), explains his view that the fundamental element of trademark law is protection against confusion and deception:

> The law of unfair trade comes down very nearly to this — as judges have repeated again and again — that one merchant shall not divert customers from another by representing what he sells as emanating from the second. This has been, and perhaps even more now is, the whole Law and the Prophets on the subject, though it assumes many guises. Therefore it was at first a debatable point whether a merchant's good will, indicated by his mark, could extend beyond such goods as he sold. How could he lose bargains which he had no means to fill? What harm did it do a chewing gum maker to have an ironmonger use his trade-mark? The law often ignores the nicer sensibilities.

> However, it has of recent years been recognized that a merchant may have a sufficient economic interest in the use of his mark outside the field of his own exploitation to justify interposition by a court. His mark is his authentic seal; by it he vouches for the goods which bear it; it carries his name for good or ill. If another uses it, he borrows the owner's reputation, whose quality no longer lies within his own control. This is an injury, even though the borrower does not tarnish it, or divert any sales by its use; for a reputation, like a face, is the symbol of its possessor and creator, and another can use it only as a mask. And so it has come to be recognized that, unless the borrower's use is so foreign to the owner's as to insure against any identification of the two, it is unlawful.

In more recent years, the property rationale has reentered center stage. The implementation of the "intent to use" registration system described above, under which rights in a mark can be reserved before use even begins, the increasing protection afforded against diminishment of the value of a mark through "dilution" and "cyber-squatting" misuse of trademarks in domain names (discussed in later chapters), as well as the property perspective analyzed in the *Florida Prepaid* decision, all reflect a disposition to value trademark rights as property, and to encourage the development and protection of that value. *See* Lemley, *The Modern Lanham Act and The Death of Common Sense*, 108 YALE L. J. 1687 (1999) (decrying trend toward "propertization" of trademark rights).

1.04　Protection of the Public Interest

T & T MANUFACTURING CO. v. A.T. CROSS CO.
United States Court of Appeals, First Circuit
587 F.2d 533 (1978), cert. denied, 441 U.S. 908 (1979)

KUNZIG, JUDGE

The sole issue presented for review in this trademark infringement appeal is the validity and enforceability of a Settlement Agreement entered into by the defendant A.T. Cross Company (Cross) and The Quill Company (First Quill) [and later assigned to T & T Mfg. Co. (Second Quill)] for the manufacture and sale of certain pens and pencils. Chief Judge Raymond J. Pettine of the United States District Court for the District of Rhode Island held, *inter alia*, the Agreement was valid and enforceable and hence estopped Cross from asserting trademark infringement and unfair competition claims as outlined *infra*. Because we agree with the district court, we affirm.

*　*　*

The principal contention of Cross [is] that the Settlement Agreement should not be enforced on grounds of public policy. Cross contends that an agreement settling a trademark dispute is to be enforced, but with one proviso, namely, that if such an agreement is likely to cause public confusion as to the respective products, then it should not be enforced.

At the outset, we note that the decisional, as well as the statutory law dealing with the area of trademarks is vitally concerned with the protection of the public interest. As was stated by this court in *General Baking Co. v. Gorman*, 3 F.2d 891 (1st Cir. 1925):

> It should never be overlooked that trade-mark and unfair competition cases are affected with a public interest. A dealer's good will is protected, not merely for his profit, but in order that the purchasing public may not be enticed into buying A's product when it wants B's product. *Id.* at 893.

Against this backdrop, Cross maintains that since the district court held that there was a likelihood of public confusion between the products of Second Quill and Cross, it follows that the Settlement Agreement allowing Second Quill to manufacture and sell such products may not be enforced.

We cannot agree with Cross that merely because the district court made a finding of likelihood of public confusion that *ipso facto* the Settlement Agreement should now not be enforced according to its terms. Rather, we agree with the district court's approach that the *degree* or *extent* of public confusion must be examined in order to ascertain whether there is any significant harm to the public by decreeing enforcement of the Settlement Agreement. Additionally, there are other considerations, most notably the policy, vital to the law of contracts, of holding people to the terms of agreements knowingly and willfully entered into. These must also be considered in resolving the question of enforcement of the Settlement Agreement.

Courts have traditionally, in disputes similar to the present case, weighed the public interest concerning trademarks against the interest in contract enforcement. *Beer Nuts, Inc. v. King Nut Co.*, 477 F.2d 326, 328–29 (6th Cir. 1973), *cert denied*, 414 U.S. 858, *rehearing denied*, 414 U.S. 1033 (1973). In *Beer Nuts*, the court concluded that a party could not challenge a trademark as a descriptive word because by contract it had lost that defense. In deciding this, the court balanced the interest in "guarding against the depletion of the general vocabulary" of descriptive words against the contract interest that "a person should be held to his undertakings." *Id.* at 329.

Similarly, in *Peyrat v. L. N. Renault & Sons, Inc.*, 247 F. Supp. 1009 (S.D.N.Y. 1965), the court reviewed a contract permitting the importation of brandy under the same name as that used by the defendant in selling its wines. Therein the court stated, "The parties to a trademark controversy may contract between themselves for any legal purpose. The agreement is for a legal purpose and is valid and enforceable so long as no injury is caused to the public." *Id.* at 1014. The court, while noting that confusion as to the source of a consumer product is the type of public injury to be prevented, concluded that any such likelihood of confusion was sufficiently abrogated by the differing channels of commerce through which the two products traveled.

In the present case, the district court, following the spirit of previous cases, correctly evaluated the competing interests of contract enforcement with any harm the public might experience due to confusion arising between the products of Second Quill and Cross.

We observe that there was no allegation that the products of First Quill were inferior to Cross, nor was the Settlement Agreement entered into with any intent to deceive the public. Moreover, the Settlement Agreement specifically consented to the manufacture of only those pens which bore a *Quill* insignia as a distinguishing characteristic. Based upon the foregoing, it is clear, as the district court found, that any harm to the public as the result of a likelihood of confusion would not be significant.

The ascertainment of what is or is not in the public interest is often a difficult and nebulous task for a court to undertake. As the court stated in *Application of E. I. Dupont DeNemours & Co.*, 476 F.2d 1357, 1362, (Cust. & Pat. App. 1973):

> Reasonable men may differ as to the *weight* to give specific evidentiary elements in a particular case. In one case it will indicate that confusion is unlikely; in the next it will not. In neither case is it helpful or necessary to inject

broad maxims or references to "the public interest" which do not aid in deciding. Only the facts can do that.

On the basis of the facts of the present case, we hold that the Settlement Agreement should be enforced according to its terms. Since we find that any harm to the public is not significant as the result of a likelihood of confusion between Second Quill's and Cross' products, the policy of holding a party to its contractual undertakings becomes dominant. Added into this balance is the judicial policy of encouraging extra-judicial settlement of trademark litigation. In the words of Chief Judge Pettine:

> Insisting that a court review a settlement to assure that no public confusion will result would make such agreements of little value to the parties. *T&T Mfg. Co.*, *supra* at 827.

Moreover, to do so would undermine the policy of giving deference to the contractual agreements of reputable businessmen-users of valuable trademarks. *See, Application of E. I. Dupont DeNemours & Co., supra.*

As a final observation, we note that Cross originally entered into the Settlement Agreement with full knowledge of a potential for immediate public confusion between its products and those of First Quill. Now, some eleven years later, Cross seeks to disaffirm the Agreement on the basis of public confusion — the same basis it was instrumental in bringing about in the first place. It appears at best incongruous that a party should be permitted to disaffirm a contract as against public policy when such grounds are the very grounds that the party itself knowingly and willfully helped to create. We decline so to do.

Accordingly, we hold upon careful consideration of all briefs and submissions and after oral argument that the judgment of the district court sustaining the validity and enforceability of the Settlement Agreement is

Affirmed.

Notes on Protection of the Public Interest

The public interest against deception is necessarily a fundamental consideration in unfair competition cases. For much of the history of trademark law, the treatment of that interest was residual to what was viewed primarily a private complaint. *See* Diamond, *Public Interest and the Trademark System*, 62 J.P.O.S. 528 (1980); *Developments In The Law — Trade-Marks And Unfair Competition*, 68 HARV. L. REV. 814, 885–893 (1955). The *Cross* case, above, turns on protection of the public interest. *See also Times Mirror Magazines, Inc. v. Field & Stream Licenses Co.*, 294 F.3d 383 (2d Cir. 2002) (holding that "in order to obtain rescission of a freely bargained trademark contract, a party must show that the public interest will be significantly injured if the contract is allowed to stand," and concluding that, "[i]n the absence of significant harm to the public, the district court [here] correctly declined to don the mantle of public interest to save plaintiff from a harm that is permitted by the contract"); *Marshak v. Green*, 746 F.2d 927 (2d Cir. 1984). However, with the rise of the Law and Economics movement, and especially through the highly influential work of William Landes and Richard Posner, the protection of the public interest has tended to take center stage in many trademark cases in recent decades.

In *Trademark Law: An Economic Perspective*, 30 J. L. & ECON. 265 (1987), Professor Landes and Judge Posner argued as follows:

> Creating [a trademark] reputation requires expenditures on product quality, service, advertising, and so on. Once the reputation is created, the firm will obtain greater profits because repeat purchases and word-of-mouth references will generate higher sales and because consumers will be willing to pay higher prices for lower search costs and greater assurances of consistent quality. . . .
> The free-riding competitor will, at little cost, capture some of the profits

associated with a strong trademark because some consumers will assume (at least in the short run) that the free holder's brands are identical. If the law does not prevent it, free riding will eventually destroy the information capital embodied in a trademark, and the prospect of free riding may therefore eliminate the incentive to develop a valuable trademark in the first place.

Under this view, rather than a property right of the tradesperson, trademark rights are more appropriately viewed as a benefit to consumers, reducing consumer search costs and giving firms the incentive to maintain consistent product quality so as to make the investment of resources in developing and maintaining a strong trade identity worthwhile. *See* Weinberg, *Is the Monopoly Theory of Trademarks Robust or a Bust?*, 13 U. GA. J. of I.P. LAW 157 (2005). This principle quickly became influential in the courts. It was stated by Judge Kozinski, in dissent, in *New Kids on the Block v. New America Publishing*, 971 F.2d 302, 305 n.2, 306 n.3 (9th Cir. 1992), as follows:

> In economic terms, trademarks reduce consumer search costs by informing people that trademarked products come from the same source. . . . Trademark protection . . . guards against the overuse of resources while also providing incentives for the creation of new combinations of resources.

See also G.S. Rasmussen & Assoc. v. Kalitta Flying Service, 958 F.2d 896, 900 (9d Cir. 1992).

In *Qualitex Co v. Jacobson Products Co.*, 514 U.S. 159, 163-64 (1995), the Supreme Court, with Justice Breyer writing for a unanimous Court, substantially adopted the Law and Economics approach to trademark law:

> In principle, trademark law, by preventing others from copying a source-identifying mark, reduce[s] the customer's costs of shopping and making purchasing decisions," 1 J. McCarthy, McCarthy on Trademarks and Unfair Competition § 2.01[2], p. 2-3 (3d ed. 1994) . . ., for it quickly and easily assures a potential customer that *this* item—the item with this mark—is made by the same producer as other similarly marked items that he or she liked (or disliked) in the past. At the same time, the law helps assure a producer that it (and not an imitating competitor) will reap the financial, reputation-related rewards associated with a desirable product. The law thereby "encourage[s] the production of quality products," *ibid.*, and simultaneously discourages those who hope to sell inferior products by capitalizing on a consumer's inability quickly to evaluate the quality of an item offered for sale. *See, e.g.*, 3 L. Altman, Callmann on Unfair Competition, Trademarks and Monopolies § 17.03 (4th ed. 1983); Landes & Posner, The Economics of Trademark Law, 78 T.M. Rep. 267, 271-272 (1988); *Park 'N Fly, Inc. v. Dollar Park & Fly, Inc.*, 469 U.S. 189, 198, 105 S.Ct. 658, 663, 83 L.Ed.2d 582 (1985); S.Rep. No. 100-515, p. 4 (1988) U.S.Code Cong. & Admin.News, 1988, pp. 5577, 5580.

Subsequently, however, the Supreme Court became more skeptical of applying Law and Economics principles to trademark law in as direct a manner as was done in *Qualitex. See Wal-Mart Stores, Inc., v. Samara Bros., Inc.*, 529 U.S. 205 (2000); *TrafFix Devices, Inc., v. Marketing Displays, Inc.*, 532 U.S. 23 (2001); *Dastar Corp. v. Twentieth Century Fox Film Corp.*, 539 U.S. 23 (2003); *KP Permanent Make-Up, Inc., v. Lasting Impression I, Inc.*, 543 U.S. 111 (2004), all of which are excerpted and explained later in this book. *See generally* Chapters 8 and 9. *See also* Doellinger, Chad J., *A New Theory of Trademarks*, 111 PENN ST. L. REV. 823-861 (2007) (criticizing the grounding of trademark law in Law and Economics theories and advocating a return to principles of fair play as the normative foundation of trademark law).

1.05 The Monopoly Phobia

A competitive economy requires clear-cut source identification for goods and services, yet the right to exclude others from any deceptive use of a mark is a form of monopoly. That right, however, is only a qualified right to exclude, extending only to the limits of likelihood of confusion or deception. Of course, antitrust problems may arise because of ancillary restraints of trade (Chapter 8,), but occasionally it has been incorrectly suggested that the objectives of trademark law and antitrust law are in conflict rather than complementary. *See United States v. Timken Roller Bearing Co.*, 83 F. Supp. 284, 315 (D. Ohio 1949); McCarthy, Trademarks and Unfair Competition, §§ 1:24, 1:32 (4th ed. 2007); 1 Gilson, Trademark Protection and Practice, § 1.03[5] (2008 ed.);Schecter, The Rational Basis of Trademark Protection, 40 Harv. L. Rev. 813 (1927).

During the 1930's and continuing for thirty years, a period of retrogression in the development of our trademark case law occurred that has been referred to as the period of "monopoly phobia." *See* Pattishall, *Trademarks and the Monopoly Phobia*, 50 Mich. L. Rev. 967 (1952). This phobia seems to have been directly incident to the anti-business philosophy that grew out of the Great Depression years and was largely fostered by the courts whose judges were appointed during the New Deal era. While the Lanham Act's protectionist philosophy and provisions were notably antithetical to such political and legal tenets, the monopoly phobia continues to the present where, fueled in part by the early cases, it is still occasionally raised as a defense in trademark litigation. To contrast the thinking of two great jurists, compare *Standard Brands, Inc. v. Smidler*, 151 F.2d 34 (2ᵈ Cir. 1945) (Frank, J.; viewing trademark protection as a judge-made monopoly justified by the benefits to consumers), *with National Fruit Product Co. v. Dwinell-Wright Co.*, 47 F. Supp. 499 (D. Mass. 1942), *aff'd*, 140 F.2d 618 (1ˢᵗ Cir. 1944) (Wyzanski, J.) (rejecting various theories that criticized trademark protection for allegedly creating undesirable monopolies).

The discussion about the possible monopolistic tendencies of trademark law largely abated after the 1950s and was put to rest, seemingly for good, with the rise of the Law and Economics movement and its adoption in trademark cases in the 1980s and 1990s, as discussed above. In *KP Permanent Make-Up, Inc., v. Lasting Impression I, Inc.*, 543, U.S. 111, 119 (2004), the Supreme Court, with Justice Souter writing for a unanimous Court, revived the notion of monopoly concerns arising from an overbroad application of the Lanham Act. This time, however, the Court's concern was more with "monopolies" on descriptive terms in the English language brought about by removing these terms from the public domain, rather than with monopolies in the commercial sense. *See* discussion in Ch. 8.

Trademark protection has progressed in this country from application of the English common law to increasingly sophisticated statutory and common law developments. Deception-based protection of the sort described above now encompasses not only word trademarks, but product shapes and packaging, color, sound, even fragrance — in short, anything that may indicate source and as to which consumers or users may experience a likelihood of confusion. This deception-based law also has evolved to apply to misrepresentations which are not trademark-based, e.g., false advertising about a product's qualities or benefits, or false disparagement of a competitor.

As mentioned above, trademark protection also exists that is not deception-based. Over half the states now have dilution statutes, under which protection is offered against trademark uses that do not necessarily cause likely confusion but instead diminish the trademark's selling power or tarnish the goodwill it symbolizes. In 1996, federal dilution provisions in the Lanham Act were enacted that afford such protection nationally for famous marks, with amendments that took effect in 2006.

New technology has raised novel legal issues. Increasing commercial use of the Internet, for example, has created difficult to resolve domain name conflicts and new forms of misrepresentation. The 1999 federal anticybersquatting statute, for example, provides remedies to trademark owners stymied by bad faith registrations of domain names that correspond to their marks. New technology also has revitalized the application of common law misappropriation theory, i.e., "reaping where one has not sown." The growing commercial significance of celebrities has resulted in the rapid evolution of another type of commercial protection, the right of publicity, which relates to individuals and the goodwill embodied in their identity. Finally, federal, state, and local governments have developed regulatory schemes intended to protect by government action the public interest in these areas. The fundamentals of protection and these various developments are addressed in the materials that follow.

CHAPTER 2
CREATION AND MAINTENANCE
OF TRADE IDENTITY RIGHTS

CONTENTS

2.01 Federal Trademark Legislation and its Constitutional Foundations

Introduction

With the rise of federal trademark regulation in the latter half of the nineteenth century, the question of use acquired a constitutional dimension that it did not possess when merely state law or common law trademark protection was at issue. Under the Lanham Act, a party that adopts a new mark will have rights to the mark only if it uses the mark "in commerce." Ultimately, this is a constitutional requirement. As the Supreme Court explained in *United States v. Morrison*, 529 U.S. 598, 606 (2000), "[e]very law enacted by Congress must be based on one or more of its powers enumerated in the Constitution. 'The powers of the legislature are defined and limited; and that those limits may not be mistaken or forgotten, the constitution is written.' *Marbury v. Madison*, 1 Cranch 137, 176 (1803) (Marshall, C. J.)." The Lanham Act is based on Congress's power to regulate commerce under the Commerce Clause of the Constitution, U.S. CONST. art. I, § 8, cl. 3, which reads: "The Congress shall have Power . . . [t]o regulate Commerce with foreign Nations, and among the several States, and with the Indian Tribes." Though we take this state of affairs for granted today, it was not always clear whether federal trademark regulation was an exercise of Congress' Commerce Clause powers, and, if so, whether that exercise was legitimate.

TRADE-MARK CASES
100 U.S. 82 (1879)

MR. JUSTICE MILLER

. . . [A]re the acts of Congress on the subject of trade-marks founded on any rightful authority in the Constitution of the United States?

The entire legislation of Congress in regard to trade-marks is of very recent origin. It is first seen in sects. 77 to 84, inclusive, of the act of July 8, 1870, entitled "'n Act to revise, consolidate, and amend the statutes relating to patents and copyrights." 16 Stat. 198. The part of this act relating to trade-marks is embodied in chap. 2, tit. 60, sects. 4937 to 4947, of the Revised Statutes.

It is sufficient at present to say that they provide for the registration in the Patent Office of any device in the nature of a trade-mark to which any person has by usage established an exclusive right, or which the person so registering intends to appropriate by that act to his exclusive use; and they make the wrongful use of a trade-mark, so registered, by any other person, without the owner's permission, a cause of action in a civil suit for damages. Six years later we have the act of Aug. 14, 1876 (19 Stat. 141), punishing by fine and imprisonment the fraudulent use, sale, and counterfeiting of trade-marks registered in pursuance of the statutes of the United States, on which the information and indictments are founded in the cases before us . . . .

As the property in trade-marks and the right to their exclusive use rest on the laws of the States, and, like the great body of the rights of person and of property, depend on them for security and protection, the power of Congress to legislate on the subject, to establish the conditions on which these rights shall be enjoyed and exercised, the period of their duration, and the legal remedies for their enforcement, if such power exist at all, must be found in the Constitution of the United States, which is the source of all powers that Congress can lawfully exercise.

In the argument of these cases this seems to be conceded, and the advocates for the validity of the acts of Congress on this subject point to two clauses of the Constitution, in one or in both of which, as they assert, sufficient warrant may be found for this legislation.

The first of these is the eighth clause of sect. 8 of the first article. That section, manifestly intended to be an enumeration of the powers expressly granted to Congress, and closing with the declaration of a rule for the ascertainment of such powers as are necessary by way of implication to carry into efficient operation those expressly given, authorizes Congress, by the clause referred to, "to promote the progress of science and useful arts, by securing for limited times, to authors and inventors, the exclusive right to their respective writings and discoveries."

As the first and only attempt by Congress to regulate the *right of trade-marks* is to be found in the act of July 8, 1870, to which we have referred, entitled "An Act to revise, consolidate, and amend the statutes relating to *patents* and *copyrights*," terms which have long since become technical, as referring, the one to inventions and the other to the writings of authors, it is a reasonable inference that this part of the statute also was, in the opinion of Congress, an exercise of the power found in that clause of the Constitution. It may also be safely assumed that until a critical examination of the subject in the courts became necessary, it was mainly if not wholly to this clause that the advocates of the law looked for its support.

Any attempt, however, to identify the essential characteristics of a trade-mark with inventions and discoveries in the arts and sciences, or with the writings of authors, will show that the effort is surrounded with insurmountable difficulties.

The ordinary trade-mark has no necessary relation to invention or discovery. The trade-mark recognized by the common law is generally the growth of a considerable period of use, rather than a sudden invention. It is often the result of accident rather than design, and when under the act of Congress it is sought to establish it by registration, neither originality, invention, discovery, science, nor art is in any way essential to the right conferred by that act. If we should endeavor to classify it under the head of writings of authors, the objections are equally strong. In this, as in regard to inventions, originality is required. And while the word *writings* may be liberally construed, as it has been, to include original designs for engravings, prints, etc., it is only such as are *original*, and are founded in the creative powers of the mind. The writings which are to be protected are *the fruits of intellectual labor*, embodied in the form of books, prints, engravings, and the like. The trade-mark may be, and generally is, the adoption of something already in existence as the distinctive symbol of the party using it. At common law the exclusive right to it grows out of its *use*, and not its mere adoption. By the act of Congress this exclusive right attaches upon registration. But in neither case does it depend upon novelty, invention, discovery, or any work of the brain. It requires no fancy or imagination, no genius, no laborious thought. It is simply founded on priority of appropriation. We look in vain in the statute for any other qualification or condition. If the symbol, however plain, simple, old, or well-known, has been first appropriated by the claimant as his distinctive trade-mark, he may by registration secure the right to its exclusive use. While such legislation may be a judicious aid to the common law on the subject of trade-marks, and may be within the competency of legislatures whose general powers embrace that class of subjects, we are unable to see any such power in the constitutional provision concerning authors and inventors, and their writings and discoveries.

The other clause of the Constitution supposed to confer the requisite authority on Congress is the third of the same section, which, read in connection with the granting clause, is as follows: 'The Congress shall have power to regulate commerce with foreign nations, and among the several States, and with the Indian tribes.'

The argument is that the use of a trade-mark—that which alone gives it any value—is to identify a particular class or quality of goods as the manufacture, produce, or property of the person who puts them in the general market for sale; that the sale of the article so distinguished is commerce; that the trade-mark is, therefore, a useful and valuable aid or instrument of commerce, and its regulation by virtue of the clause belongs to Congress, and that the act in question is a lawful exercise of this power.

* * *

The question, therefore, whether the trade-mark bears such a relation to commerce in general terms as to bring it within congressional control, when used or applied to the classes of commerce which fall within that control, is one which, in the present case, we propose to leave undecided. . . . Governed by this view of our duty, we proceed to remark that a glance at the commerce clause of the Constitution discloses at once what has been often the subject of comment in this court and out of it, that the power of regulation there conferred on Congress is limited to commerce with foreign nations, commerce among the States, and commerce with the Indian tribes. While bearing in mind the liberal construction, that commerce with foreign nations means commerce between citizens of the United States and citizens and subjects of foreign nations, and commerce among the States means commerce between the individual citizens of different States, there still remains a very large amount of commerce, perhaps the largest, which, being trade or traffic between citizens of the same State, is beyond the control of Congress.

When, therefore, Congress undertakes to enact a law, which can only be valid as a regulation of commerce, it is reasonable to expect to find on the face of the law, or from its essential nature, that it is a regulation of commerce with foreign nations, or among the several States, or with the Indian tribes. If not so limited, it is in excess of the power of Congress. If its main purpose be to establish a regulation applicable to all trade, to commerce at all points, especially if it be apparent that it is designed to govern the commerce wholly between citizens of the same State, it is obviously the exercise of a power not confided to Congress. . . . It is therefore manifest that [the Act's] broad purpose was to establish a universal system of trade-mark registration, for the benefit of all who had already used a trade-mark, or who wished to adopt one in the future, without regard to the character of the trade to which it was to be applied or the residence of the owner, with the solitary exception that those who resided in foreign countries which extended no such privileges to us were excluded from them here.

*   *   *

The questions in each of these cases being an inquiry whether these statutes can be upheld in whole or in part as valid and constitutional, must be answered in the negative; and it will be

So certified to the proper circuit courts.

U.S. PRINTING & LITHOGRAPH v. GRIGGS, COOPER & CO.
279 U.S. 156 (1929)

HOLMES, JUSTICE

This is a suit brought by the respondent, a corporation of Minnesota, against the petitioner, a corporation of Ohio, alleging that the plaintiff has a trade-mark 'Home Brand,' registered in the Patent Office for various grocers' goods which it sells at wholesale in certain named States of the Northwest; and that the defendant is printing and selling labels for similar grocers' goods, containing the word 'Home,' which labels are used by the purchasers in States other than those in which the plaintiff has established a market. No interference with interstate or foreign commerce is alleged. The bill seeks an injunction against printing and selling such labels for any groceries that the plaintiff sells. The trial court found that facts to be as above stated and the Supreme Court held that the 'purpose and effect of the (Trade-Mark Act of February 20, 1905, c. 592, s 16; 33 Stat. 728, (Code tit. 15, s 96; 15 USCA s 96)) was to project the trade mark rights of the registrant and owner thereof into all the states even in advance of the establishment of trade therein, and to afford full protection to such registrant and owner.' If affirmed a judgment for the plaintiff giving the relief prayed and a writ of certiorari was granted by this Court.

In the *Trade-Mark Cases*, 100 U. S. 82, 25 L. Ed. 550, it was held that the earlier acts attempting to give these unlimited rights were beyond the power of Congress. Soon after that decision an Act of March 3, 1881 (21 Stat. 502), gave remedies for the wrongful use of a registered trademark in foreign commerce or commerce with Indian Tribes. It was said that obviously the Act was passed in view of the above-mentioned case, that only the trade-mark used in such commerce was admitted to registry and that the registered mark could only be infringed when used in that commerce. *Warner v. Searle & Hereth Co.*, 191 U. S. 195, 204, 24 S. Ct. 79, 48 L. Ed. 145 (*see United Drug Co. v. Theodore Rectanus Co.*, 248 U. S. 90, 99, 39 S. Ct. 48, 63 L. Ed. 141) and the constitutionality of the Act even when so limited was left open. 191 U. S. 206 (24 S. Ct. 79). The Act of 1905 goes a little farther and gives remedies against reproduction, etc., of the registered trade-mark "in commerce among the several States" as well as in commerce with foreign nations, etc., section 16. A remedy for such infringement was given in Thaddeus Davids Co. v. Davids, 233 U. S. 461, 34 S. Ct. 648, 58 L. Ed. 1046. *See also American Steel Foundries v. Robertson*, 262 U. S. 209, 43 S. Ct. 541, 67 L. Ed. 953;*Baldwin Co. v. Robertson*, 265 U. S. 168, 44 S. Ct. 508, 68 L. Ed. 962. But neither authority nor the plain words of the Act allow a remedy upon it for infringing a trademark registered under it, within the limits of a State and not affecting the commerce named. More obviously still it does not enlarge common-law rights within a State where the mark has not been used. *General Baking Co. v. Gorman* (C. C. A.) 3 F.(2d) 891, 894. Some attempt was made to support the decision upon other grounds, but we do not think them presented by the record, and they are not mentioned by the Ohio Court. *Judgment reversed.*

Notes on Federal Trademark Legislation and its Constitutional Foundations

1. A Brief History of Federal Trademark Legislation

The United States trademark statutes have had a substantial effect upon the evolution of the law of trademarks and unfair competition by liberalizing the interpretation of what is needed for a cause of action. Congress's first foray into federal trademark regulation was the Act of 1870. However, in the *Trade-Mark Cases*, 100 U.S. 82 (1879), the Supreme Court held that Congress *lacked* the constitutional power either under the patent and copyright clause or under the commerce clause (given the then-controlling narrow reading of Congress's commerce clause powers) to pass the Act of 1870. See discussion *infra*. Congress then passed the Act of 1881, and then the Act under which the foundations of modern trademark law developed, the Act of 1905. The Act of 1920 was supplementary to the Act of 1905 and was adopted primarily to establish a form of limited rights registration so that United States enterprises whose marks were not registrable under the 1905 Act (e.g., surname marks) could obtain a domestic trademark registration as a basis for obtaining foreign registrations in countries where domestic registration was a prerequisite (see Chapter 3). In 1946, Congress passed the Lanham Act which, as amended, is the federal trademark law that is currently in force (see the Appendix at the end of this book).

The Act of 1905 especially encouraged the disappearance of both the earlier requirement of intent to deceive and the earlier confinement of causes of action to those involving essentially the same goods and the same names. The Lanham Act (1946), which — with various amendments — remains in force today, further liberalized and expanded the concept of infringement. It also introduced a statutory prohibition of unfair competition in its Section 43(a) (Chapter 9). Perhaps its most significant innovations, however, were its provisions that federal registration of a trademark constitutes "constructive notice of the registrant's claim of ownership thereof" and for incontestability (Chapter 3).

The Lanham Act has been amended several times since its passage. In 1984 and 1996, provisions were added to combat the burgeoning problem of trademark counterfeiting (P.L. 98-473; P.L. 104-153), with a related amendment to the criminal counterfeiting statute in 2006 (P.L. 109-181). In 1988, the Trademark Law Revision Act of 1988 (the "Revision Act") was passed by Congress. The Act of November 16, 1988, Pub. L. 100-667, Title I Section 132, 102 Stat. 3935, amending 15 U.S.C. § 1051 *et. seq.* The most notable change the Revision Act brought about was the provision for an "intent to use" federal registration system. U.S. applicants may now apply for federal trademark registration based on a "bona fide intention to use the mark in commerce," as an alternative to basing the application on actual use, which was the only valid basis for application prior to the Revision Act. An intent-based application confers upon the applicant nationwide "constructive use" rights as of the date of application, which become viable once the applicant actually begins use of the mark and the registration issues. In 1999, the Act was revised again to add anticybersquating provisions necessitated by the growth of the internet, and directed to bad faith registration of domain names that correspond to trademarks owned by others. In 2003, revisions to the Lanham Act were made to implement U.S. entry into a multi-national registration system under the Madrid Protocol. In 2006 the Act was amended to clarify and strengthen its provisions for protection against the dilution of famous marks.

2. Trademark Legislation and the Commerce Clause

In the *Trade-Mark Cases*, the Supreme Court famously concludes that federal trademark legislation must be based on Congress's powers under the Commerce Clause *because* such legislation is based on the notion of use in commerce. No one has put the use rationale clearer or more succinctly than Edward S. Rogers (later the principal drafter of the Lanham Act) in his 1914 book, GOOD WILL, TRADE-MARKS AND UNFAIR TRADING 54. "[A trademark] is not a grant from the government or from a governmental bureau. It is not dependent upon invention or discovery, or evidenced by imposing documents embellished with red seals and red tape. It depends upon one thing only, priority of adoption and use, and continuous occupancy of the market with goods bearing the mark." In *Amoskeag Mfg. Co. v. Trainer*, 101 U.S. 51, 53 (1879), the Supreme Court gave a more detailed explanation.

> The general doctrines of the law as to trade-marks, the symbols or signs which may be used to designate products of a particular manufacture, and the protection which the courts will afford to those who originally appropriated them, are not controverted. Every one is at liberty to affix to a product of his own manufacture any symbol or device, not previously appropriated, which will distinguish it from articles of the same general nature manufactured or sold by others, and thus secure to himself the benefits of increased sale by reason of any peculiar excellence he may have given to it. The symbol or device thus becomes a sign to the public of the origin of the goods to which it is attached, and an assurance that they are the genuine article of the original producer. In this way it often proves to be of great value to the manufacturer in preventing the substitution and sale of an inferior and and different article for his products. It becomes his trade-mark, and the courts will protect him in its exclusive use, either by the imposition of damages for its wrongful appropriation or by restraining others from applying it to their goods and compelling them to account for profits made on a sale of goods marked with it.

To the present day, and notwithstanding certain attenuations such as intent-to-use federal trademark applications, use in commerce remains the normative, doctrinal, and constitutional underpinning of all of trademark law.

For almost 60 years after publication of the *Trade-Mark Cases*, the Supreme Court cited to the principles set forth therein as an accurate statement of its Commerce Clause jurisprudence. In passing subsequent federal trademark legislation, Congress tried to stay within the Commerce Clause powers. Under this reading of the Commerce Clause, then, substantive federal regulation of trademark rights was not feasible. As the Supreme Court stated in 1932, "Congress, by virtue of the commerce clause, has no power to regulate upon the substantive law of trade-marks . . . ." *American Trading Co. v. H.E. Heacock Co.*, 285 U.S. 247, 256 (1932). All that changed in 1937. In that year, President Roosevelt threatened to pack the Supreme Court that had refused to endorse the New Deal, using a narrow interpretation of the Commerce Clause to strike down one New Deal federal law after the other. President Roosevelt's court-packing scheme did not succeed, but in short order the Supreme Court made massive adjustments to its Commerce Clause jurisprudence. The Court's famous "switch in time" was embodied in cases such as *West Coast Hotel Co. v. Parrish*, 300 U.S. 379 (1937) and *Wickard v. Filburn*, 317 U.S. 111 (1942). *Wickard*, in fact, cited the *Trade-Mark Cases* as an example of the Commerce Clause interpretation it was abandoning. Under this new interpretation of the Commerce Clause, Congress was empowered to regulate essentially all commercial activity taking place anywhere within the U.S. (No Supreme Court case between 1937 and 1995 invalidated an act of Congress as being beyond Congress's powers under the Commerce Clause). Thus, no constitutional impediment stood in the way of Congress's passing comprehensive, substantive trademark legislation. The Lanham Act, passed in 1946, is one outgrowth of this new, essentially limitless understanding of the reach of the Commerce Clause.

In recent years, in cases such as *United States v. Lopez*, 514 U.S. 549 (1995) and *United States v. Morrison*, 529 U.S. 598 (2000), the Supreme Court limited the reach of Commerce Clause for the first time since *West Coast Hotel* and *Wickard*. In doing so, the Court explained that "[w]hether particular operations affect interstate commerce sufficiently to come under the constitutional power of Congress to regulate them is ultimately a judicial rather than a legislative question, and can be settled finally only by this Court." *Lopez*, 514 U. S., at 557, n. 2 (quoting *Heart of Atlanta Motel*, 379 U. S., at 273 (Black, J., concurring)). It remains to be seen whether these more recent adjustments to the hitherto reigning Commerce Clause jurisprudence will compromise or affect the constitutional viability of the Lanham Act, if at all.

Should a trademark used solely *intrastate* be registrable on the federal register if its use *affects* interstate or foreign commerce? For a court that answered "yes;" *see In re Silenus Wine*, 557 F.2d 506 (C.C.P.A. 1977). Is it conceivable that an intrastate use of a mark is of such limited commercial significance that it does not meet the Lanham Act's constitutional "in commerce" requirement? What situations might arise where the Supreme Court's revisiting of its New Deal interpretation of the Commerce Clause in cases such as *Lopez* and *Morrison*, *supra*, might remove an otherwise sufficient use of a trademark from the purview of the Lanham Act on constitutional grounds? Could that ever happen with respect to use of a mark on the Internet? Is internet use of a mark by definition use of the mark in interstate commerce? Recall also that the Commerce Clause does not only speak to interstate commerce, but also to commerce with foreign nations and the Indian Tribes. What situations are imaginable where trademark use does not take place in interstate commerce but nevertheless meets the requirements of the Commerce Clause? Are the answers to any of these questions influenced by the holding in *Lopez* that determining whether a given conduct falls under the purview of the Commerce Clause is a judicial rather than a legislative task? How would such a situation be affected by state unfair competition laws? *See also* discussion on concurrent use in Chapter 7.

2.02   Adoption and Use

Introduction

Trademark rights in the United States, traditionally have been based upon first and continuous use in commerce in connection with one's goods or services. *See* the discussion in Chapter 1. The rationale is that (1) use of indicia of source engenders marketplace awareness; (2) awareness results in symbolized goodwill; and (3) use of an indicia by others should be restricted to the extent it may be likely to result in a deceptive diversion of that symbolized goodwill.

While first and continuous use of a trademark in connection with goods and services remains a valid basis for establishing trademark rights in this country, the Revision Act, which became effective November 16, 1989, provides an alternative means. It rewards the first to apply to register a mark based on a bona fide intent to use with an inchoate ownership right as of the application date that will become viable when the registration issues. Under Section 1(b) of the Lanham Act, the registration will not issue until actual use has begun, and a non-registrant prior user will still have rights superior to the registrant in its geographical area of use established prior to the registrant's filing date. However, under Sections 44 and 66 of the Lanham Act, a foreign party can obtain a trademark registration without any actual use of the mark in U.S. commerce. Use is ultimately required to maintain the registration because a declaration of use must be filed within six years of the date of the registration. A registration that is unsupported by actual use of the mark — a "naked registration," as Judge Easterbrook calls it in *Zazu designs v. L'Oreal, S.A.*, 979 F.2d 499 (7th Cir. 1992), set forth *infra* — is not enforceable in court. See the discussion on foreign registrations in Chapter 3 and on concurrent rights in Chapter 7.

The sections in this chapter discuss the major criteria in establishing trademark rights. Set forth below are definitions of the basic terms in this field from the Lanham Act (15 U.S.C. § 1127):

Trade Name; Commercial Name. The terms "trade name" and "commercial name" mean any name used by a person to identify his or her business or vocation.

Trademark. The term "trademark" includes any word, name, symbol, or device, or any combination thereof—

(1) used by a person, or

(2) which a person has a bona fide intention to use in commerce and applies to register on the principal register established by this Act, to identify and distinguish his or her goods, including a unique product, from those manufactured or sold by others and to indicate the source of the goods, even if that source is unknown.

Service Mark. The term "service mark" means any combination thereof—

(1) used by a person, or

(2) which a person has a bona fide intention to use in commerce and applies to register on the principal register established by this Act, to identify and distinguish the services of one person, including a unique service, from the services of others and to indicate the source of the services, even if that source is unknown. Titles, character names and other distinctive features of radio or television programs may be registered as service marks notwithstanding that they, or the programs, may advertise the goods of the sponsor.

Certification Mark. The term "certification mark" means any word, name, symbol, or device, or any combination thereof—

(1) used by a person other than its owner, or

(2) which its owner has a bona fide intention to permit a person other than the owner to use in commerce and files an application to register on the principal register established by this Act, to certify regional or other origin, material, mode of manufacture, quality, accuracy, or other characteristics of such person's goods or services or that the work or labor on the goods or services was performed by members of a union or other organization.

Collective Mark. The term "collective mark" means a trademark or service mark—

(1) used by the members of a cooperative, an association, or other collective group or organization, or

(2) which such cooperative, association, or other collective group or organization has a bona fide intention to use in commerce and applies to register on the principal register established by this Act, and includes marks indicating membership in a union, an association, or other organization.

Mark. The term "mark" includes any trademark, service mark, collective mark, or certification mark.

The word "commerce" means all commerce which may lawfully be regulated by Congress.

Use in Commerce. The term "use in commerce" means a bona fide use of a mark in the ordinary course of trade, and not made merely to reserve a right in a mark. For purposes of this Act, a mark shall be deemed to be in use in commerce —

(1) on goods when —

(A) it is placed in any manner on the goods or their containers or the displays associated therewith or on the tags or labels affixed thereto, or if the nature of the goods makes such placement impracticable, then on documents associated with the goods or their sale, and

(B) the goods are sold or transported in commerce, and

(2) on services when it is used or displayed in the sale or advertising of services and the services are rendered in commerce, or the services are rendered in more than one State or in the United States and a foreign country and the person rendering the services is engaged in commerce in connection with the services.

Four noteworthy treatises on the law of trademarks are: McCarthy, Trademarks and Unfair Competition, Gilson, Trademark Protection and Practice, Callmann, Unfair Competition, Trademarks and Monopolies, Hilliard, Welch, and Marvel, Trademarks and Unfair Competition

The "use in commerce" requirement for establishing trademark rights is not a formality. As the definition of "use in commerce" in Section 1127 of the Lanham Act shows, the use requirement has real bite. Since the issue of use tends to be highly fact-contingent there is no ready-made formula as to what constitutes sufficient use to establish enforceable trademark rights. However, it can be generalized from the — extremely extensive — case law on sufficiency of use that in order to support trademark rights, a party's use has to constitute a commercial market reality, must be clearly perceived by the relevant group of consumers in connection with the goods and services offered under the mark, and must not be in the nature of token use or *de minimis* use. The following cases discuss situations where the plaintiff's use was, for a variety of reasons, insufficient to establish enforceable rights.

ZAZÚ DESIGNS v. L'ORÉAL, S.A.
United States Court of Appeals, Seventh Circuit
979 F.2d 499 (1992)

Easterbrook, Circuit Judge

In 1985 Cosmair, Inc., concluded that young women craved pink and blue hair. To meet the anticipated demand, Cosmair developed a line of "hair Cosmetics" — hair coloring that is easily washed out. These inexpensive products, under the name ZAZÚ, were sold in cosmetic sections of mass merchandise stores. Apparently the teenagers of the late 1980s had better taste than Cosmair's marketing staff thought. The product flopped, but its name gave rise to this trademark suit. Cosmair is the United States licensee of L'Oréal, S.A., a French firm specializing in perfumes, beauty aids and related products. Cosmair placed L'Oréal marks on the bottles and ads. For reasons the parties have not explained, L'Oréal rather than Cosmair is the defendant even though the events that led to the litigation were orchestrated in New York rather than Paris. L'Oréal does not protest, so for simplicity we refer to Cosmair and L'Oréal collectively as "L'Oréal."

L'Oréal hired Wordmark, a consulting firm, to help it find a name for the new line of hair cosmetics. After checking the United States Trademark Register for conflicts, Wordmark suggested 250 names. L'Oréal narrowed this field to three, including ZAZÚ, and investigated their availability. This investigation turned up one federal registration of ZAZÚ as a mark for clothing and two state service mark registrations including that word. One of these is Zazú Hair Designs; the other was defunct.

Zazú Hair Designs is a hair salon in Hinsdale, Illinois, a suburb of Chicago. We call it "ZHD" to avoid confusion with the ZAZÚ mark. (ZHD employs an acute accent and L'Oréal did not; no one makes anything of the difference.) The salon is a partnership between Raymond R. Koubek and Salvatore J. Segretto, hairstylists who joined forces in 1979. ZHD registered ZAZÚ with Illinois in 1980 as a trade name for its salon. L'Oréal called the salon to find out if ZHD was selling its own products. The employee who answered reported that the salon was not but added, "we're working on it." L'Oréal called again; this time it was told that ZHD had no products available under the name ZAZÚ.

L'Oréal took the sole federal registration, held by Riviera Slacks, Inc., as a serious obstacle. Some apparel makers have migrated to cosmetics, and if Riviera were about to follow Ralph Lauren (which makes perfumes in addition to shirts and skirts) it might have a legitimate complaint against a competing use of the mark. *Sands, Taylor & Wood Co. v. Quaker Oats Co.*, 24 U.S.P.Q.2d 1001, 1011 (7th Cir. 1992). Riviera charged L'Oréal $125,000 for a covenant not to sue if L'Oréal used the ZAZÚ mark on cosmetics. In April 1986, covenant in hand and satisfied that ZHD's state trade name did not prevent the introduction of a national product, L'Oréal made a small interstate shipment as the basis of an application for federal registration, filed on June 12, 1986. By August L'Oréal had advertised and sold its products nationally.

Unknown to L'Oréal, Koubek and Segretto had for some time aspired to emulate Vidal Sassoon by marketing shampoos and conditioners under their salon's trade name. In 1985 Koubek began meeting with chemists to develop ZHD's products. Early efforts were unsuccessful; no one offered a product that satisfied ZHD. Eventually ZHD received acceptable samples from Gift Cosmetics, some of which Segretto sold to customers of the salon in plain bottles to which he taped the salon's business card. Between November 1985 and February 1986 ZHD made a few other sales. Koubek shipped two bottles to a friend in Texas, who paid $13. He also made two shipments to a hair stylist friend in Florida — 40 bottles of shampoo for $78.58. These were designed to interest the Floridian in the future marketing of the product line. These bottles could not have been sold to the public, because they lacked labels listing the ingredients and weight. *See* 21 U.S.C. § 362(b); 15 U.S.C. §§ 1452, 1453(a); 21 C.F.R. §§ 701.3, 701.13(a). After L'Oréal's national marketing was under way, its representatives thrice visited ZHD and found that the salon still had no products for sale under the ZAZÚ name. Which is not to say that ZHD was supine. Late in 1985 ZHD had ordered 25,000 bottles silk-screened with the name ZAZÚ. Later it ordered stick-on labels listing the ingredients of its products. In September 1986 ZHD began to sell small quantities of shampoo in bottles filled (and labeled) by hand in the salon. After the turn of the year ZHD directed the supplier of the shampoo and conditioner to fill some bottles; the record does not reveal how many.

After a bench trial the district court held that ZHD's sales gave it an exclusive right to use the ZAZÚ name nationally for hair products. 9 U.S.P.Q.2d 1972 (N.D. Ill. 1988). The court enjoined L'Oréal from using the mark (a gesture, since the product had bombed and L'Oréal disclaimed any interest in using ZAZÚ again). It also awarded ZHD $100,000 in damages on account of lost profits and $1 million more to pay for corrective advertising to restore luster to the ZAZÚ mark. Finding that L'Oréal had infringed ZHD's mark intentionally and used "oppressive and deceitful" tactics in the litigation, the court awarded an additional $1 million in punitive damages, topped off with $76,000 to cover ZHD's legal expenses. (L'Oréal has changed law firms for the appeal; its current counsel did not participate in the events that the district judge found to be unethical.)

*   *   *

Federal law permits the registration of trademarks and the enforcement of registered marks. Through § 43(a) of the Lanham Act, 15 U.S.C. § 1125(a), a provision addressed to deceit, it also indirectly allows the enforcement of unregistered marks. But until 1988 federal law did not specify how one acquired the rights that could be registered or enforced without registration.[*] That subject fell into the domain of state

---

[*] The Trademark Law Revision Act of 1988 added provisions allowing for registration of a mark on a showing that the applicant has a "bona fide intention . . . to use a trademark in commerce." 15 U.S.C. § 1051(b). Filing such an intent-to-use application establishes priority as of the date of filing (except as against

law, plus federal common law elaborating on the word "use" in § 43(a). *Two Pesos, Inc. v. Taco Cabana, Inc.*, 112 S. Ct. 2753, 2757 (1992); *id.* 112 S. Ct. at 2766–67 (Thomas J., concurring). *See also* 15 U.S.C. § 1127 ("trademark includes any word . . . used by a person"). At common law, "use" meant sales to the public of a product with the mark attached. *Trade-Mark Cases*, 100 U.S. 82, 94–95 (1879); *Menendez v. Holt*, 128 U.S. 514, 520–21 (1888). *See also Hanover Star Milling Co. v. Metcalf*, 240 U.S. 403, 414 (1916); *United Drug Co. v. Theodore Rectanus Co.*, 248 U.S. 90, 97 (1918).

"Use" is neither a glitch in the Lanham Act nor a historical relic. By insisting that firms use marks to obtain rights in them, the law prevents entrepreneurs from reserving brand names in order to make their rivals' marketing more costly. Public sales let others know that they should not invest resources to develop a mark similar to one already used in the trade. *Blue Bell, Inc. v. Farah Manufacturing Co.*, 508 F.2d 1260, 1264–65 (5th Cir. 1975); *see also* William M. Landes and Richard A. Posner, *Trademark Law: An Economic Perspective*, 30 J.L. & Econ. 265, 281–84 (1987). Only active use allows consumers to associate a mark with particular goods and notifies other firms that the mark is so associated.

Under the common law, one must win the race to the marketplace to establish the exclusive right to a mark. *Blue Bell v. Farah; La Societe Anonyme des Parfums LeGalion v. Jean Patou, Inc.*, 495 F.2d 1265, 1271–74 (2d Cir. 1974). Registration modifies this system slightly, allowing slight sales plus notice in the register to substitute for substantial sales without notice. 15 U.S.C. § 1051(a). (The legislation in 1988 modifies the use requirement further, but we disregard this.) ZHD's sales of its product are insufficient use to establish priority over L'Oréal. A few bottles sold over the counter in Hinsdale, and a few more mailed to friends in Texas and Florida, neither link the ZAZÚ mark with ZHD's product in the minds of consumers nor put other producers on notice. As a practical matter ZHD had no product, period, until months after L'Oréal had embarked on its doomed campaign.

In finding that ZHD's few sales secured rights against the world, the district court relied on cases such as *Department of Justice v. Calspan Corp.*, 578 F.2d 295 (C.C.P.A. 1978), which hold that a single sale, combined with proof of intent to go on selling, permit the vendor to register the mark. *See also Axton-Fisher Tobacco Co. v. Fortune Tobacco Co.*, 82 F.2d 295 (C.C.P.A. 1936); *Maternally Yours, Inc. v. Your Maternity Shop, Inc.*, 234 F.2d 538, 542 (2d Cir. 1956); *Community of Roquefort v. Santo*, 443 F.2d 1196 (C.C.P.A. 1971). But use sufficient to register a mark that soon is widely distributed is not necessarily enough to acquire rights in the absence of registration. The Lanham Act allows only trademarks "used in commerce" to be registered. 15 U.S.C. § 1051(a). Courts have read "used" in a way that allows firms to seek protection for a mark before investing substantial sums in promotion. *See Fort Howard Paper Co. v. Kimberly-Clark Corp.*, 390 F.2d 1015 (C.C.P.A. 1972) (party may rely on advertising to show superior registration rights); *but see Weight Watchers International, Inc. v. I. Rokeach & Sons, Inc.*, 211 U.S.P.Q. 700, 709 (T.M.T.A.B. 1981) (more than minimal use is required to register because the statute allows only "owner[s]" to register, and ownership of a mark depends on commercial use). Liberality in registering marks is not problematic, because the registration gives notice to latecomers, which token use alone does not. Firms need only search the register before embarking on development. Had ZHD registered ZAZÚ, the parties could have negotiated before L'Oréal committed large sums to marketing.

ZHD applied for registration of ZAZÚ after L'Oréal not only had applied to register the mark but also had put its product on the market nationwide. Efforts to register came too late. At oral argument ZHD suggested that L'Oréal's knowledge of ZHD's plan to

---

those already using the mark), but a statement of actual use must be filed within 6 months, which may be extended to 24. 15 U.S.C. § 1051(d). At the same time the statute was revised to provide that " use in commerce means the bona fide use of a mark in the ordinary course of trade, and not made merely to reserve a right in a mark. " 15 U.S.C. § 1127.

enter the hair care market using ZAZÚ; establishes ZHD's superior right to the name. Such an argument is unavailing. Intent to use a mark, like a naked registration, establishes no rights at all. *Hydro-Dynamics, Inc. v. George Putnam & Co.*, 811 F.2d 1470, 1472 (Fed. Cir. 1987). Even under the 1988 amendments (see note *), which allow registration in advance of contemplated use, an unregistered *plan* to use a mark creates no rights. Just as an intent to buy a choice parcel of land does not prevent a rival from closing the deal first, so an intent to use a mark creates no rights a competitor is bound to respect. A statute granting no rights in bare registrations cannot plausibly be understood to grant rights in "intents" divorced from either sales or registrations. Registration itself establishes only a rebuttable presumption of use as of the filing date. *Roley, Inc. v. Younghusband*, 204 F.2d 209, 211 (9th Cir. 1953). ZHD made first use of ZAZÚ; in connection with hair *services* in Illinois, but this does not translate to a protectable right to market hair *products* nationally. The district court construed L'Oréal's knowledge of ZHD's use of ZAZÚ; for salon services as knowledge "of [ZHD's] superior rights in the mark." 9 U.S.P.Q.2d at 1978. ZHD did not, however, have superior rights in the mark as applied to hair products, because it neither marketed such nor registered the mark before L'Oréal's use. Because the mark was not registered for use in conjunction with hair products, any knowledge L'Oréal may have had of ZHD's plans is irrelevant. *Cf. Weiner King, Inc. v. Wiener King Corp.*, 615 F.2d 512 (C.C.P.A. 1980).

Imagine the consequences of ZHD's approach. Businesses that knew of an intended use would not be entitled to the mark even if they made the first significant use of it. Businesses with their heads in the sand, however, could stand on the actual date they introduced their products, and so would have priority over firms that intended to use a mark but had not done so. Ignorance would be rewarded — and knowledgeable firms might back off even though the rivals' "plans" or "intent" were unlikely to come to fruition. Yet investigations of the sort L'Oréal undertook prevent costly duplication in the development of trademarks and protect consumers from the confusion resulting from two products being sold under the same mark. *See Natural Footwear Ltd. v. Hart, Shaffner & Marx*, 760 F.2d 1383, 1395 (3d Cir. 1985). L'Oréal should not be worse off because it made inquiries and found that, although no one had yet used the mark for hair products, ZHD intended to do so. Nor should a potential user have to bide its time until it learns whether other firms are serious about marketing a product. The use requirement rewards those who act quickly in getting new products in the hands of consumers. Had L'Oréal discovered that ZHD had a product on the market under the ZAZÚ; mark or that ZHD had registered ZAZÚ; for hair products, L'Oréal could have chosen another mark before committing extensive marketing resources. Knowledge that ZHD planned to use the ZAZÚ; mark in the future does not present an obstacle to L'Oréal's adopting it today. *Selfway, Inc. v. Travelers Petroleum, Inc.*, 579 F.2d 75, 79 (C.C.P.A. 1978).

* * *

The district court erred in equating a use sufficient to support registration with a use sufficient to generate nationwide rights in the absence of registration. Although whether ZHD's use is sufficient to grant it rights in theZAZÚ; mark is a question of fact on which appellate review is deferential, *California Cedar Products*, 724 F.2d at 830; *cf. Scandia Down Corp. v. Euroquilt, Inc.*, 772 F.2d 1423, 1428-29 (7th Cir. 1985), the extent to which ZHD used the mark is not disputed. ZHD's sales of hair care products were insufficient as a matter of law to establish national trademark rights at the time L'Oréal put its electric hair colors on the market.

* * *

Reversed and remanded.

IN RE CANADIAN PACIFIC LIMITED

United States Court of Appeals, Federal Circuit

754 F.2d 992 (1985)

DAVIS, CIRCUIT JUDGE

[Appeal from a decision of the Trademark Trial and Appeal Board refusing to register CANADIAN PACIFIC ENTERPRISES LIMITED, LES ENTREPRISES CANADIEN PACIFIQUE LIMITEE for a shareholder dividend reinvestment plan.]

This appeal raises a question of first impression in the elusive quest to find an appropriate definition of "services" under the Lanham Act. The Act defines "service mark," but fails to define "services." A further difficulty is that the legislative history reveals little bearing on the definition of "services." Our predecessor court has reasoned that "no attempt was made to define 'services' simply because of the plethora of services that the human mind is capable of conceiving." *American International Reinsurance Co. v. Airco, Inc.*, 570 F.2d 941, 943, 197 U.S.P.Q. 69, 71 (C.C.P.A.), *cert. denied*, 439 U.S. 866 (1978). Under that principle, appellant points out, the statute is entitled to a liberal interpretation.

In the absence of persuasive reasons to the contrary, words in a statute are to be given their ordinary and common meaning. *Banks v. Chicago Grain Trimmers Assn., Inc.*, 390 U.S. 459, 465 *reh. denied*, 391 U.S. 929 (1968). Appellant states that the accepted dictionary definition of "services" is "the performance of labor for the benefit of *another*." (Citing *Webster's Collegiate Dictionary* (5th Ed.)) (emphasis added). We do not take exception to this definition. On the contrary, that definition is consistent with the Trademark Manual of Examining Procedure § 1301.01, which, in suggesting certain criteria for determining what constitutes a service, states that "a service must be performed to the order of or for the *benefit of others* than the applicant." (Emphasis added). Hence, our concern here lies in who is to be considered "other" or "another," consonant with the policies of trademark law. When the Lanham Trademark Act was enacted, Congress was concerned with protecting the purchasers of a service or product. The Committee on Patents stated its belief that the Bill accomplished two purposes:

> One is to protect the *public* so it may be confident that, in purchasing a product bearing a particular trade-mark which it favorably knows, it will get the product which it asks for and wants to get. Secondly, where the owner of a trade-mark has spent energy, time, and money in presenting to the *public* the product, he is protected in his investment from its misappropriation. . . . [Emphasis added.]

S.Rep. No. 1333, 79th Cong., 2d Sess. 3, *reprinted in* 1946 U.S.Code Cong.Service 1274. Thus, it is this goodwill, established in the minds of the relevant buying public, which is protected by the registration of a service mark. *See* 1 McCarthy, *Trademarks and Unfair Competition*, § 2.7 (3d ed. 1992). Since it is a segment of the public which "purchases" and "benefits" from a service provided by the owner of the mark, then it is from the viewpoint of a "public" to which we direct our inquiry. The question then becomes whether the shareholders under the Plan are to be considered as members of a "public" for purposes of registrability of these marks.

Because the Plan is available *only* to Enterprises' own stockholders in connection with their further investment or participation in Enterprises' own activities, we think that no person or entity "other" than Enterprises (and its 75% parent Canadian Pacific, which has made the applications) is at all involved, and therefore that there is no "public" — which by definition must consist of at least some group of the greater public that is separate from the applicant — to which (or to whom) the asserted service mark can be directed and be useful. Enterprises' shareholders are, in fact and in law, its owners, i.e., all together they *are* Enterprises, and there is no other such owner.

In support of the contrary proposition that Enterprises' shareholders are the "other" in the definition of "services," and therefore members of a "public," appellant directs our attention to *American International Reinsurance Co. v. Airco, Inc., supra.* In that case, the applicant, whose principal business was the manufacture of sundry products, offered its *employees* a Retirement Income Plan. It was for this latter service that the applicant sought to register a service mark. In holding that such an activity constituted a "service" within the meaning of the Act, the CCPA stated that the "fact that the services in question are offered only to applicant's employees . . . is of no moment; the Act does not preclude registration simply because the services are offered only to a limited segment of the public." 570 F.2d at 943, 197 USPQ at 71. The court added that being employed by the applicant did not strip the employees of their status as members of the public. Appellant contends that by analogy its shareholders are the same as employees, and therefore that its marks are registrable.

A . . . critical distinction between *American International* and this case is that, unlike an employee, a shareholder has the right to participate proportionately in all profits, management, and the distribution of net assets on liquidation. *Freese v. United States*, 323 F. Supp. 1194, 1197 (N.D. Okla. 1971), *aff'd*, 455 F.2d 1146 (10th Cir.), *cert. denied*, 409 U.S. 879 (1972). A shareholder has an ongoing, fractional, equitable and proprietary interest in the property and assets of a corporation. 11 *Fletcher Cyc. Corp.* § 5100 (Perm.Ed.). In a word, he or she is the owner of an undivided portion of the corporation. *Id.* It follows, of course, that the "owner" of a corporation is the body of shareholders as a whole.

Appellant says that reinvestment, which in turn increases capitalization, benefits the shareholder and not just the corporation. The answer is that in this particular respect shareholders and corporations are inseparably tied together. The Plan's offer to the shareholders, as a whole, to increase their ownership in Enterprises is akin to an offer to the owner of the corporation, and thus is equivalent to an offer of a service to the corporation itself. The increased capitalization inures not only to the benefit of the corporate entity, but also to *all* the shareholders, who, as we have said, are the equitable owners of the corporation. Such a plan is analogous to a sole proprietor's, or a partnership's, offering a plan of reinvestment to himself or itself. There is no benefit or service conferred upon "another," and no benefit to be conferred on any member of the relevant buying "public." Instead, every service is rigidly limited to further ownership by the very family of owners of the marks sought to be registered. The Lanham Act does not afford this kind of intramural or internal protection.

Appellant has failed to convince us that its shareholders should be considered as members of the public, apart from appellant itself. Consequently, the Trademark Act does not apply to their activities, and we agree with the Board's decision that the applicant's marks are not registrable as service marks.

Affirmed.

Notes on Adoption and Use

As a general rule, one must use a mark in order to acquire trademark rights. *Hanover Star Milling Co. v. Metcalf*, 240 U.S. 403 (1916). Unlike patent rights, trademark and other trade identity rights result from actual use and not from invention and registration. *Trade-Mark Cases*, 100 U.S. 82 (1879). Commercial activity is necessary to establish trademark rights. Ideas for products do not establish such rights. *Keane v. Fox TV Stations, Inc.*, 129 Fed. Appx. 874 (5th Cir. 2005) (unpublished) (affirming dismissal of American Idol trademark claim because plaintiff's use of the name without a commercial enterprise did not establish trademark rights). The common-law rationale for this prescription stems from the very nature of trademarks themselves. The value of a trademark is no greater than what it symbolizes. With each sale of goods or services, goodwill, or what Mr. Justice Frankfurter called "commercial magnetism" (*Mishawaka Rubber*, § 1.03), may be built up; in the absence of such use, nothing is symbolized and nothing exists which calls for legal protection. *See United*

Drug Co. v. Theodore Rectanus Co., 248 U.S. 90, 97 (1918) ("There is no such thing as property in a trade-mark except as a right appurtenant to an established business or trade in connection with which the mark is employed").

Courts generally find trademark use on goods only where goods are sold with the trademark clearly affixed thereto, *Persha v. Armour & Co.*, 239 F.2d 628 (5ᵗʰ Cir. 1957), or displayed with the goods, packages or containers so that the mark can be seen by purchasers in close proximity to the product. *See, e.g. Matrix Motor Co. v. Toyota Motor Sales, U.S.A., Inc.*, 120 Fed. Appx. 30 (9ᵗʰ Cir. 2005), in which the Ninth Circuit affirmed that plaintiff Matrix Motors had not engaged in sufficient use of the mark on automobiles to establish trademark rights. Matrix had "never sold a car in the United States that bears the MATRIX name on its exterior." At most, Matrix had only used MATRIX "on interior car parts that were not visible to the public."

See also Dept. of Parks & Rec. v. Bazaar DelMundo, Inc., 448 F.3d 1118 (9ᵗʰ Cir. 2006) (use in brochures and history books was not commercial trademark use); *ETW Corp. v. Jireh Publishing*, 332 F.3d 915 (6ᵗʰ Cir. 2003) (no consistent trademark use on specific goods); *Herbko Int'l v. Kappa Books*, 308 F.3d 1156 (Fed. Cir. 2002) ("the title of a single book cannot serve as a source identifier," but a title for a multiple book series can). The question of trademark use in the internet context has raised additional issues, which are discussed in Chapter 6.

A nickname for a product or service may acquire trademark significance through adoption and use by the public, rather than by the trademark owner. *See, e.g., National Cable Television Association v. American Cinema Editors, Inc.*, 937 F.2d 1572 (Fed. Cir. 1991) (ACE used by the public as an acronym for the name of an association of film editors); *Anheuser-Busch, Inc. v. Power City Brewery, Inc.* 28 F. Supp. 740 (W.D.N.Y. 1939) ("BUD"); *Volkswagenwerk A.G. v. Advanced Welding & Mfg. Co.*, 193 U.S.P.Q. 673 (T.T.A.B. 1976) ("BUG"); *Coca-Cola Co. v. Busch*, 44 F.Supp. 405 (E.D. Pa. 1942) ("COKE"). These cases are generally regarded as exceptions to the general rules regarding adoption and use, in that there is no affixation and sale, *see, e.g., Digicom, Inc. v. Digicon, Inc.*, 328 F. Supp. 631, 634 (S.D. Tex. 1971). Can one reconcile this "exception" with the purpose of the adoption and use rule? What role should public usage play in this area of the law? Brody, *What's In a Nickname? Or Can Public Use Create Private Rights?* 95 TMR 1123 (2005). Does this really fall within the ambit of unfair competition protection rather than strict trademark law protection?

In many countries registration of a trademark, irrespective of use, is the act which creates trademark rights, whereas in the United States registration for many years constituted governmental recognition of rights which have previously been acquired by use. *See* Pattishall, *The Use Rationale and the Trademark Registration Treaty*, 11 A.P.L.A.J. 97 (1974). As stated above, intent-to-use applications for federal registration in the United States now establish inchoate trademark rights as of the date of application, which become viable once actual use is made and the registration issues (keep in mind, though, that this is not true for the registrations available for non-U.S. parties uncer Sections 44 and 66, which can be obtained — though not maintained for more than six years — without a showing of actual use). Use-based applications similarly establish inchoate rights as of the date of application, in addition to any common law rights that may exist.

2.03 Priority

It frequently happens that two parties introduce the same or similar goods or services under the same or similar trademarks. This may be the result of deliberate copying, or it may be perfectly innocent. In either case, the question as to who has the superior rights must be resolved. Superior rights go to the party with "priority." Priority is a term of art in trademark law. It is strongly, but not completely, related to the temporal question of first adoption and use of a mark in commerce. That issue itself can be complex, with court decisions often hinging on what constitutes bona fide use. The inquiry is further complicated by intent-to-use applications recognized in the modern Lanham Act, which can confer priority but are not initially based on use at all.

P   appellee   *D, appellant*

WARNERVISION ENTERTAINMENT INC. v. EMPIRE OF CAROLINA, INC.
United States Court of Appeals, Second Circuit
101 F.3d 259 (1996)

VAN GRAAFEILAND, CIRCUIT JUDGE

Empire of Carolina, Inc., Empire Industries, Inc. and Empire Manufacturing, Inc. (hereafter "Empire") and Thomas Lowe Ventures, Inc. d/b/a Playing Mantis (hereafter "TLV") appeal from orders of the United States District Court for the Southern District of New York (Baer, J.) preliminarily enjoining appellants from violating WarnerVision Entertainment Inc.'s trademark "REAL WHEELS," and denying Empire's cross-motion for injunctive relief.

Appellants contend that the grant of preliminary relief in WarnerVision's favor should be reversed on any of several grounds. We limit our holding to one — the district court's misapplication of 15 U.S.C. § 1057(c), part of the intent-to-use ("ITU") provisions of the Lanham Act, to the facts of the instant case. This error constitutes an abuse of discretion. *See Reuters Ltd. v. United Press Int'l, Inc.,* 903 F.2d 904, 907 (2[d] Cir.1990).

Prior to 1988, an applicant for trademark registration had to have used the mark in commerce before making the application. Following the enactment of the ITU provisions in that year, a person could seek registration of a mark not already in commercial use by alleging a bona fide intent to use it. *See* 15 U.S.C. § 1051(b). Registration may be granted only if, absent a grant of extension, the applicant files a statement of commercial use within six months of the date on which the Commissioner's notice of allowance pursuant to 15 U.S.C. § 1063(b) is issued. *See* 15 U.S.C. § 1051(d); *see also Eastman Kodak Co. v. Bell & Howell Document Management Prods. Co.,* 994 F.2d 1569, 1570 (Fed. Cir. 1993). The ITU applicant is entitled to an extension of another six months, and may receive further extensions from the Commissioner for an additional twenty four months. 15 U.S.C. § 1051(d)(2). If, but only if, the mark completes the registration process and is registered, the ITU applicant is granted a constructive use date retroactive to the ITU filing date. 15 U.S.C. § 1057(c). This retroactive dating of constructive use permits a more orderly development of the mark without the risk that priority will be lost. The issue we now address is whether the creator of a mark who files an ITU application pursuant to 15 U.S.C. § 1051(b) can be preliminarily enjoined from engaging in the commercial use required for full registration by 15 U.S.C. § 1051(d) on motion of the holder of a similar mark who commenced commercial use of its mark subsequent to the creator's ITU application but prior to the ITU applicant's commercial use. A brief statement of the pertinent facts follows.

On September 9, 1994, TLV sent the Patent and Trademark Office ("PTO") an ITU application for the mark "REAL WHEELS," stating an intent-to-use the mark in commerce on or in connection with "the following goods/services: wheels affiliated with 1/64th and 1/43rd scale toy vehicles." The application was filed under September 23, 1994. Around the same time, two other companies, apparently acting in innocence and good faith, decided that the "REAL WHEELS" mark would fit the products they were preparing to market. One of them, Buddy L, a North Carolina manufacturer that had been marketing toy replicas of vehicles for many years, selected the name for its 1995 line of vehicle replicas. The other, WarnerVision Entertainment Inc., found the name suitable for certain of its home videos which featured motorized vehicles. The videos and vehicles were shrink-wrapped together in a single package. Both companies ordered trademark searches for conflicts in the name, but, because TLV's application had not yet reached the PTO database, no conflict was found.

Both companies then filed for registration of their mark. However, because

WarnerVision's application was filed on January 3, 1995, three days before Buddy L's, it was approved, and Buddy L's was rejected. . . .

. . . On October 20, 1995, Empire purchased from TLV all of TLV's title and interest in and to the REAL WHEELS product line, trademarks and good will associated therewith, including the September 23, 1994 ITU application. At the same time, Empire licensed TLV to use the REAL WHEELS mark for toy automobiles. On November 13, 1995, WarnerVision brought the instant action.

. . . Section 1057(c) of Title 15, the statute at issue, provides that, "[c]ontingent on the registration of a mark . . . the filing of the application to register such mark shall constitute constructive use of the mark, conferring a right of priority, nationwide in effect . . . ." Empire is not claiming constructive use based on registration. Registration will not take place until after the section 1051(d) statement of use is filed and further examination is had of the application for registration. *See Eastman Kodak, supra*, 994 F.2d at 1570. Empire contends that the district court erred in granting the preliminary injunction which bars it from completing the ITU process by filing a factually supported statement of use.

We agree. Empire does not contend that the filing of its ITU application empowered it to seek affirmative or offensive relief precluding WarnerVision's use of the REAL WHEELS mark. It seeks instead to assert the ITU filing as a defense to WarnerVision's effort to prevent it from completing the ITU registration process. In substance, Empire requests that the normal principles of preliminary injunction law be applied in the instant case. This accords with the stated intent of Congress that the Lanham Act would be governed by equitable principles, which Congress described as "the core of U.S. trademark jurisprudence." *See S.Rep. No. 515, 100th Cong., 2nd Sess. 30 (1988), reprinted in 1988 U.S.C.C.A.N. 5577, 5592.*

* * *

As the International Trademark Association ("ITA") correctly notes at page 9 of its amicus brief, if Empire's ITU application cannot be used to defend against WarnerVision's application for a preliminary injunction, Empire will effectively be prevented from undertaking the use required to obtain registration. In short, granting a preliminary injunction to WarnerVision would prevent Empire form ever achieving use, registration and priority and would thus effectively and permanently terminate its rights as the holder of the ITU application. Quoting 2 McCarthy on Trademarks and Unfair Competition,

> § 19.08[1][d] at 19–59 (3d ed. 1992) the ITA said "this result 'would encourage unscrupulous entrepreneurs to look in the record for new [intent-to-use] applications by large companies, rush in to make a few sales under the same mark and sue the large company, asking for a large settlement to permit the [intent-to-use] applicant to proceed on its plans for use of the mark.' " This vulnerability to pirates is precisely what the ITU enactments were designed to eliminate. *See S.Rep. No. 151, supra, at 5592.*

The Trademark Trial and Appeal Board believes that an ITU applicant should be able to defend against piratical acts despite the fact that full registration has not yet been given. *See Larami Corp. v. Talk to Me Programs Inc.*, 36 U.S.P.Q.2d 1840 (T.T.A.B. 1995); *Zirco Corp. v. American Tel. & Tel. Co.*, 21 U.S.P.Q.2d 1542 (T.T.A.B.1992) . . . .

The ITU provisions permit the holder of an ITU application to use the mark in commerce, obtain registration, and thereby secure priority retroactive to the date of the filing of the ITU application. Of course, this right or privilege is not indefinite; it endures only for the time allotted by the statute. But as long as an ITU applicant's privilege has not expired, a court may not enjoin it from making the use necessary for registration on the grounds that another party has used the mark subsequent to the filing of the ITU application. To permit such an injunction would eviscerate the ITU provisions and defeat their very purpose.

This is not to say that a holder of a "live" ITU application may never be enjoined from using its mark. If another party can demonstrate that it used the mark before the holder filed its ITU application or that the filing was for some reason invalid, then it may be entitled to an injunction. WarnerVision says that it had made analogous use of the REAL WHEELS mark before TLV filed its ITU application and also that the assignment to Empire of TLV's ITU application was invalid. But the district court did not pass on these contentions, and we will not consider them in the first instance.

We vacate that portion of the district court's orders that grants WarnerVision preliminary injunctive relief and remand to the district court for further proceedings not inconsistent with this opinion.

* * *

Notes on Priority

1. Pre-Sale Use

Traditionally, rights have been established via affixation of the mark to a product and bona fide sales. It is possible, however, through advertising and promotion, to associate a particular mark with a particular product in the mind of the public *before* any actual sale takes place. During the gap between that created association and any actual sale, another company may enter the market with the same product bearing the same trademark, intentionally or unintentionally taking advantage of the promotional efforts of the first advertiser. Which company should have ownership rights to the trademark? The Ninth and First Circuits have favored the first adopter and *advertiser*, the one who first created the association. ". . . [U]se in a way sufficiently public to identify or distinguish the marked goods in an appropriate segment of the public mind as those of the adopter of the mark, is competent to establish ownership, even without evidence of actual sales." *New West Corp. v. NYM Co. of Cal., Inc.*, 595 F.2d 1194, 1200 (9th Cir. 1979) (quoting *New England Duplicating Co. v. Mendes*, 190 F.2d 415, 418 (1st Cir. 1951)), cited in *Walt Disney v. Kusan Inc.*, 204 U.S.P.Q. 284, 287 (C.D. Cal. 1979). How, if at all, would the outcome be affected by evidence that media advertising may make a greater impression on buyers than symbols physically imprinted on the product?

E-mail correspondence to a few potential customers prior to actual sales may be insufficient to constitute use in commerce under this test, but "trademark rights can vest even before any goods or services are actually sold if 'the totality of [one's] prior actions, taken together, [can] establish a right to use the trademark.'" *Brookfield Communications, Inc. v. West Coast Entertainment Corp.*, 174 F.3d 1036 (9th Cir. 1999), citing *New West*, 595 F.2d at 1200. To similar effect is *Planetary Motion, Inc. v. Techsplosion, Inc.*, 261 F.3d 1188 (11th Cir. 2001), in which the plaintiff's widespread, free distribution of its COOLMAIL e-mail software over the Internet was sufficient to establish trademark rights under the "totality of circumstances" test. *See also Chance v. Pac-Tel Teletrac, Inc.*, 242 F.3d 1151, 1159 (9th Cir. 2001) (holding the totality of circumstances test "must be employed to determine whether a service mark has been adequately used in commerce so as to gain the protection of the Lanham Act").

Prior use of a mark to promote a product in advertising or catalogues, although insufficient to fulfill the requirements of first use in commerce for registration, may prevent a subsequent user from obtaining a federal registration. *See, e.g., Sears, Roebuck & Co. v. Mannington Mills, Inc.*, 38 U.S.P.Q. 261 (T.T.A.B. 1963), in which Sears' prior use of VINYL-THRIFT for floor coverings in catalogs and newspaper advertisements was held to constitute "use at least analogous to trademark use serving to indicate origin thereof in Sears" and preclude registration of THRIFT-VINYL for floor coverings. Section 2(d) of the Lanham Act bars federal registration of any mark which is confusingly similar to a mark or trade name previously used by another. 15

U.S.C. § 1052(d). *See Missouri Silver Pages Directory v. Southwestern Bell Media*, 6 U.S.P.Q.2d 1028 (T.T.A.B. 1988) (solicitation of "listees" for directory might constitute sufficient use). Is this result consistent with the general purposes of the creation and protection of trademark rights? *Cf. Hart v. New York Yankees Partnership*, 184 Fed. Appx. 972 (Fed. Cir. 2006) (affirming refusal to register BABY BOMBERS for clothing and athletic wear where the Yankees for many years had referred to their minor league baseball affiliate by that term in promotional materials and the media for many years had referred to both the Yankees' major and minor league teams by that term, in addition to the Yankees being known as the "Bronx Bombers" for seventy years).

The Federal Circuit has determined that priority cannot be established through such analogous use unless the "activities claimed to constitute analogous use . . . have substantial impact on the purchasing public." *T.A.B. Systems v. PacTel Teletrac*, 77 F.3d 1372, 1375 (Fed. Cir. 1996). In *T.A.B. Systems* it held that opposer failed to establish priority through analogous use because opposer did not prove that its press releases, press kits, slide show presentations, and brochures announcing its TELETRAC automobile tracking service had a substantial impact on the relevant market; it had failed to present any evidence on the scope of dissemination or the size of the relevant market. *See id.* at 1375–76. Such use must be "of sufficient clarity and repetition to create the required identification [and] must have reached a substantial portion of the public that might be expected to purchase the service." *Id.* at 1377. Accordingly, the Federal Circuit remanded for factual findings on the consumer impact of opposer's marketing efforts.

Upon remand of the Federal Circuit's *T.A.B. Systems* decision, T.A.B. moved to suspend that Patent and Trademark Office proceeding and proceeded with an action in federal district court. After consideration of the fuller evidentiary record in that proceeding, the Ninth Circuit affirmed summary judgment in favor of Pac-Tel. *Chance d/b/a T.A.B. Systems v. Pac-Tel Teletrac, Inc.*, 242 F.3d 1151 (9th Cir. 2001). T.A.B.'s mailing of 35,000 postcards which generated 128 responses to its 800 number and no sales was insufficient to establish rights under a "totality of circumstances" test, while in contrast Pac-Tel's various activities *were* sufficient to establish prior rights. Pac-Tel's activities included trade name use, a public relations campaign using the mark to introduce its new services, interviews with major newspapers that resulted in a number of published stories mentioning the mark, and direct marketing to potential customers under the mark.

Similar standards have been applied in other circuits. In *Lucent Information Management, Inc. v. Lucent Technologies, Inc.*, 186 F.3d 311 (3[d] Cir. 1999), the court held that a party asserting priority over a federal registrant must show use prior to the application date sufficient "to pose the real likelihood of confusion among consumers in that area." Applying a "market penetration" test involving sales volume, growth trends, amount of advertising, and number of actual purchasers versus number of potential purchasers, the court determined that plaintiff's announcement letter, one sale and a few sales presentations were insufficient to establish priority in the mark LUCENT for telecommunications goods and services. *See also Warren K. Smith v. Ames Department Stores, Inc.*, 988 F. Supp. 827 (D.N.J. 1997), *aff'd per curiam*, 172 F.3d 860 (3[d] Cir. 1998) (sale of one thousand t-shirts and hats bearing the mark through sixteen stores in seven states constituted insufficient market penetration to establish priority).

Similarly, in *Circuit City Stores, Inc. v. Carmax, Inc.*, 165 F.3d 1047 (6th Cir. 1999), in which use of CARMAX for used car businesses was at issue, defendants' prior use of the mark in financial and sales statements, in listings under the mark in an association's automobile dealers' directory and its monthly reports, and dealer testimony that defendants were "known and recognized in the trade and automobile dealership community [under the mark]," were all insufficient. The court observed that "defendants repeatedly failed to use the CarMax mark in basic commercial contexts such as their telephone listings, store signs, newspaper ads and other customer information," and that there was no evidence of public awareness of the mark's association with defendant's business. The court distinguished a previous Sixth Circuit decision on those grounds. *Allard Enterprises, Inc. vs. Advanced Programming Resources, Inc.*, 146 F.3d 350 (6th Cir 1998) (use of the mark for employment services "on at least one fax, on at least one resume, and in numerous [oral] solicitations" before plaintiff's application date was sufficient under the circumstances to establish priority). In *Johnny Blastoff, Inc. v. Los Angeles Rams Football Co.*, 188 F.3d 427 (7th Cir. 1999), the Court affirmed summary judgment that the defendant owner of an NFL football team was the prior user and owner of rights in team name "St. Louis Rams," primarily based on extensive publicity surrounding announcement of the change to that name from "Los Angeles Rams," and affirmed an injunction against plaintiff (and counterclaim-defendant) who had filed a state trademark application for that name for a fictional, cartoon sports team shortly after the announcement, and subsequently had filed two federal intent-to-use applications. *Compare Silberstein v. John Does 1-10*, 82 U.S.P.Q. 2d 1958 (2d Cir. 2007), in which plaintiff unsuccessfully asserted priority in "Sqrat" for a cartoon character; the district court "properly found that, despite Silberstein's promotion of Sqrat, she never actually sold Sqrat products as a course of business."

Prior to the 1988 amendments to the Lanham Act, corporations sometimes expended months or years and substantial money in developing a new product, only to discover that another company had begun to use their intended trademark. *Ginseng-Up Corporation v. American Ginseng Co., Inc.*, 215 U.S.P.Q. 471 (S.D. N.Y. 1981) ("a gap between the initial foray into the market and the resumption of sales of the product has been recognized as a fact of life in marketing"). To avoid such problems, some companies relied upon elaborate and expensive "token-use" programs. These programs commonly involved the special printing of a few labels bearing the proposed trademark, which were then affixed to a prototype of the product or substituted as labels for similar products and sent to cooperating retailers for sale to the public. Some token-use programs involved dozens of marks with periodic shipments to cooperating retailers in every state. Such programs resulted in considerable litigation, and strong doubt was cast on their validity. The disjunction between the federal trademark registration system and the commercial realities of developing a product for the market, which caused many applicants to resort to such questionable token use in an effort to establish rights, provided much of the impetus for the 1988 revision of the Lanham Act which included intent-to-use registration provisions. For some of the historical debate which led up to that change, see Pattishall, *The Use Rationale and the Trademark Registration Treaty*, 61 A.B.A. J. 83, 84 (1975). For further discussion of the intent–to–use federal registration system, see Chapter 3, and Smith, *Intent-To-Use Practice* (1992 ed.).

An intent-to-use application which has not matured to registration does not confer upon the applicant any offensive right to an injunction against others' use of the mark. *Cf. Zazu Designs v. L'Oreal, S.A.*, 979 F.2d 499, 504 (7th Cir. 1992) (noting, in dicta, that "[e]ven under the [intent-to-use provisions] . . . an unregistered *plan* to use a mark creates no rights"). However, the court in *Warnervision Entertainment Inc. v. Empire of Carolina, Inc.*, *supra*, determined that an ITU applicant can use an application date defensively in a priority contest to establish superior, albeit contingent, rights. *See also Humetrix, Inc. v. Gemplus, S.C.A.*, 268 F.3d 910 (9th Cir. 2001) (in breach of contract case, affirming that plaintiff owned the trademark rights based on the earlier filing date for its ITU application); *Larami Corp. v. Talk to Me Programs Inc.*, 36 U.S.P.Q.2d 1840, 1845 (T.T.A.B. 1995) (allowing intent-to-use applicant to make defensive use of an ITU application date to establish priority in an opposition proceeding).

When a trademark is formally abandoned, a race to acquire rights to it may develop between competitors. In *Manhattan Industries, Inc. v. Sweater Bee* by Banff, 627 F.2d 628 (2d Cir. 1980), the court elected not to follow the priority of use principle in resolving such a contest. Using a "balancing of equities" test instead, the court found that significant shipments and investment by the latecomer weighed evenly as against the first user's priority in time, and that in the interests of equity both parties should be allowed to use the mark. The case was remanded to the district court for the fashioning of an order which would sufficiently distinguish the labels of the parties. Are any problems created by such an approach? In a subsequent decision, the defendant was held in contempt for failing to use the mark in the manner ordered, *Manhattan Industries, Inc. v. Sweater Bee by Banff, Ltd.*, 885 F.2d 1 (2ᵈ Cir. 1989). *Compare California Cedar Products v. Pine Mountain Corp.* 724 F.2d 827 (9ᵗʰ Cir. 1984), in which the court awarded rights to one company based on a strict application of first use principles, despite three parties commencing use of a formally abandoned mark within days of each other.

2. Tacking

"Tacking on" to prior use of a different mark to establish priority normally requires that the prior mark create the same commercial impression as the later– used mark. The issue is whether consumer goodwill survives alterations when a company decides to change its trademark. If the change is substantial, courts may hold that there is no continued consumer association of the "new" mark with the company's goods or services. In *Data Concepts, Inc. vs. Digital Consulting, Inc.*, 150 F.3d 620 (6ᵗʰ Cir. 1998), Data originally owned the domain name "DCI.com" and sued Digital and Network Solutions, Inc. (NSI), the registrar of domain names, to prevent NSI from reassigning the "DCI.com" domain name to Digital, owner of the federally registered trademark DCI for computer consulting and software development. Digital counterclaimed for trademark infringement, unfair competition, and dilution. The district court had summarily held that Digital had superior rights in its registered mark for consulting services and that Data was infringing those rights.

On appeal, Data argued it was the prior user based on a "tacking" theory. It cited its prior use of the lowercase letters "d," "c," and "i" as a stylized unregistered mark five years prior to Digital's registration of DCI and before Data adopted the "DCI.com" domain name. The Sixth Circuit determined that Data's previous use of the stylized letters "dci" did not create the "same continuing commercial impression" as its later use of "DCI.com," and, therefore, could not be "tacked" on to establish prior use. Data's two uses of "dci" did not look alike and, therefore, were not legal equivalents for purposes of establishing a prior use date. Concluding, however, that evidence of third party use and other flaws in the lower court's analysis created genuine factual disputes as to likelihood of confusion, it reversed the district court's grant of summary judgment and remanded.

Prior use of a mark may establish prior rights in an abbreviation of that mark. In *Forum Corp. of North America v. Forum, Ltd.*, 903 F.2d 434 (7ᵗʰ Cir. 1990), plaintiff had superior rights in the abbreviation FORUM for business training program services based on its past use of THE FORUM CORPORATION OF NORTH AMERICA and THE FORUM CORPORATION, even though defendant alleged that it was the first to use FORUM as a mark for similar services. *Compare First Bank v. First Bank Sys.*, 84 F.3d 1040 (8ᵗʰ Cir. 1996) (allowing defendant to use its federally registered FIRST BANK in region where plaintiff alleged prior common law rights in FIRST NATIONAL BANK because plaintiff had not demonstrated secondary meaning in FIRST BANK prior to defendant's federal registration).

Should the right of the prior user of a mark be foreclosed by bad faith adoption and use? What factors should be considered in determining bad faith on the part of the prior user? See the discussion on Intent in Chapter 5.

Note that only lawful use gives rise to protectable rights. *See, e.g., CreAgri, Inc. v. USANA Health Sciences, Inc.*, 474 F.3d 625 (9ᵗʰ Cir. 2007) (sales of falsely labeled dietary supplement did not establish priority).

3. Use in Foreign Country

Prior use in a foreign country, even if well known, may not establish prior rights in the United States. In *Person's Co. v. Christman*, 9 U.S.P.Q.2d 1477 (T.T.A.B. 1988), *aff'd*, 900 F.2d 1565 (Fed. Cir. 1990), a cancellation action brought by a Japanese company, the registrant had become aware during a trip to Japan of the cancellation petitioner's use there of the mark PERSON'S for clothing. Subsequently, the registrant began using the same mark in the United States for clothing. The TTAB held, however, that the petitioner's foreign use did not have an "effect on U.S. commerce." Therefore, the registrant was held to have superior rights in the U.S., and the petition was dismissed. *Compare Buti v. Perosa S.R.L.*, 139 F.3d 98 (2d Cir. 1998), in which the informal, domestic promotion of a foreign restaurant was insufficient "use in commerce" to establish trademark rights. The defendant *Perosa* had opened a Fashion Café in Milan, Italy in 1987, registered the FASHION CAFÉ trademark in Italy in 1988, and subsequently informally distributed promotional merchandise for the Italian restaurant to members of the fashion industry in the United States. In May 1993, plaintiff Buti opened a Fashion Café in Miami Beach, Florida and another in April 1995, in New York City. In 1994, upon learning of Buti's use of the name, Perosa attempted to obtain a federal registration for FASHION CAFÉ and sent a cease and desist letter to Buti, who responded by filing a declaratory judgment action. In affirming the holding for Buti, the Second Circuit held that Perosa's informal promotion in the U.S. of the Milan Fashion Café was insufficient "use in commerce" to establish rights here and justify barring Buti's use.

In *Int'l Bancorp, LLC v. Societe Des Bains De Mer*, 329 F.3d 359 (4th Cir. 2003), the court affirmed summary judgment that the declaratory judgment plaintiffs had infringed a foreign corporation's trademark rights by plaintiffs' registration and use of forty-three domain names, even though the foreign company's services under the mark were only rendered abroad. The foreign company, SBM, had operated a casino under the trademark "Casino de Monte Carlo" in Monte Carlo, Monaco since 1863. The mark was registered in Monaco, but not in the U.S. Plaintiffs operated on-line gambling websites under the infringing domain names, which all incorporated some portion of SBM's mark. The critical question was whether SBM had "used its mark in commerce" so as to be entitled to relief. SBM had a New York office that promoted its various resorts, but "[t]he Lanham Act and the Supreme Court . . . make clear that a mark's protection may not be based on mere advertising." The court concluded, however (329 F.3d at 366):

> while SBM's promotions within the United States do not on their own constitute a use in commerce of the 'Casino de Monte Carlo' mark, the mark is nonetheless used in commerce because United States citizens purchase casino services sold by a subject of a foreign nation, which purchases constitute trade with a foreign nation that Congress may regulate under the Commerce Clause. And SBM's promotions "use [] or display[] [the mark] in the sale or advertising of [these] services . . . rendered in commerce."

In support, the Fourth Circuit quoted the Supreme Court from the nineteenth century case, *Gibbons v. Ogden*, 22 U.S. 1, 193-94 (1824) (C.J. Marshall): "It has, we believe, been universally admitted, that [the foreign commerce clause] comprehends every species of commercial intercourse between the United States and foreign nations. No sort of trade can be carried on between this country and any other, to which this power does not extend." The Court distinguished *Buti v. Perosa, S.R.L.*, 139 F.3d 98 (2th Cir. 1998) (discussed above), because the plaintiff there conceded that "the food and drink services [it sells] form no part of the trade between Italy and the United States", and also conceded that plaintiff undertook no "formal advertising or public relations campaign [aimed at U.S. citizens]." Similarly, it distinguished *Person's Co. Ltd. v. Christman*, 900 F.2d 1565 (Fed. Cir. 1990), because the Japanese manufacturer in that case "had never used or displayed its mark to advertise or sell its products in the United States."

Here, SBM had provided proof of substantial advertising expenditures and significant sales success within the U.S., as well as "substantial unsolicited media coverage of the casino; frequent attempts by others to plagiarize the mark; and a long history of continuous, if not exclusive use of the mark." Furthermore, "SBM met its burden of proving secondary meaning [in the U.S.] because it had established that the plaintiff companies directly and intentionally copied the 'Casino de Monte Carlo' mark." "This case presents a record replete with demonstrations of SBM's singularly impressive commitment to building brand identity in the United States." Because confusion was likely, the lower court's order transferring the forty–three domain names to SBM was affirmed.

In contrast, in *General Healthcare Ltd. v. Qashat*, 364 F.3d 332 (1st Cir. 2004), defendant's "Kent Creme Bleach" hair-lightening product was made in the U.S., shipped to the U.K., and then sold in the Middle East. Because the element of public use of the mark in the U.S. was lacking, defendant did not establish rights in this country.

See also Grupo Gigante S.A. de C.V. v. Dallo Co., Inc., 391 F.3d 1088 (9th Cir. 2004), in which the plaintiff had used the mark GIGANTE for grocery stores in Mexico, and contested defendant's subsequent use of that mark for grocery stores in San Diego. The Ninth Circuit held that there is a famous marks exception to the territoriality principle. That principle essentially provides that trademark rights exist independently in different countries. Such a principle, however, ignores that "commerce crosses borders." "Trademark is, at its core, about protecting against consumer confusion and fraud. There can be no justification for using trademark law to fool immigrants into thinking that they are buying from the store they liked back home." *Id.* at 1095.

Plaintiff first needed to show secondary meaning in the U.S., i.e., "by a preponderance of the evidence that a *substantial* percentage of consumers in the relevant American market is familiar with the foreign mark. The relevant American market is the geographic area where the defendant uses the alleged infringing mark." *Id.* at 1098 (emphasis in the original). The Ninth Circuit vacated and remanded for application of this test. A concurring opinion would have required a showing of more than 50 percent consumer recognition in the relevant area to show that Grupo Gigante's mark was famous, instead of the 20 to 22 percent recognition that the rest of the panel accepted.

The Ninth Circuit nonetheless continues to endorse the territoriality principle, as it stated in *Am. Circuit Breaker Corp. v. Or. Breakers, Inc.*, 406 F.3d 577 (9th Cir. 2005). There, American Circuit Breaker Corp. ("ACBC") owned the U.S. trademark STAB-LOK for circuit breakers, and contracted with a Canadian manufacturer that owned the same trademark for the same goods in Canada. The Canadian company manufactured identical circuit breakers (except for their color) for both markets, and defendant Oregon Breakers imported the circuit breakers manufactured under the Canadian trademark into the U.S. for sale, in competition with ACBC's goods. ACBC sued Oregon Breakers for federal trademark infringement. While denying summary judgment for ACBC because of fact issues, the Ninth Circuit noted that, under the territoriality principle, a trademark is considered to be a separate legal entity in each country and is afforded the specific protections offered by that country. Although the territoriality principle is increasingly under fire due to globalization and the difficulty of geographically locating information products, the court concluded that the leading territoriality case, *A. Bourjois & Co. v. Katzel*, 260 U.S. 689 (1923), is still good law. *See also* the discussion on gray market goods in Chapter 7.

Compare ITC Ltd. v. Punchgini, Inc., 482 F.3d 135 (2th Cir. 2007), in which plaintiffs ITC asserted U.S. rights in BUKHARA for restaurants based in large part on the "measure of international renown" the mark had acquired from use outside the United States. While ITC once had operated BUKHARA restaurants in New York and Chicago, any U.S. rights had been abandoned by lengthy non-use (see Chapter 4).

Former employees of ITC's BUKHARA restaurants in New Delhi, India had opened an Indian restaurant in New York named BUKHARA GRILL that "mimic[ked] the ITC Bukhara logos, décor, staff uniforms, wood-slab menus, and red-checkered customers' bibs". *Punchgini*, 482 F.3d at 144. ITC nonetheless was unsuccessful in asserting trademark infringement and related claims because, "absent some use of its mark in the United States, a foreign mark holder generally may not assert priority rights under federal law, even if a United States competitor has knowingly appropriated that mark for his own use." *Id* at 156.

The Second Circuit disagreed with *Grupo Gigante*, above, to the extent the Ninth Circuit appeared to recognize a U.S. "famous marks doctrine" without Congressional endorsement. While therefore denying relief under federal law, the Second Circuit nonetheless certified the question under New York law to the New York Court of Appeals as follows: 1) Does New York common law permit the owner of a famous mark or trade dress to assert property rights therein by virtue of the owner's prior use of the mark or dress in a foreign country? 2) If so, how famous must a foreign mark be to permit a foreign mark owner to bring a claim for unfair competition?

The Court of Appeals' answer to the first question was a qualified yes, based on "our time-honored misappropriation theory, which prohibits a defendant from using a plaintiff's property right or commercial advantage. . . to compete unfairly against the plaintiff in New York." It emphasized that it was *not* recognizing a famous marks doctrine; instead, "we simply reaffirm that when a business, through renown in New York, possesses goodwill. . . [that] goodwill is protected from misappropriation under New York unfair competition law. This is so whether the business is domestic or foreign." As to the second question, "at a minimum, consumers of the goods or services provided by defendant in New York must primarily associate the mark with the foreign plaintiff." Defendant's bad intent, consumer surveys and any overlap in the parties' customers were among the relevant evidence in determining that association.

In *Empresa Cubana Del Tabaco v. Culbro Corp.*, 399 F.3d 462 (2th Cir. 2005), plaintiff Cubatobaco for many years had owned the mark COHIBA in Cuba but had never sold cigars in the United States because such sales were embargoed. Defendant General Cigar ("General") sold cigars under the mark in the U.S. Cubatabaco claimed that it owned the COHIBA mark here because General abandoned its rights in 1987 and that, by the time General began re-using the mark, COHIBA was famous in the U.S. as a Cubatabaco mark. The district court enjoined General from further use of the COHIBA mark, but the Second Circuit reversed. The court held that, even if it were to apply the famous marks doctrine, Cubatabaco was barred by the embargo from acquiring rights in U.S. trademarks. While the court in that case acknowledged that foreign marks may be protected in the U.S. if they achieve sufficient fame here, in any conflict between the Paris Convention treaty and the embargo, the embargo prevails.

2.04　Distinctive and Descriptive Terms

Introduction

The cases in this section demonstrate the problems of maintaining rights in trademarks that are inherently nondistinctive, generally because they are descriptive in some way of the goods or services which they are supposed to identify as to source. Note the discussion in the opinions of secondary meaning and trademarks referred to as "narrow" or "weak."

"Narrow or weak" trademarks are those which, by virtue of their primary significance or connotation, the relevant public does not originally associate with any particular, albeit anonymous, source. Secondary meaning is the term applied to the source-indicating significance of a mark as contrasted with its *primary* or language significance. See discussion in Chapter 6. Thus, IVORY has acquired a *secondary*

secondary
meaning
=
distinctive

meaning signifying a particular manufacturer's soap, whereas its *primary* meaning is the substance of an elephant's tusk. The Lanham Trademark Act substituted the word "distinctive" for the common-law phrase "secondary meaning" (15 U.S.C. § 1052(f)) as being more readily understandable, but the term of art "secondary meaning" retains its legal vitality. A mark which would not have been registrable under the 1905 Trademark Act because it was essentially descriptive, laudatory, geographically descriptive, or primarily merely a surname (15 U.S.C. § 85) became registrable under the present Act upon a showing that it had acquired distinctiveness through use as a trademark (15 U.S.C. § 1052(f)), i.e., had become distinctive of the source of the goods or services to which it was applied. See Chapter 3.

No Phils: how to determine
"secondary meaning"?

UNION CARBIDE CORP. v. EVER-READY, INC.
United States Court of Appeals, Seventh Circuit
531 F.2d 366 (1976)

WILBUR F. PELL, JR., CIRCUIT JUDGE

[After an initial treatment of the issue of incontestability (see discussion in Chapter 3,), the Court analyzed the source-indicating significance of plaintiff's trademark EVEREADY for electrical products, the district court having declared the trademark invalid.]

* * *

A mark is invalid if it is merely descriptive of the ingredients, qualities, or characteristics of an article of trade, *Warner & Co. v. Lilly & Co.*, 265 U.S. 526, 528 (1924). Suggestive marks, however, have long been distinguished from descriptive ones. *Watkins Products, Inc. v. Sunway Fruit Products Inc.*, 311 F.2d 496 (7th Cir. 1962), *cert. denied*, 373 U.S. 904 (1963); *Independent Nail & Packing Co., Inc. v. Stronghold Screw Products, Inc.*, 205 F.2d 921 (7th Cir. 1953), *cert. denied*, 346 U.S. 886; Restatement of the Law of Torts § 721 Comment(a) (1938). They may be thought of as a middle ground between arbitrary or fanciful names and descriptive names. *E.g., General Shoe Corporation v. Rosen*, 111 F.2d 95, 98 (4th Cir. 1940). The line between descriptive and suggestive marks is scarcely "pikestaff plain." Various tests have been used by courts to make the distinction. The district court, citing *General Shoe Corporation v. Rosen, supra; WG. Reardon Laboratories, Inc. v. B & B Exterminators*, 71 F.2d 515 (4th Cir. 1934); and *Stewart Paint Manufacturing Co. v. United Hardware Distributing Co.*, 253 F.2d 568 (8th Cir. 1958), stated:

> Suggestive terms "suggest," but do not describe the qualities of a particular product. The distinction threatens to be one without a difference. Essentially, however, the common and ordinary meaning of the term to the public and the incongruous use of it as it relates to the product determine whether a term is suggestive.

392 F. Supp. at 286. Another test which has been used and which was footnoted by the district court is whether competitors would be likely to need the terms used in the trademark in describing their products. *See* McCarthy, *supra*, § 11:21 at 391-92 (1973); Restatement of the Law of Torts § 721 Comment (a) (1938).

This court has not adopted a particular test for distinguishing between suggestive and descriptive marks. We disagree with the district court that it is a distinction without a difference, although it is often a difficult distinction to draw and is, undoubtedly, often made on an intuitive basis rather than as the result of a logical analysis susceptible of articulation. This only emphasizes the need to give due respect to the determination of the patent office if the distinction is to be drawn in a consistent manner. Perhaps the best statement of the distinction appears in A. Seidel, S. Dalroff, and E. Gonda, *Trademark Law and Practice* § 4.06 at 77 (1963):

> Generally speaking, if the mark imparts information directly, it is descrip-

tive. If it stands for an idea which requires some operation of the imagination to connect it with the goods, it is suggestive.

The information imparted may concern a characteristic, quality, or ingredient of the product. . . . Incongruity is not essential for a mark to be suggestive, rather than descriptive; but incongruity is a strong indication of non-descriptiveness, and it is probably the unusual case where a mark will be suggestive but not descriptive where there is no incongruity. The more imagination that is required to associate a mark with a product the less likely the words used will be needed by competitors to describe their products.

In analyzing Carbide's mark, the district court noted the dictionary definitions of "ever" and "ready" and concluded: "Thus, the combination of 'ever' and 'ready' means constantly prepared or available for service." Dissecting marks often leads to error. Words which could not individually become a trademark may become one when taken together. . . .

. . . The mark EVEREADY . . . suggests the quality of long life, but no one in our society would be deceived into thinking that this type of battery would never wear out or that its shelf life was infinite. There is less incongruity with regard to flashlight bodies. Nevertheless, we need not decide whether the mark's reference is too direct for the mark to be considered nondescriptive or whether the district court's holding to that effect should be overruled because of what we consider overwhelming evidence in the record of secondary meaning.

Secondary meaning need only be shown if a mark sought to be registered or sustained is found to be or is conceded to be descriptive.

* * *

. . . To establish secondary meaning it is not necessary for the public to be aware of the name of the manufacturer from which a product emanates. It is sufficient if the public is aware that the product comes from a single, though anonymous, source. . . .

We agree with the district court's summary of the factors relevant on the issue of secondary meaning: "The amount and manner of advertising, volume of sales, the length and manner of use, direct consumer testimony and consumer surveys." The district court also summarized the evidence in this case relating these factors to Carbide:

> The evidence shows that Carbide and its predecessors have distributed and sold electrical products under the EVEREADY mark since 1909; that in 1915 10 million dry cell batteries marked EVEREADY alone were sold with an advertising cost of approximately $225,000; that Carbide's sales of electrical products under the EVEREADY mark from 1963 to 1973 exceeded $100,000,000 each year; that during the 1963-1973 period Carbide advertised in magazines and trade journals, on radio and television and through point of sale displays and that the cost of the 1963-67 advertising was $50,000,000.

392 F. Supp. at 288.

Advertising expenditures, of course, are a measure of the input by which a company attempts to establish a secondary meaning. In issue is the success of this effort. The chief inquiry is directed toward purchasers' attitudes toward a mark. *Carter-Wallace Inc. v. Procter & Gamble Co.*, 434 F.2d 794, 802 (9th Cir. 1970). The public's attitude is more directly indicated by remarks of counsel for Ever-Ready. In his opening statement he said, "All right. We don't sell batteries, and that's what everybody thinks of when you mention the name EVEREADY." Later during the trial he made a similar remark.

Two surveys were taken in anticipation of this litigation. . . . In each of the surveys an insignificant number of persons named Carbide as the maker of defendants' products, but in excess of 50% of those interviewed associated Carbide products, such as batteries and flashlights, with defendants' mark. The only conclusion that can be drawn from these results is that an extremely significant portion of the population associates Carbide's products with a single anonymous source. The survey questions were not designed to establish secondary meaning: but once the issue of descriptiveness was improperly considered, the survey results could not be ignored.

Additionally, we find it difficult to believe that anyone living in our society, which has daily familiarity with hundreds of battery-operated products, can be other than thoroughly acquainted with the EVEREADY mark. While perhaps not many know that Carbide is the manufacturer of EVEREADY products, few would have any doubt that the term was being utilized other than to indicate the single, though anonymous, source. A court should not play the ostrich with regard to such general public knowledge.

We hold that the district court's determination that there was inadequate evidence to find that EVEREADY had acquired a secondary meaning is clearly erroneous.

[The Court went on to hold that the district court was also clearly erroneous in its finding of no likelihood of confusion, and directed the lower court to enter an appropriate injunction against defendants should the defendants fail to sustain their antitrust affirmative defenses upon remand.]

INVESTACORP, INC. v. ARABIAN INVESTMENT BANKING CORPORATION (INVESTCORP) E.C.

United States Court of Appeals, Eleventh Circuit
931 F.2d 1519 (1991)

EDWARD S. SMITH, SENIOR CIRCUIT JUDGE

*   *   *

. . . Appellant, Investacorp, is a Florida corporation whose primary business is providing financial services as a broker/dealer and as a financial intermediary between individuals, corporations and institutions seeking investment opportunities. There are two appellees in this case: Investcorp E.C., the parent corporation, and its wholly owned subsidiary, Investcorp International. Investcorp E.C. is an investment bank headquartered in Bahrain which began doing business in the United States under that name in 1983. Investcorp International was created by Investcorp E.C. in November of 1986 to continue conducting the business of its parent in the United States. Hereinafter, the two co-appellees will be referred to as "Investcorp."

. . . Investacorp sued Investcorp on several counts of service mark infringement and unfair competition. The district court granted summary judgment in favor of defendant on all counts of the complaint, because it determined that plaintiff does not have a proprietary interest in the mark "Investacorp" . . . .

*   *   *

In order for defendant to infringe on plaintiff's mark, plaintiff must have a protectable property interest in the mark "Investacorp". Ordinarily, such an interest is derived when a business uses a mark to represent its services. Each time a business uses a mark, it enhances the customer recognition of the mark and its association with the service, thereby inuring to the business greater rights in the mark. However a business does not automatically obtain rights in a mark by using it. A business will obtain rights in a mark upon first use only if the mark is "inherently distinctive." If the mark is not inherently distinctive, a business may obtain rights in the mark when it attains a secondary meaning . . . .

*   *   *

Investacorp is a corporation in the business of advertising their customers in corporate investment opportunities. Pursuant to a customer's desires, Investacorp sells stocks, bonds and other securities which are often initially issued by corporations. The two key formatives in the term "Investacorp" are "invest" and "corp." "Invest" is the verb "to commit (money) in order to earn a financial return," and "corp" is the widespread abbreviation for a corporation. It is beyond doubt that the term "Investacorp" bears a relationship to the type of services being offered by plaintiff. Hence, it cannot be an arbitrary or fanciful term. The only two categories remaining that are eligible for service mark protection are the descriptive and suggestive categories. Thus, we must determine whether the mark is descriptive or suggestive.

To determine whether a term is descriptive, third party usage by competitors is probative. We reject appellant's argument that third party usage is not relevant to the distinctiveness inquiry because there is a plethora of authority embracing the relevancy of third party usage.

The likelihood of prospective use by competitors is high. Both of the two formatives "invest" and "corp" pervade the lexicon of business terminology. Because the two formatives are indispensable to the investment services industry, we agree that it is very likely that competitors will need to use these terms.

Moreover, the popularity of actual use of the two key formatives also indicates that the mark is descriptive. Over eighty competing broker-dealers use the word "invest" in their mark, and there are a handful of businesses who use some combination of the formatives "invest" and "corp" in their mark. We find the popularity of use by competitors is extreme.

Also probative of the descriptiveness of a mark is the idea that is conveyed to the observer by the plain dictionary definition of the formatives comprising the mark. In this case, the two formatives combined in the term "Investacorp" literally convey to the observer that appellant is in the business of investing in corporations. Because the customer who observes the term can readily perceive the nature of plaintiff's services, without having to exercise his imagination, the term cannot be considered a suggestive term. The only remaining categorization that is eligible for protection is the descriptive category. Accordingly, "Investacorp" must be merely descriptive.

* * *

Because the term is not inherently distinctive, for appellant to have a protectable interest in the term "Investacorp," it must have attained secondary meaning before the date that appellee used the similar term "Investcorp" . . . .

* * *

Secondary meaning is the connection in the consumer's mind between the mark and the provider of the service. Plaintiff has the burden of sustaining a high degree of proof *burden* in establishing a secondary meaning for a descriptive term. This requisite high degree of proof must be considered by the court when ruling on a motion of summary judgment. Absent consumer survey evidence, as is the case here, four factors can be considered in determining whether a particular mark has acquired a secondary meaning:

> (1) [T]he length and manner of its use; (2) the nature and extent of advertising and promotion; (3) the efforts made by the plaintiff to promote a conscious connection in the public's mind between the name and the plaintiff's . . . business; and (4) the extent to which the public actually identifies the name with the plaintiff's [service].

Appellant began designating their services with the "Investacorp" mark in January of 1978. Thus, the length of appellant's use of the mark was five years prior to the appellee's use of their mark. However, there is nothing significant about the manner of appellant's use of the mark, other than appellant merely "displayed its service mark on nearly all of its transactional documents."

The nature and extent of appellant's advertisement and promotion and its achievement of a conscious connection in the public mind between the mark and the appellant's business during the relevant time period is far short of spectacular. During this period, appellant's advertising expenditures did not exceed one-hundred dollars per month. Although appellant emphasizes that they had expansive growth and showed a high ratio of sales dollars to advertising dollars during the relevant period, this fact does not indicate that appellant's bantam advertising campaigns made major inroads to the consumer psyche.

The evidence that the public actually identifies the mark with appellant's business is also lacking. Although instances of consumer confusion are probative of secondary meaning, the few isolated instances cited by appellant are not adequate to present a genuine issue of material fact. Consequently, we agree that the undisputed facts show that the mark "Investacorp" did not acquire secondary meaning before the end of the relevant time period.

. . . *Affirmed.*

MARILYN MIGLIN MODEL MAKEUP, INC. v. JOVAN, INC.
United States District Court, Northern District of Illinois
224 U.S.P.Q. 178 (1984)

McGarr, District Judge

Plaintiff Marilyn Miglin Model Makeup, Inc. ("Miglin") brought an action against defendant Jovan, Inc. ("Jovan") for trademark infringement and false advertisement arising out of Jovan's use of the word "pheromone" in connection with one of its fragrance lines. In a memorandum opinion and order dated September 28, 1983, this court granted Jovan's motion for summary judgment as to all counts of the complaint. The action is currently before the court on Jovan's motion for summary judgment on its counterclaim which seeks a declaratory judgment that Miglin does not have any trademark rights in the word "pheromone" and cancellation of Miglin's federal trademark registration. . . .

*   *   *

Jovan does not allege that the term "pheromone" is generic, which would preclude trademark registration regardless of secondary meaning; while this court has found "pheromone" to be generic for "an organic substance used for communication between individuals of the same species," *see* Mem. Op. & Order, Sept. 28, 1983, at 3, it cannot be seriously claimed to be generic for perfume, as it is used by Miglin. Rather, Jovan claims that if Miglin's product is a pheromone or contains a pheromone, the mark "Pheromone" is merely descriptive; if it is not a pheromone or does not contain a pheromone, the mark is deceptively misdescriptive.[2] In either event, proper trademark registration would be dependent on the acquisition of secondary meaning.

The court will accept as true Miglin's own statements that, in effect, it does not know or care whether "Pheromone" perfume contains pheromones, and thus will assume that "Pheromone" perfume does not contain pheromones and does not purport to be a pheromone itself. That assumption disposes of the argument that the mark is merely descriptive and moves the court on to a determination of whether the mark is deceptively misdescriptive.

---

[2] In its counterclaim, Jovan raises only the grounds of merely descriptive and deceptively misdescriptive, while in its memoranda, it also contends that Miglin's use of the mark is deceptive which, under 15 U.S.C. § 1052(a), would preclude trademark registration regardless of secondary meaning. "[D]eception is found when an essential and material element is misrepresented, is distinctly false, and is the very element upon which the customer reasonably relies in purchasing one product over another." *Gold Seal Co. v. Weeks,* 129 F. Supp. 928, 934, 105 U.S.P.Q. 407 (D.D.C. 1955), *aff'd per curiam sub nom. S.C. Johnson & Son v.* Gold Seal Co., 230 F.2d 832, 108 U.S.P.Q. 400 (D.C. Cir.), *cert. denied,* 352 U.S. 829 (1956). At the very least, a question of fact exists as to whether customers purchased Miglin's "Pheromone" perfume in reliance on a mistaken belief that it contains pheromones. For that reason, to the extent the court feels compelled to address a ground not raised in the counterclaim, the ground of deception is not susceptible at this time to summary judgment.

Unlike the category of deceptive marks, *see* note 2 *supra*, which deceive consumers into purchasing a product based on a misrepresentation of the product's ingredients, a deceptively misdescriptive mark is one in which customer confusion as to ingredients, rather than mistaken reliance, is at issue. A classic example of a deceptively misdescriptive mark is "Glass Wax" for a glass and metal cleaning product containing no wax. *See Gold Seal Co. v. Weeks*, 129 F. Supp. 928, 105 U.S.P.Q. 407 (D.D.C. 1955), *aff'd per curiam sub nom. S.C. Johnson & Son v. Gold Seal Co.*, 230 F.2d 832, 108 U.S.P.Q. 400 (D.C. Cir.), *cert. denied*, 352 U.S. 829 (1956). In *Gold Seal*, the district court rejected the contention that the mark was deceptive, finding that customers were satisfied with the product whether it contained wax or not. 129 F. Supp. at 934 & n.10, 105 U.S.P.Q. at 411 & n.10. Nevertheless, the court found it to be deceptively misdescriptive, stating, inter alia, "that customers might justifiably believe it does contain the element wax, whether or not it was significant to them in purchasing the product." *Id.* at 935, 105 U.S.P.Q. at 411–12 (footnote omitted).

The court is persuaded by that reasoning to find that the name "Pheromone" for a fragrance which does not purport to be a pheromone or to contain pheromones is deceptively misdescriptive, particularly in light of the fact that fragrance products, such as Jovan's "Andron," *do* exist and *do* purport to contain pheromones. In further support of this finding are instances of consumer and industry confusion, raised in the Miglin depositions, as to whether "Pheromone" perfume contains pheromones.

Miglin falls back on its contention that, were it not for Jovan's efforts to educate the public as to the scientific meaning of the term "pheromone," consumer confusion would not exist; consumers would know the word "pheromone" only as the source designation of Miglin's fragrance products. This argument merely begs the question. In this age when "sex sells," it was only a matter of time before a recently-coined term with sexual connotations, tailor-made for a product in the "romantic field" of fragrances, would make its way into the common vocabulary.

Having determined that Miglin's "Pheromone" mark for perfume is deceptively misdescriptive, the court must now address the question of secondary meaning, which, if determined to exist, would save Miglin's trademark registration from cancellation. "In other words, although the term's 'primary' meaning was [deceptively misdescriptive], if through use the public had come to identify the terms with plaintiff's product in particular, the [term] would have become a valid trademark." *Gimix, Inc. v. JS&A Group, Inc.*, 699 F.2d 901, 907, 217 U.S.P.Q. 677, 682–83 (7th Cir. 1983).

The ultimate issue regarding secondary meaning — what impact has the term had on the public consciousness? — can be determined by considering the following factors: the amount and manner of advertising, volume of sales, length and manner of use, direct consumer testimony and consumer surveys. *Union Carbide Corp. v. Ever-Ready, Inc.*, 531 F.2d 366, 380, 188 U.S.P.Q. 623, 635–36 (7th Cir.), *cert. denied*, 429 U.S. 830, 191 U.S.P.Q. 416 (1976). The owner of the challenged trademark bears "the burden of establishing a genuine issue of material fact as to whether its mark has attained secondary meaning in the mind of the public." *Gimix*, 699 F.2d at 908, 217 U.S.P.Q. at 683–84.

* * *

In the instant case, the most telling factor to be considered is the length of Miglin's use of the mark. Although the court can envision extraordinary circumstances under which a mark could obtain secondary meaning within a short period of time, nothing of that magnitude is evident in this case. The Seventh Circuit has placed considerable emphasis on length of use; in its recent decision in *Gimix, Inc. v. JS&A Group, Inc.*, 699 F.2d 901, 217 U.S.P.Q. 677 (7th Cir. 1983), the court stated:

> [T]he period of time involved here, from the introduction of plaintiff's product in 1975 until the introduction of [defendant's] similar product in 1980, is so brief as to cast serious doubt upon the very possibility of having established a strong

secondary meaning; by way of contrast, the Ever-Ready [sic] battery, for example, had been marketed under that name for over fifty years.

Id. at 907, 217 U.S.P.Q. at 682-83 (citing *Union Carbide Corp. v. Ever-Ready Inc.*, 531 F.2d 366, 380, 188 U.S.P.Q. 623, 635-36 (7th Cir.), *cert. denied*, 429 U.S. 830, 191 U.S.P.Q. 416 (1976)). In the instant case, even less time elapsed between Miglin's first use of the mark and Jovan's introduction of its "Andron" fragrance using the term "pheromone-based."

In light of the above discussion, Miglin has failed to establish a genuine issue of material fact as to whether its "Pheromone" mark has attained secondary meaning.

For the foregoing reasons, defendant-counterplaintiff Jovan's motion for summary judgment on its counterclaim is granted.

Notes on Distinctive and Descriptive Terms

1. Taxonomy of Trademarks

The court in *Big O Tire Dealers, Inc. v. The Goodyear Tire & Rubber Company*, 408 F. Supp. 1219 (D. Col. 1976), *aff'd*, 561 F.2d 1365 (10th Cir. 1977), gave the following explanatory jury instruction on the taxonomy of terms used as trademarks:

In trademark usage, words can be classified according to the degree of their distinctiveness. A "coined" word is an artificial word which has no language meaning except as a trademark.

EXXON is a coined word used by an oil company.

A fanciful word is like a coined word in that it is invented for the sole purpose of functioning as a trademark and it differs from the coined word only in that it may bear a relationship to another word or it may be an obsolete word.

FAB is a shortened version for fabulous and is a fanciful word used for detergent.

An "arbitrary" word is one which is in common linguistic use but when used with the goods in issue it neither suggests nor describes any ingredient, quality or characteristic of those goods.

OLD CROW for whiskey is an example of an arbitrary word.

A "suggestive" word is one which suggests what the product is without actually being descriptive of it.

STRONGHOLD for threaded nails is suggestive of their superior holding power.

A merely "descriptive" word is one which draws attention to the ingredients, quality or nature of the product.

TENDER VITTLES as applied to cat food is descriptive.

A "generic" word is one which is the language name for the product.

BUTTER is the language word for butter. There can be no trademark rights in a generic term. They remain in the public domain as a part of our language.

The right to protection of a trademark comes from its use to identify the product.

We speak of strong and weak marks in terms of the amount of use necessary to create protected rights. Words which are coined, fanciful or arbitrary are distinctive almost from their first use. Suggestive words are also protected as trademarks when used distinctively for particular products.

Words which are merely descriptive do not obtain protection solely from their use as a trademark. Such words must first acquire distinctiveness from the effect of the owner's efforts in the market place. This is what is called the development of secondary meaning; that is a merely descriptive term used as a trademark must have been so used that its primary significance in the minds of the consuming public is not the product itself but the identification of it with a single source. . . .

*   *   *

Another example of jury instructions can be found in *B&B Hardware, Inc. v. Hargis Industries, Inc.*, 252 F.3d 1010 (8th Cir. 2001) ("[e]xamples of a suggestive mark include Gleem for the name of a toothpaste and Roach Motel for the name of a pesticide"; affirming jury's verdict for defendant which found SEALTIGHT for self-sealing fasteners merely descriptive). *See also U.S. Search LLC v. U.S. Search.com, Inc.*, 300 F.3d 517 (4th Cir. 2002), in which the court stated "Coppertone, Orange Crush, and Playboy are good examples of suggestive marks because they conjure images of the associated products without directly describing [them] . . . Examples of merely descriptive marks include After Tan post-tanning lotion, 5 Minute Glue, and Yellow Pages phone directory." The court affirmed that plaintiff's use of "U.S. Search" for an executive recruiting and placement firm was at best descriptive, and that secondary meaning had not been shown.

2.   Distinguishing Suggestive and Descriptive Terms

Descriptive terms are protectable only upon a showing of secondary meaning. In contrast, no secondary meaning need be shown for a "suggestive" term as, in the particular use made of it, it is not perceived by the public according to its ordinary meaning, i.e. as simply describing the product in some way. Because secondary meaning need not be proved for suggestive marks and such marks are considered entitled to a broader scope of protection, that line of distinction is often the focus of much attention in trademark litigation. In many instances, however, the attempt to pigeonhole the term in issue and to determine the presence or absence of secondary meaning unnecessarily distracts from the basic test of likelihood of confusion. But see discussion of the *Taco Cabana* decision in Chapter 5.

Descriptive marks are those which describe to potential customers the characteristics, nature, qualities, or ingredients of goods or services. They have generally been denied trademark protection, in the absence of proven source-indicating significance (secondary meaning or distinctiveness), in the equitable belief that the number of such appropriate terms is limited and that all merchants should equally be allowed to describe (or praise) their own goods while competing for customers. A mark "may still be merely descriptive even if it only describes one quality or characteristic of the good." *In re Innovation Dev. Group, Inc.* ,126 Fed. Appx. 471 (Fed. Cir. 2005) (unpub.) (affirming refusal to register the mark TICK TAPE for a "hand tool for removing insects attached to human or animal hosts.") *See also In re Steelbuilding.com*, 415 F.3d 1293 (Fed. Cir. 2005) (STEELBUILDING.COM for "online retail services in the field of pre-engineered metal buildings and roofing systems" was descriptive and applicant failed to show requisite secondary meaning).

"Suggestive" marks are said to fall into a category between those that are merely descriptive and those that are fanciful and arbitrary. Thus, it is said that trademark protection may be afforded to suggestive terms which shed some light upon the qualities or characteristics of goods but which are not descriptive of such goods in that an effort of the imagination would be required to know their nature. *Playtex Prods v. Georgia-Pacific Corp.*, 390 F.3d 158 (2d Cir. 2004) ("WET ONES" for pre-moistened towellettes was suggestive because it could describe "a wide variety of products," not just this one); *Express Services Inc. v. Careers Express Staffing Services*, 176 F.3d 183 (3d Cir. 1999) (reversed and remanded where lower court erroneously placed EXPRESS for employment agency services in the non-existent category "generic descriptive"; the appellate court further observed that, to associate the mark with such services, consumers would need to make "an imaginative leap that may be large enough to transform 'express' from descriptive to. . . suggestive"); *Estee Lauder, Inc. v. Gap, Inc.*, 932 F. Supp. 595 (S.D.N.Y. 1996), *rev'd on other grounds*, 108 F.3d 1503 (2[d] Cir. 1997) ("100%" suggestive for skin care products labeled "100% TIME RELEASE MOISTURIZER"; "a mark that consists of a double or triple entendre, at least one meaning of which is suggestive, is protectable without proof of secondary meaning"); *Blendco, Inc. v. Conagra Foods, Inc.*, 132 Fed. Appx. 520 (5th Cir. 2005) (unpub.) (BETTER-N-BUTTER was suggestive, as it was not a dictionary term, and under the "imagination test," survey evidence showed that only about one-third of respondents thought that the term would denote a butter substitute. "Better" was not necessary to describe the products at issue, and only plaintiff and defendant had used "better than butter" for a nondairy butter-flavored oil). *Compare Frosty Treats, Inc. v. Sony Computer Entm't Am., Inc.*, 426 F.3d 1001 (8th Cir. 2005) (FROSTY TREATS descriptive for ice cream products sold from ice cream trucks); *Igloo Prods. Corp. v. Brantex, Inc.*, 202 F.3d 814 (5th Cir. 2000) ("Kool Pak" descriptive and lacking secondary meaning for portable insulated beverage coolers); *20th Century Wear, Inc. v. Sanmark-Stardust, Inc.*, 747 F.2d 81, 88 (2[d] Cir. 1984) (what might have taken a "step of the imagination" in 1973 or 1975 no longer did in more energy conservation conscious 1981 for "Cozy Warm ENERGY-SAVERS" women's pajamas). Does this "suggestive" mark test aid the objectivity of the courts or predictability in the law in this area? *See* Irani, *The Importance of Record Evidence to Categorize Marks as Generic, Descriptive or Suggestive*, 83 TRADEMARK REP. 571 (1993).

Is a better test one which inquires whether competitors need the term to describe their goods? *See Minnesota Mining & Mfg. Co. v. Johnson & Johnson*, 454 F.2d 1179, 1180 (C.C.P.A. 1972) ("[T]hey have been able to describe that product and advertise it without the use of the term coined by their competitor.") *Cf. Murphy v. Provident Mutual Life Insurance Company*, 923 F.2d 923, 927 (2d Cir. 1990), *cert. denied*, 502 U.S. 814 (1991) (advertising use of "hot" and thermometer graphic held descriptive; "If Ford Motor Company advertised its car as 'hot' and used a thermometer in its advertisements, would the thermometer be protected absent a showing of secondary meaning. We think not.") *Compare Star Indus. v. Bacardi & Co.*, 412 F.3d 373 (2d Cir. 2005), in which the court found that a stylized letter "O" was inherently distinctive. "Trademark protection of a sufficiently stylized version of a common shape or letter will not hamper effective competition because competitors remain free to use nonstylized forms or their own alternative stylizations of the same shape or letter." Is this "need" test fair? Does it have any inherent bias? Is it more objective and predictable? Does it have any inherent drawbacks? Is it a valid criterion to determine whether a term is commercially needed to describe goods to inquire whether it is in fact being used by competitors? *See Investacorp, Inc. v. Arabian Investment Banking Corp.*, *supra* (INVESTACORP merely descriptive for financial services). The Ninth Circuit held in *Yellow Cab Co. v. Yellow Cab of Elk Grove, Inc.*, 419 F.3d 925 (9th Cir. 2005), that there was an issue of fact as to whether the term "Yellow Cab" was descriptive for taxi cabs. The court rejected defendant's argument that the use of the term "yellow cab" in the New York City area was "dispositive in determining the distinctiveness of a mark used by a small business claiming territorial rights in Sacramento, California." *Yellow Cab*, 419 F.3d at 930, n.4. The court noted in particular that all licensed taxicabs in New York City were required to be yellow in order to distinguish them from taxicabs operated by smaller, independent companies.

What criteria should a court apply in determining whether a term is being used in a trademark sense, i.e., to identify as to source? *See Venetianaire Corp. v. A&P Import Co.*, 429 F.2d 1079, 1082 (2[d] Cir. 1970) ("[D]efendant obviously used the term 'as a symbol to attract public attention.' "). Does the presence of a word on a product label necessarily constitute a trademark use?

3. Proof of Secondary Meaning

Should the courts, in determining whether secondary meaning exists, simply employ the basic test of trade identity unfair competition, i.e., likelihood of confusion? *See Transgo, Inc. v. Ajac Transmission Corp.*, 768 F.2d 1001, 1015 (9th Cir. 1985) ("secondary meaning can also be established by evidence of likelihood of confusion"); *Interpace Corp. v. Lapp, Inc.*, 721 F.3d 460 (3[d] Cir. 1983) (the tests for secondary meaning and likelihood of confusion are "indistinguishable in practice"). How would you prove that an alleged trademark has source-indicating significance? In *Healthcare Advocates, Inc. v. Health Advocate, Inc.*, 169 Fed. Appx. 99 (3[d] Cir. 2006) (unpub'd), the plaintiff failed to show that secondary meaning had developed in HEALTHCARE ADVOCATES over a five year period, during which it admittedly only had limited, "ineffective" local advertising and *de minimis* sales.

In *Pabst Blue Ribbon v. Decatur Brewing Co.*, 284 F. 110 (7th Cir. 1922), plaintiff, the manufacturer of Pabst Blue Ribbon beer, was unsuccessful in its attempt to prevent the defendant from selling packages of ingredients for home brewed beer under the name "Blue Ribbon." The court observed that "Blue Ribbon" was a term signifying "high merit," which was used at the time on over sixty widely varying products, and that it was therefore only entitled to limited protection. Should we automatically assume that the public gives such marks little significance as indicators of source? In *In re Wileswood, Inc.*, 201 U.S.P.Q. 400 (T.T.A.B. 1978) the Trademark Trial and Appeal Board rejected applications to register "America's Best Popcorn" and "America's Favorite Popcorn," stating that "the phrases in question are only self-awarded laudations of applicant's product, which others might be equally entitled to use, for whatever they are worth, for the same product." Similarly, in *In re Boston Beer*, 198 F.3d 1370 (Fed. Cir. 1999), the Federal Circuit concluded that "The Best Beer in America" was unregistrable because it was nothing more than a claim of superiority, and was so highly laudatory that it was incapable of functioning as a trademark. PLATINUM was held to be a self-laudatory mark lacking secondary meaning when a denial of preliminary relief was affirmed in *Platinum Home Mortgage Corp. v. Platinum Financial Group*, 149 F.3d 722 (7th Cir. 1998). Plaintiff offered mortgage services under the name Platinum Home Mortgage Corporation, and defendant offered financial services, including mortgage services, under the name Platinum Financial Group. "[I]t requires little imagination to associate 'platinum' with superiority and quality service." In affirming the finding of no secondary meaning, the court emphasized "the minimal length of time" plaintiff had been operating under the name — three years.

In a strong dissent in favor of finding secondary meaning, Judge Wood observed that in the three years prior to suit plaintiff had opened six offices, had closed more than $700 million in mortgages, had spent almost $650,000 promoting its business, including a large illuminated billboard on a major highway near Chicago, and had become the third largest offeror of government-backed mortgages in Illinois. Plaintiff also had submitted substantial evidence of actual confusion among both potential purchasers seeking mortgages and real estate professionals.

4. Deceptive Terms

Deceptive terms that are used as trademarks will not be protected on the ground that the public will likely be misled as to the nature and qualities of the product. In *Warner-Lambert v. BreathAsure, Inc.*, 204 F.3d 87 (3[d] Cir. 2000), for example, the appellate court enjoined defendant's use of the trade name BreathAsure because it conveyed the literally false message "that its capsules could assure fresh breath." "[D]eception is found when an essential and material element is misrepresented, is distinctly false, and is the very element upon which the customer reasonably relies in purchasing one product over another." *Gold Seal Co. v. Weeks*, 129 F. Supp. 928, 934, *aff'd* per curiam *sub nom. S.C. Johnson & Son v. Gold Seal Co.*, 230 F.2d 832 (D.C. Cir.) *cert. denied,*352 U.S. 829 (1956).

"Deceptively misdescriptive" marks may be registered and protected, however, because of the lack of materiality to the purchaser's decision. Proof of secondary meaning is required. In *Marilyn Miglin Model Makeup, Inc. v. Jovan, Inc., supra,* "Pheromone" was found to be deceptively misdescriptive in part because plaintiff admittedly did not know or care whether or not its perfumes actually contained pheromones, the organic substances that allegedly attract other members of the same species.

5. Actual Confusion and Distinctiveness

Does proof of actual confusion as to source implicitly and necessarily also constitute proof of secondary meaning or distinctiveness? *See Adray v. Adry-Mart Inc.*, 37 U.S.P.Q.2d 1872 (9th Cir. 1996) (failure to instruct jury that actual confusion is a factor to consider in ascertaining secondary meaning was reversible error); *International Kennel Club, Inc. v. Mighty Star, Inc.*, 846 F.2d 1079, 1086–87 (7th Cir. 1988); *American Scientific Chemical, Inc. v. American Hospital Corp.*, 690 F.2d 791, 793 (9th Cir. 1982) ("actual confusion is an indicium of secondary meaning"). *Compare Decorations for Generations, Inc. v. Home Depot USA, Inc.*, 128 Fed. Appx. 133 (Fed. Cir. 2005) (unpublished), in which the Federal Circuit stated that actual confusion must occur among potential purchasers to be relevant to a finding of secondary meaning. In that case, the plaintiff showed only that "a few Home Depot and DFG employees and associates may have been confused as to the origins of the tree stands at issue" and that was "not substantial evidence of actual consumer confusion," i.e. confusion among potential purchasers. Should bad faith copying by a defendant raise a presumption that secondary meaning exists? *Osem Food Industries Ltd. v. Sherwood Foods Inc.*, 917 F.2d 161, 164 (4th Cir. 1990). See the discussion of Intent in Chapter 5.

6. Slogans

Can a slogan acquire trademark significance through extensive advertising and use? The question turns on whether the slogan is actually being used as a trademark. In *MicroStrategy Inc. v. Motorola, Inc.*, 245 F.3d 335, 342-43 (4th Cir. 2001), the court analyzed whether plaintiff could assert trademark protection for a slogan that it identified as its "mission statement":

> On its business card and elsewhere, MicroStrategy characterizes "Intelligence Everywhere" as the company "mission," . . . "vision," . . . "effort," . . . "motto" . . . or "dream" . . . . Although in the proper context, a mission statement, like a slogan, can serve as a trademark, a company mission statement or slogan is certainly not by definition a trademark. Rather, mission statements, like "[s]logans *often* appear in such a context that they do not identify and distinguish the source of goods or services. In such cases, they are neither protectable nor registrable as trademarks." *See* 1 McCarthy § 7:20 (emphasis added). So it is here. MicroStrategy has not demonstrated that it has used the mission statement to identify and distinguish the source of its products or services. If anything, the phrase has been used to advertise MicroStrategy's goods, without identifying the source of those goods. Unless used in a context whereby they take on a dual function, advertisements are not trademarks.
>
> Moreover, the record does not bear out MicroStrategy's claim that the company "for years has used the mark consistently in widely distributed sales brochures [and] product manuals sold with the software, and advertising for its Broadcaster software"; the mark "is commonly placed right next to the name, Broadcaster." . . . The two items that MicroStrategy provides to support this proposition are a Broadcaster product brochure, copyrighted in 2000, and a

Broadcaster administrator guide, which indicates it was published in September 1999. Nothing in the record indicates precisely how "widely" these items have been distributed. What is clear is that not even in these two documents did MicroStrategy use "Intelligence Everywhere" "consistently" as a trademark "right next to the name, Broadcaster." For example, in the text-filled three-page Broadcaster product brochure, the phrase "MicroStrategy Broadcaster" appears 19 times. . .; "Intelligence Everywhere" does not "commonly appear right next to" it, rather "Intelligence Everywhere" appears just once. . . . "Microstrategy Broadcaster" appears twice on the cover of the brochure; "Intelligence Everywhere" is nowhere on the cover. . . . "Broadcaster," in large letters, heads the top of the second page of the brochure, in much smaller letters "MicroStrategy Broadcaster" is repeated underneath, and next to that, also in the same much smaller print, is "Intelligence Everywhere." . . . While "MicroStrategy Broadcaster" is repeated several more times on the page, "Intelligence Everywhere" is not. Moreover, on the last page of the brochure, when MicroStrategy lists its trademarks, including "MicroStrategy Broadcaster" and fourteen other marks, it does not list "Intelligence Everywhere." . . .

What appears to have eluded MicroStrategy is that "[e]ven though a word, name, symbol, device, or a combination of words [a slogan] *may be used* in the sale or advertising of services or on or in connection with goods" it is not protectable as a trademark "unless it *is used* as a mark." *In re Morganroth*, 208 U.S.P.Q. at 287; *see also In re Int'l Paper Co.*, 142 U.S.P.Q. 503, 505 (T.T.A.B. 1964) (noting that the "question here is not whether a slogan can perform the function of a trademark" but whether it does perform this function, i.e., "identify and distinguish" the owner's goods from those of others). "Intelligence Everywhere" could function as a trademark, but MicroStrategy has not clearly demonstrated that it has, in fact, used the phrase as a mark.

*   *   *

Can a slogan be inherently distinctive, or must secondary meaning always be shown before it is protectable as a trademark? Is there a principled distinction between a slogan, or a "mission statement" as in the *MicroStrategy* case, and a suggestive or laudatory trademark?

7. Distinctiveness and Priority

Proof that a descriptive mark has acquired secondary meaning will not automatically confer protection against other users of confusingly similar marks. Instead, plaintiff must also demonstrate that its mark acquired secondary meaning prior to the other's first use. *Testmasters Educ. Servs. v. Singh*, 428 F.3d 559 (9th Cir. 2005) (four advertisements in college newspaper were insufficient to show secondary meaning in TESTMASTERS before opposing party began use); *Investacorp, Inc. v. Arabian Investment Banking Corp.*, *supra*; *Co-Rect Products, Inc. v. Marvy! Advertising Photography, Inc.*, 780 F.2d 1324, 1330 (8th Cir. 1985); *G. Herlman Brewing Co. v. Anheuser Busch, Inc.*, 676 F. Supp. 1436 (E.D. Wis. 1987); RESTATEMENT (THIRD) OF UNFAIR COMPETITION § 19 comment b, Reporter's Note (1995). The rationale for this is that a descriptive mark without secondary meaning does not designate source. If the senior user cannot demonstrate that its mark had acquired secondary meaning prior to the junior user's first use, then the senior user cannot prove any infringement because "there was no likelihood of confusion when the junior user arrived on the scene." J. THOMAS MCCARTHY, TRADEMARKS AND UNFAIR COMPETITION § 16:34 (4th ed. 2007). However, a plaintiff may not have to prove that its mark acquired secondary meaning prior to infringer's first use in each and every geographical pocket if plaintiff can demonstrate that its mark acquired secondary meaning "among some substantial portion of consumers nationally" and as long as the junior user was aware of the senior user's mark. *Fuddruckers, Inc. v. Doc's B.R. Others, Inc.*, 826 F.2d 837, 844 (9th Cir. 1987).

8. Nascent Goodwill

Some New York district courts had protected nascent goodwill under an equitable theory of "secondary meaning in the making." *See, e.g., National Lampoon, Inc. v. American Broadcasting Cos.*, 376 F. Supp. 733 (S.D.N.Y. 1974), *aff'd per curiam*, 497 F.2d 1343 (2th Cir. 1974). The theory was criticized as unclear and unnecessary, *see* McCarthy, Trademarks and Unfair Competition, § 15.21 (4th ed. 2007), and for focusing upon the intent of the seller while neglecting the response to the symbol by the consuming public, *Black & Decker Mfg. Co. v. Ever-Ready Appliance Mfg. Co.*, 684 F.2d 546 (8th Cir. 1982). After considering the theory in *Laureyssens v. Idea Group, Inc.*, 964 F.2d 131, 137 (2[d] Cir. 1992), the Second Circuit rejected it, stating, "Where there is no actual secondary meaning in a trade dress, the purchasing public simply does not associate the trade dress with a particular producer. Therefore a subsequent producer who adopts an imitating trade dress will not cause confusion." Is it fair to permit a competitor deliberately to preempt developing secondary meaning? On the other hand, is fairness a relevant inquiry here? What would be the consequences if the theory of secondary meaning in the making were universally adopted in U.S. trademark law, particularly in terms of "[e]verybody['s] . . . right to the use of the English language and [the] right to assume that nobody is going to take that English language away from him?" Hearings on H.R. 102 et al. before the Subcommittee on Trade-Marks of the House Committee on Patents, 77th Cong., 1st Sess., 72 (1941), quoted in *KP Permanent Make-Up, Inc., v. Lasting Impression I, Inc.*, 543 U.S. 111, n.5 (2004). What economic consequences would follow?

2.05   Geographical Terms

Introduction

Geographical terms, such as Scotch, American, California, and Allegheny, may be broadly considered as being "descriptive" trademarks, although they fall within a particular category of that designation. Generally, descriptive terms are assumed to be in the public domain. *see, e.g, KP Permanent Make-Up, Inc., v. Lasting Impression I, Inc.*, 543 U.S. 111 (2004) (noting there is "no indication that the [Lanham Act] was meant to deprive commercial speakers of the ordinary utility of descriptive words"). Because of the threshold impression that descriptive terms such as geographic indicators are or should be universally available to all residents of the locality involved, because the number of such terms applicable to a locality is limited, and because their use for trade identity purposes is generally so common, the problems of defining rights and the scope of exclusivity are particularly difficult.

AMERICAN WALTHAM WATCH CO. v. UNITED STATES WATCH CO.
Massachusetts Supreme Judicial Court
173 Mass. 85, 53 N.E. 141 (1899)

Holmes, Justice

This is a bill brought to enjoin the defendant from advertising its watches as the "Waltham Watch" or "Waltham Watches," and from marking its watches in such a way that the word "Waltham" is conspicuous. The plaintiff was the first manufacturer of watches in Waltham, and had acquired a great reputation before the defendant began to do business. It was found at the hearing that the word "Waltham," which originally was used by the plaintiff in a merely geographical sense, now, by long use in connection with the plaintiff's watches, has come to have a secondary meaning as a designation of the watches which the public has become accustomed to associate with the name. This is recognized by the defendant so far that it agrees that the preliminary injunction, granted in 1890, against using the combined words "Waltham Watch" or "Waltham Watches" in advertising its watches, shall stand, and shall be embodied in the final decree.

The question raised at the hearing, and now before us, is whether the defendant shall be enjoined further against using the words "Waltham" or "Waltham, Mass.," upon plates of its watches, without some accompanying statement which shall distinguish clearly its watches from those made by the plaintiff. The judge who heard the case found that it is of considerable commercial importance to indicate where the defendant's business of manufacturing is carried on, as it is the custom of watch manufacturers so to mark their watches, but, nevertheless, found that such an injunction ought to issue. He also found that the use of the word "Waltham," in its geographical sense, upon the dial, is not important, and should be enjoined.

The defendant's position is that, whatever its intent and whatever the effect in diverting a part of the plaintiff's business, it has a right to put its name and address upon its watches; that to require it to add words which will distinguish its watches from the plaintiff's in the mind of the general public is to require it to discredit them in advance; and that if the plaintiff, by its method of advertisement, has associated the fame of its merits with the city where it makes its wares, instead of with its own name, that is the plaintiff's folly, and cannot give it a monopoly of a geographical name, or entitle it to increase the defendant's burden in advertising the place of its works.

In cases of this sort, as in so many others, what ultimately is to be worked out is a point or line between conflicting claims, each of which has meritorious grounds, and would be extended further were it not for the other. *Ferrule Co. v. Hills*, 159 Mass. 147, 149, 150, 34 N.E. 85. It is desirable that the plaintiff should not lose custom by reason of the public mistaking another manufacturer for it. It is desirable that the defendant should be free to manufacture watches at Waltham, and to tell the world that it does so. The two desiderata cannot both be had to their full extent, and we have to fix the boundaries as best we can. On the one hand, the defendant must be allowed to accomplish its desideratum in some way, whatever the loss to the plaintiff. On the other, we think, the cases show that the defendant fairly may be required to avoid deceiving the public to the plaintiff's harm, so far as is practicable in a commercial sense. It is true that a man cannot appropriate a geographical name; but neither can he a color, or any part of the English language, or even a proper name to the exclusion of others whose names are like his. Yet a color in connection with a sufficiently complex combination of other things may be recognized as saying so circumstantially that the defendant's goods are the plaintiff's as to pass the injunction line. *New England Awl & Needle Co. v. Marlborough Awl & Needle Co.*, 168 Mass. 154, 156, 46 N.E. 386. So, although the plaintiff has no copyright on the dictionary, or any part of it, he can exclude a defendant from a part of the free field of the English language, even from the mere use of generic words, unqualified and unexplained, when they would mislead the plaintiff's customers to another shop. *Reddaway v. Banham* [1896] App. Cas. 199. So, the name of a person may become so associated with his goods that one of the same name coming into the business later will not be allowed to use even his own name without distinguishing his wares. *Brinsmead v. Brinsmead*, 13 Times Law R. 3; *Reddaway v. Bonham* [1896] App. Cas. 199, 210. *See Singer Mfg. Co. v. June Mfg. Co.*, 163 U.S. 169, 204, 16 Sup. Ct. 1002; *Cream Co. v. Keller*, 85 Fed. 643. And so, we doubt not, may a geographical name acquire a similar association with a similar effect. *Montgomery v. Thompson* [1891] App. Cas. 217.

Whatever might have been the doubts some years ago, we think that now it is pretty well settled that the plaintiff, merely on the strength of having been first in the field, may put later comers to the trouble of taking such reasonable precautions as are commercially practicable to prevent their lawful names and advertisements from deceitfully diverting the plaintiff's custom.

We cannot go behind the finding that such a deceitful diversion is the effect, and intended effect, of the marks in question. We cannot go behind the finding that it is practicable to distinguish the defendant's watches from those of the plaintiff, and that it ought to be done.

Decree for plaintiff.

COMMUNITY OF ROQUEFORT v. WILLIAM FAEHNDRICH, INC.

United States Court of Appeals, Second Circuit
303 F.2d 494 (1962)

KAUFMAN, CIRCUIT JUDGE

The Community of Roquefort (hereafter sometimes referred to as Community), a municipality in France, is the holder of a certification mark "Roquefort" for cheese, which is registered in the United States Patent Office under Section 4 of the Lanham Trade-Mark Act of 1946, 15 U.S.C.A. § 1054. Together with a French cheese exporter, another French agent, and an American cheese packaging concern, the Community filed a complaint against William Faehndrich, Inc. (hereafter referred to as Faehndrich), a New York cheese importer. The complaint alleged, *inter alia*, that Faehndrich was infringing the Community's "Roquefort" certification mark; and, in general, it sought to enjoin Faehndrich from selling cheese not produced in accordance with that mark but labeled or represented as "Imported Roquefort Cheese." Plaintiffs moved for summary judgment. At the same time they announced that if relief were granted on the Community's cause of action for infringement, the other claims would be withdrawn. The defendant denied infringement, and filed a cross motion for summary judgment. From a judgment in favor of the Community of Roquefort, and the issuance of a permanent injunction against continued infringement of the certification mark, the defendant Faehndrich appeals.

It appears that for centuries there has been produced and cured in the natural limestone caves in and about the municipality of Roquefort a sheep's milk blue-mold cheese, which has been marketed in this country for many years as "Roquefort Cheese." In an effort to protect themselves against unfair competition, producers of such French "Roquefort Cheese" frequently have asked our courts to prevent misleading use of the "Roquefort" designation. *See, e.g., Douglas v. Mod-Urn Cheese Packing Co., Inc.,* 161 Misc. 21, 290 N.Y.S. 368 (Sup. Ct. 1936); *Douglas v. Newark Cheese Co., Inc.,* 153 Misc. 85, 274 N.Y.S. 406 (Sup. Ct. 1934). For similar reasons the Community of Roquefort, in 1953, obtained a certification mark so that the term "Roquefort," as applied to cheese, would be used exclusively:

> . . . to indicate that the same has been manufactured from sheep's milk only, and has been cured in the natural caves of the Community of Roquefort, Department of Aveyron, France, in accordance with the historic methods and usages of production, curing and development which have been in vogue there for a long period of years.

Since that time the Community has been diligent in protecting the mark.

Nevertheless, in 1960, Faehndrich imported into the United States a quantity of sheep's milk blue-mold cheese, labeled "Imported Roquefort Cheese" (at Faehndrich's direction), which had been produced in Hungary and Italy. Of course, it was not (and could not be) produced by authority of the Community of Roquefort under its mark. When imported, Faehndrich's cheese was packaged in a manner clearly indicating the countries of origin. On the other hand, when Faehndrich prepared the cheese for re-sale, the labels prominently displaying the words "Product of Italy" and "Product of Hungary" were replaced with new wrappers printed "Imported Roquefort Cheese" and "Made from Pure Sheep's Milk Only," *without any indication of origin.* Hence, there was nothing on the wrappers which would suggest to the retail-buying public that Faehndrich's cheese came from Hungary or Italy.

In order to clarify our discussion of the single question presented by this appeal, i.e., whether Judge Metzner was correct in granting the Community of Roquefort's motion for summary judgment, it will be helpful to summarize the law applicable to certification marks such as the mark involved in this case, and by way of explanation, to point out certain distinctions between *trade-marks* on the one hand, and *certification marks* on the other.

Until the Lanham Act of 1946, a geographical name could not be registered as a *trade-mark*. This prohibition operated to prevent a single producer from appropriating the name of a particular place or area in which he was located to the exclusion of other and similarly situated producers. *Canal Co. v. Clark*, 80 U.S. 311 581 (1872). "If the name was to be found in an atlas . . ., that was sufficient to preclude registration." Robert, *Commentary on the Lanham Trade-Mark Act, 15 U.S.C.A. following § 1024*, 265, 271 (1948). Nevertheless, if a geographical name which had become distinctive of certain goods was registered by oversight, it was protected against infringement, *Baglin v. Cusenier Co.*, 221 U.S. 580, 591-593 (1911); moreover, if the name acquired such new significance as an indication of origin of goods, i.e., a secondary meaning, its use was protected from unfair competition even though it could not be registered as a trademark. *Elgin National Watch Co. v. Illinois Watch Case Co.*, 179 U.S. 665 (1901); Vandenburgh, *Trademark Law and Procedure* §§ 4.60, 4.70 (1959).

Section 2(e) of the Lanham Act continued to prohibit registration of a geographical name as a trade-mark, if "when applied to the goods of the applicant [it] is primarily geographically descriptive . . .," 15 U.S.C.A. § 1052(e)(2), *unless* such a name "has become distinctive of the applicant's goods . . .," 15 U.S.C.A. § 1052(f). Under the Lanham Act, therefore, if a geographical name acquires a secondary meaning, it can be registered as a trade-mark. Vandenburgh, op. cit. *supra*.

In addition to this extension of trade-mark law, the Lanham Act created an entirely new registered mark which was denominated a "certification mark." 15 U.S.C.A. § 1054; Robert, op. cit. *supra*, at p. 270.

> The term "certification mark" means a mark used upon or in connection with the products . . . of one or more persons other than the owner of the mark to certify regional or other origin, material, mode of manufacture, quality, accuracy or other characteristics of such goods . . . 15 U.S.C.A. § 1127.

A geographical name does not require a secondary meaning in order to qualify for registration as a certification mark. It is true that section 1054 provides that certification marks are "subject to the provisions relating to the registration of trademarks, so far as they are applicable. . . ." But Section 1052(e)(2), which prohibits registration of names primarily geographically descriptive, specifically excepts "indications of regional origin" registrable under section 1054. Therefore, a geographical name may be registered as a certification mark even though it is primarily geographically descriptive. This distinction, i.e., that a geographical name cannot be registered as a *trademark* unless it has secondary meaning, but can be registered as a *certification mark* without secondary meaning, has significance. A trade-mark gives a producer exclusive rights; but a certification mark, owned by a municipality, such as Roquefort, must be made available without discrimination "to certify the goods . . . of *any* person who maintains the standards or conditions which such mark certifies." (Italics added.) 15 U.S.C.A. § 1064(d)(4). *See* 4 Callmann, *Unfair Competition and Trade Marks* § 98.4(c)(2 ed. 1950).

On the other hand, a geographical name registered as a certification mark must continue to indicate the regional origin, mode of manufacture, etc. of the goods upon which it is used, just as a trade-mark must continue to identify a producer.

> When the meaning of a mark that had previously served as an indication of origin changes so that its principal significance to purchasers is that of indicating the nature or class of goods and its function as an indication of origin

is subservient thereto, it is no longer a mark but rather is a generic term. Vandenburgh, op. cit. *supra*, § 9.20.

Therefore, if a geographical name which has been registered as a certification mark, identifying certain goods, acquires principal significance as a description of those goods, the rights cease to be incontestable, 15 U.S.C.A. § 1065(4), and the mark is subject to cancellation, 15 U.S.C.A. § 1064(c); Robert, op. cit. *supra*, at pp. 280-281.

In the present case Faehndrich does not contest the validity of the mark's registration, as to which the Community's certificate of registration is prima facie proof. 15 U.S.C.A. § 1057(b). Instead, Faehndrich argues that there is a genuine issue of fact concerning the existence of generic meaning, i.e., whether the term "Roquefort" has acquired principal significance as a description of blue-mold sheep's milk cheese, regardless of its origin and without reference to the method of curing employed in the limestone caves of Roquefort, France. The difficulty with Faehndrich's position, however, is that nowhere in the affidavits submitted below on the motion for summary judgment is there any allegation of facts which suggests that such a genuine issue exists; nor does Faehndrich make any allegation that it could prove such facts at a trial. The affidavits are barren of any allegations or facts that consumers understand the word "Roquefort" to mean nothing more than blue-mold cheese made with sheep's milk. Indeed, the Community's affidavits indicate the contrary. They allege that the only other cheese of this nature commercially sold in the United States, a product of Israel, is marketed as "Garden of Eden — Heavenly Cheese — Sheep's Milk Blue-Mold Cheese"; that a similar Tunisian product is marketed abroad as "Bleu de Brebis"; and that the same cheese which Faehndrich imports from Hungary and sells with the label "Imported Roquefort Cheese" is sold in Belgium as "Merinofort." Moreover, we have already noted that producers of French Roquefort cheese have diligently protected the name from unfair competition in this country.

The purpose of summary judgment is to dispose of cases in which "there is no genuine issue as to any material fact and . . . the moving party is entitled to a judgment as a matter of law." Rule 56(c), Fed.R.Civ.P., 28 U.S.C.A.; *see* 6 Moore, *Federal Practice*, ¶ 56.04 (2 ed. 1953). Since the object is to discover whether one side has no real support for its version of the facts, the Rule specifically states that affidavits shall "set forth such facts as would be admissible in evidence." Rule 56(e), Fed.R.Civ.P. In view of this, we agree with Judge Metzner that Faehndrich "has failed to show . . . that there is any possibility on a trial that he can raise an issue of fact" in regard to generic meaning.

Moreover, since Faehndrich's wrappers indisputably bore the inscription "Imported Roquefort Cheese," we believe that the District Court was justified in finding, as a matter of law, that appellant's use of an identical mark on substantially identical goods was "likely to cause confusion or mistake or to deceive purchasers as to the source of the origin of the goods." 15 U.S.C.A. § 1114. *Accord Triumph Hosiery Mills, Inc. v. Triumph International Corp.*, 191 F. Supp. 937, 940 (S.D.N.Y. 1961).

We are well aware of the dangers involved in haphazard use of summary judgment procedures. However, summary judgment cannot be defeated where there is no indication that a genuine issue of fact exists; to permit that would be to render this valuable procedure wholly inoperative and to place a "devastating gloss" on the rule. *See* Clark, *Clarifying Amendments to the Federal Rules?*, 14 Ohio St. L.J. 241, 249-250 (1953).

Affirmed.

IN RE LES HALLES DE PARIS J.V.
United States Court Of Appeals For the Federal Circuit
334 F.3d 1371 (2003)

RADER, CIRCUIT JUDGE

* * *

On July 14, 1999. Les Halles filed its application to register the service mark LE MARAIS in connection with "restaurant services" in International Class 42. The application documented use of the mark from as early as June 4, 1995, as the name for Les Halles' restaurant in New York that serves French kosher cuisine. The United States Patent and Trademark Office (PTO) concluded that the mark is primarily geographically deceptively misdescriptive under section 2(e) (3) and refused to register it on the Principal Register. After rejecting Les Halles' request for reconsideration, the PTO made its refusal to register the mark final on September 12, 2000.

Les Halles appealed to the Board, which affirmed the PTO's refusal to register Les Halles' mark. As evidence that the mark uses misdescriptive geographic terms, the Board referred to articles and travel brochures about the Jewish quarter or neighborhood in Paris known as Le Marais. This record evidence included various statements about Le Marais being a fashionable Jewish area in Paris with fine restaurants. For example, one articles stated: "Over the years Le Marais has moved from obscurity into a gilded age of offbeat and referenced Le Maria as "the old Jewish Quarter . . . [which] blends chic apartment renovations with tiny cafes, fine new restaurants and ancient synagogues, all on narrow, sinuous streets."

Based on this record, the Board concluded: The primary significance of [LE MARAIS], at least to an appreciable segment of applicant's restaurant patrons, will be of the geographic location in Paris. In addition, the Board reasoned that because Les Halles' restaurants "are touted as being French kosher steakhouses . . . actual and potential customers of applicant's restaurants will believe that there is a connection between applicant's restaurants and the [Jewish Quarter] in Paris known as Le Marais." The Board emphasized that it was "not finding that the Examining Attorney has shown that Le Marais is noted for its restaurants or cuisines." Ultimately, however, the Board affirmed the PTO's refusal to register Les Halles' mark under section (e) (3) because it is primarily geographically deceptively misdescriptive.

* * *

This court recently addressed the legal standard for primarily geographically deceptively misdescriptive marks under section (e) (3). *See In re California Innovations, Inc.*, 329 F.3d 1334 (Fed. Cir. 2003). In that case, this court took the opportunity provided by the NAFTA amendments to the Landham Act to reexamine the legal test for geographically deceptively misdescriptive marks. *See North American Free Trade Agreement*, Dec. 17, 1992, art. 1712, 32 I.L.M. 605, 698, as implemented by NAFTA Implementation Act, Pub. L. No. 103-182, 107 Stat. 2057 (1993). This court concluded that the test applied in the past overlooked that a mark only invokes the prohibitions of section 2(e) (3) by deceiving the public with a geographic misdescription. The NAFTA amendments placed the emphasis on the statutory requirement to show deception by imposing the same restrictions on section 2(e) (3) marks that apply to other deceptive marks. *California Innovations*, 329 F.3d at 1338-40. Thus, this court applied a test for section 2(e) (3) required by the statute with a focus on whether the public is deceived, rather than solely on whether the mark was distinctive. *Id.*

This court stated: "To ensure a showing of deceptiveness . . . the PTO may not deny registration [under section 2(e) (3)] without a showing that the goods-place association made by the consumer is material to the consumer's decision to purchase those goods." *Id.* at 1340. Under section 2(e) (3), therefore, a mark is primarily geographically deceptively misdescriptive if:

(1) the primary significance of the mark is a generally known geographic location, (2) the consuming public is likely to believe the place identified by the mark indicates the origin of the goods [or services] bearing the mark, when in fact the goods [or services] do not come from that place, and (3) the misrepresentation was a material factor in the consumer's decision.

Id. at 1341.

While California Innovations involved a mark to identify the source of goods, the analysis under section 2(e) (3) applies to service marks as well. Application of the second prong of this test — the services-place association — requires some consideration. A customer typically receives services, particularly in the restaurant business, at the location of the business. Having chosen to come to that place for the services, the customer is well aware of the geographic location of the service. This choice necessarily implies that the customer is less likely to associate the services with the geographic location invoked by the mark rather than the geographic location of the service, such as a restaurant. In this case, the customer is less likely to identify the services with a region of Paris when sitting in a restaurant in New York.

Although the services-place association operated somewhat differently than a goods-place association, the second prong nonetheless continues to operate as part of the test for section 2(e) (3). In a case involving goods, the goods-place association often requires little more than a showing that the consumer identifies the place as a known source of the product. *See In re Loew's Theatres, Inc.*, 769 F.2d 764, 767-69 (Fed. Cir. 1985); *California Innovations*, 329 F.3d at 1340. Thus, to make a goods-place association, the case law permits an inference that the consumer associates the product with the geographic location in the mark because that place is known for producing the product. *Id.* In the case of a services-place association, however, a mere showing that the geographic location in the mark is known for performing the service is not sufficient. Rather the second prong of the test requires some additional reason for the consumer to associate the services with the geographic location invoked by the mark. *See In re Municipal Capital Markets, Corp.*, 51 USPQ2d 1369, 1370-71 (TTAB 1999) ("Examining Attorney must present evidence that does something more than merely establish that services as ubiquitous as restaurant services are offered in the pertinent geographic location."). Thus, a services-place association in a case dealing with restaurant services, such as the present case, requires a showing that the patrons of the restaurant are likely to believe the restaurant services have their origin in the location indicated by the mark. In other words, to refuse registration under section 2(e) (3), the PTO must show that patrons will likely be misled to make some meaningful connection between the restaurant (the service) and the relevant place.

For example, the PTO might find a services-place association if the record shows that patrons, though sitting in New York, would believe the food served by the restaurant was imported from Paris, or that the chefs in New York received specialized training in the region in Paris, or that the New York menu is identical to a known Parisian menu, or some other heightened association between the services and the relevant place. This court does not decide whether these similarities would necessarily establish a services-place association or presume to limit the forms of proof for a services-place association with these examples. Rather, this court only identifies some potential showings that might give restaurant patrons an additional reason beyond the mark itself to identify the services as originating in the relevant place.

This court recognizes that the standard under section 2(e) (3) is more difficult to satisfy for service marks than for marks on goods. In fact, for the reasons discussed above, geographic marks in connection with services are less likely to mislead the public than geographic marks on goods. Thus, a different application of the services-place association prong is appropriate, especially in the context of marks used for restaurant services — "some of the very most ubiquitous of all types of services." *Municipal Capital Markets*, 51 USPQ2d at 1370.

Beyond the second prong, however, the misleading services-place association must be a material factor in the consumer's decision to patronize the restaurant. This materiality prong, as noted by *California Innovations*, provides some measure for the statutory requirement of deception. *California Innovations*, 329 F.3d at 1340 (citing *In re House of Windsor*, 221 USPQ 53, 56-57 (TTAB 1983) for the materiality test). For goods, the PTO may raise an inference in favor of materiality with evidence that the place is famous as a source of the goods at issue. *See id.* at 1341.

To raise an inference of deception or materiality for a service mark, the PTO must show some heightened association between the services and the relevant geographic denotation. Once again, this court does not presume to dictate the form of this evidence. For restaurant services, the materiality prong might be satisfied by a particularly convincing showing that identifies the relevant place as famous for providing the specialized culinary training exhibited by the chef, and that this fact is advertised as a reason to choose this restaurant. In other words, an inference of materiality arises in the event of a very strong services-place association. Without a particularly strong services-place association, an inference would not arise, leaving the PTO to seek direct evidence of materiality. In any event, the record might show that customers would patronize the restaurant because they believed the food was imported from, or the chef was trained in, the place identified by the restaurant's mark. The importation of food and culinary training are only examples, not exclusive methods of analysis, as already noted.

In this case, the PTO and the Board did not apply the necessary standard to conclude that Les Halles' mark is primarily geographically deceptively misdescriptive. The Board concluded that the mark is primarily geographic in nature, and that patrons of Les Halles' restaurant would believe the restaurant services bear some connection to the Le Marais area of Paris. The Board's decision, however, does not show a services-place association or the materiality of that association to a patron's decision to patronize Les Halles' restaurant. To be specific, the record does not show that a diner at the restaurant in question in New York City would identify the region in Paris as a source of those restaurant services. Further, the record does not show that a material reason for the diner's choice of this restaurant in New York City was its identity with the region in Paris. At best, the evidence in this record shows that Les Halles' restaurant conjures up memories or images of the Le Marais area of Paris. This scant association falls far short of showing a material services-place association. Accordingly, this court vacates the Board's decision and remands for application of the appropriate standard in accordance with this opinion.

Notes on Geographical Terms

1. The Classification of Geographical Terms

Geographical terms are protectable as trademarks if they have acquired secondary meaning. However, they are not protectable if they are deceptive, or if they are deceptively misdescriptive of the geographical origin of the goods or services. *See Elgin National Watch Co. v. Illinois Watch Case Co.*, 179 U.S. 665 (1901); Kane, *The Unfortunate Fusion of Geographic Term Analysis Under Section 2 and Section 43(a) of the Lanham Act*, 82 VIRGINIA L. REV. 543 (1996). The Lanham Act provides in § 2(a) that a "deceptive" and in § 2(e)(2) that a "primarily geographically descriptive or deceptively misdescriptive" mark may not be registered, but § 2(f) provides that a mark which originally was geographically descriptive may be registered if it has become distinctive of the goods or services in commerce. *See, e.g., Resorts of Pinehurst, Inc. v. Pinehurst Nat'l Corp.*, 148 F.3d 417 (4th Cir. 1998) (plaintiff's PINEHURST mark for resort and golf services had acquired secondary meaning because consumers would primarily associate its use of the mark with the source of its services and not a geographic location; defendant's use of PINEHURST for golf services enjoined); Brauneis and Schechter, *Geographic Trademarks and the Protection of Competitor*

Communication, 96 TMR 782 (2006). What is the purpose of this difference? Why is CAMBRIDGE a potentially protectable trademark for Florida oranges while CALIFORNIA is not? In *Scotch Whisky Association v. United States Distilled Products Co.*, 952 F.2d 1317 (Fed. Cir. 1991), the dismissal of an opposition under § 2(a) was reversed because the Scottish surname McADAMS for whisky might deceptively suggest Scottish origin for applicant's Canadian whisky.

Following the United States' entry into the North American Free Trade Agreement with Canada and Mexico, President Clinton in December 1993 signed implementing legislation, HR3450, which amended §§ 2(f) and 23(a) to preclude registration of "primarily geographically deceptively misdescriptive" marks. *See e.g., In re Save Venice New York, Inc.*, 259 F.3d 1346 (Fed. Cir. 2001) ("The Venice Collection" refused registration as primarily geographically deceptively misdescriptive for art prints, paper and textile products, and other products); *In re Wada*, 194 F.3d 1297 (Fed. Cir. 1999) (upholding refusal to register NEW YORK WAYS GALLERY for leather goods as primarily geographically deceptively misdescriptive under NAFTA amendment). Such a mark previously was registrable under § 2(f) if it had become distinctive. A grandfather clause permits registration on the principal register if the mark became distinctive prior to the date of the bill's enactment.

In the *In re Save Venice New York* case, the Federal Circuit identified a two-part test for whether a mark is primarily geographically deceptively misdescriptive, *i.e.,* whether "(1) the mark's primary significance is a generally known geographic location; and (2) consumers would reasonably believe the applicant's goods are connected with the geographic location in the mark, when in fact they are not." "The Venice Collection" for art prints and other products was refused registration under that test. The Court also extended the test's scope to include related goods and services, holding, "the registrability of a geographic mark may be measured against the public's association of that region with both its traditional goods and any related goods or services that the public is likely to believe originate there." In the *Save Venice* case, furniture and dinnerware were among those products found to be related to the more traditional art, textile and printing industries associated with Venice. *See also Daesang Corp. v. Rhee bros., Inc.*, 77 U.S.P.Q. 2d 1753 (D. Md. 2005), in which defendant had fraudulently registered a Korean alphabet depiction of SOON CHANG, the name of a town in Korea, for a spicy condiment, without informing the Patent and Trademark Office that the town Soon Chang was well known for its high-quality production of that condiment. Defendant's registration for SOON CHANG was cancelled, and defendant was enjoined from interfering with plaintiff's use of SOON CHANG for such condiment products.

In *In re California Innovations, Inc.*, 329 F.3d 1334 (Fed. Cir. 2003), cited in *In re Les Halles De Paris J.V.*, the Federal Circuit clarified that, in such cases, materiality also needs to be shown:

> [T]he relatively easy burden of showing a naked goods-place association without proof that the association is material to the consumer's decision is no longer justified, because marks rejected under § 1052(e)(3) can no longer obtain registration through acquired distinctiveness under § 1052(f). To ensure a showing of deceptiveness and [that the geographical term is] misleading before imposing the penalty of non-registrability, the PTO may not deny registration without a showing that a goods-place association made by the consumer is material to the consumer's decision to purchase those goods.

The court opined that, although materiality was not explicitly mentioned, in both *In Re Save Venice* and *In re Wada* the court implicitly found that the applied for mark made a geographical misrepresentation that was material to consumers. Here, for the applied mark CALIFORNIA INNOVATIONS, "the evidence of a connection between California and insulated bags and wraps is tenuous. Even if the evidence supported a finding of a goods-place association, the PTO has yet to apply the materiality test in this case." The Board's refusal to register therefore was vacated and the case remanded for consideration under the proper standard.

Compare In re MBNA Am. Bank, 340 F.3d 1328 (Fed. Cir. 2003), in which the court rejected intent-to-use applications to register MONTANA SERIES and PHILADEL-PHIA CARD for "credit card services feature credit cards depicting scenes or subject matter of, or relating to" those geographic areas. While not raising traditional geographic issues, the applied for marks were found to be merely descriptive, because their consumer appeal rested on their ability to "immediately convey information about the specific regional affinity."

Before the NAFTA amendment, in *In re Nantucket, Inc.*, 677 F.2d 95 (C.C.P.A. 1982), the Court of Customs and Patent Appeals reversed a refusal to register because people would not expect shirts bearing the trademark NANTUCKET to have been made there. Judge Nies emphasized in her concurring opinion that the lack of commercial activity on Nantucket was what made the trademark arbitrary and registrable without proof of secondary meaning. She pointed out that the use of a trademark like CHICAGO would have presented a much different problem. This concurrence was cited, and its reasoning followed in *In re Handler Fenton Westerns, Inc.*, 214 U.S.P.Q. 848 (T.T.A.B. 1982), in refusing registration of DENVER WEST-ERNS for western-style shirts.

> . . . [Applicant's] shirts have their geographic origin in Denver, one of the largest and best-known cities of the American west, and applicant cannot reasonably expect that its mark is used in an arbitrary manner with respect to its goods or that purchasers would not believe its western-style shirts marked "DENVER WESTERNS" have their geographic origin in Denver.

Applying the two-part *Save Venice* test in *Japan Telecom, Inc. v. Japan Telecom America, Inc.*, 287 F.3d 866 (9th Cir. 2002), the appellate court held that the district court had erred in finding the trade name "Japan Telecom" primarily geographically deceptively misdescriptive for plaintiff's California-based company, because it had ignored "evidence that consumers might understand the word in [that] name as referring to a specific ethnic community, rather than the country," i.e., as indicating that the company "caters to the Japanese community." Concluding the Japan Telecom name nonetheless lacked secondary meaning and was unprotectable, the court affirmed summary judgment for defendant. *Cf. Institut National Des Appellations D'Origine v. Vinters Int'l Co.*, 958 F.2d 1574 (Fed. Cir. 1992), in which the Federal Circuit affirmed that CHABLIS WITH A TWIST did not deceptively suggest French origin because "Chablis" is generic in this country and *In re John Harvey & Sons Ltd.*, 32 U.S.P.Q.2d 1451 (T.T.A.B. 1994) in which the Board held that the public will not associate BRISTOL CREAM on sherry wine flavored cakes with Bristol, England. In *In re Jacques Bernier, Inc.*, 894 F.2d 389 (Fed. Cir. 1990), the Federal Circuit reversed the Board's refusal to register RODEO DRIVE for perfume. The court found no evidence in the record that the trademark would cause consumers to believe that applicant's perfume originated on Rodeo Drive in Beverly Hills. Subsequently, in *Fred Hayman Beverly Hills Inc. v. Jacques Bernier, Inc.*, 38 U.S.P.Q.2d 1691, 1694 (T.T.A.B. 1996), the Board again refused to register the RODEO DRIVE mark, finding that opposer had sufficiently demonstrated that a significant number of consumers identify certain Rodeo Drive retailers with "prestige" fragrances. Consider whether a materiality requirement would have affected those cases above, like *Nantucket*, where registration was refused.

What factors should be considered in determining whether the following marks are descriptive, or deceptively misdescriptive: IRISH SPRING for soap; DUTCH CLEANSER; ENGLISH LEATHER for after-shave lotion; ITALIAN MAIDE for canned vegetables? How would you determine whether these marks are entitled to trademark protection? *See Hamilton-Brown Shoe Co. v. Wolf Bros. & Co.*, 240 U.S. 251 (1916) (AMERICAN GIRL for shoes). In *Singer Mfg. Co. v. Birginal-Bigsby Corp.*, 319 F.2d 273 (C.C.P.A. 1963), Singer's opposition to registration of AMERICAN BEAUTY for Japanese–made sewing machines was sustained on the ground that such a mark would be primarily geographically deceptively misdescriptive under § 2(e)(2) of the Lanham Act. Although Singer did not use AMERICAN as a trademark itself, it was the principal domestic manufacturer of sewing machines and had emphasized in its advertising that its sewing machines were made in America by American craftsmen. It was on this basis that the court granted Singer standing to oppose. The court stated that "the continuing use of AMERICAN BEAUTY by appellee in the manner disclosed by the record is very likely to damage Singer by bringing about the sale of Japanese made machines to those who, if not deceived as to their origin, would, instead, purchase a Singer machine." *See also Scotch Whisky Ass'n v. Consolidated Distilled Products, Inc.*, 210 U.S.P.Q. 639 (N.D. Ill. 1981), in which the court enjoined use of LOCH-A-MOOR as a trademark for American-made liqueur because potential purchasers would be misled to believe that the liqueur was a product of Scotland, endowing it, unjustifiably, with added prestige and salability.

The Lanham Act specifically provides that collective and certification marks "including indications of regional origin used in commerce" are registrable. (15 U.S.C. § 1054). *See generally* Bengedkey & Mead, *International Protection of Appellations of Origin and Other Geographic Designations*, 82 TRADEMARK REP. 765 (1992). 15 U.S.C. § 1127 defines a certification mark as "a mark used upon or in connection with the products or services of one or more persons *other than the owner of the mark* to certify regional or other origin. . . ." This has been interpreted to mean that a producer of the goods in question cannot own a certification mark. *See Black Hills Jewelry Manufacturing Co. v. Gold Rush, Inc.*, 633 F.2d 746, 750 (8th Cir. 1980). Defendant in that case was nonetheless enjoined from using the trademark BLACK HILLS GOLD, as their jewelry was not manufactured in South Dakota, and the court found that purchasers would be misled as to origin.

2. Certification Marks

In contrast to trademarks that signify product source, certification marks are deemed to indicate product quality and not necessarily source. Because "any person who meets the standards and conditions which the mark certifies" must be permitted to use a certification mark, and because there is a "public interest in free and open competition among producers and distributors of the certified product" as well as in protection of "the market players from the influence of the certification mark owner", the Second Circuit in *Idaho Potato Comm'n v. M&M Produce Farm & Sales*, 335 F.3d 130 (2d Cir. 2003) permitted an ex-licensee on remand to challenge the validity of various IDAHO-derivative certification marks for potatoes. The court found that the need to protect the public interest outweighed the equitable principle of licensee estoppel that might otherwise have precluded such a challenge to a trademark license by an ex-licensee. To similar effect: *Idaho Potato Comm'n v. G&T Terminal Packaging, Inc.*, 425 F.3d 708 (9th Cir. 2005). See also the discussion on licensee estoppel in Chapter 4.

2.06 Surnames

Introduction

Like geographical terms, yet differently, surnames as trademarks or as identifying portions of trademarks pose special problems of protectibility. The notion that everyone should be able to use their name to identify their goods or business is deeply rooted in American mores even though perhaps unconsciously. Should everyone born with the name Ford be entitled to manufacture and sell automobiles under that name? The courts have historically revealed a distaste for unqualifiedly prohibiting the use of one's own name in commerce, but when pressed with hard cases, they have generally relied upon the basic test of likelihood of confusion. The cases that follow delineate some of the problems and their judicial treatment.

L.E. WATERMAN CO. v. MODERN PEN CO.
235 U.S. 88 (1914)

MR. JUSTICE HOLMES delivered the opinion of the court:

This suit was brought by the L. E. Waterman Company to enjoin the Modern Pen Company from using in connection with the manufacture and sale of fountain pens, other than those of the plaintiff's make, the name "A. A. Waterman" or any name containing the word "Waterman" in any form, and for an account. . . . The defendant's appeal is from the requirements that it use the name "Arthur A. Waterman & Co." instead of "A. A. Waterman & Co.," and that it juxtapose the words "not connected with the L. E. Waterman Co." After the finding of two courts and upon the evidence it must be assumed that the defendant had used the name Waterman in such a way as to mislead the public and to interfere with the plaintiff's rights unless the defendant had the right to use the name as matter of law, because it was the selling agent of a firm calling itself "A. A. Waterman & Co.," and deriving its name from a man who started in business long after the plaintiff had acquired whatever rights it has. . . . [I]t now is established that when the use of his own name upon his goods by a later competitor will and does lead the public to understand that those goods are the product of a concern already established and well known under that name, and when the profit of the confusion is known to, and, if that be material, is intended by, the later man, the law will require him to take reasonable precautions to prevent the mistake. . . . There is no distinction between corporations and natural persons in the principle, which is to prevent a fraud. . . .

* * *

The plaintiff's appeal is from the failure of the decree to prohibit the use of the name "Arthur A. Waterman & Co." even with the suffix required by the court. The ground upon which it claims this broader relief is that the agreement with A. A. Waterman by which he purported to become a partner in the firm of A. A. Waterman & Co. was a sham, that the firm does not make the pens sold by the defendant, and that all the arrangements between Waterman, the firm, and the defendant were merely colorable devices to enable the defendant to get the name upon its pens. If we were to adopt this view of the facts the nature of the parties' rights and powers perhaps might need a more careful discussion than, so far as we are aware, it has received as yet. Under the decree in its present form the plaintiff gets all the protection to which it is entitled as against another Waterman who has established himself in the business, even though one of his motives for going into it was the hope of some residual advantages from the use of his own name. . . .

We are not prepared to say as matter of law that a man who for years has been trying to do business may not join a partnership for a time long enough to start it with his name and whatever good will he has . . . . The obvious motive is met by the protection given in the decree, but does not deprive him of all rights in his name. . . .

Decree affirmed.

* * *

WYATT EARP ENTERPRISES, INC. v. SACKMAN, INC.
United States District Court, Southern District of New York
157 F. Supp. 621 (1958)

EDELSTEIN, DISTRICT JUDGE

* * *

Plaintiff is a producer of motion pictures for television and is the proprietor of a very successful series entitled "The Life and Legend of Wyatt Earp," nationally and internationally televised over the facilities of the American Broadcasting Company. The defendant has been in the business of manufacturing children's playsuits for many years, and, after the commencement of the "Wyatt Earp" television program by the plaintiff, entered into a license agreement with it purporting to grant the right to defendant to use "the name and likeness of Hugh O'Brian in the characterization of Wyatt Earp," O'Brian being the star of the program, portraying the title character. The agreement was not renewed by the plaintiff upon its expiration, another manufacturer having been licensed in place of defendant. The defendant has, after the expiration of its rights under the agreement, continued to manufacture and market children's playsuits under the name, mark and symbol of "Wyatt Earp," although without using the name and likeness of Hugh O'Brian and without specific reference to "ABC-TV."

The plaintiff seeks to enjoin the defendant's use of the name, mark and symbol "Wyatt Earp" on its playsuits on the ground that, by plaintiff's efforts, the name has come to have a secondary meaning indicative of origin, relationship and association with the television program; and that the public is likely to attribute the use of the name "Wyatt Earp" by the defendant to the plaintiff as a source of sponsorship and buy defendant's merchandise in this erroneous belief. The defendant denies the possibility of secondary meaning attaching to the name, arguing that it belonged to a living person out of the nation's history, and hence has become a part of the public domain not subject to commercial monopolization by anyone. Such a contention, I believe, overstates the law. Certainly the defendant, along with the plaintiff and everyone else, has some interest in a name out of history, as they have in words of common speech. "The only protected private interest in words of common speech is after they have come to connote, in addition to their colloquial meaning, provenience from some single source of the goods to which they are applied." *Adolph Kastor & Bros. v. Federal Trade Commission*, (2 Cir.) 138 F.2d 824, 825, 60 U.S.P.Q. 154, 155. The question is, in determining whether there is a protected private interest, whether the name "Wyatt Earp" has come to have such a connotation of provenience. If it has, the plaintiff has a cognizable interest in preventing the likelihood of consumer confusion, and it is such an interest as the law will protect against an opposing interest no greater than that of all persons in the use of the names in history. It is true that where a symbol is not fanciful but merely descriptive, the plaintiff bears a very heavy burden of proving confusion is likely. *See* dissenting opinion of Judge Frank in *Triangle Publications v. Rohrlich*, (2 Cir.) 167 F.2d 969, 974, 976, 77 U.S.P.Q. 196, 200, 201. Or it may be that a non-fanciful, real name is such a part of the national fabric that all have a measurable interest in its use, to the extent that it acquires no secondary meaning extending into a defendant's field so as to cause a likelihood of confusion. *Durable Toy & Novelty Corp. v. J. Chein & Co.*, (2 Cir.) 133 F.2d 853, 56 U.S.P.Q. 339, *cert. denied*, 320 U.S. 211, 57 U.S.P.Q. 568. ". . . [E]ach case presents a unique problem which must be answered by weighing the conflicting interests against each other." *Id.* at 855, 56 U.S.P.Q. at 341. Although "Wyatt Earp" is the name of an historical person, the defendant's interest in it is, I feel, not so strong as was the defendant's interest in the name "Uncle Sam" in the toy case, nor is the possibility of a secondary meaning attaching to "Wyatt Earp" so unlikely. If the plaintiff can show that it is likely to succeed, at trial, in proving that it invested the name of Wyatt Earp with a commercial significance and good will that is attributable to itself and that is likely to be appropriated by the defendant by way of consumer confusion, it will be entitled to the relief it seeks.

It is perhaps not too much to say, even at this preliminary stage of the proceedings, that the name of Wyatt Earp has been battered into the public consciousness by the television program to an extent far beyond any fame or notoriety ever previously attached to the marshall's name. Between September of 1955 and the end of November 1957, 102 motion picture films have been produced under the general title, "The Life and Legend of Wyatt Earp," which is also a service mark owned by the plaintiff and registered in the United States Patent Office. The films have been televised each week, 52 weeks a year, on the transcontinental release facilities of the American Broadcasting Company. More than $3,000,000 has been spent by the plaintiff in producing the films, and more than $3,500,000 has been received by the television network for its time and facility charges during the two year period commencing in September of 1955 and ending in August of 1957. Such charges continue to be made and received at the rate of more than $2,000,000 per year. By reason of the popularity of the production, enormous publicity has been generated in other media of mass communication. Popularly known as the "Wyatt Earp Program," it has from its inception been among the most popular television entertainments in the nation, viewed weekly on millions of television receivers by additional millions of persons. As an indication of the public acceptance of the program, there has been a great and increasing nationwide demand for articles and products sponsored by the plaintiff and bearing the name, mark and symbol of "Wyatt Earp." It has been asserted without denial or other comment that goods and merchandise marketed under the name of "Wyatt Earp" were unheard of prior to the first telecast of the show. The finding is nearly inescapable that the commercial value now enjoyed by the name is attributable almost entirely to the program. The plaintiff, as a result, has entered into the business of licensing merchandise rights in connection with the program under agreements controlling the nature and quality of the goods licensed so as to maintain high standards and to preserve the integrity of its good will. Under these agreements the royalties to be received for the year 1957 will exceed $100,000. The merchandise so promoted, in no way unique aside from its program identification, obviously sells much more readily than the same merchandise would sell without the program identification, as borne out by the fact that manufacturers pay substantial sums of money for the privilege of sponsorship, by way of licensing agreements. It can be found preliminarily, therefore, that the name and characterization of "Wyatt Earp" as televised by the plaintiff has become identified in the mind of the consumer public with merchandise upon which the name had been imprinted; that this identification and good will has extended to the field of children's playsuits sold and distributed under the name, mark and symbol "Wyatt Earp"; and that defendant is merchandising "Wyatt Earp" playsuits because of a popular demand for merchandise identified with the program and the plaintiff.

Since the expiration of its privileges under the licensing agreement with the plaintiff, the defendant has marketed its play clothes without the names and likeness of the star of the television program and without specific reference to "ABC-TV." It further has made certain modifications in the design of its suits. Samples of suits made by the defendant under its license and made after the expiration of its license, as well as a sample made by the current licensee, together with their boxes were handed up to the court as exhibits. Defendant's present outfit, despite the changes, appears to bear a striking resemblance to the outfit it previously made under license and to the one made by the present licensee; and these costumes, approximating the one worn by the television "Wyatt Earp," indeed seem to be markedly different from other "western" costumes. The defendant continues to mark on its boxes the name "Wyatt Earp" together with the legend "official outfit." Moreover, in its catalogue, the Wyatt Earp outfit is advertised in a context with three "TV personality" western outfits, all of them being characterized as "official," but with the "TV personality" designation omitted from the Wyatt Earp display. The text and layout are presented in such a manner as to convey the impression of an identification of defendant's Wyatt Earp playsuit with the Wyatt Earp television program. Indeed, it is so difficult to understand how any other impression could be conveyed that the finding of an intent to convey an erroneous notion of association with the program is highly probable. Unless the word "official" is passed over as sheer gibberish, the idea of sponsorship is inescapably implied.

The "critical question" in a case of secondary meaning "always is whether the public is moved in any degree to buy the article because of its source and what are the features by which it distinguishes that source." *Charles D. Briddell, Inc. v. Alglobe Trading Corp.,* (2 Cir.) 194 F.2d 416, 419, 92 U.S.P.Q. 100, 102. For under the common law of unfair competition, as well as under the Lanham Act, the likelihood of consumer confusion is the test of secondary meaning. *Id.* at p. 421, 92 U.S.P.Q. at 104. I find that, for the purposes of preliminary injunctive relief, plaintiff has met the burden of proving the likelihood of consumer-confusion. The public is moved to buy merchandise because of an identification with the name "Wyatt Earp" as developed by the plaintiff's television program. The defendant's use of the name created a likelihood that the public would believe, erroneously, that its playsuits were licensed or sponsored by the plaintiff, to the injury of the plaintiff's good will and to the hazard of its reputation. There is a high probability that, upon the trial of the issues, plaintiff will be able to establish that the name, mark and symbol "Wyatt Earp" has acquired a secondary meaning in the minds of the public as identified and associated with the television program and the plaintiff, and extending into the field of children's playsuits.

It is true that the plaintiff and defendant are not direct competitors in the same field of endeavor. The plaintiff does not manufacture children's playsuits. But where secondary meaning and consumer confusion are established, use of a trade name even upon noncompeting goods may be enjoined. *See Triangle Publications v. Rohrlich,* (2 Cir.) 167 F.2d 969, 972, 77 U.S.P.Q. 196, 198. And as held by the Court of Appeals in that case, the same principle applies to the situation of confusion about sponsorship. "In either case, the wrong of the defendant consisted in imposing upon the plaintiff a risk that the defendant's goods would be associated by the public with the plaintiff, and it can make no difference whether that association is based upon attributing defendant's goods to plaintiff or to a sponsorship by the latter when it has been determined that plaintiff had a right to protection of its trade name." *Id.* at p. 973, 77 U.S.P.Q. at 199. *See also Hanson v. Triangle Publications,* (8 Cir.) 163 F.2d 74, 74 U.S.P.Q. 280, *cert. denied,* 332 U.S. 855, 76 U.S.P.Q. 621; *Adolph Kastor & Bros v. Federal Trade Commission, supra; Esquire, Inc. v. Esquire Bar,* 37 F. Supp. 875, 49 U.S.P.Q. 592. Furthermore, in the case at bar, it would seem that something more than mere sponsorship is involved, something that very closely approaches direct competition. The plaintiff does not manufacture children's playsuits, but it licenses another to do so on a royalty basis. Any customers purchasing from the defendant on the strength of the "Wyatt Earp" name are customers diverted from plaintiff's licensee, to its direct pecuniary injury, in addition to any danger to its reputation.

While there is little doubt that the violation of plaintiff's rights by a diversion of purchasers to the defendant could readily be compensated for in a judgment for money damages, it also appears that a denial of preliminary injunctive relief would work irreparable and serious injury to the plaintiff by jeopardizing the entire licensing system it has built at great effort and expense. On a balance of the harms, the plaintiff stands to suffer much greater injury by a denial of injunctive relief than any which can befall defendant by granting such relief. Accordingly, the motion for a preliminary injunction will be granted.

* * *

PEACEABLE PLANET, INC. v. TY, INC.

362 F.3d 986 (7th Cir. 2004)

POSNER, CIRCUIT JUDGE

* * *

In the Spring of 1999, Peaceable Planet began selling a [toy] camel that it named "Niles." The name was chosen to evoke Egypt, which is largely desert except for the ribbon of land bracketing the Nile. The camel is a desert animal, and photos juxtaposing a camel with an Egyptian pyramid are common. The price tag fastened to Nile's ear contains information both about camels and about Egypt, and the Egyptian flag is stamped on the animal.

A small company, Peaceable Planet sold only a few thousand of its camels in 1999. In March of the following year, Ty began selling a camel also named "Niles." It sold a huge number of its "Niles" camels — almost two million in one year — precipitating this suit. The district court ruled that "Niles," being a personal name, is a descriptive mark that the law does not protect unless and until it has acquired secondary meaning, that is, until there is proof that consumers associate the name with the plaintiff's brand. Peaceable Planet did not prove that consumers associate the name "Niles" with its camel.

The general principle that formed the starting point for the district court's analysis was unquestionably sound. A descriptive mark is not legally protected unless it has acquired secondary meaning. [citations omitted]. An example is "All Bran." The name describes the product. If the first firm to product an all-bran cereal could obtain immediate trademark protection, and thus prevent all other producers of all-bran cereal from describing their product as all bran, it would be difficult for competitors to gain a foothold in the market. They would be as if speechless. Had Peaceable Planet named its camel "Camel," that would be a descriptive mark in a relevant sense, because it would make it very difficult for Ty to market its own camel — it wouldn't be satisfactory to have to call it "Dromedary" or "Bactrian."

Although cases and treatises commonly describe personal names as a subset of descriptive marks . . . it is apparent that the rationale for denying trademark protection to personal names without proof of secondary meaning can't be the same as the rationale just sketched for marks that are "descriptive" in the normal sense of the word. Names, as distinct from nicknames like "Red" or "Shorty," are rarely descriptive. "Niles" may evoke but it certainly does not describe a camel, any more than "Pluto" describes a dog, "Bambi" a fawn, "Garfield" a cat, or "Charlotte" a spider. (In the *Tom and Jerry* comics, "Tom," the name of the cat, could be thought descriptive, but "Jerry," the name of the mouse, could not be.) So anyone who wanted to market a toy camel, dog, fawn, cat, or spider would not be impeded in doing so by having to choose another name.

The reluctance to allow personal names to be used as trademarks reflect valid concerns (three such concerns, to be precise), but they are distinct from the concern that powers the rule that descriptive marks are not protected until they acquire secondary meaning. One of the concerns is a reluctance to forbid a person to use his own name in his own business. [Citations omitted]. Supposing a man named Brooks opened a clothing store under his name, should this prevent a second Brooks from opening a clothing store under his own (identical) name even though consumers did not yet associate the name with the first Brooks's store? It should not. [Citations omitted.]

Another and closely related concern behind the personal-name rule is that some names are so common — such as "Smith," "Jones," "Schwartz," "Wood," and "Jackson" — that consumers will not assume that two products having the same name therefore have the same source, and so they will not be confused by their bearing the same name. [Citations omitted]. If there are two bars in a city that are named "Steve's," people will not infer that they are owned by the same Steve.

The third concern, which is again related but brings us closest to the rule regarding descriptive marks, is that preventing a person from using his name to denote his business may deprive consumers of useful information. Maybe "Steve" is a well-known neighborhood figure. If he can't call his bar "Steve's" because there is an existing bar of that name, he is prevented from communicating useful information to the consuming public. [Citations omitted].

The scope of a rule is often and here limited by its rationale. Or, to make the same point differently, one way of going astray in legal analysis is to focus on the semantics of a rule rather than its purpose. Case 1 might say that a personal name could not be [protected] in the circumstances of that case without proof of secondary meaning. Case 2 might say that personal names cannot be [protected] without proof of secondary meaning but might leave off the qualifications implicit in the circumstances of the case. And then in Case 3 the court might just ask, is the trademark at issue a personal name? As we observed in *AM Int'l, Inc. v. Graphic Management Associates, Inc.*, 44 F 3d 572, 575 (7th Cir. 1995), "rules of law are rarely as clean and strict as statements of them make them seem. So varied and unpredictable are the circumstances in which they are applied that more often than not the summary statement of a rule — the terse formula that judges employ as a necessary shorthand to prevent judicial opinions from turning into treatises — is better regarded as a generalization than as the premise of a syllogism." The "rule" that personal names are not protected as trademarks until they acquire secondary meaning is a generalization, and its application is to be guided by the purposes that we have extracted from the case law. When none of the purposes that animate the "personal name" rule is present, and application of the "rule" would impede rather than promote competition and consumer welfare, an exception should be recognized. And will be; for we find cases holding, very sensibly — and with inescapable implications for the present case — that the "rule" does not apply if the public is unlikely to understand the personal name as a personal name. *Lane Capital Management, Inc. v. Lane Capital Management, Inc.*, 192 F.3d 337, 345-46 (2d Cir. 1999); *Circuit City Stores, Inc. v. CarMax, Inc.*, 165 F.3d 1047, 1054 (6th Cir. l999).

The personal-name "rule," it is worth noting, is a common law rather than statutory doctrine. All that the Lanham Act says about personal names is that a mark that is "primarily merely a surname" is not registrable in the absence of secondary meaning. 15 U.S.C. §§ l052(e)(4), (f). There is no reference to first names. The reason for the surname provision is illustrated by the Brooks example. The extension of the rule to first names is a judicial innovation and so needn't be pressed further than its rationale, as might have to be done if the rule were codified in inflexible statutory language. Notice too the limitation implicit in the statutory term "primarily."

In thinking about the applicability of the rationale of the personal-name rule to the present case, we should notice first of all that camels, whether real or toy, do not go into business. Peaceable Planet's appropriation of the name "Niles" for its camel is not preventing some hapless camel in the Sahara Desert who happens to be named "Niles" from going into the water-carrier business under its own name. The second thing to notice is that "Niles" is not a very common name; in fact it is downright rare. And the third thing to notice is that if it were a common name, still there would be no danger that precluding our hypothetical Saharan water carrier from using its birth name "Niles" would deprive that camel's customers of valuable information. In short, the rationale of the personal-name rule is wholly inapplicable to this case.

What is more, if one wants to tie the rule in some fashion to the principle that descriptive marks are not protectable without proof of second meaning, then one must note that "Niles," at least when affixed to a toy camel, is a suggestive mark, like "Microsoft" or "Business Week," or — coming closer to this case — like "Eor" used as the name of a donkey, or the proper names in *Circuit City Stores, Inc. v, CarMax, Inc.*, supra 165 F.3d at 1054, rather than being a descriptive mark. Suggestive marks are protected by trademark law without proof of secondary meaning. [Citations omitted]. Secondary meaning is not required because there are plenty of alternatives to any given suggestive mark. There are many more ways of suggesting than of describing. Suggestive names for camels include "Lawrence [of Arabia]" (one of Ty's other Beanie Babies is a camel named "Lawrence"); "Desert Taxi," "Sopwith" (the Sopwith Camel was Snoopy's World War I fighter plane), "Camelia," "Traveling Oasis," "Kamelsutra," "Cameleon," and "Humpy-Dumpy."

If "Niles" cannot be a protected trademark, it must be because to give it legal protection would run afoul of one of the purposes of the common law rule that we have identified rather than because it is a descriptive term, which it is not. But we have seen that it does not run afoul of any of those purposes. "Niles" is not the name of the defendant — it's not as if Peaceable Planet had named its camel "Ty Inc." or "H. Ty Warner." It also is not a common name, like "Smith" or "Jackson." And making Ty use a different name for its camel would not deprive the consumer of valuable information about Ty or its camel.

Treating the personal-name rule as a prohibition against ever using a personal name as a trademark (in the absence of secondary meaning) would lead to absurd results, which is a good reason for hesitating to press a rule to its logical limit, its semantic outer bounds. It would mean that the man who invented "Kitty Litter" could not [protect] the name ("Kitty" is a more common first name than "Niles") until it had acquired secondary meaning. So as soon as "Kitty Litter" hit the market, a much larger producer of cat litter could appropriate the name, flood the market with its product, and eventually obtain an enforceable trademark in the name by dint of having invested it with secondary meaning, squashing the originator. This is not an entirely fanciful example. Kitty Litter was invented (and named) in 1947 by a young man, Ed Lowe, in Cassopolis, Michigan, a town of notable obscurity. (As recently as July 2002, its population was only 1,703. We do not know what it was in 1947.) At first he sold the new product mainly to neighbors. On Ty's conception of the personal-name rule, without a patent Lowe could not have prevented a large company from selling the same product under the same name, thus squashing him. We cannot see what purpose of trademark law would be served by encouraging such conduct. Ty marks its "Niles" camel with the trademark symbol, and given the ratio of its sales to those of Peaceable Planet's "Niles," the Ty Niles may be well on its way to acquiring secondary meaning — at which point it will be able to enjoin Peaceable Planet from using the name on Peaceable's camel even though Peaceable thought of naming a camel "Niles" before Ty did. For all we know, Ty may have copied the idea from Peaceable, though Peaceable has not proved that.

Ty argues (we are quoting from its brief) that "one competitor should not be allowed to impoverish the language of commerce by monopolizing descriptive names," and "there are a limited number of personal names that are recognized as such by the public." All true. But the suggestion that "Niles" belongs to the limited class of "recognized" names or that "Niles" is the only way to name a camel is ridiculous.

And there is more: as both *Lane Capital Management, Inc. v. Lane Capital Management, Inc.*, and *Circuit City Stores, Inc. v. CarMax, Inc.*, which we cited earlier, point out, a word that is used as a person's name can be understood as something else ("Kitty," again), in which event the personal-name rule falls by the wayside. On the question whether "Niles" is likely to be understood by the plush-toy consuming public as a personal name rather than as a play on "Nile" the river, Ty conducted a survey in which about half the respondents indicated that they consider "Niles" a personal name. That is not an impressive fraction; imagine the response if one asked whether "William" is a personal name, or "Michael" or "Judith." Moreover, the survey was limited to adults even though Ty's primary market is children, and the questions posed to the respondents were slanted by obsessive repetition of the term "person's name," as in (we are quoting from the survey) "Do you think of the word on this card mainly as a person's name, mainly as something other than a person s name, or as both a person's name and as something else, or don't you have an opinion?" The intention doubtless was to create a subliminal association between "Niles" and "person's name." But the survey was not merely devoid of probative value, unprofessional, and probably inadmissible under the *Daubert* standard; it was irrelevant. If people were asked what came to mind when they saw the word "Niles" and they said a camel, there would be an argument that "Niles" was a descriptive mark, and Peaceable Planet would be sunk. The fact that "Niles" can be a person's name (as can almost any combination of letters) — although according to Ty's own statistics only about one resident of Illinois in 50,000 is named "Niles" — does not bear on whether "Niles" is a descriptive mark as applied to a plush toy camel. It is not.

There is a town named "Niles" in Illinois and another one in Michigan, and this is a reminder of the importance of context in characterizing a trademark. "Apple" is a generic term when used to denote the fruit, but a fanciful mark (the kind that receives the greatest legal protection) when used to denote a computer. If a gas station in Niles, Michigan, calls itself the "Niles Gas Station," it cannot before acquiring secondary meaning enjoin another firm from opening the "Niles Lumber Yard" in the town, on the ground that people will think that the firms are under common ownership. [Citations omitted]. In a town named Niles, firms bearing the name are sharing a name that is too common to be appropriable without proof of secondary meaning. That is not the case when the name is applied to a camel. And while both Niles, Illinois, and Niles, Michigan, are fine towns, neither is the place of origin of the camel or identified with that animal in some other way.

We conclude that Peaceable Planet has a valid trademark in the name "Niles" as applied to its camel, and so the case must be returned to the district court, where Peaceable Planet [will have] to prove infringement of its trademark . . .

end 1/23/09

* * *

Notes on Surnames

1. The Right to Use One's Surname

It is now generally recognized that there is no paramount "right" to use a surname in business where it is likely to be confused with a name that has already acquired source-indicating significance. However, "[i]n fashioning injunctive relief in a trademark case where, as here, a surname is the subject of the dispute, this Court is mindful that such injunctive relief is generally limited. . . . .Nevertheless, the old notion that an individual has an absolute right to use her surname as a mark when someone else has adopted the name first and established a secondary meaning is dead." R.J. Toomey Co. v. Toomey, 683 F. Supp. 873, 879 (D. Mass. 1988). When a surname has become strongly connected in the public mind with a certain product (e.g., STETSON hats), and a latecomer bearing the surname attempts to use the name in selling a competing product, the courts will sometimes allow the latecomer use of the name so long as it is accompanied by a prefix, suffix or disclaimer designed to allow the public to distinguish between sources. *See Taylor Wine Co. v. Bully Hill Vineyards*, 569 F.2d 731 (2[d] Cir. 1978) (Walter J. Taylor permitted to use his signature on his wines or in advertising but only with a disclaimer so as to avoid confusion with TAYLOR wines); *Caesar's World, Inc. v. Caesar's Palace*, 490 F. Supp. 818 (D.N.J. 1980) (New Jersey beauty salon owner enjoined from trademark use of "Palace" and from such use of his first name "Caesar," unless in conjunction with his last name, to avoid confusion with the Las Vegas hotel "CAESAR'S PALACE").

In *Sullivan v. Ed Sullivan Radio & TV, Inc.*, 152 N.Y.S.2d 227 (App. Div. 1956), the strength of the general public's identification of the then popular television variety show host with radio and television convinced the court that the defendant must be enjoined from using his own name, Ed Sullivan, in that form, for his business of selling and repairing radio and television sets. A lack of competition between plaintiff and defendant and the fact that defendant only owned an isolated store in Buffalo, New

York did not deter the court from its holding.

> . . . The state of facts may so change as to encompass a situation where there may be a series or a chain of similar stores throughout the country, in which case indeed, unless appellant had taken this present, prompt, action, he might at a later date encounter great difficulty in obtaining an injunction because of his own laches.

The court further noted the possibility that defendant might sell his store to a corporation in more direct competition with the television host. Plaintiff's use of "Sullivan," "E.J. Sullivan," or "Edward J. Sullivan," however, specifically was not enjoined.

2. Distinctiveness of Surnames

Section 2(e) of the Lanham Act (15 U.S.C. § 1502(e)) precludes registration of a trademark which "is primarily merely a surname" unless it "has become distinctive of the applicant's goods in commerce." *See In re Darty*, 759 F.2d 15 (Fed. Cir. 1985) (the section "reflects the common law that exclusive rights in a surname *per se* can not be established without evidence of long and exclusive use, which changes its significance from a surname of an individual to a mark for particular goods or services;" registration was refused where DARTY was the surname of a principal of the applicant, was used as such in the company name "Darty et Fils" (Darty and Son), and evidence showed it was not so unusual that it would not be recognized as a surname by a substantial number of persons); *Societe Civile Des Domaines Dourthe Freres v. S.A. Consortium Vinicole De Bordeaux Et De La Garonde*, 6 U.S.P.Q.2d 1205 (T.T.A.B. 1998) (DOURTHE for wine refused registration). As with descriptive marks, a surname is registrable and protectable if secondary meaning is shown, i.e., if it no longer is primarily merely a surname. *In re Rath*, 402 F.3d 1207 (Fed. Cir. 2005) (affirming refusal to register because German doctor's purported marks DR RATH and RATH were primarily merely surnames; although the marks were registered in Germany, the Paris Convention treaty did not require the U.S. to ignore its own requirements for registration). *Cf. In re Hutchinson Technology*, 825 F.2d 552 (Fed. Cir. 1988) (HUTCHINSON TECHNOLOGY for computer components in its entirety held registrable, even though part of the mark was primarily merely a surname).

Why should a surname be treated any differently from an arbitrary mark which is registrable upon adoption and use? What is primarily merely a surname? Should a common surname be treated differently from an uncommon one? What if a common surname also has a dictionary meaning? *See, e.g., Lane Capital Management, Inc. v. Lane Capital Management, Inc.*, 192 F.3d 337 (2th Cir. 1999) (noting that surnames such as "King" and "Cotton" are not viewed as primarily merely surnames due to their well-known dictionary meanings, and upholding a summary judgment that due to its alternative dictionary meaning, "Lane," in the mark LANE CAPITAL MANAGEMENT for financial services, had not been shown to be primarily merely a surname). *Cf. Peaceful Planet, Inc. v. Ty, Inc.*, excerpted above, in which Judge Posner explained that, "[w]hen none of the purposes that animate the personal name rule is present, and application of the rule would impede rather than promote competition and consumer welfare, an exception should be recognized." Note that § 2(a) of the Lanham Act prohibits registration of a mark "which may disparage or falsely suggest a connection with persons living or dead" and § 2(c) prohibits registration of a mark "identifying a particular living individual except by his written consent."

3. Surnames and Trademark Infringement

The courts ordinarily enjoin any surname use by the junior user where such use is not in good faith. *Société Vinicole de Champagne v. Mumm*, 143 F.2d 240 (2th Cir. 1944) (change of name); *R. W. Rogers Co. v. William Rogers Mfg. Co.*, 70 F. 1017 (2th Cir.

1895) (corporate use of a shareholder's name).

Absent intent, as indicated above, many courts have simply required the addition of a prefix, suffix, initials or first name, or the use of color, type style, or further clarifying language. See the discussion on disclaimers in the Remedies section of Chapter 10. Why should the courts seek such compromise solutions respecting surnames? Do such additions really avoid the basic problem of consumer deception? How can a court insure that the consumer will know "which Dobbs is 'his' Dobbs?" *Hat Corp. of America v. D.L. Davis Corp.*, 4 F.Supp. 613 (D. Conn 1933) ("The name has become a purely impersonal symbol. . . . For one who has known one Dobbs only [for hats], suddenly confronted with the suggestion that there are varieties of the species, is not informed which Dobbs is 'his' Dobbs"). *Cf. John B. Stetson Co. v. Stephen L. Stetson Co.*, 128 F.2d 981 (2th Cir. 1942), where the defendant had been ordered to place notices on his hat labels that he was NEVER CONNECTED IN ANY WAY with the famous manufacturer of Stetson hats. Defendant's response over time was progressively to shrink the disclaimer on the labels until its impact on purchasers was negligible. The court responded to defendant's claim of literal compliance by stating that it had plainly violated the spirit of the injunction and enjoined all use of STETSON except in the notice of differentiation. What other devices or sanctions might be utilized to balance the interest of the parties and the public? *See* Jacoby & Raskopf, *Disclaimers in Trademark Infringement Litigation: More Trouble Than They're Worth?*, 76 TRADEMARK REP. 35 (1986); Radin, *Disclaimers as Remedies for Trademark Infringement: Inadequacies and Alternatives*, 76 TRADEMARK REP. 59 (1986).

When a business enterprise makes authorized trademark use of a person's surname, should it be able to prevent subsequent trademark use of the name by that person in connection with a separate but similar enterprise? In *Holiday Inns, Inc. v. Trump*, 617 F. Supp. 1443 (D.N.J. 1985), defendant had contracted for plaintiff to use defendant's surname "Trump" in connection with plaintiff's casino hotels. Defendant then began using his surname in connection with his own casino hotel. Despite a finding of "substantial evidence in the record of actual confusion" (*Holiday Inns*, 617 F. Supp. at 1474), the court denied plaintiff relief, citing plaintiff's failure to contractually reserve exclusive rights, defendant's long-standing practice of using his name in connection with his business projects, the public's association of his name with high quality services, and the public's consequent interest in defendant's continued use of that name.

In *John Curry Skating Co. v. John Curry Skating Co.*, 626 F. Supp. 611 (D.D.C. 1985), renowned ice skater John Curry and his new marketing corporation as defendants obtained summary judgment against his former marketing corporation when the plaintiff failed to demonstrate that the public associated the mark with plaintiff rather than defendants. *Compare John Zink Co. v. Zink*, F.3d 1256 (10th Cir. 2001), in which the court held defendant in contempt for violating an injunction against use of his JOHN ZINK name in competition with plaintiff. Plaintiff had acquired the rights in that name from defendant's father for use in connection with gas and liquid fuel burners. "The purpose [of the injunction] was to permit Mr. Zink [the son] to continue to operate and to act as an individual using his proper name as he is known and has been known, but to prevent it from being linked to competitive sales endeavors in the particular business." In *Doeblers' Pa. Hybrids, Inc. v. Doebler*, 442 F.3d 812 (3[d] Cir. 2006), the court reversed and remanded the district court's summary judgment for plaintiff in a dispute over a family surname. The court cautioned that family companies should carefully consider trademark ownership issues. "[A] family surname used by family companies with a high degree of overlapping ownership and management is ripe with potential for [a dispute regarding trademark ownership.]" *See also Stilson & Assocs. v. Stilson Consulting Group, LLC*, 129 Fed. Appx. 993 (6th Cir. 2005) (unpub.) (successor in interest to "Stilson" name prevailed in trademark infringement suit against grandson of founder Stilson).

4.   Historical Surnames

Surnames that are primarily historical are said to be inherently distinctive arbitrary marks not requiring proof of secondary meaning, thus removing them from the general category of surnames. What is the rationale for this distinction? Why should the use of RAMESES or ROBIN HOOD have trademark significance upon adoption and use, while use of O'REILLY is not protectable until secondary meaning is shown? *See Lucien Piccard Watch Corp. v. Since 1868 Crescent Corp.*, 314 F. Supp. 329, 331 (S.D.N.Y. 1970) (DA VINCI); and the *Wyatt Earp* case excerpted above.

2.07   Colors

Introduction

Despite the considerable practical role that color plays in many trademarks, the protection to be accorded it often poses judicial dilemmas. It may be perfectly clear and demonstrable that color similarities result in confusion and likelihood of confusion, but courts have traditionally been concerned that the color spectrum is too limited to admit trademark protection. The *Qualitex* case and the notes that follow it discuss some of the difficulties the law has encountered in this area, and their modern resolution based in substantial part on the Law and Economics approach adopted by the *Qualitex* court. Consider what consumer products stand out to you because of their color or color combinations on the packaging or labeling of a product, or on the product itself. How much protection should be given such identifying features? How should consumer protection concerns (preventing confusion) and concerns about the depletion of practically available color marks be balanced? How well-taken is the concern that "colors are in limited supply," as *Qualitex* puts it?

QUALITEX CO. v. JACOBSON PRODUCTS CO., INC.
514 U.S. 159 (1995)

BREYER, JUSTICE

The question in this case is whether the Lanham Trademark Act of 1946 (Lanham Act), 15 U.S.C. §§ 1051–1127 (1988 ed. and Supp. V), permits the registration of a trademark that consists, purely and simply, of a color. We concluded that, sometimes, a color will meet ordinary legal trademark requirements. And, when it does so, no special legal rule prevents color alone from serving as a trademark.

I

The case before us grows out of petitioner Qualitex Company's use (since the 1950's) of a special shade of green-gold color on the pads that it makes and sells to dry cleaning firms for use on dry cleaning presses. In 1989 respondent Jacobson Products (a Qualitex rival) began to sell its own press pads to dry cleaning firms; and it colored those pads a similar green-gold. In 1991, Qualitex registered the special green-gold color on press pads with the Patent and Trademark Office as a trademark. Registration No. 1,633,711 (Feb. 5, 1991). Qualitex subsequently added a trademark infringement count, 15 U.S.C. § 1114(1), to an unfair competition claim, § 1125(a), in a lawsuit it had already filed challenging Jacobson's use of the green-gold color.

Qualitex won the lawsuit in the District Court . . . . But, the Court of Appeals for the Ninth Circuit set aside the judgment in Qualitex's favor on the trademark infringement claim because, in that Circuit's view, the Lanham Act does not permit Qualitex, or anyone else, to register "color alone" as a trademark. 13 F.3d 1297, 1300, 1302 (1994).

The courts of appeals have differed as to whether or not the law recognizes the use of color alone as a trademark. *Compare NutraSweet Co. v. Stadt Corp.*, 917 F.2d 1024, 1028 (CA7 1990) (absolute prohibition against protection of color alone), with *In re*

Owens-Corning Fiberglas Corp., 774 F.2d 1116, 1128 (CA Fed. 1985) (allowing registration of color pink for fiberglass insulation), and *Master Distributors, Inc. v. Pako Corp.,* 986 F.2d 219, 224 (CA8 1993) (declining to establish *per se* prohibition against protecting color alone as a trademark). Therefore, this Court granted certiorari . . . . We now hold that there is no rule absolutely barring the use of color alone, and we reverse the judgment of the Ninth Circuit.

II

The Lanham Act gives a seller or producer the exclusive right to "register" a trademark, 15 U.S.C. § 1052 (1988 ed. and Supp. V), and to prevent his or her competitors from using that trademark, § 1114(1). Both the language of the Act and the basic underlying principles of trademark law would seem to include color within the universe of things that can qualify as a trademark. The language of the Lanham Act describes that universe in the broadest of terms. It says that trademarks "includ[e] any word, name, symbol, or device, or any combination thereof." § 1127. Since human beings might use as a "symbol" or "device" almost anything at all that is capable of carrying meaning, this language, read literally, is not restrictive. The courts and the Patent and Trademark Office have authorized for use as a mark a particular shape (of a Coca-Cola bottle), a particular sound of (NBC's three chimes), and even a particular scent (of plumeria blossoms on sewing thread). [Citations omitted]. If a shape, a sound, and a fragrance can act as symbols why, one might ask, can a color not do the same?

A color is also capable of satisfying the more important part of the statutory definition of a trademark, which requires that a person "us[e]" or "inten[d] to use" the mark

> to identify and distinguish his or her goods, including a unique product, from those manufactured or sold by others and to indicate the source of the goods, even if that source is unknown.

15 U.S.C. § 1127. True, a product's color is unlike "fanciful," "arbitrary," or "suggestive" words or designs, which almost automatically tell a customer that they refer to a brand . . . . The imaginary word "Suntost," or the words "Suntost Marmalade," on a jar of orange jam immediately would signal a brand or a product "source"; the jam's orange color does not do so. But, over time, customers may come to treat a particular color on a product or its packaging (say, a color that in context seems unusual, such as pink on a firm's insulating material or red on the head of a large industrial bolt) as signifying a brand. And, if so, that color would have come to identify and distinguish the goods — i.e. to "indicate" their "source" — much in the way that descriptive words on a product (say, "Trim" on nail clippers or "Car-Freshener" on deodorizer) can come to indicate a product's origin . . . . In this circumstance, trademark law says that the word (e.g. "Trim"), although not inherently distinctive, has developed "secondary meaning." *See Inwood Laboratories, Inc. v. Ives Laboratories, Inc.,* 456 U.S. 844, 851, n. 11, 102 S.Ct. 2182, 2187, n. 11, 72 L.Ed.2d 606 (1982) ("secondary meaning" is acquired when "in the minds of the public, the primary significance of a product feature . . . is to identify the source of the product rather than the product itself"). Again, one might ask, if trademark law permits a descriptive word with secondary meaning to act as a mark, why would it not permit a color, under similar circumstances, to do the same?

. . . In principle, trademark law, by preventing others from copying a source-identifying mark, "reduce[s] the customer's costs of shopping and making purchasing decisions," 1 J. McCarthy, McCarthy on Trademarks and Unfair Competition § 2.01[2], p. 2-3 (3d ed. 1994) (hereinafter McCarthy), for it quickly and easily assures a potential customer that this item — the item with this mark — is made by the same producer as other similarly marked items that he or she liked (or disliked) in the past. At the same time, the law helps assure a producer that it (and not an imitating competitor) will reap the financial, reputation-related rewards associated with a desirable product. The law thereby "encourage[s] the production of quality products," *ibid.*, and simultaneously discourages those who hope to sell inferior products by capitalizing on a consumer's inability quickly to evaluate the quality of an item offered for sale . . . . It is the source-distinguishing ability of a mark — not its ontological status as color, shape, fragrance, word, or sign — that permits it to serve these basic purposes. *See* Landes & Posner, Trademark Law: An Economic Perspective, *30 J.Law & Econ.* 265, 290 (1987). And, for that reason, it is difficult to find, in basic trademark objectives, a reason to disqualify absolutely the use of a color as a mark.

Neither can we find a principled objection to the use of color as a mark in the important "functionality" doctrine of trademark law. The functionality doctrine prevents trademark law, which seeks to promote competition by protecting a firm's reputation, from instead inhibiting legitimate competition by allowing a producer to control a useful product feature. It is the province of patent law, not trademark law, to encourage invention by granting inventors a monopoly over new product designs or functions for a limited time, 35 U.S.C. §§ 154, 173, after which competitors are free to use the innovation. If a product's functional features could be used as trademarks, however, a monopoly over such features could be obtained without regard to whether they qualify as patents and could be extended forever (because trademarks may be renewed in perpetuity) . . . . *See, e.g., Kellogg Co., supra,* 305 U.S., at 119–120, 59 S.Ct., at 113-114 (trademark law cannot be used to extend monopoly over "pillow" shape of shredded wheat biscuit after the patent for that shape had expired). This Court consequently has explained that, "[i]n general terms, a product feature is functional," and cannot serve as a trademark, "if it is essential to the use or purpose of the article or if it affects the cost or quality of the article," that is, if exclusive use of the feature would put competitors at a significant non-reputation-related disadvantage. *Inwood Laboratories, Inc.,* 456 U.S., at 850, n. 10, 102 S.Ct., at 2186, n. 10. Although sometimes color plays an important role (unrelated to source identification) in making a product more desirable, sometimes it does not. And, this latter fact — the fact that sometimes color is not essential to a product's use or purpose and does not affect cost or quality — indicates that the doctrine of "functionality" does not create an absolute bar to the use of color alone as a mark. *See Owens-Corning,* 774 F.2d, at 1123 (pink color of insulation in wall "performs no nontrademark function").

It would seem, then, that color alone, at least sometimes, can meet the basic legal requirements for use as a trademark. It can act as a symbol that distinguishes a firm's goods and identifies their source, without serving any other significant function . . . . Indeed, the District Court, in this case, entered findings (accepted by the Ninth Circuit) that show Qualitex's green-gold press pad color has met these requirements. The green-gold color acts as a symbol. Having developed secondary meaning (for customers identified the green-gold color as Qualitex's), it identifies the press pads' source. And, the green-gold color serves no other function. (Although it is important to use some color on press pads to avoid noticeable stains, the court found "no competitive need in the press pad industry for the green-gold color, since other colors are equally usable." (21 U.S.P.Q.2d, at 1460.) Accordingly, unless there is some special reason that convincingly militates against the use of color alone as a trademark, trademark law would protect Qualitex's use of the green-gold color on its press pads.

III

Respondent Jacobson Products says that there are four special reasons why the law should forbid the use of color alone as a trademark. We shall explain, in turn, why we, ultimately, find them impersuasive.

First, Jacobson says that, if the law permits the use of color as a trademark, it will produce uncertainty and unresolvable court disputes about what shades of a color a competitor may lawfully use. Because lighting (morning sun, twilight mist) will affect perceptions of protected color, competitors and courts will suffer from "shade confusion" as they try to decide whether use of a similar color on a similar product does, or does not, confuse customers and thereby infringe a trademark. Jacobson adds that the "shade confusion" problem is "more difficult" and "far different from" the "determination of the similarity of words or symbols." Brief for Respondent 22.

nope

We do not believe, however, that color, in this respect, is special. Courts traditionally decide quite difficult questions about whether two words or phrases or symbols are sufficiently similar, in context, to confuse buyers. They have had to compare, for example, such words as "Bonamine" and "Dramimine" (motion-sickness remedies); "Huggies" and "Dougies" (diapers); "Cheracol" and "Syrocol" (cough syrup); "Cyclone" and "Tornado" (wire fences); and "Mattres" and "1-800-Mattres" (mattress franchisor telephone numbers). [Citations omitted]. Legal standards exist to guide courts in making such comparisons. *See, e.g., 2 McCarthy* § 15.08; *1 McCarthy* §§ 11.24-11.25 ("[S]trong" marks, with greater secondary meaning, receive broader protection than "weak" marks). We do not see why courts could not apply those standards to a color, replicating, if necessary, lighting conditions under which a color product is normally sold. *See* Ebert, *Trademark Protection in Color: Do It By the Numbers!*, 84 TRADEMARK. REP. 379, 405 (1994). Indeed, courts already have done so in cases where a trademark consists of a color plus a design, i.e., a colored symbol such as a gold stripe (around a sewer pipe), a yellow strand of wire rope, or a "brilliant yellow" band (on ampules). [Citations omitted].

Second, Jacobson argues, as have others, that colors are in limited supply. *See, e.g., NutraSweet Co.*, 917 F.2d, at 1028; *Campbell Soup Co. v. Armour & Co.*, 175 F.2d 795, 798 (CA3 1949). Jacobson claims that, if one of many competitors can appropriate a particular color for use as a trademark, and each competitor then tries to do the same, the supply of colors will soon be depleted. Put in its strongest form, this argument would concede that "[h]undreds of color pigments are manufactured and thousands of colors can be obtained by mixing." L. Sheskin, *Colors: What They Can Do For You* 47 (1947). But, it would add that, in the context of a particular product, only some colors are usable. By the time one discards colors that, say, for reasons of customer appeal, are not usable, and adds the shades that competitors cannot use lest they risk infringing a similar, registered shade, then one is left with only a handful of possible colors. And, under these circumstances, to permit one, or a few, producers to use colors as trademarks will "deplete" the supply of usable colors to the point where a competitor's inability to find a suitable color will put that competitor at a significant disadvantage.

color depletion theory

nope

This argument is unpersuasive, however, largely because it relies on an occasional problem to justify a blanket prohibition. When a color serves as a mark, normally alternative colors will likely be available for similar use by others. *See e.g., Owens-Corning*, 774 F.2d, at 1121 (pink insulation). Moreover, if that is not so — if a "color depletion" or "color scarcity" problem does arise — the trademark doctrine of "functionality" normally would seem available to prevent the anticompetitive consequences that Jacobson's argument posits, thereby minimizing that argument's practical force.

. . . Although we need not comment on the merits of specific cases, we note that lower courts have permitted competitors to copy the green color of farm machinery (because customers wanted their farm equipment to match) and have barred the use of black as a trademark on outboard boat motors (because black has the special functional attributes of decreasing the apparent size of the motor and ensuring compatibility with many different boat colors). [Citations omitted]. The Restatement (Third) of Unfair Competition adds that, if a design's "aesthetic value" lies in its ability to "confe[r] a significant benefit that cannot practically be duplicated by the use of alternative designs," then the design is "functional." Restatement (Third) of Unfair Competition § 17, Comment c., p. 175–176 (1995). The "ultimate test of aesthetic functionality," it explains, "is whether the recognition of trademark rights would significantly hinder competition." *Id.*, at 176.

The upshot is that, where a color serves a significant nontrademark function — whether to distinguish a heart pill from a digestive medicine or to satisfy the "noble instant for giving the right touch of beauty to common and necessary things," G.K. Chesterton, Simplicity and Tolstoy 61 (1912) — courts will examine whether its use as a mark would permit one competitor (or a group) to interfere with legitimate (nontrademark-related) competition through actual or potential exclusive use of an important product ingredient. That examination should not discourage firms form creating aesthetically pleasing mark designs, for it is open to their competitors to do the same. *See, e.g. W.T. Rogers Co. v. Keene,* 778 F.2d 334, 343 (CA7 (1985) (Posner, J.). But, ordinarily, it should prevent the anticompetitive consequences of Jacobson's hypothetical "color depletion" argument, when, and if, the circumstances of a particular case threaten "color depletion."

Third, Jacobson points to many older cases — including Supreme Court cases — in support of its position. In 1878, this Court described the common-law definition of trademark rather broadly to "consist of a name, symbol, figure, letter, form, or device, if adopted and used by a manufacturer or merchant in order to designate the goods he manufactures or sells to distinguish the same from those manufactured or sold by another." *McLean v. Fleming,* 96 U.S. 245, 254, 24 L.Ed. 828. Yet, in interpreting the Trademark Acts of 1881 and 1905, 21 Stat. 502, 33 Stat. 724, which retained that common-law definition, the Court questioned "[w]hether mere color can constitute a valid trade-mark," *A. Leschen & Sons Rope Co. v. Broderick & Bascom Rope Co.,* 201 U.S. 166, 171, 26 S.Ct. 425, 50 L.Ed. 710 (1906), and suggested that the "product including the coloring matter is free to all who make it." *Coca-Cola Co. v. Koke Co. of America,* 254 U.S. 143, 41 S.Ct. 113, 114, 65 L.Ed. 189 (1920). Even though these statements amounted to dicta, lower courts interpreted them as forbidding protection for color alone. *See, e.g., Campbell Soup Co.,* 175 F.2d at 798, and n. 9; *Life Savers Corp. v. Curtiss Candy Co.,* 182 F.2d 4, 9 (CA7 1950) (quoting *Campbell Soup*).

* * *

. . . Much of the pre-1985 case law rested on statements in Supreme Court opinions that interpreted pre-Lanham Act trademark law and were not directly related to the holdings in those cases. Moreover, we believe the Federal Circuit was right in 1985 when it found that the 1946 Lanham Act embodied crucial legal changes that liberalized the law to permit the use of color alone as a trademark (under appropriate circumstances). At a minimum, the Lanham Act's changes left the courts free to reevaluate the preexisting legal precedent which had absolutely forbidden the use of color alone as a trademark. Finally, when Congress re-enacted the terms "word, name, symbol, or device" in 1988, it did so against a legal background in which those terms had come to include color, and its statutory revision embraced that understanding.

Fourth, Jacobson argues that there is no need to permit color alone to function as a trademark because a firm already may use color as part of a trademark, say, as colored circle or colored letter or colored word, and may rely upon "trade dress" protection, under § 43(a) of the Lanham Act, if a competitor copies its color and thereby causes consumer confusion regarding the overall appearance of the competing products or their packaging, *see* 15 U.S.C. § 1125(a) (1988 ed., Supp. V). The first part of this argument begs the question. One can understand why a firm might find it difficult to place a usable symbol or word on a product (say, a large industrial bolt that customers normally see from a distance); and, in such instances, a firm might want to use color, pure and simple, instead of color as part of a design. Neither is the second portion of the argument convincing. Trademark law helps the holder of a mark in many ways that "trade dress" protection does not. *See* 15 U.S.C. § 1124 (ability to prevent importation of confusingly similar goods); § 1072 (constructive notice of ownership); § 1065 (incontestable status);

§ 1057(b) (prima facie evidence of validity and ownership). Thus, one can easily find reasons why the law might provide trademark protection in addition to trade dress protection.

. . . [T]he judgment of the Ninth Circuit is

Reversed.

* * *

Notes on Colors

1. The Traditional Rule

The general rule used to be that color was accorded trademark protection only when it was employed as an element of a distinctive design. *A. Leschen & Sons Rope Co. v. Broderick & Bascom Rope Co.*, 201 U.S. 166 (1906); *Barbasol Co. v. Jacobs*, 160 F.2d 336 (7th Cir. 1947) (holding that a shaving cream box having diagonal blue, white, and red stripes forming a border for a blue panel was a distinctive design) *But see Luxor Cab Mfg. Corp. v. Leading Cab Co.*, 125 Misc. 764, 211 N.Y.S. 866 (1925), *aff'd*, 215 A.D. 798, 213 N.Y.S. 847 (1925), where the color of taxicabs was held entitled to trademark protection. *See also* Samuels & Samuels, *Color Trademarks: Shades of Confusion*, 83 TRADEMARK REP. 554 (1991); *American Chiclet Co. v. Topps Chewing Gum*, 208 F.2d 560 (2d Cir. 1953) (L. Hand, J.). The reason often stated for the general rule that color alone should not have trademark significance was the limited number of colors available. It was said that if color *per se* could be appropriated, all primary colors would soon be subject to monopoly. *See, e.g., Campbell Soup Co. v. Armour & Co.*, 175 F.2d 795 (7th Cir. 1949). Recall in this context the discussion about the "monopoly phobia" in Chapter 1.

2. The Post-*Qualitex* Rule

The *Qualitex* decision, *supra*, arose because of a split among the circuits regarding the protection of color. At least one court in recent years had relied on the old general rule that color alone is not protectable. *NutraSweet Co. v. Stadt Corp.*, 917 F.2d 1024 (7th Cir. 1990), *cert. denied*, 499 U.S. 983 (1991) (affirming summary judgment that defendant's use of a blue packet for its SWEET ONE sugar substitute did not infringe plaintiff's rights in its blue packet for its EQUAL sugar substitute). *Compare In Re Owens-Corning Fiberglas Corp.*, 227 U.S.P.Q. 417 (Fed. Cir. 1985) (the color pink for insulation was registrable as a trademark given its nonfunctionality and the company's strong showing that the color had secondary meaning among consumers). *See also Forschner Group v. Arrow Trading Co.*, 124 F.3d 402 (2d Cir. 1997) (color red not protectable for handle of plaintiff's pocket knives where third parties had used red on pocket knife handles for many years); *Brunswick Corp. v. British Seagull*, 35 F.3d 1527 (Fed. Cir. 1994), *cert. denied*, 514 U.S. 1050 (1995) (refusing to register the color black for outboard marine motors because to do so would hinder competition; the color was held functional because outboard engine manufacturers used it to coordinate with a wide variety of boat colors, and the color made the engine appear smaller than lighter colors did); *Master Distributors, Inc. v. Pako Corp.*, 986 F.2d 219 (8th Cir. 1993) (endorsing the *Owens-Corning* decision and rejecting the color depletion theory as applied to plaintiff's shade of blue for splicing tape); *Keds Corp. v. Renee International Trading Corp.*, 888 F.2d 215 (1st Cir. 1989) (preliminary injunction upheld for incontestably registered blue rectangle label for sneakers, the court opining that the color depletion theory was somewhat out of date); *Black & Decker v. Pro-Tech Power, Inc.*, 26 F.Supp. 2d 834 (E.D. Va. 1998) (plaintiff awarded $1.7 million where defendant intentionally copied the yellow and black color scheme and significant design features of plaintiff's DeWalt line of power tools). For a historical overview of the cases leading up to *Qualitex* and an assessment of its impact, *see* Baker, *Correcting a Chromatic*

Aberration: Qualitex Co. v. Jacobson Products Co., 9 Harvard J.L. & Tech. 547–564 (1996). *See generally* Coleman, *Color as Trademarks: Breaking Down The Barriers of the Mere Color Rule*, 74 J. Pat. & Trademark Office Soc'y 345 (1992). On related issues of protection, such as protecting scent or sound as a trademark, see Gilson, § 2.11 (2008 ed.); Roth, *Something Old, Something New, Something Borrowed, Something Blue: A New Tradition in Nontraditional Trademark Registrations*, 27 Cardozo L. Rev. 457 (2006) (proposed use of an international color code for color registrations and suggested improvements in the registration process for other nontraditional marks); Gilson & Lalonde, *Cinnamon Buns, Marching Ducks and Cherry-Scented Race Car Exhaust: Protecting Nontraditional Trademarks*, 95 TMR 773 (2005).

In a subsequent decision, the Supreme Court reiterated the holding in *Qualitex* that color alone can never be inherently distinctive; secondary meaning must be shown before it receives trademark protection. *Wal-Mart Stores, Inc. v. Samara Brothers, Inc.* 529 U.S. 205 (2000). *Compare* Jordan and Jordan, *Qualitex v. Jacobson Products Co., The Unanswered Question: Can Color Ever Be Inherently Distinctive?*, 85 Trademark Rep. 371 (1995). The *Qualitex* court also relied in part on the doctrine of aesthetic functionality, a controversial doctrine previously embraced only by a few circuits. See the discussion in Chapter 5.

As indicated in the *Qualitex* decision, "functional" colors will not be protected. In *Life Savers Corp. v. Curtiss Candy Co.*, 182 F.2d 4 (7th Cir. 1950), the court held "the use of color, including colored stripes, as background on labels is functional and indicates the color and flavor of candy the package contains." In *North Shore Laboratories Corp. v. Cohen*, 721 F.2d 514, 523 (5th Cir. 1983), the court found that tire repair products at issue were necessarily brown in color and that "plaintiff occupies the same position as a cola manufacturer attempting to prohibit other cola manufacturers from selling brown cola." What if the color is merely ornamental? *See American Basketball Ass'n v. AMF Voit, Inc.*, 358 F. Supp. 981 (S.D.N.Y. 1973), aff'd, 487 F.2d 1393 (2d Cir. 1974), *cert. denied*, 416 U.S. 986 (1974), where the court held that "mere coloration of the various panels of the ordinary basketball is not sufficiently distinctive to be the subject of a statutory trademark. . . . I find that the colors are merely a decoration or embellishment." *American Basketball Ass'n.*, 358 F. Supp. at 985. *But see Ideal Toy Corp. v. Plawner Toy Mfg. Corp.*, 685 F.2d 78 (3dCir. 1982) (arrangement of color patches similar to that on a Rubik's Cube preliminarily enjoined).

For an example of how far courts have gone to find a color functional, see *Norwich Pharmacal Co. v. Sterling Drug, Inc.*, 271 F.2d 569 (2dCir. 1959), *cert. denied*, 362 U.S. 919 (1960), wherein the court inferred that the color pink used in a stomach upset remedy (PEPTO-BISMOL) served as a psychosomatic soothing element characterized as "functional."

A rival dealer may not appropriate another's mark by merely changing its color. *See National Ass'n of Blue Shield Plans v. United Bankers Life Ins. Co.*, 362 F.2d 374 (5th Cir. 1966), where two distinctive designs (Blue and Red Shields) differed only as to the color used. The court held that the use of different colors could not prevent a likelihood of confusion with respect to the public.

CHAPTER 3
TRADEMARK REGISTRATION
AND ADMINISTRATIVE PROCEEDINGS

CONTENTS

3.01 The Purpose of the Lanham Act

The federal law of trademarks is governed by the Trademark Act of 1946, 15 U.S.C. § 1051 *et seq.*, popularly known as the Lanham Act. The intent of the Act is stated in § 45, as follows:

> The intent of this Act is to regulate commerce within the control of Congress by making actionable the deceptive and misleading use of marks in such commerce; to protect registered marks used in such commerce from interference by State, or territorial legislation; to protect persons engaged in such commerce against unfair competition; to prevent fraud and deception in such commerce by the use of reproductions, copies, counterfeits, or colorable imitations of registered marks; and to provide rights and remedies stipulated by treaties and conventions respecting trademarks, trade names, and unfair competition entered into between the United States and foreign nations.

(15 U.S.C. § 1127.) This policy is implemented in large part by a federal registration system through which marks, when registered, are entitled to the various benefits of the Act. Although federal registration was provided for in both the Acts of 1881 and 1905, the Lanham Act broadened registrability and strengthened its effect in an effort to

respond to the needs of commerce. While federal registration of a trademark confers many benefits, as discussed in this chapter, it is important to remember that protectable common law rights can be established in this country by use alone. *See, e.g., JCW Investments, Inc., v. JCW Novelty, Inc.,* 482 F.3d 910 (7th Cir. 2007) (rejecting defendant's contention that the Lanham Act preempted state law). See also Chapter 1 above. The Lanham Act is reproduced in its entirety in the Appendix. That Act provides a cause of action for infringement of unregistered marks under § 43(a), 15 U.S.C. 1125(a). *See, e.g., Waymark Corp. v. Porta Sys. Corp.,* 334 F.3d 1358 (Fed. Cir. 2003) (although plaintiff's BATTSCAN mark had not been registered at time lawsuit was filed, registration was not required under § 43(a)).

3.02   The Benefits of Federal Registration

PARK'N FLY, INC. v. DOLLAR PARK AND FLY, INC.
469 U.S. 189 (1985)

JUSTICE O'CONNOR delivered the opinion of the Court.

* * *

I

Petitioner operates long-term parking lots near airports. After starting business in St. Louis in 1967, petitioner subsequently opened facilities in Cleveland, Houston, Boston, Memphis, and San Francisco. Petitioner applied in 1969 to the United States Patent and Trademark Office (Patent Office) to register a service mark consisting of the logo of an airplane and the words "Park'N Fly." The registration issued in August 1971. Nearly six years later, petitioner filed an affidavit with the Patent Office to establish the incontestable status of the mark. As required by § 15 of the Trademark Act of 1946 (Lanham Act), 60 Stat. 433, as amended, 15 U.S.C. § 1065, the affidavit stated that the mark had been registered and in continuous use for five consecutive years, that there had been no final adverse decision to petitioner's claim of ownership or right to registration, and that no proceedings involving such rights were pending. Incontestable status provides, subject to the provisions of § 15 and § 33(b) of the Lanham Act, "conclusive evidence of the registrant's exclusive right to use the registered mark . . ." § 33(b), 15 U.S.C. § 1115(b).

Respondent also provides long-term airport parking services, but only has operations in Portland, Oregon. Respondent calls its business "Dollar Park and Fly." Petitioner filed this infringement action in 1978 in the United States District Court for the District of Oregon and requested the court permanently to enjoin respondent from using the words "Park and Fly" in connection with its business. Respondent counterclaimed and sought cancellation of petitioner's mark on the grounds that it is a generic term. *See* § 14(c), 15 U.S.C. § 1064(c). Respondent also argued that petitioner's mark is unenforceable because it is merely descriptive. *See* § 2(e), 15 U.S.C. § 1052(e). . . .

After a bench trial, the District Court found that petitioner's mark is not generic and observed that an incontestable mark cannot be challenged on the grounds that it is merely descriptive. . . . The District Court permanently enjoined respondent from using the words "Park and Fly" and any other mark confusingly similar to "Park'N Fly."

The Court of Appeals for the Ninth Circuit reversed. 718 F.2d 327 (1983). The District Court did not err, the Court of Appeals held, in refusing to invalidate petitioner's mark. *Id.,* at 331. The Court of Appeals noted, however, that it previously had held that incontestability provides a defense against the cancellation of a mark, but it may not be used offensively to enjoin another's use. *Ibid.* Petitioner, under this analysis, could obtain an injunction only if its mark would be entitled to continued registration without regard to its incontestable status. Thus, respondent could defend the infringement action by showing that the mark was merely descriptive. Based on its own examination of the record, the Court of Appeals then determined that petitioner's mark is in fact merely descriptive, and therefore respondent should not be enjoined from using the name "Park and Fly." *Ibid.*

The decision below is in direct conflict with the decision of the Court of Appeals for the Seventh Circuit in *Union Carbide Corp. v. Ever-Ready Inc.*, 531 F.2d 366, *cert. denied*, 429 U.S. 830 (1976). We granted certiorari to resolve this conflict, 465 U.S. —, 104 S. Ct. 1438 (1984), and we now reverse.

*   *   *

This case requires us to consider the effect of the incontestability provisions of the Lanham Act in the context of an infringement action defended on the grounds that the mark is merely descriptive. Statutory construction must begin with the language employed by Congress and the assumption that the ordinary meaning of that language accurately expresses the legislative purpose. *See American Tobacco Co. v. Patterson*, 456 U.S. 63, 68 (1982). With respect to incontestable trade or service marks, § 33(b) of the Lanham Act states that "registration shall be conclusive evidence of the registrant's exclusive right to use the registered mark" subject to the conditions of § 15 and certain enumerated defenses.[1] Section 15 incorporates by reference subsections (c) and (e) of § 14, 15 U.S.C. § 1064. An incontestable mark that becomes generic may be cancelled at any time pursuant to § 14(c). That section also allows cancellation of an incontestable mark at any time if it has been abandoned, if it is being used to misrepresent the source of the goods or services in connection with which it is used, or if it was obtained

---

[1] Section 33(b) of the Lanham Act, as set forth in 15 U.S.C. § 1115(b), provides:

If the right to use the registered mark has become incontestable under section 1065 of this title, the registration shall be conclusive evidence of the registrant's exclusive right to use the registered mark in commerce or in connection with the goods or services specified in the affidavit filed under the provisions of said section 1065 subject to any conditions or limitations stated therein except when one of the following defenses or defects is established:

(1) That the registration or the incontestable right to use the mark was obtained fraudulently; or

(2) That the mark has been abandoned by the registrant; or

(3) That the registered mark is being used, by or with the permission of the registrant or a person in privity with the registrant, so as to misrepresent the source of the goods or services in connection with which the mark is used; or

(4) That the use of the name, term, or device charged to be an infringement is a use, otherwise than as a trade or service mark, of the party's individual name in his own business, or of the individual name of anyone in privity with such party, or of a term or device which is descriptive of and used fairly and in good faith only to describe to users the goods or services of such party, or their geographic origin; or

(5) That the mark whose use by a party is charged as an infringement was adopted without knowledge of the registrant's prior use and has been continuously used by such party or those in privity with him from a date prior to registration of the mark under this chapter or publication of the registered mark under subsection (c) of section 1062 of this title: *Provided, however*, That this defense or defect shall apply only for the area in which such continuous prior use is proved; or

(6) That the mark whose use is charged as an infringement was registered and used prior to the registration under this chapter or publication under subsection (c) of section 1062 of this title of the registered mark of the registrant, and not abandoned: *Provided, however*, That this defense or defect shall apply only for the area in which the mark was used prior to such registration or such publication of the registrant's mark; or

(7) That the mark has been or is being used to violate the antitrust laws of the United States.

Editor's note: Section 1115(b) the Lanham Act subsequently was amended to add two new defenses to incontestability:

(8) That the mark is functional; or

(9) That equitable principles, including laches, estoppel and acquiescence, are applicable.

fraudulently or contrary to the provisions of § 4, 15 U.S.C. § 1054, or §§ 2(a)–(c), 15 U.S.C. §§ 1052(a)–(c).[2]

One searches the language of the Lanham Act in vain to find any support for the offensive/defensive distinction applied by the Court of Appeals. The statute nowhere distinguishes between a registrant's offensive and defensive use of an incontestable mark. On the contrary, § 33(b)'s declaration that the registrant has an "exclusive right" to use the mark indicates that incontestable status may be used to enjoin infringement by others. A conclusion that such infringement cannot be enjoined renders meaningless the "exclusive right" recognized by the statute. Moreover, the language in three of the defenses enumerated in § 33(b) clearly contemplates the use of incontestability in infringement actions by plaintiffs. *See* §§ 33(b)(4)–(6), 15 U.S.C. §§ 1115(b)(4)–(6).

The language of the Lanham Act also refutes any conclusion that an incontestable mark may be challenged as merely descriptive. A mark that is merely descriptive of an applicant's goods or services is not registrable unless the mark has secondary meaning. Before a mark achieves incontestable status, registration provides prima facie evidence of the registrant's exclusive right to use the mark in commerce. § 33(a), 15 U.S.C. § 1115(a). The Lanham Act expressly provides that before a mark becomes incontestable an opposing party may prove any legal or equitable defense which might have been asserted if the mark had not been registered. *Ibid.* Thus, § 33(a) would have allowed respondent to challenge petitioner's mark as merely descriptive if the mark had not become incontestable. With respect to incontestable marks, however, § 33(b) provides that registration is *conclusive* evidence of the registrant's exclusive right to use the mark, subject to the conditions of § 15 and the seven defenses enumerated in § 33(b) itself. Mere descriptiveness is not recognized by either § 15 or § 33(b) as a basis for challenging an incontestable mark.

*   *   *

Nothing in the legislative history of the Lanham Act supports a departure from the plain language of the Statutory provisions concerning incontestability. Indeed, a conclusion that incontestable status can provide the basis for enforcement of the registrant's exclusive right to use a trade or service mark promotes the goals of the statute. The Lanham Act provides national protection of trademarks in order to secure to the owner of the mark the good will of his business and to protect the ability of consumers to distinguish among competing producers. *See* S. Rep. No. 1333, at 3, 5. National protection of trademarks is desirable, Congress concluded, because trademarks foster competition and the maintenance of quality by securing to the producer the benefits of good reputation. *Id.*, at 4. The incontestability provisions, as the proponents of the Lanham Act emphasized, provide a means for the registrant to quiet title in the ownership of his mark. . . . The opportunity to obtain incontestable status by satisfying the requirements of § 15 thus encourages producers to cultivate the good will associated with a particular mark. This function of the incontestability provisions would be utterly frustrated if the holder of an incontestable mark could not enjoin infringement by others so long as they established that the mark would not be registrable but for its incontestable status.

*   *   *

The dissent echoes arguments made by opponents of the Lanham Act that the incontestable status of a descriptive mark might take from the public domain language that is merely descriptive. As we have explained, Congress has already addressed concerns to prevent the "commercial monopolization," of descriptive language. The Lanham Act allows a mark to be challenged at any time if it becomes generic, and, under

---

[2] Sections 2(a)–(c) prohibit registration of marks containing specified subject matter, *e.g.*, the flag of the United States. Sections 4 and 14(e) concern certification marks and are inapplicable to this case.

certain circumstances, permits the non-trademark use of descriptive terms contained in an incontestable mark. Finally, if "monopolization" of an incontestable mark threatens economic competition, § 33(b)(7), 15 U.S.C. § 1115(b)(7), provides a defense on the grounds that the mark is being used to violate federal antitrust laws. At bottom, the dissent simply disagrees with the balance struck by Congress in determining the protection to be given to incontestable marks.

* * *

We conclude that the holder of a registered mark may rely on incontestability to enjoin infringement and that such an action may not be defended on the grounds that the mark is merely descriptive. . . .

[*Reversed and remanded.*]

JUSTICE STEVENS, dissenting.

* * *

If the registrant of a merely descriptive mark complies with the statutory requirement that prima-facie evidence of secondary meaning must be submitted to the Patent and Trademark Office, it is entirely consistent with the policy of the Act to accord the mark incontestable status after an additional five years of continued use. For if no rival contests the registration in that period, it is reasonable to presume that the initial prima-facie showing of distinctiveness could not be rebutted. But if no proof of secondary meaning is ever presented, either to the Patent and Trademark Office or to a court, there is simply no rational basis for leaping to the conclusion that the passage of time has transformed an inherently defective mark into an incontestable mark.

No matter how dedicated and how competent administrators may be, the possibility of error is always present, especially in nonadversary proceedings. . . .

On the basis of the record in this case, it is reasonable to infer that the operators of parking lots in the vicinity of airports may make use of the words "park and fly" simply because those words provide a ready description of their businesses, rather than because of any desire to exploit petitioner's good will. There is a well-recognized public interest in prohibiting the commercial monopolization of phrases such as "park and fly." When a business claims the exclusive right to use words or phrases that are a part of our common vocabulary, this Court should not depart from the statutorily mandated authority to "rectify the register," 15 U.S.C. § 1119, absent a clear congressional mandate. Language, even in a commercial context, properly belongs to the public unless Congress instructs otherwise. In this case we have no such instruction; in fact, the opposite command guides our actions: Congress' clear insistence that a merely descriptive mark, such as "Park'N Fly" in the context of airport parking, remain in the public domain unless secondary meaning is proved.

The Court suggests that my reading of the Act "effectively emasculates § 33(b) under the circumstances of this case." But my reading would simply require the owner of a merely descriptive mark to prove secondary meaning before obtaining any benefit from incontestability. If a mark is in fact "distinctive of the applicant's goods in commerce" as § 2(f) requires, that burden should not be onerous. If the mark does not have any such secondary meaning, the burden of course could not be met. But if that be the case, the purposes of the Act are served, not frustrated, by requiring adherence to the statutory procedure mandated by Congress.

* * *

Notes on the Benefits of Federal Registration

1. General

The right to registration flows from use in commerce. For U.S. registrants, federal registration of a mark cannot be had until it is in use; federal registration generally does not enlarge the common-law right to its protection. Even foreign registrants, who can obtain registrations without any use in commerce under Sections 44 and 66, must submit proof of use within six years after the registration issues. There are substantial benefits that accrue from federal registration, including: (a) constructive notice of the registrant's claim of ownership of the mark, 15 U.S.C. § 1072; (b) nationwide constructive use as of the date of application, 15 U.S.C. § 1057(c); (c) prima facie evidence of the registration's validity, of the registrant's ownership of the mark, and of the registrant's exclusive right to use the mark in commerce in connection with the goods or services specified in the registration certificate, 15 U.S.C. § 1057(b); (d) the right to institute a trademark action in the federal courts without regard to diversity of citizenship or the amount in controversy, 15 U.S.C. § 1121; (e) the right to request Customs officials to bar the importation of goods bearing infringing trademarks, 15 U.S.C. § 1124; (f) provision for treble damages, attorneys' fees and other remedies in civil actions for infringement, 15 U.S.C. §§ 1116–1120; and (g) the right, after continuous use of the mark for five years after registration, to have the registradtion become incontestable and thereby constitute conclusive evidence of registrant's exclusive right to use the mark in commerce for the identified goods or services, 15 U.S.C. § 1065, subject to certain defenses, including fraud, abandonment, genericness, functionality, misrepresentation, prior use, use in violation of antitrust laws, fair use, and equitable defenses, such as laches, 15 U.S.C. § 1115(b). *See, e.g., Marshak v. Treadwell*, 240 F.3d 184 (3ᵈ Cir. 2001) (sustaining jury verdict for cancellation of incontestable registration due to fraudulent procurement where there was "strong evidence" that the registrant "actually knew or believed that someone else had a right to the mark"); *Orient Express Trading Co. v. Federated Department Stores, Inc.*, 842 F.2d 650 (2d Cir. 1988) (incontestable registrations cancelled because plaintiff had committed fraud on the Patent and Trademark Office by greatly exaggerating its claims of use in its §§ 8 and 15 affidavits).

The most important of the Lanham Act's benefits in pragmatic impact are constructive use and constructive notice, incontestability, and the right to a federal cause of action, the last being discussed in Chapter 10. Note that the federal cause of action provided in the Lanham Act applies to both registered and unregistered (common-law) marks. *See* GILSON, § 1.04, 3.04 and 4.01. Upon registration, the public is charged with constructive notice of the claim of ownership of the trademark, and non-owner use of it subsequent to that registration cannot be justified or defended by claim of innocence, good faith or lack of knowledge. Thus, a principal registration has nationwide effect, preserving the registrant's right to expand at a later date without fear of having that right usurped by a newcomer. *Dawn Donut Co. v. Hart's Food Stores, Inc.*, 267 F.2d 358 (2ᵈ Cir. 1959); See also Chapter 7 (discussion of concurrent rights). Under the Revision Act, this nationwide priority right will date back to the time of application. 15 U.S.C. § 1057(c); *Warnervision Entertainment, Inc. v. Empire of Carolina, Inc.*, 101 F.3d 259 (2ᵈ Cir. 1996).

In *United States Jaycees v. Chicago Junior Ass'n of Commerce & Industry*, 505 F. Supp. 998 (N.D. Ill. 1981), the court observed that "the effect of incontestability is to foreclose *all* defenses [in infringement suits] except the seven defenses specifically enumerated in the statute." *See Park'N Fly, infra*, setting out these defenses. *See also Dakota Indus., Inc. v. Ever Best Ltd.*, 28 F.3d 910 (8ᵗʰ Cir. 1994) (federal registrant's rights in incontestable DAKOTA mark for blue jeans is a question of law, not a question of fact for the jury). An expired registration normally does not provide constructive notice, however. *First Savings Bank F.S.B. v. First Bank Sys. Inc.*, 101 F.3d 645 (10ᵗʰ

Cir. 1996) (expired registration for FIRST BANK SYSTEM did not provide constructive notice to a junior user of FIRST BANK). PTO findings reflected in a registration also may be given significant evidentiary effect in litigation. In *RFE Indus., Inc. v. SPM Corp.*, 105 F.3d 923, 926 (4th Cir. 1997) for example, PTO had issued a certificate of registration for POPCORN for popcorn-shaped silver anodes without requiring proof of secondary meaning. The appellate court concluded, "the PTO's taking of such an action is powerful evidence that the registered mark is suggestive and not descriptive." Note, however, that the weight federal courts accord PTO findings and actions widely varies. *See, e.g., Te-Ta-Ma Truth Foundation — Family of URI, Inc., v. World Church of the Creator*, 297 F.3d 662, 665-6 (7th Cir. 2002) (undertaking *de novo* review of genericness issue and according the incontestable federal registration of a challenged mark merely a "bubble-bursting presumption . . . [rather than] the sort of indomitable presumption that the Foundation seeks").

2. Incontestability

The Revision Act has resolved a conflict among the courts by providing that, in addition to the previously identified § 1115(b) defenses, equitable defenses (such as laches and estoppel) may be raised in actions involving incontestable registrations. The Revision Act also revised 15 U.S.C. § 1115(b) expressly to confirm that protection of an incontestably registered mark is still "subject to proof of infringement." In other words, as stated by the Tenth Circuit in *Coherent, Inc. v. Coherent Technologies, Inc.*, 935 F.2d 1122 (10th Cir. 1991), the incontestable status of a plaintiff's registration does not mean "any use by another party automatically constitutes infringement."

Under *Park'N Fly* the *validity* of an incontestably registered trademark cannot be challenged on descriptiveness grounds. A number of courts have recognized, however, that the *strength* of the incontestably registered mark, which may involve its descriptiveness, may be considered in determining how broad the scope of protection should be in assessing likelihood of confusion. *See, e.g., CareFirst of Md, Inc. v. First Care P.C.*, 434 F.3d 263 (9th Cir. 2006) ("incontestability alone does not establish that the trademark is strong"; "First" and "Care" were commonly used in the healthcare industry, and the evidence did not show that CAREFIRST "has conceptual or commercial strength," so that confusion with defendant's FIRST CARE mark was unlikely); *Munters Corp. v. Matsui America, Inc.*, 909 F.2d 250, 252 (7th Cir.), *cert. denied*, 498 U.S. 1016 (1990) (assessing descriptiveness of incontestably registered mark for strength and likelihood of confusion purposes "is correct practice in the Seventh Circuit"); *Miss World (UK), Ltd. v. Mrs. America Pageant, Inc.*, 856 F.2d 1445, 1449 (9th Cir. 1988) ("incontestable status does not alone establish a strong mark"); *Oreck Corp. v. U.S. Floor Systems, Inc.*, 803 F.2d 166, 171 (5th Cir.) ("[i]ncontestable status does not make a weak mark strong"), *cert. denied*, 481 U.S. 1069 (1987). *But see Dieter v. B&H Industries*, 880 F.2d 322, 329 (11th Cir. 1989) (incontestably registered mark "presumed to be at least descriptive with secondary meaning," and thus "relatively strong"), *cert. denied*, 498 U.S. 950 (1990). *See* Razzano, *Incontestability: Should It Be Given Any Effect In A Likelihood Of Confusion Determination*, 82 TRADEMARK REP. 409 (1992). The Supreme Court has clarified that the incontestability of a mark's registration in no way exempts the owner from having to prove all aspects of a trademark infringement case, including likelihood of confusion. *See KP Permanent Make-Up, Inc., v. Lasting Impression I, Inc.*, 543 U.S. 111 (2004). ~burden~

A defendant therefore may contest the *breadth* of protection accorded an incontestably registered mark (e.g., against marks used for different goods or services) by challenging its strength. See § 5.04. Incontestably registered marks also can be challenged on the grounds that the claimed mark is generic (Chapter 4) or, in the case of trade dress such as packaging and product configurations, functional (Chapter 6). *See Retail Services v. Freebies Publishing*, 364 F.3d 535 (9th Cir. 2004) (FREEBIES found generic for items offered for free; "incontestability is never a shield for a mark that is generic"); *Wilhelm Pudenz GmbH v. Littlefuse, Inc.*, 177 F.3d 1204 (11th Cir. 1999) (affirming cancellation of registrations for automobile fuse configurations based on functionality); the Trademark Law Treaty Implementation Act of 1998, Pub. L. No. 105-330, 112 Stat. 3064 (expressly identifying functionality as a defense to incontestability and basis for opposition and cancellation); 15 U.S.C. §§ 1065, 1115. The benefits of incontestability underscore the importance of an examining attorney's initial decision concerning an applied for mark. *Cf. In re Anylens Acquisition LLC*, 61 Fed. Appx. 698 (Fed. Cir. 2003) (NATIONALCONTACTLENSES.COM refused registration because "national" described the geographical extent of the proposed services, "contact lenses" was descriptive of several of the proposed services and ".com" was nothing more than "a reference to a top level domain designation").

Good faith *non*-trademark descriptive use of a mark by another is permitted under the "fair use" provision of 15 U.S.C. § 1115(b), as discussed in Chapter 7. *See, e.g., Institute for Scientific Information, Inc. v. Gordon & Breach Science Publishers, Inc.*, 931 F.2d 1002 (3d Cir. 1991), *cert. denied*, 502 U.S. 909 (1991) (descriptiveness of plaintiff's incontestably registered mark may be considered in context of defendant's § 1115(b) fair use defense).

In *Watec Co. v. Liu*, 403 F.3d 645 (9th Cir. 2005), the court applied the prior use exception to incontestability contained in Lanham Act section 15 (15 U.S.C. § 1065). That section provides:

> [E]xcept to the extent, if any, to which the use of a mark registered on the principal register infringes a valid right acquired under the law of any State or Territory by use of a mark or trade name continuing from a date prior to the date of registration under this Act of such registered mark, the right of the registrant to use such registered mark . . . shall be incontestable. . . .

After a jury found Watec America liable for intentional trademark infringement, Watec America appealed, alleging in part that Watec Japan did not make the requisite showing to overcome Watec America's incontestable rights in WATEC and WAC. The court held that "a litigant claiming § 1065 senior rights must show: (1) that his or her 'use of the mark began before its registration and publication' and (2) 'that there has been continuing use since that time.' " 403 F.3d at 653, citing *Casual Corner Assocs., Inc. v. Casual Stores of Nevada, Inc.*, 493 F.2d 709, 712 (9th Cir. 1974). After finding that the plaintiff had shown such prior and continuous use, the court affirmed the jury verdict of trademark infringement. *See also* the section on Concurrent Rights in Chapter 7.

3.03 Acquisition and Maintenance of Federal Registrations

General

The right to registration flows from use in commerce. Section 45 of the Lanham Act, 15 U.S.C. § 1127, provides that use of a mark on goods sufficient to obtain federal registration occurs when the mark "is placed in any manner on the goods or their containers or the displays associated therewith or on the tags or labels affixed thereto, or if the nature of the goods makes such placement impracticable, then on documents associated with the goods or their sale . . . and the goods are sold or transported in commerce." *See Chapter 2.* When the claimed use on goods is based on display rather than affixation, it is generally required that the display be point-of-purchase material designed to attract the attention of prospective purchasers. *In re ITT Rayonier, Inc.*, 208 U.S.P.Q. 86, 87 (T.T.A.B. 1980). *But see In re Ultraflight, Inc.*, 221 U.S.P.Q. 903, 906 (T.T.A.B. 1984), where the Board noted that in some instances inserts may be part of the goods themselves, and held that use of the mark in issue on an instruction manual inserted in a powered hand-glider assembly kit was affixation adequate for registration purposes. A website page can be such a point-of-purchase display sufficient for registration if the page displays the product and a means to order it. *In re Dell, Inc.*, 71 U.S.P.Q. 2d. 1725 (T.T.A.B. 2004).

A trademark used solely intrastate may be registrable on the federal register if its use affects interstate or foreign commerce. *In re Silenus*, 557 F.2d 506 (C.C.P.A. 1977). *See generally* Hellwig, *Acquisition of Trademark Rights Under the Trademark Law Revision Act of 1988*, 80 T.M.R. 311 (1990); Sacoff, *The Trademark Use Requirement In Trademark Registration, Opposition and Cancellation Proceedings*, 76 T.M.R. 99 (1986).

The sufficiency of use of a claimed service mark requires a different analysis since there is nothing physical to which the mark can be affixed. "Service" has been defined as "the performance of labor for the benefit of another," *In re Canadian Pacific Ltd.*, 754 F.2d 992, 994 (Fed. Cir. 1985) (the court noting the term is not defined in the Lanham Act). Valid use of a service mark requires that it be "used or displayed in the sale or advertising of services" rendered in commerce. 15 U.S.C. §§ 1127, 1052, 1053. Therefore, acceptable service mark use under § 45:

> extends beyond the narrow concept of trademark use of a mark in the accepted manner of affixation to the goods . . . and encompasses a broad spectrum of use including business cards, stationery, circulars, direct mailing pieces, advertisements in the various media including radio and television commercials, store signs, and any other method that may be employed in promoting one's service . . . [S]uch use must be an open and notorious public use directed to the segment of the purchasing public for whom the services are intended . . . and [must] inform or apprise prospective purchasers of the present or future availability of the adopter's service under the mark.

Computer Food Stores, Inc. v. Corner Store Franchises, Inc., 176 U.S.P.Q. 535, 538 (T.T.A.B. 1973). For example, use in a newspaper advertisement to identify real estate services was sufficient in *Hovnanian Estates, Inc. v. Covered Bridge Estates, Inc.*, 195 U.S.P.Q. 658 (T.T.A.B. 1977), as was use on handbills to identify entertainment in *In re Florida Cypress Gardens, Inc.*, 208 U.S.P.Q. 288 (T.T.A.B. 1980).

A trade name, as defined in § 45, can be registered under the Act, but only if used as a trademark to identify the source of goods or services, and not merely as a company or organizational name. "[T]rade names qua trade names do not qualify for registration," and where an asserted mark is a trade name, "there is a presumption that the present usage is also that of a trade name" and not a trademark. *Application of Pennsylvania Fashion Factory, Inc.*, 588 F.2d 1343, 1345 (C.C.P.A. 1978) (use of retail store name on shopping bags held insufficient).

Like a trade name, trademark rights are not automatically conferred upon a domain name. *See* Tanenbaum, *Rights and Remedies For Three Common Trademark-Domain Name Disputes: (1) Domain Name vs. Trademark, (2) Shared Trademarks, and (3) Domain Name Hijacking*, 545 PLI/Pat 297, 301 (1999). A domain name can be registered under the Lanham Act only if it is used as a trademark. The domain name must be used to identify and distinguish the source of the goods or services, in addition to identifying the web site's location. *See* MCCARTHY § 7:17.1 (4th ed. 2007); *In re Eilberg*, 49 U.S.P.Q.2d 1955, 1956 (T.T.A.B. 1998). A domain name is subject to the same requirements as any other potential mark, *see PTO Examination Guide No. 2-99*, Appendix E (Sept. 29, 1999); so the PTO may, among other things, apply the § 2(e) bars of descriptiveness, geographical descriptiveness, and surname significance in considering trademark registration of it. Moreover, the PTO does not consider the URL or the TLD in its evaluation of a domain name, as neither acts as a source indicator. *See PTO Examination Guide No. 2-99*, Appendix E (Sept. 29, 1999). Thus, a TLD like "com" cannot turn an unregisterable mark into a registrable trademark. *See, e.g. In re Anylens Acquisition LLC*, 62 Fed. Appx. 698 (Fed. Cir. 2003) (NATIONALCONTACTLENSES.COM refused registration because "national" and "contact lenses" were descriptive, and ".com" was nothing more than "a reference to a top level domain designation").

Compare In re Eddie Z's Blinds and Drapery, Inc., 74 U.S.P.Q.2d 1037 (T.T.A.B. 2005) (refusing to register generic BLINDSANDDRAPERY.COM where evidence showed "blinds and drapery" was the phrase used by many businesses to indicate they make and sell those products) with *In re Steelbuilding.com*, 415 F.3d 1293 (Fed. Cir. 2005) (STEELBUILDING.COM not generic for "online retail services in the field of pre-engineered metal buildings and roofing systems" because of ambiguity in whether the term referred to actual building or the act of building with steel).

A domain name placed inconspicuously in small lettering on business letterhead or advertisements, for example, may be insufficiently used as a source identifier to constitute trademark use, particularly where the goods or services are not identified. SEE TRADEMARK MANUAL OF EXAMINING PROCEDURE, § 1301.04; *In re Eilberg*, 49 U.S.P.Q.2d at 1956. Nevertheless, use on letterhead or business cards may be acceptable if the goods or services are clearly indicated on them and the domain name is used in a trademark manner. TRADEMARK MANUAL OF EXAMINING PROCEDURE, § 1301.04. The key is whether the domain name has been used as a symbol of product origin rather than simply informing the viewer where to find the web site in cyberspace. *In re Eilberg*, 49 U.S.P.Q.2d at 1957 (holding that the domain name merely indicated the location of the web site in cyberspace and did not separately identify the applicant's services); *Lockheed Martin Corp. v. Network Solutions, Inc.*, 985 F. Supp. 949, 956 (C.D. Cal. 1997) (noting the difference between the technical function of a domain name—locating a web site—and the potential trademark function—source identification).

A mark used to identify a collective group, e.g., a union label, is registrable as a "collective mark" when properly used in a like manner to a trademark or service mark. *See, e.g., Schroeder v. Lotito*, 221 U.S.P.Q. 812, 819 (D.R.I. 1983) (holding that suit for infringement may be brought by the collective mark owner organization on behalf of its members). A certification mark, or a mark used in connection with goods or services to certify, inter alia, region of origin, or quality, or characteristics of the goods or services, is also registrable under the Lanham Act. The Underwriters Laboratories "UL" mark and the Good Housekeeping seal of approval are examples of certification marks. *See also Community of Roquefort*, in Chapter 2, (ROQUEFORT for cheese). Registration of collective and certification marks is authorized by 15 U.S.C. § 1054.

The Principal Register

The Lanham Act provides for two Registers, the Principal (15 U.S.C. § 1051) and the Supplemental (15 U.S.C. § 1091). As noted above, a mark is not registrable or protectable if it is generic or functional. A mark also is not registrable on either the Principal Register or Supplemental Register if it consists or is comprised of (1) immoral, deceptive, scandalous, or disparaging matter; (2) the flag or insignia of any nation, state, or municipality or any simulation thereof; (3) a name, portrait, or signature identifying any living individual or deceased President without written consent; or (4) a mark likely to be confused with a previously used or registered mark. A mark which is merely descriptive, deceptively misdescriptive, or primarily merely a surname is not registrable on the Principal Register unless it "has become distinctive of the applicant's goods in commerce," that is, if it has acquired secondary meaning, but such a mark may be registrable on the Supplemental Register without such showing. 15 U.S.C. §§ 1052, 1091.

A trademark "search" is usually desirable to determine whether a proposed mark has been anticipated by a previously used or registered one. Ordinarily, a search for confusingly similar marks should examine (1) federal registrations and applications; (2) state registrations; (3) Internet usage; and (4) common-law usage disclosed by trade directories and the like. Complete records of federal registrations and applications are maintained at the United States Patent and Trademark Office in Arlington, Va. In addition, private trademark search services provide computerized searches for federal and state registrations, as well as most common-law and Internet domain name uses.

Note that trade dress (see Chapter 5) searches, e.g. for a product or packaging design, can pose practical problems, as it is much more difficult for search firms to find common law uses of trade dress, as opposed to uses of word marks. Feisthamel, Kelly & Sistek, *Trade Dress 101: Best Practices for the Registration of Product Configuration Trade Dress With the USPTO*, 93 TMR 1357 (2005). If no confusingly similar prior registrations or uses are found in the trademark search, an application may be filed. Use in commerce will be necessary before the registration will issue. 15 U.S.C. § 1051; *Larry Harmon Pictures Corp. v. Williams Restaurant Corp.*, 929 F.2d 662 (Fed. Cir. 1992) (use in interstate commerce required).

Federal registration of a trademark on the Principal Register is obtained by filing a verified written application with the Trademark Division of the United States Patent and Trademark Office accompanied by a drawing of the mark, three specimen labels or facsimiles of the mark as actually used if appropriate (i.e., for a use-based application), and the statutory filing fee. The application can be based on either actual use or intent to use. The application confers upon the applicant a nationwide right of priority, as of the filing date of the application, against all competing claimants except prior users, prior applicants, and foreign treaty applicants with an earlier priority filing date. (As to the last, see the discussion in the Foreign Registration section, below at 3.05). That nationwide right of priority is contingent upon use being made and the registration issuing, at least for U.S. applicants. 15 U.S.C. § 1057(c).

Descriptive marks are registrable if they have acquired secondary meaning (or "distinctiveness"). Secondary meaning may be shown by circumstantial proof, such as proof of substantial sales and advertising and by direct evidence, such as surveys. Until 1989, the law allowed the Commissioner to accept as prima facie evidence of distinctiveness proof (e.g., an affidavit) of substantially exclusive and continuous use in commerce of the mark during the five years preceding the filing of the application. In 1989, the Revision Act changed the law to allow the proof of acquired distinctiveness to be based on the five-year period preceding the date on which the *claim* of distinctiveness is made. This is important because such claims are often made during the sometimes lengthy post-filing period after a finding of descriptiveness by the examining attorney.

If the Trademark Division determines that no prior registrations of marks exist that are likely to cause confusion and that the mark is otherwise entitled to registration, the mark and the other particulars specified in the application are published in the *Official Gazette* of the Patent and Trademark Office. This publication notifies the public of the application in order to enable possible opposition by any person who believes he or she would be damaged by the issuance of registration for that mark. 15 U.S.C. § 1062(a).

If no opposition proceeding is instituted against a use-based application within the time allowed after publication in the *Gazette*, a Certificate of Registration is issued. If no opposition is instituted within the time allowed after the publication in the *Gazette* against an intent-to-use application for which no amendment alleging use has been filed, the applicant receives a Notice of Allowance, and only after the applicant timely files a statement that use in interstate commerce has begun is a Certificate of Registration issued. The registrant is then entitled to use notice of such registration, including the symbol "R," in association with its mark, so as to inform the public of its federal registration.

The intent-to-use applicant must have a *bona fide* intent to use the mark in connection with the identified goods and services at the time of application. *See Caesars World, Inc. v. Milanian*, 126 Fed. Appx. 775 (9th Cir. 2005) (unpublished) (defendant lacked requisite bona fide intent to use COLOSSEUM for gaming and hotel–related services; he never applied for a gaming license, lacked experience in the hotel industry and engaged in actions that indicated he intended to sell or license the mark to others instead of using it in commerce); *Commodore Electronics Ltd. v. CBM Kabushiki Kaisha*, 26 U.S.P.Q.2d 1503 (T.T.A.B. 1993) (without an adequate explanation, the absence of any documentary evidence supporting applicant's claim that it possessed a *bona fide* intent under Section 1(b) to use its mark in commerce was sufficient to prove that applicant lacked this requisite intent); *Salacuse v. Ginger Spirits Inc.*, 44 U.S.P.Q.2d 1415 (T.T.A.B. 1997) (petitioner had filed numerous ITU applications for SOUTH BEACH for products ranging from food and beverages to luggage, motor vehicles and wine, as well as ITU applications for the similar marks SOBE and SO-BE-IT in the same class; petitioner's "multiple and repeat filings of intent-to-use applications" raised a reasonable inference that petitioner lacked the requisite *bona fide* intent at the time of filing its application). *Cf. Lane Ltd. v. Jackson International Trading Co.*, 33 U.S.P.Q.2d (T.T.A.B 1994) (applicant's evidence of the formulation and implementation of a business and licensing program constituted credible objective corroboration of its intent to use the mark). The intent-to-use applicant must commence use of the mark and file a statement of use, plus specimens, within six months of the date the Patent and Trademark Office issues the "Notice of Allowance" for the application, or obtain an extension of time for filing the statement. The initial six-month period will be extended for an additional six months upon written application reconfirming the bona fide intent to use, and payment of any applicable fees. Additional six-month extensions may be obtained, not to exceed a total of three years from the date the notice of allowance is issued, upon similar applications and fee payments plus showings of good cause. Failure to file a timely statement of use will result in a ruling of abandonment of the application.

gotta use the TM

Registration of a trademark on the Principal Register remains in force under the Revision Act for ten years provided that the registrant files an affidavit or declaration of use "within one year next preceding the expiration of . . . six years" from the date of registration. 15 U.S.C. § 1058(a). The affidavit must show, with support by specimens, that the mark is still in use in connection with all the specified goods or services, or that nonuse is due to special circumstances and not due to any intention to abandon the mark. *Id.* If the affidavit is not filed, the registration will be cancelled by the Patent and Trademark Office. Each registration may be renewed for periods of ten years (twenty years under pre-Revision Act law) upon application duly filed. 15 U.S.C. § 1059. *See generally* HAWES & DWIGHT, TRADEMARK REGISTRATION PRACTICE (2006 ed.); SMITH, INTENT-TO-USE TRADEMARK PRACTICE (1992 ed.).

term

The Supplemental Register

The Supplemental Register had its origins in the Act of 1920 which provided for the registration of marks not registrable under the 1905 Act (e.g., surnames). Among the intentions of the 1920 Act was enabling the users of such marks to obtain registrations in those foreign countries whose laws required as a prerequisite registration in the applicant's country of origin. The Lanham Act in effect continued this Register as a means of registering "marks capable of distinguishing applicant's goods or services and not registrable on the principal register." 15 U.S.C. § 1091.

A registration on the Supplemental Register confers none of the presumptions or prima facie evidence benefits afforded by a registration on the Principal Register. It does, however, afford the right to potential recovery of treble damages for infringement. In addition, it entitles the registrant to use a notice of registration (the "®" sign) in connection with the mark. Also, in many countries, a foreign applicant must have a registration in its country of origin as a prerequisite for registering a mark. A registration on the supplemental register meets that requirement for U.S. trademark owners applying to register their marks in other countries. Intent-to-use applications to register on the Supplemental Register are not permitted.

3.04   State Registrations

Every state provides for the registration of trademarks, and many have adopted the Model State Trademark Bill. When use of a mark is not "in commerce," such registration may be all that is available. Generally, the state statutes specify what may be registered, what constitutes infringement (likelihood of confusion), and remedies. Their actual substantive legal effect in addition to the common law is limited in most circumstances. *National Ass'n for Healthcare Communs. v. Central Ark. Area on Aging, Inc.,* 59 U.S.P.Q.2d 1352 (8th Cir. 2001)(despite state registration, relief granted only in six county region of actual use). *See generally* INTERNATIONAL TRADEMARK ASSOCIATION, STATE TRADEMARK AND UNFAIR COMPETITION LAW (2007 ed.) McCARTHY, TRADEMARKS AND UNFAIR COMPETITION, § 22:1.

3.05   Foreign Registrations

General

Almost every nation of the world provides for the registration of trademarks. Trade identity law, and the rules and regulations respecting registration differ markedly, however, from country to country. Most other countries do not require use of the mark as a prerequisite to registration. Several multicountry treaty arrangements exist which encompass trademark-trade identity rights, the principal ones being the Paris Convention, The Madrid Protocol, and the Madrid Agreement. The United States is a member of the first two but not the last. For general commentaries on trademark registration abroad, *see* INTERNATIONAL CONTRIBUTORS, TRADEMARKS THROUGHOUT THE WORLD, (4th ed. 2006); HOROWITZ, WORLD TRADEMARK LAW AND PRACTICE, (2d ed. 2007)

Section 44 of the Lanham Act, 15 U.S.C. § 1126, allows an applicant to register a mark in the United States based upon an application to register the mark in a foreign country which is a party to a trademark treaty with the United States (Sec. 44(d)), or upon a registration for the mark in that country (Sec. 44(e)). The United States application must be filed within six months of filing the foreign application for § 44(d) to apply. *See, e.g.,* Casagrande, *What Must a Foreign Service Mark Holder Do to Create and Maintain Service Mark Rights in the United States,* 93 TMR 1354 (2003). No such time constraint applies with respect to Sec. 44(e). However, a foreign registrant's mark is not eligible for registration under Section 44 unless it is registrable under U.S. law. *See In re Rath,* 402 F.3d 1207 (Fed. Cir. 2005) (refusing registration where alleged mark was primarily merely a surname, despite its registration under German law).

The implementation of an intent-to-use registration system in this country has decreased the advantage foreign applicants have over domestic applicants. Section 44 nonetheless provides a privilege to certain foreign applicants that is unavailable to domestic applicants, who must use a mark in U.S. commerce prior to obtaining a registration. A foreign registrant's continued failure to use the mark for a period of years *after* registration, however, may result in a finding of abandonment. *Rivard v. Linville,* 133 F.3d 1446 (Fed. Cir. 1998)(ULTRACUTS registration for salon services based on Canadian registration cancelled due to five years of unexcused non-use in U.S.); *Imperial Tobacco v. Philip Morris, Inc.,* 899 F.2d 1575 (Fed. Cir. 1990) (registration cancelled for abandonment based on five years of non-use).

Multi-National Registrations — The Madrid Protocol

The United States became a member of the Madrid Protocol on November 2, 2003, as codified in Sections 1141 to 1141(n) of the Lanham Act. The Madrid Protocol creates a centralized filing system by which trademark owners in member countries can obtain and maintain trademark rights in other member countries. Unlike the Community Trade Mark System, which provides a unitary registration for all of the European

Union, the Madrid Protocol sets up a streamlined operation for registering marks in individual foreign countries. Samuels and Samuels, *International Trademark Prosecution Streamlined: The Madrid Protocol Comes into Force in the United States*, 12 J. INTELL. PROP. L. 151-162 (2004); Hines and Weinstein, *Using the Madrid Protocol After U.S. Accession*, 93 TMR 1003 (2003). Therefore, the Madrid Protocol does not itself create trademark rights but is merely a process by which national trademark rights in multiple countries may be obtained. More than seventy jurisdictions are parties to the Madrid Protocol, including Australia, China, France, Germany, Japan, the Netherlands, Spain, Turkey, and the United Kingdom.

If the member country refuses registration within the set time period, the country sends its objections to The World Intellectual Property Organization ("WIPO") and WIPO forwards them to the applicant. The applicant then must appoint local counsel to respond to the objections.

If the member country issues the registration in its country, the mark receives the same protection as other national marks. The Madrid Registrations enjoy the right of priority found in Article 4 of the Paris Convention. Therefore, the date of the Madrid Registration will be the date of filing the Madrid Application in the Office of Origin, provided that WIPO receives the Madrid Application, without deficiency, within two months of the filing date. If WIPO does not receive the application without deficiency within two months of the filing, the effective Madrid Registration date will be the day WIPO receives the last piece of missing information.

To obtain protection of a trademark in other member countries, a trademark owner must first own a trademark application or registration in a member country. This application or registration will form the "basic" application or registration. In addition, the trademark owner must be either a national of that member country, be domiciled there, or have a real and effective place of business in that country.

The trademark owner can then file a single Madrid Application based on the basic application with the basic application's trademark office ("Office of Origin"). Under the Madrid Protocol, an applicant may freely choose his or her Office of Origin on the basis of establishment, domicile, or nationality, with the understanding that there is to be only one Office of Origin. For example, a trademark owner in the United States could file its Madrid Application with the United States Patent and Trademark Office. The applicant pays one fee based on the number of countries designated and the application then can be expanded to include any number of additional member countries.

The Office of Origin examines the Madrid Application and certifies that the information in the Madrid Application is the same information contained in the basic application or registration. The trademark owner's Office of Origin then forwards the Madrid Application to the International Bureau of WIPO. WIPO examines the application to make certain it conforms with the minimal established formalities, e.g., the appropriate fee is paid. If the requirements have been met, WIPO publishes the Madrid Application in the *WIPO Gazette of International Marks* and conveys the information in the application to all of the member countries which the trademark owner has designated.

The member countries that receive the Madrid Application information from WIPO are to treat the application as a properly filed national application. Those member countries independently examine the application under the same standards they use to examine national applications. If the member country is going to refuse registration in its country, it must do so within a set period of time. The Madrid Protocol sets this time period as twelve months, with possible extension to eighteen months and even longer if the national office notifies WIPO of a possible refusal based on an opposition. If the member country fails to act within this time period, the Madrid Registration takes effect and the trademark owner enjoys the same rights as if the application had passed through the national registration system. If the member country refuses registration within the set time period, the country sends its objections to WIPO and WIPO forwards them to the applicant. The applicant then must appoint local counsel to respond to the objections.

If the member country issues the registration in its country, the mark receives the same protection as other national marks. The Madrid Registrations enjoy the right of priority found in Article 4 of the Paris Convention. Therefore, the date of the Madrid Registration will be the date of filing the Madrid Application in the Office of Origin, provided that WIPO receives the Madrid Application, without deficiency, within two months of the filing date. If WIPO does not receive the application without deficiency within two months of the filing, the effective Madrid Registration date will be the day WIPO receives the last piece of missing information.

For the first five years, the existence of the Madrid Registration depends on the fate of the basic registration. For example, if a U.S. trademark owner's federal registration was canceled or limited in any way, the Madrid Registration would be likewise canceled or limited. If such a cancellation or limitation occurs, it is known as a "central attack." There is a three month window, however, after a central attack, during which a Madrid Registration can be transformed into corresponding national rights in the various designated countries and retain the priority in those other countries that was established by the failed Madrid Registration. If, after five years, the Madrid Registration is not canceled or limited in any way, it becomes independent of the basic registration.

The Madrid Registration's term is ten years. Trademark owners can renew the Madrid Registration for another ten years through a single filing with WIPO. This renews any national rights the trademark owner obtained in member countries. A single filing with WIPO can also accomplish any post-registration modifications such as changes of name or address.

Notices of assignments of Madrid Registrations are filed with WIPO as well. Under the Madrid Protocol, any assignment must be made to a party that itself is qualified to file for a Madrid Registration. Parties may assign the basic application, the entire Madrid Registration, or any of the individual country designations. National laws govern the assignments. Therefore, under U.S. trademark law, a mark may not be assigned without its respective goodwill. (See the discussion on assignments in Chapter 4). There is no such requirement under the Madrid Protocol, however, so to ascertain whether an assignment document contained a transfer of goodwill, a search of the records of the relevant national offices would be necessary.

Any infringement actions have to be prosecuted and defended individually in the courts of the respective member countries. Therefore trademark clearance searches should normally include a search of the WIPO database. Possible conflicting marks may exist in that database which either bear earlier filing dates, or may not yet have been notified to the USPTO and entered into its database.

1. Benefits of the Madrid Protocol

- The Madrid Protocol provides streamlined, cost-effective protection in more than 70 jurisdictions. Filings are made in a single office, for one fee, in one currency, and in a single language, which can be English.
- There is no need to obtain legal representation in every country in which the applicant wants trademark protection. Local representation, however, may be needed if member countries raise issues during the registration process.
- Renewals, changes in addresses or ownership, and changes in goods and services can be made by one filing and one fee.
- Obtaining protection through the Madrid Protocol is ordinarily faster than obtaining rights by filing an individual national application, because of the set

amount of time members have to respond in connection with Madrid Registrations.

- Designations of protection to additional member countries may be made to the Madrid Application after registration. These additional registrations, as long as they are not refused in the respective countries, will be effective from the date on which WIPO records the application for territorial expansion. Therefore, the Madrid Protocol facilitates the expansion of use of trademarks into new markets.

2.   Drawbacks of the Madrid Protocol

- The USPTO currently requires a more detailed and less broad description of goods and services than many other Madrid Protocol countries require. Therefore, because Madrid Registrations are dependent on the basic application, trademark owners who register their Madrid Application through the USPTO may receive narrower protection than they would have received had they filed individual national applications in the respective jurisdictions. Conversely, many foreign trademark owners using the Madrid Protocol to apply for U.S. registrations rely on the description of goods and services of their basic applications, which tend to be far too broad to conform to the strict USPTO rules. The result is that such applications are frequently held unacceptable and have to be revised, often by hiring a U.S. attorney, which negates some of the efficiency gains that the Madrid Protocol is meant to confer.
- If the basic application is amended or refused, or the registration cancelled in the Office of Origin during the first five years, that same action is taken against the Madrid Registration, unless it is transformed into corresponding national rights within three months.
- The trademarks in Madrid Registrations cannot be amended after registration.
- Madrid Registrations can only be assigned to a party that itself is qualified to file a Madrid Application.

It appears that a U.S. company that has a real and effective place of business in another member country may file a basic application and Madrid Application there. Trademark owners are free to choose their Offices of Origin, as long as the owner is a national, domicile, or has a place of real and effective business in a member country.

3.06   Federal Administrative Proceedings

Trademark Trial and Appeal Board

Inter partes proceedings may be brought before the Trademark Trial and Appeal Board (T.T.A.B.) of the United States Patent and Trademark Office and are concerned only with whether or not a mark is registrable, or, if registered, whether or not the registration should be cancelled. The four basic inter partes proceedings are opposition, cancellation, interference, and concurrent use. They are quasi-judicial proceedings and generally follow the format of a civil action as to pleadings, motion practice, discovery, record, argument, and decision. Following joinder of issue, periods are set for discovery, deposition testimony by the party in the position of plaintiff and then by the defending party, followed by rebuttal and briefing. Oral hearing may be had before the Board, corresponding to oral summation in a court action.

A final decision of the T.T.A.B. may either be appealed to the Federal Circuit or to a federal district court for review in a trial de novo. While the district court may consider new evidence in such cases, it must give the T.T.A.B.'s findings of fact deference under the standards of the Administrative Procedure Act ("APA"), 5 U.S.C.

§ 706, and accept them unless they are unsupported by substantial evidence. *Dickinson v. Zurko*, 527 U.S. 150, 162-63 (1999) (noting that the difference between the substantial evidence standard and the clearly erroneous standard is "subtle" and "so fine" that the Court could not find a single case where the result would have been different if one standard rather than the other was applied); *CAE, Inc. v. Clean Air Engineering, Inc.*, 267 F.3d 660, 676 (7th Cir. 2001) (affirming the district court's judgment, based on new evidence, that confusion was likely, after the T.T.A.B. had held to the contrary). For a good discussion of the different avenues of appeal of T.T.A.B. decisions, and their procedural and evidentiary consequences, see the *CAE, Inc. v. Clean Air Engineering* decision at 674-676.

1. Opposition Proceedings

A Notice of Opposition may be filed by "any person who believes that he or she would be damaged by the registration of a mark . . . ." 15 U.S.C. § 1063. If the registration is successful, the trademark will not be registered. 15 U.S.C. § 1063. The opposition must be filed within thirty (30) days of the application being published in the *Official Gazette*, although extensions of time to oppose, within limits, may be obtained. 15 U.S.C. § 1063(a). *See, e.g., In re Stoller*, 203 Fed. Appx. 333 (Fed. Cir. 2006) (dismissing appeal of Patent and Trademark Office sanctions against individual for "his conduct in filing more than 1,400 extensions of time to oppose trademark applications," including two year prohibition against his filing any additional extensions).

The Trademark Rules of Practice (T.R.P.-37 C.F.R.) specify that "The opposition must set forth a short and plain statement showing how the opposer would be damaged by the registration of the opposed mark and state the grounds for opposition." 37 C.F.R. 2.104. An opposition may thus be initiated by a registrant opposing registration of a confusingly similar mark, *China Healthways Institute, Inc. dba Chi Institute v. Wang*, 491 F.3d 1337 (Fed. Cir. 2007), by one who has prior use but not registration of a trademark for which registration is now sought by another, *Towers v. Advent Software, Inc.*, 913 F.2d 942, 945 (Fed. Cir. 1990), or by one who uses, in a descriptive, generic, or geographic manner, and without claiming trademark rights thereto, a word or term now sought to be registered by another, *Quaker Oil Corp. v. Quaker State Oil Refining Corp.*, 161 U.S.P.Q. 547 (T.T.A.B. 1969), *aff'd*, 453 F.2d 1296 (C.C.P.A. 1972) (descriptive use); *Continental Airlines, Inc. v. United Airlines, Inc.*, 53 U.S.P.Q.2d 1385 (T.T.A.B. 1999) (ETICKET generic for electronic ticket service). Opposition may also be based on trade name or advertising use of a term or mark, *Knickerbocker Toy Co. v. Faultless Starch Co.*, 467 F.2d 501 (C.C.P.A. 1972). Thus, it is not necessary that the opposer show exclusive use or exclusive right to use a word or term. First use by an opposer *after* the filing of an intent-to-use application of an allegedly confusingly similar mark apparently is insufficient grounds for opposition under the Revision Act. In *Zirco v. American Telephone and Telegraph Co.*, 1991 T.T.A.B. LEXIS 43 (T.T.A.B. 1991), an opposition by a post-filing-date common law user against an intent-to-use applicant was dismissed, contingent upon registration issuing, the Board confirming that an intent-to-use applicant may successfully rely on its constructive use priority filing date in opposition proceedings. An additional basis for opposition was provided in the 1999 Trademark Reform Bill, S. 1259, Pub. L. No. 106-43, which authorized opposition and cancellation of trademark registrations on the ground of dilution. *See NASDAQ Stock Market, Inc. v. Anartica*, 69 U.S.P.Q.2d 1718 (T.T.A.B. 2003) (opposer's famous NASDAQ mark likely to be diluted by NASDAQ for sports equipment and clothing), and the discussion on trademark dilution in Chapter 8.

Neither the rules nor the statute specify the nature or amount of the damage which must be shown by the opposer. *See Young v. AGB Corp.*, 152 F.3d 1377 (Fed. Cir. 1998) (where an application to register a fiberglass steer statue for restaurant services was opposed by manufacturer of fiberglass steer statues, the opposition was dismissed because opposer only alleged that his ability to sell such statues would be impeded, and did not claim likely confusion or any other valid ground for opposition). Upon a showing of likelihood of confusion, damage will be presumed, *Daggett & Ramsdell v. Procter & Gamble Co.*, 275 F.2d 955 (C.C.P.A. 1960). Registrations on the Supplemental Register cannot be opposed but may be cancelled. *Kwik-Kopy Franchise Corp. v. Dimensional Lithographers, Inc.*, 165 U.S.P.Q. 397 (T.T.A.B. 1970).

The grounds generally relied upon for opposing the registration of a mark are those enumerated in § 2 of the Lanham Act, 15 U.S.C. § 1052. The most common basis for opposition is § 2(d), whereby the opposer claims that the applicant's mark resembles either opposer's registered or common-law trademark. In such cases the test is likelihood of confusion between the two marks. *See* Murphy, *Playing the Numbers: A Quantitive Look at Section 2(d) Cases Before the Trademark Trial and Appeal Board*, 94 TMR 800 (2004).

It is important, however, to distinguish the likelihood of confusion test in an infringement action from that in an opposition proceeding. In an opposition, because the ultimate issue is not infringement but whether the applicant's mark qualifies for federal registration, the test is based on similarities of the marks as they appear in the application and as registered or used by opposer. *See, e.g., In re Dixie Restaurants, Inc.*, 105 F.3d 1405, 1408 (Fed. Cir. 1997) (PTO may refuse to register DELTA CAFE for restaurant services based on likely confusion with the federally registered mark DELTA for hotel, motel, and restaurant services without regard to whether the registrant actually uses its mark in connection with restaurant services). *Cf. Levy v. Kosher Overseers Ass'n of America Inc.*, 104 F.3d 38 (2d Cir. 1997) (plaintiff not collaterally estopped from bringing an infringement lawsuit based on its unregistered certification mark after defendant had successfully opposed plaintiff's application, because in the opposition proceeding the T.T.A.B. did not examine the commercial use of the marks). T.T.A.B. decisions have been given varied deference in subsequent federal court infringement actions. Note, *Passing the Standard of Review Puzzle: How Much Deference Should Federal District Courts Afford Trademark Trial and Appeal Board Decisions*, 12 FED. CIR. B.J. 490 (2003).

Unlike the TTAB in a typical registration proceeding, a court in an action for federal trademark infringement must consider "the context of the marketplace." *Miguel Torres, S.A. v. Cantine Mezzacorona, S.C.A.R.L.*, 108 Fed. Appx. 816 (4th Cir. 2004) (unpublished; per curiam). In *Torres*, plaintiff sued for trademark infringement after plaintiff had successfully opposed defendant's application by showing defendant's mark was confusingly similar to plaintiff's. There, the Fourth Circuit determined that TTAB findings in the opposition could be given controlling effect if "the TTAB or the Federal Circuit . . . have taken into account, in a meaningful way, the context of the marketplace." *Torres*, 108 Fed. Appx. at 820, quoting *Levy v. Kosher Overseers Ass'n of Am., Inc.*, 104 F.3d 38, 41 (2d Cir. 1997). In the *Torres* case, the court concluded: "Although the TTAB's analysis of whether [defendant's] mark was 'likely to cause confusion' was not sufficient to settle the infringement question, it engaged in more than a cursory analysis with respect to whether the marks were visually similar or similar in terms of pronunciation." 120 Fed. Appx. at 820. The court of appeals distinguished the TTAB's factual findings that the parties' goods were "identical," "traveled in the same channels of trade," and were "purchased by the same end users," because those findings were based, not on actual use, but on the lack of any limitation in Cantine's application that would differentiate them.

Conversely, a prior trademark suit does not automatically have preclusive effect in a TTAB proceeding. In *Mayer/Berkshire Corp. v. Berkshire Fashions, Inc.*, 424 F.3d 1229 (Fed. Cir. 2005), the TTAB dismissed an opposition as barred by res judicata and collateral estoppel arising from prior litigation between the parties in which the jury found that Berkshire Fashions' use of the mark BERKSHIRE for clothing did not create a likelihood of confusion. The Federal Circuit vacated the dismissal and remanded it to the PTO for further proceedings. Citing an earlier decision, the court noted that "a trademark action in the district court is not automatically of preclusive effect in a cancellation proceeding in the PTO, for a claim for trademark infringement may not be based on the same transactional facts as a petition to cancel a registered mark, or the facts relevant to infringement may not be sufficiently applicable to trademark registration to warrant preclusion." *Mayer/Berkshire*, 424 F.3d 1232. Similarly, " '[i]n Board proceedings, likelihood of confusion is determined independent of the context of actual usage. In an infringement action, on the other hand, the context of the use of the mark is relevant.' " *Mayer/Berkshire*, 424 F.3d at 1233.

In the opposition proceeding, Mayer/Berkshire had offered evidence of actual confusion, which it argued arose after the prior litigation when Berkshire Fashions changed its marketing strategies. This evidence, the Federal Circuit concluded, "can constitute a change in transactional facts that avoids preclusion based on the earlier non-infringement decision," and was sufficient to "negate the grant of summary judgment based on preclusion." *Mayer/Berkshire*, 424 F.3d at 1233. Mayer/Berkshire had also successfully argued that the prior litigation did not include items of clothing that were included in Berkshire Fashions' application.

In the past, such matters as label, package, or wrapper similarities were neither material nor relevant in an opposition proceeding, although they ordinarily would be in an action for infringement. However, in *Kenner Parker Toys, Inc. v. Rose Art Indus., Inc.*, 963 F.2d 350 (Fed. Cir. 1992), the court found that "the trade dress of the marks enhances their inherently similar commercial impression" in holding that FUNDOUGH was confusingly similar to PLAY-DOH for modeling compounds. Trade dress has been considered in opposition proceedings to help determine the connotation a word mark imparts. *Specialty Brands, Inc. v. Coffee Bean Distributors, Inc.*, 748 F.2d 669 (Fed. Cir. 1984) (applicant's claim that its SPICE VALLEY mark for tea conveyed a country valley image was rebutted by square rigged sailing ship on its label; confusion held likely with SPICE ISLANDS for tea); *American Rice, Inc. v. H.I.T. Corp.*, 231 U.S.P.Q. 793 (T.T.A.B. 1986) (contrary to applicant's contentions, trade dress demonstrated its GOLDEN RIBBON mark imparted a "contest award" image like that of opposer's BLUE RIBBON mark; confusion held likely).

An opposition proceeding is governed by the Federal Rules of Civil Procedure and the Trademark Rules of Practice, 37 C.F.R. 2.116(a). An answer is required of the applicant in response to a notice of opposition, and these two pleadings correspond to the complaint and answer in a court action. 37 C.F.R. 2.116(c). In its answer to an opposition based on a prior registration, the applicant may not raise a defense attacking the validity of opposer's registration except by way of a counterclaim for cancellation which must be verified and be accompanied by the required fee. 37 C.F.R. 2.106(b). The defenses of laches, estoppel or acquiescence normally will be considered "only if there is a reasonable doubt [that] likelihood of confusion exists." *White Heather Distillers, Ltd. v. American Distilling Co.*, 200 U.S.P.Q. 466, 469 (T.T.A.B. 1980). *Accord CBS, Inc. v. Man's Day Publishing Co.*, 205 U.S.P.Q. 470, 475 (T.T.A.B. 1980). The Federal Circuit has held, however, that in registration cases, laches begins to run from the time that the applicant's application to register the mark is published in the *Official Gazette*, since that is the point in time at which a party can object to the applicant's registration of the mark. *National Cable Television Ass'n v. America Cinema Editors, Inc.*, 937 F.2d 1572, 1581 (Fed Cir. 1991). Acquiescence may be accorded similar treatment. *Cf. Coach House Restaurant v. Coach & Six Restaurants Inc.*, supra, 934 F.2d at 1563–64 (acquiescence as to use compared with acquiescence as to registration). Testimony is taken by deposition, and documentary evidence is authenticated and offered during periods set by the Board corresponding to the trial in court proceedings. Subsequent to the taking and filing of testimony and other evidence, the parties may submit briefs and be heard in final argument before the Board.

2. Cancellation Proceedings

A cancellation petition may be filed by "any person who believes that he is or will be damaged by the registration of a mark." 15 U.S.C. § 1064. The proceeding is essentially the same as an opposition and, with certain exceptions, must be brought within five years of the date of registration. Within that period, it may be based on the same grounds as would have supported an opposition. If a potential opposer misses the final date within which a notice of opposition must be filed, the attack must be by way of a cancellation. Although the issues are normally the same, the cancellation petitioner theoretically bears a heavier burden, since he or she must overcome the prima facie rights of the registrant evidenced by the registration certificate. 15 U.S.C. § 1057(b). If cancellation is sought after five years of registration, it then may be based only on the grounds specified in § 14 of the Lanham Act (15 U.S.C. § 1064), namely, that the mark has become the generic name of the product or service or is functional, the mark has been abandoned, the registration was fraudulently obtained, the mark is being used so as to misrepresent the source of the goods or services, or the registration was obtained contrary to the provisions of §§ 4 and 2(a), (b), or (c) of the Act. Partial cancellation or modification of the registration by limitation of the goods and services specified also may be obtained under the proper circumstances. 15 U.S.C. §§ 1064, 1068. A federal court has the authority to cancel or partially cancel a registration under 15 U.S.C. § 1119. *See Central Mfg., Inc. v. Brett*, 492 F.3d 876 (7th Cir. 2007) (cancelling registration based on other party's prior rights).

Failure to use the mark on all the goods identified in the application (or to amend the application to delete those not subject to use) may result in cancellation of the issued registration for fraud. For example, in *J.E.M. Int'l Inc. v. Happy Rompers Creations Corp.*, 74 U.S.P.Q.2d 1526 (TTAB 2005) (nonprecedential), the TTAB ordered cancellation of a registration for "a wide variety of clothing items," because the registrant, Happy Rompers, did not use the mark on "all of the goods identified in the application, Notice of Allowance, Statement of Use and subsequent registration." Happy Rompers had not been using the mark on at least 100 of the 150 goods listed in its application, and therefore "[n]on-use on this great a number of items in a long list of items must be accorded significance when filling in a form requiring a verification stating that respondent was using the mark on 'all' of the goods (or allowing respondent to delete those goods or divide out those goods upon which it is not using the mark)." *Id.* Happy Rompers' knowledge that the mark was not being used on at least two-thirds of the listed goods was sufficient to establish intent to commit fraud. To similar effect is *Standard Knitting Ltd. v. Toyota Jidosha Kabushiki Kaisha*, 77 USPQ2d 1917 (T.T.A.B. 2006) (cancelling three registrations due to fraud on the PTO).

As in an opposition proceeding, damage must be alleged by the cancellation petitioner (15 U.S.C. § 1064) and may be shown by proving likelihood of confusion, dilution or that the registration does or will interfere with the free operation of petitioner's business. Also as in an opposition proceeding, a cancellation proceeding is jurisdictionally confined to the continuing right of a party to the federal registration of its mark — not the right to use the mark. *Hammermill Paper Co. v. Gulf States Paper Corp.*, 337 F.2d 662 (C.C.P.A. 1964).

3. Interference Proceedings

Section 16 of the Lanham Act, 15 U.S.C. § 1066, provides:

> Whenever application is made for the registration of a mark which so resembles a mark previously registered by another, or for the registration of which another has previously made application, as to be likely when applied to the goods or when used in connection with the services of the applicant to cause confusion or mistake or to deceive, the Commissioner may declare that an interference exists. No interference shall be declared between an application

and the registration of a mark the right to use of which has become incontestable.

Prior to 1972, an interference proceeding was declared and instituted by the Commissioner of Patents and Trademarks when there were two applications pending for conflicting trademarks or, on petition by the applicant, when an application alleged priority of use of a mark which conflicted with a subsisting registration which had not become incontestable. In 1972, the Trademark Rules of Practice were changed, virtually eliminating interference proceedings. An interference will now be declared only on petition to the Commissioner of Patents and Trademarks and "only upon a showing of extraordinary circumstances which would result in a party being unduly prejudiced without an interference." 37 C.F.R. § 2.91(a). No undue prejudice will exist if an opposition or cancellation proceeding is available. *See* however, *In re Family Inns of America, Inc.*, 180 U.S.P.Q. 332 (Comm'r 1974), where extraordinary circumstances were shown as multiple applications had been filed for similar marks which would have required successive opposition proceedings.

An interference will be declared only between marks which have been determined to be otherwise registrable by the Examiner. 37 C.F.R.§ 2.92. The primary issue considered is priority of use, and, hence, the right to federal registration. The party whose application was filed last will be designated as the junior party and has the burden of proof as to priority. 37 C.F.R. § 2.96. The proceeding is before the Trademark Trial and Appeal Board, and the procedures are generally the same as in an opposition or cancellation proceeding.

4. Concurrent Use Proceedings

While the benefits of federal registration are national in scope, there are occasional innocent concurrent uses of the same or similar marks for the same or similar goods which, because they are used in different territories in the United States, do not give rise to a likelihood of confusion. In these situations, concurrent registrations may be obtained under § 2(d) of the Lanham Act by persons having made lawful use of the same or similar marks in commerce, provided such use is prior to the earliest filing date of any pending applications or subsisting registrations for conflicting marks. 15 U.S.C. § 1052(d). The Commissioner may also issue concurrent registrations when a court of competent jurisdiction finds more than one person entitled to use the same or similar mark in commerce. 15 U.S.C. § 1052(d).

One who believes that he or she is entitled to such a concurrent use registration may file an application which specifies, to the extent of his or her knowledge, the particulars and areas respecting the concurrent lawful use by others, and the area, goods and mode of use for which the applicant seeks registration. T.R.P. 2.42. The Patent and Trademark Office will then notify the other parties concerned and will institute a proceeding which generally follows the practice in an interference. T.R.P. 2.99(c). If concurrent registrations are issued, the Commissioner prescribes the conditions and limitations for the use of the mark thereunder by the respective parties. 15 U.S.C.§ 1052(d). *See generally* Rice, *Concurrent Use Applications and Proceedings*, 72 TRADEMARK REP. 403 (1982), and the discussion on Concurrent Rights in Chapter 7.

3.07 International Trade Commission

Under 15 U.S.C. § 1124 and 19 C.F.R. § 133.0 *et seq.*, federal registrants may record their registered trademark with the Bureau of Customs and Border Protection, and thereby cause Customs to take steps to prohibit entry of infringing imports. *See* McCARTHY, TRADEMARKS AND UNFAIR COMPETITION, § 29:38 (4th ed. 2007). Owners of unregistered trademarks and trade dress may litigate before the International Trade Commission ("ITC") under 19 U.S.C. § 1337 ("§ 337") to obtain similar relief. Registrants in some instances may also find it advantageous to seek remedial orders from the

ITC. *See, e.g., In re Certain Airtight Cast-Iron Stoves*, 215 U.S.P.Q. 963 (I.T.C. 1980).

The International Trade Commission is an administrative body authorized under § 337 to take action against unfair methods of competition and unfair acts in the importation of articles into the United States. Section 337(a) provides in pertinent part:

(1) Subject to paragraph (2), the following are unlawful, and when found by the Commission to exist shall be dealt with, in addition to any other provision of law, as provided in this section:

(A) Unfair methods of competition and unfair acts in the importation of articles (other than articles provided for in subparagraphs (B), (C), and (D)) into the United States, or in the sale of such articles by the owner, importer, or consignee, the threat or effect of which is -

(i) to destroy or substantially injure an industry in the United States;

(ii) to prevent the establishment of such an industry; or

(iii) to restrain or monopolize trade and commerce in the United States.

. . ..

* * *

The "unfair methods of competition and unfair acts" provision has been interpreted broadly to include numerous activities, including statutory and common law trademark and trade dress infringement, patent infringement, misappropriation of trade secrets, false designation of origin, false representation, palming off, false advertising, copyright infringement, and tortious interference with contractual relations. *See* Lupo & Davis, *The Use of Customs' Regulations and/or the International Trade Commission to Protect Against International Counterfeiting and Trademark Infringement*, 251 PLI/Pat 435, 441 (1988).

Complainants in an ITC proceeding are given a hearing before a Commission Administrative Law Judge (ALJ) who also exercises authority over discovery disputes and prehearing conferences. Prehearing and hearing procedures generally parallel pretrial and trial procedures of the federal courts, although they usually advance to and through trial more rapidly. The procedural rules are set forth in 19 C.F.R. Part 210. The ALJ's decision as to whether a violation has occurred and whether a remedy should be ordered is presented to the Commission as a recommendation. The Commission then makes a final determination and, if appropriate, issues a remedial order. Four of the Commission's six Commissioners must favor complainant for it to prevail.

A final determination of the Commission becomes effective immediately; however, the President of the United States has sixty days in which to disapprove the decision for policy reasons or to approve it by taking no action. The power to disapprove is rarely exercised. *But see In the Matter of Certain Alkaline Batteries*, 225 U.S.P.Q. 862 (Pres. Reagan, Jan. 4, 1985), *appeal dismissed*, 778 F.2d 1578 (Fed. Cir. 1985); *Young Engineers, Inc. v. ITC*, 721 F.2d 1305 (Fed. Cir. 1983). If the sixty days pass without action by the President, an appeal then may be taken to the Court of Appeals for the Federal Circuit. *Bourdeau Bros., Inc. v. ITC*, 444 F.3d 1317 (Fed. Cir. 2006); *Tanabe Seiyaku Co., Ltd. v. ITC*, 109 F.3d 726 (Fed. Cir. 1997), *cert. denied*, 522 U.S. 1027 (1997)(court noting that it has exclusive jurisdiction to review a final determination of the ITC).

An initial and important advantage to litigating before the ITC rather than in federal court is that a demonstration of personal jurisdiction over foreign manufacturers, which may not have the requisite "minimum contacts," is not required in § 337 actions. This is because the statute permits *in rem* orders, which act against goods, not parties, and therefore creates a separate subject matter jurisdiction independent of personal jurisdiction. *Sealed Air Corp. v. ITC*, 645 F.2d 976, 986 (C.C.P.A. 1981). Moreover, the immediate delivery of goods into the U.S. is not necessary, as the statutory phrase, "sale for importation" has been construed for jurisdictional purposes to include "the situation in which a contract for goods has been formed in accordance with section 2-204(1) of the U.C.C." *Enercom GmbH v. ITC*, 151 F.3d 1376 (Fed. Cir. 1998), *cert. denied*, 526 U.S. 1130 (1999).

The Commission is authorized to issue: (1) a general exclusion order directed against all infringing products; (2) a cease and desist order directed against a party; and (3) temporary relief during the pendency of an ITC proceeding in the form of an exclusion or cease and desist order. 19 U.S.C. §§ 1337(d), (e), (f). The commission has a great deal of discretion in shaping remedies. *See* Lafuze & Stanford, *An Overview of Section 337 of the Tariff Act of 1930: A Primer for Practice Before the ITC*, 25 J. MARSHALL L. REV. 459, 468-69 (1992). It cannot, however, award damages. Nonetheless, violations of exclusion orders can result in seizures, forfeitures and penalties. Likewise, violations of cease and desist orders can result in daily fines up to the greater of $100,000 or twice the domestic value of the articles entered or sold. *See* Lafuze & Stanford at 469, 472.

Section 337 is particularly useful to a complainant plagued by many infringers of a popular product. It affords the opportunity to stop all infringing imports in one action through a general exclusion order. A general exclusion order will cause the exclusion of all manufacturers' infringing imported goods when it is either "necessary to prevent circumvention of an exclusion order limited to products of named persons . . . [or] there is a pattern of violation . . . and it is difficult to identify the source of the infringing products." 19 U.S.C. § 1337(d)(2) (1994). All ITC exclusion orders, including general exclusion orders, are enforced by the Customs Service at U.S. ports of entry and are largely not subject to the jurisdictional constraints that can make a federal court's *in personam* decree against a foreign manufacturer difficult to enforce. Cease and desist orders are effective against domestic importers of the infringing goods, and are enforceable in federal court. 19 U.S.C. § 1337(f).

Another advantage to ITC proceedings is the dispatch with which they are conducted. Section 337 previously required completion of the proceedings within 12 months of publication of the notice of investigation in the Federal Register or, for more complicated cases, within 18 months. The statute was amended in 1994, and now requires completion at "the earliest practicable time," rather than within fixed time limits. 19 U.S.C.A. § 1337(b)(1). Nonetheless, as expressed in the accompanying Senate Joint Report, it is expected the Commission will "complete its investigations in approximately the same amount of time as is currently the practice." S. Rep. No. 412, 103d Cong., 2d Sess. 118, 119 (1994). Consequently, a complainant must be prepared for a concomitant extreme expedition of discovery and hearing schedules in prosecuting its case.

Respondents who attempt to impede the discovery process risk sanctions and evidentiary presumptions against them. Respondents are allowed to raise "[a]ll legal and equitable defenses" under § 337(c) including, presumably, all defenses found in trademark law, see, e.g., Ch. 8. Under the 1994 amendments, a respondent may file counterclaims before the ITC, but must immediately remove them to federal court. The Commission apparently may consider judicial rulings on such counterclaims as part of its "public interest" determination, discussed further below. However, because "action on . . . [a removed] counterclaim shall not delay or affect [an ITC] proceeding," 19 U.S.C. § 1337(c) (1994), the ITC "earliest practicable time" requirement mandates that the ITC not delay adjudicating a complaint pending the resolution of a removed counterclaim in federal court. Moreover, under the 1994 amendments, a respondent in an ITC action who is also a party to a federal district court proceeding can seek a mandatory stay of any federal district court proceeding that raises the same issues involved in the ITC action. *See generally* Shriver, *Separate But Equal: Intellectual Property Importation and the Recent Amendments to Section 337*, 5 MINN. J. GLOBAL TRADE 441 (1996). The stay remains in effect until the ITC action is completed, at which time the ITC record is transmitted to the district court for its use. *Minnesota Mining and Mfg. v. Beautone Specialties*, 82 F. Supp. 2d 997 (D. Minn. 2000), *app. dismissed*, 243 F.3d 556 (Fed. Cir. 2000).

For trade dress and unregistered marks, a successful complainant must prove (1) that it has a protectable trademark or trade dress (2) with which a likelihood of confusion among consumers is created by the trademark or trade dress of the imported goods at issue, and (3) that the effect or tendency of importation of the goods is to substantially injure or destroy (4) a domestic industry (5) that is efficiently and economically operated. Nos. (1) and (2) generally present typical trademark protection problems encountered in the federal courts. Since nationwide rights are being asserted under the statute, however, if the claimed mark or trade dress is not inherently distinctive, nationwide secondary meaning must be shown. *See In re Sneakers with Fabric Uppers & Rubber Soles*, 223 U.S.P.Q. 536, 539 (I.T.C. 1983). Domestic corporations with less than national areas of sale or reputation thus may be precluded from successfully bringing a complaint before the ITC.

The complainant also has the burden of demonstrating that the claimed trademark is not generic, *Sneakers with Fabric Uppers*, 223 U.S.P.Q. at 540, or that the claimed trade dress is not functional, *New England Butt Co. v. U.S. ITC*, 756 F.2d 874 (Fed. Cir. 1985).

A domestic industry typically "consists of that part of complainant's business devoted to the manufacture, distribution and sale of the product bearing the allegedly infringed trademark," *Sneakers with Fabric Uppers*, 223 U.S.P.Q. at 543, but may consist of other domestic activities respecting the product bearing the trademark or trade dress at issue. The 1988 Amendment greatly expanded the definition of what constitutes an industry. An industry, for example, can be deemed to exist in the United States, even if licensing activity is all that is occurring. *See* McCarthy, Trademarks and Unfair Competition, § 29:55 (4th ed. 2007). *Compare Schaper Mfg. Co. v. ITC*, 717 F.2d 1368, 1372-73 (Fed. Cir. 1983) (complainant's performance of some packaging, warehousing, distribution, advertising and quality control regarding toy trucks manufactured abroad held insufficient to constitute a domestic industry) *with In re Certain Cube Puzzles*, 219 U.S.P.Q. 322, 334-35 (I.T.C. 1982) (complainant's repair and packaging of, and extensive quality control over, cube puzzles manufactured abroad, which added value to them, held significant enough to constitute a domestic industry). *See also Bally/Midway Mfg. Co. v. ITC*, 714 F.2d 1117, 1120-23 (Fed. Cir. 1983), where the court reversed an ITC finding of no domestic industry, holding that complainant did have such an industry for its RALLY-X video games at the time the complaint was filed, if not subsequently as a result of respondent's acts, and that "there is nothing in the statute which requires that an industry must be of any particular size."

Once the existence of a domestic industry has been established, the "efficiently and economically operated" statutory requirement is easily met. In *Sneakers with Fabric Uppers*, 223 U.S.P.Q. at 544, the ITC stated: "Indicia of efficient and economic operation include: Use of modern equipment, effective quality control programs, competitiveness, successful sales efforts, and profitability of the subject product." To date no respondent has ever successfully demonstrated "inefficient and uneconomic" operation of a domestic industry.

"Substantial injury" or "tendency to substantially injure" is proven by evidence of lost sales, lost profits or lost customers. *See, e.g., In re Certain Cube Puzzles*, 219 U.S.P.Q. 322, 336 (I.T.C. 1982) (lost accounts and profits established requisite injury; "it does not matter that [complainant] did not suffer a loss or had increasing profits, so long as it lost profits to the imported [products]"); *Sneakers with Fabric Uppers*, 223 U.S.P.Q. at 544 (complainant successfully relied on "declining sales and profits, a deteriorating cash flow situation, employee layoffs and production cutbacks").

In *Bally/Midway*, 714 F.2d at 1124, the court stated that "[w]here the unfair practice is the importation of products that infringe a domestic industry's copyright, trademark or patent right, even a relatively small loss of sales may establish, under Section 337(a), the requisite injury to the portion of the complainant's business devoted to the exploitation of those intellectual property rights." In a subsequent case, however, the same court rejected complainant's contention that injury should be inferred any time the ITC finds infringement, regardless of whether damage to the domestic industry is shown, stating, "Section 337 does not function merely as the international extension of our patent, trademark and copyright laws." *Textron, Inc. v. ITC*, 224 U.S.P.Q. 625, 631 (Fed. Cir. 1985). Instead, "[e]ven in the context of patent, trademark or copyright infringement, the domestic industry must normally establish that the infringer holds, or threatens to hold, a significant share of the domestic market in the covered articles or has made a significant amount of sales of the articles." *Id.* at 632). *Compare Bourdeau Bros., Inc. v. ITC*, 444 F.3d 1317 (Fed. Cir. 2006) (remanded for determination of whether trademark owner authorized some U.S. sales of allegedly gray market harvesters). *SKF USA, Inc. v. ITC*, 423 F.3d 1307 (Fed. Cir. 2005) (gray market ball bearings lacked sufficiently material differences to warrant relief); *Gamut Trading Co. v. Int'l Trade Comm'n*, 200 F.3d 775 (Fed. Cir. 1999) (prohibiting the importation of gray market tractors, and noting, "direct competition between substantially identical goods is a factor to be considered, but is not prerequisite to trademark infringement"), and the discussion on gray market goods in Chapter 7.

In 1988, the Tariff Act was amended to delete the requirements to prove injury to a domestic industry, and efficient and economic operation of the domestic industry, where the plaintiff seeks to protect a *federally registered* trademark. As a result, the owner of the registered trademark need only prove the validity of the registration and infringement, and that a domestic industry relating to the goods bearing the mark exists or "is in the process of being established." The period of determining whether to grant temporary relief also was shortened.

The ITC also is statutorily obligated to consider the public interest in every case. Section 337(d) requires the Commission to consider "the effect of [the] exclusion [of imports] upon the public health and welfare, competitive conditions in the United States economy, the production of like or directly competitive articles in the United States and United States consumers. . . ." A staff attorney represents the public interest in all ITC proceedings, and even where the Commission finds a violation of § 337, the public's interest in an open economy may dictate that no remedy be ordered. *See, e.g., In re Certain Automatic Crankpin Grinders*, 205 U.S.P.Q. 71, 80 (I.T.C. 1979) (due to public interest considerations, no remedy ordered for violation of § 337 via patent infringement). An ITC finding that public interest considerations outweigh a complainant's need for relief is extremely rare, and will normally occur only when there is a strong public interest in having an adequate supply of the goods under investigation which is being insufficiently met by the domestic industry.

As a result of the statutory public interest element, a complainant must establish the economic side of the case and prove infringement even when a respondent defaults:

> A finding of a violation of section 337 requires something more than a mere showing that a respondent has defaulted. The remedy of an exclusion order, unlike the relief available in the federal courts, sometimes affects persons other than the named parties' respondent. For that reason, a default does not per se establish complainant's right to relief. . . . [Instead] reasonable effort . . . to produce substantial, reliable and probative evidence to establish a prima facie case of violation [is required].

In re Certain Food Slicers, 219 U.S.P.Q. 176, 178-79 (I.T.C. 1981). *See also In re Sneakers with Fabric Uppers & Rubber Soles*, 223 U.S.P.Q. 536, 537-38 (I.T.C. 1983) (default proceeding).

In the past, the ITC rarely issued temporary relief orders (similar to preliminary injunctions) because of the already expedited nature of its proceedings. This, coupled with the Commission's inability to award damages, led many respondents simply to default and sell off their inventory during the 12- or 18-month investigation period rather than incur the expense of defending themselves. A Second Circuit decision may have discouraged this practice among some respondents. In *Union Mfg. Co., Inc. v. Hans Baek Trading Co.*, 763 F.2d 42, 45 (2^d Cir. 1985), the court held that ITC trademark decisions have *res judicata* effect in federal court where the parties are the same and "when the issues raised and the procedures available in the ITC proceeding are in all important respects the same as those in District Court." Consequently, a respondent that defaults or loses before the ITC may be deemed already to have lost on the infringement issue in a subsequent federal court action, with only the issue of damages remaining for trial. The practice also may be affected by the 1988 amendment to the Tariff Act shortening the period for determining whether to grant temporary relief, which resulted in the ITC procedures being modeled after procedures for considering federal preliminary injunctions. LaFuze & Stanford, *An Overview of Section 337 of the Tariff Act of 1930: A Primer for Practice Before the International Trade Commission*, 25 J. MARSHALL L. REV. 459, 468–469 (1992).

Nonetheless, under some circumstances a complainant needing fast relief from the widespread infringing imports may prefer moving for preliminary injunctions in federal court against the major offenders while simultaneously seeking from the ITC a general exclusion order as well as cease and desist orders against domestic importers. *See, e.g., In re Certain Cube Puzzles*, 219 U.S.P.Q. 322, 325, 337 (I.T.C. 1982).

See generally DUVALL, FEDERAL UNFAIR COMPETITION ACTIONS: PRACTICE & PROCEDURE UNDER SECTION 337 OF THE TARIFF ACT (2006 ed.); GILSON, § 8.15; MCCARTHY, TRADEMARKS AND UNFAIR COMPETITION, § 29:55; Ritscher et al., *The Status of Dual Path Litigation in the ITC and the Courts: Issues of Jurisdiction, Res Judicata and Appellate Review*, 18 AIPLA Q. J. 155 (1990).

CHAPTER 4
LOSS OF RIGHTS

CONTENTS

THE ORIGINAL GREAT AMERICAN CHOCOLATE CHIP COOKIE COMPANY v. RIVER VALLEY COOKIES, LIMITED 970 F.2d 273 (7th Cir. 1992)

Notes on Licensing and Franchising

4.01   The Contingency of Trademark Rights

Unlike property rights, trademark rights are mutable. The law protects trademarks because, and only insofar as, they have "commercial magnetism," *Mishawaka Rubber & Woolen Mfg. Co. v S.S. Kresge Co.*, 316 U.S. 203 (1942) or "source-distinguishing ability," *Qualitex Co v. Jacobson Products Co.*, 514 U.S. 159, 164 (1995). A term or device that does not have that source-distinguishing ability is, quite simply, not a trademark, and a term that loses it ceases to be one. Trademark rights are lost when the mark no longer signifies the source of the goods or services. Section 45 of the Lanham Act, 15 U.S.C. § 1127, provides that a mark shall be deemed to be abandoned "when its use has been discontinued with intent not to resume such use" or "when any course of conduct of the registrant, including acts of omission as well as commission, causes the mark to become the generic name for the goods or services on or in connection with which it is used, or otherwise to lose its significance as a mark." Under this provision, then, rights in a mark are lost when the mark becomes generic, that is, when it comes to signify or denominate the product itself, or when, by acts of omission or commission, it is abandoned, assigned without goodwill or licensed in gross.

4.02   Generic Terms

TRADEMARK PROBLEMS AND HOW TO AVOID THEM

Brand names can be over-sold. If your product is way ahead of all its competitors, this may be the time to look around for danger signals and take preventive action if necessary. When a product is so successful that the public adopts the brand name as the name of the product itself — as distinguished from one particular manufacturer's version of that product — then the brand name has passed into the language and the manufacturer who originated it no longer has the exclusive right to use it.

Some horrible examples of valuable brand names actually lost in this way are: aspirin, cellophane, linoleum, milk of magnesia and shredded wheat. Each of these once represented the product of a single manufacturer, who obviously invested substantial sums in building up the brand. Each of them reached the point where it came to mean

---

the product rather than merely a source for the product, and competitors won the right to use the name for their own versions of it. Technically, the brand name had become a generic term for the product, and generic terms are incapable of functioning as trademarks.

There are ways of guarding against this result. Explanatory footnotes in advertising are a common technique for putting the public on notice that the manufacturer claims trademark rights in his brand name, and that it is not just the name of the product itself. Du Pont, for example, has used this: " Orlon' is Du Pont's registered trademark for its acrylic fiber." RCA Victor footnoted Victrola with the legend: "RCA Trademark for record players." Slogans can perform a similar function, perhaps even more effectively. The Eastman Kodak Company from time to time used: "If it isn't an Eastman, it isn't a Kodak." At a later period, its advertisements carried, underneath the Kodak logo, a line reading: "— a trade-mark since 1888." Another typical footnote reads: "TABASCO is the registered trademark for the brand of pepper sauce made by McIlhenny Co."

Some companies place advertisements devoted specifically to education for proper trademark usage in consumer and trade publications. Minnesota Mining (for Scotch), Du Pont (for Orlon) and the Technicolor Corporation have used such campaigns; Du Pont also issues instruction booklets on the correct manner of using its registered marks.

The appearance of a company's brand name editorially in lower case type is a specific danger signal. Many manufacturers react by sending a form letter to the editor pointing out the unfavorable implication that the brand name has become just a word in the language, and requesting initial caps and quotation marks in all future uses.

The problem discussed here is particularly acute when a new product is to be introduced. Care must be taken that the brand name coined for the new item is used in such a way that it identifies the source of the product and that it does not become the name by which the public identifies the product itself. This can be done by using the words "brand" or "trademark" to show the manufacturer's intention. But that is only a beginning, because the purchasing public may not keep such a fine point in mind.

A superior method is to use the brand name in association with the name of the general type of product involved. For example, the family medicine cabinet displays: "BISODOL Antacid Tablet" and "CORICIDIN Cold Relief Tablets." Legal commentators are fond of suggesting that if the Bayer Company had marked its famous product "ASPIRIN brand of acetylsalicylic acid" or even just "ASPIRIN headache pills" — instead of "BAYER ASPIRIN" — it probably never would have lost its trademark rights. Q-Tips, Inc., which was forced to defend its trademark in court and did so successfully against the claim that it had become generic, labels its packages: "QTIPS Cotton Swabs."

Another way to guard against public misuse or misunderstanding of a brand name is to apply it to more than a single item. Johnson & Johnson, for example, has a whole line of Band-Aid products. And Vaseline is a well-known brand of hair preparation as well as the trademark for various types of petroleum jelly.

* * *

A special aspect of this question is the patented product. The existence of a patent means that the manufacturer has a legal monopoly for seventeen years;* nobody else can make the product without his consent. If that manufacturer exercises his monopoly, his planning should include both a brand name for the product and some additional word or words by which the public can identify it. Otherwise, the brand name will be the only designation the product has; when the patent expires and competitors become free to

---

* Editor's Note: Now twenty years.

make the product, they will automatically acquire the right to use the brand name too. This is precisely what happened in the case of shredded wheat, among others. The reason for this rule of law is that the original manufacturer would be able to get the effect of an illegal extension of his patent monopoly unless competitors were free to call the product by its name — otherwise they would be unable to identify it in the way the public had learned to call for it.

* * *

BAYER CO. v. UNITED DRUG CO.,
272 F. 505 (S.D.N.Y. 1921)

L. Hand, Judge

* * *

[T]he question is whether the buyers merely understood that the word "Aspirin" meant this kind of drug, or whether it meant that and more than that; i.e., that it came from the same single, though, if one please anonymous, source from which they had got it before. Prima facie I should say, since the word is coined and means nothing by itself, that the defendant must show that it means only the kind of drug to which it applies. . . . In the case at bar the evidence shows that there is a class of buyers to whom the word "Aspirin" has always signified the plaintiff, more specifically indeed than was necessary for its protection. I refer to manufacturing chemists, to physicians, and probably to retail druggists.

* * *

The crux of this controversy, however, lies not in the use of the word to these buyers, but to the general consuming public, composed of all sorts of buyers from those somewhat acquainted with pharmaceutical terms to those who knew nothing of them. The only reasonable inference from the evidence is that these did not understand by the word anything more than a kind of drug to which for one reason or another they had become habituated. It is quite clear that while the drug was sold as powder this must have been so. It was dispensed substantially altogether on prescription during this period, and, although physicians appear to have used the terms, "Aspirin" or "acetyl salicylic acid" indifferently, it cannot be that such patients as read their prescriptions attributed to "Aspirin" any other meaning than as an ingredient in a general compound, to which faith and science might impart therapeutic virtue. Nor is there any evidence that such as may have seen both terms identified them as the same drug. I cannot speculate as to how many in fact did so. No packages could possibly have reached the consumer, nor was any advertising addressed to them; their only acquaintance with the word was as the name for a drug in whose curative properties they had got confidence.

In 1904, however, they began to get acquainted with it in a different way, for then all the larger manufacturing chemists began to make tablets, and the trade grew to extraordinary proportions. The consumer, as both sides agree, had long before the autumn of 1915 very largely abandoned consultation with physicians and assumed the right to drug himself as his own prudence and moderation might prescribe. In all cases— omitting for the moment the infringing product— the drug was sold in bottles labeled "Aspirin" with some indication of the name of the tablet maker, but none of the plaintiff. It is probable that by far the greater part of the tablets sold were in dozens or less, and that the bottles so labeled did not generally reach the hands of the consumer, but, even so, a not inconsiderable number of bottles of 100 were sold, and as to the rest they were sold only under the name "Aspirin." The consumer did not know and could not possibly know the manufacturer of the drug which he got, or whether one or more chemists made it in the United States. He never heard the name "acetylsalicylic acid" as applied to it, and without some education could not possibly have kept it in his mind, if he had. So far as any means of information at all were open to him, they indicated that it was made by most large chemists indiscriminately. . . .

After the autumn of 1915 the plaintiff totally changed its methods, and thereafter no tablets reached the consumer without its own name. But it is significant that even then it used the word "Aspirin" as though it was a general term, although it is true that there was ample notice upon the bottles and boxes that "Aspirin" meant its manufacture. The most striking part of the label read, "Bayer— Tablets of Aspirin." While this did not show any abandonment of the name, which there has never been, it did show how the plaintiff itself recognized the meaning which the word had acquired, because the phrase most properly means that these tablets were Bayer's make of the drug known as "Aspirin." It presupposes that the persons reached were using the word to denote a kind of product. Were it not so, why the addition of "Bayer," and especially why the significant word "of?"

* * *

The case, therefore, presents a situation in which, ignoring sporadic exceptions, the trade is divided into two classes, separated by vital differences. One, the manufacturing chemists, retail druggists, and physicians, has been educated to understand that "Aspirin" means the plaintiff's manufacture, and has recourse to another and an intelligible name for it, actually in use among them. The other, the consumers, the plaintiff has, consciously I must assume, allowed to acquaint themselves with the drug only by the name "Aspirin," and has not succeeded in advising that the word means the plaintiff at all. If the defendant is allowed to continue the use of the word of the first class, certainly without any condition, there is a chance that it may get customers away from the plaintiff by deception. On the other hand, if the plaintiff is allowed a monopoly of the word as against consumers, it will deprive the defendant, and the trade in general, of the right effectually to dispose of the drug by the only description which will be understood. It appears to me that the relief granted cannot in justice to either party disregard this division; each party has won, and each has lost. . . .

As to the first class the question arises whether the injunction should be absolute or conditional. A strong case may be made for the defendant's present labels. They all bear the letters "U.D. Co." in juxtaposition with "Aspirin" and of equal size. These letters are universally known by the trade to signify the plaintiff, because the custom is general for manufacturing chemists in this way to mark their goods. I think that the plaintiff would be adequately protected but for the 10 years' history of the tablet trade. However, the fact is that during that time such legends were used to indicate that the manufacturing chemist who signed, as it were, the label, was making the tablets from the plaintiff's powder. Probably at present that belief has largely disappeared, but, since we are dealing with customers who are presumably aware of that history, and who have been repeatedly told that "Aspirin" signifies the plaintiff, I can see no reason for subjecting it to the chance. The phrase "acetyl salicylic acid" to them is intelligible; it means the same drug as "Aspirin," and its use ought not unduly to hamper the trade in its business. Besides, the case in this aspect is one of trade-mark proper. Therefore I will grant an injunction against direct sales of the drug under the name "Aspirin" to manufacturing chemists, physicians, and retail druggists. This will, of course, include invoices and correspondence.

In sales to consumers there need, however, be no suffix or qualification whatever. In so far as customers came to identify the plaintiff with "Aspirin" between October, 1915, and March, 1917, this may do it some injustice, but it is impracticable to give any protection based on that possibility. Among consumers generally the name has gone into the public domain.

* * *

KELLOGG CO. v. NATIONAL BISCUIT CO.

305 U.S. 111 (1938)

MR. JUSTICE BRANDEIS delivered the opinion of the Court.

This suit was brought in the federal court for Delaware by National Biscuit Company against Kellogg Company to enjoin alleged unfair competition by the manufacture and sale of the breakfast food commonly known as shredded wheat. The competition was alleged to be unfair mainly because Kellogg Company uses, like the plaintiff, the name shredded wheat and, like the plaintiff, produces its biscuit in pillow-shaped form.

* * *

The plaintiff concedes that it does not possess the exclusive right to make shredded wheat. But it claims the exclusive right to the trade name "Shredded Wheat" and the exclusive right to make shredded wheat biscuits pillow-shaped. It charges that the defendant, by using the name and shape, and otherwise, is passing off, or enabling others to pass off, Kellogg goods for those of the plaintiff. Kellogg Company denies that the plaintiff is entitled to the exclusive use of the name or of the pillow-shape; denies any passing off; asserts that it has used every reasonable effort to distinguish its product from that of the plaintiff; and contends that in honestly competing for a part of the market for shredded wheat it is exercising the common right freely to manufacture and sell an article of commerce unprotected by patent.

First. The plaintiff has no exclusive right to the use of the term "Shredded Wheat" as a trade name. For that is the generic term of the article, which describes it with a fair degree of accuracy; and is the term by which the biscuit in pillow-shaped form is generally known by the public. Since the term is generic, the original maker of the product acquired no exclusive right to use it. As Kellogg Company had the right to make the article, it had, also, the right to use the term by which the public knows it. *Compare Saxlehner v. Wagner,* 216 U.S. 375; *Holzapfel's Compositions Co. v. Rahtien's American Composition Co.,* 183 U.S. 1. Ever since 1894 the article has been known to the public as shredded wheat. For many years, there was no attempt to use the term "Shredded Wheat" as a trade-mark. When in 1905 plaintiff's predecessor, Natural Food Company, applied for registration of the words "Shredded Whole Wheat" as a trademark under the so-called "ten year clause" of the Act of February 20, 1905, c. 592, § 5, 33 Stat. 725, William E. Williams gave notice of opposition. Upon the hearing it appeared that Williams had, as early as 1894, built a machine for making shredded wheat, and that he made and sold its product as "Shredded Whole Wheat." The Commissioner of Patents refused registration. The Court of Appeals of the District of Columbia affirmed his decision, holding that "these words accurately and aptly describe an article of food which . . . has been produced . . . for more than ten years. . . ." *Natural Food Co. v. Williams,* 30 App. D.C. 348.

Moreover, the name "Shredded Wheat," as well as the product, the process and the machinery employed in making it, has been dedicated to the public. The basic patent for the product and for the process of making it, and many other patents for special machinery to be used in making the article, issued. . . . In those patents the term "shredded" is repeatedly used as descriptive of the product. The basic patent expired October 15, 1912; the others soon after. Since during the life of the patents "Shredded Wheat" was the general designation of the patented product, there passed to the public upon the expiration of the patent, not only the right to make the article as it was made during the patent period, but also the right to apply thereto the name by which it had become known. . . .

It is contended that the plaintiff has the exclusive right to the name "Shredded Wheat," because those words acquired the "secondary meaning" of shredded wheat made at Niagara Falls by the plaintiff's predecessor. There is no basis here for applying the doctrine of secondary meaning. The evidence shows only that due to the long period in which the plaintiff or its predecessor was the only manufacturer of the product, many people have come to associate the product, and as a consequence the name by which the product is generally known, with the plaintiff's factory at Niagara Falls. But to establish a trade name in the term "shredded wheat" the plaintiff must show more than a subordinate meaning which applies to it. It must show that the primary significance of the term in the minds of the consuming public is not the product but the producer. This it has not done. The showing which it has made does not entitle it to the exclusive use of the term shredded wheat but merely entitles it to require that the defendant use reasonable care to inform the public of the source of its product.

The plaintiff seems to contend that even if Kellogg Company acquired upon the expiration of the patents the right to use the name shredded wheat, the right was lost by delay. The argument is that Kellogg Company, although the largest producer of breakfast cereals in the country, did not seriously attempt to make shredded wheat or to challenge plaintiff's right to that name until 1927, and that meanwhile plaintiff's predecessor had expended more than $17,000,000 in making the name a household word and identifying the product with its manufacture. Those facts are without legal significance. Kellogg Company's right was not one dependent upon diligent exercise. Like every other member of the public, it was, and remained, free to make shredded wheat when it chose to do so; and to call the product by its generic name. The only obligation resting upon Kellogg Company was to identify its own product lest it be mistaken for that of the plaintiff.

Second. The plaintiff has not the exclusive right to sell shredded wheat in the form of a pillow-shaped biscuit — the form in which the article became known to the public. That is the form in which shredded wheat was made under the basic patent. The patented machines used were designed to produce only the pillow-shaped biscuits. And a design patent was taken out to cover the pillow-shaped form. Hence, upon expiration of the patents the form, as well as the name, was dedicated to the public. As was said in *Singer Mfg. Co. v. June Mfg. Co.*, [163 U.S. 169], p. 185:

> It is self evident that on the expiration of a patent the monopoly granted by it ceases to exist, and the right to make the thing formerly covered by the patent becomes public property. It is upon this condition that the patent is granted. It follows, as a matter of course, that on the termination of the patent there passes to the public the right to make the machine in the form in which it was constructed during the patent. We may, therefore, dismiss without further comment the complaint, as to the form in which the defendant made his machines.

Where an article may be manufactured by all, a particular manufacturer can no more assert exclusive rights in a form in which the public has become accustomed to see the article and which, in the minds of the public, is primarily associated with the article rather than a particular producer, than it can in the case of a name with similar connections in the public mind. Kellogg Company was free to use the pillow-shaped form, subject only to the obligation to identify its product lest it be mistaken for that of the plaintiff.

Third. The question remains whether Kellogg Company in exercising its right to use the name "Shredded Wheat" and the pillow-shaped biscuit, is doing so fairly. Fairness requires that it be done in a manner which reasonably distinguishes its product from that of plaintiff.

Each company sells its biscuits only in cartons. The standard Kellogg carton contains fifteen biscuits; the plaintiff's twelve. The Kellogg cartons are distinctive. They do not resemble those used by the plaintiff either in size, form, or color. And the difference in the labels is striking. The Kellogg cartons bear in bold script the names "Kellogg's Whole Wheat Biscuit" or "Kellogg's Shredded Whole Wheat Biscuit" so sized and spaced as to strike the eye as being a Kellogg product. It is true that on some of its cartons it had a picture of two shredded wheat biscuits in a bowl of milk which was quite *more distinction*

similar to one of the plaintiff's registered trade-marks. But the name Kellogg was so prominent on all of the defendant's cartons as to minimize the possibility of confusion.

Some hotels, restaurants, and lunchrooms serve biscuits not in cartons and guests so served may conceivably suppose that a Kellogg biscuit served is one of the plaintiff's make. But no person familiar with plaintiff's product would be misled. The Kellogg biscuit is about two thirds the size of plaintiff's; and differs from it in appearance. Moreover, the field in which deception could be practiced is negligibly small. Only 2.5 percent of the Kellogg biscuits are sold to hotels, restaurants and lunchrooms. Of those so sold 98 per cent are sold in individual cartons containing two biscuits. These cartons are distinctive and bear prominently the Kellogg name. To put upon the individual biscuit some mark which would identify it as the Kellogg product is not commercially possible. Relatively few biscuits will be removed from the individual cartons before they reach the consumer. The obligation resting upon Kellogg Company is not to insure that every purchaser will know it to be the maker but to use every reasonable means to prevent confusion.

It is urged that all possibility of deception or confusion would be removed if Kellogg Company should refrain from using the name "Shredded Wheat" and adopt some form other than the pillow-shape. But the name and form are integral parts of the goodwill of the article. To share fully in the goodwill, it must use the name and the pillow-shape. And in the goodwill Kellogg Company is as free to share as the plaintiff. *Compare William R. Warner & Co. v. Eli Lilly & Co.*, 265 U.S. 526, 528, 530. Moreover, the pillow-shape must be used for another reason. The evidence is persuasive that this form is functional — that the cost of the biscuit would be increased and its high quality lessened if some other form were substituted for the pillow-shape.

Kellogg Company is undoubtedly sharing in the goodwill of the article known as "Shredded Wheat"; and thus is sharing in a market which was created by the skill and judgment of plaintiff's predecessor and has been widely extended by vast expenditures in advertising persistently made. But that is not unfair. Sharing in the goodwill of an article unprotected by patent or trade-mark is the exercise of a right possessed by all and in the free exercise of which the consuming public is deeply interested. There is no evidence of passing off or deception on the part of the Kellogg Company; and it has taken every reasonable precaution to prevent confusion or the practice of deception in the sale of its product.

Fourth. By its "clarifying" decree, the Circuit Court of Appeals enjoined Kellogg Company from using the picture of the two shredded wheat biscuits in the bowl only in connection with an injunction against manufacturing the pillow-shaped biscuits and the use of the term shredded wheat, on the grounds of unfair competition. The use of this picture was not enjoined on the independent ground of trade-mark infringement. Since the National Biscuit Company did not petition for certiorari, the question whether use of the picture is a violation of that trade-mark although Kellogg Company is free to use the name and the pillow-shaped biscuit is not here for review.

Decrees reversed with direction to dismiss the bill.

FILIPINO YELLOW PAGES, INC. v. ASIAN JOURNAL PUBLICATIONS, INC.
198 F.3d 1143 (9th Cir. 1999)

O'SCANNLAIN, CIRCUIT JUDGE

We must decide whether the publisher of a telephone directory for the Filipino-American community can establish that the term "Filipino Yellow Pages" is protectible under trademark law.

*   *   *

On August 2, 1996, FYP filed a complaint against AJP, Oriel, and Macabagdal-Oriel (collectively, "AJP") in the Central District of California. FYP alleged the following causes of action: (1) trademark infringement; (2) false designation of origin and false description of sponsorship or affiliation; (3) unfair competition and misappropriation of goodwill, reputation, and business properties; (4) misappropriation of FYP's right of publicity; (5) injury to business relationships; (6) unfair competition under California state law; and (7) trademark dilution under California state law.

AJP moved for summary judgment, arguing that the term "Filipino Yellow Pages" is generic and as such incapable of trademark protection. . . . In opposing the motion for summary judgment, FYP contended that "Filipino Yellow Pages," rather than being generic, is protectible under trademark law as a descriptive mark with a secondary meaning in the minds of consumers (i.e., as specifically referring to FYP's telephone directory). . . .

On November 26, 1997, the district court granted AJP's motion for summary judgment. The district court held that (1) the term "Filipino Yellow Pages" is generic, and as such incapable of serving as a trademark; and (2) even if the term were descriptive, AJP would still be entitled to summary judgment because FYP had failed to produce any admissible evidence of secondary meaning. On January 16, 1998, the district court entered a judgment in which it dismissed FYP's trademark claims with prejudice and dismissed FYP's other claims without prejudice, subject to refiling in state court. . . .

The first issue presented is whether the term "Filipino Yellow Pages" is generic with respect to telephone directories targeted at the Filipino-American community. If the term is generic, it cannot be the subject of trademark protection under any circumstances, even with a showing of secondary meaning. . . .

Before proceeding to the merits, a word on the burden of persuasion is appropriate. In cases involving properly registered marks, a presumption of validity places the burden of proving genericness upon the defendant. *See* 15 U.S.C. § 1057(b) ("A certificate of registration of a mark . . . shall be prima facie evidence of the validity of the registered mark. . . ."). If a supposedly valid mark is not federally registered, however, the plaintiff has the burden of proving nongenericness once the defendant asserts genericness as a defense. . . .

Case law recognizes "four different categories of terms with respect to trademark protection: (1) generic, (2) descriptive, (3) suggestive, and (4) arbitrary or fanciful." *Surgicenters of America, Inc. v. Medical Dental Surgeries Co.*, 601 F.2d 1011, 1014 (9th Cir.1979) (citing *Abercrombie & Fitch Co. v. Hunting World, Inc.*, 537 F.2d 4, 9 (2[d] Cir.1976) (Friendly, J.)). Only the first two of these four categories are at issue in the present appeal. AJP contends that "Filipino Yellow Pages" is a generic term and as such incapable of trademark protection, while FYP argues that the term is protectible as a descriptive term with secondary meaning. . .

"A 'generic' term is one that refers, or has come to be understood as referring, to the genus of which the particular product or service is a species. It cannot become a trademark under any circumstances." *Surgicenters*, 601 F.2d at 1014 (citing *Abercrombie*, 537 F.2d at 9-10). As explained by one commentator, a generic term is "the name of the product or service itself-what [the product] is, and as such . . . the very antithesis of a mark." 2 J. Thomas McCarthy, *Trademarks and Unfair Competition* § 12:1[1] (4th ed.1997). Courts sometimes refer to generic terms as "common descriptive" names, the language used in the Lanham Act for terms incapable of becoming trademarks. *Park ' N Fly, Inc., v. Dollar Park and Fly, Inc.*, 718 F.2d 327, 329 (9th Cir.1983), *rev'd on other grounds,* 469 U.S. 189, 105 S.Ct. 658, 83 L.Ed.2d 582 (1985). . . .

In determining whether a term is generic, we have often relied upon the "who-are-you/what-are-you" test: "A mark answers the buyer's questions 'Who are you?' 'Where do you come from?' 'Who vouches for you?' But the [generic] name of the product answers the question 'What are you?' " *Official Airline Guides, Inc. v. Goss*, 6 F.3d 1385, 1391 (9[th]Cir.1993) (quoting 1 J. Thomas McCarthy, *Trademarks and Unfair Competition* § 12.01 (3d ed.1992)). Under this test, "[i]f the primary significance of the trademark is to describe the *type of product* rather than the *producer,* the trademark [is] a generic term and [cannot be] a valid trademark." *Anti-Monopoly, Inc. v. General Mills Fun Group,* 611 F.2d 296, 304 (9th Cir.1979) (emphases added).

Here the parties do not dispute that "Filipino" and "yellow pages" are generic terms. The word "Filipino" is a clearly generic term used to refer to "a native of the Philippine islands" or "a citizen of the Republic of the Philippines." *Webster's Ninth New Collegiate Dictionary* 462 (1986). The term "yellow pages" has been found to be a generic term for "a local business telephone directory alphabetized by product or service." *AmCan Enters., Inc. v. Renzi,* 32 F.3d 233, 234 (7th Cir.1994) (Posner, J.) (citing cases, and noting that "yellow pages," which originally was not a generic term, has become generic over time); *see also Webster's Ninth New Collegiate Dictionary* 1367 (defining "yellow pages" as "the section of a telephone directory that lists businesses and professional firms alphabetically by category and that includes classified advertising"). The district court further noted, as shown by FYP's application for trademark registration, that the PTO requires the use of a disclaimer regarding rights to the term "yellow pages" whenever it is used as part of a registered trademark.

The issue then becomes whether combining the generic terms "Filipino" and "yellow pages" to form the composite term "Filipino Yellow Pages" creates a generic or a descriptive term. AJP argues, and the district court concluded, that "Filipino Yellow Pages" is generic based on this court's analysis in *Surgicenters of America, Inc. v. Medical Dental Surgeries Co.,* 601 F.2d 1011 (9[th]Cir.1979). In *Surgicenters,* we held that the term "surgicenter" was generic and that the plaintiff's registered service mark had to be removed from the trademark register. In our discussion in *Surgicenters,* we summarized (but did not explicitly adopt) the analysis of the district court in that case, which reasoned that "surgicenter," created by combining the generic terms "surgery" and "center," retained the generic quality of its components. *Id.* at 1015. We distinguished "surgicenter" from the composite term "Startgrolay," upheld as a valid mark for poultry feed, by noting that the combination of terms in "surgicenter" did not constitute a "deviation from normal usage" or an "unusual unitary combination." *Id.* at 1018. Nowhere in *Surgicenters* did we hold, however, that a composite term made up of generic components is automatically generic unless the combination constitutes a "deviation from normal usage" or an "unusual unitary combination."

In reaching our conclusion of genericness in *Surgicenters,* we placed significant but not controlling weight on the dictionary definitions and generic nature of "surgery" and "center." We explained that "[w]hile not determinative, dictionary definitions are relevant and often persuasive in determining how a term is understood by the consuming public, the ultimate test of whether a trademark is generic." *Id.* at 1015 n. 11.But we also based our genericness finding upon detailed information in some 45 exhibits that, taken collectively, suggested that the consuming public considered the composite term "surgicenter" to mean a surgical center generally speaking, as opposed to a surgical center maintained and operated by the plaintiff specifically. *See id.* at 1017. These exhibits included letters from potential consumers and several publications that used the term "surgicenter" in a clearly generic sense. The finding of genericness in *Surgicenters* cannot be separated from the uniquely well-developed record in that case. *See Park ' N Fly,* 718 F.2d at 330-31.

In this case, the district court cited *Surgicenters* for the proposition that "a combination of two generic words is also generic, unless the combination is a 'deviation from natural usage' or an 'unusual unitary combination.' " The court then stated that "[u]nder this analysis, the term 'Filipino Yellow Pages' seems to be neither a 'deviation from natural usage,' nor an 'unusual unitary combination.' " The district court's reading of *Surgicenters* appears somewhat troubling insofar as it oversimplifies our opinion. First, it overlooks our explicit recognition that "words which could not individually become a trademark may become one when taken together." 601 F.2d at 1017 (internal quotation marks omitted). Second, it effectively makes dictionary definitions the crucial factor in assessing genericness, even though *Surgicenters* makes clear that such definitions are "not determinative" and that the "ultimate test" of genericnessness is "how a term is understood by the consuming public." *Id.* at 1015 n. 11.Finally, it severs our *Surgicenters* analysis from its unique factual context, in which a wealth of exhibits supported a finding that the term "surgicenter" was generic even when taken as a whole (as opposed to the sum of generic parts).

Furthermore, reading the *Surgicenters* opinion for the rather broad (and somewhat reductionist) principle that "a generic term plus a generic term equals a generic term" would give rise to an unnecessary conflict between that decision and several other cases, decided both before and after *Surgicenters,* in which we have adopted a more holistic approach to evaluating composite terms. . . . [The court then goes on to discuss in depth a number of prior decisions on genericness.]

As the foregoing discussion illustrates, several pre- and post-*Surgicenters* cases have announced what could be described as an "anti-dissection rule" for evaluating the trademark validity of composite terms. *Official Airline Guides, Inc.,* 6 F.3d at 1392 (noting that under this rule, "the validity and distinctiveness of a composite trademark is determined by viewing the trademark as a whole, as it appears in the marketplace"). When *Surgicenters* is examined in light of these later cases, it becomes clear that *Surgicenters* should not be read over broadly to stand for the simple proposition that "generic plus generic equals generic." Rather, *Surgicenters* must be read in its proper context. First, it must be noted that *Surgicenters* explicitly recognizes that generic individual terms can be combined to form valid composite marks. *See* 601 F.2d at 1017. Second, it must be recalled that we found the term "surgicenter" generic based in large part on a well-developed record of 45 exhibits showing that the term "surgicenter," considered as a whole, was generic (i.e., understood by the consuming public as referring simply to a center at which surgery was performed).

In light of the foregoing discussion, the district court here may have oversimplified matters somewhat when it stated that "[t]he Ninth Circuit has held that a combination of two generic words is also generic, unless the combination is a 'deviation from natural usage' or an 'unusual unitary combination.' " Any arguable imprecision in the district court's application of *Surgicenters* was harmless, however, because the term "Filipino Yellow Pages" would be unprotectable in any event.

In finding "Filipino Yellow Pages" generic, the district court did not rely solely upon the generic nature and presence in the dictionary of "Filipino" and "yellow pages." The district court also considered other evidence tending to suggest that "Filipino Yellow Pages," even when considered as an entire mark, is generic with respect to telephone directories. The district court took note of the following facts: (1) Jornacion himself appeared to use the term "Filipino Yellow Pages" in a generic sense in the Shareholders' Buy Out Agreement with Oriel, when he "agree[d] not to compete in the Filipino Directory (Filipino Yellow Pages) in California"; (2) FYP did not bring suit to challenge the marketing of a second *Filipino Yellow Pages* to the Filipino-American community on the East Coast; and (3) a *Los Angeles Times* article, in discussing a trend toward specialized yellow pages, appeared to use the term in a generic sense; the article referred to a directory published by one Virgil Junio as "his Filipino yellow pages" instead of using the actual title of Junio's publication.

These three pieces of evidence are not as weighty as the 45 exhibits presented in *Surgicenters,* in which the record established generic use of the term "surgicenter" by *Newsweek* magazine, six medical publications, and the Department of Health, Education and Welfare. *See* 601 F.2d at 1013, 1017 n. 17. An important difference between *Surgicenters* and the instant case should be noted, however. The mark at issue in *Surgicenters* was a federally-registered mark, and thus the burden of proving genericness rested upon the party challenging the mark's validity. *See id.* at 1012, 1014. The mark at issue in this case, in contrast, is not registered; thus FYP, as trademark plaintiff, must prove that "Filipino Yellow Pages" is *not* generic. It does not appear that

FYP has offered evidence of nongenericness sufficient to rebut even the fairly modest evidence of genericness offered by AJP. In light of the evidence presented by AJP, it would seem that under the "who-are-you/what-are-you" test, the term "Filipino Yellow Pages" is generic. If faced with the question "What are you?", FYP's *Filipino Yellow Pages*, AJP's *Filipino Consumer Directory*, and the *Filipino Directory of the U.S.A. and Canada* could all respond in the same way: "A Filipino yellow pages." Giving FYP exclusive rights to the term "Filipino Yellow Pages" might be inappropriate because it would effectively "grant [FYP as] owner of the mark a monopoly, since a competitor could not describe his goods as what they are." *Surgicenters*, 601 F.2d at 1017 (internal quotation marks omitted).

Even assuming that AJP's other evidence of genericness would be insufficient to sustain a genericness finding by itself, it certainly suggests that "Filipino Yellow Pages," if descriptive, would be the feeblest of descriptive marks-in the words of one court, "perilously close to the 'generic' line." *Computerland Corp. v. Microland Computer Corp.*, 586 F.Supp. 22, 25 (N.D.Cal.1984). Such a weak descriptive mark could be a valid trademark only with a strong showing of strong secondary meaning. To this component of the trademark analysis we now turn. . . .

A descriptive term can be protected as a valid trademark only with a showing of secondary meaning. *See Surgicenters*, 601 F.2d at 1014. Secondary meaning can be established in many ways, including (but not limited to) direct consumer testimony; survey evidence; exclusivity, manner, and length of use of a mark; amount and manner of advertising; amount of sales and number of customers; established place in the market; and proof of intentional copying by the defendant. *See* 2 J. Thomas McCarthy, *Trademarks and Unfair Competition* § 15:30 (4th ed.1997). In this case, the only evidence of secondary meaning offered by FYP was contained in the declaration of its founder and president, Oscar Jornacion. . . .

FYP's evidence of secondary meaning was inadmissible, lacking in substantial probative value (as emanating from a far-from-objective source), or both. The district court did not err in concluding that FYP had failed to establish secondary meaning for "Filipino Yellow Pages." Thus "Filipino Yellow Pages," even if descriptive rather than generic, is not a valid and protectible trademark with respect to a telephone directory for the Filipino-American community. . . .

For the foregoing reasons, FYP was unable to establish the trademark protectibility of "Filipino Yellow Pages" as a descriptive mark with secondary meaning. The grant of summary judgment in favor of AJP was proper.

Affirmed.

*   *   *

Notes on Generic Terms

1. Generally

A term is generic when its principal significance to the public is to indicate the product or service itself, rather than its source. As stated by Judge Friendly in *Abercrombie & Fitch Co. v. Hunting World, Inc.*, 537 F.2d 4, 9 (2[d] Cir. 1976), "[a] generic term is one that refers, or has come to be understood as referring, to the genus of which the particular product is a species." It is the *public's* perception of the trademark which determines the extent of the rights possessed by its owner. What effect on a determination of genericness should the availability of other generic terms for the product have? In

2. Evidence of Genericness

Courts often examine the usage of a term in print media as evidence of its significance to the public. In *Mil-Mar Shoe Co. v. Shonac Corp.*, 75 F.3d 1153, 1158 & n.10 (7th Cir. 1996), the Seventh Circuit used three dictionary meanings of "warehouse" to support its holding that WAREHOUSE SHOES and SHOE WAREHOUSE are generic for high volume, retail shoe stores. The court rejected the plaintiff's argument that the adjectival use of "warehouse" in WAREHOUSE SHOES was descriptive rather than generic; "[the] generic components produce a generic composite and signify nothing more than a warehouse-type store that sells shoes," *id.* at 1161. *See also Stuhlbery Int'l Sales Co. v. John D. Brush Co.*, 240 F.3d 832 (9th Cir. 2001), in which "Fire-safe" was found likely to be generic, as "thirteen competitors use the term 'fire safe' to refer to a type of category of safe, Brush itself used the term in a generic sense, and the term is included in at least one dictionary"; *Door Sys. Inc. v. Pro-Line Door Sys. Inc.*, 83 F.3d 169 (7th Cir. 1996), in which the court noted that the absence of "door systems" in the yellow pages and a dictionary is evidence that the term is not generic; and *Eastern Airlines, Inc. v. New York Airlines, Inc.*, 218 U.S.P.Q. 71 (S.D.N.Y. 1983), in which dictionaries, Shakespeare and Walt Whitman were cited in support of the court's finding that "Air Shuttle" is generic. Expert witnesses also may be successfully utilized in establishing that a term is generic. In *WSM, Inc. v. Hilton*, 724 F.2d 1320 (8th Cir. 1984), for example, an expert in the field of regional English helped establish that "opry" was a dialectical variation of "opera" used as a generic term for a show consisting of country music, dancing and comedy routines.

While the critical issue is public perception of the term, the trademark owner's own way of using the term can be evidence of genericness. *See, e.g., Loglan Instititute., Inc. v. Logical Language Group, Inc.*, 962 F.2d 1038, 1041 (Fed. Cir. 1992)(registration canceled where "[t]he evidence indicates that Dr. Brown himself has used the term Loglan only in a generic sense" and encouraged others to do so).

3. Recapture of Generic Terms

Could a trademark which became generic ever regain its source-indicating significance? In *Singer Mfg. Co. v. June Mfg. Co.*, 163 U.S. 169, 203 (1886), the Supreme Court held SINGER for sewing machines generic, stating that the word "had become public property, and the defendant had a right to use it." Years later in *Singer Mfg. Co. v. Briley*, 207 F.2d 519, 521 n.3 (5th Cir. 1953), the court held that the Singer Company had "recaptured from the public domain the name 'Singer' . . . [and it] has thus become a valid trademark." 207 F.2d at 521 n. 3. *Compare Harley-Davidson, Inc. v. Grottanelli*, 164 F.3d 806 (2[d] Cir. 1999), in which the Second Circuit held "hog" generic for motorcycle products and services, and rejected plaintiff's attempt to invoke the "doctrine whereby trademark use can be reacquired in a generic term." The Court opined that the Singer-type situation was limited to cases involving "words that were originally proper names of the manufacturer, and [those cases] do not stand for the proposition that a commonly used name of an article like 'computer,' 'typewriter' or 'flashlight' can be appropriated by one seller as a trademark." Is the court right? Could a term which is generic ab initio, e.g., "chair," ever gain source-indicating significance? *See Kellogg Co. v. National Biscuit Co., supra.*

4. Examples of Genericness Holdings

In *Yellow Cab Co. v. Yellow Cab of Elk Grove, Inc.*, 419 F.3d 925 (9th Cir. 2005), the court of appeals reversed the district court's finding that YELLOW CAB for taxi cabs was either generic or descriptive without secondary meaning. The court applied the "who-are-you/what-are-you" test for genericness, it developed in *Filipino Yellow Pages*, excerpted above, i.e., that a trademark answers " 'the buyer's questions 'Who are you?' 'Where do you come from?' 'Who vouches for you?' But the generic name of the product answers the question 'What are you?' " *Filipino Yellow Pages*, 198 F.3d at 1147 (internal citations omitted). The court found summary judgment was not proper because there was a genuine issue of material fact with regard to the genericness of "yellow cab"; the term "appears to answer the 'who are you?' rather than the 'what are you?' question, demonstrating its nongenericness." *Yellow Cab Co.*, 419 F.3d at 929.

Judge Friendly once observed that "no matter how much money and effort the user of a generic term has poured into promoting the sale of its merchandise and what success it has achieved in securing public identification, it cannot deprive competing manufacturers of the right to call an article by its name." *Abercrombie & Fitch Co. v. Hunting World, Inc.*. In *Miller Brewing Co. v. G. Heilemann Brewing Co.*, 561 F.2d 75 (7th Cir. 1977), the court found that the term "lite" or "light" as applied to a low calorie beer was generic and therefore could not be appropriated as a trademark. It reasoned that:

> other brewers whose beers have qualities that make them "light" as that word has commonly been used remain free to call their beer "light." Otherwise a manufacturer could remove a common descriptive word from the public domain by investing his goods with an additional quality, thus gaining the exclusive right to call his wine "rose," his whiskey "blended," or his bread "white."

Compare In re Reed Elsevier Properties, Inc., 482 F.3d 1376 (Fed. Cir. 2007) (LAWYERS.COM generic for website with links to law- and lawyer-related websites); *Donchez v. Coors Brewing Co.*, 392 F.3d 1211 (10th Cir. 2004) (evidence failed to show that consumers viewed "beerman" as anything but a generic term for a beer vendor); *Anheuser-Busch, Inc. v. The Stroh Brewery Co.*, 750 F.2d 631 (8th Cir. 1984) ("LA" for reduced or low alcohol beer). *See also In re Miller Brewing Co.*, 226 U.S.P.Q. 666 (T.T.A.B. 1985) (Applicant's distinctive display of LITE for low calorie beer granted registration).

There is nothing immutable about words. Their meanings change not infrequently. Samuel Johnson put it best in the preface to his celebrated 1755 Dictionary of the English Language, where he discussed "the exuberance of signification" that causes a word to pass "from its primitive to its remote and accidental signification," so that "[t]he original sense of words is often driven out of use by their metaphorical acceptations . . . ." Jack Lynch (ed.), Samuel Johnson's Dictionary, at 34 (2002). If a word is generic, then it does not signify source; confusion as to source cannot result from its use by another, and such use will not be prohibited. *See Schwan's IP LLC v. Kraft Pizza Co.*, 79 U.S.P.Q.2d 1790 (8th Cir. 2006) (BRICK OVEN generic for frozen pizza made, or of style made, in a brick oven); *Hunt Masters, Inc. v. Landry's Seafood Restaurant*, 240 F.3d 251 (4th Cir. 2001) ("Crab House" generic for class of restaurants serving crab dishes, citing prior decision holding "Ale House" generic); and *America Online, Inc. v. AT&T Corp.*, 243 F.3d 812 (4th Cir. 2001) (holding "You Have Mail" generic for alerting customers about mail in their electronic mailbox, and "IM" generic for an instant messaging service).

Compare KP Permanent Make-Up, Inc. v. Lasting Impression I, Inc., 328 F.3d 1061 (9th Cir. 2003), *overruled on other grounds*, 543 U.S. 111 (2004) ("Micro colors" not shown to be a generic abbreviation for a skin micro pigmentation process similar to tattooing); *In re Dial-A-Mattress*, 240 F.3d 1341 (Fed. Cir. 2001) (1-888-MATTRES not generic; "[t]here is no record evidence that the relevant public refers to the class of shop-at-home telephone mattress retailers" by this mnemonic phone number); *In re American Fertility Society*, 188 F.3d 1341, 1345 (Fed. Cir. 1999) (remanded because the PTO used wrong test in assessing whether "Society for Reproductive Medicine" was generic; the test is not whether components of the mark are generic, but whether the relevant public understands the entire mark "to primarily refer to the genus of services provided"); *Sara Lee Corp. v. Kayser-Roth Corp.*, 81 F.3d 455, 464 (4th Cir.), *cert. denied*, 519 U.S. 976 (1996) (L'EGGS not generic for pantyhose; "the mark at issue is neither 'leg eggs' nor 'legs,' but L'EGGS, a word that represents a singular concept associated with

— but very different from — pantyhose . . . . [I]t is unquestionably suggestive . . . ."); *Texas Pig Stands, Inc. v. Hard Rock Cafe Int'l, Inc.*, 951 F.2d 684 (5th Cir. 1992) (PIG SANDWICH not generic for barbecued pork sandwich). *See* Under appropriate circumstances, even graphic designs can become generic in a particular industry. *See, e.g., Kendall-Jackson Winery Ltd. v. E&J Gallo Winery*, 150 F.3d 1042 (9th Cir. 1998) (although initially suggestive and protectable, "[b]ecause the grape leaf is widely used in the industry [on wine labels], it has lost the power to differentiate brands" and become a "generic emblem" for wines).

5. Prevention and Education

Measures may be taken to help prevent a distinctive term from becoming generic. *See, e.g., E.I. DuPont de Nemours & Co. v. Yoshida International, Inc.*, 393 F. Supp. 502, 507 (E.D.N.Y. 1975), in which the court cited the plaintiff's successful and "vigilant trademark education and protection program" for TEFLON for a non-stick finish included instruction of salespeople, industrial buyers and others as to correct usage in advertising and business correspondence; a publication on correct usage distributed to customers; "extensive surveillance by its legal and advertising departments as well as the outside advertising agency," with misuses promptly responded to; and "protective trademark advertising to impart to the general public the understanding that TEFLON symbolizes DuPont's non-stick finish"; and *Selchow & Righter Co. v. McGraw Hill Book Co.*, 580 F.2d 25, 27 (2d Cir. 1978), where the court granted a preliminary injunction "at least in part" because defendant's book entitled THE COMPLETE SCRABBLE DICTIONARY might render generic plaintiff's mark SCRABBLE for a word game. *But cf. Illinois High School Ass'n, supra*, in which the court noted in dicta that even the federal antidilution statute (discussed in Chapter 8) will not "resurrect a [generic mark], since if a mark becomes generic it is no longer distinctive" . . . and *Ty, Inc. v. Perryman*, 306 F.3d 509 (7th Cir. 2002), in which a judgment under dilution law against alleged generic misuse of "beanies" for stuffed toys was vacated, with Judge Posner observing that ordinary language becomes enriched by the addition of generic terms derived from brand names. In what ways might the public be educated as to the intended trademark significance of a term in advertising and on labels?

In *King-Seeley Thermos Co. v. Aladdin Industries, Inc.*, 321 F.2d 577 (2d Cir. 1963), King-Seeley's belated attempts to educate the public and rescue its registered THERMOS trademark from the public domain were unsuccessful. King-Seeley argued that the availability of an easily used generic name, vacuum bottle, distinguished its case from the *Aspirin* case, *supra*. The Court rejected this argument, stating, "the test is not what is available as an alternative to the public, but what the public's understanding is of the word it uses." Despite its finding that "Thermos" was a generic term, the Court allowed King-Seeley to use "Thermos" as it had in the past, with a capital "T" and the federal registration symbol, while defendant was ordered to always use the lower case "t," preceded by defendant's company name, and also to refrain from using "original" and "genuine" in conjunction with "thermos." In *Windsurfing International v. Fred Ostermann GmbH*, 613 F. Supp. 933 (S.D.N.Y. 1985), *modified*, 782 F.2d 995 (Fed. Cir. 1986), the owner of patent rights realized too late that "windsurfer" had become a generic term for sailboards. Subsequent efforts to educate the public and police the mark were held unsuccessful. Furthermore, a patent license provision restraining anyone but WSI from producing any product using the term "Windsurfer" was held unlawful trademark misuse, being an attempt to inhibit competition beyond the scope of WSI's patent monopoly. See the discussion on Antitrust law in Chapter 7.

Is the following from the *Thermos* opinion an overstatement: "Of course, it is obvious that the fact that there was no suitable descriptive word for either aspirin or cellophane made it difficult, if not impossible, for the original manufacturers to prevent their trademark from becoming generic." Would the decisions in the *Aspirin* and *Cellophane* cases have been the same had the manufacturers themselves not used their trademarks generically or acquiesced in such use by others? For a discussion of practices that lead to a trademark's becoming generic and those that help to prevent it, see Oddi, *Assessing "Genericness": Another View,* 78 TRADEMARK REP. 560 (1988); and McLeod, *The Status of So Highly Descriptive And Acquired Distinctiveness,* 82 TRADEMARK REP. 607 (1992).

There is no type of word or term immune to becoming generic. The issue is entirely one of the state of the public mind. Thus, the problem for the trademark user is one of educating the public. Trademarks consisting of arbitrary terms, *Saxlehner v. Wagner,* 216 U.S. 375 (1910) (HUNYADI for bitter water), surnames, *Ludlow Valve Mfg. Co. v. Pittsburgh Mfg Co.,* 166 F. 26 (3^d Cir. 1908) (LUDLOW for valves), and geographic names, *French Republic v. Saratoga Vichy Spring Co.,* 191 U.S. 427 (1903) (VICHY for water), have become generic. In *Dan Robbins & Associates, Inc. v. Questor Corp.,* 599 F.2d 1009, 1014 (C.C.P.A. 1979), the court stated: "Whether the relevant purchasing public regards a term as a common descriptive [i.e., generic] name is a question of fact to be resolved on the evidence (citation omitted). Purchaser testimony, consumer surveys, and listings in dictionaries, trade journals, newspapers and other publications, are useful evidence." *See also Anheuser-Busch Inc. v. John Labatt Ltd.,* 89 F.3d 1339 (8th Cir. 1996), *cert. denied,* 519 U.S. 1109 (1997) (upholding jury verdict that ICE BEER is generic based in part on consumer surveys showing that consumers understood the term "ice" to be the name of a beer category).

Compare Illinois High School Ass'n v. GTE Vantage, Inc., supra, in which the Seventh Circuit upheld dual use of MARCH MADNESS in connection with basketball tournaments by two different parties, with *Glover v. Ampak Inc.,* 74 F.3d 57, 60 (4th Cir. 1996), holding that WHITE TAIL for pocket knives is not generic even though it "has not been used exclusively by [registrant] and . . . the association between hunting knives and deer is easily and commonly made." The court nonetheless noted that "others' use might be probative of . . . dilution or . . . abandonment." *See also* Barsade, *Distinct Classes of Consumers of a Single Product — Accommodating Competing Perceptions of Genericness of the Same Identification,* 86 TRADEMARK REP. 56 (1996). Recognizing the enforcement problems against third parties created by the *Illinois High School Ass'n v. GTE Vantage, Inc.* decision, the parties in that case subsequently agreed to form a joint venture company, March Madness Athletic Association, L.L.C., to consolidate ownership in the MARCH MADNESS mark and eliminate the "dual usage" rights described by Judge Posner. As sole owner of rights, that company then licensed each of the parties to use the mark and proceeded to police third party use. *See, e.g., March Madness Athletic Ass'n v. Netfire, Inc.,* 162 F. Supp. 2d 560 (N.D. Tex 2001) (describing the formation of the plaintiff and enforcement efforts against third parties misusing the MARCH MADNESS mark), aff'd 120 Fed. Appx. 540 (5th Cir. 2005). *See also Note, "Mark Madness: How Brent Musberger and the Miracle Bra May Have Led to a More Equitable and Efficient Understanding of the Reverse Confusion Doctrine in Trademark Law,* 86 VA. L. REV. 597 (2000), and the discussion on licensing later in this chapter.

6. Foreign Terms

A foreign word can be generic if it translates into English as the generic word for a product or even if it has no English translation. *See Enrique Bernat F. v. Guada Lajara, Inc.,* 210 F.3d 439, 444 (5th Cir. 2000) (vacating preliminary injunction where third party use showed "chupa" was Spanish generic equivalent of "lollipop"; allowing plaintiff to monopolize the term would impede other Mexican candy makers from effectively entering U.S. lollipop market); *Otokoyama Co. Ltd. v. Wine of Japan Import, Inc.,* 175 F.3d 266, 268, 270-71 (2^d Cir. 1999) (because evidence raised sufficient doubt as to whether "otokoyama" was generic in Japanese for a type of sake, preliminary injunction vacated; "the assumption [is] that there are . . . customers in the United States who speak that foreign language" and granting exclusivity would "prevent competitors from designating a product as what it is in the foreign language their customers know best").

A word can be generic in one country while retaining its source-indicating significance in others. ASPIRIN is not protectible in the United States, but remains a valid trademark in Canada and a number of other countries. *Cf. In re Aktiengesellschaft*, 488 F.3d 960 (Fed. Cir. 2007) (ASPIRINA refused registration for analgesic goods as a merely descriptive variation or misspelling of aspirin; there also was evidence it was a Spanish language equivalent for aspirin). *See Keebler Co.*, supra (EXPORT SODAS is a generic term for crackers in Puerto Rico); *Carcione v. The Greengrocers, Inc.*, 205 U.S.P.Q. 1075 (E.D. Cal. 1979) (GREENGROCER is a generic term in Britain for retailers of fresh vegetables and fruit, but may not be in the United States).

7. Purchaser Motivation

In 1982, the Ninth Circuit held that "Monopoly" is a generic term for board games which have the creation of a monopoly as the winner's goal. *Anti-Monopoly, Inc. v. General Mills Fun Group, Inc.*, 684 F.2d 1316 (9th Cir. 1982), *cert. denied*, 459 U.S. 1227 (1983). Despite impressive evidence of the public's association of "Monopoly" with a board game manufactured by Parker Brothers, the Court was persuaded that the mark was generic by survey evidence indicating that consumers were not *motivated* to buy the game *because* it was made by Parker Brothers. How would other well-known products fare under such a test? How does this "motivation test" compare with Learned Hand's test for trademark significance in the "Aspirin" case, supra, i.e., that buyers understand the word to mean that the product came from the same single, though perhaps anonymous, source with which they are familiar? The *Anti-Monopoly* decision has been much criticized. Interestingly, a shortly subsequent Ninth Circuit decision made no reference to it in holding that the Coca-Cola Company's trademark "Coke" had not become generic. *Coca-Cola Co. v. Overland, Inc.*, 692 F.2d 1250 (9th Cir. 1982). *See* Zeisel, *The Surveys That Broke Monopoly*, 50 U. Chi. L. Rev. 896 (1983). In 1984, Congress amended the Lanham Act to prevent a recurrence of the motivation test enunciated in the *Anti-Monopoly* case. 15 U.S.C. § 1064(c); 15 U.S.C. § 1127.

4.03 Abandonment

Introduction

Abandonment of trademark rights occurs when nonuse is coupled with the absence of an intention to continue or resume the use of a previously used name or mark. For example, if it can be proved that a claimant at some period has in fact discontinued use without the intention to resume, the claimant will be held to have abandoned and forfeited to the public domain, as of the date of the intended discontinuance, all prior rights to exclusivity. Any rights he or she may subsequently possess will be newly acquired and their priority will run only from the new date when use is resumed with intention to continue such use. Section 45 of the Lanham Act provides that three years nonuse of a registered mark constitutes prima facie abandonment, but that presumption is frequently rebutted merely by a convincing demonstration of a state of mind to resume use. *See Zelinski v. Columbia 300, Inc.*, 335 F.3d 633 (7th Cir. 2003) (plaintiff's discussions with companies interested in producing his branded bowling balls sufficiently showed an intent to resume use).

The legal and logical propriety of resolving the important questions of whether trademark rights exist on the basis of the claimant's subjective state of mind is discussed in Pattishall, *The Impact of Intent In Trade Identity Cases*, 65 Nw. U. L.

Rev. 421, 434–438 (1970). Cf. Micheletti, *Preventing Loss of Trademark Rights: Quantitative and Qualitative Assessments of "Use" and Their Impact on Abandonment Determinations*, 94 TMR 634 (2004).

EXXON CORP. v. HUMBLE EXPLORATION CO., INC.
United States Court of Appeals, Fifth Circuit
695 F.2d 96 (1983)

HIGGINBOTHAM, CIRCUIT JUDGE

Humble Exploration Company, Inc. appeals from an order of the district court, 524 F. Supp. 450, enjoining its use of "Humble" as a trade name. The main issue on appeal is whether the district court erred in finding that Exxon Company, U.S.A. had not abandoned the use of the trademark HUMBLE. Because we find that the limited arranged sales of HUMBLE products as part of Exxon's trademark maintenance program are insufficient uses to avoid prima facie abandonment under 15 U.S.C. § 1127, we reverse and remand to the district court for a determination of Exxon's intent to resume use of the trademark.

Humble Oil and Refining Company was founded as a Texas corporation in 1917. Its activities included oil exploration, refining and marketing. In 1959, that company and the other regional affiliated oil companies owned by Standard Oil Company of New Jersey merged to form a larger Humble Oil & Refining Company, a Delaware corporation.

In the early 1960s, the newly expanded Humble Oil & Refining Company introduced a new branding system for its products and service stations. Throughout the country, large HUMBLE signs were erected on the company's service stations, totaling over 20,000 by 1972. At each station, a second sign in an oval located at the roadside carried a regional house mark: ENCO in Texas and other western states, ESSO in the eastern states and HUMBLE in the state of Ohio. From the early 1960's through 1972, the Humble Oil & Refining Company name appeared on all of the Company's packaged products, sometimes accompanied by the trademark ESSO, ENCO or HUMBLE, depending on the intended area of sale.

Because its management concluded that the use of three trade names, HUMBLE, ESSO and ENCO, was confusing to customers, in late 1972 Humble Oil & Refining Company adopted the name EXXON as its sole primary brand name and on January 1, 1973, Humble Oil & Refining Company became Exxon Company, U.S.A. Exxon spent in excess of twelve million dollars in advertising its name change in television and print media. EXXON signs replaced the three regional signs and all packaged products were relabeled with EXXON labels before distribution. Except for inventory at the service station level, the changeover was complete by mid-1973.

On April 12, 1972, the Board of Directors of Humble Oil & Refining Company passed a resolution calling for continued use of HUMBLE after the changeover to EXXON "in ways other than as a primary brand name." Company publications expressed the intention to protect the name HUMBLE. To do so, Exxon instituted a trademark maintenance program for the mark.

*   *   *

The district court framed the abandonment issue thus: "Is the limited use of a famous trademark solely for protective purposes a use sufficient to preclude abandonment under the common law and the Lanham Act?" It answered the question in the affirmative. Plaintiff-Appellee withdrew its Texas and common law claims in the district court, so the resolution of the abandonment issue must focus on the federal standards for abandonment set forth in the Lanham Act.

Under the Act,

A mark shall be deemed to be abandoned—

(a) When its use has been discontinued with intent not to resume use. Intent not to resume may be inferred from circumstances. Nonuse for two consecutive years shall be prima facie abandonment.[*]

15 U.S.C. § 1127 (1982). The burden of proof is on the party claiming abandonment, but when a prima facie case of trademark abandonment exists because of nonuse of the mark for over two consecutive years, the owner of the mark has the burden to demonstrate that circumstances do not justify the inference of intent not to resume use. *See Sterling Brewers, Inc. v. Schenley Industries, Inc.*, 441 F.2d 675, 679 (Cust. & Pat. App. 1971).

Appellant argues that Exxon has not used the HUMBLE mark since its changeover program. Since that time, Exxon has 1) sold existing inventory of packaged products bearing the name "Humble Oil and Refining Company"; 2) made periodic sales of nominal amounts of Exxon gasoline, motor oil and grease in pails bearing the names HUMBLE and EXXON; 3) sold Exxon bulk gasoline and diesel fuel to selected customers, who received HUMBLE invoices, through three corporations organized for that purpose; and 4) sold 55-gallon drum products from the Baytown, Texas refinery, all bearing a stencil with the names HUMBLE and EXXON.

The existing inventory was depleted by mid-1974; the sale of 55-gallon drums began in 1977. Whether or not these sales are "uses" for the purposes of 15 U.S.C. § 1127, the period between those sales was longer than two years, and under the Lanham Act, "nonuse for two consecutive years is prima facie abandonment." 15 U.S.C. § 1127. During that period between sales of inventory and sales of 55-gallon drum products, Exxon can point to only two types of sales as possible uses. As earlier described, Exxon made limited sales of packaged products with both EXXON and HUMBLE on the labels to targeted customers in these amounts: $9.28 in 1973, $.0 in 1974, $140.12 in 1975 and $42.05 in 1976. Second, products in bulk form and not bearing a trade name or mark were sold to selected customers who received the explanation that they were receiving Exxon products. The only use of HUMBLE in connection with these sales was on the invoices sent to the customers. The issue, thus, is whether these two categories of arranged sales through the trademark protection program during that period constitute "use" sufficient to avoid prima facie abandonment.

Appellant relies primarily on *La Societe Anonyme des Parfums LeGalion v. Jean Patou, Inc.*, 495 F.2d 1265 (2d Cir. 1974), and *Procter and Gamble v. Johnson & Johnson, Inc.*, 485 F. Supp. 1185 (S.D.N.Y. 1979), *aff'd without opinion*, 636 F.2d 1203 (2d Cir. 1980), to support its argument that arranged sales are nonuse. In *Jean Patou*, the plaintiff LeGalion, a French perfume manufacturer, had sold its perfume under the trademark SNOB in a number of foreign countries but was unable to sell its product in the United States because of Patou's registration for the mark in this country. Claiming that Patou had not established rights in the mark, LeGalion filed suit. The facts revealed that Patou had made 89 sales of perfume over a 20-year period and engaged in no advertising. The court found that Patou's real purpose in making the 89 sales was to keep a competitor at bay and that this "purely defensive" token use was insufficient to obtain enforceable rights in the mark. *Id.* at 1273–74. The court observed: "The token sales program engaged in here is by its very nature inconsistent with a present plan of commercial exploitation." *Id.* at 1273. It continued: "A trade mark maintenance program obviously cannot in itself justify a minimal sales effort, or the requirement of good faith commercial use would be read out of the trademark law altogether." *Id.* at 1273, n. 10.

In *Procter and Gamble*, the plaintiff maintained a "Minor Brands Program" for the purpose of protecting its ownership rights in brand names not being actively used in commerce on its products. Employees not normally involved in Procter and Gamble's (P & G's) merchandising operation took an active P & G product, labeled it with a minor

---

[*] Editor's note: The Lanham Act subsequently was revised to provide that nonuse for *three* consecutive years (not two) shall be prima facie abandonment.

brand, and shipped it to customers. For example, P & G's Prell shampoo was bottled under thirteen different minor brand labels. Fifty units of each were shipped annually to at least ten states. The court held that the plaintiff had no enforceable rights in the mark SURE for tampons on the basis of its inclusion in this minor brands program.

The district court below distinguished these cases because they treat the acquisition or adoption of a trademark that has not developed goodwill. According to the court, Exxon's use of the HUMBLE mark "in commerce for protective purposes is a good faith use" because of the residual goodwill built up in the mark. Despite the trial court's distinction, § 1127 of the Lanham Act, without mentioning goodwill, requires continued use of a mark or intent to resume use to avoid a finding of abandonment. The first requirement is not present on this record. The limited sales of packaged products to targeted customers and the arranged sales of bulk products through the three shell corporations were not sufficient uses to avoid prima facie proof of abandonment under the statute. The HUMBLE trademark was not used to identify the source of the goods. The packaged products were Exxon products with HUMBLE used as a secondary name. Of course, "the fact that a product bears more than one mark does not mean that each cannot be a valid trademark." *Old Dutch Foods, Inc. v. Dan Dee Pretzel & Potato Chip Co.*, 477 F.2d 150, 154 (6th Cir.1973). For example, in *Old Dutch* the defendant had used concurrent marks, OLD DUTCH and DAN DEE, on all his products for over thirty years. Each mark must, however, be a bona fide mark. *See Blue Bell, Inc. v. Farah Manufacturing Company, Inc.*, 508 F.2d 1260, 1267 (5th Cir.1975).

In this case, the mark HUMBLE was used only on isolated products or selected invoices sent to selected customers. No sales were made that depended upon the HUMBLE mark for identification of source. To the contrary, purchasers were informed that the selected shipments would bear the HUMBLE name or be accompanied by an HUMBLE invoice but were the desired Exxon products. That is, the HUMBLE mark did not with these sales play the role of a mark. That casting, however, is central to the plot that the Lanham Act rests on the idea of registration of marks otherwise born of use rather than the creation of marks by the act of registration. That precept finds expression in the Lanham Act requirement that to maintain a mark in the absence of use there must be an intent to resume use. That expression is plain. The Act does not allow the preservation of a mark solely to prevent its use by others. Yet the trial court's reasoning allows precisely that warehousing so long as there is residual good will associated with the mark. Exxon makes the same argument here. While that may be good policy, we cannot square it with the language of the statute. In sum, these arranged sales in which the mark was not allowed to play its basic role of identifying source were not "use" in the sense of § 1127 of the Lanham Act.

* * *

This court recognizes that the goodwill associated with the mark HUMBLE has immense value to Exxon. That fact, coupled with the efforts under the trademark maintenance program, could suggest Exxon's intent to resume use of the mark, but the trial court did not make that finding. The court found that the trademark protection program evidenced "an intent not to relinquish HUMBLE" and "an intent not to abandon HUMBLE," but it did not specifically address Exxon's intent to resume use as required by § 1127 the Lanham Act . . . . There is a difference between intent not to abandon or relinquish and intent to resume use in that an owner may not wish to abandon its mark but may have no intent to resume its use.

. . . In the context of a challenge strictly under the Lanham Act to an alleged warehousing program, as the facts of this case present, the application of the statutory language is critical. That is, this court having found that the two types of uses under the trademark maintenance program were not sufficient uses to avoid prima facie proof of abandonment, the district court must specifically address Exxon's intent to resume use of the HUMBLE trademark. An "intent to resume" requires the trademark owner to have plans to resume commercial use of the mark. Stopping at an "intent not to abandon" tolerates an owner's protecting a mark with neither commercial use nor plans to resume commercial use. Such a license is not permitted by the Lanham Act.

The judgment is reversed and the case is remanded for further proceedings consistent with this opinion. In doing so, we emphasize that we do not decide here whether the present record would support a finding that Exxon had sufficient intent to resume use of the Humble mark so as to avoid its loss, nor do we here address Exxon's rights under the common law to block any present use of the mark in a confusing manner. Finally, we leave to the trial court the decision whether additional evidence on the issue of intent to resume use ought to be heard.

*   *   *

AMBRIT, INC. v. KRAFT, INC.
United States Court Appeals, Eleventh Circuit
805 F.2d 974 (1986)

WISDOM, SENIOR CIRCUIT JUDGE

The plaintiff in this action, the Isaly Company, Inc., ("Isaly"),[1] is a Delaware corporation with its principal place of business in Clearwater, Florida. The defendant, Kraft, Inc. ("Kraft"), is a Delaware corporation with its principal place of business in Glenview, Illinois. The parties are competitors in the stickless, five ounce, square, chocolate-covered ice cream bar market. Isaly sells its bar under the trademark "Klondike", and Kraft sells its bar under the trademark "Polar B'ar." The crux of the controversy concerns the packaging of those two products.

Isaly began in the last century as a family-owned dairy business operating in Eastern Ohio and Western Pennsylvania. In 1928 Isaly started making and selling five ounce, chocolate-covered, stickless ice cream bars under the name "Klondike". Isaly now sells three versions of the Klondike bar: plain, crispy, and chocolate/chocolate. The plain Klondike bar has been wrapped in pebbled foil featuring the colors silver, blue, and white since the 1940s. Since at least 1956 the wrapper has featured a 3 x 3 inch panel of silver, white, and blue, the words "Isaly's" and "Klondike", and the figure of a polar bear.

*   *   *

Until 1978, Isaly sold the Klondike bar in a tri-state area composed of Western Pennsylvania, Eastern Ohio, and Northern West Virginia. Isaly advertised in newspapers and in point-of-sales materials in stores, both of which featured the polar bear emblem found on the bar's wrapper. Isaly also advertised on television in a commercial featuring a polar bear and prospector in a supermarket.

In 1978, Isaly began to investigate the possibility of expanding the market for the Klondike bar. Isaly decided to introduce the bar into supermarkets and convenience stores in various expansion markets. To augment the expansion it achieved on its own, Isaly approached Kraft, an international manufacturer and distributor of food products, concerning a distribution arrangement between the two parties . . . . The parties agreed that Kraft would distribute the Klondike bar in Florida and that Isaly would be responsible for most of the advertising in that market.

*   *   *

In late 1979, Kraft began to develop its own five ounce chocolate-covered ice cream bar. Kraft attempted to duplicate the exact size and taste of the Klondike bar. Kraft chose the name "Polar B'ar" after finding that name on a list of unused trademarks. A predecessor of Kraft, Southern Dairies, Inc., had sold an ice cream bar under that

---

[1] Since instituting this action in 1982, Isaly has changed its name to AmBrit, Inc. We shall refer to the company as "Isaly" throughout this opinion.

trademark from 1929 to 1932, and periodically renewed the trademark registration. Through merger, Kraft acquired it.

Kraft employed two firms to design the packaging for the Polar B'ar product, making clear to these firms that the functional features of the Polar B'ar package were to resemble as closely as possible the Klondike bar package. The bars were to be wrapped in foil and sold in six-pack trays over wrapped in transparent plastic. Kraft supplied these design firms with samples of the Klondike packaging to aid them in their efforts.

*   *   *

In 1980 Kraft sold Polar B'ars in two forms: plain and "crunchy". The colors of the triangle and block letters on the wrappers varied with each version. Plain wrappers used royal blue and "crunchy" wrappers used red. Later, Kraft introduced four new versions of the bar: chocolate, mint, heavenly hash, and peanut butter, using the colors brown, green, light blue, and golden brown respectively.

*   *   *

Kraft was the exclusive distributor of the Klondike bar in Florida from 1979 to 1982. In February 1982 Kraft notified Isaly in writing of its intention to terminate its distribution of Klondike as of April 1982. In May 1982 Isaly initiated this suit.

*   *   *

On cross-appeal, Isaly argues that the district court erred in refusing to cancel Kraft's trademark for the word mark "Polar B'ar." Isaly asserted below and again on appeal that Kraft abandoned this trademark. We agree with Isaly and therefore reverse the ruling of the district court on this issue.

From 1929 to 1932, Southern Dairies, Inc. sold an ice cream novelty under the name "Polar B'ar." Based on that use, Southern was issued trademark registration No. 254,111 for the "Polar B'ar" word mark. The trademark registration was periodically renewed and, through merger, Kraft acquired it. There is no evidence that Kraft or its predecessor used the trademark at any time between 1932 and 1980. In late 1979 or early 1980, Kraft chose to use the name "Polar B'ar" for its new ice cream novelty after a Kraft new product development manager noticed the name on a list of unused Kraft trademarks. Since 1980, Kraft has used the word mark "Polar B'ar" extensively in connection with the sale of ice cream novelties.

Whether Kraft's Polar B'ar trademark should be canceled due to abandonment presents a novel question of law. Section 45 of the Lanham Act provides:

> A mark shall be deemed to be "abandoned" - (a) When its use has been discontinued with intent not to resume. Intent not to resume may be inferred from circumstances. Non use for two consecutive years shall be prima facie abandonment.[*]

Section 14 of the Lanham Act provides for the cancellation of abandoned marks. In most cases, the abandonment issue involves a situation in which, at the time of the petition for cancellation, the use of the mark by its owner is nonexistent or virtually nonexistent. This case is novel because Kraft was using the mark extensively at the time Isaly petitioned for cancellation. Isaly does not argue that Kraft's current use of the mark is insignificant and, indeed it is beyond dispute that abandonment would be out of the question had Kraft used the mark continuously from 1932 and 1980 in the same manner that it is now using the mark. Rather, Isaly contends that Kraft's nonuse between 1932 and 1980 caused the mark to be abandoned and Kraft's registration to be void. Isaly

---

[*] Editor's note: The Lanham Act subsequently was revised to provide that nonuse for *three* consecutive years (not two) shall be prima facie abandonment.

asserts that Kraft's subsequent use beginning in 1980 does not retroactively cure its past abandonment. We agree.

For purposes of illustration, we examine what rights Kraft had in the Polar B'ar trademark as of 1978. There is no question that Isaly would have been successful if it had sought to cancel Kraft's Polar B'ar trademark on abandonment grounds in 1978. At that time, neither Kraft nor its predecessor had used the mark since 1932, almost half a century. Thus, Kraft had discontinued use and the only question would be whether Kraft intended to resume use. Kraft's nonuse establishes a prima facie case of abandonment, thereby placing the burden on Kraft to establish its intent to resume use.

At the outset, Kraft contends that it never intended to abandon the mark. That is, however, irrelevant. The proper inquiry is whether Kraft intended to resume meaningful commercial use of the mark, not whether it intended to abandon the mark. Trademark rights flow from use, not from intent to protect rights. Were the rule otherwise, a party could hold trademarks that it never intended to use but did not want to allow others to use. The Lanham Act does not permit such warehousing of trademarks.

The only evidence Kraft presented to establish its intent to resume use was that it had renewed the registration of the mark in 1949 and 1969. Given the circumstances, however, this is insufficient to rebut the prima facie proof of abandonment. Therefore, were we to turn the clock back to 1978 and examine Kraft's Polar B'ar trademark at that time, cancellation due to abandonment would be required because Kraft discontinued use with intent not to resume use.

Kraft asserts, however, that its resumption of use of the trademark in 1980 precludes our canceling the registration of the mark. This argument can be broken down into two parts. First, Kraft may be arguing that its use in 1980 negatives the conclusion that as of 1978 Kraft did not intend to resume use. This argument deserves short shrift. That Kraft in fact used the mark in 1980 does not mean that Kraft intended to use the mark in 1978. Not until one of Kraft's personnel noticed the mark on a list of unused trademarks in 1979 did Kraft have any present intention to use the mark. Therefore, our previous conclusion that Isaly would have prevailed had it sought cancellation in 1978 is not changed by Kraft's resumption of use in 1980.

A more difficult question is whether in 1986 Kraft's 1980 use precludes our canceling its registration because of abandonment. In *Mission Dry Corp. v. Seven-Up Co.*, [193 F.2d 201 (C.C.P.A. 1951)], the Court of Customs and Patent Appeals held that, once abandoned, a mark may be canceled even after its holder resumes commercial use. The propriety of this position is bolstered by the analogous case presented when a competitor that has used the mark in question in the interim between the discontinuance and resumption of use by the holder of the registered trademark petitions for cancellation. In *Conwood Corp. v. Loews Theatres, Inc.*, [173 U.S.P.Q. 829 (T.T.A.B. 1972)], the Trademark Trial and Appeal Board was confronted with that scenario and ruled that if the holder's initial discontinuance of use is an abandonment, the competitor may cancel the registration notwithstanding subsequent use. The rationale for the holding in the case involving an intervening use by a competitor makes clear that cancellation is proper even in the absence of such a use. In a case involving intervening use, the competitor's right to cancel the registration flows not from the competitor's use of the mark but from the holder's abandonment. Irrespective of whether a competitor has used the mark in question, a registered trademark, once abandoned, may be canceled even after the holder resumes use of the mark.

The ruling of the district court denying Isaly's petition to cancel Kraft's trademark registration is therefore reversed.

Notes on Abandonment

1. Mitigating Circumstances

Trademark rights may survive even a substantial period of nonuse of the mark if the failure to use is involuntary. In 1903 the Congregation of the Chartreuser, an order of monks in France, was held to be dissolved by operation of law and its properties were seized and liquidated. The liquidator then began manufacturing a liqueur, intended to match the flavor and appeal of that made by the monks, under their famous trademark CHARTREUSE.

Forced to set up new facilities in Spain and barred from using their old marks and symbols in France, the monks imported the necessary French herbs and resumed manufacture of the liqueur under a new designation, "Liqueur des Peres Chartreux." The labels for the liqueur also stated that it was the only one identical to the liqueur previously manufactured by secret process in France. In a subsequent infringement suit by the monks against a New York corporation importing French "chartreuse" the defendant claimed abandonment. *Baglin, Superior General of the Order of Carthusian Monks v. Cusenier Co.*, 221 U.S. 580 (1911). In the opinion authored by Justice Hughes, the Supreme Court quoted *Saxlehner v. Eisner & Mendelsohn Co.*, 179 U.S. 19, 31 (1900), observing, "Acts which unexplained would be sufficient to establish an abandonment may be answered by showing that there never was an intention to give up and relinquish the right claimed." Finding that they had acted reasonably under the circumstances, and that their efforts to prevent use of the old mark in France and other countries clearly demonstrated that there was no intent to abandon, the Court concluded that the monks retained their trademark ownership rights. *See Kardex Systems, Inc. v. Sistenco N.V.*, 583 F. Supp. 803 (D. Me. 1984) (financial difficulties); *Cuban Cigar Brands N.V. v. Upmann International, Inc.*, 199 U.S.P.Q. 193 (S.D.N.Y. 1978) (government action); *The General Tire & Rubber Co. v. Greenwold*, 127 U.S.P.Q. 240 (S.D. Cal. 1960) (production difficulties). *Cf. Havana Club Holdings, S.A. v. Galleon S.A.*, 203 F.3d 116 (2^d Cir.), *cert. denied*, 531 U.S. 918 (2000)(denying protection under U.S. law to Cuban company asserting trademark rights acquired from business confiscated by the communist government in Cuba).

If rights in a mark are held for a period by a trustee in bankruptcy who is simply liquidating the assets of a dormant business, does the mark become abandoned because the trustee has no intent to resume its use but only to sell the rights in it? *See Merry Hull*, 243 F. Supp. 45 (S.D.N.Y 1965); *Johanna Farms, Inc. v. Citrus Bowl, Inc.*, 199 U.S.P.Q. 16 (E.D.N.Y. 1978). *Compare Hough Manufacturing Corp. v. Virginia Metal Industries, Inc.*, 203 U.S.P.Q. 436 (E.D. Va. 1978); *Haymaker Sports, Inc. v. Turian*, 581 F.2d 257 (C.C.P.A. 1978).

2. Intent to Resume Use

In *General Healthcare Ltd. v. Qashat*, 364 F.3d 332 (1st Cir. 2004), defendant was found to have abandoned its rights in "Kent Creme Bleach" for a hair-lightening product. The presumption of abandonment was raised by three years non-use, and the lower court had "properly concluded that [defendant's] noncommittal, indefinite of intent to resume use was insufficient as a matter of law to rebut the presumption." Similarly, in *Sloan v. Auditron Elec. Corp.*, 68 Fed. Appx. 386 (4th Cir. 2003), plaintiff was found to have abandoned his rights in AUDITRON for "book keeping and accounting and tax services" when he failed to provide any "concrete evidence" that he had made any bona fide use of the mark during the previous fifteen years or had made any definite plans to do so. As the court stated there, a mark owner "cannot defeat an abandonment claim by simply asserting a vague, subjective intent to resume use of a mark at some unspecified future date." *See also Emergency One, Inc. v. Am. Fire Engine Co.*, 332 F.3d 264 (4th Cir. 2003) (after being properly instructed on remand that, "in order to avoid abandonment, a trademark owner who discontinues use of the mark must have an intent to resume use *in the reasonably foreseeable future*" (emphasis in original), a new jury determined that plaintiff lacked the requisite intent to resume use of AMERICAN EAGLE for fire engines and rescue vehicles, and had abandoned its rights). *Cf. Grocery Outlet, Inc. v. Albertson's, Inc.*, 2007 U.S. App. LEXIS 1884 (9th Cir. 2007) ("ALBERTSON'S offered sufficient evidence of its intent to resume use of the LUCKY mark [for retail grocery store services] within the reasonably foreseeable future during the short period of alleged non-use"); *ITC Ltd., v. Punchgini, Inc.*, 482 F.3d 135 (2[d] Cir. 2007) (the India-based plaintiff unsuccessfully argued that its intent to resume use of BUKHARA for restaurant services could be inferred from, among other things, its efforts to develop a Dal Bukhara line of packaged foods, its attempts to identify potential U.S. franchisees, and its continued use of BUKHARA for non-U.S. restaurants).

In *Tumblebus Inc. v. Cranmer*, 399 F.3d 754 (6th Cir. 2005), the court ruled on the geographic scope of abandonment. There, plaintiff Tumblebus sold one of its TUMBLEBUS retrofitted buses (designed to serve as a mobile children's gym) to a third party for use outside Louisville, Kentucky. That third party then sold it to defendant Cranmer, who proceeded to use it in the Louisville area. The court noted that partial geographic abandonment (i.e. abandonment outside of Louisville only) may occur, but that "[s]o long as the TUMBLEBUS mark retains its significance in the greater Louisville area," Tumblebus could continue to assert its rights there. Prior decisions "would be turned on their heads if we were to conclude that, because trademark rights may extend beyond the area in which a particular business operates, a trademark holder may also lose any rights it has in a mark anywhere in the United States by abandoning the mark in one part of the country or by failing to establish a mark with national significance."

In *Stilson & Assocs. v. Stilson Consulting Group*, 129 Fed. Appx. 993 (6th Cir. 2005) (unpub.) the court held that plaintiff DLZ did not abandon the Stilson name when it merged Stilson company into DLZ. The district court found no abandonment, given that clients who approached DLZ and its predecessor companies, thinking that it was Stilson & Associates, were provided services; that DLZ intended to invoke the Stilson name if it helped the business; that Stilson & Associates continued to work on pre-merger contracts;and that business was conducted under the Stilson & Associates name.

3. Persisting Goodwill

Might protectable goodwill in a mark persist even after use of the mark has ceased? *See Ferrari S.p.A. Esercizio Fabbriche Automobili E Corse v. McBurnie*, 11 U.S.P.Q.2d 1843 (S.D. Cal. 1989) (despite 13 years non-use of FERRARI DAYTONA SPIDER automobile body style and no intention to resume use, proof of persisting goodwill and ongoing parts support sufficiently demonstrated no abandonment of trade dress rights); *Seidelmann Yachts, Inc. v. Pace Yacht Corp.*, 14 U.S.P.Q.2d 1497 (D. Md. 1989), *aff'd without publ. op.*, 13 U.S.P.Q.2d 2025 (4th Cir. 1990) (persisting goodwill after use ends may be weighed in considering abandonment); *Defiance Button Machine Co. v. C & C Metal Products Corp.*, 759 F.2d 1053 (2d Cir.), *cert. denied*, 474 U.S. 844 (1985) (the question is whether the goodwill symbolized by the mark dissipated during the period of non-use); Bowker, *The Song Is Over But The Melody Lingers On: Persistence Of Goodwill And The Intent Factor In Trademark Abandonment*, 56 FORDHAM L. REV. 1003, 1022 (1988).

In *Cumulus Media, Inc. v. Clear Channel Comm'ns, Inc.*, 304 F.3d 1167 (11th Cir. 2002), after the plaintiff radio station had announced it was changing its name from "The Breeze," the defendant, a competitor, began using that name along with a logo similar to plaintiff's. Defendant also advertised "The Breeze is Back and on the air at 107.1 FM." In considering the lower court's grant of a preliminary injunction, the appellate court observed that, despite the announcement of a name change, plaintiff had continued making commercial use of the name in promotional materials that went "beyond mere token use." "While such an announcement is the type of circumstance from which intent not to resume may be inferred . . . it does not alone serve to make a prima facie showing of abandonment. A defendant must also introduce evidence of non-use."

The court rejected defendant's offer to make "curative" types of use designed to dispel any confusion with plaintiff. "Curative steps are sometimes required when a new user wants to use a mark that has been abandoned but is still associated by the public with its former holder." However, here there was evidence that defendant intended to divert listeners based on its deceptive use of the name, and the district court was "well within the bounds of its discretion" in prohibiting defendant from making *any* use of "The Breeze."

Can a trademark owner abandon trademark rights by failing to take action against imitators? In *Herman Miller, Inc. v. Palazzetti Imports and Exports, Inc.*, 270 F.3d 298, 317 (6th Cir. 2001), the appellate court directed the lower court on remand to consider whether plaintiff had abandoned trade dress rights in its Eames furniture designs because it allegedly had permitted the sale of third party reproductions for more than thirty years. "Although it appears unlikely that failure to prosecute [third party users], by itself, can establish that trade dress has been abandoned, it is possible that, in extreme circumstances, failure to prosecute may cause trade dress rights to be extinguished by causing a mark to lose its significance as an indication of source." *Compare L. & J.G. Stickley, Inc. v. Canal Dover Furniture Co.*, 79 F.3d 258, 264–65 and n.5 (2[d] Cir. 1996), in which the court vacated a preliminary injunction, finding that the plaintiff abandoned its trade dress rights in its MISSION furniture design through seventy years of nonuse despite renewed, contemporary public interest in the plaintiff's original design.

4. Modernizing the Mark

What factors should a manufacturer consider before modernizing a mark used successfully for years? Abandonment may result if the modernized mark is too different from the old mark, and priority will then be measured from first use of the new mark. The key in trademark modernization is maintaining the continuity of the commercial impression between the old and new marks. *In re Nuclear Research Corp.*, 16 U.S.P.Q.2d 1316, 1317 (T.T.A.B. 1990) *See* Radin, *Selected Issues Arising Under the Doctrine of Trademark Abandonment*, 79 TRADEMARK REP. 433 (1989); Pattishall, *The Goose and the Golden Egg — Some Comments About Trademark Modernization*, 47 TRADEMARK REP. 801 (1957). *Compare Ilco Corp. v. Ideal Security Hardware Corp.*, 527 F.2d 1221 (C.C.P.A. 1976) (HOME PROTECTION CENTER found not to create the same continuous commercial impression as HOME PROTECTION HARDWARE, causing defendant to lose priority of use, resulting in cancellation of registration) *with Drexel Enterprises, Inc. v. J.R. Richardson*, 312 F.2d 525 (10th Cir. 1962) (trademark rights in HERITAGE for furniture not abandoned when slant script changed to block letters and mark combined with "Henredon"). The same principle applies when marks are altered during the application process in seeking federal registration. *See, e.g., In re CTB, Inc.*, 52 U.S.P.Q.2d 1471, 1473 (T.T.A.B. 1999) ("the touchstone for permissible amendments to the mark is that the mark retains the same overall commercial impression"). *See generally* Krebs and Raju, *Has the Rule Against Material Alteration of Trademark Drawings Been Materially Altered?* 90 T.M.R. 770 (2000). *Compare Time, Inc. v. Petersen Publishing Co.*, 173 F.3d 113 (2[d] Cir. 1999), in which the court affirmed judgment for Time, Inc. after a jury found "Teen People" did not infringe "Teen" for magazines. A key jury instruction was not reversible error where it explained that Petersen's federal registration was for a stylized design of "TEEN" with an apostrophe at the beginning and the word in italicized capital letters, and not for the new logo Peterson changed to in 1997, which had no apostrophe and only a single, initial capital letter. The jury was instructed to determine whether Peterson had common law rights in that new logo and the strength of any such rights.

Should trademark rights be held abandoned if the use is changed from one product to another? Should it make any difference whether the products are closely related? In *Beech-Nut Packing Co. v. P. Lorillard Co.*, 273 U.S. 629 (1926), plaintiff sought to enjoin defendant's use of BEECHNUT for tobacco. Plaintiff had continuously used the trademark BEECH-NUT for chewing gum, peanut butter, and other foods since before 1900. Mr. Justice Holmes wrote as follows:

> The defendant claims the mark "Beechnut" for tobacco through successive assignments from the Harry Weissinger Tobacco Company, of Louisville, Kentucky, which used it from and after 1897. The plaintiff does not contest the original validity of this mark or suggest any distinction on the ground that it originated in a different State, but says that the right has been lost by abandonment. It appears that brands of tobacco have their rise and fall in popular flavor, and that the Beechnut had so declined that in 1910 only twenty-five pounds were sold, and the trade-mark was left dormant until after the dissolution of the American Tobacco Company which then held it. This was in 1911, and the Lorillard Company took over the mark with many others. Then, in connection with an effort to get a new brand that would hit the present taste, this mark was picked out, some of the adjuncts were changed, and in 1915 the new tobacco was put upon the market. Nothing had happened in the meantime to make the defendant's position worse than if it had acted more promptly, and we see no reason to disturb the finding of two Courts that the right to use the mark had not been lost. The mere lapse of time was not such that it could be said to have destroyed the right as matter of law. A trade-mark is not only a symbol of an existing good will, although it commonly is thought of only as that. Primarily it is a distinguishable token devised or picked out with the intent to appropriate it to a particular class of goods and with the hope that it will come to symbolize good will. Apart from nice and exceptional cases, and within the limits of our jurisdiction, a trade-mark and a business may start together, and in a qualified sense the mark is property, protected and alienable, although as with other property its outline is shown only by the law of torts, of which the right is a prophetic summary. Therefore the fact that the good will once associated with it has vanished does not end at once the preferential right of the proprietor to try it again upon goods of the same class with improvements that renew the proprietor's hopes.

Has the law as disclosed in the subsequent cases in this section followed or departed from such a rule?

5. Hoarding and Warehousing

Trademarks cannot be reserved or "hoarded" without trademark use or genuine intent to resume such use. *Imperial Tobacco, Ltd. v. Philip Morris, Inc.*, 899 F.2d 1575, 1581 (Fed. Cir. 1990) ("the Lanham Act was not intended to provide a warehouse for unused marks"); *Silverman v. CBS, Inc.*, 870 F.2d 40 (2d Cir.), *cert. denied*, 492 U.S. 907 (1989) (AMOS N ANDY abandoned for TV show characters). *Accord: E. Remy Martin & Co. v. Shaw-Ross International Imports, Inc.*, 756 F.2d 1525 (11th Cir. 1985); *Highland Potato Chip Co. v. Culbro Snack Foods*, 720 F.2d 981 (8th Cir. 1983). *Compare Electro Source LLC v. Brandess-Kalt-Aetna Group*, 458 F.3d 931 (9th Cir. 2006) (prior user's sporadic good faith sales of branded backpacks constituted use sufficient to avoid abandonment; "unless the trademark use is actually terminated, the intent not to resume use prong of abandonment does not come into play"). *See also West Florida Seafood Inc. v. Jet Restaurants Inc.*, 31 F.3d 1122 (Fed. Cir. 1994) (party responding to a cancellation petitioner's claim of prior use and alleging abandonment bears the burden of proving that the petitioner abandoned its mark); *Stetson v. Howard D. Wolf & Associates*, 955 F.2d 847, 850 (2ᵈ Cir. 1992) (the lower court erred in applying a "no intent to abandon" test; the correct test was whether there was "no intent . . . to resume use in the reasonably foreseeable future"); *Roulo v. Russ Berrie & Co.*, 886 F.2d 931, 939 (7ᵗʰ Cir. 1989), *cert. denied*, 493 U.S. 1075 (1990) (it was within jury's prerogative to credit plaintiff's testimony that she intended to resume use of mark after three years of non-use); *Cerveceria Centroamericana, S.A. v. Cerveceria India, Inc.*, 892 F.2d 1021 (Fed. Cir. 1989) (discussing parties' burdens of proof respecting abandonment). *Cf. Kareem Abdul-Jabbar v. General Motors Corp.*, 85 F.3d 407 (9ᵗʰ Cir. 1996) (former basketball star did not abandon his birth name, Lew Alcindor, despite extended period of nonuse because — in contrast to trademarks — state law right of publicity in a name is not contingent upon commercial use).

4.04   Assignment Without Goodwill

Introduction

Trademark rights are "assignable with the goodwill of the business in which the mark is used, or with that part of the goodwill of the business connected with the use of and symbolized by the mark." This is the modern view of trademark assignability, which was codified in the Lanham Act (15 U.S.C. § 1060). "[F]ollowing a proper assignment, the assignee steps into the shoes of the assignor," and may assert the same rights the assignor could have. *Premier Dental Products Co. v. Darby Dental Supply Co.*, 794 F.2d 850 (3ᵈ Cir.), *cert. denied*, 479 U.S. 950 (1986).

The concept of assigning trade identity rights appurtenant to the business which they represent is derived from the rationale of trade identity protection which limits that protection to the source-indicating function. Historically, in Anglo-American law, the concept was rigidly applied to the extent of requiring that the mark could only be transferred with the entire physical business with which it was associated. Some commentators noted that the physical transfer of machines, customer lists, of factories and plants might be required. *See* McCarthy, *Trademarks and Unfair Competition*, § 18:10.

This rule was followed in the United Kingdom with little flexibility until recent times. In the United States, however, the practical needs of commerce for more freedom of alienability for trademarks resulted, starting in the 1930s, in considerable relaxation of the doctrine in actual practice and in permitting an element of legal fiction for assignments of marks so long as the assignment instrument included the approved formal (or fictional) language: "with the goodwill of the business . . . symbolized by the mark." (15 U.S.C. § 1060.)

PEPSICO, INC. v. GRAPETTE CO.
United States Court of Appeals, Eighth Circuit
416 F.2d 285 (1969)

Lᴀʏ, Cɪʀᴄᴜɪᴛ Jᴜᴅɢᴇ

PepsiCo, Inc., a holding company of several subsidiaries including Pepsi Cola Co., a national soft drink bottler, sought an injunction against Grapette-Aristocrat, Inc. and its holding company Grapette Co. (hereinafter referred collectively as Grapette) on the alleged infringement of its trademark "Pepsi." In 1965 Grapette purchased the mark "Peppy" and intended to bottle a soft "pepper" drink with that name. The district court found that the mark "Peppy" was confusingly similar to "Pepsi" and as such would constitute infringement under 15 U.S.C. § 1114 (1964). However, not withstanding this finding of infringement, the court denied the plaintiff injunctive relief on the ground that it was guilty of laches. 288 F. Supp. at 937, 159 U.S.P.Q. at 410. PepsiCo., Inc. appeals. We reverse.

The evidence shows that Pepsi Cola Co. has bottled beverages duly registered under trademarks "Pepsi Cola," "Pepsi" and "Pep-Kola" for many years. *See* 15 U.S.C. § 1065. Grapette is a national bottler and distributor of soft drinks, concentrates and syrups. In 1965 it developed a formula for a new syrup to be used in a pepper type bottled beverage as opposed to a cola beverage. In searching for a name to market the new product, defendant discovered the 1926 registration of the mark "Peppy" by H. Fox and Co., a partnership. The mark had been renewed by Fox in 1946 and 1966. Sometime between 1932 and 1937 Fox began to use the mark "Peppy" in conjunction with a cola flavored syrup which was distributed on a local basis, confined mostly to the Eastern states of New York, New Jersey and Connecticut. The cola distribution was sold exclusively as syrup. Since 1958, Fox's syrup has been sold only to jobbers in 28 ounce consumer size bottles. Some ten to twelve years prior to this time it was sold also to the fountain trade as a syrup in gallon containers.

In 1965, Grapette Co. entered into an agreement with Fox Corp. in which the trademark "Peppy" was assigned to defendant for a consideration of $7,500. At this time Fox Corp. was in a Chapter 11 bankruptcy proceeding. Although Fox Corp. made a formal assignment of "goodwill," it is conceded by defendant that none of Fox Corp.'s physical assets or plant were transferred with the trademark; no inventory, customer lists, formulas, etc. Upon acquisition of the "Peppy" mark, Grapette began arrangements to have this mark placed upon its new pepper flavored soft drink. Fox Corp. continued to sell its cola syrup under the mark "Fox Brand" as well as agreeing to act as a distributor of defendant's "Peppy." In 1965, plaintiff warned the defendant of possible litigation if it did not stop the use of its mark. On April 21, 1966, this action was begun.

Plaintiff contends (1) that the transfer of the trademark "Peppy" by Fox Corp. was invalid because it was an assignment in "gross" and that therefore, Grapette cannot stand in the shoes of its predecessor in order to assert the defense of laches; and (2) that the defense of laches is not supported by sufficient evidence.

It is not disputed that Grapette must stand in the place of Fox Corp. Without a valid assignment, Grapette's rights to the use of "Peppy" accrue only as of November 1965 and it could not assert the defense of laches. PepsiCo, Inc. asserts that the 1965 assignment of the trademark by Fox Corp. to Grapette was a legal nullity in that the trademark was transferred totally disconnected from any business or goodwill of the assignor. We must agree.

Section 1060 of the Lanham Act provides:

> A registered mark or a mark for which application to register has been filed shall be assignable with the goodwill of the business in which the mark is used, or with that part of the goodwill of the business connected with the use of and symbolized by the mark, and in any such assignment it shall not be necessary to include the goodwill of the business connected with the use of and symbolized by any other mark used in the business or by the name or style under which the business is conducted. . . .

15 U.S.C. § 1060.

The early common law rule that a trademark could not be assigned "in gross" was recognized in this circuit in *Macmahan Pharmacal Co. v. Denver Chem. Mfg. Co.*, 113 F. 468 (8 Cir. 1901), and in *Carroll v. Duluth Superior Milling Co.*, 232 F. 675 (8 Cir. 1916). This court in *Carroll* observed that a trademark could only be transferred "in connection with the assignment of the particular business in which it has been used, with its goodwill, and for continued use upon the same articles or class of articles." *Id.* at 680. We later explained "that there is no property in a trademark except as a right appurtenant to an established business or trade, when it becomes an element of goodwill." *Atlas Beverage Co. v. Minneapolis Brewing Co.*, 113 F.2d 672, 674–675, 46 U.S.P.Q. 395, 397–398 (8 Cir. 1940). The rule found derivation in *Kidd v. Johnson*, 100

U.S. 617 (1879). The necessity to assign more than the naked mark was premised upon the primary object of the trademark "to indicate by its meaning or association the *origin* of the article to which it is affixed." (Emphasis ours.) 100 U.S. at 620. This court recently observed in *Sweetarts v. Sunline, Inc.*, 380 F.2d 923, 926, 154 U.S.P.Q. 459, 462 (8 Cir. 1967): "A trademark is generally any name, sign, or mark which one adopts to denominate commercial goods originating from him."

As pointed out in the *Restatement (Second) of Torts*, § 756, comment a at 136 (Tent. Draft No. 8, 1963):

> A trademark or trade name is not itself an independent object of property, nor is the right to use such mark or name. The designation is only a means of identifying particular goods, services, or a business associated with a particular commercial source, whether known or anonymous . . . Goodwill is property, and since it is transferable the symbol of the property is transferable along with it.

Strict adherence to this rule has been vigorously criticized as impractical and legalistic. Schecter, *The Rational Bases of Trademark Protection*, 40 HARV. L. REV. 813 (1926); Grismore, *The Assignment of Trademarks and Trade Names*, 30 MICH. L. REV. 489 (1932); Callmann, *Unfair Competition, Trademarks and Monopolies*, § 78 (3d ed.); Note, *Trademark Protection Following Ineffective Assignment*, 88 U. PA. L. REV. 863 (1940). According to these commentators, the continuum of the rule fails to comprehend the modern image of the trademark to the consuming public. Strict application of the rule undoubtedly fails to recognize the function of the trademark as representing as well (1) a guaranty of the product and (2) the inherent advertising value of the mark itself. *Id.*

Some recent cases have given recognition that in certain situations a naked assignment might be approved. Grapette emphasizes the case of *Hy-Cross Hatchery v. Osborne*, 303 F.2d 947, 133 U.S.P.Q. 687 (C.C.P.A. 1962), as being controlling.

There, the plaintiff sought cancellation of the trademark "Hy-Cross" solely on the basis that the assignee of the original registrant took nothing but the naked mark. The evidence showed that all the assignee received was the mark itself. Osborne, the assignor, did not continue in the same business of raising chickens. The court in discussing the issue of naked assignment stated the following [133 U.S.P.Q. at 689–690]:

> Unlike the cases relied on, Osborne, so far as the record shows, was using the mark at the time he executed the assignment of it. He had a valid registration which he also assigned. With these two legal properties he also assigned, in the very words of the statute, "that part of the goodwill of the business connected with the use of and symbolized by the mark. . . ." He was selling chicks which his advertising of record shows were designated as "No. 111 HY-CROSS (Trade Mark) AMERICAN WHITES." As part of his assignment, by assigning the goodwill, he gave up the right to sell "HY-CROSS" chicks. This had been a part of his "business." By the assignment, Welp, the assignee, acquired that right. The record shows that he began selling "Hy-Cross Hatching Eggs" and chicks designated as "HY-CROSS 501," "HY-CROSS 610," and "HY-CROSS 656." Thus, what had once been Osborne's business in "HY-CROSS" chicks became Welp's business. We do not see what legal difference it would have made if a crate of eggs had been included in the assignment, or a flock of chickens destined to be eaten.
>
> As for the argument that the transfer should have been held illegal because Osborne sold one kind of chick and Welp sold another under the mark, whereby the public would be deceived, we think the record does not support this. The *type* of chick appears to have been otherwise indicated than by the trademark, as by the numbers above quoted as well as by name. Osborne, moreover, was not under any obligation to the public not to change the breed of chicks he sold under the mark from time to time.

In the instant case we need not decide whether the strict common law rule must apply or whether the approach, as suggested by Hy-Cross, should prevail. Inherent in the rules involving the assignment of a trademark is the recognition of protection against consumer deception. Basic to this concept is the proposition that any assignment of a trademark and its goodwill (with or without tangibles or intangibles assigned) requires the mark itself be used by the assignee on a product having substantially the same characteristics. *See, e.g., Independent Baking Powder Co. v. Boorman*, 175 F. 448 (C.C.D.N.J. 1910) (alum baking powder is distinctive from phosphate baking powder); *Atlas Beverage Co. v. Minneapolis Brewing Co.*, 113 F.2d 672, 46 U.S.P.Q. 395 (8 Cir. 1940) (whiskey is a different product than beer); *H.H. Scott, Inc. v. Annapolis Electroacoustic Corp.*, 195 F. Supp. 208, 130 U.S.P.Q. 48 (D. Md. 1961) (audio reproduction equipment is distinctive from hi-fidelity consoles). *Cf. W.T. Wagner's Sons Co. v. Orange Snap Co.*, 18 F.2d 554 (5 Cir. 1927) (No infringement: ginger ale is in a different class than fruit flavored soft drinks).

Historically, this requirement is founded in the early case of *Filkins v. Blackman*, 9 Fed. Case 50 (No. 4786) (C.C.D. Conn. 1876), wherein the court observed:

> If the assignee should make a different article, he would not derive, by purchase from Jonas Blackman, a right which a court of equity would enforce, to use the name which the inventor had given to his own article, because such a use of the name would deceive the public. The right to the use of a trademark cannot be so enjoyed by an assignee that he shall have the right to affix the mark to goods differing in character or species from the article to which it was originally attached.

Id. at 52.

*   *   *

Where a transferred trademark is to be used on a new and different product, any goodwill which the mark itself might represent cannot legally be assigned. "A trademark owner does not have the right to a particular word but to the use of the word as the symbol of particular goods." Callmann, § 78.1(a) at 426. To hold otherwise would be to condone public deceit. The consumer might buy a product thinking it to be of one quality or having certain characteristics and could find it only too late to be another. To say that this would be remedied by the public soon losing faith in the product fails to give the consumer the protection it initially deserves.

It is here that Grapette's use of the mark "Peppy" meets terminal difficulty. Grapette's intended use of the mark is one to simply describe its new pepper beverage.[4] The evidence is clear that Grapette did not intend to adopt or exploit any "goodwill" from the name "Peppy" and Fox's long association and use of it *with a cola syrup*. When one considers that Grapette did not acquire any of the assets of Fox, did not acquire any formula or process by which the Fox syrup was made, *cf. Mulhens & Kropff Inc. v. Fred Muelhens, Inc.*, 38 F.2d 287 (2ᵈ Cir. 1929), *rev'd*, 43 F.2d 937, 6 U.S.P.Q. 144 (2ᵈ Cir. 1930), *mandate clarified*, 48 F.2d 206, 9 U.S.P.Q. 182 (2ᵈ Cir. 1931), and then changed the type of beverage altogether, the assignment on its face must be considered void. It seems fundamental that either the defendant did not acquire any "goodwill" as required by law or if it did, assuming as defendant argues the mark itself possesses "goodwill," by use of the mark on a totally different product, Grapette intended to deceive the public. Either ground is untenable to the validity of the assignment.

---

[4] Mr. Fooks, Chairman of the Board of Grapette, testified:

> We went into his office (Mr. Fox's) office and I told him just frankly my situation, and I had this product ready for the market with no name, and I thought his name was a very suitable name, and if it wasn't too valuable I would like to purchase it.

Record at 176a–177a.

We hold that the assignment to Grapette of the trademark "Peppy" is void and that Grapette possesses no standing to raise the equitable defense of laches.

Judgment reversed and remanded for further relief to be determined by the district court.

BLACKMUN, CIRCUIT JUDGE, concurring.

I concur, but on the ground that *Hy-Cross Hatchery, Inc. v. Osborne*, 303 F.2d 947, 133 U.S.P.Q. 687 (C.C.P.A. 1962), the case relied upon by the district court here, is not, or should not be, helpful authority for Grapette. *Hy-Cross* is a peculiar case factually in that, among other aspects, live baby chicks were the product of both assignor and assignee. The court did place some reliance on what it seemed to regard as a genuine transfer of goodwill, 303 F.2d at 950, 133 U.S.P.Q. at 689–690, and, accordingly, saw little legal significance in the absence of an assignment of tangible chicks themselves. *See J. C. Hall Co. v. Hallmark Cards, Inc.*, 340 F.2d 960, 963, 144 U.S.P.Q. 435, 437–438 (C.C.P.A. 1965), where the same court apparently relates the significance of *Hy-Cross* to the absence of a transfer of tangible assets.

But if, as Grapette urges, the *Hy-Cross* holding has greater import than its peculiar facts suggest for me, then I would regard it as aberrational to settled authority. I prefer to stay with the usual rule, long established I thought, that a trademark may not validly be assigned in gross. And product difference is only an aspect of this traditional rule. A naked assignment is all that Fox and Grapette attempted and effected. It is not enough.

* * *

MARSHAK v. GREEN
United States Court of Appeals, Second Circuit
746 F.2d 927 (1984)

MILTON POLLACK, SENIOR DISTRICT JUDGE

David Rick, the appellant, manages and promotes musical groups for entertainment under the registered trade name, "VITO AND THE SALUTATIONS." Shortly before the entry of the order complained of on this appeal, Rick was preparing to proceed to trial of his pending suit for infringement of his trade name by a competitor musical group. It was at that point that Larry Marshak, the appellee, holder of an unsatisfied monetary judgment procured three years earlier in this suit against David Rick, obtained ex parte, in the Court below, an Order of Attachment and Sale of Rick's trade name.

The Order of the District Court directed the United States Marshal "to attach whatever proprietary interest the judgment debtor, David Rick, may have or claim to have in the registered name VITO AND THE SALUTATIONS and to sell same at public auction forthwith to satisfy plaintiff's [Marshak's] judgment against said defendant [Rick], to the extent of $17,683, plus accrued interest . . . ." By an amendment to the initial order, the Court directed one day's advertising notice in a newspaper of general circulation in New York City and that such sale may take place at the offices of the attorneys for the judgment creditor.

The sale was advertised and the Marshal auctioned the appellant's trade name to the plaintiff, and he bought it in for the nominal sum of $100. In fact, no money was received by the Marshal.

Prior to the sale, the defendant, having been apprised of plaintiff's proceedings, moved the Court for a stay of the attachment, execution and sale. In his supporting affidavit he notified the Court of his pending infringement suit against his competitors and of the imminence of its trial. He asserted that the competitive group now represented by Marcus, the attorney who had obtained the money judgment against Rick in 1981, was attempting to effectuate a judicial sale of his rights to the trade name to reap an unfair advantage in the impending infringement trial. Rick's ownership of the trade name had been made an issue in the infringement suit. Rick claimed that Marcus, the attorney for the defendants in the infringement suit had placed the collection of the judgment with the attorneys who had obtained the order below, and that this creates a conflict of interest on the part of Marcus, to the prejudice of Rick's rights in the infringement suit. He urged, moreover, that his right to use the trade name "cannot be the subject of a forced sale."

Rick requested of the Court below protection by a stay of the execution on "that which belongs only to me."

Rick's application herein for a stay of the sale was denied and the Court ordered that the sale of the appellant's interest in the trade name may go forward, but that the purchaser must be given notice that the validity of the trade name was now the subject of litigation before another Judge of the same Court.

On this appeal, the judgment debtor contends that a trade name or mark per se is not a type of property which can be attached or sold at execution auction and that the order directing the same and the action taken thereunder were invalid.

Although no case has been found precisely such as this in which a Federal Court has confronted the issue of whether a trade name by itself may be subjected to a forced sale, courts have held that registered trade names or marks may not be validly assigned in gross. A sale of trade name or mark divorced from its goodwill is characterized as an "assignment in gross."

A trade name or mark is merely a symbol of goodwill; it has no independent significance apart from the goodwill it symbolizes. "A trademark only gives the right to prohibit the use of it so far as to protect the owner's goodwill." *Prestonettes, Inc. v. Coty,* (1924) 264 U.S. 359, 44 S.Ct. 350,68 L.Ed. 731; a trademark cannot be sold or assigned apart from the goodwill it symbolizes, *Lanham Act,* § 10, 15 U.S.C.S. § 1060. There are not rights in a trademark apart from the business with which the mark has been associated; they are inseparable, *Pepsico, Inc. v. Grapette Company,* 416 F.2d 285 (8th Cir.1969); *Avon Shoe Co. v. David Crystal, Inc.,* 171 F.Supp. 293, 301, *aff'd* 279 F.2d 607, *cert. denied,* 364 U.S. 909, 81 S.Ct. 271, 5 L.Ed.2d 224 (1960). Use of the mark by the assignee in connection with a different goodwill and different product would result in a fraud on the purchasing public who reasonably assume that the mark signifies the same thing, whether used by one person or another. "[T]he consumers might buy a product thinking it to be of one quality or having certain characteristics and could find only too late to be another. To say that this would be remedied by the public soon losing faith in the product fails to give the consumer the protection it initially deserves." *Pepsico, Inc. v. Grapette Co.,* 416 F.2d 285, 289 (8th Cir.1969). See also 1 J. McCarthy, *Trademark and Unfair Competition,* § 18.1, p. 794 (2d ed. 1984).

In a case which touches the issue present herein, *Ward-Chandler Bldg. Co. v. Caldwell,* 8 Cal.App.2d 375, 47 P.2d 758, 760 (1935), a judgment creditor attempted to force the sale of a trademark and goodwill of the debtor's beauty parlor. The attempt was turned aside. The Court there held that a judgment creditor could not force the sale of the trademark and goodwill of the debtor's beauty parlor. "The reason for this is that if the bare right of user could be transferred the name or mark would no longer serve to point out and protect the business with which it has become identified, or to secure the public against deception, but would tend to give a different business the benefit of the reputation established by the business to which the name had previously been applied." *Id.* 47 P.2d at 760. *See also* 33 C.J.S. *Executions,* § 25, p. 158; 74 *Am.Jur.2d Trademarks,* § 23, pp. 718-19. *Cf. Haymaker Sports, Inc. v. Turian,* 581 F.2d 257 (C.C.P.A.1978) (trademark cannot be given as collateral in security agreements).

It has been pointed out that in the case of a service mark, confusion of the public and consumers would result if an assignee offered a service different from that offered by the assignor of the mark. *See Money Store v. Harris Corp. Finance, Inc.,* 689 F.2d 666 at 678 (7th Cir.1982).

Exceptions do exist. The courts have upheld such assignments if they find that the assignee is producing a product or performing a service substantially similar to that of the assignor and that the consumers would not be deceived or harmed. *See, e.g., Visa U.S.A., Inc. v. Birmingham Trust Nat'l. Bank*, 696 F.2d 1371 (Fed.Cir.1982) (mark signifying a promise to guarantee a check can be assigned from a supermarket chain to a credit card organization); *Money Store v. Harris Corp. Finance, Inc.*, 689 F.2d 666 (7th Cir.1982); *Glamorene Products Corp. v. Proctor & Gamble & Co.*, 538 F.2d 894 (C.C.P.A.1976).

Courts have also upheld such assignments if there is a continuity of management. For example, in *Marshak v. Green*, 505 F.Supp. 1054 (S.D.N.Y.1981), defendant unsuccessfully claimed that the assignment of the service mark, "The Drifters," to plaintiff was an invalid assignment in gross. The plaintiff had been the manager of the group prior to the assignment and continued in that capacity after the assignment. The Court found that the plaintiff had promised to protect the mark from infringement and had continued to provide the same singing style. "[T]he essence of what [plaintiff] acquired was the right to inform the public that [he] is in possession of the special experience and skill symbolized by the name of the original concern, and of the sole authority to market its services." *Id.* at 1061.

There was no evidence that this case fits into either of the above exceptions. Entertainment services are unique to the performers. Moreover, there is neither continuity of management nor quality and style of music. If another group advertised themselves as VITO AND THE SALUTATIONS, the public could be confused into thinking that they were about to watch the group identified by the registered trade name.

* * *

Accordingly, the appellee was not entitled to an order directing a levy of execution and sale of the appellant's registered trademark. The order appealed from is reversed and the purported sale is set aside.

Notes on Assignment Without Goodwill

1. Transfer of Goodwill

Some courts have construed the requirement that the assignment include the goodwill of the business represented by the mark to mean that the assignee must also acquire tangible assets to establish the transfer of goodwill. *PepsiCo, Inc. v. Grapette Co.*, supra; *G's Bottom's Up Social Club v. F.P.M. Industries, Inc.*, 574 F. Supp. 1490 (S.D.N.Y. 1983). *See also Hough Manufacturing Corp. v. Virginia Metal Industries, Inc.*, 203 U.S.P.Q. 436 (E.D. Va. 1978) (separate earlier sale of defunct business's tangible assets rendered later sale of trademark and goodwill invalid as an assignment in gross). Recognizing that the central purpose of the assignment rules is to prevent consumers from being misled as to the source of the product, many courts instead have accepted a mere recitation of transfer of goodwill as sufficient without any transfer of tangible assets, so long as a substantial similarity exists between the products or services of the assignor and assignee.

In *Int'l Cosmetics Exchange, Inc. v. Gapardis Health & Beauty, Inc.*, 303 F.3d 1242 (11th Cir. 2002), specifically noting that "there need not be any transfer of tangible assets," the court concluded that "the assignment was not in gross because it continued the association of the FAIR & WHITE trademark with the very goods [cosmetics] which created its reputation." Similarly, in *Vittoria North America, L.L.C. v. Euro-Asia Imports, Inc.*, 278 F.3d 1076 (10th Cir. 2001) the court deserved that the "[t]ransfer of assets is not a sine qua non of transferring the goodwill associated with a trademark". Because the bicycle tires sold by the assignee were substantially similar to the assignor's and the defendant did not allege "any sort of disruption in the kind or quality" of the tires, the assignment was valid. *See also Sugar Busters LLC v. Brennan*, 177 F.3d 258 (5th Cir. 1999) (holding assignment invalid because assignee's SUGAR BUSTERS diet book was not sufficiently similar to assignor's SUGAR BUSTERS retail store featuring products for diabetics); *VISA, U.S.A., Inc. v. Birmingham Trust National Bank*, 696 F.2d 1371 (Fed. Cir. 1982); *Money Store v. Harriscorp Finance, Inc.*, 689 F.2d 666 (7th Cir. 1982).

Compare Berni v. International Gourmet Restaurants, Inc., 838 F.2d 642, 646–47 (2[d] Cir. 1988), holding the assignment invalid where there was no evidence goodwill was transferred and operations did not resume within a reasonable time; and *Marshak v. Green, supra*, where the court reversed an order forcing sale of a musical group's service mark to satisfy a debt, concluding that the public would be confused if another group used the mark; and *Haymaker Sports, Inc. v. Turian*, 581 F.2d 257 (C.C.P.A. 1978), where the assignment was held invalid since assignee-escrowee never used the mark itself and never acquired any tangible assets or goodwill of assignor. *See also* Caboli, *Trademark Assignment "With Goodwill": A Concept Whose Time Has Gone*, 57 FLA. L. REV. 771 (2005) (arguing that trademark rights should be freely assignable with or without goodwill, with assignees required to avoid deception and to disclose to the public any product changes). In *Robi v. Reed*, 173 F.3d 736 (9th Cir.) *cert. denied*, 120 S. Ct. 375 (1999), involving an assignment of rights in the name "The Platters" for a singing group and questions of ownership, the court observed that other courts previously had held that "a person who remains continuously involved with the group and is in a position to control the quality of its services retains the right to use of the mark, even when that person is a manager rather than a performer." Defendant was the one who had remained continuously involved and therefore the one who owned the rights, having founded the group, given it its name, managed it, and been the only member who continuously performed with it. An assignment of rights in the name to plaintiff by a former member of the group therefore was invalid.

The Court in the *PepsiCo* case discusses legal recognition of the "advertising" and "guarantee" functions of trademarks. Are these consistent with the rationale of the Anglo-American system of trademark protection which focuses on protecting the source-indicating function of marks? Would legal recognition of "advertising" or "guarantee" functions — permitting in-gross assignment of trade marks — result in a more commercially viable assignment law? If the law permitted assignment in entire disregard or derogation of the source-indicating function of trademarks, would new problems of trademark protection based upon confusion as to source be created? Assuming the correctness of the propositions that a trademark is a guarantee and a symbol of goodwill, is there, nevertheless, a fraud on, or deception of, the public or purchasers incident to entirely uninhibited alienability of marks?

How long should goodwill survive the cessation of business? *See Defiance Button Machine Co. v. C. & C. Metal Products Corp.*, 759 F.2d 1053 (2th Cir. 1985); *Hough Manufacturing Corp., supra*; *Johanna Farms, Inc. v. Citrus Bowl, Inc.*, 199 U.S.P.Q. 16 (E.D.N.Y. 1978). Is the new user obligated to maintain a character or quality of goods equivalent to those previously produced? Is the new user burdened to employ some means to distinguish his product so as to avoid misleading the public into the belief that the goods still emanate from the original source? *Compare Manhattan Medicine Co. v. Wood*, 108 U.S. 218, 223 (1883) *with* the cases in this section.

2. Assignment and License Back

An assignment of rights with a license back to the assignor has become an accepted means of resolving disputes and quieting title. *E. & J. Gallo Winery v. Gallo Cattle Co.*, 967 F.2d 1280, 1290 (9th Cir. 1992) ("a simultaneous assignment and license back of a mark is valid where . . . it does not disrupt continuity of the products or services associated with a given mark:); *Sands, Taylor & Wood Co. v. The Quaker Oats Co.*, 978 F.2d 947, 956–57 (7th Cir. 1992), *cert. denied*, 113 S. Ct. 1879 (1993); *VISA U.S.A., Inc.*

v. Birmingham Trust Nat'l Bank, 696 F.2d 1371, 1377 (Fed. Cir. 1982) ("well-settled commercial practice"), *cert. denied*, 464 U.S. 826 (1983). In *E. & J. Gallo*, the Court reasoned that the requisite goodwill had been assigned in settlement of an infringement suit because the goodwill the plaintiff believed the defendant wrongfully appropriated was returned (assigned) to the plaintiff. *Compare Greenlon, Inc. of Cincinnati v. Greenlawn, Inc.*, 542 F. Supp. 895 (S.D. Ohio 1982), where the court found that while "no tangible assets must be transferred to the assignee to validate the assignment of a mark," the assignment at issue was invalid where assignor transferred no part of his business in effecting assignment and receiving license back.

3. Lanham Act Requirements

Respecting the assignment of federal trademark registrations, note that § 10 of the Lanham Act, 15 U.S.C. § 1060, provides that a trademark assignment document may be recorded and that such recordation ". . . shall be prima facie evidence of execution." The section further provides, "An assignment shall be void as against any subsequent purchaser for a valuable consideration without notice, unless it is recorded in the Patent Office within three months after the date thereof or prior to such subsequent purchase." Assignment of an intent to use application prior to filing a verified statement of use is invalid *and* voids the application unless the assignment is made to a successor of the applicant's ongoing and existing business under the intended mark. *Clorox Co. v. Chemical Bank*, 40 U.S.P.Q.2d 1098 (T.T.A.B. 1996).

4. Split Rights

Can trademark rights be "split" where confusion is likely? For example, where a trademark is used by a manufacturer for two related products, can the manufacturer assign to another the mark and goodwill as to one of the products? *See Gentry Canning Co. v. Blue Ribbon Growers, Inc.*, 138 U.S.P.Q. 536 (T.T.A.B. 1963); *McCane v. Mims*, 187 F.2d 163, 167 (C.C.P.A. 1951) ("we know of no law which prevents a seller from reserving from a sale of a business a line or lines of merchandise that he wishes to continue to exploit himself."); What consideration should be given to the public's interest in not being deceived? *See California Fruit Growers Exchange v. Sunkist Baking Co.*, Chapter 6, in which two plaintiffs agreed not to dispute each other's rights in the trademarks SUNKIST and SUN-KIST for fruits and vegetables respectively and then sued to enjoin a third party's use of SUNKIST for bread. The court felt the plaintiffs' agreement between themselves was inconsistent with and tarnished their claim that there was a likelihood of confusion caused by a third party's use of the same mark. Does this "Sunkist Doctrine" conflict with the general policy of courts favoring settlement of disputes through agreement? Compare the discussion on the public interest in enforcing agreements in Chapter 1.

4.05 Licensing and Franchising

Introduction

A trademark may be licensed for use by another where the licensor controls the nature and quality of the goods or services in connection with which it is used. The concept of licensing is simply that the licensee is an arm of the licensor. Thus, use by the licensee does not violate the source-indicating function of the trademark. Licensing without such control is called licensing in gross. In the absence of real and effective control by the licensor the trademark will no longer symbolize a particular source and the licensor may no longer have a protectable interest in the trademark. The principle of valid trademark licensing is frequently unknown to, and overlooked by, businesspeople and even their counsel. They are inclined to treat the trade identity rights as ordinary property rights, and particularly as patent rights, which they are not.

P, appellee　　*D, appellant*

DAWN DONUT CO. v. HART'S FOOD STORES, INC.

United States Court of Appeals, Second Circuit

267 F.2d 358 (1959)

TC: D's counterclaim dismissed

counterclaim　*AC: affirmed*

LUMBARD, CIRCUIT JUDGE

* * *

I

The final issue presented is raised by defendant's appeal from the dismissal of its counterclaim for cancellation of plaintiff's registration on the ground that the plaintiff failed to exercise the control required by the Lanham Act over the nature and quality of the goods sold by its licensees.

R We are all agreed that the Lanham Act places an affirmative duty upon a licensor of a registered trademark to take reasonable measures to detect and prevent misleading uses of his mark by his licensees or suffer cancellation of his federal registration. The Act, 15 U.S.C.A. § 1064, provides that a trademark registration may be cancelled because the trademark has been "abandoned." And "abandoned" is defined in 15 *R* U.S.C.A. § 1127 to include any act or omission by the registrant which causes the trademark to lose its significance as an indication of origin.

Prior to the passage of the Lanham Act many courts took the position that the licensing of a trademark separately from the business in connection with which it had been used worked an abandonment. *Reddy Kilowatt, Inc. v. Mid-Carolina Electric Cooperative, Inc.*, 4 Cir., 1957, 240 F.2d 282, 289; *American Broadcasting Co. v. Wahl Co.*, 2 Cir., 1941, 121 F.2d 412, 413; *Everett O. Fisk & Co. v. Fisk Teachers' Agency, Inc.*, 8 Cir., 1924, 3 F.2d 7, 9. The theory of these cases was that:

> A trade-mark is intended to identify the goods of the owner and to safeguard his good will. The designation if employed by a person other than the one whose business it serves to identify would be misleading. Consequently, "a right to the use of a trade-mark or a trade-name cannot be transferred in gross."

American Broadcasting Co. v. Wahl Co., *supra*, 121 F.2d at page 413.

Other courts were somewhat more liberal and held that a trade-mark could be licensed separately from the business in connection with which it had been used provided that the licensor retained control over the quality of the goods produced by the licensee. *E. I. DuPont de Nemours & Co. v. Celanese Corporation of America*, 1948, 167 F.2d 484, 35 C.C.P.A. 1061, 3 A.L.R.2d 1213; *see also* 3 A.L.R.2d 1226, 1277–1282 (1949) and cases there cited. But even in the *DuPont* case the court was careful to point out that naked licensing, viz. the grant of licenses without the retention of control, was invalid. *E. I. DuPont de Nemours & Co. v. Celanese Corporation of America*, *supra*, 167 F.2d at page 489.

The Lanham Act clearly carries forward the view of these latter cases that controlled licensing does not work an abandonment of the licensor's registration, while a system of naked licensing does. 15 U.S.C.A. § 1055 provides:

> *R* Where a registered mark or a mark sought to be registered is or may be used legitimately by related companies, such use shall inure to the benefit of the registrant or applicant for registration, and such use shall not affect the validity of such mark or of its registration, provided such mark is not used in such manner as to deceive the public.

defn And 15 U.S.C.A. § 1127 defines "related company" to mean "any person who legitimately controls or is controlled by the registrant or applicant for registration in respect to the nature and quality of the goods or services in connection with which the mark is used."[*]

---

[*] Editor's Note: Section 1127 has since been amended to refer to the owner of the mark, rather than registrant or applicant for registration. See the Appendix.

reasoning.

Without the requirement of control, the right of a trademark owner to license his mark separately from the business in connection with which it has been used would create the danger that products bearing the same trademark might be of diverse qualities. *See American Broadcasting Co. v. Wahl Co., supra; Everett O. Fisk & Co. v. Fisk Teachers' Agency, Inc., supra.* If the licensor is not compelled to take some reasonable steps to prevent misuses of his trademark in the hands of others the public will be deprived of its most effective protection against misleading uses of a trademark. The public is hardly in a position to uncover deceptive uses of a trademark before they occur and will be at best slow to detect them after they happen. Thus, unless the licensor exercises supervision and control over the operations of its licensees the risk that the public will be unwittingly deceived will be increased and this is precisely what the Act is in part designed to prevent. *See* Sen. Report No. 1333, 79th Cong. 2d Sess. (1946). Clearly the only effective way to protect the public where a trademark is used by licensees is to place on the licensor the affirmative duty of policing in a reasonable manner the activities of his licensees.

I dissent [Note, author of opinion is disagreeing with part of the majority opinion] from the conclusion of the majority that the district court's findings are not clearly erroneous because while it is true that the trial judge must be given some discretion in determining what constitutes reasonable supervision of licensees under the Lanham Act, it is also true that an appellate court ought not to accept the conclusions of the district court unless they are supported by findings of sufficient facts. It seems to me that the only findings of the district judge regarding supervision are in such general and conclusory terms as to be meaningless. . . .

Plaintiff's licensees fall into two classes: (1) those bakers with whom it made written contracts providing that the baker purchase exclusively plaintiff's mixes and requiring him to adhere to plaintiff's directions in using the mixes; and (2) those bakers whom plaintiff permitted to sell at retail under the "Dawn" label doughnuts and other baked goods made from its mixes although there was no written agreement governing the quality of the food sold under the Dawn mark.

The contracts that plaintiff did conclude, although they provided that the purchaser use the mix as directed and without adulteration, failed to provide for any system of inspection and control. Without such a system plaintiff could not know whether these bakers were adhering to its standards in using the mix or indeed whether they were selling only products made from Dawn mixes under the trademark "Dawn."

The absence, however, of an express contract right to inspect and supervise a licensee's operations does not mean that the plaintiff's method of licensing failed to comply with the requirements of the Lanham Act. Plaintiff may in fact have exercised control in spite of the absence of any express grant by licensees of the right to inspect and supervise.

The question then, with respect to both plaintiff's contract and non-contract licensees, is whether the plaintiff in fact exercised sufficient control.

Here the only evidence in the record relating to the actual supervision of licensees by plaintiff consists of the testimony of two of plaintiff's local sales representatives that they regularly visited their particular customers and the further testimony of one of them, Jesse Cohn, the plaintiff's New York representative, that "in many cases" he did have an opportunity to inspect and observe the operations of his customers. The record does not indicate whether plaintiff's other sales representatives made any similar efforts to observe the operations of licensees.

Moreover, Cohn's testimony fails to make clear the nature of the inspection he made or how often he made one. His testimony indicates that his opportunity to observe a licensee's operations was limited to "those cases where I am able to get into the shop" and even casts some doubt on whether he actually had sufficient technical knowledge in the use of plaintiff's mix to make an adequate inspection of a licensee's operations.

The fact that it was Cohn who failed to report the defendant's use of the mark "Dawn" to the plaintiff casts still further doubt about the extent of the supervision Cohn exercised over the operations of plaintiff's New York licensees.

Thus I do not believe that we can fairly determine on this record whether plaintiff subjected its licensees to periodic and thorough inspections by trained personnel or whether its policing consisted only of chance, cursory examinations of licensees by technically untrained salesmen. The latter system of inspection hardly constitutes a sufficient program of supervision to satisfy the requirements of the Act.

Therefore it is appropriate to remand the counterclaim for more extensive findings on the relevant issues rather than hazard a determination on this incomplete and uncertain record. I would direct the district court to order the cancellation of plaintiff's registrations if it should find that the plaintiff did not adequately police the operations of its licensees.

But unless the district court finds some evidence of misuse of the mark by plaintiff in its sales of mixes to bakers at the wholesale level, the cancellation of plaintiff's registration should be limited to the use of the mark in connection with sale of the finished food products to the consuming public. Such a limited cancellation is within the power of the court. Section 1119 of 15 U.S.C.A. specifically provides that "In any action involving a registered mark the court may . . . order the cancellation of registrations, in whole or in part, . . ." Moreover, partial cancellation is consistent with § 1051(a)(1) of 15 U.S.C.A., governing the initial registration of trademarks which requires the applicant to specify "the goods in connection with which the mark is used and the mode or manner in which the mark is used in connection with such goods. . . ."

The district court's denial of an injunction restraining defendant's use of the mark "Dawn" on baked and fried goods and its dismissal of defendant's counterclaim are affirmed.

STANFIELD v. OSBORNE INDUSTRIES, INC.,
United States Court of Appeals, Tenth Circuit
52 F.3d 867 (1995)

Tacha, Circuit Judge

*   *   *

In 1972, plaintiff developed several agricultural products including a fiberglass heating pad for newborn hogs. He presented these ideas in a letter to the president of First State Bank in Osborne, Kansas. Although plaintiff was not in the business of manufacturing these products at the time of this letter, he indicated that he would call his business "Stanfield Products" if he went into business. Osborne community leaders subsequently created defendant OII to manufacture plaintiff's products. OII was incorporated in May 1973.

*   *   *

In April 1974, defendant Ronald Thibault, Stanley's brother, undertook several special design projects for OII. Ronald became a full-time employee of OII in April 1975 when he took the position of vice president in charge of marketing and engineering. Ronald decided that OII needed to reduce its dependence on the company that distributed OII's products and develop its own markets. He concluded that OII would need its own trademark to foster its independence. When plaintiff learned of OII's plan to develop a trademark, he insisted that OII use the word "Stanfield" in its mark. OII agreed, and the parties entered into the following agreement (the 1975 agreement):

LICENSE AGREEMENT

THIS AGREEMENT, made and entered into as of this 5th day of July, 1975, by and between Phillip W. Stanfield, of the County of Osborne, State of Kansas, hereinafter referred to as First Party, and Osborne Industries, Inc., hereinafter referred to as Second Party:

WITNESSED THAT:

WHEREAS, Second Party is manufacturing certain products of which First Party is the inventor as enumerated in a certain License Agreement by and between said parties dated the 3rd day of October, 1973, and

WHEREAS, Second Party is manufacturing certain products other than invented by First Party, and

WHEREAS, Second Party desires to use the name "Stanfield" on all or part of the products manufactured by Second Party whether or not the same be invented by First Party, as a distinctive mark on said products in conjunction with the name of said products, and

WHEREAS, Second Party desires to use the name "Stanfield" as a distinctive mark on all or part of its products manufactured, at its discretion for a period of Fifteen (15) years from the date of this agreement and that said design of the distinctive mark bearing the name "Stanfield" shall be at the sole discretion of said party of the Second Part as to the design of the same, and

WHEREAS, both parties agree that all products manufactured by Second Party shall bear a distinctive mark and shall bear all marks required by the patent laws pertaining to and in conjunction with a License Agreement between the parties entered into on the 3rd day of October, 1973, and in the event that any of those distinctive marks referring specifically to "Stanfield" products or used in connection with "Stanfield" products shall be registered as a trademark, Second Party will be entitled to use said trademark in connection with the License Agreement dated the 3rd day of October, 1973 by and between the parties and shall use said mark in accordance with the trademark laws.

WHEREAS, in consideration of the use of the name "Stanfield" as above described in this Agreement in regard to any or all products manufactured by Second Party, the sum of $75.00 shall be paid to First Party by Second Party for the use of said name as above described.

This Agreement shall inure to the benefit of and be binding upon the Parties hereto, their respective heirs, legal representatives, successors and assigns.

IN WITNESS WHEREOF, the parties have hereunto executed this Agreement as of the day and year first above written.

OII commissioned an artist to design two trademarks. One mark consisted of the word "Stanfield"; the other mark was a circle design incorporating the word "Stanfield." By September 1976 OII was using both trademarks. OII applied for registration of these trademarks in March 1977. The United States Patent and Trademark Office registered the circle design mark on the principal register of trademarks on January 24, 1978.

In September 1991, plaintiff requested that OII discontinue use of the Stanfield trademark, basing his request on his understanding that the 1975 license agreement had expired. OII continued using the trademark, and plaintiff filed this action alleging (1) that defendant's use of the Stanfield trademark violated 15 U.S.C. § 1125, (2) that defendant fraudulently procured the registration of the trademark, and (3) that defendants were liable to plaintiff under several state law theories.

As a preliminary matter, we must determine the nature of the parties' 1975 agreement, which is at the core of their dispute. Plaintiff contends that the 1975 agreement was a limited license permitting OII to use the "Stanfield" marks for fifteen years. Defendants argue, and the district court agreed, that the 1975 agreement was a naked license, meaning that plaintiff abandoned any rights in the trademark.

Naked (or uncontrolled) licensing of a mark occurs when a licensor allows a licensee to use the mark on any quality or type of good the licensee chooses. *2 J. Thomas McCarthy, McCarthy on Trademarks and Unfair Competition* § 18.15, at 69 (3d ed. 1992). Such uncontrolled licensing can cause the mark to lose its significance. *Id.* When "a trademark owner engages in naked licensing, without any control over the quality of goods produced by the licensee, such a practice is inherently deceptive and constitutes abandonment of any rights to the trademark by the licensor." *First Interstate Bancorp v. Stenquist,* 16 U.S.P.Q.2d (BNA) 1704, 1706, 1990 WL 300321 (N.D.Cal. July 13, 1990). Thus, the licensor must "take some reasonable steps to prevent misuse of his trademark in the hands of others." *Dawn Donut Co. v. Hart's Food Stores, Inc.,* 267 F.2d 358, 367 (2^d Cir. 1959). "The critical question . . . is whether the plaintiff sufficiently policed and inspected its licensee['s] operations to guarantee the quality of the products [the licensee] sold." *Id.* Because a finding of insufficient control results in the forfeiture of a mark, a party asserting insufficient control by a licensor must meet a high burden of proof. *Transgo, Inc. v. Ajac Transmission Parts Corp.,* 768 F.2d 1001, 1017 (9th Cir. 1985), *cert. denied,* 474 U.S. 1059, 106 S.Ct. 802, 88 L.Ed.2d 778 (1986).

We first review the agreement between the parties for evidence of control. *See Dawn Donut,* 267 F.2d at 368. The 1975 agreement did not give plaintiff an express contractual right to inspect or supervise OII's operations in any way. OII had the right to use the "Stanfield" marks on any of the products it manufactured, including products not developed by plaintiff. Moreover, OII had the "sole discretion" to design the mark. The agreement, then, did not contemplate that plaintiff would have any control of OII's use of the "Stanfield" marks.

The absence of an express contractual right of control does not necessarily result in abandonment of a mark, as long as the licensor in fact exercised sufficient control over its licensee. *Id.; see also First Interstate Bancorp,* 16 U.S.P.Q.2d (BNA) at 1705-06. In the instant case, it is undisputed that plaintiff had no contact whatsoever with OII after his employment terminated. Plaintiff contends that he exercised control over OII's use of the "Stanfield" marks by examining one swine heating pad produced by OII, by looking at several pet pads, and by occasionally reviewing OII's promotional materials and advertising. He also contends that his lack of knowledge of any quality control problems is evidence of his control. None of this, however, is evidence that plaintiff actually exercised control over OII.

Plaintiff next maintains that he relied on OII for quality control and argues that his reliance on the licensee's quality control is sufficient for him to avoid a finding of a naked license. We disagree.

In cases in which courts have found that a licensor justifiably relied on a licensee for quality control, some special relationship existed between the parties. *See, e.g., Taco Cabana Int'l, Inc. v. Two Pesos, Inc.,* 932 F.2d 1113, 1121 (5th Cir. 1991), *aff'd on other grounds,* 505 U.S. 763, 112 S. Ct. 2753, 120 L.Ed.2d 615 (1992); *Transgo,* 768 F.2d at 1017-18; *Land O'Lakes Creameries, Inc. v. Oconomowoc Canning Co.,* 330 F.2d 667, 670 (7th Cir. 1964). In *Taco Cabana,* the court examined a cross-license between two brothers who had run a chain of restaurants together for a number of years. When the brothers decided to divide the business, they agreed that both would continue to use the same trade dress in their respective restaurants. Because the parties had maintained a close, long-term working relationship, the court held that they could justifiably rely on each other to maintain quality. *Taco Cabana,* 932 F.2d at 1121. In *Transgo,* the licensor itself manufactured at least ninety percent of the goods sold by its licensee, utilizing its own procedures to maintain quality. 768 F.2d at 1017. And in *Land O'Lakes,* the court found that the licensor reasonably relied on the licensee to maintain quality because the parties had maintained a successful association with no consumer complaints for over forty years. 330 F.2d at 670.

In contrast, the relationship between plaintiff and defendant here was neither close nor successful. Since 1975, the parties have had no contact with each other except as adversaries in litigation. Under these circumstances, plaintiff could not rely on OII's quality control as a substitute for his own control as a licensor.

Finally, plaintiff argues that defendants are barred from challenging the validity of the license by the equitable doctrine of licensee estoppel. Plaintiff did not, however, present this argument to the district court. "As a general rule we refuse to consider arguments raised for the first time on appeal unless sovereign immunity or jurisdiction is in question." *Daigle v. Shell Oil Co.,* 972 F.2d 1527, 1539 (10th Cir. 1992). Because neither sovereign immunity nor jurisdiction is implicated by plaintiff's licensee estoppel argument, we will not consider the argument here.

The terms of the parties' agreement, and their subsequent actions, compel us to hold that the 1975 agreement between plaintiff and OII was a naked license, by which plaintiff abandoned all his rights in the "Stanfield" marks. Having so held, we now turn to plaintiff's claims.

*   *   *

Here, plaintiff argues that he has a commercial interest in the mark allegedly misused by OII. But he abandoned any rights he may have had in the trademark under the 1975 agreement with OII. *See Georgia Carpet Sales, Inc. v. SLS Corp.,* 789 F.Supp. 244, 246 (N.D.Ill. 1992) ("[A]ny claim under Section 1125(a) for the asserted infringement of any trade name that has been the subject matter of a naked license" is "doom[ed].") Although plaintiff asserts that he has plans to compete with OII and would like to use his name in a trademark, the mere potential of commercial interest in one's family name is insufficient to confer standing. *See Dovenmuehle,* 871 F.2d at 700. Thus, he has no reasonable interest to be protected under the Lanham Act. Without a protectible interest, plaintiff lacks standing to bring this claim under section 1125. *See id.* at 701.

*   *   *

For the reasons stated herein, the order of the district court granting defendants summary judgment is AFFIRMED.

THE ORIGINAL GREAT AMERICAN CHOCOLATE CHIP COOKIE COMPANY v. RIVER VALLEY COOKIES, LIMITED
United States Court of Appeals, Seventh Circuit
970 F.2d 273 (1992)

POSNER, CIRCUIT JUDGE

*   *   *

This case arises from a squabble between a franchisor that we shall call the "Cookie Company" and the Sigels, who had a franchise to operate a Cookie Company store in a shopping mall in Aurora, Illinois. The company terminated the Sigels' franchise but they continued to sell cookies under the company's trademark, using batter purchased elsewhere after their supply of Cookie Company batter ran out. So the company sued them (and their corporate entity) to enjoin their violating the Trademark Act, 15 U.S.C. §§ 1051 *et seq.*, and moved for a preliminary injunction. The Sigels counterclaimed, charging that their franchise agreement had been terminated in violation both of the franchise agreement and of the Illinois Franchise Disclosure Act, Ill. Rev. Stat. ch. 121, ¶ 1719, and moving for preliminary injunction directing the Cookie Company to restore their franchise. (Both parties had additional grounds for their motions, but these need not be discussed.) The district court granted the Sigels' motion and denied that of the Cookie Company.

*   *   *

The Sigels received the franchise in 1985. Between 1987 and the issuance of the preliminary injunction last year, they committed a number of material breaches. They repeatedly failed to furnish insurance certificates indicating that the Cookie Company was an additional insured on the Sigels' liability insurance policy. They paid four invoices (aggregating either $13,000 or $30,000 — the record is unclear) more than 10 days after they were due, which meant more than 20 or more than 40 days after billing, because the agreement gave the Sigels either 10 or 30 days to pay their bills, depending on what kind of bill it was. (The average delay beyond the due date was either 28 days or 31 days; again the record is unclear.) They made five other late payments. Seven times they sent the Cookie Company checks that bounced. They flunked several inspections by the company's representatives, who found oozing cheesecake, undercooked and misshapen cookies, runny brownies, chewing gum stuck to counters, and ignorant and improperly dressed employees. An independent auditor found that in a three-year period the Sigels had underreported their gross sales by more than $40,000 (a nontrivial 2.8 percent of the total — almost three times the allowed margin of error); the result was to deprive the Cookie Company of almost $3,000 in royalties. After the company terminated the franchise, the Sigels pretended it was still in effect, refused to vacate the premises, and violated the franchise agreement by selling unauthorized products — cookies made with batter not supplied by the Cookie Company.

After most of these violations the company sent the Sigels a notice of default and the violations were then cured, though not always within 5 days as required by the franchise agreement. The company relies on the alternative ground for termination — three or more violations within a 12-month period, a ground that does not require notice or an opportunity to cure. By the Sigels' own account, most of the violations occurred within an even shorter period in 1989 and 1990 when the store was being mismanaged by the person whom the Sigels (who live in St. Louis) had hired to run it.

The fact that the Cookie Company may, as the Sigels argue, have treated other franchisees more leniently is no more a defense to a breach of contract than laxity in enforcing the speed limit is a defense to a speeding ticket. The fact particularly pressed by the Sigels that their violations may have been the fault not of the Sigels themselves but of their manager and that they ceased when the manager was replaced is similarly irrelevant. Liability for breach of contract is strict. *Patton v. Mid-Continent Systems, Inc.*, 841 F.2d 742, 750 (7th Cir. 1988). It does not require proof of inexcusable neglect or deliberate wrongdoing. Even if it did, the Sigels would lose because the misconduct of a manager within the scope of his employment is attributed to the owner even in a negligence case. The case must be treated as if they had managed the store in person. We do not share the popular prejudice against absentee ownership but the Sigels cannot be allowed to obtain a legal advantage by virtue of being absentee owners.

* * *

That does not end our inquiry. Illinois like other states requires, as a matter of common law, that each party to a contract act with good faith, and some Illinois cases say that the test for good faith "seems to center on a determination of commercial reasonability." *Dayan v. McDonald's Corp.*, 466 N.E.2d 958, 973 (Ill. App. 1984); *Kawasaki Shop of Aurora, Inc. v. Kawasaki Motors Corp.*, 544 N.E.2d 457, 463 (Ill. App. 1989); *see also Lippo v. Mobil Oil Corp.*, 776 F.2d 706, 714 n. 14 (7th Cir. 1985). The equation, tentative though it is ("seems to center on") makes it sound as if, contrary to our earlier suggestion, the judges have carte blanche to declare contractual provisions negotiated by competent adults unreasonable and to refuse to enforce them. We understand the duty of good faith in contract law differently. There is no blanket duty of good faith; nor is reasonableness the test of good faith.

Contract law does not require parties to behave altruistically toward each other; it does not proceed on the philosophy that I am my brother's keeper. That philosophy may animate the law of fiduciary obligations but parties to a contract are not each other's fiduciaries, *Continental Bank, N.A. v. Everett*, 964 F.2d 701, 704–06 (7th Cir. 1992);

Dyna-Tel, Inc. v. Lakewood Engineering & Mfg. Co., 946 F.2d 539, 543 (7th Cir. 1991); *Market Street Associates Limited Partnership v. Frey*, 941 F.2d 588, 593-95 (7th Cir. 1991); *Kham & Nate's Shoes No. 2, Inc. v. First Bank of Whiting*, 908 F.2d 1351, 1357 (7th Cir. 1990) — even if the contract is a franchise. *Murphy v. White Hen Pantry*, 691 F.2d 350, 354 (7th Cir. 1982). Contract law imposes a duty, not to "be reasonable," but to avoid taking advantage of gaps in a contract in order to exploit the vulnerabilities that arise when contractual performance is sequential rather than simultaneous. *Market Street Associates Limited Partnership v. Frey, supra*, 941 F.2d at 593–96. Suppose A hires B to paint his portrait to his satisfaction and B paints it and A in fact is satisfied but says he is not in the hope of chivvying down the agreed-upon price because the portrait may be unsaleable to anyone else. This, as we noted in *Morin Building Products Co. v. Baystone Construction, Inc.*, 717 F.2d 413, 415 (7th Cir. 1983), would be bad faith, not because any provision of the contract was unreasonable and had to be reformed but because a provision had been invoked dishonestly to achieve a purpose contrary to that for which the contract had been made. The same would be true here, we may assume, if the Sigels had through their efforts built the Aurora cookie store into an immensely successful franchise and the Cookie Company had tried to appropriate the value they had created by canceling the franchise on a pretext: three (or four, or five or for that matter a dozen) utterly trivial violations of the contract that the company would have overlooked but for its desire to take advantage of the Sigels' vulnerable position. *Wright-Moore Corp. v. Ricoh Corp.*, 908 F.2d 128, 136–37 (7th Cir. 1990). This has not been shown. Not only were many of the violations not trivial, but there is no suggestion of exceptional performance by the Sigels. True, it was a new franchise, and it has been doing well ever since the incompetent manager was booted out; but it is in a prime location, and the company in negotiating the terms of the franchise rated it a "good" franchise — one very likely to do well.

*   *   *

The preliminary injunction should have been denied for the additional reason that the Sigels had infringed the Cookie Company's trademarks, in violation of the Trademark Act. (The Sigels do not, and cannot, *S & R Corp. v. Jiffy Lube Int'l, Inc.*, 968 F.2d 371, 374–75, 376, 377–78 (3[d] Cir. 1992), deny the violation.) Unclean hands is a traditional defense to an action for equitable relief. The purpose is to discourage unlawful activity, and is as relevant to preliminary as to final relief. *Shondel v. McDermott*, 775 F.2d 859, 868 (7th Cir. 1985). It is true that a modern chancellor unlike his medieval forbears does not have uncabined discretion to punish moral shortcomings by withholding equitable relief. *Polk Bros., Inc. v. Forest City Enterprises, Inc.*, 776 F.2d 185, 193 (7th Cir. 1985); *Proimos v. Fair Automotive Repair, Inc.*, 808 F.2d at 1275. Modern equity is a system of entitlements. But equitable relief is costly to the judicial system, especially in a case such as this where the relief sought would cast the court in a continuing supervisory role. It would make no sense to incur that cost on behalf of someone who was trying to defraud the person against whom he was seeking the court's assistance. "One who has defrauded his adversary to his injury in the subject matter of the action will not be heard to assert a right in equity." *Fruhling v. County of Champaign*, 420 N.E.2d 1066, 1071 (Ill. App. 1981), quoted in *Polk Bros., Inc. v. Forest City Enterprises, Inc., supra*, 776 F.2d at 193; *see also id.* at 194.

The Sigels argue that they had no choice but to infringe the Cookie Company's trademarks surreptitiously, because, had they stopped selling cookies under the company's trademarks after the company stopped shipping batter to them, they would have been forced to default on their promissory note. They are wrong. They had a choice. They could have sued the company for breach of contract and violation of the disclosure law and moved for a preliminary injunction in that action. Instead of following that route, the open and honorable one, they infringed the company's trademarks covertly and did not move for an injunction until they were discovered and sued for infringement. They should not be rewarded with a preliminary injunction for their putting their franchisor to the expense of suing them for trademark infringement. Although, as we explained in *Polk Bros.*, the course of decisions in Illinois (it is Illinois' version of the doctrine of unclean hands that we must apply in this diversity case) has not run entirely true, 776 F.2d at 194, we think an Illinois court would deny an injunction to a firm that by its fraudulent conduct had precipitated the very suit in which it was seeking the injunction. "If the plaintiff creates or contributes to the situation on which it relies, the court denies equitable relief in order to deter the wrongful conduct." *Id.* at 193.

In pooh-poohing their misconduct the Sigels place too much weight on our decision in *Lippo*. That decision held that the particular franchise agreement, which did not have the terms as the one here, made the sale of misbranded product a curable violation. The decision, interpreted narrowly in *Beermart, Inc. v. Stroh Brewery Co.*, 804 F.2d 409, 412 (7th Cir. 1986), should not be understood to stand for the broader proposition that trademark infringement by a franchisee is a trivial offense that should never entitle the franchisor to cancel the franchise, or for the still broader proposition that in a dispute between franchisee and franchisor the judicial thumb should be on the franchisee's pan of the balance. All other objections to one side (for example, the judicial oath, which, echoing Deuteronomy, requires judges to judge "without respect to persons"), such a tilt is hardly likely to help franchisees as a group. James A. Brickley, Frederick H. Dark & Michael S. Weisbach, *The Economic Effects of Franchise Termination Laws*, 34 J. LAW & ECON. 101 (1991). The more difficult it is to cancel a franchise, the higher the price that franchisors will charge for franchises. So in the end the franchisees will pay for judicial liberality and everyone will pay for the loss of legal certainty that ensues when legal principles are bent however futilely to redistributive ends.

The idea that favoring one side or the other in a class of contract disputes can redistribute wealth is one of the most persistent illusions of judicial power. It comes from failing to consider the full consequences of legal decisions. Courts deciding contract cases cannot durably shift the balance of advantages to the weaker side of the market; they can only make contracts more costly to that side in the future, because franchisors will demand compensation for bearing onerous terms. *Amoco Oil Co. v. Ashcraft, supra*, 791 F.2d at 522.

The Cookie Company appealed not only from the grant of the Sigels' motion for a preliminary injunction but also from the denial of its motion for a preliminary injunction against the Sigels' violation of its trademarks. To this part of the company's appeal the Sigels do not deign to reply. We take this to be a concession that they have no defense to the motion. The Cookie Company is entitled to the injunction that it sought, and we remand for its entry.

Reversed and remanded, with directions.

Notes on Licensing and Franchising

1. Generally

Originally, at common law, the licensing of a trademark to another ordinarily worked an abandonment of trademark rights. *See, e.g., MacMahan Pharmacal Co. v. Denver Chem. Mfg. Co.*, 113 F. 468 (8th Cir. 1901); Rogers, *Good Will, Trade Marks and Unfair Trading*, 106 (1914). It gradually developed, however, that trade identity rights could be licensed for use by another as long as the licensor controlled the nature and quality of the goods and services with which they are used. In 1946, the Lanham Act codified the existing common law by providing that a registration is not invalidated where a mark is used by a "related company" (15 U.S.C. § 1055). As amended in 1988, the Lanham Act defines a related company as "any person whose use of a mark is controlled by the owner of the mark with respect to the nature and quality of the goods or services on or in connection with which the mark is used" (15 U.S.C. § 1127).

While a license can be oral, a separate written license agreement is an important foundation for proof of the licensor's control of the nature and quality of the goods or services in connection with which the licensed trademark is used. Such agreements are an important requirement for any effective licensing program. *See, e.g., Matrix Group Limited, Inc. v. Rawling Sporting Goods Company*, 477 F.3d 583 (8th Cir. 2007) ($8.5 award to licensee where licensor terminated the license without complying with its provisions that allowed licensee thirty days to cure its alleged breach); *Tandy Corp. v. Marymac Industries, Inc.*, 213 U.S.P.Q. 702 (S.D. Tex. 1981) (licensee's use of mark for mail order services violated license agreement and was enjoined under § 43(a) of the Lanham Act). The License agreement should describe (a) the mark or other means for trade identity involved; (b) the goods or services in connection with which it is to be used; (c) the standards of quality for the goods or services; (d) the methods of supervision and control (regular submission of samples, rights of inspection, maintenance of test records, etc.); (e) any limitations on territory, sublicensing, or the sale of competing goods (*but see* the section on antitrust law in Chapter 8); (f) the time period or duration of the license and reversion of all rights after termination; and (g) the termination of rights of both parties for breach of the license agreement. For a discussion of the interface between legal and business considerations in licensing, see Feldman, *What Every Trademark Attorney Should Know About Business Motivations to License*, 86 TRADEMARK REP. 47 (1996). *See also A&L Laboratories Inc. v. Bou-Matic LLC*, 429 F.3d 775 (8th Cir. 2005) (despite defendant's contentions that contract was not meant to be a license, its provisions confirmed that it was, and that plaintiff was entitled to use the mark under that license).

2. Quality Control

Quality control, actively exercised, is the *sine qua non* of valid licensing or franchising arrangements. Failure of a licensor or franchisor to take reasonable measures to control the activities of a licensee or franchisee with respect to the nature and quality of the goods or services bearing the mark can result in the loss of trademark rights. 15 U.S.C. §§ 1055, 1127. In *Universal City Studios, Inc. v. Nintendo Co.*, 578 F. Supp. 911, 929 (S.D.N.Y. 1983), *aff'd*, 746 F.2d 112 (2d Cir. 1984), the Court held that the plaintiff's rights in KING KONG were forfeited and denied any relief by virtue of uncontrolled licensing:

> Uncontrolled licensing of a mark results in abandonment of the mark by the licensor. [citations omitted] "The critical question . . . is whether the plaintiff sufficiently policed and inspected its licensees' operations to guarantee the quality of the products they sold under its trademarks to the public." [citations omitted].

To the same effect is *First Interstate Bancorp v. Stenquist*, 16 U.S.P.Q.2d 1704 (N.D. Cal. 1990), in which plaintiff, owner of the registered mark FIRST INTERSTATE for banking services, sued defendant, who used the same mark for real estate services. The court granted plaintiff summary judgment on defendant's infringement counterclaim. The court found that: "[D]efendant's grant of a license to use his trademark without any significant control over the quality of the services provided by the licensee constituted a naked license, and resulted in abandonment of the rights to the trademark." Informal contacts and a seven-year professional and social relationship between the licensor and licensee were not enough to establish control over the quality of the licensee's work. *See also Dept. of Parks & Rec. v. Bazaar Del Mundo, Inc.*, 448 F.3d 1118 (9th Cir. 2006) (rejecting plaintiff's claim that it owned the trademark rights because defendant allegedly was its licensee, given that the parties clearly intended "to lease premises — not to license trademarks", and plaintiff never supervised or controlled defendant's restaurant services); *Ritchie v. Williams*, 395 F.3d 283 (6th Cir. 2005) (music promoter abandoned any rights in the contested mark by failing to assert any control over defendant's use of the mark); *Secular Orgs. For Sobriety, Inc. v. Ullrich*, 213 F.3d 1125

(9th Cir. 2000)(plaintiff unsuccessfully argued that defendant's prior use of "Secular Organizations for Sobriety" was only as a licensee of plaintiff; the court noted the absence of any evidence of a licensing relationship or control exerted over defendant by plaintiff, and enjoined plaintiff's use of the name).

There is variation as to what constitutes "adequate" control. It is clear, however, that it is the exercise of control, not merely the right to exercise control, which will be evaluated by the courts to determine whether the licensor has lost its trademark rights. *See General Motors Corp. v. Gibson Chemical & Oil Corp.*, 786 F.2d 105, 110 (2[d] Cir. 1986). The traditional rule is that no relief ordinarily can be had if the licensor fails to exercise control over both the nature of the goods and their quality. It has been held that a license which gives a licensee *carte blanche* to manufacture any kind of product under the licensed mark is void as against public policy. *Cartier, Inc. v. Three Sheaves Co.*, 465 F. Supp. 123, 129 (S.D.N.Y. 1979). The licensor may itself perform the necessary inspection and testing to determine compliance with its quality standards, or it may delegate such authority to a third party. *Accurate Merchandising, Inc. v. American Pacific*, 186 U.S.P.Q. 197, 200 (S.D.N.Y. 1975). In either case, the quality standards must be prescribed by the licensor.

In some situations, if there is a sufficiently close relationship between the licensor and licensee, *e.g.*, where they share the same officers, sufficient quality control may result from that relationship alone. *Taco Cabana Int'l, Inc. v. Two Pesos, Inc.*, 932 F.2d 1113, 1121 (5th Cir. 1991), *aff'd*, 113 S. Ct. 20 (1992); (cross-licensing of Mexican restaurant trade dress which created two sources for same mark did not result in abandonment given family relationship of owners and reasonable expectation of consistent quality under the circumstances); *Doeblers' Pa. Hybrids, Inc. v. Doebler*, 442 F.3d 812 (3[d] Cir. 2006) (a sufficiently special relationship to satisfy quality control obligation may have existed because the litigants were closely-held business entities owned and managed by family members with interlocking ownership and control); *Transgo, Inc. v. Ajac Transmission Corp.*, 768 F.2d 1001, 1017-18 (9th Cir. 1985) (jury finding of adequate control affirmed, in part due to longstanding close working relationship of the licensor and licensee, and their working together on the prototype for the product at issue). In *In re Raven Marine, Inc.*, 217 U.S.P.Q. 68 (T.T.A.B. 1983), however, the Trademark Trial and Appeal Board held that merely having the same stockholders, directors or officers, without proof of effective licensing controls, did not constitute a valid licensing arrangement.

In *Barcamerica Int'l USA Trust v. Tyfield Importer, Inc.*, 289 F.3d 589 (9th Cir. 2002), plaintiff's lawsuit against defendant's use of the mark "Leonardo Da Vinci" for wine failed because plaintiff had licensed a third party to use that mark for wine without exercising any quality control. In contending there had been sufficient quality control, plaintiff unsuccessfully tried to rely on its principal's occasional tasting of the licensee's wine, which he deemed "good", and on the licensee's own quality control efforts. The former was insufficient, and as to the latter, plaintiff and the licensee did not have "the type of close working relationship" that might support such reliance on the licensee's own efforts. As a result of its naked licensing, plaintiff was "estopped from asserting any rights in the mark." "Whether [the licensee's wine] was objectively 'good' or 'bad' is simply irrelevant. What matters is that [plaintiff, the licensor] played no meaningful role in holding the wine to a standard of quality — good, bad, or otherwise." *See also CNA Financial Corp. v. Brown*, 922 F. Supp. 567, 574 (M.D. Fla. 1996), *aff'd*, 162 F.3d 1334 (11th Cir. 1998)(holding company engaged in naked licensing and abandoned rights in CNA for insurance underwriting services because it allowed each subsidiary-licensee to control its own services under the mark). In a few cases, courts have held that a licensor properly relied on the efforts of a licensee to protect the quality of the goods. *See, e.g.*, *Syntex Laboratories, Inc. v. Norwich Pharmacal Co.*, 315 F. Supp. 45, 56 (S.D.N.Y. 1970), *aff'd*, 437 F.2d 566 (2d Cir. 1971); *Embedded Moments, Inc. v. International Silver Co.*, 648 F. Supp. 187 (E.D.N.Y. 1986). To maintain the validity of its mark, however, a licensor should not rely on the licensee's efforts to insure compliance with the licensor's standards. McCarthy, Trademarks and Unfair Competition, § 18:55–18:60.

3. Judicial Reluctance

Notwithstanding the strong language in the decisions requiring supervision and control, some courts have been reluctant to hold that valuable trade identity rights have been lost unless the failure to exercise control has in fact resulted in deception or injury. *Taco Cabana Int'l, Inc. v. Two Pesos, Inc.*, 932 F.2d 1113, 1121 (5th Cir. 1991), *aff'd on other grounds*, 112 S. Ct. 2753 (1992) (holding there need not be formal quality control where "the particular circumstances of the licensing arrangement indicate the public will not be deceived"); *Transgo, Inc. v. Ajac Transmission Parts Corp.*, 768 F.2d 1001, 1017–18 (9th Cir. 1985); *United States Jaycees v. Philadelphia Jaycees*, 639 F.2d 134 (3d Cir. 1981); *Dawn Donut, supra; University Book Store v. University of Wis. Board of Regents*, 33 U.S.P.Q.2d 1385 (T.T.A.B. 1994) (finding no abandonment of registrant's several WISCONSIN BADGERS marks for college sports merchandise despite decades of unpoliced third party uses of the marks under implied licenses; "the subject marks were not abandoned by applicant since the quality of the apparel imprinted with such marks remained at an acceptable level . . . ."). *But see Yamamoto & Co. (America) v. Victor United, Inc., supra; Sheila's Shine Products, Inc. v. Sheila Shine, Inc.*, 486 F.2d 114 (5th Cir. 1973); *First Interstate Bancorp. v. Stenquist, supra* (naked license); *Universal City Studios v. Nintendo Co., supra. Cf.* Park, *"Naked" Licensing Is Not A Four Letter Word: Debunking The Myth of the Quality Control Requirement in Trademark Licensing*, 82 Trademark Rep. 531 (1992).

4. Phase-Out of Use

Courts have been uniformly unwilling to penalize settlement efforts where a trademark owner granted an infringer a "phase-out period" during which the infringer phases out use of the infringing mark and disposes of inventory in settlement of a dispute. Attempts in subsequent litigation to characterize such agreements as naked licenses have failed. *See, e.g., Exxon Corp. v. Oxxford Clothes, Inc.*, 109 F.3d 1070, 1080, n.13 (5th Cir.), *cert. denied*, 522 U.S. 915 (1997) in which the court noted that "any resultant consumer confusion might well be abated more rapidly under the phase out agreements" than through "the delays which are part of conventional civil litigation between entrenched corporate opponents."

5. New Use by Licensee

Can a licensor authorize a licensee to extend use of a trademark to new or different products or services? *See Alligator Co. v. Robert Bruce*, 176 F. Supp. 377 (E.D. Pa. 1959) (answering yes, if quality control is exercised); *Yamamoto & Co. (America) v. Victor United, Inc.*, supra. Must a licensor use the trademark before licensing its use by others? The Revision Act confirmed that use solely by a licensee is adequate to bestow rights on a licensor. 15 U.S.C. § 1056.

6. Licensee Estoppel

A licensee normally will be estopped from denying the licensor's exclusive rights in the mark where there is a valid license agreement. *Smith v. Dental Prod. Co.*, 140 F.2d 140 (7th Cir. 1944), *cert. denied*, 322 U.S. 743 (1944); *E.F Prichard Co. v. Consumers Brewing Co.*, 136 F.2d 512 (6th Cir. 1943), *cert. denied*, 321 U.S. 763 (1944). And use of the mark by an ex-licensee after license termination normally will constitute infringement. *Klipsch, Inc. v. WWR Technology*, 127 F.3d 729 (8th Cir. 1997) (plaintiff granted summary judgment on infringement claim where license terminated for failure to make timely payments and defendant continued to use mark); *Church of Scientology International v. Elmira Mission of The Church of Scientology*, 794 F.2d 38 (2th Cir. 1986).

Should a licensee be estopped as well from contesting the validity of the trademark during the course of the licensing agreement? *Compare Edwin K. Williams & Co. v. Williams*, 542 F.2d 1053 (9th Cir. 1976), in which the Court held that a licensee who resisted any supervision of quality control "should not be permitted" to assert abandonment of the mark by licensor due to lack of sufficient control, with *Professional Golfers Ass'n v. Banker's Life Co.*, 186 U.S.P.Q. 447 (5th Cir. 1975), in which the Court adopted the "intermediate view" that "after expiration of the license, a former trademark licensee may challenge the licensor's title on facts which arose after the contract has expired." *See also Westowne Shoes Inc. v. Brown Group Inc.*, 104 F.3d 994, 997 (7th Cir.), *cert. denied*, 522 U.S. 861(1997), which held that absent an express, applicable contractual provision, the licensee shoe-store owner could not sue to enjoin licensor, a shoe manufacturer, from affixing the licensed mark to an allegedly inferior line of shoes, and *Twentieth Century Fox Film Corp. v. Marvel Enterprises, Inc.*, 277 F.3d 253 (2[d] Cir. 2002), which held that the licensee was not estopped from claiming that the licensor had falsely advertised the licensed product, but denied preliminary relief for failure to prove that the licensor had done so.

In *Creative Gifts, Inc. v. UFO*, 235 F.3d 540, 548 (10th Cir. 2000)(Shadur, J. by designation), the court determined that defendants' accusation of naked licensing was barred by licensee estoppel and, quoting fromCALLMAN, UNFAIR COMPETITION, TRADEMARK & MONOPOLIES, § 19:48 (Altman 4th ed. 2004), summarized the doctrine as follows:

> The licensee is estopped from claiming any rights against the licensor which are inconsistent with the terms of the license. This is true even after the license expires. He is estopped from contesting the validity of the mark,. . .or challenging the license agreement as void or against public policy, e.g., because it granted a naked license. But he may challenge the licensor's title to the mark based on events which occurred after the license expired.

In *Idaho Potato Comm'n v. M&M Produce Farm & Sales*, 335 F.3d 130 (2[d] Cir. 2003), licensee estoppel did not apply to an ex-licensee for a *certification mark*. Unlike trademarks, certification marks signify product quality and not necessarily product source, so that unrelated entities who meet the standards and conditions certified by the mark have a right to use it. This principle and the public interest in open competition exempted the ex-licensee's challenge from estoppel. To the same effect is *Idaho Potato Comm'n v. G&T Terminal Packaging, Inc.*, 425 F.3d 708 (9th Cir. 2005) (citing *McCarthy on Trademarks* § 19:91 for the proposition that "[t]rademarks protect the public from confusion by accurately indicating the source of a product. . . . A certification mark, on the other hand, is a mark used by someone other than its owner to signify that a product or service has a certain characteristic"; the licensee therefore was not estopped from challenging the license).

7. Licensee Standing

Under 15 U.S.C. § 1114(1), the owner of a registered mark, including a licensor, has standing to sue for infringement of that mark. There has been a split of authority, however, as to whether a *licensee* should have such standing. *Compare DEP Corp. v. Interstate Cigar Corp. Inc.*, 622 F.2d 621, 623–624 (2[d] Cir. 1980), reasoning that a licensee should not, with *Wynn Oil Co. v. Thomas*, 839 F.2d 1183, 1189–1190 (6th Cir. 1988), where the court concluded, without discussion, that an exclusive licensee has standing to sue for infringement of a registered mark.

Some courts have found standing for exclusive and nonexclusive licensees under the broader language of § 43(a) of the Lanham Act, 15 U.S.C. § 1125(a), which provides that an infringer "shall be liable in a civil action by any person who believes that he or she is or is likely to be damaged by such act." *See, e.g., Frisch's Restaurants, Inc. v. Elby's Big Boy, Inc.*, 670 F.2d 642, 649 (6th Cir. 1982) (exclusive licensee-franchisee had standing to sue under § 43(a)); *Ferrero U.S.A., Inc. v. Ozark Trading, Inc.*, 753 F. Supp.

1240, 1245 (D.N.J. 1991), *aff'd*, 19 U.S.P.Q.2d 1468 (3ᵈ Cir. 1991) (exclusive U.S. distributor had standing under § 43(a) to sue parallel importer; "use of the broad phraseology 'any person' in the Lanham Act . . . denotes an intent not to limit enforcement to merely the trademark owner"). It still may be necessary, however, under some circumstances to join the licensor as a party. .

8. Tax Consequences

Characterization of a transfer of trademark rights can have tax consequences as well. If the transfer is characterized as an assignment, the money made from the assignment by the assignor will be considered a capital gain; if the transfer is found to be a license, the money made will be treated as ordinary income. *See Consolidated Foods Corp. v. United States*, 196 U.S.P.Q. 664 (7ᵗʰ Cir. 1978) (royalty arrangement found to be inconsistent with the characteristics of an assignment). The 1986 tax law eliminated the preferential corporate capital gains rate, but the concept of capital gains remains important in that corporate capital losses are still only deductible to the extent of corporate capital gains. *See generally* Bell, Smith & Simensky, *A State Tax Strategy for Trademarks*, 81 Trademark Rep. 445 (1991); Reed, *Trademarks In the Sale of Part of a Business: Concurrent Use and Licensing*, 80 Trademark Rep. 514 (1990).

9. Franchising

In the 1960s, the concept of licensing became the basis for a new industry for exploiting goodwill: franchising. In the early stages of this franchising boom, some enterprises and their promoters were primarily concerned with the sale of franchises rather than their successful operation. For this and other reasons, the franchisee was often left with few rights under the franchise agreement, which led to federal and state regulation of the industry. *See generally* Glickman, Business Organizations: Franchising (2007).

In the 1970's, various state franchising laws were enacted and the Federal Trade Commission's Trade Regulation Rule on Franchising was adopted as a new means to protect prospective franchisees. Bus. Franchise Guide (CCH) ¶¶ 3000–4530.03; 16 C.F.R. § 436 (1979). In 2007, the Federal Trade Commission amended its Franchise Rule at 16 C.F.R. 436 and 437, effective on a voluntary basis as of July 1, 2007 and mandatory as of July 1, 2008. The amendment is intended "to streamline the Rule, minimize compliance costs, and to respond to changes in new technologies and market conditions in the offer and sale of franchises." Billing Code 6750-01-P at www.ftc.gov (the FTC Report on the Final Rule). The focus is on pre-sale disclosures to prospective franchisees, and the amendment largely adopts the requirements and format of the Uniform Franchise Offering Circular ("UFOC") used by the 15 states that have pre-sale franchise disclosure laws. However, in some ways it is narrower than the UFOC (e.g. in not requiring detailed disclosures pertaining to computer equipment requirements), and in some ways it is broader (e.g., in requiring identification of franchisor-initiated litigation against franchisees pertaining to the franchise relationship). Unless the particular state has adopted this FTC Rule format for disclosures, franchisors must comply with separate federal and state disclosure requirements. The FTC and most states seek to enhance franchisee rights through disclosure of specific categories of information which may bear upon the desirability of a franchise. Enforcement to date has been largely limited to cases involving affirmative, false and fraudulent disclosures. Bus. Franchise Guide (CCH) ¶¶ 8354, 8807. *See, e.g., U.S. v. American Coin-Op Services, Inc.*, No. 00-CV0126S(M) (W.D.N.Y. 2001), and *U.S. World Wide Coffee, Inc.*, No. 00-8137-CIV-GRAHAM (S.D. Fla. 2000), in which the franchisors, to settle FTC charges that they had failed to provide certain pre-sale disclosures to prospective franchisees, agreed not to make false and misleading representations in connection with future sales, and to pay monetary penalties for past conduct. Private remedies are not available under the FTC Rule but can be had under several of the state statutes. *Freedman v. Meldy's, Inc.*, 587 F. Supp. 658 (E.D. Pa. 1984); Bus. Franchise Guide (CCH), supra.

A license does not need to be officially labeled as a franchise agreement for a court to find that it is one, so that franchise disclosure and other obligations apply. *See, e.g., To-Am Equipment Co., Inc. v. Mitsubishi Caterpillar Forklift America, Inc.*, 152 F.3d 658 (7th Cir. 1998), where a $1.5 million award for wrongful franchise termination was affirmed. A jury had found that the plaintiff, a dealer of Mitsubishi forklift trucks, had paid "indirect" franchise fees via the required purchase of various manuals, and that the agreement gave plaintiff "the right to conduct its business under a marketing plan prescribed or suggested in substantial part by Mitsubishi, making the dealership a franchise under Illinois law."

10. Post-Termination Use

In litigation, the tension is often between the franchisor's claim of a right to protection under the trademark laws and the franchisee's claim of rights under the franchise agreement and federal and state compliance laws. Ordinarily, courts give precedence to the need for protection under the trademark laws, and use of a mark by an ex-franchisee after termination of the franchise will constitute infringement. This result comports with the fundamental trademark principle that such unlicensed use is likely to confuse and irreparably harm the public. 15 U.S.C. § 1127; *Re/Max North Central, Inc. v. Cook*, 272 F.3d 424 (7th Cir. 2001) (affirming preliminary injunction against ex-franchisee's use of well-known "Re/Max" mark; "a franchisee cannot hold hostage a franchisor's marks to force it to negotiate terms more favorable to the franchisee"); *Pappan Enter's, Inc. v. Hardee's Food Sys., Inc.* 143 F.3d 800 (3d Cir. 1998) (preliminary injunction granted franchisor against ex-franchisee's post-termination use of the mark due to the franchisor's "loss of control of reputation and the inevitable likelihood of confusion to customers"); *Costello v. Lungaro*, 37 U.S.P.Q.2d 1121, 1124 (th Cir. 1995) (affirming summary judgment against franchisee who made unauthorized use of franchisor's marks after the franchise agreement terminated); *S&R Corp. v. Jiffy Lube Int'l, Inc.*, 968 F.2d 371, 374–378 (3d Cir. 1992) (preliminary injunction granted)

11. Good Faith and Fair Dealing

Franchisees may make a wide range of contract claims after termination directed to such issues as wrongful termination and such remedies as recission and the reallocation of any wrongful gains by the franchisor. *Compare General Motors Corp. v. The New A.C. Chevrolet, Inc.*, 263 F.3d 296 (3d Cir. 2001), which affirmed that GM had good cause to terminate the franchisee's Chevrolet dealership when, in violation of the franchisee agreement, the franchisee added, without authorization, a Volkswagen dealership, with *Century 21 Real Estate Corp. v. Meraj Int'l Inv. Corp.*, 315 F.3d 1271 (10th Cir. 2003), in which the franchisor's error in failing to credit a royalty payment meant that termination was improper, and the franchisee's post-termination use of plaintiff's CENTURY 21 mark therefore was not infringing.

Fundamental to many of these claims is the implied covenant of good faith and fair dealing, a talisman often invoked by terminated franchisees. Ordinarily, however, no obligation should be implied which will obliterate a right expressly given under a written contract. In *Hubbard Chevrolet Co. v. General Motors Corp.*, 873 F.2d 873 (5th Cir.), *cert. denied*, 493 U.S. 978 (1989), for example, the Fifth Circuit refused to apply an "implied" covenant of good faith and fair dealing to the actions taken by General Motors in a dispute regarding the relocation of an automobile dealership and held that the District Court erred when it instructed the jury on that implied covenant. The Court noted that it would not imply the good faith covenant where the parties have unmistakably expressed their respective rights. *Hubbard*, 873 F.2d at 877. *See also The Original Great American Chocolate Chip Cookie Co. v. River Valley Cookies, Ltd.*, *supra. Compare McDonald's Corp. v. Robertson*, 147 F.3d 1301 (11th Cir. 1998) (court concluded that "some type of showing" that the franchise termination was proper was necessary and that franchisor had sufficiently done so, given defendant's repeated failure to meet quality standards; preliminary injunction affirmed).

Courts favoring implied covenants of good faith and fair dealing do so in part because the concept evokes ethical principles of fair play. Strong support exists in state and federal compliance laws. Bus. Franchise Guide (CCH) ¶¶ 8354, 8807; 16 CFR § 436 (1979), and the requirements of good faith under the Uniform Commercial Code § 2-103 and the Restatement of Contracts § 205. In *Dayan v. McDonald's Corp.*, 466 N.E.2d 958 (Ill. App. Ct. 1984), for example, the Court ruled that:

> a party vested with contractual discretion must exercise that discretion reasonably and with proper motive, and may not do so arbitrarily, capriciously or in a manner inconsistent with the reasonable expectations of the parties.

Id. at 972. *See also In re Vylene Enterprises, Inc.*, 90 F.3d 1472, 1477 (9th Cir. 1996) (holding that a franchisor's opening of a competing franchise within two miles of franchisee's restaurant breached an implied covenant of good faith even though there was no express territorial restriction in the franchise agreement); *Carvel Corp. v. Diversified Management Group, Inc.*, 930 F.2d 228 (2^{d} Cir. 1991) (holding that the jury was inadequately instructed on the implied good faith obligation in the performance of an area development agreement); *Beraha v. Baxter Health Care Corp.*, 956 F.2d 1436, 1443–45 (7th Cir. 1992) (not a duty "to be nice or to behave decently — but requiring exercise of its discretion" consistent with reasonable expectations of the parties).

Defendant franchisor's cancellation of *all* its UNION 76 gasoline dealership franchises was upheld in *Draeger Oil Co. v. Uno-Ven Co.*, 314 F.3d 299 (7th Cir. 2002), based on the dissolution of defendant's trademark holding company and its decision to exit the petroleum marketing business. "[I]t is hardly to be expected that Unocal would want to support a retail trademark, necessarily at some cost, after it had left the retail business." In holding that the franchisor was not liable to the plaintiff gasoline dealers for the cancellations, the court concluded, "[i]t is reasonable as a matter of law for a business to abandon a property that has no value to it, and if the abandonment is lawful it has no duty (unless it has voluntarily assumed one) to compensate suppliers or customers who may be harmed by its decision. That is all that happened here when Unocal withdrew from the refinery and marketing business."

12.   Franchisor Liability

Trademark franchisors have been held liable for personal injuries and property damage resulting from defective products and services supplied by franchisees. In *Kosters v. Seven-Up Co.*, 595 F.2d 347, 353 (6th Cir. 1979), the Sixth Circuit stated the principle in dicta as follows: "Liability is based on the franchisor's control and the public's assumption, induced by the franchisor's conduct, that it does in fact control and vouch for the product." *See Oberlin v. Marlin American Corp.*, 596 F.2d 1322 (7th Cir. 1979). In contrast, franchisor was not liable for the alleged negligence of its franchisee's delivery driver in a car accident in *Pizza k, Inc. v. Santagata*, 249 Ga. App. 36 (2004). "[A] franchisor is faced with the problem of exercising sufficient control over a franchisee to protect the franchisor's national identity and professional reputation, while at the same time foregoing such a degree of control that would make it vicariously liable for the acts of the franchisee and its employees." Here, "PIZZA k is not authorized under the agreement to exercise supervisory control over the daily activities of [the franchisee's] employees." *Compare also* the following cases holding that traditional franchisor controls do not create an agency agreement: *Hayman v. Ramada Inn, Inc.*, Bus. Franchise Guide (CCH) ¶ 893 (N.C. Ct. App. 1987) *and Robert Broock v. Nutri/System, Inc.*, 654 F. Supp. 7 (S.D. Ohio 1986).

Vicarious liability nonetheless may exist where there is apparent authority of the franchisor over the franchisee. In *Gizzi v. Texaco, Inc.*, 437 F.2d 308, 310 (3^{d} Cir.), *cert.*

denied, 404 U.S. 829 (1971), the Court ruled the "apparent authority" of Texaco over its franchisee was a question for the jury. *Cf. Yoder v. Honeywell*, 104 F.3d 1215 (10th Cir. 1997) (declining to "impose liability on a corporation that provides a trademark for a product under an 'apparent manufacturer' theory"). *See also Crinkley v. Holiday Inns, Inc.* 844 F.2d 156 (4th Cir. 1988) (franchisor held vicariously liable under apparent agency theory for failure to provide adequate security); *Case v. Holiday Inns, Inc.*, 851 F.2d 356 (4th Cir. 1988); *Giger v. Mobil Oil Corp.*, 823 F.2d 181 (7th Cir. 1987). These developments in the case law increase the risks to the franchisor of vicarious liability where the ex-franchisees retain for any period of time the trade identity of the franchisor. Customarily, franchisors require indemnification by franchisees, but such protection might well be ineffective against an ex-franchisee, so that the franchisor would need its own insurance and other liability protection. *See* Laufer & Gurnick, *Minimizing Vicarious Liability of Franchisors for Acts of Their Franchisees*, 6 FRANCHISE L.J. 3 (1987); Hawes, *Trademark Licensing Can Lead To Product Liability*, 34 PRAC. LAW. 23 (1988).

CHAPTER 5
TRADE DRESS PROTECTION

5.01 Product Design as Trademark

Recall the statement in *Qualitex Co v. Jacobson Products Co.*, 514 U.S. 159, 163-64 (1995), that the characteristic feature of a trademark is its "source-distinguishing ability . . . — not its ontological status as color, shape, fragrance, word, or sign . . . ." It follows that just as color and other visual indicia can serve a trademark function in indicating product source, so can product design and shape, packaging and the like. Collectively, these are known as "trade dress." Protecting trade dress, however, has raised a host of issues not encountered with word marks. While the principles of establishing and protecting rights described in earlier chapters generally apply to trade dress as well, some trade dress issues are unique, and raise different concerns, particularly as to potential anti-competitive effects of trade dress protection, and conflicts with patent and copyright law. Are there special rules for determining which trade dress is inherently distinctive, and which is protectable only upon a showing of secondary meaning? Can trade dress be protected that pertains to a utilitarian or functional aspect of the product at issue, or that is or was protected by a utility patent or design patent? What is the relationship of trade dress protection to patent law?

5.02 Trade Dress Protection and Patent Law

One of the most long-standing and controversial issues in the area of trade dress protection pertains to the ability of states to protect certain trade dress under state unfair competition law. The Supreme Court has repeatedly held that state unfair competition law that protects trade dress too stringently comes into conflict with the federal patent scheme and is preempted under the supremacy clause of the Constitution. When you read the following three cases, note the Supreme Court's high level of awareness in the most recent case, *Bonito Boats*, of the controversies its earlier holdings in *Sears* and *Compco* on this issue had engendered. Does *Bonito Boats* resolve the perceived problems of *Sears* and *Compco*? Were there actually any problems to be resolved?

SEARS ROEBUCK & CO. v. STIFFEL CO.
376 U.S. 225 (1964)

Mr. Justice Black

The question in this case is whether a State's unfair competition law can, consistently with the federal patent laws, impose liability for or prohibit the copying of an article which is protected by neither a federal patent nor a copyright. The respondent, Stiffel Company, secured design and mechanical patents on a "pole lamp" — a vertical tube having lamp fixtures along the outside, the tube being made so that it will stand upright between the floor and ceiling of a room. Pole lamps proved a decided commercial success, and soon after Stiffel brought them on the market Sears, Roebuck & Company put on the market a substantially identical lamp, which it sold more cheaply, Sears' retail price being about the same as Stiffel's wholesale price. Stiffel then brought this action against Sears in the United States District Court for the Northern District of Illinois, claiming in its first count that by copying its design Sears had infringed Stiffel's patents and in its second count that by selling copies of Stiffel's lamp Sears had caused confusion in the trade as to the source of the lamps and had thereby engaged in unfair competition under Illinois law. There was evidence that identifying tags were not attached to the Sears lamps although labels appeared on the cartons in which they were delivered to customers, that customers had asked Stiffel whether its lamps differed from Sears, and that in two cases customers who had bought Stiffel lamps had complained to Stiffel on learning that Sears was selling substantially identical lamps at a much lower price.

The District Court, after holding the patents invalid for want of invention, went on to find as a fact that Sears lamp was "a substantially exact copy" of Stiffel's and that the two lamps were so much alike, both in appearance and in functional details, "that confusion between them is likely, and some confusion has already occurred." On these findings the court held Sears guilty of unfair competition, enjoined Sears "from unfairly competing with [Stiffel] by selling or attempting to sell pole lamps identical to or confusingly similar to" Stiffel's lamp, and ordered an accounting to fix profits and damages resulting from Sears' "unfair competition."

The Court of Appeals affirmed. 313 F.2d 115, 136 U.S.P.Q. 292. That court held that, to make out a case of unfair competition under Illinois law, there was no need to show that Sears had been "palming off" its lamps as Stiffel lamps; Stiffel had only to prove that there was a "likelihood of confusion as to the source of the products" — that the two articles were sufficiently identical that customers could not tell who had made a particular one. Impressed by the "remarkable sameness of appearance" of the lamps, the Court of Appeals upheld the trial court's findings of likelihood of confusion and some actual confusion, findings which the appellate court construed to mean confusion "as to the source of the lamps." The Court of Appeals thought this enough under Illinois law to sustain the trial court's holding of unfair competition, and thus held Sears liable under Illinois law for doing no more than copying and marketing an unpatented article.

We granted certiorari to consider whether this use of a State's law of unfair competition is compatible with the federal patent law. 374 U.S. 826.

* * *

The grant of a patent is the grant of a statutory monopoly; indeed, the grant of patents in England was an explicit exception to the statute of James I prohibiting monopolies. Patents are not given as favors, as was the case of monopolies given by the Tudor monarchs, *see Case of the Monopolies (Darcy v. Allein)*, 11 Co. 84, 77 Eng. Rep. 1260 (K.B. 1602), but are meant to encourage invention by rewarding the inventor with the right, limited to a term of years fixed by the patent, to exclude others from the use of his invention. . . . [W]hen the patent expires the monopoly created by it expires, too, and the right to make the article — including the right to make it in precisely the shape it carried when patented — passes to the public, *Kellogg Co. v. National Biscuit Co.*, 305 U.S. 111, 120–122, 39 U.S.P.Q. 296, 300–301(1938); *Singer Mfg. Co. v. June Mfg. Co.*, 163 U.S. 169, 185 (1896).

Thus the patent system is one in which uniform federal standards are carefully used to promote invention while at the same time preserving free competition. Obviously a State could not, consistently with a Supremacy Clause of the Constitution, extend the life of a patent beyond its expiration date or give a patent on an article which lacked the level of invention required for federal patents. To do either would run counter to the policy of Congress of granting patents only to true inventions, and then only for a limited time. Just as a State cannot encroach upon the federal patent laws directly, it cannot, under some other law, such as that forbidding unfair competition, give protection of a kind that clashes with the objectives of the federal patent laws.

In the present case the "pole lamp" sold by Stiffel has been held not to be entitled to the protection of either a mechanical or a design patent. An unpatentable article, like an article on which the patent has expired, is in the public domain and may be made and sold by whoever chooses to do so. What Sears did was to copy Stiffel's design and to sell lamps almost identical to those sold by Stiffel. This it had every right to do under the federal patent laws. That Stiffel originated the pole lamp and made it popular is immaterial. "Sharing in the goodwill of an article unprotected by patent or trademark is the exercise of a right possessed by all — and in the free exercise of which the consuming public is deeply interested." *Kellogg Co. v. National Biscuit Co.*, *supra*, 305 U.S., at 122, 39 U.S.P.Q. at 300–301. To allow a State by use of its law of unfair competition to prevent the copying of an article which represents too slight an advance to be patented would be to permit the State to block off from the public something which federal law has said belongs to the public. The result would be that while federal law grants only 14 to 17 years' protection to genuine inventions, *see* 35 U.S.C. §§ 154, 173, States could allow perpetual protection to articles too lacking in novelty to merit any patent at all under federal constitutional standards. This would be too great an encroachment on the federal patent system to be tolerated.

Sears has been held liable here for unfair competition because of a finding of likelihood of confusion based only on the fact that Sears' lamp was copied from Stiffel's unpatented lamp and that consequently the two looked exactly alike. Of course there could be "confusion" as to who had manufactured these nearly identical articles. But mere inability of the public to tell two identical articles apart is not enough to support an injunction against copying or an award of damages for copying that which the federal patent laws permit to be copied. Doubtless a State may, in appropriate circumstances, require that goods, whether patented or unpatented, be labeled or that other precautionary steps be taken to prevent customers from being misled as to the source, just as it may protect businesses in the use of their trademarks, labels, or distinctive dress in the packaging of goods so as to prevent others, by imitating such markings, from misleading purchasers as to the source of the goods. But because of the federal patent laws a State may not, when the article is unpatented and uncopyrighted, prohibit the copying of the article itself or award damages for such copying. *Cf. G. Ricordi & Co. v.*

Haendler, 194 F.2d 914, 916, 92 U.S.P.Q. 340, 341 (2[d] Cir. 1952). The judgment below did both and in so doing gave Stiffel the equivalent of a patent monopoly on its unpatented lamp. That was error, and Sears is entitled to a judgment in its favor.

Reversed.

COMPCO CORP. v. DAY-BRITE LIGHTING, INC.
376 U.S. 234 (1964)

MR. JUSTICE BLACK delivered the opinion of the Court.

As in *Sears, Roebuck & Co. v. Stiffel Co.*, 376 U.S. 225, 84 S.Ct. 784, the question here is whether the use of a state unfair competition law to give relief against the copying of an unpatented industrial design conflicts with the federal patent laws. Both Compco and Day-Brite are manufacturers of fluorescent lighting fixtures of a kind widely used in offices and stores. Day-Brite in 1955 secured from the Patent Office a design patent on a reflector having cross-ribs claimed to give both strength and attractiveness to the fixture. Day-Brite also sought, but was refused, a mechanical patent on the same device. After Day-Brite had begun selling its fixture, Compco's predecessor . . . began making and selling fixtures very similar to Day-Brite's. This action was then brought by Day-Brite. One count alleged that Compco had infringed Day-Brite's design patent; a second count charged that the public and the trade had come to associate this particular design with Day-Brite, that Compco had copied Day-Brite's distinctive design so as to confuse and deceive purchasers into thinking Compco's fixtures were actually Day-Brite's, and that by doing this Compco had unfairly competed with Day-Brite. The complaint prayed for both an accounting and an injunction.

* * *

Notwithstanding the thinness of the evidence to support findings of likely and actual confusion among purchasers, we do not find it necessary in this case to determine whether there is 'clear error' in these findings. They, like those in *Sears, Roebuck & Co. v. Stiffel Co.*, 376 U.S. 225, 84 S.Ct. 784, were based wholly on the fact that selling an article which is an exact copy of another unpatented article is likely to produce and did in this case produce confusion as to the source of the article. Even accepting the findings, we hold that the order for an accounting for damages and the injunction are in conflict with the federal patent laws. Today we have held in *Sears, Roebuck & Co. v. Stiffel* Co., 376 U.S. 225, 84 S.Ct. 784, that when an article is unprotected by a patent or a copyright, state law may not forbid others to copy that article. To forbid copying would interfere with the federal policy, found in Art. I, s 8, cl. 8, of the Constitution and in the implementing federal statutes, of allowing free access to copy whatever the federal patent and copyright laws leave in the public domain. Here Day-Brite's fixture has been held not to be entitled to a design or mechanical patent. Under the federal patent laws it is, therefore, in the public domain and can be copied in every detail by whoever pleases. It is true that the trial court found that the configuration of Day-Brite's fixture identified Day-Brite to the trade because the arrangement of the ribbing had, like a trademark, acquired a "secondary meaning" by which that particular design was associated with Day-Brite. But if the design is not entitled to a design patent or other federal statutory protection, then it can be copied at will.

As we have said in *Sears*, while the federal patent laws prevent a State from prohibiting the copying and selling of unpatented articles, they do not stand in the way of state law, statutory or decisional, which requires those who make and sell copies to take precautions to identify their products as their own. A State of course has power to impose liability upon those who, knowing that the public is relying upon an original manufacturer's reputation for quality and integrity, deceive the public by palming off their copies as the original. That an article copied from an unpatented article could be made in some other way, that the design is 'nonfunctional' and not essential to the use of either article, that the configuration of the article copied may have a 'secondary meaning' which identifies the maker to the trade, or that there may be 'confusion' among purchasers as to which article is which or as to who is the maker, may be relevant evidence in applying a State's law requiring such precautions as labeling; however, and regardless of the copier's motives, neither these facts nor any others can furnish a basis for imposing liability for or prohibiting the actual acts of copying and selling. *Cf. Kellogg Co. v. National Biscuit Co.*, 305 U.S. 111, 120, 59 S.Ct. 109, 114, 83 L.Ed. 73 (1938). And of course a State cannot hold a copier accountable in damages for failure to label or otherwise to identify his goods unless his failure is in violation of valid state statutory or decisional law requiring the copier to label or take other precautions to prevent confusion of customers as to the source of the goods. . . .

Since the judgment below forbids the sale of a copy of an unpatented article and orders an accounting for damages for such copying, it cannot stand.

Reversed.

BONITO BOATS, INC, v. THUNDER CRAFT BOATS, INC.
489 U.S. 141 (1989)

JUSTICE O'CONNOR delivered the opinion of the Court.

We must decide today what limits the operation of the federal patent system places on the States' ability to offer substantial protection to utilitarian and design ideas which the patent laws leave otherwise unprotected. In *Interpart Corp. v. Italia*, 777 F.2d 678 (1985), the Court of Appeals for the Federal Circuit concluded that a California law prohibiting the use of the "direct molding process" to duplicate unpatented articles posed no threat to the policies behind the federal patent laws. In this case, the Florida Supreme Court came to a contrary conclusion. It struck down a Florida statute which prohibits the use of the direct molding process to duplicate unpatented boat hulls, finding that the protection offered by the Florida law conflicted with the balance struck by Congress in the federal patent statute between the encouragement of invention and free competition in unpatented ideas. 515 So.2d 220 (1987). We granted certiorari to resolve the conflict, 486 U.S. 1004, 108 S.Ct. 1727, 100 L.Ed.2d 192 (1988), and we now affirm the judgment of the Florida Supreme Court.

* * *

The pre-emptive sweep of our decisions in *Sears* and *Compco* has been the subject of heated scholarly and judicial debate. . . . Read at their highest level of generality, the two decisions could be taken to stand for the proposition that the States are completely disabled from offering any form of protection to articles or processes which fall within the broad scope of patentable subject matter. . . . Since the potentially patentable includes "anything under the sun that is made by man," *Diamond v. Chakrabarty*, 447 U.S. 303, 309, 100 S.Ct. 2204, 2207, 65 L.Ed.2d 144 (1980) (citation omitted), the broadest reading of *Sears* would prohibit the States from regulating the deceptive simulation of trade dress or the tortious appropriation of private information.

That the extrapolation of such a broad pre-emptive principle from *Sears* is inappropriate is clear from the balance struck in *Sears* itself. The *Sears* Court made it plain that the States "may protect businesses in the use of their trademarks, labels, or distinctive dress in the packaging of goods so as to prevent others, by imitating such markings, from misleading purchasers as to the source of the goods." *Sears, supra*, 376 U.S., at 232, 84 S.Ct., at 789 (footnote omitted). Trade dress is, of course, potentially the subject matter of design patents. *See W.T. Rogers Co. v. Keene*, 778 F.2d 334, 337 (CA7 1985). Yet our decision in *Sears* clearly indicates that the States may place limited regulations on the circumstances in which such designs are used in order to prevent consumer confusion as to source. Thus, while *Sears* speaks in absolutist terms, its conclusion that the States may place some conditions on the use of trade dress indicates an implicit recognition that all state regulation of potentially patentable but unpatented subject matter is not *ipso facto* pre-empted by the federal patent laws.

* * *

At the heart of *Sears* and *Compco* is the conclusion that the efficient operation of the federal patent system depends upon substantially free trade in publicly known, unpatented design and utilitarian conceptions. In *Sears*, the state law offered "the equivalent of a patent monopoly," 376 U.S., at 233, 84 S.Ct., at 789, in the functional aspects of a product which had been placed in public commerce absent the protection of a valid patent. While, as noted above, our decisions since *Sears* have taken a decidedly less rigid view of the scope of federal pre-emption under the patent laws, . . . we believe that the *Sears* Court correctly concluded that the States may not offer patent-like protection to intellectual creations which would otherwise remain unprotected as a matter of federal law. Both the novelty and the nonobviousness requirements of federal patent law are grounded in the notion that concepts within the public grasp, or those so obvious that they readily could be, are the tools of creation available to all. They provide the baseline of free competition upon which the patent system's incentive to creative effort depends. A state law that substantially interferes with the enjoyment of an unpatented utilitarian or design conception which has been freely disclosed by its author to the public at large impermissibly contravenes the ultimate goal of public disclosure and use which is the centerpiece of federal patent policy. Moreover, through the creation of patent-like rights, the States could essentially redirect inventive efforts away from the careful criteria of patentability developed by Congress over the last 200 years. We understand this to be the reasoning at the core of our decisions in *Sears* and *Compco*, and we reaffirm that reasoning today.

We believe that the Florida statute at issue in this case so substantially impedes the public use of the otherwise unprotected design and utilitarian ideas embodied in unpatented boat hulls as to run afoul of the teaching of our decisions in *Sears* and *Compco*. . . . In contrast to the operation of unfair competition law, the Florida statute is aimed directly at preventing the exploitation of the design and utilitarian conceptions embodied in the product itself.

* * *

By offering patent-like protection for ideas deemed unprotected under the present federal scheme, the Florida statute conflicts with the "strong federal policy favoring free competition in ideas which do not merit patent protection." *Lear, Inc.*, 395 U.S., at 656, 89 S.Ct., at 1903. We therefore agree with the majority of the Florida Supreme Court that the Florida statute is preempted by the Supremacy Clause, and the judgment of that court is hereby affirmed.

It is so ordered.

* * *

Notes on Trade Dress Protection and Patent Law

Sears and *Compco* precipitated an immediate and disturbed reaction within bar and academia. The decisions appeared to weaken an area which had been the subject of well-developed, although frequently problematical, unfair competition common law prohibiting product simulation where secondary meaning had attached to a product configuration and likelihood of confusion could be shown. The decisions are likewise notable for their apparent refueling of the monopoly phobias of the New Deal era. See Chapter 1. *Sears* and *Compco* also raised an apparent problem in protecting distinctive packaging and similar trade dress under unfair competition principles. As stated in *Compco*, "to forbid copying would interfere with the federal policy . . . of allowing free access to copy whatever the federal patent and copyright laws leave in the public domain." *See Spangler Candy Co. v. Crystal Pure Candy Co.*, 353 F.2d 641 (7th Cir.

1965). Notwithstanding this pronouncement, the lower courts generally confined the doctrine of *Sears* and *Compco* to product copying and did not extend it to distinctive packaging or similar trade dress.

In *Goldstein v. California*, 412 U.S. 546 (1973), the Supreme Court held that the preemption doctrine expressed in the *Sears* and *Compco* cases does not preclude state action against unauthorized duplication of uncopyrighted recordings by so-called tape pirates. Some thought the *Goldstein* decision indicated some limitation of the *Sears* and *Compco* rationale. *See* GILSON, § 7.04 (2008); MCCARTHY, TRADEMARKS AND UNFAIR COMPETITION § 1:9 (4th ed. 2007). Subsequent federal court and Supreme Court decisions have found such limitations in affording protection to product designs under trade dress law.

If a nonfunctional design acts as a trademark, serving to indicate source to the public, might *Sears* and *Compco* nonetheless preclude its protection from copying under § 43(a)? In *Truck Equipment Service Co. v. Fruehauf Corp.*, 536 F.2d 1210 (8th Cir. 1976), the court rejected such an argument by the defendant, characterizing the cited language from the above *Compco* decision as dictum and noting that "[t]he law of trademark and the issues of functionality and secondary meaning were not before the Court" in that case. Finding that plaintiff's nonfunctional exterior design for its semitrailer had acquired secondary meaning and that defendant's copying of that design created a likelihood of confusion, the Court awarded injunctive relief and defendant's profits to plaintiff. *Accord Dallas Cowboys Cheerleaders, Inc. v. Pussycat Cinema, Ltd.*, 604 F.2d 200, 204 (2ᵈ Cir. 1979) ("it is clear that *Sears-Compco* did not redefine the permissible scope of the law of trademarks insofar as it applies to origin and sponsorship"); *Rolls-Royce Motors Ltd. v. A&T Fiberglass, Inc.*, 428 F. Supp. 689 (N.D. Ga. 1976); *see also Ideal Toy Corp. v. Plawner Toy Mfg. Corp.*, 685 F.2d 78, 81 (3ᵈ Cir. 1982) ("*Sears* and *Compco* do not preclude a court from affording protection from infringement of a design element that has achieved secondary meaning and is non-functional, notwithstanding the absence of a patent"). *Cf. Litton Systems, Inc. v. Whirlpool Corp.*, 728 F.2d 1423 (Fed. Cir. 1984), where the allegedly infringing copying of a patented design was held analogous to the uses in *Sears* and *Compco* precluding protection under state law, and *Gemveto Jewelry Co. v. Jeff Cooper, Inc.*, 800 F.2d 256 (Fed. Cir. 1986), where the court held that under *Sears* and *Compco* defendant could be prohibited only from palming off defendant's jewelry as plaintiff's.

In his textbook, UNFAIR COMPETITION AND TRADE-MARKS (4th ed. 1947) at page 390, Nims explained the difference between the legal protections afforded patents and trademarks:

> The good will of the patentee survives the patent. His popularity as manufacturer or merchant may create a demand for the product as made by him which may be represented by a trade-mark, by non-functional decorative features which have acquired a secondary meaning, or by dress such as a label or wrapper of peculiar design by which the article and its maker have become associated in the public mind. These features have nothing to do with the patent rights. They are property of the patentee which survives the patent. As to them, the general rules with regard to trade-marks and the dress of the goods apply as though no patent were involved. As a manufacturer, one may make any unpatented article, but as a vendor, he may be restricted in the interest of fair competition.

This explanation was cited approvingly by the Court in *In re Mogen David Wine Corp.*, 328 F.2d 925 (C.C.P.A. 1964), in which it held registrable a bottle configuration as a trademark for wines, and further held that use of the configuration during the life of its design patent was valid trademark use. The Court observed:

> In our opinion, trademark rights, or rights under the law of unfair competition, which happen to continue beyond the expiration of a design patent, do not "extend" the patent monopoly. They exist independently of it, under different

law and for different reasons. The termination of either has no legal effect on the continuance of the other. When the patent monopoly ends, it ends. The trademark rights do not extend it. We know of no provision of patent law, statutory or otherwise, that guarantees to anyone an absolute right to copy the subject matter of any expired patent. Patent expiration is nothing more than the cessation of the patentee's right to exclude held under the patent law. Conversely, trademarks conceivably could end through non-use during the life of a patent. We doubt it would be argued that the patent rights should also expire so as not to "extend" them.

In his concurrence, Judge Rich found "[w]hether competition would in fact be hindered" to be "the crux of the matter," and concluded, "Others can meet any real or imagined demand for wine in decanter-type bottles — assuming there is any such thing — without being in the least hampered in competition in inability to copy the Mogen David bottle design. They might even excel in competition by producing a more attractive design under the stimulus of a prohibition against copying under the principles of unfair competition law."

Two district court "lamp" decisions make for an interesting comparison with the *Sears* decision, undertaking the type of analysis that was absent there. In *PAF S.r.l. v. Lisa Lighting Co.*, 712 F. Supp. 394 (S.D.N.Y. 1989), plaintiff's DOVE desk lamp design was held nonfunctional, the court noting the existence of hundreds of other lamp configurations, and was held to possess secondary meaning, based on evidence of extensive sales and advertising, unsolicited media coverage, and defendant's intentional copying. Defendant consequently was enjoined under § 43(a) from marketing its SWAN lamp, a low quality Taiwanese imitation. In *Remcraft Lighting Products, Inc. v. Maxim Lighting, Inc.*, 706 F. Supp. 855, 857 (S.D. Fla. 1989), defendant's summary judgment motion was denied because disputed fact issues existed over whether plaintiff's lamp configuration was primarily functional, and, if not, whether the configuration was distinctive, with the court noting that it was not the "shades, swivels or canopies which the plaintiff seeks to protect, but the plaintiff's unique *design* of these elements."

Consider the interplay between the law as to simulating product configurations and that as to simulating distinctive product packaging. Do the public policy reasons for permitting copying in *Sears* and *Compco* apply to distinctive packages, bottles, containers, and the like, where a public benefit from copying is more difficult to discern? In *Sicilia Di R. Biebow & Co. v. Cox*, 732 F.2d 417, 426 n.7 (5th Cir. 1984), the court stated, "The need to avoid monopolization of a design lessens . . . in the area of distinctive trade dress. The wide range of available packaging and design options allows a producer to appropriate a distinctive identity without unduly hindering his competitor's ability to compete." In *Johnson & Johnson v. Quality Pure Mfg., Inc.*, 484 F. Supp. 975 (D.N.J. 1979), defendant had copied the trade dress of three different products of plaintiff's for use in the sale of defendant's apparently less expensive products. The court observed *Johnson & Johnson*, (484 F. Supp. at 980–81):

> In and of itself, competition, on a price basis is entirely lawful and, in fact, is encouraged. It is what the better mousetrap concept is all about. But it is not fair play to sell a competing product on the basis of a lower price and at the same time use a trade dress designed and calculated to fool the customer into the belief that he is getting someone else's product.

In *Bonito Boats*, the Court noted that under *Sears*, even in the absence of a patent, the states may protect nonfunctional design aspects that have acquired secondary meaning "where consumer confusion is likely to result." *Bonito Boats*, 489 U.S. at 158. The Court also noted that in enacting § 43(a), Congress gave "*federal* recognition to many of the concerns which underlie the state tort of unfair competition." *Id.* at 166 (emphasis added). Federal registration of a particular product design, of course, also supplies a basis for federal protection. Such federal protection, of course, eliminates the preemption concerns underlying the decisions in *Sears*, *Compco*, and *Bonito Boats*.

Feisthamel, Kelly & Sistek, *Trade Dress 101: Best Practices for Registration of Product Configuration Trade Dress eith the USPTO*, 95 TMR 1357 (2005). *Cf. Gibson Guitar Corp. v. Paul Reed Smith Guitars, LP*, 423 F.3d 539 (6th Cir. 2005) (determining that the lower court improperly expanded plaintiff's registered rights in a guitar's body shape to other design features such as the placement and style of knobs and switches).

Note that it is precisely the gravamen of trademark infringement claims –consumer confusion — that allows states to provide unfair competition protection to trade dress owners. Trademark infringement is discussed below in Chapters 6 and 7. Does this mean that state law dilution claims — which, as explained in Chapter 8, do not have a confusion requirement — *might* conflict with the federal patent scheme? If not, why not? How about federal dilution claims?

After the Supreme Court struck down the Florida statute in *Bonito Boats*, boatmakers successfully sought assistance from U.S. legislators, and the Vehicle Hull Protection Act was enacted as Chapter 13 of the Copyright Act. Under 17 U.S.C. § 1301, a sufficiently original design of a "vessel hull, including a plug or mold" can be protected from copying, even if it has a utilitarian function.

5.03   Functionality

IN RE MORTON-NORWICH PRODUCTS, INC.
United States Court of Customs and Patent Appeals
671 F.2d 1332 (1982)

RICH, JUDGE

This appeal is from the ex parte decision of the United States Patent and Trademark Office (PTO) Trademark Trial and Appeal Board (board), 209 U.S.P.Q. 437 (T.T.A.B. 1980), in application serial No. 123,548, filed April 21, 1977, sustaining the examiner's refusal to register appellant's container configuration on the principal register. We reverse the holding on "functionality" and remand for a determination of distinctiveness.

Appellant's application seeks to register the following container configuration as a trademark for spray starch, soil and stain removers, spray cleaners for household use, liquid household cleaners and general grease removers, and insecticides:

Appellant owns U.S. Design Patent 238,655, issued Feb. 3, 1976, on the above configuration, and U.S. Patent 3,749,290, issued July 31, 1973, directed to the mechanism in the spray top.

*   *   *

A trademark is defined as "any word, name, symbol, or device or any combination thereof adopted and used by a manufacturer or merchant *to identify his goods* and distinguish them from those manufactured or sold by others" (emphasis ours). 15 U.S.C. § 1127 (1976). Thus, it was long the rule that a trademark must be something other than, and separate from, the merchandise to which it is applied. . . .

Aside from the trademark/product "separateness" rationale for not recognizing the bare design of an article or its container as a trademark, it was theorized that all such designs would soon be appropriated, leaving nothing for use by would-be competitors. One court, for example, feared that "The forms and materials of packages to contain articles of merchandise . . . would be rapidly taken up and appropriated by dealers, until some one, bolder than the others, might go to the very root of things, and claim for his goods the primitive brown paper and tow string, as a peculiar property." *Harrington v. Libby*, 11 F. Cas. 605, 606 (C.C.S.D.N.Y.1877) (No. 6,107). *Accord, Diamond Match Co. v. Saginaw Match Co.*, 142 F. 727, 729–30 (6th Cir. 1906).

This limitation of permissible trademark subject matter later gave way to assertions that one or more features of a product or package design could legally function as a trademark. *E.g., Alan Wood Steel Co. v. Watson*, 150 F. Supp. 861, 863, 113 U.S.P.Q. 311, 312 (D.D.C. 1957); *Capewell Horse Nail Co. v. Mooney, supra.* It was eventually held that the entire design of an article (or its container) could, without other means of identification, function to identify the source of the article and be protected as a trademark. *E.g., In re Minnesota Mining and Manufacturing Co.*, 51 C.C.P.A. 1546, 1547–48, 335 F.2d 836, 837, 142 U.S.P.Q. 366, 367 (1964).

That protection was limited, however, to those designs of articles and containers, or features thereof, which were "nonfunctional." . . . This requirement of "nonfunctionality" is not mandated by statute, but "is deduced entirely from court decisions." *In re Mogen David Wine Corp.*, 51 C.C.P.A. 1260, 1269, 328 F.2d 925, 932, 140 U.S.P.Q. 575, 581 (1964) (Rich, J., concurring).* It has as its genesis the judicial theory that there exists a fundamental right to compete through imitation of a competitor's product, which right can only be *temporarily* denied by the patent or copyright laws:

> If one manufacturer should make an advance in effectiveness of operation, or in simplicity of form, or in utility of color; and if that advance did not entitle him to a monopoly by means of a machine or process or a product or a design patent; and if by means of unfair trade suits he could shut out other manufacturers who plainly intended to share in the benefits of unpatented utilities . . . he would be given gratuitously a monopoly more effective than that of the unobtainable patent in the ratio of eternity to seventeen years. [*Pope Automatic Merchandising Co. v. McCrum-Howell Co.*, 191 F. 979, 981–82 (7th Cir. 1911).] [Additional citations omitted.]

An exception to the right to copy exists, however, where the product or package design under consideration is "nonfunctional" and serves to identify its manufacturer or seller, and the exception exists even though the design is not temporarily protectible through acquisition of patent or copyright. Thus, when a design is "nonfunctional," the right to compete through imitation gives way, presumably upon balance of that right with the originator's right to prevent others from infringing upon an established symbol of trade identification.

This preliminary discussion leads to the heart of the matter — how do we define the concept of "functionality," and what role does the above balancing of interests play in that definitional process?

---

* Editor's Note: The Lanham Act has since been amended to expressly mandate nonfunctionality. See the Notes to this Section.

I. Functionality Defined

*   *   *

A. "Functional" means "utilitarian"

From the earliest cases, "functionality" has been expressed in terms of "utility." In 1930, this court stated it to be "well settled that the configuration of *an article having utility* is not the subject of trade-mark protection." (Emphasis ours.) *In re Dennison Mfg. Co.*, 39 F.2d 720, 721, 5 U.S.P.Q. 316, 317, 17 C.C.P.A. 987, 988 (1930) (Arbitrary urn or vase-like shape of reinforcing patch on a tag.). *Accord, Sparklets Corp. v. Walter Kidde Sales Co.*, 26 C.C.P.A. 1342, 1345; 104 F.2d 396, 399; 42 U.S.P.Q. 73, 76 (1939); *In re National Stone-Tile Corp.*, 57 F.2d 382, 383, 13 U.S.P.Q. 11, 12, 19 C.C.P.A. 1101, 1102 (1932). This broad statement of the "law," that the design of an article "having utility" cannot be a trademark, is incorrect and inconsistent with later pronouncements.

We wish to make it clear — in fact, we wish to characterize it as the *first* addition to the *Deister* "truisms" — that a discussion of "functionality" is *always* in reference to the *design* of the thing under consideration (in the sense of its appearance) and *not* the thing itself. One court, for example, paraphrasing Gertrude Stein, commented that "a dish is a dish is a dish." *Hygienic Specialties Co. v. H. G. Salzman, Inc.*, 302 F.2d 614, 621, 133 U.S.P.Q. 96, 103 (2^d Cir. 1962). No doubt, by definition, a dish always functions as a dish and has its utility, but it is the appearance of the dish which is important in a case such as this, as will become clear.

Assuming the *Dennison* court intended that its statement reference an article whose *configuration* "has utility," its statement is still too broad. Under that reasoning, the design of a particular article would be protectable as a trademark only where the design was useless, that is, wholly unrelated to the function of the article. For example, where a merchant sought to register on the supplemental register the overall configuration of a triangular chemical cake for use in a process of metal plating, this court stated that the shape was capable of becoming a trademark because it "is entirely arbitrary and, except for its solidity (*all* shapes being solid), has no functional significance whatever." *In re Minnesota Mining and Mfg. Co.*, 51 C.C.P.A. *supra* at 1551, 335 F.2d at 840, 142 U.S.P.Q. at 369.

Most designs, however, result in the production of articles, containers, or features thereof which are indeed utilitarian, and examination into the possibility of trademark protection is not to the mere *existence* of utility, but to the degree of *design* utility. The ore concentrating and coal cleaning table shape in *Deister*, for example, was refused registration as a trademark because its shape was "*in essence* utilitarian," 48 C.C.P.A. *supra* at 968, 289 F.2d at 506, 129 U.S.P.Q. at 322. Likewise, the design of a cast aluminum fitting for joining lengths of tubing together was denied registration because it was held to be "in essence utilitarian or functional." *In re Hollaender Mfg. Co.*, 511 F.2d 1186, 1189, 185 U.S.P.Q. 101, 103 (C.C.P.A. 1975). The configuration of a thermostat cover was also refused registration because a round cover was "probably the most utilitarian" design which could have been selected for a round mechanism. *In re Honeywell, Inc.*, 532 F.2d 180, 182, 189 U.S.P.Q. 343, 344 (C.C.P.A. 1976).

Thus, it is the "utilitarian" *design* of a "utilitarian" *object* with which we are concerned, and the manner of use of the term "utilitarian" must be examined at each occurrence. The latter occurrence is, of course, consistent with the lay meaning of the term. But the former is being used to denote a *legal consequence* (it being synonymous with "functional"), and it therefore requires further explication.

B. "Utilitarian" means "superior in function (de facto) or economy of manufacture," which "superiority" is determined in light of competitive necessity to copy

*   *   *

. . . [I]t is clear that courts in the past have considered the public policy involved in this area of the law as, not the *right* to slavishly copy articles which are not protected by patent or copyright, but the *need* to copy those articles, which is more properly termed the right to compete *effectively*. Even the earliest cases, which discussed protectability in terms of exhaustion of possible packaging forms, recognized that the real issue was whether "the effect would be to gradually throttle trade." *Harrington v. Libby, supra* at 606.

More recent cases also discuss "functionality" in light of competition. One court noted that the "question in each case is whether protection against imitation will hinder the competitor in competition."*Truck Equipment Service Co. v. Fruehauf Corp.*, 536 F.2d 1210, 1218, 191 U.S.P.Q. 79, 85 (8th Cir. 1976). Another court, upon suit for trademark infringement (the alleged trademark being plaintiff's building design), stated that "enjoining others from using the building design [would not] inhibit competition in any way." *Fotomat Corp. v. Cochran*, 437 F. Supp. 1231, 1235, 194 U.S.P.Q. 128, 131 (D. Kan. 1977). This court has also referenced "hinderance of competition" in a number of the "functionality" cases which have been argued before it.

II. Determining "Functionality"

A. In general

Keeping in mind, as shown by the foregoing review, that "functionality" is determined in light of "utility," which is determined in light of "superiority of design," and rests upon the foundation "essential to effective competition," *Ives Laboratories, Inc. v. Darby Drug Co.*, 601 F.2d 631, 643, 202 U.S.P.Q. 548, 558 (2[d] Cir. 1979), and cases cited *supra*, there exist a number of factors, both positive and negative, which aid in that determination.

Previous opinions of this court have discussed what evidence is useful to demonstrate that a particular design is "superior." In *In re Shenango Ceramics, Inc.*, 362 F.2d 287, 291, 150 U.S.P.Q. 115, 119, 53 C.C.P.A. 1268, 1273 (1966), the court noted that the existence of an expired utility patent which disclosed the *utilitarian advantage of the design* sought to be registered as a trademark was *evidence* that it was "functional." [Citations omitted]. It may also be significant that the originator of the design touts its utilitarian advantages through advertising. [Citations omitted].

Since the effect upon competition "is really the crux of the matter," it is, of course, significant that there are other alternatives available. Nims, *Unfair Competition and Trade-Marks* at 377. *Compare Time Mechanisms, Inc. v. Qonaar Corp.*, 422 F. Supp. 905, 913, 194 U.S.P.Q. 500, 506 (D.N.J. 1976) ("the parking meter mechanism can be contained by housings of many different configurations") *and In re World's Finest Chocolate, Inc.*, 474 F.2d 1012, 1014, 177 U.S.P.Q. 205, 206 (C.C.P.A. 1973) ("We think competitors can readily meet the demand for packaged candy bars by use of other packaging styles, and we find no utilitarian advantages flowing from this package design as opposed to others as was found in the rhomboidally-shaped deck involved in *Deister*.") *and In re Mogen David Wine Corp.*, C.C.P.A. *supra* at 1270, 328 F.2d at 933, 140 U.S.P.Q. at 581 (Rich, J., concurring. "Others can meet any real or imagined demand for wine in decanter-type bottles — assuming there is any such thing — without being in the least hampered in competition by inability to copy the Mogen David bottle design.") *and In re Minnesota Mining and Mfg. Co.*, 51 C.C.P.A. *supra* at 1551, 335 F.2d at 840, 142 U.S.P.Q. at 369 (It was noted to be an undisputed fact of record that the article whose design was sought to be registered "could be formed into almost any shape.") *and Fotomat Corp. v. Cochran*, 437 F. Supp. *supra* at 1235, 194 U.S.P.Q. at 131 (The court noted that the design of plaintiff's building functioned "no better than a myriad of other building designs.") *with In re Honeywell, Inc.*, 532 F.2d at 182, 189 U.S.P.Q. at 344 (A portion of the board opinion which the court adopted noted that there "are only so many basic shapes in which a thermostat or its cover can be made," but then concluded that, "That fact that thermostat covers may be produced in other forms or shapes does not and cannot detract from the functional character of the configuration here involved.").

It is also significant that a particular design results from a comparatively simple or cheap method of manufacturing the article. In *Schwinn Bicycle Co. v. Murray Ohio Mfg. Co.*, 339 F. Supp. 973, 980, 172 U.S.P.Q. 14, 19 (M.D. Tenn. 1971), *aff'd*, 470 F.2d 975, 176 U.S.P.Q. 161 (6th Cir. 1972), the court stated its reason for refusing to recognize the plaintiff's bicycle rim surface design as a trademark:

> The evidence is uncontradicted that the various manufacturers of bicycle rims in the United States consider it commercially necessary to mask, hide or camouflage the roughened and charred appearance resulting from welding the tubular rim sections together. The evidence represented indicates that the only other process used by bicycle rim manufacturers in the United States is the more complex and more expensive process of grinding and polishing.

[Citations omitted].

B. The case at bar

1. The evidence of functionality

We come now to the task of applying to the facts of this case the distilled essence of the body of law on "functionality" above discussed. The question is whether appellant's plastic spray bottle is de jure functional; is it the best or one of a few superior designs available? We hold, on the basis of the evidence before the board, that it is not.

The board thought otherwise but did not state a single supporting reason. In spite of her strong convictions about it, neither did the examiner. Each expressed mere opinions and it is not clear to us what either had in mind in using the terms "functional" and "utilitarian." Of course, the spray bottle is highly useful and performs its intended functions in an admirable way, but that is not enough to render the *design* of the spray bottle — which is all that matters here — functional.

As the examiner appreciated, the spray bottle consists of two major parts, a bottle and a trigger-operated, spray-producing pump mechanism which also serves as a closure. We shall call the latter the spray top. In the first place, a molded plastic bottle can have an infinite variety of forms or designs and still *function* to hold liquid. No one form is *necessary* or appears to be "superior." Many bottles have necks, to be grasped for pouring or holding, and the necks likewise can be in a variety of forms. The PTO has not produced one iota of evidence to show that the shape of appellant's bottle was *required* to be as it is for any de facto functional reason, which might lead to an affirmative determination of de jure functionality. The evidence, consisting of competitor's molded plastic bottles for similar products, demonstrates that the same functions can be performed by a variety of other shapes with no sacrifice of any functional advantage. There is no necessity to copy appellant's trade dress to enjoy any of the functions of a spray-top container.

As to the appearance of the spray top, the evidence of record shows that it too can take a number of diverse forms, all of which are equally suitable as housings for the pump and spray mechanisms. Appellant acquired a patent on the pump mechanism (No. 3,749,290) the drawings of which show it embodied in a structure which bears not the slightest resemblance to the appearance of appellant's spray top. The pictures of the competition's spray bottles further illustrate that no particular housing *design* is necessary to have a pump-type sprayer. Appellant's spray top, seen from the side, is rhomboidal, roughly speaking, a design which bears no relation to the shape of the pump mechanism housed within it and is an arbitrary decoration — no more de jure functional than is the grille of an automobile with respect to its under-the-hood power plant. The evidence shows that even the shapes of pump triggers can and do vary while performing the same function.

What is sought to be registered, however, is no single design feature or component but the overall composite design comprising both bottle and spray top. While that design must be *accommodated* to the functions performed, we see no evidence that it was *dictated* by them and resulted in a functionally or economically superior design of such a container.

Applying the legal principles discussed above, we do not see that allowing appellant to exclude others (upon proof of distinctiveness) from using this trade dress will hinder competition or impinge upon the rights of others to compete effectively in the sale of the goods named in the application, even to the extent of marketing them in *functionally* identical spray containers. The fact is that many others are doing so. Competitors have apparently had no need to simulate appellant's trade dress, in whole or in part, in order to enjoy all of the *functional* aspects of a spray top container. Upon expiration of any patent protection appellant may now be enjoying on its spray and pump mechanism, competitors may even copy and enjoy all of its functions without copying the external appearance of appellant's spray top.

If the functions of appellant's bottle can be performed equally well by containers of innumerable designs and, thus, no one is injured in competition, why did the board state that appellant's *design* is functional and for that reason not registrable?

2. *The relationship between "functionality" and distinctiveness*

*   *   *

The issues of distinctiveness and functionality may have been somewhat intermixed by the board. The design in issue appears to us to be relatively simple and plain, and the board, although not ruling upon appellant's contention that its design has acquired secondary meaning, discussed only distinctiveness before reaching its conclusion that the design was "functional." The unexpressed (and perhaps unconscious) thought may have been that if something is not inherently distinctive (appellant admits that its design is not), perhaps even austere, then, since it does not at a particular time function as a legally recognized indication of source, it probably never will. And since it is so plain that one may believe it is not and never will be a trademark, it will be perceived — not that the design is not inherently distinctive — but that it is "functional," without analysis of why it is believed to be "functional." The sole criterion seems to have been that the design is ordinary.

While it is certainly arguable that lack of distinctiveness may, where appropriate, permit an inference that a design was created primarily with an eye toward the utility of the *article*, that fact is by no means conclusive as to the "functionality" of the *design* of that article. Whether in fact the design is "functional" requires closer and more careful scrutiny. We cannot say that there exists an inverse proportional relationship in all cases between distinctiveness of design and functionality (de facto or de jure).

*   *   *

[Reversed and remanded on issue of distinctiveness or secondary meaning].

*   *   *

TRAFFIX DEVICES, INC. V. MARKETING DISPLAYS, INC.
532 U.S. 23 (2001)

Justice Kennedy

Temporary road signs with warnings like "Road Work Ahead" or "Left Shoulder Closed" must withstand strong gusts of wind. An inventor named Robert Sarkisian obtained two utility patents for a mechanism built upon two springs (the dual-spring design) to keep these and other outdoor signs upright despite adverse wind conditions. The holder of the now-expired Sarkisian patents, respondent Marketing Displays, Inc. (MDI), established a successful business in the manufacture and sale of sign stands incorporating the patented feature. MDI's stands for road signs were recognizable to buyers and users (it says) because the spring design was visible near the base of the sign.

This litigation followed after the patents expired and a competitor, TrafFix Devices, Inc., sold sign stands with a visible spring mechanism that looked like MDI's. MDI and TrafFix products looked alike because they were. When TrafFix started in business, it sent an MDI product abroad to have it reverse engineered, that is to say copied . . . .

*　*　*

It is well established that trade dress can be protected under federal law. The design or packaging of a product may acquire a distinctiveness which serves to identify the product with its manufacturer or source; and a design or package which acquires this secondary meaning, assuming other requisites are met, is a trade dress which may not be used in a manner likely to cause confusion as to the origin, sponsorship, or approval of the goods. In these respects protection for trade dress exists to promote competition. As we explained just last Term, *see Wal-Mart Stores, Inc. v. Samara Bothers, Inc.*, 529 U.S. 205, 120 S. Ct. 1339, 146 L. Ed. 2d 182 (2000), various Courts of Appeals have allowed claims of trade dress infringement relying on the general provision of the Lanham Act which provides a cause of action to one who is injured when a person uses "any word, term name, symbol, or device, or any combination thereof . . . which is likely to cause confusion as to the origin, sponsorship, or approval of his or her goods." 15 U.S.C. § 1125(a)(1)(A). Congress confirmed this statutory protection for trade dress by amending the Lanham Act to recognize the concept. Title 15 U.S.C. § 1125(a)(3) (1994 ed., Supp. V) provides: "In an action for trade dress infringement under this chapter for trade dress not registered on the principal register, the person who asserts trade dress protection has the burden of proving that the matter sought to be protected is not functional." This burden of proof gives force to the well-established rule that trade dress protection may not be claimed for product features that are functional. *Qualitex*, 514 U.S. at 164-165; *Two Pesos, Inc. v. Taco Cabana, Inc.*, 505 U.S. 763, 775, 112 S. Ct. 2753, 120 L. Ed. 2d 615 (1992). And in *Wal-Mart, supra*, we were careful to caution against misuse or over-extension of trade dress. We noted that "product design almost invariably serves purposes other than source identification." 529 U.S. at 213.

Trade dress protection must subsist with the recognition that in many instances there is no prohibition against copying goods and products. In general, unless an intellectual property right such as a patent or copyright protects an item, it will be subject to copying. As the Court has explained, copying is not always discouraged or disfavored by the laws which preserve our competitive economy. *Bonito Boats, Inc. v. Thunder Craft Boats, Inc.*, 489 U.S. 141, 160, 103 L. Ed. 2d 118, 109 Ct. 971 (1989). Allowing competitors to copy will have salutary effects in many instances. "Reverse engineering of chemical and mechanical articles in the public domain often leads to significant advances in technology." *Ibid.*

The principal question in this case is the effect of an expired patent on a claim of trade dress infringement. A prior patent, we conclude, has vital significance in resolving the trade dress claim. A utility patent is strong evidence that the features therein claimed are functional. If trade dress protection is sought for those features the strong evidence of functionality based on the previous patent adds great weight to the statutory presumption that features are deemed functional until proved otherwise by the party seeking trade dress protection. Where the expired patent claimed the features in question, one who seeks to establish trade dress protection must carry the heavy burden of showing that the feature is not functional, for instance by showing that it is merely an ornamental, incidental, or arbitrary aspect of the device.

In the case before us, the central advance claimed in the expired utility patents (the Sarkisian patents) is the dual-spring design; and the dual-spring design is the essential feature of the trade dress MDI now seeks to establish and to protect. The rule we have explained bars the trade dress claim, for MDI did not, and cannot, carry the burden of overcoming the strong evidentiary inference of functionality based on the disclosure of the dual-spring design in the claims of the expired patents.

The rationale for the rule that the disclosure of a feature in the claims of a utility patent constitutes strong evidence of functionality is well illustrated in this case. The dual-spring design serves the important purpose of keeping the sign upright even in heavy wind conditions; and, as confirmed by the statements in the expired patents, it does so in a useful manner. As the specification of one of the patents recites, prior art "devices, in practice, will topple under the force of a strong wind." U.S. Patent No. 3,662,482, col. 1. The dual-spring design allows sign stands to resist toppling in strong winds. Using a dual-spring design rather than a single spring achieves important operational advantages. For example, the specifications of the patents note that the "use of a pair of springs . . . as opposed to the use of a single spring to support the frame structure prevents canting or twisting of the sign around a vertical axis," and that, if not prevented, twisting "may cause damage to the spring structure and may result in tipping of the device." U.S. Patent No. 3,646,696, col. 3. In the course of patent prosecution, it was said that "the use of a pair of spring connections as opposed to a single spring connection . . . forms an important part of this combination" because it "forces the sign frame to tip along the longitudinal axis of the elongated ground-engaging members." App. 218. The dual-spring design affects the cost of the device as well; it was acknowledged that the device "could use three springs but this would unnecessarily increase the cost of the device." App. 217. These statements made in the patent applications and in the course of procuring the patents demonstrate the functionality of the design. MDI does not assert that any of these representations are mistaken or inaccurate, and this is further strong evidence of the functionality of the dual-spring design.

Inwood Test

. . . . Discussing trademarks, we have said " 'in general terms, a product feature is functional,' and cannot serve as a trademark, 'if it is essential to the use or purpose of the article or if it affects the cost or quality of the article.' " *Qualitex*, 514 U.S. at 165 (quoting *Inwood Laboratories, Inc. v. Ives Laboratories, Inc.*, 456 U.S. 844, 850, n. 10, 102 S. Ct. 2182, 72 L. Ed. 2d 606 (1982)). Expanding upon the meaning of this phrase, we have that a functional feature is one the "exclusive use of [which] would put competitors at a significant non-reputation-related disadvantage." 514 U.S. at 165. The Court of Appeals in the instant case seemed to interpret this language to mean that a necessary test for functionality is "whether the particular product configuration is a competitive necessity." 200 F.3d at 940. *See also Vornado*, 58 F.3d at 1507("Functionality, by contrast, has been defined both by our circuit, and more recently by the Supreme Court, in terms of competitive need"). This was incorrect as a comprehensive definition. As explained in *Qualitex, supra* and *Inwood, supra*, a feature is also functional when it is essential to the use or purpose of the device or when it affects the cost or quality of the device. The *Qualitex* decision did not purport to displace this traditional rule. Instead, it quoted the rule as *Inwood* had set it forth. It is proper to inquire into a "significant non-reputation-related disadvantage" in cases of aesthetic functionality, the question involved in *Qualitex*. Where the design is functional under the *Inwood* formulation there is no need to proceed further to consider if there is a competitive necessity for the feature. In *Qualitex*, by contrast, aesthetic functionality was the central question, there having been no indication that the green-gold color of the laundry press pad had any bearing on the use or purpose of the product or its cost of quality

The Court has allowed trade dress protection to certain product features that are inherently distinctive. *Two Pesos*, 505 U.S. at 774. In *Two Pesos*, however, the Court at the outset made the explicit analytic assumption that the trade dress features in question (decorations and other features to evoke a Mexican theme in a restaurant) were not functional. 505 U.S. at 767, n. 6. The trade dress in those cases did not bar competitors from copying functional product design features. In the instant case, beyond serving the purpose of informing consumers that the sign stands are made by MDI (assuming it does so), the dual-spring design provides a unique and useful mechanism to resist the force of the wind. Functionality having been established, whether MDI's dual-spring design has acquired secondary meaning need not be considered.

There is no need, furthermore, to engage, as did the Court of Appeals, in speculation about other design possibilities, such as using three or four springs which might serve the same purpose. 200 F.3d at 940. Here, the functionality of the spring design means that competitors need not explore whether other spring juxtapositions might be used. The dual-spring design is not an arbitrary flourish in the configuration of MDI's product; it is the reason the device works. Other designs need not be attempted.

Because the dual-spring design is functional, it is unnecessary for competitors to explore designs to hide the springs, say by using a box or framework to cover them, as suggested by the Court of Appeals. *Ibid.* The dual-spring design assures the user the device will work. If buyers are assured the product serves its purpose by seeing the operative mechanism that in itself serves an important market need. It would be at cross-purposes to those objectives, and something of a paradox, were we to require the manufacturer to conceal the very item the user seeks.

In a case where a manufacturer seeks to protect arbitrary, incidental, or ornamental aspects of features of a product found in the patent claims, such as arbitrary curves in the legs or an ornamental pattern painted on the springs, a different result might obtain. There the manufacturer could perhaps prove that those aspects do not serve a purpose within the terms of the utility patent. The inquiry into whether such features, asserted to be trade dress, are functional by reason of their inclusion in the claims of an expired utility patent could be aided by going beyond the claims and examining the patent and its prosecution history to see if the feature in question is shown as a useful part of the invention. No such claim is made here, however. MDI in essence seeks protection for the dual-spring design alone. The asserted trade dress consists simply of the dual-spring design, four legs, a base, an upright, and a sign. MDI has pointed to nothing arbitrary about the components of its device or the way they are assembled. The Lanham Act does not exist to reward manufacturers for their innovation in creating a particular device; that is the purpose of the patent law and its period of exclusivity. The Lanham Act, furthermore, does not protect trade dress in a functional design simply because an investment has been made to encourage the public to associate a particular functional feature with a single manufacturer or seller. The Court of Appeals erred in viewing MDI as possessing the right to exclude competitors from using a design identical to MDI's and to require those competitors to adopt a different design simply to avoid copying it. MDI cannot gain the exclusive right to produce sign stands using the dual-spring design by asserting that consumers associate it with the look of the invention itself. Whether a utility patent has expired or there has been no utility patent at all, a product design which has a particular appearance may be functional because it is "essential to the use or purpose of the article" or "affects the cost or quality of the article." *Inwood*, 456 U.S. at 850, n. 10.

TrafFix and some of its *amici* argue that the Patent Clause of the Constitution, Art. I, § 8, cl. 8, of its own force, prohibits the holder of an expired utility patent from claiming trade dress protection. Brief for Petitioner 33-36; Brief for Panduit Corp. as *Amicus Curiae* 3; Brief for Malla Pollack as *Amicus Curiae* 2. We need not resolve this question. If, despite the rule that functional features may not be the subject of trade dress protection, a case arises in which trade dress becomes the practical equivalent of an expired utility patent, that will be time enough to consider the matter. The judgment of the Court of Appeals is reversed, and the case is remanded for further proceedings consistent with this opinion.

It is so ordered.

Notes on Functionality

1. Assessing Functionality

What should be the test of functionality? Must a product shape or other trade dress be essentially or primarily utilitarian to be functional? *See Morton-Norwich, supra.* In *Warner Bros., Inc. v. Gay Toys, Inc.*, 724 F.2d 327, 331 (2ᵈ Cir. 1983), the court stated:

> The functionality defense . . . was developed to protect advances in functional design from being monopolized. It is designed to encourage competition and the broadest dissemination of useful design features. The question posed is whether by protecting the [plaintiff's] symbols we are creating an eternal monopoly on the shape or form of some useful object, thereby limiting the sharing of utilitarian refinements in useful objects.

See also Hartford House, Ltd. v. Hallmark Cards, Inc., 846 F.2d 1268, 1273 (10th Cir. 1988) ("the issue of functionality turns on whether protection of the *combination* [of elements] would hinder competition or impinge on the rights of others to compete effectively"); *Truck Equipment Service Co. v. Fruehauf Corp.*, 536 F.2d 1210, 1218 (8th Cir. 1976) ("The question in each case is whether protection against imitation will hinder the competitor in competition"); *Sicilia Di R. Biebow, supra*, 732 F.2d at 429 ("To achieve the status of "functional" a design or feature must be superior or optimal in terms of engineering, economy or manufacture, or accommodation of utilitarian function or performance"); *Deere & Co. v. Farmhand, Inc.*, 560 F. Supp. 85, 95 (S.D. Iowa 1982), *aff'd*, 721 F.2d 253 (8th Cir. 1983) (distinguishing *Fruehauf* as having found the feature functional because it was "based on sound engineering principles . . . [and chosen for its] utilitarian functionality").

In *W.T. Rogers, Inc. v. Keene*, 778 F.2d 334, 339 (7th Cir. 1985), the court explained functionality as follows:

> [A] functional feature is one which competitors would have to spend money not to copy but to design around, as they would have to do if they wanted to come up with a non-oval substitute for a football. It is something costly to do without (like the hood [of a car] itself), rather than costly to have (like the statue of Mercury [on the hood of a car]).

See also Incredible Techs. v. Virtual Techs., 400 F.3d 1007, 1011 (7th Cir. 2005) ("The video displays contain many common aspects of the game of golf. . . the trade dress is functional because something similar is essential to the use and play of the video game"); *Eco Mfg., LLC v. Honeywell Int'l, Inc.*, 357 F.3d 649 (7th Cir. 2003) (affirming preliminary finding that Honeywell's round thermostat shape was functional, in part because the round shape could reduce injuries and be easier to operate by people with disabilities); *Epic Metals Corp. v. Souliere*, 99 F.3d 1034 (11th Cir. 1996) (geometric shape of composite floor deck held functional because president's testimony extolled the shape as enhancing the strength of the deck sections); *Elmer v. ICC Fabricating*, 67 F.3d 1571, 1579-80 (Fed. Cir. 1995) (vehicle mounted advertising sign held functional because each of its constituent elements was functional and it was patented); *Merchant & Evans, Inc. v. Roosevelt Building Products Co.*, 963 F.2d 628 (3ᵈ Cir. 1992) (roofing seam design held functional where it improved watertightness and durability and was one of only two basic designs available on the market); *Woodsmith Pub. Co. v. Meredith Corp.*, 904 F.2d 1244 (8th Cir. 1990) (plaintiff's alleged how-to magazine trade dress, common to many publications in the field, summarily held functional); McDonald & Smith, *Proving Non-Functionality of Product Shapes: Honeywell Wins "Round II" on Thermostat Shape*, 79 T.M.R. 62 (1989). *Compare Tools USA & Equip. Co. v. Champ Frame Straightening Equip.*, 87 F.3d 654 (4ᵈ Cir. 1996) (upholding jury verdict for plaintiff; combination of elements in mail-order catalog non-functional where, though the information conveyed in the catalog was useful, competitors did not need to imitate plaintiff's presentation).

Some courts focused their inquiry on whether there were viable alternative designs in the marketplace. *See, e.g., Brandir Int'l, Inc. v. Cascade Pacific Lumber Co.*, 834 F.2d 1142, 1148 (2^d Cir. 1987); *Leatherman Tool Group, Inc. v. Cooper Industries Inc.*, 199 F.3d 1009, 1023 (9th Cir. 1999). ("Leatherman does not have rights under trade dress law to compel its competitors to resort to alternative designs which have a different set of advantages and disadvantages"; permanent injunction reversed).

The Supreme Court re-endorsed application of the *Inwood* test ("essential to the use or purpose or the article or affects the cost or quality of the article"), in assessing functionality in the *Traffix Devices* case excerpted above. It opined that "[w]here the design is functional under the *Inwood* formulation there is no need to proceed further to consider if there is a competitive necessity for the feature," and that in such a case, "speculation about other design possibilities" is unnecessary. This directive of *Traffix Devices* was applied in *Eppendorf-Netholer-Hinz GmbH v. Ritter GmbH*, 289 F.3d 251 (5th Cir. 2002), in which the designs of plaintiff's disposable pipette tips and certain dispenser syringes were held functional under the *Inwood* test. The Fifth Circuit did note that, if a functionality determination cannot be made under *Inwood*, then the competitive necessity test ("exclusive use . . . would put competitors at a significant non-reputation-related disadvantage") may be used. The Federal Circuit made a similar observation regarding the consideration of alternative designs in *Valu Engineering v. Dexnord Corp.*, 278 F.3d 1268, 1276 (Fed. Cir. 2002):

> Nothing in *Traffix* suggests that consideration of alternative designs is not properly part of the overall mix, and we do not read the Court's observations in *Traffix* as rendering the availability of alternative designs irrelevant. Rather, we conclude that the Court merely noted that once a product feature is found functional based on other considerations there is no need to consider the availability of alternative designs, because the feature cannot be given trade dress protection merely because there are alternative designs available. But that does not mean that the availability of alternative designs cannot be a legitimate source of evidence in the first place.

In the end, the Court in *Valu Engineering* affirmed that Valu's cross-sectional design for conveyor guide rails was functional. Its decision was based on the utilitarian advantages of the design and application of the *Morton-Norwich* factors, i.e. an abandoned utility patent application, advertising touting the utilitarian advantages of the design, available alternative designs dictated solely by function, and Valu's design resulting in "a comparatively simple or cheap method of manufacturing." The Federal Circuit similarly confirmed that the Supreme Court's *Traffix* decision does not alter the *Morton-Norwich* functionality analysis in *In re Bose Corp.*, 81 U.S.P.Q.2d 1748 (Fed. Cir. 2007). *See also Fuji Kogyo Co., Ltd. v. Pacific Bay Int'l, Inc.*, 461 F.3d 675 (6th Cir. 2006) (post-*Traffix* case applying *Morton-Norwich* factors in determining that design for fishing line guides was functional); *Clicks Billiards v. Sixshooters, Inc.*, 251 F.3d 252 (9th Cir. 2002) (reversing summary judgment for defendant where fact issues remained as to whether the overall image of plaintiff's pool hall was nonfunctional, distinctive and infringed, citing *Traffix Devices* and *Inwood*, but applying a *Morton-Norwich*– type of analysis). *Cf. Tie Tech, Inc. v. Kinedyne, Inc.*, 296 F.3d 778 (9th Cir. 2002) (design of "web-cutter" device used to release handicapped individuals from securement in emergencies was functional; "it is semantic trickery to say that there is still some sort of separate 'overall appearance' which is non-functional" and "there exists a fundamental right to compete through imitation of a competitor's product").

In *Talking Rain Beverage Co. v. South Beach Beverage Co.*, 349 F.3d 601 (9th Cir. 2003), the court applied a multifactor analysis combined with the Supreme Court's guidance in *Traffix* in concluding that plaintiff's registered bottle design was functional. Both parties' bottles "resemble a typical 'bike bottle' [having] smooth sides and a recessed grip area." In determining that plaintiff's design was functional, the court observed that: (1) plaintiff's "Get a Grip" advertising touted the utilitarian advantages of a recessed grip design; (2) both parties conceded that the grip feature gave the bottle structural support; as a consequence, "trademark law does not prohibit [defendant] from also using this efficient manufacturing process"; and (3) the bottle design provided utilitarian advantages, because the recessed grip fit easily into standard bicycle beverage holders. Finally, while the court noted that defendant "could have achieved the same functionality by adopting a bike bottle design other than the design embodied by [plaintiff's] trademark", it concluded that "under the Supreme Court's decision in *Traffix*, the mere existence of alternatives does not render a product nonfunctional." Similarly, in *Antioch Co. v. Western Trimming Corp.*, 347 F.3d 150 (6th Cir. 2003), the court noted *Traffix's* admonition that competitors need not "adopt a different design simply to avoid copying" functional product designs, in holding that plaintiff's padded, dual-hinged scrapbook design was functional. *See also Frosty Treats, Inc. v. Sony Computer Entm't Am., Inc.*, 426 F.3d 1001 (8th Cir. 2005) ("[t]here is no evidence that the exclusive use of the Safety Clown graphic [on the side of an ice cream truck] would deny Frosty Treats' competitors the ability to compete effectively or place competitors at any non-reputational disadvantage"; however, summary judgment for defendant was affirmed because confusion was unlikely); *Bretford Mfg. v. Smith Sys. Mfg. Co.*, 419 F.3d 576 (7th Cir. 2005) (plaintiff's v-shaped table leg was functional despite customers specifically asking for it; otherwise, "new entry would be curtailed unduly by the risk and expense of trademark litigation, for *every* introducer of a new design could make the same sort of claim").

Occasionally genericness principles are applied in trade dress cases. *See, e.g., Sunrise Jewelry Mfg. Corp. v. Fred S.A.*, 175 F.3d 1322 (Fed. Cir. 1999) (a product design or configuration can be generic under the Lanham Act's cancellation provision; remanded for determination of whether a "metallic nautical rope design" for clocks, watches and jewelry was generic); *Kendall-Jackson Winery Ltd. v. E & J Gallo Winery*, 150 F.3d 1042 (9th Cir. 1998) (design of grape leaf widely used in the industry had become a "generic emblem" for wines).

For many years functionality was not expressly included in the Lanham Act as a defense against an incontestably registered mark. *See, e.g., Shakespeare Co. v. Silstar Corp. of Am.*, 110 F.3d 234 (4th Cir. 1997), *cert. denied*, 522 U.S. 1046 (1998). That was changed by the Trademark Law Treaty Implementation Act of 1998, Pub. L. No. 105-330, 112 Stat. 3064. It amended the Lanham Act to expressly identify functionality as a defense to incontestability and a basis for opposition and cancellation in registration proceedings, and to give plaintiff the burden to prove that an unregistered trade dress is not functional. *See, e.g.*, 15 U.S.C. § 1125(a)(3).

On general issues of trade dress protection and the functionality doctrine, see MITCHELL, WADYKA, JACOBS & LEE, U.S. TRADE DRESS LAW (2007 ed.);LEVIN, TRADE DRESS PROTECTION (2007 ed,); Gleiberman, *From Fast Food to Fast Cars: Overbroad Protection of Product Trade Dress Under Section 43(a) of the Lanham Act*, 45 STAN. L. REV. 2037 (1993); DORR & MUNCH, PROTECTING TRADE DRESS (1997 ed.); Gifford, *The Interplay of Product Definition, Design and Trade Dress*, 75 MINN. L. REV. 769 (1991).

2. Design Patents

Because they have a different basis for protection than utilit patents, design patents have been held to raise a presumption of *non*-functionality. *See, e.g., Talking Rain Beverage v. South Beach Beverage Co.* above (plaintiff's design patent for its bike bottle design raises a presumption of nonfunctionality).

Can a configuration that has been or could have been the subject of a design patent be subject to trade dress protection? A number of courts have answered yes. *See Kohler Co. v. Moen, Inc.*, 12 F.3d 632 (7th Cir. 1993) (upholding T.T.A.B.'s decision to register trade dress of plaintiff's unpatented LEGEND faucet design); *Ferrari S.p.A. Esercizio Fabriche Automobile E Corse v. Roberts*, 944 F.2d 1235, 1240 (6th Cir. 1991), *cert. denied*, 505 U.S. 1219 (1992) (protecting the trade dress of plaintiff's unpatented

FERRARI sports car design and noting that "[c]ourts have consistently rejected [the] . . . argument that the availability of design patent protection precludes . . . Lanham Act [trade dress protection]"); *Winning Ways, Inc. v. Holloway Sportswear, Inc.*, 903 F. Supp. 1457 (D. Kan. 1995) (denying defendant's motion for summary judgment; prior design patent for plaintiff's jacket design does not preclude trade dress protection for jacket features); *Hubbell Inc. v. Pass & Seymour, Inc.*, 883 F. Supp. 955 (S.D.N.Y. 1995) (denying defendant's motion to dismiss plaintiff's trade dress infringement claim for its plugs and connectors; "the expiration of the design patent does not preclude a party from seeking [trade dress] protection"). *Cf. W.T. Rogers v. Keene*, 778 F.2d 334, 337 (7th Cir. 1985) (upholding special jury verdict finding plaintiff's unpatented tray design functional, but noting that "the courts that have considered the issue have concluded, rightly in our view, that [the design patent provision] does not prevent the enforcement of a common law trademark in a design feature").

Design patent protection has one advantage over trade dress protection: secondary meaning is not required. However, "[d]esign patent protection is very narrow, covering only what is shown in the drawings in the patent." *U. Hartco Engineering, Inc. v. Wang Int'l, Inc.*, 142 Fed Appx. 455 (Fed. Cir. 2005). Trade dress protection, extending to where confusion or dilution (see Chapter 8) is likely, may be broader, and is not limited to a statutory term. *See also Lawman Armor Corp. v. Winner Int'l, LLC*, 437 F.3d 1383 (Fed. Cir. 2006) (finding no design patent infringement because the alleged "points of novelty" were disclosed in the prior art).

Third party design patents for similar designs may be probative as to the lack of distinctiveness of an allegedly protectable trade dress. In *In re Pacer Tech*, 338 F.3d 1348 (Fed. Cir. 2003), several design patents for container cap designs similar to the applicant's were considered evidence of a lack of distinctiveness. Relevant factors included "whether [the design] was a 'common' basic shape or design, whether it was unique or unusual in a particular field." and "whether it was capable of creating a commercial impression distinct from the accompanying words." Here, the other design patents for similar cap designs created a prima facie case that the applied for design was not "unique or unusual" in the field that was not rebutted. "Pacer could successfully rebut the prima facie case, for example, with evidence showing that the container caps shown in the design patents were not actually being sold in the relevant market," but had not done so.

3. Pharmaceutical Cases

A number of generic drug cases involving the practice of copying the capsule size, shape and color of prescription drugs have also presented a legal forum for addressing trade dress and functionality issues under § 43(a). In *Ives Laboratories, Inc. v. Darby Drug Co.*, 488 F. Supp. 394 (E.D.N.Y. 1980), a generic drug manufacturer was sued under § 43(a) for allegedly copying the capsule colors used by the plaintiff, a brand name manufacturer of a similar drug. The plaintiff sued in the alternative for contributory infringement, alleging that the similarity in appearance caused pharmacists to mislabel defendant's generic drug with plaintiff's registered trademark. The district court held there was no § 43(a) violation in the copying of functional drug capsule colors. The functionality was said to lie in the reliance patients, doctors, hospitals, wholesalers and pharmacies placed on colors in determining correct drug and dosage. The court also found that the defendant was not liable for contributory infringement. The Court of Appeals subsequently reversed the latter holding, concluding that the district court had failed to give sufficient weight to plaintiff's evidence of a "pattern of illegal substitution and mislabeling in New York . . ." *Ives Laboratories, Inc. v. Darby Drug Co.*, 638 F.2d 538, 543 (2d Cir. 1981).

Addressing, on certiorari, the issue of contributory infringement, Justice O'Connor stated the general rule:

[I]f a manufacturer or distributor intentionally induces another to infringe a trademark, or if it continues to supply its product to one whom it knows or has reason to know is engaging in trademark infringement, the manufacturer or distributor is contributorily responsible for any harm done as a result of the deceit.

Inwood Laboratories, supra, 456 U.S. at 854. Finding that the Court of Appeals had substituted its own interpretation of the evidence for that of the lower court without adequate justification, and that the trial court's findings on the issues were not clearly erroneous, the Supreme Court reversed the Court of Appeals' holding with directions that the appellate court consider on remand the district court's decision regarding plaintiff's § 43(a) claim. That holding of no § 43(a) violation was later affirmed by the Court of Appeals in an unpublished memorandum, reproduced at 71 TRADEMARK REP. 117 (1982), with the appellate court expressly declining to grant the decision future *stare decisis* effect. *See also An Analysis of the Ives Case: A TMR Panel* (Kranzow, McCarthy, Palladino, Pattishall, Swann), 72 TRADEMARK REP. 118 (1982).

In *SK&F Co. v. Premo Pharmaceutical Laboratories,* 625 F.2d 1055 (3ᵈ Cir. 1980), the Third Circuit preliminarily enjoined such copying under § 43(a). The court concluded (at page 1064) that the copied shape and color scheme had "nothing to do with the purpose or performance of the drug, or with its processing. The only value of the trade dress was in identifying the goods with their source . . . ." It further concluded that defendant intended that its product would be associated with plaintiff's and that it acted with the awareness that unscrupulous pharmacists would pass off defendant's product as plaintiff's. Similar § 43(a) violations were found in *Ciba-Geigy Corp. v. Balor Pharmaceutical Co.,* 747 F.2d 844 (3ᵈ Cir. 1984); *Par Pharmaceutical, Inc. v. Searle Pharmaceuticals, Inc.,* 227 U.S.P.Q. 1024 (N.D. Ill. 1985); *A.H. Robins Co. v. Medicine Chest Corp.,* 206 U.S.P.Q. 1015 (E.D. Mo. 1980), and *Boehringer Ingelhein G.m.b.H. v. Pharmadyne Laboratories,* 532 F. Supp. 1040 (D.N.J. 1980). *Compare Shire U.S., Inc. v. Barr Labs, Inc.,* 329 F.3d 348 (3ᵈ Cir. 2003), affirming a denial of preliminary relief on functionality grounds. Defendant sold a generic equivalent of plaintiff's prescription stimulant used in treating attention deficit hyperactivity disorder (ADHD). Defendant imitated the shape and colors of plaintiff's tablets, although with some differences in the shape and markings. The appellate court observed that, "we have the benefit of the Supreme Court's most recent decisions which caution against the over-extension of trade dress protection." The district court's conclusion, based on expert testimony, that "the similarity in tablet appearance enhances patient safety by promoting psychological acceptance" was upheld, and it "did not clearly err in finding that plaintiff had failed to show that its product configuration was non-functional." *See also* McGough, *Reassessing the Protectability of Prescription and OTC Drug Trade Dress,* 81 TRADEMARK REP. 255 (1991); and the discussion on Contributory Infringement in Chapter 6.

4. Expired Utility Patents

Would it be better to have a bright line rule precluding trade dress protection for a product configuration disclosed in an expired utility patent? *See* Geremia, *Protecting the Right to Copy: Trade Dress Claims for Configurations in Expired Utility Patents,* 92 Nw. U. L. REV. 2 (1998), in which the author contends that the doctrine of functionality "no longer adequately works to preclude the subject matter of expired utility patents from trade dress protection," and that such a bright line rule is needed. *Compare* Mohr, *At the Interface of Patent and Trademark Law: Should a Product Configuration Disclosed in a Utility Patent Ever Quality for Trade Dress Protection?,* 19 HASTINGS COMM. & ENT. L. J. 339 (1997), also advocating a strict rule precluding trade dress protection for any feature or configuration disclosed anywhere in a patent, so that the public gets the benefit of its bargain under patent law.

The Supreme Court clarified the role of expired utility patents in *TrafFix Devices, Inc. v. Marketing Devices, Inc., supra.* Justice Kennedy for a unanimous court noted, among other things, that under Section 43(a)(3) of the Lanham Act, a person who asserts protection for unregistered trade dress "has the burden of proving that the matter sought to be protected is not functional," and that in the Court's *Wal-Mart v. Samara* decision, the Court had cautioned against "misuse or over-extension of trade dress." Similary, in *Bonito Boats, Inc. v. Thunder Craft Boats, Inc.*, 489 U.S. 141, 160 (1989), the Court had observed that in many instances the copying of a product design is not prohibited and may benefit the public.

Against this background, the *TrafFix* Court concluded that an expired utility patent has "vital significance in resolving the trade dress claim," and "is strong evidence that the features therein claimed are functional." This "adds great weight to the statutory presumption that features are deemed functional until proved otherwise." In that case the plaintiff failed to overcome the presumption, and its dual-spring traffic sign design was held functional.

5. Aesthetic Functionality

THE RESTATEMENT (THIRD) OF UNFAIR COMPETITION § 17 (1995) defines aesthetic functionality as follows:

> A design is functional because of its aesthetic value only if it confers a significant benefit that cannot be duplicated by the use of alternative designs. Because of the difficulties inherent in evaluating the aesthetic superiority of a particular design, a finding of aesthetic functionality generally will be made only when objective evidence indicates a lack of adequate alternative designs. Such evidence typically exists only when the range of adequate alternative designs is limited by either the nature of the design feature or the basis of its aesthetic appeal. The ultimate test of functionality, as with utilitarian designs, is whether the recognition of trademark rights would significantly hinder competition.

The Supreme Court cited the RESTATEMENT (THIRD) in *Qualitex v. Jacobson Products Co., Inc.*, 514 U.S. 159 (1995) (holding that color alone may serve as a protectable trademark), in giving a qualified endorsement to application of the aesthetic functionality doctrine "when, and if, the circumstances of a particular case threaten 'color depletion,' " i.e., if the depletion of available colors in that market would mean that protection would hinder competition. In *Traffix Devices, Inc. v. Marketing Displays, Inc.*, supra, the Supreme Court reiterated that it is proper to inquire whether trade dress protection of a design feature "would put competitors at a significant non-reputation-related disadvantage" in an aesthetic functionality case, quoting from its *Qualitex* decision.

In *Keene Corp. v. Paraflex Industries, Inc.*, 653 F.2d 822, 825 (3^d Cir. 1981), the court stated that "The difficulty with . . . a broad view of aesthetic functionality . . . is that it provides a disincentive for development of imaginative and attractive design. The more appealing the design, the less protection it would receive." Nonetheless, the court held the district court was not clearly erroneous in finding that plaintiff's distinctive, source-indicating design for its outdoor wall-mounted luminaire was so compatible architecturally with modern structures that the court could not grant a trademark monopoly without stifling competition. The appellate court referred to the limited number of such designs for a luminaire as distinguishing the factual situation from "the selection of a wine bottle or ashtray design." *Keene Corp.*, 653 F.2d at 827. *Followed: Standard Terry Mills, Inc. v. Shen Mfg. Co.*, 803 F.2d 778, 781 (3^d Cir. 1986) (weave and check pattern of plaintiff's kitchen towel served to make it "strong, durable and compatible with contemporary kitchen decor" and was therefore functional). *See also H. Hi. Ltd. Partnership v. Winghouse of Fla, Inc.*, 451 F.3d 1300 (11th Cir. 2006) (key elements of Hooters servers' outfits, e.g. white tank tops and orange running shorts, designed to help the servers "titillate, entice and arouse," were functional and unprotectable against defendant's outfits with black tank tops and black running shorts); *Publications Int'l Ltd. v. Landoll, Inc.*, 164 F.3d 337 (7th Cir. 1998) (affirming summary judgment for defendant; plaintiff's cookbook trade dress, comprised of "the [large] size of the pages, the gilded edges of the pages, and the covers, which are oilcloth or the equivalent", was entirely functional, and the gold color of the gilding was "a prime example of aesthetic functionality"); *Schwinn Bicycle Co. v. Ross Bicycles, Inc.*, 870 F.2d 1176, 1191 (7th th Cir. 1989) (reversing preliminary injunction grant for failure to properly consider aesthetic functionality defense; "there may come a point where the design feature is so important to the value of the product to consumers that continued trademark protection would deprive them of competitive alternatives"); and *Deere & Co.*, supra, where, because farmers like to match the color of separately bought loaders with the color of their tractors, plaintiff's "John Deere green" color was found aesthetically functional and copying of it permissible, despite the secondary meaning the color had acquired.

Compare Au-Tomotive Gold, Inc. v. Volkswagen of Am., Inc., 457 F.3d 1062 (9th Cir. 2006) (famous Volkswagen and Audi marks as used on defendant's key chains, license plate frames and related goods were not aesthetically functional; "[a]ny disadvantage Auto Gold claims in not being able to sell [the branded products] is tied to the reputation and association with Volkswagen and Audi"); and *Sicilia Di R. Biebow & Co. v. Cox.*, 732 F.2d 417 (5th Cir. 1984), where the case was remanded after the lower court used too broad a definition of aesthetic functionality, i.e., "an important ingredient in the commercial success of" a product. *See generally* Wong, *The Aesthetic Functionality Doctrine and the Law of Trade Dress*, 83 Cornell L. Rev. 1116 (1998); Harriman, *Aesthetic Functionality: The Disarray Among Modern Courts*, 86 Trademark Rep. 276 (1996); Gilson § 2A.04 (2008 ed.).

In *Knitwaves Inc. v. Lollytogs Ltd.*, 71 F.3d 996 (2[d] Cir. 1995), the court found that a knitted sweater design was not aesthetically functional because the defendant failed to establish that the plaintiff's exclusive use of the design foreclosed the relevant market. However, because the plaintiff adopted the design for aesthetic purposes, the court held that the design did not serve "primarily as a designator of origin" and, thus, was not protectable trade dress under § 43(a). *Compare Abercrombie & Fitch Stores, Inc. v. American Eagle Outfitters, Inc.*, 280 F.3d 619 (6th Cir. 2002), in which certain sport symbols on clothing were held aesthetically functional. The court reasoned that protecting "suggestive symbols like lacrosse sticks and the ski patrol cross on clothing [used] to convey the product's athletic nature or capacity to invoke images of athleticism . . . would deny consumers the benefits of a competitive market . . . [t]hese design features are something that other producers of [casual clothing] have to have as part of the product in order to be able to compete effectively in the market". Competitors had only "a limited range of sports and sporting equipment to choose from in attempting to convey this idea in this manner of clothing". Arguably, in that case widespread third party use of such symbols would have prevented their indicating a single source in any event, but in an instance where third party use is not widespread, resort to the theory of aesthetic functionality may be necessary.

In *Wallace Int'l Silversmiths, Inc. v. Godinger Silver Art Co.*, 916 F.2d 76 (2[d] Cir. 1990), *cert. denied*, 499 U.S. 976 (1991), the court held that elements such as scrolls and flowers in plaintiff's GRANDE BAROQUE silverware were aesthetically functional and necessary to a competitor in the Baroque silverware market. Only plaintiff's "precise expression" could be protected; otherwise it would obtain an unlawful monopoly on a decorative style. *Id.* at 80-81. *Compare Godinger Silver Art Co. v. International Silver Co.*, 37 U.S.P.Q.2d 1453, 1454-55, 1458 & n.3 (S.D.N.Y. 1995) (granting preliminary injunction against defendant's infringement of plaintiff's *copyright* in its 20th CEN-TURY BAROQUE silverware, the same silverware unsuccessfully alleged to infringe the *Wallace* plaintiff's trade dress).

5.04 Distinctiveness

TWO PESOS, INC. v. TACO CABANA, INC.
United States Supreme Court
505 U.S. 763 (1992)

WHITE, JUSTICE

The issue in this case is whether the trade dress[1] of a restaurant may be protected under § 43(a) of the Trademark Act of 1946 (Lanham Act), 60 Stat. 441, 15 U.S.C. § 1125(a) (1982 ed.), based on a finding of inherent distinctiveness, without proof that the trade dress has secondary meaning.

I.

Respondent Taco Cabana, Inc., operates a chain of fast-food restaurants in Texas. The restaurants serve Mexican food. The first Taco Cabana restaurant was opened in San Antonio in September 1978, and five more restaurants had been opened in San Antonio by 1985. Taco Cabana describes its Mexican trade dress as:

> "a festive eating atmosphere having interior dining and patio areas decorated with artifacts, bright colors, paintings and murals. The patio includes interior and exterior areas with the interior patio capable of being sealed off from the outside patio by overhead garage doors. The stepped exterior of the building is a festive and vivid color scheme using top border paint and neon stripes. Bright awnings and umbrellas continue the theme." 932 F.2d 1113, 1117 (CA 5 1991).

In December 1985, a Two Pesos, Inc. restaurant was opened in Houston. Two Pesos adopted a motif very similar to the foregoing description of Taco Cabana's trade dress. Two Pesos restaurants expanded rapidly in Houston and other markets, but did not enter San Antonio. In 1986, Taco Cabana entered the Houston and Austin markets and expanded into other Texas cities, including Dallas and El Paso where Two Pesos was also doing business.

In 1987, Taco Cabana sued Two Pesos in the United States District Court for the Southern District of Texas for trade dress infringement under § 43(a) of the Lanham Act, 15 U.S.C. § 1125(a) (1982 ed.), and for theft of trade secrets under Texas common law. The case was tried to a jury, which was instructed to return its verdict in the form of answers to five questions propounded by the trial judge. The jury's answers were: Taco Cabana has a trade dress; taken as a whole, the trade dress is nonfunctional; the trade dress is inherently distinctive;[2] the trade dress has not acquired a secondary meaning[4] in the Texas market; and the alleged infringement creates a likelihood of

---

[1] The District Court instructed the jury: " '[T]rade dress' is the total image of the business. Taco Cabana's trade dress may include the shape and general appearance of the exterior of the restaurant, the identifying sign, the interior kitchen floor plan, the decor, the menu, the equipment used to serve food, the servers' uniforms and other features reflecting on the total image of the restaurant." 1 App. 83–84. The Court of Appeals accepted this definition and quoted from *Blue Bell Bio-Medical v. Cinbad, Inc.*, 864 F.2d 1253, 1256 (CA 5 1989): "The 'trade dress' of a product is essentially its total image and overall appearance." *See* 932 F.2d 1113, 1118 (CA5 1991). It "involves the total image of a product and may include features such as size, shape, color or color combinations, texture, graphics, or even particular sales techniques." *John H. Harland Co. v. Clarke Checks, Inc.*, 711 F.2d 966, 980 (CA11 1983). Restatement (Third) of Unfair Competition § 16, Comment *a* (Tent. Draft No. 2, Mar. 23, 1990).

[2] The instructions were that to be found inherently distinctive, the trade dress must not be descriptive.

[4] Secondary meaning is used generally to indicate that a mark or dress "has come through use to be uniquely associated with a specific source." Restatement (Third) of Unfair Competition § 13, Comment *e* (Tent. Draft No. 2, Mar. 23, 1990). "To establish secondary meaning, a manufacturer must show that, in the minds of the public, the primary significance of a product feature or term is to identify the source of the product

confusion on the part of ordinary customers as to the source or association of the restaurant's goods or services. Because, as the jury was told, Taco Cabana's trade dress was protected if it either was inherently distinctive or had acquired a secondary meaning, judgment was entered awarding damages to Taco Cabana. In the course of calculating damages, the trial court held that Two Pesos had intentionally and deliberately infringed Taco Cabana's trade dress.[5]

The Court of Appeals ruled that the instructions adequately stated the applicable law and that the evidence supported the jury's findings. In particular, the Court of Appeals rejected petitioner's argument that a finding of no secondary meaning contradicted a finding of inherent distinctiveness.

*   *   *

We granted certiorari to resolve the conflict among the Courts of Appeals on the question whether trade dress which is inherently distinctive is protectable under § 43(a) without a showing that it has acquired secondary meaning. 502 U.S. —, 112 S. Ct. 964 (1992). We find that it is, and we therefore affirm.

*   *   *

Petitioner argues that the jury's finding that the trade dress has not acquired a secondary meaning shows conclusively that the trade dress is not inherently distinctive. Brief for Petitioner 9. The Court of Appeals' disposition of this issue was sound:

> Two Pesos' argument — that the jury finding of inherent distinctiveness contradicts its finding of no secondary meaning in the Texas market — ignores the law in this circuit. While the necessarily imperfect (and often prohibitively difficult) methods for assessing secondary meaning address the empirical question of current consumer association, the legal recognition of an inherently distinctive trademark or trade dress acknowledges the owner's legitimate proprietary interest in its unique and valuable informational device, regardless of whether substantial consumer association yet bestows the additional empirical protection of secondary meaning. 932 F.2d, at 1120, n. 7.

Although petitioner makes the above argument, it appears to concede elsewhere in its briefing that it is possible for a trade dress, even a restaurant trade dress, to be inherently distinctive and thus eligible for protection under § 43(a). Brief for Petitioner 10–11, 17–18; Reply Brief for Petitioner 10–14. Recognizing that a general requirement of secondary meaning imposes "an unfair prospect of theft [or] financial loss" on the developer of fanciful or arbitrary trade dress at the outset of its use, petitioner suggests that such trade dress should receive limited protection without proof of secondary meaning. Reply Brief for Petitioner 10. Petitioner argues that such protection should be only temporary and subject to defeasance when over time the dress has failed to acquire a secondary meaning. This approach is also vulnerable for the reasons given by the Court of Appeals. If temporary protection is available from the earliest use of the trade dress, it must be because it is neither functional nor descriptive but an inherently distinctive dress that is capable of identifying a particular source of the product. Such a trade dress, or mark, is not subject to copying by concerns that have an equal opportunity to choose their own inherently distinctive trade dress. To terminate protection for failure to gain secondary meaning over some unspecified time could not be based on the failure of the dress to retain its fanciful, arbitrary, or suggestive nature, but on the failure of the user of the dress to be successful enough in the marketplace. This

---

rather than the product itself." *Inwood Laboratories, Inc. v. Ives Laboratories, Inc.*, 456 U.S. 844, 851, n. 11 (1982).

[5] The Court of Appeals agreed: "The weight of the evidence persuades us, as it did Judge Singleton, that Two Pesos brazenly copied Taco Cabana's successful trade dress, and proceeded to expand in a manner that foreclosed several important markets within Taco Cabana's natural zone of expansion." 932 F.2d at 1127, n. 20.

is not a valid basis to find a dress or mark ineligible for protection. The user of such a trade dress should be able to maintain what competitive position it has and continue to seek wider identification among potential customers.

*   *   *

It would be a different matter if there were textual basis in § 43(a) for treating inherently distinctive verbal or symbolic trademarks differently from inherently distinctive trade dress. But there is none. The section does not mention trademarks or trade dress, whether they be called generic, descriptive, suggestive, arbitrary, fanciful, or functional. Nor does the concept of secondary meaning appear in the text of § 43(a). Where secondary meaning does appear in the statute, 15 U.S.C. § 1052 (1982 ed.), it is a requirement that applies only to merely descriptive marks and not to inherently distinctive ones. We see no basis for requiring secondary meaning for inherently distinctive trade dress protection under § 43(a) but not for other distinctive words, symbols, or devices capable of identifying a producer's product.

Engrafting onto § 43(a) a requirement of secondary meaning for inherently distinctive trade dress also would undermine the purposes of the Lanham Act. Protection of trade dress, no less than of trademarks, serves the Act's purpose to "secure to the owner of the mark the goodwill of his business and to protect the ability of consumers to distinguish among competing producers. National protection of trademarks is desirable, Congress concluded, because trademarks foster competition and the maintenance of quality by securing to the producer the benefits of good reputation." *Park'N Fly*, 469 U.S., at 198, citing S. Rep. No. 1333, 79th Cong., 2d Sess., 3–5 (1946) (citations omitted). By making more difficult the identification of a producer with its product, a secondary meaning requirement for a nondescriptive trade dress would hinder improving or maintaining the producer's competitive position.

Suggestions that under the Fifth Circuit's law, the initial user of any shape or design would cut off competition from products of like design and shape are not persuasive. Only nonfunctional, distinctive trade dress is protected under § 43(a). The Fifth Circuit holds that a design is legally functional, and thus unprotectable, if it is one of a limited number of equally efficient options available to competitors and free competition would be unduly hindered by according the design trademark protection. *See Sicilia Di R. Biebow & Co. v. Cox*, 732 F.2d 417, 426 (CA 5 1984). This serves to assure that competition will not be stifled by the exhaustion of a limited number of trade dresses.

On the other hand, adding a secondary meaning requirement could have anticompetitive effects, creating particular burdens on the start-up of small companies. It would present special difficulties for a business, such as respondent, that seeks to start a new product in a limited area and then expand into new markets. Denying protection for inherently distinctive nonfunctional trade dress until after secondary meaning has been established would allow a competitor, which has not adopted a distinctive trade dress of its own, to appropriate the originator's dress in other markets and to deter the originator from expanding into and competing in these areas.

As noted above, petitioner concedes that protecting an inherently distinctive trade dress from its inception may be critical to new entrants to the market and that withholding protection until secondary meaning has been established would be contrary to the goals of the Lanham Act. Petitioner specifically suggests, however, that the solution is to dispense with the requirement of secondary meaning for a reasonable, but brief, period at the outset of the use of a trade dress. Reply Brief for Petitioner 11–12. If § 43(a) does not require secondary meaning at the outset of a business' adoption of trade dress, there is no basis in the statute to support the suggestion that such a requirement comes into being after some unspecified time.

III

We agree with the Court of Appeals that proof of secondary meaning is not required to prevail on a claim under § 43(a) of the Lanham Act where the trade dress at issue is inherently distinctive, and accordingly the judgment of that court is affirmed.

WAL-MART STORES, INC. v. SAMARA BROTHERS, INC.
529 U.S. 205 (2000)

JUSTICE SCALIA delivered the opinion of the Court.

In this case, we decide under what circumstances a product's design is distinctive, and therefore protectible, in an action for infringement of unregistered trade dress under § 43(a) of the Trademark Act of 1946 (Lanham Act), 60 Stat. 441, as amended, 15 U.S.C. § 1125(a).

I

Respondent Samara Brothers, Inc., designs and manufactures children's clothing. Its primary product is a line of spring/summer one-piece seersucker outfits decorated with appliqués of hearts, flowers, fruits, and the like. A number of chain stores, including JCPenney, sell this line of clothing under contract with Samara.

Petitioner Wal-Mart Stores, Inc., is one of the nation's best known retailers, selling among other things children's clothing. In 1995, Wal-Mart contracted with one of its suppliers, Judy-Philippine, Inc., to manufacture a line of children's outfits for sale in the 1996 spring/summer season. Wal-Mart sent Judy-Philippine photographs of a number of garments from Samara's line, on which Judy-Philippine's garments were to be based; Judy-Philippine duly copied, with only minor modifications, 16 of Samara's garments, many of which contained copyrighted elements. In 1996, Wal-Mart briskly sold the so-called knockoffs, generating more than $1.15 million in gross profits.

In June 1996, a buyer for JCPenney called a representative at Samara to complain that she had seen Samara garments on sale at Wal-Mart for a lower price than JCPenney was allowed to charge under its contract with Samara. The Samara representative told the buyer that Samara did not supply its clothing to Wal-Mart. Their suspicions aroused, however, Samara officials launched an investigation, which disclosed that Wal-Mart and several other major retailers — Kmart, Caldor, Hills, and Goody's — were selling the knockoffs of Samara's outfits produced by Judy-Philippine.

After sending cease-and-desist letters, Samara brought this action in the United States District Court for the Southern District of New York against Wal-Mart, Judy-Philippine, Kmart, Caldor, Hills, and Goody's for copyright infringement under federal law, consumer fraud and unfair competition under New York law, and — most relevant for our purposes — infringement of unregistered trade dress under § 43(a) of the Lanham Act, 15 U.S.C. § 1125(a). All of the defendants except Wal-Mart settled before trial.

After a weeklong trial, the jury found in favor of Samara on all of its claims. Wal-Mart then renewed a motion for judgment as a matter of law, claiming, *inter alia*, that there was insufficient evidence to support a conclusion that Samara's clothing designs could be legally protected as distinctive trade dress for purposes of § 43(a). The District Court denied the motion, 969 F. Supp. 895 (SDNY 1997), and awarded Samara damages, interest, costs, and fees totaling almost $1.6 million, together with injunctive relief, *see* App. to Pet. for Cert. 56-58. The Second Circuit affirmed the denial of the motion for judgment as a matter of law, 165 F.3d 120 (1998), and we granted certiorari, 528 U.S. (1999).

II

The Lanham Act provides for the registration of trademarks, which it defines in § 45 to include "any word, name, symbol, or device, or any combination thereof [used or intended to be used] to identify and distinguish [a producer's] goods . . . from those manufactured or sold by others and to indicate the source of the goods. . . ." 15 U.S.C. § 1127. Registration of a mark under § 2 of the Act, 15 U.S.C. § 1052, enables the owner to sue an infringer under § 32, 15 U.S.C. § 1114; it also entitles the owner to a presumption that its mark is valid, *see* § 7(b), 15 U.S.C. § 1057(b), and ordinarily renders the registered mark incontestable after five years of continuous use, see § 15, 15 U.S.C. § 1065. In addition to protecting registered marks, the Lanham Act, in § 43(a), gives a producer a cause of action for the use by any person of "any word, term, name, symbol, or device, or any combination thereof . . . which. . . is likely to cause confusion. . . as to the origin, sponsorship, or approval of his or her goods. . . ." 15 U.S.C. § 1125(a). It is the latter provision that is at issue in this case.

The breadth of the definition of marks registrable under § 2, and of the confusion-producing elements recited as actionable by § 43(a), has been held to embrace not just word marks, such as "Nike," and symbol marks, such as Nike's "swoosh" symbol, but also "trade dress" — a category that originally included only the packaging, or "dressing," of a product, but in recent years has been expanded by many courts of appeals to encompass the design of a product. *See, e.g., Ashley Furniture Industries, Inc. v. Sangiacomo N.A., Ltd.* 187 F.3d 363 (CA4 1999) (bedroom furniture); *Knitwaves, Inc. v. Lollytogs, Ltd.*, 71 F.3d 996 (CA2 1995) (sweaters); *Stuart Hall Co., Inc. v. Ampad Corp.*, 51 F.3d 780 (CA8 1995) (notebooks). These courts have assumed, often without discussion, that trade dress constitutes a "symbol" or "device" for purposes of the relevant sections, and we conclude likewise. "Since human beings might use as a 'symbol' or 'device' almost anything at all that is capable of carrying meaning, this language, read literally, is not restrictive." *Qualitex Co. v. Jacobson Products Co.*, 514 U.S. 159, 162 (1995). This reading of § 2 and § 43(a) is buttressed by a recently added subsection of § 43(a), § 43(a)(3), which refers specifically to "civil action[s] for trade dress infringement under this chapter for trade dress not registered on the principal register." 15 U.S.C.A. § 1125(a)(3) (Oct. 1999 Supp.).

The test of § 43(a) provides little guidance as to the circumstances under which unregistered trade dress may be protected. It does require that a producer show that the allegedly infringing feature is not "functional," *see* § 43(a)(3), and is likely to cause confusion with the product for which protection is sought, *see* § 43(a)(1)(A). Nothing in § 43(a) explicitly requires a producer to show that its trade dress is distinctive, but courts have universally imposed that requirement, since without distinctiveness the trade dress would not "cause confusion . . . as to the origin, sponsorship, or approval of [the] goods," as the section requires. Distinctiveness is, moreover, an explicit prerequisite for registration of trade dress under § 2, and "the general principles qualifying a mark for registration under § 2 of the Lanham Act are for the most part applicable in determining whether an unregistered mark is entitled to protection under § 43(a)." *Two Pesos, Inc. v. Taco Cabana, Inc.*, 505 U.S. 763, 768 (1992) (citations omitted).

In evaluating the distinctiveness of a mark under § 2 (and therefore, by analogy, under § 43(a)), courts have held that a mark can be distinctive in one or two ways. First, a mark is inherently distinctive if "[its] intrinsic nature serves to identify a particular source." *Ibid.* In the context of word marks, courts have applied the now-classic test originally formulated by Judge Friendly, in which word marks that are "arbitrary" ("Camel" cigarettes), "fanciful" ("Kodak" film), or "suggestive" ("Tide" laundry detergent) are held to be inherently distinctive. *See Abercrombie & Fitch Co. v. Hunting World, Inc.*, 537 F.2d 4, 10-11 (CA2 1976). Second, a mark has acquired distinctiveness, even if it is not inherently distinctive, if it has developed secondary meaning, which occurs when, "in the minds of the public, the primary significance of a [mark] is to identify the source of the product rather than the product itself." *Inwood Laboratories,*

Inc. v. Ives Laboratories, Inc., 456 U.S. 844, 851, n. 11 (1982).*

The judicial differentiation between marks that are inherently distinctive and those that have developed secondary meaning has solid foundation in the statute itself. Section 2 requires that registration be granted to any trademark "by which the goods of the applicant may be distinguished from the goods of others" — subject to various limited exceptions. 15 U.S.C. § 1052. It also provides, again with limited exceptions, that "nothing in this chapter shall prevent the registration of a mark used by the applicant which has become distinctive of the applicant's goods in commerce" — that is, which is not inherently distinctive but has become so only through secondary meaning. § 2(f), 15 U.S.C. § 1052(f). Nothing in § 2, however, demands the conclusion that *every* category of mark necessarily includes some marks "by which the goods of the applicant may be distinguished from the goods of others" *without* secondary meaning — that in every category some marks are inherently distinctive.

Indeed, with respect to at least one category of mark-colors-we held that no mark can ever be inherently distinctive. *See Qualitex*, 514 U.S., at 162–163. In *Qualitex* petitioner manufactured and sold green-gold dry-cleaning press pads. After respondent began selling pads of a similar color, petitioner brought suit under § 43(a), then added a claim under § 32 after obtaining registration for the color of its pads. We held that a color could be protected as a trademark, but only upon a showing of secondary meaning. Reasoning by analogy to the *Abercrombie & Fitch* test developed for word marks, we noted that a product's color is unlike a "fanciful," "arbitrary," or "suggestive" mark, since it does not "almost *automatically* tell a customer that [it] refer[s] to a brand," *ibid.*, and does not "immediately . . . signal a brand or a product 'source,' " *id.*, at 163. However, we noted that, "over time, customers may come to treat a particular color on a product or its packaging . . . as signifying a brand." *Id.*, at 162-163. Because a color, like a "descriptive" word mark, could eventually "come to indicate a product's origin," we concluded that it could be protected *upon a showing of secondary meaning. Ibid.*

It seems to us that design, like color, is not inherently distinctive. The attribution of inherent distinctiveness to certain categories of word marks and product packaging derives from the fact that the very purpose of attaching a particular word to a product, or encasing it in a distinctive packaging, is most often to identify the source of the product. Although the words and packaging can serve subsidiary functions — a suggestive word mark (such as "Tide" for laundry detergent), for instance, may invoke positive connotations in the consumer's mind, and a garish form of packaging (such as Tide's squat, brightly decorated plastic bottles for its liquid laundry detergent) may attract an otherwise indifferent consumer's attention on a crowded store shelf — their predominant function remains source identification. Consumers are therefore predisposed to regard those symbols as indication of the producer, which is why such symbols "almost *automatically* tell a customer that they refer to a brand," *id.*, at 162-163, and "immediately . . . signal a brand or a product 'source,' " *id.*, at 163. And where it is not reasonable to assume consumer predisposition to take an affixed word or packaging as indication of source — where, for example, the affixed word is descriptive of the product ("Tasty" bread) or of a geographic origin ("Georgia" peaches) — inherent distinctiveness will not be found. That is why the statute generally excludes, from those word marks that can be registered as inherently distinctive, words that are "merely descriptive" of the goods, § 2(e)(1), 15 U.S.C. § 1052(e)(1), or "primarily geographically descriptive of them," *see* § 2(e)(2), 15 U.S.C. § 1052(e)(2). In the case of product design, as in the case of color, we think consumer predisposition to equate the feature with the

---

* The phrase "secondary meaning" originally arose in the context of word marks, where it served to distinguish the source-identifying meaning from the ordinary, or "primary," meaning of the word. "Secondary meaning" has since come to refer to the acquired, source-identifying meaning of a non-word mark as well. It is often a misnomer in that context, since non-word marks ordinarily have no "primary" meaning. Clarity might well be served by using the term "acquired meaning" in both the word-mark and the non-word-mark contexts — but in this opinion we follow what has become the conventional terminology.

source does not exist. Consumers are aware of the reality that, almost invariably, even the most unusual of product designs — such as a cocktail shaker shaped like a penguin — is intended not to identify the source, but to render the product itself more useful or more appealing.

The fact that product design almost invariably serves purposes other than source identification not only renders inherent distinctiveness problematic; it also renders application of an inherent-distinctiveness principle more harmful to other consumer interests. Consumers should not be deprived of the benefits of competition with regard to the utilitarian and esthetic purposes that product design ordinarily serves by a rule of law that facilitates plausible threats of suit against new entrants based upon alleged inherent distinctiveness. How easy it is to mount a plausible suit depends, of course, upon the clarity of the test for inherent distinctiveness, and where product design is concerned we have little confidence that a reasonably clear test can be devised. Respondent and the United States as *amicus curiae* urge us to adopt for product design relevant portions of the test formulated by the Court of Customs and Patent Appeals for product packaging in *Seabrook Foods, Inc.v Bar-Well Foods, Ltd.*, 568 F.2d 1342 (1977). That opinion, in determining the inherent distinctiveness of a product's packaging, considered, among other things, "whether it was a 'common' basic shape or design, whether it was unique or unusual in a particular field, [and] whether it was a mere refinement of a commonly-adopted and well-known form of ornamentation for a particular class of goods viewed by the public as a dress or ornamentation for the goods." *Id.*, at 1344 (footnotes omitted). Such a test would rarely provide the basis for summary disposition of an anticompetitive strike suit. Indeed, at oral argument, counsel for the United States quite understandably would not give a definitive answer as to whether the test was met in this very case, saying only that "[t]his is a very difficult case for that purpose." Tr. of Oral Arg. 19.

It is true, of course, that the person seeking to exclude new entrants would have to establish the nonfunctionality of the design feature, *see* § 43(a)(3), 15 U.S.C.A. § 1125 (a)(3) (Oct. 1999 Supp.) — a showing that may involve consideration of its esthetic appeal, *see Qualitex*, 514 U.S., at 170. Competition is deterred, however, not merely by successful suit but by the plausible threat of successful suit, and given the unlikelihood of inherently source-identifying design, the game of allowing suit based upon alleged inherent distinctiveness seems to us not worth the candle. That is especially so since the producer can ordinarily obtain protection for a design that *is* inherently source identifying (if any such exists), but that does not yet have secondary meaning, by securing a design patent or a copyright for the design — as, indeed, respondent did for certain elements of the designs in this case. The availability of these other protections greatly reduces any harm to the producer that might ensue from our conclusion that a product design cannot be protected under § 43(a) without a showing of secondary meaning.

Respondent contends that our decision in *Two Pesos* forecloses a conclusion that product-design trade dress can never be inherently distinctive. In that case, we held that the trade dress of a chain of Mexican restaurants, which the plaintiff described as "a festive eating atmosphere having interior dining and patio areas decorated with artifacts, bright colors, paintings and murals," 505 U.S., at 765 (internal quotation marks and citation omitted), could be protected under § 43(a) without a showing of secondary meaning, *see id.*, at 776. *Two Pesos* unquestionably establishes the legal principle that trade dress can be inherently distinctive, *see, e.g., id.*, at 773, but it does not establish that *product-design* trade dress can be. *Two Pesos* is inapposite to our holding here because the trade dress at issue, the decor of a restaurant, seems to use not to constitute product *design*. It was either product packaging — which, as we have discussed, normally *is* taken by the consumer to indicate origin — or else some *tertium quid* that is akin to product packaging and has no bearing on the present case.

Respondent replies that this manner of distinguishing *Two Pesos* will force courts to draw difficult lines between product-design and product-packaging trade dress. There will indeed be some hard cases at the margin: a classic glass Coca-Cola bottle, for instance, may constitute packaging for those consumers who drink the Coke and then discard the bottle, but may constitute the product itself for those consumers who are bottle collectors, or part of the product itself for those consumers who buy Coke in the classic glass bottle, rather than a can, because they think it more stylish to drink from the former. We believe, however, that the frequency and the difficulty of having to distinguish between product design and product packaging will be much less than the frequency and the difficulty of having to decide when a product design is inherently distinctive. To the extent there are close cases, we believe that courts should err on the side of caution and classify ambiguous trade dress as product design, thereby requiring secondary meaning. The very closeness will suggest the existence of relatively small utility in adopting an inherent-distinctiveness principle, and relatively great consumer benefit in requiring a demonstration of secondary meaning.

* * *

We hold that, in an action for infringement of unregistered trade dress under § 43(a) of the Lanham Act, a product's design is distinctive, and therefore protectible, only upon a showing of secondary meaning. The judgment of the Second Circuit is reversed, and the case is remanded for further proceedings consistent with this opinion.

Notes on Distinctiveness

1. Inherent Distinctiveness

In the past, some courts had held that if a trade dress was arbitrary and inherently distinctive, its owner was entitled to protection without showing secondary meaning, just as would be the case for word trademarks. As stated in *Chevron Chemical Co. v. Voluntary Purchasing Groups, Inc.*, 659 F.2d 695, 702 (5th Cir. 1981), *cert. denied*, 457 U.S. 1126 (1982):

> If the features of the trade dress sought to be protected are arbitrary and serve no function either to describe the product or assist in its effective packaging, there is no reason to require a plaintiff to show consumer connotations associated with such arbitrarily selected features.

Accord Blau Plumbing, Inc. v. S.O.S. Fix-It, Inc., 781 F.2d 604, 608 (7th Cir. 1986) (but "location box" in yellow pages advertisement held functional); *Wiley v. American Greetings Corp.*, 762 F.2d 139, 141 (1st Cir. 1985) (but red heart affixed to breast of teddy bear held not inherently distinctive and lacking secondary meaning); *Animal Fair, Inc. v. Amfesco Industries, Inc.*, 620 F. Supp. 175, 190 (D. Minn. 1985), *aff'd* 794 F.2d 678 (1986) ("bearpaw" slipper design held inherently distinctive). *Cf. Metro Kane Imports, Ltd. v. Rowoco, Inc.*, 618 F. Supp. 273, 276-277 (S.D.N.Y. 1985), *aff'd*, 800 F.2d 1128 (2d Cir. 1986) (showing of secondary meaning in trade dress necessary under Lanham Act but not under New York common law of unfair competition).

The Supreme Court confirmed the validity of this analysis in *Two Pesos, Inc. v. Taco Cabana Inc.*, supra. It found no reversible error in the district court instruction that allowed the jury to find plaintiff's restaurant trade dress inherently distinctive and protectable without proof of secondary meaning. Cases following *Taco Cabana* include: *Fun-Damental Too Ltd. v. Gemmy Indus. Corp.*, 111 F.3d 993, 1001 (2d Cir. 1997) (upholding district court finding that triangular-shaped, "open-style" packaging for novelty coin bank was inherently distinctive and infringed); *Computer Care v. Service Systems Enterprises, Inc.*, 982 F.2d 1063 (7th Cir. 1992) (trade dress of plaintiff's auto care reminder letters, sales brochure and monthly reports held inherently distinctive and infringed despite presence of some descriptive or generic elements); *George Basch Co. v. Blue Coral, Inc.*, 982 F.2d 1532 (2d Cir.), *cert. denied*, 506 U.S. 991 (1992) (defendant's assertion that plaintiff failed to show secondary meaning in its metal polish trade dress rendered moot by *Taco Cabana*, since jury had found the trade dress inherently distinctive); *Cf. Echo Travel, Inc. v. Travel Associates, Inc.*, 870 F.2d 1264 (7th Cir. 1989) (affirming that plaintiff's promotional poster depicting a beach scene was merely descriptive of its vacation services and lacked secondary meaning), and Dillon *Two Pesos: More Interesting for What it Did Not Decide*, 83 TRADEMARK REP. 77 (1993).

Over time, a division developed among the federal courts as to whether the test for inherent distinctiveness in packaging design should be the same for product configuration. Some courts advocated a different test, or higher standard, for product configurations. *See, e.g., Duraco Prods. v. Joy Plastic Enterprises*, 40 F.3d 1431 (3d Cir. 1994) (because configuration "is not a symbol according to which one can relate the signifier . . . to the signified", the court determined that an inherently distinctive configuration must be (1) unusual and memorable; (2) conceptually separable from the product; and (3) likely to serve primarily as a designator of origin); *Knitwaves Inc. v. Lollytogs Ltd.*, 71 F.3d 996, 1008 (2d Cir. 1995) (adopting *Duraco* standard). *Cf. Seabrook Foods, Inc. v. Bar-Well Foods, Ltd.*, 568 F.2d 1342, 1344 (C.C.P.A. 1977) (in product packaging case, creating new test later applied by Federal Circuit and other courts in configuration cases).

Other courts concluded that the traditional means of analysis should apply to both product design and product packaging. *See, e.g., Ashley Furniture Industries, Inc. v. San Giacomo N.A. Ltd.*, 187 F.3d 363 (4th Cir. 1999) (endorsing application of traditional word mark distinctiveness categories (generic, descriptive, suggestive, arbitrary or fanciful) to configurations in bedroom furniture case, and concluding the *Seabrook* analysis could be used to further clarify the application of those categories in a particular case); *Stuart Hall Company v. Ampad Corp.*, 51 F.3d 780 (8th Cir. 1995) (interpreting Supreme Court's *Taco Cabana* decision to mean that the tests for product design and for packaging should be the same).

In *Wal-Mart Stores v. Samara Brothers, supra*, the Supreme Court provided a bright line resolution of this split among the circuits, holding that, "product-design trade dress can never be inherently distinctive." This decision raises a number of questions. For example, as the decision is directed to unregistered trade dress, should heightened deference be given to the registration decisions of examining attorneys at the Patent and Trademark Office? (See Chapter 3). That office and the Federal Circuit now follow *Wal-Mart v. Samara* in requiring proof of secondary meaning for product configurations. *See, e.g., In re Slokevage*, 441 F.3d 957 (Fed. Cir. 2006) (affirming that applicant's product design for clothing was not inherently distinctive, and that proof of acquired distinctiveness therefore was required). What happens to existing product configuration registrations that were granted based on inherent distinctiveness? Does it matter whether the registration is incontestable? What if the *Taco Cabana* case had first gone to trial *after* the *Samara* decision? Would the trial court have had to "err on the side of caution" and treat the restaurant trade dress as a product design, and require a showing of secondary meaning? What happens to the new market entrants the Court was concerned about in *Taco Cabana* i.e, "adding a secondary meaning requirement could have anticompetitive effects, creating particular burdens on the start-up of small company"? *Taco Cabana*, 505 U.S. at 775. *See also* Smith, *Trade Distinctiveness: Solving Scalia's Tertium Quid Trade Dress Conundrum*, 2005 MICH. ST. L. REV. 243 (2005).

Did the Supreme Court in *Taco Cabana, supra*, correctly assume that whatever is "inherently distinctive" also indicates source? An inherently distinctive trade dress perhaps may come to indicate source sooner than other subject matter through its use in commerce. But until a trade dress has come to signify source by virtue of use that has penetrated the consciousness of an appreciable number of relevant persons, there can be no deception. When source–signifying awareness has been generated, something exists deserving the law's protection, but not until then. Might the protection of various appearance features, characteristics, combinations or creations as being inherently distinctive amount to the equivalent of a perpetual copyright privilege? "Secondary meaning," in the context of trade identity law, describes a state of mind of persons who have come to perceive or recognize something as signifying a particular (known or unknown by name) source. Secondary meaning is not inherent distinctiveness. Instead, it is a particular acquired distinctiveness.

The words "secondary meaning" were well known and understood in trademark law when the Lanham Trademark Act was being drafted by Edward S. Rogers of Chicago. Courts, however, frequently were unfamiliar with trademark law, and some had trouble with the arcane term "secondary meaning." The word "distinctive" was substituted for the term "secondary meaning" in the Lanham Act. "Secondary meaning" does not appear anywhere in the Act, which may have contributed to the rationale of *Taco Cabana.*, as well as *Wal-Mart.*

As indicated in *Taco Cabana,* even the shape of a building may possess trademark significance under the proper circumstances. *See* Burgunder, *Commercial Photographs of Famous Buildings: The Sixth Circuit Fails to Make The Hall of Fame,* 89 TRADEMARK REP. 791 (1999); Fletcher, *Buildings as Trademarks: The Fotomat Cases,* 69 TRADEMARK REP. 229-64 (1979). *Compare Clicks Billiards, Inc. v. Sixshooters, Inc.,* 251 F.3d 1252 (9th Cir. 2001) (reversing summary judgment for defendant due to fact issues as to whether the overall image of plaintiff's pool hall was nonfunctional, distinctive and infringed), *with Prufrock Ltd., Inc. v. Lasater,* 781 F.2d 129 (8th Cir. 1986) (plaintiff's "down home country cooking" trade dress for its restaurant was held functional and unprotectable) and *Rock and Roll Hall of Fame and Museum, Inc. v. Gentile Productions,* 45 U.S.P.Q. 1412 (6th Cir. 1998) (defendant's poster photograph of a museum was preliminarily held non-infringing where plaintiff's "irregular" and "disparate" uses of the museum building design on a variety of products was not a "consistent and repetitive use of a designation as an indicator of source," and did not create protectable trademark rights). Qualifying building designs also can be registered as trademarks with the U.S. Patent and Trademark Office. For example, the designs of the Citicorp Center in Manhattan, the Sears Tower in Chicago, and the Transamerica Tower in San Francisco, all have been registered.

2. Acquired Distinctiveness or Secondary Meaning

If a product design or other trade dress is not inherently distinctive, then acquired distinctiveness, or secondary meaning, must be shown. Secondary meaning may be demonstrated for nonfunctional trade dress in a manner similar to word marks, i.e., by satisfying such factors as: (1) length and manner of use; (2) nature and extent of advertising and promotion; (3) volume of sales; (4) the efforts made to promote a conscious connection in the public's mind between the trade dress and the plaintiff's product or service; and (5) the extent to which the public actually identifies the trade dress with plaintiff's product or service. *Echo Travel, Inc. v. Travel Associates, Inc.,* 870 F.2d 1264, 1267 (7th Cir. 1989)(promotional poster lacked secondary meaning). The unusualness of the design and the extent that it has been advertised and promoted can play particularly significant roles in determining whether secondary meaning exists. As the court observed in connection with packaging in *Willie W. Gray v. Meijer, Inc.,* 295 F.3d 641 (6th Cir. 2002):

> [T]he most mundane packaging may be infused with meaning by advertising and promotional tools, rendering a strong trade dress. Likewise, particularly unique packaging even without any artificial efforts to establish a secondary meaning for the product may result in a strong trade dress. The combination of these two factors determines the relative strength or weakness of the trade dress.

Advertising that shows a picture of the claimed trade dress but does not emphasize it as a source indicator, however, may be insufficient to support a claim of secondary meaning. In *The Yankee Candle Co., v. The Bridgewater Candle Co., LLC,* 259 F.3d 25

(1st Cir. 2002), for example, plaintiff's advertising "did not emphasize any particular element of its [claimed] trade dress, and thus could not be probative of secondary meaning." *See also Mennen Co. v. Gillette Co.*, 565 F. Supp. 648 (S.D.N.Y. 1983) (stripe design lacked secondary meaning, the court noting that the advertising did not tell consumers to "look for" the stripe), *aff'd without op.*, 742 F.2d 1437 (2d Cir. 1984); *Turtle Wax, Inc. v. First Brands Corp.*, 781 F. Supp. 1314 (N.D. Ill. 1991) ("the Court is unpersuaded . . . that [plaintiff] can establish secondary meaning simply by means of an advertising and promotional campaign which only displays but does not emphasize the trade dress of its product").

Where a showing of secondary meaning in trade dress is necessary, could proof of intentional copying by the defendant be sufficient? *See Herman Miller, Inc. v. Palazetti Imports and Exports, Inc.*, 270 F.3d 298 (6th Cir. 2001) (including intentional copying among the factors probative of secondary meaning); *Clicks Billiards, Inc. v. Sixshooters, Inc.*, 251 F.3d 1252, 1264, 1266 (9th Cir. 2001) ("in appropriate circumstances, deliberate copying may suffice to support an inference of secondary meaning"; in this pool hall trade dress case, evidence of deliberate copying also was entitled to "great weight" on the issue of likely confusion); *Osem Food Industries, Ltd. v. Sherwood Foods, Inc.*, 917 F.2d 161 (4th Cir. 1990) (defendant's intentional copying of plaintiff's soup packaging raised presumptions of secondary meaning and likely confusion which defendant failed to rebut). *See also Gasser Chair Co. v. Infanti Chair Mfg. Corp.*, 943 F. Supp. 201, 214 (E.D.N.Y. 1996) (buttressing a finding of secondary meaning in stackable chairs with evidence of defendant's intentional copying).

Where, however, a competitor intentionally copies a product feature because consumers desire that feature apart from its value as a signifier of source, intentional copying may be considered legitimate competitive activity. *See, e.g., The Yankee Candle Co., v. The Bridgewater Candle Co., LLC*, 259 F.3d 25 (1stCir. 2002) (plaintiff's evidence of intentional copying was not probative of secondary meaning, given "the highly functional nature of certain elements of Yankee's claimed combination trade dress"; *Shakespeare Co. v. Silstar Corp. of Am.*110 F.3d 234, 241 (4th Cir. 1997), *cert. denied*, 522 U.S. 1046 (1998); (defendant's copying of a functional clear tip on plaintiff's fishing rod did not give rise to presumption of likelihood of confusion); *Libman Co. v. Vining Indus. Inc.*, 69 F.3d 1360, 1363 (7th Cir. 1995), *cert. denied*, 517 U.S. 1234 (1996) (Posner, C.J.) (use of allegedly imitative contrasting color scheme for broom bristles was not infringing because, among other reasons, the defendant could have adopted the scheme in an attempt to cater to consumers' desires, not to confuse them as to the source of the defendant's broom); *Thomas & Betts Corp. v. Panduit Corp.*, 65 F.3d 654, 660–61 (7th Cir. 1995), *cert. denied*, 516 U.S. 1159 (1996); ("the magistrate judge did not distinguish between goodwill toward the producer — all that trade dress law protects — and goodwill toward the article — 'the attractive features . . . that the product holds for consumers' — which is freely appropriable by second comers"); *Duraco Prods. v. Joy Plastic Enters., Ltd.*, 40 F.3d 1431, 1445 (3d Cr. 1994) ("[e]xploiting the goodwill of the article — the attractiveness features . . . that the product holds for consumers — is robust competition; only deceiving consumers, or exploiting the goodwill of another producer, is unfair competition").

3. Family of Trade Dress

Several courts have remarked on the significant challenge facing plaintiffs who assert trade dress rights in a "line" or "family" of products. See also the discussion on families of word marks in Chapter 6. In *AM General Corp. and General Motors Corp. v. DaimlerChrysler Corp.*, 311 F.3d 796, 804 (7th Cir. 2002), citing an earlier Federal Circuit decision, the Seventh Circuit defined a "family of marks" as a group of marks having "a recognizable common characteristic . . . used in such a way that the public associates not only the individual marks, but the common characteristic of the family, with the trademark owner." It held that defendant "can't be said to have infringed a family of marks that did not exist when its [automotive] grille entered the market, or at least had not acquired secondary meaning when the [defendant's] grille entered the market." *In Regal Jewelry Co., Inc. v. Kingsbridge International, Inc.*, 999 F. Supp. 477 (S.D.N.Y. 1998), the plaintiff seller of novelty items claimed infringement of an alleged family of packaging trade dress encompassing "gray teal blue" boxes having a photograph that overlapped a white frame, with the product name above the photograph. In denying relief, the court found that plaintiff's trade dress had been inconsistently used and insufficiently articulated to receive protection. In addition, the trade dress was at best descriptive, and had not achieved secondary meaning.

Consistent presentation across the line of products is critical. In a case involving an alleged family of outdoor furniture products — the Second Circuit held that the plaintiff had failed to "indicate what unique combination of features makes the trade dress of the ten items in the Petoskey line inherently distinctive." *Landscape Forms, Inv. v. Columbia Cascade Co.*, 113 F.3d 373, 381 (2^d Cir. 1997). Plaintiff had claimed rights in metal tubing furniture "bent in gentle turns" which "in combination with the various seating surfaces gives the viewer a floating or suspended feeling." Similarly, in *Yurman Design, Inc. v. PAJ, Inc.*, 262 F.3d 101 (2^d Cir. 2001), plaintiff successfully obtained relief for five of its jewelry designs under copyright law, but was unsuccessful in asserting rights in a larger family of trade dress under the Lanham Act. The fatal flaw in the trade dress claim was "try as it might, the Court [could not] divine precisely what [plaintiff's] specific trade dress was . . . [W]e hold that a plaintiff asserting that a trade dress protects an entire line of different products must articulate the specific common elements sought to be registered." *See also Rose Art Industries Inc. v. Raymond Geddes & Co.*, 31 F. Supp.2d 367, *amended* 1998 U.S. Dist. LEXIS 21616 (D.N.J. 1998) ("the multiple background color combinations that [plaintiff] utilized[d] to package its crayon, marker and colored pencil products and [plaintiff]'s inconsistent use" of its labeling features, as well as "the variations in the appearance of Rose Arts' logo" did not constitute an identifiable family of trade dress); *Al-Site Corp. v. VSI Int'l Inc.*, 174 F.3d 1308 (Fed. Cir. 1999) (plaintiff's color coding system changed from time to time, so that it lacked the "stable visual appearance" necessary for trade dress protection). Compare *Alpha Kappa Alpha Sorority, inc., v. Converse, nc.*, 175 Fed. Appx. 672 (5th Cir. 2006), in which the Fifth Circuit, in reversing, distinguished *Landscape Forms*. The plaintiff fraternities and sororities had sufficiently pled the trademarks and trade dress, some of which contained the "founding year(s), colors and identification "of plaintiffs' organizations that defendant Converse allegedly had infringed in its GREEKPAK line of shows. In the court's view, the *Landscape Forms* analysis "actually supports our holding that the complaint sufficiently articulated the elements of the plaintiff's unregistered trademarks and trade dress."

4. Historical Designs

Where a *plaintiff* intentionally copies a "historical design" — a design previously introduced, but no longer marketed, by a third party — and subsequently claims infringement of its alleged trade dress rights in that design, it may be difficult for the plaintiff to establish secondary meaning. *See L. & J.G. Stickley, Inc. v. Canal Dover Furniture Co.*, 79 F.3d 258, 265 (2^d Cir. 1996) (reversing preliminary injunction and holding that plaintiff had not established secondary meaning in the design of its replicas of "Mission furniture" sold during the 1920s; "[i]n a case of exact reproductions of historical designs, we think that [the secondary meaning requirement] presents a high hurdle to a Lanham Act plaintiff"); *see also EFS Mkt'g v. Russ Berrie & Co.*, 76 F.3d 487 (2^d Cir. 1996) (holding that plaintiff's replica of a troll doll in the public domain since 1961 is neither inherently distinctive nor capable of acquiring secondary meaning).

CHAPTER 6
INFRINGEMENT OF TRADEMARK RIGHTS

CONTENTS

6.01 Introduction

Likelihood of consumer confusion is the touchstone of trademark infringement. It is an empirical inquiry, and it constitutes the central issue contested in the vast majority of trademark infringement litigation. As we have seen, Anglo-American trademark law was built upon two concepts. The first is prior use; the second is source-identifying significance deserving of protection against a likelihood of confusion. The former provides the basis for rights, and the latter the scope within which they may be asserted. Deceptively simple, likelihood of confusion is at the heart of trademark infringement law under the common law and the federal statute. The plaintiff in a trademark infringement action — the prior user — must prove by factual evidence that the defendant's conduct causes an actionable likelihood of confusion. In all circumstances, "the burden of proving likelihood of confusion rests with the plaintiff." *KP Permanent Make-Up, Inc. v. Lasting Impression I, Inc.*, 543 U.S. 111, 121 (2004).

Proving trademark infringement under the 1905 Act required the plaintiff to show that plaintiff's and defendant's marks were both "confusingly similar" and used on goods "of the same descriptive properties." Under the 1946 Act, the plaintiff originally had to prove that the defendant's mark was "likely to cause confusion or mistake or to deceive *purchasers* as to the source of origin of such goods or services." In 1962 the Act was amended to delete the word "purchasers." The evolution of the test for likelihood of confusion demonstrates the emergence of a better understanding of the commercial realities of trademark use. As you work through the materials, consider the purposes for each step in this evolution.

Determining whether confusion is likely is not an ordinary question. It concerns the state of mind of numberless individuals under particular conditions. Rarely, if ever, can its resolution be utterly black or white. A determination must be made whether appreciable confusion of source will result from the use of an accused mark or other means for trade identity. This determination or prediction should be derived from evidence, rather than the subjective reaction of the fact-finder.

All Circuits use multi-factor tests to analyze the likelihood of confusion issue. Those tests reflect many of the considerations discussed in earlier chapters. The first two sections of this Chapter delineate the likelihood of confusion test and demonstrate its application to individual cases. This includes factors such as similarity of appearance, sound, connotation, goods, and marketing environment.

The vast variety of factual situations encountered in trademark infringement trials has given rise to a number of judicially created infringement doctrines that evolved to aid both the court and the finder of fact in assessing the particulars of given factual situations. This includes doctrines such as initial interest confusion, reverse confusion, and post-sale confusion. One of the factors of the confusion test, intent, can be outcome-determinative in trademark infringement litigation. The application of this intent factor can be complex; it is analyzed in detail below.

We then discuss counterfeiting, which is fully intentional copying of another party's trademark on products that typically are of inferior quality. As is well known, counterfeiting constitutes a substantial global threat not only to intellectual property owners, but often also to the health and safety of consumers.

The final section in this Chapter pertains to consumer surveys and expert witnesses. It has become common to use surveys and expert witnesses to assist the finder of fact in the proof of infringement. A variety of different survey formats are accepted by the courts. Courts generally demand certain safeguards to assure the scientific validity of surveys.

When reading the materials in this Chapter, consider the interplay and varying relative importance of these considerations in each of the cases. Note that the general framework of inquiry must encompass many considerations which may arise in some individual cases but not others, such as intentional infringement, use of a family of marks, use of several marks on a product or natural expansion of a business into related product areas. Note also that some courts reach their conclusions as to likelihood of confusion, and thus infringement, subjectively and based upon their own reactions as to similarity rather than objectively and based upon evidence of confusion introduced by the parties. Is this a deficiency? Of the court? Of counsel? Or can it be an appropriate factfinding inquiry given the circumstances of certain cases?

Diverse factual considerations are subsumed under the likelihood of confusion inquiry. What relationship among goods or services is relevant to the test? What persons are relevant to the test? What weight should be given to similarities in the way marks are perceived, such as appearance or pronunciation? To similarities in the meaning of marks? To what degree is the issue one of fact, and to what extent is it a mixed issue of fact and law?

6.02   Federal Court Multifactor Tests

All circuits have developed multi-factor tests to capture the rich empirical issues arising in trademark infringement cases. Perhaps the best known is the test developed by Judge Friendly in *Polaroid Corp. v. Polarad Electronics Corp.*, 287 F.2d 492, 495 (2d Cir. 1961). It retains its precedential force in the Second Circuit. Both with regard to the substantive factors and with regard to its deliberately open-ended nature, the *Polaroid* test is a good example of such tests throughout the circuits:

> . . . Where the products are different, the prior owner's chance of success is a function of many variables: the strength of his mark, the degree of similarity between the two marks, the proximity of the products, the likelihood that the prior owner will bridge the gap, actual confusion, and the reciprocal of defendant's good faith in adopting its own mark, the quality of defendant's product, and the sophistication of the buyers. Even this extensive catalogue does not exhaust the possibilities — the court may have to take still other variables into account.

Other circuits use variations of the *Polaroid* test to determine whether the defendant's conduct creates a likelihood of confusion. *See, e.g., GMC v. Lanard Toys, Inc.*, 468 F.3d 405 (6th Cir. 2006) (because district court failed to discuss Eighth Circuit's eight confusion factors, appellate court had to analyze them *de novo*); *Ford Motor Co. v. Summit Motor Products, Inc.*, 930 F.2d 277, 293 (3d Cir.), *cert. denied*, 502 U.S. 939 (1991) (listing ten relevant factors); *Schwinn Bicycle Co. v. Ross Bicycles, Inc.*, 870 F.2d 1176, 1185 (7th Cir. 1989) (referring to the factors as "digits" of confusion); *Boston Athletic Ass'n v. Sullivan*, 867 F.2d 22, 29 (1st Cir. 1989); *Conagra, Inc. v. Singleton*, 743 F.2d 1508, 1514 (11th Cir. 1984).

The most extensive list of factors is used in the Patent and Trademark Office, and was set forth in *In re E. I. Du Pont de Nemours & Co.*, 476 F.2d 1357, 1361 (C.C.P.A. 1973):

> In testing for likelihood of confusion under Sec. 2(d), therefore the following, when of record, must be considered:

> (1) The similarity or dissimilarity of the marks in their entireties as to appearance, sound, connotation and commercial impression.

> (2) The similarity of dissimilarity and nature of the goods or services as described in an application or registration or in connection with which a prior mark is in use.

> (3) The similarity or dissimilarity of established, likely-to-continue trade channels.

> (4) The conditions under which and buyers to whom sales are made, i.e. "impulse" vs. careful, sophisticated purchasing.

> (5) The fame of the prior mark (sales, advertising, length of use).

> (6) The number and nature of similar marks in use on similar goods.

> (7) The nature and extent of any actual confusion.

> (8) The length of time during and conditions under which there has been concurrent use without evidence of actual confusion.

> (9) The variety of goods on which a mark is or is not used (house mark, "family" mark, product mark).

> (10) The market interface between applicant and the owner of a prior mark:

>> (a) a mere "consent" to register or use.

>> (b) agreement provisions designed to preclude confusion, i.e. limitations on continued use of the marks by each party.

(c) assignment of mark, application, registration and good will of the related business.

(d) laches and estoppel attributable to owner of prior mark and indicative of lack of confusion.

(11) The extent to which applicant has a right to exclude others from use of its mark on its goods.

(12) The extent of potential confusion, i.e., whether de minimis or substantial.

(13) Any other established fact probative of the effect of use.

The *Du Pont* factors continue to be used by that court's successor, the Federal Circuit, *see, e.g., Specialty Brands, Inc. v. Coffee Bean Distributors Inc.*, 748 F.2d 669, 671–72 (Fed. Cir. 1984).

Originally developed for non-competing goods cases, the *Polaroid* test from 1961, set forth above, now applies in competing goods cases as well. *Thompson Medical Co. v. Pfizer, Inc.*, 753 F.2d 208, 214 (2^d Cir. 1985). In vacating the lower court's denial of preliminary relief in *New Kayak Pool Corp. v. R&P Pools, Inc.*, 246 F.3d 183, 185 (2^d Cir. 2001) for failure to apply or even mention the Polaroid factor test, the appellate court quoted a previous decision in explaining its importance:

> The steady application of Polaroid is critical to the proper development of trademark law, for it is only when the Polaroid factors are applied consistently and clearly over time that the relevant distinctions between different factual configurations can emerge. Litigants are entitled to the illumination and guidance this common-law process affords, and appellate courts depend on it for the performance of their assigned task of review. . . . The efficacy of the multi-factor approach . . . depends on thorough, careful, and consistent application of the doctrine by district courts.

Depending upon the circumstances of the case, a particular confusion factor may be accorded greater or lesser weight. The factor tests are only aids in determining the ultimate issue of likelihood of confusion. "When balancing the factors, district courts generally should not treat any single factor as dispositive (with some exceptions, as discussed immediately below); nor should a court treat the inquiry as a mechanical process by which the party with the greatest number of factors wins. Instead, the court should focus on the ultimate question of whether consumers are likely to be confused." *Playtex Prods. v. Georgia-Pacific Corp.*, 390 F.3d 158, 162 (2^d Cir. 2004) (citations and quotation marks omitted).

In appropriate circumstances, therefore, a single factor may decide the outcome of a trademark infringement claim. The next case demonstrates this adaptability of the likelihood of confusion text to the facts of particular cases.

CHAMPAGNE LOUIS ROEDERER, S.A. v. DELICATO VINEYARDS
148 F.3d 1373 (Fed. Cir. 1998)

Champagne Louis Roederer, S.A. ("Roederer") appeals from a decision in an opposition proceeding by the Trademark Trial and Appeal Board of the Patent and Trademark Office (the "Board"). *See Champagne Louis Roederer, S.A. v. Delicato Vineyards*, Opposition No. 80,932 (TTAB June 25, 1997). Delicato Vineyards' ("Delicato") predecessor in interest filed application serial no. 73/701,485 to register the word mark "CRYSTAL CREEK" for wine. Roederer filed an opposition to the registration based on its two marks-the word mark "CRISTAL," and the mark "CRISTAL CHAMPAGNE" with accompanying graphic design. The Board dismissed Roederer's opposition after determining that the application mark was not confusingly similar to either of Roederer's marks. Because we conclude that Roederer failed to demonstrate any error in the Board's legal analysis or ultimate legal conclusion regarding likelihood of confusion, or clear error with respect to any of its findings on the individual *DuPont* factors, we must affirm. . . .

The Board . . . treated the dissimilarity of the marks with respect to appearance, sound, significance, and commercial impression as the dispositive *DuPont* factor, concluding that this dissimilarity alone precluded any reasonable likelihood of confusion. *See id.* at 11. Specifically, as to significance, the Board found that the word marks "CRISTAL" and "CRYSTAL CREEK" evoked very different images in the minds of relevant consumers: while the former suggested the clarity of the wine within the bottle or the glass of which the bottle itself was made, the latter suggested "a very clear (and hence probably remote from civilization) creek or stream." . . . The Board then found that the appearance and sound of the competing marks were also dissimilar.. . . .Based on these three underlying findings on this single *DuPont* factor, the Board dismissed the opposition because of the difference in commercial impressions it found were created by the marks. . . .

Roederer suggests, first, that it was an error of law for the Board to rely solely on the dissimilarity of the marks in evaluating the likelihood of confusion and to fail to give surpassing weight to the other *DuPont* factors, all of which were found to favor Roederer. We note, however, that we have previously upheld Board determinations that one *DuPont* factor may be dispositive in a likelihood of confusion analysis, especially when that single factor is the dissimilarity of the marks. *See, e.g., Kellogg Co. v. Pack'em Enters.,* 951 F.2d 330, 332-33, 21 USPQ2d 1142, 1144-45 (Fed.Cir.1991) (stating that "[w]e know of no reason why, in a particular case, a single *DuPont* factor may not be dispositive" and holding that "substantial and undisputed differences" between two competing marks justified a conclusion of no likelihood of confusion on summary judgment); *Keebler Co. v. Murray Bakery Prods.,* 866 F.2d 1386, 1388, 9 U.S.P.Q.2d 1736, 1739 (Fed.Cir.1989) (agreeing with the Board that the "more important fact for resolving the issue of likelihood of confusion . . . is the dissimilarity in commercial impression between the marks"). We have not been persuaded that, on this record, the Board erred in concluding that the marks' dissimilarities were dispositive, notwithstanding due weight being accorded to the *DuPont* factors found in Roederer's favor.

Second, Roederer has failed to demonstrate any instance of clear error in the Board's factual findings with respect to the dissimilarities of the marks in appearance, sound, significance, or overall commercial impression. Although Roederer disagrees, chiefly, with the Board's interpretation of the commercial impression of the marks, even reasoned disagreement with such a finding does not, without more, establish that it is clearly erroneous. . . . Thus, because Roederer has failed to demonstrate any reversible factual or legal error, we must

AFFIRM.

6.03 Applying the Multi-Factor Test

The *Roederer* case excerpted above was decided against appellant Roederer despite the fact that, as the court noted, the majority of *Du Pont* factors actually favored Roederer. This can be seen as a virtue because of the open-minded, nondoctrinal focus on the reality of whether consumers are likely to be confused. On the other hand, it may be seen as undermining predictability. When Roederer initiated the litigation, could it have anticipated that the court would focus on one confusion factor disfavoring it, to the near-exclusion of most other factors (under which Roederer might have actually prevailed)? How is planning possible in such a situation? If the elaborate multi-factor tests developed by the circuits can be reduced to a single factor, how can the likelihood of confusion inquiry be prevented from being based simply on a gut reaction by the court, rather than a principled and evidence-based analysis? The following decisions, in which the lower court is reversed and then reversed again after remand, exemplify this tension between objective inquiry and subjective reaction, which is frequently encountered in trademark infringement litigation.

BEER NUTS, INC, v. CLOVER CLUB FOODS CO. [BEER NUTS I]
711 F.2d 934 (10th Cir. 1983)

SEYMOUR, CIRCUIT JUDGE

Beer Nuts, Inc. (Beer Nuts) sued Clover Club Foods (Clover Club) alleging trademark infringement under 15 U.S.C. § 1114 (1976), unfair competition under 15 U.S.C. § 1125 (1976), and a pendent claim of state law trademark infringement. These claims arose from Clover Club's use of the words "Brew Nuts" with a picture of an overflowing stein on packages containing a sweetened, salted peanut product virtually identical to a product sold by Beer Nuts.

*   *   *

Infringement of a trademark occurs when the use of the similar mark is likely to cause confusion in the marketplace concerning the source of the different products. *Vitek Systems, Inc. v. Abbott Laboratories*, 675 F.2d 190, 192 (8th Cir. 1982). "The resolution of this issue requires the court to consider numerous factors to determine whether, under all the circumstances, there is a likelihood of confusion." *Id.* In making this determination, this court has used the criteria set out in Restatement of Torts § 729 (1938):

> (a) the degree of similarity between the designation and the trade-mark or trade name in
>
> (i) appearance;
>
> (ii) pronunciation of the words used;
>
> (iii) verbal translation of the pictures or designs involved;
>
> (iv) suggestion;
>
> (b) the intent of the actor in adopting the designation;
>
> (c) the relation in use and manner of marketing between the goods or services marketed by the actor and those marketed by the other;
>
> (d) the degree of care likely to be exercised by purchasers.

Other courts have used some formulation of this same test. [Citations omitted]. The above list is not exhaustive and no one factor is determinative. The facts of a particular case may require consideration of other variables as well. *McGregor-Doniger*, 599 F.2d at 1130; *Polaroid Corp. v. Polarad Electronics Corp.*, 287 F.2d 492, 495 (2[d] Cir.), *cert. denied*, 368 U.S. 820 (1961).

As set forth above, "[s]imilarity of the marks is tested on three levels: sight, sound, and meaning . . . Each must be considered as [it] is encountered in the marketplace. Although similarity is measured by the marks as entities, similarities weigh more heavily than differences." *AMF Inc.*, 599 F.2d at 351; *Vitek Systems, Inc.*, 675 F.2d at 192.

> It is not necessary for similarity to go only to the eye or the ear for there to be infringement. The use of a designation which causes confusion because it conveys the same idea, or stimulates the same mental reaction, or has the same meaning is enjoined on the same basis as where the similarity goes to the eye or the ear. Confusion of origin of goods may be caused alone by confusing similarity in the meaning of the designations employed. The whole background of the case must be considered.

Standard Oil Co. v. Standard Oil Co., 252 F.2d 65, 74 (10th Cir. 1958) (footnotes omitted).

In evaluating similarity, "[i]t is axiomatic in trademark law that 'side-by-side' comparison is not the test." *Levi Strauss & Co. v. Blue Bell, Inc.*, 632 F.2d 817, 822 (9th Cir. 1980); *American Home Products Corp. v. Johnson Chemical Co.*, 589 F.2d 103, 107 (2[d] Cir. 1978); *James Burrough Ltd. v. Sign of Beefeater, Inc.*, 540 F.2d 266, 275 (7th Cir.

1976); *Fotomat Corp.*, 437 F. Supp. at 1244. The marks "must be compared in the light of what occurs in the marketplace, not in the courtroom." *James Burrough Ltd.*, 540 F.2d at 275. "A prospective purchaser does not ordinarily carry a sample or specimen of the article he knows well enough to call by its trade name, he necessarily depends upon the mental picture of that which symbolizes origin and ownership of the thing desired." *Avrick v. Rockmont Envelope Co.*, 155 F.2d 568, 573 (10th Cir. 1946). Therefore, the court must determine whether the alleged infringing mark will be confusing to the public when singly presented. *Id.* at 572–73; *American Home Products*, 589 F.2d at 107; *James Burrough Ltd.*, 540 F.2d at 275; *Union Carbide*, 531 F.2d at 382.

"Intent on the part of the alleged infringer to pass off its goods as the product of another raises an inference of likelihood of confusion . . ." *Squirtco v. Seven-Up Co.*, 628 F.2d 1086, 1091 (8th Cir.1980); *Alpha Industries v. Alpha Steel Tube & Shapes, Inc.*, 616 F.2d 440, 446 (9th Cir.1980). "[P]roof that a defendant chose a mark with the intent of copying plaintiff's mark, standing alone, may justify an inference of confusing similarity." *Sun-Fun Products, Inc. v. Suntan Research & Development, Inc.*, 656 F.2d 186, 190 (5th Cir.1981). One who adopts a mark similar to another already established in the marketplace does so at his peril, *Fotomat Corp.*, 437 F. Supp. at 1243, because the court presumes that he "can accomplish his purpose: that is, that the public will be deceived." *AMF Inc.*, 599 F.2d at 354; *Fotomat Corp.*, 437 F. Supp. at 1243. All doubts must be resolved against him. *American Home Products*, 589 F.2d at 107.

Also relevant to likelihood of confusion are the means by which the products are marketed. "Converging marketing channels increase the likelihood of confusion." *AMF Inc.*, 599 F.2d at 353. The possibility of confusion is greatest when products reach the public by the same retail outlets. *See generally Exxon Corp. v. Texas Motor Exchange*, 628 F.2d 500, 505–06 (5th Cir. 1980); *Scott Paper Co. v. Scott's Liquid Gold, Inc.*, 589 F.2d 1225, 1229 (3d Cir.1978). Confusing similarity is most likely when the products themselves are very similar. *Exxon Corp.*, 628 F.2d at 505; *see Fotomat Corp.*, 437 F. Supp. at 1243–44.

Finally, the court must examine the degree of care with which the public will choose the products in the marketplace. " "The general impression of the ordinary purchaser, buying under the normally prevalent conditions of the market and giving the attention such purchasers usually give in buying that class of goods, is the touchstone.' " *McGregor-Doniger*, 599 F.2d at 1137 (quoting 3 R. Callmann, *The Law of Unfair Competition, Trademarks and Monopolies* § 81.2 at 577 (3d ed. 1969) (footnote omitted)); *see Squirtco*, 628 F.2d at 1091. Buyers typically exercise little care in the selection of inexpensive items that may be purchased on impulse. Despite a lower degree of similarity, these items are more likely to be confused than expensive items which are chosen carefully. *Sun-Fun Products*, 656 F.2d at 191; *Fotomat Corp.*, 437 F. Supp. at 1244.

In this case, the district court's resolution of the infringement claim was improperly based solely on a side-by-side package comparison, although the parties presented evidence on other relevant factors, including Clover Club's intent in adopting the trademark "Brew Nuts," the manner in which Beer Nuts and Brew Nuts are marketed, and the degree of care purchasers exercise when buying the products. *See* Restatement of Torts, § 729(b), (c), (d). Moreover, the court erroneously equated likelihood of confusion with similarity. *See AMF Inc.*, 599 F.2d at 350. Similarity must be considered along with the other factors set out in the Restatement to determine whether, under all the circumstances of the marketplace, confusion is likely. The court's failure to weigh all of the relevant factors in determining likelihood of confusion constitutes reversible error. Although we offer no opinion regarding the merits of this case, we remand for a proper evaluation of similarity and a reconsideration of likelihood of confusion under the correct legal standards and the evidence presented.

*   *   *

The case is reversed and remanded for reconsideration of the likelihood of confusion under the legal standards set forth in this opinion . . . .

BEER NUTS, INC. v. CLOVER CLUB FOODS CO. [BEER NUTS II]
605 F.Supp. 855 (D. Utah 1985)

JENKINS, CHIEF JUDGE

This is an action for trademark infringement under the Lanham Act, 15 U.S.C. § 1114 (1976). Beer Nuts, Inc., asserts that the defendant Clover Club Food Company's use of the term BREW NUTS and a drawing of an overflowing stein on a package of sweetened and salted peanuts infringes the plaintiff's registered trademark BEER NUTS®. After a trial on the merits, this court ruled that because there was no likelihood of confusion concerning the origin of the competing products, Clover Club had not infringed Beer Nuts' trademark. *Beer Nuts, Inc. v. Clover Club Foods Co.*, 520 F. Supp. 395 (D. Utah 1981). The United States Court of Appeals for the Tenth Circuit, after concluding that this court based its decision "solely on a side-by-side comparison of the Beer Nuts and Brew Nuts packages," reversed and remanded. *Beer Nuts, Inc., v. Clover Club Foods Co.*, 711 F.2d 934, 941 (10th Cir.1983). . . .

Like the BEER NUTS® trademark, the BREW NUTS mark conveys more than one message: One is to mark origin; another, to suggest a use of the product. However, the court does not hold that Clover Club has established a fair use defense. *See Beer Nuts* 711 F.2d at 937-38. Rather, the court holds that a trademark, such as BEER NUTS®, that uses words from the common reservoir of language and that describes the principal use of the product it represents, is not entitled to the same degree of protection to which a trademark that uses an arbitrary, fanciful word or that does not describe the principal use of the product is entitled. . . . Otherwise, the trademark owner whose trademark both identifies origin and describes the principal use of the product would be at a competitive advantage not intended by the Lanham Act. He would be the only competitor entitled to describe as well as to identify. . .

Accordingly, the court finds that the BREW NUTS package is not so similar to the trademark BEER NUTS® as to create a likelihood of confusion about the source of Clover Club's nuts. This finding is based on both a comparison of the individual features of the BREW NUTS package with the words "Beer Nuts," and on a comparison of the total effect of the BREW NUTS package with the words "Beer Nuts.". . .

The words "Brew Nuts" and "Beer Nuts" are not similar in pronunciation. Aside from the common word "nuts," the two word pairs are not phonetically similar. Clover Club's use of the words "Brew Nuts" does not create a likelihood of confusion about the origin of BREW NUTS. . . .

One of Beer Nuts' principal contentions is that Clover Club's use of an overflowing stein on its package creates a likelihood of confusion about BREW NUTS' origin. Beer Nuts does not object that Clover Club's stein is similar to Beer Nuts' stein because Beer Nuts does not use a stein in its packaging or advertising. Rather, Beer Nuts argues that the verbal translation of the picture creates the confusion.

Obviously, the picture has no sound. If one translates the picture into the word "stein," or "cask," or "mug," or "cup," and compares it with the words "Beer Nuts," one cannot help but note that the appearance, sound, and meaning are different. Beer Nuts argues that it is not the stein that is objectionable, but what is inside the stein, assuming that one knows what is inside. Even if the court assumes that beer is inside the stein, rather than some other brew, such as root beer or even coffee, the verbal translation of the picture at plaintiff's best is "beer," or perhaps "beer stein"-not "Beer Nuts."

Clover Club is not precluded from using language to suggest to its customers that its honey coated nuts are good with beer, so long as the suggestion does not create a likelihood of confusion about the origin of those nuts. Similarly, Clover Club is not precluded from using a picture to make the same suggestion. The court finds that the picture of an overflowing stein has two functions: one is to mark origin; the other, to suggest that Clover Club's nuts are good with beverages, including beer. In marking origin, there is nothing about the stein that suggests the nuts come from Beer Nuts, Inc., or from any source other than Clover Club. The picture does not create a probability that prospective customers will be confused about the origin of Clover Club's nuts. . . .

. . . Beer Nuts argues that because Clover Club was aware of Beer Nuts' trademark and packaging, and because Clover Club adopted packaging that, according to Beer Nuts, is confusingly similar to Beer Nuts' trademark, it follows that Clover Club must have intended to pass BREW NUTS off as the product of Beer Nuts. The court has rejected the premise to Beer Nuts argument-that the BREW NUTS packaging is deceptively similar to the BEER NUTS®) trademark. Accordingly, Clover Club's use of the BREW NUTS packaging does not justify an inference that Clover Club intended to confuse the public. . . .

Clover Club did intend to market a product very similar to BEER NUTS®. Clover Club also intended to market that product in packages that suggest what company officials believed to be the best use of that product-consumption with beverages, including beer. Beer Nuts argues repeatedly that Clover Club's choice of the words "Brew Nuts" over the alternative suggested by its ad agency, "Ah Nuts," is evidence of intent to create confusion. The court disagrees. Clover Club's decision to market its nuts as BREW NUTS rather than Ah Nuts was based on Clover Club's belief that BREW NUTS was a better mark than Ah Nuts would be. . . . The court is unwilling to infer from that decision that Clover Club intended to pass its nuts off as the product of a competitor. . . .

The final factor that the Tenth Circuit has designated as important in the analysis is "the degree of care with which the public will choose the products in the marketplace." *Id.* . . . None of the evidence on the degree of care likely to be exercised by purchasers is at all conclusive. The court finds, however, that an ordinary purchaser who exercises reasonable prudence in purchasing BREW NUTS would view the entire package front, including the Clover Club® trademark, sufficiently long enough to read the words BREW NUTS, see the picture of the stein, and recognize the Clover Club® trademark. Indeed, a purchaser would be careless to purchase the nuts so quickly that he or she would not see the Clover Club®) trademark. . . .

Although it is not one of the factors specifically identified by the Court of Appeals, the court finds the lack of evidence of actual confusion to be probative. . . . BREW NUTS and BEER NUTS® were marketed in the same area for at least three years. Both companies sold tens of thousands of packages of their nuts in the same area during those three years. Throughout the trial, not a single witness testified that he or she had been confused by the BREW NUTS package. . . .

CONCLUSION.

. . .[T]he court finds by a preponderance of the evidence that Clover Clubs' use of its BREW NUTS package does not create a likelihood of confusion about the source of BREW NUTS. That finding is reinforced by the lack of actual confusion during the three years BREW NUTS were marketed in the same area as the plaintiff's product, BEER NUTS®. Accordingly, Clover Club has not infringed Beer Nuts' trademark. . . .

BEER NUTS, INC. v. CLOVER CLUB FOODS CO. [BEER NUTS III]
United States Court of Appeals, Tenth Circuit
805 F.2d 920 (1986)

TACHA, CIRCUIT JUDGE

In our prior opinion, we held that marks may be confusingly similar if, as entities, they look or sound similar or convey the same idea or meaning. We directed the district court to consider appearance, pronunciation of words used, verbal translation of the pictures or designs involved, and suggestion. These factors are not to be considered in isolation; they must be examined in the context of the marks as a whole as they are encountered by consumers in the marketplace. Similarities are to be weighed more heavily than differences, especially when the trademarks are used on virtually identical products packaged in the same manner. 711 F.2d at 940–41. The district court erred in focusing almost exclusively on the differences between the trademarks. The district court found that the BEER NUTS and BREW NUTS trademarks are not similar in appearance because the words do not look alike, the meaning of the word "brew" is broader than the word "beer," and the Clover Club trademark appears on the BREW NUTS package. The district court also found that the words in the trademarks are not similar in pronunciation and that Clover Club's use of the overflowing stein with the words BREW NUTS does not give rise to a verbal translation that equates BEER NUTS with BREW NUTS. 605 F. Supp. at 860.

Although there are clearly differences between the marks, the phonetic and semantic similarities outweigh these differences. The words "brew" and "beer" are not identical, but they have a similar sound. They are both one syllable words having four letters three of which are the same, and they both begin with the same letter. Moreover, the evidence shows that the word "brew" is a common synonym for "beer." Clover Club's marketing manager admitted at trial that the word "brew" in Clover Club's mark connotes "beer." Because Clover Club joined the term "brew" with a representation of a stein which has an overflowing head of foam, the word "brew" in Clover Club's trademark cannot reasonably be taken to mean coffee or tea or beverages in general; it can only be understood to mean beer. BREW NUTS thus necessarily conveys the same meaning or idea as BEER NUTS. The presence of the smaller Clover Club trademark is not enough to eliminate the likelihood of confusion in this case where the products and their marks are similar because consumers typically do not engage in side by side comparison of the products. 711 F.2d at 941. Moreover, a secondary trademark on a small, inexpensive item such as a package of nuts does not eliminate the possibility of confusion because consumers exercise little care in purchasing these products. *Id.*

We previously instructed the district court that similarities in the marketing of the products and the degree of care exercised by purchasers are factors to be weighed in light of the similarity of the marks. 711 F.2d at 940–41. Both Beer Nuts and Clover Club use their marks on sweetened salted peanuts. There is no dispute that the products are marketed in the same manner. The district court correctly understood the effect which we held those facts should have on its consideration of the issue of likelihood of confusion, stating:

> Accordingly, less similarity between the BREW NUTS package and the BEER NUTS trademark may lead to a likelihood of confusion than when the goods themselves are different or when the goods themselves are marketed differently. The court recognizes that "[t]he possibility of confusion is greatest when products reach the public by the same retail outlets," *Beer Nuts*, at 941, and that "[c]onfusing similarity is most likely when the products are themselves very similar." *Id.*

605 F. Supp. at 863. Nevertheless, the district court failed to give the virtual identity of the parties' products and marketing methods proper weight. Because the marks are very similar in many respects, the virtual identity of the products and marketing

methods adds strength to the position that the products are likely to be confused.

Regarding the degree of care exercised by purchasers, this court stated that "[b]uyers typically exercise little care in the selection of inexpensive items that may be purchased on impulse. Despite a lower degree of similarity, these items are more likely to be confused than expensive items which are chosen carefully." 711 F.2d at 941 (citations omitted). The district court noted that BREW NUTS and BEER NUTS are both relatively inexpensive snack foods. 605 F. Supp. at 863. Furthermore, Clover Club's president admitted that Clover Club's BREW NUTS are purchased as impulse items in that they are not generally on a shopper's grocery list. According to this evidence and the law of this case, the district court should have concluded that the two products are purchased with little care and are thus likely to be confused. The district court failed to reach this conclusion and instead found that consumers exercise substantial care in purchasing the parties' products and are not likely to be confused.[1] 605 F. Supp. at 863–64. We find that the district court's conclusion is erroneous.

Clover Club's intent in adopting BREW NUTS with an overflowing stein as a trademark is also a factor in assessing likelihood of confusion. . . . We thus instructed the district court that deliberate adoption of a similar mark may lead to an inference of intent to pass off goods as those of another which in turn supports a finding of likelihood of confusion.

The inference of intent is especially strong when the parties have had a prior relationship. Such a relationship provides evidence of the alleged infringer's intent to trade on the plaintiff's goodwill. *Sicilia Di R. Biebow & Co. v. Cox*, 732 F.2d 417, 432 (5th Cir. 1984). Beer Nuts' use of its trademark predated by two decades the use of the BREW NUTS trademark. Clover Club distributed BEER NUTS for many years prior to developing BREW NUTS. BEER NUTS is a very successful product. Clover Club cannot deny knowledge of the BEER NUTS trademark and the popularity of the product. Clover Club sells its product in the same markets as Beer Nuts. The names of the products are similar. The packages are similar. Clover Club's advertising agency advised against the use of the BREW NUTS trademark. The combination of these factors makes clear that Clover Club deliberately adopted a mark similar to the BEER NUTS mark.

Notwithstanding this evidence, the district court refused to draw any inference of intent, stating that "Beer Nuts presented no direct evidence that Clover Club intended to pass BREW NUTS off as the product of another and thus derive benefit from another's reputation." 605 F. Supp. at 862. The district court concluded that no inference of intent could be drawn from the similarities between the trademarks because the marks are not similar. *Id.* However, as we have previously noted, the district court erred in concluding that the marks are not similar, and intent should have been inferred from that similarity.

The district court also relied on Clover Club's assertion that Frito Lay, not Beer Nuts, is its competition. 605 F. Supp. at 863. However, the inference of intent which results from the deliberate adoption of a similar trademark is not rebutted by evidence as to who the infringer's competitors might be. The ultimate question is whether there

---

[1] In reaching its conclusion, the district court relied on testimony of Clover Club's president that consumers often exercise great care in purchasing potato chips. 605 F. Supp. at 863–64. The testimony concerned a study Clover Club had conducted fifteen years earlier. The study itself was not introduced into evidence. The witness testified that the study consisted of videotapes of customers selecting potato chips in the snack food aisle of a Salt Lake City grocery store. He further testified that from the study he concluded that many people carefully examined the packages and compared them with competitors' packages before they made a selection. Given the applicable law, this testimony cannot outweigh the uncontested fact that BEER NUTS and BREW NUTS are both inexpensive snack foods purchased as impulse items.

BEER NUTS contends that the testimony concerning the study is inadmissible. Since this testimony cannot overcome the other evidence in the case, we need not rule on BEER NUTS' contention.

is a likelihood of confusion between the trademarks; it does not matter who the infringer identifies as its chief competitor in the market.

Because of the similarity of the marks and the inferences that should have been drawn therefrom, all doubts should have been resolved against the alleged infringer Clover Club. 711 F.2d at 941. We find no indication in the trial court opinion that this legal standard was applied to the factual inquiry.

In deciding whether likelihood of confusion exists, the district court noted that Beer Nuts presented no evidence of actual confusion. The court stated that this absence of evidence "supports the conclusion that confusion about the source of BREW NUTS is unlikely." 605 F. Supp. at 864.

While evidence of actual confusion supports a finding of likelihood of confusion, *Soweco*, 617 F.2d at 1186; *Union Carbide*, 531 F.2d at 383, absence of such evidence does *not* necessarily support a finding of *no* likelihood of confusion, especially when the products involved are inexpensive, *Sicilia Di R. Biebow & Co.*, 732 F.2d at 433. "It would be exceedingly difficult to detect instances of actual confusion when . . . the goods are relatively inexpensive and their actual properties are exactly identical. . . ." *Chevron Chem. Co. v. Voluntary Purchasing Groups*, 659 F.2d 695, 705 (5th Cir.1981), *cert. denied*, 457 U.S. 1126 (1982). Purchasers are unlikely to bother to inform the trademark owner when they are confused about an inexpensive product. *Union Carbide*, 531 F.2d at 383.

In the present case, it is undisputed that the products are inexpensive and virtually identical. Therefore, the district court erred in finding that the absence of evidence of actual confusion supports a conclusion that there is no likelihood of confusion.

* * *

Reversed and remanded.

6.04   Similarity of Appearance, Sound or Connotation

Similarity of appearance has always been the paramount criterion in determining likelihood of confusion. If anything, its importance has been augmented in recent decades by the impact of new communication technologies such as the Internet, television, cell phones, mass media advertising and self-service marketing. Generally, similarity of sound has been accorded less weight by the courts and less attention by the infringers. Even in a visual and graphic age, however, it remains a principal trademark consideration. The problem of similarity of connotation also raises difficult and subtle semantic questions. As with questions of appearance and pronunciation, however, the issue in cases of similar connotation remains not what is the dictionary definition (although that can be probative evidence), but what is likely to be the understanding of an appreciable number of those who may encounter the marks.

Appearance

In deciding whether the appearance of two marks is likely to result in confusion, consideration must be given to the visual impression created by each mark as a whole in the marketplace. It is not a question of similarity or dissimilarity of the various parts considered in a vacuum. At issue is whether or not consumers or potential consumers are likely to be confused in their general recollection of the marks, rather than the resemblance, or lack of it, disclosed by a side-by-side comparison by the court. *Malletier v. Burlington Coat Factory Warehouse Corp.*, 426 F.3d 532, 538 (2[d]Cir. 2005) ("a district court must ask not whether differences are easily discernable on simultaneous viewing, but whether they are likely to be memorable enough to dispel confusion on serial viewing"); *Louis Vuitton Malletier v. Dooney & Bourke, Inc.*, 454 F.3d 108 (2[d] Cir. 2006) (to the same effect). *See International Ass'n of Machinists & Aero Workers v. Winship Green Nursing Center*, 103 F.3d 196, 201 (1st Cir. 1996) ("any meaningful inquiry into the likelihood of confusion necessarily must replicate the circumstances in which the ordinary consumer actually confronts. . . the conflicting mark"); *Beer Nuts, Inc. v. Clover Club Foods Company*, 805 F.2d 920 (10th Cir. 1986). A side-by-side comparison may be more likely to encourage subjective, "visceral" judicial reactions to marks. *See Libman Co. v. Vining Indus., Inc.*, 69 F.3d 1360, 1362 (7th Cir. 1995), *cert. denied*, 517 U.S. 1234 (1996) (reversing lower court judgment for plaintiff after noting plaintiff's failure to object to appellate court's side-by-side comparison of the parties' products at oral argument). *Cf. McNeil Nutritional, LLC v. Heartland Sweeteners*, LLC 511 F.3d 350 (3d Cir. 2007) ("if buyers typically see the two products side-by-side, as is true in this case, then a side-by-side comparison may be appropriate.")

Since rights in trademarks arise out of use, they necessarily exist in the entire mark as used, and not as segmented or dissected. *Joseph Schlitz Brewing Co. v. Houston Ice & Brewing Co.*, 250 U.S. 28, 29 (1919) (Holmes, J.: "It is a fallacy to break the fagot stick by stick"); *Beckwith v. Commissioner of Patents*, 252 U.S. 538, 545, 546 (1920); *Duluth News-Tribune v. Mesabi Publ. Co.*, 84 F.3d 1093, 1097 (8th Cir. 1996) ("[r]ather than consider the similarities between component parts of the marks, we must evaluate the impression that each mark in its entirety is likely to have on a purchaser exercising the attention usually given by purchasers of such products").

A predominant or salient feature of a mark nonetheless may be entitled to extra weight in determining likelihood of confusion where consumers or potential consumers are more likely to have a general recollection of the principal feature than the mark as a whole. *See Ty, Inc. v. The Jones Group*, 237 F.3d 891 (7th Cir. 2001) (appropriate to consider "salient portion of mark" in finding confusion likely between "Beanie Babies" for plush toy animals and "Beanie Racers" for plush toy racing cars). *Compare Packard Press, Inc. v. Hewlett-Packard, Inc.*, 227 F.3d 1352 (Fed. Cir. 2000) (by focusing only on the "Packard" portion of the parties' "Hewlett-Packard" and "Packard Technology" marks, the Board had improperly dissected them; "it is proper to indicate that more weight is given to a particular component of the mark . . . [but] that does not excuse consideration of the other components of the mark as a whole"). After the district court in this case conducted the proper analysis on remand, its holding of confusing similarity was affirmed, based on "Packard" being the "dominating and distinguishing element" of the latter mark. *Hewlett-Packard v. Packard Press, Inc.*, 281 F.3d 1261 (Fed. Cir. 2002).

The mere repositioning or changing of one letter in a well-known trademark commonly will not avoid a likelihood of confusion and a determination of infringement. *See Royal Appliance Mfg. Co. v. Minuteman Int'l, Inc.*, 30 Fed. Appx. 964 (Fed. Cir. 2002) (MVP for domestic and industrial vacuum cleaners held confusingly similar to MPV for commercial and industrial vacuum cleaners, where both began with "M", were made up of the same letters, and sounded alike); *Squirt Co. v. Seven-Up Co.*, 480 F.Supp. 789 (E.D. Mo. 1979), *aff'd on infringement finding*, 628 F.2d 1086 (8th Cir. 1980) (QUIRST infringes SQUIRT for soft drinks); *Cartier, Inc. v. Three Sheaves Co., Inc.*, 465 F.Supp. 123 (S.D.N.Y. 1979) (CATTIER infringes CARTIER for cosmetics).

In *Vornado, Inc. v. Breuer Electrical Mfg. Co.*, 390 F.2d 724 (C.C.P.A. 1968), the manufacturer of TORNADO vacuum cleaners and other electrical machines opposed an application for registration of VORNADO for electrical appliances. Despite the fact that TORNADO is a common well-known word and VORNADO was a coined mark, the court found confusion likely based upon the striking similarity in sound and appearance of the two marks, and affirmed the denial of registration. Applicant had contended that the differing styles of presentation would adequately distinguish the two, but the court held that "the display of a mark is of no material significance since the display may be changed at any time as may be dictated by the fancy of the applicant or the owner of the mark."

In dissent, Judge Rich argued that the public was likely to remember the marks as different, and distinguish their sources, because VORNADO is "an irritating trade mark."

> I will amplify my meaning by saying that my first impulse was to call it an "itchy" mark, that word denoting a "mild stimulation of pain receptors." This may be a personal reaction to the mark which I have to many marks which are just enough different from common words to make one brood about them and their possible origins. The one thing I am certain about with respect to such marks is that they are not the words they resemble. That is why I hold the opinion I do in this case that confusion is unlikely.

Because of the nature of the Internet, consumer perception of the appearance of domain names may differ from their perception of the appearance of any related trademarks. For example, the domain names "entrepreneur.com" owned by the plaintiff publisher of Entrepreneur magazine and entrepreneurpr.com owned by defendant's Entrepreneur PR public relations business were at issue in *Entrepreneur Media, Inc. v. Smith*, 279 F.3d 1135 (9th Cir. 2002). The court noted their similarity but observed that, "[i]n the Internet context, consumers are aware that domain names for different websites are quite often similar, because of the need for language economy, and that very small differences matter." Finding issues of fact as to whether confusion was likely, the court reversed the summary judgment granted plaintiff and remanded that portion of the case. *See also NVST.com v. Nvest L.L.P.*, 32 Fed. Appx. 207 (9th Cir. 2002) (the owner of mark NVST for investment services and the domain name nvst.com was denied preliminary relief against defendant mutual fund's use of domain names such as nvestfunds.com and nvestlp.com, because of, among other things, the presence of the "e" in defendant's domain names and "the additional words alongside the nvest letter string").

Sound

Two marks, hardly similar in appearance or meaning, may be so similar in sound as to result in a likelihood of confusion, particularly where the products are ordinarily purchased by spoken word. *Kimberly-Clark Corp. v. H. Douglas Enterprises*, 774 F.2d 1144 (Fed. Cir. 1985) (HUGGIES v. DOUGIES for disposable diapers); *Crown Radio Corp. v. Soundscriber Corp.*, 506 F.2d 1392 (C.C.P.A. 1974) (CROWNSCRIBER v. SOUNDSCRIBER for tape recorders); *Grotrian, Helfferich, Schulz, etc. v. Steinway & Sons*, 523 F.2d 1331 (2[d] Cir. 1975) (GROTRIAN-STEINWEG v. STEINWAY for German-made pianos); *Dr. Ing h.f.c. Porsche Ag. v. Zin*, 481 F. Supp. 1247 (N.D. Tex. 1979) (PORSHA for automobile sales and repair of PORSCHE cars v. PORSCHE for automobile manufacture). *Cf. Surfvivor Media, Inc. v. Survivor Prods.*, 406 F.3d 625 (9th Cir. 2005) (SURFVIVOR for Hawaiian beached-themed products, and SURVIVOR for a reality TV series and its collateral merchandise; "[p[honetically, [the two marks] are nearly identical. . .[h]owever, 'surfvivor', a coined term, connotes a more precise reference to surfing"; because of that, and other differences in the parties' uses, confusion held unlikely).

In considering similarity of sound, the "correct" pronunciation of a trademark is not the issue. The issue is the pronunciation used by potential purchasers, even if it is incorrect. *See J.B. Williams Co. v. Le Conte Cosmetics, Inc.*, 523 F.2d 187 (9th Cir. 1975); *National Distillers and Chemical Corp. v. Wm. Grant & Sons, Inc.*, 505 F.2d 719, 721 (C.C.P.A. 1974); *Lebow Bros, Inc. v. Lebole Euroconf S.p.A.*, 503 F.Supp. 209, 212 (E.D. Pa. 1980).

Connotation

APPLE COMPUTER, INC v. FORMULA INTERN. INC.
725 F.2d 521 (9th Cir. 1984)

FERGUSON, CIRCUIT JUDGE

Formula International, Inc. (Formula) appeals from the district court's grant of a preliminary injunction in favor of the plaintiff, Apple Computer, Inc. (Apple). The injunction prohibits Formula from copying computer programs having copyrights registered to Apple, from importing, selling, distributing, or advertising those copies, and from using the mark "Pineapple" or any other mark or name confusingly similar to the trademarks used by Apple. Because we find that the district court did not abuse its discretion or rely on erroneous legal premises in issuing the injunction, we affirm.

FACTS:

Formula is a wholesaler and retailer of electronic parts and electronic kits. In May 1982, Formula entered the computer market, selling a computer kit under the trademark "Pineapple." The computer was designed to be compatible with application software written for the home computer manufactured by Apple, the Apple II. . . . Apple brought suit against Formula claiming copyright, trademark, and patent infringement, as well as unfair competition. Formula counterclaimed for antitrust violations and unfair competition and sought declaratory relief as to the validity of certain patents and copyrights. After a brief period of discovery, Apple moved for a preliminary injunction based on its copyright and trademark infringement claims, and on its unfair competition claims. The district court granted the motion on April 12, 1983, and the district court's opinion is reported at 562 F.Supp. 775 (C.D.Cal.1983).

* * *

II. DID THE DISTRICT COURT ABUSE ITS DISCRETION IN PRELIMINARILY ENJOINING FORMULA FROM USING THE TRADEMARK "PINEAPPLE" ON ITS COMPUTER PRODUCTS?

A. *Likelihood of Success on the Merits*

Formula contends that the trial court abused its discretion in preliminarily enjoining Formula from using the trademark "Pineapple" because it failed to consider the eight factors set forth in *AMF v. Sleekcraft Boats*, 599 F.2d 341, 348-49 (9th Cir.1979) in determining whether a likelihood of confusion of the parties' trademarks existed. . . . We cannot say that the trial court abused its discretion in concluding that the use of the name "Pineapple" is confusingly similar to the Apple trademark when used on related goods. Formula concedes that both Apple and Formula sell similar products through similar marketing channels and also that Formula intended to expand its product line into assembled computers. Under these circumstances, it was not a clear abuse of discretion for the trial court to conclude that the addition of the prefix "Pine" to the trademark "Apple" presented a likelihood of confusion. One of the possible effects of the use of the prefix may be to suggest that the computer kits are manufactured by licensees or subsidiaries of Apple. *See Goodyear Tire & Rubber Co. v. H. Rosenthal Co.*, 246 F.Supp. 724 (D.Minn.1965).

B. *Irreparable Injury*

Once Apple demonstrated a likelihood of success on the merits of its trademark infringement claim, the district court could have reasonably concluded that continuing infringement would result in loss of control over Apple's reputation and loss of goodwill.

See, e.g., Black Hills Jewelry Mfg. Co. v. Gold Rush, Inc., 633 F.2d 746, 753 (8th Cir.1980); *St. Ives Lab., Inc. v. Nature's Own Lab.*, 529 F.Supp. 347, 350 (C.D.Cal.1981). Formula, on the other hand, has only recently entered the computer market and its computer sales constitute a minor percentage of its total sales. Thus, it cannot be said that the district court abused its discretion in concluding that continuing infringement by Formula presented a possibility of irreparable harm to Apple and that the balance of the hardships tipped in Apple's favor.

CONCLUSION:

The district court did not abuse its discretion or rely on erroneous legal premises in issuing the preliminary injunction.

AFFIRMED.

*   *   *

Confusion as to source may arise primarily as a result of the mental associations evoked by two marks. *AMF Inc. v. Sleekcraft Boats*, 599 F.2d 341 (9th Cir. 1979) (SLEEKCRAFT v. SLICKCRAFT for recreational boats); *American Home Products Corp. v. Johnson Chemical Co.*, 589 F.2d 103 (2[d] Cir. 1978) (ROACH MOTEL v. ROACH INN for insect traps). *But see National Distiller's and Chemical Corp. v. William Grant & Sons, Inc.*, 505 F.2d 719 (C.C.P.A. 1974) where the court held DUET for prepared alcoholic cocktails not likely to be confused with DUVET for French brandy and stated, "[t]he familiar is readily distinguishable from the unfamiliar; DUET is a familiar word; DUVET is not." *Accord Jacobs v. International Multifoods Corp.*, 688 F.2d 1234 (C.C.P.A. 1982) (BOSTON TEA PARTY for tea not infringed by BOSTON SEA PARTY for restaurant services). In affirming the dismissal of a petition to cancel the registration of HUNGRY HOBO based on HOBO JOE'S, both for restaurant services, the court in *Colony Foods, Inc. v. Sagemark, Ltd.*, 735 F.2d 1336, 1339 (Fed. Cir. 1984) approvingly cited the following analysis by the Trademark Trial and Appeal Board:

> Comparing them in their entireties we find petitioner's mark [HOBO JOE'S] to designate a particular person of the itinerant or vagrant persuasion while respondent's mark [HUNGRY HOBO] gives the impression of an anonymous person of that kind in need of a meal. Thus, customers would leave petitioner's restaurants with an image of a particular individual hobo named Joe, as opposed to the concept of an anonymous hobo whose distinguishing characteristic is that he happens to be hungry, as would be the case with respondent's mark. Stated otherwise, the fact that both marks play on the hobo theme is not enough to make confusion likely, in light of the differences in the marks as a whole.

See also Playtex Prods. v. Georgia-Pacific Corp., 390 F.3d 158 (2[d] Cir. 2004) (while "wet" and "moist" were "almost synonymous," the dissimilarities in sound and appearance made confusion unlikely between WET ONES and QUILTED NORTHERN MOIST ONES, for pre-moistened wipes); *Luigino's Inc. v. Stouffer Corp.*, 170 F.3d 827 (8th Cir. 1999) (LEAN 'N TASTY did not infringe LEAN CUISINE for low-fat frozen food; shared use of the descriptive term "lean" was insufficient to create confusing similarity, and "tasty" and "cuisine" have dissimilar meanings). Courts normally emphasize what the words mean to the particular segment of the public allegedly confused. *Cf. Earthquake Sound Corp. v. Bumper Indus.*, 352 F.3d 1210 (9th Cir. 2003) (CARQUAKE likely to be confused with EARTHQUAKE and BASS-QUAKE, all for car audio products; while "visually distinct", the marks "have an obvious aural and connotative similarity"); *TBC Corp. v. Holsa, Inc.*, 126 F.3d 1470 (Fed. Cir. 1997) (GRAND SLAM for tires likely to be confused with GRAND AM for tires; meaning of the former in the fields of bridge and sports would be unfamiliar to many tire buyers and "will have no effect on their minds in seeing the term on tires"; marks were too closely similar in sound, in particular, and in appearance).

Synonymous Marks

MOBIL OIL CORP. v. PEGASUS PETROLEUM CORP.
818 F.2d 254 (2d Cir. 1987)

LUMBARD, CIRCUIT JUDGE

Mobil Oil Corporation brought this action in the Southern District charging Pegasus Petroleum Corporation with trademark infringement and unfair competition, 15 U.S.C. § 1114(1); false designation of origin, 15 U.S.C. § 1125(a); and trademark dilution, N.Y.Gen.Bus.Law § 368-d. On July 8, 1986, after a three-day bench trial, Judge MacMahon entered judgment for Mobil on each of its claims, dismissed Pegasus Petroleum's counterclaims seeking to cancel Mobil's trademark registration, and enjoined Pegasus Petroleum from using the mark "Pegasus" in connection with the petroleum industry or related businesses. We affirm.

Mobil, one of the world's largest corporations, manufactures and sells a vast array of petroleum products to industrial consumers and to the general public. Since 1931, Mobil has made extensive use of its well known "flying horse" symbol-representing Pegasus, the winged horse of Greek mythology-in connection with its petroleum business. . . . As the district court explained, it is "undisputed that Mobil's extensive use of the flying horse symbol for such a long period of time in connection with all of Mobil's commercial activity has rendered it a very strong mark. Indeed, counsel for [Pegasus Petroleum] could think of few trademarks, if any, that were stronger trademarks in American commerce today." . . .

Pegasus Petroleum, incorporated in 1981, confines its activities to oil trading, and does not sell directly to the general public. Its founder, Gregory Callimanopulos, testified that he selected the name "Pegasus Petroleum" because he wanted a name with both mythical connotations and alliterative qualities. Callimanopulos admitted that he knew of Mobil's flying horse symbol when he picked the name, but claimed that he did not know that the symbol represented Pegasus or that Mobil used the word "Pegasus" in connection with its petroleum business. . . .

* * *

Pegasus Petroleum does not dispute the district court's conclusion that the strength of Mobil's flying horse mark is "without question, and perhaps without equal." As an arbitrary mark-there is nothing suggestive of the petroleum business in the flying horse symbol-Mobil's symbol deserves "the most protection the Lanham Act can provide." *Lois Sportswear, U.S.A., Inc. v. Levi Strauss & Co.*, 799 F.2d 867, 871 (2d Cir.1986). On the other hand, Pegasus Petroleum vigorously attacks the district court's finding of similarity between the two marks, arguing that the district court erred by blindly equating the word "Pegasus" with its pictorial representation-Mobil's flying horse. While we agree that words and their pictorial representations should not be equated as a matter of law, a district court may make such a determination as a factual matter. *See, e.g., Beer Nuts, Inc. v. King Nut Co.*, 477 F.2d 326, 329 (6th Cir.) ("It is well settled that words and their pictorial representation are treated the same in determining the likelihood of confusion between two marks."), *cert. denied*, 414 U.S. 858, 94 S.Ct. 66, 38 L.Ed.2d 108 (1973); *Izod, Ltd. v. Zip Hosiery Co.*, 405 F.2d 575, 577 (C.C.P.A.1969) ("Members of the purchasing public viewing appellant's pictorial representation of a feline animal as applied to men's and women's outer shirts and appellee's literal designation TIGER HEAD for men's work socks might well and reasonably conclude that the respective goods of the parties emanated from the same source."): *Instrumentalist Co. v. Marine Corps League*, 509 F.Supp. 323, 328 (N.D.Ill.1981) ("the fact that defendants' certificate most prominently displays a picture of Sousa (rather than a literal transcription of his name) does not preclude a finding of infringement"). *See generally* 2 J. McCarthy, *Trademarks and Unfair Competition,* § 23:8 at 68 & n. 10 (2d ed. 1984) (citing cases). Judge MacMahon made such a determination here:

> "[W]e find that the similarity of the mark exists in the strong probability that prospective purchasers of defendant's product will equate or translate Mobil's symbol for "Pegasus" and vice versa. We find that the word "Pegasus" evokes the symbol of the flying red horse and that the flying horse is associated in the mind with Mobil. In other words, the symbol of the flying horse and its name "Pegasus" are synonymous." That conclusion finds support in common sense as well as the record .

*   *   *

Mobil's ubiquitous presence throughout the petroleum industry further increases the likelihood that a consumer will confuse Pegasus Petroleum with Mobil. *See Armco, Inc. v. Armco Burglar Alarm Co.,* 693 F.2d 1155, 1161 (5ᵗʰ Cir.1982) ("Diversification makes it more likely that a potential customer would associate the non-diversified company's services with the diversified company, even though the two companies do not actually compete."). Finally, the great similarity between the two marks-the district court concluded that they were "synonymous"-entitles Mobil's mark to protection over a broader range of related products. *Cf. Squirtco v. Seven-Up Co.,* 628 F.2d 1086, 1091 (8ᵗʰ Cir.1980) (closely related products require less similarity to support a finding of trademark infringement). . . .

For the foregoing reasons, we agree with the district court's finding that Pegasus Petroleum infringed on Mobil's registered flying horse trademark and therefore affirm its judgment. Mobil's "unfair competition claim is governed by essentially the same considerations as its infringement claim." *Steinway & Sons, supra,* 523 F.2d at 1342 n. 21. Therefore, we also affirm the district court on Mobil's unfair competition claim. As the judgment finds full support in the district court's findings on Mobil's first two claims, we need not consider Mobil's other two claims-false designation of origin, and trademark dilution under New York law.

AFFIRMED.

*   *   *

In *Mobil Oil,* the record contained substantial fact evidence supporting a finding of likelihood of confusion, including evidence that defendant's use of the word mark PEGASUS had actually confused consumers. What are the outer limits of the synonymous mark doctrine? Should its application be confined to cases where the factual evidence in favor of likelihood of confusion is strong? A winged horse looks nothing like the letter combination PEGASUS. In what situations should similarity of meaning among marks trump their dissimilar appearance?

Should there be any legal presumptions as to whether the consumer goodwill associated with a mark resides more in its appearance or its meaning?

The connotations of words and symbols involve psychological and environmental as well as strictly semantic and communicative considerations. In one of the many legal disputes over the years following the historic order that the Standard Oil Trust be dissolved, *Standard Oil v. United States,* 221 U.S. 1 (1911), Humble Oil, a wholly owned subsidiary of Standard Oil of New Jersey, sought a declaratory judgment allowing it to use its ESSO mark in a five-state area historically inhabited by defendant Standard Oil of Kentucky. *Standard Oil Co. (Kentucky) v. Humble Oil & Refining Co.,* 363 F.2d 945 (5ᵗʰ Cir. 1966). The district court perceived dissimilarities in sound between the pronunciation of ESSO and SO (short for "Standard Oil") and between the appearance of the party's signs, and held that there was no likelihood of confusion as to source. In reversing, the appellate court noted that courts in other parts of the country had found no dissimilarity in sound, and went on to state that:

> The test is not whether an ordinary buyer can on normal inspection tell that "ESSO" as shown on signs looks different from "Standard" or "Standard Oil" when shown on signs. Rather the test is whether some normally intelligent buyers think that "ESSO" is another name for Standard Oil or think it is in fact a Standard Oil designation, and therefore, believe ESSO stations are Standard Oil stations.

> The long history of Standard Oil litigation and the many and varied instances of confusion in the record led the appellate court to conclude that "the public believes that all of the pseudonyms for Standard Oil [*e.g.* SOHIO] belong to the same or related companies."

See also Standard Oil Co. v. Standard Oil Co., 252 F.2d 65 (10th Cir. 1958)

Foreign Terms

Even a foreign word may create likely confusion with an American trademark if the connotation is similar. *In re American Safety Razor Co.*, 2 U.S.P.Q.2d 1459 (T.T.A.B. 1987) (GOOD MORNING for shaving cream confusingly similar to BUENOS DIAS for soap). *Compare In re Sarkil, Ltd.*, 721 F.2d 353 (Fed. Cir. 1983), in which the court held that the French word REPECHAGE, which has various meanings including "make-up examination," was not confusingly similar in connotation to registered mark SECOND CHANCE, and *Pizzeria Uno Corp. v. Temple*, 747 F.2d 1522 (4th Cir. 1984), in which the appellate court reversed a lower court holding that PIZZERIA UNO for restaurant services was the equivalent of "Number One [or Best] Pizzeria," a weak descriptive mark not infringed by TACO UNO for similar services. The correct translation, according to the appellate court, was "merely" "one", no more and no less, making plaintiff's mark suggestive and, ultimately, infringed. In *Morrison Entertainment Group, Inc. v. Nintendo of Am., Inc.*, 56 Fed. Appx. 782 (9th Cir. 2003), POKEMON for a popular toy character was held unlikely to be confused with plaintiff's MONSTER IN MY POCKET mark, despite "po-kay-mon" being an abbreviation in Japanese for "pocket monster." Casual American observers would not know the origin of the word, and even if the "foreign equivalents doctrine" were applied, "any similarity in meaning between the two marks is not sufficient to overcome the very significant difference in the sight and sound of the marks." *Cf. Attrezzi, LLC v. Maytag Corp.*, 436 F.3d 32 (1st Cir. 2006) (while "attrezzi" is Italian for "tools", it was not merely descriptive for either plaintiff's kitchen products retail store or defendant's kitchen appliances, and confusion was likely).

6.05 Marketing Environment

Courts tend to presume that consumers are unlikely to assume that widely divergent products (infant care products and automobile parts, for example, or plumbing services and investment banking services) would emanate from the same source. This presumption often applies despite the same or similar marks being used in connection with such goods or services. Our experience as consumers conditions our conscious or subconscious thought process in concluding, correctly or not, that products come from the same or a related source. All conceivable factors and circumstances affecting both the physical environment where particular goods are purchased, or the thought patterns of the people themselves who customarily make such purchases, are a part of the marketing environment. All of that environment bears upon the issue of likelihood of confusion. Courts have long recognized this psychological dimension of trademarks: "The creation of a market through an established symbol implies that people float on a psychological current engendered by the various advertising devices which give a trade-mark its potency. It is that which [trademark law] protects." *Mishawaka Rubber & Woolen Mfg. Co. v. S. S. Kresge Co.*, 316 U.S. 203, 208 (1942).

CALIFORNIA FRUIT GROWERS EXCHANGE v. SUNKIST BAKING CO.
166 F.2d 971 (7th Cir. 1947)

MINTON, CIRCUIT JUDGE

*   *   *

. . . [T]he plaintiff Exchange is a non-profit co-operative marketing association incorporated under the laws of California and is engaged primarily in marketing and selling citrus fruits throughout the United States and in foreign countries. The plaintiff Corporation is a New York corporation engaged in the selection, preparing, padding, and marketing of canned and dried fruits and vegetables, including raisins, throughout the United States and in foreign countries.

Exchange has employed the trade-mark "Sunkist" in the sale of over two billion dollars worth of goods and has expended over forty million dollars in advertising the trade-mark. Certificates of registration for the trade-mark "Sunkist" have been issued to Exchange by the United States Patent Office for oranges, lemons, citrus fruits, oils and acids, pectin, citrus-flavored non-alcoholic maltless beverages as soft drinks, and concentrates for making soft drinks. Corporation has employed the trade-mark "Sun-Kist" since 1907 and has sold approximately fifty million dollars worth of goods bearing such trade-mark and has expended in excess of $350,000 in advertising it. Certificates of registration for the trade-mark "Sun-Kist" have been issued by the Patent Office to Corporation for canned and dried fruits and vegetables, milk, butter, walnuts, catsup, pickles, olive oil, jams, jellies, olives, coffee, tea, beans, pineapple juice, grape juice, tomato juice, raisins, grapes, and various other products. The joint and concurrent use of the trade-marks "Sunkist" and "Sun-Kist" by both plaintiffs has eventuated under and by virtue of an agreement between them whereby each has granted the other the right to employ the mark on the goods aforesaid.

The defendant Sunkist Baking Company is . . . engaged in baking and selling bread and buns, including white bread, whole-wheat bread, "Weet-Hart" bread and raisin bread, in interstate commerce, under the firm name and style of "Sunkist Baking Co.," in and about Rock Island and adjacent cities. Each loaf of bread sold by the defendants is enclosed in a wrapper bearing the name "Sunkist Baking Co." and also the words "Sunkist Bread. . . ."

The court found that the plaintiffs' and the defendants' goods are sold in the same channels and may be consumed together, and that the defendants have endeavored to appropriate and capitalize upon the plaintiffs' trade-marks. . . .

*   *   *

Unless "Sunkist" covers everything edible under the sun, we cannot believe that anyone whose I.Q. is high enough to be regarded by the law would ever be confused or would be likely to be confused in the purchase of a loaf of bread branded as "Sunkist" because someone else sold fruits and vegetables under that name. The purchaser is buying bread, not a name. If the plaintiffs sold bread under the name "Sunkist," that would present a different question; but the plaintiffs do not, and there is no finding that the plaintiffs ever applied the word "Sunkist" to bakery products.

*   *   *

We do not think there is a finding that there is likelihood of confusion as to the source of origin of the products, as required by the Lanham Act.

The court made the following finding as a part of Finding 12: "Defendants' bread bearing the word 'Sunkist' as used by defendants would naturally or reasonably be supposed to come from plaintiffs."

Let us assume that this finding can be separated from its context in Finding 12, which we do not think it can be, and that it is a finding that there is likelihood of confusion among the public as to the source of origin. Then this finding is not sustained by substantial evidence. The only evidence to support this finding is the testimony of two so-called experts who testified on behalf of the plaintiffs, and the fact that bread is sold in the same class of stores and to the same class of customers as the plaintiffs' fruits and vegetables. Against this finding is the difference in the nature of the products themselves — they are not of the same descriptive properties. As to this difference, its weight and significance is as open to us as to the District Courts. Certainly the stores where the products of the parties are sold and the customers to whom they are sold are as well-known to us as to the District Court, and such subsidiary facts are of little or no significance, according to an eminent authority who says:

> However, it has been pointed out, with reason, that modern stores sell all sorts of commodities, and a rule that all goods sold in the same stores are to be considered related goods, would have the practical effect of creating universal trade-marks independent of the nature of the goods on which they are used.

Nims, *Unfair Competition and Trade-Marks, Fourth ed.*, 1947, Vol. I, p. 693.

There is another strange aspect about this confusion which the plaintiffs contend is likely to occur. It will be observed that the plaintiffs have launched into the market two classes of goods under the marks "Sunkist" and "Sun-Kist," which goods are much more nearly of the same class and descriptive properties than the defendants' bread is of the same class and descriptive properties as any of the products of the two plaintiffs; and this is all done without confusion because the parties have agreed, forsooth, there shall be no confusion. Granted the plaintiffs had a right to contract away the public's likelihood of confusion from their closely related products sold all over the United States and in foreign countries, their cry that there is a likelihood of confusion of the source of a loaf of bread put out by a local bakery at Rock Island, Illinois, with their products because they market fruits and vegetables under the same name, is hardly audible to us. When a customer bought a jar of jelly under the name "Sunkist," he could not be confused as to whether it came from California Fruit Growers Exchange or California Packing Corporation. The plaintiffs had taken care of that by contract. We are supposed to believe that when a customer bought fruits or vegetables under the name "Sunkist," he was not confused as to whether the fruit came from the California Fruit Growers Exchange or the vegetables from the California Packing Corporation; but if he bought a loaf of bread under the name "Sunkist," he was likely to think that he bought it from one or the other of the plaintiffs because they sold fruits and vegetables, but never bread. With the plaintiffs practicing such hocus-pocus with the trade-name "Sunkist," we shall ask to be excused when we are admonished by these dividers of confusion by contract to hear their vice president and advertising manager shout confusion on behalf of the purchasing public.

* * *

For the reasons above set forth, the judgment of the District Court is reversed and the causes remanded, with directions to dismiss the complaint.

* * *

IN RE MARTIN'S FAMOUS PASTRY SHOPPE, INC.
748 F.2d 1565 (Fed. Cir. 1984)

PAULINE NEWMAN, CIRCUIT JUDGE

This appeal is from the January 17, 1984 decision of the Trademark Trial and Appeal Board of the U.S. Patent and Trademark Office (Board), affirming the ex parte rejection of appellant's application, Ser. No. 280,013, to register the word-mark MARTIN'S for "wheat bran and honey bread." We affirm.

The refusal to register rests on section 2(d) of the Lanham Act, 15 U.S.C. § 1052(d). The Board held, in a two-to-one decision, that there would be a likelihood of confusion between applicant's mark and Reg. No. 1,032,429 for the mark MARTIN'S for "cheese." 221 USPQ 364 (TTAB 1984) . . . .

. . . The first factor to be considered is the similarity or dissimilarity of the marks in their entireties as to appearance, sound, connotation, and commercial impression. This factor weights heavily against applicant, as the two word marks are identical: MARTIN'S. MARTIN'S is not suggestive or descriptive of either bread or cheese.

We look next to the named goods in connection with which each mark is used. We agree with the Board that applicant's baked goods and registrant's cheese "exhibit cognizable differences." 221 USPQ at 366. The goods in question, bread and cheese, nevertheless travel in the same channels of trade and are sold by the same retail outlets. Although dairy products generally need to be refrigerated and may be kept in a separate area of a market, it was not error for the Board to take notice of the fact that "a wide variety of baked goods are now stored and sold in supermarkets in frozen or refrigerated form" or that "deli counters may well display bread and rolls in close proximity to the cold cuts and cheeses purveyed there." *Id.* Bread and cheese are staple, relatively inexpensive comestibles, subject to frequent replacement. Purchasers of such products have long been held to a lesser standard of purchasing care. *Walter Baker & Co. v. Altamay Chocolate Co.,* 37 F.2d 957, 958, 4 USPQ 159, 161 (CCPA 1930); *Specialty Brands, Inc. v. Coffee Bean Distributors, Inc.,* 748 F.2d 669, -USPQ- (Fed.Cir. 1984).

The record is silent as to whether MARTIN'S for cheese is or may be a well-known or famous trademark. We do however observe that the registration of the MARTIN'S trademark for use with cheese states that the mark has been in use since 1891. There was no evidence presented of use of similar marks by others, or of actual confusion in the marketplace.

The Board considered the fact that bread and cheese are likely to be used together as relevant to the question of likelihood of confusion. 221 USPQ at 366. Applicant contends that the "complementary use" test has no utility in food cases as the number of food products which can be used in combination is so great as to render this test meaningless. Applicant maintains that the Board gave its finding of complementary use controlling weight and that but for this factor it would not have affirmed the Trademark Examiner's refusal to register its mark.

Applicant thus argues that food products should be an exception to the complementary use test, and that the fact that identical marks are used on different but related food products should not be considered in a determination of likelihood of confusion. We find no basis in law or experience for creating such an exception. Evidence of complementary use may be given more or less weight depending on the nature of the goods, but this evidence may not be ignored. The extent to which particular food products are deemed related will depend on the facts of each individual case. In the instant case, we take notice that the products "bread" and "cheese" are often used in combination. Such complementary use has long been recognized as a relevant consideration in determining a likelihood of confusion . . . .

. . . We agree with the Board that the complementary nature of bread and cheese cannot be ignored, and that the association of identical trademarks with these products is likely to produce confusion when the products are not common origin.

In the case at bar, there is an extensive pattern of complementary interests: the channels of trade, the types of stores, the commonality of purchasers, and the conjoint use. These facts are distinguished from those of *In re Mars, Inc.,* 741 F.2d 395, 222 USPQ 938 (Fed.Cir.1984), in which we found no likelihood of confusion between the applicant's mark CANYON for candy bars and a prior registrant's identical mark for fresh citrus fruit. The cumulative effect of all contributing factors must be weighed, as each case is decided on its own facts. *Massey Junior College, Inc. v. Fashion Institute of Technology,* 492 F.2d 1399, 1404, 181 USPQ 272, 275-76 (CCPA 1974). To the extent that any doubts may remain, it is proper that they be resolved in favor of the prior registrant. *In re Pneumatiques, Caoutchouc Manufacture et Plastiques Kelber-*

Colombes, 487 F.2d 918, 179 USPQ 729 (CCPA 1973).

After reviewing the entire record and weighing all relevant factors, we hold that there is a likelihood of confusion within the meaning of 15 U.S.C. § 1052(d) between the marks MARTIN'S for wheat bran and honey bread and MARTIN'S for cheese.

The decision of the Board is affirmed.

AFFIRMED.

Notes on Marketing Environment

1.   Generally

The environment in which marks are actually and usually encountered by the purchasing public is an important psychological conditioning factor that may contribute to or detract from a likelihood of confusion. *Avon Shoe Co. v. David Crystal, Inc.*, 171 F. Supp. 293 (S.D.N.Y. 1959), *aff'd*, 279 F.2d 607 (2d Cir. 1960), *cert. denied*, 364 U.S. 909 (1960). Where goods are sold through the same channels of trade, or in the same type of store or specialty shop, likelihood of confusion is enhanced because one is thereby mentally conditioned toward assuming a single source. *See M2 Software, Inc. v. Madacy Entm't*, 421 F.3d 1073 (9th Cir. 2005) (confusion unlikely between M2 for film and music industry management and media products, and M2 for a record label, where, among other things, "it was doubtful that M2 Software would expand into general retail distribution of audio CDs" like defendant), and *H. Lubovsky, Inc. v. Esprit de Corp.*, 627 F. Supp. 483 (S.D.N.Y. 1986), in which the court found that non-sports shoes and sportswear are sold in different stores or departments.

2.   Supermarkets and Department Stores

What is the effect if the products of both parties are sold in supermarkets or department stores? *See California Fruit Growers, supra*; *Canada Dry Corp. v. American Home Prods. Corp.*, 468 F.2d 207 (C.C.P.A. 1972). *Compare Meat Indus. Suppliers, Inc. v. Kroger Co.*, 130 U.S.P.Q. 434, 439 (N.D. Ill. 1961) ("It has been asserted that the average purchaser undergoes, while in a supermarket, an experience not unlike that of hypnosis"). Should such stores be viewed as amalgams of separate and distinct product selling areas? In *Federated Foods, Inc. v. Fort Howard Paper Co.*, 544 F.2d 1098, 1103 (C.C.P.A. 1976), the court stated its view as follows:

> A wide variety of products, not only from different manufacturers within an industry but also from diverse industries, have been brought together in the modern supermarket for the convenience of the customers. The mere existence of such an environment should not foreclose further inquiry into the likelihood of confusion arising from the use of similar marks on any goods so displayed.

See, e.g. Star Indus. v. Bacardi & Co., 412 F.3d 373 (2d Cir. 2005) (although vodka and rum are sold in the same stores to the same consumers, they are sold in "distinct submarkets of the market for alcoholic beverages"); *Pure Gold, Inc. v. Syntex (U.S.A.), Inc.*, 739 F.2d 624 (Fed. Cir. 1984), in which FERMODYL PURE GOLD for hair treatment preparations was held not likely to be confused with PURE GOLD for citrus fruits and juices; *Scott Paper Co. v. Scott's Liquid Gold, Inc.*, 589 F.2d 1225 (3d Cir. 1978) (SCOTT'S LIQUID GOLD for household cleaner not likely to be confused with SCOTT for paper products). The same might be said for goods and services sold on the Internet. *Compare* the discussion in *GoTo.com, Inc. v. The Walt Disney Company*, in § 6.06 below.

Some courts have made retail shelving location part of their analysis in such cases. In *Procter & Gamble Co. v. Johnson & Johnson, Inc.*, 485 F. Supp. 1185 (S.D.N.Y. 1979), the court found there was a "competitive distance" between the products whose trade marks were in issue; "while the two types of products are sold in the same outlets, they are not sold side by side or on the same shelf. In drug stores, supermarkets and discount houses, deodorants have one shelving section and women's menstrual protection products another." *See also Lever Brothers Co. v. American Bakeries Co.*, 693 F.2d 251 (2ᵈ Cir. 1982) (no side-by-side sales could possibly occur, since margarine must be kept in refrigeration compartments and bread is not). *Compare In re Martin's Famous Pastry Shoppe, Inc., supra*, in which the court found that although bread and cheese may be kept in different areas of market, often they are displayed in close proximity.

3. The Internet

The Internet also has made a wide variety of products and services available to customers in one place — the user's computer. Like the Internet itself, judicial analysis of this marketing environment has continued to evolve since its advent. In *GoTo.com, Inc. v. The Walt Disney Company*, 202 F.3d 1199 (9ᵗʰ Cir. 2000), excerpted in the next section, for example, both parties operated search engines under a similar traffic light logo, and used "the web as a substantial marketing and advertising channel". In concluding that confusion was likely, the court observed "the web, as a marketing channel, is particularly susceptible to a likelihood of confusion since, as it did in this case, it allows for competing marks to be encountered at the same time, on the same screen". *Compare NVST.com v. Nvest, L.L.P.*, 32 Fed. Appx. 207 (9ᵗʰ Cir. 2002), where confusion was unlikely between the parties' domain names for their investment-related services. The court distinguished the *GoTo.com* decision because the parties' "web pages look considerably different and offer entirely different products." Similarly, in *Therma-Scan, Inc. v. Thermoscan, Inc.*, 295 F.3d 623 (6ᵗʰ Cir. 2002), confusion was held unlikely for the parties' health care products. There the court observed that, "a non-specific reference to Internet use is no more proof of a company's marketing channels than the fact that it is listed in the Yellow Pages of the telephone directory." *Compare also Planetary Motion, Inc. v. Techsplosion, Inc.*, 261 F.3d 1188 (11ᵗʰ Cir. 2001), in which COOLMAIL for email-related software was found likely to be confused with COOLMAIL for an email service. Consumers "reasonably could attribute [plaintiff's] software and an email service under the same name to the same source."

4. Channels of Trade

How important in determining likelihood of confusion is the fact that one party sells only at retail and the other only at wholesale? *See Cadbury Beverages Inc. v. Cott Corp.*, 73 F.3d 474 (2ᵈ Cir. 1996) (reversing summary judgment for defendant; plaintiff's use of COTT for retail beverages and defendant's affixation of trade name Cott Corp. on wholesale beverages raised factual question as to likelihood of confusion); *Pierce Foods Corp. v. Tyson Foods, Inc.*, 231 U.S.P.Q. 287 (D.N.J. 1986).

In *Electronic Design & Sales, Inc. v. Electronic Data Systems Corp.*, 954 F.2d 713 (Fed. Cir. 1992), confusion was held unlikely between EDS and Design for battery chargers and power supplies and EDS for computer services despite the products being sold to many of the same corporate customers; the court found the products were sufficiently different and there was no demonstration that the same person within each corporation bought both parties' products. As the Eighth Circuit explained in *Checkpoint Systems, Inc. v. Check Point Software Technologies, Inc.*, 269 F.3d 270 (3ᵈ Cir. 2001), "[t]he relatedness analysis is intensely factual. Goods may fall under the same general product category but operate in distinct niches." In that case both parties sold security–related products under the trademark CHECKPOINT, but plaintiff's products were physical alarm systems while defendant sold software for keeping electronic information secure. The same large corporations purchased products from each company, but confusion was found unlikely, in part because the evidence failed to show that "the same security professionals within these corporations have knowledge of these different technologies and are responsible for purchasing them." The court also noted that "[p]laintiff's and defendant's products are not impulse purchases, but rather are subject to long sales efforts and careful customer decision making . . . consumers take care in making purchasing decisions [in the security market] and are not likely to be confused by the parties' similar marks."

What significance, if any, should be given to how the products in question are ordinarily purchased: Over the counter? By self-service? In busy stores without opportunity for visual comparison? On-line? At little expense? To be consumed in use? By telephone? On impulse? In haste? By the foreign-born? By children? By lip-movers? By illiterates? What if the products are ordinarily bought as a personal matter with great care? By experts? By purchasing agents? At great expense? After careful comparison? By prescription?

5. Degree of Purchaser Care

Purchaser care in the marketing environment can affect the issue of whether confusion is likely. In *Jet, Inc. v. Sewage Aeration Systems*, 165 F.3d 419 (6th Cir. 1999) AEROB-A-JET was held unlikely to be confused with JET, both being used for sewage treatment devices for homes. The court observed that, "the very high degree of care that purchasers in this market – both contractors with the skills and responsibility for installing home sewage treatment systems and homeowners spending hundreds or thousands of dollars to buy or repair such systems – [could] be expected to exercise, eliminated virtually any possibility that [defendant's] use of [its mark would] cause confusion." *See also, Playmakers LLC v. ESPN, Inc.*, 71 U.S.P.Q. 2d 1759 (9th Cir. 2004) (PLAYMAKERS for agency representing professional athletes unlikely to be confused with defendant's PLAYMAKERS cable television series because of the different marketing channels, the "degree of care professional and aspiring professional athletes are likely to exercise before choosing an agent," and because PLAYMAKERS was in common use); *NVST.com v. Nvest L.L.P.*, 32 Fed. Appx. 207 (9th Cir. 2002) (confusion unlikely where plaintiff's customers "who are considering large investments — can certainly be expected to plan their purchases carefully").

Compare Incredible Techs. v. Virtual Techs., 400 F.3d 1007 (7th Cir. 2005) (rejecting confusion claim that relied on hazy perceptions of bar and tavern patrons consuming alcohol; "[o]ne wonders how different the [videogame] control panels would have to be to avoid confusing such users"); *Kemp v. Bumble Bee Seafoods, Inc.*, 398 F.3d 1049 (8th Cir. 2005) (confusion among professional buyers of food products "serves as strong evidence that the average consumer, who exercises less scrutiny, is likely to be confused"); *Frehling Enterprises Inc. v. International Select Group, Inc.*, 192 F.3d 1330 (11th Cir. 1999) (holding confusion was likely between OGGETTI and BELL' OGGETTI for home furniture products, and rejecting district court's conclusion that plaintiff was in a different channel of trade ("higher end department stores like Macy's and Bloomingdale's") than defendant ("mass market retail outlets like Circuit City and Sears" for "less affluent consumers"), with the court noting that many consumers "cross-shop" and frequent both types of retailers). *Compare Estee Lauder Inc. v. Gap, Inc.*, 108 F.3d 1503 (2d Cir. 1997), in which the court held that confusion was not likely between the parties' "100%" skin care products because, among other reasons, defendant's OLD NAVY retail stores marketed to the "mass middle" while plaintiff marketed to upscale retail purchasers; *Duluth News-Tribune v. Mesabi Publishing Co.*, 84 F.3d 1093, 1099 (8th Cir. 1996), in which the court found no likely confusion between DULUTH NEWS-TRIBUNE and DAILY TRIBUNE partly because more than 90% of defendant's sales were to subscribers who presumably were more likely to exercise care when choosing between competing newspapers than newsstand customers; *Specialty Brands, Inc. v. Coffee Bean Distributors, Inc.*, 748 F.2d 669 (Fed. Cir. 1984), in which purchasers of relatively inexpensive products were held to a lesser standard of purchasing care; *Lindy Pen Co. v. Bic Pen Corp.*, 725 F.2d 1240, 1245 (9th Cir. 1984), in which the court held there was no likelihood of confusion in the visual marketplace, but remanded the case on the issue of confusion created by oral telephone solicitations; *Pocket Books, Inc. v. Dell Publishing Co.*, 49 Misc. 2d 596, 368 N.Y.S.2d 46 (1966) (lip-movers).

What is the effect of developments in advertising, the Internet, radio, television, and other media on the marketing environment? *See* Hartman, *Subliminal Confusion: The Misappropriation of Advertising Value*, 78 TRADEMARK REP. 506 (1988).

6.06   Similarity of Goods and Services

Courts tend to presume that where goods sold under the same or similar marks are themselves similar, the same, or in some way closely related, the likelihood that they may be attributed to the same or a related source is enhanced. This presumption is founded on an empirical, or perhaps a psychological, premise, namely, that consumers have been conditioned to assume that manufacturers and merchants usually manufacture and market their goods and services within related fields. Thus, courts assume that it is reasonable and likely for consumers to believe that if similar marks are applied to similar goods or services they probably come from the same, or a related, source. What circumstances might justify abandoning that presumption in a given case?

DREAMWERKS   PRODUCTION   GROUP   INC.   v.   SKG   STUDIO,   dba   DreamWorks, SKG
142 F.3d 1127 (9th Cir. 1998)

KOZINSKI, CIRCUIT JUDGE

*   *   *

Dreamwerks, a company hardly anyone has heard of, sues entertainment colossus DreamWorks SKG, claiming trademark infringement. This is the reverse of the normal trademark infringement case, where the well-known mark goes after a look-alike, sound-alike, feel-alike unknown which is trying to cash in on the famous mark's goodwill. The twist here is that Dreamwerks, the unknown, was doing business under that name long before DreamWorks was a twinkle in Hollywood's eye. Dreamwerks is therefore the senior mark, and it argues that its customers will mistakenly think they are dealing with DreamWorks, the junior mark.

Facts

Everyone — or most everyone — has heard of DreamWorks SKG, established in 1994 by what many consider the three hottest names in Hollywood: Steven Spielberg, Jeffrey Katzenberg and David Geffen (each of whom graciously contributed an initial to form the SKG part of the trademark). DreamWorks is a film studio, having produced such well-advertised movies as *The Peacemaker, Amistad* and *Mouse Hunt.* Like other movie studios, DreamWorks participates more generally in the entertainment business, having created DreamWorks Interactive (a joint venture with software giant Microsoft); GameWorks (described in the press as a micropub and virtual reality video arcade for the 90s); and DreamWorks Toys (a joint venture with toy maker Hasbro).

Less well-known is Dreamwerks Production Group, Inc., a small Florida company that since 1984 has been in the business of organizing conventions in the Northeast and Midwest, mostly with a Star Trek theme. At a typical Star Trek convention, Dreamwerks draws customers with a star like DeForest Kelly (Bones), Leonard Nimoy (Spock) or Michael Dorn (Worf from *The Next Generation*). For an admission fee of $25 or so, customers get autographs, meet fellow trekkies, compete in costume contests, listen to pitches for upcoming movies and browse the products of vendors who have rented space at the convention. Dreamwerks sometimes presents previews of science fiction and adventure/fantasy movies produced by the major studios, such as *Batman Returns, Dracula, Aladdin* and *Jurassic Park.* Dreamwerks clearly caters to the pocket-protector niche, and its convention business has never really taken off. But the longevity of the enterprise illustrates its remarkable resilience, not unlike the starship itself.

Because Dreamwerks registered its mark with the United States Patent and Trademark Office in 1992, it holds the senior mark and is the plaintiff here. It claims that DreamWorks SKG is causing confusion in the marketplace by using a mark too similar to its own and is doing so with respect to goods and services that are too similar to those it (Dreamwerks) is offering.

Pshaw, one might say. What could be better for Dreamwerks than to have people confuse it with a mega movie studio? Many an infringer has tried to manufacture precisely such confusion and thereby siphon off the goodwill of a popular mark. *See, e.g., E. & J. Gallo Winery v. Gallo Cattle Co.* 967 F.2d 1280, 1293 (9th Cir. 1992) ("Gallo" wine and "Joseph Gallo" cheese). Not so, answers Dreamwerks, apparently in earnest. It is not interested in fooling consumers, and it claims to suffer ill will when people buy tickets under the misimpression that they are dealing with DreamWorks rather than Dreamwerks. Dreamwerks also frets that its own goodwill will be washed away by the rising tide of publicity associated with the junior mark. Dreamwerks points out (somewhat wistfully) that it hopes to expand its business into related fields, and that these avenues will be foreclosed if DreamWorks gets there first. Finally, Dreamwerks notes that whatever goodwill it has built now rests in the hands of DreamWorks; if the latter should take a major misstep and tarnish its reputation with the public, Dreamwerks too would be pulled down.

These are not fanciful or unreasonable concerns, though they may be somewhat exaggerated by the hope of winning an award or settlement against an apparently very solvent DreamWorks. We are not, however, in a position to judge the extent to which these harms are likely, nor whether they are somehow offset by any extra goodwill plaintiff may inadvertently reap as a result of the confusion between its mark and that of the defendant. These are matters for the trier of fact. The narrow question presented here is whether Dreamwerks has stated a claim for trademark infringement sufficient to survive summary judgment. The district court held that Dreamwerks had not because the core functions of the two businesses are so distinct that there is no likelihood of confusion as a matter of law. Dreamwerks appeals, and it is that ruling we review de novo. *See Americana Trading, Inc. v. Russ Berrie & Co.*, 966 F.2d 1284, 1287 (9th Cir. 1992).

Discussion

*   *   *

. . . The question in such cases is whether consumers doing business with the senior user might mistakenly believe that they are dealing with the junior user. More specifically, the question here is whether a reasonable consumer attending a Dreamwerks-sponsored convention might do so believing that it is a convention sponsored by DreamWorks.

Before performing a Vulcan mind meld on the "reasonably prudent consumer," we note that if this were an ordinary trademark case rather than a reverse infringement case — in other words if DreamWorks had been there first and Dreamwerks later opened up a business running entertainment—related conventions—there would be little doubt that DreamWorks would have stated a case for infringement sufficient to survive summary judgment. The reason for this, of course, is that a famous mark like DreamWorks SKG casts a long shadow. Does the result change in a reverse infringement case because the long shadow is cast by the junior mark? We think not.

. . . "Dreamwerks" is an arbitrary and fictitious mark deserving of strong protection. Had Dreamwerks chosen a descriptive mark like Sci-Fi Conventions Inc., or a suggestive mark like Sci-Fi World, some confusion with the marks of legitimate competitors might be expected. DreamWorks argues that the word "Dream" makes the

Dreamwerks mark suggestive of a company which brings sci-fi dreams to life. But "Dream" is used in too many different ways to suggest any particular meaning to the reasonable consumer.

At best, "Dreamwerks" conjures images related to fantasy, hope or reverie. It's too great a mental leap from hopes to Star Trek conventions for us to treat the mark as suggestive. The Dreamwerks mark deserves broad protection.

Sight, sound and meaning is easy. There is perfect similarity of sound, since "Dreamwerks" and "DreamWorks" are pronounced the same way. There is also similarity of meaning: Neither literally means anything, and to the extent the words suggest a fantasy world, they do so equally. Similarity of sight presents a slightly closer question. The man-in-the-moon DreamWorks logo, when presented in the full regalia of a movie trailer, is quite distinctive. But "DreamWorks" often appears in the general press and in industry magazines without the logo, leaving only the slight difference in spelling. Spelling is a lost art; many moviegoers might think that Mirimax and Colombia Pictures are movie studios. Moreover, a perceptive consumer who does notice the "e" and lower-case "w" in Dreamwerks might shrug off the difference as an intentional modification identifying an ancillary division of the same company. While we recognize that spelling matters, we're not sure substituting one vowel for another and capitalizing a middle consonant dispels the similarity between the marks.

The clincher is the relatedness of the goods. Twenty years ago DreamWorks may have had an argument that making movies and promoting sci-fi merchandise are different businesses promoting different products.

But movies and sci-fi merchandise are now as complementary as baseball and hot dogs. The main products sold at Dreamwerks conventions are movie and TV collectibles and memorabilia; the lectures, previews and appearances by actors which attract customers to Dreamwerks conventions are all dependent, in one way or another, on the output of entertainment giants like DreamWorks.

The district court emphasized that Dreamwerks has carved out a narrow niche in the entertainment marketplace, while DreamWorks controls a much broader segment. Dreamwerks targets trekkies; DreamWorks targets everyone. But the relatedness of each company's prime directive isn't relevant. Rather, we must focus on Dreamwerks' customers and ask whether they are likely to associate the conventions with Dream-Works the studio. Entertainment studios control all sorts of related industries: publishing, clothing, amusement parks, computer games and an endless list of toys and kids' products. In this environment it's easy for customers to suspect DreamWorks of sponsoring conventions at which movie merchandise is sold. Other studios are rapidly expanding their merchandising outlets: Universal Studios has theme parks in California, Florida and Japan with dozens of stores selling movie-related products, and Disney is helping transform New York's Times Square into a G-rated shopping center. Dream-werks convention-goers might well assume that DreamWorks decided to ride the coattails of Spielberg's unparalleled reputation for sci-fi/adventure films (*Jaws, E.T., Close Encounters, Raiders, Jurassic Park*) into the sci-fi merchandising business.

Conclusion

. . . A clever new trademark diversifies both the marketplace and the marketplace of ideas; a takeoff or copy of a mark, even if accidental, adds nothing but confusion. This dispute could have been avoided had DreamWorks been more careful, or a tad more creative, in choosing its name.

We REVERSE and REMAND for further proceedings consistent with this opinion.

GOTO.COM, INC. v. THE WALT DISNEY COMPANY
202 F.3d 1199 (9th Cir. 2000)

O'SCANNLAIN, CIRCUIT JUDGE.

We must decide whether two remarkably similar logos used commercially on the World Wide Web are likely to confuse consumers under federal trademark law.

The Walt Disney Company ("Disney") appeals the district court's grant of a preliminary injunction against it that was sought by GoTo.com ("GoTo"). The injunction prohibits Disney from using a logo confusingly similarly to GoTo's mark. GoTo operates a web site that contains a pay-for-placement search engine, which allows consumers to locate items on the Web using a search algorithm weighted in favor of those advertisers who have paid to have their products given a priority by the engine. In December 1997, GoTo began using on its web site one of the two logos at issue in this appeal. The GoTo logo consists of the words "GO" and "TO" in a white font stacked vertically within a green circle. Although this green circle has been displayed against backgrounds of various *colors*, it is very often rendered against a square yellow background. To the right of the word "TO" are the characters ".com" in black, spilling out of the green circle onto the background color.

In preparing to launch a web site of its own, Disney commissioned a design firm, U.S. Web/CKS ("CKS"), to devise a logo for its Web portal, the Go Network in April 1998. The Go Network is an interconnected collection of web sites, all belonging to Disney properties, designed to provide an easy starting point for consumers who use the Web. The Go Network integrates sites such as <disney.com>, <abc.com>, <abcnews.com>, <abcsports.com>, <espn.com>, <family.com>, and <infoseek.com>. CKS designed a logo that resembles a traffic light: it contains a green circle within a yellow square, with details and contouring that is suggestive of a traffic light with a single lens. Within the green circle, the word "GO" appears in a white font, and next to the traffic light, the word "Network" appears in a black font.

Michael Eisner, the chairman of Disney, approved the CKS logo at the end of August 1998. Then, in December 1998, Disney beta-launched the Go Network, displaying its logo prominently on all of the interconnected sites. On December 22, 1998, shortly after this beta launch and more than a fortnight before the formal launch, GoTo complained to Disney about its use of the logo on its Go Network web sites. Disney did not cease using the logo, and GoTo subsequently filed this lawsuit on February 18, 1999, alleging inter alia a violation of § 43(a)(1)(A) of the Lanham Act, 15 U.S.C. § 1125(a)(1)(A). . . .

On November 12, 1999, the district court granted GoTo's motion for a preliminary injunction.

*   *   *

Obviously, the greater the similarity between the two marks at issue, the greater the likelihood of confusion. We have developed certain detailed axioms to guide this comparison: first, the marks must be considered in their entirety and as they appear in the marketplace, *see Filipino Yellow Pages, Inc. v. Asian Journal Publications, Inc.*, 198 F.3d 1143, 1147-50 (9th Cir. 1999); second, similarity is adjudged in terms of appearance, sound, and meaning, *see, e.g., Dreamwerks Prod. Group v. SKG Studio*, 142 F.3d 1127, 1131 (9th Cir. 1998); and third, similarities are weighed more heavily than differences, *see Goss*, 6 F.3d at 1392.

With a single glance at the two images, one is immediately struck by their similarity. Both logos consist of white capital letters in an almost identical sans serif font rendered on a green circle. The circle in turn is matted by a square yellow background.

Quibbles over trivial distinctions between these two logos are unimpressive. The logos are glaringly similar.

*   *   *

The first of the other two controlling . . . considerations is that "[r]elated goods are generally more likely than unrelated goods to confuse the public as to the producers of the goods." *Brookfield*, 174 F.3d at 1055. With respect to Internet services, even services that are not identical are capable of confusing the public. Although even Web tyros can distinguish between a web site that for example, provides discounted travel tickets and one that provides free Web-based e-mail, a user would almost certainly assume a common sponsorship if the sites' trademarks were the same. The <Yahoo.com> web site is just one example of Web genies that coordinate a bevy of distinct services under a common banner. Indeed, Disney's own portal shows the potential for one company to provide a host of unrelated services. Whereas in the world of bricks and mortar, one may be able to distinguish easily between an expensive restaurant in New York and a mediocre one in Los Angeles, *see, e.g., Sardi's Restaurant*, 755 F.2d at 723-24, the Web is a very different world.

Our ever-growing dependence on the Web may force us eventually to evolve into increasingly sophisticated users of the medium, but, for now, we can safely conclude that the use of remarkably similar trademarks on different web sites creates a likelihood of confusion amongst Web users. The ever-growing number of tentacled conglomerates may force us to conclude that even one hundred and one products could all be sponsored by a single consortium.

In this case, the services offered by GoTo and Disney are very similar. Both entities operate search engines and are, therefore, direct competitors on this score. In *Fleischmann Distiling Corp. v. Maier Brewing Co.*, 314 F.2d 149, 153-55 (9th Cir. 1963), we concluded that beer and whiskey were sufficiently similar products to create a likelihood of confusion regarding the source of origin when sold under the same trade name. Competing Internet search engines are even more similar services.

Both GoTo and Disney use the Web as a substantial marketing and advertising channel, and we have given special consideration to that forum. In *Brookfield*, we stated that the use of the Web is a factor "that courts have consistently recognized as exacerbating the likelihood of confusion." 174 F.3d at 1057 (citations omitted). We now reiterate that the Web, as a marketing channel, is particularly susceptible to a likelihood of confusion since, as it did in this case, it allows for competing marks to be encountered at the same time, on the same screen.

In determining whether there is a likelihood of confusion, we rely heavily on the fact that the marks are similar, that Disney and GoTo offer very similar services, and that they both use the web as their marketing channel.

*   *   *

In its analysis of the degree of care that users of the Internet take, at least one federal court has ascribed a certain sophistication to Web denizens. *See Alta Vista v. Digital Equipment Corp.*, 44 F.Supp.2d 72, 77 (D. Mass. 1998). Although the use of computers may once have been the exclusive domain of an elite intelligentsia, even modern-day Luddites are now capable of navigating cyberspace. Furthermore, the question in this analysis is not how sophisticated web surfers are but, rather, how high the cost is of choosing one service — that is, one web site — over another on the Web. We agree with our previous conclusion that this cost is negligible: it is simply a single click of a mouse.

> In the Internet context, in particular, entering a web site takes little effort — usually one click from a linked site or a search engine's list; thus, Web surfers are more likely to be confused as to the ownership of a web site than traditional patrons of a brick-and-mortar store would be of a store's ownership.

Brookfield, 174 F.3d at 1057.

Navigating amongst web sites involves practically no effort whatsoever, and arguments that Web users exercise a great deal of care before clicking on hyperlinks are unconvincing. Our conclusion is further supported by the Third Circuit's rule that "the standard of care to be exercised by the reasonably prudent purchaser will be equal to that of the least sophisticated consumer." *Ford Motor Co. v. Summit Motor Prods., Inc.,* 930 F.2d 277, 293 (3ᵈ Cir. 1991).

From our analysis of the *Sleekcraft* factors, we conclude that GoTo has demonstrated a likelihood of success on its claim that Disney's use of its logo violates the Lanham Act. From this showing of likelihood of success on the merits in this trademark infringement claim, we may presume irreparable injury. *See Brookfield,* 174 F.3d at 1066; *Metro Pub.,* 987 F.2d at 640. GoTo has therefore demonstrated the combination of success on the merits and the possibility of irreparable injury necessary to entitle it to a preliminary injunction in a trademark case.

*   *   *

AFFIRMED.

Notes on Similarity of Goods and Services

1.   Relationship of Goods and Services

It is now well settled, and in fact codified in the Lanham Act, 15 U.S.C. § 1114, that trademark rights afford protection against not only the use of similar marks on similar goods or services, but also against use on other goods or services that might naturally be supposed to emanate from the same source. *Yale Elec. Corp. v. Robertson,* 26 F.2d 972, 973–974 (2ᵈ Cir. 1928); *Triangle Pub'ns, Inc. v. Rohrlich,* 167 F.2d 969 (2ᵈ Cir. 1948)(confusion likely between MISS SEVENTEEN for girdles and SEVENTEEN for young women's magazine through public perception of sponsorship). *See also* the discussion at the beginning of this chapter, of the multifactor tests applied by the federal courts in assessing likelihood of confusion.

In *Scarves by Vera, Inc. v. Todo Imports Ltd.,* 544 F.2d 1167 (2ᵈ Cir. 1976), the court noted that many if not most fashion designers sell perfumes and cosmetics under their own trademarks, indicating that such products are closely related. Similarly, in *Helene Curtis Industries v. Church & Dwight Co.,* 560 F.2d 1325 (7ᵗʰ Cir. 1977), the court viewed underarm deodorant and baking soda as related goods where plaintiff had long promoted its ARM & HAMMER baking soda for use as a deodorant. *Compare Federated Foods, Inc. v. Fort Howard Paper Co.,* 544 F.2d 1098 (C.C.P.A. 1976) (HY-TOP plastic bags, aluminum foil and sponges were held not so related to HY-TEX toilet tissue that confusion would be likely, the only link established being that they might be found in the same area of the supermarket) *and In re Mars, Inc.,* 741 F.2d 395 (Fed. Cir. 1984) (candy bars and fresh citrus fruits held insufficiently related).

Goods or services that are used together (complementary goods) may be considered related in a confusion analysis. *See, e.g., In re Martin's Famous Pastry Shoppe, Inc.,* 748 F.2d 1565 (Fed Cir. 1984)(bread and cheese). However, such a finding is not automatic. In *Packard Press v. Hewlett-Packard Co.,* 227 F.3d 1352 (Fed. Cir. 2000), for example, the court explained, "the test is not that goods and services must be related if used together, but merely that finding is part of the underlying factual inquiry as to whether the goods and services at issue . . . can be related in the mind of the consuming public as to the origin of the goods." Confusion was held unlikely between two BLUE MOON marks for beer and restaurant services in *In re Coors Brewing Co.,* 343 F.3d 1340 (Fed. Cir. 2003); "the fact that restaurants serve food and beverages is not enough to render food and beverages related to restaurant services for purposes of determining the likelihood of confusion." Federal registrations indicated "it is uncommon for restaurants and beer to share the same trademarks," and the evidence of record showed only a "de minimis" overlap, with only "a tiny percentage of all restaurants also serv[ing] as a source of beer." The court analogized to some department stores selling private label automotive parts. In its view, that would not establish "that department store services in general are sufficiently related to automotive lubrication services" to make confusion likely when a similar mark was used for oil change services and for department store services. *See also Shen Mfg. Co. v. Ritz Hotel Ltd.*, 393 F.3d 1238 (Fed. Cir. 2004) (confusion unlikely between RITZ for cooking classes and for textiles; "although a student of cooking classes would undoubtedly use kitchen textiles, it does not follow that the consuming public would understand those products to have originated from the same source"; confusion similarly held unlikely between RITZ KIDS for children's clothing and RITZ for kitchen textiles because consumers would not likely mistakenly believe that the producer of the latter had expanded into children's clothing). In *Bose Corp. v. QSC Audio Products, Inc.*, 293 F.3d 1367 (Fed. Cir. 2002), the court reached a different result. Bose sold ACOUSTIC WAVE and WAVE loudspeaker systems, compact disc players and the like, while QSC sold POWERWAVE amplifiers which were components used in sound systems. Noting that Bose's marks were famous, that "amplification of sound is at the heart" of Bose's products, and that Bose had marketed a component product, the Court held that the products were sufficiently related and confusion was likely.

The fact that both products at issue may be generally stated to be in one field, one market, or one product category, does not necessary mean that they are sufficiently related for confusion to be likely. In *Therma-scan, Inc. v. Thermoscan, Inc.*, 295 F.3d 623 (6th Cir. 2002), the parties used the similar marks THERMA-SCAN and THERMOSCAN for products that might be said to "co-exist in a very broad industry of medical applications of thermology and infra-red identification of heat". However, plaintiff's infra-red thermal-imaging examinations of the human body and defendant's electronic ear thermometers "utilize similar technology in very different ways". The court found the parties "market their goods and services to different segments of the population" and "do not compete," so that confusion was unlikely. In *Astra Pharmaceutical Products, Inc. v. Beckman Instruments, Inc.*, 718 F.2d 1201 (1st Cir. 1983), the court similarly found that use of defendant's ASTRA blood analyzer laboratory instrument and plaintiff's ASTRA drugs in the health care field was not enough to make them related goods. The Eighth Circuit explained in *Checkpoint Systems, Inc. v. Check Point Software Technologies, Inc.*, 269 F.3d 270 (3d Cir. 2001) that, "[t]he relatedness analysis is intensely factual. Goods may fall under the same general product category but operate in distinct niches." In that case both parties sold security-related products under the same CHECKPOINT mark, but plaintiff's products were commercial security systems such as devices to prevent merchandise theft, while defendant sold software for keeping electronic information secure. While the same large corporations purchased products from each company, confusion was unlikely, in part because the evidence failed to show that "the same security professionals within these corporations have knowledge of these different technologies and are responsible for purchasing them." *See also NVST.com v. Nvest L.L.P.*, 32 Fed. Appx. 207 (9th Cir. 2002), a domain name case in which, although both parties offered investment services, plaintiff targeted wealthy investors looking to research emerging companies and merger and acquisition opportunities, while defendant targeted investors looking for advice on retirement or mutual funds; *and Alpha Industries, Inc. v. Alpha Steel Tube & Shapes, Inc.*, 616 F.2d 440 (9th Cir. 1980), in which ALPHA for steel tubes was held not to infringe ALPHA for steel making machinery because the items were expensive, the purchasers sophisticated and from two distinct groups, and the mark weak.

Conversely, even if goods or services are not competitive, it is still possible for the public to become confused and the plaintiff to be damaged. *See Team Tires Plus, Ltd. v. Tires Plus, Inc.*, 394 F.3d 831 (10th Cir. 2005) (TIRES PLUS for retail tire stores held confusingly similar to the same mark for rendering technical assistance in the establishment of automobile tire stores, with the court observing that trademark infringement is not limited to competing uses of the mark). *Spring Mills, Inc. v.*

Ultracashmere House, Ltd., 689 F.2d 1127 (2ᵈ Cir. 1982); *James Burrough Ltd. v. Sign of the Beefeaters, Inc.*, 572 F.2d 574 (7ᵗʰ Cir. 1978) where, in both cases, the courts found no direct diversion of customers but instead deception of the public (BEEFEATER'S) and loss of goodwill or tarnishment of reputation (ULTRACASHMERE).

2. Natural Area of Expansion

Some courts have recognized enforceable trademark rights for a trademark owner in a "natural area of expansion." In *Tiffany & Co. v. Parfums Lamborghini*, 214 U.S.P.Q. 77 (S.D.N.Y. 1981), the court held that a demonstrated intention to enter the perfume field and recent purchase of plaintiff by a cosmetics and perfume company entitled plaintiff to trademark protection in the noncompeting perfume field. Similarly, in *Exquisite Form Industries, Inc. v. Exquisite Fabrics of London*, 378 F. Supp. 403 (S.D.N.Y. 1974), the court stated that "if it is demonstrated that plaintiff has continuously expanded its product line in the past, and has further plans to expand into defendant's area, a court may be justified in finding a likelihood of confusion even between dissimilar products." *Compare* the failure to expand in *Patsy's Brand, Inc. v. I.O.B. Reality, Inc.*, 317 F.3d 209 (2ᵈ Cir. 2003), in which two unrelated New York restaurants had co-existed for decades under the names "Patsy's Italian Restaurant" (plaintiff), and "Patsy's Pizzeria" (defendant). Plaintiff opened its restaurant after defendant, but was the first to sell pasta sauce at retail, which it sold under its "Patsy's PR" brand. Plaintiff built up substantial national sales of its pasta sauce, and federally registered the mark. In claiming superior rights in "Patsy's" for such a product, defendant damaged its case by submitting false evidence in an attempt to show prior use on pasta sauce. Rejecting defendant's assertion of prior rights for pasta sauce based on its prior use of "Patsy's" in connection with its restaurant, the Second Circuit concluded that in a case of such lengthy co-existence, "protection for the use of the common feature of the two names in the related field belongs to the first entrant to that field," regardless of who first used the mark overall. Plaintiff was the first entrant for this retail product.

In the Second Circuit this potential expansion has been described as a potential for "bridging the gap." *Lever Bros. v. American Bakeries Co.*, 693 F.2d 251, 258 (2ᵈ Cir. 1982). *Mushroom Makers, supra*, 580 F.2d at 49; *Lever Bros.*, supra, 693 F.2d at 258; *Vitarroz, supra*, 644 F.2d at 969. Goods across the gap and goods in the natural area of expansion presumably are not related goods. If the court finds that the goods *are* related, is the natural area of expansion irrelevant? *Helene Curtis Industries, Inc.*, supra, 560 F.2d at 1331. In *Cadbury Beverages Inc. v. Cott Corp.*, 73 F.3d 474, 482 (2ᵈ Cir. 1996), plaintiff, a retail marketer of COTT soda, had no intention to enter the wholesale soda market. However, due to defendant's use of plaintiff's trademark in defendant's Cott Corp. trade name in the wholesale market, wholesale purchasing agents might suppose that plaintiff had already bridged the gap. According to the court, assessing the "bridging the gap" factor therefore requires a fact-finder to resolve whether consumers may perceive that the plaintiff already has bridged the gap. *Compare Commerce Nat'l Ins. Services, Inc. v. Commerce Ins. Agency, Inc.*, 214 F.3d 432 (3ᵈ Cir. 2000), in which the parties had co-existed for years using the mark COMMERCE in the banking and insurance respectively, until the first user of the mark, having used it for banking, entered the insurance market through a subsidiary and alleged prior rights. The court determined that establishing rights in the banking market did not do so in the insurance market, and that the first to use the mark in the insurance market had superior rights in that market. *See also Heartsprings, Inc. v. Heartspring, Inc.*, 143 F.3d 550 (10ᵗʰ Cir.), *cert. denied*, 525 U.S. 964 (1998), affirming that confusion was unlikely between "Heartsprings" for a for-profit corporation that provided educational materials for children, and "Heartspring" for a non-profit organization that ran a school for disabled children. The court observed that there was little overlap between the parties' products, services or marketing strategies.

3. Strength and Famous Marks

"Famous" or "celebrated" marks are sometimes afforded greater protection than those less well-known. Should they be? *See, e.g., CPC International, Inc. v. Skippy, Inc.*, 231 U.S.P.Q. 811, 814 (E.D. Va. 1986) ("consumers in today's world will automatically connect any product bearing the mark 'SKIPPY' with SKIPPY peanut butter and the company that manufactures it"); *Hallmark Cards, Inc. v. Hallmark Dodge, Inc.*, 229 U.S.P.Q. 882 (W.D. Mo. 1986) (HALLMARK DODGE for automobile dealership infringes HALLMARK for greeting cards); *John Walker & Sons, Ltd. v. Bethea*, 305 F. Supp. 1302 (D.S.C. 1969) (JOHNNY WALKER Motel held to infringe JOHNNY WALKER Scotch Whiskey).

The fame of plaintiff's VIRGIN mark and the breadth of products and services sold under it were critical to plaintiff's successful suit against defendant's use of VIRGIN WIRELESS for wireless telephones and related goods in *Virgin Enterprises, Ltd. v. Nawab*, 335 F.3d 141 (2ᵈ Cir. 2003). The Second Circuit emphasized the diversity of plaintiff's VIRGIN businesses, including an airline, large-scale record stores called Virgin Megastores, an Internet information service, music recordings, computer games, books, and luggage. The district court, in denying plaintiff preliminary relief, had "accorded plaintiff too narrow a scope of protection for its famous, arbitrary and distinctive mark." Instead, the mark was entitled to "a broad scope of protection, precisely because the use of the mark by others in connection with stores selling reasonably closely related merchandise would inevitably have a high likelihood of causing consumer confusion." Here, among other things, wireless phones were closely enough related to CD players, and the plaintiff had already formulated a plan to license its mark for wireless devices.

A "famous" or "celebrated" mark often will be protected regardless of dissimilarity of goods or services. What is the rationale, if any, for such disparate treatment? In *James Burrough Ltd. v. Sign of the Beefeater, Inc.*, 540 F.2d 266, 276 (7ᵗʰ Cir. 1976), the court stated: "A mark that is strong because of its fame or its uniqueness, is more likely to be remembered and more likely to be associated in the public mind with a greater breadth of products or services, than is a mark that is weak." Similarly, in *Recot, Inc. v. M.C. Becton*, 214 F.3d 1322, 1327 (Fed Cir. 2000), the court vacated and remanded the dismissal of an opposition to FIDO LAY for edible dog treats based on FRITO LAY for snack foods, stating, "[w]hen an opposer's mark is a strong, famous mark, it can never be 'of little consequence'. The fame of a trademark may affect the likelihood purchasers will be confused inasmuch as less care may be taken in purchasing a product under a famous name." The fame of opposer's NASDAQ mark for its stock market allowed it to successfully oppose registration of NASDAQ for sporting goods and clothing in *The NASDAQ Market v. Anartica, S.r.i.*, 69 U.S.P.Q. 2d 1718 (T.T.A.B. 2003). "[O]pposer's mark is accorded more protection precisely because it is more likely to be remembered and associated in the public mind."

Compare Kellogg Co. v. Toucan Golf Co., 337 F.3d 616 (6ᵗʰ Cir. 2003), in which Kellogg unsuccessfully tried to prevent registration of TOUCAN GOLD for golf equipment, based on Kellogg's TOUCAN SAM logo and word mark used in connection with its FROOT LOOPS cereal. Golf products were "in an industry far removed from that of Kellogg." The court discounted Kellogg's evidence that it had used the mark on golf shirts and balls in its limited circulation promotional catalog, and had depicted the TOUCAN SAM character as a golfer in some advertisements. "Kellogg's presence in the golf industry was insignificant, and nothing more than a marketing tool to boost sales of its cereal . . . [O]ne thirty second advertisement does not render TOUCAN SAM a golfer, nor does a novelty catalog make Kellogg a player in the golfing industry."

Fame worked against the owner of prior rights in *B.V.D. Licensing Corp. v. Body Action Design, Inc.*, 846 F.2d 727 (Fed. Cir. 1988), where the court held confusion was unlikely between the famous mark B.V.D. for men's underwear and the mark B.A.D for clothing, including undergarments. It reasoned that the better known a mark is, the more readily the public becomes aware of even a small deviation from it. In *Kenner Parker Toys, Inc. v. Rose Art Industries, Inc.*, 963 F.2d 350 (Fed. Cir. 1992), the Federal Circuit distinguished *B.V.D.* and held that FUNDOUGH was confusingly similar to PLAY-DOH for modelling compounds. In doing so, it reemphasized the traditional rule that famous marks are entitled to greater protection, stating (at 1457):

> If investors forfeit legal protection by increasing a mark's fame, the law would then countenance a disincentive for investments in trademarks. The law is not so schizophrenic. In consonance with the purposes and origins of trademark protection, the Lanham Act provides a broader range of protection as a mark's fame grows.

Finding *B.V.D.* to be an unusual decision, it stated, "[t]he holding of *B.V.D.*, to the extent it treats fame as a liability, is confined to the facts of that case." *Id.* at 1457. *See also Bose Corp. v. QSC Audio Products, Inc.*, 293 F.3d 1367 (Fed. Cir. 2002) (defendant's POWERWAVE amplifiers were likely to be confused with Bose's famous ACOUSTIC WAVE and WAVE marks for loudspeaker systems, radios, CD players and the like); *Palm Bay Imps., Inc. v. Veuve Clicquot Ponsardin Maison Fondee En 1772*, 396 F.3d 1369 (Fed. Cir. 2005) (VEUVE ROYALE for sparkling wine likely to be confused with VEUVE CLICQUOT, among other marks, for champagne; "[f]ame for confusion purposes arises as long as a significant portion of the relevant consuming public, namely, purchasers of champagne and sparkling wine, recognizes the mark as a source indicator"). *See generally* McCarthy, Trademarks and Unfair Competition, § 11:73 (4th ed. 2007).

4. Family of Marks

Rights in a mark may be strengthened if the mark, or its salient component, is used in connection with a range of products or services. This is sometimes referred to as a "family" of marks. In *J & J Snack Foods Corp. v. McDonald's Corp.*, 932 F.2d 1460 (Fed. Cir. 1991), the Federal Circuit explained (at 1462):

> A family of marks is a group of marks having a recognizable common characteristic, wherein the marks are composed and used in such a way that the public associates not only the individual marks, but the common characteristic of the family, with the trademark owner. Simply using a series of similar marks does not of itself establish the existence of a family. There must be a recognition among the purchasing public that the common characteristic is indicative of a common origin of the goods. . . .

> Recognition of the family is achieved when the pattern of usage of the common element is sufficient to be indicative of the origin of the family. It is thus necessary to consider the use, advertisement, and distinctiveness of the marks, including assessment of the contribution of the common feature to the recognition of the marks as of common origin.

For example, the court in *Quality Inns Int'l v. McDonald's Corp.*, 695 F. Supp. 198, 212 (D. Md. 1988), found that McDonald's had created a famous "Mc" family of marks:

> "As part of its promotion, McDonald's created a language that it called "McLanguage" from which it developed a family of marks for its products such as McChicken, McNugget, McPizza, as well as marks outside the food area related to its business such as McStop, McKids, and McShuttle. There is no evidence that this language or these marks existed before McDonald's created them or that, outside of McDonald's sphere of promotion and presence, anyone would understand these words to mean anything. "Mc" obviously is a Scottish or Irish surname used in proper names. The use to form words, however, was unique at the time. The marks that are owned by McDonald's and that were formulated by combining "Mc" and a generic word are fanciful and enjoy a

meaning that associates the product immediately with McDonald's and its products and service."

The court also found that this "family of marks may have a synergistic recognition that is greater than the sum for each mark. Due to the strength of that family of marks, the court enjoined defendant's use of "McSleep Inn" for economy motels. Likewise, the owner of Toys 'R Us was found to have created a family of "R Us" marks: *Geoffrey, Inc. v. Stratton*, 16 U.S.P.Q.2d 1691 (C.D. Cal. 1990) (enjoining PHONES-R-US for retail store selling phones, accessories and answering machines; "[w]hether spoken or written, PHONES-R-US is virtually indistinguishable from plaintiff's family of 'R US' marks"); and Miles Laboratories (subsequently acquired by Bayer Corporation) created a family of "STIX" suffix marks for chemical reagent strips, transforming an arguably weak component into a strong mark entitled to broad protection: *International Diagnostic Technology, Inc. v. Miles Labs, Inc.*, 746 F.2d 798 (Fed. Cir. 1984) (affirming refusal to register STIQ for a sampler used in conjunction with test tubes in medical laboratories). Similarly, see *Han Beauty, Inc. v. Alberto-Culver Co.*, 236 F.3d 1333 (Fed. Cir. 2001) (applicant's TREVIVE mark for hair care products likely to be confused with Alberto-Culver's family of "TRES" prefix marks for hair care products).

It also is possible to create a family of trade dress. See the discussion in Chapter 5.

5. Trade Dress

Is prevention of product simulation socially or economically desirable in a competitive economy? Can differentiation as to source of copied products satisfactorily be achieved through labeling? In *Sunbeam Products Inc. v. West Bend Co.*, 123 F.3d 246, 259 (5th Cir. 1997), the court found confusion likely between the parties' food mixers despite dissimilar labeling, and observed that, "the mere labeling of a product will not automatically alleviate likelihood of confusion." Similarly, in *Fun-Damental Too Ltd. v. Gemmy Indus. Corp.*, 111 F.3d 993, 1003 (2d Cir. 1997), the court granted preliminary relief against defendant's CURRENCY CAN novelty bank as infringing plaintiff's TOILET BANK, in part because the trade names on the packaging were not well-known and, "consumers are more likely to remember the coinbank's packaging than its name"; and in *Clamp Mfg. Co. v. Enco Mfg. Co.*, 870 F.2d 512 (9th Cir.), *cert. denied*, 493 U.S. 872 (1989), defendant's C-clamp device was held to infringe even though it bore defendant's name. *Compare Litton Systems, Inc. v. Whirlpool Corp.*, *supra*, in which the parties' prominent uses of their respective trademarks dispelled any likely confusion between their microwave ovens; *Beverage Marketing USA, Inc. v. South Beach Beverage Co.*, 33 Fed. Appx. 12 (2d Cir. 2002) and *Nora Beverages, Inc. v. Perrier Group of America, Inc.*, 269 F.3d 114,119 (2d Cir. 2001), two cases involving bottle designs where "prominent and distinctive" labels made confusion unlikely; and *Bristol-Myers Squibb Co. v. McNeil-P.P.C., Inc.*, 973 F.2d 1033 (2d. Cir. 1992), in which the prominent presence of defendant's well-known TYLENOL mark on its pain reliever packaging made confusion with plaintiff's EXCEDRIN PM packaging unlikely. In *Antioch Co. v. Western Trimming Corp.*, 347 F.3d 150 (6th Cir. 2003), plaintiff's scrapbook design was held functional, but the court also noted that defendant used "its own distinctive logo, scrollwork, stickers, and face sheet" to "provide sufficient signals to scrapbook buyers" that its product did not originate with plaintiff, making confusion unlikely.

Initial interest confusion, discussed in more detail below, may also apply in trade dress cases, even when the infringing product label bears language disassociating it from plaintiff's product, because the confusingly similar trade dress induces the consumer to reach for the infringing product on the shelf. *See McNeil-PPC v. Guardian Drug Co.*, 984 F. Supp. 1066, 1074 (E.D. Mich. 1997). *But cf. Dorr-Oliver, Inc. v. Fluid-Quip, Inc.*, 94 F.3d 376, 382 (7th Cir. 1996) (rejecting initial interest confusion argument because "where product configurations are at issue, consumers are generally more likely to think that a competitor has entered the market with a similar product").

In *Conopco, Inc. v. May Department Stores Co.*, 46 F.3d 1556 (Fed. Cir. 1994), *cert. denied*, 545 U.S. 1078 (1995) plaintiff relaunched its VASELINE Intensive Care Lotion, using a new formula and unusual package design. Defendants created and sold a similar-looking private label version through Venture stores, with a label bearing a "compare to" statement and the diagonally-striped VENTURE logo. The district court found willful trademark and trade dress infringement and awarded treble damages of over $280,000. The Federal Circuit reversed. It noted the lower court's failure to properly consider the effect of the VENTURE house logo, which appeared not only on the label and in advertisements, but on other private label products, employee uniforms, and signs throughout the store. The court held the use of this logo was sufficient to eliminate confusion, noting that "the marketing device employed by defendants is neither new nor subtle," and opining that the purchasing public knows private labels are different from national brands. *Compare Badger Meter v. Grinnell Corp.*, 13 F.3d 1145 (7th Cir. 1994) (upholding jury verdict that defendant's water meter trade dress infringed plaintiff's, and rejecting argument that distinguishing marks made confusion unlikely, noting that purchasers might erroneously think defendant was selling a private label version of plaintiff's product), *with Merriam-Webster, Inc. v. Random House*, 35 F.3d 65 (2[d] Cir. 1994), *cert. denied*, 513 U.S. 1190 (1995) (reversing a jury's finding of infringement of plaintiff's dictionary trade dress where primary similarities were common, generic or descriptive and there were distinguishing house marks and logos) and *Libman Co. v. Vining Indus. Inc.*, 69 F.3d 1360, 1362–63 (7th Cir. 1995), *cert. denied*, 517 U.S. 1234 (1996) (reversing finding of infringement of registered contrasting color scheme for broom bristles because, among other reasons, the mark was weak; the parties' color schemes were not identical; and their word marks and advertising were dissimilar). *See also Continental Plastic Containers v. Owens Brockway Plastic Products, Inc.*, 141 F.3d 1073 (Fed. Cir. 1998), in which confusion with plaintiff's gallon-size plastic fruit juice bottles was held unlikely among wholesalers, because sales resulted from long-term negotiations and direct, ongoing communications between the parties. Analysis of the consumer market was found unnecessary, because plaintiff only sold empty bottles to wholesalers, without lids or labels, and the wholesalers then presumably had them filled with juice, lidded and labeled for retail sale.

Can product configuration infringe a word trademark, *e.g.*, can "turtle-shaped" candy infringe the trademark TURTLE for candy? What factors of law and evidence are relevant to such a determination? Should the test in this situation be simply likelihood of confusion? *Compare Laura Secord Candy Shops Ltd. v. Barton's Candy Corp.*, 179 U.S.P.Q. 715 (N.D. Ill. 1973) *with* the discussion above on Similarity of Appearance, Sound or Connotation.

In appropriate cases, dilution law may afford trade dress protection, even in the absence of any likelihood of confusion, as discussed in Chapter 8. *See, e.g., Sunbeam Prods. v. West Bend Co.*, 123 F.3d 246 (5th Cir. 1997), *cert. denied*, 523 U.S. 1118 (1998) (dilution of plaintiff's unregistered trade dress for its MIXMASTER mixer); *Nabisco, Inc. v. PF Brands, Inc.*, 191 F.3d 208 (2[d] Cir. 1999) (preliminary injunction against dilution of Pepperidge Farm's famous goldfish cracker configuration). For a scathing criticism of the *Sunbeam* decision, *see* Heald, *The Worst Intellectual Property Opinion Ever Written: Sunbeam Products, Inc. v. West Bend Co.: Exposing the Malign Application of the Federal Dilution Statute to Product Configuration*, 5 U. of GA. J. of INTELL. PROP. L. 415 (1998).

6. Weak Marks

A descriptive or laudatory mark may be considered intrinsically "weak" and therefore entitled to only a narrow scope of protection against uses of similar marks. *See, e.g., Petro Stopping Centers, L.P. v. James River Petroleum,* 130 F.3d 88 (4th Cir. 1997) (PETRO STOPPING CENTER for truck stop services was descriptive and entitled to only a narrow scope of protection; confusion held unlikely with defendant's PETRO CARD payment card for self-service filling stations). With substantial sales and advertising, or other means, of course, an intrinsically weak mark can become strong and even famous. *See, e.g., Union Carbide Corp. v. Ever-Ready, Inc.,* 531 F.2d 366 (7th Cir. 1976) (reversing district court's holding that plaintiff's EVEREADY mark for batteries was descriptive and invalid; "we find it difficult to believe that anyone in our society. . . can be other than thoroughly acquainted with [plaintiff's] EVEREADY mark . . . A court should not play the ostrich with regard to such general public knowledge").

As discussed in Chapter 3, while the *validity* of an incontestably registered mark cannot be challenged on the ground that the mark is merely descriptive, the descriptiveness and intrinsic weakness of a mark nonetheless can be considered in assessing the mark's strength and the breadth of protection it is afforded. *See, e.g., Therma-Scan, Inc. v. Thermoscan, Inc.,* 295 F.3d 623 (6th Cir. 2002), in which the plaintiff did not attempt to show that its THERMASCAN mark was widely recognized, but instead relied on its incontestable registration to raise a presumption of strength. The court explained that this reliance was misplaced. "Even where a trademark is incontestable and 'worthy of full protection', the significance of its presumed strength will depend on its recognition among members of the public. . . . [Plaintiff's] trademark, although valid and incontestable, is not an especially strong mark. Not only is the mark descriptive, but it also lacks strong public recognition." Similarly, in *Entrepreneur Media, Inc. v. Smith,* 279 F.3d 1135 (9th Cir. 2002), an incontestable registration of ENTREPRENEUR for a magazine did not preclude considering its descriptiveness in assessing the mark's strength or weakness for likelihood of confusion purposes. "Entrepreneur" described the subject matter and the intended audience of the magazine, and "[t]he need of others in the marketplace to use the term 'entrepreneur' to describe their goods or services confirms that [the] mark is descriptive."

7. Third Party Uses

The existence of third party uses of the same or a similar mark for other products can weaken a trademark owner's rights and narrow the scope of its protection. Words like "Sun" or "National", for example, are incorporated into the marks of many different trademark owners. As the Federal Circuit's predecessor court explained in *King Candy Co. v. Eunice King's Kitchen, Inc.,* 496 F.2d 1400, 1401 (C.C.P.A. 1974), this narrowed scope of protection simply means that when weak marks are at issue, confusion may be unlikely because the public easily distinguishes between the different uses:

> The expressions "weak" and "entitled to limited protection" are but other ways of saying . . . that confusion is unlikely because the marks are of such non-arbitrary nature or so widely used that the public easily distinguishes slight differences in the marks under consideration as well as differences in the goods to which they are applied, even though the goods of the parties may be considered "related."

The owner of a mark in such a "crowded field" therefore has a limited ability to prevent the use of similar marks. As stated by Professor McCarthy, "In such a crowd, customers will not likely be confused between any two of the crowd and may have learned to carefully pick out one from another." McCARTHY, TRADEMARKS AND UNFAIR COMPETITION, § 11:85 (4th ed. 2007).

In the *Entrepreneur Media, Inc. v. Smith* case above, for example, many third party uses of "Entrepreneur" created a "crowded field of marks and plaintiff obtained only very limited relief." Similarly, in *Taj Mahal Enterprises, Ltd. v. Trump*, 742 F. Supp. 892 (D.N.J. 1990), *summary judgment gr.*, 745 F. Supp. 240 (D.N.J. 1990), numerous third-party uses made plaintiff's TAJ MAHAL mark for its restaurant weak. Conversely, Donald Trump's TRUMP surname was very strong, and confusion was held unlikely with his TRUMP TAJ MAHAL casino and hotel. To similar effect are: *Willie W. Gray v. Meijer, Inc.*, 295 F.3d 641 (6th Cir. 2002) (third party packaging uses of the phrase "Chicago Style" and depictions of the Chicago skyline for a wide variety of products over many years made those elements unprotectable, and confusion unlikely between the parties' popcorn packages); *Bliss Salon Day Spa v. Bliss World*, 268 F.3d 494 (7th Cir. 2001) ("Bliss marks are a glut on the market in hair styling and beauty care. . . . [This] makes it all but impossible to imagine a consumer seeing the mark Bliss would assume the product or service came from the Bliss Day Spa of Wilmette"). *Al-Site Corp. v. VSI International Inc.*, 174 F.3d 1308, 1330 (Fed. Cir. 1999) (reversing grant of permanent injunction after jury wrongly found MAGNA DOT likely to be confused with MAGNIVISION for nonprescription glasses, the appellate court observing that "the MAGNA/MAGNI prefix as well as the VISION suffix enjoy wide use in the eyeglass industry on similar goods and services" and that such "common usage . . . weighs strongly against a finding of likelihood of confusion"); *Streetwise Maps, Inc. v. Vandam, Inc.*, 159 F.3d 739, 743-44 (2d Cir. 1998) ("Streetwise" was not "particularly strong" for maps even though it was inherently distinctive; other map makers used "street," and both "street" and "wise" were extensively used in connection with other products).

Compare In Sports Authority Inc. v. Prime Hospitality Corp., 89 F.3d 955, 961 (2d Cir. 1996), in which the court acknowledged that extensive, unchallenged, third party use of the incontestably registered mark, SPORTS AUTHORITY, might be relevant in ascertaining the mark's strength. In that case, however, the evidence did not support a summary judgment determination that the mark was weak because many of the third party uses were abandoned or were significantly different from plaintiff's mark. *Id.* at 961. Similarly, in *Playboy Enterprises Int'l v. Netscape Comm'ns Corp.*, 354 F.3d 1020 (9th Cir. 2004), the court observed that, "'[e]vidence of third-party use in markets similar to the markholders' is more compelling than evidence of third-party use in unrelated markets", and in *Morningside Group Ltd. v. Morningside Capital Group L.L.C.*, 182 F.3d 133, 139 (2d Cir. 1999), the appellate court concluded the lower court had wrongly found plaintiff's MORNINGSIDE mark was weak based on unrelated third party uses. "Here the relevant market is the relatively small world of financial investment professionals . . . [u]se of a like mark in a different market for different products or services need not undermine the mark's strength in its own market". *See also Committee for Idaho's High Desert v. Yost*, 92 F.3d 814, 820 (9th Cir. 1996) (finding third party use prior to plaintiff's adoption of CIHD not probative on whether plaintiff established priority over defendant; "a third party's prior use of a trademark is not a defense in an infringement action"). Marks that are both in a "crowded field" and expressive of "trade puffery" may be especially weak. *See, e.g., First Savings Bank F.S.B. v. First Bank Sys. Inc.*, 101 F.3d 645, 655 (10th Cir. 1996) (noting that FIRST BANK is a weak mark because it is expressive of "trade puffery"; "[w]hen the primary term is weakly protected to begin with, minor alterations may effectively negate any confusing similarity between the two marks").

6.07   Ornamental Use of Trademarks

BOSTON PROFESSIONAL HOCKEY ASS'N, INC. v. DALLAS CAP & EMBLEM MFG., INC.,
510 F.2d 1004 (5th Cir. 1975)

RONEY, CIRCUIT JUDGE

Nearly everyone is familiar with the artistic symbols which designate the individual teams in various professional sports. The question in this case of first impression is whether the unauthorized, intentional duplication of a professional hockey team's symbol on an embroidered emblem, to be sold to the public as a patch for attachment to clothing, violates any legal right of the team to the exclusive use of that symbol. Contrary to the decision of the district court, we hold that the team has an interest in its own individualized symbol entitled to legal protection against such unauthorized duplication.

* * *

The Facts

The controlling facts of the case at bar are relatively uncomplicated and uncontested. Plaintiffs play ice hockey professionally. In producing and promoting the sport of ice hockey, plaintiffs have each adopted and widely publicized individual team symbols. . . .

Plaintiffs have authorized National Hockey League Services, Inc. (NHLS) to act as their exclusive licensing agent. NHLS has licensed various manufacturers to use the team symbols on merchandise and has granted to one manufacturer, Lion Brothers Company, Inc., the exclusive license to manufacture embroidered emblems depicting the marks in question. In the spring of 1972, NHLS authorized the sale of NHL team emblems in connection with the sale of Kraft candies. That promotion alone was advertised on more than five million bags of candy.

Defendant Dallas Cap & Emblem Manufacturing, Inc., is in the business of making and selling embroidered cloth emblems. In August of 1968 and June of 1971, defendant sought to obtain from NHLS an exclusive license to make embroidered emblems representing the team motifs. Although these negotiations were unsuccessful, defendant went ahead and manufactured and sold without authorization emblems which were substantial duplications of the marks. During the month of April 1972, defendant sold approximately 24,603 of these emblems to sporting goods stores in various states. Defendant deliberately reproduced plaintiffs' marks on embroidered emblems and intended the consuming public to recognize the emblems as the symbols of the various hockey teams and to purchase them as such.

* * *

The Case

The difficulty with this case stems from the fact that a reproduction of the trademark itself is being sold, unattached to any other goods or services. The statutory and case law of trademarks is oriented toward the use of such marks to sell something other than the mark itself. The district court thought that to give plaintiffs protection in this case would be tantamount to the creation of a copyright monopoly for designs that were not copyrighted. The copyright laws are based on an entirely different concept than the trademark laws, and contemplate that the copyrighted material, like patented ideas, will eventually pass into the public domain. The trademark laws are based on the needed protection of the public and business interests and there is no reason why trademarks should ever pass into the public domain by the mere passage of time. . . .

Underlying our decision are three persuasive points. First, the major commercial value of the emblems is derived from the efforts of plaintiffs. Second, defendant sought and ostensibly would have asserted, if obtained, an exclusive right to make and sell the emblems. Third, the sale of a reproduction of the trademark itself on an emblem is an accepted use of such team symbols in connection with the type of activity in which the business of professional sports is engaged. We need not deal here with the concept of whether every artistic reproduction of the symbol would infringe upon plaintiffs' rights. We restrict ourselves to the emblems sold principally through sporting goods stores for informal use by the public in connection with sports activities and to show public allegiance to or identification with the teams themselves.

As to 15 U.S.C.A. § 1114

Plaintiffs indisputably have established the first three elements of a § 1114 cause of action. Plaintiffs' marks are validly registered and defendant manufactured and sold emblems which were (1) substantial duplications of the marks, (2) without plaintiffs' consent, and (3) in interstate commerce. The issue is whether plaintiffs have proven elements four and five of an action for mark infringement under the Lanham Act, i.e., whether the symbols are used in connection with the sale of goods and whether such use is likely to cause confusion, mistake or deception.

The fourth requisite of a § 1114 cause of action is that the infringing use of the registered mark must be in connection with the sale, offering for sale, distribution or advertising of any goods. Although the district court did not expressly find that plaintiffs had failed to establish element four, such a finding was implicit in the court's statement that 'in the instant case, the registered trade mark is, in effect, the product itself.'

Defendant is in the business of manufacturing and marketing emblems for wearing apparel. These emblems are the products, or goods, which defendant sells. When defendant causes plaintiffs' marks to be embroidered upon emblems which it later markets, defendant uses those marks in connection with the sale of goods as surely as if defendant had embroidered the marks upon knit caps. *See Boston Professional Hockey Association, Inc. v. Reliable Knitting Works, Inc.*, 178 USPQ 274 (E.D.Wis.1973). The fact that the symbol covers the entire face of defendant's product does not alter the fact that the trademark symbol is used in connection with the sale of the product. The sports fan in his local sporting goods store purchases defendant's fabric and thread emblems because they are embroidered with the symbols of ice hockey teams. Were defendant to embroider the same fabric with the same thread in other designs, the resulting products would still be emblems for wearing apparel but they would not give trademark identification to the customer. The conclusion is inescapable that, without plaintiffs' marks, defendant would not have a market for his particular product among ice hockey fans desiring to purchase emblems embroidered with the symbols of their favorite teams. It becomes clear that defendant's use of plaintiffs' marks is in connection with the sale, offering for sale, distribution, or advertising of goods and that plaintiffs have established the fourth element of a § 1114 cause of action.

The fifth element of a cause of action for mark infringement under 15 U.S.C.A. § 1114 is that the infringing use is likely to cause confusion, or to cause mistake or to deceive. . . . The confusion question here is conceptually difficult. It can be said that the public buyer knew that the emblems portrayed the teams' symbols. Thus, it can be argued, the buyer is not confused or deceived. This argument misplaces the purpose of the confusion requirement. The confusion or deceit requirement is met by the fact that the defendant duplicated the protected trademarks and sold them to the public knowing that the public would identify them as being the teams' trademarks. The certain knowledge of the buyer that the source and origin of the trademark symbols were in plaintiffs satisfies the requirement of the act. The argument that confusion must be as to the source of the manufacture of the emblem itself is unpersuasive, where the trademark, originated by the team, is the triggering mechanism for the sale of the emblem. . . .

As to 15 U.S.C.A. § 1125.

The district court held that plaintiffs failed to prove a cause of action under 15 U.S.C.A. § 1125 for false designation of origin of the goods in question or for false description by means of symbols. Because all plaintiffs, with the exception of Toronto, have established a cause of action for registered mark infringement, the district court's decision in regard to a § 1125 cause of action only affects plaintiff Toronto. The district court based its denial of a § 1125 cause of action on two findings of fact: (1) there was no likelihood of confusion as to the source of the emblems and (2) defendant did not make any false representations concerning the origin of the emblems. Our decision that confusion is self-evident from the nature of defendant's use of plaintiffs' marks applies with equal force in plaintiff Toronto's case. We reverse. . . .

In the case sub judice, defendant did not merely copy a product of the Toronto team. Defendant reproduced Toronto's common law mark on embroidered emblems with the intent that the public recognize and purchase the emblems as the symbol of the Toronto team. In the language of § 1125, defendant used a symbol, Toronto's mark, which tended falsely to represent goods, the embroidered emblems, in commerce. Where the consuming public had the certain knowledge that the source and origin of the trademark symbol was in the Toronto team, the reproduction of that symbol by defendant constituted a violation of § 1125. . . .

As to Unfair Competition.

Although the district court denied plaintiffs relief under the applicable provisions of the Lanham Act, the court found that the actions of defendant constituted unfair competition. The court stated that defendant's use of plaintiffs' marks had '. . . the prospect of trading on the competitive advantage the mark originator has to the public which desires the 'official' product.' Unfair competition is a question of fact, Volkswagenwerk Aktiengesellschaft v. Rickard, 492 F.2d 474 (5th Cir. 1974). Our review is narrowly circumscribed by F.R.Civ.P. 52(a). We find that there is substantial evidence which reflects that defendant competed unfairly with plaintiffs and, accordingly, we affirm the decision of the district court in this regard.

The unfair competition cannot, however, be rendered fair by the disclaimer ordered by the district court. The exact duplication of the symbol and the sale as the team's emblem satisfying the confusion requirement of the law, words which indicate it was not authorized by the trademark owner are insufficient to remedy the illegal confusion. Only a prohibition of the unauthorized use will sufficiently remedy the wrong.

Reversed and remanded.

* * *

Stacey L. Dogan and Mark A. Lemley
The Merchandising Right: Fragile Theory or
Fait Accompli?
54 EMORY L.J. 461 (Winter 2005)

Trademark merchandising is big business. One marketing consultant estimated the global market for licensing and marketing sports-related merchandise at $17 billion in 2001. The college-logo retail market was estimated at $3 billion in 2003. The 2002 Salt Lake Olympics generated $500 million in gross sales—and $34 million in licensing revenues—from sale of "Olympics" attire. Even municipal police departments want a piece of the action, applying to register their names as trademarks and demanding royalties from television programs designed to evoke their image. Want to wear a hat showing your support for your college or favorite baseball team? Want to wear a t-shirt emblazoned with the word "Barbie" or the "Harley-Davidson" logo? You may have no choice but to get an officially licensed piece of gear, at least if trademark owners have their way.

With this much money at stake, it's no surprise that trademark holders demand royalties for use of "their" marks on shirts, key chains, jewelry, and related consumer products. After all, the value of these products comes largely from the allure of the trademarks, and it seems only fair to reward the party that created that value . . . doesn't it?

It turns out that the answer is more complicated than this intuitive account predicts. Historically, trademark law has existed primarily to protect against consumer deception that occurs when one party attempts to pass off its products as those of another. Trademark law makes sense because it promotes the flow of truthful product information and leads to more efficient and competitive markets. From an economic and policy perspective, it is by no means obvious that trademark holders should have exclusive rights over the sale of products that use marks for their ornamental or "intrinsic" value, rather than as indicators of source or official sponsorship. Trademark law seeks to promote, rather than hinder, truthful competition in markets for products sought by consumers. If a trademark is the product, giving one party exclusive rights over it runs in tension with the law's procompetitive goals— frequently without any deception-related justification. If competition brings the best products to consumers at the lowest prices, departure from the competitive market requires a compelling justification.

On the other hand, there may be circumstances in which consumers expect that trademark holders sponsored or produced the products bearing their mark, in which case use of the mark by others—even as a part of a product— might result in genuine confusion. When this happens, the procompetitive goal of promoting marketplace clarity runs in tension with the objective of ensuring competition in product features. At the very least, the fact that the trademark constitutes part of the product, rather than purely an indication of source, complicates the analysis, creating tension between the dual goals of trademark law.

Given these complexities, together with the economic interests at stake, it would be reasonable to expect the law and practice of merchandising rights to be well-settled and reflect a considered balancing of the interests of trademark holders and their competitors. In reality, however, much of the multi-billion dollar industry of merchandise licensing has grown around a handful of cases from the 1970s and 1980s that established merchandising rights with little regard for the competing legal or policy concerns at stake. Those cases are far from settled law—indeed, many decisions decline to give trademark owners the right to control sales of their trademarks as products. We think it is high time to revisit that case law and to reconsider the theoretical justifications for a merchandising right.

That review provides little support for trademark owners' assumptions about merchandising. Doctrinally, the most broad-reaching merchandising cases—which presumed infringement based on the public recognition of the mark as a trademark —were simply wrong in their analysis of trademark infringement and have been specifically rejected by subsequent decisions. Philosophically, even a merchandising right that hinges on likelihood of confusion raises competition-related concerns that should affect courts' analysis of both the merits of and the appropriate remedies in merchandising cases. Most importantly, recent Supreme Court case law suggests that, if the Supreme Court had the opportunity to evaluate the merchandising theory (something it has never done), it would deny the existence of such a right. Further, the Court would be right to do so. When a trademark is sold, not as a source indicator, but as a desirable feature of a product, competition suffers—and consumers pay—if other sellers are shut out of the market for that feature. . . .

* * *

[W]e consider the theory of unjust enrichment or free riding that seems to underlie the instincts of courts and trademark owners in many of the merchandising cases.

Advocates of the merchandising right justify it by referring to the "free riding" that would occur if competitors could sell t-shirts featuring protected marks. Competitors would be "trading on their goodwill" and therefore presumably taking something that ought as a matter of right to belong to the trademark owners. Courts sometimes talk loosely about appropriation of a trademark owner's goodwill as the harm to be prevented. . . .

These justifications are circular and ultimately empty. The moral claim for ownership of a merchandising right presumes that someone must control this particular segment of the market. If courts begin their analysis on that basis, it might make sense that the trademark owner is the logical entity to exercise that control. But there is no reason to start from that presumption. Courts do not assume that the trademark owner has the right to control parodies, criticism, referential uses of the mark, or "uses" of a mark that call attention to features of competing products. Trademark rights have never given exclusive rights to control all uses of a mark. Instead, they have traditionally given trademark owners the right only to prevent uses that confuse consumers, or blur the distinctive significance of the mark, in order to minimize consumer search costs and facilitate the functioning of large-scale markets. Uses of a mark that do not raise these concerns are reserved to the free market. The merchandising theory expands the rights of trademark owners, giving them a new form of control over uses of "their" mark at the expense of the background norm of competition. That expansion requires some justification: In a market economy it is not reasonable to simply assume that someone must own the right to compete in a particular way.

This justification cannot be found in the notion of "free riding" or of appropriation of goodwill. Those notions too assume rather than demonstrate that someone is entitled to own a right on which another might free ride. No one thinks newspapers are "free riding" on trade names when they report news about the companies that use those names, even though one can imagine a world in which the trademark owner licensed such use. Similarly, we don't think of gas stations as free riding on competitors when they locate across the street from that competitor, or of stores free riding on the anchor tenant of a shopping mall by deciding to lease space in that mall. Companies engaging in all these activities are free riding in some sense; they are using the name or reputation of another company without paying. But the world is full of free riding. The question is whether a particular type of conduct causes the kind of harm that trademark law ought to address. Simply announcing that a particular use of a trademark is an improper appropriation of the trademark owner's goodwill assumes the conclusion.

The problem is not simply the absence of a good reason to grant trademark owners a merchandising right. A merchandising right can actually interfere with the fundamental goals of trademark law, as we discuss in the next section.

Why not grant trademark owners a right to control merchandising of their logos? The answer begins with the fundamental justification of trademark law: improving the functioning of the market by reducing consumer search costs. From a search costs perspective, a general merchandising right unmoored from confusion conflicts with, rather than promoting, trademark law's procompetitive goals. If consumers are not duped into believing that a trademark-bearing product was either sponsored or made by the trademark holder, then the quality of product-related information in the marketplace has not suffered from the use. And the overarching goal of market competition will only gain: The unlicensed product will presumably compete in the marketplace with any licensed versions, bringing prices down, letting consumers choose higher-quality products with identical logos, and generally benefiting the consumer. On balance, then, nonconfusing uses of marks on merchandise serve rather than impede competition in the marketplace and thus promote the overall goals of trademark and unfair competition law.

Trademark law facilitates market competition by permitting consumers to find products cheaply and quickly by relating advertising and their own experiences to the products they buy. An infringement of a trademark is one that increases consumer search costs, normally by confusing consumers. Trademarks can extend not only to words and logos, but also to trade dress and even the color or shape of a product. But trademark law does not give rights over an entire product class, because doing so would short-circuit the very market competition trademark law is supposed to protect. Similarly, a merchandising right would give rights over irreplaceable product features, which inevitably increases the cost of those products. If only one company controls the sale of Seattle Seahawks t-shirts, those shirts will cost more and be of worse quality than if the market competes to provide those shirts. Consumers lose something tangible—they pay more for the shirt, they are unable to express their support for the Seahawks because they can't afford the shirt, or they get a lower quality shirt. There must be some reason for the law to compel that loss.

The Boston Hockey approach has no logical stopping point. It conflicts with the text of the Lanham Act, which makes infringement turn not on a mental association between the defendant's product and the trademark holder, but on confusion, deception, or mistake. More significantly, it leaves courts without an effective standard for determining when the use of a trademark is legal. The merchandising right cases seem to stem from the unjust enrichment instinct that "if value, then right." But as we have explained elsewhere, that instinct has no solid basis in public policy. It would make each of the countless "nominative uses" trademark law permits into infringements. Additionally, it would turn trademark law from a right designed to facilitate commerce into a right to control language, something the courts have repeatedly warned against given its troubling implications for both competition and free speech. College students and football fans could not support their team unless they paid the required fee. Newspapers might be at risk for using brand names or logos in connection with their stories. Aqua couldn't sing the song "Barbie Girl," or Walking Mountain create art using Barbie dolls, even though consumers were not confused. Individuals might even be liable for wearing tattoos or jewelry containing trademarked logos, or tattoo parlors for applying them. . . .

Even absent a good theoretical justification for a broad merchandising right, advocates might fall back on practical concerns. It seems clear that trademark owners assume they have a right to control merchandising. Wouldn't it upset the settled expectations of those trademark owners to suddenly nullify the right? Similarly, might consumers be confused if they too believe that any t-shirt bearing a corporate logo is licensed by the corporation? Trademark owner expectations provide no real reason to continue a merchandising right, but the law may have to take consumer expectations into account. It does not need a broad merchandising right to do so, however.

1. Trademark Owner Expectations

The first concern need not detain us long. First, based on our review of the cases in Part I, it is far from clear that trademark owners are reasonable in assuming the existence of such a right. The case law support for it has never been strong or unequivocal. Second, there is no obvious investment that will be lost if the broad merchandising theory is rejected. Trademark owners won't lose their protection against consumer confusion or dilution. Nor can the trademark owner make a plausible case that a competing sale of, say, Dallas Cowboys hats will weaken the connection between the mark and the team. True, the Cowboys might make less money than they would if trademarks were absolute property rights, and they might argue that this "discourages investment" in football. But so what? The point of trademark law has never been to maximize profits for trademark owners at the expense of competitors and consumers. The investment at issue in these cases is not investment in the quality of the underlying product (the team), but investment in merchandising the brand itself. As Ralph Brown quite sensibly suggested, this is not the goal of the law.

For similar reasons, we can reject the argument that a merchandising right provides needed financial support for the trademark owner. This is a slightly altered form of the argument that merchandising rights serve as incentives—an argument that has been soundly refuted elsewhere. Merchandise may be an indirect way of subsidizing colleges and other trademark owners, though we are skeptical that the argument has much persuasive force when applied to corporations such as Nike or Coca-Cola rather than to universities. But if the goal of consumers is to contribute to the school, there are other, more direct ways of doing so. Indeed, if consumers do in fact value obtaining goods from the trademark owner itself—perhaps because it supports the school or team—then we would expect the market to reflect that by developing a distinction between ordinary merchandise and officially licensed merchandise. This may be the best of all worlds, because consumers will learn whether merchandise is sponsored by the trademark owner or not, and can choose their goods accordingly. The emphasis in merchandising inquiries would appropriately shift, then, to whether the defendant had deceptively suggested that its goods were officially licensed by the trademark holder. That is something within the traditional competence of trademark law, and a task courts are well equipped to perform.

2. Consumer Expectations

The consumer concern is a more significant one. It is possible that consumers have come to expect that San Francisco Giants jerseys are licensed by the Giants, not because they serve a brand-identifying function but simply because the law has sometimes required such a relationship. Indeed, the NFL cases discussed above found evidence of this. If this expectation exists, consumers may be confused if the law changes. If so, a law based on eliminating consumer confusion may be obliged to give trademark owners the right to prevent such uses in order to avoid this confusion.

Or perhaps not. . . .The idea that once-legal conduct becomes illegal simply because the public believes it is illegal seems like bootstrapping. Nor would it justify a general right, rather than one based on particularized findings of consumer confusion. There are many famous marks and icons for which we have not granted merchandising rights. No one controls the exclusive right to make "Statue of Liberty" t-shirts or paperweights, for example. And while consumers might assume a licensing relationship in the context of some famous marks, particularly in the field of professional sports, there are many more marks for which there is no evidence that consumers expect the trademark owner to be the only manufacturer. Even if courts decide they cannot undo what some cases have done in the sports context, there is no reason to extend the merchandising right any further, since it is hard to find any theoretical or statutory basis for the property approach to trademarks.

If trademark law is committed to basing trademark doctrine on consumer reactions, however, we might be stuck with those reactions in particular cases even if bad legal decisions initially helped create them. The real underlying issue is whether the trademark law should act here as a creator or as a reflector of societal norms. In the context of likelihood of confusion analysis, trademark law has traditionally adapted itself to reflect societal norms, rendering a use illegal if but only if it confuses consumers. In other areas, however, trademark law acts as a norms creator, establishing standards that shape rather than merely respond to consumer beliefs. The law creates certain limiting doctrines—genericide, trademark use, and fair use, for example—that constrain the scope of trademark rights and that exist whether or not the public is aware of them. Trademark's norm-creation role is important because it prevents a downward spiral in which the court focuses on the most gullible consumers, lowering the standards and expectations of others. Rigorous application of these doctrines can affect consumer perceptions. In effect, the law is leading rather than following consumer expectations.

. . . . As Robert Denicola pointed out, the role of trademark law as a norms creator may be especially important in merchandising cases: Unlike the ordinary trademark case, in which an infringing defendant can simply choose another mark and compete fairly in the relevant market, "a defendant enjoined from using a well-known insignia on T-shirts or caps is effectively excluded from the market for such products. It can sell to no one, including those who care not the slightest whether their Boston Red Sox cap is licensed or approved." On the other hand, if it is correct that consumers now believe t-shirts are sponsored by the owner of the logos emblazoned on them, that assumption seems to fit within the likelihood of confusion analysis, as to which trademark law has traditionally been a norms reflector.

We are inclined to believe that merchandising is a case in which the law should act as a norms creator, setting aspirational goals rather than responding to current consumer expectations. In part this is because any consumer confusion is itself an artifact of legal cases that seem to create a new merchandising right; arguably it should be up to the courts, not consumers, to undo the problems a few ill-considered decisions may have created. This is particularly so when consumers believe that the law requires permission to use a logo, which may not matter at all to their assessment of the quality of the merchandise at issue, such as when the product prominently identifies its manufacturer. If individuals don't "care one way or the other whether the [trademark holder] sponsors or endorses such products or whether the products are officially licensed," then the competitive process certainly does not suffer from their assumption that the use required a license.

Undoubtedly, however, in some cases trademark holders could establish likely confusion as to sponsorship among people who actually cared about such sponsorship, and the courts in such cases would have to decide upon appropriate relief. Where there is such confusion, courts can probably cure it without eliminating competition simply by requiring a conspicuous disclaimer. Some courts have taken this approach, permitting merchandising uses but requiring that the user take all reasonable steps to try to reduce confusion both at the point of purchase and postsale. Robert Bone suggests that the law should aggressively create norms here and declare disclaimers the sole remedy in all merchandising cases. We would not go that far. As we note in the next section, there may be rare instances of postsale confusion that would not be cured by a disclaimer. But it is at least a useful starting point.

Three factors persuade us that disclaimers, rather than injunctions against use, should suffice in most merchandising cases. First, the competition-oriented concerns discussed above make these cases special and suggest that courts should try, if at all possible, to address consumer confusion in a way that preserves consumer choice. Second, given that the vast majority of these cases involve "licensing confusion"—i.e., whether the trademark holder officially licensed the use rather than whether it produced, manufactured, or sold the product—a prominent disclaimer should be more capable of addressing such confusion than in the typical case of confusion as to the origin of goods. Finally, disclaimers will facilitate the process of norms creation: As consumers grow more accustomed to competition between licensed and unlicensed products, they will adjust their expectations and make a product's officially licensed status just another piece of information that factors into their purchasing decisions.

We conclude, therefore, that the fact that consumers may believe trademark owners have a right to control merchandise bearing their brands does not itself justify a merchandising right. The issue is certainly not free from doubt, and we can readily imagine a court concluding that even if the merchandising theory is unpersuasive, perhaps the law has gone too far down that road to turn back now. But even if a court were to take that position, a limited, likelihood-of-confusion rationale for keeping a bad law intact is quite different from a theoretical justification for cementing and extending the merchandising right.

* * *

Conclusion

[T]he Supreme Court seems to have a firm idea of what trademark law is about, a vision that leaves no room for a merchandising right. It is likely, therefore, that courts considering merchandising claims in the future will not be inclined to uphold them absent special circumstances.

We do not believe this should be cause for alarm or for congressional intervention. The merchandising theory has not been persuasive to courts in large measure because its justifications lack persuasive force. The arguments normally advanced for a merchandising right are circular and ultimately rather empty. Most of the good a merchandising right might do can be accomplished more directly using existing trademark doctrines such as postsale confusion. Thus, we would eliminate the presumption of a merchandising right and put courts to the task of determining whether, under the circumstances, a particular use was in fact likely to confuse consumers as to source or sponsorship. If not, the competitor ought to have access to the mark as product without incurring the cost of labeling itself as an "unofficial" product. If confusion is likely, a disclaimer will ordinarily resolve it. We can imagine some circumstances in which the risk of postsale confusion would justify an injunction, but those will be rare cases. Most cases of consumer confusion can be solved without a merchandising right. And when there is no consumer confusion at all, the assertion of a pure right to control use of a mark for no other reason than because it is "mine" is at odds with trademark theory and good public policy. Consumers do not need it, the statute does not support it, and we are well rid of it.

*   *   *

Notes on Ornamental Use of Trademarks

Trademarks, configurations and other trade dress sometimes acquire a prestige or attractiveness in the public eye which gives them a commercial value of their own, apart from their value to their owner as an indicator of product source. This appeal may create a market for products such as clothing or glassware which feature these source indicators as ornamentation. When such devices are intentionally used by others as ornamentation only, the issue of whether confusion is likely may prove problematic.

Should a prior user be entitled to stop such use by others regardless of source confusion? What should be the result if consumers believe there is only a remote connection between the products or services of the plaintiff and the defendant, e.g., sponsorship? When it comes to merchandise and apparel related to professional sports teams, such as t-shirts, balls, watches and jewelry, wall decorations, and so on, what do consumers in fact believe about the provenance of such merchandise? Does it matter whether consumers believe that the merchandise is "officially licensed," or that the sellers have permission or authorization from the respective sports teams? If we reject, with Professors Dogan and Lemley, the assertion of expansive "merchandising rights" by holders of popular marks, what is the limiting principle to that rejection? Put another way, it is universally accepted in U.S. trademark law that marks can be licensed. *See* Chapter 4. Limiting "merchandising rights" means limiting the ability to license. What doctrinal basis is available to decide which licenses are permissible and which are not? Dogan and Lemly maintain that "a disclaimer will ordinarily resolve" consumer confusion." Some empirical studies disagree. *See* Jacoby & Raskopf, *Disclaimers in Trademark Infringement Litigation: More Trouble Than They Are Worth?* 76 TRADEMARK REP. 35 (1986) (consumer studies show that disclaimers do not cure consumer confusion); *ProFitness Physical Therapy Center v. Pro-Fit Orthopedic and Sports Physical Therapy P.C.*, 314 F.3d 62, 70 (2ᵈ Cir. 2002) ("a growing body of academic literature has concluded that disclaimers, especially those . . . which employ brief negator words such as 'no' or 'not,' are generally ineffective") (citation and quotation marks omitted).

In *Dallas Cowboys Cheerleaders v. Pussycat Cinema, Ltd.*, 604 F.2d 200 (2ᵈ Cir. 1979), the defendant was preliminarily enjoined from distributing or exhibiting the "sexually depraved" movie "Debbie Does Dallas" because use of the plaintiff's cheerleader uniform would likely mislead the public into believing that plaintiff sponsored the movie. Similarly in *Gucci Shops, Inc. v. R.H. Macy & Co.*, 446 F. Supp. 838 (S.D.N.Y. 1977), the court found that use of GUCCI GOO on a diaper bag could mislead the public into believing plaintiff Gucci was somehow associated with the product's manufacture, promotion and sale, and in *Coca-Cola Co. v. Gemini Rising, Inc.*, 346 F. Supp. 1183 (E.D.N.Y. 1972), defendant was enjoined from use of ENJOY COCAINE in famous Coca-Cola script on its posters. Are there any reasons other than confusion that should entitle the trademark owner to protection against these types of uses? *See* ᴳⁱˡˢᵒⁿ, § 5.05[8]; the discussion on parody in Chapter 7, and the section on Dilution and domain name misuse in Chapter 8.

Cases adopting the approach of *Boston Hockey* include *University of Georgia Athletic Ass'n v. Laite*, 756 F.2d 1535 (11ᵗʰ Cir. 1985) (representation of school mascot on beer can label violated § 43(a)); *Rolls-Royce Motors, Ltd. v. A & A Fiberglass, Inc.*, 428 F. Supp. 689 (N.D. Ga. 1977) (customizing kits for putting imitation Rolls-Royce front grill and hood ornamentation on a Volkswagen Beetle automobile infringed the registered designs of plaintiff and violated § 43(a)).

Compare International Order of Job's Daughters v. Lindeburg & Co., 633 F.2d 912 (9ᵗʰ Cir. 1980), *cert. denied*, 452 U.S. 941 (1981), in which the court rejected the reasoning of *Boston Hockey* and held that the nontrademark jewelry use of plaintiff fraternal organization's name and emblem did not infringe the organization's trademark rights and did not violate § 43(a): "The name and emblem were functional aesthetic components of the product, not trademarks. There could be, therefore, no infringement." *Id.* at 920. *Cf. WSM, Inc. v. Tennessee Sales Co.*, 709 F.2d 1084, 1087 (6th Cir. 1983) (distinguishing *Job's Daughters*). *See also Application of Penthouse International, Ltd.*, 565 F.2d 679 (C.C.P.A. 1977), where the Trademark Trial and Appeal Board's refusal to register applicant's trademark as a jewelry design was reversed (565 F.2d at 682):

> Depriving the public of the right to copy the Penthouse key logo for jewelry (1) does not hinder competition and (2) does not take from the goods (jewelry) something of substantial value. Moreover . . . the public is already prevented from making unauthorized copies of the mark in the form of a piece of jewelry.

Could a particular word or design element serve both a trademark and a functional purpose? If so, what would be the standard for protection? In *Plasticolor Molded Products v. Ford Motor Co.*, 713 F. Supp. 1329 (C.D. Cal. 1989), the court found Plasticolor's automotive floor mats bearing Ford's trademarks such as MUSTANG were "mixed-use articles," with Ford's trademarks serving both a trademark and a functional purpose on them, the functional purpose being to show the purchaser's allegiance to Ford. The Court held that established trademark principles were inapplicable to claims involving such "mixed-use articles" because total protection "defeats much of the feature's functionality," but that denying any protection "would be decimating a cause of action explicitly provided by Congress." *Plasticolor Molded Products*, 713 F. Supp. at 1337, 1338. The court therefore sought "a solution that permits trademarks to be copied as functional features, but minimizes the likelihood the public will associate the copied mark with the registrant." *Id.* at 1339.

The Court's proposed solution was to require sufficient disclaimers at the point-of-purchase to avoid likelihood of confusion, but to tolerate some post-sale confusion, by only requiring "all reasonable steps" be taken to eliminate such confusion. The tolerance of some post-purchase confusion as based on the court's conclusion that few customers would be attracted to a "floor mat whose upper surface reads 'FORD (not authorized by Ford Motor Company)'," *Plasticolor Molded Products*, 713 F. Supp. at 1339 (C.D. Cal. 1991). After articulating its new standard for "mixed-use articles," the Court held that it could not dispose of the issue on summary judgment. This decision subsequently was vacated pursuant to an agreement of the parties. 767 F. Supp. 1036 (C.D. Cal. 1991). *Cf. Au-Tomotive Gold, Inc. v. Volkswagen of Am., Inc.*, 457 F.3d 1062 (9th Cir. 2006) (use of plaintiff's Volkswagen and Audi marks on key chains, license plate frames and the like was not functional; "consumers want 'Audi' and 'Volkswagen' accessories, not beautiful accessories").

6.08 Initial Interest Confusion

D, appellant *P, appellee*

GROTRIAN, HELFFERICH, SCHULZ, ETC. v. STEINWAY & SONS
523 F.2d 1331 (2d Cir. 1975)

TC: found fo. P
Ac: affirmed

TIMBERS, CIRCUIT JUDGE

* * *

It is undisputed that the parties are in direct competition for a rather limited class of customer [namely, purchasers and potential purchasers of pianos]. Few people in the United States ever have heard of a Grotrian-Steinweg [piano]. Whatever reputation Grotrian's products may enjoy outside the United States and whatever may be the competition between the two pianos in other countries, Steinway is the renowned name here. We think it is inescapable that a potential American purchaser of the kind of piano which the parties sell, upon hearing the name "Grotrian-Steinweg," would associate Grotrian's product with Steinway. . . .

Turning to the issue of actual confusion, we hold that the court's finding that such confusion existed is not clearly erroneous but is supported by substantial evidence. . . .

The [district] court found that, despite the high price of the pianos and the sophistication of the purchasers, the likelihood of confusion resulting from the factors discussed above could not be eliminated by the degree of care taken in selection:

> "It is the subliminal confusion apparent in the record as to the relationship, past and present, between the corporate entities and the products that can transcend the competence of even the most sophisticated consumer. Misled into an initial interest, a potential Steinway buyer may satisfy himself that the less expensive Grotrian-Steinweg is at least as good, if not better, than a Steinway. Deception and confusion thus work to appropriate defendant's good will. This confusion, or mistaken beliefs as to the companies' interrelationships, can destroy the value of the trademark which is intended to point to only one company." 365 F.Supp. at 717 (footnote omitted).

Grotrian contends that in considering the issue of the degree of care exercised by purchasers the court failed to give sufficient weight to the nature of the products, their cost, and the conditions under which they are purchased. It argues that there was no proof, and inferentially in view of the above three factors that there could be no proof, that anyone ever had bought or would buy a Grotrian-Steinweg piano thinking it was a Steinway or was guaranteed by Steinway. Therefore, according to Grotrian, no infringement was shown.

We recognize that in a trademark infringement action the kind of product, its cost and the conditions of purchase are important factors in considering whether the degree of care exercised by the purchaser can eliminate the likelihood of confusion which would otherwise exist. We decline to hold, however, that actual or potential confusion at the time of purchase necessarily must be demonstrated to establish trademark infringement under the circumstances of this case.

The issue here is not the possibility that a purchaser would buy a Grotrian-Steinweg thinking it was actually a Steinway or that Grotrian had some connection with Steinway and Sons. The harm to Steinway, rather, is the likelihood that a consumer, hearing the "Grotrian-Steinweg" name and thinking it had some connection with "Steinway", would consider it on that basis. The "Grotrian-Steinweg" name therefore would attract potential customers based on the reputation built up by Steinway in this country for many years. The harm to Steinway in short is the likelihood . . . that potential piano purchasers will think that there is some connection between the Grotrian-Steinweg and Steinway pianos. . . .

We hold that the district court correctly concluded that Grotrian consciously and intentionally infringed Steinway's trademarks. . . .

BROOKFIELD COMMUNICATIONS INC. v. WEST COAST ENTERTAINMENT CORP.
174 F.3d 1036 (9th Cir. 1999)

O'SCANNLAIN, DISTRICT JUDGE

We must venture into cyberspace to determine whether federal trademark and unfair competition laws prohibit a video rental store chain from using an entertainment-industry information provider's trademark in the domain name of its web site and in its web site's metatags.

Brookfield Communications, Inc. ("Brookfield") appeals the district court's denial of its motion for a preliminary injunction prohibiting West Coast Entertainment Corporation ("West Coast") from using in commerce terms confusingly similar to Brookfield's trademark, "MovieBuff."

* * *

Sometime in 1996, Brookfield attempted to register the World Wide Web ("the Web") domain name "moviebuff.com" with Network Solutions, Inc. ("Network Solutions"), but was informed that the requested domain name had already been registered by West Coast.

* * *

Given the virtual identity of "moviebuff.com" and "MovieBuff," the relatedness of the products and services accompanied by those marks, and the companies' simultaneous use of the Web as a marketing and advertising tool, many forms of consumer confusion are likely to result. People surfing the Web for information on "MovieBuff" may confuse "MovieBuff" with the searchable entertainment database at "moviebuff.com" and simply assume that they have reached Brookfield's web site. *See, e.g.*, Cardservice Int'l, 950 F. Supp. at 741. In the Internet context, in particular, entering a web site takes little effort - usually one click from a linked site or a search engine's list; thus, Web surfers are more likely to be confused as to the ownership of a web site than traditional patrons of a brick-and-mortar store would be of a store's ownership. Alternatively, they may incorrectly believe that West Coast licensed "MovieBuff" from Brookfield, *see, e.g., Indianapolis Colts, Inc. v. Metropolitan Baltimore Football Club Ltd.*, 34 F.3d 410, 415-416 (7th Cir. 1994), or that Brookfield otherwise sponsored West Coast's database, *see E. Remy Martin*, 756 F.2d at 1530; *Fuji Photo Film Co. v. Shinohara Shoji Kabushike Kaisha*, 754 F.2d 591, 596 (5th Cir. 1985). Other consumers may simply believe that West Coast bought out Brookfield or that they are related companies.

Yet other forms of confusion are likely to ensue. Consumers may wrongly assume that the "MovieBuff" database they were searching for is no longer offered, having been replaced by West Coast's entertainment database, and thus simply use the services at West Coast's web site. *See, e.g., Cardservice Int'l*, 950 F. Supp. At 741. And even where people realize, immediately upon accessing "moviebuff.com," that they have reached a site operated by West Coast and wholly unrelated to Brookfield, West Coast will still have gained a customer by appropriating the goodwill that Brookfield has developed in its "MovieBuff" mark. A consumer who was originally looking for Brookfield's products or services may be perfectly content with West Coast's database (especially as it is offered free of charge); but he reached West Coast's site because of its use of Brookfield's mark as its second-level domain name, which is a misappropriation of Brookfield's good-will by West Coast.

* * *

So far we have considered only West Coast's use of the domain name "moviebuff-.com." Because Brookfield requested that we also preliminarily enjoin West Coast from using marks confusingly similar to "MovieBuff" in metatags and buried code, we must also decide whether West Coast can, consistently with the trademark and unfair competition laws, use "MovieBuff" or "moviebuff.com" in its HTML code.[23]

* * *

Although entering "MovieBuff" into a search engine is likely to bring up a list including "westcoastvideo.com" if West coast has included that therm in its metatags, the resulting confusion is not as great as where West Coast uses the "moviebuff.com" domain name. First, when the user inputs "MovieBuff" into an Internet search engine, the list produced by the search engine is likely to include both West Coast's and Brookfield's web sites. Thus, in scanning such a list, the Web user will often be able to find the particular web site he is seeking. Moreover, even if the Web user chooses the web site belonging to West Coast, he will see that the domain name of the web site he selected is "westcoastvideo.com." Since there is no confusion resulting from the domain address, and since West Coast's initial web page prominently displays its own name, it is difficult to say that a consumer is likely to be confused about whose site he has reached or to think that Brookfield somehow sponsors West Coast's web site.

Nevertheless, West Coast's use of "moviebuff.com" in metatags will still result in what is known as initial interest confusion. Web surfers looking for Brookfield's "MovieBuff" products who are taken by a search engine to "westcoastvideo.com" will find a database similar enough to "MovieBuff" such that a sizeable number of consumers who were originally looking for Brookfield's product will simply decide to utilize West Coast's offerings instead. Although there is no source confusion in the sense that consumers know they are patronizing West Coast rather than Brookfield, there is nevertheless initial interest confusion in the sense that, by using "moviebuff.com" or "MovieBuff" to divert people looking for "MovieBuff" to its web site, West Coast improperly benefits from the goodwill that Brookfield developed in its mark. Recently in *Dr. Seuss*, we explicitly recognized that the use of another's trademark in a manner calculated "to capture initial consumer attention, even though no actual sale is finally completed as a result of the confusion, may be still an infringement." *Dr. Seuss*, 109 F.3d at 1405 (citing *Mobil Oil Corp. v. Pegasus Petroleum Corp.*, 818 F.2d 254, 257-58 (2ᵈ Cir. 1987)).

* * *

Using another's trademark in one's metatags is much like posting a sign with another's trademark in front of one's store. Suppose West Coast's competitor (let's call it "Blockbuster") puts up a billboard on a highway reading "West Coast Video: 2 miles ahead at Exit 7" where West Coast is really located at Exit 8 but Blockbuster is located at Exit 7. Customers looking for West Coast's store will pull off at Exit 7 and drive around looking for it. Unable to locate West Coast, but seeing the Blockbuster store

---

[23] As we explained in Part II, metatags are HTML code not visible to Web users but used by search engines in determining which sites correspond to the keywords entered by a Web user. Although Brookfield never explained what it meant by "buried code," the leading trademark treatise explains that "buried code" is another term for the HTML code that is used by search engines but that is not visible to users. *See* 3 McCarthy, supra, at § 25:69 n. 1. We will use the term metatags as encompassing HTML code generally.

right by the highway entrance, they may simply rent there. Even consumers who prefer West Coast may find it not worth the trouble to continue searching for West Coast since there is a Blockbuster right there. Customers are not confused in the narrow sense: they are fully aware that they are purchasing from Blockbuster and they have no reason to believe that Blockbuster is related to, or in any way sponsored by, West Coast. Nevertheless, the fact that there is only initial consumer confusion does not alter the fact that Blockbuster would be misappropriating West Coast's acquired goodwill. *See Blockbuster*, 869 F. Supp. at 513 (finding trademark infringement where the defendant, a video rental store, attracted customer' initial interest by using a sign confusingly to its competitors even though confusion would end long before the point of sale or rental); *see also Dr. Seuss*, 109 F.3d at 1405; *Mobil Oil*, 818 F.2d at 260; *Green Prods.*, 992 F. Supp at 1076.

*   *   *

We agree that West Coast can legitimately use an appropriate descriptive term in its metatags. But "MovieBuff" is not such a descriptive term. Even though it differs from "Movie Buff" by only a single space, that difference is pivotal. The term "Movie Buff" is a descriptive term, which is routinely used in the English Language to describe a movie devotee. "MovieBuff" is not. The term "MovieBuff" is not in the dictionary. *See Merriam-Webster's Collegiate Dictionary*, 762 (10th ed. 1998); *American Heritage College Dictionary*, 893 (3d ed. 1997); *Webster's New World College Dictionary*, 889 (3d ed. 1997); *Webster's Third New Int'l Dictionary*, 1480 (unabridged 1993). Nor has that term been used in any published federal or state court opinion. In light of the fact that it is not a word in the English Language, when the term "MovieBuff" is employed, it is used to refer to Brookfield's products ad services, rather than to mean "motion picture enthusiast." The proper term for the "motion picture enthusiast" is "Movie Buff," which West Coast certainly can use. It cannot, however, omit the space.

Moreover, West Coast is not absolutely barred from using the term "MovieBuff." As we explained above, that term can be legitimately used to describe Brookfield's product. For example, its web page might well include an advertisement banner such as "Why pay for MovieBuff when you can get the same thing here for FREE?" which clearly employs "MovieBuff" to refer to Brookfield's products. West Coast, however, presently uses Brookfield's trademark not to reference Brookfield's products, but instead to describe its own product (in the case of the domain name) and to attract people to its web site (in the case of the metatags). That is not fair use.

*   *   *

As we have seen, registration of a domain name for a Web site does not trump long-established principles of trademark law. When a firm uses a competitor's trademark in the domain name of its web site, users are likely to be confused as to its source or sponsorship. Similarly, using a competitor's trademark in the metatags of such a web site is likely to cause what we have described as initial interest confusion. These forms of confusion are exactly what the trademark laws are designed to prevent.

Accordingly, we reverse and remand this case to the district court with instructions to enter a preliminary injunction in favor of Brookfield in accordance with this opinion.

REVERSED and REMANDED.

PLAYBOY ENTERPRISES, INC. v. NETSCAPE COMMUNICATIONS CORPORATION
354 F.3d 1020 (9th Cir. 2004)

T.G. NELSON, CIRCUIT JUDGE

Playboy Enterprises International, Inc. (PEI) appeals from the district court's grant of summary judgment in favor of Netscape Communications Corporation and Excite, Inc. PEI sued defendants for trademark infringement and dilution. We have jurisdiction pursuant to 28 U.S.C. § 1291. Because we conclude that genuine issues of material fact preclude summary judgment on both the trademark infringement and dilution claims, we reverse and remand.

I. FACTS

This case involves a practice called "keying" that defendants use on their Internet search engines. Keying allows advertisers to target individuals with certain interests by linking advertisements to pre-identified terms. To take an innocuous example, a person who searches for a term related to gardening may be a likely customer for a company selling seeds. Thus, a seed company might pay to have its advertisement displayed when searchers enter terms related to gardening. After paying a fee to defendants, that company could have its advertisements appear on the page listing the search results for gardening-related terms: the ad would be "keyed" to gardening-related terms. Advertisements appearing on search result pages are called "banner ads" because they run along the top or side of a page much like a banner. . . .

Defendants have various lists of terms to which they key advertisers' banner ads. Those lists include the one at issue in this case, a list containing terms related to sex and adult-oriented entertainment. Among the over-400 terms in this list are two for which PEI holds trademarks: "playboy" and "playmate." . . . Defendants *require* adult-oriented companies to link their ads to this set of words. Thus, when a user types in "playboy," "playmate," or one of the other listed terms, those companies' banner ads appear on the search results page. . . .

PEI introduced evidence that the adult-oriented banner ads displayed on defendants' search results pages are often graphic in nature and are confusingly labeled or not labeled at all. In addition, the parties do not dispute that buttons on the banner ads say "click here." When a searcher complies, the search results page disappears, and the searcher finds him or herself at the advertiser's website. PEI presented uncontroverted evidence that defendants monitor "click rates," the ratio between the number of times searchers click on banner ads and the number of times the ads are shown. Defendants use click rate statistics to convince advertisers to renew their keyword contracts. The higher the click rate, the more successful they deem a banner ad.

PEI sued defendants, asserting that they were using PEI's marks in a manner that infringed upon and diluted them. The district court denied PEI's request for a preliminary injunction, and this court affirmed in an unpublished disposition. . . .On remand, the parties filed cross-motions for summary judgment. The district court granted summary judgment in favor of defendants. We reverse.

*   *   *

III. DISCUSSION

A. Trademark Infringement

*   *   *

PEI's strongest argument for a likelihood of confusion is for a certain kind of confusion: initial interest confusion. . . . Initial interest confusion is customer confusion that creates initial interest in a competitor's product. . . . Although dispelled before an actual sale occurs, initial interest confusion impermissibly capitalizes on the goodwill associated with a mark and is therefore actionable trademark infringement. . . .

PEI asserts that, by keying adult-oriented advertisements to PEI's trademarks, defendants actively create initial interest confusion in the following manner. Because banner advertisements appear immediately after users type in PEI's marks, PEI asserts that users are likely to be confused regarding the sponsorship of un-labeled banner advertisements. . . . In addition, many of the advertisements instruct users to "click here." Because of their confusion, users may follow the instruction, believing they will be connected to a PEI cite. Even if they realize "immediately upon accessing" the competitor's site that they have reached a site "wholly unrelated to" PEI's, the damage has been done: Through initial consumer confusion, the competitor "will still have gained a customer by appropriating the goodwill that [PEI] has developed in its [ ] mark." . . .

PEI's theory strongly resembles the theory adopted by this court in *Brookfield Communications, Inc. v. West Coast Entertainment Corporation*. . . . In *Brookfield*, a video rental company, West Coast Entertainment Corporation, planned on using "moviebuff.com" as a domain name for its website and using a similar term in the metatags for the site. . . . Brookfield had trademarked the term "MovieBuff," however, and sued West Coast for trademark infringement. . . . The court ruled in favor of Brookfield. It reasoned that Internet users entering Brookfield's mark (plus ".com") or searching for Brookfield's mark on search engines using metatags, would find themselves at West Coast's website. Although they might "realize, immediately upon accessing 'moviebuff.com,' that they have reached a site operated by West Coast and wholly unrelated to Brookfield," some customers who were originally seeking Brookfield's website "may be perfectly content with West Coast's database (especially as it is offered free of charge)." . . . Because those customers would have found West Coast's site due to West Coast's "misappropriation of Brookfield's goodwill" in its mark, the court concluded that Brookfield withstood summary judgment. . . .

In this case, PEI claims that defendants, in conjunction with advertisers, have misappropriated the goodwill of PEI's marks by leading Internet users to competitors' websites just as West Coast video misappropriated the goodwill of Brookfield's mark. Some consumers, initially seeking PEI's sites, may initially believe that unlabeled banner advertisements are links to PEI's sites or to sites affiliated with PEI. Once they follow the instructions to "click here," and they access the site, they may well realize that they are not at a PEI-sponsored site. However, they may be perfectly happy to remain on the competitor's site, just as the *Brookfield* court surmised that some searchers initially seeking Brookfield's site would happily remain on West Coast's site. The Internet user will have reached the site because of defendants' use of PEI's mark. Such use is actionable.

*   *   *

IV. CONCLUSION

Genuine issues of material fact exist as to PEI's trademark infringement and dilution claims. Accordingly, we reverse the district court's grant of summary judgment in favor of defendants and remand for further proceedings.

REVERSED AND REMANDED.

BERZON, CIRCUIT JUDGE, concurring.

I concur in Judge Nelson's careful opinion in this case, as it is fully consistent with the applicable precedents. I write separately, however, to express concern that one of those precedents was wrongly decided and may one day, if not now, need to be reconsidered *en banc*.

I am struck by how analytically similar keyed advertisements are to the metatags found infringing in *Brookfield Communications v. West Coast Entertainment Corp.*, 174 F.3d 1036 (9th Cir.1999). In *Brookfield*, the court held that the defendant could not use the trademarked term "moviebuff" as one of its metatags. Metatags are part of the HTML code of a web page, and therefore are invisible to internet users. Search engines use these metatags to pull out websites applicable to search terms. *See also Promatek*

Indus., Ltd. v. Equitrac Corp., 300 F.3d 808, 812-13 (7ᵗʰ Cir.2002) (adopting the *Brookfield* holding).

Specifically, *Brookfield* held that the use of the trademarked terms in metatags violated the Lanham Act because it caused "initial interest confusion." *Brookfield*, 174 F.3d at 1062-66. The court explained that even though "there is no source confusion in the sense that consumers know[who] they are patronizing, . . . there is nevertheless initial interest confusion in the sense that, by using 'moviebuff.com' or 'MovieBuff' to divert people looking for 'MovieBuff' to its website, [the defendant] improperly benefits from the goodwill that [the plaintiff] developed in its mark." *Id.* at 1062.

As applied to this case, *Brookfield* might suggest that there could be a Lanham Act violation *even if* the banner advertisements were clearly labeled, either by the advertiser or by the search engine. I do not believe that to be so. So read, the metatag holding in *Brookfield* would expand the reach of initial interest confusion from situations in which a party is initially confused to situations in which a party is never confused. I do not think it is reasonable to find initial interest confusion when a consumer is never confused as to source or affiliation, but instead knows, or should know, from the outset that a product or web link is not related to that of the trademark holder because the list produced by the search engine so informs him.

There is a big difference between hijacking a customer to another website by making the customer think he or she is visiting the trademark holder's website (even if only briefly), which is what may be happening in this case when the banner advertisements are not labeled, and just distracting a potential customer with another *choice*, when it is clear that it is a choice. True, when the search engine list generated by the search for the trademark ensconced in a metatag comes up, an internet user might *choose* to visit westcoastvideo.com, the defendant's website in *Brookfield*, instead of the plaintiff's moviebuff.com website, but such choices do not constitute trademark infringement off the internet, and I cannot understand why they should on the internet.

For example, consider the following scenario: I walk into Macy's and ask for the Calvin Klein section and am directed upstairs to the second floor. Once I get to the second floor, on my way to the Calvin Klein section, I notice a more prominently displayed line of Charter Club clothes, Macy's own brand, designed to appeal to the same people attracted by the style of Calvin Klein's latest line of clothes. Let's say I get diverted from my goal of reaching the Calvin Klein section, the Charter Club stuff looks good enough to me, and I purchase some Charter Club shirts instead. Has Charter Club or Macy's infringed Calvin Klein's trademark, simply by having another product more prominently displayed before one reaches the Klein line? Certainly not. *See* Gregory Shea, Note, *Trademarks and Keyword Banner Advertising*, 75 S. CAL. L. REV. 529, 554 (2002) (comparing keyed banner advertisements to a customer entering a supermarket, requesting Tylenol, and then being directed to the pain reliever section which includes generic Acetaminophen, along with other generic and name-brand pain relievers); Julie A. Rajzer, Comment, *Misunderstanding the Internet: How Courts are Overprotecting Trademarks Used in Metatags*, 2001 MICH. ST. L. REV. 427, 462-63 (2001) (highlighting the brick-and-mortar world in which Kellogg's Raisin Bran and Post Raisin Bran both appear next to one another on the same aisle).

Similarly, suppose a customer walks into a bookstore and asks for Playboy magazine and is then directed to the adult magazine section, where he or she sees Penthouse or Hustler up front on the rack while Playboy is buried in back. One would not say that Penthouse or Hustler had violated Playboy's trademark. This conclusion holds true even if Hustler paid the store owner to put its magazines in front of Playboy's.

One can test these analogies with an on-line example: If I went to Macy's website and did a search for a Calvin Klein shirt, would Macy's violate Calvin Klein's trademark if it responded (as does Amazon.com, for example) with the requested shirt and pictures of other shirts I might like to consider as well? I very much doubt it.

Accordingly, I simply cannot understand the broad principle set forth in *Brookfield*.

Even the main analogy given in *Brookfield* belies its conclusion. The Court gives an example of Blockbuster misdirecting customers from a competing video store, West Coast Video, by putting up a highway billboard sign giving directions to Blockbuster but telling customers that a West Coast Video store is located there. *Brookfield*, 174 F.3d at 1064. Even though customers who arrive at the Blockbuster realize that it is not West Coast Video, they were initially misled and confused. *Id.*

But there was no similar misdirection in *Brookfield*, nor would there be similar misdirection in this case were the banner ads labeled or otherwise identified. The *Brookfield* defendant's website was described by the court as being accurately listed as westcoastvideo.com in the applicable search results. Consumers were free to choose the official moviebuff.com website and were not hijacked or misdirected elsewhere. I note that the billboard analogy has been widely criticized as inapplicable to the internet situation, given both the fact that customers were not misdirected and the minimal inconvenience in directing one's web browser back to the original list of search results. *See* J. Thomas McCarthy, *McCarthy on Trademarks & Unfair Competition* § 25:69 (4th ed.2003); Shea, *supra* at 552.

* * *

Notes on Initial Interest Confusion

Prior to its application in the Internet context, the doctrine of initial interest confusion was used relatively rarely. One example is *Elvis Presley Enter., Inc. v. Capece*, 141 F.3d 188, 204 (5th Cir. 1998), where the court enjoined use of "The Velvet Elvis" as a night club service mark and in related advertising because consumers likely would initially be confused that defendant was endorsed by the Elvis Presley estate; this was "even more significant because the defendant's bar sometimes charges a cover charge for entry, which allows the defendants to benefit from initial-interest confusion before it can be dissipated by entry into the bar."

A substantial number of Internet-related decisions have turned on this issue of initial interest confusion. Besides *Brookfield* and *Playboy v. Netscape*, excerpted above, other relevant decisions include *Stilson & Assocs. v. Stilson Consulting Group*, 129 Fed. Appx. 993 (6th Cir. 2005) (unpub.) (the Lanham Act "forbids a competitor from luring potential customers away from a producer by initially passing off its goods or services as those of the producer even if confusion as to the source of the goods is dispelled by the time any sales are consummated"); *PACCAR, Inc. v. Telescan Techs., L.L.C.*, 319 F.3d 243 (6th Cir. 2003) (use of plaintiff's PETERBILT and KENWORTH trademarks for trucks in the domain names for defendant's truck locator websites created initial interest confusion; disclaimer of affiliation on defendant's website would appear too late in accessing process to dispel it); *Promatek Industries, Inc. v. Equitrac Corp.*, 300 F.3d 808 (7th Cir. 2002) ("Customers believing they are entering the first store rather than the second are still likely to hang around before they leave. The same theory is true for websites. Consumers who are directed to Equitrac's website are likely to learn more about Equitrac and its products before beginning a new search for Promatek and Copitrak"); and *Interstellar Starship Services, Ltd. v. Epix, Inc.*, 184 F.3d 1107, 1111 (9th Cir. 1999) (domain name use of trademark held likely to cause initial interest confusion, "permitting ISS to capitalize on the goodwill Epix developed in its trademark — even if the customer is never confused about Epix's lack of connection to epix.com'"). *Compare*, however, *TeleTech Customer Care Management (California) v. Tele-Tech Co.*, 977 F. Supp. 1407 (C.D. Cal. 1997), which enjoined defendant's use of plaintiff's trademark as a domain name on dilution grounds (see Chapter 8), but found that the proof of initial interest confusion was insufficient to demonstrate likelihood of confusion, with the court opining that the "brief confusion" was "not cognizable under the trademark laws."

1. Non-Competitive Products

Should initial interest confusion be viewed differently if the parties' goods or services are non-competitive? Might other factors come into play? In *Bigstar Entertainment Inc. v. Next Big Star, Inc.*, 105 F. Supp. 2d 185, 207-211 (S.D.N.Y. 2000), plaintiff sold videos through its "bigstar.com" website, and sued to stop defendant from using "nextbigstar.com" to conduct an entertainment talent search. In considering plaintiff's motion for preliminary relief, the court distinguished the *Brookfield Communications* decision above and cited several factors supporting denial:

> [T]his court declines to apply this initial interest confusion doctrine in the context of the Internet in a case involving (1) non-competitors; (2) web addresses not virtually identical; (3) weak marks without sufficient evidence of secondary meaning; (4) substantially different products; (5) similar names and trademarks used by third parties; (6) no intentional use of plaintiff's marks by defendant's in defendants' metatags; and (7) no evidence of bad faith efforts by defendants to divert patronage by trading on any name, goodwill or reputation plaintiff may have established.

Similarly, in *Checkpoint Systems, Inc. v. Check Point Software Technologies, Inc.*, 269 F.3d 270 (3ᵈ Cir. 2001), because "the markets for the parties' products are not converging," plaintiff's evidence of temporary initial interest confusion was "entitled to less weight than it might be in a case where the parties compete or are strongly interrelated, or where there is evidence or even an inference that a defendant was trying to trade on plaintiff's goodwill." *See also Hasbro, Inc. v. Clue Computing, Inc.*, 66 F. Supp. 2d 117, 125 (D. Mass. 1999), *aff'd* 232 F.3d 1 (1ˢᵗ Cir. 2000) (owner of famous CLUE mark for the board game unsuccessfully sued Clue Computing, a computer consulting firm, over its use of the domain name "clue.com"; initial confusion among people who then realize they are at the wrong site "may rise to the level of inconvenience [but] is not substantial enough to be legally significant"). *See generally* Doellinger, *Internet, Metatags and Initial Interest Confusion: A Look to the Past to Reconceptualize the Future*, 41 IDEA 173 (2001).

Compare Gibson Guitar Corp. v. Paul Reed Smith Guitars, LP, 423 F.3d 539 (6ᵗʰ Cir. 2005), in which the Sixth Circuit declined to find initial interest confusion in a product configuration case involving the shape of a guitar. The court noted that no circuit had applied an initial interest confusion theory to find infringement of a product shape. It concluded that "many legitimately competing product shapes are likely to create some initial interest in the competing product due to the competing product's resemblance to the better-known product when viewed from afar." The court went on to state that such a finding of likelihood of confusion in such circumstances would create a "penumbra" of protection for shapes that would not otherwise qualify for trademark protection. The court did state, however, that it was not creating a rule that product-shape trademarks could never be subject to initial interest confusion, just that it could not imagine such a case. *See also* the discussions on Permitted Use in Chapter 7 and on Misrepresentation in Chapter 8.

2. Commentators

Judge Berzon's concurrence in *Playboy v. Netscape*, which is excerpted above, is a notable judicial critique of a broad application of initial interest confusion analysis in the Internet context. The application of initial interest confusion analysis has also been the subject of much debate among scholarly commentators, particularly with regard to the Internet. *See, e.g.*, Rothman, *Initial Interest Confusion: Standing at the Crossroads of Trademark Law*, 27 CARDOZO L. REV. 105-192 (2005); *Dogan & Lemley, Trademarks and Consumer Search Costs on the Internet*, 41 HOUS. L. REV. 777 (2005); *Recent Development, Making Your Mark on Google*, 18 HARV. J.L. & TECH. 479 (2005); *McCarthy, Metatags and the Sale of Keywords in Search Engine Advertising*, 9 INTELL. PROP. L. BULL. 137-158 (2005); *Suh, Intellectual Property Law and Competitive*

Internet Advertising Technologies: Why Legitimate Pop-up Advertising Practices Should be Protected, 79 St. John's L. Rev. 161 (2005); *Grynberg, The Road Not Taken: Initial Interest Confusion, Consumer Search Costs, and the Challenge of the Internet*, 28 Seattle U.L. Rev. 97-144 (2004); *Widmaier, Use, Liability, and the Structure of Trademark Law*, 33 Hofstra L. Rev. 603 (2004); Stuckey, Online and Internet Law, Ch. 7 (2006).

6.09 Post-Sale Confusion

FERRARI S.P.A. ESERCIZIO FABRICHE AUTOMOBILI E CORSE v. ROBERTS
944 F.2d 1235 (6th Cir. 1991)

Ryan, Circuit Judge

This is a trademark infringement action brought pursuant to the Lanham Act, 15 U.S.C. § 1051, et seq. The principal issue is whether the district court correctly concluded that plaintiff Ferrari enjoyed unregistered trademark protection in the exterior shape and appearance of two of its automobiles and, if so, whether defendant Roberts' replicas of Ferrari's designs infringed that protection, in violation of section 43(a) of the Lanham Act. . . .

The Facts

Ferrari is the world famous designer and manufacturer of racing automobiles and upscale sports cars. Between 1969 and 1973, Ferrari produced the 365 GTB/4 Daytona. Because Ferrari intentionally limits production of its cars in order to create an image of exclusivity, only 1400 Daytonas were built; of these, only 100 were originally built as Spyders, soft-top convertibles. Daytona Spyders currently sell for one to two million dollars. Although Ferrari no longer makes Daytona Spyders, they have continuously produced mechanical parts and body panels, and provided repair service for the cars.

Ferrari began producing a car called the Testarossa in 1984. To date, Ferrari has produced approximately 5000 Testarossas. Production of these cars is also intentionally limited to preserve exclusivity: the entire anticipated production is sold out for the next several years and the waiting period to purchase a Testarossa is approximately five years. A new Testarossa sells for approximately $230,000.

Roberts is engaged in a number of business ventures related to the automobile industry. One enterprise is the manufacture of fiberglass kits that replicate the exterior features of Ferrari's Daytona Spyder and Testarossa automobiles. Roberts' copies are called the Miami Spyder and the Miami Coupe, respectively. The kit is a one-piece body shell molded from reinforced fiberglass. It is usually bolted onto the undercarriage of another automobile such as a Chevrolet Corvette or a Pontiac Fiero, called the donor car. Roberts marketed the Miami Spyder primarily through advertising in kit-car magazines. Most of the replicas were sold as kits for about $8,500, although a fully accessorized "turnkey" version was available for about $50,000. . . .

The district court found, and it is not disputed, that Ferrari's automobiles and Roberts' replicas are virtually identical in appearance.

Ferrari brought suit against Roberts in March 1988 alleging trademark infringement, in violation of section 43(a) of the Lanham Act, and obtained a preliminary injunction enjoining Roberts from manufacturing the replica cars. . . .

Ferrari's Lanham Act claim in this case is a "trade dress" claim. Ferrari charges, and the district court found, that the unique and distinctive exterior shape and design of the Daytona Spyder and the Testarossa are protected trade dress which Roberts has infringed by copying them and marketing his replicas.

* * *

Roberts argues that his replicas do not violate the Lanham Act because he informed his purchasers that his significantly cheaper cars and kits were not genuine Ferraris and thus there was no confusion at the point of sale. The Lanham Act, however, was intended to do more than protect consumers at the point of sale. When the Lanham Act was enacted in 1946, its protection was limited to the use of marks "likely to cause confusion or mistake or to deceive purchasers as to the source of origin of such goods or services." In 1967, Congress deleted this language and broadened the Act's protection to include the use of marks "likely to cause confusion or mistake or to deceive." Thus, Congress intended "to regulate commerce within [its control] by making actionable the deceptive and misleading use of marks in such commerce; [and] . . . to protect persons engaged in such commerce against unfair competition. . . ." 15 U.S.C. § 1127. Although, as the dissent points out, Congress rejected an anti-dilution provision when recently amending the Lanham Act, it made no effort to amend or delete this language clearly protecting the confusion of goods in commerce. The court in [*Rolex Watch, U.S.A., Inc. v. Canner*, 645 F.Supp. 484, 492 (S.D.Fla.1986)] explicitly recognized this concern with regulating commerce:

> The real question before this Court is whether the alleged infringer has placed a product in commerce that is "likely to cause confusion, or to cause mistake, or to deceive." . . . The fact that an immediate buyer of a $25 counterfeit watch does not entertain any notions that it is the real thing has no place in this analysis. Once a product is injected into commerce, there is no bar to confusion, mistake, or deception occurring at some future point in time.

Rolex Watch, 645 F.Supp. at 492-93 (emphasis in original). The *Rolex Watch* court noted that this interpretation was necessary to protect against the cheapening and dilution of the genuine product, and to protect the manufacturer's reputation. *Id.* at 495 . . . . As the court explained:

> Individuals examining the counterfeits, believing them to be genuine Rolex watches, might find themselves unimpressed with the quality of the item and consequently be inhibited from purchasing the real time piece. Others who see the watches bearing the Rolex trademarks on so many wrists might find themselves discouraged from acquiring a genuine because the items have become too common place and no longer possess the prestige once associated with them.

Rolex Watch, 645 F.Supp. at 495 . . . . Such is the damage which could occur here. As the district court explained when deciding whether Roberts' former partner's Ferrari replicas would be confused with Ferrari's cars:

> Ferrari has gained a well-earned reputation for making uniquely designed automobiles of quality and rarity. The DAYTONA SPYDER design is well-known among the relevant public and exclusively and positively associated with Ferrari. If the country is populated with hundreds, if not thousands, of replicas of rare, distinct, and unique vintage cars, obviously they are no longer unique. Even if a person seeing one of these replicas driving down the road is not confused, Ferrari's exclusive association with this design has been diluted and eroded. If the replica Daytona looks cheap or in disrepair, Ferrari's reputation for rarity and quality could be damaged. . ..

Ferrari, 11 U.S.P.Q.2d at 1848. . . .

Since Congress intended to protect the reputation of the manufacturer as well as to protect purchasers, the Act's protection is not limited to confusion at the point of sale. Because Ferrari's reputation in the field could be damaged by the marketing of Roberts' replicas, the district court did not err in permitting recovery despite the absence of point of sale confusion.

* * *

For the foregoing reasons, the judgment of the district court is AFFIRMED.

* * *

Notes on Post-Sale Confusion

A number of courts have recognized likely post-sale nonpurchaser confusion as actionable under the Lanham Act. Originally, § 32(1) of the Lanham Act only proscribed likelihood of confusion, mistake or deception of "purchasers as to the source of origin of such goods and services." In 1962, however, Congress amended the Act to delete the quoted portion from the section. 15 U.S.C. § 1114(1), amended 1962, 76 Stat. 769. The result was a much expanded confusion test encompassing nonpurchasers.

The injury derives in part from the fact that post-sale nonpurchasers may be prospective purchasers, with the confusion potentially affecting their future purchasing decisions. *Lois Sportswear, U.S.A., Inc. v. Levi Strauss & Co.*, 799 F.2d 867, 872–73 (2d Cir. 1986) ("The confusion the Act seeks to prevent in this context is that a consumer seeing [appellant's] familiar stitching pattern will associate the jeans with appellee and that association will influence his buying decisions."). *See also Academy of Motion Picture Arts & Sciences v. Creative House Promotions, Inc.*, 944 F.2d 1446 (9th Cir. 1991) (post-sale confusion likely between corporate award statuette and OSCAR movie award statuette); *Keds Corp. v. Renee International Trading Corp.*, 888 F.2d 215, 222 (1st Cir. 1989) (confusion of prospective consumers); *Polo Fashions, Inc. v. Craftex, Inc.*, 816 F.2d 145, 148 (4th Cir. 1987) (in the after–sale context, "it is likely that the observer would identify [defendant's] shirt with the plaintiff, and the plaintiff's reputation would suffer damage if the shirt appeared to be of poor quality"). *Compare with Dorr-Oliver, Inc. v. Fluid-Quip, Inc.*, 94 F.3d 376, 383 (7th Cir. 1996) (finding that defendant's labeled replacement part used on plaintiff's machine did not cause post-sale confusion because "[w]here product configurations are at issue, consumers are generally more likely to think that a competitor has entered the market with a similar product"). *But see Insty' Bit, Inc. v. Poly-Tech Indus. Inc.*, 95 F.3d 663, 672 (8th Cir. 1996), *cert. denied*, 117 S. Ct. 1085 (1997) (vacating summary judgment for defendant, noting that the post-sale confusion doctrine is applicable to configuration trade dress claims). In *Gibson Guitar Corp. v. Paul Reed Smith Guitars, LP*, 423 F.3d 539 (6th Cir. 2005), the Sixth Circuit declined to find post-sale confusion in a product configuration case. The court distinguished *Ferrari*, its only prior post-sale confusion decision (excerpted above), because there the Sixth Circuit had been concerned that the defendant's cheap replica cars would be confused with Ferrari's expensive and exclusive cars and damage Ferrari's reputation. In *Gibson*, the parties admitted that their guitars were of similar high quality. The court therefore treated plaintiff's allegation of post-sale confusion as an insupportable substitute for evidence of point-of-sale confusion. *See generally Tichane, The Maturing Trademark Doctrine of Post-Sale Confusion*, 85 TRADEMARK REP. 399 (1995); *Allen, Who Must Be Confused and When?: The Scope of Confusion Actionable Under Federal Trademark Law*, 26 WAKE FOREST L. REV. 321 (1991); *Erhlich, When Should Post-Sale Confusion Prevent Use or Registration of Marks?*, 81 TRADEMARK REP. 267 (1991).

Post-sale confusion also is an important consideration in trademark counterfeiting cases, as discussed *infra*.

6.10   Reverse Confusion

BIG O TIRE DEALERS, INC. v. GOODYEAR TIRE & RUBBER CO.
561 F.2d 1365 (10th Cir. 1977)

LEWIS, CHIEF JUDGE

This civil action was brought by Big O Tire Dealers, Inc. ("Big O") asserting claims of unfair competition against The Goodyear Tire & Rubber Co. ("Goodyear") based upon false designation of origin under 15 U.S.C. § 1125(a) and common law trademark infringement. . . . Filing a comprehensive post-trial opinion the United States District Court for the District of Colorado entered judgment on the jury's verdict, permanently enjoined Goodyear from infringing on Big O's trademark, and dismissed Goodyear's counterclaim for equitable relief. 408 F.Supp. 1219. Goodyear appeals that judgment.

Big O is a tire-buying organization which provides merchandising techniques, advertising concepts, operating systems, and other aids to approximately 200 independent retail tire dealers in 14 states who identify themselves to the public as Big O dealers. These dealers sell replacement tires using the Big O label on "private brand" tires. They also sell other companies' brands such as B. F. Goodrich and Michelin Tires. At the time of trial Big O's total net worth was approximately $200,000.

Goodyear is the world's largest tire manufacturer. In 1974 Goodyear's net sales totaled more than $5.25 billion and its net income after taxes surpassed $157 million. In the replacement market Goodyear sells through a nationwide network of company-owned stores, franchise dealers, and independent retailers.

In the fall of 1973 Big O decided to identify two of its lines of private brand tires as "Big O Big Foot 60" and "Big O Big Foot 70." These names were placed on the sidewall of the respective tires in raised white letters. The first interstate shipment of these tires occurred in February 1974. Big O dealers began selling these tires to the public in April 1974. Big O did not succeed in registering "Big Foot" as a trademark with the United States Patent and Trademark Office.

In the last three months of 1973 Goodyear began making snowmobile replacement tracks using the trademark "Bigfoot." From October 1973 to August 1975 Goodyear made only 671 "Bigfoot" snowmobile tracks and sold only 411 tracks. In December 1973 Goodyear filed an application to register "Bigfoot" as a trademark for snowmobile tracks with the United States Patent and Trademark Office; the registration was granted on October 15, 1974.

In July 1974 Goodyear decided to use the term "Bigfoot" in a nationwide advertising campaign to promote the sale of its new "Custom Polysteel Radial" tire. . . .

On August 24, 1974, Goodyear first learned of Big O's "Big Foot" tires [and attempted, unsuccessfully, to secure Big O's permission to continue use of the "Bigfoot" mark.] . . . [O]n September 16, 1974, Goodyear launched its nationwide "Bigfoot" promotion on ABC's Monday Night Football telecast. By August 31, 1975, Goodyear had spent $9,690,029 on its massive, saturation campaign.

*   *   *

IV.

The district court charged the jury:

> A trademark is infringed when a second person (later user) uses it in a manner which is likely to cause confusion among ordinarily prudent purchasers or prospective purchasers as to the source of the products. The test is not one of actual confusion; it is the likelihood of confusion.

The effect of this instruction was to permit the jury to base liability on a likelihood of any kind of confusion. Big O does not claim nor was any evidence presented showing Goodyear intended to trade on the goodwill of Big O or to palm off Goodyear products as being those of Big O. Instead, Big O contends Goodyear's use of Big O's trademark created a likelihood of confusion concerning the source of Big O's "Big Foot" tires.

The facts of this case are different from the usual trademark infringement case. As the trial judge stated, the usual trademark infringement case involves a claim by a plaintiff with a substantial investment in a well established trademark. The plaintiff would seek recovery for the loss of income resulting from a second user attempting to trade on the goodwill associated with that established mark by suggesting to the consuming public that his product comes from the same origin as the plaintiff's product. The instant case, however, involves reverse confusion wherein the infringer's use of plaintiff's mark results in confusion as to the origin of plaintiff's product. Only one reported decision involves the issue of reverse confusion. In *Westward Coach Mfg. Co. v. Ford Motor Co.*, 7 Cir., 388 F.2d 627, cert. denied, 392 U.S. 927, 88 S.Ct. 2286, 20 L.Ed.2d 1386, the court held reverse confusion is not actionable as a trademark infringement under Indiana law.

Consequently, Goodyear argues the second use of a trademark is not actionable if it merely creates a likelihood of confusion concerning the source of the first user's product. Since both parties agree Colorado law is controlling in this case, we must decide whether this so-called reverse confusion is actionable under Colorado law. To our knowledge, the Colorado courts have never considered whether a second use creating the likelihood of confusion about the source of the first user's products is actionable. However, the Colorado Court of Appeals in deciding a trade name infringement case involving an issue of first impression, cogently pointed out that the Colorado Supreme Court has consistently recognized and followed a policy of protecting established trade names and preventing public confusion and the tendency has been to widen the scope of that protection.*Wood v. Wood's Homes, Inc.*, 33 Colo.App. 285, 519 P.2d 1212, 1215–16.

Using that language as a guiding light in divining what Colorado law is on this issue of first impression, we hold that the Colorado courts, if given the opportunity, would extend its common law trademark infringement actions to include reverse confusion situations. Such a rule would further Colorado's "policy of protecting trade names and preventing public confusion" as well as having "the tendency (of widening) the scope of that protection."

The district court very persuasively answered Goodyear's argument that liability for trademark infringement cannot be imposed without a showing that Goodyear intended to trade on the goodwill of Big O or to palm off Goodyear products as being those of Big O's when it said:

> The logical consequence of accepting Goodyear's position would be the immunization from unfair competition liability of a company with a well established trade name and with the economic power to advertise extensively for a product name taken from a competitor. If the law is to limit recovery to passing off, anyone with adequate size and resources can adopt any trademark and develop a new meaning for that trademark as identification of the second user's products. The activities of Goodyear in this case are unquestionably unfair competition through an improper use of a trademark and that must be actionable.

408 F.Supp. at 1236.

Goodyear further argues there was no credible evidence from which the jury could have found a likelihood of reverse confusion. A review of the record demonstrates the lack of merit in this argument. Big O presented more than a dozen witnesses who testified to actual confusion as to the source of Big O's "Big Foot" tires after watching a Goodyear "Bigfoot" commercial. The jury could have reasonably inferred a likelihood of confusion from these witnesses' testimony of actual confusion. Moreover, two of Goodyear's executive officers, Kelley and Eaves, testified confusion was likely or even inevitable.

* * *

[T]he judgment is affirmed.

Notes on Reverse Confusion

Reverse confusion is another type of confusion receiving growing recognition under the Lanham Act. As discussed in the *Big O* case above, reverse confusion occurs when the legitimate prior user's goods or services become likely to be perceived as those of the junior user. In *M2 Software, Inc. v. Madacy Entm't*, 421 F.3d 1073, 1088 (9th Cir. 2005), the district court's jury instructions properly provided that reverse confusion occurs when "(1) a senior user of a mark seeks to protect its business identity from being overwhelmed by a larger junior user that has saturated the market with publicity and/or advertising; and (2) consumers doing business with the senior user mistakenly believe that they are dealing with the larger junior user." *See, e.g., DreamWerks Production Group, Inc. v. SKG Studio dba Dreamworks SKG*, 142 F.3d 1127 (9th Cir. 1998) (reversing summary judgment for defendant where reverse confusion was likely between science fiction convention producer and "entertainment colossus"); *Fisons Horticulture Inc. v. Vigoro Indus. Inc.*, 30 F.3d 466 (3d Cir. 1994) (vacating judgment for defendant and remanding to district court to determine whether reverse confusion was likely where a large company adopted FAIRWAY GREEN for fertilizers after a smaller company had already adopted FAIRWAY for peat moss); *Sands, Taylor & Wood Co. v. Quaker Oats Co.*, 978 F.2d 947, 958 (7th Cir. 1992) ("Protecting the trademark owner's interest in capitalizing on the goodwill associated with its mark by moving into new markets is especially compelling in . . . a reverse confusion case, where the junior user so overwhelms the *senior* user's mark that the senior user may come to be seen as the infringer"), *cert. denied*, 113 S. Ct. 1879 (1993); *Banff Ltd. v. Federated Dept. Stores, Inc.*, 841 F.2d 486, 490–91 (2[d] Cir. 1988) (reverse confusion held likely between Bloomingdale's use of B-WEAR for women's apparel and plaintiff's prior use of BEE WEAR for similar goods; "Were reverse confusion not a sufficient basis to obtain Lanham Act protection, a larger company could with impunity infringe the senior mark of a smaller one"); *Fuddrucker's Inc. v. Doc's B.R. Others, Inc.*, 826 F.2d 837, 845 (9th Cir. 1987) ("The potential for harm is equally great if the consumers believe that the infringer runs the original user"); *Ameritech, Inc. v. American Information Technologies Corp.*, 811 F.2d 960, 966 (6th Cir. 1987) ("senior user's interest in the trademark can be suffocated by the junior user"). *Compare Custom Vehicles Inc. v. Forest River Inc.*, 476 F.3d 481 (7th Cir. 2007) in which the court rejected a reverse confusion claim for failure of the senior user to show secondary meaning before his mark was "drowned out" by the junior user's mark. "[I]t is difficult, maybe impossible, for a small seller of an unpopular brand — a seller who has negligible sales — to acquire secondary meaning for its brand name. Such a seller is better off adopting a fanciful or arbitrary mark, which is enforceable without proof of secondary meaning."

6.11   Actual Confusion

BEACON MUTUAL INSURANCE COMPANY v. ONEBEACON
INSURANCE GROUP
376 F.3d 8 (1st Cir. 2004)

LYNCH, CIRCUIT JUDGE

This is a case of first impression for this circuit on several issues under the Lanham Act, 15 U.S.C. § 1051 et seq.

The plaintiff, formerly known as the State Compensation Insurance Fund, was chartered in 1990 by the Rhode Island legislature as the workers' compensation insurer of last resort in the state. In 1992, it adopted the name The Beacon Mutual Insurance Company ("Beacon Mutual") and, since then, has sold workers' compensation insurance in Rhode Island under the marks "The Beacon Mutual Insurance Company," "Beacon Insurance," and "The Beacon," with an accompanying lighthouse logo. The name change was brought about by increased competition following the resolution of a crisis in the state workers' compensation market.

In June 2001, the defendant OneBeacon Insurance Group ("OneBeacon"), which sells various forms of commercial insurance nationwide, switched to its current name and adopted a lighthouse logo as well, albeit in a different font and arrangement. The name change resulted from the sale of the company, then called CGU Corporation, to another company; the terms of the sale required CGU to change its name. OneBeacon is a direct competitor of Beacon Mutual in the Rhode Island market for workers' compensation insurance.

Beacon Mutual brought suit one month after OneBeacon's name change, alleging violations of the Lanham Act, 15 U.S.C. §§ 1125(a), and state trademark laws. On November 14, 2003, the district court granted summary judgment in favor of OneBeacon on all counts on the ground that Beacon Mutual had not demonstrated a substantial likelihood of confusion. *Beacon Mut. Ins. Co. v. OneBeacon Ins. Group*, 290 F.Supp.2d 241, 252 (D.R.I.2003). Beacon Mutual now appeals. . . .

We hold that the type of commercial injury actionable under § 43(a) of the Lanham Act, 15 U.S.C. §§ 1125(a), is not restricted to the loss of sales to actual and prospective buyers of the product in question. Confusion is relevant when it exists in the minds of persons in a position to influence the purchasing decision or persons whose confusion presents a significant risk to the sales, goodwill, or reputation of the trademark owner. This holding is consistent with our existing case law, under which post-sale confusion is actionable. *See I.P. Lund Trading, ApS v. Kohler Co.*, 163 F.3d 27, 44 (1st Cir.1998). We also hold that relevant commercial injury includes not only loss of sales but also harm to the trademark holder's goodwill and reputation.

*   *   *

A. Evidence of Actual Confusion

We turn first to . . . evidence of actual confusion. On summary judgment, OneBeacon, for its part, has not disputed the accuracy of the 249 instances of actual confusion listed in the Confusion Matrix.

Instead, OneBeacon argued to the district court that confusion is relevant only if it (1) involved actual or potential purchasers and (2) caused the trademark holder to lose sales. . . .

We join those courts holding that actual confusion is commercially relevant if the alleged infringer's use of the mark could inflict commercial injury in the form of . . . a diversion of sales, damage to goodwill, or loss of control over reputation on the trademark holder. . . . The fact that the injury is to a company's reputation or goodwill, rather than directly to its sales, does not render the confusion any less actionable. . . .

It is true that when a Lanham Act case involves directly competing goods, as here, the usual harm from confusion is both the potential purchase of the defendant's product rather than the plaintiff's and the loss of goodwill and reputation occasioned when the defendant's product is inferior. . . . But nothing in the statute suggests that demonstrable harm to plaintiff's goodwill and reputation resulting from confusion of marks is restricted to this classic situation. This case does not, as we understand it, raise a claim that the defendant's product is inferior.

We also hold that the likelihood of confusion inquiry is not limited to actual or potential purchasers, but also includes others whose confusion threatens the trademark owner's commercial interest in its mark. . . . Relevant confusion among non-purchasers may well extend beyond the confusion of those persons positioned to influence directly the decisions of purchasers.

*   *   *

Misdirected premium payments, one could reasonably infer, cause delays in crediting those payments. One could infer that those delays, in turn, cause the coverage of Beacon Mutual's customers (i.e., employers) to lapse or to be cancelled if the error is not corrected in time. That, in turn, one could further infer, places those employers in violation of Rhode Island laws requiring employers to maintain workers' compensation insurance. R.I. Gen. Law§ 28-29-6. Indeed, according to the Confusion Matrix (the accuracy of which has not been challenged), at least one Beacon Mutual customer has had its policy lapse because of such an error. Moreover, even if the error is corrected before a lapse or cancellation in coverage occurs, it is reasonable to infer that the customer, in many instances, would be displeased by the error or by being wrongly accused of missing a premium payment. Whether or not a particular policy is actually cancelled, one could reasonably infer that Beacon Mutual's goodwill and reputation for good service has been harmed.

Similarly, a factfinder could infer that misdirected claim forms from health care providers cause delays in payments to those providers. As Chief Judge Arrigan of the Rhode Island Workers' Compensation Court noted, Beacon Mutual maintains an approved preferred provider network. delayed payments, one could infer, make providers less inclined to remain in that network. When providers drop out of the network, injured workers covered by Beacon Mutual's workers' compensation insurance have a smaller pool of doctors and hospitals from which to choose, a result that one could infer harms Beacon Mutual's goodwill and reputation for providing good coverage.

A factfinder could further infer that injured workers will be upset when their confidential medical records are sent to the wrong insurer. Some health care providers, one could also infer, will attempt to avoid such situations, which potentially give rise to liability under Rhode Island statutes prohibiting the disclosure of such information without written consent, R.I. Gen. Law§ 5-37.3-4, by refusing to accept patients insured by Beacon Mutual. Either of those consequences could reasonably be viewed as detracting from Beacon Mutual's goodwill and reputation.

Misdirected communications from third-party insurance agencies, one could also infer, increase the costs of claims processing, leading to lower profits (if premiums stay the same) or lower sales (if premiums go up). Where disputes with third-party insurers must be resolved before an injured worker is reimbursed, one could also infer that such misdirected communications delay reimbursement, again harming Beacon Mutual's goodwill and reputation.

Further, a factfinder could infer, as Chief Judge Arrigan did in his letter to Beacon Mutual, that employers and injured workers will not receive timely notice of legal proceedings if service of process and other legal notices are sent to the wrong insurer and that those employers' and employees' rights could be compromised as a result. It is no great leap to infer that such problems would harm Beacon Mutual's goodwill and reputation.

Given that reasonable inferences must be drawn in Beacon Mutual's favor on summary judgment, we find that Beacon Mutual has presented sufficient evidence of actual confusion relevant to its commercial interests for this factor to count in its favor on summary judgment. That leaves OneBeacon fighting an uphill battle in arguing that no reasonable factfinder could find a substantial likelihood of confusion. Evidence of actual confusion is often considered the most persuasive evidence of likelihood of confusion because past confusion is frequently a strong indicator of future confusion. *See* 3 McCarthy § 23:13; see also *KOS Pharms., Inc. v. Andrx Corp.*, 369 F.3d 700, 720 (3[d] Cir. 2004) ("even a few incidents" of actual confusion are "highly probative of the likelihood of confusion" (internal quotation marks omitted)); *Thane Int'l, Inc. v. Trek Bicycle Corp.*, 305 F.3d 894, 902 (9th Cir. 2002) ("Evidence of actual confusion constitutes persuasive proof that future confusion is likely." (internal quotation marks omitted)).

* * *

Beacon Mutual must still prove its case at trial; this opinion holds only that it must be given the chance to do so. The grant of summary judgment in favor of OneBeacon is reversed, and the case is remanded for further proceedings consistent with this opinion. Costs are awarded to Beacon Mutual.

Notes on Actual Confusion

While proof of actual confusion is not required to prove likelihood of confusion, when such evidence exists it is often given great weight. As one court has stated, "There can be no more positive or substantial proof of the likelihood of confusion than proof of actual confusion." *World Carpets, Inc. v. Dick Littrell's New World Carpets*, 438 F.2d 482, 489 (5th Cir. 1971). The treatment of actual confusion evidence varies, however, according to the particular circumstances of the case. *See, e.g., Playtex Prods. v. Georgia-Pacific Corp.*, 390 F.3d 158, 167 (2[d] Cir. 2004) (search engine results associating the marks at issue were not evidence of actual confusion: "the fact that the computer associates 'moist ones' with 'wet ones' reflects little, if anything, about whether consumers are actually confused"); *Daddy's Junky Music Stores Inc. v. Big Daddy's Family Music Ctr.*, 109 F.3d 275, 284 (6th Cir. 1997) (reversing summary judgment for defendant; one instance of actual confusion was not insignificant given lack of evidence that parties' mailing lists overlapped); *Duluth News-Tribune v. Mesabi Publishing Co., supra*, at 1098 ("several isolated incidents" of actual confusion between DULUTH NEWS-TRIBUNE and SATURDAY NEWS & TRIBUNE manifested inattentiveness rather than actual confusion; some temporary confusion might be expected upon the adoption of a similar mark); *Woodsmith Publishing Co. v. Meredith Corp.*, 904 F.2d 1244 (8th Cir. 1990) (summary judgment for defendant affirmed in magazine trade dress case; evidence of confusion of a few inattentive readers held insufficient to create a factual dispute); *Berkshire Fashions, Inc. v. Sara Lee Corp.*, 725 F. Supp. 790 (S.D.N.Y. 1989), *aff'd*, 904 F.2d 33 (2[d] Cir. 1990) (actual confusion in the trade is highly probative of likely confusion, since the trade is more sophisticated than average consumers); *Universal Money Centers, Inc. v. American Telephone & Telegraph Co.*, 17 U.S.P.Q.2d 1435, 1440 (D. Kan. 1990) (approximately one hundred mistaken attempts to use defendant's credit cards in plaintiff's automatic teller machines found "numerically insignificant in light of the four million AT&T cards that are in circulation and in light of the 15,000 daily . . . transactions" in defendant's machines).

Proof of actual confusion is not necessary for injunctive relief; however, some courts require such proof as a basis for awarding monetary damages. *See, e.g., Resource Developers, Inc. v. Statue of Liberty-Ellis Island Foundation, Inc.*, 926 F.2d 134, 139 (2[d] Cir. 1991), and the discussion on damages in Chapter 10.

Might a lack of any actual confusion evidence over a substantial period of time indicate that confusion is *unlikely*? The RESTATEMENT OF THE LAW THIRD, UNFAIR COMPETITION (American Law Institute 1995) provides in Section 23:

(1) A likelihood of confusion may be inferred from proof of actual confusion.

(2) An absence of likelihood of confusion may be inferred from an absence of proof of actual confusion when the actor and the other have made significant use of their respective designations in the same geographic market for a substantial period of time.

See also Pignons S.A. de Mecanique v. Polaroid Corp., 657 F.2d 482, 490 (1st Cir. 1981) (lack of evidence of actual confusion, "when the marks have been side by side, for a substantial period of time, [raises] a strong presumption that there is little likelihood of confusion," quoting Callmann, *The Law of Unfair Competition, Trademarks and Monopolies*, § 82.3(a)). *Followed: Greentree Laboratories, Inc. v. G.G. Bean, Inc.*, 718 F. Supp. 998, 1000 (D. Me. 1989). *Compare Beer Nuts, Inc. v. Clover Club Foods Co.*, 805 F.2d 920, 928 (10th Cir. 1986) ("Purchasers are unlikely to bother to inform the trademark owner when they are confused about an inexpensive product").

In *Checkpoint Systems, Inc. v. Check Point Software Technologies, Inc.*, 269 F.3d 270 (3d Cir. 2001) the court affirmed the denial of relief where, among other things, there had been no reported actual confusion despite the lengthy co-existence of the marks at issue in connection with corporate physical and computer security products. It observed that, when that happens, "one can infer that continued marketing will not lead to consumer confusion in the future. The longer the challenged product has been in use, the stronger this inference will be."*Compare CAE, Inc. v. Clean Air Engineering, Inc.*, 267 F.3d 660 (7th Cir. 2001), where confusion was held likely between parties' uses of the mark CAE for process engineering and data acquisition systems despite no reported actual confusion during the parties' twenty-five year co-existence. "[B]ecause . . . instances of actual confusion may be difficult to discover, the most that the absence of evidence of actual confusion can be said to indicate is that the record does not contain any evidence of actual confusion known to the parties." Which is the better view? Should it depend on whether actual confusion evidence would be expected to surface under the particular circumstances?

6.12   Intent

Pattishall, THE IMPACT OF INTENT IN TRADE IDENTITY CASES*
65 NW. U. L. REV. 421 (1970)

It has been said that "[t]he protection of trademarks is the law's recognition of the psychological function of symbols." The axiomatic depth of this statement by the late Mr. Justice Frankfurter soon becomes apparent in any encounters with the law of trade identity. The pragmatic impact of another judicial statement reveals itself much later. It was Judge Learned Hand who wrote of proven intent to compete unfairly in *My-T-Fine Corp. v. Samuels*:

But when it appears, we think that it has an important procedural result; a late comer who deliberately copies the dress of his competitors already in the field, must at least prove that his effort has been futile. Prima facie the court will treat his opinion so disclosed as expert and will not assume that it was erroneous. He may indeed succeed in showing that it was; that, however bad his purpose, it will fail in execution; if he does, he will win. . . . But such an intent raises a presumption that customers will be deceived.

The essence of this reasoning had been expressed several decades earlier in more

---

* Reprinted by special permission of Northwestern University School of Law, *Northwestern University Law Review*, Volume 65, pp. 421–422 (1970).

earthly language by Master of the Rolls Cozens-Hardy:

> If I find that a man, taking a particular name under which to trade, is a knave, I give him credit for not being also a fool, and I assume that there is a reasonable probability that his knavish purpose will succeed.

The presumption of infringement doctrine of the *My-T-Fine* case and of decisions which both preceded and followed it expressing the same rationale has long been familiar. The extraordinary impact which a showing of wrongful intent has exercised in the entire field of trade identity law, however, appears to have been inadequately recognized. Courts today frequently and correctly comment that the intent element is not legally requisite in either trademark infringement or unfair competition law. The body of decided cases reveals, nonetheless, that in an astonishingly high percentage of trade identity decisions in which relief was granted, the defendant was found guilty, either directly or circumstantially, of intended poaching if not outright fraud. Indeed, empirical observation indicates that something in the nature of this form of *animus furandi* remains virtually an essential ingredient for a winning plaintiff's suit in the area of trade identity law.

MY-T-FINE CORPORATION v. SAMUELS
69 F.2d 76 (2d Cir. 1934)

L. HAND, CIRCUIT JUDGE

The plaintiff is the manufacturer of a confection of chocolate and sugar, used in making a kind of pudding, and sold in small cardboard boxes. The suit, which is founded upon diversity of citizenship, is to protect its make-up which the defendant is alleged to have copied. . . .

. . . The suit is to protect the box of 1929. By 1933 the plaintiff's sales had grown to an enormous total, over 100,000,000 in all; it had spent more than a million and a half dollars in advertisement; its trade had spread very extensively through the Union. To some extent its product has become known as the "Red and Green package," but by far the greater number of customers ask for it by its name, "My-T-Fine."

The defendants sell a similar product under the name, "Velmo." Before July 1, 1931, when they first introduced it into New York City, the body of their box, which was of substantially the same size as the plaintiff's, was solidly of about the same shade of green, but had no red stripes along the edges. At the top of the front was a black, instead of a white, chevron on which in large red letters was the word, "Velmo." Below in black was the word, "Chocolate," and below that in red on a white stripe, "Dessert." The back was also of green, on which the directions for using were printed in black; these were in part a literal copy of the plaintiff's. In July, 1931, the defendants added red stripes around all the edges of this box, of substantially the same width as the plaintiff's, and a white tablet on the back to contain the printed matter. They sold it very generally throughout the city of New York, so generally that they insist it must have come to the plaintiff's notice very soon after it was first put on sale. The suit was filed on July 7, 1933, and the plaintiff at once moved for a preliminary injunction. The judge, thinking the similarity between the packages too little, and the delay too long, denied the motion.

It would be impossible on this record to say that any one who meant to buy the plaintiff's pudding has hitherto been misled into taking the defendants' by a mistake in the appearance of the box. Indeed such evidence is usually hard to get even after a trial, and upon this motion the affidavits are too hazy and unreliable, even if undisputed. The plaintiff has proved no more than that the boxes look a good deal alike, and that confusion may well arise; and were it not for the evidence of the defendants' intent to deceive and so to secure the plaintiff's customers, we would scarcely feel justified in interfering at this stage of the cause. We need not say whether that intent is always a necessary element in such causes of suit; probably it originally was in federal courts.

McLean v. Fleming, 96 U.S. 245; *Lawrence Mfg. Co. v. Tennessee Mfg. Co.*, 138 U.S. 537; *Elgin National Watch Co. v. Illinois Watch Case Co.*, 179 U.S. 665. But when it appears, we think that it has an important procedural result; a late comer who deliberately copies the dress of his competitors already in the field, must at least prove that his effort has been futile. Prima facie the court will treat his opinion so disclosed as expert and will not assume that it was erroneous. *Fairbank Co. v. R. W. Bell Mfg. Co.*, 77 F. 869, 877 (C.C.A. 2); *Capewell Horse Nail Co. v. Green*, 188 F. 20, 24 (C.C.A. 2); *Wolf Bros. & Co. v. Hamilton*, 165 F. 413, 416 (C.C.A. 8); *Thum Co. v. Dickinson*, 245 F. 609, 621, 622 (C.C.A. 6); *Wesson v. Galef*, (D.C.) 286 F. 621, 626. He may indeed succeed in showing that it was; that, however bad his purpose, it will fail in execution; if he does, he will win. *Kann v. Diamond Steel Co.*, 89 F. 706, 713 (C.C.A. 8). But such an intent raises a presumption that customers will be deceived.

In the case at bar, it seems to us fairly demonstrated that the defendants have copied the plaintiff's make-up as far as they dared.

. . . At the very outset the directions were lifted bodily from the back of the plaintiff's box; and although the defendants were within their rights as to that, still the circumstance is relevant because it proves that the box had been before them when they designed their own make-up, and that it had been their point of departure. In addition they took solid green for the body, and put on a chevron; and while perhaps they did not choose a general combination of red and green, at least they adopted a red lettering. Whether or not they meant to get hold of the plaintiff's customers by that make-up, their next step was bolder, and put their intent beyond question; they added the red stripes at every edge; so that the real differences that remained were only in the name and the color of the chevron. As they had not the slightest original interest in the colors chosen and their distribution, they could only have meant to cause confusion, out of which they might profit by diverting the plaintiff's customers. This being the intent, the dissimilarities between the two do not in our judgment rebut the presumption.

The delay of two years before beginning suit does not seem to us of importance, even upon this application. There is indeed some question as to just when the plaintiff learned of the defendants' second box; but we see nothing in that to give us pause; we are ready to assume that it learned of its appearance at once. Again, were it not for the intent of trade unfairly, we might hesitate, but advantages built upon a deliberately plagiarized make-up do not seem to us to give the borrower any standing to complain that his vested interests will be disturbed. . . .

The decree is reversed; the plaintiff may take an injunction against the use of the second box, i.e., that with the red edges. For the present and until trial, the earlier box will not be enjoined.

KEMP v. BUMBLE BEE SEAFOODS, INC.
398 F.3d 1049 (8th Cir. 2005)

MELLOOY CIRCUIT JUDGE

Defendant-Appellant Bumble Bee Seafoods, Inc. ("Bumble Bee") appeals the district court's adverse rulings following a bench trial on the trademark issues of likelihood of confusion and dilution. Because we find that confusion was likely, we reverse and remand for entry of judgment in favor of Bumble Bee.

I. Background

Plaintiff-Appellee Louis E. Kemp ("Mr.Kemp") is from a family that had been engaged in the wholesale and retail seafood business since 1930. In 1985, Mr. Kemp started Kemp Foods, Inc., which made and sold artificial crab products containing surimi, a low-fat, processed fish product. In 1987, Mr. Kemp sold the seafood business to Oscar Mayer Foods Corporation for $4 million pursuant to a Stock Acquisition

Agreement. Under the Agreement, Mr. Kemp transferred all trademarks used in his business, including KEMP, KEMP'S and KEMP'S & Design to Oscar Mayer. . . .

[The parties subsequently amended the Agreement to include, among other things, a reservation of rights for Mr. Kemp to utilize the mark KEMP under certain conditions.]

In 1992, Oscar Mayer sold the surimi business to Tyson Foods, Inc., who in turn sold the business to Bumble Bee. Con Agra Foods subsequently acquired Bumble Bee. Before October 1995, Bumble Bee and its predecessors spent over $49 million to promote and advertise the LOUIS KEMP marks. By October 1995, the LOUIS KEMP marks had achieved a brand awareness of 47%, Bumble Bee's Louis Kemp Seafood Company held a 77% share of the market for retail pre-packaged seafood and LOUIS KEMP was the number one surimi seafood brand with a 55% market share. It is undisputed that Bumble Bee owns numerous registered trademarks for KEMP . . . .

In October 1995, Mr. Kemp began commercial use of the mark LOUIS KEMP on wild rice, chicken and wild rice soup, and wild rice with stir fry vegetables. . . .

On March 13, 1996, Tyson, then owner of the LOUIS KEMP marks, sent Mr. Kemp a cease and desist letter. Tyson alleged infringement and likelihood of confusion. On March 21, 1996, Mr. Kemp responded by explaining that he believed the amended Agreement permitted his use of the trademark LOUIS KEMP on non-surimi products. Mr. Kemp then filed this suit to seek a declaratory judgment regarding a contractual right to use the trademark LOUIS KEMP. Mr. Kemp also brought tortious interference and unfair competition claims against Tyson and Bumble Bee. Tyson and Bumble Bee filed trademark infringement and dilution counterclaims against Mr. Kemp based on federal and Minnesota law. . . .

[T]he only issues remaining in the present litigation are whether the use by Kemp of the trademark LOUIS KEMP or any formative of this mark in connection with rice products, including without limitation "seasoned wild rice, chicken wild rice soup, and wild rice with stir fried vegetables" as well as "southwestern white and wild rice, cooked and seasoned white and wild rice and wild and white rice stir fry" (all as identified by Kemp in response to Tyson's Interrogatory No. 1) infringes and/or dilutes Tyson's rights in the Louis Kemp Marks. . . .

[D]uring trial, Mr. Kemp . . . made clear his intention to take advantage of the goodwill and brand equity that Bumble Bee and its predecessors had built in the trademark LOUIS KEMP:

Q: Well, isn't it a fact that you used the mark LOUIS KEMP on you[r] wild rice products solely to take advantage of the huge investment that Oscar Mayer and Tyson invested in the brand?

A: Absolutely true and that's because the agreement I made with them and they made with me.

The district court applied the six factor test from *SquirtCo v. Seven-Up Co.*, 628 F.2d 1086, 1091 (8th Cir.1980) (listing the following as factors to consider in assessing the likelihood of confusion: (1) the strength of the owner's mark; (2) the similarity of the owner's mark and the alleged infringer's mark; (3) the degree to which the products compete with each other; (4) the alleged infringer's intent to "pass off" its goods as those of the trademark owner; (5) incidents of actual confusion; and (6) the type of product, its costs and conditions of purchase (the "*SquirtCo* factors")). . . .

II. Analysis-Likelihood of Confusion

We review application of the *SquirtCo* factors and the ultimate determination of a likelihood of confusion for clear error. . . . Mr. Kemp argues that minor differences in trade dress, as previously described, establish that the marks are dissimilar. He argues further that he did not have an intent to misappropriate the goodwill consumers associate with Bumble Bee's mark and that his receipt of advice from counsel proves this fact. . . .

*   *   *

Turning to the fourth factor, the alleged infringer's intent to pass off his goods as those of the trademark owner, we believe the evidence supports only one permissible view of Mr. Kemp's admission, namely, his desire to cause consumers to associate his brand with that of Bumble Bee. The evidence of this clear intention to appropriate for his own benefit the considerable equity, i.e., the trademark goodwill, of the LOUIS KEMP brand name was undisputed. Further, this intention did not change over time. Rather, Mr. Kemp noted his intent in his solicitation letters to Mr. Paulucci and again testified at trial that his subsequent, actual use of the name was designed to take advantage of the investment Oscar Mayer and Tyson had made in the mark.

Rarely will a junior user admit such an intention. Mr. Kemp apparently did so in this case because he believed contract rights entitled him to use the trademark LOUIS KEMP. His subjective opinions regarding his contract rights, however, in no way diminish the effect of his statement. He openly admitted his intention to market his products to take advantage of the considerable equity of the Oscar Mayer and Tyson investments. The only way to take advantage of this brand equity is to cause consumers to mistakenly believe there is, at a minimum, an association between the sources of the products.

*   *   *

We cannot discount this intent based on the fact that Mr. Kemp believed the contract entitled him to play on the goodwill of Bumble Bee's marks. As noted, the contract conditioned Mr. Kemp's right to use a related mark upon Oscar Mayer's prior approval, which Mr. Kemp did not seek. Further, we cannot discount this intent based on the fact that Mr. Kemp received advice of counsel and slightly modified his presentation of his LOUIS KEMP mark. Discounting a showing of intent based on minor changes in presentation is inappropriate because:

> [f]ew businesspeople are foolhardy enough to be so blatant in their attempt to increase profits. To find trademark infringement only by exact identity and not where the junior user makes some slight modification would be in effect to reward the cunning infringer and punish only the bumbling one.

J. Thomas McCarthy, *Trademarks and Unfair Competition* § 23.20 (4th ed.2002) (citations and internal quotations omitted). Clearly, Mr. Kemp attempted to minimize his legal risk. His desire to minimize his legal risk, however, cannot be equated with a diminution of his desire to "take advantage of the considerable equity" of Bumble Bee's trademark.

It is important to note that intent as a *SquirtCo* factor is relevant not because trademark infringement requires intent, bad faith, or any other *mens rea.* Instead, this *SquirtCo* factor is relevant because it demonstrates *the junior user's true opinion* as to the dispositive issue, namely, whether confusion is likely. Accordingly, it is irrelevant that he may have believed contract rights excused his use.[5] He adopted the mark LOUIS KEMP specifically to take advantage of the "considerable equity" Bumble Bee and its predecessors had built in the mark. He admitted this regarding his prospective intentions in his letter to solicit Mr. Paulucci as a partner, and he admitted this under examination regarding his intentions surrounding his actual use. We believe this evidence permits only one possible conclusion, namely, that Mr. Kemp believed consumers would associate his products with those of the senior user. Accordingly, this factor weighs very strongly in favor of finding that confusion was likely.

*   *   *

In summary, a balancing of the *SquirtCo* factors support a finding that consumer

---

[5] As noted previously, the only issue before us is the issue of infringement. Based on the stipulation of the parties and the related California litigation, there is no contractual right to use an infringing mark.

confusion was likely and Mr. Kemp's use was infringement. Having found infringement due to a likelihood of confusion, and there being no remedies for dilution separate from the available remedies for infringement, we need not address the issue of dilution. The judgment of the district court is reversed and this case is remanded for determination of an appropriate remedy.

Notes on Intent

1. Presumption of Infringement

While the intent of an alleged infringer is a relevant consideration in determining likelihood of confusion, it is not requisite that a complainant establish wrongful intent in order to prevail in a trademark action. *See Daddy's Junky Music Stores Inc. v. Big Daddy's Family Music Ctr.*, 109 F.3d 275, 287 (6th Cir. 1997) ("[T]he presence of intent can constitute strong evidence of confusion . . . . [But] the lack of intent by a defendant is 'largely irrelevant in determining if consumers likely will be confused . . . .' "); *Lois Sportswear, U.S.A., Inc. v. Levi Strauss & Co.*, 799 F.2d 867, 875 (2d Cir. 1986).

As a practical matter, however, courts more readily find a trademark tort where evidence of wrongful intent is presented. *See* Pattishall, *The Impact of Intent, supra*. In *Perfect Fit Industries v. Acme Quilting Co.*, 618 F.2d 950 (2d Cir. 1980), the court noted that secondary meaning for plaintiff's mattress pad trade dress had not been shown, but confusing similarity could be presumed from defendant's intentional copying. Similarly, in *HMH Publishing Co. v. Brincat*, 504 F.2d 713 (9th Cir. 1974), the court stated it would have found no likelihood of confusion as to sponsorship by plaintiff publisher of Playboy magazine of defendant's automotive products and services sold under the mark PLAYBOY except for the "somewhat weak" evidence of defendant's intent. *See also Fuji Photo Film Co. v. Shinohara Shoji*, 754 F.2d 591, 596 (5th Cir. 1985), where the court stated, "Good faith is not a defense to trademark infringement . . . the reason for this is clear: if potential purchasers are confused, no amount of good faith can make them less so. Bad faith, however, may, without more, prove infringement." Similarly, in *Sally Beauty Co., Inc. v. Beautyco, Inc.*, 304 F.3d 964, 973 (10th Cir. 2002), the court confirmed that "[p]roof that a defendant chose a mark with the intent of copying the plaintiff's mark may, standing alone, justify an inference of likelihood of confusion." It explained, "[o]ne who adopts a mark similar to another already established in the marketplace does so at his peril, because the court assumes that he can accomplish his purpose: that is that the public will be deceived. All doubts must be resolved against him." *See* GILSON, § 5.07 (2008 ed.).

Usually, sufficient evidence of intent is held to raise a rebuttable presumption of likelihood of confusion. *See Sara Lee Corp. v. Kayser-Roth Corp.*, 81 F.3d 455, 466 (4th Cir.), *cert. denied*, 519 U.S. 976 (1996) ("If there is intent to confuse the buying public, this is strong evidence establishing likelihood of confusion . . . . In other words, we presume that a person who sets out to infringe on another's trademark has more brains than scruples, and will likely succeed"). One court held that presumption to be rebutted when it found that, "[d]efendants, while acting with an improper intent, carried out their promotional scheme in such an inept fashion — whether deliberately or not — that plaintiff's rights were not disturbed." *Johnny Carson Apparel, Inc. v. Zeeman Manufacturing Co.*, 203 U.S.P.Q. 585, 595 (N.D. Ga. 1978). *See also Alberto Culver Co. v. Andrea Dumon, Inc.*, 466 F.2d 705, 709–710 (7th Cir. 1972).

2. Proof of Intent

Generally, proof of intent is based upon circumstantial evidence, direct evidence rarely being available (the *Kemp* case excerpted above being one of those rare, and often outcome-determinative, exceptions). Thus, in *Spring Mills, Inc. v. Ultracashmere House, Ltd.*, 689 F.2d 1127 (2d Cir. 1982), the court found: "No motive other than a desire for a free ride would appear to explain the slavish copying of the Ultrasuede hand tag by defendants." *See also Eli Lilly & Co. v. Natural Answers, Inc.*, 233 F.3d 456 (7th Cir. 2000)(defendant's use of plaintiff's famous PROZAC mark in defendant's website metatags was significant evidence of defendant's wrongful intent to confuse consumers regarding defendant's HERBOZAC product); *Fun-Damental Too Ltd. v. Gemmy Indus. Corp.*, 111 F.3d 993, 1004 (2[d] Cir. 1997) (defendant's "false markdown" on its novelty change banks — crossing out a marked price comparable to the price of plaintiff's product and displaying a "discount" price — supported an inference that defendant intentionally copied plaintiff's distinctive product packaging); *Washington Speaker's Bureau, Inc. v. Leading Authorities, Inc.*, 33 F. Supp. 2d 488 (E.D. Va. 1999) (defendant's domain name "www.washingtonspeakers.com" and similar names in the "com" and "net" top level domains held likely to be confused with plaintiff's unregistered mark "Washington Speaker's Bureau"; evidence of defendant's intentional appropriation of plaintiff's mark was "crucial" and "conclusive evidence" that confusion was likely, and partly was shown by defendant's registration of other domain names similar to marks of other competitors).

Courts often draw a presumption of bad faith merely from proof that defendant knew of plaintiff's mark at the time of adoption. *Nabisco Brands v. Kaye*, 760 F. Supp. 25, 27 (D. Conn. 1991) (confusion held likely where, while claiming non-infringement, defendant admitted his A-2 mark for steak sauce was designed to draw on the market recognition of plaintiff's A-1 mark); *Caesars World, Inc. v. Caesar's Palace*, 490 F. Supp. 818 (D.N.J. 1980) (Defendant's "innocent adoption" defense must fail in light of visit to plaintiff's resort hotel nine months before the opening of defendant's beauty salon with similar trade name). *Compare Century 21 Real Estate Corp. v. Magee*, 19 U.S.P.Q.2d 1530, 1534–35 (C.D. Cal. 1991) (defendant used CENTURY 31 for real estate brokerage services and claimed he had never heard of plaintiff's CENTURY 21 mark; the court nonetheless inferred an intent to benefit from plaintiff's goodwill and enjoined defendant); *Brooks Bros. v. Brooks Clothing of California Ltd.*, 60 F. Supp. 442 (S.D. Cal. 1945), *aff'd*, 158 F.2d 798 (9th Cir. 1947) (innocent adoption became wrongful intent when defendant began to advertise falsely in source-confusing manner).

In assessing whether plaintiff should be awarded defendant's profits, the Second Circuit in one case concluded that bad faith might be inferred from defendant's failure to follow its attorney's advice to obtain a full trademark search which would include common law users, rather than relying on a limited search of federal registrations. *International Star Class Yacht Racing Ass'n. v. Tommy Hilfiger U.S.A.*, 80 F.3d 749, 753–54 (2[d] Cir. 1996) ("[The defendant's] choice not to perform a full search under these circumstances reminds us of two of the famous trio of monkeys who, by covering their eyes and ears, neither saw nor heard any evil."); *Compare Star Indus. v. Bacardi & Co.*, 412 F.3d 373 (2[d] Cir. 2005) (because plaintiff did not attempt to register its design until after the litigation began, "no trademark search, no matter how perfect, would have discovered [plaintiff's] 'O' design trademark"). *See also Everest Capital Ltd. v. Everest Funds Mgmt. L.L.C.*, 393 F.3d 755 (8th Cir. 2005) (affirming jury finding of no likelihood of confusion; while plaintiff presented evidence that defendant's owner was aware of plaintiff when defendant formed its company, "knowledge of a competitor does not prove an intent to mislead consumers as to product origins"); *Playtex Prods. v. Georgia-Pacific Corp.*, 390 F.3d 158, 166 (2[d] Cir. 2004) ("Prior knowledge of a senior user's mark does not, without more, create an inference of bad faith"); *Surfvivor Media, Inc. v. Survivor Prods.*, 406 F.3d 625 (9th Cir. 2005) (defendant's insistence that they lacked intent to infringe even though they were aware of plaintiff's mark was "not dispositive"). *Barbecue Marx, Inc. v. Ogden*, 235 F.3d 1041, 1046 (7th Cir. 2000) (defendant's knowledge of plaintiff's SMOKE DADDY restaurant before opening defendant's BONE DADDY restaurant did not show bad intent where inspiration for defendant's restaurant name was an animated film and the restaurants had significant differences).

However, a competitor is not precluded from intentionally copying functional or otherwise unprotectable elements of a mark or trade dress, as discussed in Chapter 5. *See, e.g., Willie W. Gray v. Meijer, Inc.*, 295 F.3d 641 (6th Cir. 2002) (plaintiff's claim of intentional copying carried no weight where the elements at issue, such as the phrase "Chicago Style" and a depiction of the Chicago skyline, were unprotectable); *The Yankee Candle Co., Inc. v. The Bridgewater Candle Co., LLC*, 259 F.3d 25 (1st Cir. 2001) (evidence of intentional copying was not probative given "the highly functional nature" of the claimed elements). *See also Estee Lauder, Inc. v. Gap, Inc.*, 932 F. Supp. 595 (S.D.N.Y. 1996), *rev'd on other grounds*, 108 F.3d 1503 (2[d] Cir. 1997) (distinguishing *Hilfiger*; defendant's refusal to "fold its tent" after learning of plaintiff's similar mark did not constitute bad faith because defendant's attorney gave colorable, albeit ultimately incorrect, advice that defendant's mark did not infringe plaintiff's); *Universal Money Centers Inc. v. American Telephone & Telegraph Co.*, 22 F.3d 1527 (10th Cir.), *cert. denied*, 513 U.S. 1052 (1994) (evidence that the junior user knew that the senior user might challenge the junior user's mark does not establish that the junior user intended to derive a benefit from the senior user's goodwill).

Can continuous use after protest from the plaintiff be evidence of wrongful intent? *See Hilfiger*, supra, at 754 (defendant's failure to stop marketing its infringing goods after receipt of plaintiff's cease-and-desist letter deemed probative of willful infringement). *Compare Isador Straus v. Notaseme Hosiery Co.*, 240 U.S. 179 (1916) *with Johnson & Johnson v. Quality Pure Mfg., Inc.*, 484 F. Supp. 975 (D.N.J. 1979), wherein the court held, "once the similarity is brought to his attention a failure or refusal to alter the trade dress to avoid the confusion is equivalent to an original and actual intent."*But see H. Lubovsky, Inc. v. Esprit de Corp.*, 627 F. Supp. 483, 490–91 (S.D.N.Y. 1986), where the court found no bad faith in defendant's use of ESPRIT for clothes despite its knowledge of plaintiff's federal registration and use of ESPRIT for shoes and its previous unsuccessful attempt to purchase plaintiff's rights.

3. Patent and Trademark Office

Historically, the United States Patent and Trademark Office has not given great weight to the intent element on the premise that it does not have jurisdiction or power to adjudicate that issue. *See Scholl Mfg. Co. v. Principle Business Enterprises, Inc.*, 150 U.S.P.Q. 217, 219 (T.T.A.B. 1966); *Coca-Cola Co. v. Fanta*, 155 U.S.P.Q. 276, 278 (T.T.A.B. 1967). Is this position consistent with the *My-T-Fine* doctrine? Where the statutory issue is likelihood of confusion, should not all evidence relevant to that issue be examined? *Compare Standard Brands, Inc. v. Peters*, 191 U.S.P.Q. 168, 171 (T.T.A.B. 1975), wherein the Board stated that intent may be a factor in proceedings "to the extent that it can . . . resolve any doubt as to the question of likelihood of confusion." If the Board initially determines that confusion is likely, however, or that there is no reasonable likelihood of confusion, proof of intent or lack thereof will not affect the decision. *Electronic Water Conditioners, Inc. v. Turbomag Corp.*, 221 U.S.P.Q. 162, 165 (T.T.A.B. 1984).

4. Intent and Secondary Meaning

Non-distinctive marks must be shown to have acquired secondary meaning before their infringement may be found. Might proof of intentional copying constitute evidence of secondary meaning as well as evidence of likelihood of confusion? *See GMC v. Lanard Toys, Inc.*, 468 F.3d 405 (6th Cir. 2006) ("Intentional copying may be used to show secondary meaning"); *Sally Beauty Co., Inc. v. Beautyco, Inc.*, 304 F.3d 964 (10th Cir. 2002) ("proof of intentional copying [is] relevant to whether a mark has acquired secondary meaning"); *Committee for Idaho's High Desert v. Yost*, 92 F.3d 814, 822 (9th Cir. 1996) (evidence that defendant "knowingly, intentionally and deliberately adopted and used" plaintiff's CIHD mark "offers strong support for the finding of secondary meaning"); *Osem Industries Ltd. v. Sherwood Foods, Inc.*, 917 F.2d 161 (4th Cir. 1990) (defendant's admission that it copied the trade dress of plaintiff's soup packages created both a presumption of secondary meaning and of likely confusion which defendant failed to rebut); *Transgo, Inc. v. Ajac Transmission Parts Corp.*, 768 F.2d 1001, 1016 (9th Cir. 1986) ("[p]roof of exact copying, without any opposing proof, can be sufficient to establish a secondary meaning"); *M. Kramer Mfg. Co. v. Andrews*, 783 F.2d 421, 448 (4th Cir. 1985) ("evidence of intentional, direct copying establishes a prima facie case of secondary meaning"). Why? Is this a sound argument in all circumstances? Is there a possibility of circular reasoning? Of proving too much?

Note in this connection the distinction some courts have drawn between (legitimate) intent to copy a desirable feature of a competitor's product and (illegitimate) intent to exploit that product's secondary meaning. As the Seventh Circuit has reasoned: "To bolster his conclusion that the oval head possessed secondary meaning, the magistrate judge found that

> 'the evidence is undisputed that [Panduit] intentionally copied the entire line of plaintiff's TY-RAP cable ties because of the advantages this product enjoyed.' . . . Far from supporting a finding of secondary meaning, this conclusion explicitly undermines it. Copying is only evidence of secondary meaning if the defendant's intent in copying is to confuse consumers and pass off his product as the plaintiff's. In that situation, the defendant's belief that plaintiff's trade dress has acquired secondary meaning-so that his copying will indeed facilitate his passing off-is some evidence that the trade dress actually has acquired secondary meaning. *See Blau Plumbing, Inc. v. S.O.S. Fix-it, Inc.*, 781 F.2d 604, 611 (7th Cir.1986). But "evidence of intent is often ambiguous," *id.*, and this is particularly true where the product itself is copied. "[T]he copier may very well be exploiting a particularly desirable feature, rather than seeking to confuse consumers as to the source." *Duraco*, 40 F.3d at 1453. The magistrate judge found that Panduit copied T & B's TY-RAP knowing that it was a successful product and seeking a piece of the market for cable ties with particular features which consumers desire and have become accustomed to, *i.e.*, oval heads and metal barbs. This copying of the 'advantages that this product enjoyed' does not support an inference that any of the copied features possessed secondary meaning.

Thomas & Betts Corp. v. Panduit Corp., 65 F.3d 654, 663 (7th Cir. 1995).

5. Intent to Capitalize

Some courts have distinguished between an (impermissible) intent to profit by confusion of consumers and a (permissible) intent only to capitalize on plaintiff's mark, without creating such confusion. In affirming the dismissal of plaintiff's claim in *Toho Co. v. Sears, Roebuck & Co.*, 645 F.2d 788 (9th Cir. 1981), the court found that Sear's use of a BAGZILLA trademark and reptilian monster on its garbage bags was intended only as a "pun," one which did not create any consumer confusion as to sponsorship by creators of the GODZILLA movie character. In *American Footwear Corp. v. General Footwear Co.*, 609 F.2d 655 (2[d] Cir. 1979), the court found that the manufacturer of a BIONIC BOOT hiking boot had the intent to capitalize on the market or fad created by a television show featuring a BIONIC MAN, but not the intent to confuse the public into the belief that the manufacturer's product was a product of the show's creators, and accordingly found that no unfair competition had resulted. *See also Philip Morris, Inc. v. R.J. Reynolds Tobacco Co.*, 188 U.S.P.Q. 289 (S.D.N.Y. 1975) (one competitor may intentionally capitalize on another's advertising investment so long as he does not attempt to confuse the public as to source); *Brooks Shoe Mfg. Co. v. Suave Shoe Corp.*, 533 F. Supp. 75 (S.D. Fla. 1981), *aff'd*, 716 F.2d 854 (11th Cir. 1983) (defendant's intentional copying of plaintiff's V design and color scheme for running shoes did not indicate likelihood of confusion where evidence showed that the design and color scheme were "fashionable" in the industry and defendant only had "an intent to copy a fashion"). *Compare Universal City Studios, Inc. v. Montgomery Ward & Co.*, 207

U.S.P.Q. 852 (N.D. Ill. 1980), in which defendant's use of JAWS, JAWS TWO and JAWS POWER for trash compactors was held to infringe plaintiff's marks for motion pictures. The court stated that intentional misappropriation is evidence of secondary meaning and likelihood of confusion — "[t]he public need only believe there is some connection or association with or approval by the producer of the movie." Is the principal concern in such cases a diminishment of the distinctiveness of plaintiff's mark, rather than likelihood of confusion? See the discussion on dilution law in Chapter 8.

In the Restatement Of The Law Third, Unfair Competition (American Law Institute 1995), Section 22 on Intent provides:

(1) A likelihood of confusion may be inferred from proof that the actor used a designation resembling another's trademark, trade name, collective mark, or certification mark with the intent to cause confusion or to deceive.

(2) A likelihood of confusion may not be inferred from proof that the actor intentionally copied the other's designation if the actor acted in good faith in circumstances that do not otherwise indicate an intent to cause confusion or to deceive.

See, for example, Holiday Inns, Inc. v. 800 Reservation, Inc., 86 F.3d 619 (6th Cir. 1996),*supra*, in which the defendant deliberately adopted its similar telephone number to attract callers intending to call Holiday Inn's 1–800–HOLIDAY reservation line, but neither promoted that telephone number nor attempted to mislead its callers into believing they had actually called Holiday Inn's reservation line. The *Holiday Inns* case is excerpted and further discussed in Chapter 8.

6. Intent and Initial Interest Confusion

Cases where trademark infringement is found on the basis of initial interest confusion often have a strong element of intent. Thus, in both *Grotrian v. Steinway* and *Brookfield*, two influential initial interest confusion cases that are excerpted in Section 6.08 above, the courts found substantial intent on defendants' part to trade off of the goodwill of plaintiffs' marks. *See also Mobil Oil Corp. v. Pegasus Petroleum Corp.*. 818 F.2d 254 (2^d Cir. 1987) (initial interest confusion may lure customers into listening to cold-call advertisements they would not otherwise entertain and is thus a sufficient trademark injury) (excerpted in this chapter)); *Dorr-Oliver, Inc. v. Fluid-Quip, Inc.*, 94 F.3d 376, 382 (7th Cir. 1996) (comparing initial interest confusion to bait-and-switch marketing practices that allow competitors to get their foot in the consumer's door via confusion). Because the damage lies in the presale appropriation of goodwill, the sophistication level of consumers typically is held to be irrelevant. *See SecuraComm Consulting, Inc. v. SecuraCom, Inc.*, 984 F. Supp. 286, 298-99 (D.N.J. 1997); *reversed on monetary award*, 166 F.3d 182 (3^dCir. 1999).

If the parties are not competitors or the products at issue are insufficiently related, the "bait and switch" aspect of initial interest confusion may be absent. *See, e.g., Checkpoint Systems, Inc. v. Check Point Software Technologies, Inc.*, 269 F.3d 270 (3rd Cir. 2001) in which the Court observed that cases "which have applied the initial interest doctrine indicate[] that the parties are either direct competitors, or strongly interrelated such that it could be expected that plaintiff would expand into defendant's market". Given that "[t]he markets for the parties' [security-related] products are not converging", the court concluded in *Checkpoint Systems* that the evidence of "temporary initial interest confusion" was entitled to less weight and that confusion between the parties' marks was unlikely. *See also Syndicate Sales, Inc. v. Hampshire Paper Corp.*, 192 F.3d 633 (7th Cir. 1999) (holding that post-sale inspection of labeling and packaging for plastic baskets used for floral bouquets at funerals, by sophisticated retailers who could return "the incorrect goods," remedied potential damage caused by initial interest confusion).

7. Intent and Progressive Encroachment

Under the doctrine of progressive encroachment it is unlawful to appropriate piecemeal a means for trade identity that could not be taken as a whole. In *O&W Thum Co. v. Dickinson*, 245 F. 609 (6th Cir. 1917), defendant, over a period of years, had gradually changed the packaging for his fly paper to more closely mimic that of plaintiff. Defendant first changed the directions on his cartons to be exactly like plaintiff's, and then copied plaintiff's methods of securing the carton corners and lid. Defendant subsequently changed the graphic design for his fly paper to again mimic plaintiff's, and finally the color to do the same. Defendant's attempts to justify the changes "as a matter of expense" failed. The court also rejected defendant's laches defense that plaintiff had unreasonable delayed in bringing suit, observing that such "a progressive course of encroachment . . . does not tend to arouse hostile action until it is fully developed." Similarly, in *Independent Nail & Packaging Co. v. Stronghold Screw Products, Inc.*, 205 F.2d 921 (7th Cir. 1953) the plaintiff had invented a ribbed nail which it named STRONGHOLD, registering that name as a trademark five years later. At the date of trial plaintiff controlled almost the entire market for "metal fasteners." Defendant began using STRONGHOLD as a trademark for screws slightly before plaintiff's registration issued, but became aware of plaintiff's registration soon thereafter. Nonetheless, defendant elected to use the mark on its letterheads, business forms and catalogs. A few years later defendant changed its name to Stronghold Screw Products, prompting the first protest from plaintiff. Independent Nail had not previously protested the use of the mark because defendant's prior name, Manufacturer's Screw Products, had always appeared prominently with any use of STRONGHOLD. The court found that defendant's incorporation of "Stronghold" into its business name constituted progressive encroachment, citing *O. & W. Thum Co.* It found plaintiff justifiably had not taken action until the encroachment was fully developed, and granted plaintiff injunctive relief.

Progressive encroachment may simply be considered as evidence disclosing a planned or contrived intent to deceive. In *Commerce Foods, Inc. v. PLC Commerce Corp.*, 504 F. Supp. 190 (S.D.N.Y. 1980), over a three-year period defendant progressively changed the design on its tins for imported hard candy to imitate the lettering, language, visual design and bordering of plaintiff's candy tin design. This was viewed as evidence of intent to confuse consumers and accordingly raised the presumption of likelihood of confusion. Progressive encroachment also may be claimed by a trademark owner in response to a defendant's allegation of unreasonable delay in assertion of trademark rights. *See* the discussion on Laches in Chapter 7.

Should there be some point in time after which a progressive encroacher is allowed to enjoy the benefits of his own goodwill? Should such problems be handled purely on a case-by-case basis? *See* Kilmer, *Progressive Encroachment: Analysis Of A Counterdefense To Laches And Acquiescence In Trademark Infringement Litigation*, 74 TRADEMARK Rep. 229 (1984).

8. Intent and Market Encroachment

Some courts have extended the theory of progressive encroachment to include the gradual encroachment on a party's market, the theory again being that "such a course does not tend to arouse hostile action until it is fully developed." *O. & W. Thum, supra.* In *Parrot Jungle, Inc. v. Parrot Jungle, Inc.*, 512 F. Supp. 266 (S.D.N.Y. 1981), the court rejected defendant's claim of laches, stating:

> [t]here is a substantial difference between plaintiff's awareness of a pet store or stores in New York and its awareness of a national franchising effort. . . . A modest encroachment is one thing, a sudden proposed national exploitation of plaintiff's name is quite another, and plaintiff's failure to challenge the former will not entirely disable plaintiffs from preventing the latter. . . .

Likewise in *John Wright, Inc. v. Casper Corp.*, 419 F. Supp. 292, 323 (E.D. Pa. 1976), *aff'd in part and rev'd in part, Donsco, Inc. v. Casper Corp.*, 587 F.2d 602 (3^d Cir. 1978), the court rejected a laches defense when the delay occurred during a time of progressive market encroachment culminating in "sudden promotional expansion aimed at the exploitation of [the] market created by the plaintiff," citing *Independent Nail, supra* . *See also Kellogg Co. v. Exxon Corp.*, 209 F.3d 562 (6th Cir. 2000) (encroachment from petroleum market into food and beverage market); *Tandy Corp. v. Malone & Hyde, Inc.*, 769 F.2d 362, 367 (6th Cir. 1985); *E-Systems, Inc. v. Monitek, Inc.*, 222 U.S.P.Q. 115, 117 (9th Cir. 1983) ("had defendant's encroachment been minimal, or its growth slow and steady, there would be no laches"); *E. & J. Gallo Winery v. Gallo Cattle Co.*, 12 U.S.P.Q.2d 1657, 1676 (E.D. Cal. 1989) ("A senior user is not required to object to a junior user's practice until the respective marks have had substantial exposure in common channels of trade so as to pose a real threat of potential confusion"), *aff'd in relevant part*, 967 F.2d 1280 (9th Cir. 1992).

6.13   Counterfeiting

A flourishing market has developed in the sale of imitative products bearing deliberately copied, or "counterfeit," trademarks. Often the imitative products are manufactured in countries where parts and labor are cheaper than elsewhere in the world. By use of the counterfeit trademark, traffickers in such products intentionally deceive purchasers into believing that the imitative product, made at less expense and often sold at a lower price, is the genuine item. Often thought of as an attempt to capitalize upon designer names such as Gucci or Christian Dior, the intentional counterfeiting of trademarks also encompasses such diverse items as computer hardware and software, drugs, medical devices, and parts for cars and airplanes. In addition to constituting blatant trademark infringement, the manufacture and sale of counterfeit merchandise may pose dangers to the public health and safety, as such merchandise is often of inferior quality. It may also result in serious damage to the business and reputation of the trademark owner, who is perceived as sponsoring inferior quality goods which fall apart or fail to function as advertised.

The "Trademark Counterfeiting Act of 1984" (P.L. 98 473, 15 U.S.C. § 1116, 18 U.S.C. § 2320) was enacted in response to this burgeoning illegal industry and provides both criminal and civil causes of action. *See generally* 73 T.M.R. 459 *et. seq.* (1983). *But see* Barnett, *Shopping for Gucci on Kanal Street: Reflections on Status Consumption, Intellectual Property and the Incentive Thesis*, 91 Va. L. Rev. 1381 (2005) (examining the fashion industry and making the counter-intuitive argument that counterfeiting may sometimes benefit the trademark owner by promoting the product's desirability and enabling the trademark owner to charge a "snob premium" for the real product). On July 2, 1996, in response to estimated losses to U.S. businesses of $200 billion dollars due to counterfeiting, the Anticounterfeiting Protection Act of 1996, (P.L. 104 153) (1996 Act) was enacted. The 1996 Act provided for even stiffer civil and criminal penalties and made it easier for trademark owners to take effective action against counterfeiters. In 2006, the Stop Counterfeiting in Manufactured Goods Act (P.L. 109-181, 120 Stat. 285), amended Title 18 to, among other things, further stiffen criminal penalties, create liability for trafficking in counterfeit labels and packaging as well as counterfeit goods, and require convicted offenders to pay restitution to the trademark owner. *See, e.g., U.S. v. Beydoun*, 461 F.3d 102 (5th Cir. 2006) (evaluating proofs for amount of mandatory restitution).

LOUIS VUITTON S.A. v. LEE
875 F.2d 584 (7th Cir. 1989)

POSNER, CIRCUIT JUDGE

Louis Vuitton S.A., the French manufacturer of swank luggage, handbags, and other merchandise, appeals the district court's refusal to award it any damages for the infringement of its registered trademark by the defendants, Mr. and Mrs. Lee. Korean immigrants, the Lees own a shop in Chicago that they call K-Econo Merchandise. The shop carries an eclectic, even ragtag, selection of merchandise ranging from gifts, toys, and electronic equipment to handbags and luggage. Mr. Lee speaks no English, Mrs. Lee speaks poor "shop-keepers' English." When the events giving rise to the suit occurred the Lees had been living in the United States for four years, had (it appears) been engaged in the retail trade for that entire time, and had been selling luggage and handbags from time to time since opening K-Econo eighteen months previously.

Concerned with the widespread sale of counterfeit Louis Vuitton goods in American cities, Vuitton's counsel engaged an investigator, Melvin Weinberg. On May 29, 1995, accompanied by an employee of Gucci (a coplaintiff, Gucci did not appeal), Weinberg visited K-Econo and bought a counterfeit Louis Vuitton camera case for $37.80 — a fraction of the price of the genuine item — and paid for it with a Master-charge credit card. The Gucci employee bought a counterfeit Gucci camera case.

Vuitton and Gucci filed this suit on June 18, seeking treble the Lees' profits from the sale of the counterfeit merchandise, a permanent injunction, and attorney's fees. *See* 15 U.S.C. §§ 1116, 1117(a), (b). Two days later, executing an ex parte order that the district judge had issued under 15 U.S.C. § 1116(d)(1)(A), the plaintiffs seized three articles of counterfeit Vuitton merchandise and three articles of counterfeit Gucci merchandise from the Lees' store. At her deposition Mrs. Lee stated through an interpreter that customers had told her before the raid (indeed, before she sold the counterfeit camera case to Weinberg) that her Vuitton and Gucci merchandise was counterfeit. And at the opening of the trial on February 24, 1986, the parties submitted to the court a written stipulation (copied from the final pretrial order) that "with at least constructive notice of plaintiffs' federal registration rights, defendants have knowingly and willfully offered for sale, sold and distributed various types of luggage, handbags and accessories upon which are imprinted imitations and copies of plaintiffs' registered trademarks. Plaintiffs have never authorized or consented in any way to the use by defendants of their registered trademarks." Shortly before the trial the district judge had issued an uncontested permanent injunction to prevent the Lees from further infringing the plaintiffs' trademarks, and the final pretrial order listed only a single issue for trial: "The parties dispute the amount of income generated by defendants as a result of the sale of counterfeit Vuitton and Gucci merchandise." . . .

* * *

[The district] judge chose to credit Mrs. Lee's testimony at trial that she hadn't known before the raid that the items were counterfeit, rather than the contrary testimony (also admitted as evidence at the trial) in her deposition. The judge waved aside the stipulation that the Lees had knowingly and willfully sold counterfeit merchandise, remarking that maybe all the stipulation meant was that the Lees had knowingly *sold* the merchandise, as opposed to knowing it was *counterfeit* merchandise. Alternatively he deemed the final pretrial order, from which the stipulation had been drawn, to have been modified by the course of the trial because the plaintiffs had not objected to the Lees' testifying contrary to the stipulation. The judge disbelieved Weinberg's testimony and indeed opined that he had come perilously close to committing perjury. The way was now prepared for the judge's conclusion (692 F. Supp. at 911–12):

> Having determined that defendants did not "intentionally us[e] a mark or designation, knowing such mark or designation [was] a counterfeit mark," § 1117(b), this court has concluded that, for reasons of equity, it should deny plaintiffs monetary relief under § 1117(a). Defendants, who speak little English, did not realize they were violating plaintiffs' rights until they were so informed in June, 1985; once they knew, they immediately agreed to terminate their misconduct. Furthermore, out of the hundreds of items at K-Econo, only eight were shown to be counterfeits of Gucci and Vuitton.

In short, nothing in this case suggests that defendants were actively engaged in palming off counterfeit products as a substantial part of their business. There simply was no need for this case to have gone to trial on the issue of monetary relief. The permanent injunction sufficed to apprise defendants of their wrongdoing and ensure that they would not violate plaintiffs' rights in the future. The trademark laws entitled plaintiffs to protect their merchandise, as they did and should, but this court need not, and will not, allow plaintiffs to use the laws as a sword, and their millions as a mace, to crush two small, unsophisticated and unwary immigrant merchants.

The master of sword and mace asks us to reverse and remand for a new trial on monetary relief before a different judge.

The district judge's handling of this case has left much to be desired . . . . He had no justification for interpreting the stipulation to mean only that the defendants had knowingly sold the merchandise in question. Selling is not an act that is done unconsciously, so a "knowing" sale must mean something more than a sale performed while the seller is awake. It is true that the statute (so far as pertinent here) is limited to the sale of counterfeit merchandise, as distinct from the private use of it, *see* S.Rep. No. 526, 98th Cong., 2d Sess. 11 (1982), and that the Lees apparently kept some of the Vuitton and Gucci counterfeits for their personal use, or at least never got around to selling them. But it would be one thing for the Lees to stipulate that they had sold some of the counterfeits without thereby conceding knowledge of their counterfeit status, and it was another to stipulate that they sold counterfeit merchandise "knowingly and willfully" — the latter stipulation, which is the one they made, could mean only that they knew they were selling counterfeits. The reference in the stipulation to constructive notice (lawyerese for no notice) signifies only that although the Lees may not have known that Vuitton and Gucci owned registered trademarks, this fact is irrelevant because section 1117(b), while imposing stiff monetary penalties only for the knowing use of counterfeit registered marks, does not require that the defendant know they are registered. *See* Joint Statement on Trademark Counterfeiting Legislation, 130 Cong.Rec. H12076–77 (daily ed. Oct. 10, 1984).

The stipulation was part of the final pretrial order; and although a pretrial order can be modified, modification shall be "by a subsequent order" and "only to prevent manifest injustice." Fed.R.Civ.P. 16(e). No subsequent order was entered here, and anyway the condition for such an order — that it be necessary to prevent manifest injustice — was not satisfied. The stipulation was in conformity with Mrs. Lee's deposition, in which she admitted having known before the raid that the merchandise was counterfeit. Her counsel had agreed to the deposition being admitted into evidence even though she hadn't signed it. Although the judge said Mrs. Lee hadn't signed it because she thought it contained mistakes, there is no evidence to support this conjecture beyond the fact that she changed her testimony at trial. We don't know whether she failed to sign her deposition because there really were mistakes in it, because her lawyer didn't give it to her to sign, because her English was so poor that she couldn't read it, or because she realized that it contained damaging admissions. The least plausible conjecture concerning her *volte-face*, as we shall see, is that the plaintiffs' translator had mistranslated Mrs. Lee. And it would be absurd to infer a mistake in a deposition from the fact that, at trial, the deponent changed her testimony. Depositions are used at trial to impeach testimony; testimony is not used at trial to impeach depositions. If Mrs. Lee's admission had been given effect, as we think it should have been, Vuitton's entitlement to damages under 15 U.S.C. § 1117(b) would have been established. More on this point later.

The judge also had no justification for berating Vuitton for seeking monetary relief rather than resting content with an injunction. As Congress well knew in beefing up the legal sanctions for counterfeiting trademarks in 1984 (even to the extent of making trafficking in counterfeit trademarks a crime, *see* 18 U.S.C. § 2320), and as is anyway obvious to even a casual consumer, the sale of counterfeit merchandise has become endemic — perhaps pandemic. *See* S.Rep. No. 526, *supra*, at 2-6. Most of the infringing sellers are small retailers, such as K-Econo. Obtaining an injunction against each and every one of them would be infeasible. Trademark owners cannot hire investigators to shop every retail store in the nation. And even if they could and did, and obtained injunctions against all present violators, this would not stop the counterfeiting. Other infringers would spring up, and would continue infringing until enjoined. To stop counterfeiting, a trademark owner must be able to invoke section 1117(b), the treble-damage (alternatively, at the plaintiff's option, treble-profit) provision that Congress added to the trademark law in 1984. Treble damages are a particularly suitable remedy in cases where surreptitious violations are possible, for in such cases simple damages (or profits) will underdeter; the violator will know that he won't be caught every time, and merely confiscating his profits in the cases in which he is caught will leave him with a net profit from infringement. From this we can see that the disparity in size between the typical owner of a trademark on fashionable goods and the typical seller of counterfeits of those trademarked goods is no reason to deny monetary relief to the former; for the smaller the violator, the less likely he is to be caught, and the more needful therefore is a heavy punishment if he is caught. The fact that "palming off counterfeit goods" is not "a *substantial* part of [the violator's] business" (692 F.Supp. at 912 (emphasis added)) is not, as the district judge believed, an extenuating circumstance.

Section 1117(b) is a severe statute. The trebling of the plaintiff's damages or the defendant's profits — whichever is greater — is mandatory (as is the award of the plaintiff's attorney's fees), subject only to the statute's exception for "extenuating circumstances," which as we shall see is extremely narrow. The other provision under which the plaintiffs sought monetary relief in this case, 15 U.S.C. § 1117(a) (plain § 1117 before the 1984 amendments), not only makes the trebling of damages or profits discretionary and the award of attorney's fees exceptional, but also makes the award of relief under it "subject to the principles of equity." It was on this ground that the district judge refused to award damages under 1117(a). But the principles of equity referred to in section 1117(a) do not in our view justify withholding all monetary relief from the victim of a trademark infringement merely because the infringement was innocent. As between the "innocent" infringer who seeks to get off scot-free, and the innocent infringed who has neither engaged in any inequitable conduct nor sought treble damages or treble profits (or indeed any part of the defendant's profits that is attributable to the defendant's superior efficiency rather than to the plaintiff's trademark), the stronger equity is with the innocent infringed. That clearly is the case here with regard to the untrebled component of the relief sought. So far as appears, Vuitton is seeking profits that are due *entirely* to its trademark, for the fakes that the Lees sold were of poor workmanship and probably were marketable only because of their fake Louis Vuitton trademark. And the district judge's scolding notwithstanding, Vuitton has not been guilty of any inequitable conduct. It is not inequitable to enforce one's legal rights, whereas the defendants were at best careless in purchasing brand-name merchandise from an itinerant peddler without inquiry as to source. There is no evidence that Vuitton or Gucci engaged in predatory discovery or otherwise abused the litigation process. In these circumstances a plaintiff is entitled at the very least either to simple damages or to the defendants' profits. "Equity" is not a roving commission to redistribute wealth from large companies to small ones. The Lanham Act was not written by Robin Hood.

In addition, this is one of those relatively rare cases in which we are left with a "definite and firm conviction," *United States v. United States Gypsum Co.*, 333 U.S. 364, 395, 68 S.Ct. 525, 542, 92 L.Ed. 746 (1948); *Anderson v. City of Bessemer City*, 470 U.S. 564, 573, 105 S.Ct. 1504, 1511, 84 L.Ed.2d 518 (1985), that the district judge erred in a finding of fact — the finding that Mrs. Lee had not known before the raid that she was selling counterfeit merchandise. The Lees had lived in the United States for four years, engaged in the retail trade, and by their own admission had been selling handbags, luggage, and related merchandise for eighteen months before Weinberg appeared. Although not a large business, K-Econo was not negligible. During the year prior to the trial, the Lees had deposited more than a quarter of a million dollars in K-Econo's bank account. They accepted major credit cards. They must have known something about the retail trade. Vuitton and Gucci are international status symbols known to everyone, whether or not proficient in the English language, who sells handbags and luggage, and to most people who buy them. It is inconceivable that Mrs. Lee had never heard of these firms, nor did she testify that she had never heard of them. She could hardly have thought she was buying the genuine article, for manufacturers of high-fashion leather goods do not distribute them to retail outlets through itinerant peddlers, do not line the goods with purple vinyl, and do not sell them at prices which permit the retailer to make money reselling them for $37.80.

* * *

A further point is that although section 1117(b) requires a showing that the defendant's violation involved "knowing such mark . . . is counterfeit," it is enough for these purposes that the defendant failed to inquire further because he was afraid of what the inquiry would yield. Willful blindness is knowledge enough. *See* Joint Statement on Trademark Counterfeiting Legislation, *supra*, 130 Cong. Rec. at H12076–77" ("Of course, if the prosecution proves that the defendant was 'willfully blind' to the counterfeit nature of the mark, it will have met its burden of showing 'knowledge' "); cf. *United States v. Josefik*, 753 F.2d 585, 589 (7th Cir. 1985); *Bosco v. Serhant*, 836 F.2d 271, 276 (7th Cir. 1987). Knowing as she must have that Vuitton and Gucci are expensive brand-name goods unlikely to display (as these did) poor workmanship, to be lined with purple vinyl, and to be sold by itinerant peddlers at bargain-basement prices, Mrs. Lee was obligated at the very least to ask her supplier whether the items he was selling her were genuine Vuitton and Gucci merchandise or counterfeit.

Even if we are wrong in believing that the judge committed clear error in finding that the use of the marks was not a knowing use, the issue had been stipulated away in the pretrial order and the judge violated Rule 16(e) in refusing to abide by it.

It remains to decide whether we should uphold the district judge's finding regarding the number of infringing items that the Lees sold, and remand simply for a determination of the profits they made on each, a trebling of that sum, an award to the plaintiff of its reasonable attorney's fees, as expressly provided for in section 1117(b), and an award to the plaintiff of this costs. We needn't worry about the defense of extenuating circumstances to treble damage or treble-profit liability under section 1117(b), because as an affirmative defense it must be pleaded or otherwise presented to the district court. It was not, and is therefore waived. It is in any event inapplicable, being intended for extreme cases — cases in which "the imposition of treble damages would mean that [the defendant] would be unable to support his or her family," Joint Statement on Trademark Counterfeiting Legislation, *supra*, 130 Cong.Rec. at H12083; *see Fendi S.A.S. di Paola Fendi e Sorelle v. Cosmetic World, Ltd.*, 642 F.Supp. 1143, 1147 (S.D.N.Y. 1986). The Lees do not argue that this is such a case.

Ordinarily the judge's decision to disbelieve Weinberg's testimony concerning the number of infringing items would be conclusive, and then Vuitton would indeed be entitled only to treble the Lees' profits on the three Vuitton fakes they say they sold, plus attorney's fees and costs. But we think the judge's handling of this proceeding has been so flawed that none of his findings should stand. Cf. *Rogers v. Richmond*, 365 U.S. 534, 547, 81 S.Ct. 735, 743, 5 L.Ed.2d 760 (1961) ("Historical facts 'found' in the perspective framed by an erroneous legal standard cannot plausibly be expected to furnish the basis for correct conclusions if and merely because a correct standard is later applied to them"). Vuitton has a right to have the veracity of its witnesses evaluated by a judge whose judgment has not been clouded by overreaction to the human dimensions of the litigation as he perceived them. For he forgot that while the Lees are human, so are the customers, employees, suppliers, and owners of Louis Vuitton. A corporation is not a thing; it is a network of relations among human beings.

*   *   *

The judgment is reversed, and the case remanded for a new trial on damages, consistent with this opinion.

REVERSED AND REMANDED, WITH DIRECTIONS.

Notes on Counterfeiting

1. Generally

The Trademark Counterfeiting Act of 1984 provides criminal and civil penalties for anyone who "intentionally traffics or attempts to traffic in goods or services and knowingly uses a counterfeit mark on or in connection with such goods or services." A "counterfeit mark" is defined as:

> a spurious mark that is used in connection with trafficking in goods or services [and] that is identical with or substantially indistinguishable from a mark registered for those goods or services on the principal register . . . and in use, whether or not the defendant knew such mark was so registered.

(15 U.S.C. § 1116.) The 1984 Act subjects individuals engaged in trademark counterfeiting to criminal penalties of up to $250,000 and/or up to five years imprisonment. Heavier fines are provided for corporate violators and stiffer penalties for repeat offenders. Laches is not a defense. *U.S. v. Milstein*, 401 F.3d 53, 64 (2^d Cir. 2005) (to apply such equitable defenses in a counterfeiting case would lead to "absurd results", and such willful infringement would preclude their application in any event). In civil actions the 1984 Act provides for treble damages or profits (whichever is greater) and attorney's fees, unless the court finds that there are "extenuating circumstances."

The 1996 Act enhanced the civil and criminal remedies for trademark counterfeiting in three principal ways. First, it added a new § 35(c) to the Lanham Act, 18 U.S.C. § 1117(c), providing for statutory damages as an alternative to actual damages incurred by trademark counterfeiting. The amended scheme allowed for statutory damages from $500 to $10,000 for each mark non-willfully infringed, and up to $1 million for each mark willfully infringed. *See, e.g., Playboy Enterprises, Inc. v. Universal Tel-A-Talk, Inc.,* 1998 U.S. Dist. Lexis 17282 (E.D. Pa. 1998) (plaintiff awarded $10,000 in statutory damages as well as attorneys' fees where defendant offered subscriptions to adult entertainment websites under Playboy's marks and portrayed the sites as endorsed by plaintiff). Second, the 1996 Act amended § 526 of the Tariff Act of 1930, 15 U.S.C. § 1526, to authorize the U.S. Customs Service to levy civil penalties on those involved in the importation of counterfeit merchandise, with the penalty amount equal to the market value of the merchandise had it been genuine. The imposition of such a civil penalty does not preclude the availability of other civil or criminal remedies for trademark counterfeiting. *Cf. U.S. v. Milstein*, 401 F.3d 53 (2^d Cir. 2005) (ordering $3.5 million in restitution to the victims of defendant's counterfeit drugs sales). Finally, the 1996 Act added trafficking in goods or services bearing counterfeit marks to the list of "predicate acts" proscribed under the federal Racketeer Influenced and Corrupt Organizations Act (RICO), 18 U.S.C. § 1961(1)(B).

The 2006 Stop Counterfeiting in Manufactured Goods Act (P.L. 109-181; 120 Stat. 285) ("SCMG") was intended to close loopholes present in the criminal statute. For example, it legislatively overruled a decision that had found no liability for trafficking in counterfeit medallions which purchasers could attach to purses and luggage to make them look like products of the trademark owner, i.e., *U.S. v. Giles*, 213 F.3d 1247 (10th Cir. 2000). Under the 2006 Act, it is a violation to traffic in counterfeit "labels, patches, stickers, wrappers, badges, emblems, medallions, charms, boxes, containers, cans, cases, hangtags, documentation or packaging of any type or nature." This also addresses a common dodge used by counterfeiters — not applying the trademark-bearing label until after the typically foreign-made fake product has been imported into this country and is ready to be sold. The SCMG also, among other things, provides for the following: (1) mandatory forfeiture and destruction of counterfeit goods, labels and packaging, etc.; (2) mandatory restitution to the trademark owner; (3) forfeiture of profits, and property and equipment used to produce the counterfeit goods; and (4) a new definition of "traffic" that encompasses possession of counterfeit goods with the intent to distribute for financial gain, as well as distribution.

2. Seizure Orders

Seizure of counterfeit industrial parts and other merchandise before they are distributed in the market understandably has become an extremely important civil remedy in this area of law. The 1984 Act authorizes federal courts to grant *ex parte* seizures of counterfeit goods and related materials in appropriate circumstances. The 1996 Act greatly expanded the types of law enforcement officers that may execute seizure orders, so that, e.g., not only U.S. Marshals but also officers from the U.S. Customs Service, Secret Service, FBI, post office, and state and local enforcement agencies may do so. The seized goods are taken into the custody of the court and the applicant for seizure must provide adequate security for payment for any damages suffered due to a wrongful seizure.

The applicant for a seizure order must, among other things, demonstrate the following under 15 U.S.C. § 1116(d)(4):

(1) that another order, such as a temporary restraining order, would not be adequate;

(2) the applicant has not publicized the requested seizure;

(3) a likelihood of success in proving that the mark in question is counterfeit, and was used "in connection with the sale, offering for sale, or distribution of goods";

(4) that "an immediate and irreparable injury" will occur without an *ex parte* seizure (this normally is satisfied by demonstrating that the counterfeit merchandise may be distributed);

(5) the matter to be seized will be at the location identified in the application;

(6) the harm to the applicant making the request for an order outweighs the possible harm to the defendant, (a relatively easy showing under most circumstances);

(7) the person against whom the order is granted would move, destroy, or conceal the counterfeit goods.

Other requirements include prior notice to the local U.S. Attorney before the seizure. 15 U.S.C. § 1116(d)(2). After the seizure, the court is bound to protect the accused party from publicity, § 1116(d)(6), and from disclosure of its trade secrets or confidential information, § 1116(d)(7). *Cf. Lorillard Tobacco Co. v. Bison Food Corp.*, 377 F.3d 313 (3[d] Cir. 2004) (refusing to enter a seizure order and instead granting a temporary restraining order where plaintiff presented no evidence that defendants could not be trusted to comply with a court order); *In re Vuitton et Fils S.A.*, 606 F.2d 1 (2[d] Cir. 1979) (pre-Counterfeiting Act decision granting plaintiff an *ex parte* temporary restraining order to preserve the status quo and prevent removal or destruction of alleged counterfeit Vuitton marks on leather products). *See generally General Motors Corp. v. Gibson Chem. & Oil Corp.*, 786 F.2d 105 (2[d] Cir. 1986) (although seizure order is not subject to interlocutory appeal, defendant's interests were protected by requiring security to be posted and conducting a prompt post-seizure hearing).

3. Limitations on Seizure Orders

The Counterfeiting Acts do have limitations. They apply only to *federally registered* trademarks. Certain goods also are exempted from the Acts. For example, gray market goods, i.e., goods bearing an authentic trademark intended for sale abroad but imported for sale in a country where the trademark signifies a domestic source (discussed in Chapter 7), are exempted because current Treasury Department regulations apply to their importation. Additionally, if a licensee manufactures too much of a product under a valid trademark licensing agreement, those "overruns" are not considered counterfeit goods because of the owner's initial approval. The overrun exception does not apply, however, if the licensee uses the mark for goods not covered by the licensing agreement. Finally, trade dress, that is, the color, shape or design of a product or its packaging (see Chapter 5), is not covered by the Counterfeiting Acts unless it is registered as a trademark.

When confronted with circumstances outside the Acts' statutory authority, however, courts have relied upon common law authority in ordering civil seizures, as well as Rule 65 of the Federal Rules of Civil Procedure, and the All Writs Act, 28 U.S.C. § 1651, which empowers judges to issue all orders necessary in aid of their jurisdiction. *See, e.g., Pepe (U.K.), Ltd. v. Ocean View Factory Outlet Corp.*, 770 F. Supp. 754 (D.P.R. 1991). Prior to passage of the Counterfeiting Acts, the courts had fashioned similar relief in a number of cases which remain important for the protection of unregistered marks against counterfeiters. *See In re Vuitton*, 606 F.2d 1 (2ᵈ Cir. 1979); *Polo Fashions, Inc. v. Dick Bruhn, Inc.*, 793 F.2d 1132 (9ᵗʰ Cir. 1986); *Ford Motor Co. v. B & H Auto Supply, Inc.*, 646 F. Supp. 975 (D. Minn. 1986). In *Reebok International Ltd. v. Marnatech Enterprises*, 970 F.2d 552, 560 (9ᵗʰ Cir. 1992), the district court issued a preliminary injunction order freezing the defendant's assets, concluding that the defendant counterfeiters might otherwise "hide their allegedly ill-gotten funds" and ultimately preclude monetary relief to plaintiff. In affirming, the Ninth Circuit held that because the Lanham Act authorizes an accounting of profits as a form of final equitable relief, the district court had the inherent power to freeze assets "to ensure the availability of that final relief." While concurring with the majority decision, Judge Fernandez described the order as a type "that could drive an opponent to the wall regardless of the ultimate merits of the action. It is a frightening example of the reach of the court's injunctive powers." 970 F.2d at 563.

The copyright laws also authorize seizures of counterfeits of copyrighted works. 17 U.S.C. § 503.

4. Wrongful Seizures

To balance the strong remedies made available to plaintiffs, the 1984 Counterfeiting Act provides a cause of action against parties who wrongfully obtain seizure orders. 15 U.S.C. § 1116(d)(11). In *General Electric Co. v. Speicher*, 676 F. Supp. 1421 (N.D. Ind. 1988), *rev'd*, 877 F.2d 531 (7ᵗʰ Cir. 1988), the district court awarded defendant wrongful seizure damages after plaintiff's representatives took unauthorized photos and seized irrelevant items as well as non-counterfeit goods. The Seventh Circuit reversed in a strongly worded opinion by Judge Posner, observing that the broad seizure order issued by the district court encompassed non-counterfeit items, and holding that the unauthorized photographs were not unlawful since everything photographed could have been seized. Similarly, in *Martin's Herend Imports Inc. v. Diamond & Gem Trading United States Co.*, 195 F.3d 765 (5ᵗʰ Cir. 1999), the court affirmed that plaintiff had not acted in bad faith in obtaining an *ex parte* seizure order and was not liable for wrongful seizure. The court noted that a seizure can be wrongful if obtained in bad faith or "if the items seized are predominantly legitimate". Here, the district court had applied the correct standard for determining whether there was bad faith, i.e., "whether [plaintiff] sought the seizure knowing it was baseless". The basis for suspecting defendant of counterfeiting submitted by plaintiff at the *ex parte* hearing demonstrated plaintiff's good faith, which defendant failed to rebut. In *Waco Int'l, Inc. v. KHK Scaffolding Houston, Inc.*, 278 F.3d 523 (5th Cir. 2002), the Fifth Circuit applied the same test for wrongful seizure, i.e., a seizure may be wrongful if where an applicant acted in bad faith in seeking the order, *or* if the goods seized are "predominantly legitimate merchandise, even if the plaintiff acted in good faith." In that case the seized scaffolding products did not bear plaintiff's WACO mark, and the court affirmed a wrongful seizure award to defendant of over $1 million in attorneys' fees and punitive damages.

5. Liability

In *Electronic Laboratory Supply v. Cullen*, 977 F.2d 798 (3d Cir. 1992), the Third Circuit held that an attorney representing a party is not an "applicant" under § 1116(d)(11), and cannot be liable for wrongful seizure under that section. However, in *Vector Research v. Howard & Howard Attys. P.C.*, 76 F.3d 692, 698 (6th Cir. 1996), the Sixth Circuit held that attorneys participating in seizures can be considered "federal actors" for purposes of imposing liability under the rule set out in *Bivens v. Six Unknown Named Agents of Federal Bureau of Narcotics*, 403 U.S. 388 (1971), which recognized a cause of action against federal agents violating constitutional rights under color of authority, the federal-actor counterpart to 42 U.S.C. § 1983 (applicable to state actors). Moreover, relying on *Wyatt v. Cole*, 504 U.S. 158 (1992) (holding that non-government employees subject to liability under § 1983 are not afforded qualified immunity), the court held that non-government employees participating in seizures subject to *Bivens* liability are not entitled to qualified immunity. Attorneys participating in seizures do retain a defense of good faith, according to the Sixth Circuit, but it is not adjudicable on a motion to dismiss.

In *Hard Rock Cafe Licensing Corp. v. Concessions Services, Inc.*, 955 F.2d 1143, 1148 (7th Cir. 1992), the court held that the owner of a flea market could be liable for the counterfeiting violations of a vendor "if it knew or had reason to know of them," citing the Supreme Court's test for contributory liability set forth in *Inwood Laboratories, Inc. v. Ives Laboratories, Inc.*, 456 U.S. 844 (1982). It also reconfirmed the Seventh Circuit's holding in *Louis Vuitton v. Lee*, supra, that "willful blindness is equivalent to actual knowledge," and further clarified that, "[t]o be willfully blind a person must suspect wrongdoing and deliberately fail to investigate." *Hard Rock Cafe*, 955 F.2d at 1149. In appropriate circumstances, simply offering to sell counterfeit goods sometime in the future can result in liability. In *Levi Strauss & Co. v. Shilon*, 121 F.3d 1309 (9th Cir. 1997) the defendant had shown samples of counterfeit tags, labels and blue jeans to plaintiff's undercover investigators, and offered to sell them 10,000 sets. Concluding the offer to sell was not "hypothetical." the Ninth Circuit held that "defendant can be liable under Section 32 for an offer to sell counterfeit goods despite the district court's conclusion that there was insufficient evidence to prove that he actually sold or produced the goods." *Compare U.S. v. Halbegger*, 370 F.3d 441 (4th Cir. 2004) (alleged counterfeiter not guilty where only shipped fake goods to a potential customer without receiving any consideration in return). The 2006 SCMG Act subsequently made possession with intent to distribute for financial gain unlawful.

See generally Bainton, *Reflections on The Trademark Counterfeiting Act of 1984: Score a Few for the Good Guys*, 82 Trademark Rep. 1 (1992).

State anti-counterfeiting statutes similar to the federal statute have been enacted in California (Cal. Bus. & Prof. Code § 14340), and some other states.

6. Criminal Counterfeiting

There are two state of mind elements of the criminal offense: intentional trafficking and knowing use of a counterfeit mark. *See, e.g., United States v. Infurnari*, 647 F. Supp. 57 (W.D.N.Y. 1986). The criminal sanctions apply to "[w]hoever intentionally traffics or attempts to traffic in goods or services and knowingly uses a counterfeit mark on or in connection with such goods or services." 18 U.S.C. § 2320(a). Whether or not the counterfeit goods are equivalent in quality to the trademark owner's is irrelevant; the trademark owner has an inviolate right to control quality. *U.S. v. Farmer*, 370 F.3d 495 (4th Cir. 2004). The purchase of counterfeit items for personal use is not penalized under the 1984 Act.

According to the sponsors of the 1984 Act, the government can prove the intentional trafficking element easily, since most people who sell goods do so "on purpose." The knowledge element is the more difficult to prove, as the prosecution must show that the defendant had "an awareness or a firm belief" that the mark was counterfeit. *See United States v. Sultan*, 115 F.3d 321 (5th Cir. 1997) (reversing conviction of an auto parts distributor accused of trafficking in counterfeit GM parts due to insufficient evidence of defendant's knowledge). The burden of proof for this element, however, can also be met if the prosecution shows that the defendant was "willfully blind" to the counterfeit nature of the mark. However, "If a person has an honest, good faith belief that the mark in question is not counterfeit, he or she will not be liable." *Joint Statement on Trademark Counterfeiting Legislation*, 130 CONG. REC. H12, 077 (daily ed. Oct. 10, 1984). For the government's view of the elements of proof in criminal counterfeiting cases, *see* U.S. Dept. of Justice, Executive Office for U.S. Attorneys, Office of Legal Education, *Prosecuting Intellectual Property Crimes*, Ch. 2 (2006).

Criminal sentencing is discretionary. The legislative history of the 1984 Act emphasizes that an appropriate deterrent would include a combination of a prison term and fine. The drafters of the 1984 Act recognized, however, that the imposition of the maximum fines would be unlikely, except for the most egregious forms of counterfeiting. *See, e.g., United States v. Hon*, 904 F.2d 803 (2[d] Cir. 1990) (defendant, convicted of selling counterfeit watches, sentenced to thirty-six months probation and assessed a $6,000 fine). *Cf. United States v. Song*, 934 F.2d 105, 109 (7th Cir. 1991) (upholding defendant's five criminal convictions for trafficking in counterfeit goods bearing five trademarks belonging to five different trademark owners; "the correct unit of prosecution under Section 2320 is the counterfeit mark"); and *United States v. Cho*, 136 F.3d 982 (5th Cir. 1998) (retail value of defendant's counterfeit designer handbags, not the loss resulting from defendant's infringement, determined sentence enhancement under the U.S. Sentencing Guidelines; because the retail value exceeded $2000, defendant was sentenced to two concurrent fourteen-month terms in prison and two concurrent three-year terms of supervised release, in addition to paying $6,633.95 in restitution to the designer handbag manufacturers).

In *U.S. v. Giles*, 213 F.3d 1247 (10th Cir. 2000), defendant sold logo-bearing patches, medallions and straps which could be attached to purses and luggage to give appearance of a Dooney & Bourke bag; emphasizing that criminal statutes must be construed narrowly, the Tenth Circuit held that, "because the statute does not so provide, we are persuaded that Section 2320 does not forbid the mere act of trafficking in counterfeit labels which are unconnected to any goods". As indicated above, this holding was legislatively overruled by the 2006 SCMG Act, which confirmed criminal liability for trafficking in counterfeit labels, patches, medallions and similar trademark-bearing attachments.

7. Counterfeiting and Post-Sale Confusion

Even if a defendant explains to the purchaser that the cheap ROLEX watch is actually a counterfeit, the defendant will still be liable under the Counterfeiting Acts. *United States v. Gantos*, 817 F.2d 41, 43 (8th Cir.), *cert. denied*, 484 U.S. 860 (1987). One reason given is that while the direct purchaser may not be confused, those who observe the wearer of the counterfeit, or who receive the counterfeit through resale or as a gift, are likely to be confused into believing it is the real thing. This usually is referred to as "post-sale confusion." *See, e.g., U.S. v. Foote*, 413 F.3d 1240 (10th Cir. 2005) (counterfeiting conviction can be based on potential third party post-sale confusion);

United States v. Hon, 904 F.2d 803 (2ᵈ Cir. 1990), *cert. denied*, 498 U.S. 1069 (1991) (jury could consider likelihood of confusion of general public, not just purchasing public); *United States v. Yamin*, 868 F.2d 130, 133 (5ᵗʰ Cir.), *cert. denied*, 492 U.S. 924 (1989) (no error where jury was instructed to find liability if general public, not just potential purchasers, likely to be confused); *United States v. Torkington*, 812 F.2d 1347, 1352–1353 (11ᵗʰ Cir. 1987) (likelihood of confusion encompasses post-sale confusion). The direct purchaser, furthermore, would be able to sell it to an unknowing third party without explaining it is counterfeit. See also the discussion on post-sale confusion in civil cases earlier in this chapter.

8. U.S. Customs Service

Under § 526 of the Tariff Act of 1930, 19 U.S.C. § 1526, it is also possible for a trademark owner to alert the U.S. Customs Service to the anticipated import of goods bearing a particular counterfeit trademark. Compliance with the requirement of 19 C.F.R. 133.0 *et seq.*, promulgated under § 526, will result in the Service barring the entrance of any such goods which it discovers. As amended by the 1996 Act, the Tariff Act requires Customs officials to destroy all imported counterfeit items unless the party whose trademark rights are infringed by the counterfeit items consents to their sale with the benefits to be distributed to a charity or government agency.

6.14 Contributory Infringement

PERFECT 10, INC. v. VISA INTERN. SERVICE ASS'N
494 F.3d 788 (9ᵗʰ Cir. 2007)

Milan D. Smith, Jr., Circuit Judge

Perfect 10, Inc. (Perfect 10) sued Visa International Service Association, MasterCard International Inc., and several affiliated banks and data processing services (collectively, the Defendants), alleging secondary liability under federal copyright and trademark law and liability under California statutory and common law. It sued because Defendants continue to process credit card payments to websites that infringe Perfect 10's intellectual property rights after being notified by Perfect 10 of infringement by those websites. The district court dismissed all causes of action under Federal Rule of Civil Procedure 12(b)(6) for failure to state a claim upon which relief can be granted. We affirm the decision of the district court.

FACTS AND PRIOR PROCEEDINGS

Perfect 10 publishes the magazine "PERFECT10" and operates the subscription website www. perfect 10. com., both of which "feature tasteful copyrighted images of the world's most beautiful natural models." Appellant's Opening Brief at 1. Perfect 10 claims copyrights in the photographs published in its magazine and on its website, federal registration of the "PERFECT 10" trademark and blanket publicity rights for many of the models appearing in the photographs. Perfect 10 alleges that numerous websites based in several countries have stolen its proprietary images, altered them, and illegally offered them for sale online.

Instead of suing the direct infringers in this case, Perfect 10 sued Defendants, financial institutions that process certain credit card payments to the allegedly infringing websites. . . .

* * *

B. Secondary Liability for Trademark Infringement

The tests for secondary trademark infringement are even more difficult to satisfy than those required to find secondary copyright infringement. *See Sony Corp. v. Universal City Studios,* 464 U.S. 417, 439 n. 19, 104 S.Ct. 774, 78 L.Ed.2d 574 (1984); *Fonovisa,* 76 F.3d at 265 (noting that "trademark infringement liability is more narrowly circumscribed than copyright infringement"). While the tests for such infringement are somewhat different in the trademark context, Perfect 10's factual allegations in support of these claims are essentially identical to those alleged in Perfect 10's copyright claims, and they fail to state a claim for similar reasons.

1. Contributory Trademark Infringement

To be liable for contributory trademark infringement, a defendant must have (1) "intentionally induced" the primary infringer to infringe, or (2) continued to supply an infringing product to an infringer with knowledge that the infringer is mislabeling the particular product supplied. *Inwood Labs., Inc. v. Ives Labs., Inc.,* 456 U.S. 844, 855, 102 S.Ct. 2182, 72 L.Ed.2d 606 (1982). When the alleged direct infringer supplies a service rather than a product, under the second prong of this test, the court must "consider the extent of control exercised by the defendant over the third party's means of infringement." *Lockheed Martin Corp. v. Network Solutions, Inc.,* 194 F.3d 980, 984 (9th Cir.1999). For liability to attach, there must be "[d]irect control and monitoring of the instrumentality used by a third party to infringe the plaintiff's mark." *Id.*

Perfect 10 has failed to plead a viable claim under either prong of Inwood Labs-and, by extension, Lockheed Martin. First, it has not pled facts showing that Defendants "intentionally induced" infringement of Perfect 10's mark. Perfect 10 has alleged that Defendants are providing critical support to websites that are using the PERFECT 10 mark in a manner that is likely to cause the public to believe that they are authorized by Perfect 10. Its factual allegations in support of this claim are identical to those it made in support of its copyright claims. These allegations, however, cite no affirmative acts by Defendants suggesting that third parties infringe Perfect 10's mark, much less induce them to do so.

Second, Perfect 10 has failed to allege facts sufficient to show "[d]irect control and monitoring of the instrumentality used by a third party to infringe the plaintiff's mark." *Lockheed Martin,* 194 F.3d at 984. Perfect 10 claims that the "product" or "instrumentality" at issue here is the credit card payment network through which Defendants process payments for infringing material. Appellant's Opening Brief at 39. As discussed at length above, this network is not the instrument used to infringe Perfect 10's trademarks; that infringement occurs without any involvement of Defendants and their payment systems. Perfect 10 has not alleged that Defendants have the power to remove infringing material from these websites or directly stop their distribution over the Internet. At most, Perfect 10 alleges that Defendants can choose to stop processing payments to these websites, and that this refusal might have the practical effect of stopping or reducing the infringing activity. This, without more, does not constitute "direct control." *See Lockheed Martin,* 194 F.3d at 985 ("While the landlord of a flea market might reasonably be expected to monitor the merchandise sold on his premises, [defendant] NSI cannot reasonably be expected to monitor the Internet.") (citation omitted).

2. Vicarious Trademark Infringement

Vicarious liability for trademark infringement requires "a finding that the defendant and the infringer have an apparent or actual partnership, have authority to bind one another in transactions with third parties or exercise joint ownership or control over the infringing product." *Hard Rock Café Licensing Corp. v. Concession Servs., Inc.,* 955 F.2d 1143, 1150 (7th Cir.1992) (internal quotations omitted), followed by *Symantec Corp.*

v. CD Micro, Inc., 286 F.Supp.2d 1265, 1275 (D.Or.2003).

Perfect 10 argues that Defendants are liable as follows: "Defendants and the Stolen Content Websites are in a symbiotic financial partnership pursuant to which the websites operate their businesses according to defendants' rules and regulations and defendants share the profits, transaction by transaction." Appellant's Opening Brief at 40. For the same reasons that this relationship does not establish "right and ability to control" for copyright purposes, neither does it establish such a "symbiotic" relationship or "joint ownership or control" for trademark purposes. Defendants process payments to these websites and collect their usual processing fees, nothing more.

Perfect 10 further argues that "Defendants' acceptance of a charge binds the Stolen Content Website to provide the infringing images to third parties." Appellant's Opening Brief at 40. Even if legally relevant, Perfect 10's allegation is legally incorrect. It is the websites' contracts with the consumers that bind the websites to provide the infringing images, not the websites' relationship with Defendants. [19] The websites' contracts with Defendants are merely a means of settling the resulting debits and credits among the websites and the relevant consumers. We hold that Perfect 10 fails to state a claim for vicarious trademark infringement.

KOZINSKI, CIRCUIT JUDGE, dissenting for the most part:

*   *   *

Trademark Infringement

. . . I disagree with the majority when it claims that defendants do not contributorily infringe on Perfect 10's trademark because they lack "[d]irect control and monitoring of the instrumentality used by a third party to infringe the plaintiff's mark." Maj. op. at 807 (internal quotation marks omitted). The Lanham Act forbids "use in commerce . . . of a registered mark in connection with the sale, offering for sale, distribution, or advertising of any goods or services on or in connection with which such use is likely to cause confusion." 15 U.S.C. § 1114(1)(a). Plaintiff alleges that the Stolen Content Websites sell images marked with Perfect 10's trademark. First Am. Compl. at 17 ¶ 65. Without defendants' payment systems, the infringers would find it much harder to peddle their infringing goods. Plaintiff thus pled facts sufficient to state a claim for contributory trademark infringement.

The cases on which the majority relies are not to the contrary. *Inwood Laboratories, Inc. v. Ives Laboratories, Inc.*, 456 U.S. 844, 102 S.Ct. 2182, 72 L.Ed.2d 606 (1982), involved a manufacturer and says nothing of consequence bearing on our situation. *Lockheed Martin Corp. v. Network Solutions, Inc.*, 194 F.3d 980, 984 (9th Cir.1999), turned on the fact that the defendant there, a registrar of Internet domain names, lacked sufficient control "over the third party's means of infringement," because it lacked "control and monitoring of the instrumentality used by a third party to infringe the plaintiff's marks." *Id.* By contrast, credit cards are directly involved in every infringing transaction; not only do they process the payment for virtually every sale of pirated images by the Stolen Content Websites, they control whether such transactions will go forward. This is more than enough to establish the "control and monitoring" that Lockheed Martin requires for contributory trademark infringement.

As to vicarious trademark infringement, the majority claims that there is neither a symbiotic partnership between the direct infringers and defendants, nor authority to bind one another in transactions with third parties. Maj. op. at 807 (*citing Hard Rock*

---

[19] The dissent claims that no contractual relationship arises between the infringers and consumers until Defendants process a payment. Dissent at 822-23. Even if true as a factual and legal matter-and given the absence of any citation, it is difficult to know whether this is true-this results from a decision of the websites to delay formation of the relationship, not from any requirement Defendants impose on the transaction.

Cafe Licensing Corp. v. Concession Servs., Inc., 955 F.2d 1143 (7th Cir. 1992)). But plaintiff alleges that the Stolen Content Websites cannot operate without the use of credit cards, First Am. Compl. at 2 ¶ 7, while defendants make huge profits by processing these illegal transactions. *See also* p. 820 *supra*. If this is not symbiosis, what is? Likewise, while "the websites' contracts with the consumers . . . bind the websites to provide the infringing images," maj. op. at 808 (emphasis removed), it is defendants' actions that bind the websites to that contract. Only after the credit cards approve and process the payment does the obligation to deliver the stolen content come into existence. The majority thus errs in absolving defendants of vicarious trademark infringement.

*   *   *

Notes on Contributory Infringement

The Supreme Court's holding in *MGM Studios, Inc. v. Grokster, Ltd.*, 125 S. Ct. 2764 (2005), regarding copyright law, is instructive with respect to all types of contributory infringement of intellectual property. In *Grokster* the Supreme Court grappled with balancing the benefits of new technology against intellectual property rights, just as it had 20 years earlier in *Sony Corp. of America v. Universal City Studios, Inc.*, 464 U.S. 417 (1984) (the "*Betamax*" case). Grokster distributed software that allowed computer users to share files through a peer-to-peer ("P2P") network. A P2P network allows computers to communicate directly without going through a central server. Grokster advertised itself as the successor to the popular Napster service, which had permitted wide-spread downloading of copyrighted music, without payment to the copyright holders. Napster's service was held to constitute copyright infringement. MGM and others sued Grokster and others, also alleging copyright infringement.

Grokster could not be liable for direct infringement because users of its software shared files directly and not through Grokster, so MGM brought claims for vicarious and contributory infringement. Grokster defended, saying its software was "capable of substantial noninfringing uses" such as downloading copyright free files, and therefore was immune from vicarious or contributory liability under *Betamax* (which held that sellers of VCRs were not contributorily liable for users' copyright infringement, namely taping television shows, in part because VCR's are capable of substantial non-infringing use.)

The Supreme Court, reversing the Ninth Circuit, ruled against Grokster. The court restated the holding in *Betamax* as follows: "[*Betamax*] barred secondary liability based on presuming or imputing intent to cause infringement solely from the design or distribution of a product capable of substantial lawful use, which the distributor knows is in fact used for infringement." 545 U.S. at 934. The court then held Grokster contributorily liable because, unlike Sony in the *Betamax* case, Grokster distributed its software "with the object of promoting its use to infringe copyright, as shown by clear expression or other affirmative steps taken to foster infringement. . . ." 545 U.S. at 937. Grokster therefore was liable for the "resulting acts of infringement by third parties." *Id.* The court found substantial evidence that Grokster intended to induce infringement including: (1) Grokster targeted Napster customers "indicat[ing] a principal, if not exclusive intent to bring about infringement"; (2) Grokster did not use filtering technology to try to stop infringement; and (3) Grokster made its profits by selling advertising space, i.e., directing ads to computers using the P2P software. Grokster's profit depended on high volume use. Ninety percent of such use was infringing, according to MGM's survey. With respect to ad sales, the court noted: "This evidence alone would not justify an inference of unlawful intent, but its import is clear in the entire record's context." 545 U.S. at 941. The court did not decide the issue of vicarious liability, limiting itself to considering contributory infringement. In *Betamax*, in contrast, there was no evidence that Sony intended to induce infringement or profit from it.

Justice Breyer wrote a concurring opinion joined by Justices O'Connor and Stevens. Justice Ginsberg also wrote a concurrence, joined by Justices Rehnquist and Kennedy. Most fundamentally, Justice Breyer disagreed with the majority's revision of the rule in *Betamax*, believing that the court's new rule served neither copyright holders nor developers of new technology. Most of them, Justice Breyer said, would find their evidentiary burden higher than under the court's prior *Betamax* holding. The latter would find it riskier to enter the market with new technology, and therefore would be deterred from developing such technology. Justice Ginsburg wrote separately to clarify why she believed the Ninth Circuit misapplied the holding of *Betamax* in granting summary judgment to Grokster. Ginsburg stated that the *Grokster* case "differs markedly from *Sony*," because there was evidence that Grokster's products were "overwhelmingly used to infringe and that this infringement was the overwhelming source of revenue from the products." 545 U.S. at 808, internal citations omitted. That evidence was "insufficient to demonstrate, beyond genuine debate, a reasonable prospect that substantial or commercially significant noninfringing uses were likely to develop over time." *Id.*

The court's *Grokster* ruling appears to be in accord with earlier Supreme Court decisions in the trademark arena: *Inwood Labs. v. Ives Labs.*, 456 U.S. 844, 854 (1982) (contributory liability exists when a manufacturer or distributor "intentionally induces another to infringe a trademark, or if it continues to supply its product to one whom it knows or has reason to know is engaging in trademark infringement"), and *William R. Warner & Co. v. El. Lilly & Co.*, 265 U.S. 526 (1924) (a manufacturer is contributorily liable if it intentionally enables or induces retailers to palm off its product as that of a competitor). *See A Panel Analysis of the Ives Case* (Kranzow, McCarthy, Palladino, Pattishall, Swann), 72 TMR 118 (1982), and the discussion on vicarious franchisor liability in Chapter 4. Should the same principles apply to trademark issues in the online environment after the *Grokster* decision? *See, e.g.*, Sunderji, *Protecting Online Auction Sites from the Contributory Trademark Liability Storm: A Legislative Solution to the Tiffany, Inc. v. eBay, Inc. Problem*, 74 FORDHAM L. REV. 909 (2005).

6.14 Surveys and Experts

Survey evidence has been employed increasingly in trademark litigation in proof of issues such as secondary meaning and likelihood of confusion. Properly conducted and presented, a survey can provide persuasive evidence of potential or actual consumer reactions. *Ab initio*, however, such evidence is hearsay in nature. There is normally no opportunity for an opposing counsel to cross-examine survey respondents, nor for the trier of fact to observe respondent demeanor and credibility. Accordingly, courts carefully scrutinize the trustworthiness and reliability of the surveying process itself. A poorly designed or sloppily administered survey may be either rejected as evidence or accorded little weight. *See, e.g., M2 Software Inc. v. Madacy Entm't*, 421 F.3d 1073 (9th Cir. 2005) (district court properly rejected plaintiff's survey because its creator did not qualify as an expert, nor was the survey shown to have adhered to acceptable methods in a "statistically correct manner").

Federal Rule of Evidence 703, which allows experts in appropriate circumstances to base their testimony on out of court hearsay information, has also contributed to the increased use of surveys in trademark litigation. "The rule . . . offers a more satisfactory basis for ruling upon the admissibility of public opinion poll evidence. Attention is directed to the validity of the techniques employed rather than to relatively fruitless inquiries into whether hearsay is involved." Notes on Advisory Committee on Proposed Rules, FRE 703. Similarly facilitating the use of survey evidence is Federal Rule of Evidence 803 (3, 5, 6). It liberalizes and codifies what had come to be known as the "shopbook rule" which permitted use of books and records kept in the ordinary course of business. *See* the extensive discussion in *Schering Corp. v. Pfizer, Inc.*, 189 F.3d 218 (2[d] Cir. 1999) (Sotomayor, J.) of survey admissibility under Rule 803, as well as Rule 807, which permits hearsay evidence not specifically covered by Rule 803 to be admitted in appropriate circumstances where there are "equivalent circumstantial guarantees of trustworthiness," and Leighton, *Using (and Not Using) the Hearsay Rules to Admit and Exclude Surveys in Lanham Act False Advertising and Trademark Cases*, 92 TMR 1305 (2002).

Requisites for a properly conducted survey are that the survey be conducted within a proper *universe* ("that segment of the population whose characteristics are relevant to the proposition in question," Note, 66 HARV. L. REV. 499 (1953)), and that subjects for the survey constitute a fair and representative *sample* of that universe. Further, the survey must contain unbiased questions, be conducted with proper security so that the interviewers do not know who they represent, and be properly tabulated, verified and interpreted by an expert. These and other factors considered by the courts in assessing the reliability and weight of a survey are illustrated by the cases below. *See also* the *Manual for Complex Litigation (Fourth)*, § 11.493 (2004), and *Reference Manual on Scientific Evidence*, pp. 223-271 (1994), both issued by the Federal Judicial Center.

THE SCOTCH WHISKEY ASS'N v. CONSOLIDATED DISTILLED PRODUCTS, INC.
210 U.S.P.Q. 639 (N.D. Ill. 1981)

MAROVITZ, DISTRICT JUDGE

Plaintiff The Scotch Whiskey Association brings this action against defendant Consolidated Distilled Products, Inc. appealing a decision rendered by the Trademark Trial and Appeal Board (the "Board") of the United States Department of Commerce's Patent and Trademark Office. The jurisdiction of the Court is invoked pursuant to 15 U.S.C. §§ 1071(b) and 1121 and 28 U.S.C. § 1338(a).

Plaintiff, a United Kingdom Corporation, is an association of Scottish whiskey distillers organized for the purpose of promoting the interests of and the trade in whiskey produced in Scotland. Defendant produces and markets alcoholic beverages. Defendant has pending an application to register the mark "Loch-A-Moor" as a trademark for an after-dinner liqueur that it produces and retails in the United States. Plaintiff opposes the registration of "Loch-A-Moor" as a trademark on the ground that the mark is allegedly deceptive as to the geographic origin of defendant's product in violation of 15 U.S.C. §§ 1051(e)(2) and § 1125(a), and the Convention of Paris of the Protection of Industrial Property, as implemented by 15 U.S.C. § 1126. Specifically, plaintiff contends that the Loch-A-Moor mark falsely describes the product as having Scotland as its place of origin.

* * *

Subsequent to the Board's decision in this matter, plaintiff retained the marketing and survey research firm of Elrick & Lavidge to conduct a survey to ascertain what, if any, place of geographic origin the Loch-A-Moor label imparts to consumers. Mr. Robert Lavidge designed the survey used and testified at trial as to its design and the manner in which it was conducted. The survey was conducted in September 1979 by way of face-to-face interviews in New York City, Chicago, and San Francisco metropolitan area shopping centers. No alcoholic beverages were sold within the shopping centers used. The survey population consisted of persons who stated that they had either bought or consumed an after-dinner liqueur within the past year.

At each location, the survey was administered by paid interviewers who were supervised by professionals. The interviewers were never informed for whom the survey was being performed. Once a person replied that he had used or consumed an after-dinner liqueur within the past year, he was shown a bottle of Loch-A-Moor bearing the Loch-A-Moor mark. Interviewers were instructed to permit a respondent to view the bottle as long as he wished, but not to allow a respondent to actually hold the bottle. After viewing the bottle, the respondents were then asked the following two questions:

(1) "Where do you think this liqueur comes from?" and (2) "Why do you think it comes from (place mentioned in response to the first question)?" Interviewers were instructed to record all responses verbatim. That the instructions were adhered to by the interviewers in the Chicago area portion of the survey was supported by the testimony of both the supervisor for the Chicago portion of the survey and one of the Chicago interviewers. Validation of all of the survey results was achieved by telephoning approximately 40 percent of the respondents to verify the responses given. This validation technique caused one response to be disregarded when calculating the survey results.

There was a total of 607 persons in the survey population: 201 in the New York City area; 206 in the Chicago area; and 200 in the San Francisco area. Scotland was the most common response given by members of the survey population to the first question. Of the total survey population, 32.7 percent unequivocally gave Scotland as their answer to the first question. Scotland was given as an unequivocal response by 37.3 percent of the New York City area respondents, by 26.7 percent of the Chicago area respondents, and by 34 percent of the San Francisco area respondents. Of those members of the survey population which unequivocally responded Scotland to the first question, the overwhelming majority gave responses to the second question that indicated that that mark's name or label or both caused them to give Scotland as their response to the first question. The second most common response to the first question was Chicago, given by 7.7 percent of the total survey population.

*   *   *

Based upon the stipulated facts as to Loch-A-Moor's mark, the Court's own observation of the mark, *see General Foods Corp. v. Borden, Inc.*, 191 U.S.P.Q. 674, 678 (N.D. Ill. 1976), and the survey evidence, the Court finds that the Loch-A-Moor mark is likely to mislead consumers to believe that the geographic origin of the product is Scotland. As stated, "loch" is a Scottish word, "moor" is a British word, and the label displays a castle and refers to a Scottish island. Further, while the Court finds Mr. Klinsky's testimony credible insofar as he testified that the mark was not chosen for the purpose of deceiving the public as to the origin of the product, the Court finds it nonetheless significant that the mark was deliberately chosen because of its Scottish connotation. . . .

In this connection, the Court finds the survey evidence presented by plaintiff to be particularly persuasive. Survey evidence can be helpful in ascertaining the likelihood of confusion for purposes of the trademark laws, *Exxon Corp. v. Texas Motor Exchange of Houston*, 628 F.2d 500, 506, 208 U.S.P.Q. 384, 388–389, (5th Cir. 1980); *James Burrough Ltd. v. Sign of the Beefeater, Inc.*, 540 F.2d 266, 279, 192 U.S.P.Q. 555, 565–566 (7th Cir. 1976); *Union Carbide Corp. v. Ever-Ready, Inc.*, 531 F.2d at 382, 188 U.S.P.Q. at 637–638; *General Foods Corp. v. Borden, Inc.*, 191 U.S.P.Q. at 678. This proposition is also particularly true when a low-cost item is involved. *Union Carbide Corp. v. Ever-Ready, Inc.*, 531 F.2d at 388, 188 U.S.P.Q. at 643–644. The weight accorded survey evidence is determined by examining, inter alia: (1) the sample size; (2) the nature of the universe; (3) the nature of the questions; and (4) by whom the survey was conducted. It is the Court's examination of these factors with regard to plaintiff's survey that causes the Court to accord great weight to the survey evidence.

First, the Court finds that the sample size of 607 persons is easily sufficient to allow the Court to extrapolate the survey responses to the national population of after-dinner liqueur consumers and purchasers. Second, the Court finds that the universe was properly defined as consumers as well as purchasers of after-dinner liqueurs because the universe should include potential purchasers as well as actual purchasers. Third, the questions were properly framed to discover the ultimate question of geographic misdescriptiveness presented to the Court for resolution. They were framed clearly and were not in any fashion leading. Fourth, the survey was scientifically conducted by impartial interviewers and qualified experts. *James Burrough Ltd. v. Sign of the*

Beefeater, Inc., 540 F.2d at 278, 192 U.S.P.Q. at 564–565. The interviewers were not aware of the purpose for which the survey was conducted, were instructed to record responses verbatim, and an effective validation technique was employed. *See id.* While the Court is mindful that the survey was not performed in an actual purchasing situation, it does not deem that fact to significantly undermine the weight of the survey findings because, as discussed above, the universe was properly defined. *See generally General Foods Corp. v. Borden, Inc.*, 191 U.S.P.Q. at 681.

*   *   *

Defendant presented evidence at trial that, it argues, casts doubt upon the validity of the 32.6 percent figure as being the percentage of the survey population that unequivocally responded Scotland to the first survey question. Specifically, defendant argues that the disparity between the number of unequivocal Scotland responses by the San Francisco and New York respondents, on the one hand, and the Chicago respondents, on the other, suggests that only the Chicago interviewers strictly adhered to the instruction to record verbatim the responses given. The Court finds unpersuasive the evidence presented in support of this argument. Moreover, the Court is unpersuaded that defendant's argument seeks to establish a significant point. An equivocal Scotland response could in many circumstances be considered evidence of a likelihood of confusion as to geographic origin. In any event, the Court finds that the Chicago portion of the survey would alone be sufficient to demonstrate a violation of §§ 1125(a).

*   *   *

[Judgement for plaintiff.]

INDIANAPOLIS COLTS, INC. v. METROPOLITAN BALTIMORE FOOTBALL CLUB LIMITED PARTNERSHIP
34 F.3d 410 (7th Cir. 1994)

POSNER, CHIEF JUDGE

The Indianapolis Colts and the National Football League, to which the Colts belong, brought suit for trademark infringement (15 U.S.C. §§ 1051 *et seq.*) against the Canadian Football League's new team in Baltimore, which wants to call itself the "Baltimore CFL Colts." (Four of the Canadian Football Leagues teams are American.) The plaintiffs obtained a preliminary injunction against the new team's using the "Colts," or "Baltimore Colts," or "Baltimore CFL Colts," in connection with the playing of professional football, the broadcast of football games, or the sale of merchandise to football fans and other buyers. The ground for the injunction was that consumers of "Baltimore CFL Colts" merchandise are likely to think, mistakenly, that the new Baltimore team is an NFL team related in some fashion to the Indianapolis Colts, formerly the Baltimore Colts. From the order granting the injunction the new team and its owners appeal to use under 28 U.S.C. § 1292(a)(1). Since the injunction was granted, the new team has played its first two games — without a name.

A bit of history is necessary to frame the dispute. In 1952, the National Football League permitted one of its teams, the Dallas Texans, which was bankrupt, to move to Baltimore, where it was renamed the "Baltimore Colts." Under that name it became one of the most illustrious teams in the history of professional football. In 1984, the team's owner, with the permission of the NFL, moved the team to Indianapolis, and it was renamed the "Indianapolis Colts." The move, sudden and secretive, outraged the citizens of Baltimore. The city instituted litigation in a futile effort to get the team back — even tried, unsuccessfully, to get the team back by condemnation under the city's power to eminent domain — and the Colts brought a countersuit that also failed . . . .

Nine years later, the Canadian Football League granted a franchise for a Baltimore team. Baltimoreans clamored for naming the new team the "Baltimore Colts." And so it was named — until the NFL got wind of the name and threatened legal action. The name was then changed to "Baltimore CFL Colts" and publicity launched, merchandise licensed, and other steps taken in preparation for the commencement of play this summer.

* * *

To help judges strike the balance, the parties to trademark disputes frequently as here hire professionals in marketing or applied statistics to conduct surveys of consumers . . . . The battle of experts that ensues is frequently unedifying. *Olympia Equipment Leasing Co. v. Western Union Telegraph Co.*, 797 F.2d 370, 382 (7th Cir. 1986). Many experts are willing for a generous (and sometimes for a modest) fee to bend their science in the direction from which their fee is coming. The constraints that the market in consultant services for lawyers places on this sort of behavior are weak, as shown by the fact that both experts in this case were hired and, we have no doubt, generously remunerated even though both have been criticized in previous judicial opinions. The judicial constraints on tendentious expert testimony are inherently weak because judges (and even more so juries, though that is not an issue in a trademark case) lack training or experience in the relevant fields of expert knowledge. But that is the system we have. It might be improved by asking each party's hired expert to designate a third, a neutral expert who would be appointed by the court to conduct the necessary studies. The necessary authority exists, *see* Fed. R. Evid. 706, but was not exercised here.

Both parties presented studies. The defendants' was prepared by Michael Rappeport and is summarized in a perfunctory affidavit by Dr. Rappeport to which the district gave little weight. That was a kindness. The heart of Rappeport's study was a survey that consisted of three loaded questions asked in one Baltimore mall. Rappeport has been criticized before for his methodology, *Jarret Int'l, Inc. v. Promotion in Motion, Inc.*, 826 F. Supp. 69, 73-74 (E.D.N.Y. 1993), and we hope that he will take these criticisms to heart in his next courtroom appearance.

The plaintiffs' study, conducted by Jacob Jacoby, was far more substantial and the district judge found it on the whole credible. The 28-page report with its numerous appendices has all the trappings of social scientific rigor. Interviewers showed several hundred consumers in 24 malls scattered around the country shirts and hats licensed by the defendants for sale to consumers. The shirts and hats have "Baltimore CFL Colts" stamped on them. The consumers were asked whether they were football fans, whether they watched football games on television, and whether they ever bought merchandise with a team name on it. Then they were asked, with reference to the "Baltimore CFL Colts" merchandise that they were shown, such questions as whether they knew what sport the team played, what teams it played against, what league the team was in, and whether the team or league needed someone's permission to use this name, and if so whose. If, for example, the respondent answered that the team had to get permission from the Canadian Football League, the interviewer was directed to ask the respondent whether the Canadian Football League had in turn to get permission from someone. There were other questions, none however obviously loaded, and a whole other survey, the purpose of which was to control for "noise," in which another group of mallgoers was asked the identical questions about a hypothetical team unappetizingly named the "Baltimore Horses." The idea was by comparing the answers of the two groups to see whether the source of confusion was the name "Baltimore Colts" or just the name "Baltimore," in which event the injunction would do no good since no one suggests that the new Baltimore team should be forbidden to use "Baltimore" in its name, provided the following word is not "Colts."

Rappeport threw darts at Jacoby's study. Some landed wide. We are especially perplexed by the argument that survey research belongs to sociology rather than psychology (we leave the reader to guess the respective disciplines to which our rival experts belong); the courtroom is a peculiar site for academic turf wars. We also do not think it was improper for Jacoby to inquire about confusion between "Baltimore CFL

Colts" and "Baltimore Colts," even though the Indianapolis Colts have abandoned "Baltimore Colts." If consumers believe that the new Baltimore team is the old Baltimore Colts, and the Indianapolis Colts some sort of upstart (the Johnny Unitas position), they will be less likely to buy merchandise stamped "Indianapolis Colts." But Rappeport was right to complain that the choice of "Horses" for the comparison team loaded the dice and that some of Jacoby's questions were a bit slanted. That is only to say, however, that Jacoby's survey was not perfect, and this is not news. Trials would be very short if only perfect evidence were admissible.

Jacoby's survey of consumers' reactions to the "Baltimore CFL Colts" merchandise found rather astonishing levels of confusion not plausibly attributable to the presence of the name "Baltimore" alone, since "Baltimore Horses" engendered much less. (We don't like the name "Baltimore Horses," as we have said; but we doubt that a more attractive "Baltimore" name, the "Baltimore Leopards," for example, would have generated the level of confusion that "Baltimore CFL Colts" did. *National Football League v. Wichita Falls Sportswear, Inc., supra,* 532 F. Supp. at 660.) Among self-identified football fans, 64 percent thought that the "Baltimore CFL Colts" was either the old (NFL) Baltimore Colts or the Indianapolis Colts. But perhaps this result is not so astonishing. Although most American football fans have heard of Canadian football, many probably are unfamiliar with the acronym "CFL," and as we remarked earlier it is not a very conspicuous part of the team logo stamped on the merchandise. Among fans who watch football on television, 59 percent displayed the same confusion; and even among those who watch football on cable television, which attracts a more educated audience on average and actually carries CFL games, 58 percent were confused when shown the merchandise. Among the minority not confused about who the "Baltimore CFL Colts" are, a substantial minority, ranging from 21 to 34 percent depending on the precise subsample, thought the team was somehow sponsored or authorized by the Indianapolis Colts or the National Football League. It is unfortunate and perhaps a bit tricky that the subsample of consumers likely to buy merchandise with a team name on it was not limited to consumers likely to buy merchandise with a *football* team's name on it; the choice of the name "Baltimore Horses" for the comparison team was unfortunate; and no doubt there are other tricks of the survey researcher's black arts that we have missed. There is the more fundamental problem, one common to almost all consumer survey research, that people are more careful when they are laying out their money than when they are answering questions.

But with all this granted, we cannot say that the district judge committed a clear error (the standard, *Scandia Down Corp. v. Euroquilt, Inc., supra,* 772 F.2d at 1427–28) in crediting the major findings of the Jacoby study and inferring from it and the other evidence in the record that the defendants' use of the name "Baltimore CFL Colts" whether for the team or on merchandise was likely to confuse a substantial number of consumers. This means — given the defendants' failure to raise any issue concerning the respective irreparable harms from granting or denying the preliminary injunction — that the judge's finding concerning likelihood of confusion required that the injunction issue.

The defendants argue, finally, that, even so, the injunction is overbroad; it should not have forbidden them to use the word "Colts," but rather confined them to using it in conjunction with "Baltimore CFL." We are baffled by the argument. If they want to use "Colts" in conjunction with anything besides a Baltimore football team, there is nothing in this lawsuit to prevent them. The objection is precisely to their use of the word in a setting that will lead many consumers to believe it designates either the old Baltimore Colts (falsely implying that the Indianapolis Colts are not the successor to the Baltimore Colts or that the new Baltimore team is an NFL team or is approved by or affiliated with the NFL) or the Indianapolis Colts.

The defendants make some other arguments but they do not have sufficient merit to warrant discussion. The judgment of the district court granting the preliminary injunction is *AFFIRMED*.

Notes on Surveys and Experts

1. Surveys Generally

Surveys afford a basis for determining likelihood of confusion by ascertaining scientifically the mental associations and reactions of consumers and potential consumers to the marks involved. *See* Gilson, § 8.11 (2008 ed.); Gunn & Evans, Jr., *Trademark Surveys*, 20 Texas Tech. L. Rev. 1 (1989); Pattishall, *Reaction Test Evidence in Trade Identity Cases*, 49 Trademark Rep. 145 (1959). Such evidence has also been found probative in determining secondary meaning, *see, e.g., President & Trustees of Colby College v. Colby College-N.H.*, 508 F.2d 804, 809 (1st Cir. 1975) ("The importance of qualified survey evidence in establishing secondary meaning is well recognized"); and whether a term is generic, *Donchez v. Coors Brewing Co.*, 392 F.3d 1211 (10th Cir. 2004) (75% of respondents viewed "beerman" as generic); *E.I. DuPont de Nemours & Co. v. Yoshida Int'l, Inc.*, 393 F.Supp. 502 (E.D.N.Y. 1975) (TEFLON not generic). Surveys also may properly be used to determine consumer reactions in false advertising cases. *See Novartis Consumer Health, Inc. v. Johnson & Johnson-Merck Consumer Pharmaceuticals Co.*, 290 F.3d 578 (3d Cir. 2002) (survey showing at least 15% of survey respondents were deceived by defendant's product label claim was sufficient to show preliminary relief was warranted), and the discussion on advertising cases in Chapter 8.

2. Examples of Survey Formats

a) Deceptive Designation Format

In *Scotch Whiskey Association, supra*, the confusion survey questions were as follows:

1. First, may I ask, have you bought or consumed any after-dinner liqueur in the past year?

Yes ( ) No ( ) Don't know, Don't remember, not sure ( )

(If "NO" or "DON'T KNOW," thank respondent and terminate interview).

If "YES", show liqueur bottle and ask:

2a. Where do you think this liqueur comes from?

(Record answer verbatim.)

(If respondent mentions a place in answer to Q2a, ASK:)

2b. Why do you think it comes from (Place mentioned in answer to Q2a).

(Record answer verbatim.)

3. Thank you. That's all there is to it. So that I may complete this interview, may I please have your name, address, and telephone number?

In this sequence, Question 1 is the screen question to obtain the proper universe, Question 2(a) is the key question to determine if there is confusion and Question 2(b) is a probe question to learn why there is confusion. Question 3 is for verification purposes. Note that the *Scotch Whiskey Association* survey was not a probability sample so that the results could not be scientifically projected to a larger universe than those actually interviewed. Nonetheless, the court found it to be persuasive evidence of the deceptively Scottish connotation imparted by the name LOCH-A-MOOR for defendant's liqueur.

b)   Standard Eveready Format

In *Union Carbide Corp. v. Ever-Ready, Inc.*, 531 F.2d 366, 385–388 (7th Cir. 1976), the following survey questions were found probative of both secondary meaning and likelihood of confusion where the defendants' EVER-READY lamp was shown as the stimulus (see Chapter 2):

(1)   Who do you think puts out the lamp shown here?
(2)   What makes you think so?
(3)   Please name any other products put out by the same concern which puts out the lamp shown here.

Ordinarily, of course, secondary meaning would be tested in such a survey by showing the respondent the product for which secondary meaning is claimed. In *Ever-Ready*, however, in excess of 50% of those interviewed associated Union Carbide products, such as batteries and flashlights, with defendants' mark. The court correctly held that these results established secondary meaning, albeit unintentionally.

c)   Genericness Format

Genericness was found based upon the following survey evidence in *E.I. DuPont de Nemours & Co. v. Yoshida International, Inc.*, 393 F. Supp. 502 (E.D.N.Y. 1975):

I'd like to read 8 names to you to get you to tell me whether you think it is a brand name or a common name; by *brand* name, I mean a word like *Chevrolet* which is made by one company; by *common* name, I mean *automobile* which is made by a number of different companies. So if I were to ask you, "Is Chevrolet a brand name or a common name?," what would you say?

[If respondent understands, continue. If not understood, explain again.]

Now, would you say   is a brand name or a common name?

[Repeat with each of eight examples]

The results were as follows:

NAME	BRAND %	COMMON %	DON'T KNOW
STP	90	5	5
THERMOS	51	46	3
MARGARINE	9	91	1
TEFLON	68	31	2
JELLO	75	25	1
REFRIGERATOR	6	94	—
ASPIRIN	13	86	—
COKE	76	24	—

The survey caused the court to find that "the public is quite good at sorting out brand names from common names and, for TEFLON, [it] answers the critical question . . .," demonstrating that TEFLON functions as a brand name. This survey tests the understanding of respondents; does it test usage?

In contrast, in *Anti-monopoly* the court rejected a similar brand name survey for the game Monopoly as irrelevant, stating that, "under the survey definition, 'Monopoly' would have to be a 'brand name' because it is made by only one company. This tells us nothing at all about the *primary* meaning of 'Monopoly' in the minds of consumers." The court instead endorsed the results of a "motivation" survey where 65% of the respondents chose, out of two statements, the response "I want a 'Monopoly' game primarily because I am interested in playing 'Monopoly,' I don't much care who makes it," while only 32% chose "I would like Parker Brothers' 'Monopoly' game primarily because I like Parker Brothers' products." The court concluded as a result that the primary significance of "Monopoly" was product, not source, and that the name was therefore generic and the trademark registration for it invalid. What criticisms can be made of the survey designs accepted by each court? Are the two cases reconcilable? *See* Zeisel, *The Surveys That Broke Monopoly*, 50 U. Chi. L. Rev. 896 (1983). In 1984, future use of such a purchaser motivation test in Lanham Act cases was legislatively barred by Congress.

d)   Mystery Shopper Format

Mystery shopper surveys are highly trustworthy because they eliminate much of the artificiality inherent in most survey methodologies and create a wallet-in-the-hand reality. First accepted in *SunAmerica Corp. v. Sun Life Assurance Co. of Canada*, 890 F. Supp. 1559 (N.D. Ga); 77 F.3d 1325 (11th Cir.), *cert. denied*, 519 U.S. 822 (1996), a court-directed mystery shopper survey sought to assess the degree to which brokers trained to sell "Sun Life of America" and "Sun Life of Canada" annuities were confused as to the source of the products or the relationship between the two companies. Trained interviewers, working with prescribed questions, telephoned randomly selected brokers pretending to be potential annuity buyers. The telephone methodology facilitated veracity (as would use of new Internet technologies). Because of the high level of confusion among brokers and the fact that brokers are the conduit through which most annuities reach consumers, the court held that the results of the mystery shopper survey proved inevitable confusion among consumers, and enjoined the junior user.

For a discussion of various survey formats, *see* Welter, Trademark Surveys (1999).

3.   Survey Methodology

What factors should a court consider before accepting a survey into evidence? A number of cases discuss this in depth, including *Brooks Shoe Mfg. Co. v. Suave Shoe Corp.*, 533 F. Supp. 75 (S.D. Fla. 1981), *aff'd*, 716 F.2d 854 (11th Cir. 1983), in which the court enumerates eight elements of a proper survey foundation and discusses how one survey failed to establish those elements while another succeeded. In *American Footwear Corp. v. General Footwear Co.*, 609 F.2d 655 (2d Cir. 1979), the court discusses inappropriate wording of questions, failure to replicate appropriate consumer environment and error in selecting survey universe as justifying the district court's rejection of survey evidence. *See also Amstar Corp. v. Domino's Pizza, Inc.*, 615 F.2d 252 (5th Cir. 1980). Often courts will admit defective surveys, but accord them diminished or minimal weight depending on the perceived magnitude of the imperfections. *McGraw-Edison Co. v. Walt Disney Productions*, 787 F.2d 1163, 1172 (7th Cir. 1986); *Jellibeans, Inc. v. Skating Clubs of Georgia, Inc.*, 716 F.2d 833, 844–45 (11th Cir. 1983); *Inc. Publishing Corp. v. Manhattan Magazine, Inc.*, 616 F. Supp. 370, 390 (S.D.N.Y. 1985), *aff'd without opinion*, 788 F.2d 3 (2d Cir. 1986). *Compare Starter Corp. v. Converse, Inc.*, 170 F.3d 286 (2d Cir. 1999) (exclusion of defendant's survey in athletic footwear case was not abuse of discretion where district found it was "little more than a memory test, testing the ability of participants to remember the names of shoes they had just been shown" and shedding no light on the issue of likelihood of confusion). *See generally* Jacoby & Handlin, *Non-Probability Sampling Designs for Litigation Surveys*, 81 Trademark Rep. 169 (1991); Weiss, *The Use of Survey Evidence in Trademark Litigation: Science, Art or Confidence Game?*, 80 Trademark Rep. 71 (1990); Jones, *Developing and Using Survey Evidence in Trademark Litigation*, 19 Mem. St. U. L. Rev. 471 (1989). As indicated in the *Indianapolis Colts* case, *supra*, the use of a control group to compare against the test group of respondents can enhance the reliability of survey results. For a response to Judge Posner's criticisms of his survey in that case, *see* Rappeport, *The Role of The Survey "Expert" — A Response to Judge Posner*, 85 Trademark Rep. 211 (1995). *See also* Welter, *A Call to Improve Survey Evidence, id.* at 205.

Are the problems inherent in survey evidence outweighed by the value of such evidence in ascertaining consumer reaction? In *Levi Strauss & Co. v. Blue Bell, Inc.,* 732 F.2d 676 (9th Cir. 1984), the Court relied heavily on survey evidence indicating minimal actual confusion and no likelihood of confusion in finding that defendant's use of an identifying pocket tab on its shirts did not infringe or unfairly compete with plaintiff's use of the same type of tab. This despite *Levi Strauss & Co. v. Blue Bell, Inc.,* 632 F.2d 817 (9th Cir. 1980), where a similar tab on pants was held to have secondary meaning and Blue Bell was enjoined from use of such a label. Subsequently a rehearing was granted and the opinion withdrawn, *Levi Strauss v. Blue Bell, Inc.,* 734 F.2d 409 (9th Cir. 1984).

4. Relevant Universe

The relevant universe as to likelihood of confusion is generally defined as "potential customers." *See Rhodes Pharmacal Co. v. FTC,* 208 F.2d 382 (7th Cir. 1953), *modified,* 348 U.S. 940 (1955). Is this necessarily correct and sufficient? In *Brooks Shoe, supra* Note (2), spectators and participants at running events in the Washington-Baltimore area constituted too narrow a universe to give a fair indication of whether the consuming public associates a "V" design with plaintiff's running shoes. Similarly, in *Vision Sports, Inc. v. Melville Corp.,* 888 F.2d 609, 615 (9th Cir. 1989), the court found the probative value of plaintiff's secondary meaning survey for its logo for clothing for skateboard enthusiasts was decreased where the universe was limited to 10–18-year-olds who attended skateboarding events or read skateboarding magazines, rather than 15–25-year-olds who purchase activewear.

In *Universal City Studios, Inc. v. Nintendo Co., Ltd.,* 746 F.2d 112, 118 (2[d] Cir. 1984), the universe was held improper where the survey was conducted among individuals who had already purchased or leased the DONKEY KONG video game machines at issue. In *Amstar, supra,* 71% of respondents thought the maker of DOMINO pizza also made DOMINO sugar — but the questions were asked of female household members at home, whereas at that time the primary purchasers of defendant's pizza were shown to be single male college students. Also, 8 of 10 cities where the interviews were conducted did not have defendant's pizza outlets and outlets only had just been opened in the remaining two. The court stated "the appropriate universe should include a fair sampling of those purchasers most likely to partake of the alleged infringer's goods or services." This one did not and was therefore fatally defective. In *National Football League Properties v. Wichita Falls Sportswear,* 532 F. Supp. 651 (W.D. Wa. 1982), plaintiff's universe was the entire U.S. population between the ages of 13 and 65. Defendant argued that this was too broad and that the relevant universe was likely purchasers of NFL football jersey replicas. Unfortunately (for defendant) plaintiff's comprehensive survey analysis included a separate data category which contained the suggested universe and accompanying response results. In a similar apparel case, *National Football League Properties, Inc. v. New Jersey Giants, Inc.,* 637 F. Supp. 507 (D.N.J. 1986), the court held proper a universe which consisted of persons 14 years or older who either: (a) in the past year had bought, or (b) within 6 months were likely to buy, a slogan or picture t-shirt, sweatshirt or other clothing.

In *Anheuser-Busch Inc. v. Stroh Brewery Co.,* 750 F.2d 631 (8th Cir. 1984), in holding that "LA" for a new low alcohol beer was neither generic nor descriptive, the Eighth Circuit was willing to rely in part on survey responses from a group of respondents who had not seen, heard of or tried plaintiff's product because of the newness of the product. In *G. Heileman Brewing Co. v. Anheuser-Busch, Inc.,* 873 F.2d 985, 995 (7th Cir. 1989), in contrast, the results of a similar survey were discounted because the survey tested "thoroughly uninformed consumers" regarding their perception of "LA" for beer. *See generally,* Bird, *Streamlining Consumer Survey Analysis: An Examination of the Concept of Universe in Consumer Surveys Offered in Intellectual Property Litigation,* 88 TMR 269 (1998).

5. Bias

What criteria would you consider in determining whether a survey is biased? *See American Footwear, supra* at 661, in which the court found the question "with whom or what do you associate a product labeled Bionic" too self-serving and suggested the more relevant inquiry should have been "with whom or what do you associate 'Bionic' boot?" In *Wuv's International, Inc. v. Love's Enterprises, Inc.*, 208 U.S.P.Q. 736 (D. Colo. 1980), the court found the question "do you believe that this restaurant is connected with or related to any other restaurants" to be unnecessarily suggestive because it limited respondent's choices to other restaurant operations, including, *inter alia*, plaintiff's. In *Philip Morris, Inc. v. R.J. Reynolds Tobacco Co.*, 188 U.S.P.Q. 289 (S.D.N.Y. 1975), the court ruled that the survey was tailored to elicit brand identification instead of whether consumers considered the word "lights" to be a descriptive term or a term associated with plaintiff. The court suggested "a neutral question would have been: 'respecting cigarettes, will you tell me what the word Lights means to you?' " It is also possible for a survey to be unbiased but too open-ended and abstract, *Exxon Corp. v. Texas Motor Exchange, Inc.*, 628 F.2d 500, 506 (5th Cir. 1980) ("Surveys that involve nothing more than showing an individual a trademark and asking if it brings anything else to mind are given little weight in this Circuit . . . [they are] little more than word-association tests"), or a survey procedure too rigorous, *Wendy's International, Inc. v. Big Bite, Inc.*, 576 F. Supp. 816, 823 (S.D. Ohio 1983) (instructions to probe respondents until no more answers were forthcoming probably resulted in more sponsorship-confusion answers than would otherwise have resulted). *See generally* 3 GILSON, TRADEMARK PROTECTION AND PRACTICE § 8.11[3][c] (2008 ed.). Can reliable survey responses be induced by flattering letters or offers of prizes in return for prompt replies? *See DuPont Cellophane Co. v. Waxed Prod. Co.*, 85 F.2d 75, 80 (2d Cir. 1936), *cert. denied*, 299 U.S. 601 (1936).

6. Environment

Must a survey be conducted in the actual marketing environment to constitute valid evidence of purchaser's state of mind? *See* the *Scotch Whisky Association* case, *supra*, in which the court found that, while the survey was not performed in an actual purchasing situation, this did not significantly undermine the weight of the survey findings because the universe was properly defined. Similarly, in *General Foods Corp. v. Borden, Inc.*, 191 U.S.P.Q. 674 (N.D. Ill. 1976), the court stated that "interviews at respondents' homes are probative of state of mind at the time of purchase. Deviation from the actual purchase situation has been considered in weighing the force of this evidence. . . ." *See also Zippo Mfg. Co. v. Rogers Imports, Inc.*, 216 F. Supp. 670, 685 (S.D.N.Y. 1963); *Inc. Publishing, supra* Note (2), 616 F. Supp. at 392. Surveys taken at a time when market conditions have changed significantly since the alleged infringement occurred may not generate the relevant consumer state of mind. *See, e.g., Zippo Mfg., supra*, 216 F. Supp. at 690; *Calvin Klein Co. v. Farah Mfg. Co.*, 229 U.S.P.Q. 795 (S.D.N.Y. 1985).

7. Agreed Survey Formats

Should the courts themselves conduct or supervise the obtaining of survey evidence? *See Triangle Publications, Inc. v. Rohrlich*, 167 F.2d 969, 976–977 (2d Cir. 1948) (Frank, J. dissenting); *Piper Aircraft Corp. v. Way– Aero Inc.*,, 741 F.2d 925, 931 (7th Cir. 1984). ("Plaintiff followed the 'commendable procedure' of submitting the survey questions, along with the results of a preliminary survey, to the district court for a ruling *in limine* on the question of admissibility"). In *Sun America Corp. v. Sun Life Assurance Co. of Canada*, 890 F. Supp. 1559 (N.D. Ga. 1994), *aff'd* 77 F.3d 1325 (11th Cir. 1996), the court ordered, with agreement of the parties, that a joint survey be designed and conducted to determine the level of confusion caused by both parties' use of "Sun Life" names in the sale of annuity products. In the "mystery shopper" survey format agreed upon by the parties, interviewers called brokers and played the role of customers asking about the parties' products. As indicated above, the court found that the confusion percentages among different cells ranging from 15% to more than 60% helped demonstrate "inevitable" and "intolerable" confusion. Would a court conducted or supervised survey virtually obviate the necessity of a trial on the issue of likelihood of confusion?

8.   Secondary Meaning Surveys

As indicated above, survey evidence has been successfully used to help demonstrate secondary meaning. *See, e.g., Zatarains, Inc. v. Oak Grove Smokehouse, Inc.*, 698 F.2d 786, 795 (5th Cir. 1983) (over 20% of respondents correctly identified plaintiff's brand as a product used for frying fish); *Vision Center v. Opticks, Inc.*, 596 F.2d 111, 119 (5th Cir. 1979), (noting failure to offer an objective survey and finding remaining secondary meaning evidence insufficient), *cert. denied*, 444 U.S. 1016 (1980); *President & Trustees of Colby College v. Colby College-New Hampshire*, 508 F.2d 804, 809 (1st Cir. 1975) ("The importance of qualified survey evidence in establishing secondary meaning is well recognized") .

In *Bose Corp. v. QSC Audio Products, Inc.*, 293 F.3d 1367 (Fed. Cir. 2002), the court indicated that survey evidence of consumer recognition may be unnecessary for a *famous* mark. "[D]irect evidence, such as surveys, is not required in order to determine whether a mark is famous. Indeed, . . . virtually all of our precedent attributing fame to a mark has done so through indirect evidence of the extent to which a mark has earned fame in the consumer marketplace". In *Bose*, the evidence of substantial sales advertising, and promotion over a number of years, as well as widespread media mentions, was sufficient to establish fame without a survey.

9.   Deceptive Advertising Surveys

Surveys often are used to demonstrate that an advertisement conveys a deceptive message to consumers. Such surveys typically ask, "What is the main [or key] message of the advertisement", accompanied by more directed questions such as, what is the product being advertised and what is being claimed about it? *See* Vodra & Miller, *"Did He Really Say That?" Survey Evidence in Deceptive Advertising Litigation*, 92 TMR 794 (2002), and the discussion on deceptive advertising in Chapter 8.

10.   Failure to Offer a Survey

The failure to offer a survey typically will not in and of itself affect the right to relief. *Tools USA & Equip. v. Champ Frame Straightening Equip. Inc.*, 87 F.3d 654, 661 (4th Cir. 1996) (upholding special verdict finding confusion likely in trade dress case; "survey evidence is not necessarily the best evidence of actual confusion and 'surveys are not required to prove likelihood of confusion' "); *Committee for Idaho's High Desert v. Yost*, 92 F.3d 814, 822 (9th Cir. 1996) ("survey evidence is not a requirement for . . . proof [of secondary meaning]"); *International Kennel Club, Inc. v. Mighty Star, Inc.*, 846 F.2d 1079, 1086 (7th Cir. 1988) (absence of survey evidence does not preclude preliminary injunctive relief) *and Charles Jacquin et Cie, Inc. v. Destileria Serralles, Inc.*, 921 F.2d 467, 476 (3[d] Cir. 1990) (upholding refusal to give a jury instruction on appellant's failure to offer a confusion survey in a trade dress case). *Compare*, however, *Star Indus. v. Bacardi & Co.*, 412 F.3d 373 (2[d] Cir. 2005) (a plaintiff's failure to present a consumer survey may weigh against a finding of consumer confusion, even if the defendant's survey is flawed); *Gucci v. Gucci Shops*, 688 F. Supp. 916 (S.D.N.Y. 1988) (absence of rebuttal survey found significant). *See also* Edelman, *Failure to Conduct A Survey in Trademark Infringement Cases: A Critique of the Adverse Inference*, 90 T.M.R. 746 (2001).

11.   Sufficient Percentage of Respondents

What percentage of survey respondent confusion should be sufficient to demonstrate consumer confusion as to product source? In *James Burrough, Ltd. v. Sign of the Beefeater, Inc.*, 540 F.2d 266, 279 (7th Cir. 1976), the Court of Appeals found the district court's characterization of 15% confusion as "small" to be erroneous, finding instead that it "evidences a likelihood of confusion, deception or mistake regarding the sponsorship of [defendant's] services sufficient on this record to establish Distiller's right to relief." Similarly, in*Novartis Consumer Health, Inc. v. Johnson & Johnson-Merck Consumer Pharmaceuticals Co.*, 290 F.3d 578 (3[d] Cir. 2002), the court noted its willingness in a false advertising case to uphold a preliminary injunction based on survey evidence showing as little as 15% deception. *Compare with Reed Union Corp. v. Turtle Wax Inc.*, 77 F.3d 909, 912 (7th Cir. 1996) (accepting defendant's survey control study which showed a noise level of confusion exceeding 20% when respondents were presented with a made-up car wax product, so that plaintiff's survey showing 25% confusion between the parties' car wax products was insufficient to prove a likelihood of confusion caused by the parties' marks). In *Henri's Food Products Co., Inc. v. Kraft, Inc.*, 220 U.S.P.Q. 386 (7th Cir. 1983), the Seventh Circuit held that the district court was correct in holding that a 7.6% confusion weighs *against* a finding of infringement. *See also Grotrian, Helfferich, Schulz, Th. Steinway Nachf. v. Steinway & Sons*, 365 F. Supp. 707 (S.D.N.Y. 1973) (8.5% confusion, 7.7% perceived connection between parties held to be strong evidence of confusion; unclear whether percentages were combined), *aff'd* 523 F.2d 1331 (2[d] Cir. 1973). *Compare Frosty Treats, Inc. v. Sony Computer Entm't, Inc.*, 75 U.S.P.Q.2d 1570 (8th Cir. 2005) (survey did not support claim that confusion was likely where over 400 survey respondents failed to recall "Frosty Treats" when asked to identify the names of ice cream trucks from which they had purchased ice cream).

What percentage of respondents should be sufficient to establish secondary meaning? The Seventh Circuit has observed that a secondary meaning survey showing 50% recognition "is regarded as clearly sufficient to establish secondary meaning [while] a figure in the thirties can only be considered marginal." *Spraying Systems Co. v. Delavan, Inc.*, 975 F.2d 387, 394 (7th Cir. 1992). Nonetheless, a figure in the thirties "is still probative of the issue of secondary meaning and the factfinder should weigh that fact with all of the other evidence to determine if secondary meaning exists". *Id. See also Zatarains v. Oak Grove Smokehouse, supra*(a percentage of 20% found probative).

12.   Other Experts

Expert witnesses can be used in a variety of ways to assist the trier of fact in deciding trademark and unfair competition cases. In *Waco Int'l, Inc. v. KHK Scaffolding Houston, Inc.*, 278 F.3d 523 (5th Cir. 2002), in considering wrongful seizure claim in a counterfeiting case, the jury properly was allowed to consider the expert testimony of an experienced lawyer on the proper procedures for considering and obtaining a seizure order. *See also, Han Beauty, Inc. v. Alberto-Culver Co.*, 236 F.3d 1333 (Fed. Cir. 2001)(in hair care product case, the Court relied on testimony of University of Illinois professor of French in finding opposer's "TRES"- prefix family of marks and applicant's TREVIVE mark would be perceived as French in sound and appearance, with TRES and TRE both pronounced "Tray"; confusion held likely); *WSM Inc. v. Hilton*, 724 F.2d 1320 (8th Cir. 1984) (relying on an expert in the field of regional English to establish that "opry" was in common use before Grand Ole Opry began using it in 1927); *G.D. Searle & Co. v. Charles Prizer & Co.*, 265 F.2d 385 (7th Cir.), *cert. denied*, 361 U.S. 819 (1959) (relying on a Northwestern University professor's testimony as to the sound similarity of the marks DRAMAMINE and BONAMINE for motion sickness pills in holding confusion likely); *Conagra, Inc. v. Geo. A. Hormel & Co.*, 784 F. Supp. 700 (D. Neb. 1992) (favoring the testimony of defendant's linguist over plaintiff's in holding HEALTHY CHOICE and HEALTHY SELECTIONS for frozen food were not confusingly similar in sound and connotation); *A-Veda Corp. v. Aura, Inc.*, 19 U.S.P.Q.2d 1864 (D. Minn. 1991) (relying on testimony of defendant's graphics expert in holding confusion unlikely between competing shampoo products).

In *Sherrell, Inc. v. Revlon, Inc.*, 205 U.S.P.Q. 250 (S.D.N.Y. 1980), defendant made the advertising claim that its copycat perfume was identical to CHANEL NO. 5 perfume, and "only your checkbook will know the difference." Chanel's chief perfumist successfully demonstrated, based on gas chromatograph and "sniff" tests, that the two were not equivalent and that there was "a noticeable difference between genuine Chanel No. 5" and the copy. Sherrell was enjoined from making claims of equivalency, including its claim that "even the most sophisticated perfume expert would have great difficulty in telling 'Ours' from the imported originals." For further discussion of the use of experts in advertising cases, see Chapter 8.

13.   Admissibility of Testimony

In *Daubert v. Merrell Dow Pharmaceuticals, Inc.*, 113 S. Ct. 2783 (1993), the Supreme Court clarified that in the federal courts the standard for admissibility of testimony by expert witnesses is contained in Federal Rule of Evidence 702, and that Rule 702 supplanted the old standard stated in *Frye v. United States*, 293 F. 1013 (D.C. Cir. 1923). Under the old *Frye* test, the judge only had to determine whether the testimony was based on principles generally accepted in the scientific community. Rule 702 provides:

> If scientific, technical or other specialized knowledge will assist the trier of fact to understand the evidence or to determine a fact in issue, a witness qualified as an expert by knowledge, skill, experience, training or education, may testify thereto in the form of an opinion or otherwise.

In *Daubert*, Justice Blackmun found that the terms "scientific" and "knowledge" require that the proposed testimony "rests on a reliable foundation" and that to satisfy Rule 702, a judge will have to make "a preliminary assessment of whether the reasoning or methodology underlying the testimony is scientifically valid and whether that reasoning or methodology properly can be applied to the facts at issue." In his dissent, Chief Justice Rehnquist complained that in focussing on methodology this way, the majority was requiring trial judges "to become amateur scientists" in order to determine the admissibility of such testimony.

In one of the first decisions applying *Daubert*, Judge Zagel in the Northern District of Illinois excluded in a product liability case an expert's testimony that defendant's miter saw was unreasonably dangerous because the expert had done no testing of his theory and had only spent "maybe an hour" thinking about the issue while examining the saw. *Paul Stanczyk v. Black & Decker and DeWalt*, No. 91 C 4054. The exclusion of expert testimony on behalf of plaintiffs was upheld under *Daubert* in *Group Health Plan, Inc. v. Phillip Morris USA, Inc.*, 344 F.3d 753 (8th Cir. 2003), because the expert's assumptions were in conflict with plaintiffs' theory of the case. Several Minneapolis HMOs had collectively sued some of the nation's largest tobacco companies for violating Minnesota's false advertising and unfair competition statutes by misleading the public about the dangers of smoking. The excluded expert testimony was based on assumptions about rates of addiction that conflicted with the plaintiffs' theory of damages allegedly caused by deceptive marketing for "low tar" and "light" cigarettes. *See also Sears, Roebuck & Co. v. Menard, Inc.*, 72 U.S.P.Q.2d 1221 (N.D. Ill. 2003) (confusion survey excluded under *Daubert* because it was leading, it distorted marketplace conditions by manipulating the survey stimulus, and it failed to ask the standard follow-up question: "Why do you say that?"); Plevan, *Daubert's Impact on Survey Experts in Lanham Act Litigation*, 95 TMR 596 (2005).

In *Kumho Tire Co. v. Carmichael*, 526 U.S. 137 (1999), the Supreme Court extended the application of *Daubert* by holding that the gatekeeping obligations on a trial judge to ensure that scientific testimony is relevant and reliable apply to testimony based on "technical" and "other specialized" knowledge as well as scientific evidence. Further, in carrying out those gatekeeping functions, the trial judge is not required to apply the *Daubert* factors themselves, but may exercise her discretion as to the applicability of individual factors or the factors as a whole. In *Betterbox Comm'ns, Ltd. v. BB Technologies, Inc.*, 300 F.3d 325, 329 (3d Cir. 2002), the Third Circuit observed that the *Kumho* decision clarified that, in cases not involving scientific testimony, the *Daubert* factors may or may not be pertinent, and "the relevant reliability concerns may focus upon personal knowledge or experience." In *Betterbox*, the expert's twenty years experience in direct marketing and other relevant areas was sufficient to make his testimony admissible.

CHAPTER 7
DEFENSES AND LIMITATIONS

CONTENTS

c. **Descriptive Fair Use**

d. **Addition of House Marks**

7.01 Introduction

In previous chapters, we discussed the foundations of trademark rights and the elements of trademark infringement claims. In litigation in federal court or the TTAB, a defendant may use a defect in any of these foundations or elements in plaintiff's trademark rights or plaintiff's infringement claim as a defense, which if true would cause defendant to prevail against plaintiff. Such defects in plaintiff's trademark rights or infringement claim may include factors such as the following: plaintiff has not used its mark in commerce; plantiff's mark lacks priority over defendant's mark; plaintiff's mark is generic or was abandoned; plaintiff's mark is descriptive and lacks secondary meaning; defendant's conduct does not create a likelihood of confusion; and so on. In other words, defects in plaintiff's case in chief can make highly effective defenses. For that reason, defendants routinely tend to assert them. These defects do not, however, exhaust the universe of defenses available to alleged infringers. There are a number of defenses that permit defendants to prevail against claims that are not technically defective or those for which the law holds that liability should not be imposed. It is to these special defenses that the present Chapter is devoted. An additional defense, arising out of the First Amendment's protection of freedom of speech, is discussed in Chapter 9.

DEVELOPMENTS IN THE LAW — TRADE-MARKS AND UNFAIR COMPETITION
68 Harv. L. Rev. 814 (1955)[*]

Since the test of injury to the trade-mark owner is likelihood of public confusion, whatever interest the public may have in the integrity of a symbol it has come to associate with a particular product or source will ordinarily be safeguarded in a private infringement suit. There are cases, however, where a mark which consumers identify exclusively with the plaintiff's product has in fact been infringed, but the plaintiff is precluded by his own conduct from asserting his claim to protection. Thus the doctrine of unclean hands has barred a plaintiff whose mark is misdescriptive of his product, who falsely advertises the trade-marked item, or who has changed the quality of the goods sold under a mark so as to deceive the public. Further, if the plaintiff, with knowledge of the defendant's use, delays an unreasonable time before protesting, or in other ways indicates acquiescence in the adverse use, he may be precluded from complaining if the defendant has relied by investing substantially in the infringing mark. And a contract between the parties allowing for joint use of a mark will be a valid defense against the prior user in an infringement proceeding, as will a release or waiver.

In many estoppel cases it is possible that the public will no longer have an interest in protecting the trade-mark, since through its continued use by more than one person the symbol may have lost distinctiveness in identifying a single source in the public mind. However, when the public is confused by the dual use of the trade-mark, the effect of applying personal defenses against its owner will be only to perpetuate this confusion. Thus in *Procter & Gamble Co. v. J. L. Prescott Co.*, the court held the plaintiff to be barred by laches and refused an injunction, although there was evidence of substantial confusion among grocers and consumers between the names "Chas-O" and "Chipso," both used on soap. Where the plaintiff's suit is dismissed because of unclean hands, not only is confusion tolerated, but the plaintiff can continue to mislabel or falsely advertise his product. Further, nothing will prevent the defendant from joining the plaintiff in practicing the same deception on the public. Thus where the plaintiff's figless laxative

---

[*] Copyright © 1955 by The Harvard Law Review Association. Reprinted by permission.

was trade-marked "Syrup of Figs," the result of the court's refusal to enjoin the defendant was that there might be two misbranded products on the market instead of one.

Strict Limitation of Equitable Defenses, and Conditional or Partial Relief. — Many courts, aware of these possible consequences, have been reluctant to apply rigorously the doctrine of unclean hands in unfair competition and trade-mark cases when the flaws in the plaintiff's action were technical and minor and the danger of public confusion was clear. Similarly, where justification for raising an estoppel is doubtful, some courts, while denying the plaintiff an accounting, will grant him injunctive relief. Furthermore, the traditional discretion of equity in framing decrees has allowed the courts a certain area of maneuver within which they can attempt to lessen this danger. Thus, where the situation causing the plaintiff's unclean hands can be corrected within a short period of time, courts have given conditional decrees; in order to safeguard the public from confusion and deception, the defendant has been enjoined from infringing the mark on condition that the plaintiff cease the undesirable practices. A similar method has been to dismiss the plaintiff's claim without prejudice, so that the plaintiff who "cleans his hands" can return to court and obtain an injunction. And some courts, while allowing the defendant to continue use of the mark, have attempted to lessen the danger of confusion by affording partial relief to a plaintiff barred by laches; defendants have been enjoined from precise imitation of the plaintiff's distinctive script and have been compelled to prefix corporate names.

7.02 Laches and Acquiescence

"The doctrine of laches is derived from the maxim that those who sleep on their rights, lose them." *Chattanoga Mfg., Inc. v. Nike, Inc.*, 301 F.3d 789 (7th Cir. 2002). Acquiescence can occur when a mark owner actively assents to another's use. If the plaintiff, having known of the defendant's use of a mark, unreasonably delays before objecting, or indicates acquiescence to the defendant's use, that plaintiff may find the prospects for relief limited, or even barred, if the defendant shows reliance through investment in the infringing mark, or shows other unfair prejudice.

BLACK DIAMOND SPORTSWEAR, INC. v. BLACK DIAMOND EQUIPMENT, LTD.
84 U.S.P.Q.2d 1758 (2d Cir. 2007)

SUMMARY ORDER

* * *

Plaintiff Black Diamond Sportswear, Inc. ("BDS") appeals from an award of summary judgment to defendant Black Diamond Equipment, Ltd. ("BDE") on BDS's claims of trademark infringement, false designation of origin, and dilution under federal common law and the Lanham Act, 15 U.S.C. §§ 1114, 1125. BDS contends that the district court erred in holding that its claims were barred by the equitable doctrine of laches because significant factual disputes exist that preclude the application of that defense. BDS also asserts that, even if laches does bar its claim for monetary damages, the district court should nevertheless have granted its request for injunctive relief. . .

* * *

A. The District Court Properly Applied Laches to Bar BDS's Claims

* * *

. . .Laches will apply where (1) plaintiff had knowledge of defendant's use of its marks, (2) plaintiff inexcusably delayed in taking action with respect to defendant's use, and (3) defendant suffered prejudice as a result. *See Saratoga Vichy Spring Co., Inc. v. Lehman*, 625 F.2d 1037, 1040 (2ᵈ Cir. 1980).

"Although laches is an equitable defense, employed instead of a statutory time-bar, analogous statutes of limitation remain an important determinant in the application of a laches defense." *Conopco, Inc. v. Campbell Soup Co.*, 95 F.3d at 191. Because the Lanham Act establishes no limitations period and because no corresponding federal statute of limitation exists, "we look to the most appropriate or the most analogous state statute of limitations for laches purposes." *Id.* (internal quotation marks omitted). That statute, in turn, determines which party has the burden of proving or rebutting the laches defense.

> [P]rior to the running of the most closely analogous state statute of limitations there is no presumption of laches and the burden remains on the defendant to prove the defense. Alternatively, once the analogous statute has run, a presumption of laches will apply and plaintiff must show why the laches defense ought not be applied in the case.

Id. In the instant case, the parties agree that Vermont's six-year statute of limitations for civil actions applies. *See* 12 V.S.A. § 511.

1. No Genuine Issues of Material Fact Exist

* * *

A plaintiff is not "obligated to sue until its right to protection has ripened such that plaintiff knew or should have known, not simply that defendant was using the potentially offending mark, but that plaintiff had a provable infringement claim against defendant." *Physical Therapy Ctr. v. Pro-Fit Orthopedic & Sports Physical Therapy*, 314 F.3d 62, 70 (2ᵈ Cir. 2002). Under the doctrine of progressive encroachment, a plaintiff has "some latitude in the timing of its bringing suit" because the laches period begins to run, not at the first sign of a de minimis infringing use, but rather, when "the likelihood of confusion looms large." *Id.* (internal quotation marks omitted). We have recognized that "any other rule would require each trademark owner to sue first and ask questions later, and would foster meritless litigation." *Id.* (internal quotation marks and alteration omitted).

In granting summary judgment to BDE on its laches defense, the district court concluded that BDS engaged in unreasonable delay in bringing suit because "BDS had to be aware by the mid-1990s that a company using a similar mark was selling goods in direct competition with it." We agree. It is undisputed that BDE began using the Black Diamond mark in 1990, that BDS was aware of that fact, and that, prior to 1998, BDE sold skiwear products — including gloves, mittens, hats, and t-shirts — that competed directly with BDS's gloves, mittens, ski hats, and t-shirts. Although BDS contends that BDE's pre-1998 products "did not directly compete with the bulk of BDS's line," Appellant's Reply Br. at 18 (emphasis added), BDS fails to identify any "hard evidence" in the record supporting this assertion, *D'Amico v. City of New York*, 132 F.3d 145, 149 (2ᵈ Cir. 1998) (noting that at summary judgment, nonmoving party "must offer some hard evidence showing that its version of the events is not wholly fanciful"). Even if BDS could identify such evidence, moreover, the doctrine of progressive encroachment only excuses delay in filing suit where "defendant, after beginning its use of the mark, redirected its business so that it more squarely competed with plaintiff." *Pro-Fit Orthopedic & Sports Physical Therapy*, 314 F.3d at 70 (emphasis added). In the instant case, BDE's products competed directly at the outset with those of BDS when it began selling skiwear in 1990. *See Tillamook Country Smoker, Inc. v. Tillamook County Creamery Ass'n*, 465 F.3d 1102, 1110 (9ᵗʰ Cir. 2006) ("A junior user's growth of its existing business and the concomitant increase in its use of the mark do not constitute progressive encroachment.") Although BDS attempts to narrow the relevant clothing category to "fleece skiwear," this claim is belied both by BDS's federal trademark registration for "ski wear" generally and by its own CEO's testimony identifying BDS's market as "outdoor ski wear."

The record also demonstrates that BDS should have known of BDE's infringing use of the mark on its pre-1998 products. A trademark owner is "chargeable with such knowledge as he might have obtained upon [due] inquiry." *Polaroid Corp. v. Polarad Electronics Corp.*, 182 F. Supp. 350, 355 (E.D.N.Y. 1960) (quoting *Johnston v. Standard Mining Co.*, 148 U.S. 360, 370, 13 S. Ct. 585, 37 L. Ed. 480 (1893)); see 6 J. Thomas McCarthy, McCARTHY ON TRADEMARKS AND UNFAIR COMPETITION, § 31:38, at 31-97 (4th ed. 2007) (noting that trademark owner has "duty to police its rights against infringers"). As noted, it is undisputed that BDS was aware of BDE's use of the Black Diamond mark on ski equipment as early as 1990. The possibility of it expanding into skiwear was hardly farfetched. Had BDS exercised due diligence in policing its mark, it would readily have learned that BDE was, in fact, selling skiwear in direct competition with plaintiff's clothing line as early as 1990. BDE marketed its products in widely distributed catalogues, at yearly trade shows in which BDS and BDE both participated, and through retail stores nationwide, including in BDS's home state of Vermont. The district court correctly found that, if BDs had policed any of these obvious distribution channels from 1990 onwards, it would have known that the likelihood of confusion with BDE's skiwear products "loom[ed] large." *Physical Therapy Ctr. v. Pro-Fit Orthopedic & Sports Physical Therapy*, 314 F.3d at 70. Accordingly, we conclude that no genuine issue of material fact exists regarding the existence of "a provable infringement claim" by the mid-1990s — and certainly well before October 15, 1997, the earliest date within the six-year analogous statute of limitations — and that a presumption in favor of laches therefore applies. *Conopco, Inc. v. Campbell Soup Co.*, 95 F.3d at 191. We further conclude that BDS failed to rebut this presumption, including the presumption of prejudice, and that the district court therefore properly relied on laches to dismiss BDS's claims.

2. BDE Did Not Act in Bad Faith

BDs also contends that the district court erred in applying laches because the record contains sufficient evidence to support a reasonable inference that BDE acted in bad faith. It is well established that a defendant must have "clean hands" to assert the equitable defense of laches. *Hermes Int'l v. Lederer de Paris Fifth Ave., Inc.*, 219 F.3d 104, 107 (2d cir. 2000); see *Precision Instrument Mfg. Co. v. Automotive Maintenance Mach. Co.*, 324 U.S. 806, 814, 65 S. Ct. 993, 89 L. Ed. 1381, 1945 Dec. Comm'r Pat. 582 (1945) (observing that "he who comes into equity must come with clean hands" (internal quotation marks omitted)). Although "[b]ad faith may be inferred from the junior user's actual or constructive knowledge of the senior user's mark," *Star Indus. v. Bacardi & Co. Ltd.*, 412 F.3d 373, 389 (2d Cir. 2005), a junior user's knowledge of the mark may still be consistent with good faith unless the evidence indicates "an intent to promote confusion or exploit good will or reputation," *id.* at 388.

As the district court correctly concluded, nothing in the record evidence supports a conclusion that BDE's selection of the Black Diamond mark related to BDS's use of the mark or that BDE ever "sought to pass off its products as those of BDS." Although the district court did not expressly address BDS's claim of reverse confusion, see id. at 388 n.3 (explaining that reverse confusion occurs where "the junior user is able to amass such trademark strength in its imitative mark that the senior user's products become associated with the junior user in the minds of consumers"), the record evidence does not support a reasonable inference that BDE intended to promote such confusion, for example, by flooding the market with its skiwear products and causing consumers to believe erroneously that BDS's goods were produced by BDE. *See Lang v. Retirement Living Publishing Co.*, 949 F.2d 576, 583 (2d Cir. 1991) (observing that "[r]everse confusion is the misimpression that the junior user is the source of the senior user's goods" (internal quotation marks omitted)); *see also Freedom Card, Inc. v. JPMorgan Chase & Co.*, 432 F.3d 463, 473 (3ᵈ Cir. 2005) ("The offender in a reverse confusion case will typically exploit confusion to push the senior user out of the market."). Accordingly, we conclude that the district court properly determined at summary judgment that BDE did not act in bad faith and that BDS's claims were barred by laches.

B. The District Court Correctly Denied Injunctive Relief

BDS contends that, even if laches bars its claim for monetary damages, the district court should still have granted its request for injunctive relief. We have recognized that, even where laches is a valid defense to damages, "a court may nonetheless grant injunctive relief if it determines that the likelihood of confusion is so great that it outweighs the effect of plaintiff's delay in bringing suit." *ProFitness Physical Therapy Ctr. v. Pro-Fit Orthopedic & Sports Physical Therapy*, 314 F.3d at 68. The purpose of this exception to laches "is to vindicate the public interest in avoiding inevitable confusion in the marketplace." *SunAmerica Corp. v. Sun Life Assurance Co.*, 77 F.3d 1325, 1334-36 (11ᵗʰ Cir. 1996). We have noted that "the public's interest is especially significant when health and safety concerns are implicated." *Conopco, Inc. v. Campbell Soup Co.*, 95 F.3d at 194. That is not this case.

Although BDS's CEO testified that consumers have mistaken BDS for BDE numerous times at numerous retail trade shows, these instances involved customers' confusion about the existence of two companies called Black Diamond, rather than confusion about "mistaken purchasing decisions." *Lang v. Retirement Living Publishing Co.*, 949 F.2d at 583 (noting that "trademark infringement protects only against mistaken purchasing decisions and not against confusion generally" (internal quotation marks omitted). The only other evidence of confusion in the record is the CEO's testimony that BDS received a pair of "Scarpa hiking boots" from a consumer who was trying to return the merchandise to BDE. Given that BDE and BDS have both been selling skiwear for seventeen years, this isolated incident of postsale confusion, coupled with the lack of any record evidence suggesting a high likelihood of confusion or the existence of a compelling public interest, is clearly insufficient to override the defense of laches so as to mandate injunctive relief in this case.

* * *

AFFIRMED.

SUNAMERICA CORP. V. SUN LIFE ASSURANCE CO. OF CANADA
890 F. Supp. 1559 (N.D. Ga. 1994)

Camp, J.

Plaintiffs are an American holding company, SunAmerica, Inc. ["SunAmerica"] and its wholly-owned subsidiary, Sun Life Insurance Company of America ["Sun Life of America" or "SLA"]. Defendants are a Canadian mutual life insurance company, Sun Life Assurance Company of Canada ["Sun Life of Canada" or "SLC"] and its wholly-owned U.S. subsidiary, Sun Life Assurance Company of Canada (U.S.). Both parties presently are in the business of selling annuity products to American consumers. Both Plaintiffs and Defendants have used the service mark "Sun Life" alone or in combination with geographic modifiers and other descriptive terms for over seventy-five years.

* * *

Evidence presented at trial showed conclusively that actual confusion between the various "Sun Life" marks is a common occurrence. Confused customers regularly call the wrong company for annuity information, or mail checks and applications to the wrong address several times each week. Poorly identified "Sun Life" advertisements create buyer interest in the competing company's product. A customer consents to a sales appointment, confusing the calling company's identity with its competitor. Confusion exists when salespeople fail to attend a seminar because they misidentify the issuer of the product; when newspapers confuse the names of the parties in reporting financial events; and when registered brokers routinely must be told which company a product manager does not represent.

Consistent with the abundance of anecdotal evidence, the parties' joint survey reveals a remarkable amount of actual confusion among those professional salespeople most likely to understand important product and issuer distinctions. Both parties agree that 57% of SLC brokers are definitely confused by the name "Sun Life of America," 59% of SLA brokers are confused by "Sun Life (U.S.)," and 35% of SLA brokers are confused by "Sun Life of Canada." Having examined the totality of the circumstances surrounding the time and type of trademark usage, the Court finds overwhelming evidence that actual confusion exists among the disputed "Sun Life" marks. *See Jellibeans,* 716 F.2d at 844.

. . .Weighing the evidence of actual confusion most heavily, the Court concludes that the parties' "Sun Life" marks are highly similar and that there is a substantial likelihood of confusion even when the companies' full names are used.

* * *

The Court finds that Sun Life of Canada is the senior user of the "Sun Life" marks, having continuously used "Sun Life of Canada" in the United States since 1895 and the "Sun Life" abbreviation at least since 1914. In addition, its commercial success after entering the United States indicates that SLC achieved secondary meaning in the "Sun Life of Canada" and "Sun Life" marks prior to Plaintiffs' adoption of its "Sun Life Insurance Company of America" name in 1916. Accordingly, Defendants have a protectable property interest in their "Sun Life" marks. *See Investacorp,* 931 F.2d at 1522 (if a mark is not inherently distinctive, a company obtains rights when the mark attains secondary meaning). *See also* 1 McCarthy § 16.12.

* * *

In response to Defendants' Lanham Act claim, SLA asserts the affirmative defense of acquiescence. In essence, Sun Life of America argues that SLC knew of and affirmatively consented to SLA's use of the "Sun Life of America" and "Sun Life Insurance Company of America" service marks. The Court agrees.

 "Acquiescence" is an equitable defense denoting active consent by the trademark owner to another use of the mark. If acquiescence is proven, the trademark owner is estopped from asserting dormant rights against an infringer. *See Coach House Restaurant, Inc. v. Coach and Six Restaurants, Inc.,* 934 F.2d 1551, 1558 (11th Cir. 1991). The acquiescence defense requires proof of three elements:

(1)   that the owner actively represented it would not assert a right or claim;
(2)   that the delay between the representation and the assertion of the right or claim was not excusable; and
(3)   that the delay caused the alleged infringer undue prejudice. *Id.* In this case, the facts show that Sun Life of Canada acquiesced to Plaintiffs' use of the allegedly infringing marks [over a period of more than sixty years].

(1)   *Affirmative Representations*

Evidence produced at trial establishes that SLC affirmatively consented to SLA's use of "Sun Life of America" through at least 1980. Nor do Defendants contest this first element of acquiescence.

* * *

While it is true that the senior user of a mark has no obligation to sue until "the likelihood of [public] confusion looms large," Defendants' Proposed Conclusions of Law

[#178], ¶ 13 (quoting *3 McCarthy* § 31.06 [2][a]), Sun Life of Canada recognized early and complained frequently about the increasing levels of public confusion caused by the similarity in names. The Court concludes from the evidence that Sun Life of Canada's delay in asserting its trademark rights through a counterclaim filed in 1989 is not excusable.

(3) *Undue Prejudice*

The third element of the acquiescence defense requires proof that Sun Life of America would suffer undue prejudice from Defendants' inexcusable delay in filing suit. Although this element presents a close question at this point in time, the Court is persuaded that SLA would lose some material amount of goodwill in its "Sun Life" name if it is forced to cease using the mark.

* * *

The Court has determined that Defendants have protectable property rights in their "Sun Life" marks; that Plaintiff's use of similar marks presents a likelihood of confusion; and that Defendants have acquiesced in Plaintiffs' use of the confusingly similar marks. As earlier noted, acquiescence will estop Sun Life of Canada from extinguishing Sun Life of America's use of its mark unless there is an inevitability of confusion. *SunAmerica Corp. v. Sun Life Assurance Co. of Canada*, 24 U.S.P.Q.2d 1505, 1510 (11th Cir. 1992). The Eleventh Circuit recently explained:

> Although petitioner has acquiesced in use of their logo by the registrant, the public interest in preventing confusion around the marketplace is paramount to any inequity caused the registrant. Consequently, if there is an inevitability of confusion, petitioner's law suit may be revived from estoppel.

Coach House Restaurant, Inc. v. Coach and Six Restaurants, Inc., 934 F.2d 1551, 1564 (11th Cir. 1991) (citing *Iodent Chem. Co. v. Dart Drug Corp.*, 207 U.S.P.Q. 602 (T.T.A.B. 1980)). Thus, even if a junior user establishes the equitable defense of acquiescence, the prior user will not be estopped to assert trademark rights "if the identity of the marks and goods of the parties are such that confusion or mistake in trade is inevitable." *Iodent*, 207 U.S.P.Q. at 606.

The standard for finding an inevitability of confusion is "an increment higher" than the standard for finding a likelihood of confusion. *Coach House*, 934 F.2d at 1564. In the present case, that additional increment is easily satisfied by the abundance of evidence provided by witnesses and by the proof of actual confusion found in the results of the joint survey.

Although by no means the only proof of confusion, the survey results provide a quantitative assessment of a "definitely confused" market even when the companies' full names are used. Courts have been willing to tolerate low levels of consumer confusion, but levels falling within the 25% to 50% range are viewed as excessive. *See generally 3 McCarthy* § 32.54 [1] [c] (citing cases). In this case, definite confusion ranged from 15% to 35% on average among brokers representing both companies, exceeded 60% among SLC's brokers asked about the American company, and averaged between 28% and 59% of SLA's registered representatives questioned about the Canadian entities. Moreover, the survey's measure of definite confusion understates the true amount of broker confusion, since it excludes those respondents who were "probably" and "possibly" confused.

In a more qualitative sense, the Court is acutely aware that annuity investments are often of critical importance to the people who make them, representing as they do the expectations of a secure retirement income derived from the proceeds of one's life savings. Consequently, the fact that even 15% to 20% of those making such an investment decision are definitely confused about the identity of the issuer is far less tolerable than if the same consumer were buying a household cleanser or a restaurant meal.

In light of these considerations, the Court concludes that the undisputed levels of definite confusion proven by the joint survey, together with other evidence of actual confusion as described above, establish inevitability of confusion even when the litigants use their full company names. Consequently, geographic modifiers will not cure the problem. Given the close similarity in service marks and the virtual identity of the parties' products, channels of trade, customers base, and advertising media, the public interest becomes the Court's dominant consideration. *See The Ultra-White Co. v. Johnson Chem. Indus., Inc.,* 465 F.2d 891, 893–94 (C.C.P.A. 1972). In this instance, the public interest in preventing intolerable confusion in the marketplace requires the revival of Defendants' prior trademark rights. Accordingly, Defendants are entitled to an injunction barring Plaintiffs' continued use of a "Sun Life" mark.

* * *

So Ordered.

Notes on Laches and Acquiescence

1. Effect of Laches

Laches may, and usually does, bar monetary relief, but generally it will not preclude injunctive relief against the continuing tort in trade identity cases. *See Menendez v. Holt,* 128 U.S. 514 (1888); *McLean v. Fleming,* 96 U.S. 245, 251 (1878). In *James Burrough Ltd. v. Sign of the Beefeater, Inc.,* 572 F.2d 574 (7th Cir. 1978), the court held that, upon a showing of laches, plaintiff may lose the right to recover past damages but may be entitled to injunctive relief and post-filing damages. To the same effect are *Herman Miller, Inc. v. Palazzetti Imports and Exports, Inc.,* 270 F.3d 298 (6th Cir. 2001) (plaintiff's laches barred pre-filing damages but not injunctive relief and post-filing damages), and *Ramada Inns, Inc. v. Apple,* 208 U.S.P.Q. 371 (D.S.C. 1980) (same). In *Houston Sports Assn., Inc. v. Astro-Card Co.,* 520 F. Supp. 1178 (S.D. Tex. 1981), the court ruled that establishing laches will only bar plaintiff from recovering past damages, and establishing *estoppel,* which requires a showing of intentional deception or gross negligence, will bar recovery of post-filing damages and injunctive relief as well. *See also Skippy, Inc. v. CPC International, Inc.,* 674 F.2d 209 (4th Cir. 1982), in which the court stated that if defendant has acted in bad faith, laches may not bar injunctive relief but will bar plaintiff's damages claim, and *University of Pittsburgh v. Champion Products, Inc.,* 686 F.2d 1040, 1044 (3[d] Cir. 1982), *cert. denied,* 459 U.S. 1088 (1982), in which the court stated that barring a claim for past damages but allowing injunctive relief is "much more common" than "that narrow class of cases where plaintiff's delay has been so outrageous, unreasonable and inexcusable as to constitute a virtual abandonment of its right."

Given the public interest in the elimination of confusion as to product source, should injunctive relief *never* be barred by a demonstration of laches? Senior users generally have not been successful in propounding such a rule. *See Prudential Insurance Co. v. Gibraltar Financial Corp.,* 694 F.2d 1150, 1152 (9th Cir. 1982); *Saratoga Vichy Spring Co., Inc. v. Lehman,* 625 F.2d 1037 (2[d] Cir. 1980). *Compare Underwriters Laboratories v. United Laboratories,* 203 U.S.P.Q. 180, 183 (N.D. Ill. 1978), in which the court stated, "application of the defense of laches to these circumstances would ignore the paramount objective of the law of trademark infringement and unfair competition which is protection of the public interest."

What if a party delays 20 or 30 years? *See Hot Wax, Inc. v. Turtle Wax, Inc.,* 191 F.3d 813 (7th Cir. 1999) (affirming summary judgment for defendant based on plaintiff's unexcused 20 year delay); *Exxon Corp. v. Oxxford Clothes Inc.,* 109 F.3d 1070, 1080–83 (5th Cir. 1997) (barring plaintiff's dilution claim under Texas law due to twenty-two year delay); *Prudential Insurance, supra,* (28-year delay constituted laches which barred all relief); *Skippy, Inc., supra,* (30-year delay barred damages recovery; injunctive relief denied on other grounds). Should it make a difference whether the products are non-competitive? *See James Burrough, supra; Polaroid Corp. v. Polarad Electronics Corp.*, 287 F.2d 492 (2ᵈ Cir. 1961).

In view of the public interest in avoiding consumer confusion, some courts have declined to bar an injunction based on laches or acquiescence where confusion is "inevitable". *See SunAmerica Corp. v. Sun Life Assurance Co. of Canada, supra; TMT N. Am., Inc. v. Magic Touch GmbH*, 124 F.3d 876 (7ᵗʰ Cir. 1997) (unless inevitable confusion could be demonstrated, acquiescence precluded preliminary relief). *Compare Resorts of Pinehurst, Inc. v. Pinehurst Nat'l Corp.*, 148 F.3d 417 (4ᵗʰ Cir. 1998) ("Resorts' strong proof of likelihood of confusion — indeed, actual confusion — trumps the defense of laches and acquiescence"). In *Tillamook Country Smoker v. Tillamook County Creamery Ass'n*, 465 F.3d 1102 (9ᵗʰ Cir. 2006), the Ninth Circuit suggested that the public interest in avoiding inevitable confusion should only "trump" or "override" laches in cases where the product allegedly was harmful or threatened the public's safety or well being. It nonetheless rejected application of the doctrine in that particular case because the complainant had contributed to the confusion problem by offering the other party's products in its "catalog, store and website."

The Trademark Trial and Appeal Board traditionally has considered "evidence of laches, estoppel, or acquiescence as a factor in determining the issue of likelihood of confusion or mistake or deception only if there is a reasonable doubt that such a likelihood exists." *White Heather Distillers Ltd. v. American Distilling Co.*, 200 U.S.P.Q. 466, 469 (T.T.A.B. 1978). *Accord CBS, Inc. v. Man's Day Publishing Co.*, 205 U.S.P.Q. 470, 475 (T.T.A.B. 1980); *Richdel, Inc. v. Mathews Co.*, 190 U.S.P.Q. 37, 41 (T.T.A.B. 1976). *Compare*, however, *Bridgestone/Firestone Research, Inc. v. Automobile Club*, 245 F.3d 1359 (Fed. Cir. 2001). There the French auto club responsible for the Le Mans car race petitoned to cancel Bridgestone/Firestone's registration of LE MANS for tires under § 2(a) of the Lanham Act, for falsely suggesting a connection with the auto club and the club's sponsorship of that race — but did so 27 years after the registration issued. The uncontroverted evidence of undue delay and economic prejudice to Bridgestone/Firestone resulted in laches barring the auto club's petition. According to the court, laches may be applied in § 2(a) cases unless there is "misrepresentation or deceit," and here there was evidence of neither.

Should laches and acquiescence begin to run when the opposer or cancellation petitioner first had knowledge of the alleged infringer's *use* of the mark, or knowledge of its attempt to obtain a registration? The Federal Circuit has held that laches in registration proceedings begin to run from the time of awareness of the *application to register* the mark, since that is the point at which a party begins to acquire rights to which an objection in the Patent and Trademark Office could be made. *National Cable Television Ass'n v. America Cinema Editors, Inc.*, 937 F.2d 1572, 1581 (Fed. Cir. 1991). *See also Bridgestone/Firestone v. Automobile Club ,supra* (same). That may be true for acquiescence as well. *Cf. Coach House Restaurant v. Coach & Six Restaurants, Inc.*, 934 F.2d 1551 (11ᵗʰ Cir. 1991) (distinguishing between acquiescence to use and acquiescence to registration).

2.   Elements of Laches

The basic elements of laches are: (1) that plaintiff had actual or constructive knowledge of defendant's use of its mark; (2) that plaintiff inexcusably delayed in taking action with respect thereto; and (3) that defendant detrimentally relied upon plaintiff's inaction or otherwise would be inequitably prejudiced were plaintiff permitted to assert its rights at the time of filing suit. *See Cuban Cigar Brands N.V. v. Upmann Int'l, Inc.* 457 F.Supp. 90, 98 (S.D.N.Y. 1978) , *aff'd* 607 F.2d 995 (2ᵈ Cir. 1979).

Knowledge

There has been some debate as to the proper standard by which to assess the first element of knowledge. *Compare Nartron Corp. v. STMicroelectronics, Inc.* 305 F.3d 397 409 (6th Cir. 2002) ("defendant unreasonably delayed after it knew or should have known of the alleged infringement") and *Armco, Inc. v. Armco Burglar Alarm Co., Inc.*, 693 F.2d 1155, 1161 (5th Cir. 1982) ("'knew or should have known' is a logical implementation of the duty to police one's mark") with *Georgia-Pacific Corp. v. Great Plains Bag Co.*, 614 F.2d 757 (C.C.P.A. 1980) (actual knowledge of the trademark use must be shown). In *Jarrow Formulas, Inc. v. Nutrition Now, Inc.*, 304 F.3d 829 (9th Cir. 2002) the Ninth Circuit stated that "knew or *should* have known" is the proper standard: "laches penalizes inexcusable dilatory behavior . . . if the plaintiff legitimately was unaware of the defendant's conduct, laches is no bar to suit."

"Knowledge" may be derived from the constructive notice of another party's actions. For example, a corporation may have imputed to it the knowledge of lower echelon employees. In *Georgia-Pacific, supra*, the court found that while knowledge of mark usage gained by bookkeepers and dock workers would not be so imputed, the knowledge of professional salespersons would be, since they were present in the marketplace and cognizant of sales factors, which included the protection of goodwill. *Cf. Plasticolor Molded Products v. Ford Motor Co.*, 698 F. Supp. 199, 202–03 (C.D. Cal. 1988) (ten years of infringement by licensee but no evidence of licensor knowledge), *summ. judgment granted in part and denied in part*, 713 F. Supp. 1329 (C.D. Cal. 1989), *vacated pursuant to settlement*, 767 F. Supp. 1036 (C.D. Cal. 1991).

In *Chattanoga Mfg., Inc. v. Nike, Inc.*, 301 F.3d 789 (7th Cir. 2002), plaintiff asserted rights in JORDAN for women's clothing against Nike's sale of "Jordan" clothing endorsed by Michael Jordan. Plaintiff was attributed with constructive knowledge at least nine years before the lawsuit, given the prominence of Nike's massive ad campaign and the media's admitted frequent reference to "Jordan products". "The law is well-settled that . . . the plaintiff is chargeable with such knowledge as he may have obtained upon inquiry, provided the facts already known by him were such as to put a man of ordinary intelligence on inquiry." *Compare Ford Motor Co. v. Catalanotte*, 342 F.3d 543 (6th Cir. 2003), in which defendant's 1997 registration of the domain name fordworld.com ("Ford World" was the name of Ford's employee newspaper) was not the date that began the "delay" period; that period instead began in 2000 when defendant first offered to sell Ford the domain name, while falsely claiming he had received several other offers for it. This shorter period did not constitute laches.

Should a successor in rights to a mark be charged with the knowledge possessed by his predecessor? *Charvet S.A. v. Dominique France, Inc.*, 568 F. Supp. 470 (S.D.N.Y. 1983), *aff'd*, 736 F.2d 846 (2[d] Cir. 1984). What effect should the constructive notice provision of the Lanham Act have on the issue of laches when the defendant's mark has been registered under the Act? *Compare Carter-Wallace, Inc. v. Procter & Gamble Co.*, 434 F.2d 794 (9th Cir. 1970) *with Valmor Prods. Co. v. Standard Prods. Corp.*, 464 F.2d 200 (1st Cir. 1972). *See also E-Systems, Inc. v. Monitek, Inc.*, 720 F.2d 604 (9th Cir. 1983), in which plaintiff had constructive notice of the claim of ownership when defendant registered its trademark, but delayed six years in filing suit. *Compare Beauty Time, Inc. v. VU Skin Systems*, 118 F.3d 140 (3[d] Cir. 1997) (vacating dismissal based on laches where filing of registration maintenance affidavits did not constitute constructive notice under 15 U.S.C. § 1072 and no actual knowledge shown).

Inexcusable Delay

Almost any length of time can constitute inexcusable delay, depending upon the circumstances and the resultant prejudice to the defendant. A mere lapse of time alone will not normally constitute laches, *Jordan K. Rand, Ltd. v. Lazoff Bros., Inc.*, 537 F. Supp. 587, 594 (D.P.R. 1982); *Hank Thorp, Inc. v. Minilite, Inc.*, 474 F. Supp. 228, 239 (D. Del. 1979); *Johanna Farms, Inc. v. Citrus Bowl, Inc.*, 199 U.S.P.Q. 16, 28 (E.D.N.Y.

1978); *Cuban Cigar Brands, supra* . The other elements must be present.

What could constitute *excusable* delay? *See Piper Aircraft Corp. v. Way-Aero, Inc.*, 741 F.2d 925, 932 (7th Cir. 1984) (settlement attempts); *Nabisco Brands Inc. v. Conusa Corp.*, 722 F. Supp. 1287, 1292 (M.D.N.C.) ("'laches should not necessarily always be measured from defendant's very first use of the contested mark, but from the date that defendant's acts first significantly impacted on plaintiff's goodwill and business reputation") (quoting McCarthy, Trademarks and Unfair Competition § 31.6 at 570), *aff'd*, 14 U.S.P.Q.2d 1324 (4th Cir. 1989); *Coco Rico, Inc. v. Fuertes Pasarell*, 738 F. Supp. 613, 619 (D.P.R. 1990) (no laches where plaintiff sued defendants as soon as defendants' use made an impact on plaintiff's sales); *Varitronics Systems, Inc. v. Merlin Equipment, Inc.*, 682 F. Supp. 1203, 1209 (S.D. Fla. 1988) (delay due to negotiations to avoid litigation did not constitute laches); *Gaston's White River Resort v. Rush*, 701 F. Supp. 1431, 1436 (W.D. Ark. 1988) (inactivity by owner's previous attorneys and delay due to seasonal nature of the business did not constitute laches); *Aluminum Fabricating Co. v. Season-All Window Corp.*, 160 F. Supp. 41 (S.D.N.Y. 1957), *aff'd*, 259 F.2d 314 (2[d] Cir. 1958) (absence of competition between the parties at the time of knowledge of use); *Haviland & Co. v. Johann Haviland China Corp.*, 269 F. Supp. 928 (S.D.N.Y. 1967) (de minimis sales by defendant).

A plaintiff normally is entitled to delay suit until a defendant's activities create a significant likelihood of confusion. *Kason Industries, Inc. v. Component Hardware Group, Inc.*, (11th Cir. 1997) ("delay is to be measured from the time at which the plaintiff knows or should know she has a provable claim for infringement . . . The senior user has no obligation to sue until 'the likelihood of confusion looms large' ", quoting McCarthy, Trademarks and Unfair Competition, § 31.19 (4th Ed. 2007)); *Sara Lee Corp. v. Kayser-Roth Corp.*, 81 F.3d 455, 462 (4th Cir. 1996) (application of laches defense was error where plaintiff "chose to delay its pursuit of a remedy until its right to protection had clearly ripened"). "To rebut a presumption of laches in a trademark case, a plaintiff generally must show that a defendant has made recent inroads on plaintiff's interests, such as entering the plaintiff's geographic market . . . altering a product to make it more similar to the plaintiff's, . . . or extending the mark to goods and services that more directly compete with the plaintiff's." *Solow Bldg. Co. LLC v. Nine West Group, Inc.*, 48 Fed. Appx. 15 (2[d] Cir. 2002). *See also Santana Prods v. Bobrick Washroom Equip., Inc.*, 401 F.3d 123 (3[d] Cir. 2005) (to rebut presumption from analogous state statute of limitations, plaintiff had to show both excusable delay and a lack of prejudice to defendant), and the discussion on progressive encroachment in Chapter 6. *See also Tillamook Country Smoker v. Tillamook County Creamery Ass'n*, 465 F.3d 1102 (9th Cir. 2006) ("[c]ommon methods of encroachment [that defeat a claim of laches] are the junior user's expansion of its business into different regions or into different markets") and the discussion on progressive encroachment in Chapter 5, *supra.*

In *NAACP v. NAACP Legal Defense Fund*, 559 F. Supp. 1337 (D.D.C. 1983), the court found that the history of the parties' relationship, the fact that plaintiff never misled defendant as to its objections to the trademark use, and plaintiff's understandable unwillingness to initiate a divisive lawsuit all made the delay excusable. The appellate court reversed, finding that thirteen years of concurrent use without any ongoing settlement negotiations constituted laches, barring plaintiff's suit. *NAACP v. NAACP Legal Defense Fund*, 753 F.2d 131 (D.C. Cir.1985). Similarly, in *Hot Wax, Inc. v. Turtle Wax, Inc.*, 191 F.3d 813 (7th Cir. 1999), a "sparse letter writing campaign" for two years in the 1990s did not excuse delay from the late 1970s, and summary judgment for defendant was affirmed. *Compare Saratoga Vichy Spring Co., Inc. v. Lehman*, 625 F.2d 1037 (2[d] Cir. 1980), in which the court found that, despite the fact that the mark was not being used by defendant's predecessor during the period of delay, plaintiff knew the mark was in the process of being revived and should have given warning of any objections, and *Charvet, S.A.*, 568 F .Supp. 470 (S.D.N.Y. 1983), *aff'd* 736 F.2d 846 (2[d] Cir. 1984), in which the court stated that "it is fatuous to suggest that year in and year out desultory conversations, some occurring during chance meetings, which achieve no result and with each party adhering to its position, excuses [sic] delay."

Some federal courts invoke "analogous" state statutes of limitations to raise a presumption of laches as was done in *Black Diamond Sportswear*, excerpted above. . In *Tandy Corp. v. Malone & Hyde, Inc.*, 769 F.2d 362 (6th Cir. 1985), the court determined that the analogous statute of limitations raised a presumption that "an action is barred if not brought within the period of the statute of limitations and is alive if brought within the period." 768 F.2d at 365. Applying the three-year Tennessee statute for "tortious injury to property," it then reversed the lower court's denial of all relief based on laches, finding plaintiff's "32-month delay may be evidence of corporate indecision but it is not so unreasonable as to overcome the presumption afforded by the analogous 3-year statute." 769 F.2d at 366. *See also Conopco Inc. v. Campbell Soup Co.*, 95 F.3d 187 (2d Cir. 1996) (barring plaintiff's false advertising claim due to laches although claim was not *presumptively* barred by laches because it was brought within the six year limit established by the "analogous" New York fraud statute).

In *Jarrow Formulas, Inc. v. Nutrition Now, Inc.* 304 F.3d 829 (9th Cir. 2002), a seven year unexcused delay, more than twice the three year period of the analogous California statute of limitations, combined with severe prejudice, constituted laches barring all relief. The court held that "the presumption of laches is triggered if any part of the claimed wrongful conduct occurred beyond the limitations period. To hold otherwise would effectively swallow the rule of laches and render it a spineless defense."*Compare Lyons P'Ship L.P. v. Morris Costumes, Inc.*, 243 F.3d 789, 797 (4th Cir. 2001) ("Although the district court was correct to hold that [plaintiff]could not recover for claims that accrued outside the limitations period, it erred to the extent that it dismissed [plaintiff's Lanham Act] claims that were premised upon acts that occurred within the applicable period"). *See also Chattanoga Mfg., Inc. v. Nike, Inc.*, 301 F.3d 789 (7th Cir. 2002) (three year statute of limitations; at least nine year inexcusable delay combined with severe prejudice barred all relief); *Herman Miller, Inc. v. Palazzetti Imports and Exports*, 270 F.3d 298 (6th Cir. 2001) (plaintiff never rebutted presumption of laches raised by Michigan statute of limitations, and district court properly granted summary judgment barring plaintiff from obtaining pre-filing damages). In *Island Steel Systems, Inc. v. Waters*, 296 F.3d 200 (3d Cir. 2002), the court affirmed that the Virgin Islands' two year statute of limitations for deceptive trade practices was applicable, and that the statutory period "begins running from the date the violation occurred, not the date the violation was discovered, as would be the case under the statute of limitations for fraud."

Is there anything wrong with the analogous statute of limitations approach? In *Hot Wax, Inc. v. Turtle Wax, Inc.*, *supra*, the court explained that "courts have used this analogous limitations period as a baseline for determining whether a presumption of laches exists,', but that a statute of limitations cannot the sole factor, because Lanham Act cases typically present a "continuing wrong" by the defendant. The court observed, "[u]nder the notion of a continuing wrong, 'only the last infringing act need be within the statutory period', [citation]. Without the availability of the application of laches to a claim arising from a continuing wrong, a party could, theoretically, delay filing suit indefinitely." This reasoning was approvingly cited in *Bridgestone/Firestone Research, Inc. v. Automobile Club*, 245 F.3d 1359, 1364 (Fed. Cir. 2001), in which the court held a 27-year delay causing economic prejudice constituted laches barring the action, despite petitioner's assertion of a "continuing wrong." *Cf. Blue Cross & Blue Shield Assn. v. Group Hospitalization & Medical Services, Inc.*, 744 F. Supp. 700, 717 (E.D. Va.) (Lanham Act claims not barred by the applicable Illinois statute of limitations, since defendant's unlawful conduct was ongoing), *aff'd in part and remanded in part*, 911 F.2d 720 (4th Cir. 1990).

Detrimental Reliance or Other Prejudice

A showing of detrimental reliance or other inequitable prejudice experienced by the party asserting the defense of laches is the final requirement. In *Conopco, supra*, the Second Circuit affirmed that detrimental reliance was shown by defendant's commitment of "massive resources" to its advertising campaign, and the commercial impossibility of adopting an alternative marketing position after plaintiff delayed five years before commencing a false advertising suit. To similar effect is *Hot Wax, Inc. v. Turtle Wax, Inc., supra*, where defendant had "invested significant amounts of time and money in product development and advertising" in establishing its market position, constituting detrimental reliance on plaintiff's unexcused delay. Detrimental reliance also was successfully demonstrated in *Chattanoga Mfg., Inc. v. Nike, Inc.*, 301 F.3d 789 (7th Cir. 2002) ("Nike has spent millions of dollars annually promoting its Michael Jordan-endorsed products and has acquired a position as a market leader. Had Chattanoga challenged Nike's use of the term Jordan in a timely manner and prevailed, Nike could have promoted its products in a number of different ways") and *Jarrow Formulas, Inc. v. Nutrition Now, Inc.*, 304 F.3d 829 (9th Cir. 2002) (defendant "has invested enormous resources in tying [the product's] identity to the challenged claims . . . If [plaintiff] had filed suit sooner, [defendant] could have invested its resources in shaping an alternative identity").

The purchasing of parts and equipment to enable the expansion of business and the incurrence of additional potential liability during the period of delay were enough in *Whitaker Corp. v. Execuair Corp.*, 736 F.2d 1341, 1347 (9th Cir. 1984), but expanded use of the allegedly infringing mark was not enough in *Citibank N.A. v. Citibanc Group, Inc.*, 724 F.2d 1540, 1546–47 (11th Cir. 1984); the defendants in *Citibank* were held not to have relied on plaintiff's delay where the expansion was "in the face of plaintiff's constant complaints." *See also American International Group, Inc. v. American International Bank*, 926 F.2d 829, 833 (9th Cir. 1991) (defendant failed to show injury or prejudice). In *Houston Sports Assn., supra* however, the court observed that a prolonged delay alone may give rise to a presumption of prejudice. One reason for this might be the law's dislike for stale claims; evidence favorable to the defendant may be expected to be lost or destroyed when prolonged delay occurs. In *Bridgestone/Firestone Research, Inc. v. Auto Club*, 245 F.3d 1359, 1363 (Fed. Cir. 2001), the court observed that "[t]wo general categories of prejudice may flow from an unreasonable delay: prejudice at trial due to loss of evidence or memory of witnesses, and economic prejudice based on loss of time or money or foregone opportunity." In that case, longstanding investment in and promotion of the brand, use on multiple products and widespread commercial use during the period of undue delay supported the finding of laches barring relief.

Are there any other factors which a court should consider in deciding whether laches constitutes a valid defense? *See Carl Zeis Stiftung v. V.E.B. Carl Zeiss, Jena*, 293 F. Supp. 892, 917 (S.D.N.Y. 1968), *aff'd*, 433 F.2d 686 (2[d] Cir. 1970) *cert. denied*, 403 U.S. 905 (1971), which lists the following among the relevant factors in the determination: (1) strength and value of the trademark rights asserted; (2) plaintiff's diligence in protecting the mark; (3) harm resulting to plaintiff if relief is denied; (4) good or bad faith of the infringer; (5) competitiveness of the uses of the mark; (6) extent of harm suffered by junior user because of the senior user's delay.

> Where the owner of the trademark fails to take any action for many years to enforce a relatively weak trademark against a junior user who has proceeded innocently to use the same or similar mark on non-competing goods in which he has invested large sums, so that denial of relief would cause relatively little harm to the senior user in contrast to the serious prejudice that would result to defendant, relief will be denied.

Id. at 917. *See also Conan Properties, Inc. v. Conans Pizza*, 752 F.2d 145, 152 (5th Cir. 1985) (laches barred relief only in Austin, Texas area). In *Grupo Gigante S.A. de C.V.*

Dallo Co., Inc., 119 F. Supp. 2d 1083 (C.D. Cal. 2000), the court found confusion likely between the parties' respective uses of the name Gigante for grocery stores in the San Diego area, but declined to award injunctive relief. Given the plaintiff's lack of diligence and the parties' co-existence for more than ten years, the court found "no threat of great harm to the plaintiffs if the status quo is maintained." It observed, however, that "[i]f the defendants at some later date change the nature or extent of their current exploitation of the Gigante name, the Court might be inclined to find that some form of injunctive relief would be appropriate." *Compare* Judge Posner's summarization in his concurrence in *Piper Aircraft*, *supra* 741 F.2d at 938: "The judge is supposed to balance the impact on the defendant of the plaintiff's delay against the reasonableness of the plaintiff's having waited as long as he did to sue and the strength of the plaintiff's case," *and* Professor McCarthy's statement that "Estoppel by laches = delay × prejudice."McCARTHY, TRADEMARKS AND UNFAIR COMPETITION § 31:12 at 31–34 (4th ed. 2007).

In *Patsy's Brand v. IOB Realty*, 317 F.3d 209, 217 (2ᵈ Cir. 2003), two unrelated New York City restaurants had co-existed under the name "Patsy's" for more than half a century. In 1994, plaintiff began selling "Patsy's Brand" pasta sauces nationally at retail and over the Internet, and obtained a federal registration in connection with sauces. Subsequently, defendants began selling pasta sauce under the mark PATSY'S with a label similar to plaintiff's. Defendants asserted they had superior rights to plaintiff because they used PATSY'S first for restaurant services, and pasta sauce was a related product. The appellate court disagreed because of defendants' laches:

> Where, as here, the senior use[r] has tolerated for decades the junior user's competition in the same market with a name similar to that of the senior user, the justification for preserving for the senior user use of a dominant component of its name in a related field vanishes entirely. In such circumstances, protection for use of the common feature of the two names in the related field belongs to the first entrant into that field. When a senior user delays in enforcing its rights, a junior user may acquire a valid trademark in a related field, enforceable against even the senior user.

A permanent injunction against the defendants, modified to permit only non-confusing, informational use of their name in small sized type, was affirmed.

3.   Effect of Bad Faith

Because laches is an equitable doctrine, bad faith infringement may preclude its application. *See, e.g., U.S. v. Milstein*, 401 F.3d 53, 64 (2ᵈ Cir. 2005) (equitable defenses like laches are not available in counterfeiting cases because willful infringement precludes their application; a contrary approach would lead to "absurd results"); *Kason Indus., Inc. v. Component Hardware Group, Inc.*, 120 F.3d 1199 (11ᵗʰ Cir. 1997) ("[g]enerally, laches will not bar an injunction against an intentional infringer"); *Black & Decker v. Pro-Tech Power, Inc.*, 26 F. Supp. 2d 834 (E.D. Va. 1998) (defendant's intentional copying of plaintiff's trade dress placed the equities in plaintiff's favor, defeating any laches claim defendant may have had). *Compare Jarrow Formulas, Inc. v. Nutrition Now, Inc.*, 304 F.3d 829 (9ᵗʰ Cir. 2002), in which, because of plaintiff's laches, the court affirmed the dismissal of its suit. The plaintiff claimed that laches should not apply because of defendant's allegedly inequitable and false advertising, which would be against the public interest. The court first observed that the public interest in accurate advertising "will trump laches only when the suit concerns allegations that the product is harmful or otherwise a threat to public safety and well-being", and "the critical question is whether consumer health will be materially affected." Otherwise, "laches in effect would not be a defense to Lanham Act false advertising claims." In rejecting plaintiff's contention, it stated, "[a] plaintiff can escape laches under the unclean hands doctrine only if the court is left with a firm conviction that the defendant acted with a fraudulent intent in making the challenged claims." The unclean hands doctrine is discussed further in the next section.

4. Effect of Delay on Preliminary Relief

Delay in assertion of rights also may result in denial of preliminary injunctive relief. In *Citibank, N.A. v. Citytrust*, 756 F.2d 273, 276 (2^d Cir. 1985), the court explained:

> Preliminary injunctions are generally granted under the theory that there is an urgent need for speedy action to protect the plaintiffs' rights. Delay in seeking enforcement of those rights, however, tends to indicate at least a reduced need for such drastic, speedy action. . . . Significant delay in applying for injunctive relief in a trademark case tends to neutralize any presumption that infringement alone will cause irreparable harm pending trial, and such delay alone may justify denial of a preliminary injunction.

The analysis of delay in the preliminary injunction context is different from that at trial. As the court observed in *Majorica S.A. v. R.H. Macy & Co.*, 762 F.2d 7 (2^d Cir. 1985):

> Lack of diligence, standing alone, is insufficient to support a claim of laches; the party asserting the claim also must establish that it was prejudiced by the delay. [Citation]. Lack of diligence, standing alone, may, however, preclude the granting of preliminary injunctive relief, because it goes primarily to the issue of irreparable harm rather than occasional prejudice.

Accord Tom Doherty Assocs. v. Saban Entertainment, 60 F.3d 27 (2^d Cir. 1995) ("A district court should consider delay in assessing irreparable harm"); *GTE Corp. v. Williams*, 731 F.2d 676 (10th Cir. 1984); *Chem-Trend Inc. v. McCarthy*, 780 F. Supp. 458, 462 (E.D. Mich. 1991) (describing plaintiff's failed attempt to prove irreparable harm in a delayed motion for preliminary injunctive relief as "trying to slam the door on the barn after the horses are long gone"). *Compare Ty, Inc. v. The Jones Group, Inc.*, 237 F.3d 891 (7th Cir. 2001) (while plaintiff's eight month delay raised questions about irreparable harm, defendant showed no negative effect on it from the delay, and defendant voluntarily assumed the risk when it decided to market "Beanie Racers" stuffed toys in the face of plaintiff's rights in "Beanie Babies"); *King v. Innovation Books*, 976 F.2d 824, (2^d Cir. 1992) (eight month delay did not undercut the sense of urgency or imminent threat where plaintiff repeatedly objected to use of his name in movie's title and had difficulty getting copy of movie from defendant; preliminary injunction granted). *See also* Edelman, *Delay in Filing Preliminary Injunction Motions: A Five Year Update*, 85 TRADEMARK REP. 1 (1995); Raskopf & Edelman, *Delay in Filing Preliminary Injunction Motions: How Long Is Too Long*, 80 TRADEMARK REP. 36 (1990).

5. Acquiescence

Acquiescence constitutes a ground for denial of relief where the plaintiff's conduct amounts to an express or implied assurance that the plaintiff will not assert trademark rights against the defendant. *See, e.g., SunAmerica Corp. v. Sun Life Assurance Co. of Canada, supra.* Acquiescence normally will only affect the prior user's rights as against the accused infringer, and will not work a forfeiture of the prior user's right to use the mark. *See, e.g., TMT North America, Inc. v. Magic Touch GmbH*, 124 F.3d 876 (7th Cir. 1997) (reversing district court's holding of forfeiture of rights due to acquiescence, and noting, "the legitimate coexisting interests of the parties in an acquiescence case counsels for minimizing the hardship on either party to the extent possible consistent with the public interest"). Laches imports a merely passive assent, while acquiescence implies active assent. For what was termed "a classic example of acquiescence," *see CBS, Inc. v. Man's Day Publishing Co.*, 205 U.S.P.Q. 470 (T.T.A.B. 1980). Could a court correctly imply acquiescence where the plaintiff remains silent with knowledge of defendant's actions for an extended period of time?

One party's extended acquiescence to another's use of a similar mark in the same market may put the two at parity in extending the mark to related markets, so that, regardless of original priority, the first entrant into the related product market may establish prior rights there. That is what happened in *Patsy's Brand, Inc. v. I.O.B. Realty, Inc.*, 317 F.3d 209 (2^d Cir. 2003). Although defendant was the first to open a restaurant in New York under a "Patsy's" name, after the parties' restaurants had co-existed in New York under their "Patsy's" names for decades, plaintiff was the first to establish rights in "Patsy's" in the related retail pasta market:

> Where, as here, the senior user has tolerated for decades the junior user's competition in the same market with a name similar to that of the senior user, the justification for preserving for the senior user of a dominant component of its name vanishes entirely. In such circumstances, protection for the use of the common feature of the two names in the related field belongs to the first entrant to that field.

In *Kellogg Co. v. Exxon Corp.*, 209 F.3d 562, 573–575 (6th Cir. 2000) both parties had used a cartoon tiger in marketing for many years, Kellogg for its Frosted Flakes cereal and Exxon to promote motor oil. In the 1980s Exxon began to phase out use of the tiger, only to change course in the 1990s, making the tiger's appearance more warm and friendly and beginning to use it to promote food, beverages and convenience stores. At that point Kellogg sued.

The district court entered summary judgment for Exxon based on Kellogg's acquiescence to Exxon's use since 1959, but the appellate court reversed. It reasoned that Kellogg never actively consented to Exxon's use of the cartoon tiger with respect to non-petroleum products, or otherwise engaged in affirmative conduct creating an estoppel for such products. To similar effect is *Westchester Media v. PRL USA Holdings, Inc.*, 214 F.3d 658, 668 (5th Cir. 2000) (there was no delay in objecting because the new Polo magazine was "an entirely new product and different from the old Polo magazine in most aspects").

Where substantial public confusion is demonstrated, the equitable doctrine may give way to the public interest in avoiding consumer deception, as discussed in the *SunAmerica Corp. v. Sun Life Assurance Co. of Canada*, decision excerpted above.

7.03 Unclean Hands

COCA-COLA CO. v. KOKE CO. OF AMERICA
254 U.S. 143 (1920)

HOLMES, J.

This is a bill in equity brought by the Coca-Cola Company to prevent the infringement of its trade-mark Coca-Cola and unfair competition with it in its business of making and selling the beverage for which the trade-mark is used. The District Court gave the plaintiff a decree. 235 Fed. Rep. 408. This was reversed by the Circuit Court of Appeals. 255 Fed. Rep. 894. Subsequently a writ of certiorari was granted by this Court. 250 U.S. 637.

It appears that after the plaintiff's predecessors in title had used the mark for some years it was registered under the Act of Congress of March 3, 1881, c. 138, 21 Stat. 502, and again under the Act of February 20, 1905, c. 592, 33 Stat. 724. Both the Courts below agree that subject to the one question to be considered the plaintiff has a right to equitable relief. Whatever may have been its original weakness, the mark for years has acquired a secondary significance and has indicated the plaintiff's product alone. It is found that defendant's mixture is made and sold in imitation of the plaintiff's and that the word Koke was chosen for the purpose of reaping the benefits of the advertising done by the plaintiff and of selling the imitation as and for the plaintiff's goods. The only obstacle found by the Circuit Court of Appeals in the way of continuing the injunction granted below was its opinion that the trade-mark in itself and the advertisements accompanying it made such fraudulent representations to the public that the plaintiff had lost its claim to any help from the Court. That is the question upon which the writ of certiorari was granted and the main one that we shall discuss.

Of course, a man is not to be protected in the use of a device the very purpose and effect of which is to swindle the public. But the defects of a plaintiff do not offer a very broad ground for allowing another to swindle him. The defense relied on here should be scrutinized with a critical eye. The main point is this: Before 1900 the beginning of the good will was more or less helped by the presence of cocaine, a drug that, like alcohol or caffein or opium, may be described as a deadly poison or as a valuable item of the pharmacopoea according to the rhetorical purposes in view. The amount seems to have been very small, but it may have been enough to begin a bad habit and after the Food and Drug Act of June 30, 1906, c. 3915, 34 Stat. 768, if not earlier, long before this suit was brought, it was eliminated from the plaintiff's compound. Coca leaves still are used, to be sure, but after they have been subjected to a drastic process that removes from them every characteristic substance except a little tannin and still less chlorophyl. The cola nut, at best, on its side furnishes but a very small portion of the caffein, which now is the only element that has appreciable effect. That comes mainly from other sources. It is argued that the continued use of the name imports a representation that has ceased to be true and that the representation is reinforced by a picture of coca leaves and cola nuts upon the label and by advertisements, which however were many years before this suit was brought, that the drink is an "ideal nerve tonic and stimulant," etc., and that thus the very thing sought to be protected is used as a fraud.

The argument does not satisfy us. We are dealing here with a popular drink not with a medicine, and although what has been said might suggest that its attraction lay in producing the expectation of a toxic effect the facts point to a different conclusion. Since 1900 the sales have increased at a very great rate corresponding to a like increase in advertising. The name now characterizes a beverage to be had at almost any soda fountain. It means a single thing coming from a single source, and well known to the community. It hardly would be too much to say that the drink characterizes the name as much as the name the drink. In other words Coca-Cola probably means to most persons the plaintiff's familiar product to be had everywhere rather than a compound of particular substances. Although the fact did not appear in *United States v. Coca Cola Co.*, 241 U.S. 265, 289, we see no reason to doubt that, as we have said, it has acquired a secondary meaning in which perhaps the product is more emphasized than the producer but to which the producer is entitled. The coca leaves and whatever of cola nut is employed may be used to justify the continuance of the name or they may affect the flavor as the plaintiff contends, but before this suit was brought the plaintiff had advertised to the public that it must not expect and would not find cocaine, and had eliminated everything tending to suggest cocaine effects except the name and the picture of the leaves and nuts, which probably conveyed little or nothing to most who saw it. It appears to us that it would be going too far to deny the plaintiff relief against a palpable fraud because possibly here and there an ignorant person might call for the drink with the hope for incipient cocaine intoxication. The plaintiff's position must be judged by the facts as they were when the suit was begun, not by the facts of a different condition and an earlier time.

The decree of the District Court restrains the defendant from using the word Dope. The plaintiff illustrated in a very striking way the fact that the word is one of the most featureless known even to the language of those who are incapable of discriminating speech. In some places it would be used to call for Coca-Cola. It equally would have been used to call for anything else having about it a faint aureole of poison. It does not suggest Coca-Cola by similarity and whatever objections there may be to its use, objections which the plaintiff equally makes to its application to Coca Cola, we see no ground on which the plaintiff can claim a personal right to exclude the defendant from using it.

The product including the coloring matter is free to all who can make it if no extrinsic deceiving element is present. The injunction should be modified also in this respect.

Decree reversed.

Decree of District Court modified and affirmed.

HÄAGEN-DAZS, INC. v. FRUSEN GLÄDJÉ LTD.
493 F. Supp. 73 (S.D.N.Y. 1980)

DUFFY, DISTRICT JUDGE

Successful commercial marketing has many rewards. Most important to the marketer are the financial rewards to be reaped. However, when a manufacturer develops a novel marketing approach — a commercial concept meeting with a receptive consumer — the concept is often imitated. This is precisely what occurred in the case at bar.

Plaintiff, Häagen-Dazs, Inc., is the producer of Häagen-Dazs ice cream. Häagen-Dazs has come to be known as a premium ice cream product. The defendants are the producers and distributors of Frusen Glädjé ice cream which, although a recent entrant into the ice cream market, is advertised as a premium ice cream product.

Plaintiff commenced the instant suit charging defendants with unfair competition in violation of the Lanham Act, 15 U.S.C. § 1125(a), and New York State Law. In addition, plaintiff charges that defendants are attempting to palm their product off as that of the plaintiff.

The essence of plaintiff's claim is that defendants have packaged their product in such a way as to "cash in on the commercial magnetism of the exclusive marketing technique developed . . . by the family which owns and operates Häagen-Dazs." Plaintiff's Memorandum at 2. In particular, plaintiff focuses upon five features on defendants' ice cream container which it charges were taken directly from its ice cream container in an effort to appeal to Häagen-Dazs customers and confuse them into believing that defendants' product is related to the Häagen-Dazs line. These features are: (i) the phraseology used in reciting the ingredients of the product in issue; (ii) a recitation of the artificial ingredients not contained in the product; (iii) the manner in which the product is to be eaten in order to enhance its flavor; (iv) a two-word germanic-sounding name having an umlaut over the letter "a" [ä]; and, (v) a map of Scandinavia.

Plaintiff concludes that defendants have intentionally packaged their product in a manner calculated to trade upon "plaintiff's unique Scandinavian marketing theme." Transcript at 4–5.

Plaintiff has now moved for a preliminary injunction to prevent defendants' continued use of the allegedly infringing container. . . .

* * *

There is no question that the names in issue, Häagen-Dazs and Frusen Glädjé, are clearly distinguishable. It is true that both names contain two words to identify an ice cream product, but so do the names "Louis Sherry" and "Dolly Madison." Plaintiff cannot hope to base its claim of infringement upon such a fortuitous similarity. It is also true that the names in issue seem to be of Swedish origin and, as is appropriate in that language, an umlaut appears over the letter "a". This, however, is a matter of grammar and not a basis upon which a claim of infringement may hinge.

This suit is grounded in plaintiff's failure to appreciate the difference between an attempt to trade off the good will of another and the legitimate imitation of an admittedly effective marketing technique. In fact, plaintiff attempts by this law suit to significantly broaden its protected "trademark" to include its so-called "unique Scandinavian marketing theme." To do so, however, would work a grave injustice not only upon the defendants in this case, but also upon late entrants into a given product market. For example, when consumers became increasingly aware of the ingredients in food products, producers rushed to extoll the virtues of their "all natural" products. It would be ludicrous, however, to suggest that in our free enterprise system, one producer and not another is permitted to take advantage of the "all natural" marketing approach to enhance consumer reception of its product.

* * *

I turn finally to consider plaintiff's allegations that defendants' container is intended to deceive the public into believing that their product is made and/or sold in Sweden. In particular, plaintiff charges:

> defendants claim their ice cream is manufactured "under the authority" of a Swedish corporation, although Frusen Glädjé is produced in Pennsylvania by an American company and is not sold in Sweden at all; defendants fail to reveal the actual manufacturer, packer or distributor, all of which are American companies, which violates the applicable statutory labelling requirements; defendants also employ three lines of Swedish language on their container to add to the false impression that their product is sold or made in Sweden; and the English translation appearing beneath the Swedish language states that the recipe for Frusen Glädjé comes "From Old Sweden," whereas, in fact, the recipe is American.

Although defendants dispute the accuracy of these charges, even if true they simply do not advance plaintiff's case at all. On the contrary, since plaintiff itself has attempted to package its product in such a way as to give the impression that it is of Scandinavian origin, although it too is, in fact, of domestic origin, it is guilty of the same deceptive trade practices of which it accuses defendants. In short, since plaintiff's hands are similarly unclean, they may not secure equitable relief simply because defendants' hands may be a shade or two less clean.

Accordingly, plaintiff's motion for a preliminary injunction is denied.

Notes on Unclean Hands

As indicated by Justice Holmes in the *Coca-Cola* case, *supra*, unclean hands is a rather narrow defense in trade identity cases: "But the defects of a plaintiff do not offer a very broad ground for another to swindle him." *Accord: Highmark Inc. v. UPMC Health Plan, Inc.*, 276 F.3d 160 (3[d] Cir. 2001) (plaintiff's "inappropriate use of a term in its 1999 advertisement does not excuse [defendant's] current deceptive and misleading advertisements to the public"). The effect of the defense is likewise limited by the court's concern that the public not be deceived. *But see Holeproof Hosiery Co. v. Wallach Bros.*, 172 F. 859 (2[d] Cir. 1909), wherein the court held HOLEPROOF was not so deceptively misdescriptive of hosiery as to constitute unclean hands, although holes might appear. *Compare Worden v. California Fig Syrup Co.*, 187 U.S. 516 (1903). What is the correct solution to the dilemma of the courts in this area? Should the courts sustain unclean hands or other equitable defenses and thereby allow confusion as to source to the public's as well as the plaintiff's detriment? In *Bell v. Streetwise Records, Ltd.*, 761 F.2d 67, 75–76 (1st Cir. 1985), rights to the name of the singing group NEW EDITION were in dispute. There the lower court's denial of a preliminary injunction on the ground of unclean hands was reversed, the appellate court stating:

> [T]he court entered a decree that, in effect, left both plaintiff and defendant free to use the trade name. Even if this result were fair as between the parties, it is not fair in respect to the public. It creates the very "source" confusion that legal trademark, and trade name, doctrine developed to avoid. When arguing parties are, in a sense, both responsible for the success of a name, a court may find it difficult to decide which, in fact, "owns" the name; the temptation may be great to say "both own it" or try to "divide" the name among them. The public interest, however, normally requires an exclusive award. . . . In short, we do

not view the "unclean hands" doctrine as sufficient, on the facts of this case, to justify continuation of public confusion.

On remand plaintiff's motion for preliminary injunction was granted. *Bell v. Streetwise Records, Ltd.*, 640 F. Supp. 575 (D. Mass. 1986). *See generally* 3 GILSON, TRADEMARK PROTECTION AND PRACTICE § 8.12[13][a] (2008 ed.); MCCARTHY, TRADEMARK PROTECTION AND UNFAIR COMPETITION §§ 31:52-31:54 (4th ed. 2007); Note, *The Besmirched Plaintiff and the Confused Public: Unclean Hands in Trademark Infringement*, 65 COLUM. L. REV. 109 (1965).

In *United States Jaycees v. Philadelphia Jaycees*, 639 F.2d 134 (3^d Cir. 1981), the lower court's holding that enforcement of plaintiff's trademark rights would unconstitutionally aid the enforcement of its sexually discriminatory membership policy was overturned on appeal because of an insubstantial relationship between the two. However, in *United States Jaycees v. Cedar Rapids Jaycees*, 794 F.2d 379 (8th Cir. 1986), the Eighth Circuit refused to uphold plaintiff's attempt to revoke defendant's license after defendant began admitting women as members. Noting that plaintiff had subsequently amended its by-laws to allow women members, the court stated, "we agree that USJ normally has a right to choose who uses its trademark, but disagree that the courts must in all instances assist and enforce those choices when the only purpose to be served is punishment of an otherwise productive and conforming member simply because the member was on the prevailing side in a past internal policy dispute." In *Kiwanis International v. Ridgewood Kiwanis Club*, 627 F. Supp. 1381 (D.N.J. 1986), the court was even more adamant in refusing to extend the court's protection to the licensor's "blatant and admitted sexist attitude." "What is truly at issue here is whether Kiwanis can, directly or indirectly, enforce its policy against women with the imprimatur of the court. This opinion concludes that it cannot. Kiwanis' trademark rights are subject to the right of women to be free of discrimination, as indeed they should be." (627 F. Supp. at 1395).

Generally, misconduct that constitutes unclean hands has involved either misrepresentations as to the quality and ingredients of the product or service, its source or geographical origin, or its efficacy. In order to be recognized, the basis for the claim of unclean hands normally must be directly related to the trademark rights at issue. *Worthington v. Anderson*, 386 F.3d 1314 (10th Cir. 2004) (affirming dismissal of plaintiff's trademark infringement claim because plaintiff's misconduct was sufficiently related; plaintiff had thrown "economic obstacles in the way of" defendants' compliance with an award of the trademark for bakeries to plaintiff when it "should have been obvious that [defendants] would incur considerable expense in divesting themselves of the trademark"). *See also* the discussion on trademark misuse in the section on antitrust violations, *infra*.

Should use of the ® (federal registration) symbol when federal registration has not been granted be grounds for applying the doctrine of unclean hands in infringement cases? *See Shatel Corp. v. Mao Ta Lumber & Yacht Corp.*, 697 F.2d 1352, 1355 (11th Cir. 1983), in which the court stated: "Because misunderstandings about the use of federal registration symbols are common . . . courts have been reluctant to find unclean hands where the misuse of the registration symbol was negligent or immaterial to the litigation." *Compare Ginseng-Up Corp. v. American Ginseng Co.*, 215 U.S.P.Q. 471 (S.D.N.Y. 1981), where the alleged misrepresentations in plaintiff's application for trademark registration were found immaterial since the action was based on common law trademark rights.

7.04 Antitrust Violations

Introduction

The antitrust laws are designed to preserve and promote competition in the marketplace. The resulting benefits from such competition are believed to include higher quality goods and services and lower prices for the consumer. A monopolization, or attempted monopolization, of the market for a product may conflict with the goals the antitrust laws are designed to serve. The applicable statutes provide as follows:

Section 1 of the Sherman Act (15 U.S.C. § 1):

Every contract, combination, in the form of trust or otherwise, or conspiracy, in restraint of trade or commerce among the several States, or with foreign nations, is declared to be illegal . . .

Section 2 of the Sherman Act (15 U.S.C. § 2):

Every person who shall monopolize, or attempt to monopolize, or combine or conspire with any other person or persons, to monopolize any part of the trade or commerce among the several States, or with foreign nations, shall be deemed guilty of a felony, and, on conviction thereof, shall be punishable by a fine not exceeding $10,000,000 if a corporation, or, if any other person, $350,000, or by imprisonment not exceeding three years, or by both said punishments, in the discretion of the court.

Section 5 of the Federal Trade Commission Act (15 U.S.C. § 45):

(a)(1) Unfair methods of competition in or affecting commerce, and unfair or deceptive acts or practices in or affecting commerce, are declared unlawful.

Section 3 of the Clayton Act (15 U.S.C. § 14):

It shall be unlawful for any person engaged in commerce, in the course of such commerce, to lease or make a sale or contract for sale of goods, wares, merchandise, machinery, supplies or other commodities . . . on the condition, agreement or understanding that the lessee or purchaser thereof shall not use or deal in the goods, wares, merchandise, machinery, supplies or other commodities of a competitor or competitors of the lessor or seller, where the effect . . . may be to substantially lessen competition or tend to create a monopoly in any line of commerce.

Civil damages and injunctive relief are authorized under 15 U.S.C. § 15(a) and § 26.

Normally the objectives of trademark and antitrust law are complementary.

The antitrust laws require competition, not piracy. The essence of competition is the ability of competing products to obtain public recognition based on their own individual merit. A product has not won on its own merit if the real reason the public purchases it is that the public believes it is obtaining the product of another company.

Standard Oil (Ky.) v. Humble Oil & Refining Co., 363 F.2d 945, 954 (5th Cir. 1966). *cert. denied*, 385 U.S. 1007 (1967). *Cf. Sanderson v. Culligan Int'l Co.*, 415 F.3d 620 (7th Cir. 2005) (the Sherman Act does not "forbid all 'unfair' business tactics, without regard to the likelihood that the adversary will achieve and retain a monopoly at consumers' expense . . . much competition is unfair, or at least ungentlemanly . . . there is no obligation to be kindly or cooperative toward other producers"). In some instances, however, agreements, licenses, distribution controls, and other limitations involving trademark use may be held to be unlawfully anticompetitive restraints of trade. Thus, a familiarity with antitrust concepts is essential in the trade identity field. *See generally* VON KALINOWKSI, SULLIVAN & MCGUIRE, ANTITRUST LAWS AND TRADE REGULATION, Ch.'s 72-75 (2d ed. 2007); , HOLMES, INTELLECTUAL PROPERTY AND ANTITRUST LAW (2007 ed.).

The fundamental test of antitrust violations is whether the conduct in issue promotes or suppresses competition in the marketplace. The Supreme Court traditionally has used one of two analytical tests to determine whether specific commercial conduct is violative of the antitrust laws.

> [T]here are certain agreements or practices which because of their pernicious effect on competition and lack of any redeeming virtue are conclusively presumed to be unreasonable and therefore illegal without elaborate inquiry as to the precise harm they have caused or the business excuse for their use. Such conduct is deemed "illegal *per se*."

Northern Pacific Ry. Co. v. United States, 356 U.S. 1, 5 (1958). The categories of trade restraints considered per se unlawful include horizontal price fixing (agreements among competitors at the same market level to fix prices), market divisions among competitors, and some group boycotts. *See, e.g., United States v. Citizens & Southern National Bank*, 422 U.S. 86, 118 (1975) (market divisions); *Northern Pacific Railway Co. v. United States*, 356 U.S. 1, 5 (1958) (price fixing); *Hahn v. Oregon Physicians' Service*, 868 F.2d 1022 (9th Cir. 1988) (price fixing, market divisions, group boycotts), *cert. denied*, 493 U.S. 846 (1989).

The second test of legality, the "rule of reason," requires more extensive analysis by a court to determine "whether the restraint imposed is such as merely regulates and perhaps thereby promotes competition or whether it is such as may suppress or even destroy competition." *Chicago Board of Trade v. United States*, 246 U.S. 231, 238 (1918). *See* Timberg, *Trademarks, Monopoly and the Restraint of Competition*, 68 HARV. L. REV. 814, 898–908 (1955); Hill, *Antitrust Violations as a Defense to Trademark Infringement*, 71 TRADEMARK REP. 148 (1981); MCCARTHY, TRADEMARKS AND UNFAIR COMPETITION, Ch. 31 (4th ed. 2007).

Many states have state antitrust statutes which authorize both governmental and private enforcement. *See generally* ABA Section of Antitrust Law, *Antitrust Law Developments* (4th ed. 2006). Many states also have "little FTC Acts" which authorize private causes of action. *See, e.g.,* 85 Ill. Comp. Stat. 510.

Trademark Misuse

Trademark litigation is occasionally defended on the ground that the plaintiff is trying to monopolize the market for the *product* via misuse of its rights in its trademark. Like any other unclean hands defense, *see* § 7.03, *supra*, trademark misuse must be directly related to the trademark rights in issue for the defense to be recognized. For many years the courts rejected the antitrust defense, reasoning that the trademark itself either was not or could not be directly used as the prime instrument to effectuate the antitrust activity. More recently the courts have held that the burden of establishing direct misuse is heavy but not insuperable.

In *Carl Zeiss Stiftung v. V.E.B. Carl Zeiss, Jena*, 298 F. Supp. 1309 (S.D.N.Y. 1969), defendants in an action for trademark infringement alleged that plaintiffs used their ZEISS camera trademarks in violation of the antitrust laws in a variety of ways, including illegal combinations, territorial restraints, tying, and price discrimination. The court stated that while an antitrust misuse defense may be available, "an essential element of the antitrust misuse defense in a trademark case is proof that the mark itself has been the basic and fundamental vehicle required and used to accomplish the violation." The court concluded that defendants failed to establish that plaintiff had used the ZEISS trademark to violate the antitrust laws. Similarly, in *Coca-Cola Co. v. Howard Johnson Co.*, 386 F. Supp. 330, 335–6 (N.D. Ga. 1974), the court rejected such a defense because an "immediate and necessary relationship" between plaintiff's passing off claim and the alleged antitrust violation was lacking; and in *Rolls-Royce Motors Ltd. v. A & A Fiberglass, Inc.*, 428 F. Supp. 689, 697 (N.D. Ga. 1976), the court summarized its view as follows: "[u]nder this test, based on judicial reluctance to permit every case for trademark infringement to expand into a major antitrust action, the antitrust defenses must fall." *See also Valley Products Company v. Landmark*, 128 F.2d 398 (6th Cir. 1997) (antitrust action dismissed where plaintiff, a former supplier of logo-bearing guest amenities to defendant hotel franchisor, could not show its injury from cancellation of its vendor agreement would not have occurred but for alleged trademark misuse by franchisor).

How can a means for trade identity be more than ancillary to an alleged antitrust violation? In *Clorox Co. v. Sterling Winthrop Inc.*, 117 F.3d 50, 57 (2[d] Cir. 1997), the court held that the defendant, the maker of LYSOL, did not violate the Sherman Act by entering into an agreement prohibiting the use of plaintiff's PINE-SOL mark on disinfectant products. The court reasoned that the agreement was not anticompetitive because it did not prevent the plaintiff from marketing a disinfectant, but only from marketing a disinfectant as a PINE-SOL product. Similarly, in *Domed Stadium Hotel, Inc. v. Holiday Inns, Inc.*, 732 F.2d 480 (5th Cir. 1984), a franchisee alleged that Holiday Inns was attempting to monopolize and restrain trade in the market for Holiday Inn hotel rooms. In granting Holiday Inns summary judgment the court stated that the relevant product market was not Holiday Inn rooms, but hotel rooms generally, and that "absent exceptional market conditions, one brand in a market of competing brands cannot constitute a relevant product market." *Domed Stadium Hotel*, 732 F.2d at 488. *See also Weber v. National Football League*, 112 F. Supp.2d 667 (N.D. Ohio 2000) (dismissing case which alleged monopolization of domain names derived from football league's "Jets" and "Dolphins" trademarks; "the market is defined in terms of domain names in general, not 'jets.com' and 'dolphins.com' "). *Compare Kellogg Co. v. National Biscuit Co.*, 71 F.2d 662 (2[d] Cir. 1934). In that case Nabisco purchased the Shredded Wheat Company and sought to protect shredded wheat as a valid trademark. Plaintiff alleged that Nabisco directed its salesmen to slander plaintiff's product, threatened distributors who carried plaintiff's product, and brought suit against plaintiff to stop plaintiff's manufacture of shredded wheat. The court denied defendant's motion to dismiss the complaint and stated the test as follows, *Kellogg*, 71 F.2d at 666: "the principal question at trial will be whether the defendant has attempted to monopolize the trade in shredded wheat or only to establish exclusive rights in certain trade names, trademarks and shapes of the manufactured product."

In *Drop Dead Co. v. S.C. Johnson & Son, Inc.*, 326 F.2d 87, 96 (9th Cir. 1963), the court rejected appellant's antitrust defense and indicated that appellee's registration of multiple marks for wax products, mass advertising of its trademarks, mass sales, and bringing of infringement suits to protect its trademarks "constitute the sort of aggressive competition and promotion that the antitrust laws seek to protect particularly within the limits of lawful monopolies granted by Congress 'in its wisdom.'" Thus, in *La Maur, Inc. v. Alberto-Culver Co.*, 496 F.2d 618 (8th Cir. 1974), the court stated that the owner of a trademark is entitled to protect its mark even if it strengthens or creates the potential monopoly which a trademark registration affords the registrant. Similarly, in *Procter & Gamble Co. v. Johnson & Johnson, Inc.*, 485 F. Supp. 1185 (S.D.N.Y. 1979), the court found plaintiff's "Minor Brands [token use] Program" was not anticompetitive, and in *Coca-Cola Co. v. Overland, Inc.*, 692 F.2d 1250 (9th Cir. 1982), the court stated that Coca-Cola Company's policy of bringing trademark infringement suits against retailers who substituted other brands for COCA-COLA was not coercive or anticompetitive. *Cf. Santana Prods. v. Bobrick Washroom Equip.*,401 F.3d 123 (3[d] Cir. 2005) (defendants' alleged "group boycott" based on allegations about the safety of plaintiff's toilet partitions was instead "classic competition on the merits of its product"; plaintiff was free to tout the superiority of its product and prove defendants wrong).

"Sham" lawsuits directed at competitors can create liability, but the test is not a subjective one. In *Professional Real Estate Investors, Inc. v. Columbia Pictures*, 508 U.S. 49 (1993), a copyright infringement action, the Supreme Court held that, regardless of a plaintiff's possible subjective anticompetitive intent, an objectively reasonable effort to litigate cannot constitute a "sham" lawsuit creating antitrust liability.

Compare Phi Delta Theta Fraternity v. J.A. Buchroeder & Co., 251 F. Supp. 968 (W.D. Mo. 1966), where defendants alleged that L.G. Balfour Co., a jewelry manufacturer, had violated the antitrust laws by securing exclusive jeweler licenses from college fraternities and sororities and thereby using federal trademark registrations of their insignia to force local chapters of the fraternities and sororities to honor the exclusive arrangement with Balfour. The court held that the stipulated facts, if proven, showed Balfour had violated the antitrust laws and that the violation was an affirmative defense to allegations of trademark infringement because the trademark itself was the instrument which effectuated the antitrust activity. In *Timken Roller Bearing Co. v. United States*, 341 U.S. 593 (1951), Timken, an Ohio corporation, combined with its British and French subsidiaries to eliminate competition in the manufacture and sale of antifriction bearings. The court rejected appellant's argument that its actions were merely reasonable steps taken to implement a trademark licensing program. The court stated, 341 U.S. at 598: "Furthermore, while a trademark merely affords protection to a name, the agreements in the present case went far beyond protection of the name TIMKEN and provided for control of the manufacture and sale of antifriction bearings whether carrying the mark or not." *See American Aloe Corp. v. Aloe Creme Labs, Inc.*, 420 F.2d 1248 (7th Cir. 1970), *cert. denied*, 398 U.S. 929 (1970) (monopoly); *Radiant Burners, Inc. v. Peoples Gas Light & Coke Co.*, 364 U.S. 656 (1961) (use of a certification mark for an illegal boycott).

See generally HOLMES, INTELLECTUAL PROPERTY AND ANTITRUST LAW (2007); VON KALINOWSKI, SULLIVAN & McGUIRL, ANTITRUST LAWS AND TRADE REGULATION, Chs. 72-75 (2d ed. 2007).

License and Distribution Controls

1. Exclusive Dealing

A supplier generally has the right to deal only with those with whom it wishes to deal. As long as it does so independently, it may refuse to deal with anyone. *Monsanto Co. v. Spray-Rite Service Corp.*, 465 U.S. 752 (1984); *H.L. Moore Drug Exchange v. Eli Lilly & Co.*, 662 F.2d 935, 946 (2d Cir. 1981), *cert. denied*, 459 U.S. 880 (1982) ("We need not consider whether Lilly's action was motivated by anticompetitive reasons, since a unilateral decision to terminate, no matter what the reason, does not constitute a violation of the antitrust laws"). Should a supplier of a trademarked product, however, ever be able to prevent its customers from purchasing the product of a competitor? Arrangements which restrict the buyer's ability to purchase similar products from a competitor are termed "exclusive dealing" arrangements. Potentially anticompetitive in their effect, exclusive dealing arrangements are subject to scrutiny under §§ 1 and 2 of the Sherman Act, § 3 of the Clayton Act, and § 5 of the Federal Trade Commission Act. Exclusive dealing arrangements are not *per se* unlawful. The Supreme Court has declared that proper analysis of such arrangements under the Sherman and Clayton Act requires:

> weigh[ing] the probable effect of the contract on the relevant area of effective competition, taking into account the relative strength of the parties, the proportionate volume of commerce involved in relation to the total volume of commerce in the relevant market area, and the probable immediate and future effects which pre-emption of that share of the market might have on effective competition therein.

Tampa Electric Co. v. Nashville Coal Co., 365 U.S. 320. 329 (1961). "The court [in *Tampa Electric*] further emphasized the significance of the possible economic justification for the accused arrangement in light of the legitimate reasons for employing such a device." *Susser v. Carvel Corp.*, 332 F.2d 505, 516 (2ᵈ Cir. 1964).

In *Jefferson Parish Hospital District No. 2 v. Hyde*, 466 U.S. 2 (1984), which principally was analyzed as a tying case, the court found no violative exclusive dealing in a hospital's exclusive contract with a group of anesthesiologists. Justice O'Connor stated in her concurrence, "Exclusive dealing is an unreasonable restraint on trade only when a significant fraction of buyers or sellers are frozen out of a market by the exclusive deal." 466 U.S. at 45. There, the contract affected "only a small fraction of the markets in which anesthesiologists may sell their services, and a still smaller fraction of the market in which hospitals may secure anesthesiological services." *Id.* at 46–47. Subsequent decisions have upheld exclusive dealing arrangements where distribution channels were not unduly restricted. *See, e.g., Seagood Trading Corp. v. Jerrico, Inc.,* 924 F.2d 1555 (11ᵗʰ Cir. 1991); Ryko Mfg. Co. v. Edens Services, 823 F.2d 1215, 1234–35 (8ᵗʰ Cir. 1987), *cert. denied*, 484 U.S. 1026 (1988). *Compare In re Independent Service Orgs. Antitrust Litigation*, 203 F.3d 1322 (Fed. Cir. 2000) (patent owner's refusal to sell or license its patented copier parts to independent service organizations did not violate antitrust law). In actions for exclusive dealing brought under § 5 of the Federal Trade Commission Act, the Supreme Court has applied a similar standard. The test is whether the exclusive dealing arrangement effectively forecloses competitors from "a significant number of outlets." *Federal Trade Comm'n v. Brown Shoe Co.*, 384 U.S. 316 (1966).

In *Susser v. Carvel Corp., supra*, plaintiffs claimed that Carvel's franchise agreement violated the Sherman and Clayton Acts by requiring trademark licensees to sell only Carvel products. The Second Circuit held (332 F.2d at 517) that the Carvel franchise agreement was not an unlawfully exclusive dealership and was economically justified:

> The requirement that only Carvel products be sold at Carvel outlets derives from the desirability that the public identify each Carvel outlet as one of a chain which offers identical products at a uniform standard of quality. The antitrust laws certainly do not require that the licensor of a trademark permit his licensees to associate with that trademark other products unrelated to those customarily sold under the mark . . . Carvel was not required to accede to the requests of one or another of the dealers that they be permitted to sell Christmas trees or hamburgers, for example, which would have thrust upon Carvel the obligation to acquaint itself with the production and sale of these items so as to establish reasonable quality controls.

In *U.S. v. Visa USA, Inc.*, 344 F.3d 229 (2ᵈ. Cir. 2003), *cert. denied* 543 U.S. 811 (2004), use of an "exclusionary rule" by Visa USA and Mastercard was enjoined as a violation of the Sherman Act. Visa USA and Mastercard "are not single entities; they are consortiums of competitors. They are owned and effectively operated by some 20,000 banks, which compete with one another . . . [and] set the policies of Visa USA and Mastercard." At issue was the rule that effectively foreclosed Amex and Discover, the two major competing brands, from issuing cards through the consortium banks. Although defendants argued that the exclusionary rule pro-competitively promoted "cohesion" in the Visa USA and Mastercard networks, allowing them to compete effectively in the marketplace, the court instead concluded that the rule harmed competition "by reducing overall card output and available card features, as well as by decreasing network services output and stunting price competition, product innovation and output."

The appellate court analogized that it was as if "Coca-Cola, Pepsi-Cola, and several other leading sellers of soft drinks joined together to form an association to contract for trucking services and exacted of contracting truckers a commitment not to carry for any soft drink maker that was not a part of the consortium," except that here the consortium members were putting the restrictions on *themselves*, with each agreeing "not to compete with the others in a manner which the consortium considers harmful to its combined interests." Such a horizontal restraint is prohibited under the Sherman Act.

2. Price Controls

The distributor or manufacturer of a trademarked product does not have the unlimited right to fix the price at which wholesalers or retailers resell that product. Such "resale price maintenance" may be prohibited under the antitrust laws. *See United States v. Bausch & Lomb Optical Co.*, 321 U.S. 707, 721 (1944):

> Soft Lite is the distributor of an unpatented article. It sells to its wholesalers at prices satisfactory to itself. Beyond that point it may not project its power over the prices of its wholesaler customers by agreement. A distributor of a trademarked article may not lawfully limit by agreement, express or implied, the price at which or the persons to whom its purchasers may resell. . . .

In *Carvel, supra*, the plaintiffs alleged that the following language in the Carvel franchise manual was unlawful price fixing: "Whenever Carvel recommends a retail price, such recommendation is based upon Carvel's experience concerning all factors that enter into a proper price, but such recommendation is in no manner binding upon the dealer." The court rejected plaintiff's argument and held that "the mere existence of a means whereby retail price levels are recommended is not sufficient to establish a violation of the Sherman Act, unless there is a showing of an attempt to enforce a price structure upon the retail tradesmen." *Carvel*, 332 F.2d at 510. The rule against resale price agreements was effectively limited over time for agreements setting *maximum* resale prices because such agreements do not lessen competition and actually benefit consumers by keeping prices down. Accordingly, courts found the requisite antitrust injury absent in such cases. *See, e.g., Atlantic Richfield Co. v. USA Petroleum Co.*, 495 U.S. 328 (1990) (no antitrust injury to competitor because inability to raise prices benefitted consumers and did not threaten competition). In *Jack Walters & Sons Corp. v. Morton Building, Inc.*, 737 F.2d 698, 708 (7th Cir. 1984), the court held that a manufacturer can advertise a retail price and "take reasonable measures to make sure the advertised price is not exceeded. These measures include trying to persuade dealers to adhere to the advertised price and checking around to make sure they are adhering." It reasoned that otherwise the advertising would mislead consumers, and, while the manufacturer could not require dealer compliance with minimum prices, a maximum price ceiling based on advertising was justifiable.

The Supreme Court subsequently reversed its previous rule that vertical maximum price fixing was *per se* unlawful, and held that such arrangements should be analyzed under the rule of reason. *State Oil Company v. Khan*, 522 U.S. 3 (1997) (O'Connor, J.). In doing so, the unanimous court observed that low prices benefit consumers regardless of how they are set, and "so long as they are above predatory levels, they do not threaten competition," quoting *Atlantic Richfield Co. v. USA Petroleum Co.*, 495 U.S. 328, 340 (1990).

The Supreme Court later decided that vertical *minimum* price-fixing should be analyzed under the rule of reason, too. In *Leegin Creative Leather Products, Inc. v. PSKS, Inc.*, 127 S.Ct. 2705 (2007), plaintiff PSKS, operator of women's apparel store Kay's Kloset, sued Leegin, alleging that Leegin's retail agreements specifying prices for its "Brighton" women's fashion accessories violated antitrust laws. Leegin had stopped selling to Kay's Kloset when the retailer refused to cease selling Brighton goods below suggested prices. Leegin sought to prohibit discounting to ensure that its products were distributed through high-service retailers that would provide a "different experience than [consumers] get in Sam's Club or in Wal-Mart." 168 L. Ed. 2d at 631. The district court relied on the rule established in *Dr. Miles Medical Co. v. John D. Park & Sons Co.*, 220 US. 373 (1911), that it is *per se* illegal under § 1 of the Sherman Act for a manufacturer and its distributor to agree on minimum resale prices for the manufacturer's goods. The district court therefore excluded as irrelevant Leegin's planned expert testimony describing the procompetitive effects of its price-fixing policy. A jury awarded PSKS $1.2 million, and the district court trebled the damages and awarded PSKS its attorneys' fees and costs, entering judgment against Leegin for $3.9 million.

The Fifth Circuit affirmed, explaining that it was bound by *Dr. Miles*. Leegin unsuccessfully argued that the "rule of reason" rather than the *per se* rule should apply. The Supreme Court granted certiorari to "determine whether vertical minimum resale price maintenance agreements should continue to be treated as *per se* unlawful." 168 L. Ed. 2d at 633.

The rule of reason requires consideration of a variety of factors, including market power and the actual effect of the restraint. *Id.* at 634. "To justify a *per se* prohibition a restraint must have 'manifestly anticompetitive' effects and 'lack . . . any redeeming virtue.' " *Id.* at 634, citing earlier decisions. The Court found that "[t]he reasoning of the Court's more recent jurisprudence has rejected the rationales on which *Dr. Miles* was based." *Id.* Citing amicus briefs and contemporary economic theory, the Court found that vertical agreements ensuring resale price maintenance are as or more likely to have procompetitive effects with respect to interbrand competition than anticompetitive effects. "[E]conomics literature is replete with procompetitive justifications for a manufacturer's use of resale price maintenance." *Id.* at 636. "Minimum resale price maintenance can stimulate interbrand competition - the competition among manufacturers selling different brands of the same type of product - by reducing intrabrand competition - the competition among retailers selling the same brand." *Id.* "The promotion of interbrand competition is important because 'the primary purpose of the antitrust laws is to protect this type of competition.' " *Id.* at 636–37, citing *State Oil Co. v. Khan*, 522 U.S. 3, 15 (1997).

Eliminating interbrand price competition through resale price maintenance encourages retailers, through an ensured margin, "to invest in tangible or intangible services or promotional efforts that aid the manufacturer's position as against rival manufacturers." 168 L. Ed. 2d at 637. The Court pointed out that "[r]esale price maintenance also has the potential to give consumers more options so that they can choose among low-price, low-service brands; high-price, high-service brands; and brands that fall in between," *Id.*, and that "[a]bsent vertical price restraints, the retail services that enhance interbrand competition might be underprovided. This is because discounting retailers can free ride on retailers who furnish services and then capture some of the increased demand those services generate." *Id.* Resale price maintenance may also be procompetitive by facilitating market entry for new firms and brands, as well as encouraging retail services that otherwise would not be provided. *Id.*

While vertical resale price-fixing agreements can be abused, this did not favor a *per se* rule: "Notwithstanding the risks of unlawful conduct, it cannot be stated with any degree of confidence that resale price maintenance 'always or almost always tends to restrict competition and decrease output." *Id.* at 639. "As the rule would proscribe a significant amount of procompetitive conduct, these agreements appear ill-suited for *per se* condemnation." 168 L. Ed. 2d at 639. "In sum, it is a flawed antitrust doctrine that serves the interests of lawyers - by creating legal distinctions that operate as traps for the unwary - more than the interests of consumers - by requiring manufacturers to choose second-best options to achieve sound business objectives." *Id.* In applying a rule of reason analysis on remand, several factors would need to be considered, including the number of manufacturers using the practice, whether the manufacturer or the retailers were the impetus for the restraint, and the manufacturer's market power.

Justice Breyer, joined in his dissent by Justices Stevens, Souter, and Ginsburg, noted that "Th[e] *per se* rule is one upon which the legal profession, business, and the public have relied for close to a century." How easily can courts identify instances in which the benefits are likely to outweigh potential harms? My own answer is, *not very easily*. For one thing, it is often difficult to identify who - producer or dealer - is the moving force behind any given resale price maintenance agreement." *Id.* at 653. Justice Breyer was also wary of potential mistakes in applying the required "complex economic criteria."

3. Tying Arrangements

When a trademark owner forces a customer to purchase a second "tied" product from the trademark owner or owner-approved source in order to obtain the initial "tying" product that the customer desires, a court may find that an illegal tying arrangement exists. The plaintiff must establish: (1) that the tying product may not be obtained unless the tied product is also purchased; (2) that the tying product and the tied product are separate and distinct; (3) that the tying product possesses sufficient economic power appreciably to restrain competition in the tied market; and (4) that a "not insubstantial" amount of commerce is affected by the arrangement. A defendant in appropriate circumstances may successfully defend against an accusation of illegal tying by showing a special justification for the particular tying arrangement in question. The Supreme Court in *Ill. Tool Works, Inc. v. Indep. Ink, Inc.*, 547 U.S. 28 (2006), held that for antitrust purposes under Section 1 of the Sherman Act, the mere fact that a tying product is patented does not necessarily confer market power, and the plaintiff therefore was required to prove the defendant's market power. This reasoning would appear to apply even more strongly to trademarks, which are not subject to a statutory monopoly.

In *Jack Walters & Sons, supra*, 737 F.2d at 704–05, the Seventh Circuit explained the difficulties inherent in a claim of trademark tying:

> . . . It is one thing to say that a manufacturer of copying machines who requires his customers to buy from him the copying paper that is used in the machines is conditioning the sale of the machines on the customer's purchase of a distinct product; it is quite another to say that General Motors lets you use the name Buick on condition that you buy the car to which the name is attached. That is a fantastical description of the transaction, and the cases reject the proposition that a tie-in claim can be based on it. . . . To accept it would be to impose in the name of antitrust a regime of compulsory licensing of trademarks — an absurd project. Moreover, since a trademark that denotes a product is rarely licensed apart from the product — and was not in this case — the separate-markets test of *Jefferson Parish* is not satisfied.

> However, some cases, including several in this circuit, do treat as tying products trademarks that name not a product manufactured by the trademark's owner but a service which he provides to consumers through a system of franchised retail outlets; the tie-in consists of requiring franchisees, as a condition of being allowed to use the trademark, to buy distinct products supplied by the franchisor.

> . . . The trademark is analytically separable from the tied product, so there is not the same absurdity in treating the trademark as a tying product as there is when the trademark is simply the name of the alleged tied product, as in our example of the Buick name and the Buick automobile. "Chicken Delight," in contrast, was the name of a fast-food franchise operation, not the name of a product; and the franchisor, the owner of the "Chicken Delight" mark, manufactured none of the things (which included mixes, fryers, and packaging supplies) that it required its franchisees to buy from it as a condition of their being allowed to use the name. *Siegel v. Chicken Delight, Inc., supra*, 448 F.2d at 48 n. 4. It was a "case of a franchise system set up not to distribute the trade-marked goods of the franchisor, but . . . to conduct a certain business under a common trademark or trade name." *Id.* at 48 (footnote omitted). The name and the tied products thus were separable in a way that the name Buick and the car sold under that name are not. Or so at least it can be argued; for the *Chicken Delight* line of cases is not universally delectated.

Compare the following justification of a tying arrangement in the *Carvel* case which required licensees to purchase directly from Carvel or from a source approved by Carvel, CARVEL ice cream mix made by a secret formula and other products used in either the preparation or sale of the end product offered to the public, 332 F.2d at 519.

> . . . The true tying item was . . . the CARVEL trademark, whose growing repute was intended to help the little band of Carvel dealers swim a bit faster than their numerous rivals up the highly competitive stream. There may, of course, be cases where a trademark has acquired such prominence that the coupling of some further item to its license would constitute a *per se* violation; but such a trademark would satisfy the market dominance test of *Times-Picayune* and *Northern Pacific*. The figures show that CARVEL is not such a mark.

> Tying arrangements differ from other *per se* violations, such as price-fixing, *United States v. Trenton Potteries Co.*, 273 U.S. 392 (1927), in that they can be justified on occasion, as by proof that "the protection of goodwill may necessitate" their use "where specifications for a substitute would be so detailed that they could not practicably be supplied," *Standard Oil Co. of Calif. and Standard Stations v. United States*, 337 U.S. 293, 306 (1949). Since the value of a trademark depends solely on the public image it conveys, its holder must exercise controls to assure himself that the mark is not shown in a derogatory light. The record affords no sufficient basis for upsetting the finding of the District Judge that "[t]o require Carvel to limit itself to advance specifications of standards for all the various types of accessory products used in connection with the mix would impose an impractical and unreasonable burden of formulation. . . ."

In *Kentucky Fried Chicken Corp. v. Diversified Packaging Corp.*, 549 F.2d 368 (5th Cir. 1977), the court stated that the appellant failed to establish that KFC's system was not a reasonable method of quality control, and in *Phonetele, Inc. v. American Telephone & Telegraph*, 664 F.2d 716, 738–739 (9th Cir. 1981), *cert. denied*, 459 U.S. 1145 (1983), the court ruled that the defendant could offer justifications for undertaking the tie. *See* McCarthy, *Trademark Franchising and Antitrust: The Trouble With Tie-Ins*, 58 CAL. L. REV. 1085 (1971).

In *Principe v. McDonald's Corp.*, 631 F.2d 303, 309 (4th Cir. 1980), the court stated:

> the proper inquiry is not whether the allegedly tied products are associated in the public's mind with the franchisor's trademark, but whether they are integral components of the business method being franchised. Where the challenged aggregation is an essential ingredient of the franchised system's formula for success, there is but a single product and no tie-in exists. . . .

See also Power Test Petroleum Distributors v. Calcu Gas, 754 F.2d 91 (2d Cir. 1985); *California Glazed Products, Inc. v. Burns & Russell Co.*, 708 F.2d 1423 (9th Cir. 1983), *cert. denied*, 464 U.S. 937 (1983); *Krehl v. Baskin-Robbins Ice Cream Co.*, 664 F.2d 1348 (9th Cir. 1982). *Compare Metrix Warehouse, Inc. v. Daimler-Benz Aktiengesellschaft*, 828 F.2d 1033 (4th Cir. 1987), *cert. denied*, 486 U.S. 1017 (1988) (less restrictive means existed to ensure quality than tying replacement parts to sale of new cars) *with Mozart Co. v. Mercedes-Benz in North America, Inc.*, 833 F.2d 1342 (9th Cir. 1987), *cert. denied*, 488 U.S. 870 (1988) (upholding jury's finding that no less restrictive alternative existed to control quality and protect goodwill than to tie the sale of replacement parts to the sale of new cars), and *Town Sound & Custom Tops, Inc. v. Chrysler Motors Corp.*, 959 F.2d 468 (3d Cir.) (en banc), *cert. denied*, 506 U.S. 868 (1992) (affirming summary judgment that Chrysler had not unlawfully tied the sale of automobile sound systems for Chrysler automobiles to the sale of the automobiles themselves, finding that "competition in the automobile market adequately protects those consumers who consider auto sound systems when buying their cars from having to pay too much").

In *Massachusetts v. Microsoft Corp.*, 373 F.3d 1199 (D.C. Cir. 2004), a consent decree required that Microsoft enable manufacturers to allow consumer use of Internet browsers other than Microsoft's Internet Explorer. The appellate court previously had upheld the district court's finding that Microsoft's integration of Internet Explorer and its Windows operating system generally "prevented OEMs from pre-installing other browsers and deterred consumers from using them." "The district court fashioned a remedy aimed at reducing the costs an OEM might face in having to support multiple internet browsers . . . We say, Well done!" *Microsoft*, 373 F.3d at 1210.

The appellate court concluded that, in the consent decree, the "district court's end-user access provision fosters competition by opening the channels of distribution to non-Microsoft middleware," i.e,. web-browsing software. *Microsoft*, 373 F.3d at 1211. The court also affirmed a requirement that Microsoft disclose certain communications protocols, i.e. languages that allowed servers and clients to communicate with one another.

Does ownership of a trademark confer economic power analogous to ownership of patents or copyrights which are constitutionally sanctioned monopolies? *See Siegel v. Chicken Delight, Inc.*, 448 F.2d 43 (9th Cir. 1971). A number of decisions have required proof of the economic power possessed by the trademark in issue. *See Kentucky Fried Chicken, supra; Capital Temporaries, Inc. v. Olsten Corp.*, 506 F.2d 658 (2d Cir. 1974); *Golden West Insulation, Inc. v. Stardust Invest. Corp.*, 615 P.2d 1048 (Or. App. 1980); Smirti, *Trademarks as Tying Products: The Presumption of Economic Power*, 69 Trademark Rep. 1 (1979). This is likely to become the rule after the Supreme Court's patent-related decision in *Ill. Tool Works, Inc. v. Indep. Ink, Inc.*, 547 U.S. 28 (2006) (the mere fact that the tying product is patented does not automatically confer market power, and the plaintiff must prove the defendant's market power).

In *Jefferson Parish Hospital District No. 2 v. Hyde*, 466 U.S. 2, 17–22 (1984), the Supreme Court held that to establish that there are two separate products capable of being tied, there must exist separate markets for each product. Secondly, the owner of the tying product must have sufficient market power to force purchase of the tied product. At issue in *Jefferson Parish* was the requirement that patients at a hospital use the services of one firm of anesthesiologists. While noting that the services unquestionably could be provided separately, the court stated,

> there is nothing inherently anticompetitive about packaged sales. Only if patients are forced to purchase [the firm's] services as a result of the hospital's market power would the arrangement have anticompetitive consequences. If no forcing is present, patients are free to enter a competing hospital and to use another anesthesiologist instead of [the firm].

The existence of numerous competing hospitals employing anesthesiologists resulted in reversal and remand of the Fifth Circuit finding of per se illegal tying.

One court concluded, "the emphasis in the Supreme Court's recent decision in *Jefferson Parish* on proving that the owner of the tying product has real market power may doom the franchise trademark cases, as they mostly involve highly competitive retail industries, such as the fast-food business." *Jack Walters, supra*, 737 F.2d at 705. *See also Will v. Comprehensive Accounting Corp.*, 776 F.2d 665 (7th Cir. 1985) (franchisees failed to establish that franchisor had market power); *cf. Midwestern Waffles, Inc. v. Waffle House, Inc.*, 734 F.2d 705, 712 (11th Cir. 1984) ("if competitors are in some way prevented from offering a franchise comparable to a Waffle House franchise, the court will find that a Waffle House franchise can be a tying product").

A subsequent Supreme Court decision gave new life to franchise tying cases. In *Eastman Kodak Co. v. Image Technical Services, Inc.*, 504 U.S. 451 (1992), the dispute involved the sale of service and replacement parts for Kodak photocopying and micrographic equipment. Kodak offered separate service contracts for its equipment. Other manufacturers' replacement parts were not compatible with Kodak's equipment. When independent service organizations (ISO's) began offering cheaper and higher quality service for Kodak equipment, with parts, Kodak sought to eliminate them as competition. For example, Kodak pressured Kodak equipment owners and independent parts distributors not to sell Kodak parts to ISO's, and parts manufacturers not to sell Kodak parts to anyone but Kodak. This succeeded in driving a number of ISO's out of business, and forcing unwilling customers to use Kodak service.

In moving for summary judgment, Kodak argued that, as in *Jefferson Parish*, the aggressive competition in the equipment market showed it did not have sufficient market power in the parts and services market to effect a tie. In affirming the Ninth Circuit's denial of summary judgment, the Supreme Court held that a reasonable trier of fact could find that parts and services were distinct products having separate markets, and that Kodak had sufficient power in the parts market to force unwanted purchases of a tied product, service. The majority was influenced by the fact that customers were "locked in" by the equipment purchase, with the cost of switching products high, and by evidence showing that Kodak might be taking advantage of this by raising prices in the service aftermarket above competitive levels. Justice Scalia dissented, stating, "If Kodak set generally supracompetitive prices for either spare parts or repair services without making an offsetting reduction on the price of its machines, national consumers would simply turn to Kodak's competitors for photocopying and micrographic systems."

After the *Kodak* decision, some franchisees claimed that they were "locked in" by the franchise agreement, and that unlawful tying occurred. In *Collins v. International Dairy Queen*, 939 F. Supp. 875 (M.D. Ga. 1996), several franchisees alleged that the DAIRY QUEEN franchisor engaged in illegal tying by forcing the franchisees to purchase supplies only from sources authorized by the franchisor. In that case, the court denied the defendant's motion for summary judgment due to evidence that Dairy Queen had 90% market share in the soft-serve ice cream business and that Dairy Queen had forced its franchisees to pay supra-competitive prices for authorized supplies.

However, some courts have held that tying arrangements are not illegal where franchisees consent to being "locked in" to supply and services markets over which the franchisor does not have sufficient control. In *Queen City Pizza, Inc. v. Domino's Pizza, Inc.*, 922 F. Supp. 1055 (E.D. Pa. 1996), *aff'd*, 124 F.3d 420 (3d Cir. 1997), the court held that the DOMINOS'S PIZZA franchisor did not illegally tie its franchises to authorized suppliers and distributors because the franchisees agreed to this restriction in the franchise agreement and the franchisor did not have sufficient power over the supply and distribution markets. *Id.* at 1062. The court reasoned that the franchisor's power over the franchisees came not from market share over the "precontract" supply and distribution markets but from the franchise agreement itself. Thus, the franchisees' claims "implicate principles of contract, and are not the concern of antitrust laws." *Id.* *See also Wilson v. Mobil Oil Corp.*, 940 F. Supp. 944, 953 (E.D. La. 1996) (denying franchisor's motion to dismiss and rejecting the defense that franchisees agreed to exclusively purchase franchisor's motor oil because "it is not at all clear . . .what was disclosed to these plaintiffs about the Mobil supply arrangements or when it was disclosed"). *Cf. PSI Repair Serv., Inc. v. Honeywell, Inc.*, 104 F.3d 811 (6th Cir.), *cert. denied*, 520 U.S. 1265 (1997) (granting summary judgment to defendant who did not illegally "lock in" consumers of industrial control replacement parts because, unlike the *Kodak* defendant, its restrictive replacement parts policy was known to consumers *before* purchasing); *Digital Equip. Corp. v. Uniq Digital Techs. Inc.*, 73 F.3d 756 (7th Cir. 1996) (Easterbrook, J.) (defendant's operating systems were not illegally tied to computers because customers agreed to this "bundling" and defendant did not have sufficient power over the operating system market).

4. Territorial Restrictions

Should a trademark owner be able to impose territorial restraints upon the use of its trademarks? "Territorial restraints" limit the geographical areas in which customers of the trademark owner may market the trademarked product. The courts have distinguished two kinds of territorial restraints: those affecting the relationships in the chain of distribution from manufacturers to the retail customer, called "vertical restraints," and those between competitors, called "horizontal restraints."

In 1977, the Supreme Court held that non-price, vertical restraints should not be considered illegal *per se* but should be analyzed under the rule of reason. *Continental T.V. Inc. v. GTE Sylvania*, 433 U.S. 36 (1977). Thus, a franchisor ordinarily can validly agree to appoint only one franchisee in a territory (*United States v. Arnold Schwinn & Co.*, 388 U.S. 365 (1967)) and can contractually restrict a franchisee to a territory of primary responsibility, provided the restraint "is likely to promote interbrand competition without overly restricting intrabrand competition." *Continental T.V., Inc. v. GTE Sylvania, Inc.*, 694 F.2d 1132, 1137 (9th Cir. 1982). In that case, on remand from the Supreme Court's *Continental T.V.* decision, *supra*, the Ninth Circuit affirmed a grant of summary judgment to the franchisor, holding the location agreement to be reasonable and lawful. Among the factors it found persuasive were the interchangeability of television products coupled with the presence of viable competitors ready to sell to any retailers in the relevant market, the fact that the agreement was not overly restrictive (e.g., plaintiff was in no way prohibited from selling non-franchise television products in the location in question) and the fact that the agreement was not adopted for the purpose of preventing price discounting.

Post-*Continental T.V.* decisions have upheld territorial restrictions under the rule of reason. *See, e.g., Murrow Furniture Galleries, Inc. v. Thomasville Furniture Industries, Inc.*, 889 F.2d 524 (4th Cir. 1989) (denying preliminary relief against prohibition of orders and advertising outside area of responsibility); *Murphy v. Business Cards Tomorrow, Inc.*, 854 F.2d 1202, 1204 (9th Cir. 1988) (territorial restrictions); *O.S.C. Corp. v. Apple Computer, Inc.*, 792 F.2d 1464 (9th Cir. 1986) (prohibition of mail order sales upheld). Typically, substantial interbrand competition has been the primary factor in court approval. *See, e.g., Vylene Enterprises, Inc. v. Naugles, Inc.*, 90 F.3d 1472, 1477 (9th Cir. 1996) (applying California contract law; franchisor's opening of a franchise restaurant within two miles of franchisee's restaurant breached the implied covenant of good faith); *Mendelovitz v. Adolph Coors Co.*, 693 F.2d 570, 576 n. 10 (5th Cir. 1982); *Muenster Butane, Inc. v. Stewart Co.*, 651 F.2d 292 (5th Cir. 1981) (substantial interbrand competition and lack of market power). *Cf.* Midwestern Waffles v. Waffle House, Inc., 734 F.2d 705, 711 (11th Cir. 1984), where the court reasoned that if the franchisor alone allocated territories a rule of reason analysis would apply to the vertical restriction; whereas if the franchisor and some franchisees agreed among themselves as to the division of territories a horizontal restriction and *per se* violation would exist. *See also Republic Tobacco Co. v. N. Atl. Trading Co.*, 381 F.3d 717 (7th Cir. 2004) (vertical exclusive distributorship agreements between roll-your-own cigarette paper company and its distributors and retailers was presumptively legal). Note also that the Soft Drink Interbrand Competition Act, 15 U.S.C. §§ 3501–3503, allows soft drink bottlers or distributors to include territorial restrictions in trademark licenses.

In *Icee Distributors, Inc. v. J&J Snack Foods Corp.*, 325 F.3d 586 (5th Cir. 2003), the plaintiff regional distributor of ICEE semi-frozen syrup beverages objected when another distributor began selling the same ICEE product in squeeze tubes in plaintiff's territory. It sued the ICEE trademark licensor for breach of the license agreement, the distributor for selling the same product in plaintiff's territory, and Wal-Mart for being the retail outlet for the squeeze tube products. After a jury found the licensor liable for breach, and the distributor and Wal-Mart liable for trademark dilution (see Chapter 8), an injunction was entered. Because plaintiff was not the owner of the trademark, the dilution holding could not be upheld on appeal. Finding, however, that the contract validly granted plaintiff an exclusive license to sell the ICEE products in its regional territory, the court affirmed the injunction against ICEE sales in that territory by the other distributor and Wal-Mart "because it is independently sustainable as a proper remedy for the breach of contract."

Should territorial agreements among competing businesses be accorded similar treatment? In *United States v. Topco Associates, Inc.*, 405 U.S. 596 (1972), the Court held that an agreement by the 25 members of the TOPCO supermarket cooperative association that members would not sell TOPCO brand products outside specifically designated territories was a per se violation of the Sherman Act. Quoting *White Motor Co. v. United States*, 372 U.S. 253, 263 (1963), the Court stated that "horizontal territorial limitations are naked restraints of trade with no purpose except stifling of competition." *Cf. Midwestern Waffles, supra*, 734 F.2d at 711, where the court reasoned that if the franchisor alone allocated territories a rule of reason analysis would apply to the vertical restriction; whereas it would be a horizontal restriction and per se violation if the franchisor and some franchisees agreed among themselves as to the division of territories.

See generally 2 GILSON, TRADEMARK PROTECTION AND PRACTICE § 6.03(4) (2008 ed.); *Altschuler, Sylvania, Vertical Restraints and Dual Distribution*, 25 ANTITRUST BULL. 1 (1980); *Zelek, Stern & Dunfree, A Rule of Reason Decision Model After Sylvania*, 68 CAL. L. REV. 13 (1980); *Posner, The Rule of Reason and the Economic Approach: Reflections on the Sylvania Decision*, 45 U. CHI. L. REV. 1 (1977).

Price Discrimination

Section 2(a) of the Robinson-Patman Act [15 U.S.C. § 13(a)], states:

> That it shall be unlawful for any person engaged in commerce . . . to discriminate in price between different purchasers of commodities of like grade and quality . . . where the effect of such discrimination may be substantially to lessen competition or tend to create a monopoly in any line of commerce, or to injure, destroy, or prevent competition. . . .

In *FTC v. Borden Co.*, 383 U.S. 637 (1966), the Borden Company was selling evaporated milk under both the BORDEN trademark and various private labels. The private label products sold at lower prices. The court found that since the products were identical the price differential was potentially discriminatory in violation of § 2(a) of the Robinson-Patman Act. Justices Stewart and Harlan dissented, arguing that the differences in the products, even if slight, and the consumer preference for the well-known brand justified the differences in price. Might consumer preference for that product compared to a "generic" product of equal quality, but lower price? *See* McCARTHY, TRADEMARKS AND UNFAIR COMPETITION §§ 3:10-3:11 (4th ed. 2007); Osgood, *The Borden Litigation — Its Impact Upon the Issues of Like Grade and Quality and Competitive Injury Under the Robinson-Patman Act*, 59 TRADEMARK REP. 423 (1969); Comment, *The Supreme Court, 1965 Term*, 80 HARV. L. REV. 91, 236 (1966). On remand of the *Borden* case, the Court of Appeals set aside the FTC's cease and desist order against Borden's dual distribution practice on various grounds, including that the private label milk was available to all customers of its premium brand. *Borden v. FTC*, 381 F.2d 175 (5th Cir. 1967). In doing so, it stated (381 F.2d at 180):

> It is easily understood why the private label milk is sold at all levels of distribution for substantially less than Borden brand milk. By increased advertising and promotional efforts over the years, Borden has created a decided consumer preference for milk bearing a Borden label. The label has come to represent a value in itself.

Remedies

What ought to be the remedies for trademark antitrust violations to redress damage caused by the violations and to restore competition? The successful assertion of civil antitrust claims can result in injunctive relief, treble damages and estoppel for trademark misuse. *See* 15 U.S.C. § 15, and the discussion on Trademark Misuse, supra. In *Ford Motor Co. v. United States*, 405 U.S. 562 (1972), the court prohibited Ford for five years from using its own trade name on spark plugs. In *United States v. Western Electric Co.*, 569 F. Supp. 1057 (D.D.C. 1983), *aff'd without op.*, 104 S. Ct. 542 (1983), the court in its plan for the reorganization of American Telephone and Telegraph (AT&T), ordered assignment of the BELL trade name and trademark to the new regional telephone operating companies. The court rejected AT&T's argument that AT&T shared a "common heritage" in the BELL trade name and trademark and prohibited AT&T from use of the BELL trade name and trademark after January 1, 1984. *Compare Switzer Bros, Inc. v. Locklin*, 297 F.2d 39, 48 (7th Cir. 1961), *cert. denied*, 369 U.S. 851 (1962) ("It seems to us that divestiture of property rights in a trademark, by injunction against the mark's continued use, is a remedy which would seldom commend itself to equity in a private suit under the antitrust laws").

Consider whether compulsory licensing of a trademark should be an alternative remedy to divestiture. In *In re Borden, Inc.*, 92 F.T.C. 669, 672–778 (1976), an FTC Administrative Law Judge ordered the Borden Company to cease activities which monopolized the processed lemon juice market and to grant licenses for a ten-year period for the use of Borden's REALEMON trademark to anyone engaged in or who wished to enter the processed lemon juice market. The FTC set aside the Administrative Law Judge's licensing requirement but noted that it may impose compulsory licensing or suspension of use of a trademark as antitrust relief in an appropriate case. *In re Borden, Inc.*, 92 F.T.C. 669, 807–808 (1978); *order to cease monopolistic activities upheld in Borden, Inc. v. FTC*, 674 F.2d 498 (6th Cir. 1982), *vacated and remanded*, 461 U.S. 940 (1983) (remanded to FTC for entry of cease-and-desist order to which the parties had agreed).

Under a compulsory licensing order, would the licensor have to maintain a quality control system in order that the public not be deceived when purchasing a product bearing the licensed trademark? How would compulsory licensing affect consumer perception of the product bearing the licensed trademark? Would restrictions on the amount of money a trademark owner could spend advertising the trademark or restrictions on the size of the trademark on product labels be more appropriate remedies? For additional commentary, see *Holmes, Trademark Licensing As Structural Antitrust Relief: An Analytical Framework*, 71 TRADEMARK REP. 127 (1981); *McCarthy, Compulsory Licensing of a Trademark: Remedy or Penalty?*, 67 TRADEMARK REP. 197 (1977); *Scherer, The Posnerian Harvest: Separating Wheat from Chaff* [Book Review], 86 YALE L.J. 974, 999 (1977); *Abuse of Trademarks: A Proposal for Compulsory Licensing*, 7 U. MICH. J.L. Ref. 644 (1974).

Section 33(b)(7) of the Lanham Act provides that incontestable rights in a trademark are lost if "the mark has been or is being used to violate the antitrust laws of the United States." *See Redd v. Shell Oil Co.*, 524 F.2d 1054 (10th Cir. 1975); Smith, *Trademarks and Antitrust: The Misuse Defense Under Section 33(b)(7) of the Lanham Act*, 4 HARV. J.L. & PUB. POL'Y 161 (1981). *But see Phi Delta Theta Fraternity v. J. A. Buchroeder & Company*, 251 F. Supp. 968 (W.D. Mo. 1966), where the court stated that § 33(b)(7) should not be read narrowly; i.e., rights also may be lost from violative use of a mark that is not incontestably registered.

7.05　Concurrent Rights

Introduction

Some of the most perplexing problems of trademark law arise when a conflict develops between two or more confusingly similar marks or trade names which have been used over a period of time in different geographical areas by unrelated companies. Similar problems develop when goods or services previously unrelated become related through technological, marketing, or other socio-economic change. In these situations the rights of each party are exceedingly difficult to evaluate on the basis of existing statutory and case law. Courts are understandably reluctant in such circumstances to deprive the junior user of its valuable goodwill or disturb the public's habits and reasonable expectations, yet they must strive to prevent, or at least minimize, likelihood of confusion. As a consequence of these dilemmas, the courts often accord great weight to considerations such as intent, actual or constructive knowledge, or strained distinctions between marks.

The common-law concept which limits the senior user's rights to the areas of actual use persists despite present day patterns of communication, travel, and migration which frequently cause marks to be known beyond such areas. The constructive notice and constructive use provisions of the Lanham Act (15 U.S.C. § 1057(c), 1072), and the courts' application of them, have had great impact upon these problem areas in statutory cases. *Cf. Emergency One, Inc. v. Am. Fire Eagle Engine Co.*, 332 F.3d 264 (4th Cir. 2003) (in the absence of federal registration, defendant's rights were "limited to the areas where [defendant] used the mark"). The cases which follow disclose some of these problems as well as the evolution of the law. A dramatic example of the perplexities generated in this area is found in the territorial division of rights in the trade name and mark STANDARD OIL, and the conflicts spawned thereby (*e.g.*, *Standard Oil Co. (Ky.) v. Humble Oil & Refining Co.*, 363 F.2d 945 (5th Cir. 1966).

UNITED DRUG CO. v. THEODORE RECTANUS CO.
248 U.S. 90 (1918)

Mr. Justice Pitney

*　*　*

The essential facts are as follows: About the year 1877 Ellen M. Regis, a resident of Haverhill, Massachusetts, began to compound and distribute in a small way a preparation for medicinal use in cases of dyspepsia and some other ailments, to which she applied as a distinguishing name the word "Rex" — derived from her surname. The word was put upon the boxes and packages in which the medicine was placed upon the market, after the usual manner of a trade-mark. At first alone, and afterwards in partnership with her son under the firm name of "E.M. Regis & Company," she continued the business on a modest scale; in 1898 she recorded the word "Rex" as a trademark under the laws of Massachusetts (Acts 1895, p. 519, c. 462, § 1); in 1900 the firm procured its registration in the United States Patent Office under the Act of March 3, 1881, c. 138, 21 Stat. 502; in 1904 the Supreme Court of Massachusetts sustained their trade-mark right under the state law as against a concern that was selling medicinal preparations of the present petitioner under the designation of "Rex-all remedies" (*Regis v. Jaynes*, 185 Massachusetts, 458); afterwards the firm established priority in the mark as against petitioner in a contested proceeding in the Patent Office; and subsequently, in the year 1911, petitioner purchased the business with the trade-mark right, and has carried it on in connection with its other business, which consists in the manufacture of medicinal preparations, and their distribution and sale through retail drug stores, known as "Rexall stores," situated in the different States of the Union, four of them being in Louisville, Kentucky.

Meanwhile, about the year 1883, Theodore Rectanus, a druggist in Louisville, familiarly known as "Rex," employed this word as a trade-mark for a medicinal preparation known as "a blood purifier." He continued this use to a considerable extent in Louisville and vicinity, spending money in advertising and building up a trade, so that — except for whatever effect might flow from Mrs. Regis' prior adoption of the word in Massachusetts, of which he was entirely ignorant — he was entitled to use the word as his trade-mark. In the year 1906 he sold his business, including the right to the use of the word, to respondent; and the use of the mark by him and afterwards by respondent was continuous from about the year 1883 until the filing of the bill in the year 1912.

Petitioner's first use of the word "Rex" in connection with the sale of drugs in Louisville or vicinity was in April, 1912, when two shipments of "Rex Dyspepsia Tablets," aggregating 150 boxes and valued at $22.50, were sent to one of the "Rexall" stores in that city. Shortly after this the remedy was mentioned by name in local newspaper advertisements published by those stores. In the previous September, petitioner shipped a trifling amount — five boxes — to a drug store in Franklin, Kentucky, approximately 120 miles distant from Louisville. There is nothing to show that before this any customer in or near Kentucky had heard of the Regis remedy, with or without the description "Rex," or that this word ever possessed any meaning to the purchasing public in that State except as pointing to Rectanus and the Rectanus Company and their "blood purifier." That it did and does convey the latter meaning in Louisville and vicinity is proved without dispute. Months before petitioner's first shipment of its remedy to Kentucky, petitioner was distinctly notified (in June, 1911) by one of its Louisville distributors that respondent was using the word "Rex" to designate its medicinal preparations, and that such use had been commenced by Mr. Rectanus as much as 16 or 17 years before that time.

* * *

The entire argument for the petitioner is summed up on the contention that whenever the first user of a trade-mark has been reasonably diligent in extending the territory of his trade, and as a result of such extension has in good faith come into competition with a later user of the same mark who in equal good faith has extended his trade locally before invasion of his field by the first user, so that finally it comes to pass that the rival traders are offering competitive merchandise in a common market under the same trade-mark, the later user should be enjoined at the suit of the prior adopter, even though the latter be the last to enter the competitive field and the former have already established a trade there. Its application to the case is based upon the hypothesis that the record shows that Mrs. Regis and her firm, during the entire period of limited and local trade in her medicine under the Rex mark, were making efforts to extend their trade so far as they were able to do with the means at their disposal. There is little in the record to support this hypothesis; but, waiving this, we will pass upon the principal contention.

The asserted doctrine is based upon the fundamental error of supposing that a trade-mark right is a right in gross or at large, like a statutory copyright or a patent for an invention, to either of which, in truth, it has little or no analogy. *Canal Co. v. Clark*, 13 Wall. 311, 322; *McLean v. Fleming*, 96 U.S. 245, 254. There is no such thing as property in a trade-mark except as a right appurtenant to an established business or trade in connection with which the mark is employed. The law of trade-marks is but a part of the broader law of unfair competition; the right to a particular mark grows out of its use, not its mere adoption; its function is simply to designate the goods as the product of a particular trader and to protect his good will against the sale of another's product as his; and it is not the subject of property except in connection with an existing business. *Hanover Milling Co. v. Metcalf*, 240 U.S. 403, 412–414.

* * *

Undoubtedly, the general rule is that, as between conflicting claimants to the right to use the same mark, priority of appropriation determines the question. *See Canal Co. v. Clark*, 13 Wall. 311, 323; *McLean v. Fleming*, 96 U.S. 245, 251; *Manufacturing Co. v. Trainer*, 101 U.S. 51, 53; *Columbia Mill Co. v. Alcorn*, 150 U.S. 460, 463. But the reason is that purchasers have come to understand the mark as indicating the origin of the wares, so that its use by a second producer amounts to an attempt to sell his goods as those of his competitor. The reason for the rule does not extend to a case where the same trade-mark happens to be employed simultaneously by two manufacturers in different markets separate and remote from each other, so that the mark means one thing in one market, an entirely different thing in another. It would be a perversion of the rule of priority to give it such an application in our broadly extended country that an innocent party who had in good faith employed a trade-mark in one State, and by the use of it had built up a trade there, being the first appropriator in that jurisdiction, might afterwards be prevented from using it, with consequent injury to his trade and good-will, at the instance of one who theretofore had employed the same mark but only in other and remote jurisdictions, upon the ground that its first employment happened to antedate that of the first-mentioned trader.

*   *   *

The same point was involved in *Hanover Milling Co. v. Metcalf*, 240 U.S. 403, 415, where we said:

> In the ordinary case of parties competing under the same mark in the same market, it is correct to say that prior appropriation settles the question. But where two parties independently are employing the same mark upon goods of the same class, but in separate markets wholly remote the one from the other, the question of prior appropriation is legally insignificant, unless at least it appear that the second adopter has selected the mark with some design inimical to the interests of the first user, such as to take the benefit of the reputation of his goods, to forestall the extension of his trade, or the like.

In this case, as already remarked, there is no suggestion of a sinister purpose on the part of Rectanus or the Rectanus Company; hence the passage quoted correctly defines the status of the parties prior to the time when they came into competition in the Kentucky market. And it results, as a necessary inference from what we have said, that petitioner, being the newcomer in that market, must enter it subject to whatever rights had previously been acquired there in good faith by the Rectanus Company and its predecessor. To hold otherwise — to require Rectanus to retire from the field upon the entry of Mrs. Regis' successor — would be to establish the right of the latter as a right in gross, and to extend it to territory wholly remote from the furthest reach of the trade to which it was annexed, with the effect not merely of depriving Rectanus of the benefit of the good-will resulting from his long-continued use of the mark in Louisville and vicinity, and his substantial expenditures in building up his trade, but of enabling petitioner to reap substantial benefit from the publicity that Rectanus has thus given to the mark in that locality, and of confusing if not misleading the public as to the origin of goods thereafter sold in Louisville under the Rex mark, for, in that market, until petitioner entered, "Rex" meant the Rectanus product, not that of Regis.

*   *   *

Here the essential facts are so closely parallel to those that furnished the basis of decision in the *Allen & Wheeler Case*, report *sub nom. Hanover Milling Co. v. Metcalf*, 240 U.S. 403, 419–420, as to render further discussion unnecessary. Mrs. Regis and her firm, having during a long period of years confined their use of the "Rex" mark to a limited territory wholly remote from that in controversy, must be held to have taken the risk that some innocent party might in the meantime hit upon the same mark, apply it to goods of similar character, and, expend money and effort in building up a trade under it; and since it appears that Rectanus in good faith, and without notice of any prior use by others, selected and used the "Rex" mark, and by the expenditure of money and effort succeeded in building up a local but valuable trade under it in Louisville and vicinity before petitioner entered that field, so that "Rex" had come to be recognized there as the "trade signature" of Rectanus and of respondent as his successor, petitioner is estopped to set up their continued use of the mark in that territory as an infringement of the Regis trade-mark. Whatever confusion may have arisen from conflicting use of the mark is attributable to petitioner's entry into the field with notice of the situation; and petitioner cannot complain of this. As already stated, respondent is not complaining of it.

Decree affirmed.

DAWN DONUT CO. v. HART'S FOOD STORES, INC.
267 F.2d 358 (2^d Cir. 1959)

LUMBARD, CIRCUIT JUDGE

*   *   *

Plaintiff, Dawn Donut Co., Inc., of Jackson, Michigan since June 1, 1922 has continuously used the trademark "Dawn" upon 25 to 100 pound bags of doughnut mix which it sells to bakers in various states, including New York, and since 1935 it has similarly marketed a line of sweet dough mixes for use in the baking of coffee cakes, cinnamon rolls and oven goods in general under that mark. In 1950 cake mixes were added to the company's line of products. Dawn's sales representatives call upon bakers to solicit orders for mixes and the orders obtained are filled by shipment to the purchaser either directly from plaintiff's Jackson, Michigan plant, where the mixes are manufactured, or from a local warehouse within the customer's state. For some years plaintiff maintained a warehouse in Jamestown, New York, from which shipments were made, but sometime prior to the commencement of this suit in 1954 it discontinued this warehouse and has since then shipped its mixes to its New York customers directly from Michigan.

Plaintiff furnishes certain buyers of its mixes, principally those who agree to become exclusive Dawn Donut Shops, with advertising and packaging material bearing the trademark "Dawn" and permits these bakers to sell goods made from the mixes to the consuming public under that trademark. These display materials are supplied either as a courtesy or at a moderate price apparently to stimulate and promote the sale of plaintiff's mixes.

The district court found that with the exception of one Dawn Donut Shop operated in the city of Rochester, New York during 1926–27, plaintiff's licensing of its mark in connection with the retail sale of doughnuts in the state of New York has been confined to areas not less than 60 miles from defendant's trading area. The court also found that for the past eighteen years plaintiff's present New York State representative has, without interruption, made regular calls upon bakers in the city of Rochester, N. Y., and in neighboring towns and cities, soliciting orders for plaintiff's mixes and that throughout this period orders have been filled and shipments made of plaintiff's mixes from Jackson, Michigan into the city of Rochester. But it does not appear that any of these purchasers of plaintiff's mixes employed the plaintiff's mark in connection with retail sales.

The defendant, Hart Food Stores, Inc., owns and operates a retail grocery chain within the New York counties of Monroe, Wayne, Livingston, Genesee, Ontario and Wyoming. The products of defendant's bakery, Starhart Bakeries, Inc., a New York corporation of which it is the sole stockholder, are distributed through these stores, thus confining the distribution of defendant's product to an area within a 45 mile radius of Rochester. Its advertising of doughnuts and other baked products over television and radio and in newspapers is also limited to this area. Defendant's bakery corporation was formed on April 13, 1951 and first used the imprint "Dawn" in packaging its products on August 30, 1951. The district court found that the defendant adopted the mark "Dawn" without any actual knowledge of plaintiff's use or federal registration of the mark, selecting it largely because of a slogan "Baked at midnight, delivered at Dawn" which was originated by defendant's president and used by defendant in its bakery operations from 1929 to 1935. Defendant's president testified, however, that no investigation was made prior to the adoption of the mark to see if anyone else was employing it. Plaintiff's marks were registered federally in 1927, and their registration was renewed in 1947. Therefore by virtue of the Lanham Act, 15 U.S.C.A. § 1072, the defendant had constructive notice of plaintiff's marks as of July 5, 1947, the effective date of the Act.

Defendant's principal contention is that because plaintiff has failed to exploit the mark "Dawn" for some thirty years at the retail level in the Rochester trading area, plaintiff should not be accorded the exclusive right to use the mark in this area.

We reject this contention as inconsistent with the scope of protection afforded a federal registrant by the Lanham Act.

Prior to the passage of the Lanham Act courts generally held that the owner of a registered trademark could not sustain an action for infringement against another who, without knowledge of the registration, used the mark in a different trading area from that exploited by the registrant so that public confusion was unlikely. *Hanover Star Milling Co. v. Metcalf*, 1916, 240 U.S. 403; *cf. White Tower System, Inc. v. White Castle System of Eating Houses Corporation*, 6 Cir., 1937, 90 F.2d 67, *certiorari denied*, 1937, 302 U.S. 720; Note, *Developments in the Law of Trade-Marks and Unfair Competition*, 68 Harv. L. Rev. 814, 857–858 (1955). By being the first to adopt a mark in an area without knowledge of its prior registration, a junior user of a mark could gain the right to exploit the mark exclusively in that market.

But the Lanham Act, 15 U.S.C.A. § 1072, provides that registration of a trade-mark on the principal register is constructive notice of the registrant's claim of ownership. Thus, by eliminating the defense of good faith and lack of knowledge, § 1072 affords nationwide protection to registered marks, regardless of the areas in which the registrant actually uses the mark.

That such is the purpose of Congress is further evidenced by 15 U.S.C.A. §§ 1115(a) and (b) which make the certificate of registration evidence of the registrant's "exclusive right to use the . . . mark in commerce." "Commerce" is defined in 15 U.S.C.A. § 1127 to include all the commerce which may lawfully be regulated by Congress. These two provisions of the Lanham Act make it plain that the fact that the defendant employed the mark "Dawn," without actual knowledge of plaintiff's registration, at the retail level in a limited geographical area of New York state before the plaintiff used the mark in that market, does not entitle it to exclude the plaintiff from using the mark in that area or to use the mark concurrently once the plaintiff licenses the mark or otherwise exploits it in connection with retail sales in the area.

Plaintiff's failure to license its trademarks in defendant's trading area during the thirty-odd years that have elapsed since it licensed them to a Rochester baker does not work an abandonment of the rights in that area. We hold that 15 U.S.C.A. § 1127, which provides for abandonment in certain cases of non-use, applies only when the registrant fails to use his mark, within the meaning of § 1127, anywhere in the nation. Since the Lanham Act affords a registrant nationwide protection, a contrary holding would create an insoluble problem of measuring the geographical extent of the abandonment. Even prior to the passage of the Lanham Act, when the trade-mark protection flowed from state law and therefore depended on use within the state, no case, as far as we have been able to ascertain, held that a trade-mark owner abandoned his rights within only part of a state because of his failure to use the mark in that part of the state. *Cf. Jacobs v. Iodent Chemical Co.*, 3 Cir., 1930, 41 F.2d 637.

Accordingly, since plaintiff has used its trademark continuously at the retail level, it has not abandoned its federal registration rights even in defendant's trading area.

We reject defendant's further claim that plaintiff is prevented by laches from enjoining defendant's use of the mark "Dawn" upon doughnuts and other baked and fried goods. Defendant argues that plaintiff's New York sales representative, one Jesse Cohn, who also represented several other companies besides plaintiff, called upon defendant on a monthly basis, and that about four years prior to the commencement of this lawsuit he observed boxes bearing the label "Dawn" on the desk of one Jack Solomon, defendant's bakery manager. At the trial Cohn denied that he ever saw any packaging in defendant's bakery for baked and fried goods bearing the label Dawn, although he admitted seeing some packages for other food products in defendant's bakery bearing the mark "Dawn." The district court held that since Cohn's contacts with the defendant were on behalf of companies other than the plaintiff, the knowledge of Cohn would not be imputed. We agree with the district court's conclusion.

*   *   *

The Lanham Act, 15 U.S.C.A. § 1114, sets out the standard for awarding a registrant relief against the unauthorized use of his mark by another. It provides that the registrant may enjoin only that concurrent use which creates a likelihood of public confusion as to the origin of the products in connection with which the marks are used. Therefore if the use of the marks by the registrant and the unauthorized user are confined to two sufficiently distinct and geographically separate markets, with no likelihood that the registrant will expand his use into defendant's market, so that no public confusion is possible, then the registrant is not entitled to enjoin the junior user's use of the mark. See *Fairway Foods, Inc. v. Fairway Markets, Inc.*, 9 Cir., 1955, 227 F.2d 193; Note, *Developments in the Law of Trade-Marks and Unfair Competition*, 68 Harv. L. Rev. 814, 857–60 (1955); *cf. Sterling Brewing, Inc. v. Cold Springs Brewing Corp., supra.*

As long as plaintiff and defendant confine their use of the mark "Dawn" in connection with the retail sale of baked goods to their present separate trading areas it is clear that no public confusion is likely.

*   *   *

The decisive question then is whether plaintiff's use of the mark "Dawn" at the retail level is likely to be confined to its current area of use or whether in the normal course of its business, it is likely to expand the retail use of the mark into defendant's trading area. If such expansion were probable, then the concurrent use of the marks would give rise to the conclusion that there was a likelihood of confusion.

The district court found that in view of the plaintiff's inactivity for about thirty years in exploiting its trademarks in defendant's trading area at the retail level either by advertising directed at retail purchasers or by retail sales through authorized licensed users, there was no reasonable expectation that plaintiff would extend its retail operations into defendant's trading area. There is ample evidence in the record to support this conclusion and we cannot say that it is clearly erroneous.

We note not only that plaintiff has failed to license its mark at the retail level in defendant's trading area for a substantial period of time, but also that the trend of plaintiff's business manifests a striking decrease in the number of licensees employing its mark at the retail level in New York state and throughout the country. In the 1922-1930 period plaintiff had 75 to 80 licensees across the country with 11 located in New York. At the time of the trial plaintiff listed only 16 active licensees not one of which was located in New York.

The normal likelihood that plaintiff's wholesale operations in the Rochester area would expand to the retail level is fully rebutted and overcome by the decisive fact that plaintiff has in fact not licensed or otherwise exploited its mark at retail in the area for some thirty years.

Accordingly, because plaintiff and defendant use the mark in connection with retail sales in distinct and separate markets and because there is no present prospect that plaintiff will expand its use of the mark at the retail level into defendant's trading area, we conclude that there is no likelihood of public confusion arising from the concurrent use of the marks and therefore the issuance of an injunction is not warranted. *A fortiori* plaintiff is not entitled to any accounting or damages. However, because of the effect we have attributed to the constructive notice provision of the Lanham Act, the plaintiff may later, upon a proper showing of an intent to use the mark at the retail level in defendant's market area, be entitled to enjoin defendant's use of the mark.

*   *   *

[*Affirmed.*]

WEINER KING, INC. v. WIENER KING CORP.
615 F.2d 512 (C.C.P.A. 1980)

RICH, J.

* * *

Weiner King was the first to adopt and use its mark WEINER KING. Later, [Wiener King Corp. of North Carolina] "WKNC" innocently adopt[ed] its mark WIENER KING in a market area remote from that of Weiner King's market area. Under such circumstances, it is settled law that each party has a right to use its mark in its own initial area of use. *United Drug Co. v. Theodore Rectanus Co.*, 248 U.S. 90 (1918); *Hanover Star Milling Co. v. Metcalf*, 240 U.S. 403 (1916). In dispute here are the *registrable rights* to the remainder of the United States possessed by each party.

This case takes on an added dimension of complexity for two reasons: WKNC, the later adopter, was the first to register its mark under the Lanham Act; and, even though an innocent adopter, WKNC underwent a large portion of its expansion after notice of the existence of Weiner King and its use of the WEINER KING mark in the Flemington, New Jersey, area.

Weiner King's major contention on appeal is that any expansion on the part of WKNC which occurred after it learned of Weiner King and the use of the WEINER KING mark was at WKNC's peril and cannot serve as a basis for a right to register as a concurrent user in any of the areas it entered after notice. We do not agree.

It is said that nature abhors a vacuum. The same may be said of equity; it must operate in a factual environment. The TTAB had the task of balancing the equities between a prior user who remained content to operate a small, locally-oriented business with no apparent desire to expand, and who, until recently, declined to seek the benefits of Lanham Act registration, and a subsequent user, whose expressed purpose has been, from its inception, to expand into a nationwide franchising operation, and who has fulfilled its purpose, taking advantage of Lanham Act registration in the process.

A crucial question brought into issue by Weiner King is the character of WKNC's expansion which occurred subsequent to its learning of Weiner King's existence. If it was in bad faith it cannot support a right to registration for use in those areas.

The District Court found that this expansion was not an attempt to "palm off" or trade on the reputation of Weiner King. "Instead, they [sought] to gain from their own goodwill, founded upon the use of 'Wiener King' throughout a large part of the United States." 407 F. Supp. at 1282. This finding was undisturbed on appeal. It is binding on the parties by stipulation.

The only basis urged by Weiner King for absence of good faith on the part of WKNC is the fact that WKNC expanded out of North Carolina with notice of Weiner King's existence and use of its WEINER KING mark. We hold that this reason is legally insufficient to support a finding of bad faith. In so holding, we caution that such a determination must always be the product of the particular fact pattern involved in each case. While an attempt to "palm off," or a motive to "box in" a prior user by cutting into its probable area of expansion, each necessarily flowing from knowledge of the existence of the prior user, might be sufficient to support a finding of bad faith, *mere knowledge of the existence of the prior user* should not, by itself, constitute bad faith.

Turning to the fundamental question in this case, i.e., who gets what territory, this court has suggested certain criteria which are helpful in resolving this question. In *In re Beatrice Foods, Co.*, 429 F.2d 466, 475 (1970), this court noted that actual use in a territory was not necessary to establish rights in that territory, and that the inquiry should focus on the party's (1) previous business activity; (2) previous expansion or lack thereof; (3) dominance of contiguous areas; (4) presently-planned expansion; and, where applicable (5) possible market penetration by means of products brought in from other areas.

In the present case, reliance on factors 1–4 weighs overwhelmingly in favor of WKNC. This is clear from the stipulated findings in the civil action alone, which demonstrate that Weiner King comes up virtually empty-handed in all of the categories. While we could stop here, there are several other reasons why, in this case, the decision of the TTAB should be affirmed.

In appropriate situations, courts have restricted a prior user to its actual trade territory in favor of a later user who has appeared on the horizon. *See Jacobs v. Iodent Chemical Co.*, 41 F.2d 637 (3ᵈ Cir. 1930). In *Zimmerman v. Holiday Inns of America*, 438 Pa. 528, 266 A.2d 87 (1970), *cert. denied*, 400 U.S. 992 (1971), the facts revealed that a local motel operator had unsuccessfully sued a nationwide franchise motel chain which he felt was encroaching on his territory, thus alerting the chain, a later user, to his existence. The later user then opened fifteen additional motels in the state. In a subsequent suit to enjoin the chain, the court, noting a lack of bad faith on the part of the chain, limited injunctive relief to an area within twenty-two miles of the local operator's motels. The Pennsylvania Supreme Court affirmed, thus acknowledging the right of the later user to operate in areas into which it had expanded after notice of the existence of the prior user.

The commentators have not been silent on this issue. Restriction of a prior user to its actual trade territory and zone of probable expansion has been noted. *See* McCarthy, *Trademarks and Unfair Competition*, § 26:8 at 218 & n. 13 (3d ed. 1992). One established authority has stated that the *Hanover* and *Rectanus* cases, *supra*, "are based on the theory that the prior user in each case abandoned its right to expand its trade when it failed to exercise that right." 1 H. Nims, *Unfair Competition and Trade Marks*, § 218(b) at 645 (4th ed. 1947). This is precisely the principle relied upon below by the TTAB. 201 U.S.P.Q. at 916.

We also find it significant that WKNC was the first to register its mark. In *Giant Foods, Inc. v. Malone & Hyde, Inc.*, 522 F.2d at 1396, 187 U.S.P.Q. at 382, a majority of this court stated:

> The winner of the race for [virgin territory], according to our system of federal registration, is the senior user at least in those instances where he is also the first to apply for a federal registration.

It was thus implicitly recognized that there is a policy of encouraging prompt registration of marks by rewarding those who first seek registration under the Lanham Act. We restated this policy again in *In re Beatrice Foods Co.*, 429 F.2d at 474 n. 13:

> [W]here the prior user does not apply for a registration before registration is granted to another, *there may be valid grounds, based on a policy of rewarding those who first seek federal registration, and a consideration of the rights created by the existing registration, for limiting his registration to the area of actual use and permitting the prior registrant to retain the nationwide protection of the act restricted only by the territory of the prior user.* [Emphasis ours.]

We deem this to be sound policy when applied in the proper case, as determined by its facts and circumstances. From our view of the facts and circumstances here, this is a proper case.

Section 2(d) of the Lanham Act (15 U.S.C. § 1052(d)) also supports the decision of the TTAB. One of the stated purposes of the act, to prevent consumer confusion, *see* H.R. Rep. No. 219, 79th Cong., 1st Sess. 2 (1945); S. Rep. No. 1333 (1946), is embodied in § 2(d), which reads in pertinent part:

> No trademark shall be refused registration unless it — (d) Consists of or comprises a mark which so resembles . . . a mark . . . previously used in the United States by another and not abandoned, as to be likely, when applied to the goods of the applicant, to cause confusion, or to cause mistake, or to deceive: *Provided,* That when the Commissioner determines that confusion, mistake, or

deception is not likely to result from the continued use by more than one person of the same or similar marks under conditions and limitations as to the mode or place of use of the marks . . . concurrent registrations may be issued to such persons . . . In issuing concurrent registrations, the Commissioner shall prescribe conditions and limitations as to the mode or place of use of the mark. . . .

Section 2(d) recognizes that, under certain conditions, more than one party may have a right to use, and hence to register, a given mark. The proviso of § 2(d) instructs the Commissioner that, when issuing concurrent registrations, he is to impose conditions and limitations to the use of the mark by the concurrent registrants. It is plain that these conditions and limitations are to be imposed for the purpose of preventing consumer confusion. The proviso exhibits no bias in favor of the prior user.

The TTAB found that "it is an inescapable conclusion that, outside of Weiner King's little enclave, 'WIENER KING' means WKNC's restaurants and to allow Weiner King to step out of its trading area, would cause confusion to the purchasing public." 201 U.S.P.Q. at 916. By finding that Weiner King's reputation zone is a circle with a 15-mile radius, the Third Circuit has made essentially the same finding. It is binding on the parties by stipulation. In light of this fact, the issuance to Weiner King of a concurrent registration which encompasses the entire United States except for the state of North Carolina would serve only to foster the very confusion which the act was meant to prevent.

We do not rely for our decision on § 22 of the Lanham Act (15 U.S.C. § 1072), which provides that a registration serves as constructive notice of the claim of ownership of the registered mark, thus cutting off the defense of subsequent good faith adoption by another party. Although such an approach has been suggested, *see* Schwartz, *Concurrent Registration Under the Lanham Trademark Act of 1946: What is the Impact on Section 2(d) of Section 22?*, 55 T.M. Rep. 413 (1965), we do not believe that a mechanical approach which always defers to the first to register comprehends all of the factors which must be taken into account in order to come to a reasoned decision. The problems of concurrent use issues must ultimately be solved by a comprehensive factual analysis, which the TTAB has both the power and the resources to make.

*   *   *

[*Modified.*]

Notes on Concurrent Rights

1. Generally

At common law, the user of a trademark cannot prevent the good faith use of a confusingly similar mark in a separate geographic market where neither the user's trade nor business reputation has reached. *See United Drug, supra; Hanover Star Milling Co. v. Metcalf*, 240 U.S. 403 (1916), *Nat'l Assn'n for Healthcare Comm'ns, Inc. v. Central Arkansas Agency on Aging, Inc.*, 59 U.S.P.Q.2d 1352 (8th Cir. 2001). Mere knowledge of a remote use may not amount to bad faith. In *C P Interests, Inc. v. California Pools, Inc.*, 238 F.3d 690 (5th Cir. 2001), for example, involving initially remote uses of the mark CALIFORNIA POOLS for swimming pool construction, the court upheld a jury instruction that "mere knowledge of the [senior user's] use of the mark does not defeat good faith, though it is a factor you may consider if you find that [the junior user] had knowledge at the time of its first use." There, the knowledge was not dispositive in the absence of evidence of an intent to benefit from the senior user's reputation or goodwill.

2. Market Penetration

How much "market penetration" is needed to establish exclusive rights in a particular territory? *See Sweetarts v. Sunline, Inc.*, 436 F.2d 705, 708 (8th Cir. 1971):

> In determining this issue the trial court should weigh all the factors including plaintiff's dollar value of sales at the time defendants entered the market, number of customers compared to the population of the state, relative and potential growth of sales, and length of time since significant sales. Though the market penetration need not be large to entitle plaintiff to protection, *Sweet Sixteen Co. v. Sweet "16" Shop*, 15 F.2d 920 (8 Cir 1926), it must be significant enough to pose the real likelihood of confusion among the consumers in that area between the products of plaintiff and the products of defendants.

(quoting *Sweetarts v. Sunline, Inc.*, 380 F.2d 923 (8th Cir. 1967)).

In *Wrist-Rocket Mfg. Co. v. Saunders Archery Co.*, 578 F.2d 727 (8th Cir. 1978), in which a prior user confronted a registrant possessing incontestability rights, the court found that the prior user had made "significant sales" (one wrist-rocket per 20-30,000 people in a state) in 25 states, and divided the country between the parties accordingly. *See also Nat'l Ass'n for Healthcare Communications, Inc. v. Central Arkansas Agency on Aging, Inc.*, 59 U.S.P.Q.2d 1352 (8th Cir. 2001) (applying *Sweetarts* factors and finding plaintiff had made insufficient penetration in defendant's six county area of use); *Natural Footwear Ltd. v. Hart, Schaffner & Marx*, 760 F.2d 1383 (3d Cir. 1985) (insufficient market penetration outside of New Jersey); *V & V Food Products, Inc. v. Cacique Cheese Co.*, 683 F. Supp. 662, 668 (N.D. Ill. 1988) (market penetration sufficient to establish rights in four states).

Should it be possible to lose exclusive rights in some marketing areas while retaining them in others? In *Sheila's Shine Products v. Sheila Shine, Inc.*, 486 F.2d 114 (5d Cir. 1973), the court held that plaintiff had lost its trademark rights either through nonuse and intent to abandon, or, alternatively, through licensing with insufficient control, in all but the seven states in which plaintiff itself continued to use the trademark. As a result, defendant was granted rights to exclusive use of the mark in the remaining forty-three states. *Compare United States Jaycees v. Philadelphia Jaycees*, 639 F.2d 134 (3d Cir. 1981), where, over a strong dissent, the court refused to apply this "regional abandonment" theory to a city-sized area. After the defendant-counterclaimant successfully showed that the plaintiff had abandoned its rights in AMERICAN EAGLE in connection with fire engines and rescue vehicles in *Emergency One, Inc. v. American Fire Eagle Engine Co.*, 332 F.3d 264 (4th Cir. 2003), the district court entered a nationwide injunction against plaintiff's use of that mark, because such use would infringe defendant's common law rights in its mark AMERICAN FIRE EAGLE in connection with similar products. The Fourth Circuit vacated the injunction, because the district court entered "without any evidence of the localities in which [defendant] used the mark". Absent federal registration, "any injunctive relief to which AFE was entitled was also limited to the areas where [defendant] used the mark." The case therefore was remanded for determination of that issue. *See generally* Gross, *The Territorial Scope of Trademark Rights*, 44 U. MIAMI L. REV. 1075 (1990).

3. Secondary Meaning and Ambulatory Clientele

A nondistinctive mark possessing secondary meaning in the territory where it long has been used subsequently may be used by its owner in a new territory where it has not yet acquired secondary meaning. Should the mark's acquired significance in the old territory affect the breadth of protection extended to it in the new? In *beef & brew, inc. v. BEEF & BREW INC.*, 389 F. Supp. 179 (D. Ore. 1974), plaintiff demonstrated secondary meaning for its merely descriptive restaurant name in the Seattle but not the Portland area. The court rejected plaintiff's zone of expansion argument and denied relief. In *A.J. Canfield Co. v. Concord Beverage Co.*, 629 F. Supp. 200, 210 (E.D. Pa.

1985), *aff'd on other grounds*, 808 F.2d 291 (3^d Cir. 1986), the court held for defendant, finding plaintiff's mark at most had acquired secondary meaning in the Chicago area, not in defendant's East Coast marketing area. *Compare A.J. Canfield Co. v. Vess Beverages, Inc.*, 612 F. Supp. 1081 (N.D. Ill. 1985) (finding substantial likelihood plaintiff would be able to demonstrate secondary meaning in Chicago area). *See also Bank of Texas v. Commerce Southwest, Inc.*, 741 F.2d 785 (5th Cir. 1984); *Shoppers Fair of Arkansas, Inc. v. Sanders Co.*, 328 F.2d 496 (8th Cir. 1964).

What is the effect of modern communication and travel on trademark rights and likelihood of confusion as to source? In *Chopra v. Kapur*, 185 U.S.P.Q. 195, 200 (N.D. Cal. 1974), the parties' closest restaurants were located in San Francisco and Chicago; nonetheless, the court found likelihood of confusion, in part because "the clientele of plaintiff's restaurants is ambulatory and plaintiff's reputation and good will have extended to the San Francisco area. In these circumstances, geographical proximity is not necessary." For one of the earliest cases applying this principle, see *Stork Restaurant, Inc. v. Sahati*, 166 F.2d 348 (9th Cir. 1948). *Compare Steak & Brew, Inc. v. Beef & Brew Restaurant, Inc.*, 370 F. Supp. 1030 (S.D. Ill. 1974), in which plaintiff unsuccessfully contended that the *United Drug* principle, which protects the innocent second party in his own market area, does not apply to hotels or restaurants, and *Maxim's Limited v. Badonsky*, 772 F.2d 388 (7th Cir. 1985) (relief denied where clientele for expensive restaurants were sophisticated and discriminating). *See also Barbecue Marx, Inc. v. 551 Ogden, Inc.*, 235 F.3d 1041 (7th Cir. 2000), in which the Court held that confusion was unlikely and that it was clear error for the district court to fail to weigh in defendant's favor the locations of the parties' restaurants in disparate neighborhoods of Chicago: "SMOKE DADDY is located in Wicker Park and BONE DADDY is located in River West. These neighborhoods are in the heart of Chicago. In such a densely populated area, 1.4 miles is quite a distance, especially in an area crowded with dozens of restaurants, as these neighborhoods are."

4.　Concurrent Use and the Internet

Geographic restrictions agreed to by the parties may be circumvented by the potentially unrestricted geographic scope of the Internet. In *Harrods Ltd. v. Sixty Internet Domain Names*, 302 F.3d 214 (4th Cir. 2002), for example, plaintiff Harrods UK had the right to use the Harrods name in connection with department store services in the United Kingdom and the U.S., and Harrods BA, a former subsidiary, had the independent right to use the Harrods name in connection with department store services in Argentina and much of South America. Harrods BA overstepped its boundaries, however, when it registered numerous Harrods-derivative domain names in the .com, .org and .net top level domains, *e.g.* harrodsstore, harrodsshopping, shoppingharrods, etc. Evidence showed that Harrods BA had done so in bad faith to divert customers of Harrods UK and extract payment from Harrods UK to purchase the domain names.

The Court affirmed an order transferring fifty-four of the domain names to Harrods UK, and remanded for consideration of whether Harrods BA had registered six other Argentina-related domain names in bad faith. In doing so it observed, "even recognizing the rights of a concurrent user of a mark, a legitimate concurrent user still violates the other user's rights if it uses the shared mark in a manner that would cause consumer confusion, such as by using the mark in the other's geographic area. . . . Thus, if a concurrent user registers a domain name with the intent of expanding its use of the shared mark beyond its geographically restricted area, then the domain name is registered in bad faith . . . ."

Compare Toys "R" Us v. Step Two, S.A., 318 F.3d 446 (3^d Cir. 2003), in which the Court ordered jurisdictional discovery against the Spanish defendant. Plaintiff operated a U.S. network of "Imaginarium" stores that sold educational toys and games, with a website at www.imaginarium.com. Defendant franchised "Imaginarium" toy stores in Spain and nine other countries, and promoted merchandise at a Spanish website at www.imaginarium.es. After defendant registered four U.S. "Imaginarium" domain names, including www.imaginariumworld.com, and began offering merchandise at those websites, plaintiff sued. Because plaintiff did not proceed on an *in rem* basis as the plaintiff had in *Harrods*, above, various jurisdictional issues were raised (*see* Chapter 10) that required additional discovery.

For discussion of some of the concurrent use issues raised by the Internet, see *Creasman, Establishing Geographic Rights in Trademarks Based on Internet Use*, 95 TMR 1016 (2005); *Dinwoodie, (National) Trademark Laws and the (Non-National) Domain Name System*, 21 U. La. J. Int'l Econ. L. 495 (2000).

5. Areas of Natural Expansion

Should a prior user's rights extend to areas of natural expansion? In *beef & brew, inc. v. BEEF & BREW INC.*, supra at 185, the court observed that the natural expansion doctrine is imprecise and potentially inconsistent with the objectives of free competition, and that the leading natural expansion cases rest each upon a finding of secondary meaning, or bad faith, or both. *See also Blue Ribbon Feed v. Farmers Union Central Exchange*, 731 F.2d 415, 422 (7th Cir. 1984) (a "mere hope of expansion beyond its trade area is insufficient to support the protection sought"), and *Raxton Corp. v. Anania Assocs., Inc.*, 635 F.2d 924, 930 (1st Cir. 1980), in which the court stated:

> A natural expansion doctrine that penalized innocent users of a trademark simply because they occupied what for them would be a largely undiscoverable path of some remote prior user's expansion strikes us as at once unworkable, unfair, and, in the light of statutory protection available today, unnecessary.

Absent a federal registration, why should any "right to natural expansion" be found to exist in trade identity law, if indeed it does? Can such a right be justified under our "protect only against likely confusion" rationale? *See* Marks, *Trademark Protection Under the "Natural Area of Business Expansion" Doctrine*, 53 Notre Dame L. Rev. 869 (1978).

6. Federal Registration and Nationwide Rights

Under the Lanham Act's current interpretation by many courts, a federal registrant acquires rights in his mark even in areas in which he does not conduct his business. As stated in the *Dawn Donut* case, *supra*, and *American Foods, Inc. v. Golden Flake, Inc.*, 312 F.2d 619 (5th Cir. 1963), once a federal registrant evidences a present prospect or likelihood of expansion, he is entitled to an injunction against a local, junior user. *See Foxtrap, Inc. v. Foxtrap, Inc.*, 671 F.2d 636 (D.C. Cir. 1982) (observing that the Lanham Act constructive notice provision removed the common-law good faith defense of *Hanover* and *Rectanus*); *Comidas Exquisitos, Inc. v. O'Malley & McGee's, Inc.*, 775 F.2d 260 (8th Cir. 1985) (relief denied where no present likelihood of expansion into defendant's area by registrant); *Pizzeria Uno Corp. v. Temple*, 747 F.2d 1522, 1536 (4th Cir. 1984) (same). Is this a sound and fair rule consistent with the basic doctrines of our trade identity law? *Compare Circuit City Stores, Inc. v. Carmax, Inc.*, 165 F.3d 1047 (6th Cir. 1999) (in the Sixth Circuit, "no particular finding of likelihood of entry or irreparable harm is necessary for injunctive relief in trademark infringement and unfair competition cases" and, once infringement was found, "the District Court was not required to find that Circuit City was about to enter the defendant's market [in Northeast Ohio] in order to grant injunctive relief").

See generally Casagrande, *The "Dawn Donut Rule": Still Standing (Article III, That Is) Even with the Rise of the Internet*, 90 T.M.R. 723 (2000); Comment, *The Scope of Territorial Protection of Trademarks*, 65 Nw. U.L. Rev. 781 (1970).

Need a federal registrant prove likelihood of expansion if he or she can show the mark has already established a reputation in a junior user's territory? *Cf. Circuit City v. Carmax, supra; Tisch Hotels, Inc. v. Americana Inn, Inc.,* 350 F.2d 609 (7th Cir. 1965).

7. Federal Registration and Common Law Prior Use

What territorial rights are acquired by a registrant who is not the first user of the mark? Should the first user's rights be limited to areas of actual use? Should the plans of either to expand business under the mark, e.g., via franchising, be considered in the determination? *See Weiner King, supra; Minute Man Press Int'l, Inc. v. MinuteMen Press, Inc.,* 219 U.S.P.Q. 426 (N.D. Cal. 1983); McCarthy, *Trademarks and Unfair Competition* § 20:84 (4th ed. 2007).

What determination of rights should result when a mark is registered by the senior user but a junior user innocently adopts the mark in a remote location prior to the first user's date of registration (or, after the 1988 revision of the Lanham Act, prior to the filing date of the application, see below) and uses it continuously after adoption? The Lanham Act provides such a junior user with a defense to an infringement claim made by a registrant possessing *incontestability* rights in a mark under 15 U.S.C. § 1115, "[p]rovided, however, that this defense . . . shall apply only for the area in which such continuous prior use is proved." 15 U.S.C. § 1115(b)(5). In *Induct-O-Matic Corp. v. Inductotherm Corp.,* 747 F.2d 358, 366 (6th Cir. 1984), and *Ace Hardware, Co. v. Ace Hardware Corp.,* 218 U.S.P.Q. 240 (N.D.N.Y. 1982), the courts held the junior user entitled to protection in the area of use that predated the registration. *Cf. Casual Corner Assocs., Inc. v. Casual Stores of Nevada, Inc.,* 493 F.2d 709 (9th Cir. 1974), where failure to use the mark for one year prevented defendant from asserting the defense of *continuous* pre-registration use, and *First Bank v. First Bank Sys. Inc.,* 84 F.3d 1040 (8th Cir. 1996), where plaintiff failed to establish secondary meaning in its unregistered use of descriptive term FIRST BANK in three Iowa counties prior to defendant's federal registration of FIRST BANK. For a discussion of the incontestability provisions of the Lanham Act, see Chapter 3, *supra.*

Should innocent adoption by a junior user before registration (or application, see below) by the senior user be a defense with regard to *contestable* registered marks? In *Golden Door, Inc. v. Odisho,* 437 F. Supp. 956, 964 (N.D. Cal. 1977), *aff'd,* 646 F.2d 347 (9th Cir. 1980), the court stated:

> [w]hether the enumerated exception constitutes a substantive defense to a claim of infringement, or merely alters the evidentiary weight accorded the presumption of plaintiff's exclusive right to use of the mark established by registration, has been a subject of confusion among the courts and authorities in the field of trademark law,

and reluctantly (*see Golden Door,* 437 F. Supp. at 864) following Ninth Circuit precedent, applied the defense to the federal but not the state trademark claim.

In *Matador Motor Inns, Inc. v. Matador Motel, Inc.,* 376 F. Supp. 385, 388 (D.N.J. 1974), the court termed "patently absurd" plaintiff's contention that the defense was inapplicable because plaintiff's mark was not yet incontestable.

> An incontestable mark, by definition, enjoys greater procedural protection than one of a lesser status. . . . If this be the case, clearly a defense to an infringement action based on an incontestable service mark must also be applicable to a contestable mark.

Similarly, in *Value House v. Phillips Mercantile Co.,* 523 F.2d 424, 429 (10th Cir. 1975), the court stated "The prior use defense in these circumstances is made available by 15 U.S.C.A. 1115(b)(5) even against a plaintiff whose mark has become incontestable and so the defense is *a fortiori* available here." *See also Wrist-Rocket Mfg. Co., supra; Money Store v. Harriscorp Finance, Inc.,* 689 F.2d 666 (7th Cir. 1982); *T-Shirts Plus v. T-Shirts Plus, Inc.,* 222 U.S.P.Q. 117 (C.D. Cal. 1983); *Allied Telephone Co. v. Allied Telephone Systems Co.,* 218 U.S.P.Q. 817 (S.D. Ohio 1982).

Under the Lanham Act before its 1988 revision, the prior use defense described above had to be based on continuous use begun before the registrant's *registration* issued. Under the Revision Act, registrants are deemed to have nationwide constructive use as of the *application* filing date. 15 U.S.C. § 1057(c). Therefore, in actions involving registrations derived from applications filed after the November 16, 1989 effective date of the Revision Act, the prior use must have begun before the registrant's application filing date for the prior use defense to apply. 15 U.S.C. § 1115(b)(5). In *Allard Enterprises, Inc. v. Advancing Programming Resources, Inc.*, 146 F.3d 350 (6th Cir. 1998), for example, the appellate court affirmed defendant's rights in its area of use of APR for employment placement services were prior to those of the federal registrant plaintiff. Relying on defendant's less than extensive activities under the mark ("on at least one fax, on at least one resume, and in numerous [oral] solicitations"), the court observed, "defendant's rights to its mark extend only as far as the area where its continuous prior use of that mark preempted plaintiff's constructive use of its mark."

The *Allard* court's apparent endorsement of rather minimal activities to establish priority subsequently was explained (and limited) by the Sixth Circuit in *Circuit City Stores, Inc. v. Carmax, Inc.*, 165 F.3d 1047, 1055 (6th Cir. 1999) as turning instead on the evidence in *Allard* of sufficient public awareness of defendant's use of the mark in connection with its business. In *Circuit City*, defendants failed to show priority over the federal registrant plaintiff where defendants "repeatedly failed to use the Carmax mark [for a used car business] in basic commercial contexts such as their telephone listing, store signs, newspaper ads and other customer information" and supplied no evidence of public awareness of their use of the mark. *See also Advance Stores Co. v. Refinishing Specialities Inc.*, 188 F.3d 408 (6th Cir. 1999) (federal registrant had nationwide rights in NAPA for auto parts stores except in Jefferson County, Kentucky where defendant established prior rights). *Compare Lucent Information Management Inc. v. Lucent Technologies*, 186 F.3d 311 (3d Cir. 1999) (plaintiff's announcement letter, one sale and a few sales presentations were insufficient to establish priority in LUCENT for telecommunications services over defendant's constructive use as of its application date).

8. Concurrent Registrations

Note that § 2(d) of the Lanham Act authorizes concurrent registrations where two or more users are each entitled to use of a mark. *See Noah's, Inc. v. Nark, Inc.*, 560 F. Supp. 1253 (E.D. Mo. 1983), *aff'd*, 728 F.2d 410 (8th Cir. 1984), in which the senior user was granted a registration for the State of Iowa, but held to have abandoned its national trademark rights to an expansionist junior user. *Cf. Holiday Inn v. Holiday Inns, Inc.*, 534 F.2d 312 (C.C.P.A. 1976), in which a prior user of "Holiday Inn" in a small local area was granted a restricted registration for that area despite potential confusion with the famous chain. See the section on concurrent use proceedings in Chapter 3.

9. Concurrent Use Agreements

Parties also may agree to divide territories of use between them, as long as source confusion remains unlikely. *In re Four Seasons Hotels Ltd.*, 987 F.2d 1565 (Fed. Cir. 1993); *Amalgamated Bank of N.Y. v. Amalgamated Trust & Savings*, 842 F.2d 1270 (Fed. Cir. 1988). *See also Houlihan v. Parliament Import Co.*, 921 F.2d 1258 (Fed. Cir. 1990) (upholding concurrent registration of BAREFOOT BYNUM for wine to two contiguous users who obtained territorial assignments from original owner; the court observed that concurrent registrants need not have products of identical quality).

7.06   Gray Market Goods

Introduction

"Parallel imports" or "gray market goods" are goods bearing an authentic trademark which are intended for distribution in foreign countries but which are instead imported and sold to the ultimate consumer in a country where the trademark signifies a domestic source. Typically, the manufacturer establishes a distribution system in which it authorizes or licenses the manufacture or sale of its products in specific foreign territories. Parallel importers purchase these products abroad and import them for domestic sale. As a result, these unauthorized goods often compete directly with goods imported and sold by the manufacturer's authorized distributor. In other instances, where the manufacturer has both domestic and foreign production facilities, the parallel imports compete with goods made domestically and intended only for domestic distribution. A number of factors including fluctuations in market conditions, currency exchange rates and disparities in costs, services or wage scales, may enable the sale of gray market goods at a price lower than that of authorized goods.

Historically, trademark law has viewed parallel imports under competing property law concepts: (1) "universal" rights in which a mark has no territorial bounds and ownership is exhausted once the product is sold, and (2) "territorial" rights in which a mark is exclusively owned by the registrant or user within each territory. *See* Hiebert, *Foundations of the Law of Parallel Importation: Duality and Universality in Nineteenth Century Trademark Law*, 80 TRADEMARK REP. 483 (1990). In the cases which follow, Justice Holmes' *Bourjois* and *Prestonettes* opinions established that in the United States the law of parallel imports is not based upon property law, but upon protection of the public from confusion or deception. If the domestic source has developed a goodwill factually independent from that of the foreign source, confusion may occur. While consideration of the relative benefits to consumers of barring or allowing parallel imports should be part of any analysis of this area of the law, the confusion principle remains fundamental.

A. BOURJOIS & CO. v. KATZEL
260 U.S. 689 (1923)

MR. JUSTICE HOLMES delivered the opinion of the Court.

This is a bill to restrain the infringement of the trade marks "Java" and "Bourjois" registered in the Patent Office of the United States. A preliminary injunction was granted by the District Court, 274 Fed. 856, but the order was reversed by the Circuit Court of Appeals, one Judge dissenting. 275 Fed. 539. A writ of certiorari was granted by this Court. 257 U.S. 630. In 1913 A. Bourjois & Cie., E. Wertheimer & Cie., Successeurs, doing business in France and also in the United States, sold to the plaintiff for a large sum their business in the United States, with their good will and their trade marks registered in the Patent Office. The latter related particularly to face powder, and included the above words. The plaintiff since its purchase has registered them again and goes on with the business that it bought, using substantially the same form of box and label as its predecessors and importing its face powder from France. It uses care in selecting colors suitable for the American market, in packing and in keeping up the standard, and has spent much money in advertising, &c., so that the business has grown very great and the labels have come to be understood by the public here as meaning goods coming from the plaintiff. The boxes have upon their backs: "Trade Marks Reg. U.S. Pat. Off. Made in France — Packed in the U.S.A. by A. Bourjois & Co., Inc., of New York, Succ'rs. in the U.S. to A. Bourjois & Cie., and E. Wertheimer & Cie."

The defendant, finding that the rate of exchange enabled her to do so at a profit, bought a large quantity of the same powder in France and is selling it here in the French boxes which closely resemble those used by the plaintiff except that they have not the last quoted statement on the backs, and that the label reads "Poudre de Riz de Java," whereas the plaintiff has found it advisable to strike out the suggestion of rice powder and has "Poudre Java" instead. There is no question that the defendant infringes the plaintiff's rights unless the fact that her boxes and powder are the genuine product of the French concern gives her a right to sell them in the present form.

We are of opinion that the plaintiff's rights are infringed. After the sale the French manufacturers could not have come to the United States and have used their old marks in competition with the plaintiff. That plainly follows from the statute authorizing assignments. Act of February 20, 1905, c. 592, § 10, 33 Stat. 727. If for the purpose of evading the effect of the transfer, it had arranged with the defendant that she should sell with the old label, we suppose that no one would doubt that the contrivance must fail. There is no such conspiracy here, but, apart from the opening of a door to one, the vendors could not convey their goods free from the restriction to which the vendors were subject. Ownership of the goods does not carry the right to sell them with a specific mark. It does not necessarily carry the right to sell them at all in a given place. If the goods were patented in the United States a dealer who lawfully bought similar goods abroad from one who had a right to make and sell them there could not sell them in the United States. *Boesch v. Graff*, 133 U.S. 697. The monopoly in that case is more extensive, but we see no sufficient reason for holding that the monopoly of a trade mark, so far as it goes, is less complete. It deals with a delicate matter that may be of great value but that easily is destroyed, and therefore should be protected with corresponding care. It is said that the trade mark here is that of the French house and truly indicates the origin of the goods. But that is not accurate. It is the trade mark of the plaintiff only in the United States and indicates in law, and, it is found, by public understanding, that the goods come from the plaintiff although not made by it. It was sold and could only be sold with the good will of the business that the plaintiff bought. *Eiseman v. Schiffer*, 157 Fed. 473. It stakes the reputation of the plaintiff upon the character of the goods. *Menendez v. Holt*, 128 U.S. 514. The injunction granted by the District Court was proper under §§ 17 and 19 of the Trade Mark Act. Act of February 20, 1905, c. 592, 33 Stat. 724, 728, 729.

Decree of Circuit Court of Appeals reversed.

PRESTONETTES, INC. v. COTY
264 U.S. 359 (1924)

Mr. Justice Holmes

This is a bill in equity brought by the respondent, Coty, a citizen of France, against Prestonettes, a New York corporation, having its principal place of business in the Southern District of New York. It seeks to restrain alleged unlawful uses of the plaintiff's registered trade-marks, "Coty" and "L'Origan" upon toilet powders and perfumes. The defendant purchases the genuine powder, subjects it to pressure, adds a binder to give it coherence and sells the compact in a metal case. It buys the genuine perfume in bottles and sells it in smaller bottles. We need not mention what labels it used before this suit as the defendant is content to abide by the decree of the District Court. That decree allowed the defendant to put upon the rebottled perfume "Prestonettes, Inc., not connected with Coty, states that the contents are Coty's — (giving the name of the article) independently rebottled in New York," every word to be in letters of the same size, color, type and general distinctiveness. It allowed the defendant to make compacts from the genuine loose powder of the plaintiff and to sell them with this label on the container: "Prestonettes, Inc., not connected with Coty, states that the compact of face powder herein was independently compounded by it from Coty's — (giving the name) loose powder and its own binder. Loose powder — per cent, Binder — per cent," every word to be in letters of the same size, color, type and general distinctiveness. The Circuit Court of Appeals, considering the very delicate and volatile nature of the perfume, its easy deterioration, and the opportunities for adulteration, issued an absolute preliminary injunction against the use of the above marks except on the original packages as marked and sold by the plaintiff, thinking that the defendant could not put upon the plaintiff the burden of keeping a constant watch. 285 Fed. 501. *Certiorari granted*, 260 U.S. 720.

The bill does not charge the defendant with adulterating or otherwise deteriorating the plaintiff's product except that it intimates rather than alleges metal containers to be bad, and the Circuit Court of Appeals stated that there were no controverted questions of fact but that the issue was simply one of law. It seemingly assumed that the defendant handled the plaintiff's product without in any way injuring its qualities and made its decree upon that assumption. The decree seems to us to have gone too far.

The defendant of course by virtue of its ownership had a right to compound or change what it bought, to divide either the original or the modified product, and to sell it so divided. The plaintiff could not prevent or complain of its stating the nature of the component parts and the source from which they were derived if it did not use the trade-mark in doing so. For instance, the defendant could state that a certain percentage of its compound was made at a certain place in Paris, however well known as the plaintiff's factory that place might be. If the compound was worse than the constituent, it might be a misfortune to the plaintiff, but the plaintiff would have no cause of action, as the defendant was exercising the rights of ownership and only telling the truth. The existence of a trade-mark would have no bearing on the question. Then what new rights does the trade-mark confer? It does not confer a right to prohibit the use of the word or words. It is not a copyright. The argument drawn from the language of the Trade-Mark Act does not seem to us to need discussion. A trade-mark only gives the right to prohibit the use of it so far as to protect the owner's good will against the sale of another's product as his. *United Drug Co. v. Theodore Rectanus Co.*, 248 U.S. 90, 97. There is nothing to the contrary in *Bourjois & Co. v. Katzel*, 260 U.S. 689. There the trade-mark protected indicated that the goods came from the plaintiff in the United States, although not made by it, and therefore could not be put upon other goods of the same make coming from abroad. When the mark is used in a way that does not deceive the public, we see no such sanctity in the word as to prevent its being used to tell the truth. It is not taboo. *Canal Co. v. Clark*, 13 Wall. 311, 327.

If the name of Coty were allowed to be printed in different letters from the rest of the inscription dictated by the District Court a casual purchaser might look no further and might be deceived. But when it in no way stands out from the statement of facts that unquestionably the defendant has a right to communicate in some form, we see no reason why it should not be used collaterally, not to indicate the goods, but to say that the trade-marked product is a constituent in the article now offered as new and changed. As a general proposition there can be no doubt that the word might be so used. If a man bought a barrel of a certain flour, or a demijohn of Old Crow whiskey, he certainly could sell the flour in smaller packages or in former days could have sold the whiskey in bottles, and tell what it was, if he stated that he did the dividing up or the bottling. And this would not be because of a license implied from the special facts but on the general ground that we have stated. It seems to us that no new right can be evoked from the fact that the perfume or powder is delicate and likely to be spoiled, or from the omnipresent possibility of fraud. If the defendant's rebottling the plaintiff's perfume deteriorates it and the public is adequately informed who does the rebottling, the public, with or without the plaintiff's assistance, is likely to find it out. And so of the powder in its new form.

This is not a suit for unfair competition. It stands upon the plaintiff's rights as owner of a trade-mark registered under the act of Congress. The question therefore is not how far the court would go in aid of a plaintiff who showed ground for suspecting the defendant of making a dishonest use of his opportunities, but is whether the plaintiff has the naked right alleged to prohibit the defendant from making even a collateral reference to the plaintiff's mark. We are of opinion that the decree of the Circuit Court of Appeals must be reversed and that that of the District Court must stand.

OSAWA & COMPANY v. B & H PHOTO
589 F. Supp. 1163 (S.D.N.Y. 1984)

LEVAL, DISTRICT JUDGE

*   *   *

Plaintiff is the duly registered owner in the United States of the Mamiya marks. . . .

The Mamiya equipment is sophisticated and expensive, designed for use by professional photographers and advanced amateurs. Accordingly it includes a wide range of peripheral equipment designed for special applications. In order to be able to supply promptly the needs of its professional photographer customers, plaintiff maintains at all times a stock of all such peripheral equipment.

Plaintiff purchases advertising and incurs other public relations expenses. To educate users, dealers and potential customers in the advantages and complex capabilities of its equipment, it organizes seminars, which are conducted in various parts of the country. To stimulate sales, it occasionally offers rebates, sometimes consisting of a free piece of peripheral equipment to one who purchases a Mamiya camera during a specified period.

Plaintiff distributes the Mamiya equipment through authorized camera dealers who apply for dealerships. Plaintiff's sales policy is based on its perception of a fundamental difference between equipment of such complexity and a simple amateur's camera. Because of the high cost and complexity of the equipment and because of the sophisticated demands of purchasers, plaintiff foresees a continuing relationship between dealer and customer involving advice, service and the future purchase of specialized peripheral equipment expanding the capabilities of the camera. According to its perception, a purchaser of a Mamiya camera who was unable to obtain such support from his dealer would soon be a dissatisfied customer. Accordingly, plaintiff has been unwilling to distribute its equipment through any camera store but will authorize and sell only to those dealers who demonstrate a willingness to take in an adequate full line stock so that they will be both able and motivated to service future needs of their customers.

Plaintiff also devotes considerable care to handling, including inspection on arrival. It offers free warranty repairs, performed either by its employees or by authorized service representatives, who must receive training in the equipment.

Defendants are discount camera dealers, offering camera equipment often at prices substantially cheaper than are available at other stores. Defendants advertise in national photography magazines. These advertisements characteristically are concerned with price; they set forth, mostly in small print, items of available equipment with prices. They sell by mail and by telephone to credit card purchasers, as well as over the counter. Defendants formerly were authorized Mamiya dealers purchasing from plaintiffs. Their dealerships were terminated as a result of the dispute over gray market merchandising.

Defendants advertise and sell Mamiya equipment that has been imported in violation of the Customs exclusion order. They are found also to have imported such merchandise. They sell this equipment at retail prices far below the prices of authorized dealers. In some cases they sell at prices cheaper than those at which plaintiff offers its merchandise to its dealers.

*   *   *

Plaintiff has shown a drastic decline in its sales in 1983 as compared with average levels over the past nine years. Concomitantly, it has laid off a large part of its personnel, including a significant part of the repair force, and has suffered consequent delays in time needed for warranty repairs. The advertising budget for the Mamiya mark has been severely slashed. Competition from gray marketers has caused demoralization, disaffection and misunderstanding among authorized dealers, 40% of whom have dropped the Mamiya line since 1980. There is evidence that some dealers have misunderstood the cause of the problem, believing that plaintiff was granting preferred price treatment to their competitors.

Another aspect of the harm is that plaintiff's advertising expenditures and public relations efforts are incurred largely for the benefit of its competitors, the gray market sellers, who free ride on plaintiff's publicity.

Also in order to avoid consumer confusion, disaffection and resentment, plaintiff has performed warranty repairs and honored rebate offers on gray market cameras, essentially furnishing free service and benefit to support the sales of its competitors.

* * *

Consumer confusion also arises from the wide price disparities between legitimate and gray imports. Consumers will wonder why the same equipment can be purchased so much more cheaply at one place than at others. Many will no doubt assume the explanation is that plaintiff is gouging, which will engender hostility to the mark.

* * *

. . . B & H has developed a new strategy in litigation and now undertakes that it will warrant the gray Mamiya merchandise that it sells. (It also offers to parallel all Mamiya rebate offers by similar offers of its own.) This ingenious stratagem, however, offers only a superficial solution. More realistically it can be seen as aggravating the problem. For the warranty is of value to the goodwill of the mark only if offered by one who has the incentive to uphold the reputation of the mark. B & H would have no such incentive. Plaintiff would have no assurance that B & H's warranty repairs would be properly performed or that the obligation would be graciously accepted. It would be constantly subject to the risk that B & H would disavow the obligation or perform inadequate repairs. Disparities between plaintiff's and defendants' performance of warranty work would further confuse the marketplace as to the standing and meaning of the Mamiya mark.

* * *

Defendants here seek to apply the principles of exhaustion on an international scale, arguing that once the goods bearing the Mamiya mark have been sold in commerce, bringing a profit to the original markholder, neither the original markholder nor his assignees may exert control over them. This position might have substantial force if no independent U.S. goodwill were represented by the Mamiya marks.

However, plaintiff has proved convincingly that, as the result of its efforts, it has developed in the United States marketplace a substantial goodwill separate and distinct from the goodwill emanating from the branded goods themselves. This local goodwill is the product of plaintiff's many U.S. activities (described above) promoting and standing behind the mark, including significantly warranty service, promotional rebates, educational activities and advertising. The Mamiya trademark in the U.S. represents a goodwill generated and importantly influenced by these activities. It is not the same trademark either in law or in fact as the Mamiya trademark at the place of manufacture, where it designates only the goodwill of the manufacturer.

Defendants rely on the turn-of-the-century cases noted above. They argue that both § 526 and the Holmes *Bourjois* decisions should be narrowly limited to situations where the domestic markholder had purchased outright the U.S. mark and goodwill and was not related to the foreign mark originator.

I find no basis for this contention either in fact or in logic. The old universality cases and the theory upon which they rest represent an incorrect analysis that has been repudiated in both statutory and decisional law, at least where the domestic markholder has developed an independent goodwill.

* * *

Defendants also argue that plaintiff's position would give plaintiff an unjustifiable monopoly on the U.S. sale of Mamiya equipment. This is simply not so. Nothing in this opinion would bar defendants from importing and selling the equipment manufactured by Mamiya Co. in Japan. What is forbidden is infringing on plaintiff's rights to the Mamiya marks. So long as defendants take steps so as not to infringe on plaintiff's trademark rights, nothing in the reasoning of this opinion would prevent them from dealing in the same equipment. . . .

[*Preliminary Injunction granted*].

LEVER BROTHERS COMPANY v. UNITED STATES
981 F.2d 1330 (D.C. 1993)

SENTELLE, CIRCUIT JUDGE

The District Court entered a judgment invalidating the "affiliate exception" of 19 C.F.R. § 133.21(c)(2) (1988) as inconsistent with the statutory mandate of the Lanham Act of 1946, 15 U.S.C. § 1124 (1988), prohibiting importation of goods which copy or simulate the mark of a domestic manufacturer, and issued a nationwide injunction barring enforcement of the regulation with respect to *any* foreign goods bearing a valid United States trademark but materially and physically differing from the United States version of the goods.

The United States appeals. We conclude that the District Court, obedient to our limited remand in a prior decision in this same case, properly determined that the regulation is inconsistent with the statute. However, because we conclude that the remedy the District Court provided is overbroad, we vacate the judgment and remand for entry of an injunction against allowing the importation of the foreign-produced Lever Brothers brand products at issue in this case.

* * *

Lever Brothers Company ("Lever US" or "Lever"), an American company, and its British affiliate, Lever Brothers Limited ("Lever UK"), both manufacture deodorant soap under the "Shield" trademark and hand dishwashing liquid under the "Sunlight" trademark. The trademarks are registered in each country. The products have evidently been formulated differently to suit local tastes and circumstances. The U.S. version lathers more, the soaps smell different, the colorants used in American "Shield" have been certified by the FDA whereas the colorants in British "Shield" have not, and the U.S. version contains a bacteriostat that enhances the deodorant properties of the soap. The British version of "Sunlight" dishwashing soap produces less suds, and the American version is formulated to work best in the "soft water" available in most American cities, whereas the British version is designed for "hard water" common in Britain.

The packaging of the U.S. and U.K. products is also somewhat different. The British "Shield" logo is written in script form and is packaged in foil wrappings and contains a wave motif, whereas the American "Shield" logo is written in block form, does not come in foil wrappings and contains a grid pattern. There is small print on the packages indicating where they were manufactured. The British "Sunlight" comes in a cylindrical bottle labeled "Sunlight Washing Up Liquid." The American "Sunlight" comes in a yellow, hour-glass-shaped bottle labeled "Sunlight Dishwashing Liquid."

Lever asserts that the unauthorized influx of these foreign products has created substantial consumer confusion and deception in the United States about the nature and origin of this merchandise, and that it has received numerous consumer complaints from American consumers who unknowingly bought the British products and were disappointed.

Lever argues that the importation of the British products was in violation of § 42 of the Lanham Act, 15 U.S.C. § 1124 which provides that with the exception of goods imported for personal use:

> [N]o article of imported merchandise which shall copy or simulate the name of the [sic] any domestic manufacture, or manufacturer . . . or which shall copy or simulate a trademark registered in accordance with the provisions of this chapter . . . shall be admitted to entry at any customhouse of the United States.

Id. The United States Customs Service ("Customs"), however, was allowing importation of the British goods under the "affiliate exception" created by 19 C.F.R. § 133.21(c)(2), which provides that foreign goods bearing United States trademarks are not forbidden when "[t]he foreign and domestic trademark or tradename owners are parent and subsidiary companies or are otherwise subject to common ownership or control."

In *Lever I*, we concluded that "the natural, virtually inevitable reading of § 42 is that it bars foreign goods bearing a trademark identical to the valid U.S. trademark but physically different," without regard to affiliation between the producing firms or the genuine character of the trademark abroad. 877 F.2d 101, 111 (D.C. Cir. 1989).

* * *

Customs' main argument from the legislative history is that § 42 of the Lanham Act applies only to imports of goods bearing trademarks that "copy or simulate" a registered mark. Customs thus draws a distinction between "genuine" marks and marks that "copy or simulate." A mark applied by a foreign firm subject to ownership and control common to that of the domestic trademark owner is by definition "genuine," Customs urges, regardless of whether or not the goods are identical. Thus, any importation of goods manufactured by an affiliate of a U.S. trademark owner cannot "copy or simulate" a registered mark because those goods are *ipso facto* "genuine."

This argument is fatally flawed. It rests on the false premise that foreign trademarks applied to foreign goods are "genuine" in the United States. Trademarks applied to physically different foreign goods are not genuine from the viewpoint of the American consumer. As we stated in *Lever I*:

> On its face . . . § [42] appears to aim at deceit and consumer confusion; when identical trademarks have acquired different meanings in different countries, one who imports the foreign version to sell it under that trademark will (in the absence of some specially differentiating feature) cause the confusion Congress sought to avoid. The fact of affiliation between the producers in no way reduces the probability of that confusion; it is certainly not a constructive consent to importation.

877 F.2d at 111.

There is a larger, more fundamental and ultimately fatal weakness in Customs' position in this case. Section 42 on its face appears to forbid importation of goods that "copy or simulate" a United States trademark. Customs has the burden of adducing evidence from the legislative history of § 42 and its administrative practice of an exception for materially different goods whose similar foreign and domestic trademarks are owned by affiliated companies. At a minimum, this requires that the specific question be addressed in the legislative history or the administrative record. It is not enough to posit that silence implies authorization, when the authorization sought runs counter to the evident meaning of the governing statute. Therefore, we conclude that § 42 of the

Lanham Act precludes the application of Customs' affiliate exception with respect to physically, materially different goods.

[*Remanded for modified injunction.*]

Notes on Gray Market Goods

1. Material Differences

Efforts to bar parallel imports have been criticized as protectionist. It is argued that "free trade" in parallel imports allegedly would promote an effective world-wide division of labor by rewarding those foreign manufacturers or importers who can produce or distribute products less expensively than their United States counterparts. Opponents of parallel imports argue, however, that the issue is not one of free trade versus protectionism if consumers are likely to be confused. This is most obvious where the parallel imports are neither identical to their domestic counterparts nor supported by equal service structures or warranties, but may be equally true where consumers are simply not informed of the non-domestic source of goods. If the domestic owner can show a separate and truly independent domestic goodwill, or material differences between the domestic and foreign products, relief against gray market importation normally will be granted. *See Davidoff & CIE, SA v. PLD Int'l Corp.* , 263 F.3d 1297 (11th Cir. 2001) (defendant's etching off of batch codes from gray market fragrance bottles, to prevent the U.S. trademark owner from identifying the seller, "degraded the appearance of the bottle" creating material differences warranting injunctive relief); *Ferrero U.S.A., Inc. v. Ozak Trading, Inc.* 21 U.S.P.Q.2d 1215 (3d Cir. 1991) (enjoining gray market importation of materially different TIC TAC breath mints); *Grupo Gamesa S.A. De C.V. v. Dulceria El Molino Inc.*, 39 U.S.P.Q.2d 1531 (C.D. Cal. 1996) (material differences in gray market GAMESA cookies and crackers, including noncompliance with FDA labeling requirements and California law requiring enriched flour, created a likelihood of confusion); *PepsiCo Inc. v. Giraud*, 7 U.S.P.Q.2d 1371 (D.P.R. 1988) (material differences in gray market PEPSI COLA created likelihood of confusion). *Cf. Bourdeau Bros., Inc. v. ITC*, 444 F.3d 1317 (Fed. Cir. 2006) (remanded to determine whether trademark owner authorized some of the allegedly infringing sales in the U.S.); *SKF USA, Inc. v. ITC*, 423 F.3d 1307 (Fed. Cir. 2005) (gray market ball bearings lacked sufficient material differences to warrant relief), and the discussion on the International Trade Commission in Chapter 3. *See generally* Goldman, *Unfair Competition, False Advertising and only Two Calories: Will the Tic Tac Case Close the Gray Market for Good?*, 83 T.M.R. 495 (1993) (discussing applications of the material differences test).

In *Gamut Trading Co. v. U.S. International Trade Commission and Kubota Tractor Corp.*, 200 F.3d 775 (Fed. Cir. 1999) the exclusive U.S. licensee of KUBOTA for tractors complained to the ITC under the Tariff Act, and obtained a general exclusion order against importation of used Japanese tractors bearing the KUBOTA mark, and cease and desist orders against sale in the U.S. of previously imported tractors. In large part because of differences in the terrain in which the tractors were intended to be used, the Japanese models materially differed in such aspects as structural strength, speed capabilities, and wheel-base and tire tread dimensions. They also were labeled in Japanese, and were difficult to service in this country, with some parts unavailable. In affirming the orders against importation and sale, the Federal Circuit emphasized the material differences. The Court also affirmed the ITC's rejection of the importer's offer to instead label the Japanese models to inform consumers of the differences. Among other reasons, the ITC was concerned that the labels could be removed prior to sale. *Compare Iberia Foods Corp. v. Romeo*, 150 F.3d 298 (3d Cir. 1998), in which the plaintiff, owner of the continental U.S. trademark rights, and the defendant importer, both bought MISTOLIN household cleaning products for resale from the same manufacturing source in Puerto Rico. Plaintiff alleged that defendant's imported

MISTOLIN products were materially different because plaintiff engaged in post-manufacturing quality control inspections that defendant did not. Rejecting plaintiff's inspections as being a "*de minimis* check" insufficient to create material differences, the Third Circuit reversed the lower court's summary judgment for plaintiff, and entered judgment for defendant.

Some parallel imports are clearly inferior to the authorized product, making exclusion under a confusion standard particularly appropriate. They may also violate U.S. law and regulations such as EPA standards or FDA labeling requirements. *See Grupo Gamesa, supra*; Minchan, *The Gray Market: A Call for Greater Protection of Consumers and Trademark Owners*, 12 U. PA. J. INT'L BUS. L. 457 (1991); Lipner, *Trademarked Goods and Their Gray Market Equivalents: Should Product Differences Result in the Barring of Unauthorized Goods from the U.S. Market?*, 18 HOFSTRA L. REV. 1029 (1990).

2. Free Riding and Protection of Goodwill

Regardless of whether source confusion is present, many opponents of parallel imports object to parallel importers' free riding on the advertising, warranty, and service efforts of the U.S. company, while selling the same product at a lower price. Should such injury be actionable even absent the basic trademark principle of protecting the public from confusion or deception? *See* Lipner, *The Legality of Parallel Imports: Trademark, Antitrust or Equity?*, 19 TEXAS INT'L L.J. 553 (1984). In *In the Matter of Certain Alkaline Batteries*, 225 U.S.P.Q. 823 (Int'l Trade Comm'n 1984), DURACELL batteries manufactured by a wholly owned Belgian subsidiary of Duracell Inc. were imported into the United States in competition with DURACELL batteries manufactured by Duracell domestically. The commission majority excluded all Belgian DURACELL batteries stating that the function of trademark law should not be limited only to preventing consumer confusion, but should, *inter alia*, ensure an equal level of quality, assist sellers in advertising and selling their goods, and protect a trademark owner's investment. In a separate opinion, two commissioners disagreed with the legal basis for the majority ruling and urged application of the doctrine established by the *Bourjois* and *Prestonettes* cases, with consequent exclusion only of improperly labelled batteries and of batteries on which use of the DURACELL trademark was likely to cause confusion. On January 4, 1985, President Reagan disapproved the ruling of the Commission in *Duracell* on the ground that "the Commission's interpretation of Section 42 of the Lanham Act (15 U.S.C. § 1124) . . . is at odds with the longstanding regulatory interpretation of the Department of Treasury" which was then under review. *In the Matter of Certain Alkaline Batteries*, 225 U.S.P.Q. 862 (Pres. 1985).

In *Bell & Howell: Mamiya Co. v. Masel Supply Co.*, 548 F. Supp. 1063 (E.D.N.Y. 1982), the plaintiff in *Osawa, supra* under its predecessor name, obtained a preliminary injunction against another gray market dealer, but the injunction was vacated and the case remanded by the Court of Appeals because there was insufficient proof of likelihood of confusion or deception and of irreparable injury, *Bell & Howell: Mamiya Co. v. Masel Supply Co.*, 719 F.2d 42, 46 (2ᵈ Cir. 1983):

> On the basis of the present record, irreparable injury may well not be present herein since there would appear to be little confusion, if any, as to the origin of goods and no significant likelihood of damage to BHMC's reputation since thus far it has not been shown that Masel's goods, which have a common origin of manufacture of BHMC's goods, are inferior to those sold by BHMC and are injuring BHMC's reputation. Further, it does not appear that the lack of warranties accompanying MAMIYA cameras sold by Masel amounts to irreparable injury, since the consumer can be made aware by, among other things, labels on the camera boxes or notices in advertisements as to whether the cameras are sold with or without warranties. Thus, less drastic means would appear to be available to avoid the claimed confusion.

In *Osawa*, 589 F. Supp. at 1165, the court found that the plaintiff had remedied the deficiencies alluded to in *Bell & Howell*, having shown likelihood of confusion and having provided "substantial proof of irreparable harm." *Cf. Model Rectifier Corp. v. Takachiho Int'l, Inc.*, 221 U.S.P.Q. 502 (9th Cir. 1983), where the court affirmed a preliminary injunction against a parallel importer stating that the damages were "by their nature irreparable."

3.   The Tariff Act

The Tariff Act § 526(a) prohibits the importation of a product "that bears a trademark owned by a citizen of . . . the United States and [that] is registered in the U.S. Patent and Trademark Office." 19 U.S.C. 1526(a). Proof of likely confusion is not expressly required. The Third Circuit, for example, upheld a lower court's preliminary injunction preventing the importation of identical goods under § 526 in *Premier Dental Products Co. v. Darby Dental Supply Co.*, 794 F.2d 850 (3[d] Cir. 1986), where the plaintiff owned the domestic trademark rights and had developed a separate goodwill from that of the foreign trademark owner and manufacturer. The appellate court rejected the lower court's basis for its finding of irreparable harm, finding no immediate danger of a decline in plaintiff's sales which might result in cancellation of its distribution contract. It instead found the requisite irreparable harm in the inevitable injury to the plaintiff's goodwill and mark created by defendant's importations. It stated (at p. 859):

> Purchasers of [plaintiff's] IMPREGUM are confident that they can obtain the same product, service and financial guaranties that they have gotten before. The continued availability of IMPREGUM through sources, like [defendant] not associated with [plaintiff] must inevitably injure [plaintiff's] reputation as the exclusive domestic source of IMPREGUM. This would constitute irreparable injury to the value of the mark because customers would no longer have that same confidence. This is true whether or not the service and financial guaranties are comparable to those offered by [plaintiff].

> . . . [W]e believe that *Bourjois* and Section 526 make it clear that an American distributor's goodwill can be harmed even by the sale of gray market goods that are *identical* to those sold by the distributor.

The court upheld the lower court's requirement that the plaintiff supply the defendant with the trademarked goods on the same terms and conditions the plaintiff supplied its other customers, in order to protect the defendant's interest. *See generally* Supnik, *The Bell and Howell: Mamiya Case — Where Now Parallel Imports?*, 74 TRADEMARK REP. 1 (1984).

In *Am. Circuit Breaker Corp. v. Or Breakers, Inc.*, 406 F.3d 577 (9th Cir. 2005), the court declined to bar gray market circuit breakers where the only difference was color, which was non-material. In the absence of any material difference, consumers were getting exactly what they expected, and there was no confusion. However, the court made special note that "the circumstances of this case suggest that ACBC would have had a remedy under the Tariff Act," because § 526 of the Act "prohibits the importation of 'foreign-made articles bearing a trademark identical with one owned by a citizen [or corporation] of the United States.'" *Id.* at 485, n.4, quoting *k Mart Corp. v. Cartier, Inc.*, 486 U.S. 288 (1988). U.S. Customs' interpretation of § 526 in its regulations is discussed below. Those regulations have been influential in the federal courts as well. *Vittoria N.A. L.L.C. v. Euro-Asia Imports, Inc.*, 278 F.3d 1076 (10th Cir. 2001) (considering Customs' regulation exemptions to § 526 and finding none applied).

4. Bureau of Customs and Border Protection

a) Customs' Regulations and the K Mart Decision

The U.S. Bureau of Customs and Border Protection ("Customs"), part of the Department of Homeland Security, will bar parallel imports under 19 U.S.C. § 1526, except under circumstances identified in 19 C.F.R. § 133.21. 19 U.S.C. § 1526(a) prohibits importing "into the United States any merchandise of foreign manufacture if such merchandise . . . bears a trademark owned by a citizen of, or by a corporation, or association created or organized within, the United States, and registered in the Patent and Trademark Office by a person domiciled in the United States . . ., unless written consent of the owner of such trademark is produced at the time of making entry." Under Customs' implementing regulation, 19 C.F.R. § 133.21, however, Customs did not prohibit parallel imports when (1) both the foreign and domestic trademark were owned by "the same person"; or (2) where the foreign and domestic trademark owners were parent and subsidiary or otherwise subject to common ownership or control; or (3) where use of the trademark by a foreign manufacturer was authorized by the U.S. trademark owner.

In *K Mart Corp. v. Cartier, Inc.*, 486 U.S. 281 (1988), the Supreme Court addressed the validity of 19 C.F.R. § 133.21 and found the third subsection invalid while upholding the validity of the first two. The majority held that given the ambiguities in the statutory terms "foreign manufacture" and "owned by" in 19 U.S.C. § 1526, subsections (1) and (2) under which Customs refused to bar importation were valid regulatory interpretations of that section. The Court found that in the subsection (1) situation either the domestic or foreign entity could be said to "own" the U.S. trademark, and in the subsection (2) situation goods manufactured by a foreign subsidiary of a domestic company could be said to be goods which are not "of foreign manufacture," so that action by Customs would not be required. However, a different majority struck down subsection (3) which had permitted importation of goods manufactured abroad by a company that is merely authorized (i.e. licensed) to use a trademark by the domestic trademark owner. Finding the above ambiguities did not apply to subsection (3), the court stated "Under no reasonable construction of the statutory language can goods made in a foreign country by an independent foreign manufacturer be removed from the purview of the statute." *Id.* at 1813. Customs therefore was required to prohibit importation of such goods. Customs subsequently deleted the third subsection from the regulation. 55 Fed. Reg. 52040 (1990) (amending 19 C.F.R. § 133.21).

b) The Federal Courts

K Mart only addressed the validity of Customs' regulations, and did not address the application of the Lanham Act to gray market issues. A number of courts have held that where the gray goods at issue are materially different from their domestic counterparts, confusion is likely and the Lanham Act is violated regardless of any "common control" or affiliation between the U.S. and foreign trademark owners. *See, e.g., Lever Brothers v. United States, supra,* (Customs enjoined from permitting importation into the U.S. of materially different British SHIELD soap and SUN LIGHT dishwashing detergent); *Martin's Herend Imports v. Diamond & Gem Trading USA Co.,* 112 F.3d 1296 (5th Cir. 1997) (plaintiff was the exclusive licensee of select HERENDI products in the U.S.; material differences — different shapes, colors, and patterns — between the plaintiff's authorized HERENDI porcelain tableware and defendant's unauthorized pieces resulted in an injunction against defendant, but one narrowly tailored to prevent defendant from marketing only those HERENDI products which were different from ones that plaintiff had marketed in the U.S.); *Societe Des Produits Nestle S.A. v. Casa Helvetia, Inc.,* 25 U.S.P.Q.2d 1256 (1st Cir. 1992) (material differences in Venezuelan PERUGINA chocolates created likely confusion with Italian PERUGINA chocolates distributed in U.S. in violation of §§ 32,

42 and 43(a)). *Original Appalachian Artworks, Inc. v. Granada Electronics, Inc.*, 816 F.2d 68 (2ᵈ Cir.), *cert. denied*, 484 U.S. 847 (1987) (enjoining the importation into the U.S. of CABBAGE PATCH KID dolls licensed for sale in Spain due to material differences in the language of the dolls' "adoption papers"). *Cf. Pepsico Inc. v. Nostalgia Products Corp.*, 18 U.S.P.Q.2d 1404, 1406 (N.D. Ill. 1990) (consent judgment entered where third-party importation of unauthorized goods produced by foreign licensee violated Tariff Act, citing *K Mart*); *Duracell, Inc. v. Global Imports, Inc.*, 12 U.S.P.Q.2d 1651, 1653 (S.D.N.Y. 1989) (refusing to vacate injunction entered before *K Mart* decision, noting that although *K Mart* held that Customs' "common control" regulations were valid, it left open the Lanham Act issues, and that in the Second Circuit goods covered by Customs' "common control" exception still may cause likely confusion in violation of the Lanham Act). *See also* Hahn, *Gray Market Goods: Has A Resolution Been Found?*, 81 TRADEMARK REP. 58 (1991).

The Ninth Circuit interpreted the Customs Service's common control exception to the exclusion of parallel imports in *United States v. Eighty-Nine (89) Bottles of Eau de Joy*, 797 F.2d 767 (9ˢᵗ Cir. 1986). The defendant had imported perfumes allegedly in violation of the Tariff Act, and the government sought forfeiture of these genuine goods. The defendant argued that the European trademark owner exercised sufficient control over the American trademark owner to bring the parties within the Customs Service's common control exception. The Ninth Circuit held that the exception applied "when the foreign and domestic entity are really the same entity," but not where the relationship between the foreign and domestic trademark owners was essentially that of licensor-licensee, as it was in *Eighty-Nine Bottles*.

In *NEC Electronics v. CAL Circuit Abco*, 810 F.2d 1506 (9ᵗʰ Cir. 1987), *cert. denied*, 484 U.S. 851 (1987), the Ninth Circuit vacated the district court's injunction prohibiting the importation of genuine goods where the plaintiff was the owner of the domestic trademark rights and the wholly-owned subsidiary of the manufacturer, a Japanese computer chip company. The defendant purchased the manufacturer's goods abroad, imported them into the United States and sold the goods. Without an analysis of the plaintiff's efforts to develop a separate domestic goodwill in the trademark for its computer chips, the court observed that plaintiff "cannot look to United States trademark law to insulate the American market or vitiate the effects of international trade." *See also Weil Ceramics & Glass, Inc. v. Dash*, 878 F.2d 659 (3ᵈ Cir.), *cert. denied*, 110 S. Ct. 156 (1989), where, without an analysis as to separate goodwill, the Third Circuit denied relief against gray market imports because plaintiff shared in profits from its foreign parent's sales to defendant, the foreign parent could stop selling to defendant, and the domestic and gray goods were identical. To similar effect is *Yamaha Corp. of America v. ABC International Traders, Inc.*, 1991 U.S. App. LEXIS 17882 (9th Cir. 1991), in which the court affirmed summary judgment against plaintiff, holding that federal trademark law affords no protection to a wholly-owned U.S. subsidiary of a foreign manufacturer against a rival company that imports and sells goods made by the foreign parent. *Compare Vittoria North America L.L.C. v. Euro-Asia Imports, Inc.*, 278 F.3d 1076 (10ᵗʰ Cir. 2001), in which the owner of U.S. rights in the mark VITTORIA for bicycle tires successfully sued under § 526 of the Tariff Act to bar defendant's importation of gray market VITTORIA tires manufactured by the owner of the Italian trademark rights. The Court observed that, "[t]he prototypical gray market victim . . . is a domestic firm that purchases from an independent foreign firm the rights to register and use the latter's trademark as a United States trademark and to sell its foreign manufactured products here." In response to defendant's assertion of the "common control" defense, the Court found that, although the U.S. and Italian trademark owners had a close business relationship, plaintiff was not controlled by the Italian company, and the two were not subject to common control.

c)   Customs and Material Differences

The Customs Service implemented a regulation in 1999, 19 C.F.R. § 133.23, which permits U.S. trademark owners to obtain some relief at Customs when the foreign and domestic trademark owners are the "same person", or subject to common control, but the U.S. trademark owner is able to show that the foreign goods are materially different. The relief is limited, however. Even such materially different goods will not be barred from entry by Customs if they bear a label stating: "This product is not a product authorized by the United States trademark owner for importation and is physically and materially different from the authorized product." Is this likely to be sufficient to obviate problems or dissatisfaction which may arise from materially different products? For a critical discussion of this Customs' regulation, *see* Goodale, *The New Customs Gray Market Regulations: Boon or Bust for U.S. Trademark Owners?*, 28 AIPLA Q.J. 335 (2000) (arguing that the regulation should be judicially struck down). *Compare Gamut Trading Co. v. U.S. International Trade Commission*, 202 F.3d 775 (Fed. Cir. 1999), in which the Federal Circuit affirmed the ITC's order excluding materially different tractors, and also affirmed rejection of the importer's preferred remedy of explanatory labeling. The rejection was based in part on concerns that the labels could be removed prior to sale.

5.   State Law Provisions

Should consumers be able to purchase less expensive gray market goods as long as they are clearly and truthfully informed of the inferiority of the products? California and New York require retailers to inform customers that gray market goods may not be accompanied by the manufacturer's U.S. warranty or may not be eligible for a manufacturer's rebate. 1986 Cal. Rev. Stat. Ch. 1497; N.Y. Gen. Bus. Law § 218aa.

6.   Involvement of the Trademark Owner

Some courts have found the parallel imports to be genuine goods and held that, as a consequence, there could be no infringement. *See, e.g., Bourdeau Bros. v. ITC*, 444 F.3d 1317 (Fed. Cir. 2006) (remanding for determination as to whether the trademark owner authorized some of the allegedly infringing sales in the U.S.). In *Monte Carlo Shirt, Inc. v. Daewo Int'l (America) Corp.*, 707 F.2d 1054 (9th Cir. 1983), parallel importation of goods ordered but subsequently rejected by the U.S. trademark owner was upheld since the goods were originally produced for the complaining trademark owner on contract for future domestic sale. A similar result was reached in *Parfums Stern, Inc. v. United States Customs Service*, 575 F. Supp. 416 (S.D. Fla. 1983), where the district court distinguished *Bourjois* and *Osawa* on the basis that the U.S. trademark owner had by its own actions placed the parallel imports into foreign markets in ways which facilitated their importation. In *Denbicare U.S.A., Inc. v. Toys "R" Us Inc.*, 84 F.3d 1143 (9th Cir.), *cert. denied*, 519 U.S. 873 (1996), the court found that allegedly inferior and improperly labelled diapers were not unlawful gray market goods because the plaintiff had consented to their sale in a U.S. foreign trade zone. Applying the copyright doctrine of "first sale" to plaintiff's trademark infringement claim, the court concluded that after the U.S. foreign trade zone sale every other party in the distribution chain, including Toys "R" Us, was authorized to sell the diapers in the U.S. *Compare El Greco Leather Products Co. v. Shoe World*, 806 F.2d 392 (2[d] Cir. 1986), where the court granted relief under the Lanham Act and enjoined importation of foreign goods manufactured for the trademark owner, finding the goods were not genuine since they had been rejected by the trademark owner. The court stated:

> The mere act of ordering a product to be labeled with a trademark does not deprive its holder of the right to control the product and the trademark. It is true that El Greco did not, at the time it cancelled the last two lots of its order, give instructions on how to dispose of the shoes that had already been

manufactured and affixed with the CANDIE'S trademark. But we do not view such a step as necessary on the facts presented here.

> Once it cancelled the order, El Greco was entitled to assume that [the manufacturer] would not dispose of the shoes without either removing the CANDIE'S trademark . . . or affording El Greco an opportunity to inspect the goods and certify their quality prior to disposal, or, at the minimum, seeking instructions from El Greco on how to dispose of them.

El Greco Leather, 806 F.2d at 395–96.

7. The Copyright Act

Section 602 of the Copyright Act prohibits the unauthorized importation of reproductions of copyrighted works, but its scope was found limited in *Quality King Distributors, Inc. v. L'anza Research Int'l, Inc.*, 523 U.S. 135 (1998). In that case involving hair care products bearing copyrighted labels, the Court held that under the first sale doctrine, once a copyright owner sells a copyrighted work "lawfully made under this title," it loses the right to bar importation. The Court noted that the importation of pirated and unlawfully possessed works can still be prevented under Section 602, as can the importation of works lawfully made "under the law of some other country." Therefore, it appears that if the copyrighted work is lawfully manufactured inside the U.S, its importation back into this country after sale cannot be prevented under copyright law, but if the work is manufactured *outside* the U.S. and is subject to U.S. copyright, importation after sale still can be prevented under Section 602. *Compare CBS, Inc. v. Scorpio Music Distributors*, 569 F. Supp. 47 (E.D. Pa. 1983), *aff'd*, 738 F.2d 421 (3d Cir. 1984) (enjoining unauthorized importation of copyrighted audiorecordings). *See also Phillips Beverage Co. v. Belvedere, S.A.*, 204 F.3d 905 (8th Cir. 2000), in which a bottle designer and manufacturer that had unsuccessfully sought a temporary restraining order in district court successfully got imported bottles detained after recording a copyright registration with Customs. It subsequently was ordered to withdraw its detention request from Customs, however, because it had initially invoked the district court's jurisdiction and the detention by Customs would have frustrated the district court's order denying relief.

7.07 Permitted Use

Introduction

The law does not prohibit the use of another's trademark on or in connection with the sale of one's own goods or services as long as such use is not deceptive. The seminal decisions on permitted use of another's trademark were those written by Justice Holmes in *Bourjois* and *Prestonettes*, *supra*. Comparative advertising of competing brands has fostered another form of such litigation, and the Lanham Act has codified the common law defense of fair use. 15 U.S.C.§ 1115(b)(4). In reconciling the following decisions, note the courts' emphasis on truthful disclosure. Consider whether a trademark or trade name can truthfully be used on repaired, damaged, deteriorated, or repackaged goods sold by other than the trademark owner if it is made clear that the goods are in fact repaired, damaged, deteriorated, repackaged, unguaranteed or otherwise varying from the trademark owner's standards. The salient principle governing the legal propriety of using another's trademark is simply that of truthfulness and the absence of any likelihood of deception. Resale by the first purchaser of an originally trademarked item generally is permitted use under the "first sale doctrine." *See Brilliance Audio, Inc. v. Haights Cross Communications, Inc.*, 474 F.3d 365 (6th Cir. 2007). However, there are exceptions to that doctrine. When the purchaser of the trademarked item repackages it without proper notice of the repackaging, the first sale doctrine will not prevent an infringement claim. *Id.* Likewise, "the first sale doctrine does not apply. . .'when an alleged infringer sells trademarked goods that are *materially different* than those sold by the trademark owner.' " *Id.* citations omitted. (emphasis in original).

CHAMPION SPARK PLUG CO. v. SANDERS
331 U.S. 125 (1947)

Mr. Justice Douglas

Petitioner is a manufacturer of spark plugs which it sells under the trade mark "Champion." Respondents collect the used plugs, repair and recondition them, and resell them. Respondents retain the word "Champion" on the repaired or reconditioned plugs. The outside box or carton in which the plugs are packed has stamped on it the word "Champion" together with the letter and figure denoting the particular style or type. They also have printed on them "Perfect Process Spark Plugs Guaranteed Dependable" and "Perfect Process Renewed Spark Plugs." Each carton contains smaller boxes in which the plugs are individually packed. These inside boxes also carry legends indicating that the plug has been renewed.[1] But respondent company's business name or address is not printed on the cartons. It supplies customers with petitioner's charts containing recommendations for the use of Champion plugs. On each individual plug is stamped in small letters, blue on black, the work "Renewed,"which at times is almost illegible.

Petitioner brought this suit in the District Court, charging infringement of its trade mark and unfair competition. *See* Judicial Code §§ 24 (1), (7), 28 U.S.C. §§ 41(1), (7). The District Court found that respondents had infringed the trade mark. It enjoined them from offering or selling any of petitioner's plugs which had been repaired or reconditioned unless (a) the trade mark and type and style marks were removed, (b) the plugs were repainted with a durable gray, brown, orange, or green paint, (c) the word "REPAIRED" was stamped into the plug in letters of such size and depth as to retain enough white paint to display distinctly each letter of the word, (d) the cartons in which the plugs were packed carried a legend indicating that they contained used spark plugs originally made by petitioner and repaired and made fit for use up to 10,000 miles by respondent company.[2] The District Court denied an accounting. *See* 56 F. Supp. 782, 61 F. Supp. 247.

The Circuit Court of Appeals held that respondents not only had infringed petitioner's trade mark but also were guilty of unfair competition. It likewise denied an accounting but modified the decree in the following respects: (a) it eliminated the provision requiring the trade mark and type and style marks to be removed from the repaired or reconditioned plugs; (b) it substituted for the requirement that the word "REPAIRED" be stamped into the plug, etc., a provision that the word "REPAIRED" or "USED" be stamped and baked on the plug by an electrical hot press in a contrasting color so as to be clearly and distinctly visible, the plug having been completely covered by permanent aluminum paint or other paint or lacquer; and (c) it eliminated the provision specifying the precise legend to be printed on the cartons and

---

[1] "The process used in renewing this plug has been developed through 10 years continuous experience. This Spark Plug has been tested for firing under compression before packing."

"This Spark Plug is guaranteed to be a selected used Spark Plug, thoroughly renewed and in perfect mechanical condition and is guaranteed to give satisfactory service for 10,000 miles."

[2] The prescribed legend read:

Used spark plug(s) originally made by Champion Spark Plug Company repaired and made fit for use up to 10,000 miles by Perfect Recondition Spark Plug Co., 1133 Bedford Avenue, Brooklyn, N.Y.

The decree also provided:

the name and address of the defendants to be larger and more prominent than the legend itself, and the name of plaintiff may be in slightly larger type than the rest of the body of the legend.

substituted therefor a more general one.[7] 156 F.2d 488. The case is here on a petition for certiorari which we granted because of the apparent conflict between the decision below and *Champion Spark Plug Co. v. Reich*, 121 F.2d 769, decided by the Circuit Court of Appeals for the Eighth Circuit.

There is no challenge here to the findings as to the misleading character of the merchandising methods employed by respondents, nor to the conclusion that they have not only infringed petitioner's trade mark but have also engaged in unfair competition. The controversy here relates to the adequacy of the relief granted, particularly the refusal of the Circuit Court of Appeals to require respondents to remove the word "Champion" from the repaired or reconditioned plugs which they resell.

We put to one side the case of a manufacturer or distributor who markets new or used spark plugs of one make under the trade mark of another. *See Bourjois & Co. v. Katzel*, 260 U.S. 689; *Old Dearborn Co. v. Seagram Corp.*, 299 U.S. 183, 194. Equity then steps in to prohibit defendant's use of the mark which symbolized plaintiff's good will and "stakes the reputation of the plaintiff upon the character of the goods." *Bourjois & Co. v. Katzel, supra* p. 692.

We are dealing here with second-hand goods. The spark plugs, though used, are nevertheless Champion plugs and not those of another make. There is evidence to support what one would suspect, that a used spark plug which has been repaired or reconditioned does not measure up to the specifications of a new one. But the same would be true of a second-hand Ford or Chevrolet car. And we would not suppose that one could be enjoined from selling a car whose valves had been reground and whose piston rings had been replaced unless he removed the name Ford or Chevrolet. . . .

Cases may be imagined where the reconditioning or repair would be so extensive or so basic that it would be a misnomer to call the article by its original name, even though the words "used" or "repaired" were added. *Cf. Ingersoll v. Doyle*, 247 F.620 But no such practice is involved here. The repair or reconditioning of the plugs does not give them a new design. It is no more than a restoration, so far as possible, of their original condition. The type marks attached by the manufacturer are determined by the use to which the plug is to be put. But the thread size and size of the cylinder hole into which the plug is fitted are not affected by the reconditioning. The heat range also has relevance to the type marks. And there is evidence that the reconditioned plugs are inferior so far as heat range and other qualities are concerned. But inferiority is expected in most second-hand articles. Indeed, they generally cost the customer less. That is the case here. Inferiority is immaterial so long as the article is clearly and distinctly sold as repaired or reconditioned rather than as new. The result is, of course, that the second-hand dealer gets some advantage from the trade mark. But under the rule of *Prestonettes, Inc. v. Coty, supra*, that is wholly permissible so long as the manufacturer is not identified with the inferior qualities of the product resulting from wear and tear or the reconditioning by the dealer. Full disclosure gives the manufacturer all the protection to which he is entitled.

The decree as shaped by the Circuit Court of Appeals is fashioned to serve the requirements of full disclosure. We cannot say that of the alternatives available the ones it chose are inadequate for that purpose. We are mindful of the fact that this case, unlike *Prestonettes, Inc. v. Coty, supra*, involves unfair competition as well as trade mark infringement; and that where unfair competition is established, any doubts as to the adequacy of the relief are generally resolved against the transgressor. *Warner & Co. v. Lilly & Co.*, 265 U.S. 526, 532. But there was here no showing of fraud or palming off. Their absence, of course, does not undermine the finding of unfair competition.

---

[7] "The decree shall permit the defendants to state on cartons and containers, selling and advertising material, business records, correspondence and other papers, when published, the original make and type numbers provided it is made clear that any plug referred to therein is used and reconditioned by the defendants, and that such material contains the name and address of defendants."

Federal Trade Commission v. Winsted Hosiery Co., 258 U.S. 483, 493–94; *G. H. Mumm Champagne v. Eastern Wine Corp.*, 142 F.2d 499, 501. But the character of the conduct giving rise to the unfair competition is relevant to the remedy which should be afforded. *See Siegel Co. v. Federal Trade Commission*, 327 U.S. 608. We cannot say that the conduct of respondents in this case, or the nature of the article involved and the characteristics of the merchandising methods used to sell it, called for more stringent controls than the Circuit Court of Appeals provided.

. . . Here, as we have noted, there has been no showing of fraud or palming off. For several years respondents apparently endeavored to comply with a cease and desist order of the Federal Trade Commission requiring them to place on the plugs and on the cartons a label revealing that the plugs were used or second-hand. Moreover, as stated by the Circuit Court of Appeals, the likelihood of damage to petitioner or profit to respondents due to any misrepresentation seems slight. In view of these various circumstances it seems to us that the injunction will satisfy the equities of the case.

Affirmed.

SOCIETE COMPTOIR DE L'INDUSTRIE COTONNIERE ETABLISSEMENTS BOUSSAC v. ALEXANDER'S DEPARTMENT STORES, INC.

299 F.2d 33 (2ᵈ Cir. 1962)

SMITH, CIRCUIT JUDGE

* * *

Plaintiffs are a group of foreign and domestic corporations who do business under the names of "Dior" and "Christian Dior," which names are registered as trademarks. Defendant is the owner of retail, discount type, department stores in a metropolitan area and is well known for its low cost retailing policies which are made possible by the use of self-service merchandising techniques and a high volume, low mark-up policy. Defendant used the name of "Dior" and "Christian Dior" extensively to promote the sale of garments copied from original creations designed by the house of Dior.

* * *

Defendant's representation that the garments being sold by it were copies of plaintiffs' original creations was apparently truthful. We do not understand plaintiffs to claim that the garments were so poorly made or executed as not to constitute copies; but in any event they have certainly failed to establish that to be the case. The merchandise was so described in the newspaper advertisements, on hang tags attached to the garments reading, "Original by Christian Dior—Alexander's Exclusive—Paris—Adaptation"; and on a television fashion show sponsored by defendant which employed a singing commercial.[1]

* * *

In any proceeding under the Lanham Act the gist of the proceeding is a "false description or representation," 15 U.S.C.A. § 1125(a), or a use of the mark which "is likely to cause confusion or mistake or to deceive purchasers as to the source of origin of such goods or services," 15 U.S.C.A. § 1114(1). The registering of a proper noun as a trade-mark does not withdraw it from the language, nor reduce it to the exclusive possession of the registrant which may be jealously guarding against any and all use by others. Registration bestows upon the owner of the mark the limited right to protect his

---

[1] "Dior, Dior, Christian Dior, the latest, latest, Chic-est, sleekest clothing you've been waiting for. That's Christian Dior. — Dior, Dior, Christian you've been waiting for. That's Christian Dior. — Dior, Dior, Christian dresses make you look like a girl. Suits fit floppier, they flatter any form, even if you're just above or just below the norm. Dior, Dior, Christian Dior, the latest, latest, Chic-est, sleekest clothing you've been waiting for. That's Christian Dior."

good will from possible harm by those uses of another as may engender a belief in the mind of the public that the product identified by the infringing mark is made or sponsored by the owner of the mark. *Champion Spark Plug Co. v. Sanders*, 331 U.S. 126 (1947), citing with approval, *Prestonettes, Inc. v. Coty*, 264 U.S. 359 (1924). The Lanham Act does not prohibit a commercial rival's truthfully denominating his goods a copy of a design in the public domain, though he uses the name of the designer to do so. Indeed it is difficult to see any other means that might be employed to inform the consuming public of the true origin of the design. *Cf.* Nims, *Unfair Competition and Trade-Marks*, § 130(a) (4th Ed. 1947).

Those cases involving sponsorship, whether trademark infringement or unfair competition, protecting the owner of the mark, are based upon a finding that the defendant's goods are likely to be thought to have originated with, or have been sponsored by, the true owner of the mark. *E.g., Triangle Publications v. Rohrlich*, 167 F.2d 969 (2 Cir. 1948); *Adolph Kastor & Bros., Inc. v. FTC.*, 138 F.2d 824 (2 Cir. 1943).

Common law unfair competition must be grounded in either deception or appropriation of the exclusive property of the plaintiff. The line of cases relied upon by plaintiffs, *e.g., International News Service v. The Associated Press*, 248 U.S. 215 (1911); [additional citations omitted], did not prohibit the defendant from informing the public as to the source of a product which he was permitted to sell. On the contrary, the defendant in each case was prohibited from pirating the intangible property of complainant. [Citations omitted].

In the case at bar it is conceded that the "pirating" of the design is lawful and proper. *Fashion Originators' Guild of America v. F.T.C.*, 114 F.2d 80 (2 Cir. 1940), *aff'd*, 312 U.S. 457 949 (1941). The only property right alleged to have been invaded is the good will embodied in the trademark. But the right of the complainant in his mark is limited to dilution which is brought about by confusion as to source or affiliation. [citations omitted]. Involved in the instant case is a conflict of values which necessarily arises in an economy characterized by competition and private property. The courts have come to recognize the true nature of the considerations often involved in efforts to extend protection of common law trade names so as to create a shield against competition. *Standard Brands v. Smidler*, 151 F.2d 34, 41 (2 Cir. 1945) (concurring opinion, Frank, C. J.). The interest of the consumer here in competitive prices of garments using Dior designs without deception as to origin, is at least as great as the interest of plaintiffs in monopolizing the name.

[Denial of a preliminary injunction affirmed].

COSMETICALLY SEALED INDUSTRIES, INC. v. CHESEBROUGH-POND'S USA CO.
125 F.3d 28 (App. Ct. 1997)

NEWMAN, CIRCUIT JUDGE

* * *

CSI manufacturers and sells a line of six cosmetic products, one of which is a lip gloss, applied over lipstick to make it, in the words of CSI's promotional materials, "Smear Proof," "Smudge Proof," and "Kiss Proof." The lip gloss is marketed under the registered trademark "SEALED WITH A KISS" and the registered trade dress symbol of a pair of bright red lips. The product was formerly called "MY LIPS ARE SEALED". CSI's other products are used to prolong the wear of various cosmetics or to conceal skin blemishes. The names of all six products contain the word "Sealed." In 1993, Chesebrough, which markets "CUTEX" personal care products, launched a promotional campaign for a new long-wearing lipstick called "CUTEX COLOR SPLASH." The promotional campaign used a fairly large countertop cardboard display holding sixty trial-size lipsticks and a number of complimentary postcards on which appeared a line drawing of a pair of lips and the message, "I thought you could use a kiss." The display invited consumers to take one of the postcards, place a lipstick imprint of her lips on it, and mail it. Beneath the slot holding the cards were the words, in small type, "Take this postcard and send it to the one you love!!" Next to the cards were the words, in slightly larger script type, "Seal it with a Kiss!!" The dominant graphic feature of the display, filling the left one-third of the display card, was a line drawing of a woman's face with bright red lips. The product name "COLOR SPLASH" appeared in the center of the display card in red block letters, at least twice the size of the lettering for "Seal it with a Kiss!!" Above this name was the brand name "CUTEX" in block letters three times the size of the "Seal it" instruction.

Judge Rakoff ruled that Chesebrough did not use "Seal it with a Kiss!!" as a mark to identify its Color Splash lipsticks, but only as an invitation for the consumer to try one of the Color Splash lipsticks and then to "seal" or imprint one of the complimentary postcards with a kiss from freshly lipsticked lips. Judge Rakoff concluded that Chesebrough used the words "Seal it with a Kiss" to convey, in their ordinary meaning, an invitation to customers, rather than as a mark to identify a product, and that Chesebrough was therefore entitled to prevail on its fair use defense.

Fair use is a defense to liability under the Lanham Act even if a defendant's conduct would otherwise constitute infringement of another's trademark. Section 33(b)(4) of the Lanham Act defines fair use as:

> a use, otherwise than as a mark, of . . .a term or device which is descriptive of . and used fairly and in good faith only to describe the goods or services of [a] party . . ..

15 U.S.C. § 1115(b)(4) (1994). The defense permits others to use protected marks in descriptive ways, but not as marks identifying their own products. *Car-Freshner Corp. v. S.C. Johnson & Son, Inc.*, 70 F.3d 267, 270 (2ᵈ Cir. 1995).

[handwritten margin note: Carved out in Lanham Act]

Though the terms of the Act recognize the fair use defense where the name or term is used "to describe the goods," that phrase has not been narrowly confined to words that describe a characteristic of the goods, such as size or quality. Instead, we have recognized that the phrase permits use of words or images that are used, in Judge Leval's helpful expression, in their "descriptive sense." *See id.* at 269. In *Car-Freshner,* though the image of a pine-tree shape communicated an aspect of the product, its pine scent, use of the image was also approved because the image referred to the Christmas season in which the products was sold. *See id.* at 270. This description (by the suggestive use of the image) of the period in which the product was sold was deemed to be a "description of the goods" within the meaning of the fair use defense. Similarly, we have held the fair use defense applicable to a clothing manufacturer's use of the words "Come on Strong" as "describing a presumably desirable effect" of its menswear. *See B & L Sales Associates v. H. Daroff & Sons, Inc.*, 421 F.2d 352, 354 (2ᵈ Cir. 1970).

In the instant case, the challenged phrase "Seal it with a Kiss" (with or without the two exclamation points) is a clear instance of a non-trademark use of words in their descriptive sense. The phrase conveys the instruction to seal by kissing the complimentary postcard to signify the amorous sentiment conveyed to the recipient of the card. Though the words "Seal it with a Kiss" do not describe a characteristic of the defendants' product, they surely are used in their "descriptive sense"- to describe an action that the sellers hope consumers will take, using their product. *See* Restatement (Third) of Unfair Competition § 28 cmt. c (1995) ("Use of a descriptive term in textual . . . instruction . . . is ordinarily a fair use.").

The defendants' phrase is assuredly close to the plaintiff's mark "SEALED WITH A KISS," differing only in the use of the imperative mood "seal," rather than "sealed," and the addition of the objective pronoun "it." If any confusion results, that is a risk the plaintiff accepted when it decided to identify its product with a mark that uses a well known descriptive phrase. *See Car-Freshner*, 70 F.3d at 270. The phrase "sealed with a kiss" is a fixture of the language, used by generations of school girls, who have given it such currency that it is readily recognized when communicated only as an acronym - SWAK.

The non-trademark use of the challenged phrase and the defendants' good faith are both evidenced by the fact that the source of the defendants' product is clearly identified by the prominent display of the defendants' own trademarks. Chesebrough's promotional display clearly and prominently connected the lipstick to the well known "CUTEX" brand name, as well as to the newer "COLOR SPLASH" product name. The challenged phrase does not appear on the lipstick itself, on its packaging, or in any other advertising or promotional materials related to Chesebrough's product. The phrase appears only in relation to the postcards that consumers are invited to use, as Chesebrough hopes, with its brand of lipstick.

Plaintiff contends that defendants' trademark use of the challenged phrase is supported, indeed admitted, by the paragraph of defendants' answer that states that the promotional display has been so successful that the phrase "has come to be associated by consumers of cosmetics products with" defendants' lipsticks. *See* Defendants' Answer ¶ 65. We disagree. So long as the defendants in good faith are using the phrase in its descriptive sense and prominently identifying the product with the defendants' marks, the defendants incur no liability simply because the materials containing the descriptive phrase are so widely disseminated as to form some degree of association in the public's mind between the phrase and the product. That too is a risk the plaintiff took in selecting as its mark a phrase that was not only descriptive but readily recognized by consumers.

The judgment of The District Court is affirmed.

THE NEW KIDS ON THE BLOCK v. NEWS AMERICA PUBLISHING, INC.
971 F.2d 302 (9th Cir. 1992)

KOZINSKI, CIRCUIT JUDGE

The individual plaintiffs perform professionally as The New Kids on the Block, reputedly one of today's hottest musical acts. This case requires us to weigh their rights in that name against the rights of others to use it in identifying the New Kids as the subjects of public opinion polls.

Background

No longer are entertainers limited to their craft in marketing themselves to the public. This is the age of multi-media publicity blitzkrieg: Trading on their popularity, many entertainers hawk posters, T-shirts, badges, coffee mugs and the like — handsomely supplementing their incomes while boosting their public images. The New Kids are no exception; the record in this case indicates there are more than 500 products or services bearing the New Kids trademark. Among these are services taking advantage of a recent development in telecommunications: 900 area code numbers, where the caller is charged a fee, a portion of which is paid to the call recipient. Fans can call various New Kids 900 numbers to listen to the New Kids talk about themselves, to listen to other fans talk about the New Kids, or to leave messages for the New Kids and other fans.

The defendants, two newspapers of national circulation, conducted separate polls of their readers seeking an answer to a pressing question: Which one of the New Kids is the most popular? *USA Today*'s announcement contained a picture of the New Kids and asked, "Who's the best on the block?" The announcement listed a 900 number for voting, noting that "any USA Today profits from this phone line will go to charity," and closed with the following:

> New Kids on the Block are pop's hottest group. Which of the five is your fave? Or are they a turn off? . . . Each call costs 50 cents. Results in Friday's Life section.

The Star's announcement, under a picture of the New Kids, went to the heart of the matter: "Now which kid is the sexiest?" The announcement, which appeared in the middle of a page containing a story on the New Kids concert, also stated:

> Which of the New Kids on the Block would you most like to move next door?
> STAR wants to know which cool New Kid is the hottest with our readers.

Readers were then directed to a 900 number to register their votes; each call cost 95 cents per minute.[1]

Fearing that the two newspapers were undermining their hegemony over their fans, the New Kids filed a shotgun complaint in federal court raising no fewer than ten claims: (1) common law trademark infringement; (2) Lanham Act false advertising; (3) Lanham Act false designation of origin; (4) Lanham Act unfair competition; (5) state trade name infringement; (6) state false advertising; (7) state unfair competition; (8) commercial misappropriation; (9) common-law misappropriation; and (10) intentional interference with prospective economic advantage. The two papers raised the First Amendment as a defense, on the theory that the polls were part and parcel of their "news-gathering activities." The district court granted summary judgment for defendants. 745 F. Supp. 1540 (C.D. Cal. 1990).

*   *   *

A . . . problem arises when a trademark also describes a person, a place or an attribute of a product. If the trademark holder were allowed exclusive rights in such use, the language would be depleted in much the same way as if generic words were protectable. Thus trademark law recognizes a defense where the mark is used only "to describe the goods or services of [a] party, or their geographic origin." 15 U.S.C. § 115(b)(4). "The 'fair use' defense, in essence, forbids a trademark registrant to appropriate a descriptive term for his exclusive use and so prevent others from accurately describing a characteristic of their goods." *Soweco, Inc. v. Shell Oil Co.*, 617 F.2d 1178, 1185 (5th Cir. 1980). Once again, the courts will hold as a matter of law that the original producer does not sponsor or endorse another product that uses his mark in a descriptive manner. *See, e.g., Schmid Laboratories v. Youngs Drug Products Corp.*, 482 F. Supp. 14 (D.N.J. 1979) ("ribbed" condoms).

With so many well-known trademarks, such as Jell-O, Scotch tape and Kleenex, there are equally informative non-trademark words describing the product (gelatin, cellophane tape and facial tissue). But sometimes there is no descriptive substitute, and a problem closely related to genericity and descriptiveness is presented when many goods and services are effectively identifiable only by their trademarks. For example, one might refer to "the two-time world champions" or "the professional basketball team from Chicago," but it's far simpler (and more likely to be understood) to refer to the Chicago Bulls. In such cases, use of the trademark does not imply sponsorship or endorsement of the product because the mark is used only to describe the thing, rather than to identify its source.

Indeed, it is often virtually impossible to refer to a particular product for purposes of comparison, criticism, point of reference or any other such purpose without using the mark. For example, reference to a large automobile manufacturer based in Michigan would not differentiate among the Big Three; reference to a large Japanese manufacturer of home electronics would narrow the field to a dozen or more companies. Much useful social and commercial discourse would be all but impossible if speakers were under threat of an infringement lawsuit every time they made reference to a person, company or product by using its trademark.

A good example of this is *Volkswagenwerk Aktiengesellschaft v. Church*, 411 F.2d 350

---

[1] The *USA Today* poll generated less than $300 in revenues, all of which the newspaper donated to the Berklee College of Music. *The Star's* poll generated about $1600.

(9th Cir. 1969), where we held that Volkswagen could not prevent an automobile repair shop from using its mark. We recognized that in "advertising [the repair of Volkswagens, it] would be difficult, if not impossible, for [Church] to avoid altogether the use of the word 'Volkswagen' or its abbreviation 'VW,' which are the normal terms which, to the public at large, signify appellant's cars." *Id.* at 352. Church did not suggest to customers that he was part of the Volkswagen organization or that his repair shop was sponsored or authorized by VW; he merely used the words, "Volkswagen" and "VW" to convey information about the types of cars he repaired. Therefore, his use of the Volkswagen trademark was not an infringing one.

* * *

To be sure, this is not the classic fair use case where the defendant has used the plaintiff's mark to describe the defendant's *own* product. Here, the New Kids trademark is used to refer to the New Kids themselves. We therefore do not purport to alter the test applicable in the paradigmatic fair use case. If the defendant's use of the plaintiff's trademark refers to something other than the plaintiff's product, the traditional fair use inquiry will continue to govern. But, where the defendant uses a trademark to describe the plaintiff's product rather than its own, we hold that a commercial user is entitled to a nominative fair use defense provided he meets the following three requirements: First, the product or service in question must be one not readily identifiable without use of the trademark; second, only so much of the mark or marks may be used as is reasonably necessary to identify the product or service; and third, the user must do nothing that would, in conjunction with the mark, suggest sponsorship or endorsement by the trademark holder.

* * *

The New Kids do not claim there was anything false or misleading about the newspapers' use of their mark. Rather, the first seven causes of action, while purporting to state different claims, all hinge on one key factual allegation: that the newspapers' use of the New Kids name in conducting the unauthorized polls somehow implied that the New Kids were sponsoring the polls. It is no more reasonably possible, however, to refer to the New Kids as an entity than it is to refer to the Chicago Bulls, Volkswagens or the Boston Marathon without using the trademark. Indeed, how could someone not conversant with the proper names of the individual New Kids talk about the group at all? While plaintiffs' trademark certainly deserves protection against copycats and those who falsely claim that the New Kids have endorsed or sponsored them, such protection does not extend to rendering newspaper articles, conversations, polls and comparative advertising impossible. The first nominative use requirement is therefore met.

Also met are the second and third requirements. Both *The Star* and *USA Today* reference the New Kids only to the extent necessary to identify them as the subject of the polls; they do not use the New Kids' distinctive logo or anything else that isn't needed to make the announcements intelligible to readers. First, nothing in the announcements suggests joint sponsorship or endorsement by the New Kids. The *USA Today* announcement implies quite the contrary by asking whether the New Kids might be a "turn off." *The Star*'s poll is more effusive but says nothing that expressly or by fair implication connotes endorsement or joint sponsorship on the part of the New Kids.

The New Kids argue that, even if the newspapers are entitled to a nominative fair use defense for the announcements, they are not entitled to it for the polls themselves, which were money-making enterprises separate and apart from the newspapers' reporting businesses. According to plaintiffs, defendants could have minimized the intrusion into their rights by using an 800 number or asking readers to call in on normal telephone lines which would not have resulted in a profit to the newspapers based on the conduct of the polls themselves.

The New Kids see this as a crucial difference, distinguishing this case from *Volkswagenwerk*, *WCBV-TV* and other nominative use cases. The New Kids' argument in support of this distinction is not entirely implausible: They point out that their fans, like everyone else, have limited resources. Thus a dollar spent calling the newspapers' 900 lines to express loyalty to the New Kids may well be a dollar not spent on New Kids products and services, including the New Kids' own 900 numbers. In short, plaintiffs argue that a nominative fair use defense is inapplicable where the use in question competes directly with that of the trademark holder.

We reject this argument. While the New Kids have a limited property right in their name, that right does not entitle them to control their fans' use of their own money. Where, as here, the use does not imply sponsorship or endorsement, the fact that it is carried on for profit and in competition with the trademark holder's business is beside the point. *See, e.g., Universal City Studios, Inc. v. Ideal Publishing Corp.*, 195 U.S.P.Q. 761 (S.D.N.Y. 1977) (magazine's use of TV program's trademark "Hardy Boys" in connection with photographs of show's stars not infringing). Voting for their favorite New Kid may be, as plaintiffs point out, a way for fans to articulate their loyalty to the group, and this may diminish the resources available for products and services they sponsor. But the trademark laws do not give the New Kids the right to channel their fans' enthusiasm (and dollars) only into items licensed or authorized by them. *See International Order of Job's Daughters v. Lindeburg & Co.*, 633 F.2d 912 (9th Cir. 1990) (no infringement where unauthorized jewelry maker produced rings and pins bearing fraternal organization's trademark). The New Kids could not use the trademark laws to prevent the publication of an unauthorized group biography or to censor all parodies or satires which use their name. We fail to see a material difference between these examples and the use here.

Summary judgment was proper as to the first seven causes of action because they all hinge on a theory of implied endorsement; there was none here as the uses in question were purely nominative.

* * *

The district court's judgment is

Affirmed.

KP PERMANENT MAKE-UP, INC. v. LASTING IMPRESSION I, INC.
543 U.S. 111 (2004)

JUSTICE SOUTER delivered the opinion of the Court.[*]

The question here is whether a party raising the statutory affirmative defense of fair use to a claim of trademark infringement, 15 U.S.C. § 1115(b)(4), has a burden to negate any likelihood that the practice complained of will confuse consumers about the origin of the goods or services affected. We hold it does not.

I

Each party to this case sells permanent makeup, a mixture of pigment and liquid for injection under the skin to camouflage injuries and modify nature's dispensations, and each has used some version of the term "micro color" (as one word or two, singular or plural) in marketing and selling its product. Petition KP Permanent Make-Up, Inc., claims to have used the single-word version since 1990 or 1991 on advertising flyers and since 1991 on pigment bottles. Respondents Lasting Impression I, Inc., and its licensee, MCN International, Inc. (Lasting, for simplicity), deny that KP began using the term that early, but we accept KP's allegation as true for present purposes; the District and Appeals Courts took it to be so, and the disputed facts do not matter to our resolution

---

[*] JUSTICE SCALIA joins all but footnotes 4 and 5 of this opinion. JUSTICE BREYER joins all but footnote 6.

of the issue. In 1992, Lasting applied to the United States Patent and Trademark Office (PTO) under 15 U.S.C. § 1051 for registration of a trademark consisting of the words "Micro Colors" in white letters separated by a green bar within a black square. The PTO registered the mark to Lasting in 1993, and in 1999 the registration became incontestable. § 1065.

It was also in 1999 that KP produced a 10-page advertising brochure using "microcolor" in a large, stylized typeface, provoking Lasting to demand that KP stop using the term. Instead, KP sued Lasting in the Central District of California, seeking, on more than one ground, a declaratory judgment that its language infringed no such exclusive right as Lasting claimed.[3] Lasting counterclaimed, alleging, among other things, that KP had infringed Lasting's "Micro Colors" trademark.

KP sought summary judgment on the infringement counterclaim, based on the statutory affirmative defense of fair use, 15 U.S.C. § 1115(b)(4). After finding that Lasting had conceded that KP used the term only to describe its goods and not as a mark, the District Court held that KP was acting fairly and in good faith because undisputed facts showed that KP had employed the term "microcolor" continuously from a time before Lasting adopted the two-word, plural variant as a mark. Without enquiring whether the practice was likely to cause confusion, the court concluded that KP had made out its affirmative defense under § 1115(b)(4) and entered summary judgment for KP on Lasting's infringement claim.

On appeal, 328 F.3d 1061 (2003), the Court of Appeals for the Ninth Circuit thought it was error for the District Court to have addressed the fair use defense without delving into the matter of possible confusion on the part of consumers about the origin of KP's goods. The reviewing court took the view that no use could be recognized as fair where any consumer confusion was probable, and although the court did not pointedly address the burden of proof, it appears to have placed it on KP to show absence of consumer confusion. *Id.*, at 1072 ("Therefore, KP can only benefit from the fair use defense if there is no likelihood of confusion between KP's use of the term 'microcolor' and Lasting's mark"). Since it found there were disputed material facts relevant under the circuit's eight-factor test for assessing the likelihood of confusion, it reversed the summary judgment and remanded the case.

We granted KP's petition for certiorari, 540 U.S. 1099 (2004), to address a disagreement among the Courts of Appeals on the significance of likely confusion for a fair use defense to a trademark infringement claim, and the obligation of a party defending on that ground to show that its use is unlikely to cause consumer confusion. Compare 328 F.3d, at 1072 (likelihood of confusion bars the fair use defense); *PACCAR, Inc. v. TeleScan Technologies, L.L.C.*, 319 F.3d 243, 256 (CA6 2003) ("[A] finding of a likelihood of confusion forecloses a fair use defense"); and *Zatarains, Inc. v. Oak Grove Smokehouse*, 698 F.2d 786, 796 (CA5 1983) (alleging infringers were free to use words contained in a trademark "in their ordinary, descriptive sense, so long as such use [did] not tend to confuse customers as to the source of the goods"), with *Cosmetically Sealed Industries, Inc. v. Chesebrough-Pond's USA Co.*, 125 F.3d 28, 30–31 (CA2 1997) (the fair use defense may succeed even if there is likelihood of confusion); *Shakespeare Co. v. Silstar Corp. of Am.*, 110 F.3d 234, 243 (CA4 1997) ("[A] determination of likely confusion [does not] preclud[e] considering the fairness of use"); *Sunmark, Inc. v. Ocean Spray Cranberries, Inc.*, 64 F.3d 1055, 1059 (CA7 1995) (finding that likelihood of

---

[3] [Footnotes 1 and 2 omitted]. We summarize the proceedings in this litigation only as they are relevant to the question before us. The District Court's findings as to the generic or descriptive nature of the term "micro color" and any secondary meaning that term has acquired by any of the parties, see SA CV 00-276-GLT (EEx) (CD Cal. May 16, 2001), pp. 3–5, 5–8, are not before us. Nor are the Court of Appeals's holdings on these issues. See 328 F.3d 1061, 1068–1071 (CA9 2003). Nor do we address the Court of Appeals's discussion of "nominative fair use." *Id.*, at 1071–1072.

confusion did not preclude the fair use defense). We now vacate the judgment of the Court of Appeals.

II

A

The Trademark Act of 1946, known for its principal proponent as the Lanham Act, 60 Stat. 427, as amended, 15 U.S.C. § 1051 *et seq.*, provides the user of a trade or service mark with the opportunity to register it with the PTO, §§ 1051, 1053. If the registrant then satisfies further conditions including continuous use for five consecutive years, "the right . . . to use such registered mark in commerce" to designate the origin of the goods specified in the registration "shall be incontestable" outside certain listed exceptions. § 1065.

The holder of a registered mark (incontestable or not) has a civil action against anyone employing an imitation or it in commerce when "such use if likely to cause confusion, or to cause mistake, or to deceive." § 1114(1). Although an incontestable registration is "conclusive evidence . . . of the registrant's exclusive right to use the . . . mark in commerce," § 1115(b), the plaintiff's success is still subject to "proof of infringement as defined in section 1114," § 1115(b). And that, as just noted, requires a showing that the defendant's actual practice is likely to produce confusion in the minds of consumers about the origin of the goods or services in question. *See Two Pesos, Inc. v. Taco Cabana, Inc.*, 505 U.S. 763, 780 (1992) (STEVENS, J., concurring); *Lone Star Steakhouse and Saloon, Inc. v. Alpha of Virginia, Inc.*, 43 F.3d 922, 935 (CA4 1995); Restatement (Third) of Unfair Competition § 21, Comment *a* (1995). This plaintiff's burden has to be kept in mind when reading the relevant portion of the further provision for an affirmative defense of fair use, available to a party whose

> "use of the name, term, or device charged to be an infringement is a use, otherwise than as a mark, . . . of a term or device which is descriptive of and used fairly and in good faith only to describe the goods or services of such party, or their geographic origin . . . ." § 1115(b)(4).

Two points are evident. Section 1115(b) places a burden of proving likelihood of confusion (that is, infringement) on the party charging infringement even when relying on an incontestable registration. And Congress said nothing about likelihood of confusion in setting out the elements of the fair use defense in § 1115(b)(4).

Starting from these textual fixed points, it takes a long stretch to claim that a defense of fair use entails any burden to negate confusion. It is just not plausible that Congress would have used the descriptive phrase "likely to cause confusion, or to cause mistake, or to deceive" in § 1114 to describe the requirement that a markholder show likelihood of consumer confusion, but would have relied on the phrase "used fairly" in § 1115(b)(4) in a fit of terse drafting meant to place a defendant under a burden to negate confusion. " '[W]here Congress includes particular language in one section of a statute but omits it in another section of the same Act, it is generally presumed that Congress acts intentionally and purposely in the disparate inclusion or exclusion.' " *Russello v. United States*, 464 U.S. 16, 23 (1983) (quoting *United States v. Wong Kim Bo*, 472 F.2d 720, 722 (CA5 1972)) (alteration in original).[4]

Nor do we find much force in Lasting's suggestion that "used fairly" in § 1115(b)(4) is an oblique incorporation of a likelihood-of-confusion test developed in the common law

---

[4] Not only that, but the failure to say anything about a defendant's burden on this point was almost certainly not an oversight, not after the House Subcommittee on Trademarks declined to forward a proposal to provide expressly as an element of the defense that a descriptive use be " '[un]likely to deceive the public.' " Hearings on H.R. 102 et al. before the Subcommittee on Trade-Marks of the House Committee on Patents, 77th Cong., 1st Sess., 167–168 (1941) (hereinafter Hearings) (testimony of Prof. Milton Handler).

384 DEFENSES AND LIMITATIONS CH. 7

of unfair competition. Lasting is certainly correct that some unfair competition cases would stress that use of a term by another in conducting its trade went too far in sowing confusion, and would either enjoin the use or order the defendant to include a disclaimer. *See, e.g., Baglin v. Cusenier Co.*, 221 U.S. 580, 602 (1911) ("[W]e are unable to escape the conclusion that such use, in the manner shown, was to serve the purpose of simulation . . ."); *Herring-Hall-Marvin Safe Co. v. Hall's Safe Co.*, 208 U.S. 554, 559 (1908) ("[T]he rights of the two parties have been reconciled by allowing the use, provided that an explanation is attached"). But the common law of unfair competition also tolerated some degree of confusion from a descriptive use of words contained in another person's trademark. *See, e.g., William R. Warner & Co. v. Eli Lilly & Co.*, 265 U.S. 526, 528 (1924) (as to plaintiffs trademark claim, "[t]he use of a similar name by another to truthfully describe his own product does not constitute a legal or moral wrong, even if its effect be to cause the public to mistake the origin or ownership of the product"); *Canal Co. v. Clark*, 13 Wall. 311, 327 (1872) ("Purchasers may be mistaken, but they are not deceived by false representations, and equity will not enjoin against telling the truth"); *see also* 3 L. Altman, Callmann on Unfair Competition, Trademarks and Monopolies § 18:2, pp. 18–8 to 18–9, n. 1 (4th ed. 2004) (citing cases). While these cases are consistent with taking account of the likelihood of consumer confusion as one consideration in deciding whether a use is fair, see Part II-B, *infra*, they do not stand for the proposition that an assessment of confusion alone may be dispositive. Certainly one cannot get out of them any defense burden to negate it entirely.

Finally, a look at the typical course of litigation in an infringement action points up the incoherence of placing a burden to show nonconfusion on a defendant. If a plaintiff succeeds in making out a prima facie case of trademark infringement, including the element of likelihood of consumer confusion, the defendant may offer rebutting evidence to undercut the force of the plaintiff's evidence on this (or any) element, or raise an affirmative defense to bar relief even if the prima facie case is sound, or do both. But it would make no sense to give the defendant a defense of showing affirmatively that the plaintiff cannot succeed in proving some element (like confusion); all the defendant needs to do is to leave the factfinder unpersuaded that the plaintiff has carried its own burden on that point. A defendant has no need of a court's true belief when agnosticism will do. Put another way, it is only when a plaintiff has shown likely confusion by a preponderance of the evidence that a defendant could have any need of an affirmative defense, but under Lasting's theory the defense would be foreclosed in such a case. "[I]t defies logic to argue that a defense may not be asserted in the only situation where it even becomes relevant." *Shakespeare Co. v. Silstar Corp.*, 110 F.3d, at 243. Nor would it make sense to provide an affirmative defense of no confusion plus good faith, when merely rebutting the plaintiff's case on confusion would entitle the defendant to judgment, good faith or not.

* * *

B

Since the burden of proving likelihood of confusion rests with the plaintiff, and the fair use defendant has no free-standing need to show confusion unlikely, it follows (contrary to the Court of Appeals's view) that some possibility of consumer confusion must be compatible with fair use, and so it is. The common law's tolerance of a certain degree of confusion on the part of consumers followed from the very fact that in cases like this one an originally descriptive term was selected to be used as a mark, not to mention the undesirability of allowing anyone to obtain a complete monopoly on use of a descriptive term simply by grabbing it first. *Canal Co. v. Clark, supra*, at 323–324, 327. The Lanham Act adopts a similar leniency, there being no indication that the statute was meant to deprive commercial speakers of the ordinary utility of descriptive words. "If any confusion results, that is a risk the plaintiff accepted when it decided to identify its product with a mark that uses a well known descriptive phrase." *Cosmetically Sealed*

Industries, Inc. v. Chesebrough-Pond's USA Co., 125 F.3d, at 30. *See also Park'N Fly, Inc. v. Dollar Park and Fly, Inc.*, 469 U.S. 189, 201, 105 S.Ct. 658, 83 L.Ed.2d 582 (1985) (noting safeguards in Lanham Act to prevent commercial monopolization of language); *Car-Freshner Corp. v. S.C. Johnson & Son, Inc.*, 70 F.3d 267, 269 (C.A.2 1995) (noting importance of "protect[ing] the right of society at large to use words or images in their primary descriptive sense").[5] This right to describe is the reason that descriptive terms qualify for registration as trademarks only after taking on secondary meaning as "distinctive of the applicant's goods," 15 U.S.C. § 1052(f), with the registrant getting an exclusive right not in the original, descriptive sense, but only in the secondary one associated with the markholder's goods, 2 McCarthy, *supra*, § 11:45 ("The only aspect of the mark which is given legal protection is that penumbra or fringe of secondary meaning which surrounds the old descriptive word").

While we thus recognize that mere risk of confusion will not rule out fair use, we think it would be improvident to go further in this case, for deciding anything more would take us beyond the Ninth Circuit's consideration of the subject. It suffices to realize that our holding that fair use can occur along with some degree of confusion does not foreclose the relevance of the extent of any likely consumer confusion in assessing whether a defendant's use is objectively fair. Two Courts of Appeals have found it relevant to consider such scope, and commentators and *amici* here have urged us to say that the degree of likely consumer confusion bears not only on the fairness of using a term, but even on the further question whether an originally descriptive term has become so identified as a mark that a defendant's use of it cannot realistically be called descriptive. *See Shakespeare Co. v. Silstar Corp., supra*, at 243 ("[T]o the degree that confusion is likely, a use is less likely to be found fair . . ." (emphasis omitted)); *Sunmark, Inc. v. Ocean Spray Cranberries, Inc.*, 64 F.3d, at 1059; Restatement (Third) of Unfair Competition, § 28; Brief for American Intellectual Property Law Association as *Amicus Curiae* 13–18; Brief for Private Label Manufacturers Association as *Amicus Curiae* 16–17; Brief for Society of Permanent Cosmetic Professionals et al. as *Amici Curiae* 8–11.

Since we do not rule out the pertinence of the degree of consumer confusion under the fair use defense, we likewise do not pass upon the position of the United States, as *amicus*, that the "used fairly" requirement in § 1115(b)(4) demands only that the descriptive term describe the goods accurately. Tr. of Oral Arg. 17. Accuracy of course has to be a consideration in assessing fair use, but the proceedings in this case so far raise no occasion to evaluate some other concerns that courts might pick as relevant, quite apart from attention to confusion. The Restatement raises possibilities like commercial justification and the strength of the plaintiff's mark. Restatement § 28. As to them, it is enough to say here that the door is not closed.

III

In sum, a plaintiff claiming infringement of an incontestable mark must show likelihood of consumer confusion as part of the prima facie case, 15 U.S.C. § 1115(b), while the defendant has no independent burden to negate the likelihood of any confusion in raising the affirmative defense that a term is used descriptively, not as a mark, fairly, and in good faith, § 1115(b)(4).

Because we read the Court of Appeals as requiring KP to shoulder a burden on the issue of confusion, we vacate the judgment and remand the case for further proceedings consistent with this opinion.[6]

---

[5] *See also* Hearings 72 (testimony of Wallace Martin, Chairman, American Bar Association Committee on Trade-Mark Legislation) ("Everybody has got a right to the use of the English language and has got a right to assume that nobody is going to take that English language away from him").

[6] The record indicates that on remand the courts should direct their attention in particular to certain factual

It is so ordered.

Notes on Permitted Use

1. Altered and Unauthorized Products

a) Repaired, Reconditioned, and Modified Products

Repaired, reconditioned, or modified products and product-related services (e.g., automotive repair shops) may display the trademark of the original maker of the product so long as there is full disclosure and the public is not likely to be confused into thinking there is an agency relationship. *See Champion, supra; Bulova Watch Co. v. Allerton Co.*, 328 F.2d 20 (7th Cir. 1964) (discussed below).

Where confusion is likely, however, such use will not be permitted. In *Karl Storz Endoscopy-America, Inc. v. Surgical Technologies, Inc.*, 285 F.3d 848 (9th Cir. 2002), for example, defendant's repair and refurbishment of plaintiff's surgical instruments raised issues of fact as to whether confusion was likely. Storz presented evidence of actual confusion among surgeons and "evidence that Surgitech's rebuilds were the construction of a different product associated with Storz's trademark." *See also Davidoff & CIE SA v. PLD Int'l Corp.*, 263 F.3d 1297 (11th Cir. 2001) (defendant's etching off of batch codes from fragrance bottles bearing plaintiff's marks degraded the appearance of the bottles so that they were materially different and confusion was likely); *Toshiba Am. Info. Sys. v. Advantage Telecom*, 19 Fed. Appx. 646 (9th Cir. 2001) (defendant's sale of products bearing plaintiff's TOSHIBA mark but not the product serial numbers would prevent customers from receiving upgrade and recall services, and void any warranty, creating material differences which justified injunctive relief).

In *Nitro Leisure Prods v. Acushnet Co.*, 341 F.3d 1356 (Fed. Cir. 2003), plaintiff Acushnet sold new golf balls under trademarks like TITLEIST and ACUSHNET. Defendant Nitro sold two categories of used golf balls at discounted rates: "recycled" balls purchased in good condition, and then washed and repackaged; and "refurbished" balls bearing stains, scuffs, or blemishes that had to be repainted (including the trademark) before being sold. The "refurbished" balls each featured the logo "USED & REFURBISHED BY SECOND CHANCE" or "USED AND REFURBISHED BY GOLFBALLSDIRECT.COM" on each ball. "Second Chance" and "Golfballsdirect.com" were retail businesses run by Nitro. Some, but not all, of the refurbished balls also featured a Nitro trademark, in addition to the original Acushnet-owned trademark indicating the ball's original source. The packaging for Nitro's balls contained a disclaimer stating that refurbished balls "are subject to performance variations from new ones," and that "this product has NOT been endorsed or approved by the original manufacturer and the balls DO NOT fall under the original manufacturer's warranty." Acushnet sued Nitro for trademark infringement, dilution and unfair competition based on the "refurbished" balls. Acushnet conceded that under the "first sale" doctrine, it had no trademark infringement claim with respect to the "recycled" balls. The district court denied preliminary relief, and Acushnet appealed.

The Federal Circuit affirmed. "[S]o long as the customer is getting a product with the expected characteristics, and so long as the goodwill built up by the trademark

---

issues bearing on the fair use defense, properly applied. The District Court said that Lasting's motion for summary adjudication conceded that KP used "microcolor" descriptively and not as a mark. SA CV 00-276-GLT (EEx) at 8, App. to Pet. for Cert. 29a. We think it is arguable that Lasting made those concessions only as to KP's use of "microcolor" on bottles and flyers in the early 1990s, not as to the stylized version of "microcolor" that appeared in KP's 1999 brochure. See Opposition to Motion for Summary Judgment in SA CV 00-276-GLT (EEx) (CD Cal.), pp. 18–19; Appellants' Opening Brief in No. 01-56055 (CA9), pp. 31–2. We also note that the fair use analysis of KP's employment of the stylized version of "microcolor" on its brochure may differ from that of its use of the term on the bottles and flyers.

owner is not eroded by being identified with inferior quality, the Lanham Act does not prevent the truthful use of trademarks, even if such use results in the enrichment of others." It might be possible that "the reconditioning or repair would be so extensive or so basic that it would be a misnomer to call the article by its original name." However, purchasers of refurbished goods "do not expect the product to be in the same condition as a new product," but rather anticipate that "products will be degraded or will show signs of wear and tear and will not measure up to or perform at the same level as if new." For these types of goods "consumers are not likely to be confused by - and indeed expect - differences in the goods compared to new, unused goods." The court affirmed the denial of relief on three grounds: (1) that "the differences between the goods were nothing more than what would be expected for used golf balls," (2) that it was "not a misnomer" to use plaintiff's marks on the refurbished balls, and (3) that plaintiff had not shown that confusion was likely. Importantly, defendant had submitted evidence that the disclaimers featured on its packaging reduced confusion in the marketplace.

Note that some states have statutes prohibiting use of an original manufacturer's trademark on rebottled or repackaged products. *See, e.g.,* 765 Ill. Comp. Stat. (1992) 1050. Can such statutes be justified if there is full disclosure and confusion is not likely? *Compare Enesco Corp. v. Price/Costco Inc.*, 146 F.3d 1083 (9th Cir. 1998), where the court held that defendant could be found liable under trademark law for failure to give consumers notice that defendant had repackaged plaintiff's "Precious Moments" porcelain bisque figurines, but that with adequate notice to the public that defendant had repackaged them, "the public would not likely be confused" as to the source of any damage to the figurines caused by the repackaging.

Should one be permitted to sell an altered product bearing another's trademark without the necessity of disclosure if the altered product is of a higher rather than lesser quality than that sold by the trademark's owner (e.g., whiskey purchased in the cask and then bottled and sold under the mark of the manufacturer from whom it was purchased)? In some instances the desired higher quality may necessitate such an alteration of the original article that continued use of the original trademark would be inappropriate and misleading. In *Bulova Watch Co. v. Allerton Co.*, 328 F.2d 20 (7th Cir. 1964), the defendant had purchased Bulova watches on the market, then recased the movements, still bearing the "Bulova" trademark, in diamond-decorated cases, which defendant then sold to retail outlets under the trade name "Treasure Mates." Deeming such a significantly altered product to constitute "a new construction," the court stated at p. 23 that "[t]he watch is no longer a Bulova watch." The court allowed proper collateral references to the source of the movement but enjoined any use of the trademark "Bulova" as such. Consequently, the court allowed collateral use with full disclosure as to defendant's role in the recasing and as the sole guarantor of the watch, for catalog inserts, displays and advertising, but enjoined any use of the "Bulova" trademark on the movement itself. *See also Rolex Watch, U.S.A., Inc. v. Michel Co.*, 179 F.3d 704 (9th Cir. 1999) (remanding for permanent injunction "completely enjoining the use of Rolex's trademarks on the altered watches that [defendant] sells", because defendant's refurbishments and alterations "are so basic it is a misnomer" to sell the watches under plaintiff's marks). *Cf. Kealoha v. E.I. du Pont de Nemours & Co.*, 82 F.3d 894, 902–903 (9th Cir. 1996) (TEFLON plastic incorporated into jaw implant which subsequently fragmented and caused injury did not make owner of TEFLON mark liable where implant manufacturer was warned of possible unsuitability for this purpose and implant manufacturer expressly assumed responsibility; while TEFLON mark was conspicuous, it identified the source of raw material and would not cause source confusion with regard to the implant itself "as it was abundantly clear that Vitek and not DuPont was responsible for the manufacture and design of the implant").

b)   Out of Date and Defective Products

Should a merchant be allowed to sell to the public "distressed merchandise" comprising defective, damaged, or out of style goods which still bear the trademark of the original manufacturer or supplier? In *J. C. Penney Co. v. Charbeth's Little General Store*, 185 U.S.P.Q. 254 (E.D.N.Y. 1975), defendant represented discontinued or out of style J.C. Penney merchandise as new, and sold it at a price lower than that charged by J.C. Penney for new merchandise; the court noted several kinds of public deception that might be expected to result and preliminarily enjoined defendant from advertising or selling any merchandise bearing plaintiff's name or trademarks. In *Adolph Coors Co. v. A. Genderson & Sons, Inc.*, 486 F. Supp. 131 (D. Col. 1980), defendant distributed plaintiff's unpasteurized beer without authorization and without following plaintiff's rigid quality control standards; the court compared the case with those where inferior or altered goods were resold under the original trademark, citing *J.C. Penney v. Charbeth's*, *supra*, and enjoined defendant from any further unauthorized distributions. *See also Warner-Lambert Co. v. Northside Dev. Corp.*, 86 F.3d 3 (2^d Cir. 1996) (preliminarily enjoining the sale of stale HALLS cough drops); *Polymer Technology Corp. v. Mimran*, 975 F.2d 58 (2^d Cir. 1992) (vacating denial of preliminary injunction; defendant's retail distribution of plaintiff's BOSTON professional lens care solution might infringe because plaintiff's professional packages do not comply with FDA labeling requirements for retail solutions); *Bill Blass, Ltd. v. SAZ Corp.*, 751 F.2d 152 (3^d Cir. 1984) (out of date designer label fashions); *J.C. Penney Co. v. Parrish Co.*, 335 F. Supp. 209 (D. Idaho 1971). *Compare Denbicare U.S.A. Inc. v. Toys "R" Us Inc.*, 84 F.3d 1143 (9th Cir.), *cert. denied*, 519 U.S. 873 (1996) (allowing the sale of allegedly inferior diapers in discontinued packaging because plaintiff previously had consented to their sale in a U.S. foreign trade zone); *Alfred Dunhill Ltd. v. Interstate Cigar Co.*, 499 F.2d 232 (2^d Cir. 1974).

c)   The Right to Inspect and Approve

The trademark owner's right to inspect and approve goods sold under its mark was upheld in *Shell Oil Co. v. Commercial Petroleum, Inc.*, 928 F.2d 104, 107 (4th Cir. 1991) in which defendant had purchased bulk oil from plaintiff and resold it under plaintiff's trademarks without adhering to plaintiff's quality control standards, the court held that this was trademark infringement because the product was not "genuine" if plaintiff's quality control standards were not followed; *C.B. Fleet Co. v. Complete Packaging Corp.*, 739 F. Supp. 393, 398–99 (N.D. Ill. 1990), in which defendant was preliminarily enjoined from selling deodorant products bearing plaintiff's trademark under a "right to inspect and approve" theory; and *Ford Motor Company v. Cook*, 35 U.S.P.Q.2d 1062 (7th Cir. 1995), affirming an injunction against defendant's sale of uninspected automotive grilles bearing plaintiff's trademarks that defendant purchased at a supplier's bankruptcy sale. *Cf. The Grateful Palate, Inc. v. Joshua Tree Imports, LLC*, 220 Fed. Appx. 635 (9th Cir. 2007) ("a product sold without the authorization of the mark holder is generally deemed non-genuine for purposes of the Lanham Act"; remanded for application of the proper legal standard); *General Motors Corp. v. Keystone Automotive Indus.*, 453 F.3d 351 (6th Cir. 2006) (finding risk of post-sale confusion where defendant used plaintiff's trademarks on replacement grilles).

In *Australian Gold, Inc. v. Hatfield, Inc.*, 436 F.3d 1228 (10th Cir. 2006), plaintiffs' tanning supplies were only sold through distributors to tanning salons. Defendants made unauthorized sales of them over the Internet, actively concealing themselves from plaintiff and changing their company name whenever plaintiff discovered them. Plaintiff required all distributors to undergo training on proper use of its products, and the distributors in turn would provide the training to the tanning salon operators. The Tenth Circuit affirmed a jury award to plaintiff of over $5 million. Defendants had misrepresented themselves on their websites as "favored or authorized dealers", and given their bad intent to cause confusion, were "not shielded by the first sale doctrine".

2.   Comparative and Nominative Fair Use

a)   Comparative Marketing

The use of another's trademark in the advertising or marketing of products or services is permitted provided there is truthful disclosure and no likelihood of confusion. *See* 2 GILSON, TRADEMARK PROTECTION AND PRACTICE § 5.09[3] (2008 ed.); McCARTHY, TRADEMARKS AND UNFAIR PROTECTION §§ 25:34–25:52 (4th ed. 2007). As stated in *Societe Comptoir De L'Industrie Cotonneire Etablissements Boussac v. Alexander's Department Stores, Inc., supra*:

> The Lanham Act does not prohibit a commercial rival's truthfully denominating his goods a copy of a design in the public domain, though he uses the name of the designer to do so. Indeed, it is difficult to see any other means that might be employed to inform the consuming public of the true origin of the design.

In essence, is the rule respecting use of another's trademark simply the familiar one that deception or its likelihood will not be permitted but such use is not per se taboo?

How may one lawfully use the trademark of another in comparative advertising? *See Smith v. Chanel, Inc.*, 402 F.2d 562 (9ᵗʰ Cir. 1968), in which one challenge in defendant's advertising was: "We dare you to try to detect any difference between Chanel #5 ($25.00) and Ta'Ron's 2nd Chance. $7.00." *Compare Chanel, Inc. v. Smith*, 178 U.S.P.Q. 630 (N.D. Calif. 1973) *and Saxony Prods., Inc. v. Guerlain, Inc.*, 513 F.2d 716, 722 (9ᵗʰ Cir. 1975), in which the court stated:

> for purposes of comparative advertising Saxony could use Guerlain's trademark SHALIMAR to apprise consumers [truthfully] that Fragrance S is "like" or "similar" to SHALIMAR. The use of Guerlain's trademark, however, constituted a violation of the Lanham Act if Saxony falsely represented that Fragrance S was "like" or "similar" to SHALIMAR or if there was a reasonable likelihood that consumers would be confused as to the source of Fragrance S."

See also the discussion in the misrepresentation section in Chapter 8, *infra*; Livermore, *On Uses of a Competitor's Trademark*, 59 TRADEMARK REP. 30 (1969).

b)   Nominative Fair Use

As explained by Judge Kozinski in *The New Kids on the Block, supra*, non-trademark owners are entitled to "nominative" fair use in which they use another's trademark to truthfully refer to a particular product for purposes of comparison, criticism, point of reference and the like. Such use must not, however, "suggest sponsorship or endorsement by the trademark holder." *Id. See also Nikkei Keizai Shimbun, Inc. v. Comline Business Data, Inc.*, 166 F.3d 65, 73 (2ᵈ Cir. 1999) (it was fair use for defendant to use plaintiff publisher's name to identify defendant's abstracts of plaintiff's news articles; "it will usually be impossible to identify the source of factual information without using a registered trademark of the source"). The *New Kids* nominative fair use test was applied in a case involving the use of Princess Diana's image on collectible jewelry, plates and dolls in *Cairns v. Franklin Mint Co.*, 292 F.3d 1139 (9ᵗʰ Cir. 2002). The court held defendant was making fair use because no adequate substitute was available ("Princess Diana's physical appearance is not readily identifiable without use of her likeness"), defendant used no more than reasonably necessary (it was doubtful defendant "would be able to sell its' Diana, Princess of Wales Porcelain Portrait Doll' without prominent reference to Princess Diana"), and defendant's use did not suggest endorsement by plaintiff, the representative of a memorial fund and executor of her estate. As to the last, the court noted that third party use of her persona without authorization had been allowed for several years, and consumers therefore had no reason to erroneously believe that defendant was making authorized use. *Compare Brother Records, Inc. v. Jardine*, 318 F.3d 900 (9ᵗʰCir 2003) (original band member's use of "The Beach Boys" trademark was not nominative fair use because it was likely to create sponsorship confusion); *United We Stand America, Inc., v. United We Stand America New York, Inc.*, 128 F.3d 86 (2ᵈ Cir.), *cert. denied*, 118 S.Ct. 1521 (1998) (use of a version of presidential candidate Ross Perot's campaign slogan UNITED WE STAND AMERICA by a Perot supporter for a local group was not protectable First Amendment use but caused likely confusion warranting injunctive relief); Doellinger, "Nominative Fair Use: Jardine and the Demise of A Doctrine," 1 Nw. J. of TECH. & I.P. 66 (2003) (criticizing the nominative fair use doctrine).

In *Century 21 Real Estate Corp. v. Lendingtree Inc.*, 425 F.3d 211 (3ᵈ Cir. 2005), the Third Circuit applied the Supreme Court's *KP Permanent* decision excerpted above, and concluded that the Supreme Court's holding that fair use may be successfully shown even where there is "some possibility of confusion" applied not just to "classic fair use," but also to nominative fair use. It further concluded that the Supreme Court's decision made the Ninth Circuit's *New Kids on the Block* decision and its offspring obsolete. It then instead adopted a "two step approach." First, the plaintiff would have to prove confusion is likely. If so, then the burden would shift to the defendant to establish nominative fair use under a modified version of the Ninth Circuit test. To do so, the defendant would need to show that the use of plaintiff's mark was necessary, that defendant only used as much of plaintiff's mark as was necessary, and that defendant's conduct or language reflected the true and accurate relationship between plaintiff's and defendant's products or services.

Some would contend that nominative fair use differs from descriptive fair use, and that these issues are better covered by the *New Kids on the Block* requirement that the alleged nominative fair use not "suggest sponsorship or endorsement by the trademark holder." Perhaps this area of the law should simply be viewed as a restatement of Justice Holmes' famous observation in *Prestonettes, Inc. v. Coty*, 264 U.S. 359 (1924) that, "When the mark is used in a way that does not deceive the public, we see no such sanctity in the word as to prevent its being used to tell the truth. It is not taboo."

Such fair use principles similarly apply to trademarks on the Internet. *See, e.g., Bally Total Fitness Holding Corp. v. Faber*, 29 F.Supp.2d 1161 (C.D. Cal. 1998) (granting defendant summary judgment in connection with its "ballysucks.com" website containing First Amendment-protected criticism of plaintiff), and the discussion of Internet-related issues in § 8.01, *infra*. In *Playboy Enterprises, Inc. v. Welles*, 279 F.3d 796 (9ᵗʰ Cir. 2002) a former Playboy Playmate of the Year made fair use of "Playboy Playmate of the Year 1981" in headings and banner ads on her website, and "Playboy" and "Playmate" in the website metatags. However, her repetitive wallpaper use of the PMOY mark was unnecessary and potentially infringing. In *Playboy Enterprises, Int'l, Inc. v. Netscape Comm'ns Corp.*, 354 F.3d 1020 (9ᵗʰ Cir. 2004), defendant sold advertisers a list of search terms, so that when users typed plaintiff's "playboy" or "playmate" trademarks into defendant's search engine, the advertisers' banner ads for sex and adult-oriented entertainment websites would appear on the search page. Defendant had been granted summary judgment, but issues of fact as to whether the advertisers' unlabeled or confusingly labeled banner ads created likely initial interest confusion caused the court to reverse and remand. In considering defendant's fair use defense, the court noted that defendant listed over 400 terms besides Playboy's mark that could trigger the banner ads, and "there is nothing indispensable, in this context, about using Playboy's marks." It was not nominative fair use, because defendant was not intending to identify Playboy or its marks by their use, but to capitalize on the association.

Similarly, defendants' use of a plaintiff's trademark on in its web sites, metatags and its purchase of promotional placement in search results for plaintiff's products was more than the mere display and stocking of trademark items protected by the first sale doctrine. In *Australian Gold, Inc. v., Hatfield*, 436 F.3d 1228(10ᵗʰ Cir. 2006), citing *Eli Lilly & Co. v. Natural Answers, Inc.*, 233 F.3d 456, 465 (7ᵗʰ Cir. 2000). "[T]he first sale doctrine does not protect resellers who use other entities trademarks to give the impression that they are favored or authorized dealers for a product when in fact they are not." *Id.*

c) Descriptive Fair Use

Non-deceptive descriptive use of a term that another has claimed as a trademark for a similar product may be permissible under appropriate circumstances. *Zatarain's Inc. v. Oak Grove Smokehouse, Inc.,* 698 F.2d 786 (5th Cir. 1983) (fair, good faith, descriptive use of "Fish Fry" on packaging of defendant's "VISKO'S Fish Fry" batter mix did not infringe plaintiff's registered FISH-FRI mark for similar product; the descriptive nature of defendant's use and dissimilarities in the parties' packaging made confusion "virtually impossible"); *Door Sys. Inc. v. Pro-Line Door Sys. Inc.,* 83 F.3d 169, 173 (7th Cir. 1996) (defendant's descriptive use of "door systems" in its mark, PRO-LINE DOOR SYSTEMS for automatic garage door products and services, was not likely to cause confusion with plaintiff's DOOR SYSTEMS mark for similar products and services). In *Packman v. Chicago Tribune Co.,* 267 F.3d 628 (7th Cir. 2001), plaintiff owned the registered mark "The Joy of Six"; the Chicago Tribune's descriptive use of "The Joy of Six" in a front page headline was fair use even when reproduced on merchandise. The use of the phrase "referred to happiness about [the Chicago Bulls'] six championships and . . . [as a play on the well-known book title, "The Joy of Sex"] the phrase is widely used to describe the joy of six of anything."

Section 33 of the Lanham Act, 15 U.S.C. § 1115(b)(4) provides that use of a term other than as a trade or service mark is not an infringement if the term is used fairly and in good faith to describe the goods or services of the party. The defense applies at common-law as well as under the statute. *William R. Warner & Co. v. Eli Lilly & Co.,* 265 U.S. 526, 528 (1924). *Venetianaire Corp. of America v. A&P Import Co.,* 429 F.2d 1079, 1081 (2d Cir. 1970) (the statute incorporates the defense previously available at common law).

If plaintiff's mark is suggestive rather than descriptive, should the defense of fair use be precluded? *Compare Seaboard Seed Co. v. Bemis Co.,* 632 F. Supp. 1133, 1138 (N.D. Ill. 1986) (QUICK GREEN for grass seed not descriptive, so defense unavailable) *with Charles of the Ritz Group, Ltd. v. Marcon, Ltd.,* 230 U.S.P.Q. 377 (S.D.N.Y. 1986) (SILK for cosmetics held suggestive, not descriptive, but fair use upheld). *See also Car-Freshner Corp. v. S.C. Johnson & Son, Inc.,* 70 F.3d 267, 269 (2d Cir. 1995) (defendant's descriptive use of plaintiff's registered pine tree shape for air fresheners held fair use and not infringing; "it should make no difference whether the plaintiff's mark is to be classed on the descriptive tier of the trademark ladder . . .. [w]hat matters is whether the *defendant* is using the protected word or image descriptively, and not as a trademark"); *Shakespeare Co. v. Silstar Corp.,* 906 F. Supp. 997 (D.S.C. 1995), *aff'd,* 110 F.3d 234 (4d Cir. 1997) (holding that defendant's "descriptive," non-trademark use of a clear tip on a fishing rod, in potential conflict with plaintiff's incontestably registered fishing rod trade dress, was fair use); *Dowbrands L.P. v. Helene Curtis, Inc.,* 863 F. Supp. 963, 966–69 (D. Minn. 1994) (fair use defense not limited to descriptive marks). If the defendant uses the term as a trademark, rather than descriptively, § 33 should not be applicable. *Lindy Pen Co. v. Bic Pen Corp.,* 725 F.2d 1240, 1248 (9th Cir. 1984), *cert. denied,* 469 U.S. 1188 (1985) (mark merely descriptive but used as trademark by defendant; district court's finding of fair use reversed); *Tree Tavern Products, Inc. v. Conagra, Inc.,* 640 F. Supp. 1263, 1268–69 (D. Del. 1986).

Decisions holding that fair use was established include *Soweco, Inc. v. Shell Oil Co.,* 617 F.2d 1178 (5th Cir. 1980) ("Larvacide" on larvae-killer fair use despite plaintiff's registration of "LARVACIDE" for similar products); *Abercrombie & Fitch Co. v. Hunting World, Inc.,* 537 F.2d 4, 12–13 (2d Cir. 1976) ("safari" with respect to boots held fair use); *B & L Sales Associates v. H. Daroff & Sons, Inc.,* 421 F.2d 352 (2d Cir. 1970) ("COME ON STRONG with Botany 500" held not to infringe registered trademark COME ON STRONG for clothing); *Kiki Undies Corp. v. Alexander's*

Department Stores, 390 F.2d 604 (2ᵈ Cir. 1968). (KIKI versus Kicky for similar clothing products; "plaintiff has offered no proof that [defendant] used "Kicky" as a trademark or other than as a descriptive adjective.") A key factor in such cases often is defendant's prominent use of its own mark. *See B & L Associates, supra.*

In *Sands, Taylor & Wood Co. v. Quaker Oats Co.*, 978 F.2d 947 (7ᵗʰ Cir. 1992), plaintiff, owner of the trademark THIRST-AID, sued defendant for using the advertising slogan "GATORADE is Thirst Aid." Although defendant's GATORADE mark was famous and plaintiff's mark was descriptive, the court nonetheless rejected a fair use defense. The court affirmed that defendant used THIRST AID prominently as an "attention-getting symbol," and with its rhyming slogan, created a unique association with defendant's mark that was likely to cause reverse confusion. 978 F.2d at 954. *Compare W.W.W. Pharmaceutical Co. v. Gillette Co.*, 984 F.2d 567 (2ᵈ Cir. 1993), where plaintiff owned the mark SPORT STICK for lip balm, and the court found no likelihood of reverse confusion with defendant's RIGHT GUARD SPORT STICK for deodorant, in large part because of the weakness of plaintiff's mark and the renown of defendant's RIGHT GUARD mark.

Should establishing that confusion is unlikely be a prerequisite to a successful fair use defense? In *KP Permanent Make-Up, Inc. v. Lasting Impression I, Inc.*, excerpted above, the Supreme Court resolved a split in the circuit courts on whether a defendant pleading fair use in a trademark infringement claim also has the burden to negate likelihood of confusion. The court held that the defendant does not have this burden. Both parties in *KP Permanent* marketed permanent makeup supplies using the term "Microcolors." Lasting Impression, the owner of a registration for a mark containing Microcolors, demanded that KP cease such use. In response, KP sued in the Central District of California seeking a declaratory judgment that KP used the term fairly only to describe the qualities of its products. The district court granted KP's summary judgment motion, finding that KP had proved its affirmative defense of fair use. The Ninth Circuit reversed, finding that there could be no fair use where confusion was probable.

The Supreme Court reversed the Ninth Circuit, concluding that construction of the Lanham Act confirmed that a defendant alleging fair use did not need to negate confusion. The court reasoned that, since it was the plaintiff's burden to prove confusion, it was nonsensical to impose on the defendant the burden to disprove it. The court did not decide what role likelihood of confusion might play in determining whether a use is fair. The court noted: "It suffices to realize that our holding that fair use can occur along with some degree of confusion does not foreclose the relevance of the extent of any likely consumer confusion in assessing whether a defendant's use is objectively fair." *Id.* at 123.

d) Addition of House Marks

Occasionally a second user defends an infringement claim by citing the use of its own well-known mark in conjunction with the term in which the plaintiff claims rights. The theory is that the second user's well-known mark, sometimes referred to as a "house mark," conveys to consumers that the second user is the source of the product, and is sufficient to dispel any likelihood of confusion. Courts often have held, however, that the addition of such a house mark actually increases the risk of confusion rather than diminishes it, by falsely suggesting an affiliation between the two users. *See, e.g., American Trading, Inc. v. Russ Berrie & Co.*, 966 F.2d 1284 (9ᵗʰ Cir. 1992) ("a purchaser could well think plaintiff had licensed defendant"), citing *Menendez v. Holt*, 128 U.S. 514, 521 (1888) (use by defendant of its house mark along with plaintiff's LA FAVORITA mark was "an aggravation and not a justification, for it is openly trading in the name of another upon the reputation acquired by the device of the true proprietor"); *International Kennel Club of Chicago, Inc. v. Mighty Star, Inc.*, 846 F.2d 1079 (7ᵗʰ Cir. 1988) (defendants' house mark argument was "a smoke screen and a poor excuse"; consumers "would necessarily believe that [plaintiff] had licensed, approved or otherwise authorized the defendants' use"). Other courts have simply declared the use of a house mark ineffective to dispel confusion in the particular case. *See, e.g., Lois Sportswear U.S.A. v. Levi Strauss & Co.*, 799 F.2d 867, 873–74 (2ᵈ Cir. 1986); (back pocket stitching pattern on jeans); *AMF Inc. v. Sleekcraft Boats*, 599 F.2d 341, 351 (9ᵗʰ Cir. 1979) (SLICKCRAFT and SLEEKCRAFT for boats). *Cf. Playtex Prods v. Georgia-Pacific Corp.*, 390 F.3d 158 (2ᵈ Cir. 2004) (while recognizing that the addition of a house mark can aggravate rather than alleviate confusion, here the marks "Quilted Northern Moist-Ones" and "Wet Ones" were too dissimilar for confusion to be likely).

Nonetheless, in cases where the common element is a descriptive or otherwise weak term or phrase, and the house mark is strong, the addition of the house mark may act to help prevent confusion from being likely. *See, e.g., Nabisco, Inc. v. Warner-Lambert Co.*, 220 F.3d 43, 47 (2ᵈ Cir. 2000) (DENTYNE ICE v. ICE BREAKERS, both for chewing gum); *W.W.W. Pharmaceutical Co. v. Gillette Co.*, 984 F.2d 567 (2ᵈ Cir. 1993) (SPORTSTICK lip balm v. RIGHT GUARD SPORT STICK deodorant); *G. Heileman Brewing Co. v. Anheuser-Busch, Inc.*, 873 F.2d 985, 999–1000 (7ᵗʰ Cir. 1989); (BLATZ L.A. and SHARP'S LA unlikely to be confused with "LA from Anheuser-Busch"). *Compare Lindy's Pen Co. v. Bic Pen Corp.*, 725 F.2d 1240, 1245 n.4 (6ᵗʰ Cir. 1985) in which the parties' prominent uses of their BIC and LINDY house marks in connection with a weak AUDITOR's mark for pens made confusion unlikely in all markets, except the telephone sales market; because pens may have been orally ordered by AUDITOR's mark alone, that market had to be reexamined on remand.

The combination of a strong house mark with other factors such as differences in the goods also has been held to dispel likely confusion in some cases. In *Worthington Foods, Inc. v. Kellogg Co.*, 732 F. Supp. 1417 (S.D. Ohio 1990), plaintiff used the mark HEARTWISE on its MORNINGSTAR FARMS vegetable protein meat substitute products, and defendant sold KELLOGG'S HEARTWISE breakfast cereal. Holding confusion unlikely, the court stated (732 F. Supp. at 1441–42):

> Certainly, the use of a house mark does not automatically preclude the defendant's liability. House marks are, nonetheless, one factor which the court must consider in the calculus of the likelihood of confusion. . . . Specifically, the house mark of a company tends to deemphasize the contested mark as a source of the goods or services. . . . Here, the defendant sells its cereal with the Kellogg's mark which the defendant prominently displays on its cereal packages directly above the Heartwise name. Therefore, the likelihood of confusion is much smaller than a comparison of the plaintiff's HEARTWISE and the defendant's Heartwise word marks alone would suggest.

House marks have helped dispel confusion in some trade dress cases, where packaging or product design similarities were at issue. See Chapter 5. *Compare Litton Systems, Inc. v. Whirlpool Corp.*, 728 F.2d 1423 (Fed. Cir. 1984), where the parties' prominent uses of their respective well-known marks dispelled any likelihood of confusion between the designs of their microwave ovens, with *Fun-Damental Too, Ltd. v. Gemmy Indus. Corp.*, 111 F.3d 993, 2003 (2ᵈ Cir. 1997), granting preliminary relief against defendant's novelty bank despite the differences in word marks, in part because the marks were not well-known and "consumers are more likely to remember the coinbank's packaging than its name."

On the effect of house marks, *See generally* KIRKPATRICK, LIKELIHOOD OF CONFUSION IN TRADEMARK LAW, § 4.8 (2007 ed.); *Beran, Likelihood of Confusion: Will That House Mark Get You 'Home Free'?*, 83 TRADEMARK REP. 336 (1993).

CHAPTER 8
UNFAIR COMPETITION LAW

8.01   Dilution and Domain Name Misuse

Introduction

The federal and state dilution statutes have been a profound development in American trademark and unfair competition law. They broaden and supplement traditional objectives by protecting the distinctive quality of marks and names notwithstanding the absence of classical likelihood of confusion as to source or of competition between the parties. Thus, a famous mark may be protected against the use of a similar mark on totally unrelated products or services. Likewise, generic use of a mark in dictionaries, directories, etc., or unauthorized use on reconditioned or otherwise altered products may be subject to restraint under dilution statutes. *See Ty, Inc. v. Perryman*, 306 F.3d 509 (7th Cir. 2002) (Posner, J.) (questioning whether dilution protection against generic use is in the public interest).

The seminal article on dilution is *Frank I. Schechter, The Rational Basis of Trademark Protection*, 40 HARV. L. REV. 813 (1927), although it does not refer to the subject as "dilution." Schechter urged that "the preservation of the uniqueness of a trademark should constitute the only rational basis for its protection." His concept has gradually borne fruit in additional statutory protection through adoption of the now numerous state dilution statutes. Section 12 of the Model State Trademark Act (U.S.T.A. 1965), from which many state statutes were derived, included the following dilution provision:

> Likelihood of injury to business reputation or of dilution of the distinctive quality of a mark registered under this Act, or a mark valid at common law, or a trade name valid at common law, shall be a ground for injunctive relief notwithstanding the absence of competition between the parties or the absence of confusion as to the source of goods or services.

Originally, the state dilution statutes were afforded exceedingly limited application by the courts. It appears, however, that the interpretive law has now developed toward comprehension and support of the concept.

The passage in 1996 of a federal dilution statute, which complements state law, is the latest evolutionary step in this important area of trademark and unfair competition law.

The statute defines dilution as follows (15 U.S.C. 1127):

> The term"dilution" means lessening of the capacity of a famous mark to identify and distinguish goods and services, regardless of the presence or absence of —

> (1) competition between the owner of the famous mark and other parties, or
> (2) likelihood of confusion, mistake or deception.

As amended by the Trademark Dilution Revision Act ("TDRA") in 2006, the statute clarifies that it encompasses both "dilution by blurring" and "dilution by tarnishment." 15 U.S.C. § 1125(c)(2)(B):

> "[D]ilution by blurring" is association arising from the similarity between a mark or trade name and a famous mark that impairs the distinctiveness of the famous mark. In determining whether a mark or trade name is likely to cause dilution by blurring, the court may consider all relevant factors, including the following:

> (i) The degree of similarity between the mark or trade name and the famous mark.

> (ii) The degree of inherent or acquired distinctiveness of the famous mark.

> (iii) The extent to which the owner of the famous mark is engaging in substantially exclusive use of the mark.

> (iv) The degree of recognition of the famous mark.

> (v) Whether the user of the mark or trade name intended to create an association with the famous mark.

> (vi) Any actual association between the mark or trade name and the famous mark.

> . . . [D]ilution by tarnishment is association arising from the similarity between a mark or trade name and a famous mark that harms the reputation of the famous mark.

The federal dilution statute provides nationwide protection against dilution, but unlike some state statutes, its protection is limited to *famous* marks. Under the TDRA, 15 U.S.C. § 1125(c), "[a] mark is famous if it is widely recognized by the general consuming public of the United States as a designation of source of the goods or services of the mark's owner." In determining whether a mark possesses the requisite degree of recognition, the court may consider all relevant factors, including the following:

> (i) The duration, extent, and geographic reach of advertising and publicity of the mark, whether advertised or publicized by the owner or third parties.

> (ii) The amount, volume, and geographic extent of sales of goods or services offered under the mark.

> (iii) The extent of actual recognition of the mark.

> (iv) Whether the mark was registered under the Act of March 3, 1881, or the Act of February 20 1905, or on the principal register.

The federal act is to be applied "regardless of the presence or absence of " competition between the parties or likelihood of confusion. 15 U.S.C. § 1125(c)(6). As specified in the TDRA, 15 U.S.C. § 1125(c)(3), its scope is limited by certain permitted use exclusions (15 U.S.C. § 1125(c)(A)):

> The following shall not be actionable as dilution by blurring or dilution by tarnishment under this subsection:

> (A) Any fair use, including a nominative or descriptive fair use, or facilitation of such fair use, of a famous mark by another person other than as a designation of source for the person's own goods or services, including use in connection with—

(i) advertising or promotion that permits consumers to compare goods or services; or

(ii) identifying and parodying, criticizing, or commenting upon the famous mark owner or the goods or services of the famous mark owner.

(B) All forms of news reporting and news commentary.

(C) Any noncommercial use of a mark.

The federal dilution statute also has become a means of obtaining relief against some unauthorized uses of Internet domain names that are identical or substantially similar to well-known trademarks. Domain names normally are allocated simply on a first-come, first-served basis. This has permitted so-called "cybersquatters" to hoard domain names which imitate well-recognized trademarks in order to profit from selling or licensing the name to marks' owners. *See, e.g.,* Quittner, *Billions Registered: Right Now. There Are No Rules to Keep You From Owning a Bitchin' Corporate Name as Your Own Internet Address,* WIRED, (Oct. 1994) (detailing the author's unauthorized acquisition of the domain name "mcdonalds.com" and encouraging others to hoard domain names).

Concerns about the limitations of the federal dilution statute in combatting cyber-squatting led in 1999 to the enactment of the Anticybersquatting Consumer Protection Act, adding a new § 43(d) in the Lanham Act, 15 U.S.C. § 1125(d). It created a cause of action against anyone who, with a bad faith intent to profit from the mark, registers, traffics in, or uses a domain name that is identical or confusingly similar to a distinctive mark, or is identical or confusingly similar to or dilutive of a famous mark. As an alternative means of obtainig relief against cybersquatters, an on-line dispute resolution process also was created. The application of dilution law in various contexts, including the on-line environment, and other avenues for addressing domain name misuse, are discussed in the cases and materials that follow.

* * *

SPORTY'S FARM L.L.C. v. SPORTSMAN'S MARKET, INC.
United States Court of Appeals, Second Circuit
202 F.3d 489 (2000)

CALABRESI, CIRCUIT JUDGE

* * *

Sportsman's is a mail order catalog company that is quite well-known among pilots and aviation enthusiasts for selling products tailored to their needs. In recent years, Sportsman's has expanded its catalog business well beyond the aviation market into that for tools and home accessories. The company annually distributes approximately 18 million catalogs nationwide, and has yearly revenues of about $50 million. Aviation sales account for about 60% of Sportsman's revenue, while non-aviation sales comprise the remaining 40%.

In the 1960s, Sportsman's began using the logo "sporty" to identify its catalogs and products. In 1985, Sportsman's registered the trademark sporty's with the United States Patent and Trademark Office. Since then, Sportsman's has complied with all statutory requirements to preserve its interest in the sporty's mark. Sporty's appears on the cover of all Sportsman's catalogs; Sportsman's international toll free number is 1-800-4sportys; and one of Sportsman's domestic toll free phone numbers is 1-800-Sportys. Sportsman's spends about $10 million per year advertising its sporty's logo.

Omega is a mail order catalog company that sells mainly scientific process measurement and control instruments. In late 1994 or early 1995, the owners of Omega, Arthur and Betty Hollander, decided to enter the aviation catalog business and, for that purpose, formed a wholly-owned subsidiary called Pilot's Depot, LLC ("Pilot's Depot"). Shortly thereafter, Omega registered the domain name sportys.com with NSI. Arthur

Hollander was a pilot who received Sportsman's catalogs and thus was aware of the sporty's trademark.

In January 1996, nine months after registering sportys.com, Omega formed another wholly-owned subsidiary called Sporty's Farm and sold it the rights to sportys.com for $16,200. Sporty's Farm grows and sells Christmas trees, and soon began advertising its Christmas trees on a sportys.com web page. When asked how the name Sporty's Farm was selected for Omega's Christmas tree subsidiary, Ralph S. Michael, the CEO of Omega and manager of Sporty's Farm, explained, as summarized by the district court, that:

> in his own mind and among his family, he always thought of and referred to the Pennsylvania land where Sporty's Farm now operates as Spotty's farm. The origin of the name. . . derived from a childhood memory he had of his uncle's farm in upstate New York. As a youngster, Michael owned a dog named Spotty. Because the dog strayed, his uncle took him to his upstate farm. Michael thereafter referred to the farm as Spotty's farm. The name Sporty's Farm was . . . a subsequent derivation.

There is, however, no evidence in the record that Hollander was considering starting a Christmas tree business when he registered sportys.com or that Hollander was ever acquainted with Michael's dog Spotty.

In March 1996, Sportsman's discovered that Omega had registered sportys.com as a domain name. Thereafter, and before Sportsman's could take any action, Sporty's Farm brought this declaratory action seeking the right to continue its use of sportys.com. Sportsman's counterclaimed and also sued Omega as a third-party defendant for, inter alia, (1) trademark infringement, (2) trademark dilution pursuant to the Federal Trademark Dilution Act, and (3) unfair competition under state law. Both sides sought injunctive relief to force the other to relinquish its claims to sportys.com. While this litigation was ongoing, Sportysman's used "sportys-catalogs.com" as its primary domain name.

After a bench trial, the court rejected Sportsman's trademark infringement claim and all related claims that are based on a "likelihood of [consumer] confusion" since "the parties operate wholly unrelated businesses [and t]herefore, confusion in the market-place is not likely to develop." *Id.* at 282–83. But on Sportsman's trademark dilution action, where a likelihood of confusion was not necessary, the district court found for Sportsman's. The court concluded (1) that sporty's was a famous mark entitled to protection under the FTDA since "the 'Sporty's' mark enjoys general name recognition in the consuming public," *id.* at 288, and (2) that Sporty's Farm and Omega had diluted sporty's because "registration of the 'sportys.com' domain name effectively compro-mises Sportsman's Market's ability to identify and distinguish its goods on the Internet . . . [by] precluding Sportsman's Market from using its 'unique identifier,'" *id.* at 289. The court also held, however, that Sportsman's could only get injunctive relief and was not entitled to "punitive damages . . . profits, and attorney's fees and costs" pursuant to the Federal Trademark Dilution Act since Sporty Farm and Omega's conduct did not constitute willful dilution under the FTDA.

*   *   *

. . . [W]hile this appeal was pending, Congress passed the Anticybersquatting Consumer Protection Act. That law was passed "to protect consumers and American businesses, to promote the growth of online commerce, and to provide clarity in the law for trademark owners by prohibiting the bad-faith and abusive registration of distinctive marks as Internet domain names with the intent to profit from the goodwill associated with such marks — a practice commonly referred to as 'cybersquatting'" S. Rep. No. 106-140, at 4. In particular, Congress viewed the legal remedies available for victims of cybersquatting before the passage of the Anticybersquatting Consumer Protection Act as "expensive and uncertain." H.R. Rep. No. 106-412, at 6. The Senate made clear its view on this point:

> While the [Federal Trademark Dilution Act] has been useful in pursuing cybersquatters, cybersquatters have become increasingly sophisticated as the case law has developed and now take the necessary precautions to insulate themselves from liability. For example, many cybersquatters are now careful to no longer offer the domain name for sale in any manner that could implicate liability under existing trademark dilution case law. And, in cases of warehousing and trafficking in domain names, courts have sometimes declined to provide assistance to trademark holders, leaving them without adequate and effective judicial remedies. This uncertainty as to the trademark law's application to the Internet has produced inconsistent judicial decisions and created extensive monitoring obligations, unnecessary legal costs, and uncertainty for consumers and trademark owners alike.

*   *   *

Under the new Act, we must first determine whether sporty's is a distinctive or famous mark and thus entitled to the Anticybersquatting Consumer Protection Act's protection. *See* 15 U.S.C. § 1125(d)(1)(A)(ii)(I), (II). The district court concluded that sporty's is both distinctive and famous. We agree that sporty's is a "distinctive" mark. As a result, and without casting any doubt on the district court's holding in this respect, we need not, and hence do not, decide whether sporty's is also a "famous" mark.

*   *   *

Distinctiveness refers to inherent qualities of a mark and is a completely different concept from fame. A mark may be distinctive before it has been used — when its fame is nonexistent. By the same token, even a famous mark may be so ordinary, or descriptive as to be notable for its lack of distinctiveness. *See Nabisco, Inc. v. PF Brands, Inc.*, 191 F.3d 208, 215–26 (2[d] Cir. 1999). We have no doubt that sporty's, as used in connection with Sportsman's catalogue of merchandise and advertising, is inherently distinctive. Furthermore, Sportsman's filed an affidavit under 15 U.S.C. § 1065 that rendered its registration of the sporty's mark incontestable, which entitles Sportsman's "to a presumption that its registered trademark is inherently distinctive." *Equine Techs., Inc. v. Equitechnology, Inc.*, 68 F.3d 542, 545 (1st Cir. 1995). We therefore conclude that, for the purposes of § 1125(d)(1)(A)(ii)(I), the sporty's mark is distinctive.

The next question is whether domain name sportys.com is "identical or confusingly similar to" the sporty's mark. 15 U.S.C. § 1125(d)(1)(A)(ii)(I). As we noted above, apostrophes cannot be used in domain names. . . . As a result, the secondary domain name in this case (sportys) is indistinguishable from the Sportsman's trademark (sporty's). Cf. *Brookfield Communications, Inc. v. West Coast Entertainment Corp.*, 174 F.3d 1036, 1055 (9th Cir. 1999) (observing that the differences between the mark "MovieBuff" and the domain name "moviebuff.com" are "inconsequential in light of the fact that Web addresses are not caps-sensitive and that the '.com' top-level domain signifies the site's commercial nature"). We therefore conclude that, although the domain name sportys.com is not precisely identical to the sporty's mark, it is certainly "confusingly similar" to the protected mark under § 1125(d)(1)(A)(ii)(I). Cf. *Wella Corp. v. Wella Graphics, Inc.*, 874 F.Supp. 54, 56 (E.D.N.Y. 1994) (finding the new mark "Wello" confusingly similar to the trademark "Wella").

We next turn to the issue of whether Sporty's Farm acted with a "bad faith intent to profit" from the mark sporty's when it registered the domain name sportys.com. 15 U.S.C. § 1125(d)(1)(A)(i). The statute lists nine [nonexclusive] factors to assist courts in determining when a defendant has acted with a bad faith intent to profit from use of a mark. . . .

*   *   *

We hold that there is more than enough evidence in the record below of "bad faith intent to profit" on the part of Sporty's Farm. . . First, it is clear that neither Sporty's Farm nor Omega had any intellectual property rights in sportys.com at the time Omega registered the domain name. *See id.* § 1125(d)(1)(B)(i)(I). Sporty's Farm was not formed until nine months after the domain name was registered, and it did not begin operations or obtain the domain name from Omega until after this lawsuit was filed. Second, the domain name does not consist of the legal name of the party that registered it, Omega. *See id.* 15 U.S.C. § 1125(d)(1)(B)(i)(II). Moreover, although the domain name does include part of the name of Sporty's Farm, that entity did not exist at the time the domain name was registered.

The third factor, the prior use of the domain name in connection with the bona fide offering of any goods or services, also cuts against Sporty's Farm since it did not use the site until after this litigation began, undermining its claim that the offering of Christmas trees on the site was in good faith. *See id.* § 1125(d)(1)(B)(i)(III). Further weighing in favor of a conclusion that Sporty's Farm had the requisite statutory bad faith intent, as a matter of law, are the following: (1) Sporty's Farm does not claim that its use of the domain name was "noncommercial" or a "fair use of the mark," *see id.* § 1125(d)(1)(B)(IV), (2) Omega sold the mark to Sporty's Farm under suspicious circumstances. . . . and, (3) as we discussed above, the sporty's mark is undoubtedly distinctive.

The most important grounds for our holding that Sporty's Farm acted with a bad faith intent, however, are the unique circumstances of this case, which do not fit neatly into the specific factors enumerated by Congress but may nevertheless be considered under the statute. We know from the record and from the district court's findings that Omega planned to enter into direct competition with Sportsman's in the pilot and aviation consumer market. As recipients of Sportsman's catalogs, Omega's owners, the Hollanders, were fully aware that sporty's was a very strong mark for consumers of those products. It cannot be doubted, as the court found below, that Omega registered sportys.com for the primary purpose of keeping Sportsman's from using that domain name. Several months later, and after this lawsuit was filed, Omega created another company in an unrelated business that received the name Sporty's Farm so that it could (1) use the sportys.com domain name in some commercial fashion, (2) keep the name away from Sportsman's, and (3) protect itself in the event that Sportsman's brought an infringement claim alleging that a "likelihood of confusion" had been created by Omega's version of cybersquatting. Finally, the explanation given for Sporty's Farm's desire to use the domain name, based on the existence of the dog Spotty, is more amusing than credible. Given these facts and the district court's grant of an equitable injunction under the FTDA, there is ample and overwhelming evidence that, as a matter of law, Sporty's Farm's acted with a "bad faith intent to profit" from the domain name sportys.com as those terms are used in the ACPA.

. . . The question that remains is what remedy is Sportsman's entitled to. The Act permits a court to "order the forfeiture or cancellation of the domain name or the transfer of the domain name to the owner of the mark," § 1125(d)(1)(C) for any "domain name[] registered before, on, or after the date of the enactment of [the] Act," Pub. L. No. 106-113, § 3010. That is precisely what the district court did here, albeit under the pre-existing law, when it directed a) Omega and Sporty's Farm to release their interest in sportys.com and to transfer the name to Sportsman's, and b) permanently enjoined those entities from taking any action to prevent and/or hinder Sportsman's from obtaining the domain name. That relief remains appropriate under the ACPA. We therefore affirm the district court's grant of injunctive relief.

We must also determine, however, if Sportsman's is entitled to damages either under the ACPA or pre-existing law. Under the ACPA, damages are unavailable to Sportsman's since sportys.com was registered and used by Sporty's Farm prior to the passage of the new law . . . .

We conclude . . . that damages [also] are not available to Sportsman's under the FTDA. The district court found that Sporty's Farm did not act willfully. . . . [G]iven the uncertain state of the law at the time that Sporty's Farm and Omega acted, we cannot say that the district court clearly erred in finding that their behavior did not amount to willful dilution. It follows that Sportsman's is not entitled to damages under the FTDA.

*   *   *

The judgment of the district court is AFFIRMED in all particulars.

MEAD DATA CENTRAL, INC. v. TOYOTA MOTOR SALES, U.S.A., INC.

LEXIS   United States Court of Appeals, Second Circuit   *LEXUS*
875 F.2d 1026 (1989)

VAN GRAAFEILAND, CIRCUIT JUDGE

*   *   *

Toyota Motor Sales, U.S.A., Inc. and its parent, Toyota Motor Corporation, appeal from a judgment of the United States District Court for the Southern District of New York (Edelstein, J.) enjoining them from using LEXUS as the name of their new luxury automobile and the division that manufactures it. The district court held that, under New York's antidilution statute, N.Y. Gen. Bus. Law § 368-d, Toyota's use of LEXUS is likely to dilute the distinctive quality of LEXIS, the mark used by Mead Data Central, Inc. for its computerized legal research service, 702 F. Supp. 1031 (1988). On March 8, 1989, we entered an order of reversal stating that an opinion would follow. This is the opinion.

Section 368-d of New York's General Business Law, which has counterparts in at least twenty other states, reads as follows:

> Likelihood of injury to business reputation or of dilution of the distinctive quality of a mark or trade name shall be a ground for injunctive relief in cases of infringement of a mark registered or not registered or in cases of unfair competition, notwithstanding the absence of competition between the parties or the absence of confusion as to the source of goods or services. . . .   The district court's finding that "to establish that LEXIS is an English word required expert testimony at trial" is clearly erroneous. Anyone with a rudimentary knowledge of English can go to a library or bookstore and find the word in one of the above-mentioned standard dictionaries.

Moreover, the record discloses that numerous other companies had adopted "Lexis" in identifying their business or its product, *e.g.*, Lexis Ltd., Lexis Computer Systems Ltd., Lexis Language and Export Information Service, Lexis Corp., Maxwell Labs Lexis 3. In sum, we reject Mead's argument that LEXIS is a coined mark which originated in the mind of its former president and, as such, is entitled *per se* to the greater protection that a unique mark such as "Kodak" would receive. *See Esquire, Inc. v. Esquire Slipper Mfg. Co.*, 243 F.2d 540, 543 (1st Cir. 1957); *Intercontinental Mfg. Co. v. Continental Motors Corp.*, 230 F.2d 621, 623 (C.C.P.A. 1956).

Nevertheless, through its extensive sales and advertising in the field of computerized legal research, Mead has made LEXIS a strong mark in that field, and the district court so found. In particular, the district court accepted studies proffered by both parties which revealed that 76 percent of attorneys associated LEXIS with specific attributes of the service provided by Mead. However, among the general adult population, LEXIS is recognized by only one percent of those surveyed, half of this one percent being attorneys or accountants. The district court therefore concluded that LEXIS is strong only within its own market.

* * *

. . . We liken LEXUS to such words as "census," "focus" and "locus," and differentiate it from such words as "axis," "aegis" and "iris."[2] If we were to substitute the letter "i" for the letter "u" in "census," we would not pronounce it as we now do. Likewise, if we were to substitute the letter "u" for the letter "i" in "axis," we would not pronounce it as we now do. In short, we agree with the testimony of Toyota's speech expert, who testified:

> Of course, anyone can pronounce "lexis" and "lexus" the same, either both with an unstressed I or both with an unstressed U, or schwa — or with some other sound in between. But, properly, the distinction between unstressed I and unstressed U, or schwa, is a standard one in English; the distinction is there to be made in ordinary, reasonably careful speech.

In addition, we do not believe that "everyday spoken English" is the proper test to use in deciding the issue of similarity in the instant case. Under the Constitution, there is a " 'commonsense' distinction between speech proposing a commercial transaction, which occurs in an area traditionally subject to government regulation, and other varieties of speech." *Central Hudson Gas & Electric corp. v. Public Service Comm'n,* 447 U.S. 557, 562 (1980) (quoting *Ohralik v. Ohio State Bar Ass'n,* 436 U.S. 447, 455–56 (1978)).

* * *

"Advertising is the primary means by which the connection between a name and a company is established . . .," *Beneficial Corp. v. Beneficial Capital Corp.,* 529 F. Supp. 445, 448 (S.D.N.Y. 1982), and oral advertising is done primarily on radio and television. When Mead's speech expert was asked whether there were instances in which LEXUS and LEXIS would be pronounced differently, he replied "Yes, although a deliberate attempt must be made to do so . . . . They can be pronounced distinctly but they are not when they are used in common parlance, in everyday language or speech." We take it as a given that television and radio announcers are more careful and precise in their diction than is the man on the street. Moreover, it is the rare television commercial that does not contain a visual reference to the mark and product, which in the instant case would be the LEXUS automobile. We conclude that in the field of commercial advertising, which is the field subject to regulation, there is no substantial similarity between Mead's mark and Toyota's.

* * *

The strength and distinctiveness of LEXIS is limited to the market for its services — attorneys and accountants. Outside that market, LEXIS has very little selling power. Because only one percent of the general population associates LEXIS with the attributes of Mead's services, it cannot be said that LEXIS identifies that service to the general public and distinguishes it from others. Moreover, the bulk of Mead's advertising budget is devoted to reaching attorneys through professional journals.

This Court has defined dilution as either the blurring of a mark's product identification or the tarnishment of the affirmative associations a mark has come to convey. *Sally Gee, Inc. v. Myra Hogan, Inc., supra,* 699 F.2d at 625 (quoting 3A Callmann, *The Law of Unfair Competition, Trademarks and Monopolies* § 84.2 at 954–55). Mead does not claim that Toyota's use of LEXUS would tarnish affirmative associations engendered by LEXIS. The question that remains, therefore, is whether LEXIS is likely to be blurred by LEXUS.

---

[2] Similarly, we liken LEXUS to NEXXUS, a nationally known shampoo, and LEXIS to NEXIS, Mead's trademark for its computerized news service. NEXXUS and NEXIS have co-existed in apparent tranquility for almost a decade.

*   *   *

It is apparent . . . .that there must be some mental association between plaintiff's and defendant's marks.

> [I]f a reasonable buyer is not at all likely to link the two uses of the trademark in his or her own mind, even subtly or subliminally, then there can be no dilution . . . . [D]ilution theory presumes *some kind of mental association* in the reasonable buyer's mind between the two party's [sic] uses of the mark.

McCarthy, *supra*, § 24.13 at 213–14.

This mental association may be created where the plaintiff's mark is very famous and therefore has a distinctive quality for a significant percentage of the defendant's market. [citations omitted]. As discussed above, such distinctiveness as LEXIS possesses is limited to the narrow market of attorneys and accountants. Moreover, the process which LEXIS represents is widely disparate from the product represented by LEXUS. For the general public, LEXIS has no distinctive quality that LEXUS will dilute.

The possibility that someday LEXUS may become a famous mark in the mind of the general public has little relevance in the instant dilution analysis since it is quite apparent that the general public associates nothing with LEXIS. On the other hand, the recognized sophistication of attorneys, the principal users of the service, has substantial relevance. *See Sally Gee, Inc. v. Myra Hogan, Inc.*, *supra*, 699 F.2d at 626. Because of this knowledgeable sophistication, it is unlikely that, even in the market where Mead principally operates, there will be any significant amount of blurring between the LEXIS and LEXUS marks.

For all the foregoing reasons, we hold that Toyota did not violate section 368-d. We see no need therefore to discuss Toyota's remaining arguments for reversal.

Sweet, District Judge, concurring:

*   *   *

The only finding that supports a likelihood of dilution is the district court's conclusion that LEXUS eventually may become so famous that members of the general public who now associate LEXIS or LEXUS with nothing at all may associate the terms with Toyota's automobiles and that Mead's customers may think first of Toyota's car when they hear LEXIS. *See* Dist. Ct. Op. at 30–31. This analysis is problematic. First, section 368-d protects a mark's selling power among the consuming public. [citations omitted]. Because the LEXIS mark possesses selling power only among lawyers and accountants, it is irrelevant for dilution analysis that the general public may come to associate LEXIS or LEXUS with Toyota's automobile rather than nothing at all. Second, the district court offered no evidence for its speculation that LEXUS's fame may cause Mead customers to associate "lexis" with Toyota's cars. It seems equally plausible that no blurring will occur — because many lawyers and accountants use Mead's services regularly, their frequent association of LEXIS with those services will enable LEXIS's mark to withstand Toyota's advertising campaign.

Therefore, even if we accept the district court's finding regarding the renown of the LEXUS mark, however, reversal still is required. The differences in the marks and in the products covered by the marks, the sophistication of Mead's consumers, the absence of predatory intent, and the limited renown of the LEXIS mark all indicate that blurring is unlikely.

*   *   *

DEERE & COMPANY v. MTD PRODUCTS, INC.
United States Court of Appeals, Second Circuit
41 F.3d 39 (1994)

JON O. NEWMAN, CHIEF JUDGE

This appeal in a trademark case presents a rarely litigated issue likely to recur with increasing frequency in this era of head-to-head comparative advertising. The precise issue, arising under the New York anti-dilution statute, N.Y. Gen. Bus. Law § 368-d (McKinney 1984), is whether an advertiser may depict an altered form of a competitor's trademark to identify the competitor's product in a comparative ad. The issue arises on an appeal by defendant-appellant MTD Products, Inc. ("MTD") from the August 9, 1994, order of the United States District Court for the Southern District of New York (Lawrence M. McKenna, Judge) granting a preliminary injunction to plaintiff-appellee Deere & Company ("Deere") and Deere's cross-appeal to broaden the scope of the injunction beyond New York State, 860 F. Supp. 113. The injunction prevents MTD from airing a television commercial that shows an animated version of the leaping deer that has become appellee's well-known logo.

Although a number of dilution cases in this Circuit have involved use of a trademark by a competitor to identify a competitor's products in comparative advertising, as well as use by a noncompetitor in a humorous variation of a trademark, we have not yet considered whether the use of an altered version of a distinctive trademark to identify a competitor's product and achieve a humorous effect can constitute trademark dilution. Though we find MTD's animated version of Deere's deer amusing, we agree with Judge McKenna that the television commercial is a likely violation of the anti-dilution statute. We therefore affirm the preliminary injunction.

Background

Deere, a Delaware corporation with its principal place of business in Illinois, is the world's largest supplier of agricultural equipment. For over one hundred years, Deere has used a deer design ("Deere Logo") as a trademark for identifying its products and services. Deere owns numerous trademark registrations for different versions of the Deere Logo. Although these versions vary slightly, all depict a static, two-dimensional silhouette of a leaping male deer in profile. The Deere Logo is widely recognizable and a valuable business asset.

MTD, an Ohio company with its principal place of business in Ohio, manufactures and sells lawn tractors. In 1993, W.B. Doner & Company ("Doner"), MTD's advertising agency, decided to create and produce a commercial — the subject of this litigation — that would use the Deere Logo, without Deere's authorization, for the purpose of comparing Deere's line of lawn tractors to MTD's "Yard-Man" tractor. The intent was to identify Deere as the market leader and convey the message that Yard-Man was of comparable quality but less costly than a Deere lawn tractor.

Doner altered the Deere Logo in several respects. For example, as Judge McKenna found, the deer in the MTD version of the logo ("Commercial Logo") is "somewhat differently proportioned, particularly with respect to its width, than the deer in the Deere Logo." Doner also removed the name "John Deere" from the version of the logo used by Deere on the front of its lawn tractors, and made the logo frame more sharply rectangular.

More significantly, the deer in the Commercial Logo is animated and assumes various poses. Specifically, the MTD deer looks over its shoulder, jumps through the logo frame (which breaks into pieces and tumbles to the ground), hops to a pinging noise, and, as a two-dimensional cartoon, runs, in apparent fear, as it is pursued by the Yard-Man lawn tractor and a barking dog. Judge McKenna described the dog as "recognizable as a breed that is short in stature," and in the commercial the fleeting deer appears to be even smaller than the dog. Doner's interoffice documents reflect that the animated deer in the commercial was intended to appear "more playful and/or confused than distressed."

* * *

Whether the use of the mark is to identify a competing product in an informative comparative ad, to make comment, or to spoof the mark to enliven the advertisement for a noncompeting or a competing product, the scope of protection under a dilution statute must take into account the degree to which the mark is altered and the nature of the alteration. Not every alteration will constitute dilution, and more leeway for alterations is appropriate in the context of satiric expression and humorous ads for noncompeting products. But some alterations have the potential to so lessen the selling power of a distinctive mark that they are appropriately proscribed by a dilution statute. Dilution of this sort is more likely to be found when the alterations are made by a competitor with both an incentive to diminish the favorable attributes of the mark and an ample opportunity to promote its products in ways that make no significant alteration.

* * *

Wherever New York will ultimately draw the line, we can be reasonably confident that the MTD commercial challenged in this case crosses it. The commercial takes a static image of a graceful, full-size deer — symbolizing Deere's substance and strength — and portrays, in an animated version, a deer that appears smaller than a small dog and scampers away from the dog and a lawn tractor, looking over its shoulder in apparent fear. Alterations of that sort, accomplished for the sole purpose of promoting a competing product, are properly found to be within New York's concept of dilution because they risk the possibility that consumers will come to attribute unfavorable characteristics to a mark and ultimately associate the mark with inferior goods and services. *See Merriam-Webster, Inc. v. Random House, Inc.*, 35 F.3d 65, 73 (2^d Cir. 1994) (injunction under section 368-d appropriate where there is likelihood that distinctive trademark will be "weakened, blurred or diluted" in its value or quality) (quoting *Miss Universe, Inc. v. Patricelli*, 753 F.2d 235, 238 (2^d Cir. 1985)); *Sally Gee*, 699 F.2d at 624–25 ("The interest protected by § 368-d is not simply commercial goodwill, but the selling power that a distinctive mark or name with favorable associations has engendered for a product in the mind of the consuming public").

Significantly, the District Court did not enjoin accurate reproduction of the Deere Logo to identify Deere products in comparative advertisements. MTD remains free to deliver its message of alleged product superiority without altering and thereby diluting Deere's trademarks. The Court's order imposes no restriction on truthful advertising properly comparing specific products and their "objectively measurable attributes." *FTC Policy Statement on Comparative Advertising*, 16 C.F.R. § 14.15 n. 1 (1993). In view of this, the District Court's finding of a likelihood of dilution was entirely appropriate, notwithstanding the fact that MTD's humorous depiction of the deer occurred in the context of a comparative advertisement.

* * *

. . . [A] number of states do not have anti-dilution laws, and even those states with such laws or similar causes of action might not restrict commercial use of trademarks that do not confuse consumers or blur or tarnish the trademark. *Cf. Rosemont Enterprises, Inc. v. Urban Systems, Inc.*, 42 A.D.2d 544, 345 N.Y.S.2d 17, 18 (1973) (restricting injunction to New York because "[i]n other jurisdictions . . ., the law with respect to the right of privacy could have other efficacy with respect to a public figure . . .both in common-law interpretation and in statutes").

Particularly at this early stage in the litigation, where the relief is preliminary, it was proper for the District Court to restrict the reach of the injunction. *See Blue Ribbon Feed Co. v. Farmers Union Central Exchange, Inc.*, 731 F.2d 415, 422 (7th Cir. 1984) (recognizing that "considerations of comity among the states favor limited out-of-state application of exclusive rights acquired under domestic law, and a district court does not err when it takes a restrained approach to the extra-territorial application of such rights"). Accordingly, we do not disturb the geographic limitation.

Conclusion

The Order of the District Court granting a preliminary injunction as to activities within New York State is affirmed.

Notes on Dilution

1. Federal Dilution Law

a) Generally

The federal dilution statute has added to existing state law and does not preempt it. As stated in the House Report 104–374 (November 30, 1995), "It is important to note that the proposed federal dilution statute would not preempt state dilution laws. Unlike patent and copyright laws, federal trademark law co-exists with state trademark law, and it is to be expected that the federal dilution statute should similarly co-exist with state dilution statutes." The Act does, however, bar some state law actions. Section 43(c)(3) provides that ownership of a federal registration for the accused mark "shall be a complete bar to an action against that person, with respect to that mark, that is brought by another person under the common law or statute of a state and that seeks to prevent dilution of the distinctiveness of a mark, label or form of advertisement." *See, e.g., Westchester Media v. PRL USA Holdings, Inc.*, 214 F.3d 658, 669 (5th Cir. 2000) (because defendant's mark was federally registered, plaintiff's dilution claim under Texas state law was barred, but its federal dilution claim was not), and *Chicoine &Visitine, The Role of State Trademark Dilution Statutes in Light of the Trademark Dilution Revision Act of 2006*, 96 TMR 1155 (2006).

Words often used to describe dilution include "corrosion," "erosion," "watering down," and "whittling away" of the distinctive character of the mark. A prevailing plaintiff is entitled to an injunction against the defendant's "commercial use in commerce" of the diluting mark. 15 U.S.C.§ 1125(c)(1). Where the defendant willfully intended to trade on the owner's reputation or to cause dilution, under federal law monetary relief may be awarded at the court's discretion and subject to the principles of equity. 15 U.S.C. § 1125(c)(2).

The Federal dilution statute exempts from its coverage fair use in comparative advertising, noncommercial use, and all forms of news reporting and news commentary. 15 U.S.C. § 1125(c)(4). In a pre-TDRA decision, *Dr. Seuss Enter. v. Penguin Books USA, Inc.*, 924 F. Supp. 1559, 1573–74 (S.D. Cal. 1996), *aff'd*, 109 F.3d 1394 (9th Cir.), *cert. dismissed*, 521 U.S. 1146 (1997), for example, the court cited this provision in denying plaintiff preliminary dilution relief against defendant's sale of its book *The Cat Not in the Hat! A Parody by Dr. Juice*, which was a parody of the *O.J. Simpson criminal trial*. Although plaintiff's marks associated with the Dr. Seuss book *A Cat in the Hat* were famous, the court held that defendant's book was the type of "noncommercial" expressive use permitted under the First Amendment and § 43(c)(4)(B). *Id.* at 1574 (quoting Sen. Hatch's statement that the § 43(c)(4)(B) exception for "noncommercial use of a mark" includes "parody, satire, and other forms of expression that are not part of a commercial expression," 141 CONG. REC. S19310 (daily ed. Dec. 29, 1995)). Sales of the book nonetheless were enjoined under the Copyright Act because the work was insufficiently transformative to avoid infringing the Dr. Seuss book. The fair use exemption in the FTDA similarly was applied in *Mattel, Inc. v. MCA Records, Inc.*, 296 F.3d 894 (9th Cir. 2002). There the Danish band Aqua had produced a song "Barbie Girl" that parodied values associated with the famous doll and attracted the ire of Barbie's owner, Mattel. Mattel's FTDA claim failed because "the song . . . lampoons the Barbie image and comments humorously on the cultural values Aqua claims she represents. Use of the Barbie mark in the song Barbie Girl therefore falls within the noncommercial use exemption to the FTDA . . . [and] use of the mark in the song's title is also exempted." The accompanying trademark infringement claim failed because confusion was unlikely. See also the discussion on Parody and Satire in Chapter 9, *supra*, and *McCarthy, The 1996 Federal Anti-Dilution Statute ("FTDA")*, 16 CARDOZO ARTS and ENT. L.J. 587 (1998).

b) Actual or Likely Dilution

There had been a split in the circuits regarding whether relief under the federal dilution statute required evidence of *actual* dilution of the trademark's distinctiveness, rather than likelihood of dilution. *Compare Ringling Bros.-Barnum & Bailey Combined Shows, Inc. v. Utah Div. of Travel Dev.*, 170 F.3d 449 (4th Cir. 1999), *cert. denied*, 528 U.S. 923 (1999), *with Nabisco, Inc. v. PF Brands, Inc.*, 191 F.3d 208 (2d Cir. 1999), Other circuits weighed in on one side or the other. The dispute arose principally because of the federal statute's provision that liability was created by acts which "cause dilution," whereas state statutes typically provide for such liability where the acts are "*likely to* cause dilution."

In rejecting the notion that proof of actual harm is required in the *Nabisco* case, the Second Circuit observed that if the famous senior mark were being exploited with continually growing success, the senior user might never be able to show diminished revenues, no matter how obvious it was that the junior use diluted the distinctiveness of the senior, and that if there were any losses, it would be highly speculative to attribute them to the dilution of the mark. *Compare also Westchester Media v. PRL USA Holdings, Inc.*, 214 F.3d 658, 670 (5th Cir. 2000) (in denying relief in a case involving the Ralph Lauren POLO mark, the Fifth Circuit adopted the Fourth Circuit's "actual harm" standard) *with Eli Lilly & Co. v. Natural Answers, Inc.*, 233 F.3d 456, 480 (7th Cir. 2000) (affirming preliminary relief against defendant's use of HERBROZAC for an herbal mood elevator as being likely to dilute the distinctiveness of plaintiff's PROZAC mark).

In *Moseley v. V Secret Catalog, Inc.*, 537 U.S. 418 (2003), the Supreme Court resolved the split in the circuits by unanimously holding that a successful action under the FTDA "requires a showing of actual dilution, rather than a likelihood of dilution."

V Secret had sued the Moseleys for infringement and dilution of V Secret's famous VICTORIA'S SECRET mark, based on the Moseleys' use of the name "Victor's Secret" which they changed to "Victor's Little Secret" for a lingerie and adult product store in Kentucky. In the district court, V Secret lost on its infringement claim, a decision it did not appeal, but was granted summary judgment on its dilution claim. Applying a likelihood of dilution standard, the Sixth Circuit affirmed the grant of summary judgment. It concluded that, "consumers who hear the name 'Victor's Little Secret' are likely automatically to think of the more famous store and link it to the Moseleys' adult toy, gag gift, and lingerie shop. This, then, is a classic instance of dilution by tarnishing (associating the Victoria's Secret name with sex toys and lewd coffee mugs) and by blurring (linking the chain with a single, unauthorized establishment)."

In considering whether a plaintiff should be required to show likely or actual dilution, the Supreme Court first considered the basic underpinnings of trademark common law, citing, PATTISHALL, HILLIARD & WELCH, TRADEMARKS AND UNFAIR COMPETITION, Ch. 1 (5th ed. 2002), and its codification in the Lanham Act. It then contrasted the "causes dilution" language of the federal statute with the "likelihood of" harm language used in the state statutes. In view of the state law antecedents and the use of "likelihood of" elsewhere in the Lanham Act, among other things, the Court concluded the failure to expressly include a "likelihood" standard demonstrated

Congress's intention that the federal standard be "actual dilution." It therefore reversed and remanded for application of the correct "actual dilution" standard.

In doing so, the Supreme Court recognized the difficulties of proving actual dilution. It underscored that "the consequences of dilution, such as an actual loss of sales or profits, need not be proved." However, "at least where the marks at issue are not identical, the mere fact that consumers mentally associate the junior user's mark with a famous mark is not sufficient," because "such mental association will not necessarily reduce the capacity of a famous mark to identify the goods of its owner" as required under the FTDA. Accepting the proposition that "consumer surveys and other means of demonstrating actual dilution are expensive and often unreliable," the Court observed that such direct evidence may not be necessary "if actual dilution can reliably be proven through circumstantial evidence — the obvious case is one where the junior and senior marks are identical." *Cf. Horphag Research Ltd. v. Garcia*, 475 F.3d 1029 (9th Cir. 2007) (post-*Moseley* decision finding that use of identical marks was circumstantial evidence of dilution). For another post-*Moseley* and pre-TDRA application of dilution law, *see Savin Corp. v. Savin Corp.*, 391 F.3d 439 (2[d] Cir. 2004) (opining that "an identity of marks creates a presumption of actual dilution," and noting that the federal dilution standard was more stringent than the New York state law dilution standard).

The type of difficulties in proving actual dilution noted by the Supreme Court in *Moseley*, particularly where the marks are non-identical, were a major impetus for the enactment of the TDRA. Under the TDRA, a plaintiff is required to prove a "likelihood of dilution" rather than actual dilution. *Starbucks Corp. v. Wolfe's Borough Coffee, Inc.*, 477 F.3d 765 (2[d] Cir. 2007) (remanded for consideration under TDRA "likelihood of dilution" standard after district court erroneously applied "actual dilution" standard). The TDRA cured other anomalies that had arisen in connection with the federal dilution statute, e.g. confirming that a famous mark with acquired as well as inherent distinctiveness is subject to its protection, as is a famous trade dress even if unregistered. 15 U.S.C. § 1125(c)(1) and (4).

Despite the *V Secret* holding, even before the TDRA, the standard for opposition proceedings in the Patent and Trademark Office remained "likelihood of dilution." In *The NASDAQ Stock Market, Inc. v. Anartica*, 69 U.S.P.Q. 2d 1718 (T.T.A.B. 2003), the Board explained that the "likelihood" standard must apply for at least two reasons: first, the lack of actual use by an intent-to-use applicant means that actual dilution could not be shown when such applications were opposed, and second, the Lanham Act expressly permits opposition when a use "would cause dilution," rather than requiring that the use actually cause dilution. In the *NASDAQ* case, the stock market opposer easily showed the requisite fame, given that it had spent "hundreds of millions" to increase awareness of its NASDAQ mark, and "there have been countless articles published which discuss the NASDAQ stock market." Confusion and dilution then were found likely. Consumers seeing applicant's NASDAQ mark "would either conclude it that it was opposer's mark being used . . . or would have to reach a contrary conclusion only by associating the mark less strongly with opposer. Either result would be a blurring and would lessen the capacity of opposer's mark to identify goods and services."

c) Tarnishment

Dilution can occur by tarnishment of the positive associations engendered by a trademark, as well as by diminishment of its distinctiveness. *See, e.g., Deere & Co. v. MTD Products, supra* ("'Tarnishment' generally arises when the plaintiff's trademark is linked to products of shoddy quality, or is portrayed in unwholesome or unsavory context likely to evoke unflattering thoughts about the product"). The TDRA confirmed that famous marks are protected under it from likelihood of dilution by tarnishment. 15 U.S.C. § 1125(c)(1).

Although the federal statute did not expressly refer to tarnishment prior to the

TDRA, several courts construed it to protect against dilution by tarnishment. *See Anheuser-Busch Inc. v. Andy's Sportswear Inc.*, 40 U.S.P.Q.2d 1542 (N.D. Cal. 1996) (BUTTWISER t-shirt dilutes plaintiff's BUDWEISER mark for beer; temporary restraining order granted); *Clinique Labs. Inc. v. Dep Corp., Inc.*, 945 F. Supp. 547 (S.D.N.Y. 1996) (holding that defendant's BASIQUE skin care products did not tarnish plaintiff's CLINIQUE skin care products under the Dilution Act); *Dr. Seuss, supra*, at 1573 (quoting legislative history); *Ringling Bros.-Barnum & Bailey Combined Shows, Inc. v. Windows Corp.*, 937 F. Supp. 204, 211 (S.D.N.Y. 1996) (defendant's GREATEST BAR ON EARTH service mark for a night club did not tarnish the "wholesome, family oriented image of [plaintiff's] GREATEST SHOW ON EARTH" mark under the Dilution Act, noting alcohol was served at venues where plaintiff's circus performs).

d) What Is Famous

Courts occasionally found marks to be "famous" and protectable from dilution without express application of the factors set forth in the pre-TDRA federal dilution statute. In *Intermatic, Inc. v Toeppen*, 947 F. Supp. 1227 (N.D. Ill. 1996), for example, the court found that plaintiff's INTERMATIC mark was famous based on plaintiff's exclusive, fifty-year use of a fanciful, federally registered mark, which defendant did not dispute. In *Wawa, Inc. v. Haaf*, 40 U.S.P.Q.2d 1629 (E.D. Pa. 1996), *aff'd*, 116 F.3d 471 (3^d Cir. 1997), the court determined that plaintiff's WAWA for food stores was regionally famous due to its operating approximately 500 such stores for ninety years in six states throughout the northeastern United States. *See also Clinique Labs., Inc. v. Dep Corp.*, 945 F. Supp 547 (S.D.N.Y. 1996) (finding plaintiff's CLINIQUE mark and trade dress for cosmetics famous because they are distinctive; the "mark and dress are distinctive for the purpose of an infringement claim under Section 43(a), and under the statutory factors, they are distinctive for purposes of Section 43(c) as well"). *Compare Golden Bear Int'l Inc. v. Bear U.S.A. Inc.*, 969 F. Supp. 742, (N.D. Ga. 1996) (plaintiff's GOLDEN BEAR mark for golf clothing and accessories not famous due to plaintiff's limited consumer base and extensive third party use of plaintiff's mark); *Novo Nordisk, Inc. v. Eli Lilly & Co.*, 1996 U.S. Dist. LEXIS 12807, at *15 n.16 (S.D.N.Y. 1996) (plaintiff's NovoPen marks for insulin injecting systems not famous because plaintiff had acquired only 1% of the relevant market); and *American Express v. CFK Inc.*, 947 F. Supp. 310 (E.D. Mich. 1996) (analyzing each of the eight factors provided in the Federal Dilution Act to determine that American Express's DON'T LEAVE HOME WITHOUT IT family of marks is famous). Professor McCarthy has suggested that a mark should not be considered famous unless it is known to more than 50 percent of defendant's potential customers. McCARTHY, TRADEMARKS AND UNFAIR COMPETITION, § 24:92 (4th ed. 2007).

Prior to the TDRA, some courts found it sufficient for dilution purposes if the mark was famous only in a particular market segment. *See Times-Mirror Magazines, Inc. v. Las Vegas Sports News, L.L.C.*, 212 F.3d 157, 166 (3^d Cir. 2000), in which plaintiff's mark "The Sporting News" for a weekly sports publication was famous in the sports periodicals market, and plaintiff was granted preliminary relief where defendant's "Las Vegas Sporting News" for a weekly betting publication was likely to dilute plaintiff's mark in that market. To similar effect are *Advantage Rent-A-Car, Inc. v. Enterprise Rent-A-Car Co.*, 238 F.3d 378, 381 (5th Cir. 2001) (but plaintiff's mark was insufficiently famous in the car rental market); *Syndicated Sales Inc. v. Hampshire Paper Corp.*, 192 F.3d 633, 640 (7th Cir. 1999) (remanding for consideration of whether plaintiff's floral basket trade dress was famous within its market). This was sometimes called "niche market dilution." The Ninth Circuit examined this concept in *Thane Int'l, Inc. v. Trek Bicycle Corp.*, 305 F.3d 894 (9th Cir. 2002), explaining, "[n]iche market fame protection is . . . limited. The statute protects a mark only when a mark is famous within a niche market *and* the alleged diluter uses the mark within that niche." In considering the use of the TREK and OrbiTrek marks at issue, the court affirmed summary judgment that there was no dilution, reasoning that a "reasonable factfinder could not . . . conclude that mobile bicycles and elliptical orbit machines operate in the same narrow market segment for purposes of the niche fame concept, although both products can be used for exercise . . . [and] it could not reasonably find that TREK is a famous mark in that [stationary exercise machine] market, as opposed to in the market segment frequented by bicycle enthusiasts."

The TDRA has changed the definition of famous: "a mark is famous if it is widely recognized by the general consuming public of the United States as a designation of source of the goods or services of the mark's owner." This likely will make it more difficult to succeed under a "niche market fame" theory.

e) Defendants' Mark and the Nature of Its Use

Courts have held that the Federal Dilution Act reaches marks that are similar, albeit not identical to, famous marks. *See, e.g., Wawa, Inc. v. Haaf,* 40 U.S.P.Q.2d 1629 (E.D. Pa 1996), *aff'd,* 116 F.3d 471 (3ᵈCir. 1997) (granting WAWA food market a preliminary injunction against HAHA 24 hour market under the Dilution Act). In *Ringling Bros.- Barnum & Bailey Combined Shows, Inc. v. B.E. Windows Corp.,* 937 F. Supp. 204, 210 (S.D.N.Y. 1996), in contrast, the court declined to preliminarily enjoin defendant's use of the service mark THE GREATEST BAR ON EARTH for a restaurant and bar, observing that the owner of a famous mark faces an "uphill battle" when it attempts to enjoin use of an alteration of its mark on unrelated goods or services. Thus, among other reasons, the court denied dilution relief because plaintiff's GREATEST SHOW ON EARTH mark for circus entertainment was not "very" or "substantially" similar to the mark that defendant used on unrelated services. *Id.* at 211 ("The word 'bar' has nothing to do with the circus or the amusement/entertainment industry. While the GREATEST SHOW ON EARTH is a famous mark, [defendant] is not using that mark"). *Cf. Mead Data Central, Inc. v. Toyota Motor Sales, U.S.A., Inc., supra* (holding that to establish dilution by blurring under New York law the two marks must be "very" or "substantially" similar).

In *Moseley v. V Secret Catalog, Inc.,* 537 U.S. 418 (2003), the Supreme Court indicated that when the marks are identical, meeting the burden of proof under the FTDA may be easier. The Court stated, "at least where the marks at issue are not identical, the mere fact that consumers mentally associate the junior user's mark with a famous mark is not sufficient" to establish dilution. That suggested that proof of such mental association alone might be sufficient where the marks *were* identical. The Court underscored this by observing that direct evidence of dilution, such as surveys, may not be necessary "if actual dilution can reliably be proven through circumstantial evidence — the obvious case is one where the junior and senior uses are identical." While it changes the standard to "likelihood of dilution," the TDRA does not directly address any differences in proof requirements for identical versus non-identical marks.

To ascertain dilution by "blurring," or diminishment, under the federal dilution statute in the past, several courts used the following six factors articulated in Judge Sweet's concurrence in *Mead Data Central,* 875 F.2d at 1035: (1) similarity of the marks; (2) similarity of the products; (3) sophistication of customers; (4) defendant's predatory intent; (5) renown of the senior mark; and (6) renown of the junior mark. *See, e.g., Clinique Labs v. Dep Corp.,* 945 F. Supp. 547 (S.D.N.Y. 1996) (holding that several of plaintiff's trademarks and its trade dress for its CLINIQUE products were diluted by defendant's BASIQUE product line); *American Express Co. v. CFK Inc.,* 947 F. Supp. 310 (E.D. Mich. 1996) (denying plaintiff's motion for summary judgment; balancing of six factors left genuine issues of fact as to whether defendant's DON'T LEAVE HOME WITHOUT ME POCKET ADDRESS BOOK diluted plaintiff's DON'T LEAVE HOME WITHOUT family of marks); *Ringling Bros. v. B.E. Windows, supra; Wawa, supra.* Other courts have criticized the *Sweet* factors as deriving from likelihood of confusion analysis rather than being particularly useful in analyzing likely dilution, and many have supplemented them with other factors such as "shared customers and geographic isolation" and the "duration of the junior use." *Times-Mirror Magazines v. Las Vegas Sporting News,* 212 F.3d 157, 168 (3^d Cir. 2000), quoting from *Nabisco, Inc. v. PF Brands, supra.*

f) Dilution of Trade Dress

Even prior to the TDRA's confirmation of trade dress protection discussed above, courts had protected trade dress under the Federal Dilution Act. *See, e.g., Nabisco, Inc. and Nabisco Brands Co. v. PF Brands, Inc. And Pepperidge Farm, Inc.,* 191 F.3d 208 (2^d Cir. 1999) (preliminary injunction against dilution of Pepperidge Farm's famous goldfish cracker configuration); *Clinique, supra* (trade dress of plaintiff's CLINIQUE cosmetics); *Sunbeam Prods. Inc. v. West Bend Co.,* 39 U.S.P.Q.2d 1545, 1555 (S.D. Miss. 1996), *aff'd,* 123 F.3d 246 (5th Cir. 1997) (summarily enjoining defendant's dilution of the unregistered trade dress of plaintiff's MIXMASTER mixer), *cert. denied* 523 U.S. 1118 (1998). Such protection also may be available under state law. *See, e.g., Merriam-Webster, Inc. v. Random House,* 35 F.3d 65 (2^d Cir. 1994) *cert. denied,* 513 U.S. 1190 (1995) (New York dilution statute also applies to trade dress). *Cf. Escada AG v. Limited, Inc.,* 810 F. Supp. 571 (S.D.N.Y. 1993) (summarily dismissing claim for dilution of distinctive perfume bottle shape because design was potentially patentable and claim therefore was preempted by federal patent law). For a scathing critique of the *Sunbeam* decision, see Heald, *The Worst Intellectual Property Opinion Ever Written:* Sunbeam Products, Inc. v. West Bend Co.: *Exposing the Malign Application of the Federal Dilution Statute to Product Configuration,* 5 U. of GA. J. INTELL. PROP. L. 415 (1998). For a discussion of trade dress protection generally, see Chapter 5.

In *I.P. Lund Trading ApS v. Kohler Co.,* 163 F.3d 27 (1st Cir. 1998), plaintiff sought infringement and dilution protection for its faucet configuration. The First Circuit affirmed the denial of a preliminary injunction against the defendants on infringement grounds, and vacated the lower court grant of preliminary relief under the Federal Trademark Dilution Act ("FTDA"). Concluding that "there was not sufficient attention paid to the heightened fame standard that the FTDA establishes," it cited the VOLA faucet's lack of renown beyond "the world of interior design and high-end bathroom fixtures." The appellate court observed that the unregistered product design was not inherently distinctive, and was not so well publicized and known that it had achieved the level of fame Congress intended. In vacating the preliminary holding of dilution by blurring, the court opined that the proper inquiry for blurring is "whether customers are likely to view the marks as essentially the same." and that in general, dilution laws "are not intended to serve as mere fallback protection for trademark owners unable to prove trademark infringement."

g) Dilution and Registration Proceedings

Dilution as such does not constitute "infringement" of a federally registered mark under the Lanham Act. *See Jean Patou, Inc. v. Jacqueline Cochran, Inc.,* 201 F. Supp. 861, 867 (S.D.N.Y. 1962), *aff'd,* 312 F.2d 125 (2^d Cir. 1963). "Dilution may overlap infringement sometimes, but if infringement were a *sine qua non,* dilution would be a pointless, merely cumulative offense." Fletcher & Weinberg, U.S.T.A. TRADEMARK LAW HANDBOOK (1986). Dilution previously had been held not to provide a ground which to oppose or cancel a federal registration of a mark. *Babson Bros. Co. v. Surge Power Corp.,* 39 U.S.P.Q.2d 1953 (T.T.A.B. 1996) (holding that federal Dilution Act does not provide a ground for opposition or cancellation); *Tiffany & Co. v. National Gypsum Co.,* 459 F.2d 527 (C.C.P.A. 1972) (same with respect to state antidilution statute). This was legislatively overruled in the 1999 Trademark Reform Bill, *S. 1259, Pub. L. No. 106-43,* which authorized dilution-based oppositions to applications and cancellations of registrations. *See, e.g., The Nasdaq Market, Inc. v. Antartica,* 69 U.S.P.Q.2d 1718 (T.T.A.B. 2003) (applicant's NASDAQ mark for clothing likely to dilute famous NASDAQ mark for the stock market); *Toro Co. v. ToroHead, Inc.,* 61 U.S.P.Q.2d 1164

(T.T.A.B. 2001) (analyzing the dilution claim at length and ultimately dismissing the opposition because, among other things, the fame of opposer's TORO mark for lawn care and similar products was not shown to extend to applicant's market for magnetic heads for computer disk drives).

h) Generic Use and Dilution

Is use of a trademark in a generic sense a form of dilution? *See Selchow & Righter Co. v. McGraw-Hill Book Co.*, 580 F.2d 25, 27 (2d Cir. 1978), where the court granted a preliminary injunction "at least in part" because of a determination that defendant's book entitled THE COMPLETE SCRABBLE DICTIONARY might render generic plaintiff's mark SCRABBLE for a word game; Robb, *Trademark Misuse in Dictionaries: Inadequacy of Existing Legal Action and a Suggested Cure*, 65 MARQ. L. REV. 179 (1981); Derenberg, *supra*, 44 CAL. L. REV. 439, 464. Does the "noncommercial use" exception in the federal statute preclude such a federal dilution cause of action against generic misuse?

Judge Posner weighed in on the issue of whether generic misuse can constitute dilution in *Ty, Inc. v. Perryman*, 306 F.3d 509 (7th Cir. 2002). There the lower court had granted dilution relief against defendant's referring to third party products by the nickname "beanies", which had become a famous mark for plaintiff's toys. It found "[t]his clearly lessens the capacity of the plaintiff to distinguish its goods from [its] competitors." The Seventh Circuit, in an opinion by Judge Posner, vacated that decision. In rejecting the application of dilution law to generic misuse, he opined that allowing such dilution actions might not be in the public interest, as ordinary language becomes enriched by the addition of generic terms that once were trademarks. The court did affirm an injunction, on deceptiveness grounds, against the defendant's website use of the heading "Other Beanies" for third party products, and suggested a disclaimer might be appropriate on remand. *Cf. Horphag Research Ltd. v. Garcia*, 475 F.3d 1029 (9th Cir. 2007) (defendant's generic use of plaintiff's PYCNOGENOL trademark caused consumers to call plaintiff asking if defendant "was selling a real PYCNOGENOL product"; actual dilution found).

i) Surveys and Dilution

What types of survey evidence might be probative in a dilution action? One of the factors under the FTDA for determining whether a mark is famous is the mark's degree of recognition in the trading areas and trade channels of the mark's owner and of the person against whom the injunction is sought. This factor may be susceptible to proof by survey evidence. A dilution plaintiff also must at least establish that there is a mental association in the buyer's mind between the famous and the junior mark. *See Mead Data, supra; Fruit of Loom, Inc. v. Girouard*, 994 F.2d 1359 (9th Cir. 1993); RESTATEMENT (THIRD) OF UNFAIR COMPETITION SURVEY § 25, comment f (1995). A survey may help in that regard, as well. In *Wawa, Inc. v. Haaf*, 40 U.S.P.Q. 2d 1629, 1632 (E.D. Pa. 1996), for example, after concluding plaintiff's "Wawa" mark for its chain of convenience stores was famous, the court found that defendant's use of the mark "HaHa" in connection with his one convenience store diluted it. *Id.* at 1633. The court applied the "Sweet" factors and approvingly cited survey evidence that "persons in HAHA's neighborhood who were interviewed about Defendant's market tended, in 29% of the cases, to associate Defendant's market with a Wawa market." *Id.* at 1632.

One commentator has recommended that corporations anxious to protect their marks from dilution should regularly administer brand equity surveys. *Bible, Defining and Quantifying Dilution Under the Federal Trademark Dilution Act of 1995: Using Survey Evidence To Show Actual Confusion*, 70 U. COLO. L. REV. 295, 327–28, 332 (Winter 1998). A brand equity survey can gauge consumer perception factors, including: "the amount and nature of a product's advertising and marketing, the amount of time the product has been in the market, the consumer's personal experience with the product, the consumer's perception of people who buy the product, and whether the brand name is used on only a single type of product or service." *Id.*, at 328. Might such survey results over time reliably show a decrease in brand equity attributable to the junior, diluting use, or might other factors come into play? What other survey designs might be used to show likely dilution? *See generally Barber, How to Do A Trademark Dilution Survey (or Perhaps How Not To Do One)*, 89 TMR 616 (1999).

2. Internet Domain Names

a) The Federal Dilution Statute

(1) Domain Names and Likelihood of Confusion

Cybersquatting (bad faith registration of a domain name which incorporates or imitates another's trademark) has not necessarily been proscribed under traditional trademark infringement law. Individuals attempting to profit from pirated domain names often do not conduct business, or even provide information, on their web sites. Therefore it can be difficult to show that unauthorized use of a trademark in a domain name would likely confuse consumers as to the source or sponsorship of the site's content. If products or services *are* offered on the website, however, relief based on likely confusion may apply. In *Paccar, Inc. v. Telescan Techs., L.L.C.*, 319 F.3d 243 (6th Cir. 2003), for example, plaintiff owned the trademarks at issue for trucks and truck parts; confusion was likely due to defendant's incorporation of plaintiff's trademarks into domain names for defendant's websites which provided truck locator services. *See, also Cardservice Int'l Inc. v. McGee*, 950 F. Supp. 737 (E.D. Va. 1997) (ordering defendant to relinquish "cardservice.com" address used to market credit and debit card processing services due to likely confusion with plaintiff's identical services sold under the registered mark CARDSERVICE INTERNATIONAL); *Planned Parenthood Fed'n of Am. Inc. v. Bucci*, 42 U.S.P.Q.2d 1430 (S.D.N.Y. 1997) (preliminarily enjoining defendant from using "plannedparenthood.com" to promote his anti-abortion book); *Actmedia, Inc. v. Active Media Int'l Inc.*, 1996 U.S. Dist. LEXIS 20814 (N.D. Ill. July 17, 1996) (enjoining defendant's use of the domain name "actmedia.com" as likely to cause confusion with plaintiff's competing services under its federally registered ACTMEDIA mark). *Compare Sloan v. Auditron Elec. Corp.*, 68 Fed. Appx. 386 (4th Cir. 2003), in which the parties' products (audio equipment for defendants, and bookkeeping and tax services for the plaintiff), were too disparate for defendant's auditron.com domain name to create likely confusion with plaintiff's AUDITRON mark, and *Taubman Co. v. Webfeats*, 319 F.3d 770 (6th Cir. 2003) (no likelihood of confusion where defendant discontinued its single commercial link to another website and had no other commercial activities).

Even geographically discrete concurrent uses can raise confusion problems when the marks are used in domain names that can be widely accessed via the Internet. In *Harrods, Ltd. v. Sixty Domain Names*, 302 F.3d 214 (4th Cir. 2002), for example, also described in Chapter 8, two companies both had legitimate rights to use the name "Harrods" in different parts of the world in connection with department store services. Harrods BA, centered in Buenos Aires, originally was a subsidiary of the British company Harrods UK, but became a separate company with the independent right to use the Harrods name in Argentina and much of South America. Harrods BA subsequently registered with a Virginia registrar numerous "harrods" derivative domain names in the .com, .net and .org top level domains, such as harrodsstore, harrodsshopping, shoppingharrods, etc. Harrods UK then filed suit.

The appellate court observed that, although both companies had legitimate rights to use the Harrods name, "even recognizing the rights of concurrent users of a mark, a legitimate concurrent user still violates the other user's rights if it uses the shared mark in a manner that would cause consumer confusion, such as by using the mark in the other's geographic area. . . . Thus, if a concurrent user registers a domain name with the intent of expanding its use of the shared mark beyond its geographically restricted area, then the domain name is registered in bad faith. . ..''

Here, there was evidence of such bad faith, including evidence showing Harrods BA had a business plan to use the domain names "to profit by deliberately confusing and diverting non-South American customers seeking to shop at Harrods U.K." The Sixth Circuit consequently affirmed the order transferring the fifty-four non-Argentina domain names to Harrods UK, and reversed and remanded to permit discovery as to six remaining domain names that were Argentina-related. For a discussion of concurrent use issues raised by domain names, see Dinwoodie, (*National) Trademark Laws and the (Non-National) Domain Name System*, 21 U. Pa. J. Int'l Econ. L. 495 (2000).

(2)　Blurring and Tarnishing

The legislative history of the (now amended) FTDA expressly refers to its use against domain name hijackers:

> [I]t is my hope that this anti-dilution statute can help stem the use of deceptive Internet addresses taken by those who are choosing marks that are associated with the products or reputations of others.

141 Cong. Rec. S.19312 (Dec. 29, 1995) (remarks of Sen. Leahy).

In the 1990s, the FTDA became a much-used weapon against the then-novel phenomenon of cybersquatting, due to its lack of a likelihood of confusion requirement. *Panavision International v. Toeppen*, 11 F.3d 1316 (9[th]Cir. 1998), the defendant had registered the domain name panavision.com. In response to a cease and desist letter from Panavision, Toeppen had offered to sell it the domain name registration. When Panavision declined, Toeppen registered Panavision's PANAFLEX mark as a domain name. Toeppen displayed a map of Pana, Illinois on the panavision.com site, and the word "hello" on the panaflex.com site. The court found Toeppen liable for dilution, concluding that obtaining domain name registrations solely in order to sell them to owners of corresponding trademarks was in itself use in commerce. The dilution derived from the interference with customers' ability to find plaintiff on the Internet under its trademark, and because "Toeppen's use . . . put Panavision's name and reputation at his mercy." The same defendant lost on similar dilution grounds in *Intermatic, Inc. v. Toeppen*, 947 F. Supp. 1227 (N.D. Ill. 1996), when it used plaintiff's famous INTER-MATIC mark in its registered domain name intermatic.com.

Compare Avery Dennison v. Sumpton, et al., 189 F.3d 868 (9th Cir. 1999), in which the defendants had registered over 12,000 common last names as Internet domain names, as part of their e-mail provider business in which they offered "vanity" e-mail addresses to users for a fee. Plaintiff owned the federally registered trademarks AVERY and DENNISON for office products and industrial fasteners, respectively. The district court had granted plaintiff summary judgment that plaintiff's marks were famous and that defendants' maintenance of the domain names avery.net and dennison.net diluted plaintiff's rights under the federal dilution act. The appellate court reversed the holding for plaintiff, and remanded for entry of summary judgment in favor of defendants.

The appellate court reasoned that, while plaintiff's marks were distinctive, they had not been shown to be famous. Third party trademark use of "Avery" and "Dennison" was "commonplace," and there was "no evidence . . . that Avery Dennison possesses any degree of recognition among Internet users or that Appellants direct their e-mail services at Avery Dennison's customer base." Defendant's use also was not "commercial use" under the federal statute because defendants "do not use trademarks qua trademarks", but rather "use words that happen to be trademarks for their non-trademark value." *Compare TCPIP Holding Co., Inc. v. Haar Comm'ns, Inc.*, 244 F.3d

88 (2[d] Cir. 2001) (involving plaintiff's descriptive mark "The Children's Place" for stores selling children's merchandise, and affirming preliminary relief against a number of defendant's closely similar domain names, e.g., thechildrensplace.com and childrensplace.com, because confusion was likely). *See generally* Ducker, *Trademark Law Lost in Cyberspace: Trademark Protection For The Internet*, 9 HARV. J.L. & TECH. 483 (1996).

A domain name that is likely to dilute by tarnishment also has been subject to injunctive relief. *See, e.g., Hasbro Inc. v. Internet Entertainment Group Ltd.*, 40 U.S.P.Q.2D 1479 (W.D. Wash. 1996) (preliminarily enjoining defendant from diluting plaintiff's federally registered CANDY LAND mark by using the domain name "candyland.com" to identify a sexually explicit web site); *Toys "R" Us Inc. v. Akkaoui*, 40 U.S.P.Q.2d 1836 (N.D. Ca. 1996) (preliminarily enjoining defendant's use of "adultsr-us.com" to sell sexual devices and clothing over the Internet).

However, the famousness requirement of the FTDA, among other things, prevented it from becoming an effective tool against cybersquatting for all but the most famous marks. This ineffectiveness of both dilution and infringement claims against cybersquatters was one of the motivating factors behind passage of the Anti-Cybersquatting Consumer Protection Act, discussed below. Moreover, with the Supreme Court in *Moseley* (excerpted above) imposing an "actual dilution" requirement and casting doubt on the viability of tarnishment claims under the FTDA, the viability of federal dilution claims for use in cybersquatting situations (and in general) was severely compromised. As discussed above, the TDRA restored that viability, at least for nationally famous marks.

(3) Internet Gripe Sites

What is the best policy toward Internet gripe sites? In the absence of commercial activity, should they be immune from trademark-based objections? Or should a gripe site operator be required to somehow distinguish the pirated domain name from the owner's trademark, e.g. with a domain name such as "[mark]sucks.com" and prominent differentiating information for those accessing the site?

In *Bally Total Fitness Holding Corp. v. Faber*, 29 F. Supp. 2d 1161 (C.D. Cal. 1998), Faber, an Internet web page designer, set up a "BallySucks" web page dedicated to complaints about Bally's business. On the web page, the BALLY TOTAL FITNESS service mark had the word "SUCKS" superimposed on it in large, red letters, with "Bally Total Fitness Complaints! Unauthorized" directly beneath it. After Bally sued Faber, the court granted Faber summary judgment. It found that there was no risk of confusion — the word "sucks" superimposed over the Bally trademark and proclamation of being "unauthorized" made it clear the site was not authorized by Bally. In addition, there was no dilution because Faber's use was non-commercial, with the First Amendment protecting such consumer commentary from allegations of product tarnishment. There is a thorough discussion of this case in *Cisneros, Bally Total Fitness Corp. v. Faber*, 15 BERKELEY TECH. L. J. 229 (2000). Similarly, in *Taubman Co. v. Webfeats*, 319 F.3d 770, 778 (6th Cir. 2003), the court found that defendant's use of plaintiff's mark in the domain name "taubmansucks.com" did not create any likelihood of confusion. "Taubman concedes that Mishkoff is 'free to shout Taubman Sucks! from the rooftops.' . . . The rooftops of our past have evolved into the Internet domain names of our present."

The Eighth Circuit held against a defendant's gripe sites in *Faegre & Benson, LLP v. Purdy*, 129 Fed. App'x. 323 (8th Cir. 2005) (unpub.) There, plaintiff Faegre & Benson LLP, a law firm, moved for preliminary relief based on defendant's alleged infringement and violations of the ACPA. The defendants registered numerous Internet domain names that incorporated and were identical or confusingly similar to the law firm's federally-registered FAEGRE & BENSON LLP mark. The sites contained statements about Faegre & Benson that the law firm considered defamatory. The district court preliminarily enjoined the defendants from using domain names identical to or confusingly similar to the firm's marks unless the protest or critical commentary nature of the attached web site was apparent from the domain name itself.

The defendants appealed, arguing that the injunction was overbroad, that the web sites were noncommercial and not likely to cause confusion, and that their speech was protected by the First Amendment. The appellate court, using a "pragmatic approach" and noting that the defendant could "express his views using domain names that do not create confusion" with Faegre's marks, upheld the preliminary injunction against the defendants, finding no abuse of discretion.

Similarly, in *Bd. of Dirs.of Sapphire Bay Conds. W. v. Simpson*, 129 Fed. App'x. 711 (3^d Cir. 2005) (unpub.), the Board of Directors of Sapphire Bay Condominiums West ("the Board") sued Simpson for trademark infringement and dilution claiming that Simpson had, without authorization, registered the domain name <sapphirebaycondos.com> and operated a web site at that domain name featuring critical statements about the Board. The district court granted the Board a preliminary injunction. With regard to the federal dilution claim, the court determined that the mark was famous and that Simpson's use of the mark caused dilution "by lessening the capacity of the mark to identify and distinguish the Board's services." *Sapphire Bay*, 129 Fed. App'x. at 714. The court also concluded that Simpson's use of the mark was commercial speech, because it was intended to cause the Board financial harm, and that therefore was not exempt from the dilution law. The Third Circuit affirmed.

In contrast, in *Lucent Technologies, Inc. v. Johnson*, 56 U.S.P.Q.2d 1637 (C.D. Cal. 2000), in which the owner of the mark LUCENT for telecommunications equipment and services sued the registrant of "lucentsucks.com". Noting that the defendant offered pornography at the website, the court denied defendant's motion to dismiss, finding fact issues as to possible tarnishment of plaintiff's mark and defendant's claim of fair use. In a UDRP proceeding (see below), *Ester Lauder, Inc. v. estelauder.com*, WIPO Case No D2000-0869, the respondent used the slightly misspelled domain names estelauder.com and estelauder.net to solicit complaints about the famous cosmetics company, and claimed fair use. In ordering the transfer of the domain names to Estee Lauder, the panel emphasized the distinction between website content and the domain name itself, concluding that the respondent had no right to use a domain name confusingly similar to complainant's trademark. *See also E&J Gallo Winery v. Spider Webs, Ltd.*, 286 F.3d 270 (5th Cir. 2002) (defendant's "Whiny Winery" website critical of plaintiff at ernestandjuliogallo.com, launched *after* the lawsuit concerning that domain name was filed, only further demonstrated defendant's bad faith). *Cf. Mattel, Inc. v. Adventure Apparel*, 2001 U.S. Dist. LEXIS 13885 (S.D.N.Y. 2001) (defendant's defense that it intended to set up parody websites at barbiesbeachwear.com and barbiesclothing.com failed since it never did so, and those domain names instead linked to defendant's commercial website), and the discussion on tarnishment in dilution cases, above. For discussion of such "cybergriping" generally, *see Creasman, Free Speech and "Sucking" - When is the Use of a Trademark in a Domain Name Fair?* 95 TMR 1034 (2005); *Kelley, Is Liability Just a Link Away? Trademark Dilution by Tarnishment under the FTDA of 1995 and Hyperlinks on the World Wide Web*, 9 J. INTELL. PROP. L. 361, 375 (2002); *Lopez, Corporate Strategies for Addressing Internet "Complaint" Sites*, 14 INT'L L. PRAC. 101, 101–102 (2001).

There are several cybergriping cases in which courts allowed defendants to use plaintiff's trademark in defendants' domain names without any "disclaimer" such as ___sucks. These decisions include *TMI, Inc. v. Maxwell*, 368 F.3d 433 (5th Cir. 2004), and *Lucas Nursery & Landscaping, Inc. v. Grosse*, 359 F.3d 806, 811 (6th Cir. 2004). They are discussed in Chapter 9. *See also Lamparello v. Falwell*, 420 F.3d 309 (4th cir. 2005) (no liability for using domain name <www.fallwell.com> for web site criticizing Reverend Falwell's positions on homosexuality, observing that initial interest confusion theory does not apply to a gripe site on which the defendant is not using the mark "to capture the markholder's customers and profits").

In another gripe site decision, the absence of commercial use did not save the defendant. In *Bosley Med. Inst., Inc. v. Kremer*, 403 F.3d 672 (9ᵗʰ Cir. 2005), Bosley Medical Institute, owner of the registered BOSLEY MEDICAL mark, sued defendant Michael Kremer for operating the gripe site <bosleymedical.com>. Kremer earned no revenue from the web site, and did not sell goods or services, or provide any commercial links, on the web site. The district court entered summary judgment for Kremer on the infringement, dilution, and ACPA claims after ruling that his use of Bosley's trademark in his domain name was noncommercial and unlikely to cause confusion.

The court of appeals affirmed the summary judgment in favor of Kremer with respect to the infringement and dilution claims, but not the ACPA claim. Bosley argued that Kremer's use of Bosley's mark was commercial because one could reach commercial sites from Bosley's site, but the court noted that any connection was attenuated because there was no link on Kremer's site directly to a commercial site. Bosley also argued that Kremer's use was commercial under *People for the Ethical Treatment of Animals v. Doughney*, 263 F.3d 359 (4ᵗʰ Cir. 2001) (the *"PETA"* case). The court stated: "To the extent that the *PETA* court held that the Lanham Act's commercial use requirement is satisfied because the defendant's use of the plaintiff's mark as the domain name may deter customers from reaching the plaintiff's site itself, we respectfully disagree with that rationale." *Id.* at 679. However, the court of appeals reversed the summary judgment with respect to the cybersquatting claim, determining that the ACPA does not contain a commercial use requirement.

b) The Anticybersquatting Consumer Protection Act

(1) The Scope of Protection and Relief

Concerns about the limitations of the federal dilution statute's application to cybersquatting problems led to the enactment of the Anticybersquatting Consumer Protection Act ("ACPA") in November, 1999, and a new Section 43(d) in the Lanham Act, 15 U.S.C. § 1125(d). "[C]ybersquatters had started to take the necessary precautions to insulate themselves from liability under the Federal Trademark Dilution Act." *Virtual Works, Inc. v. Volkswagen of Am., Inc.*, 238 F.3d 264 (4ᵗʰ Cir. 2001) (transferring defendant's "vw.net" domain name to plaintiff under the ACPA where defendant, among other things, "foresaw the ability to profit from the natural association of 'vw.net' with plaintiff's VW mark"). It created a cause of action against anyone who, with bad faith intent to profit from the mark, registers, traffics in, or uses a domain name that is identical or confusingly similar to a distinctive mark, or is identical or confusingly similar to or dilutive of a famous mark.

The Act was passed "to protect consumers and American business, to promote the growth of online commerce, and to provide clarity in the law for trademark owners by prohibiting the bad-faith and abusive registration of distinctive marks as Internet domain names with the intent to profit from the goodwill associated with such marks — a practice commonly referred to as 'cybersquatting.'" ₛ. ᵣₑₚ. ₙₒ. 106–140 at 4. The Senate explained:

> While the [Federal Trademark Dilution Act] has been useful in pursuing cybersquatters, cybersquatters have become increasingly sophisticated as the case law has developed and now take the necessary precautions to insulate themselves from liability. For example, many cybersquatters are now careful to no longer offer the domain name for sale in any manner that could implicate liability under existing trademark dilution case law. And, in cases of warehousing and trafficking in domain names, courts have sometimes declined to provide assistance to trademark holders, leaving them without adequate and effective judicial remedies. This uncertainty as to the trademark law's application to the Internet has produced inconsistent judicial decisions and created extensive

monitoring obligations, unnecessary legal costs, and uncertainty for consumers and trademark owners alike.

The statute contains a non-exhaustive list of factors that a court may consider in determining whether there is bad faith, including: (1) any trademark or other intellectual property rights the alleged violator has in the domain name; (2) whether the domain name is a legal name of the person or a name commonly used to identify them; (3) the person's prior use of the domain name in connection with a *bona fide* offering of goods or services; (4) the person's intent to create likely confusion and divert customers from the mark owner either for commercial gain or to tarnish or disparage the mark; (5) any offer by the person to sell or transfer the domain name rights either to the mark owner or a third party; (6) the use of false or misleading contact information when applying for registration; (7) the person's registration or acquisition of multiple domain names that the person knows are identical or confusingly similar to the distinctive marks of others or dilutive of others' famous marks; and (8) the person's legitimate non-commercial or fair use of the domain name in a site accessible under the domain name.

See *Ford Motor Co. v. Catalanotte*, 342 F.3d 543 (6th Cir. 2003), a straightforward ACPA decision awarding Ford injunctive and monetary relief where defendant had registered the domain name "fordworld.com" while knowing that "Ford World" was the name of Ford's employee newspaper. After registration, defendant had e-mailed Ford's officers falsely claiming that he had received other offers for the domain name, and urging Ford to purchase it before those others did. "[R]egistering a famous trademark as a domain name and then offering it for sale to the trademark owner is exactly the wrong Congress intended to remedy when it passed the ACPA." Similarly, in *DaimlerChrysler v. Net Inc.*, 388 F.3d 201 (6th Cir. 2004), the Sixth Circuit affirmed summary judgment of cybersquatting where the defendants had used a fictitious name to register <www.foradodge.com> and "dozens of other domain names that are similar to various trademarks," with such overall conduct that "no rational trier of fact could find that the defendants did not violate the ACPA." *Compare Intersteller Starship Servs. v. Epix, Inc.*, 304 F.3d 936, 947 (9th Cir. 2002), in which the requisite bad faith was not shown under ACPA. Defendant had registered the epix.com domain name "as a descriptive term to connote" the website's content, *i.e.* "electronic pictures" (e-pictures), and only offered to sell the domain name to plaintiff in the context of settlement negotiations. How would the defendant in *Panavision v. Toeppen, supra*, fare under the ACPA? *See* Lipton, *Beyond Cybersquatting: Taking Domain Name Disputes Past Trademark Policy*, 40 WAKE FOREST L. REV. 1361 (2005); Martin, *"Too Famous To Live Long"* — *The Anticybersquatting Consumer Protection Act Sets its Sights to Eliminate Cybersquatter Opportunistic Claims on Domain Names*, 31 ST. MARY'S L.J. 797 (2000).

In *Virtual Works, Inc. v. Volkswagen of America, Inc.*, noted above, defendant had registered vw.net and notified Volkswagen's trademark department "that unless Volkswagen bought the rights of vw.net, Virtual Works would sell the domain name to the highest bidder." It then gave Volkswagen twenty-four hours to respond. Volkswagen instead filed suit. Calling cybersquatting "the Internet version of a land grab", the court observed that the ACPA was enacted in part because "cybersquatters had started to take the necessary precautions to insulate themselves from liability under the Federal Trademark Dilution Act." Here there was other evidence of defendant's bad faith, including that "it foresaw the ability to profit from the natural association of vw.net with the VW mark." Summary judgment against defendant and the transfer of the domain name to plaintiff were affirmed under the ACPA. Consequently, the issues of likelihood of confusion or dilution did not have to be addressed. In another action under the ACPA, *Shields v. Zuccarini*, 254 F.3d 476 (3d Cir. 2001), the defendant had registered spelling variations of the domain name for a popular artist's site (joecartoon.com). Through this "typosquatting", defendant's sites "mousetrapped" visitors into having to click through a series of advertisements before exiting. After the artist filed suit under the ACPA, the defendant tried to escape liability by redesigning his site as a "political protest" against the contents of the artist's cartoons. Agreeing with the district court that defendant's registration of thousands of domain names identical or confusingly similar to the distinctive marks of others demonstrated bad faith, and that defendant's claim of good faith commentary was "a spurious explanation cooked up purely for this suit," the appellate court affirmed summary judgment for plaintiff. The same defendant was held liable for an identical typosquatting scheme in *Electronics Boutique Holdings Corp. v. Zuccarini*, 56 U.S.P.Q.2d 1705 (C.D. Pa. 2000). *Compare Northern Light Technology, Inc. v. Northern Lights Club*, 236 F.3d 57 (1ˢᵗCir. 2001) (defendants' numerous registrations of domain names containing the trademarks of others constituted "powerful evidence" of defendants'bad faith, bolstered by defendants' implausible and "myriad explanations" for its use of the offending domain name, but court affirmed liability for trademark infringement rather than cybersquatting because of concerns about retroactive application of the ACPA); *March Madness Ath. Ass'n LLC v. Netfire, Inc.*, 120 Fed. App'x. 540 (5ᵗʰ Cir. 2005) (registrant of marchmadness.com demonstrated "bad faith intent to profit" from renown of plaintiff's MARCH MADNESS mark for basketball tournaments); and *Intersteller Starship Servs. v. Epix, Inc.*, 304 F.3d 936, 947 (9ᵗʰ Cir. 2002) (requisite bad faith not shown under ACPA where defendant registered the domain name "as a descriptive term to connote" the website's content, and only offered to sell the domain name in the context of settlement negotiations).

Should a registrar or domain name auctioneer be responsible for the activities of a bad faith registrant? *See Bird v. Parsons*, 289 F.3d 865 (6ᵗʰ Cir. 2002) (affirming dismissal of complaint against domain name registrar and domain name auction website that offered the domain name for sale on behalf of the registrant).

The statute allows a court to order the forfeiture or cancellation of the domain name or the transfer of the name to the mark owner. In *Porsche Cars North America, Inc. v. porschenet*, 302 F.3d 248, 261–262 (4ᵗʰ Cir. 2002), the court refused to transfer ownership of a domain name in a dilution case, concluding that it is not an authorized remedy under the FTDA. In contrast, "[t]he ACPA 'was adopted specifically to provide courts with a preferable alternative to stretching federal dilution law when dealing with cybersquatting cases.'". In addition to the traditional monetary remedies available under Section 34(a) of the Lanham Act, this amendment also provides for elective statutory damages ranging from $1000 to $100,000 per domain name. *See, e.g., Shields v. Zuccarini*, 254 F.3d 476 (3ᵈ Cir. 2001) (awarding $10,000 for each violative domain name plus attorneys' fees); *Electronics Boutique Holdings Corp. v. Zuccarini*, 59 U.S.P.Q.2d 1705 (E.D. Pa. 2000) ($100,000 per violative domain name plus attorneys' fees). The Act applies to domain names registered before its passage, but the complainant cannot recover damages for pre-Act activities. Martin, *"Too Famous To Live Long" - The Anticybersquatting Consumer Protection Act Sets its Sights to Eliminate Cybersquatter Opportunistic Claims on Domain Names*, 31 Sᴛ. Mᴀʀʏ's L.J. 797 (2000).

The Act also creates liability for registration of another individual's name, or one confusingly similar to it, as a domain name with the intent to profit by selling the domain name. This problem can arise, for example, in connection with celebrity names. See the discussion in the section on ICANN's dispute resolution policy, below. An exception exists if the name is used in, affiliated with, or related to a work of authorship under the Copyright Act. In actions brought against registration of another individual's name, the Act provides for a discretionary award of costs and attorneys' fees to the prevailing party. 15 U.S.C. § 1129.

Some states, such as California, Louisiana and Hawaii, have enacted their own state legislation concerning bad faith domain name registration. *See* Cal. Stat. § 17525; La. Rev. Stat. 51:300:12 and Haw. Rev. Stat. § 481B.

(2) *In Rem* Jurisdiction

In the past, cybersquatters have frequently used aliases or otherwise supplied false identifying information in registering domain names. Prior to the Anticybersquatting Act, trademark owners seeking relief often were stymied by an inability to locate cybersquatters or to establish personal jurisdiction over them. The Act now authorizes *in rem* actions against the domain name itself. An *in rem* action may be brought when the owner either is unable to establish personal jurisdiction over the alleged violator, or is unable to find that person through due diligence. However, in such *in rem* actions, the remedy is limited to forfeiture or cancellation of the domain name. In *Harrods Ltd. v. Sixty Internet Domain Names*, *Harrods*, 302 F.3d 214 (4th Cir. 2002), *in rem* jurisdiction was upheld where plaintiff could not establish personal jurisdiction over the Argentine registrant; the court also concluded that a plaintiff bringing an *in rem* action under § 1125(d) "may, in appropriate circumstances, pursue infringement and dilution claims as well." *See also* Jennings, *Significant Trademark/Domain Name Issues in Cyberspace*, 663 PLI/Pat 649 (2001) (cited approvingly by the court in *Harrods* for the proposition that infringement and dilution claims also may be brought in appropriate Lanham Act *in rem* cases). In the *Porsche Cars v. porschenet* case described above, the Fourth Circuit upheld *in rem* jurisdiction over domain names owned by a British citizen despite the latter's last minute consent to personal jurisdiction in California. 302 F.3d at 255–258. *Compare* the filing of an *in rem* suit in the wrong court in *Fleetboston Financial Corp. v. Fleetbostonfinancial.com*, 138 F. Supp. 2d 121 (D. Mass. 2001). The court in that case observed that the ACPA "allows a plaintiff to bring an *in rem* action only in the judicial district in which the registrar, registry or other domain name authority is located as specified" in 15 U.S.C. § 1125(d)(2)(A). Because none of those was located in Massachusetts where plaintiff sued, the case was dismissed. *See generally* Lee, *In Rem Jurisdiction in Cyberspace*, 57 WASHINGTON L. REV. 97 (2000).

(3) Reverse Domain Name Hijacking

As a balance against its potential misuse by plaintiffs, the ACPA authorizes actions against what is sometimes called "reverse domain name hijacking." 15 U.S.C. § 1114(2)(D)(v) allows a domain name registrant to sue a trademark owner to establish that the registrant's registration or use of the domain name is not unlawful, and to prevent its transfer or to cause reactivation of the registrant's ownership of it. In *Barcelona.com, Inc. v. Excelentisimo Ayuntamiento de Barcelona*, 330 F.3d 617 (4th Cir. 2003), the Fourth Circuit explained:

> If a domain name registrant cybersquats in violation of the ACPA, he "hijacks" the domain name from a trademark owner who ordinarily would be expected to use the domain name involving his trademark. But when a trademark owner overreaches in exercising rights under the ACPA, he "reverse hijacks" the domain name from the domain name registrant. Thus, § 1114(2)(D)(v), enacted to protect domain name registrants against overreaching trademark owners, may be referred to as the "reverse domain name hijacking provision".

Because the domain name registrant had registered "barcelona.com" in good faith as a purely geographical designation, the Court held for the registrant over the objections of the City Council of Barcelona, Spain.

Such a cause of action was discussed and reinstated in *Hawes v. Network Solutions, Inc.*, 337 F.3d 377 (4th Cir. 2003). In *Storey v. Cello Holdings L.L.C.*, 347 F.3d 370 (2d Cir. 2003), an individual who had registered "cello.com" along with other musical instrument-based domain names was able at the district court level to have his ownership restored under this section after an adverse decision from a UDRP panel. However, the Second Circuit vacated and remanded because, while the original registration may have been in good faith, the registrant's subsequent offer to sell the domain name to Cello Holdings may or may not have shown a bad faith intent to profit that would create liability. In *Dluhos v. Strasberg*, 321 F.3d 365 (3d Cir. 2003) the court confirmed that a domain name registrant facing an adverse decision under the UDRP "may sue for a declaration that the registrant is not in violation of [the ACPA], as well as for an injunction returning the domain name." It remanded "with a direction that the court review the dispute-resolution award *de novo*" under the ACPA.

c)   ICANN'S Dispute Resolution Policy

(1)   UDRP Procedures and Requirements

An on-line dispute resolution process was created in 1999 as another means to combat cybersquatters. In the early 1990s, Congress had contracted with Network Solutions, Inc. (NSI) (which subsequently was acquired by Verisign, Inc.) to create and manage an information center to assign new domain names and operate the main root server. The growth of the Internet, increasingly international use and some criticisms of NSI, led the United States government to create a plan for privatization of the domain name system. As a result, additional registrars were authorized to register domain names and the Internet Corporation for Assigned Names and Numbers (ICANN), a non-profit corporation, was formed to take over responsibility for the IP address space allocation, protocol parameter assignment, domain name system management, and root server system management functions.

The purpose of the ICANN Policy was explained in the Second Staff Report on Implementation Documents for the Uniform Dispute Resolution Policy (Oct. 25, 1999), available at www.icann.org:

> [The Policy] calls for administrative resolution for only a small, special class of disputes. . . . The adopted policy establishes a stream-lined, inexpensive administrative dispute-resolution procedure intended only for the relatively narrow class of cases of "abusive registrations". . . . The policy relegates all "legitimate" disputes - such as those where both disputants had longstanding trademark rights in the name when it was registered as a domain name - to the courts.

ICANN possesses no inherent authority, but instead derives its effectiveness from the voluntary participation of those registrars it purports to regulate. For a detailed history of the Internet and the creation of ICANN, see, *The Domain Name System: A Case Study of The Significance of Norms To Internet Governance*, 112 HARV. L. REV. 1657 (May 1999). *See also www.icann.org; www.iana.org.* Cybersquatting was one of the first major issues to be confronted by ICANN, which it addressed in August, 1999, by adopting a Uniform Domain Name Dispute Resolution Policy (the "Policy").

The Policy is incorporated by reference into all registration agreements with registrars that have adopted it. In applying to register, an applicant makes representations that a) the statements made in the Registration Agreement are complete and accurate; b) to the applicant's knowledge, the registration of the domain name will not infringe upon or violate the rights of a third party; c) the applicant is not registering the domain name for an unlawful purpose; and d) the applicant will not knowingly use the domain name in violation of laws and regulations. The policy provides that the registrar will cancel, transfer or otherwise make changes to domain name registrations upon receipt of:

1.   authorization from registrant;
2.   an order from a court or arbitral tribunal;
3.   an Administrative Panel decision in accordance with the procedures outlined in the Policy.

The Policy requires registrants to submit to a mandatory administrative proceeding when a third party asserts that the registrant's domain name is identical or confusingly similar to a mark in which the complainant has rights, and either that the registrant has no rights or legitimate interests in the domain name, or that the registrant's domain name has been registered and is being used in bad faith. Bad faith may be established by evidence that registrant has:

1.   registered or acquired the domain name primarily for the purpose of selling, renting, or otherwise transferring the domain name registration to the mark

owner for valuable consideration in excess of documented out-of-pocket costs related to the domain name;

2. registered or acquired the domain name to prevent the owner of the mark from reflecting the mark in a corresponding domain name, provided registrant has engaged in a pattern of such conduct;

3. registered the domain name primarily for the purpose of disrupting the business of a competitor; or

4. by using the domain name, intentionally attempted to attract, for commercial gain, Internet users to registrant's web site or other on-line location, by creating a likelihood of confusion with the complainant's mark as to the source, sponsorship, affiliation, or endorsement of registrant's web site or location, or of a product or service on registrant's web site or location.

In *National Association of Professional Baseball Leagues, Inc. v. Zuccarini*, WIPO No. D2002-1, 67 U.S.P.Q. 2d 1315 (Jan. 21, 2003), for example, a repeat "typosquatter" lost again after the owner of the federally registered trademark MINOR LEAGUE BASEBALL challenged the typosquatter's registration of the slightly misspelled domain name "minorleaugebaseball.com." "[T]yposquatting . . . is the intentional misspelling of words with intent to intercept and siphon off traffic from its intended destination, by preying on Internauts who making common typing errors. Typosquatting is inherently parasitic and of itself evidence of bad faith." The panel noted defendant's "long history of registering as domain names the trademarks of others or slight misspellings of them", citing, among others, *Shields v. Zuccarini*, 254 F.3d 476 (3ᵈ Cir. 2001). Defendant had no legitimate interest in the confusingly similar domain name, and used it in bad faith for a pornography website which children seeking baseball information might accidentally access.

True Blue Production, Inc. v. Hoffman, 73 U.S.P.Q. 2d 1512 (WIPO 2004) was a UDRP proceeding concerning Hoffman's registration of the domain name <fatactress-.com>. Hoffman used the disputed domain name to re-direct site visitors to his web site at plannedchildhood.com>, which was devoted to a negative portrayal of abortion, among other things. True Blue first used FAT ACTRESS on July 21, 2004, in an article announcing a television series starring Kirstie Alley. Hoffman registered the domain name on July 22, 2004. The panel found that, given Kirstie Alley's fame and the publicity associated with the series, it was "eminently reasonable" to conclude that the article established trademark rights. *True Blue*, 73 U.S.P.Q.2d at 1518. The panel also concluded Hoffman intended to cause confusion between his web site and the series. Given findings of Hoffman's bad faith in previous UDRP proceedings, the panel found that Hoffman's "apparent intent of opportunistic use" constituted bad faith registration and use in this case. The panel found "such opportunistic exploitation constitutes bad faith in and of itself" and ordered the domain name transferred to True Blue. *Id.* at 1520.

A panel again found bad faith in *June Bug Enterprises Inc. v. Kyamko*, 73 U.S.P.Q.2d 1310 (NAF Nov. 2004). Complainant June Bug Enterprises, holder of the rights to the MAGIC JOHNSON mark, filed a UDRP complaint requesting that Kyamko's domain name "magicjohnson.com" be transferred to June Bug. June Bug had previously registered the MAGICJOHNSON.COM domain name, but inadvertently let the registration expire. Kyamko then registered the domain name to exhibit pornography on the web.

The Panel ordered Kyamko to transfer the domain name for the following reasons: 1) the domain name was virtually identical to June Bug's MAGIC JOHNSON mark; 2) Kyamko had no rights in the mark and was appropriating it to exhibit pornography (which is not a "bona fide offering of goods or services" nor a "legitimate noncommercial or fair use of the domain name" under the UDRP); 3) Kyamko was not commonly known by the domain name; 4) use of the domain name to divert users to pornography creates a presumption of bad faith; 5) Kyamko's conduct in "snapping-up" expired domain names was predatory, in that Kyamko offered no evidence to refute the distinctiveness of June Bug's mark; 6) Kyamko had no need to use the mark to link to pornography; and 7) June Bug's failure to maintain the domain name registration did not mitigate Kyamko's bad faith.

A UDRP proceeding may be inappropriate if the dispute is highly factual or involves non-UDRP issues. *See, e.g., Estate of Marlon Brando v. Whoisguard*, 77 U.S.P.Q.2d 1229 (NAF 2005) (dismissing proceeding involving issues of whether Marlon Brando intended to make an inter vivos gift of the disputed domain name and completed the gift prior to his death; these were highly factual inquiries beyond the scope of the UDRP and ill-suited to the summary nature of UDRP proceedings).

(2) Defenses in UDRP Proceedings

Defenses include prior use of the domain name in connection with a bona fide offering of goods or services, or a legitimate non-commercial or fair use of the domain name without intent to divert customers or tarnish the mark at issue. The Policy does not prevent any party from seeking relief in a court, before, during, or after the administrative proceeding. As can be seen, it has similarities to the Anticybersquatting Act discussed above, and a party may in appropriate circumstances seek relief under either or both. In *Mess Enterprises v. Scott Enterprises Ltd.*, 74 U.S.P.Q.2d 1289 (WIPO, January 25, 2005), for example, the panel found that Mess had engaged in reverse domain name hijacking by filing a trademark application more than two years after Scott had registered the domain name <mess.com>, with Mess aware of Scott's prior registration. The panel determined that Mess intended to register the trademark and then acquire the domain name from Scott via the UDRP proceeding. Such intent, coupled with Scott's good-faith registration of the domain name, led the panel to note that this "case exhibits one of the most egregious examples of reverse domain name hijacking that any of the Panelists has thus far ever seen." *Mess*, 74 U.S.P.Q.2d at 1296. *See generally* Emerson, *Wasting Time in Cyberspace: The UDRP's Inefficient Approach Toward Arbitrating Domain Name Disputes*, 34 U. BALT. L. REV. 161 (2004); Solomon, *Two New Tools to Combat Cyberpiracy - A Comparison*, 90 T.M.R. 679 (2000).

(3) Precedential Weight in Federal Court

What weight should a UDRP decision be given in a subsequent federal court action? *See Weber-Stephen Products co. v. Armitage Hardware and Building Supply*, 54 U.S.P.Q.2d 1766 (N.D.Ill.2000) (Aspen, J.) (staying federal court action pending outcome of UDRP proceeding; however, "at this time we decline to determine the precise standard by which we would review the pending decision, and what degree of deference (if any), we would give that decision"). Judicial review is contemplated in the UDRP. In *Parisi v. Netlearning, Inc.*, 139 F. Supp.2d 745 (E.D. Va. 2001), the declaratory judgment plaintiff contested an adverse ICANN decision. The defendant moved to dismiss, contending that plaintiff was improperly attempting to vacate an arbitration award in violation of the Federal Arbitration Act ("FAA"). In declining to dismiss, the court reasoned that ICANN clearly intended to provide for judicial review of panel decisions, and that the FAA therefore did not apply. Similarly, in *Sallen v. Corinthians Licenciamentos Ltda.*, 273 F.3d 14 (1st Cir. 2001), the loser of an ICANN proceeding sought a declaration that he was not in violation of the ACPA and was not required to transfer the domain name. In reversing the lower court's dismissal, the First Circuit confirmed that such an action is authorized under 15 U.S.C. § 1114(D)(V). The Second Circuit in *Storey v. Cello Holdings L.L.C.*, 347 F.3d 370 (2d Cir. 2003), concurred with the First and Fourth Circuit's decisions in *Sallen v. Corinthians*, 273 F.3d 14, 19 (1st Cir. 2001) and *Hawes v. Network Solutions, Inc.*, 337 F.3d 377, 386 (4th Cir. 2003), that a UDRP decision has no binding precedential or res judicata effects on subsequent ACPA actions. *See also Barcelona.com, Inc. v. Excelentisimo Ayuntamiento de Barcelona*, 330 F.3d 617 (4th Cir. 2003), calling the UDRP

" 'adjudication lite' as a result of its streamlined nature and loose rules regarding applicable law," and observing that "the UDRP itself contemplates judicial intervention." *See generally* Holstein-Childress, *Lex Cyberus: The UDRP as a Gatekeeper to Judicial Resolution of Competing Rights to Domain Names*, 109 PENN ST. L. REV. 565 (2004).

(4) Celebrity Decisions

While trademark owners generally have been successful under the ICANN procedures, celebrities have received mixed results. Actress Julia Roberts was able to retrieve the domain name juliaroberts.com in *Julia Fiona Roberts v. Russell Boyd*, WIPO Case No. D2000-210, and actress Nicole Kidman had similar success in *Nicole Kidman v. John Zuccarini*, WIPO Case No. D2000-1415, as did Madonna in *Madonna Ciccone v. Dan Parisi*, WIPO Case No. D2000-847. *See also* the "Fat Actress" and "Magic Johnson" cases discussed above. However, the singer "Sting" failed to retrieve sting.com where there was evidence the registrant had made *bona fide* use of the name Sting prior to obtaining the domain name registration, and there was no evidence he was seeking to trade on the goodwill of the well-known singer. Bruce Springsteen similarly was unsuccessful in *Bruce Springsteen v. Jeff Burger and Bruce Springsteen Club*, WIPO Case No. D2000-1532. There the arbitration panel observed that "[a]n Internet search using the words 'Bruce Springsteen' gives rise to literally thousands of hits. It is perfectly apparent to any Internet user that not all of those hits are 'official' or 'authorized' sites." The panel also observed that the registrant had not registered brucespringsteen.net and brucespringsteen.org, and that Springsteen was operating an official site at the brucespringsteen.net address. How would other initial interest confusion cases (*see, e.g.*, the discussion in Chapter 6) fare under this type of analysis? *See generally* Badgley, *Improving ICANN in Ten Easy Steps*, 2001 J. TECH.L. & POL'Y 109.

Use of a celebrity's name in a domain name for an informational website about that celebrity may be a fair use. In *Morris v. Unofficial Fan Club*, 78 U.S.P.Q.2d 1360 (NAF 2005), a case involving the domain name steviewonder.com, the panelist explained that, "[a]n active and clearly non-commercial fan site may have rights and legitimate interests in the domain name that includes the complainant's trademark. The site should be noncommercial and clearly distinctive from any official site." In this case, however, the site had been inactive for six years, displaying only an invitation to send an e-mail to join the Unofficial Stevie Wonder Fan Club, and was expanded to link to some information about the club only after the UDRP complaint was filed. Because the inactive site barred the famous singer/songwriter from registering the desirable ".com" domain name for himself, and because respondent's history of registering over one hundred celebrity-name domain names helped establish his bad faith, the respondent was ordered to transfer the domain name. *See also Bogart Inc. v. Humphrey Bogart Club*, Case No. FA0306000162770 (NAF 2003), brought by a company that promoted and licensed third-party uses of the late actor's name, likeness and image, in which the registrant lost because his "primary purpose here is not to provide an informational site about Humphrey Bogart, but rather to link to his business site." and registrant, pre-litigation, had indicated he might sell the domain name to complainant for an exorbitant price.

(5) Additional Top Level Domains

To enable use of additional website addresses in this country, in 2001 ICANN began introducing seven new global top level domains:.biz,.info,.pro,.name,.zero,.coop and.museum. The.biz domain, for example, is intended to be dedicated exclusively to the business community. Registrants in these domains are subject to the UDRP.

In 2002, the top level domain ".us" became available for domain name registration by

U.S. citizens, residents, businesses and others with a *bona fide* presence in the United States.

3. State Dilution Law

a) Generally

The rationale behind the state dilution statutes has been the protection of the distinctive quality of a mark, even in the absence of likelihood of confusion, against such use by another as may degrade or decrease that distinctiveness. *See* Pattishall, *Dawning Acceptance of the Dilution Rationale For Trademark-Trade Identity Protection,* 74 TRADEMARK REP. 289 (1984). "The essence of dilution is the watering down of the potency of a mark and the gradual debilitation of its selling power." *Toys "R" Us, Inc. v. Canarsie Kiddie Shop, Inc.,* 599 F. Supp. 1189, 1208 (E.D.N.Y. 1983). In *Exxon Corp. v. Exxene Corp.,* 696 F.2d 544, 590 (7th Cir. 1982), Judge Posner explained, as follows, one of the earliest decisions based on state dilution law, *Polaroid Corp. v. Polaraid, Inc.,* 319 F.2d 830 (7th Cir. 1963):

> No longer would the word "Polaroid" call immediately to mind the highly regarded cameras made by the Polaroid Corporation. The mental image would be blurred, at least to anyone who had dealt with Polaroid or seen its ads, by recollection of Polaraid's refrigeration services. It is the same kind of disso-nance that would be produced by selling cat food under the name "Romanoff," or baby carriages under the name "Aston Martin."

In *Ameritech, Inc. v. American Information Technologies,* 811 F.2d 960 (6th Cir. 1987), the court described dilution as use that causes a "gradual diminution of the mark's distinctiveness, effectiveness and, hence, value. This kind of infringement corrodes the senior user's interest in the trademark by blurring its product identification or by damaging positive associations that have attached to it." *See generally* McCARTHY, TRADEMARKS AND UNFAIR COMPETITION §§ 24:67–24:79 (4th ed. 2007); *Hartman, Brand Equity Impairment - The Meaning of Dilution,* 87 TRADEMARK REP. 418 (1997); Leimer, *Trademark Dilution in the United States,* TRADEMARK WORLD (November, 1993); *Welkowitz, Reexamining Trademark Dilution,* 44 VAND. L. REV. 531 (1991).

Dilution statutes exist in more than half the states, including Alabama, Alaska, Arizona, Arkansas, California, Connecticut, Delaware, Florida, Georgia, Idaho, Illinois, Iowa, Louisiana, Maine, Massachusetts, Minnesota, Mississippi, Missouri, Montana, Nebraska, New Hampshire, New Jersey, New Mexico, New York, Oregon, Pennsylva-nia, Rhode Island, South Carolina, Tennessee, Texas, Washington, West Virginia, and Wyoming. Additionally, Ohio has recognized common law dilution claims.

b) State Law and Tarnishment

The state dilution statutes typically also protect against "tarnishment." Such tarnishment may be due to "unwholesome associations" with plaintiff's mark. *Community Federal Savings & Loan Assoc. v. Orondorff,* 678 F.2d 1034 (11th Cir. 1982) (enjoining use of COOKIE JAR on topless bar across the street from bank bearing that name). *See, e.g., American Express Co. v. Vibra Approved Laboratories Corp.,* 10 U.S.P.Q.2d 2006 (S.D.N.Y. 1989) (defendant enjoined from marketing a "condom card" bearing the name AMERICAN EXPRESS and slogan "Never leave home without it," because it was likely to dilute plaintiff's AMERICAN EXPRESS credit card mark and its slogan "Don't leave home without it"); *Eastman Kodak Co. v. Rakow,* 739 F. Supp. 116 (W.D.N.Y. 1989) (nationwide injunction against comedian's use of stage name "Kodak" for off-color comedy); *Coca-Cola Company v. Alma-Leo U.S.A.,* 719 F.Supp. 725 (N.D. Ill. 1989) (defendant enjoined from marketing white powder bubble gum resembling cocaine in a plastic simulation of Coca-Cola's famous bottle). Or the tarnishment may occur because of association with a lower quality product. *See, e.g., Steinway & Sons v. Demars & Friends,* 210 U.S.P.Q. 954 (C.D. Cal. 1981) (STEIN-WAY for clip-on beer handles dilutes the "quality and prestige" symbolized by STEINWAY piano mark). *Cf. Sally Gee, Inc. v. Myra Hogan, Inc.,* 699 F.2d 621 (2ᵈ Cir. 1983), where the court held there was no dilution of mass-produced SALLY GEE clothing by high quality handmade SALLY GEE garments.

Tarnishment normally will not be found in the absence of negative associations, or where the use is a sufficiently protected parody. *Hormel Foods Corp. v. Jim Henson Prods., Inc.,* 73 F.3d 497, 507 (2ᵈCir. 1996) (holding that defendant's use of Muppet character "Spa'am" did not tarnish plaintiff's SPAM canned ham under New York statute; "[t]he sine qua non of tarnishment is a finding that plaintiff's mark will suffer negative associations through defendant's use").

Is the *John Deere* case excerpted above merely a different type of tarnishment case? *See Hormel Foods* 73 F.3d at 507. *Compare People for the Ethical Treatment of Animals v. Doughney,* 2001 U.S. App. LEXIS 19028 (4ᵗʰ Cir. 2001) (use of plaintiff's famous PETA name for an animal rights' organization in defendant's peta.org domain name could not be parody even if defendant's "People Eating Tasty Animals" website were parody because the two "were not simultaneous" and the domain name was likely to confuse those seeking plaintiff's website).

c)   Application to Competitors

Virtually all the state dilution statutes contain the proviso entitling an injured party to relief "notwithstanding the absence of competition between the parties or the absence of confusion as to the source of goods or services." Some courts nonetheless have interpreted this to mean the statute does not apply to competitors. *See, e.g,. AHP Subsidiary Holding Co. v. Stuart Hale Co.,* 1 F.3d 611 (7ᵗʰ Cir. 1993) ("the protection of the Illinois Anti-Dilution statute is not available to competitors under Illinois case law"). In *Nikon, Inc. v. Ikon Corp.,* 987 F.2d 91 (2ᵈ Cir. 1993), in contrast, the Second Circuit confirmed that the New York dilution statute applies to both competitors and noncompetitors.

d)   Distinctiveness and Fame

Many state statutes have not required a "strong" or "well-known" mark for the dilution doctrine to apply, but some judicial opinions seem to have "read in" such a requirement. *See, e.g., Fruit of the Loom, Inc. v. Girouard,* 994 F.2d 1359 (9ᵗʰ Cir. 1993) ("'FRUIT' [for clothing] is far from being in the class we have recognized"); *Accuride International, Inc. v. Accuride Corp.,* 871 F.2d 1531 (9ᵗʰ Cir. 1989) (ACCURIDE for drawer slides insufficiently distinctive to be diluted); *Miss Universe, Inc. v. Patricelli,* 753 F.2d 235 (2ᵈ Cir. 1985) (MISS U.S.A. not strong enough to be diluted by MISS VENUS U.S.A.); *Freedom Savings & Loan Ass'n. v. Way,* 757 F.2d 1176 (11ᵗʰ Cir. 1985), *cert. denied,* 474 U.S. 845 (1985) (FREEDOM for savings and loan not strong enough to be diluted by FREEDOM for real estate service); *Astra Pharmaceutical Products, Inc. v. Beckman Instruments, Inc.,* 718 F.2d 1201 (1ˢᵗ Cir. 1983) (ASTRA for local anesthetic too weak to be diluted by ASTRA for blood analyzer); *American Dairy Queen Corp. v. ROT Inc.,* 16 U.S.P.Q.2d 1077 (N.D. Ill. 1990) (slogan WE TREAT YOU RIGHT for fast food restaurants too weak for preliminary relief against defendant's use of same slogan for renting television and stereo equipment); *Oxford Industries, Inc. v. JBJ Fabrics, Inc.,* 6 U.S.P.Q.2d 1756 (S.D.N.Y. 1988) (JBJ for wearing apparel not strong enough to be diluted); *Allied Maintenance Corp. v. Allied Mechanical Trades, Inc.,* 369 N.E.2d 1162 (N.Y. 1977) (ALLIED MAINTENANCE for maintenance of large office buildings not diluted by ALLIED MECHANICAL TRADES, INC. for installation and repair of heating, ventilating and air conditioning equipment where "Allied" was used by at least 300 New York City businesses and plaintiff failed to show its name had acquired secondary meaning). *Cf. Dreyfus Fund v. Royal Bank of*

Canada, 525 F.Supp. 1108 (S.D.N.Y. 1981) (plaintiffs' "lion" logo strong and diluted by defendant's use in the same financial field).

The dilution provision of the Model State Trademark Bill ("MSTB"), as revised in 1992, is patterned after the federal dilution statute and limits its protection to famous marks. It authorizes state law protection of "a mark which is famous in this state," whether registered or unregistered. Illinois adopted the MSTB, effective January 1, 1998. 765 ILCS 1036/65.

Where should the line be drawn as to distinctiveness and fame? *See, e.g. Advantage Rent-A-Car, Inc. v. Enterprise Rent-A-Car Co.*, 238 F.3d 378, 381 (5th Cir. 2001) (slogan insufficiently famous for federal dilution statute, but case remanded for determination whether it was sufficiently distinctive under that jurisdiction's state law, which "requires only distinctiveness, not fame"). What if a mark is distinctive only in a small, local area? *See Wedgwood Homes, Inc. v. Lund*, 639 P.2d 277 (1983) (state dilution protection is not limited to nationally famous marks; WEDGWOOD for retirement apartments in one Oregon county likely to dilute WEDGWOOD for homes in the same area); *Community Federal Savings & Loan Ass'n v. Orondoff*, 678 F.2d 1034 (11th Cir. 1982) (enjoining tarnishing use of COOKIE JAR for topless bar across the street from bank with an ATM featuring the same name).

e) Likelihood of Confusion and Dilution

If likelihood of confusion is established, can dilution exist? *Nabisco, Inc. v. PF Brands, Inc.*, 191 F.3d 208 (2[d] Cir. 1999) (enjoining sale of goldfish-shaped crackers that diluted famous Pepperidge Farm configuration under federal dilution statute; "consumer confusion would undoubtedly dilute the distinctive selling power of a trademark. . . . A junior use that confuses customers as to which mark is which surely dilutes the distinctiveness of the senior mark"); *James Burrough Ltd. v. Sign of the Beefeater, Inc.*, 540 F.2d 266, n. 16 (7th Cir. 1976) ("A trademark likely to confuse is necessarily a trademark likely to dilute"); *Champions Golf Club Inc. v. Sunrise Land Corp.*, 846 F.Supp. 742, 758 (W.D. Ark. 1994) (having first found apparent competition and likely confusion, in enjoining defendant, the court alternatively noted that, under its equitable powers and Arkansas law, even if the defendant's CHAMPIONS golf course in Texas did not compete with plaintiff's Arkansas CHAMPIONS course, the court could prevent defendant's use of CHAMPIONS which had begun to "eat away at and dilute and weaken the value of plaintiff's name"). *Compare Three Blind Mice Designs Co. v. Cyrk*, 892 F. Supp. 303 (D. Mass. 1995), in which the court held that where the parties' goods were competitive and likely confusion was established, the state dilution law claim was preempted by § 43(a) of the Lanham Act. In a particular case, might not a significant number of consumers likely make the mental connection of source confusion, while a significant number of others instead likely make the type of mental connection warranting dilution relief?

f) State Law Relief

In most cases where plaintiff prevailed on its state law dilution claim, the courts have provided only injunctive relief. *See, e.g., Ringling Bros.-Barnum & Bailey Combined Shows, Inc. v. Celozzi-Ettelson Chevrolet, Inc.*, 855 F.2d 480 (7th Cir. 1988) (defendant enjoined from using GREATEST USED CAR SHOW ON EARTH to advertise used cars because the slogan diluted Ringling Bros.' GREATEST SHOW ON EARTH slogan); *Hyatt Corp. v. Hyatt Legal Services*, 736 F.2d 1153 (7[th]Cir. 1984), *cert. denied*, 469 U.S. 1019 (1985) (HYATT for legal services chain diluted well-known HYATT mark of hotel chain; in subsequent settlement Hyatt Legal Services agreed to state at the bottom of all advertisements: "Hyatt Legal Services is named after its founder, Joel L. Hyatt"); *Golden Door, Inc. v. Odisho*, 437 F.Supp. 956 (N.D. Cal. 1977), *aff'd*, 646 F.2d 347 (9th Cir. 1980). Would an award of damages or of the cost of "corrective" advertising ever be warranted in a dilution case? The federal dilution statute, as discussed above, does provide for damages in cases of "willful" dilution. 15 U.S.C. § 1125(c)(2).

4. Restatement (Third) of Unfair Competition

THE RESTATEMENT (THIRD) OF UNFAIR COMPETITION, § 25 (1995) provides:

(1) One may be subject to liability under the law of trademarks for the use of a designation that resembles the trademark, trade name, collective mark, or certification mark of another without proof of a likelihood of confusion only under an applicable antidilution statute. An actor is subject to liability under an antidilution statute if the actor uses such a designation in a manner that is likely to associate the other's mark with the goods, services, or business of the actor and:

(a) the other's mark is highly distinctive and the association of the mark with the actor's goods, services, or business is likely to cause a reduction in that distinctiveness; or

(b) the association of the other's mark with the actor's goods, services, or business, or the nature of the actor's use, is likely to disparage the other's goods, services, or business or tarnish the images associated with the other's mark.

(2) One who uses a designation that resembles the trademark, trade name, collective mark, or certification mark of another, not in a manner that is likely to associate the other's mark with the goods, services, or business of the actor, but rather to comment on, criticize, ridicule, parody, or disparage the other or the other's goods, services, business, or mark, is subject to liability without proof of a likelihood of confusion only if the actor's conduct meets the requirements of a cause of action for defamation, invasion of privacy, or injurious falsehood.

Note that liability for a likely reduction in distinctiveness under part 1(a) requires that the owner's mark be "highly distinctive," while liability for likely disparagement or tarnishment under part 1(b) does not. Why the difference? For an application of the Restatement's part 1(a) distinctiveness standard, *see Tower Publications, Inc. v. MTS Inc.,* 21 U.S.P.Q.2d 1303, 1305 (N.D. Ill. 1991) in which the court held that "Tower Records of Illinois" for a company that published decisions and opinions of Illinois government commissions was insufficiently distinctive for dilution protection from defendant's use of TOWER RECORDS for music stores.

In a dilution case, what is the mental connection between the parties' marks that needs to be made by consumers? According to the Restatement (Third) of Unfair Competition, § 25, comment f (1995):

The connection . . . is not that which serves as the basis of trademark infringement — the mistaken belief that the plaintiff is in some way associated with defendant's goods — but rather is the accurate recognition that a mark once associated exclusively with the plaintiff is now also in use as an identifying symbol by others.

Is it necessary under state law that the plaintiff's mark be known (or well-known) among a significant percentage of potential purchasers of defendant's product for dilution to occur? *See Mead Data v. Toyota,* supra.

8.02 Misrepresentation

Introduction

The scope of the law, both private and public, respecting misrepresentation and false description of goods or services is in active evolution. The courts increasingly have found a clearly defined "federal law of unfair competition" expressed in § 43(a) of the

Lanham Act (15 U.S.C. § 1125(a)(1), which, as revised by the 1988 Act, provides in part as follows:

> Any person who, on or in connection with any goods or services, or any container for goods, uses in commerce any word, term, name, symbol, or device, or any combination thereof, or any false designation of origin, false or misleading description of fact, or false or misleading representation of fact, which —
>
> (A) is likely to cause confusion, or to cause mistake, or to deceive as to the affiliation, connection, or association of such person with another person, or as to the origin, sponsorship, or approval of his or her goods, services, or commercial activities by another person, or
>
> (B) in commercial advertising or promotion, misrepresents the nature, characteristics, qualities, or geographic origin of his or her or another person's goods, services, or commercial activities, shall be liable in a civil action by any person who believes that he or she is or is likely to be damaged by such act.

Section 43(a) was primarily intended by the framers of the Act to provide a remedy for the use of a geographic name, or "appellation of origin" in connection with goods not actually from that locality. ROBERT, THE NEW TRADE-MARK MANUAL 186–188 (1947). Interpretation of the language of the section has evolved, however, to provide a federal cause of action not only against deception as to geographic origin but also against a variety of misrepresentations and false descriptions, and against a variety of acts deceptive as to the identity of the manufacturer, seller, or servicer. It is now also established that such actions can be based on likelihood of damage without the necessity of actual damage. The cases which follow demonstrate the course and current extent of this evolution, but its full scope probably has not yet developed. See also the discussion on trade dress protection in Chapter 5.

GILLIAM v. AMERICAN BROADCASTING COMPANIES, INC.
United States Court of Appeals, Second Circuit
538 F.2d 14 (1976)

LUMBARD, CIRCUIT JUDGE

Plaintiffs, a group of British writers and performers known as "Monty Python," appeal from a denial by Judge Lasker in the Southern District of a preliminary injunction to restrain the American Broadcasting Company (ABC) from broadcasting edited versions of three separate programs originally written and performed by Monty Python for broadcast by the British Broadcasting Corporation (BBC).

Since its formation in 1969, the Monty Python group has gained popularity primarily through its thirty-minute television programs created for BBC as part of a comedy series entitled "Monty Python's Flying Circus." . . .

In October 1973, Time-Life Films acquired the right to distribute in the United States certain BBC television programs, including the Monty Python series. . . .

* * *

ABC broadcast the first of the specials on October 3, 1975. Appellants did not see a tape of the program until late November and were allegedly "appalled" at the discontinuity and "mutilation" that had resulted from the editing done by Time-Life for ABC. Twenty-four minutes of the original 90 minutes of recording had been omitted. Some of the editing had been done in order to make time for commercials; other material had been edited, according to ABC, because the original programs contained offensive or obscene matter.

* * *

Here, the appellants claim that the editing done for ABC mutilated the original work and that consequently the broadcast of those programs as the creation of Monty Python violated the Lanham Act § 43(a), 15 U.S.C. § 1125(a). This statute, the federal counterpart to state unfair competition laws, has been invoked to prevent misrepresentations that may injure plaintiff's business or personal reputation, even where no registered trademark is concerned. *See Mortellito v. Nina of California*, 335 F. Supp. 1288, 1294 (S.D.N.Y. 1972). It is sufficient to violate the Act that a representation of a product, although technically true, creates a false impression of the product's origin. *See Rich v. RCA Corp.*, 390 F. Supp. 530 (S.D.N.Y. 1975) (recent picture of plaintiff on cover of album containing songs recorded in distant past held to be a false representation that the songs were new); *Geisel v. Poynter Products, Inc.*, 283 F. Supp. 261, 267 (S.D.N.Y. 1968).

These cases cannot be distinguished from the situation in which a television network broadcasts a program properly designated as having been written and performed by a group, but which has been edited, without the writer's consent, into a form that departs substantially from the original work. "To deform his work is to present him to the public as the creator of a work not his own, and thus makes him subject to criticism for work he has not done." *Roeder, supra*, at 569. In such a case, it is the writer or performer, rather than the network. who suffers the consequences of the mutilation, for the public will have only the final product by which to evaluate the work. Thus, an allegation that a defendant has presented to the public a "garbled," *Granz v. Harris, supra* (Frank, J., concurring), distorted version of plaintiff's work seeks to redress the very rights sought to be protected by the Lanham Act, 15 U.S.C. § 1125(a), and should be recognized as stating a cause of action under that statute. *See Autry v. Republic Productions, Inc.*, 213 F.2d 667 (9th Cir. 1954); *Jaeger v. American Int'l Pictures, Inc.*, 330 F. Supp. 274 (S.D.N.Y. 1971), which suggest the violation of such a right if mutilation could be proven.

During the hearing on the preliminary injunction, Judge Lasker viewed the edited version of the Monty Python program broadcast on December 26 and the original, unedited version. After hearing argument of this appeal, this panel also viewed and compared the two versions. We find that the truncated version at times omitted the climax of the skits to which appellants' rare brand of humor was leading and at other times deleted essential elements in the schematic development of a story line. We therefore agree with Judge Lasker's conclusion that the edited version broadcast by ABC impaired the integrity of appellants' work and represented to the public as the product of appellants what was actually a mere caricature of their talents. We believe that a valid cause of action for such distortion exists and that therefore a preliminary injunction may issue to prevent repetition of the broadcast prior to final determination of the issues.

* * *

FASHION BOUTIQUE OF SHORT HILLS, INC. v. FENDI USA, INC.
United States Court Of Appeals, Second Circuit
314 F.3d 48 (2003)

WALKER, JOHN M.., CHIEF JUDGE

* * *

BACKGROUND

I. Overview

Between 1983 and July 1991, Fashion Boutique sold products bearing the internationally-renowned Fendi trademark in an upscale mall in Short Hills, New Jersey. Fashion Boutique was the only freestanding Fendi boutique in the greater New York metropolitan area until Fendi Stores opened on Fifth Avenue in New York City in

October 1989. Both Fashion Boutique and Fendi Stores carried only the international line of Fendi products. This "exclusive" line is considered superior in quality to the domestic line sold in American department stores.

Two months after Fendi opened its Fifth Avenue Store, Fashion Boutique experienced a sharp decline in its sales and, by July 1991, Fashion Boutique closed its retail operations. Fashion Boutique alleged in its complaint that the precipitous fall in its sales was caused by a corporate policy carried out by Fendi to misrepresent the quality and authenticity of the products sold at Fashion Boutique.

Fashion Boutique conceded in the district court that it could not show that many of its customers heard disparaging statements first-hand at the Fifth Avenue store. Rather, its theory was and is that Fendi employees made misrepresentations to some customers at the Fifth Avenue store, those customers relayed the comments to others, and the false rumors were thus spread throughout Fashion Boutique's customer base. Prior to the close of its business, Fashion Boutique maintained a mailing list of over 8,000 customers.

Fashion Boutique claims that the actions by Fendi led to the destruction of its retail business, violated Section 43(a)(l)(B) of the Lanham Act, 15 U.S.C. § 1125(a) (1994), which prohibits misrepresentation of another person's goods or services in "commercial advertising or promotion," and violated New York law on product disparagement and slander.

II. Motion for Summary Judgment on the Lanham Act Claim

After the close of discovery, Fendi moved for summary judgment on Fashion Boutique's Lanham Act claim. Following certain pre-trial evidentiary rulings, the district court granted defendants' motion. *See Fashion Boutique I*, 942 F. Supp. at 217.

In challenging the district court's grant of partial summary judgment, Fashion Boutique relies primarily on reported conversations between Fendi personnel and nine undercover investigators hired to pose as shoppers and on declarations by forty Fashion Boutique customers. In none of the proffered interactions did employees at the Fifth Avenue store initiate conversations about Fashion Boutique. They commented on Fashion Boutique only after the customers mentioned plaintiff. For example, several customers who reported their conversations with Fendi employees went to the Fifth Avenue store seeking to repair or exchange products or were wearing Fendi products as they shopped at that store. After the customer informed Fendi personnel that the item had been bought at Fashion Boutique, the employee reacted by making critical comments about the quality of Fashion Boutique's merchandise and, on several occasions, refused to exchange or repair the product.

(1) Incidents Prior to the Close of Fashion Boutique

Prior to Fashion Boutique's demise, Fendi personnel told a total of eleven customers that Fashion Boutique carried an inferior, "department store" line of products or that Fashion Boutique sold "fake" or "bogus" merchandise. During four visits to Fendi's Fifth Avenue store, undercover investigators were told that Fashion Boutique's merchandise was of inferior quality. Five shoppers and several undercover investigators related incidents in which Fendi employees described Fashion Boutique's goods as a "different line" from that sold at the Fifth Avenue store. In addition, Fendi employees made critical comments about the customer service at Fashion Boutique to six investigators and one customer.

Sixteen Fashion Boutique customers reported having "heard rumors" that Fashion Boutique sold fake Fendi merchandise "during the period 1990-1991." One shopper heard similar rumors but could not remember when she heard them.

(2) Statements Made After the Close of Fashion Boutique

Eight customers identified statements made after Fashion Boutique's demise in July 1991. Fendi employees told four of them that Fashion Boutique sold a "different line" of products, three others that Fashion Boutique sold inferior or fake Fendi goods, and one other that Fashion Boutique closed because it caused trouble or was too costly to maintain. In addition, a Fendi employee told one investigator that the owners of Fashion Boutique were filing for bankruptcy.

(3) Caroline Clarke Deposition

As evidence of the alleged policy of disparagement, plaintiff presented the deposition of Caroline Clarke, a former employee of Fendi USA. Although Clarke's superiors never explicitly told her of a policy to disparage Fashion Boutique, she learned from speaking to managers and salespersons at Fendi Stores that salespersons followed a practice of disparaging the customer service at Fashion Boutique.

(4) The District Court's Decisions

After carefully reviewing the evidence, Judge Cedarbaum determined that most of the evidence submitted by Fashion Boutique failed to support the Lanham Act claim. Specifically, the district court found that (1) the statements suggesting that Fashion Boutique sold a "different" line were not disparaging because "different" does not impugn the quality of the product; (2) the declarations by customers alleging to have "heard rumors" that Fashion Boutique sold fake items was inadmissable hearsay and thus could not be considered on a motion for summary judgment; and (3) disparaging remarks made after Fashion Boutique closed were not actionable under the Lanham Act and, because plaintiff and defendants were no longer competitors, were not relevant. *See id.* at 215.

Judge Cedarbaum concluded that the remaining evidence was insufficient to withstand a motion for summary judgment because it did not fall within the meaning of "commercial advertising or promotion" as set forth in the Lanham Act. The district court held that the Lanham Act is violated when the defendants proactively pursue customer contacts and disparage the plaintiff's goods or services. *See id.* at 215–16 (listing cases). Because each disparaging comment was made only after the customer initiated a discussion about Fashion Boutique, the district court concluded that the communications were reactive and not proactive. *See id.* at 216.

Moreover, relying on the four-part test announced in *Gordon & Breach Sci. Publishers S.A. v. Am. Inst. of Physics*, 859 F. Supp. 1521, 1535–36 (S.D.N.Y. 1994) ("Gordon & Breach I"), the district court held that to constitute "commercial advertising or promotion" the statements must be sufficiently disseminated to the relevant purchasing public. *See Fashion Boutique I*, 942 F. Supp. at 216. The district court concluded that plaintiff had failed to prove sufficient dissemination because it presented only a dozen admissible comments within a purchasing public universe consisting of thousands of customers.

*   *   *

[The Lanham Act] does not define the phrase "commercial advertising or promotion." In determining whether representations qualify as "commercial advertising or promotion," most courts have adopted the four-part test set forth in *Gordon & Breach I*. Under the test, in order to qualify as "commercial advertising or promotion," the contested representations must be "(1) commercial speech; (2) by a defendant who is in commercial competition with plaintiff; (3) for the purpose of influencing consumers to buy defendant's goods or services"; and, (4) although representations less formal than those made as part of a classic advertising campaign may suffice, they must be disseminated sufficiently to the relevant purchasing public. [Citations omitted]. . . .[W]e easily accept the first and third elements of the Gordon & Breach test that define the term "commercial" as referring to "commercial speech" that is made for the purpose of influencing the purchasing decisions of the consuming public. *See Gordon & Breach I*, 859 F. Supp. at 1536.

The precise meaning of "advertising or promotion" has been subject to various interpretations. *Compare Gordon & Breach Sci. Publishers S.A.. v. Am. Inst. of Physics*, 905 F. Supp. 169, 182 (S.D.N.Y. 1995) (holding that "any promotional statement directed at actual or potential purchasers falls within the reach" of the Lanham Act), and *Mobius Mgmt. Sys., Inc. v. Fourth Dimension Software, Inc.*, 880 F. Supp. 1005, 1020–21 (S.D.N.Y. 1994) (holding that single letter addressed to one purchaser constitutes "advertising or promotion"); with *Garland Co. v. Ecology Roof Sys., Corp.*, 895 F. Supp. 274, 279 (D. Kan. 1995) (rejecting *Mobius* and holding that the Lanham Act is violated only where the misrepresentations are widely disseminated within the relevant purchasing public), and *Med. Graphics Corp. v. Sensormedics Corp.*, 872 F. Supp. 643,650–51 (D. Minn. 1994). The statute's disjunctive wording compels us to give meanings to both "advertising" and "promotion" that do not render either term superfluous. *See Connecticut ex rel Blumenthal v. United States Dep't of the Interior* 228 F.3d 82, 88 (2d Cir. 2000). We conclude that the distinction between advertising and promotion lies in the form of the representation. Although advertising is generally understood to consist of widespread communication through print or broadcast media, "promotion" may take other forms of publicity used in the relevant industry, such as displays at trade shows and sales presentations to buyers. *See, e.g., Seven-Up*, 86 F.3d at 1386 (finding sales presentation to a significant percentage of industry customers constitutes advertising under the Lanham Act).

The Seventh Circuit has recently limited the scope of the Lanham Act to advertising defined as "a form of promotion to anonymous recipients, as distinguished from face-to-face communication, . . . [and] a subset of persuasion [that relies on] dissemination of prefabricated promotional material." *See First Health Group Corp. v. BCE Emergis Corp.*, 269 F.3d 800, 803 (7th Cir. 2001) (internal quotations omitted). The problem with the Seventh Circuit's focus on the term "advertising" is that it fails to define the term "promotion" in any meaningful way.

Although the Lanham Act encompasses more than the traditional advertising campaign, the language of the Act cannot be stretched so broadly as to encompass all commercial speech. *See, e.g., Sports Unlimited, Inc v. Lankford Enters., Inc.*, 275 F.3d 996, 1005 (10th Cir. 2002); *First Health Group*, 269 F.3d at 803. The ordinary understanding of both "advertising" and "promotion" connotes activity designed to disseminate information to the public. *Cf. Garland*, 895 F. Supp. at 276. Thus, the touchstone of whether a defendant's actions may be considered "commercial advertising or promotion" under the Lanham Act is that the contested representations are part of an organized campaign to penetrate the relevant market. Proof of widespread dissemination within the relevant industry is a normal concomitant of meeting this requirement. Thus, businesses harmed by isolated disparaging statements do not have redress under the Lanham Act; they must seek redress under state-law causes of action. *See, e.g., id.* at 279; *Am. Needle & Novelty, Inc. v. Drew Pearson Mktg., Inc.*, 820 F. Supp. 1072, 1078 n.2 (N.D. Ill. 1993).

In determining whether a defendant's misrepresentations are designed to reach the public, we find the district court's proactive-reactive distinction instructive, but not necessarily dispositive. Although most reactive statements will doubtless consist of off-the-cuff comments that do not violate the Lanham Act because no broad dissemination is intended or effected, we leave open the possibility that a cause of action might exist where a defendant maintains a well-enforced policy to disparage its competitor each time it is mentioned by a customer, if such a policy of reactive disparagement successfully reaches a substantial number of the competitor's potential customers.

In sum, we adopt the first, third and fourth elements of the Gordon & Breach test. To decide this appeal, we need not decide [ ] the second element - that defendant and plaintiff be competitors. We note that the requirement is not set forth in the text of Section 43(a) and express no view on its soundness.

C. Fashion Boutique's Lanham Act Claim

Based on the foregoing principles, we easily conclude that Fashion Boutique failed to put forward sufficient evidence that defendants' actions constituted "commercial advertising or promotion" under the Lanham Act.

Turning first to plaintiff's evidentiary claims, we believe that the district court did not abuse its discretion in excluding the evidence of rumors. *See Nora Beverages, Inc. v. Perrier Group of Am., Inc.*, 164 F.3d 736, 746 (2^d Cir. 1998) (stating that evidentiary rulings, even those made at the summary judgment stage, are reviewed for "manifest error"). Regardless of whether the rumor evidence was properly rejected as hearsay, the district court later decided, in any event, that its prejudicial effect outweighed its minimal probative value. We find no "manifest error" in this decision given the absence of proof connecting defendants to the rumors.

There is no evidence to suggest that the remaining statements were part of an organized campaign to penetrate the marketplace. Even including the "different line" statements, post- closing statements, and comments made to undercover investigators, Fashion Boutique has presented a total of twenty-seven oral statements regarding plaintiff's products in a marketplace of thousands of customers. Such evidence is insufficient to satisfy the requirement that representations be disseminated widely in order to constitute "commercial advertising or promotion" under the Lanham Act. *See Sports Unlimited*, 275 F.3d at 1004–05 (finding evidence of dissemination of information to two customers, where plaintiff made up to 150 bids per year, insufficient to constitute "commercial advertising or promotion"); *cf. Coastal Abstract*, 173 F.3d at 735 (upholding jury's verdict on Lanham Act where misrepresentation was made to one of three potential clients); *Seven-Up*, 86 F.3d at 1386 (finding evidence of dissemination sufficient where statements were made to eleven out of seventy-four potential customers). The Clark deposition was specifically limited to disparagement of the customer service at Fashion Boutique, as distinct from the products sold there, and there is nothing to suggest that the comments were anything more than individual reactions to particular customers' mention of Fashion Boutique.

*   *   *

Conclusion

For the foregoing reasons, we affirm the judgment of the district court.

*   *   *

VIDAL SASSOON, INC. v. BRISTOL-MYERS CO.
United States Court of Appeals, Second Circuit
661 F.2d 272 (1981)

IRVING R. KAUFMAN, CIRCUIT JUDGE

*   *   *

. . . In the spring of 1980, appellant Bristol-Myers Co. ("Bristol"), a pharmaceutical manufacturer, decided to wage an aggressive, new advertising campaign on behalf of its shampoo product, "Body on Tap," so named because of its high beer content. Accordingly, Bristol began in June to broadcast on national television a commercial "starring" the high fashion model Cristina Ferrare. The commercial depicts a turbaned Miss Ferrare, apparently fresh from shampooing her hair, holding a bottle of Body on Tap. She claims: "[I]n shampoo tests with over nine hundred women like me, Body on

Tap got higher ratings than Prell for body. Higher than Flex for conditioning. Higher than Sassoon for strong, healthy looking hair." As is well known to the consuming public, Prell, Flex, and Sassoon are shampoo competitors of Body on Tap. Sassoon is the product of appellee Vidal Sassoon, Inc. ("Sassoon"). As Miss Ferrare refers in turn to each of the shampoos, the product is flashed on the television screen. The commercial ends as Miss Ferrare, now brushing her dry hair, states: "Now I use Body on Tap for fuller body and for clean, strong, beautifully conditioned hair. Body on Tap. It's great shampoo."

It is undisputed that 900 women did not, after trying both shampoos, make product-to-product comparisons between Body on Tap and Sassoon, or, for that matter, between Body on Tap and any of the other shampoos mentioned in the advertisements. Rather, groups of approximately 200 women, in what the advertising trade terms "blind monadic testing," each tested *one* shampoo and rated it on a qualitative scale ("outstanding," "excellent," "very good," "good," "fair," or "poor") with respect to 27 attributes, such as body and conditioning. Thus, no woman tried more than one shampoo. The data for an attribute of a particular shampoo were combined by category of qualitative rating, so that a percentage figure for each qualitative rating could be derived. The "outstanding" and "excellent" ratings were then added, and the lower four ratings were discarded. Following this procedure, MISI determined that 36% of the women who tested Body on Tap found it "outstanding" or "excellent" with relation to "strong, healthy looking hair," whereas only 24% of the separate group of women who tested Sassoon gave it such ratings. These results are the basis of Bristol's advertising claim that the women preferred Body on Tap to Sassoon. When the "very good" and "good" ratings are combined with the "outstanding" and "excellent" ratings, however, there is only a statistically insignificant difference of 1% between the ratings of the two shampoos respecting "strong, healthy looking hair."

The propriety of blind monadic testing for the purpose of comparative advertising claims is in some doubt. Dr. Edwin N. Berdy, President of MISI, stated by deposition that such testing is typically employed "where one would like an absolute response to the product . . . without reference to another specific product." In his affidavit, Dr. Ben Kajioka, Sassoon's Vice President of Research and Development, stated that blind monadic testing cannot support comparative advertising claims. And indeed, Bristol initially conducted the 1978 tests not with the intention of using their results in comparative advertising, but to determine consumer reaction to the recent national introduction of Body on Tap. On the other hand, Dr. Berdy testified that blind monadic testing had been used in connection with comparative advertising in the past.

The 900 "women like" Cristina Ferrare had tried the shampoos might suggest, at the very least, that 900 adult women participated in the test. In actuality, approximately one-third of the "women" were ages 13–18. This fact is noteworthy in light of the testimony of Alfred Lowman, the advertising executive who created the "Ferrare 900 Women" campaign, that the commercial was designed to attract a larger portion of the adult women's shampoo market to Body on Tap. Sassoon had always fared well among adult women, whereas Body on Tap had appealed disproportionately to teenagers. Bristol's marketing studies have revealed that the advertisements were successful in increasing usage and awareness of Body on Tap among adult women.

There is also some question concerning the methodology of the tests. Dr. Kajioka stated that Bristol instructed the women who tested Sassoon to use it contrary to Sassoon's own instructions. Bristol also allowed the women to use other brands while they were testing Sassoon. Thus, the women's responses may not accurately reflect their reaction to Sassoon as distinct from other shampoos.

In September, 1980 Sassoon commenced this action, claiming that the several "Ferrare-900 Women" advertisements violated the prohibition of § 43(a) of the Lanham Trademark Act, 15 U.S.C. § 1125(a) against false and misleading advertising. . . .

* * *

Sassoon submitted, together with other evidence, a consumer perception study prepared for it by ASI Market Research, Inc. ("ASI"). Participants in the ASI test were asked to view the "Ferrare-900 Women" commercial twice, following a screening of entertainment and other advertisement materials. Members of the test group were then asked to answer one multiple-choice and three open-ended questions. The multiple-choice question was "How many different brands mentioned in the commercial did *each* of the 900 women try?" (emphasis in original). A choice of five responses followed — "one," "two," "three," "four," or "five or more." Ninety-five percent of those who answered the question said that each of the 900 women had tried two or more brands. Answering the open-ended question, "This commercial described the results of shampoo tests. What did these tests show?", 62% of the participants indicated that the tests showed that Body on Tap was competitively superior, either in a general way (38%), or as specifically compared with one or more other brands (24%). In answer to another question, 53% stated that the primary message of the commercial was Body on Tap's competitive superiority.

On the basis of the evidence submitted to him, Judge Stewart concluded that Sassoon had demonstrated a probability of success on the merits and a possibility of irreparable injury if the dissemination of the advertisements did not cease. Accordingly, he granted Sassoon's motion for a preliminary injunction.

* * *

We have previously endorsed the ASI format as probative of the meaning consumers derive from commercial advertising. *American Home Products Corp. v. Johnson & Johnson*, 577 F.2d 160, 167–69, 167 n.15 (2d Cir. 1978). The results of the test ASI conducted for Sassoon suggest that most potential purchasers would incorrectly believe that the 900 women in the MISI survey made product-to-product comparisons among two or more shampoos. The study also presents evidence that consumers, after viewing the "Ferrare-900 Women" television commercial, would assume that Body on Tap was competitively superior when a combination of qualitative rating categories different from the one used by Bristol would yield no more than a showing of virtual competitive parity between Body on Tap and Sassoon. Whether or not the statements made in the advertisements are literally true, § 43(a) of the Lanham Act encompasses more than blatant falsehoods. It embraces "innuendo, indirect intimations, and ambiguous suggestions" evidenced by the consuming public's misapprehension of the hard facts underlying an advertisement. *American Home Products Corp. v. Johnson & Johnson, supra*, 577 F.2d at 165. Based largely on his evaluation of the ASI test results, Judge Stewart properly concluded, therefore, that Sassoon had made a showing of a probable § 43(a) violation. We also note that at least one statement made by Bristol, that 900 "women like" Cristina Ferrare tried the shampoo (when in fact only two-thirds of the sample were adult women), appears to be facially false, and may therefore be enjoined without regard to consumer reaction. *Id.*

Bristol asserts that the misrepresentations alleged by Sassoon are only misstatements concerning the test results and the manner in which the tests were conducted, not the "inherent quality," *Fur Information & Fashion Council, Inc. v. E. F. Timme & Son, Inc.*, 501 F.2d 1048, 1051 (2ᵈ Cir.), *cert. denied*, 419 U.S. 1022, of Body on Tap. Misleading statements regarding consumer test methodology, Bristol argues, do not fall within § 43(a). We agree that Bristol has not in so many words falsely described the quality of Body on Tap. It has not, to give a hypothetical example, baldly stated that the shampoo smells like roses when it in fact does not. The inaccuracies alleged concern the number and age of the women in the tests, how the comparisons were made, and how the results were tabulated. After a careful review of cases interpreting the Lanham Act and its legislative history, however, we are persuaded that § 43(a) does prohibit the misrepresentations alleged here.

* * *

[T]he alleged untruths concerning the MISI tests were at least "in connection with" Body on Tap, and, as the ASI study reveals, they quite probably created the impression that Body on Tap was superior. Judge Stewart could appropriately find, moreover, that this view was probably false because, if the qualitative rating categories were combined in a different manner, there would be no significant statistical difference between Sassoon and Body on Tap. While we recognize that § 43(a) encompasses only misrepresentations with reference to the "inherent quality or characteristic" of defendant's product, *see Fur Information & Fashion Council, Inc. v. E. F. Timme & Son, Inc., supra*, 501 F.2d at 1051, we are nevertheless convinced that Judge Stewart was correct in concluding that Sassoon would probably succeed in showing that the intent and total effect of the advertisements were to lead consumers into believing that Body on Tap was competitively superior, surely a representation regarding its "inherent quality." *See R. J. Reynolds Tobacco Co. v. Loew's Theatres, Inc.*, 511 F. Supp. 867 (S.D.N.Y. 1980) (bias in defendant's consumer test caused deception as to the quality of defendant's goods and thereby established action pursuant to § 43(a)).

In a case like this, where many of the qualities of a product (such as "body") are not susceptible to objective measurement, it is difficult to see how the manufacturer can advertise its product's "quality" more effectively than through the dissemination of the results of consumer preference studies. In such instances, the medium of the consumer test truly becomes the message of inherent superiority. We do not hold that every misrepresentation concerning consumer test results or methodology can result in liability pursuant to § 43(a). But where depictions of consumer test results or methodology are so significantly misleading that the reasonably intelligent consumer would be deceived about the product's inherent quality or characteristics, an action under § 43(a) may lie.

Finally, we believe that Sassoon made an adequate showing of the possibility of irreparable injury. Although the likelihood of injury and causation cannot be presumed, *Johnson & Johnson v. Carter-Wallace, Inc.*, 631 F.2d 186, 190 (2[d] Cir. 1980), Judge Stewart properly concluded that Sassoon had offered "proof providing a reasonable basis for the belief that . . . [it] is likely to be damaged as a result of the false advertising." *Id.* Sassoon and Body on Tap compete in the same market, and it is quite likely that the apparently effective suggestions of competitive superiority, if repeatedly communicated to consumers, would eventually result in loss of sales to Sassoon. *McNeilab, Inc. v. American Home Products Corp.*, 501 F. Supp. 517, 530 (S.D.N.Y. 1980). Although Sassoon offered no evidence of actual sales loss directly traceable to the alleged misrepresentations, proof of diversion of sales is not required for an injunction to issue pursuant to § 43(a). *See Johnson & Johnson v. Carter Wallace, Inc., supra*, 631 F.2d at 192. We also note that Bristol's own "Shampoo Tracking Study" reveals that awareness and purchases of Body on Tap among women ages 18-34 increased significantly shortly after the commencement of the "Ferrare-900 Women" advertising campaign. Judge Stewart properly inferred that Sassoon might be damaged if the advertisements did not cease.

Accordingly, we affirm the order of the district court.

* * *

TIME WARNER CABLE, INC. V. DIRECTV, INC.
497 F.3d 144 (2[d] Cir. 2007)

STRAUB, CIRCUIT JUDGE

* * *

DIRECTV began running a television commercial in October 2006 featuring celebrity Jessica Simpson. In the commercial, Simpson, portraying her character of Daisy Duke from the movie *The Dukes of Hazzard*, tells some of her customers at the local diner:

Simpson: Y'all ready to order?

Hey, 253 straight days at the gym to get this body and you're not gonna watch me on DIRECTV HD?

You're just not gonna get the best picture out of some fancy big screen TV without DIRECTV.

It's broadcast in 1080i. I totally don't know what that means, but I want it.

The original version of the commercial concluded with a narrator saying, "For picture quality that beats cable, you've got to get DIRECTV."

In response to objections by Times Warner Cable, Inc. ("TWC") and pursuant to agreements entered into by the parties, DIRECTV pulled the original version of the commercial and replaced it with a revised one ("Revised Simpson Commercial"), which began airing in early December 2006. The Revised Simpson Commercial is identical to the original, except that it ends with a different tag line: "For an HD picture that can't be beat, get DIRECTV."

DIRECTV debuted another commercial in October 2006, featuring actor William Shatner as Captain James T. Kirk, his character from the popular *Star Trek* television show and film series. The following conversation takes place on the Starship Enterprise:

Mr. Chekov: Should we raise our shields, Captain?

Captain Kirk: At ease, Mr. Chekov.

Again with the shields. I wish he'd just relax and enjoy the amazing picture clarity of the DIRECTV HD we just hooked up.

With what Starfleet just ponied up for this big screen TV, settling for cable would be illogical.

Mr. Spock: [Clearing throat.]

Captain Kirk: What, I can't use that line?

The original version ended with the announcer saying, "For picture quality that beats cable, you've got to get DIRECTV."

DIRECTV agreed to stop running the Shatner commercial in November 2006. In January 2007, DIRECTV released a revised version of the commercial ("Revised Shatner Commercial") with the revamped tag line, "For an HD picture that can't be beat, get DIRECTV."

DIRECTV also waged its campaign in cyberspace, placing banner advertisements on various websites to promote the message that when it comes to picture quality, "source matters." The banner ads have the same basic structure. They open by showing an image that is so highly pixelated that it is impossible to discern what is being depicted. On top of this indistinct image is superimposed the slogan, "SOURCE MATTERS." After about a second, a vertical line splits the screen into two parts, one labeled "OTHER TV" and the other "DIRECTV." On the OTHER TV side of the line, the picture is extremely pixelated and distorted, like the opening image. By contrast, the picture on the DIRECTV side is exceptionally sharp and clear. The DIRECTV screen reveals that what we have been looking at all along is an image of New York Giants quarterback Eli Manning; in another ad, it is a picture of two women snorkeling in tropical waters. The advertisements then invite browsers to "FIND OUT WHY DIRECTV's picture beats cable" and to "LEARN MORE" about a special offer. In the original design, users who clicked on the "LEARN MORE" icon were automatically directed to HDTV section of DIRECTV's website.

* * *

1. Television Commercials

Two different theories of recovery are available to a plaintiff who brings a false advertising action under § 43(a) of the Lanham Act. First, the plaintiff can demonstrate that the challenged advertisement is literally false, *i.e.*, false on its face. *See GAC Int'l, Inc.*, 862 F.2d at 977. When an advertisement is shown to be literally or facially false, consumer deception is presumed and "the court may grant relief without reference to the advertisement's [actual] impact on the buying public." *Coca-Cola Co.*, 690 F.2d at 317. "This is because plaintiffs alleging a literal falsehood are claiming that a statement, on its face, conflicts with reality, a claim that is best supported by comparing the statement itself with the reality it purports to describe." *Schering Corp. v. Pfizer, Inc.*, 189 F.3d 218, 229 (2ᵈ Cir. 1999).

Alternatively, a plaintiff can show that the advertisement, while not literally false, is nevertheless likely to mislead or confuse consumers. *See Coca-Cola Co.*, 690 F.2d at 317.

"[P]laintiffs alleging an implied falsehood are claiming that a statement, whatever its literal truth, has left an impression on the listener [or viewer] that conflicts with reality" - - a claim that "invites a comparison of the impression, rather than the statement, with the truth." *Schering Corp.*, 189 F.3d at 229. Therefore, whereas "plaintiffs seeking to establish a literal falsehood must generally show the substance of what is conveyed, . . . a district court *must* rely on extrinsic evidence [of consumer deception or confusion] to support a finding of an implicitly false message." *Id.* (internal quotation marks omitted).

* * *

Here, TWC chose to pursue only the first path of literal falsity, and the District Court granted the preliminary injunction against the television commercials on that basis. In this appeal, DIRECTV does not dispute that it would be a misrepresentation to claim that the picture quality of DIRECTV HD is superior to that of cable HD. Rather, it argues that neither commercial explicitly makes such a claim and therefore cannot be literally false.

a. Revised Simpson Commercial

DIRECTV's argument is easily dismissed with respect to the Revised Simpson Commercial. In the critical lines, Simpson tells audiences, "You've just not gonna get the best picture out of some fancy big screen TV without DIRECTV. It's broadcast in 1080i." These statements make the explicit assertion that it is impossible to obtain "the best picture" - - i.e., a "1080i"-resolution picture - - from any source other than DIRECTV. This claim is flatly untrue; the uncontroverted factual record establishes that viewers can, in fact, get the same "best picture" by ordering HD programming from their cable service provider. We therefore affirm the District Court's determination that the Revised Simpson Commercial's contention "that a viewer cannot 'get the best picture' without DIRECTV is . . . likely to be proven literally false." *Time Warner Cable, Inc.*, 475 F. Supp. 2d at 306.

b. Revised Shatner Commercial

The issue of whether the Revised Shatner Commercial is likely to be proven literally false requires more analysis. When interpreting the controversial statement, "With what Starfleet just ponied up for this big screen TV, settling for cable would be illogical," the District Court looked not only at that particular text, but also at the surrounding context. In light of Shatner's opening comment extolling the "amazing picture quality of . . . DIRECTV HD" and the announcer's closing remark highlighting the unbeatable "HD picture" provided by DIRECTV, the District Court found that the line in the middle - - "settling for cable would be illogical" - - clearly referred to cable's HD picture quality. Since it would only be "illogical" to "settle" for cable's HD picture if it was materially inferior to DIRECTV's HD picture, the District Court concluded that TWC was likely to establish that the statement was literally false.

DIRECTV argues that the District Court's ruling was clearly erroneous because the actual statement at issue, "settling for cable would be illogical," does not explicitly compare the picture quality of DIRECTV *HD* with that of cable *HD*, and indeed, does not mention *HD* at all. In DIRECTV's view, the District Court based its determination of literal falsity not on the words actually used, but on what it subjectively perceived to be the general message conveyed by the commercial as a whole. DIRECTV contends that this was plainly improper under this Court's decision in *American Home Products Corp. v. Johnson & Johnson*, 577 F.2d 160 (2d Cir. 1978).

TWC, on the other hand, maintains that the District Court properly took context into account in interpreting the commercial, as directed by this Court in *Avis Rent A Car System, Inc. v. Hertz Corp.*, 782 F.2d 381 (2d Cir. 1986). TWC argues that under *Avis Rent A Car*, an advertisement can be literally false even though no "combination of words between two punctuation signals" is untrue, if the clear meaning of the statement, considered in context, is false. Given the commercial's repeated references to "HD picture," TWC contends that the District Court correctly found that "settling for cable would be illogical" literally made the false claim that cable's HD picture quality is inferior to DIRECTV's.

* * *

At first glance, *American Home Products* and *Avis Rent A Car* may appear to conflict. *American Home Products* counsels that when an advertisement is not false on its face, but instead relies on indirect intimations, district courts should look to consumer reaction to determine meaning, and not rest on their subjective impressions of the advertisement as a whole. *Avis Rent A Car*, on the other hand, instructs district courts to consider the overall context of an advertisement to discern its true meaning, and holds that the message conveyed by an advertisement may be viewed as not false in the context of the business at issue, even the written words are not literally accurate.

On closer reading, however, the two cases can be reconciled. In *American Home Products*, we did not say that context is irrelevant or that courts are myopically bound to the explicit words of an advertisement. Rather, we held that where it is "clear that . . . the language of the advertisement [] is not unambiguous," the district court should look to consumer response data to resolve the ambiguity. *Am. Home Prods.*, 577 F.2d at 164. In *Avis Rent A Car*, we concluded that there was no ambiguity to resolve because even though the statement, "Hertz has more new cars than Avis has cars," did not expressly qualify the comparison, given the surrounding context, it "unmistakably" referred to the companies' rental fleets. *Avis Rent A Car*, 782 F.2d at 384.

These two cases, read together, compel us to now formally adopt what is known in other circuits as the "false by necessary implication" doctrine (citations omitted). Under this doctrine, a district court evaluating whether an advertisement is literally false "must analyze the message conveyed in full context," *Pennzoil Co.*, 987 F.2d at 946, i.e., it "must consider the advertisement in its entirety and not . . . engage in disputatious dissection," *Avis Rent A Car*, 782 F.2d at 385 (internal quotation marks omitted). If the words or images, considered in context, necessarily imply a false message, the advertisement is literally false and no extrinsic evidence of consumer confusion is required. *See Novartis Consumer Health, Inc. v. Johnson & Johnson-Merck Pharm. Co.*, 290 F.3d 578, 586–87 (3d Cir. 2002). ("A 'literally false' message may be either explicit or 'conveyed by necessary implication when, considering the advertisement in its entirety, the audience would recognize the claim as readily as if it had been explicitly stated.'" (quoting *Clorox Co. Puerto Rico*, 228 F.3d at 35)). However, "only an *unambiguous* message can be literally false." *Id.* at 587. Therefore, if the language or graphic is susceptible to more than one reasonable interpretation, the advertisement cannot be literally false. *See Scotts Co.*, 315 F.3d at 275 (stating that a literal falsity argument fails if the statement or image "can reasonably be understood as conveying different messages"); *Clorox Co. Puerto Rico*, 228 F.3d at 35 ("[A] factfinder might conclude that the message conveyed by a particular advertisement remains so balanced between several plausible meanings that the claim made by the advertisement is too uncertain to serve as the basis of a literal falsity claim . . ."). There may still be a "basis for a claim that the advertisement is misleading," *Clorox Co. Puerto Rico*, 228 F.3d at 35, but to resolve such a claim, the district court must look to consumer data to determine what "the person to whom the advertisement is addressed find[s] to be the message," *Am. Home Prods.*, 577 F.2d at 166 (citation omitted). In short, where the advertisement does not unambiguously make a claim, "the court's reaction is at best not determinative and at worst irrelevant." *Id.*

Here, the District Court found that Shatner's assertion that "settling for cable would be illogical," considered in light of the advertisement as a whole, unambiguously made the false claim that cable's HD picture quality is inferior to that of DIRECTV's. We cannot say that this finding was clearly erroneous, especially given that in the immediately preceding line, Shatner praises the "amazing picture clarity of DIRECTV HD." We accordingly affirm the District Court's conclusion that TWC established a likelihood of success on its claim that the Revised Shatner Commercial is literally false.

2. Internet Advertisements

It is uncontroverted that the images used in the Internet Advertisements to represent cable are inaccurate depictions of the picture quality provided by cable's digital or analog service. The Internet Advertisements are therefore explicitly and literally false. *See Coca-Cola Co.*, 690 F.2d at 318 (reversing the district court's finding of no literal falsity in an orange juice commercial where "[t]he visual component of the ad makes an explicit representation that Premium Pack is produced by squeezing oranges and pouring the freshly-squeezed juice directly into the carton. This is not a true representation of how the product is prepared. Premium Pack juice is heated and sometimes frozen prior to packaging.").

DIRECTV does not contest this point. Rather, it asserts that the images are so grossly distorted and exaggerated that no reasonable buyer would take them to be accurate depictions "of how a consumer's television picture would look when connected to cable." Consequently, DIRECTV argues, the images are obviously just puffery, which cannot form the basis of a Lanham Act violation. . . . "Puffery is an exaggeration or overstatement expressed in broad, vague and commendatory language. 'Such sales talk, or puffing, as it is commonly called, is considered to be offered and understood as an expression of the seller's opinion only, which is to be discounted as such by the buyer . . . The 'puffing' rule amounts to a seller's [*35] privilege to lie his head off, so long as he says nothing specific.' " *Pennzoil Co.*, 987 F.2d at 945 (quoting W. Page Keeton, et al., *Prosser and Keeton on the Law of Torts* § 109, at 756–57 (5th ed. 1984)). . . . [I]f a visual representation is so grossly exaggerated that no reasonable buyer would take it at face value, there is no danger of consumer deception and hence, no basis for a false advertising claim.

Our review of the record persuades us that the District Court clearly erred in rejecting DIRECTV's puffery defense. The "OTHER TV" images in the Internet Advertisements are - - to borrow the words of Ronald Boyer, TWC's Senior Network Engineer - - "unwatchably blurry, distorted, and pixelated, and . . . nothing like the images a customer would ordinarily see using Time Warner Cable's cable service." Boyer further explained that

> the types of gross distortions shown in DIRECTV's Website Demonstrative and Banner Ads are not the type of disruptions that could naturally happen to an analog or non-HD digital cable picture. These advertisements depict the picture quality of cable television as a series of large colored square blocks, laid out in a grid like graph paper, which nearly entirely obscure the image. This is not the

type of wavy or "snowy" picture that might occur from degradation of an unconverted analog cable picture, or the type of macro-blocking or "pixelization" that might occur from degradation of a digital cable picture. Rather, the patchwork of colored blocks that DIRECTV depicts in its advertisement appears to be the type of distortion that would result if someone took a low-resolution photograph and enlarged it too much or zoomed in too close. If DIRECTV intended the advertisement to depict a pixelization problem, this is a gross exaggeration of one.

*   *   *

For the foregoing reasons, we AFFIRM the preliminary injunction [against the television commercials] and REMAND for further proceedings consistent with this opinion.

*   *   *

DASTAR CORP. V. TWENTIETH CENTURY FOX FILM CORP.
United States Supreme Court
539 U.S. 23 (2003)

JUSTICE SCALIA delivered the opinion of the Court.

*   *   *

In this case, we are asked to decide whether § 43(a) of the Lanham Act, *15 U.S.C. § 1125(a)*, prevents the unaccredited copying of a work, and if so, whether a court may double a profit award under *§ 1117(a)*, in order to deter future infringing conduct.

I

In 1948, three and a half years after the German surrender at Reims, General Dwight D. Eisenhower completed Crusade in Europe, his written account of the allied campaign in Europe during World War II. Doubleday published the book, registered it with the Copyright Office in 1948, and granted exclusive television rights to an affiliate of respondent Twentieth Century Fox Film Corporation (Fox). Fox, in turn, arranged for Time, Inc., to produce a television series, also called Crusade in Europe, based on the book, and Time assigned its copyright in the series to Fox. The television series, consisting of 26 episodes, was first broadcast in 1949. It combined a soundtrack based on a narration of the book with film footage from the United States Army, Navy, and Coast Guard, the British Ministry of Information and War Office, the National Film Board of Canada, and unidentified "Newsreel Pool Cameramen." In 1975, Doubleday renewed the copyright on the book as the " 'proprietor of copyright in a work made for hire.' " App. to Pet for Cert. 9a. Fox, however, did not renew the copyright on the Crusade television series, which expired in 1977, leaving the television series in the public domain.

In 1988, Fox reacquired the television rights in General Eisenhower's book, including the exclusive right to distribute the Crusade television series on video and to sub-license others to do so. Respondents SFM Entertainment and New Line Home Video, Inc., in turn, acquired from Fox the exclusive rights to distribute Crusade on video. SFM obtained the negatives of the original television series, restored them, and repackaged the series on videotape; New Line distributed the videotapes.

Enter petitioner Dastar. In 1995, Dastar decided to expand its product line from music compact discs to videos. Anticipating renewed interest in World War II on the 50th anniversary of the war's end, Dastar released a video set entitled World War II Campaigns in Europe. To make Campaigns, Dastar purchased eight beta cam tapes of the *original* version of the Crusade television series, which is in the public domain, copied them, and then edited the series. Dastar's Campaigns series is slightly more than half as long as the original Crusade television series. Dastar substituted a new opening sequence, credit page, and final closing for those of the Crusade television series; inserted new chapter-title sequences and narrated chapter introductions; moved the "recap" in the Crusade television series to the beginning and retitled it as a "preview"; and removed references to and images of the book. Dastar created new packaging for its Campaigns series and (as already noted) a new title.

Dastar manufactured and sold the Campaigns video set as its own product. The advertising states: "Produced and Distributed by: *Entertainment Distributing*" (which is owned by Dastar), and makes no reference to the Crusade television series. Similarly, the screen credits state "DASTAR CORP presents" and "an ENTERTAINMENT DISTRIBUTING Production," and list as executive producer, producer, and associate producer, employees of Dastar. Supp. App. 2–3, 30. The Campaigns videos themselves also make no reference to the Crusade television series, New Line's Crusade videotapes, or the book. Dastar sells its Campaigns videos to Sam's Club, Costco, Best Buy, and other retailers and mail-order companies for $ 25 per set, substantially less than New Line's video set.

In 1998, respondents Fox, SFM, and New Line brought this action alleging that Dastar's sale of its Campaigns video set infringes Doubleday's copyright in General Eisenhower's book and, thus, their exclusive television rights in the book. Respondents later amended their complaint to add claims that Dastar's sale of Campaigns "without proper credit" to the Crusade television series constitutes "reverse passing off"[1] in violation of § 43(a) of the Lanham Act, 15 U.S.C. § 1125(a), and in violation of state unfair-competition law. App. to Pet. for Cert. 31a. On cross-motions for summary judgment, the District Court found for respondents on all three counts, *id.*, at 54a-55a, treating its resolution of the Lanham Act claim as controlling on the state-law unfair-competition claim because "the ultimate test under both is whether the public is likely to be deceived or confused," *id.*, at 54a. The court awarded Dastar's profits to respondents and doubled them pursuant to § 35 of the Lanham Act, 15 U.S.C. § 1117(a), to deter future infringing conduct by petitioner.

The Court of Appeals for the Ninth Circuit affirmed the judgment for respondents on the Lanham Act claim, but reversed as to the copyright claim and remanded. *34 Fed. Appx. 312, 316 (2002)*. (It said nothing with regard to the state-law claim.) With respect to the Lanham Act claim, the Court of Appeals reasoned that "Dastar copied substantially the entire *Crusade in Europe* series created by Twentieth Century Fox, labeled the resulting product with a different name and marketed it without attribution to Fox [,and] therefore committed a 'bodily appropriation' of Fox's series." *Id., at 314.* It concluded that "Dastar's 'bodily appropriation' of Fox's original [television] series is sufficient to establish the reverse passing off." *Ibid.*[2] The court also affirmed the District Court's award under the Lanham Act of twice Dastar's profits. We granted certiorari. *Dastar Corp. v. Twentieth Century Fox Film Corp.*, 537 U.S. 1099, 123 S. Ct. 816, 154 L. Ed. 2d 767 (2003).

II

The Lanham Act was intended to make "actionable the deceptive and misleading use of marks," and "to protect persons engaged in . . . commerce against unfair competi-

---

[1] Passing off (or palming off, as it is sometimes called) occurs when a producer misrepresents his own goods or services as someone else's. See, e.g., O. & W. Thum Co. v. Dickinson, 245 F. 609, 621 (CA6 1917). "Reverse passing off," as its name implies, is the opposite: The producer misrepresents someone else's goods or services as his own. See, e.g., Williams v. Curtiss-Wright Corp., 691 F.2d 168, 172 (CA3 1982).

[2] As for the copyright claim, the Ninth Circuit held that the tax treatment General Eisenhower sought for his manuscript of the book created a triable issue as to whether he intended the book to be a work for hire, and thus as to whether Doubleday properly renewed the copyright in 1976. See 34 Fed. Appx., at 314. The copyright issue is still the subject of litigation, but is not before us. We express no opinion as to whether petitioner's product would infringe a valid copyright in General Eisenhower's book.

tion." *15 U.S.C. § 1127.* While much of the Lanham Act addresses the registration, use, and infringement of trademarks and related marks, § 43(a), *15 U.S.C. § 1125(a)* is one of the few provisions that goes beyond trademark protection. As originally enacted, *§ 43(a)* created a federal remedy against a person who used in commerce either "a false designation of origin, or any false description or representation" in connection with "any goods or services." 60 Stat. 441. As the Second Circuit accurately observed with regard to the original enactment, however — and as remains true after the 1988 revision — *§ 43(a)* "does not have boundless application as a remedy for unfair trade practices," *Alfred Dunhill, Ltd. v. Interstate Cigar Co., 499 F.2d 232, 237 (1974).* "Because of its inherently limited wording, *§ 43(a)* can never be a federal 'codification' of the overall law of 'unfair competition,' " 4 J. McCarthy Trademarks and Unfair Competition § 27:7, p. 27–14 (4th ed. 2002) (McCarthy), but can apply only to certain unfair trade practices prohibited by its text.

Although a case can be made that a proper reading of *§ 43(a)*, as originally enacted, would treat the word "origin" as referring only "to the geographic location in which the goods originated," *Two Pesos, Inc. v. Taco Cabana, Inc., 505 U.S. 763, 777, 112 S. Ct. 2753, 120 L. Ed. 2d 615 (1992)* (STEVENS, J. concurring in judgment), the Courts of Appeals considering the issue, beginning with the Sixth Circuit, unanimously concluded that it "does not merely refer to geographical origin, but also to origin of source or manufacture," *Federal-Mogul-Bower Bearings, Inc. v. Azoff, 313 F.2d 405, 408 (1963)*, thereby creating a federal cause of action for traditional trademark infringement of unregistered marks. *See* 4 McCarthy § 27:14; *Two Pesos, supra, at 768.* Moreover, every Circuit to consider the issue found *§ 43(a)* broad enough to encompass reverse passing off. *See, e.g., Williams v. Curtiss-Wright Corp., 691 F.2d 168, 172 (CA3 1982); Arrow United Indus., Inc. v. Hugh Richards, Inc., 678 F.2d 410, 415 (CA2 1982); F. E. L. Publications, Ltd. v. Catholic Bishop of Chicago, 214 USPQ 409, 416 (CA7 1982); Smith v. Montoro, 648 F.2d 602, 603 (CA9 1981); Bangor Punta Operations, Inc. v. Universal Marine Co., 543 F.2d 1107, 1109 (CA5 1976).* The Trademark Law Revision Act of 1988 made clear that *§ 43(a)* covers origin of production as well as geographic origin. Its language is amply inclusive, moreover, of reverse passing off — if indeed it does not implicitly adopt the unanimous court-of-appeals jurisprudence on that subject. *See, e.g., Alpo Petfoods, Inc. v. Ralston Purina Co., 913 F.2d 958, 963, 286 U.S. App. D.C. 192-964, n. 6 (CADC 1990)* (Thomas, J.).

Thus, as it comes to us, the gravamen of respondents' claim is that, in marketing and selling Campaigns as its own product without acknowledging its nearly wholesale reliance on the Crusade television series, Dastar has made a "false designation of origin, false or misleading description of fact, or false or misleading representation of fact, which . . . is likely to cause confusion . . . as to the origin . . . of his or her goods." *See, e.g.,* Brief for Respondents 8, 11. That claim would undoubtedly be sustained if Dastar had bought some of New Line's Crusade videotapes and merely repackaged them as its own. Dastar's alleged wrongdoing, however, is vastly different: it took a creative work in the public domain — the Crusade television series — copied it, made modifications (arguably minor), and produced its very own series of videotapes. If "origin" refers only to the manufacturer or producer of the physical "goods" that are made available to the public (in this case the videotapes), Dastar was the origin. If, however, "origin" includes the creator of the underlying work that Dastar copied, then someone else (perhaps Fox) was the origin of Dastar's product. At bottom, we must decide what *§ 43(a)(1)(A) of the Lanham Act* means by the "origin" of "goods."

III

The dictionary definition of "origin" is "the fact or process of coming into being from a source," and "that from which anything primarily proceeds; source." Webster's New International Dictionary 1720–1721 (2d ed. 1949). And the dictionary definition of "goods" (as relevant here) is "wares; merchandise." *Id.,* at 1079. We think the most natural understanding of the "origin" of "goods" — the source of wares — is the producer of the tangible product sold in the marketplace, in this case the physical Campaigns videotape sold by Dastar. The concept might be stretched (as it was under the original version of *§ 43(a)* to include not only the actual producer, but also the trademark owner who commissioned or assumed responsibility for ("stood behind") production of the physical product. But as used in the Lanham Act, the phrase "origin of goods" is in our view incapable of connoting the person or entity that originated the ideas or communications that "goods" embody or contain. Such an extension would not only stretch the text, but it would be out of accord with the history and purpose of the Lanham Act and inconsistent with precedent.

Section 43(a) of the Lanham Act prohibits actions like trademark infringement that deceive consumers and impair a producer's goodwill. It forbids, for example, the Coca-Cola Company's passing off its product as Pepsi-Cola or reverse passing off Pepsi-Cola as its product. But the brand-loyal consumer who prefers the drink that the Coca-Cola Company or PepsiCo sells, while he believes that that company produced (or at least stands behind the production of) that product, surely does not necessarily believe that that company was the "origin" of the drink in the sense that it was the very first to devise the formula. The consumer who buys a branded product does not automatically assume that the brand-name company is the same entity that came up with the idea for the product, or designed the product — and typically does not care whether it is. The words of the Lanham Act should not be stretched to cover matters that are typically of no consequence to purchasers.

It could be argued, perhaps, that the reality of purchaser concern is different for what might be called a communicative product — one that is valued not primarily for its physical qualities, such as a hammer, but for the intellectual content that it conveys, such as a book or, as here, a video. The purchaser of a novel is interested not merely, if at all, in the identity of the producer of the physical tome (the publisher), but also, and indeed primarily, in the identity of the creator of the story it conveys (the author). And the author, of course, has at least as much interest in avoiding passing-off (or reverse passing-off) of his creation as does the publisher. For such a communicative product (the argument goes) "origin of goods" in *§ 43(a)* must be deemed to include not merely the producer of the physical item (the publishing house Farrar, Straus and Giroux, or the video producer Dastar) but also the creator of the content that the physical item conveys (the author Tom Wolfe, or — assertedly — respondents).

The problem with this argument according special treatment to communicative products is that it causes the Lanham Act to conflict with the law of copyright, which addresses that subject specifically. The right to copy, and to copy without attribution, once a copyright has expired, like "the right to make [an article whose patent has expired] — including the right to make it in precisely the shape it carried when patented — passes to the public." *Sears, Roebuck & Co. v. Stiffel Co., 376 U.S. 225, 230, 84 S. Ct. 784, 11 L. Ed. 2d 661, 1964 Dec. Comm'r Pat. 425 (1964); see also Kellogg Co. v. National Biscuit Co., 305 U.S. 111, 121–122, 59 S. Ct. 109, 83 L. Ed. 73, 1939 Dec. Comm'r Pat. 850 (1938).* "In general, unless an intellectual property right such as a patent or copyright protects an item, it will be subject to copying." *TrafFix Devices, Inc. v. Marketing Displays, Inc., 532 U.S. 23, 29, 121 S. Ct. 1255, 149 L. Ed. 2d 164 (2001).* The rights of a patentee or copyright holder are part of a "carefully crafted bargain," *Bonito Boats, Inc. v. Thunder Craft Boats, Inc., 489 U.S. 141, 150–151, 109 S. Ct. 971, 103 L. Ed. 2d 118 (1989),* under which, once the patent or copyright monopoly has expired, the public may use the invention or work at will and without attribution. Thus, in construing the Lanham Act, we have been "careful to caution against misuse or over-extension" of trademark and related protections into areas traditionally occupied by patent or copyright. *TrafFix, 532 U.S., at 29.* "The Lanham Act," we have said, "does not exist to reward manufacturers for their innovation in creating a particular device; that is the purpose of the patent law and its period of exclusivity." *Id., at 34.* Federal trademark law "has no necessary relation to invention or discovery," *Trade-Mark Cases, 100 U.S. 82,*

94, 25 L. Ed. 550, 1879 Dec. Comm'r Pat. 619 (1879), but rather, by preventing competitors from copying "a source-identifying mark," "reduces the customer's costs of shopping and making purchasing decisions," and "helps assure a producer that it (and not an imitating competitor) will reap the financial, reputation-related rewards associated with a desirable product," *Qualitex Co. v. Jacobson Products Co., 514 U.S. 159, 163–164, 115 S. Ct. 1300, 131 L. Ed. 2d 248 (1995)* (internal quotation marks and citation omitted). Assuming for the sake of argument that Dastar's representation of itself as the "Producer" of its videos amounted to a representation that it originated the creative work conveyed by the videos, allowing a cause of action under *§ 43(a)* for that representation would create a species of mutant copyright law that limits the public's "federal right to 'copy and to use,'" expired copyrights, *Bonito Boats, supra, at 165*.

When Congress has wished to create such an addition to the law of copyright, it has done so with much more specificity than the Lanham Act's ambiguous use of "origin." The *Visual Artists Rights Act of 1990, § 603(a), 104 Stat. 5128*, provides that the author of an artistic work "shall have the right . . . to claim authorship of that work." *17 U.S.C. § 106A(a)(1)(A)*. That express right of attribution is carefully limited and focused: It attaches only to specified "works of visual art," *§ 101*, is personal to the artist, *§§ 106A(b) and (e)*, and endures only for "the life of the author," at *§ 106A(d)(1)*. Recognizing in *§ 43(a)* a cause of action for misrepresentation of authorship of noncopyrighted works (visual or otherwise) would render these limitations superfluous. A statutory interpretation that renders another statute superfluous is of course to be avoided. *E.g., Mackey v. Lanier Collection Agency & Service, Inc., 486 U.S. 825, 837, 100 L. Ed. 2d 836, 108 S. Ct. 2182*, and n. 11 (1988).

Reading "origin" in *§ 43(a)* to require attribution of uncopyrighted materials would pose serious practical problems. Without a copyrighted work as the basepoint, the word "origin" has no discernable limits. A video of the MGM film Carmen Jones, after its copyright has expired, would presumably require attribution not just to MGM, but to Oscar Hammerstein II (who wrote the musical on which the film was based), to Georges Bizet (who wrote the opera on which the musical was based), and to Prosper Merimee (who wrote the novel on which the opera was based). In many cases, figuring out who is in the line of "origin" would be no simple task. Indeed, in the present case it is far from clear that respondents have that status. Neither SFM nor New Line had anything to do with the production of the Crusade television series — they merely were licensed to distribute the video version. While Fox might have a claim to being in the line of origin, its involvement with the creation of the television series was limited at best. Time, Inc., was the principal if not the exclusive creator, albeit under arrangement with Fox. And of course it was neither Fox nor Time, Inc., that shot the film used in the Crusade television series. Rather, that footage came from the United States Army, Navy, and Coast Guard, the British Ministry of Information and War Office, the National Film Board of Canada, and unidentified "Newsreel Pool Cameramen." If anyone has a claim to being the *original* creator of the material used in both the Crusade television series and the Campaigns videotapes, it would be those groups, rather than Fox. We do not think the Lanham Act requires this search for the source of the Nile and all its tributaries.

Another practical difficulty of adopting a special definition of "origin" for communicative products is that it places the manufacturers of those products in a difficult position. On the one hand, they would face Lanham Act liability for *failing* to credit the creator of a work on which their lawful copies are based; and on the other hand they could face Lanham Act liability for *crediting* the creator if that should be regarded as implying the creator's "sponsorship or approval" of the copy, *15 U.S.C. § 1125(a)(1)(A)*. In this case, for example, if Dastar had simply "copied [the television series] as Crusade in Europe and sold it as Crusade in Europe," without changing the title or packaging (including the original credits to Fox), it is hard to have confidence in respondents' assurance that they "would not be here on a Lanham Act cause of action," Tr. of Oral Arg. 35.

Finally, reading *§ 43(a) of the Lanham Act* as creating a cause of action for, in effect, plagiarism — the use of otherwise unprotected works and inventions without attribution — would be hard to reconcile with our previous decisions. For example, in *Wal-Mart Stores, Inc. v. Samara Brothers, Inc., 529 U.S. 205, 120 S. Ct. 1339, 146 L. Ed. 2d 182 (2000)*, we considered whether product-design trade dress can ever be inherently distinctive. Wal-Mart produced "knockoffs" of children's clothes designed and manufactured by Samara Brothers, containing only "minor modifications" of the original designs. *Id., at 208.* We concluded that the designs could not be protected under *§ 43(a)* without a showing that they had acquired "secondary meaning," *id., at 214*, so that they " 'identify the source of the product rather than the product itself,' " *id., at 211* (quoting *Inwood Laboratories, Inc. v. Ives Laboratories, Inc., 456 U.S. 844, 851, n. 11, 102 S. Ct. 2182, 72 L. Ed. 2d 606 (1982))*. This carefully considered limitation would be entirely pointless if the "original" producer could turn around and pursue a reverse-passing-off claim under exactly the same provision of the Lanham Act. Samara would merely have had to argue that it was the "origin" of the designs that Wal-Mart was selling as its own line. It was not, because "origin of goods" in the Lanham Act referred to the producer of the clothes, and not the producer of the (potentially) copyrightable or patentable designs that the clothes embodied.

Similarly under respondents' theory, the "origin of goods" provision of *§ 43(a)* would have supported the suit that we rejected in *Bonito Boats, 489 U.S. 141, 109 S. Ct. 971, 103 L. Ed. 2d 118*, where the defendants had used molds to duplicate the plaintiff's unpatented boat hulls (apparently without crediting the plaintiff). And it would have supported the suit we rejected in *TrafFix, 532 U.S. 23, 121 S. Ct. 1255, 149 L. Ed. 2d 164*: The plaintiff, whose patents on flexible road signs had expired, and who could not prevail on a trade-dress claim under *§ 43(a)* because the features of the signs were functional, would have had a reverse-passing-off claim for unattributed copying of his design.

In sum, reading the phrase "origin of goods" in the Lanham Act in accordance with the Act's common-law foundations (which were *not* designed to protect originality or creativity), and in light of the copyright and patent laws (which *were*), we conclude that the phrase refers to the producer of the tangible goods that are offered for sale, and not to the author of any idea, concept, or communication embodied in those goods. Cf. *17 U.S.C. § 202* (distinguishing between a copyrighted work and "any material object in which the work is embodied"). To hold otherwise would be akin to finding that *§ 43(a)* created a species of perpetual patent and copyright, which Congress may not do. *See Eldred v. Ashcroft, 537 U.S. 186, 208, 123 S. Ct. 769, 154 L. Ed. 2d 683 (2003)*.

The creative talent of the sort that lay behind the Campaigns videos is not left without protection. The original film footage used in the Crusade television series could have been copyrighted, *see 17 U.S.C. § 102(a)(6)*, as was copyrighted (as a compilation) the Crusade television series, even though it included material from the public domain, *see § 103(a)*. Had Fox renewed the copyright in the Crusade television series, it would have had an easy claim of copyright infringement. And respondents' contention that Campaigns infringes Doubleday's copyright in General Eisenhower's book is still a live question on remand. If, moreover, the producer of a video that substantially copied the Crusade series were, in advertising or promotion, to give purchasers the impression that the video was quite different from that series, then one or more of the respondents might have a cause of action — not for reverse passing off under the "confusion . . . as to the origin" provision of *§ 43(a)(1)(A)*, but for misrepresentation under the "misrepresents the nature, characteristics [or] qualities" provision of *§ 43(a)(1)(B)*. For merely saying it is the producer of the video, however, no Lanham Act liability attaches to Dastar.

Because we conclude that Dastar was the "origin" of the products it sold as its own, respondents cannot prevail on their Lanham Act claim. We thus have no occasion to consider whether the Lanham Act permitted an award of double petitioner's profits. The judgment of the Court of Appeals for the Ninth Circuit is reversed, and the case is remanded for further proceedings consistent with this opinion.

It is so ordered.

JUSTICE BREYER took no part in the consideration or decision of this case.

* * *

Notes on Misrepresentation

1. Generally

The statutory predecessor of § 43(a) of the Lanham Act, 15 U.S.C. § 123 (1920), applied only to "a false designation of origin" affixed to "an article or merchandise . . . willfully and with intent to deceive" and only persons "doing business in the locality falsely indicated as that of origin" had standing to sue under the section. Accordingly, the obstacles presented to a plaintiff attempting to prevent such deception in the marketplace under the old Trademark Act of 1920 often were formidable. *See California Apparel Creators v. Wieder of California, Inc.*, 162 F.2d 893 (2ᵈ Cir. 1947). The passage of the Lanham Act dramatically broadened the scope of "false designation of origin" to include "any false or misleading description or representation" "use[d] in connection with any goods or services . . .," such action to be brought "by any person who believes he or she is or is likely to be damaged by the use of such false description or representation." The goal of Congress was "to modernize the trademark statutes so that they will conform to legitimate present-day business practice." S. Rep. No. 1333, 79th Cong., 2d Sess. (1946), reprinted in 1946 U.S. Code Cong. Service, at 1276.

Response to this Congressional intent, however, was slow in developing. Early decisions limited the scope of § 43(a) to those trademark uses likely to cause confusion as to geographical origin, passing-off cases, and traditional trademark-engendered deception. *Samson Crane Co. v. Union National Sales, Inc.*, 87 F. Supp. 218 (D. Mass. 1949), *aff'd per curiam*, 180 F.2d 896 (1ˢᵗ Cir. 1950). In *Maternally Yours, Inc. v. Your Maternity Shop, Inc.*, 234 F.2d 538, 546 (2d Cir. 1956), Judge Clark, in a concurring opinion, referred to § 43(a), which had not even been cited by the parties, and noted: "Indeed, there is indication here and elsewhere that the bar has not yet realized the potential impact of this statutory provision."

Since that time the application of the section has gradually expanded and courts have relied upon § 43(a) to apply the principles of unfair competition law to the constantly changing and evolving practices in the business world.

2. The Broad Scope of § 43(a)

a) Types of Misrepresentation

Some examples of the broad implementation of § 43(a)'s prohibitions against a "false designation of origin" and "any false or misleading description or representation" are: *Playboy Enters. v. Netscape Comm'ns*, 354 F.3d 1020 (9ᵗʰ Cir. 2004) (use of plaintiff's trademarks in Internet search engines to trigger potentially confusing competitive banner ads); *Johnson v. Jones*, 47 U.S.P.Q. 2d 1481, 1488 (6ᵗʰ Cir. 1998) (replacing plaintiff architect's name with defendant's name on architectural plans); *Nintendo of Am., Inc. v. Dragon Pac. Int'l*, 40 F.3d 1007 (9ᵗʰ Cir. 1994) (representing unlawfully copied software to be authorized by Nintendo); *PPX Enterprises, Inc. v. Audiofidelity Enterprises*, 818 F.2d 266 (2ᵈ Cir. 1987) (misrepresenting that record album featured performances by Jimi Hendrix); *Boston Professional Hockey Ass'n v. Dallas Cap & Emblem Mfg., Inc.*, 510 F.2d 1004 (5ᵗʰ Cir. 1975) (unlicensed manufacturing for sale of emblems and insignias of professional hockey teams); *Potato Chip Inst. v. General Mills, Inc.*, 333 F. Supp. 173 (D. Neb. 1971), *aff'd*, 461 F.2d 1088 (8ᵗʰ Cir. 1972) (using the term "potato chips" without explanation for a product made from dried potato granules); *Union Tank Car Co. v. Lindsay Soft Water Corp.*, 257 F. Supp. 510 (D. Neb. 1966), *aff'd*, 387 F.2d 477 (8th Cir. 1967) (falsely claiming authorized dealership); *Bohsei Enterprises Co., U.S.A. v. Porteous Fastener Co.*, 441 F. Supp. 162 (C.D. Cal. 1977) (falsely suggesting product is of domestic manufacture by omission of foreign origin identification).

Compare, however, *Norton Tire Co. v. Tire Kingdom Co.*, 858 F.2d 1533 (11th Cir. 1988), where defendant's alleged "bait and switch" advertising techniques did not violate § 43(a) because, with persistence, a customer could obtain the advertised low priced tires instead of the high priced tires promoted in the store by defendant's salespeople; *Lipton v. Nature Co.*, 71 F.3d 464, 473 (2[d] Cir. 1995), where the court held that defendant's affixation of false copyright notices to material that infringed plaintiff's copyrights was not a false designation of origin under § 43(a); *Nature's Way Products, Inc. v. Nature-Pharma, Inc.*, 736 F. Supp. 245 (D. Utah 1990), where a claim against alleged imitation of plaintiff's marketing techniques such as promoting chaparral as a dietary supplement was dismissed as "frivolous"; *Masdea v. Scholz*, 742 F. Supp. 713 (D. Mass. 1990), where mere imitation of plaintiff's drumming style on a recording did not violate § 43(a); and *Paramount Pictures Corp. v. Video Broadcasting Systems, Inc.*, 724 F. Supp. 808 (D. Kan. 1989), where preliminary relief was denied under § 43(a) even though defendant had recorded advertisements which overlapped or obliterated the original pre-recorded Pepsi commercials and FBI warnings. *See also* MCKENNEY & LONG, FEDERAL UNFAIR COMPETITION: LANHAM ACT § 43(a) (2007 ed.); *Pinover, The Rights of Authors, Artists, and Performers Under Section 43(a) of the Lanham Act*, 83 TRADEMARK REP. 38 (1993); *Bauer, A Federal Law of Unfair Competition: What Should Be The Reach of Sec. 43(a) of the Lanham Act?*, 31 UCLA L. REV. 671 (1984). What other possible torts of misrepresentation might fall within the expanding purview of § 43(a)?

As with the other remedial provisions of the Lanham Act (§ 32), it is not necessary under § 43 to prove that a false designation of origin or false description or representation was intentional. *Parkway Baking Co. v. Freihofer Baking Co.*, 255 F.2d 641, 648 (3d Cir. 1958). Neither is it necessary that the representation or description be literally false but only that it convey a false impression. *See American Home Products Corp. v. Johnson & Johnson*, 577 F.2d 160, 165 (2[d] Cir. 1978) ("Were it otherwise, clever use of innuendo, indirect intimations and ambiguous suggestions could shield the advertisement from scrutiny precisely when protection against such sophisticated deception is most needed"); *followed*: *McNeilab, Inc. v. American Home Products Corp.*, 501 F. Supp. 517 (S.D.N.Y. 1980).

b) Standing

A competitive relationship between the parties is not requisite for an action under § 43(a). *National Lampoon, Inc. v. American Broadcasting Co.*, 376 F. Supp. 733 (S.D.N.Y. 1974); *Mortellito v. Nina of Cal., Inc.*, 335 F. Supp. 1288 (S.D.N.Y. 1972). However, the absence of a commercial competitive relationship nonetheless is often cited in denying standing. Does a consumer "who believes that he or she is or is likely to be damaged" by acts prohibited under § 43(a) have standing to sue? *Compare Arnesen v. Raymond Lee Organization, Inc.*, 333 F. Supp. 116 (C.D. Cal. 1971), holding that consumers had standing to bring a class action under § 43(a), *with Colligan v. Activities Club of New York, Ltd.*, 442 F.2d 686 (2[d] Cir.), *cert. denied*, 404 U.S. 1004 (1971), in which the court dismissed a § 43(a) consumer class action, stating at p. 692:

> The Act's purpose, as defined in § 45, is exclusively to protect the interests of a purely commercial class against unscrupulous commercial conduct.

The *Colligan* decision was rejected as contrary to the plain language of § 43(a) by the Third Circuit in *Thorn v. Reliance Van Co.*, 736 F.2d 929, 932 (3[d] Cir. 1984), which granted standing to an investor in a bankrupt company in a suit against a competitor of that company.

The Third Circuit subsequently clarified that in that circuit a plaintiff, to have standing, must allege that he or she is either a direct competitor of the defendant, or is acting as a surrogate for a direct competitor. *Conte Bros. Automotive, Inc. et al. v. Quaker State-Slick 50, Inc. et al.*, 992 F. Supp. 709 (D.N.J. 1998), *aff'd*, 165 F.3d 221 (3ᵈ Cir. 1998). It held that Section 43(a) did not confer standing upon retailers to sue a manufacturer for allegedly falsely advertising a product that competed with products sold by the retailers. The plaintiff retailers had alleged that the defendants used a nationwide campaign to advertise and promote their Slick 50 motor oil substitute products in an intentionally misleading manner. Plaintiffs claimed that this advertising harmed sales of competing engine additives, and sued on behalf of themselves and "all persons in the United States who have offered for sale, either as retailers or wholesalers, motor oil product that directly compete with Slick 50." Plaintiffs in this case were not in competition with the defendants, nor acting as surrogates for a competitor. As the plaintiffs were simply retailers of competing engine additives, they lacked standing. *See also Jack Russell Terrier Network v. Am. Kennel Club*, 407 F.3d 1027 (9ᵗʰ Cir. 2005) (no standing where dog-breeding club terminated one plaintiff, a regional chapter, and blacklisted two plaintiff members for signing up with another club, because the plaintiffs had not suffered a "competitive injury"); *American Ass'n of Orthodontists v. Yellow Book USA, Inc.*, 434 F.3d 1100 (8ᵗʰ Cir. 2006) (no standing for Orthodontists Association to sue publisher of yellow-pages directory for its dental listings where "neither the AAO nor its members are competitors of the alleged wrongdoer").

See generally Keller & Trunko, *Consumer Use of RICO to Challenge False Advertising Claims*, C674 ALI-ABA 51 (1991); Thompson, *Consumer Standing Under Section 43(a): More Legislative History, More Confusion*, 79 TRADEMARK REP. 341 (1989); and *Ames Publishing Co. v. Walker-David Publications, Inc.*, 372 F. Supp. 1 (E.D. Pa. 1974), a § 43(a) case in which the court refused to apply an unclean-hands defense against a plaintiff who was a "vicarious avenger" of a particular class of consumers lacking standing to bring the suit.

3.   Misrepresentations on the Internet

a)   Metatags

The Internet has engendered new forms of misrepresentation, including the use of another's trademark as a website metatag or key word to attract search engine users. As discussed in § 5.05 on Intent and § 6.02, such metatag and key word trademark use can create likely initial interest confusion which courts have held actionable. *See, e.g., Brookfield Communications Inc. v. West Coast Entertainment Corp.*, 174 F.3d 1036 (9ᵗʰ Cir. 1999) (affirming preliminary injunction against defendant video rental store chain's metatag use of plaintiff's "moviebuff" trademark); *SNA, Inc. v. Array*, 51 F. Supp. 2d 554 (E.D. Pa. 1999), *appeal dismissed*, 172 F.3d 41 (3ᵈ Cir. 1999) (enjoining metatag use of plaintiff's "seawind" mark; "defendants intentionally use plaintiff's mark in this way to lure Internet users to their site instead of SNA's official site . . . [t]his is true whether the metatagging is visible or hidden in the code, and no matter what the website's domain name is"); *Playboy Enters., Inc. v. Calvin Designer Label*, 985 F. Supp. 1220 (N.D. Cal. 1997) (preliminarily enjoining metatag use of plaintiff's PLAYBOY and PLAYMATE marks). *See also Eli Lilly & Co. v. Natural Answers, Inc.*, 233 F.3d 456 (7ᵗʰ Cir. 2000) (finding that defendant's use of plaintiff's mark in defendant's metatags was highly persuasive evidence of a wrongful intent to confuse consumers); *Interstellar Starship Services, Ltd. v. Epix, Inc.*, 184 F.3d 1107 (9ᵗʰ Cir. 1999) (reversing summary judgment that "epix.com" domain name did not infringe plaintiff's EPIX mark, citing concerns about initial interest confusion).

In *Promatek Industries, Ltd. v. Equitrac Corp.*, 300 F.3d 808 (7ᵗʰ Cir. 2002), the parties competed in selling cost-recovery equipment. Defendant also provided maintenance and service for plaintiff's equipment, and because of that put plaintiff's Copitrak trademark (misspelled as "Copitrack") in its metatags. When it learned plaintiff had sued, defendant contacted all of the search engines known to it, and requested that they remove any link between the term Copitrack and defendant's website. Defendant also removed the Copitrack metatag from its website.

The district court granted a preliminary injunction mandating that, in addition to the actions defendant already had taken, defendant put the following language on its website:

If you were directed to this site through the term "Copitrack,'," that is in error as there is no affiliation between [defendant] Equitrac and that term. The mark "Copitrak" is a registered trademark of Promatek Industries, Ltd., which can be found at www.promatek.com or www.copitrak.com.

On appeal, defendant unsuccessfully contended that the ordered language unfairly informed consumers of its competitor and encouraged them to go to plaintiff's website. The court viewed it differently: "the remedial language on the website is more informative than it is harmful. Equitrac's speculative argument that Promatek may gain a competitive advantage by inclusion of the remedial language is rejected."

In *Horphag Research, Ltd. v. Pellegrini*, 328 F.3d 1108 (9th Cir. 2003), defendant, allegedly to compare his product to Horphag's, repeatedly used Horphag's registered trademark "Pycnogenol" in defendant's text and web site metatags. Pycnogenol is a pine bark extract product, and through his web site defendant sold that product along with other pharmaceutical products, including one he called "the Original French Pycnogenol." In affirming the district court's judgment of trademark infringement, the court rejected defendant's fair use defense (328 F.3d at 1112):

By using the mark so pervasively, not just in the text of his web sites but also in the metatags used to link others to his web sites, [defendant] exceeds any measure of reasonable necessity in using the Pycnogenol mark. Moreover, the constant use of Horphag's Pycnogenol trademark and variants thereof, such as "the Original French Pycnogenol", likely suggests that Horphag sponsors or is associated with [defendant's] web sites and products.

Noting the district court's finding that defendant had "expressly admitted that [by the metatag use of the mark] he intended for his web sites to gain priority in an Internet search for Pycnogenol," the appellate court also affirmed the award of attorneys' fees to plaintiff.

Fair use principles apply. (See Chapter 7). *Bihari v. Gross*, 119 F. Supp. 2d 309 (S.D.N.Y. 2000), for example, after relinquishing the domain names "bihari.com" and "bihariinteriors.com" for sites critical of plaintiff, defendant used plaintiff's "Bihari Interiors" name in the metatags for defendant's "designscam.com" site which again criticized plaintiff. In denying preliminary relief the court found that the metatags fairly identified the contents of the website and disclaimers on the site showed defendant's good faith. Similarly, in *Playboy Enters. Inc. v. Welles*, 7 F. Supp. 2d 1098 (S.D. Cal. 1998), *aff'd*, 279 F.3d 796 (9th Cir. 2002) in which a former Playboy playmate was not enjoined from metatag use of the mark PLAYBOY where she had used it in good faith "to index the content of her website" and "it not only references her identity as '*Playboy*' Playmate of the Year 1981 but it may also reference the legitimate editorial uses of the term" in her website and *Interactive Prods. Corp. v. a2z Mobile Office Solutions, Inc.*, 326 F.3d 687 (6th Cir. 2003), (defendant's apparent holdover use of plaintiff's "Lap Traveler" mark, from previously selling plaintiff's product, in an address for a page in defendant's web site, was not infringing; "[b]ecause post-domain paths do not typically signify source, it is unlikely that the presence of another's trademark in a post-domain path of a URL would ever violate trademark law").

b) Keywords

Search engines commonly use website elements such as metatags for compiling their listings, but many also offer the opportunity simply to purchase the right to be prominently listed when a user types in a particular search term or "keyword." Keywords also can be purchased and used to trigger pop-up ads. In *Nissan Motor Co. v. Nissan Computer Corp.*, 204 F.R.D. 460 (C. D. Cal. 2000), for example, defendant counterclaimed that plaintiff had unlawfully paid search engines to list plaintiff's website when searchers typed in "nissan" or "nissan.com". Both parties had legitimate rights in the mark NISSAN; plaintiff for automobiles and other vehicles, and defendant for computer sales and services. Defendant owned the domain name www.nissan.com. The court initially reasoned that that "[t]here appears to be no good cause for not extending" the law respecting improper use of metatags, "to cases where one infringes or dilutes another's mark by purchasing a search term — as opposed to using another's mark in one's metatag for the purpose of manipulating a search engine's results list." However, that law did not apply in this case because plaintiff had valid rights in "Nissan," and by extension, the right to purchase as a search term that mark with the ".com" top level domain name added. *Cf. Picture It Sold!, Inc. v. I Sold It, LLC*, 199 Fed. Appx. 631 (9th Cir. 2006) (if, on remand, plaintiff could show defendants purchased key word advertising based on plaintiff's trademark as a search term, the lower court would have to "resolve the somewhat difficult question of whether this activitiy is sufficiently analogous to metatag use so as to be prohibited").

In *Playboy Enters. v. Netscape Communs. Corp.*, 354 F.3d 1020 (9th Cir. 2004), in which Netscape had engaged in keying third party banner ads to searches for Playboy's marks on Netscape's search engine. Netscape sold advertisers a list of search terms related to sex and adult-oriented entertainment, including "playboy" and "playmate," and required the advertisers to link their banner ads to the terms. Consequently, when a user typed in "playboy" or "playmate" or another listed term, the advertiser's banner ad would appear on the search page. The ads had "Click Here" buttons that linked to the advertiser's web site. The district court had granted summary judgment to Netscape, but the appellate court concluded that Playboy had shown that the ads were often confusingly labeled or not labeled at all, and that there were issues of fact as to whether the practice created initial interest confusion. The appellate court also rejected Netscape's fair use defense, noting that it listed over 400 terms for the advertisers and "there is nothing indispensable, in this context", about using Playboy's marks.

Some decisions have turned on whether the keyword triggering of pop-up advertisements is actionable "use" of the trademark under the Lanham Act. In *1-800 Contacts, Inc. v. WhenU.com, Inc.*, 414 F.3d 400 (2[d] Cir. 2005), for example, Plaintiff 1-800 Contacts, Inc. ("1-800") distributed contact lenses. Defendant WhenU.com, Inc. ("WhenU") used proprietary software to monitor and provide content-relevant pop-up advertisements to Internet users. WhenU's software "randomly selects an advertisement from the corresponding product or service category to deliver to a [consumer's] computer screen at roughly the same time the web site or search result sought by the [consumer] appears." *1-800-Contacts*, 414 F.3d at 400. 1-800 sued WhenU, claiming WhenU infringed its trademarks by causing competitor's pop-up ads to appear whenever the consumer accessed 1-800's web site. 1-800 claimed that the pop-up ads infringed because: the ads changed the appearance of 1-800's web site; they appeared to be authorized by 1-800; and the ads interfered with the design and function of the web site. The district court preliminarily enjoined WhenU from using 1-800's trademarks in connection with WhenU's contextual advertising. WhenU filed an interlocutory appeal.

The Second Circuit reversed and remanded, holding that "as a matter of law, WhenU does not 'use' 1-800's trademarks within the meaning of the Lanham Act, 15 U.S.C. § 1127, when it (1) includes 1-800's web site address, which is almost identical to 1-800's trademark, in an unpublished directory of terms that trigger delivery of

WhenU's contextually relevant advertising to [computer users]; or (2) causes separate, branded pop-up ads to appear on a [computer user's] computer screen either above, below, or along the bottom edge of the 1-800 web site window." *1–800–Contacts*414 F.3d at 403. The court therefore did not need to address whether confusion was likely. The court noted that "WhenU does not 'place' 1-800 trademarks on any goods or services in order to pass them off as emanating from or authorized by 1-800," and WhenU, unlike other providers of pop-up advertisements, "does not disclose the proprietary contents of [its] directory to its advertising clients nor does it permit these clients to request or purchase specified keywords to add to the directory." *1–800–Contacts*414 F.3d at 408–409. "A company's internal utilization of a trademark in a way that does not communicate it to the public is analogous to a[n] individual's private thoughts about a trademark. Such conduct simply does not violate the Lanham Act, which is concerned with the use of trademarks in connection with the sale of goods or services in a manner likely to lead to consumer confusion as to the source of the goods or services." *Id.*

The court analogized WhenU's pop-up ad scheme to a commonly used marketing technique:

> [A] drug store typically places its own store-brand generic products next to the trademarked products they emulate in order to induce a customer who has specifically sought out the trademarked product to consider the store's less-expensive alternative. WhenU employs the same marketing strategy by informing [computer users] who have sought out a specific trademarked product about available coupons, discounts, or alternative products that may be of interest to them." *1–800–Contacts* 414 F.3d at 411.

The court also concluded that computer users who had downloaded WhenU's software had implicitly authorized the pop-ups.

See also Gator.com Corp. v. L.L. Bean, Inc., 398 F.3d 1125 (9th Cir. 2005) (pop-up ad provider Gator.com settled claim for infringement filed by L.L .Bean regarding Gator.com's placement of ads for other vendors on L.L. Bean web site).

Many courts, in contrast, have followed the reasoning of *Playboy v. Netscape*, above, and *Brookfield Communications, Inc. v. West Coast Entertainment Corp.*, 174 F.3d 1036 (9th Cir. 1999) (affirming preliminary injunction against defendant's metatag use of plaintiff's "moviebuff" trademark; case excerpted in Chapter 6), in finding the sale and purchase of another's brands as keywords constitute trademark use. These courts have interpreted "use in commerce" broadly to mean commercial uses in which defendants realize commercial benefits through the keyword sale or purchase. Such findings have allowed these courts to proceed to determine whether confusion is likely. This has been applied in cases brought against defendant search engines for selling keywords and promoting third party infringement, as well as in cases brought against competitors of plaintiffs that have purchased plaintiffs' trademarks for use in keyword advertising.

In *Government Employees Insurance Co. v. Google, Inc.*, 330 F. Supp. 2d 700 (E.D. Va. 2004), plaintiff alleged numerous Lanham Act trademark claims arising out of the sale by defendants Google and Overture of plaintiff's trademarks as keywords for sponsored links. Defendants moved to dismiss the complaint, arguing that the plaintiff did not sufficiently allege use "in commerce" or "in connection with the sale, offering for sale, or advertising of goods and services" because it failed to allege that defendants used the marks as source identifiers. *Id.* at 702. Further, defendants claimed that because they used the marks only in internal computer algorithms that never appeared to the user, the user could not be confused. *Id.* The court denied defendants' motion to dismiss the Lanham Act claims, finding that GEICO sufficiently pled trademark use by including allegations that defendants sold keywords that triggered links to sponsored advertisements. *Id.* at 704. It further ruled that "when defendants sell the rights to link advertising to plaintiff's trademarks, defendants are using the trademarks in commerce in a way that may imply that defendants have permission from the trademark holder to do so." *Id.* The court opted for this interpretation of "use in commerce" employed in

Playboy over the narrow one espoused in the WhenU.com cases, believing the former line of cases to be "better reasoned." *Id.* at 703. The court left open the factual issue of whether confusion was likely. *Id.* at 704.

Other district courts subsequently applied this broad reading of "use in commerce" for keyword transactions. In *800-JR Cigar, Inc. v. GoTo.com, Inc.*, 437 F. Supp. 2d 273 (D.N.J. 2006), plaintiff cigar dealer sued defendant, a "pay-for-priority Internet search engine," for its unauthorized sale of plaintiff's trademarks. *Id.* at 277. Relying on the GEICO analysis, the court concluded as a matter of law that defendant was making trademark use of plaintiff's marks. *Id.* at 285. It found that defendant was using the marks in commerce in three ways: 1) by accepting bids from plaintiff's competitors to pay for prominence in the search results, defendant traded on the value of plaintiff's marks; 2) by ranking sponsored links above naturally occurring search results, defendant "injected itself into the marketplace, acting as a conduit to steer potential customers away from [plaintiff] to [plaintiff's] competitors"; and 3) through its Search Term Suggestion Tool, defendant specifically marketed plaintiff's marks to third parties. *Id.* The court found material issues of fact as to whether confusion was likely and denied defendant's motion for summary judgment on the Lanham Act claims. *Id.* at 292.

Subsequent cases in other districts relied on GEICO and JR Cigar to rule similarly. *See, e.g., Buying for the Home, LLC v. Humble Abode, LLC*, 459 F. Supp. 2d 310 (D.N.J. 2006) (purchasing keywords for AdWords meets the Lanham Act's use requirement); *Int'l Profit Assocs. v. Paisola*, 461 F. Supp. 2d 672 (N.D. Ill. 2006) (granting plaintiff temporary restraining order upon finding that purchasing keywords for AdWords was a trademark use that was likely to create confusion); *Edina Realty, Inc. v. TheMLSonline.com*, 2006 U.S. Dist. LEXIS 13775 (D. Minn. March 20, 2006) ("While not a conventional 'use in commerce,' defendant nevertheless uses [plaintiff's] mark commercially [by purchasing the mark as a search term]").

How should courts weigh these concerns about the statutory requirement of "use in commerce" and the public interest in having courts assess whether confusion is likely?

See generally , Welch, Google v. American Blind & Wallpaper: Settled Case Doesn't End National Keyword Debate, Lexis Expert Commentary, 2007; STUCKEY, INTERNET AND ONLINE LAW, Ch. 7 (2006); Barrett, *Internet Trademark Suits and the Demise of Trademark Use*, 39 U.C. DAVIS L. REV. 371 (2006); *Suh, Intellectual Property Law and Competitive Internet Advertising Technologies: Why Legitimate Pop-Up Advertising Practices Should Be Protected*, 79 ST. JOHN'S L. REV. 161 (2005); *Rothman, Initial Interest Confusion: Standing at the Crossroads of Trademark Law*, 27 CARDOZO L. REV. 105 (2005); McCarthy, *Metatags and the Sale of Keywords in Search Engine Advertising: Confusing Consumer Confusion with Choice*, 9 INTELL. PROP. L. BULL. 137 (2005); *Recent Development, Making Your Mark on Google*, 18 HARV. J.L. & TECH. 479 (2005); Widmaier, *Use, Liability, and the Structure of Trademark Law*, 33 HOFSTRA L. REV. 603 (2004); *Dogan & Lemley, Trademarks and Consumer Search Costs on the Internet*, 41 HOUS. L. REV. 777 (2004); Grynberg, *The Road Not Taken: Initial Interest Confusion, Consumer Search Costs, and the Challenge of the Internet*, 28 SEATTLE U.L. REV. 97 (2004); *Doellinger, "Internet, Metatags and Initial Interest Confusion: A Look to the Past to Reconceptualize the Future"*, 41 IDEA 173 (2001); *Kucala, Jr., Putting the Meat Back in Meta-Tags*, 2001 J.L., TECH. & POL'Y (2001).

c) Linking

The Internet practices of linking and framing also have, on occasion, run afoul of the Lanham Act and unfair competition laws. Linking and framing are techniques that can be used on websites to provide access to other sites. Hypertext links, generally referred to as links, are active buttons and text on web pages that, when selected, can immediately take the user to another website. Deep linking involves linking to "an internal or subsidiary page of a website located at a lower level or several levels down from the home page." Tsilas, *Minimizing Potential Liability Associated With Linking and Framing on the World Wide Web*, 8 COMM. LAW CONSPECTUS 85, 86 (2000). Thus, deep linking involves the circumvention of the other site's home page or any other intervening pages. Unlike linking, framing allows a user to view content from another website without ever leaving the first site. Content from the second site is brought into the first site, and thus the content from the second site is viewed through some of the original website's content - the frame.

Linking to other web pages has become a fundamental means of navigating the Internet and is generally viewed as legally permissible. Nevertheless, linking has been held unlawful in some contexts. For example, in *Nissan Motor Co., Ltd. v. Nissan Computer Corp.*, 89 F. Supp. 2d 1134 (C.D. Cal. 2000), *aff'd without op.*, 246 F.3d 675 (9th Cir. 2003), the defendant, a computer services company, offered computer-related information and services at its websites at nissan.com and nissan.net, where computer-related information and services were offered. While the initial use apparently was in good faith, subsequently defendant's website at nissan.com began displaying car-related advertisements and links to various car merchandisers like "cartrackers.com." The district court preliminarily enjoined the defendant from posting car-related advertisements and car-related Internet links on either of the websites. As the court noted, "by posting automobile related links and advertisements, the defendant derives advertising revenue due to the diversion of a consumer's initial interest in [plaintiff's] Nissan vehicles." *Nissan*, 89 F. Supp. 2d at 1164. Defendant was further directed to prominently display a disclaimer of affiliation with plaintiff, which also would identify plaintiff's correct website address. A link to plaintiff's site was not required, and defendant was permitted to continue use of "Nissan" in its metatags.

d)   Deep Linking

Website owners often consider deep linking to their site problematic, because it reduces the amount of time spent on the site and can bypass disclaimers and advertisements. An additional concern with deep linking is the implication it may produce that the two sites are associated and involved in some form of business relationship. *See* Tontodonato, *Deep-Linking: Sure You Can Exploit My Trademark, Weaken Its Strength, and Make Yourself Money While Doing it*, 22 T. JEFFERSON L. REV. 201, 202 (2000). Deep linking has not yet been squarely addressed by an appellate court, but a few cases have raised the issue.

For example, in *Ticketmaster Corp. v. Microsoft Corp.*, No. 97-3055 DDP (C.D. Cal.), the defendant operated a Seattle Sidewalk website that linked directly to the plaintiff's ticket purchasing page, several layers within the Ticketmaster website. Ticketmaster objected to this deep link, in part, because the bypassed pages contained much of Ticketmaster's advertising. Unfortunately, the suit did not resolve any of the legal issues surrounding deep linking, as the case was settled with the defendant agreeing to link to Ticketmaster's home page rather than deep linking to the purchasing page. *Compare Ticketmaster Corp. v. Tickets.com, Inc.*, 54 U.S.P.Q.2d 1344 (C.D. Cal. 2000), in which the court found insufficient harm to Ticketmaster from the deep linking by Tickets.com to warrant preliminary relief, particularly given the benefit to Ticketmaster of ticket sales through the link. *See generally* Tsilas, *Minimizing Potential Liability Associated with Linking and Framing on the World Wide Web*, 8 COMM. LAW CONSPECTUS 85, 88 (2000). A Scottish court did issue an interim interdict (analogous to a preliminary injunction) preventing deep linking. *Shetland Times Ltd. v. Wills*, Court of Sessions, Edinburg (Oct. 24, 1996). Nevertheless, the issue remains unsettled in the United States. *See generally*, Docking, *Internet Links: The Good, the Bad, the Tortious, and a Two-Part Test*, 36 U. TOL. L. REV. 367 (2005).

The Georgia legislature passed a Criminal Linking Act in 1996. *See* Ga. Code Ann. § 16-9-93.1 (1996). The statute prohibited the creation of links that contained another's trademark without the express permission of the trademark owner. However, a Georgia district court permanently enjoined enforcement of the act because it contained content-based restrictions and was not narrowly tailored. *American Civil Liberties Union of Georgia v. Miller*, 977 F. Supp. 1228 (N.D. Ga. 1997).

e) Framing

Framing can create likely confusion as to the source of the content displayed on the framing site, or the relationship between the framed and framing sites. Framing also will often cover up the advertisements displayed on the framed site, potentially affecting the advertising revenue of the framed site. One of the first cases addressing the issue of framing was *Washington Post Co. v. Total News*, No. 97 Civ. 1190 (S.D.N.Y. 1997). The defendant's website had a news directory that framed the content of numerous online news services. The framing brought the content of the external sites within the frame of the defendant's site, which included the defendant's trademark, URL address, and commercial banners. Before the court was able to address the issue, a settlement was reached that prohibited the defendant from framing the content. *See* Chan, *Internet Framing-Complement or Hijack?*, 5 MICH. TELECOMM. & TECH. L. REV. 143, 149 (1998-99). In *Hard Rock Café v. Morton*, 1999 U.S. Dist. LEXIS 8340 (S.D.N.Y. 1999), the court ordered defendants to cease framing another site, but did so in the context of a licensing agreement between the parties. The decision therefore may have little precedential value outside of such agreements. Defendant's proposal to cure the problem by instead linking to a third party site was rejected at 1999 U.S. Dist. LEXIS 13760 (S.D.N.Y. 1999) ("By erecting a link to CDNOW in return for a commission, Hard Rock Hotel uses the Hard Rock Hotel Marks to direct Internet traffic and promotes and profits from the sale of CDs" in violation of the parties' contract). *See also* Tsilas, *Minimizing Potential Liability Associated with Linking and Framing on the World Wide Web, supra* at 93.

Compare Kelly v. Arriba Soft Corp., 280 F.3d 934 (9th Cir. 2002), a copyright-based decision in which defendant operated an Internet image search engine that displayed its image results as small, low resolution "thumbnails". The thumbnails linked to the actual images on other people's websites, and were framed by defendant's web page's text and advertising. Defendant had thirty-five of the plaintiff photographer's images in its database, and plaintiff sued for copyright infringement.

The appellate court upheld the use of the thumbnails as fair use, concluding users were unlikely to enlarge them to a more standard size because of the low resolution, and that defendant's use served a different function than plaintiff's, i.e., improving access to Internet information rather than artistic expression, with no harm to plaintiff's market or the value of the photographs. The court did hold that defendant's display of full-size images of plaintiff's photographs was copyright infringement, violating plaintiff's exclusive right to their public display.

Notes on False and Misleading Advertising

1. Comparative Use

Unauthorized comparative advertising use of a competitor's trademark will not create liability under § 43(a) in the absence of misrepresentations or likelihood of confusion as to source. In *Diversified Marketing, Inc. v. Estee Lauder, Inc.*, 705 F. Supp. 128 (S.D.N.Y. 1988), the court held that Diversified's BEAUTY USA advertising slogan "If you like ESTEE LAUDER . . . You'll love BEAUTY USA" was permissible comparative advertising. Similarly, in *Smith v. Chanel, Inc.*, 402 F.2d 562 (9th Cir. 1968), defendant was held entitled to advertise "We dare you to detect any difference between Chanel #5 (25.00) and Ta'Ron's 2nd Chance. $7.00." See also the discussion in Permitted Use in Chapter 8, *supra. Compare Tyco Industries, Inc. v. Lego Systems, Inc.*, 5 U.S.P.Q.2d 1023 (D.N.J. 1987), in which the court enjoined Tyco's false comparative claim that its toy building block set "looks and feels like Lego," *Sony*

Computer Ent. Am., Inc. v. Bleem, 214 F.3d 1022 (9th Cir. 2000) (unauthorized use of screen shots from plaintiff's video game for comparison of clarity of defendant's video game screen display was fair use), and *Highmark Inc. v. UPMC Health Plan, Inc.*, 276 F.3d 160 (3[d] Cir. 2001) (defendant liable for false statements in comparative newspaper advertisement).

Defendant's comparative advertising was enjoined in *Charles of the Ritz Group Ltd v. Quality King Distributors*, 832 F.2d 1317 (2[d] Cir. 1987), where the court affirmed a preliminary injunction against use of the phrases "If you like OPIUM, you'll love OMNI" for a low-priced "smell-alike", and the substitute phrase proffered by defendant, "If You Like OPIUM, a fragrance by Yves Saint Laurent, You'll Love OMNI, a fragrance by Deborah Intl'l Beauty. Yves Saint Laurent and Opium are not related in any manner to Deborah Int'l Beauty and Omni." As to the latter, the disclaimer failed to indicate that OPIUM and OMNI were competing products sold by competitors, instead using the ambiguous phrase "not related to." Furthermore, defendant failed to introduce any evidence that the disclaimer would reduce consumer confusion.

To successfully challenge a "tests prove that my product is better than yours" claim, however, a plaintiff must only prove that the tests upon which the claim is based were not sufficiently reliable. *See, e.g., Southland Sod Farms v. Stover Seed Co.*, 108 F.3d 1134, 1139 (9th Cir. 1997); *Rhone-Poulenc Rorer Pharmaceuticals v. Marion Merrell Dow*, 93 F.3d 511, 514–15 (8th Cir. 1992) (citing cases). *See also BASF Corp. v. Old World Trading Co.*, 41 F.3d 1081 (7th Cir. 1994) (plaintiff successfully challenged defendant's ad making test-based claims by proving that the tests were never actually performed). A test-based claim was not preliminarily enjoined in *Johnson & Johnson Vision Care, Inc. v. 1-800 Contacts, Inc.*, 299 F.3d 1242 (11th Cir. 2002). In challenging the ad's test-based claim about the superiority of defendant's contact lenses, plaintiff needed to show "that the tests were not sufficiently reliable to permit [that] conclusion". The preliminary injunction was vacated where plaintiff only showed that the test design was not perfect and that the claim was potentially misleading. Alternatively, plaintiff would have needed to provide evidence of actual consumer deception, and had not done so.

A completely unsubstantiated claim may be enjoined under appropriate circumstances. *See, e.g., Novartis Consumer Health, Inc. v. Johnson & Johnson-Merck Consumer Pharmaceuticals Co.*, 290 F.3d 578 (3[d] Cir. 2002), in which the court observed that, "although the plaintiff normally has the burden to demonstrate that the defendant's advertising claim is false, a court may find that a completely unsubstantiated advertising claim by the defendant is per se false without additional evidence from the plaintiff to that effect." A preliminary injunction was affirmed against the unsubstantiated use of "Night Time Strength" in the brand name for defendant's heartburn medicine. Defendant's product name and label had conveyed to twenty–five percent of survey respondents an unsubstantiated message of all-night relief from heartburn.

2. Disparagement

Prior to the passage of the Revision Act in 1988, some courts limited § 43(a) by recognizing actions under it based on a defendant's misrepresentations about its own products, but holding the section inapplicable to misrepresentations by a defendant about *plaintiff's* products. *See, e.g., Bernard Food Industries, Inc. v. Dietene Co.*, 415 F.2d 1279 (7th Cir. 1969), *cert. denied*, 397 U.S. 912 (1970); *Oil Heat Institute v. Northwest Natural Gas*, 708 F. Supp. 1118 (D. Or. 1988).

The Revision Act expressly made misrepresentations about "*another person's* goods, services or commercial activities" actionable under § 43(a). In *U.S. Healthcare, Inc. v. Blue Cross of Greater Philadelphia*, 898 F.2d 914 (3[d] Cir.), *cert. denied*, 498 U.S. 816 (1990), for example, the court found actionable alleged advertising misrepresentations made about one another by two health care competitors, and *Holmsten Ice Rinks, Inc. v. Burley's Rink Supply, Inc.*, 14 U.S.P.Q.2d 1492 (D. Minn. 1990), defendant's false representations about plaintiff in defendant's product catalog were preliminarily enjoined.

In *National Artists Management Co. v. Weaving, National Artists*, 769 F. Supp. 1224 (S.D.N.Y. 1991), plaintiff was a leading theatrical booking agency and defendant was an ex-employee who planned to form her own booking agency. After leaving plaintiff's employ, defendant told a number of plaintiff's clients that "she was forced to terminate her relationship with [plaintiff] because of certain illegal and improper business practices engaged in by [plaintiff's] principals." *National Artists*, 769 F. Supp. at 1226. Plaintiff subsequently lost business from some of those she had contacted.

In considering defendant's motion to dismiss, the court set forth a four-prong test for stating a cause of action under § 43(a)(2): (1) "that defendant made false or misleading factual representations of the nature, characteristics, or qualities of plaintiff's services"; (2) "in commerce"; (3) "in the context of commercial advertising or commercial promotion"; and (4) "that defendants' actions made plaintiffs believe that they were likely to be damaged by such false or misleading factual misrepresentations." *Id.* at 1230. The Court then found that, aside from the truth or falsity of the representations which would have to be determined at trial, the test was satisfied. The "commercial advertising or promotion" prong was satisfied because defendant "had taken sufficient steps toward her new business for the Lanham Act to apply," (769 F. Supp. at 1234), and because her conversations had the commercial purpose of promoting that business. *See generally* Stevens, *Commercial Disparagement under Section 43(a)(1)(B) of the Lanham Act*, 7 Tul. J. Tech. & Intell. Prop. 267 (2005).

3. Dissemination

In *Fashion Boutique of Short Hills, Inc. v. Fendi USA, Inc.*, excerpted above, the Second Circuit explained that:

> the touchstone of whether a defendant's actions may be considered "commercial advertising or promotion" under the Lanham Act is that the contested representations are part of an organized campaign to penetrate the relevant market. Proof of widespread dissemination within the relevant industry is a normal concomitant of meeting this requirement. Thus, businesses harmed by isolated disparaging statements do not have redress under the Lanham Act; they must seek redress under state-law causes of action.

In *Podiatrist Ass'n v. La Cruz Azul de P.R., Inc.*, 332 F.3d 6 (1st Cir. 2003), the plaintiffs asserted that Blue Cross "falsely disparaged the health care services provided by podiatrists and actively encouraged patients to seek services from medical doctors instead." However, "a plaintiff at the very least must identify some medium or means through which the defendant disseminated information to a particular class of consumers." Plaintiff failed to plead "the use of any particular advertising or promotion medium," and dismissal therefore was affirmed. In *Rice v. Fox Broad. Co.*, 330 F.3d 1170 (9th Cir. 2003), plaintiff contended that defendant's television programs falsely claimed that they would reveal the secrets of several magic tricks "for the first time on television". Because the statements were "part of the show itself, and [were] not made in promotion or marketing" of the show, the statements were "not actionable as commercial advertising or promotion under the Lanham Act." In a Second Circuit decision after the *Fashion Boutique v. Fendi* case above, summary judgment for defendants on the federal claim was affirmed where defendants' statements in an art magazine article repudiating the authenticity of certain paintings were not "commercial advertising or promotion", and similar statements in a disseminated letter had not been shown to be false or misleading. *Boule v. Hutton*, 328 F.3d 84 (2d Cir. 2003). On remand, plaintiffs nonetheless successfully proved common law business disparagement where defendants' statements suggested that plaintiff's had unwittingly purchased fakes, or had sought to deliberately deceive prospective purchasers. *Boule v. Hutton*, 71 U.S.P.Q.2d 1691 (S.D.N.Y. 2004). *See also Aviation Charter, Inc. v. Aviation Research Group/U.S.*, 416 F.3d 864 (8th Cir. 2005) (airline charter company's commercial disparagement claim against an aviation ratings company rejected because the parties were not in competition, and also because plaintiff failed to show the statements were false and disparaging).

How much dissemination is sufficient to bring the conduct within the scope of § 43(a) normally depends on the size of the relevant market. In *Seven-Up Co. v. Coca-Cola Co.*, 86 F.3d 1379 (5th Cir. 1996), sales presentations made to bottlers by the defendant, Coca-Cola, were found actionable under § 43(a). Noting the "broad remedial purpose" of the Lanham Act, the court found that the relevant "consuming public" for Coca-Cola's sales presentations was the bottling companies that it hoped to persuade to bottle Coca-Cola's SPRITE soft drink instead of plaintiff's 7-UP. Thus, even though Coca-Cola only presented its allegedly misleading sales presentation to two of seventy-four targeted bottlers, the court held that the presentations were "disseminated sufficiently to the relevant purchasing public" for the plaintiff to properly state a claim under § 43(a). *Id.* at 1386. However, because the plaintiff failed to prove that Coca-Cola's presentations were material to several bottlers' decision to switch from Seven-Up to Coca-Cola, the court overturned the jury's liability determination. *Id.* at 1389.

See also Coastal Abstract Service, Inc. v. First American Title Insurance Co., 165 F.3d 658 (9th Cir. 1998) (a title insurance company's representation to a lender that another company was not paying its bills on time was sufficiently disseminated to be an actionable "promotion", given there were only two or three nationwide refinancing operations like that of the lender receiving the misrepresentation); *Mobius Mgmt. Sys., Inc. v. Fourth Dimension Software, Inc.*, 880 F. Supp. 1005 (S.D.N.Y. 1994) (single letter from a computer software manufacturer constituted "commercial advertising or promotion" given small market); *Gordon & Breach Science Publishers v. American Inst. of Physics*, 859 F. Supp. 1521 (S.D.N.Y. 1994) (non-profit publisher's distribution of misleading comparative surveys of scientific journals to librarians deemed "promotion" where "librarians represent the core consumers of those products"). Compare with *Sanderson v. Culligan Int'l Co.*, 415 F.3d 620, 624 (7th Cir. 2005) (allegedly false person-to-person communications at an industry trade show were potentially actionable under state law, but not the Lanham Act); *Fashion Boutique of Short Hills, Inc. v. Fendi USA, Inc.*, supra (alleged disparagement of New Jersey FENDI store by employee comments to a few inquiring customers at New York City FENDI store not "advertising or promotion"); *American Needle & Novelty v. Drew Pearson Mktg.*, 820 F. Supp. 1072 (N.D. Ill. 1993) (an allegedly false letter about plaintiff's hat business circulated to NBA team executives not "commercial advertising or promotion"); *Licata & Co. v. Goldberg*, 812 F. Supp. 403, 408 (S.D.N.Y. 1993) (concluding that the Lanham Act "would be trivialized if it were applied to statements . . . by an individual sales representative to an individual customer concerning matters which an ordinary listener would recognize as personal opinion").

In *ISI Int'l v. Borden Ladner LLP*, 316 F.3d 731 (7th Cir. 2003), defendant's allegedly disparaging letters to plaintiff's customers concerning patent rights did not constitute "commercial advertising or promotion" under § 43. Similarly, in *Sports Unlimited, Inc. v. Lankford Enterprises, Inc.*, 275 F.3d 996 (10th Cir. 2002), defendant floor installer's distribution of unfavorable competitive information about plaintiff to two persons associated with a particular project was held insufficient to constitute commercial advertising or promotion under the Lanham Act.

The Seventh Circuit analyzed whether direct oral solicitations constituted "commercial advertising or promotion" under the Lanham Act in affirming dismissal in *First Health Group Corp. v. BCE Emergis Corp.*, 269 F.3d 800 (7th Cir. 2001). It concluded that "[a]dvertising is a form of promotion to anonymous recipients, as distinguished from face-to-face communication." Consequently, "statements by a firm's sales force could not be called advertising; likewise, it is hard to see how statements of [defendant's] executives and lawyers, made over a conference table in effort to negotiate a contract . . . could be called 'commercial advertising or promotion' ". Plaintiff also failed to show that the accused statements were false or that hospital personnel were deceived by them. *Compare* this with the analysis of oral statements in the excerpt above from the Second Circuit's *Fashion Boutique v. Fendi* decision.

4. First Amendment Considerations

Are there any First Amendment constitutional limitations on preventing misrepresentations under § 43(a)? *See Consumers Union of U.S. v. General Signal Corp.*, 724 F.2d 1044, 1051–53 (2^d Cir. 1983), where the court refused to preliminarily enjoin a vacuum cleaner manufacturer's television commercials featuring accurate reference to a *Consumer Report's* magazine rating of its product, despite the plaintiff-publisher's longstanding policy against advertising use of its ratings. *Cf. Serio-US Indus. v. Plastic Recovery Techs. Corp.*, 459 F.3d 1311, 1321 (Fed. Cir. 2006) (no liability for plaintiff's communications that defendant had infringed its patents; they were "objectively reasonable," and such "marketplace statements" would create liability only if they were made in bad faith); *World Wide Ass'n of Specialty Programs v. Pure, Inc.*, 450 F.3d 1132 (10th Cir. 2006) (plaintiff had thrust "itself in the national spotlight" with respect to "the public controversy on how to deal with troubled teens," and had not shown the requisite actual malice under state law in connection with defendant's negative statements about plaintiff, nor had plaintiff shown the requisite falsity and injury under the Lanham Act).

The court dismissed a § 43(a) claim against dissemination of a pamphlet which disparaged plaintiff's paintings and sculptures as sacrilegious in *Wojnarowicz v. American Family Association*, 745 F. Supp. 130, 141–42 (S.D.N.Y. 1990). In doing so, the court cited the following legislative history:

> [T]he proposed changes in Section 43(a) should not be read in any way to limit political speech, consumer or editorial comment, parodies, satires, or other constitutionally protected material. . . . The section is narrowly drafted to encompass only clearly false and misleading commercial speech. S. 1883, 101st Cong., 1st Sess., 135 Cong. Rec. 1207, 1217 (April 13, 1989).

The court summarily held for defendant on First Amendment grounds in *Rogers v. Grimaldi*, 695 F. Supp. 112 (S.D.N.Y. 1988), *aff'd*, 875 F.2d 994 (2^d Cir. 1989). Ginger Rogers had sued under § 43(a) and state right of publicity law over an Italian film entitled "Ginger and Fred," which was about two cabaret performers who imitated her and Fred Astaire. In affirming, the Second Circuit for the first time articulated a balancing test for Lanham Act claims involving artistic expression. It stated that enjoining the distribution of artistic works does not violate the First Amendment where the public interest in avoiding consumer confusion outweighs the public interest in free expression. For movie titles using a celebrity's name, the Court held that unless the title had no artistic relevance to the underlying work or was expressly misleading, no injunction should issue. Here the title was artistically relevant to the film, and it was not expressly misleading. The Court also held that the use of Ms. Roger's name in the title was not actionable under Oregon right of publicity law.

The *Rogers v. Grimaldi* test was followed in *Mattel, Inc. v. MCA Records, Inc.*, 296 F.3d 894 (9th Cir. 2002). Under *Rogers v. Grimaldi*, the title "Barbie Girl" had relevance to the underlying song that parodied values associated with the famous doll, and was not explicitly misleading. "The *only* indication that Mattel might be associated with the song is the use of Barbie in the title; if this were enough to satisfy this prong of the *Rogers* test, it would render *Rogers* a nullity." Summary judgment against plaintiff was affirmed where the public interest in avoiding confusion did not outweigh the public interest in free expression. *Mattel* is excerpted in Chapter 9.

In *ETW v. Jireh Publishing, Inc.*, 332 F.3d 915 (6th Cir. 2003), the court used a

Rogers v. Grimaldi analysis in permitting defendant's use of golfer Tiger Woods' name on the inside flap of an envelope containing an art print featuring his image, and in the narrative description for the print. A *Rogers v. Grimaldi* defense was considered in *Parks v. LaFace Records*, 329 F.3d 437 (6th Cir. 2003), in considering the use of civil rights icon Rosa Parks' name as a song title. The appellate court was skeptical that the title had the necessary relevance to the song's content because: the key "back of the bus" phrase in the song "has absolutely nothing to do with Rosa Parks," the song could be considered "antithetical to the qualities identified with Rosa Parks," and her name may have been "appropriated solely because of the vastly increased marketing power" it would bring. The court nonetheless remanded for the lower court to determine whether the song title had the requisite artistic relevance to sustain a *Rogers* defense. *Parks* is excerpted in Chapter 9. *See also* Blackburn, *Title Blanding: How the Lanham Act Strips Artistic Expression from Song Titles*, 22 CARDOZO ARTS & ENT. L.J. 837 (2005); Zimdahl, *A Celebrity Balancing Act: An Analysis of Trademark Protection under the Lanham Act and the First Amendment Artistic Express Defense*, 99 NW. J.L. REV. 1817 (2005), and the discussion of permitted use in artistic works in Chapter 7.

> *Compare* the following footnote in *Vidal Sassoon, supra*:
>
> Bristol argues that, because its advertisements are supposedly protected by the First Amendment to the Constitution, Judge Stewart should have imposed a higher burden on Sassoon. This argument is without merit. Misleading commercial speech is beyond the protective reach of the First Amendment, *Central Hudson Gas & Electric Co. v. Public Service Comm'n.*, 447 U.S. 557, 566 (1980). The Lanham Act's content-neutral prohibition of false and misleading advertising does not arouse First Amendment concerns that justify alteration of the normal standard for preliminary injunctive relief. *Dallas Cowboys Cheerleaders, Inc. v. Pussycat Cinema, Ltd.*, 604 F.2d 200, 206 (2[d] Cir. 1979).

Compare American Diary Queen Corporation v. New Line Productions, Inc., 35 F. Supp. 2d 727 (D. Minn. 1998), in which defendant was preliminarily enjoined from using the name "Dairy Queens" as the title for its new movie. Described as a "mock documentary, satirizing beauty contests in rural Minnesota," the film contained no references to plaintiff's famous DAIRY QUEEN trademark other than in its proposed title. The court found that confusion was likely as to the source of the film, or that consumers would likely believe that New Line had received plaintiff's endorsement or permission to use the mark. The court also found plaintiff would likely succeed on its federal dilution by tarnishment claim, because of the association of "the enormous goodwill created and possessed, by [plaintiff] and represented by its 'Dairy Queen' mark" with the "unwholesome content of the film." Despite defendant's assertions that its marketing and advertising would clarify that plaintiff was not connected in any way with the film, the court found that in the word-of-mouth context of film publicity "even the best efforts to append a distinguishing disclaimer would be of no account". As to defendant's First Amendment defense, "[t]here is no effort of any kind to modify or muzzle New Line's views or expressions concerning the midwest beauty contests, 'dairy country,' or the film's asserted objectionable sexual, racial or religious content. ADQ simply wants to keep the public from developing the sense that it is a sponsor or endorser of New Line's film, or has voluntarily lent its name to it."

First Amendment considerations are discussed in greater detail in Chapter 9.

5. Proof of False and Misleading Advertising

a) Literally False Claims

Increasingly sophisticated methods of marketing and advertising have in turn made possible more sophisticated methods of misleading the public as to relative qualities of products in the market. When the representation is literally or "facially" false, a number of courts have held that injunctive relief may be granted under § 43(a) without reference to the advertisement's impact on the buying public. *Warner-Lambert Co. v. BreathAsure, Inc.*, 204 F.3d 87, 96 (3ᵈ Cir. 2000) (because defendant's claim "that its capsules could assure fresh breath was literally false, Warner-Lambert did not have to introduce consumer testimony, marketing surveys or proof of lost profits to enjoin [its] use"); *S.C. Johnson & Sons, Inc. v. The Clorox Co.*, 241 F.3d 232 (2ᵈ Cir. 2001), (defendant's television ads showing goldfish in distress as plaintiff's food storage bag rapidly leaked water were "literally false based on the evidence presented at trial of the real risk and rate of leakage from [plaintiff's] bags"); *Coca-Cola Co. v. Tropicana Products, Inc.*, 690 F.2d 312 (2ᵈ Cir. 1982) (visual and aural components of television ad suggesting defendant's pasteurized and sometimes frozen orange juice comes fresh-squeezed from the orange held blatantly false).

b) Literally True but Misleading Claims

When the claims made are literally true but nonetheless have the potential to mislead, confuse or deceive, it becomes necessary for a court to consider evidence of public reaction to the advertisement. *Porous Media Corp. v. Pall Corp.*, 110 F.3d 1329, 1334 (8ᵗʰ Cir. 1997); "The question in such cases is — what does the person to whom the advertisement is addressed find to be the message?" *American Brands, Inc. v. R.J. Reynolds Tobacco Co.*, 413 F. Supp. 1352, 1357 (S.D.N.Y. 1976). *Compare Rhone-Poulenc Rorer Pharmaceuticals v. Marion Merrell Dow*, 93 F.3d 511, 516 (8ᵗʰ Cir. 1992), where the court found that advertisements featuring images of two gasoline pumps and two identical airline tickets available at different prices accompanied by the rhetorical question "Which one would you choose?" implicitly made a false claim that the two drugs at issue were comparable when they were not. Because this "implicit message was literally false," the court did not require proof of actual consumer confusion to support a finding of false advertising liability. *Id. Compare also United Industries Corporation v. Clorox*, 140 F.3d 1175 (8ᵗʰ Cir. 1998), in which Clorox and United Industries had produced competing cockroach bait insecticide products. Clorox claimed that United falsely advertised that its "Maxattrax" product "Kills Roaches in 24 Hours." The appellate court found no reversible error in the district court's denial of preliminary relief because Maxattrax did, in fact, kill roaches in 24 hours, and the lower court's conclusion that there was no implicit message of complete control of an infestation problem within 24 hours was not clearly erroneous. In *Scott Co. v. United Industries Corp.*, 315 F.3d 264 (4ᵗʰ Cir. 2002), the depiction of mature crabgrass on defendant's product packaging did not convey a literally false message that the product killed mature crabgrass, in part because prominent accompanying text conveyed a different message. Plaintiff's consumer reaction evidence was found unreliable and preliminary relief was denied.

In appropriate cases, a presumption of public deception will arise if the defendant intended such deception. *See, e.g., Cashmere & Camel Hair M'frs Institute v. Saks Fifth Avenue*, 284 F.3d 302 (1ˢᵗ Cir. 2002) ("[i]t is well-established that if there is proof that a defendant *intentionally* set out to deceive or mislead consumers, a presumption arises that consumers in fact have been deceived").

c) Literally False by Necessary Implication

A claim also may be literally false "by necessary implication." *See* the *Time Warner Cable v. Directv* case excerpted above. In *Novartis Consumer Health, Inc. v. Johnson & Johnson-Merck Consumer Pharmaceuticals Co.*, 290 F.3d 578 (3ᵈ Cir. 2002) the name "Mylanta Night Time Strength" for defendant's heartburn medicine was literally false by necessary implication because it falsely conveyed the message that the product "was specially made to work at night". *See also Clorox Co. Puerto Rico v. Proctor & Gamble Commercial Co.*, 228 F.3d 24, 35 (1ˢᵗ Cir. 2000) ("Whiter is not possible" for detergent in ad's context might make a literally false claim, by necessary implication, of equality or superiority to a detergent and bleach combination); *Zoller Labs, LLC v. NBTY, Inc.*, 111 Fed. Appx. 978 (10 [th] Cir. 2004) (unpub'd) ("Compare to the Ingredients of Zantex-3" was not literally false by necessary implication because "only an unambiguous message can be literally false", and defendant's statement could be interpreted in more than one way); *and Rhone-Poulenc Rorer Pharmaceuticals v. Marion Merrell Dow*, 93 F.3d 511, 516 (8th Cir. 1992), where the court found that advertisements featuring images of two gasoline pumps and two identical airline tickets available at different prices accompanied by the rhetorical question "Which one would you choose?" implicitly made a false claim that the two drugs at issue were comparable when they were not. Because this "implicit message was literally false," the court did not require proof of actual consumer confusion to support its finding of false advertising liability. *Compare United Indus. Corp. v. Clorox Co.*, 140 F.3d 1175 (8th Cir. 1998), in which Clorox and United Industries had produced competing cockroach bait insecticide products. Clorox claimed that United falsely advertised that its "Maxattrax" product "Kills Roaches in 24 Hours." The appellate court found no reversible error in the district court's denial of preliminary relief because Maxattrax did, in fact, kill roaches in 24 hours, and the lower court's conclusion that there was no implicit message of complete control of an infestation problem within 24 hours was not clearly erroneous.

d) Materiality

If a plaintiff establishes that a claim is literally false, should it also have to show that the claim is material to consumers? In *Pizza Hut, Inc. v. Papa John's Int'l, Inc.*, 227 F.3d 489, 487 (5th Cir. 2000), the Fifth Circuit determined a showing of materiality was not required: "with respect to materiality, when the statements of fact at issue are shown to be literally false, the plaintiff need not introduce evidence of the impact the statement had on consumers. In such a circumstance, the court will assume that the statements actually misled consumers." *Followed: James P. Logan, Jr. v. Burgers Ozark Country Cured Hams, Inc.*, 263 F.3d 447 (5th Cir. 2001) (enjoining defendant's literally false claim that it sold spiral sliced meat products when it no longer did). *Compare Johnson & Johnson Vision Care, Inc. v. 1-800 Contacts, Inc.*, 299 F.3d 1242 (11th Cir. 2002), in which the court concluded, "[t]he plaintiff must establish materiality even when a court finds that the defendant's advertisement is literally false." In that case, although the defendant contact lens manufacturer falsely claimed that it contracted with "eye doctors" rather than accurately claiming that it did so with "eye care practitioners," plaintiff failed to show that this was material to consumer decisions. *See also Cashmere & Camel Hair Mfg. Inst. v. Saks Fifth Ave.*, 284 F.3d 302, 311 (1st Cir. 2002) (to show materiality, the plaintiff must establish that "the defendant's deception is likely to influence [the] purchasing decision"); *Pelman v. McDonald's Corp.*, 396 F.3d 508, 511 (2[d] Cir. 2005) (New York state law does not require proof of actual reliance on the deceptive acts or practices). In an unusual case, *B. Sanfield, Inc. v. Finlay Fine Jewelry Corp.*, 258 F.3d 578 (7th Cir. 2001), the Seventh Circuit found that defendant's claim of offering a 50% reduction from some higher price for its jewelry was literally false because the sale price was its regular price, but affirmed the denial of relief because plaintiff failed to show "either financial injury in the past or any likelihood of future business losses." Is this an example of a deceptive practice so entrenched that it has no demonstrable effect on the market? *See generally* Leighton, *Materiality and Puffing in Lanham Act False Advertising Cases: The Proofs, Presumptions and Pretexts*, 94 TMR 979 (2004).

e) Market Research and Surveys

Market research studies have played an increasingly important role in demonstrating public reaction to accused advertising claims which are not literally false. In *American Home Products Corp. v. Johnson & Johnson*, 577 F.2d 160 (2[d] Cir. 1978) a declaratory judgment action brought under § 43(a), plaintiff's television ads claimed that plaintiff's Anacin aspirin product was superior to defendant's Tylenol pain reliever in reducing inflammation. The district court was unable to reach a definitive conclusion on the truthfulness of this claim, but agreed with defendant that the ads also implicitly and falsely claimed pain-relieving superiority. Relying heavily on consumer reaction test data, the court enjoined the advertisement of such claims. In affirming, the Court of Appeals stated,

> What the ASI test shows, then, is the powerful "subliminal" influence of modern advertisements . . . . The survey reveals that the word "inflammation" triggers pain association, and pain association is what both advertisements are all about. The district court properly relied on these conclusions in finding that the commercial claimed general analgesic superiority.

The Court of Appeals also found that such an implicit claim clearly was intended by plaintiff. *Id.* at 166, n.12.

As discussed in Chapter 6, , surveys may be conducted during, or in anticipation of, litigation, to help prove the truth or falsity of advertising claims as perceived by consumers. *See, e.g., Novartis Consumer Health, Inc. v. Johnson & Johnson-Merck Consumer Pharmaceuticals Co.*, 290 F.3d 578 (3th Cir. 2002) (defendant's product name and label conveyed to twenty-five percent of survey respondents a deceptive message of all-night relief from heartburn). The practice has become so common that the Tenth Circuit has observed that, in cases involving "ambiguous or true-but-misleading statements . . . [s]uccessful plaintiffs usually present evidence of the public's reaction through consumer surveys." *American Council of Certified Podiatric Physician and Surgeons v. American Board of Podiatric Surgery, Inc.*, 185 F.3d 606, 616–617 (10th Cir. 1999). In that case, a jury found for plaintiff, but the district court nonetheless granted defendant judgment as a matter of law. Plaintiff had failed to introduce sufficient evidence that the ambiguous or allegedly misleading advertising claims had caused actual deception. In affirming, the appellate court noted that plaintiff had not followed the usual course for such claims by submitting a consumer survey or other market research.

Compare, however, *Mead Johnson & Co. v. Abbott Laboratories*, 201 F.3d 883 (7th Cir. 1999), in which the claim "1st Choice of Doctors" on packaging for defendant's infant formula product was held to truthfully convey "that more physicians preferred this product than any of its rivals." In granting a preliminary injunction, the district court had relied on a survey which purportedly showed that consumers understood the phrase to mean that at least a majority of physicians preferred the product, when in reality only a plurality did. Rejecting that survey evidence, the Seventh Circuit held that, while surveys are "accepted ways to probe for things such as confusion as to source", they should not be used to determine the meaning of words when the ordinary meaning is plain. The court observed that defendant's product *was* "the '1st Choice of Doctors' according to ordinary usage. . . . When [as here] the absolute preference for the leading product is high, and the difference in support from the medical profession substantial, it is all but impossible to call the claim of 'first choice' misleading."

f)   Examples of False Advertising Decisions

In *McNeil-P.C.C., Inc. v. Bristol-Myers Squibb Co.*, 938 F.2d 1544, 1549, 1551 (2[d] Cir. 1991), the court stated that a plaintiff must show the alleged substantiation for a defendant's advertising claim is "not sufficiently reliable to conclude with reasonable certainty that [it] established the claim made" and, finding plaintiff had done so, enjoined defendant's claim that its pain relieving product "works better" than plaintiff's. In *ALPO Petfoods, Inc. v. Ralston Purina Co.*, 913 F.2d 958 (D.C. Cir. 1990), both defendant's advertising claim that its dog food prevented canine hip dysplasia, and plaintiff's advertising claim that its dog food contained the formula most preferred by veterinarians, were held material and false; the case was remanded for reassessment of each party's damages. *See also BASF Corp. v. Old World Trading Co.*, 41 F.3d 1081 (7th

Cir. 1994) (enjoining unsubstantiated claim that plaintiff's private label antifreeze met certain industry specifications and awarding plaintiff $4.5 million); *Grove Fresh Distributors v. New England Apple Products*, 969 F.2d 552 (7th Cir. 1992) (defendant falsely advertised its orange juice as "100% Florida" when the juice was adulterated with sugar and pulpwash); *Castrol, Inc. v. Quaker State Corp.*, 977 F.2d 57 (2[d] Cir. 1992) (defendant falsely advertised that tests proved its motor oil provided better protection against engine wear); *U-Haul Int'l, Inc. v. Jartran, Inc.*, 681 F.2d 1159 (9th Cir. 1982) (various advertising claims as to the superiority of defendant's trucks and trailers over those of plaintiff preliminarily enjoined); *American Home Products Corp. v. Abbott Laboratories*, 522 F. Supp. 1035 (S.D.N.Y. 1981) (advertising claims that hemorrhoid preparation was "new" and stopped pain immediately preliminarily enjoined); *Toro Co. v. Textron, Inc.*, 499 F. Supp. 241 (D. Del. 1980) (various advertising claims as to the superiority of defendant's snow thrower over that of plaintiff preliminarily enjoined).

Compare Pizza Hut, Inc. v. Papa John's Int'l, Inc., 227 F.3d 489, 499 (5th Cir. 2000) (slogan "Better Ingredients, Better Pizza" was non-actionable puffery; "[e]ach half of the slogan amounts to little more than an exaggerated opinion of superiority that no consumer would be justified in relying upon"); *Lipton v. Nature Co.*, 71 F.3d 464, 474 (2[d] Cir. 1995), (defendant's promotional claim that he had conducted "thorough[] research" in compiling a list of terms that he allegedly copied from plaintiff was held "mere puffing"); *Johnson & Johnson-Merck Cons. Pharm. Co. v. Rhone Poulenc Rohrer Pharm.*, 19 F.3d 125 (3[d] Cir. 1994), in which the court concluded that defendant's claim that Extra Strength Maalox Plus was "the strongest antacid there is" was not sufficiently shown to mislead, stating "although there is evidence of intent to mislead, it is of a kind regrettably pervasive throughout the antacid industry and does not reach the egregious proportions that would warrant a presumption shifting the burden of proof"; *Avis Rent A Car System, Inc. v. Hertz Corp.*, 782 F.2d 381 (2[d] Cir. 1986), in which the court held that defendant's advertising claim that "Hertz has more new cars than Avis has cars," while literally false as to car ownership, was not false in context, where the public would perceive it to refer to cars available for rental by the companies, and *Procter & Gamble Co. v. Chesebrough-Pond's, Inc.*, 747 F.2d 114 (2[d] Cir. 1984), where on cross-motions for preliminary injunction neither party established a likelihood of successfully demonstrating the unreliability of the other's supporting tests for "test-proven" product superiority claims and consequent claim falsity.

The plaintiff in a false advertising case must show that defendant's false advertising caused the plaintiff's injury. *Air Turbine Tech., Inc. v. Atlas Copco AB*, 410 F.3d 701 (Fed. Cir. 2005) (affirming summary judgment for defendant because plaintiff did not provide evidence sufficient to allow a reasonable juror to find that defendant's false advertising caused the alleged injuries to plaintiff.)

See generally Albert & Bochino, Jr., *Trade Libel: Theory and Practice Under the Common Law, the Lanham Act, and the First Amendment*, 89 TRADEMARK REP. 826 (1999); BeVier, *Competitor Suits for False Advertising under Section 43(a) of the Lanham Act: A Puzzle in the Law of Deception*, 78 VA. L. REV. 1 (1992); Tepper, *False Advertising Claims and the Revision of the Lanham Act: A Step in Which Direction?*, 59 U. CINN. L. REV. 957 (1991); Singdahlsen, *The Risk of Chill: A Cost of the Standards Governing the Regulation of False Advertising Under Section 43(a) of the Lanham Act*, 77 VA. L. REV. 339 (1991).

g) Standing

In accordance with the broad judicial construction given the rest of the section some courts have stated that for standing under § 43(a) a plaintiff need only have "a reasonable interest to be protected against [the alleged] false advertising." *New West Corp. v. NYM Co. of Cal, Inc.*, 595 F.2d 1194, 1198 (9th Cir. 1979); *Quabaug Rubber Co. v. Fabiano Shoe Co.*, 567 F.2d 154, 160 (1st Cir. 1977). Because of the difficulty of showing any actual diversion of sales created by allegedly false advertising, courts have also been willing to grant injunctive relief upon a relatively minimal showing of likelihood of damage. Should damage sufficient to satisfy the statute be presumed once a plaintiff shows that the parties compete in a relevant market and that defendant's ads are false? Such an argument was rejected by the court in *Johnson & Johnson v. Carter-Wallace, Inc.*, 631 F.2d 186 (2^d Cir. 1980), yet the court found likelihood of damage on very limited evidence.

A plaintiff that only intends to compete, but does not yet actually compete, with the defendant may not be able to demonstrate a "reasonable interest" sufficient to establish standing to sue under § 43(a). In *PDK Labs Inc. v. Friedlander*, 103 F.3d 1105, 1111–13 (2^d Cir. 1997), the Second Circuit determined that a declaratory judgment defendant did not have standing to bring a false advertising counterclaim against the declaratory plaintiff because he did not currently sell a retail weight loss product that competed with the plaintiff's product. Moreover, in the court's view, the defendant's allegation of losing potential investors and royalties as a result of plaintiff's conduct did not constitute "sufficient pecuniary interest" to confer standing in the absence of direct competition. Similarly, plaintiffs lacked standing in *The Joint Stock Society v. UDV North America, Inc.*, 266 F.3d 164 (3^d Cir. 2001). The plaintiffs alleged that the U.S. defendants misrepresented Smirnoff Vodka as being made in Russia, but lacked standing because "[t]he defendants' allegedly false advertising cannot have harmed the plaintiffs by channeling their customers toward Smirnoff when the plaintiffs have not even begun offering their product for sale in the United States."

h) National Advertising Division of the Better Business Bureau

An alternative forum for resolving advertising disputes is the National Advertising Division, or NAD. This arm of the Council of Better Business Bureaus (CBBB) was founded in 1971 by the advertising community as a forum in which advertisers could arbitrate disputes over "national" advertising. Since its inception, the NAD has resolved thousands of cases involving the truth and accuracy of advertising. While the NAD has the power to initiate an investigation of claims, most cases are brought to the division's attention by competitors. Consumers also may initiate challenges at the NAD.

In a typical case, a competitor or individual sends the NAD a letter and supporting materials challenging the truth of the claims made in a company's advertisement. An NAD examining attorney then reviews the challenge to determine, in his or her discretion, whether it is appropriate for NAD resolution. For example, although the advertisement need not be "national" in the sense of dissemination to all fifty states, it normally should encompass more than one state.

Once the challenge is accepted by the NAD, the advertiser is given a limited amount of time to respond, with additional briefing by both parties permitted. After reviewing the briefs and, in appropriate cases, meeting with the parties separately, the NAD issues a written decision. The NAD's decision may be appealed for a panel review by the National Advertising Review Board (NARB). The five member reviewing panel consists of one "public" member, one "advertising agency" member, and three "advertiser" members. CBBB Code of Advertising, § 3.2. On appeal each party may summarize the facts and arguments which were presented to the NAD and answer questions from the panel. The panel will then issue a written decision.

An NAD proceeding normally is less expensive than federal court litigation, and can be much faster. Typically, the NAD's decision is issued two or three months after a challenge is filed. There is no discovery in NAD cases, and the NAD will assess any alleged implicit falsity of an advertisement without requiring survey or other consumer reaction evidence. Because the NAD is not a court, however, it cannot award monetary damages, or issue an injunction. The NAD commonly will require discontinuance or modification of misleading advertising claims. Compliance with NAD decisions is voluntary. If an advertiser fails to voluntarily comply with an NAD decision, the NAD may refer the matter to the Federal Trade Commission. *See, e.g., Council for Better*

Business Bureaus, Advertising Topics, Supp. 578, p. 2 (Jan. 1998) (announcing NAD had referred allegedly deceptive advertising by manufacturer of swimming pool safety covers to FTC, where the advertiser declined to participate in the NAD regulatory process or to provide substantiation for its superiority and performance claims). The FTC has its own remedies as well as the authority to file a civil complaint (See Chapter 11).

Notes on Passing Off

1. Traditional Passing Off

Another form of misrepresentation, with its roots in the common law, is called "passing off". As used in Great Britain and in some of the older American cases, the term is broadly synonymous with trademark and unfair competition. In the United States today, the term "passing off" (or, as it is sometimes called, "palming off"), usually has a narrower meaning: the unexplained substitution of one party's product when the product of another is expected or sought. Passing off frequently is accomplished with the assistance of deceptive representations or a confusingly similar trade identity.

In *William R. Warner & Co. v. Eli Lilly & Co.*, 265 U.S. 526 (1924), defendant encouraged or enabled passing off where its salespeople encouraged druggists to substitute defendant's cheaper Quin-Coco chocolate quinine preparation when asked for plaintiff's Coco-Quinine product. *See also Inwood Laboratories v. Ives Laboratories*, 454 U.S. 844 (1982); *Larsen v. Terk Technologies Corp.*, 151 F.3d 140 (4th Cir. 1998) (defendant, a distributor of plaintiff's compact disk holders, copied them, affixed unregistered marks to the copies, and passed them off as plaintiff's); *Accurate Leather & Novelty Co. v. LTD Commodities*, 18 U.S.P.Q.2d 1327 (N.D. Ill. 1990) (preliminarily enjoining defendant's catalog use of a photograph of plaintiff's handbag to sell defendant's inferior handbag); *The Coca-Cola Co. v. Scrivener*, 117 U.S.P.Q. 394 (S.D. Cal. 1958) (defendants wrongfully substituted Pepsi when customers asked for Coke, and failed to provide adequate notice of that practice). In *Sealy, Inc. v. Easy Living, Inc.*, 743 F.2d 1378 (9th Cir. 1984), the court found defendant liable for contributory infringement for selling bed foundations with fabric patterns identical to those on plaintiff's mattresses. The court held that defendant could reasonably foresee that retailers would pass off the foundations and mattresses as a matching set, even though they were made by two different manufacturers. In *Cooper Industries, Inc. v. Leatherman Tool Group, Inc.*, 532 U.S. 424 (2001) a jury found Cooper liable for passing off for using photographs and a modified drawing of Leatherman's multi-function pocket tool (with Leatherman's trademark whited out) in marketing materials and catalogs for defendant's similar product. The Supreme Court remanded the case for reassessment of punitive damages award under the proper standard. See the discussion of the Supreme Court's follow-up decision on punitive damages in Chapter 10.

A retailer may be required to police the activities of its agents and employees when passing off can be anticipated. *See Scotch Whisky Ass'n v. Barton Distilling Co.*, 170 U.S.P.Q. 455 (N. D. Ill. 1971), *aff'd*, 179 U.S.P.Q. 712 (7th Cir. 1973). Note that in the *Sealy, Warner and Scotch Whisky Ass'n* cases, passing off should have been anticipated by the defendants both because of their own enabling acts, and the reasonably probable conduct of their customers distributing the product.

Although "generic" terms normally are not entitled to trademark protection, protection may be had from another's deceptive use of the term, *i.e.*, if the competitor is using it to help pass off his product as that of the generic term user. *See Technical Publishing Co. v. Lebhor-Friedman, Inc.*, 729 F.2d 1136 (7th Cir. 1984); *Miller Brewing Co. v. Joseph Schlitz Brewing Co.*, 605 F.2d 990, 997 (7th Cir. 1979) ("The absence of trademark protection [for LITE for beer] does not mean that Miller must submit to a competitor's palming off of its product as the product of Miller"). Such passing off will typically occur via misleading advertising involving use of the generic term. *See for example, Leon Finker, Inc. v. Schlussel*, 469 F. Supp. 674 (S.D.N.Y. 1979), and *Eastern Airlines, Inc. v. New York Airlines, Inc.*, 218 U.S.P.Q. 71 (S.D.N.Y. 1983). Or it may result from the concurrent blatant imitation of the product itself; *see Metric & Multistandard Components v. Metric's Inc.*, 635 F.2d 710 (8th Cir. 1980). *Compare Courtenay Comm'ns v. Itall*, 334 F.3d 210 (2d Cir. 2003), where the court concluded that, even if the words "iMarketing News" were found generic, defendant's graphic composite mark containing those words might be protectable against defendant's similar use. It therefore vacated the dismissal and remanded the case.

2) Reverse Passing Off

Traditional "passing off" of "palming off" occurs when parties attempt to deceptively substitute goods or services for those of another. A different form of unfair competition has been found to occur when a purchaser of goods removes the original trademark, substitutes another trademark of the purchaser's choosing, and then offers the product for resale. Such conduct has been termed "reverse passing [or palming] off." This cause of action is discussed in the *Twentieth Century Fox v. Dastar* case excerpted above.' Since the original trademark owner made its profit on the initial sale, the damage to it from such resales is not at once apparent. One court described the injury in this manner:

> in reverse palming off cases, the originator of the misidentified product is involuntarily deprived of the advertising value of its name and of the goodwill that otherwise would stem from public knowledge of the true source of the satisfactory product. The ultimate purchaser is also deprived of knowing the true source of the product and may even be deceived into believing that it comes from another source.

Smith v. Montoro, 648 F.2d 602 (9th Cir. 1981).

Accordingly, one normally may not lawfully place one's own trademark on another's product for such deceptive resales, nor may one use such a rebranded product as a sample for sales of one's own product. *FRA S.p.A. v. SURG-O-FLEX of America, Inc.*, 415 F. Supp. 607 (S.D.N.Y. 1976); *Matsushita Electric Corp. v. Solar Sounds Systems, Inc.*, 381 F. Supp. 64, 67 (S.D.N.Y. 1974) ("The use of a misbranded product in soliciting orders for a different product seems as clear a false designation of origin' as could be conceived"); *Johnson v. Jones*, 149 F.3d 494, 504 (6th Cir. 1998) (defendant's replacing of plaintiff architect's name on architectural plans with defendant's name constituted "quintessential reverse passing off"); *Blank v. Pollack*, 916 F. Supp. 165, 170 (N.D.N.Y. 1996) (declining to dismiss reverse passing off claim where defendant's advertising allegedly falsely claimed defendant developed plaintiff's window crank concept); *Nike, Inc. v. Rubber Manufacturers Ass'n. Inc.*, 509 F. Supp. 919 (S.D.N.Y. 1981) (rebranding running shoes for promotional purposes).

Compare Syngenta Seeds, Inc. v. Delta Cotton Corp., 457 F.3d 1269 (Fed. Cir. 2006) (plaintiff failed to show injury from alleged reverse passing off of wheat seed; "we question whether a Lanham Act claim for reverse passing off is even cognizable when the rebranded product is used for a different purpose than, and thus does not compete with, the trademarked product"); *Stromback v. New Line Cinema*, 384 F.3d 283 (6th Cir. 2004) (screenplay and movie at issue were not substantially similar; "a finding of no substantial similarity on the copyright claim precludes the Lanham Act claim"); *Danielson v. Winchester-Conant Props.*, 322 F.3d 26 (1st Cir. 2003) (First Circuit has not yet recognized claim for "reverse passing off," but even if it did, plaintiff did not seek injunctive relief regarding substituted name on residential development site plans, and made insufficient showing for monetary relief); *Cavalier v. Random House, Inc.*, 297 F.3d 815 (9st Cir. 2002) (no reverse passing off where books at issue significantly differed; "without substantial similarity there can be no claim for reverse passing off");

Lipscher and Kehoe v. LRP Pubs., Inc., 266 F.3d 1305 (11th Cir. 2001) (affirming dismissal of reverse passing off claim where plaintiff presented no evidence of likely confusion caused by defendant allegedly taking false credit for plaintiff's database); *Murray Hill Pubs., Inc. v. ABC Comm'ns, Inc.*, 264 F.3d 622 (6th Cir. 2001) (no reverse passing off where plaintiff's copyright infringement claim failed and, rather than false credit, no writing credit at all was given for the song at issue).

In the *Dastar* case, the Supreme Court ostensibly invalidated an obscure subdoctrine of trademark law ("bodily appropriation," a subset of the "reverse passing off" subdoctrine used to establish a likelihood of confusion). Many observers were puzzled at the time as to why the court had chosen to grant *certiorari* in a seemingly unimportant case dealing with a decidedly esoteric and technical point of law. In retrospect, it appears the court's true concern again was a potential overbreadth of protection under the trademark laws which would be inconsistent with, in this case, copyright law. The *Dastar* court invalidated the "bodily appropriation" subdoctrine at issue in the case, not because of its obvious lack of a connection with the Lanham Act, but rather on constitutional grounds. Citing *Bonito Boats*, the court held that using trademark law as a *"species of mutant copyright law* that limits the public's federal right to copy and use expired copyrights" is unconstitutional because it extends indefinitely the limited monopoly granted by copyright law. *Dastar*, 539 U.S. 23 (emphasis added). Congress or the courts thus may not use trademark law to create "perpetual copyright." *Id.* Both patent and copyright law are founded on Art. I, § 8, cl. 8 of the Constitution with its "Limited Times" provision. In *Dastar* the Supreme Court remanded the state law unfair competition claim, and that claim subsequently was dismissed in *Twentieth Century Fox Film Corp. v. Dastar Corp.*, 68 U.S.P.Q. 2d 1536 (C.D. Cal. 2003) because "the Ninth Circuit has consistently held that claims brought under California unfair competition law are substantially congruent to claims brought under the Lanham Act." Interestingly, after remand, the Ninth Circuit affirmed that Dastar had infringed the copyright in plaintiffs' World War II videotape series. *Dastar*, 429 F.3d 869 (9th Cir. 2005).

The Seventh Circuit interpreted *Dastar* in *Bretford Mfg. v. Smith Sys. Mfg. Co.*, 419 F.3d 576 (7th Cir. 2005). There, Bretford manufactured computer tables featuring a V-shaped leg assembly. Smith Systems, a competitor, decided to copy Bretford's leg assembly, but its metal fabricator could not fashion it in time for a major client demonstration. Smith first attached an actual Bretford assembly to its table top for the demonstration, then shipped the client's tables with its own copied leg assembly. Bretford sued, claiming that Smith infringed its trade dress and that Smith engaged in reverse passing off when it used an actual Bretford leg assembly for the client demonstration. The district court initially found for Bretford, but then reversed its decision in light of the Supreme Court's decisions in *Wal-Mart Stores, Inc. v. Samara Bros., Inc.*, 529 U.S. 205 (2000), and *Dastar Corp. v. Twentieth-Century Fox Film Corp.*

On appeal, the Seventh Circuit affirmed in Smith's favor, noting that *Dastar* meant there must be a trademark-specific injury, so the relevant question was whether the consumer likely would be confused as to who produced the finished product. However, as far as Smith's client was concerned, "the table's 'origin' was Smith System, no matter who made any component or assembly." *Bretford*, 419 F.3d at 581. The court cited examples such as Ford cars, which "include Fram oil filters, Goodyear tires, Owens-Corning glass, Bose radios, Pennzoil lubricants, and many other constituents," and said that the reverse passing-off doctrine "does not condemn the way in which all products are made."

Despite its potentially wide-ranging holding, the Supreme Court's *Dastar* opinion did not invalidate the principle of reverse passing off. The Court expressly noted that the reverse passing off claim "would undoubtedly be sustained if Dastar had bought some of New Line's Crusade videotapes and merely repackaged them as its own." Cf. *Thompkins v. Li'l Joe Records, Inc.*, 476 F.3d 1294 (11th Cir. 2007) (where plaintiff did not allege that defendant was selling his rap records under another artist's name, but only that defendant (correctly) indicated that defendant was the creator of the physical recordings, *Dastar* explicitly precluded relief for reverse passing off). *See generally* Connor, *After Dastar: Can a Right of Attribution Still Exist Under § 43(a) of the Lanham Act?*, 9 INTELL. PROP. L. BULL. 11 (2004).

8.03   Misappropriation

Introduction

Another category of unfair competition is misappropriation. The misappropriation cause of action, sometimes described as "reaping where one has not sown." was first enunciated by the Supreme Court in the still-controversial case, *International News Service v. Associated Press*, 248 U.S. 215 (1918), discussed in the excerpted case below and in the notes following.

THE NATIONAL BASKETBALL ASSOCIATION v. MOTOROLA, INC.

United States Court of Appeals, Second Circuit
105 F.3d 841 (1997)

WINTER, CIRCUIT JUDGE

Motorola, Inc. and Sports Team Analysis and Tracking Systems ("STATS") appeal from a permanent injunction entered by Judge Preska. The injunction concerns a handheld pager sold by Motorola and marketed under the name "SportsTrax," which displays updated information of professional basketball games in progress. The injunction prohibits appellants, absent authorization from the National Basketball Association and NBA Properties, Inc. (collectively the "NBA"), from transmitting scores or other data about NBA games in progress via the pagers, STATS's site on America On-Line's computer dial-up service, or "any equivalent means."

The crux of the dispute concerns the extent to which a state law "hot-news" misappropriation claim based on *International News Service v. Associated Press*, 248 U.S. 215, 39 S. Ct. 68, 63 L. Ed. 211 (1918) ("*INS*"), survives preemption by the federal Copyright Act and whether the NBA's claim fits within the surviving *INS* -type claims.

. . .

*   *   *

The facts are largely undisputed. Motorola manufactures and markets the Sports-Trax paging device while STATS supplies the game information that is transmitted to the pagers. The product became available to the public in January 1996, at a retail price of about $200. SportsTrax's pager has an inch-and-a-half by inch-and-a-half screen and operates in four basic modes: "current," "statistics," "final scores" and "demonstration." It is the "current" mode that gives rise to the present dispute. In that mode, SportsTrax displays the following information on NBA games in progress: (i) the teams playing; (ii) score changes; (iii) the team in possession of the ball; (iv) whether the team is in the free-throw bonus; (v) the quarter of the game; and (iv) time remaining in the quarter. The information is updated every two to three minutes, with more frequent updates near the end of the first half and the need of the game. There is a lag of approximately two or three minutes between events in the game itself and when the information appears on the pager screen.

SportsTrax's operation relies on a "data feed" supplied by STATS reporters who watch the games on television or listen to them on the radio. The reporters key into a personal computer changes in the score and other information such as successful and missed shorts, fouls, and clock updates. The information is relayed by modem to STATS's host computer, which compiles, analyzes, and formats the data for retransmission. The information is then sent to a common carrier, which then sends it via satellite to various local FM radio networks that in turn emit the signal received by the individual SportsTrax pagers.

Although the NBA's complaint concerned only the SportsTrax device, the NBA offered evidence at trial concerning STATS's America On-Line ("AOL") site. Starting in January, 1996, users who accessed STATS's AOL site, typically via a modem attached to a home computer, were provided with slightly more comprehensive and detailed real-time game information than is displayed on a SportsTrax pager. On the AOL site, game scores are updated every 15 seconds to a minute, and the player and team statistics are updated each minute . . . . [W]e regard the legal issues as identical with respect to both products, and our holding applies equally to SportsTrax and STATS's AOL site.

The issues before us are ones the have arisen in various forms over the course of this century as technology has steadily increased the speed and quantity of information transmission. Today, individuals at home, at work, or elsewhere, can use a computer, pager, or other device to obtain highly selective kinds of information virtually at will. *International News Service v. Associated Press,* 248 U.S. 215, 39 S. Ct. 68, 63 L. Ed. 211 (1918) ("*INS*") was one of the first cases to address the issues raised by these technological advances, although the technology involved in that case was primitive by contemporary standards. *INS* involved two wire services, the Associated Press ("AP") and the International News Service ("INS"), that transmitted newsstories by wire to member newspapers. *Id.* INS would lift factual stories from AP bulletins and send them by wire to INS papers. *Id.* at 231, 39 S. Ct. at 69–70. INS would also take factual stories from east coast AP papers and wire them to INS papers on the west coast that had yet to publish because of time differentials. *Id.* at 238, 39 S. Ct. at 72. The Supreme Court held that INS's conduct was common-law misappropriation of AP's property. *Id.* at 242, 39 S. Ct. at 73–74.

With the advance of technology, radio stations began "live" broadcasts of events such as baseball games and operas, and various entrepreneurs began to use the transmissions of others in one way or another for their own profit. In response, New York courts created a body of misappropriation law, loosely based on INS, that sought to apply ethical standards to the use by one party of another's transmissions of events.

* * *

In our view, the elements central to an *INS* claim are: (i) the plaintiff generates or collects information at some cost or expense, [citations omitted]; (ii) the value of the information is highly time-sensitive, [citations omitted]; (iii) the defendant's use of the information constitutes free-riding on the plaintiff's costly efforts to generate or collect it, [citations omitted]; (iv) the defendant's use of the information is in direct competition with a product or service offered by the plaintiff, [citations omitted]; (v) the ability of other parties to free-ride on the efforts of the plaintiff would so reduce the incentive to produce the product or service that its existence or quality would be substantially threatened, . . . *INS*, 248 U.S. at 241, 39 S. Ct. at 73 ("[INS's conduct] would render [AP's] publication profitless, or so little profitable as in effect to cut off the service by rendering the cost prohibitive in comparison with the return.")[8]

---

[8] Some authorities have labeled this element as requiring direct competition between the defendant and the plaintiff between the defendant and the plaintiff in a primary market. "[I]n most of the small number of cases in which the misappropriation doctrine has been determinative, the defendant's appropriation, like that in INS, resulted in direct competition in the plaintiffs' primary market . . . Appeals to the misappropriation doctrine are almost always rejected when the appropriation does not intrude upon the plaintiff's primary market." *Restatement (Third) of Unfair Competition,* § 38 cmt. c., at 412–13; *see also National Football League v. Governor of State of Delaware,* 435 F. Supp. 1372 (D. Del. 1977). In that case, the NFL sued Delaware over the state's lottery game which was based on NFL games. In dismissing the wrongful misappropriation claims, the court states:

While courts have recognized that one has a right to one's own harvest, this proposition has not been

INS is not about ethics; it is about the protection of property rights in time-sensitive information so that the information will be made available to the public by profit seeking entrepreneurs. If services like AP were not assured of property rights in the news they pay to collect, they would cease to collect it. The ability of their competitors to appropriate their product at only nominal cost and thereby to disseminate a competing product at a lower price would destroy the incentive to collect news in the first place. The newspaper-reading public would suffer because no one would have an incentive to collect "hot news."

We therefore find the extra elements — those in addition to the elements of copyright infringement — that allow a "hot-news" claim to survive preemption are: (i) the time-sensitive value of factual information, (ii) the free-riding by a defendant, and (iii) the threat to the very existence of the product or service provided by the plaintiff.

*   *   *

We conclude that Motorola and STATS have not engaged in unlawful misappropriation under the "hot-news" test set out above. To be sure, some of the elements of a "hot-news" *INS* claim are met. The information transmitted to SportsTrax is not precisely contemporaneous, but it is nevertheless time-sensitive. Also, the NBA does provide, or will shortly do so, information like that available through SportsTrax. It now offers a service called "Gamestats" that provides official play-by-play game sheets and half-time and final box scores within each arena. It also provides such information to the media in each arena. In the future, the NBA plans to enhance Gamestats so that it will be networked between the various arenas and will support a pager product analogous to SportsTrax. SportsTrax will of course directly compete with an enhanced Gamestats.

However, there are critical elements missing in the NBA's attempt to assert a "hot-news" *INS* -type claim. As framed by the NBA, their claim compresses and confuses three different informational products. The first product is generating the information by playing the games; the second product is transmitting live, full descriptions of those games; and the third product is collecting and retransmitting strictly factual information about the games. The first and second products are the NBA's primary business: producing basketball games for live attendance and licensing copyrighted broadcasts of those games. The collection and retransmission of strictly factual material about the games is a different product: *e.g.*, box-scores in newspapers, summaries of statistics on television sports news, and real-time facts to be transmitted to pagers. In our view, the NBA has failed to show any competitive effect whatsoever from SportsTrax on the first and second products and a lack of any free-riding by SportsTrax on the third.

With regard to the NBA's primary products — producing basketball games with live attendance and licensing copyrighted broadcasts of those games — there is no evidence that anyone regards SportsTrax or the AOL site as a substitute for attending NBA games or watching them on television. In fact, Motorola markets SportsTrax as being designed "for those times when you cannot be at the arena, watch the game on TV, or listen to the radio . . .. "

The NBA argues that the paper market is also relevant to a "hot-news" *INS* -type claim and that SportsTrax's future competition with Gamestats satisfies any missing element. We agree that there is a separate market for the real-time transmission of factual information to pagers or similar devices, such as STATS's AOL site. However,

---

construed to preclude others from profiting from demands for collateral services generated by the success of one's business venture.

Id. at 1378. The court also noted, "It is true that Delaware is thus making profits it would not make but for the existence of the NFL, but I find this difficult to distinguish from the multitude of charter bus companies who generate profit from servicing those of plaintiff's fans who want to go to the stadium or, indeed, the sidewalk popcorn salesman who services the crowd as it surges towards the gate." *Id.*

we disagree that SportsTrax is in any sense free-riding off Gamestats.

An indispensable element of an *INS* "hot-news" claim is free riding by a defendant on a plaintiff's product, enabling the defendant to produce a directly competitive product for less money because it has lower costs. SportsTrax is not such a product. The use of pagers to transmit real-time information about NBA games requires: (i) the collecting of facts about the games; (ii) the transmission of these facts on a network; (iii) the assembling of them by the particular service; and (iv) the transmission of them to pagers or an on-line computer site. Appellants are in no way free-riding on Gamestats. Motorola and STATS expend their own resources to collect purely factual information generated in NBA games to transmit to SportsTrax pagers. They have their own network and assemble and transmit data themselves.

To be sure, if appellants in the future were to collect facts from an enhanced Gamestats pager to retransmit them to SportsTrax pagers, that would constitute free-riding and might well cause Gamestats to be unprofitable because it had to bear costs to collect facts that SportsTrax did not. If the appropriation of facts from one pager to another pager service were allowed, transmission of current information on NBA games to pagers or similar devices would be substantially deterred because any potential transmitter would know that the first entrant would quickly encounter a lower cost competitor free-riding on the originator's transmissions.[9]

However, that is not the case in the instant matter. SportsTrax and Gamestats are each bearing their own costs of collecting factual information on NBA games, and, if one produces a product that is cheaper or otherwise superior to the other, that producer will prevail in the marketplace. This is obviously not the situation against which *INS* was intended to prevent: the potential lack of any such product or service because of the anticipation of free-riding.

* * *

We vacate the injunction entered by the district court and order that the NBA's claim for misappropriation be dismissed . . ..

Notes on Misappropriation

The viability of the misappropriation theory has waxed and waned since the *INS* decision in 1918. After the Supreme Court's decision in *Erie v. Tompkins,* 304 U.S. 64 (1938) (abolishing federal courts' subject matter jurisdiction to hear claims based upon federal common law), misappropriation was no longer viewed as a valid federal cause of action, and some states explicitly repudiated it as a state law cause of action. *See, e.g., Addressograph-Multigraph Corp. v. American Expansion Bolt & Mfg. Co.,* 124 F.2d 706, 708–09 (7th Cir. 1941), *cert. denied,* 316 U.S. 682 (1942) (stating at that time that Illinois courts rejected the theory of misappropriation). *But see Metropolitan Opera Ass'n v. Wagner-Nichols Recorder Corp.,* 101 N.Y.S.2d 483, 492 (N.Y. Sup. Ct. 1950), *aff'd,* 279 A.2d 632 (1951) (noting that misappropriation law in New York is "broad and flexible" and "deal[s] with business malpractices offensive to the ethics of society"). Moreover, after the decisions in *Sears* and *Compco, see* Chapter 5, some courts and commentators questioned whether the federal patent and copyright laws preempted state law misappropriation claims. *See Columbia Broadcasting Sys., Inc. v. De Costa,* 377 F.2d 315 (1st Cir.), *cert. denied,* 389 U.S. 1007 (1967); Treece, *Patent Policy and Preemption: The Stiffel and Compco Cases,* 32 U. CHI. L. REV. 80 (1964). Then, the

---

[9] It may well be that the NBA's product, when enhanced, will actually have a competitive edge because its Gamestats system will apparently be used for a number of in-stadium services as well as the pager market, resulting in a certain amount of cost sharing. Gamestats might also have a temporal advantage in collecting and transmitting official statistics. Whether this is so does not affect our disposition of this matter, although it does demonstrate the gulf between this case and *INS*, where the free-riding created the danger of no wire service being viable.

Supreme Court's decision in *Goldstein v. California*, 412 U.S. 546, 569–70 (1973), revitalized the misappropriation theory through its recognition that the 1909 Copyright Act did not preempt a California statute which made it a criminal offense to "pirate" others' performances recorded on tapes and records. *See also United States Golf Ass'n v. St. Andrew's Sys. Data-Max, Inc.*, 749 F.2d 1028, 1036 (3[d] Cir. 1984) (noting that "[*Goldstein*] ha[s] made clear . . . that the misappropriation doctrine has not been completely eviscerated" in the wake of *Sears* and *Compco*). In 1976, however, Congress amended the Copyright Act to preempt all common law or state statutes which confer "legal or equitable rights that are equivalent to any of the exclusive rights within the general scope of copyright . . . and come within the subject matter of copyright." 17 U.S.C. § 301. As a result, some courts have held that the 1976 Copyright Act supersedes the *Goldstein* decision. *See, e.g., Crow v. Wainwright*, 720 F.2d 1224, 1225 (11th Cir. 1983), *cert. denied*, 469 U.S. 819 (1984) (noting that section 301 "clearly evinces Congress' intent to overrule by statute cases such as *Goldstein* . . ..").

In the wake of the 1976 Copyright Act some courts have determined that a misappropriation cause of action survives preemption when an "extra element" is alleged. *See National Basketball Ass'n v. Motorola, supra* (specific "hot news" misappropriation claim from *INS* survives preemption.) *See also Harper & Row Publishers, Inc. v. Nation Enter.*, 723 F. 2d 195, 200 (2[d] Cir. 1983) (propounding the "extra element" test), *rev'd on other grounds*, 471 U.S. 539 (1985), and Silverstein, *Impact of the INS Misappropriation Doctrine in the Cyberspace/Information Age*, 30 Bus. L. Rev. 73 (1997).

In analyzing the *INS* decision, the court in *United States Golf Ass'n v. St. Andrews Systems*, 749 F.2d 1028, 1038 (3[d] Cir. 1984), characterized INS's activities as potentially destructive of AP's incentive to create the news reports, since INS was directly competing in AP's market — the sale of newspapers. This in turn was against the public interest in having the information created. It found such direct competition to be essential to a successful misappropriation claim. "[T]he direct competition requirement protects the public interest in free access to information except where protection of the creator's interest is required in order to assure that the information is produced." 749 F.2d at 1038. Since the parties in *United States Golf Ass'n* competed only indirectly, the court found that defendant's marketing of a computerized handicapping system using plaintiff's golf handicapping formula was not a disincentive to plaintiff, the governing body of amateur golf in this country, to maintain and update that formula. It accordingly rejected the misappropriation claim.

Compare the Third Circuit's decision in *United States Golf Ass'n v. St. Andrews Systems* with *United States Golf Association v. Arroyo Software Corp.*, 81 Cal.App. 4th 607 (1999). There the California Court of Appeal affirmed judgment enjoining defendant, a producer of computer software, under California misappropriation law from using plaintiff's golf handicap formulas and service marks in defendant's handicap calculating software program. Plaintiff had guarded its proprietary interest in its Handicap System and its related Formulas and marks, barring others who were not golf associations or golf clubs from use without consent. The court observed that "there is a virtually unlimited number of possible handicap formulas" and found "substantial evidence" to support "the trial court's conclusion that protection of the USGA handicapping business is necessary to protect the basic incentive for the production of the idea or information involved". It denied defendants' claim of collateral estoppel, in which they argued plaintiffs were barred from relitigating the same issues litigated fourteen years earlier in *U.S. Golf Ass'n v. St. Andrews Systems.* The present case involved a "completely changed" and "unique" Handicap System, "created through the efforts of many people laboring for thousands of hours over more than two decades" after the creation of plaintiff's former handicapping formula in the prior case. Also, under California misappropriation law, plaintiff did not have to show the parties were in direct competition. There was no preemption by federal copyright law because the Handicap System and Formulas were "processes" and "systems" excluded from copyright protection under § 102(b) of the Copyright Act, and therefore were "not works of authorship that come within the subject matter of copyright". Also, defendant's use and appropriation was not equivalent to "simply copying" them. *Id.* at 621–623. *See also Dow Jones & Co. v. Int'l Secs. Exch.*, 451 F.3d 295 (2^d Cir. 2006) in which it was not misappropriation of any intellectual property right, or trademark infringement or dilution, for defendant to create, list and facilitate the trading of options in plaintiffs' DIAMONDS exchange traded fund designed to track a proprietary market index; by creating the fund using their proprietary formulas and selling shares to the public, plaintiffs forfeited any right to control resale and public trading of the shares.

Notwithstanding the 1976 Copyright Act, the unusual facts of the *INS* case and the uncertain parameters of its equitable theory condemning "reaping where one has not sown," have led to varying and sometimes restrictive applications among the courts. As summarized in the *Restatement (Third) of Unfair Competition* § 38 cmt. c (1995):

> The facts of the INS decision are unusual and may serve, in part, to limit its rationale . . . . The limited extent to which the INS rationale has been incorporated into the common law of the states indicate [sic] that the decision is properly viewed as a response to unusual circumstances rather than as a statement of generally applicable principles of common law. Many subsequent decisions have expressly limited the INS case to its facts.

One Internet case drew on hoary principles of law to resolve an information appropriation dispute. In *eBay, Inc. v. Bidder's Edge, Inc.*, 100 F. Supp. 2d 1058 (N.D. Cal. 2000), defendant's website contained an aggregate auction database which included information from plaintiff's auction database. To create the portion of the database relating to plaintiff, the defendant sent robotic "web crawlers" on to plaintiff's auction website to retrieve the information. The court granted a preliminary injunction, concluding that plaintiff was likely to succeed under the theory that defendant committed "trespass to chattels" by appropriating plaintiff's auction information in this way. The court noted that "[i]f BE's activity is allowed to continue unchecked, it would encourage other auction aggregators to engage in similar recursive searching of the eBay system such that eBay would suffer irreparable harm from reduced system performance, system unavailability, or data losses." *Compare Creative Computing v. Getloaded.com LLC*, 386 F.3d 930 (9th Cir. 2004), in which the defendant, who had misappropriated source code and customer information from its competitor's cargoloading-related website, was liable for damages and enjoined from ever accessing plaintiff's website, like "one who has repeatedly shoplifted from a particular store, so the judge prohibits him from entering it again"; *EF Cultural Travel BV v. Zefer*, 318 F.3d 58 (1st Cir. 2003), in which the court affirmed a preliminary injunction against defendant's use of a "scraper tool" automated searching program to compile (and undercut) the travel tour pricing information on plaintiff's website, because the scraper tool had been unlawfully constructed using confidential information from plaintiff's former employees, and *Kremen v. Cohen*, 314 F.3d 1127 (9th Cir. 2003), in which the Ninth Circuit certified to the California Supreme Court the question of whether the defendant domain name registrar's unauthorized conveyance of the plaintiff's domain name to another party constituted unlawful conversion under California state law. Much computer-accessing misconduct also is subject to the provisions of the Computer Fraud and Abuse Act, 18 U.S.C. § 1030.

For an interesting discussion of the *eBay v. Bidder's Edge* case, *see* Chang, *Bidding on Trespass: eBay, Inc. v.* Bidder's *Edge, Inc. and the Abuse of Trespass Theory in Cyberspace Law*, 29 AIPLA QUARTERLY J. 445 (2001). The author expresses concern that "[c]yber trespass to chattels is on its way to becoming the 'cure-all' remedy for unwanted Internet contacts", and concludes that plaintiff should be required to show "that either actual and tangible harm was done to the chattel, or that the chattel's value to the plaintiff was substantially diminished." Because neither was shown in the *eBay* case, in the author's view trespass to chattels should not have been found by the court.

8.04   Distinctive Advertising and Merchandising

Introduction

Unfair competition cases respecting distinctive advertising and commercial characters basically involve the familiar principles of likelihood of deception as to source or sponsorship. With the development of mass communication, particularly with the advent of television, and the Internet, distinctive advertising motifs, commercial characters, and similar devices have become important mechanisms by which businesses both generate and symbolize goodwill. The trademark and unfair competition law decisions which follow demonstrate the application of the basic principles to what are often highly ingenious and effectively deceptive means for trading on another's good will.

DECOSTA v. COLUMBIA BROADCASTING SYSTEM, INC.
United States Court of Appeals, First Circuit
520 F.2d 499 (1975)

Coffin, Chief Judge

Plaintiff, a dozen years ago, began this suit against the Columbia Broadcasting System, Inc. and allied corporations (CBS) to seek compensation for their unauthorized use of a character concept he had developed, embodying a costume, slogan, name, and symbol. A mechanic living in Cranston, Rhode Island, his avocation had been to don an all black cowboy suit, with a St. Mary's medal affixed to his flat crowned black hat, a chess symbol to his holster, and an antique derringer secreted under his arm, and make public appearances at rodeos and other events, meeting innumerable children, and passing out his card, inscribed with a chess set knight, proclaiming "Have Gun Will Travel, Wire Paladin, N. Court St., Cranston, R.I." . . . As every well versed television viewer of the late fifties and early sixties knows, the gestalt conveyed by plaintiff's costume and accessories found its way into defendants' television series, "Have Gun Will Travel," which enjoyed enormous popularity for over eight years in its initial run, grossing in excess of fourteen million dollars.

*   *   *

. . . Our first inquiry is whether plaintiff's marks and dress are protectable under either the broad concept of unfair competition or that part of unfair competition dealing with trade and service mark infringement. As to plaintiff's dress, this may have had less claim to protection against infringement than his card. For there is no question but that the photograph of plaintiff in full regalia which he widely distributed was copyrightable [but bore no copyright notice]. 17 U.S.C. § 5(j), *Burrow-Giles Lithographic Co. v. Sarony*, 111 U.S. 53 (1884). The card is less vulnerable on copyright preemption grounds. Its three components — the slogan, "Have Gun Will Travel," the name in the phrase "Wire Paladin," and the knight chess piece — are in categories protectable as common law trade or service marks. *See, e.g.*, Callmann, *The Law of Trademarks*, Vol. 3, § 77.4(g) (slogans); § 66.1 (trade names).

What is not clear is whether plaintiff's activities in connection with his marks entitle him to the protection of trade and service mark law. As we said in *DeCosta I*, 377 F.2d at 316, "[t]his was perhaps one of the purest promotions ever staged, for plaintiff did not seek anything but the entertainment of others." Plaintiff testified that he never used the name "Paladin," the slogan or the chess piece for any business use, and never published any advertisements; that he did not even receive his expenses for appearances at horse shows and rodeos; and that the distribution and mailing of pictures and cards was costly to him. . . .

* * *

. . . It is not a big step in theory to say that an individual who develops and promotes for entertainment purposes a specialty character associated with a distinctive name, costume, slogan, and other marks, but who never charges a fee, is also entitled to protection under the common law doctrine relating to trademarks and unfair competition. But, if the step were taken, what principle should both guide and limit? If plaintiff is recognized as one who performs services in commerce, what about the hobbyist magician, square dance caller, story teller, amateur actor, singer, barbershop quartet, standup comic? How frequent must be the appearances? How prominent the mark? How often must the performer appear in other states to enjoy Lanham Act protection? We know of no logical or obvious line of demarcation. The price of an open-ended extension of protection for some creative activity is, pro tanto, a curtailment of the borrowing, poaching, imitation which underlie so much other innovative activity.

Protection at present has the merits of inherent limitations: the existence of a trade, business, or profession where the "good will" to be protected has been subject to the acid test of the willingness of people to pay for goods or services; or, in the case of nonprofit institutions, the voluntary investment in time, effort, and money of many individuals to create and maintain a program of sufficient interest to consumers, members, and sponsors to warrant protection. We hesitate to take the step of offering common law unfair competition protection to eleemosynary individuals. Whether legislatures are better equipped than courts to deal with this problem, we cannot clearly say, but in our posture of doubt would prefer to see expansion of protection come from that source.

Having exposed our misgivings, we do not rely on a holding that the absence of a profit-oriented enterprise disqualifies plaintiff from protection. We shall assume, therefore, that plaintiff's marks meet the requirements of common law service marks. We also shall assume that they are distinctive enough so that proof of secondary meaning is not essential. In the alternative, we shall accept the finding of the magistrate, adopted by the district court, that, at least among some people, plaintiff's name and card had come to be associated with him.

* * *

. . . There is another factor, we think, which should guide a judgment as to likelihood of confusion — the time when the evidence is submitted. There is ample reason, at the incipiency of an alleged infringement, in a suit seeking injunctive relief, for a plaintiff to argue and a court to rule that the similarity of marks is such that confusion is all too likely to ensue. Plaintiff should not be expected to stand by and await the dismal proof. Callmann, Vol. 3, § 80.6, pp. 559–560. "[C] onversely," adds Callmann, "after the lapse of substantial time if no one appears to have been actually deceived that fact is strongly probative of the defense that there is no likelihood of deception arising out of the use of the mark in question." *Id.* at 562. Defendants have urged that plaintiff, having delayed for almost the entire limitations period before bringing suit, should be barred by the doctrine of estoppel by laches from further prosecution of this litigation. Plaintiff's rejoinder is that he was, during this period, going from attorney to attorney, seeking assistance before he was able to make progress. We do not find in the authorities sufficient support, where defendants' action was found by the jury to be deliberate and knowing, to invoke this doctrine. Nevertheless, we do say that the delay, for reasons stated, increases the quantum of proof of confusion which the plaintiff has the obligation to supply.

. . . When we examine the magistrate's opinion on this issue, we find only a finding as to the identical nature of the marks used by plaintiff and defendants and the resulting "great likelihood of confusion" therefrom, and another that "At least 6 witnesses testified that they had at first thought, on viewing the television program, that Richard Boone was the plaintiff Mr. DeCosta until they learned the contrary from viewing the credits of the show, or otherwise." The paucity of these findings takes on some significance when we note that after remand of the case to the district court in 1968, following our decision in *DeCosta I*, the plaintiff was given the opportunity to supplement the record in support of his second and third causes of action. The quoted findings are the result.

. . . The magistrate's findings being treated as final, they are here subject to the same standard of review as are district court findings under Fed. R. Civ. Pro. 52(a). They must be accepted unless clearly erroneous. On this issue, however, we see no alternative to saying the finding is not supported. If the identity of the marks settled the question of likelihood of confusion, there was no need for further evidence after *DeCosta I*; we had taken some pains to make the point. But, in fact (rather, in law) extrinsic evidence, as we have noted, should be considered. Here, the disparities are substantial. Plaintiff's enterprise was localized; defendants' was nationwide. Plaintiff's appearances were simple happenings, passing out cards and pictures, riding, occasionally walking his horse, and executing a quick draw gun maneuver; defendant's extrinsic television series portrayed an elegant hired gun on manifold missions. Plaintiff's customers were attendees at rodeos and parades, patients at hospitals, etc.; defendants' purchasers were its program's sponsors, who in turn were responsive to the nation's television audience. Moreover, plaintiff's suit was not brought in 1957 when the alleged infringement began; the testimony as to likelihood of confusion was introduced by affidavit eleven years later, when the first run of defendants' series had terminated. After this lapse of time, the testimony of six witnesses that they thought, on first viewing the program, that the television character Paladin was plaintiff, seems to us either no evidence at all or such minimal evidence as not to support a finding of likelihood of confusion requiring an accounting of defendants' profits from a highly successful, 225-episode series grossing over fourteen million dollars. We do not blame plaintiff or counsel; we suspect that the most exacting search for proof would not have produced more.

. . . We recognize that plaintiff has lost something of value to him. The very success of defendants' series saturated the public consciousness and in time diluted the attractiveness of plaintiff's creation, although he continued his appearances longer than defendants' first run. While he was not injured financially, there can be no doubt that he has felt deprived. As a commentator has observed, "[I]t could be argued that the most appropriate measure of damages would be the emotional harm that he suffered when CBS exploited his character and lured his audience away." 66 MICH. L. REV. at 1034. But to give any relief, however tailored, we need a predicate of liability. Absent the ultimate fact of confusion, we cannot find a basis for liability for common law service mark infringement or unfair competition.

Judgment reversed. Remanded with instructions to enter judgment for defendants.

EVEREADY BATTERY COMPANY, INC. v. ADOLPH COORS COMPANY
United States District Court, N.D. Illinois
765 F.Supp. 440 (1991)

NORGLE, DISTRICT JUDGE

* * *

This case arises from a recently made (and not yet aired) beer commercial by defendant Adolph Coors Company ("Coors") which spoofs a popular series of Eveready battery commercials featuring a pink mechanical toy bunny (the "Energizer Bunny"). Eveready seeks to enjoin Coors' use of the disputed beer commercial, alleging copyright infringement, trademark infringement under the Lanham Act, and trademark dilution under the Illinois Anti-Dilution Act.

The "Energizer Bunny" ad campaign began approximately three years ago in an apparent response to a television commercial aired by Eveready's primary competitor, Duracell. The Duracell commercial depicts a large number of mechanical toy bunnies beating horizontally-held "snare drums." In the Duracell commercial, the bunny running on Duracell batteries continues to operate and beat on its drum while all of the other bunnies stop running. The voice-over on the Duracell commercial states that in comparison tests, the Duracell battery outlasted its competitors.

Subsequently, from late 1988 to early 1989, Eveready ran a television commercial containing similar mechanical toy bunnies. Eveready's commercial also begins with a scene depicting a number of these bunnies, beating on horizontally-held "snare drums." The voice-over, speaking over the tinny "rat-atat-tat" tattoo of the drums, states: "Don't be fooled by commercials where one battery company's toy outlasts the others." At this point, the toy bunny in the first row turns its head and opens its eyes wide as the camera focuses in on the Energizer logo emblazoned on a large, vertical bass drum, carried by the toy Energizer Bunny as it enters the picture from screen right. The Energizer Bunny, adorned with sporty sunglasses and beach thongs, strolls across the screen in front of the other bunnies, striking deep, booming notes on its bass drum. The voice-over continues: "The fact is, Energizer was never invited to their playoffs . . . because nothing outlasts the Energizer. They keep going and going and going . . . ." As the voice-over speaks, the Energizer Bunny, which apparently has turned around, pauses in the middle of the picture, leans back while beating on its drum, then exits screen right.

After airing the initial Energizer Bunny commercial, Eveready hired a new ad agency, Chiat/Day/Mojo Inc. Advertising ("Chiat/Day"), which developed an ad campaign revolving around the Energizer Bunny. The series of television commercials created by Chiat/Day as part of this campaign use the Eveready Bunny in a "commercial within a commercial" format. Each spot begins with what at first appears to be a typical television advertisement (which the viewer later realizes is for a fictitious product or service). At some point during the spot, an off-camera drum beat appears to distract the actors in the bogus commercial while the Energizer Bunny-which virtually always appears in its characteristic beach thongs and sunglasses-strolls onto screen beating his bass drum. The actors of the bogus commercial stare incredulously as the intruding mechanical toy bunny nonchalantly propels across the screen, beating the drum and often knocking over props from the fictitious commercial's set. In many of these Energizer commercials, the bunny spins around once and twirls his drum mallets before proceeding to propel out of the picture. Each of the commercials ends with a voice-over which states: "Still going. Nothing outlasts the Energizer. They keep going and going . . . [voice fades out]."

In the past two years, Eveready has produced approximately twenty Energizer Bunny commercials with the interruptive "commercial within a commercial" motif. Although these commercials have cost Eveready approximately $55,000,000 over the past two years (apparently a very modest sum by current advertising standards), they have become among the most popular television commercials in the country and are deemed "break through" ads among those in the advertising industry.

On September 11, 1989, Eveready filed for trademark registration of its Energizer Bunny with the United States Patent and Trademark Office ("PTO"). An illustration of the mark submitted by Eveready appears in the August 21, 1990 Official Gazette of the PTO. This illustration is a sketch of the Eveready Bunny wearing beach thongs, sunglasses, a vertically held bass drum, and wielding a drum mallet behind its head. The sketch does not designate any colors associated with mark, and the bass drum held by the bunny contains no writing or design.

* * *

In late 1990 . . . Foote, Cone and Belding Communications, Inc. ("FCB"), the advertising agents for Coors, was given the job of creating a humorous commercial involving Leslie Nielsen, a well-known actor[7] who has been featured in previous Coors Light commercials . . . .

The Coors commercial begins with a background voice, speaking over a classical music score, heartily describing the attributes of an unidentified beer. As the voice speaks, the visual shows an extreme closeup of beer pouring into a glass. The voice and music then grind to a halt as a drum beat is heard and Mr. Nielsen appears walking across the visual. Mr. Nielsen wears a conservative, dark business suit, fake white rabbit ears, fuzzy white tail and rabbit feet (which look like rectangular pink slippers). He carries a life-sized bass drum imprinted with the COORS LIGHT logo. After beating the drum several times, Mr. Nielsen spins rapidly seven or so times and, after recovering somewhat from his apparent dizziness, resumes walking. He says "thank you" before exiting off the screen. As Mr. Nielsen exits, another background voice states: "Coors Light, the official beer of the nineties, is the fastest growing light beer in America. It keeps growing and growing and growing . . . [voice fades out]." At the end of the spot, a visual appears depicting Coors' "Silver Bullet" logo-a horizontal Coors Light can-streaking across the bottom of the screen, leaving in its wake the mark "Coors Light."

* * *

Thus, the sole question at issue in the present Lanham Act analysis is whether Coors' presentation of Leslie Nielsen in bunny ears, tail and feet, while banging on a bass drum, is sufficient "to cause confusion, or to cause mistake, or to deceive as to the affiliation, connection, or association" of Mr. Nielsen or Coors Light with Eveready or the Energizer Bunny symbol. In other words, does the Coors commercial cause its viewers to correlate Coors and its products or symbols with Eveready and its products and symbols in terms of origin, sponsorship, or approval?

* * *

The only factor in this analysis which weighs in favor of plaintiff is the strength of its mark. During the approximately two years of the Energizer Bunny ad campaign, Eveready has produced some twenty commercials featuring its bunny, and these commercials have met with tremendous success. The pink drumming mechanical toy bunny may have developed secondary meaning in the marketplace as a symbol for Energizer products. However, the very strength of the Energizer Bunny mark in this case seems to weigh against a likelihood of confusion, particularly in light of the obvious parody depicted in defendant's use. The degree of similarity between the "marks" in appearance and suggestion is slight. Indeed, the unmistakable differences between the Energizer Bunny and Leslie Nielsen in modified rabbit attire arguably generate much of the humor in the Coors parody. Next, the products at issue here are completely dissimilar and do not overlap in any significant manner. No consumer is likely to mistake Coors as the source of origin for Energizer batteries or Eveready as the source of origin for Coors beer. It is also apparent that Coors did not intend to create in consumers the impression that its beer is endorsed or otherwise affiliated with Energizer batteries.[20]

Further, the court notes that Coors' parody defense would likely defeat Eveready's Lanham Act claim in any event. Parody has been recognized as a defense to a trademark infringement action . . . . To the extent that the Coors commercial conveys the message "that it is the original," it emphatically conveys "that it is not the original." Thus, this court construes the Coors commercial as a permissible parody which does not violate the provisions of the Lanham Act.

---

[7] Mr. Nielsen has starred in recent popular movies such as "Airplane," "The Naked Gun," and "Police Squad." Each of these movies are "slapstick" comedies which are saturated with parody.

[20] Originally, plaintiff argued that the juxtaposition of their "wholesome" bunny with the sale of a beer product might create an improper impression or negative association in the minds of consumers.. . . However, it abandoned this argument at the preliminary injunction hearing after defendant played the Eveready "Chateau Marmoset" commercial - in which the Eveready Bunny disrupts a fictitious wine commercial.

. . . In order to succeed on a dilution claim under this [Illinois] Act, a plaintiff must show: 1) that the mark is distinctive, and 2) that the subsequent user's use dilutes that distinctiveness. *Ringling Bros.*, 855 F.2d at 482 (quoting *Hyatt Corp. v. Hyatt Legal Services*, 736 F.2d 1153, 1157 (7th Cir. 1984)).

In the present case, the plaintiff has established the distinctiveness of the Energizer Bunny mark. Energizer provided evidence that a recent advertising survey listed the Energizer Bunny spots as the seventh-best remembered ad among consumers in the U.S. There is little doubt that the highly touted Eveready Bunny campaign has succeeded in creating an association, in the minds of America's consumers, between the Energizer Bunny and Energizer batteries. However, Energizer has not established a likelihood that Coors' commercial is likely to dilute the distinctiveness of its mark or the power of the association which that mark has created.

* * *

Eveready argues that Coors' use of its mark was "deceptively similar" because Coors, like the defendant in *Ringling Bros.*, used the "entire" mark. "Coors has used the entire 'bunny' trademark: the drum, the drumming, the spinning, the interruption of a 'commercial,' as well as the deceptively similar phrase 'It keeps growing and growing and growing . . . ' " Plaintiff's Supplemental Memorandum, p. 9. However, as the court noted above, while each of the elements mentioned by Eveready may be copyrightable expressions under the Copyright Act, they do not all constitute protectible elements of Eveready's *trademark*. Rather, Eveready's trademark protection is circumscribed by the boundaries of the mark itself, which here is the bunny symbol illustrated in Eveready's trademark application. *See* Appendix A.

Given the limited coverage of plaintiff's mark, and the nature of defendant's taking, the court finds that Eveready's reliance on *Ringling Bros.*, is misplaced. Unlike the defendant in *Ringling Bros.*, Coors clearly did not use the entire Eveready Bunny mark. . . . This court finds that the Nielsen character in the Coors commercial is neither identical, nor "deceptively similar," to Eveready's mark. Consequently, Eveready has not established a likelihood of success on its trademark dilution claim.

. . . For all the reasons stated above, Eveready's motion for preliminary injunction is denied.

APPENDIX

TM 104   OFFICIAL GAZETTE   AUGUST 21, 1990

CLASS 9—(Continued).   CLASS 9—(Continued).

SN 73–823,590. VIDEONICS, INC., CAMPBELL, CA. FILED 9–5–1989.

SN 73–824,785. EVEREADY BATTERY COMPANY, INC., ST. LOUIS, MO. FILED 9–11–1989

VIDEONICS

FOR VIDEO CONTROL UNITS AND REMOTE CONTROL APPARATUS FOR VIDEO CONTROL UNITS (U.S. CL. 26).
FIRST USE 8–24–1987; IN COMMERCE 8–24–1987.

SN 73–823,747. LEYBOLD AG, KOLN, FED REP GERMANY, FILED 9–6–1989.

THE STIPPLING SHOWN IN THE DRAWING IS A FEATURE OF THE MARK AND IS NOT INTENDED TO INDICATE COLOR.
THE MARK CONSISTS OF A RABBIT WITH A DRUM.
FOR BATTERIES (U.S. CL. 21).
FIRST USE 10–30–1988; IN COMMERCE 10–30–1988.

VIGIVAC

PRIORITY CLAIMED UNDER SEC. 44(D) ON FED REP GERMANY APPLICATION NO. L32496/9WZ, FILED 7–12–1989, REG. NO. 1146203, DATED 9–15–1989, EXPIRES 7–12–1999.
FOR MONITORS AND CONTROLS FOR VACUUM PUMPS; METERS FOR CHECKING THE OPERATION OF VACUUM PUMPS; OIL FLOW MONITORS FOR USE WITH LUBRICATED VACUUM PUMPS (U.S. CL. 26).

SN 73–825,118. METROHM LTD., HERISAU, SWITZERLAND, FILED 9–11–1989.

TITRINO

PRIORITY CLAIMED UNDER SEC. 44(D) ON SWITZERLAND APPLICATION NO. 2112, FILED 3–16–1989, REG. NO. 371365, DATED 3–16–1989, EXPIRES 3–16–2009.
FOR MEASURING AND CHECKING APPARATUS, NAMELY AUTOMATIC TITRATING APPARATUS (U.S. CL. 26).

SN 73–824,186. LASER MAGNETIC STORAGE INTERNATIONAL COMPANY, COLORADO SPRINGS, CO. FILED 9–8–1989.

SN 73–826,405. CLARK EQUIPMENT COMPANY, SOUTH BEND, IN. FILED 9–19–1989.

INDEPENDENCE

BOBCAT

FOR MAGNETIC TAPE DRIVE FOR USE WITH COMPUTERS (U.S. CL. 26).
FIRST USE 5–0–1989; IN COMMERCE 5–0–1989.

OWNER OF U.S. REG. NOS. 670,566, 1,153,505 AND OTHERS.
FOR BATTERIES FOR OFF-ROAD MACHINERY (U.S. CL. 21).
FIRST USE 6–0–1986; IN COMMERCE 6–0–1986.

Notes on Distinctive Advertising and Merchandising

As a matter of policy, should trademark significance be accorded to fanciful advertising characters when they are not used on or in immediate connection with the sale of products? Should proof of secondary meaning, i.e., source of goods or services association, be required? What is the effect of modern media advertising upon the marketing and economic significance of fanciful advertising characters? *See* BATTERSBY & GRIMES, THE LAW OF MERCHANDISE AND CHARACTER LICENSING (2007 ed.); *Nickles, The Conflicts Between Intellectual Property Protections When a Character Enters the Public Domain,* 7 UCLA ENT. L. REV. 133 (1999).

What should the limits on the Lanham Act protection be in this area? *See* the section on Misrepresentation, supra, and Proctor, *Distinctive and Unusual Marketing Techniques: Are They Protectable Under Section 43(a) of The Lanham Act? Should They Be?*, 77 TRADEMARK REP. 4 (1987). The copying or imitation of a distinctive character created by another may result in liability under either unfair competition law or copyright law. Even when such copying does not facilitate the palming off of a particular product as that of the character's creator, § 43(a) of the Lanham Act may apply because the character itself has become associated with plaintiff or its product in the public mind. *See DC Comics, Inc. v. Filmation Associates*, 486 F. Supp 1273 (S.D.N.Y. 1980) (although "plaintiff's remedy more properly lies under the Copyright Act," defendant's animated television series using characters identical to those created by plaintiff infringed plaintiff's Lanham Act and state law rights in its characters; injunctive relief granted and damages awarded); *Frederick Warne & Co. v. Book Sales, Inc.*, 481 F. Supp. 1191, 1196–97 (S.D.N.Y. 1979); *Edgar Rice Burroughs, Inc. v. Manns Theatres*, 195 U.S.P.Q. 159 (C.D. Cal. 1976). In *DC Comics, Inc. v. Powers*, 465 F. Supp. 843 (S.D.N.Y. 1978), the defendant was preliminarily enjoined from titling its newspaper "Daily Planet" on the motion of the plaintiff owner of the rights in the Superman story, a story which includes a newspaper of that title. The court found that although plaintiff had never specifically licensed rights in that element of the Superman story, it had "demonstrated an association of . . . duration and consistency with the Daily Planet sufficient to establish a common law trademark therein." 465 F. Supp. at 847. Defendant's continued use of the title was found likely to cause irreparable injury to plaintiff, making injunctive relief necessary.

Compare, however, *Comedy III Productions Inc. v. New Line Cinema*, 200 F.3d 593 (9th Cir. 2000) (as amended), in which the court declined to find trademark rights in a clip from a Three Stooges movie used in another movie, *The Long Kiss Goodnight*. The copyright in the Three Stooges film had long expired, and "Comedy III has not . . . explain[ed] how the film footage could contain a distinctive mark or how footage of the Three Stooges' name, voices, images and act can have secondary meaning." The Court opined that Comedy III might have a trademark claim "[h]ad New Line used the likeness of the Three Stooges on t-shirts which it was selling . . . [b]ut we will not entertain this expedition of trademark protection squarely into the dominion of copyright law." Plaintiff was in fact successful in a subsequent case against a defendant selling t-shirts bearing a likeness of The Three Stooges, but under right of publicity law rather than trademark law. *Comedy III Productions, Inc. v. Saderup*, 58 U.S.P.Q.2d 1823 (Cal. 2001). See the discussion on right of publicity law in the following section.

The active market in licensing toys and other products based on created characters inevitably has led to attempts to manufacture and sell imitative products without license from, or payment to, the creators of the characters or their assignees. The Second and Seventh Circuit were both called upon to determine whether the sale of toy cars imitative of the distinctive "General Lee" Dodge Charger on the "Dukes of Hazzard" television series infringed the rights of the series' producer under § 43(a). Based in part upon plaintiff's evidence indicating that eight out of every ten children surveyed immediately associated defendant's toy car with the "General Lee" of the television show, the Second Circuit reversed the lower court's denial of plaintiff's motion for a preliminary injunction. The appellate court found that "many of the consumers . . . assumed that the car was sponsored by Warner Bros. This is sufficient to invoke the protection of this Court." *Warner Bros., Inc. v. Gay Toys, Inc.*, 658 F.2d 76, 79 (2d Cir. 1981). In a later decision the Seventh Circuit noted that the Second Circuit's references to consumer perception of direct sponsorship by plaintiff may have overstated the case: "it is sufficient if the public assumes that the product comes from a single though anonymous, source." *Processed Plastic Co. v. Warner Communications*, 675 F.2d 852, 856 (7th Cir. 1982).

Compare Ideal Toy Corp. v. Kenner Products Div., 443 F. Supp. 291 (S.D.N.Y. 1977), where "Star Team" toys somewhat similar in appearance and theme to characters in the popular "Star Wars" movie were found not to infringe the rights of that movie's producer. On the copyright issue in the declaratory judgment action the court stated,

> The defendants have no more right to a monopoly in the theme of a black robed, helmeted, evil figure in outer space conflict with a humanoid and a smaller nonhumanoid robot than Shakespeare would have in the theme of a "riotous knight who kept wassail to the discomfort of the household," and who had conflicts with "a foppish steward who had become amorous of his mistress."

Ideal Toy, 443 F. Supp. at 304. On the unfair competition issue it stated, "A finding of general 'association' — that the toys 'look like' the movie or remind someone of the movie — does not mean that the prospective purchaser thinks that the toys are derived from the movie or 'sponsored' by the movie." *Ideal Toy*, 443 F. Supp. at 308.

The *De Costa* decision, supra, (relief denied creator of "Paladin" character against broadcasting company that based TV series on that character), was roundly criticized after it came down. Mr. DeCosta subsequently persisted in attempting to vindicate his rights. After the 1975 decision, he succeeded in obtaining a federal registration for the Paladin mark over CBS's opposition, with the Trademark Trial and Appeal Board stating: "This seems to us to be a bald-face argument that opposer, already branded a pirate, should be allowed to make off with additional plunder unhindered by any inconvenience that might result from the recognition of applicant's lawful rights." *Columbia Broadcasting System, Inc. v. De Costa*, 192 U.S.P.Q. 453, 457 (T.T.A.B. 1976). In *DeCosta v. Viacom International, Inc.*, 758 F. Supp. 807 (D.R.I. 1991), the court found that CBS's assignment of its rights to defendant and De Costa's acquisition of trademark registrations created new "clusters of conduct" and new rights for De Costa justifying a new trial. A jury in the new trial then awarded De Costa $200,000. The First Circuit, however, reversed the district court and dismissed the case, holding De Costa was collaterally estopped by its prior decision. *DeCosta v. Viacom Int'l, Inc.*, 25 U.S.P.Q.2d 1187 (1st Cir. 1992).

8.05   Right of Publicity

Introduction

The right of publicity is the exclusive right of an individual to the commercial exploitation of his or her identity, including name, likeness and other identity attributes. As the court stated in *Carson v. Here's Johnny Portable Toilets, Inc.*, 698 F.2d 831 (6th Cir. 1983): "A celebrity's right of publicity is invaded whenever his identity is intentionally misappropriated for commercial purposes." The commercial invocation of a person's identity can take many forms. *Landham v. Lewis Galoob Toys, Inc.*, 227 F.3d 619, 624 (6th Cir. 2000) ("Although the right began as a protection for a celebrity's 'name and likeness', i.e. physical features, it is now generally understood to cover anything that suggests the plaintiff's personal identity"). The right of publicity developed as an offshoot from the law of the right of privacy, under which a person's feelings and private affairs are afforded protection. *See* McCarthy, Rights of Publicity AND Privacy §§ 1.5, 1.7 (4th ed. 2007).

Recognition of the right of publicity is a relatively recent legal development. It was first referred to as such in *Haelan Laboratories, Inc. v. Topps Chewing Gum, Inc.*, 202 F.2d 866 (2d Cir.), *cert. denied*, 346 U.S. 816 (1953). There the plaintiff had asserted an exclusive right to use baseball players' photographs in connection with the sales of plaintiffs' chewing gum. In recognizing the right, the court observed that ballplayers "would feel sorely deprived if they no longer received money for authorizing advertisements popularizing their countenances . . . . This right of publicity would usually yield them no money unless it could be made the subject of an exclusive grant which barred any other advertiser from using their pictures." 202 F.2d at 868. *See also Pavesich v. New England Life Insurance Co.*, 50 S.E. 68 (Ga. 1905) (early case extending individual's right of privacy to the prevention of the unauthorized, nondefamatory advertising use of a name or likeness). *Cf. Roberson v. Rochester Folding Box Co.*, 64 N.E. 442 (N.Y. 1902) (rejecting common law right of privacy claim and permitting nonlibelous use of plaintiff's portrait on advertising posters).

Is the right of publicity more properly viewed as an economic incentive for the type of achievement that brings commercial value to a person's name or likeness, or as a means of preventing unjust enrichment by theft of goodwill? *See Zacchini v. Scripps-Howard Broadcasting Co.*, 433 U.S. 562 (1977). What difference might this make? If a court considers the right to be an economic incentive, and in the particular fact situation there is no deception as to source or sponsorship, a countervailing public interest in having information about the famous personality or in viewing performances or having souvenirs that evoke that personality might be found to outweigh the individual's right of publicity. If, however, the individual was deemed to have created a protectable goodwill subject to the individual's exclusive control, any commercial use by another of that goodwill without permission would be unjust enrichment if not an unlawful theft, presumably making a balancing test inapplicable.

Would the elimination of right of publicity law and the consequent economic benefits to the individual really affect the efforts individuals make to achieve fame, or act to reduce the number of persons willing to make the necessary effort? Should public acclaim result in an individual being protected from *any* unauthorized use of his or her name or likeness when the use has some commercial ramifications (e.g., use of a famous person's name in an novel or movie)? In the material that follows consider the function of, and the basis and necessity for, right of publicity law, and compare it with the law of unfair competition as discussed earlier in this chapter.

WHITE v. SAMSUNG ELECTRONICS AMERICA, INC.
United States Court of Appeals, Ninth Circuit
971 F.2d 1395 (1992)

GOODWIN, SENIOR CIRCUIT JUDGE

*   *   *

This case involves a promotional "fame and fortune" dispute. In running a particular advertisement without Vanna White's permission, defendants Samsung Electronics America, Inc. (Samsung) and David Deutsch Associates, Inc. (Deutsch) attempted to capitalize on White's fame to enhance their fortune. White sued, alleging infringement of various intellectual property rights, but the district court granted summary judgment in favor of the defendants. We affirm in part, reverse in part, and remand.

Plaintiff Vanna White is the hostess of "Wheel of Fortune," one of the most popular game shows in television history. An estimated forty million people watch the program daily. Capitalizing on the fame which her participation in the show has bestowed on her, White markets her identity to various advertisers.

The dispute in this case arose out of a series of advertisements prepared for Samsung by Deutsch. The series ran in an least half a dozen publications with widespread, and in some cases national, circulation. Each of the advertisements in the series followed the same theme. Each depicted a current item from popular culture and a Samsung electronic product. Each was set in the twenty-first century and conveyed the message that the Samsung product would still be in use by that time. By hypothesizing outrageous future outcomes for the cultural items, the ads created humorous effects. For example, one lampooned current popular notions of an unhealthy diet by depicting a raw steak with the caption: "Revealed to be health food. 2010 A.D." Another depicted irreverent "news"-show host Morton Downey Jr. in front of an American flag with the caption: "Presidential candidate. 2008 A.D."

The advertisement which prompted the current dispute was for Samsung videocassette recorders (VCRs). The ad depicted a robot, dressed in a wig, gown, and jewelry which Deutsch consciously selected to resemble White's hair and dress. The robot was posed next to a game board which is instantly recognizable as the Wheel of Fortune game show set, in a stance for which White is famous. The caption of the ad read: "Longest-running game show. 2012 A.D." Defendants referred to the ad as the "Vanna White" ad. Unlike the other celebrities used in the campaign, White neither consented to the ads nor was she paid.

*   *   *

I. Section 3344

White first argues that the district court erred in rejecting her claim under [California Civil Code] § 3344. Section 3344(a) provides, in pertinent part, that "[a] ny person who knowingly uses another's name, voice, signature, photograph, or likeness, in any manner, . . . for purposes of advertising or selling, . . . without such person's prior consent . . . shall be liable for any damages sustained by the person or persons injured as a result thereof."

White argues that the Samsung advertisement used her "likeness" in contravention of § 3344. In *Midler v. Ford Motor Co.*, 849 F.2d 460 (9th Cir. 1988), this court rejected Bette Midler's § 3344 claim concerning a Ford television commercial in which a Midler "sound-alike" sang a song which Midler had made famous. In rejecting Midler's claim, this court noted that "[t]he defendants did not use Midler's name or anything else whose use is prohibited by the statute. The voice they used was [another person's], not hers. The term 'likeness' refers to a visual image not a vocal imitation." *Id.* at 463.

In this case, Samsung and Deutsch used a robot with mechanical features, and not, for example, a manikin molded to White's precise features. Without deciding for all purposes when a caricature or impressionistic resemblance might become a "likeness," we agree with the district court that the robot at issue here was not White's "likeness" within the meaning of § 3344. Accordingly, we affirm the court's dismissal of White's § 3344 claim.

II. Right of Publicity

White next argues that the district court erred in granting summary judgment to defendants on White's common law right of publicity claim. In *Eastwood v. Superior Court*, 149 Cal. App. 3d 409, 198 Cal. Rptr. 342 (1983), the California court of appeal stated that the common law right of publicity cause of action "may be pleaded by alleging (1) the defendant's use of the plaintiff's identity; (2) the appropriation of plaintiff's name or likeness to defendant's advantage, commercially or otherwise; (3) lack of consent; and (4) resulting injury." *Id.* at 417 (citing Prosser, *Law of Torts* (4th ed. 1971) § 117 pp. 804–807). The district court dismissed White's claim for failure to satisfy *Eastwood's* second prong, reasoning that defendants had not appropriated White's "name or likeness" with their robot ad. We agree that the robot ad did not make use of White's name or likeness. However, the common law right of publicity is not so confined.

*   *   *

Since Prosser's early formulation, the case law has borne out his insight that the right of publicity is not limited to the appropriation of name or likeness. In *Motschenbacher v. R.J. Reynolds Tobacco Co.*, 498 F.2d 821 (9th Cir. 1974), the defendant had used a photograph of the plaintiff's race car in a television commercial. Although the plaintiff appeared driving the car in the photograph, his features were not visible. Even though the defendant had not appropriated the plaintiff's name or likeness, this court held that plaintiff's California right of publicity claim should reach the jury.

In *Midler*, this court held that, even though the defendants had not used Midler's name or likeness, Midler had stated a claim for violation of her California common law right of publicity because "the defendants . . . for their own profit in selling their product did appropriate part of her identity" by using a Midler sound-alike. *Id.* at 463–64.

In *Carson v. Here's Johnny Portable Toilets, Inc.*, 698 F.2d 831 (6th Cir. 1983), the defendant had marketed portable toilets under the brand name "Here's Johnny" — Johnny Carson's signature "Tonight Show" introduction — without Carson's permission. The district court had dismissed Carson's Michigan common law right of publicity claim because the defendants had not used Carson's "name or likeness." *Id.* at 835. In reversing the district court, the sixth circuit found "the district court's conception of the right of publicity . . . too narrow" and held that the right was implicated because the defendant had appropriated Carson's identity by using, *inter alia*, the phrase "Here's Johnny." *Id.* at 835–37.

* * *

Although the defendants in these cases avoided the most obvious means of appropriating the plaintiffs' identities, each of their actions directly implicated the commercial interests which the right of publicity is designed to protect. As the *Carson* court explained:

> [t]he right of publicity has developed to protect the commercial interest of celebrities in their identities. The theory of the right is that a celebrity's identity can be valuable in the promotion of products, and the celebrity has an interest that may be protected from the unauthorized commercial exploitation of that identity.. . . If the celebrity's identity is commercially exploited, there has been an invasion of his right whether or not his "name or likeness" is used.

Carson, 698 F.2d at 835. It is not important *how* the defendant has appropriated the plaintiff's identity, but *whether* the defendant has done so. *Motschenbacher*, *Midler*, and *Carson* teach the impossibility of treating the right of publicity as guarding only against a laundry list of specific means of appropriating identity. A rule which says that the right of publicity can be infringed only through the use of nine different methods of appropriating identity merely challenges the clever advertising strategist to come up with the tenth.

* * *

Consider a hypothetical advertisement which depicts a mechanical robot with male features, an African-American complexion, and a bald head. The robot is wearing black hightop Air Jordan basketball sneakers, and a red basketball uniform with black trim, baggy shorts, and the number 23 (though not revealing "Bulls" or "Jordan" lettering). The ad depicts the robot dunking a basketball one-handed, stiff-armed, legs extended like open scissors, and tongue hanging out. Now envision that this ad is run on television during professional basketball games. Considered individually, the robot's physical attributes, its dress, and its stance tell us little. Taken together, they lead to the only conclusion that any sports viewer who has registered a discernible pulse in the past five years would reach: the ad is about Michael Jordan.

Viewed separately, the individual aspects of the advertisement in the present case say little. Viewed together, they leave little doubt about the celebrity the ad is meant to depict. The female-shaped robot is wearing a long gown, blond wig, and large jewelry. Vanna White dresses exactly like this at times, but so do many other women. The robot is in the process of turning a block letter on a game-board. Vanna White dresses like this while turning letters on a game-board but perhaps similarly attired Scrabble-playing women do this as well. The robot is standing on what looks to be the Wheel of Fortune game show set. Vanna White dresses like this, turns letters, and does this on the Wheel of Fortune game show. She is the only one. Indeed, defendants themselves referred to their ad as the "Vanna White" ad. We are not surprised.

Television and other media create marketable celebrity identity value. Considerable energy and ingenuity are expended by those who have achieved celebrity value to exploit it for profit. The law protects the celebrity's sole right to exploit this value whether the celebrity has achieved her fame out of rare ability, dumb luck, or a combination thereof. We decline Samsung and Deutsch's invitation to permit the evisceration of the common law right of publicity through means as facile as those in this case. Because White has alleged facts showing that Samsung and Deutsch had appropriated her identity, the district court erred by rejecting, on summary judgment, White's common law right of publicity claim.

III. The Lanham Act

* * *

[T]he district court [also] erred in rejecting White's Lanham Act claim at the summary judgment stage. In so concluding, we emphasize two facts, however. First, construing the motion papers in White's favor, as we must, we hold only that White has raised a genuine issue of material fact concerning a likelihood of confusion as to her endorsement. *Cohen v. Paramount Pictures Corp.*, 845 F.2d 851, 852–53 (9th Cir. 1988). Whether White's Lanham Act claim should succeed is a matter for the jury. Second, we stress that we reach this conclusion in light of the peculiar facts of this case. In particular, we note that the robot ad identifies White and was part of a series of ads in which other celebrities participated and were paid for their endorsement of Samsung's products.

IV. The Parody Defense

In defense, defendants cite a number of cases for the proposition that their robot ad constituted protected speech. The only cases they cite which are even remotely relevant to this case are *Hustler Magazine v. Falwell*, 485 U.S. 46 (1988) and *L.L. Bean, Inc. v. Drake Publishers, Inc.*, 811 F.2d 26 (1st Cir. 1987). Those cases involved parodies of advertisements run for the purpose of poking fun at Jerry Falwell and L.L. Bean, respectively. This case involves a true advertisement run for the purpose of selling Samsung VCRs. The ad's spoof of Vanna White and Wheel of Fortune is subservient and only tangentially related to the ad's primary message: "buy Samsung VCRs." Defendants' parody arguments are better addressed to non-commercial parodies. The difference between a "parody" and a "knock-off" is the difference between fun and profit.

* * *

[Remanded].

WHITE v. SAMSUNG ELECTRONICS AMERICA, INC.
United States Court of Appeals, Ninth Circuit
989 F.2d 1512 (1993)

KOZINSKI, CIRCUIT JUDGE, with whom CIRCUIT JUDGES O'SCANNLAIN and KLEINFELD join, dissenting from the order rejecting the suggestion for rehearing en banc.

I.

Saddam Hussein wants to keep advertisers from using his picture in unflattering contexts. Clint Eastwood doesn't want tabloids to write about him. Rudolf Valentino's heirs want to control his film biography. The Girl Scouts don't want their image soiled by association with certain activities. George Lucas wants to keep Strategic Defense Initiative fans from calling it "Star Wars." Pepsico doesn't want singers to use the word "Pepsi" in their songs.[6] Guy Lombardo wants an exclusive property right to ads that

---

[6] Pepsico Inc. claimed the lyrics and packaging of grunge rocker Tad Doyle's "Jack Pepsi" song were "offensive to [it] and [. . .] likely to offend [its] customers," in part because they "associate [Pepsico] and its Pepsi marks with intoxication and drunk driving." Deborah Russell, *Doyle Leaves Pepsi Thirsty for*

show big bands playing on New Year's Eve. Uri Geller thinks he should be paid for ads showing psychics bending metal through telekinesis. Paul Prudhomme, that household name, thinks the same about ads featuring corpulent bearded chefs. And scads of copyright holders see purple when their creations are made fun of.

Something very dangerous is going on here. Private property, including intellectual property, is essential to our way of life. It provides an incentive for investment and innovation; it stimulates the flourishing of our culture; it protects the moral entitlements of people to the fruits of their labors. But reducing too much to private property can be bad medicine. Private land, for instance, is far more useful if separated from other private land by public streets, roads and highways. Public parks, utility rights-of-way and sewers reduce the amount of land in private hands, but vastly enhance the value of the property that remains.

So too it is with intellectual property. Overprotecting intellectual property is as harmful as underprotecting it. Creativity is impossible without a rich public domain. Nothing today, likely nothing since we tamed fire, is genuinely new: Culture, like science and technology, grows by accretion, each new creator building on the works of those who came before. Overprotection stifles the very creative forces it's supposed to nurture.

The panel's opinion is a classic case of overprotection. Concerned about what it sees as a wrong done to Vanna White, the panel majority erects a property right of remarkable and dangerous breadth: Under the majority's opinion, it's now a tort for advertisers to *remind* the public of a celebrity. Not to use a celebrity's name, voice, signature or likeness; not to imply the celebrity endorses a product; but simply to evoke the celebrity's image in the public's mind. This Orwellian notion withdraws far more from the public domain than prudence and common sense allow. It conflicts with the Copyright Act and the Copyright Clause. It raises serious First Amendment problems. It's bad law, and it deserves a long, hard second look.

Compensation, Billboard, June 15, 1991, at 43. Conversely, the Hell's Angels recently sued Marvel Comics to keep it from publishing a comic book called "Hell's Angel," starring a character of the same name. Marvel settled by paying $35,000 to charity and promising never to use the name "Hell's Angel" again in connection with any of its publications. *Marvel, Hell's Angels Settle Trademark Suit*, L.A. Daily J., Feb. 2, 1993, § II, at 1.

Trademarks are often reflected in the mirror of our popular culture. *See* Truman Capote, *Breakfast at Tiffany's* (1958); Kurt Vonnegut, Jr., *Breakfast of Champions* (1973); Tom Wolfe, *The Electric Kool-Aid Acid Test* (1968) (which, incidentally, includes a chapter on the Hell's Angels); Larry Niven, *Man of Steel, Woman of Kleenex* in *All the Myriad Ways* (1971); *Looking for Mr. Goodbar* (1977); *The Coca-Cola Kid* (1985) (using Coca-Cola as a metaphor for American commercialism); *The Kentucky Fried Movie* (1977); *Harley Davidson and the Marlboro Man* (1991); *The Wonder Years* (ABC 1988–present) ("Wonder Years" was a slogan of Wonder Bread); Tim Rice and Andrew Lloyd Webber, *Joseph and the Amazing Technicolor Dream Coat* (musical).

Hear Janis Joplin, *Mercedes Benz*, on *Pearl* (CBS 1971); Paul Simon, *Kodachrome*, on *There Goes Rhymin' Simon* (Warner 1973); Leonard Cohen, *Chelsea Hotel*, on *The Best of Leonard Cohen* (CBS 1975); Bruce Springsteen, *Cadillac Ranch*, on *The River* (CBS 1980); Prince, *Little Red Corvette*, on *1999* (Warner 1982); dada, *Dizz Knee Land*, on *Puzzle* (IRS 1992) ("I just robbed a grocery store — I'm going to Disneyland/I just flipped off President George — I'm going to Disneyland"); Monty Python, *Spam*, on *The Final Rip Off* (Virgin 1988); Roy Clark, *Thank God and Greyhound [You're Gone]*, on *Roy Clark's Greatest Hits Volume I* (MCA 1979); Mel Tillis, *Coca-Cola Cowboy*, on *The Very Best of* (MCA 1981) ("You're just a Coca-Cola cowboy/You've got an Eastwood smile and Robert Redford hair. . . .").

Dance to Talking Heads, *Popular Favorites 1976–92: Sand in the Vaseline* (Sire 1992); Talking Heads, *Popsicle*, on *id. Admire* Andy Warhol, *Campbell's Soup Can. Cf.* REO Speedwagon, 38 Special, and Jello Biafra of the Dead Kennedys.

The creators of some of these works might have gotten permission from the trademark owners, though it's unlikely Kool-Aid relished being connected with LSD, Hershey with homicidal maniacs, Disney with armed robbers, or Coca-Cola with cultural imperialism. Certainly no free society can *demand* that artists get such permission.

* * *

The majority isn't, in fact, preventing the "evisceration" of Vanna White's existing rights; it's creating a new and much broader property right, a right unknown in California law. It's replacing the existing balance between the interests of the celebrity and those of the public by a different balance, one substantially more favorable to the celebrity. Instead of having an exclusive right in her name, likeness, signature or voice, every famous person now has an exclusive right to *anything that reminds the viewer of her.* After all, that's all Samsung did. It used an inanimate object to remind people of White, to "evoke [her identity]." 971 F.2d at 1399.

Consider how sweeping this new right is. What is it about the ad that makes people think of White? It's not the robot's wig, clothes or jewelry; there must be ten million blond women (many of them quasi-famous) who wear dresses and jewelry like White's. It's that the robot is posed near the "Wheel of Fortune" game board. Remove the game board from the ad, and no one would think of Vanna White. *See* Appendix. But once you include the game board, anybody standing beside it — a brunette woman, a man wearing women's clothes, a monkey in a wig and gown — would evoke White's image, precisely the way the robot did. It's the "Wheel of Fortune" set, not the robot's face or dress or jewelry that evokes White's image. The panel is giving White an exclusive right not in what she looks like or who she is, but in what she does for a living.

This is entirely the wrong place to strike the balance. Intellectual property rights aren't free: They're imposed at the expense of future creators and of the public at large. Where would we be if Charles Lindbergh had an exclusive right in the concept of a heroic solo aviator? If Arthur Conan Doyle had gotten a copyright in the idea of the detective story, or Albert Einstein had patented the theory of relativity? If every author and celebrity had been given the right to keep people from mocking them or their work? Surely this would have made the world poorer, not richer, culturally as well as economically.

This is why intellectual property law is full of careful balances between what's set aside for the owner and what's left in the public domain for the rest of us. The relatively short life of patents; the longer, but finite, life of copyrights; copyright's idea-expression dichotomy; the fair use doctrine; the prohibition on copyrighting facts; the compulsory license of television broadcasts and musical compositions; federal preemption of overbroad state intellectual property laws; the nominative use doctrine in trademark law; the right to make soundalike recordings. All of these diminish an intellectual property owner's rights. All let the public use something created by someone else. But all are necessary to maintain a free environment in which creative genius can flourish.

The intellectual property right created by the panel here has none of these essential limitations: No fair use exception; no right to parody; no idea-expression dichotomy. It impoverishes the public domain, to the detriment of future creators and the public at large. Instead of well-defined, limited characteristics such as name, likeness or voice, advertisers will now have to cope with vague claims of "appropriation of identity," claims often made by people with a wholly exaggerated sense of their own fame and significance. *See* pp. 1512–13 & notes 1–10 *supra.* Future Vanna Whites might not get the chance to create their personae, because their employers may fear some celebrity will claim the persona is too similar to her own. The public will be robbed of parodies of celebrities, and our culture will be deprived of the valuable safety valve that parody and mockery create.

* * *

Notes on Right of Publicity

1. Generally

The right of publicity exists only under state statutory and common law. Some states, like New York, statutorily restrict the scope of the right of publicity. *See Hampton v. Guare*, 22 U.S.P.Q.2d 1713 (N.Y. Sup. Ct. 1992), *aff'd*, 600 N.Y.S.2d 57 (N.Y. Ct. App.), *appeal denied*, 625 N.E.2d 590 (1993) (defendant's unauthorized use in the play, "Six Degrees of Separation," of events from plaintiff's life did not violate plaintiff's right of publicity because it was not use of plaintiff's "name, portrait or picture" as required by applicable New York statute); *Stephano v. News Group Publications, Inc.*, 474 N.E.2d 580 (N.Y. 1984) (protection restricted to names and likenesses). Other states, generally through their courts, have been more expansive, so that commercial use of any attribute, characteristic or object associated by the public with the individual may be actionable. *See, e.g., Carson v. Here's Johnny Portable Toilets, Inc.*, 698 F.2d 831 (6th Cir. 1983) (phrase "Here's Johnny" associated with celebrity Johnny Carson); *Motschenbacher v. R. J. Reynolds Tobacco Co.*, 498 F.2d 821, 827 (9th Cir. 1974) (concluding there was a common law right of publicity claim for use of identifiable race car associated with famous driver, even though the driver himself was not shown). *Compare Matthews v. Wozencraft*, 15 F.3d 432, 437 (5th Cir. 1994) (unauthorized use of defendant's life story in book and movie, "Rush," not a misappropriation of name or likeness under Texas common law; "life story . . .is not a name or likeness'").

Whether a particular non-identical use constitutes use of a person's name or likeness is an issue of fact. See, e.g., *Donchez v. Coors Brewing Co.*, 392 F.3d 1211 (10th Cir. 2004) (even if Colorado recognized a right of publicity, none of the characters in Coors' commercials resembled plaintiff's alleged "Bob the Beerman" character and plaintiff failed to prove Coors had used his likeness to its commercial advantage); *Newcombe v. Adolf Coors Company*, 157 F.3d 686 (9th Cir. 1998) (reversing summary judgment granted beer company and advertising agency, where beer ad featured redrawn newspaper photograph of former major league baseball all-star, and recovering alcoholic, Don Newcombe; "we hold that a triable issue of fact has been raised as to whether Newcombe is readily identifiable as the pitcher in the advertisement"); *Wendt v. Host International, Inc.*, 125 F.3d 806 (9th Cir. 1997) (district court had granted defendant summary judgment, finding that animatronic robots placed in airport bars modeled after the set for the Cheers television show had "no similarity at all" to plaintiff actors who had starred in that show; in reversing, the appellate court concluded, "[a]ppellants have raised genuine issues of material fact concerning the degree to which the figures look like them", and "[t]he ultimate issue for the jury to decide is whether the defendants are commercially exploiting the likeness of the figures to Wendt and Ratzenberger to engender profits to their enterprises").

In *Nurmi v. Peterson*, 10 U.S.P.Q.2d 1775 (C.D. Cal. 1989), plaintiff's publicity claim was dismissed because she did not claim that the actual features of her VAMPIRA character, a 1950s horror movie TV hostess, had been used for commercial purposes, but only that defendant had created a new character that resembled VAMPIRA. *Compare Nurmi* with the *White* decision, *supra*, in which, arguably, a "resemblance" of Vanna White was used for commercial purposes. *See Gigliotti, Beyond Name and Likeness: Should California's Expansion of the Right of Publicity Protect Non-Human Identity*, 83 TRADEMARK REP. 64 (1993) (analyzing the *White* decision).

As digital imaging becomes more sophisticated and widely used, novel right of publicity issues are likely to arise. Might a digitally created virtual person have a right of publicity? What if a portion of a celebrity's anatomy, e.g., Bette Davis' eyes, is digitally "borrowed" and used in a depiction of someone else? An interesting discussion of the potential legal ramifications of this developing technology may be found in Beard, "*Clones, Bones and Twilight Zones: Protecting the Digital Persona of the Quick, the*

Dead, and the Imaginary," 16 BERKELEY TECH. L. J. 1165 (2001).

At least forty states now provide some protection for the right of publicity, by statute or common law — or both. *See generally* MCCARTHY, RIGHT OF PUBLICITY AND PRIVACY, Ch. 6 (2ᵈ ed. 2006). *Cf. Donchez v. Coors Brewing Co.*, 392 F.3d 1211 (10ᵗʰ Cir. 2004) (Colorado had not yet recognized a right of publicity). Because the right of publicity exists under state rather than federal law, conflict of law principles often must be applied in publicity cases. *See, e.g., Groucho Marx Productions, Inc. v. Day & Night Co.*, 689 F.2d 317, 319–20 (2ᵈ Cir. 1982); *Bi-Rite Enterprises, Inc. v. Bruce Miner Co.*, 757 F.2d 440 (1ˢᵗ Cir. 1985) (considering British and American law). Should there be a federal right of publicity statute? *See, e.g.*, Haemmerli, *Whose Who? The Case for a Kantian Right of Publicity*, 49 DUKE L. J. 383 (1999) (arguing the time is right for such a federal statute); Robinson, *Preemption, the Right of Publicity, and a New Federal Statute*, 16 CARDOZO ARTS & ENT. L.J. 183 (1998).

Articles discussing the right of publicity include: Symposium, *Trademark and Publicity Rights of Athletes*, 15 FORDHAM INTELL. PROP. MEDIA & ENT. L. J. 49 (2005); Lloyd, *Who Should Profit - The Balancing Act between a Celebrity's Right of Publicity and The Public's Right of Freedom of Expression in a Capitalist Society*, 15 SETON HALL J. SPORTS & ENT. L. 85 (2005); Goddenough, *Go Fish: Evaluating The Restatement's Formulation of the Law of Publicity*, 47 S. C. L. REV. 709 (1996) (including a good discussion of the history of publicity law); McCarthy, *The Human Persona as Commercial Property: The Right of Publicity*, 19 COLUM-VLA JL & ARTS 129 (1995); Bloom, *Preventing the Misappropriation of Identity: Beyond the Right of Publicity*, 13 HASTINGS COMM. & ENT. L.J. 489 (1991); Armstrong, *The Reification of Celebrity: Persona as Property*, 51 LA. L. REV. 443 (1991).

2. The Zacchini Case

In *Zacchini v. Scripps-Howard Broadcasting Co.*, 433 U.S. 562 (1977), an Ohio television station had shown a film of the entirety of plaintiff's 15-second "human cannonball" circus act on a newscast. In holding that the First and Fourteenth Amendments did not require the state to grant a privilege to the press from liability under Ohio's right of publicity law, the Court observed (p. 573) that: "the state's interest in permitting a 'right of publicity', is . . . closely analogous to the goals of patent and copyright law, focusing on the right of the individual to reap the reward of his endeavors and having little to do with protecting feelings or reputation." The Court found that the broadcast went "to the heart of [plaintiff's] ability to earn a living as an entertainer" and therefore constituted "what may be the strongest case for a 'right of publicity' — involving, not the appropriation of an entertainer's reputation to enhance the attractiveness of a commercial product, but the appropriation of the very activity by which the entertainer acquired his reputation in the first place." *Id.* at 576.

The Court referred to the prevention of "unjust enrichment by the theft of goodwill" as a rationale for protecting the right of publicity, but rested its decision on the basis of the state's legitimate interest in providing an economic incentive for entertainers "to make the investment required to produce a performance of interest to the public." *Id.* *Compare Cardtoons, L.C. v. Major League Baseball Players Ass'n*, 95 F.3d 959, 973–76 (10ᵗʰ Cir. 1996) (discussing, and finding unpersuasive, the economic and non-economic justifications for enforcing a right of publicity to proscribe defendant's baseball card parodies of major league baseball players). *See* Note, *Human Cannonballs and the First Amendment: Zacchini v. Scripps-Howard Broadcasting Co.*, 30 STAN. L. REV. (1978).

3. First Amendment Concerns

a) Dissemination of Information and Ideas

If the primary purpose of the unauthorized use is dissemination of ideas or information, the right of publicity may give way to the First Amendment. *Rosemont Enterprises, Inc. v. Random House, Inc.*, 58 Misc. 2d 1, 6 (N.Y. Sup. Ct. 1968), *aff'd*, 301 N.Y.S.2d 948 (App. Div. 1969) ("Just as a public figure's 'right of privacy' must yield to the public interest so too must the 'right of publicity' bow where such conflicts with the free dissemination of thought, ideas, newsworthy events, and matters of public interest"); *Matthews v. Wozencraft*, 15 F.3d 432 (5th Cir. 1994) (unauthorized use in book and movie "Rush" of events from plaintiff's life held permissible because defendant's work did not demonstrate a "reckless disregard for the truth" under the applicable public figure standard); *Rogers v. Grimaldi*, 875 F.2d 994 (2d Cir. 1989) (right of publicity will not bar use of celebrity's name in a movie title unless it is "wholly unrelated" or simply a disguised advertisement for collateral goods or services); *Hicks v. Casablanca Records*, 464 F. Supp. 426 (S.D.N.Y. 1978) (no liability for novel and movie portrayal of fictionalized account of incident in author Agatha Christie's life). *Compare Eastwood v. National Enquirer, Inc.*, 123 F.3d 1249, 1256 (9th Cir. 1997) (false publication of "exclusive interview" with actor Clint Eastwood met "actual malice" standard for a public figure to recover damages from a news organization; "the editors intended to convey the impression — known by them to be false — that Eastwood willfully submitted to an interview by the [National] Enquirer" and the jury award of $150,000 was justified because the jury could have found his fans would either think him a hypocrite for doing so, or that he was "essentially washed up as a movie star if he was courting publicity in a sensationalist tabloid."); *Elvis Presley Enterprises, Inc. v. Elvisly Yours, Inc.*, 936 F.2d 889 (6th Cir. 1991) (scope of injunction limited to prohibit only unauthorized *commercial* use of Elvis Presley's name, image or likeness, as opposed to *all* use).

b) The Information Need Not Have Great Significance

The protected informational content need not have great social or political significance. *Lerman v. Flynt Distributing Co.*, 745 F.2d 123, 128 (2d Cir. 1984), *cert. denied*, 471 U.S. 1054 (1985) (no liability for nude photograph of person misidentified as plaintiff); *Michaels v. Internet Entertainment Group*, 48 U.S.P.Q.2d 1891 (C.D. Cal. 1998) (no liability where entertainment news show broadcast excerpts of videotape showing actress Pamela Anderson Lee *en flagrante*); *Ann-Margret v. High Soc. Magazine, Inc.*, 498 F. Supp. 401 (S.D.N.Y. 1980) (no liability for use of semi-nude photograph of actress; First Amendment protection applies even when media is being "trivial or . . . obnoxious"); *Montana v. San Jose Mercury News, Inc.*, 35 U.S.P.Q.2d 1783 (Cal. Ct. App. 1995) (First Amendment protected a newspaper publisher from liability for selling a reproduced drawing of football star Joe Montana that originally appeared in the newspaper's "Souvenir Section").

c) Predominantly Commercial Use

In *Hoffman v. Capital Cities*, 255 F.3d 1180 (9th Cir. 2001), *Los Angeles Times Magazine* had published a "Fabulous Hollywood Issue" which included a "Grand Illusions" article. In the article sixteen famous movie stills had been altered to show the actors wearing 1997 fashions, including one with plaintiff Dustin Hoffman playing a woman in the movie, "Tootsie." The lower court awarded Hoffman $3 million in compensatory and punitive damages, plus attorneys' fees. The appellate court reversed.

While the use of his image was in an article, Hoffman pointed out that a "Shopper's Guide" in the back provided stores and prices for the shoes and gown superimposed on his image. The appellate court countered that his image was not used in a traditional advertisement for the purpose of selling a product, that the magazine was not paid by the designers for featuring their clothing in the article, and that the article was the cover article for the issues' theme, combining "fashion photography, humor, and visual and verbal editorial comment on classic films and famous actors." It concluded that the use of photograph was "not commercial speech" and was "entitled to full First Amendment protection," thus defeating Hoffman's claim.

Conversely, where the predominant purpose of the use is commercial, First Amendment rights may give way to a plaintiff's right of publicity. *See, e.g., Downing v. Abercrombie & Fitch*, 265 F.3d 994 (9th Cir. 2001) (although clothing catalogue had a surfing theme, depiction of plaintiff professional surfers was used in advertising context to sell clothing and violated their right of publicity, distinguishing *Hoffman*); *Abdul-Jabbar v. General Motors Corp.*, 85 F.3d 407 (9th Cir. 1996) (no First Amendment right to feature basketball star's former name and his college championship history in conjunction with an automobile advertisement despite informational content); *Tellado v. Time-Life Books, Inc.*, 643 F. Supp. 904, 910, 913 (D.N.J. 1986) (defendant's motion for summary judgment denied; First Amendment claim rejected where defendant's use of a photograph of plaintiff veteran to advertise a book series on the Viet Nam War appeared to be a "predominantly commercial" use designed to "stimulate profits"); *Mendonsa v. Time, Inc.*, 678 F. Supp. 967, 971–72 (D.R.I. 1988) (original magazine publication of famous "kissing sailor" photograph featuring plaintiff on V-J Day was protected by First Amendment, but plaintiff stated a publicity cause of action for the magazine's subsequent offer to sell readers copies of the photograph for $1,600 each). *Compare with Page v. Something Weird Video*, 40 U.S.P.Q.2d 1196, 1200 (C.D. Cal. 1996) (First Amendment protected defendant's use of unauthorized drawings resembling plaintiff to advertise videos featuring plaintiff; "[b]ecause the films themselves are protected by the First Amendment, the incidental advertising is also protected").

d)　Transformative Use

In *Comedy III Productions, Inc. v. Saderup*, 58 U.S.P.Q.2d 1823 (Cal. Supreme Ct. 2001), involving t-shirts bearing the likenesses of The Three Stooges, the court endorsed "a balancing test between the First Amendment and the right of publicity based on whether the work in question adds significant creative elements so as to be transformed into something more than a mere celebrity likeness or imitation." It reasoned that when a work "contains significant transformative elements," like a parody, for example, "it is also less likely to interfere with the economic interest protected by the right of publicity," and does not "generally threaten [the] markets for celebrity memorabilia that the right of publicity is designed to protect." It observed that a useful subsidiary inquiry, particularly in close cases, was whether "the marketability and economic value of the challenged work derive primarily from the fame of the celebrity depicted." In this case, plaintiff's "literal, conventional depictions of The Three Stooges" were insufficiently transformative, and defendant's sale of t-shirts bearing them was enjoined.

The California Supreme Court's "transformative test," first articulated in the *Comedy III v. Saderup* decision was applied again by that court in *Winter v. DC Comics*, 66 U.S.P.Q. 2d 1954 (Cal. Supreme Ct. 2003). Plaintiffs Johnny and Edgar Winter, "well-known performing and recording musicians originally from Texas." sued DC Comics under right of publicity law for featuring in its comic books the characters Johnny and Edgar Autumn as "villainous half-worm, half-human offspring." The half-human portions bore a strong resemblance to the Winter Brothers.

The trial court entered summary judgment in favor of defendant. On appeal, the California Supreme Court explained that the *Comedy III* transformative test emphasizes the lack of commercial harm created by truly transformative works: "Works of parody or other distortions of the celebrity figure are not, from the celebrity fan's viewpoint, good substitutes for conventional depictions of the celebrity, and therefore do not generally threaten markets for celebrity memorabilia that the right of publicity is designed to protect." The transformative test requires the court to determine "whether a product containing a celebrity's likeness is so transformed that it has become primarily the defendant's own expression rather than the celebrity's likeness." While in *Comedy III* the defendant's depiction of the Three Stooges on t-shirts was insufficiently transformative, in this case the distorted parody depiction of the Winter Brothers featured in one small section of a "quite expressive" comic book series *was* sufficiently transformative, with the result that it would be a poor market substitute for actual Winter Brothers memorabilia. The court did remand plaintiff's claim that defendant's advertising misleadingly suggested that the plaintiffs were connected with or endorsed the comic books.

The *Comedy III* test was applied by the Sixth Circuit in *ETW Corp. v. Jireh Publishing*, 332 F.3d 915 (6th Cir. 2003). Plaintiff ETW was the licensing agent for professional golfer Tiger Woods, and held the exclusive rights to exploit his commercial identity through use of his name, likeness, etc., as well as to use the registered mark TIGER WOODS in connection with art prints and other products. The licensing agent sued over the defendant publisher's sale of a limited edition art print depicting Woods' 1997 victory at the Masters Tournament. Applying *Comedy III*, the print was protected by the First Amendment from plaintiff's right of publicity claims. The art print contained transformative elements in its portrayal of "a historic sporting event" (including the images of past golf legends looking down on Woods from the sky), and no serious economic harm to plaintiff was likely to result. Given the balance of harms and the public's interest in expressive communications, the court concluded that whatever rights plaintiff possessed in Woods name and likeness "must yield to the First Amendment." For a further discussion of this case, see Chapter 9.

In *Cardtoons L.C. v. Major League Baseball Players Ass'n*, 95 F.3d 959 (10th Cir. 1996), the court held an Oklahoma right of publicity statute unconstitutional because it did not provide a parody exception as necessary under the First Amendment. Parodies, the Tenth Circuit reasoned, convey valuable information criticizing an idea or person. Well-known persons are unlikely to authorize parodies of themselves, and a right of publicity broad enough to protect against unauthorized parodies could suppress an effective and age-old form of criticism. Thus, the court held that the Major League Baseball Players Association's right of publicity claim must yield to the defendant's First Amendment right to market parody baseball trading cards. *See generally* Coyne, *Toward a Modified Fair Use Defense In Right of Publicity Cases*, 29 Wm. & Md. L. Rev. 781 (1988).

4. Incidental Commercial Use

First Amendment considerations aside, if the commercial benefit from the use is only incidentally or indirectly commercial, then a commercial purpose is not predominant, and the use is lawful. *Benavidez v. Anheuser Busch, Inc.*, 873 F.2d 102 (5th Cir. 1989) (increased goodwill Anheuser-Busch might obtain via war hero documentary with Anheuser-Busch's name at the end of the credits was only incidental and insufficiently commercial to warrant publicity relief); *Faloona v. Hustler Magazine, Inc.*, 607 F. Supp. 1341, 1360 (N.D. Tex. 1985), *aff'd*, 799 F.2d 1000 (5th Cir. 1986), *cert. denied*, 479 U.S. 1088 (1987).

5. First Sale Doctrine

In considering the right's commercial underpinnings, one court has held that the right of publicity is limited by the first sale doctrine. *Allison v. Vintage Sports Plaques*, 136 F.3d 1443 (11th Cir. 1998). The defendant had purchased trading cards bearing the likenesses of race car driver Clifford Allison and professional baseball pitcher Orel Hershiser and, after mounting and framing them, sold the plaques as a "Limited

Edition" and "Authentic Collectible." In affirming summary judgment for defendant, the court held that plaintiff's right of publicity did not extend beyond the first sale. It noted that failure to apply the first sale doctrine "would render tortious the resale of sports trading cards and memorabilia and thus would have a profound effect on the market for trading cards, which now supports a multi-billion dollar industry." including, presumably, "prevent[ing] a child from selling to his friend a baseball card that he had purchased, a consequence that undoubtedly would be contrary to the policies supporting" the right of publicity. Even with the doctrine's application, "a celebrity would continue to enjoy the right to license the use of her image in the first instance — and thus enjoy the power to determine when, or if, her image will be distributed." *Id.* at 1449. It also approvingly cited the district court's observation that, "Vintage would probably violate the right of publicity if [it] attached the trading card to a baseball glove and sold it 'as an official Orel Hershiser glove' or if [it] affixed a Clifford Allison card onto a model car and sold it as 'an official Clifford Allison car.'"*Id.* at 1450.

6. Lanham Act

How does right of publicity law differ from unfair competition law and § 43(a) of the Lanham Act? *Compare Carson v. Here's Johnny Portable Toilets, Inc.*, 698 F.2d 831 (6th Cir. 1983) (Johnny Carson's right of publicity held invaded by the intentional appropriation of his identity ("Here's Johnny") for use in connection with defendant's corporate name and product but lower court's holding of no § 43(a) violation affirmed) *with Allen v. National Video, Inc.*, 610 F. Supp. 612 (S.D.N.Y. 1985) (Woody Allen look-alike held liable under § 43(a) without resolving publicity claims under New York's statute). *See also Brown v. Twentieth Century Fox Film Corp.*, 799 F. Supp. 166 (D.D.C. 1992) (one-time mention of plaintiff's name, James Brown, in film "The Commitments" and promotional trailer held not a "wholesale misappropriation" giving rise to a right of publicity claim and did not create a false impression of sponsorship under § 43(a)), *aff'd without op.*, 15 F.3d 1159 (D.C. Cir. 1994); Lemley & Dogan, *What the Right of Publicity Can Learn from Trademark Law*, 58 STANFORD L. REV. 1161 (2006); Dreitler, *The Tiger Woods' Case - Has the Sixth Circuit Abandoned Trademark Law - ETW Corp. v. Jireh Publishing, Inc.*, 38 AKRON L. REV. 337 (2005); Soloman, *Can the Lanham Act Protect Tiger Woods? An Analysis of Whether the Lanham Act is a Proper Substitute for a Federal Right of Publicity*, 94 TMR 1202 (2004); Goldman, *Elvis Is Alive, But He Shouldn't Be: The Right of Publicity Revisited*, 1992 B.Y.U. L. REV. 597 (1992) (arguing celebrities should not have their right of publicity protected unless confusion is likely).

One plaintiff was unsuccessful in asserting a right of publicity in its corporate trademark, "Eagle's Eye," for the sale and manufacture of women's clothing. *The Eagle's Eye, Inc. v. Ambler Fashion Shop, Inc.*, 227 U.S.P.Q. 1018, 1022 (E.D. Pa. 1985). It remains to be seen whether the right of publicity might apply to a more famous corporate trademark embodying a more recognizable "persona" than that presented in *Eagle's Eye*. *See* Winner, *Right of Identity: Right of Publicity and Protection for a Trademark's "Persona,"* 71 TRADEMARK REP. 193 (1981).

Could an entertainer's name function as a service mark? This question was answered in the affirmative in *Five Platters, Inc. v. Purdie*, 419 F. Supp. 372 (D. Md. 1976) (entertainment provided by singing group The Platters); *In re Carson*, 197 U.S.P.Q. 554 (T.T.A.B. 1977) (entertainment provided by comedian and talk show host Johnny Carson); and *Estate of Presley v. Russen, supra*. *See also* McGeehan, *Trademark Registration of a Celebrity Persona*, 87 TRADEMARK REP. 351 (1997); Heneghan & Wansley, *The Service Mark Alternative to the Right of Publicity: Estate of Presley v. Russen*, 14 PAC. L.J. 181 (1983).

7. Economic Loss

Should a plaintiff asserting violation of his right of publicity be required to show an identifiable economic loss? *See Estate of Presley v. Russen*, 513 F. Supp. 1339 (D.N.J. 1981) ("Because the doctrine of the right of publicity emphasizes the protection of the commercial value of the celebrity's name or likeness, the plaintiff must demonstrate sufficiently that the defendant's use . . . has or is likely to result in an identifiable economic loss," the court noting in particular the absence of a public deception element in right of publicity claims); *Bi-Rite Enterprises, Inc. v. Button Master*, 555 F. Supp. 1188 (S.D.N.Y. 1983), *Supp. Opinion*, 578 F. Supp. 59 (S.D.N.Y. 1983) (damages). In *Landham v. Lewis Galoob Toys, Inc.*, 227 F.3d 619 (6th Cir. 2000), plaintiff was, in the words of the court, a "fringe actor" who appeared as "Billy, the Native American Tracker" in the action movie Predator. When defendant came out with set of toys based on the movie that included a "Billy" action figure that bore no resemblance to plaintiff, plaintiff claimed his right of publicity was infringed. The court pointedly observed, "to assert the right of publicity, a plaintiff must demonstrate that there is value in associating an item of commerce with his identity." Plaintiff did not, and summary judgment against him was affirmed.

8. Voice Misappropriation

Should commercial use of an imitation of a professional entertainer's style of vocal delivery create liability for unfair competition or right of publicity infringement? *See Lahr v. Adell Chem. Co.*, 300 F.2d 256 (1st Cir. 1962) (enjoining use of imitation of Bert Lahr's voice for cartoon duck). *Cf. Oliveira v. Frito-Lay, Inc.*, 251 F.3d 56 (2d Cir. 2001) (plaintiff's widely known vocal recording of the 1964 song "The Girl from Ipanema" used in a snack commercial); *Sinatra v. Goodyear Tire & Rubber Co.*, 435 F.2d 711 (9th Cir. 1970), *cert. denied*, 402 U.S. 906 (1971) (tire advertisement featuring Nancy Sinatra's rendition of "These Boots Are Made For Walking"); *Booth v. Colgate-Palmolive Co.*, 362 F. Supp. 343 (S.D.N.Y. 1973) (voice for "Hazel" cartoon character in a television commercial imitated the voice developed and made famous by plaintiff in the "Hazel" television series). Over $2.5 million was awarded to singer Tom Waits in *Waits v. Frito-Lay*, 978 F.2d 1093 (9th Cir. 1992), *cert. denied*, 506 U.S. 1080 (1993), where defendant's use of an imitation of his distinctive voice in a snack food commercial constituted voice misappropriation and also violated § 43(a), and in *Midler v. Ford Motor Co.*, 849 F.2d 460 (9th Cir. 1988), *cert. denied*, 503 U.S. 951 (1992), Bette Midler's unfair competition claims were rejected but use of an imitation of her voice in a car commercial constituted common law misappropriation. *Compare Laws v. Sony Music Entertainment, Inc.*, 78 U.S.P.Q.2d 1910 (9th Cir. 2006), in which, in denying relief, the court distinguished the Tom Waits and Bette Midler cases as "plainly different" because here an actual recording of plaintiff's voice was used, and copyright law preempted plaintiff's right of publicity claim.

9. Transfer and Descendibility

Is the right of publicity a property right? Should it be assignable? Should the right survive the death of the person originally possessing it? Some jurisdictions recognize a post-mortem right of publicity, while others do not. *See, e.g., Cairn v. Franklin Mint Co.*, 292 F. 3d 1139 (9th Cir. 2002) (affirming dismissal of right of publicity claim regarding Princess Diana; while California recognized a post-mortem right of publicity, Great Britain, the domicile of Princess Diana, did not). *See also Martin Luther King, Jr., Center for Social Change v. American Heritage Products, Inc.*, 694 F.2d 674 (11th Cir. 1983); *Acme Circus Operating Co. v. Kuperstock*, 711 F.2d 1538 (11th Cir. 1983) (applying California law); *Estate of Presley, supra* (New Jersey law); *Price v. Hal Roach Studios, Inc.*, 400 F. Supp. 836, 844 (S.D.N.Y. 1975). *Compare Hagen v. Dahmer*, 38 U.S.P.Q.2d 1146, 1149 (E.D. Wis. 1995) (holding that Wisconsin statute only recognizes a right of publicity in living persons); *Reeves v. United Artists*, 572 F. Supp.

1231 (N.D. Ohio 1983), *aff'd*, 765 F.2d 79 (6th Cir. 1985); *Lugosi v. Universal Pictures*, 160 Cal. Rptr. 323, 329 (Cal. 1979) ("We hold that the right to exploit name and likeness is personal to the artist and must be exercised, if at all, by him during his lifetime"); *but see* Cal. Civ. Code § 990; GILSON, TRADEMARK PROTECTION AND PRACTICE, § 2.15 (2008 ed.).

In *Memphis Development Foundation v. Factors Etc., Inc.*, 616 F.2d 956 (6th Cir. 1980), a declaratory judgment action, the plaintiff non-profit foundation had solicited contributions for a large statue of Elvis Presley to be erected in Memphis, and had given contributors small pewter replicas of the statue in exchange for contributions of $25 or more. Defendant licensee of the deceased Presley's right of publicity sought to enjoin distribution of the replicas, claiming that they were actually being sold for $25 a piece. Having to determine the descendibility of the right of publicity under Tennessee law in the absence of precedent in that state, the court reviewed the question in the light of such factors as "policy considerations" and "moral presuppositions." *Memphis Development*, 616 F.2d at 958. It observed (616 F.2d at 959):

> Fame is an incident of . . . strong [psychological] motivation. . . . The desire to exploit fame for the commercial advantage of one's heirs is by contrast a weak principle of motivation. . . .

> On the other hand, there are strong reasons for declining to recognize the inheritability of the right. A whole set of practical problems of judicial line-drawing would arise should the court recognize such an inheritable right. How long would the "property" interest last? Is the right of publicity taxable? At what point does the right collide with the right of free expression guaranteed by the first amendment? Does the right apply to elected officials and military heroes whose fame was gained on the public payroll, as well as to movie stars, singers and athletes?. . . .

*   *   *

> . . . The intangible and shifting nature of fame and celebrity status, the presence of widespread public and press participation in its creation, the unusual psychic rewards and income that often flow from it during life and the fact that it may be created by bad as well as good conduct combine to create serious reservations about making fame the permanent right of a few individuals to the exclusion of the general public. Heretofore, the law has always thought that leaving a good name to one's children is sufficient reward in itself for the individual, whether famous or not. Commercialization of this virtue after death in the hands of heirs is contrary to our legal tradition and somehow seems contrary to the moral presuppositions of our culture.

Should the right of publicity survive after death only *if* the decedent commercially exploited his identity in promoting products or services during his lifetime? Should it only attach, in a manner analogous to trademark use, to those types of products or services actually promoted by the decedent? *See Groucho Marx Productions v. Day and Night Co.*, 689 F.2d 317, 323 (2[d] Cir. 1982) ("Even if there is a limited descendible right [under California law], applicable to a product or service promoted by the celebrity, the defendants are not using the names or likeness of the Marx brothers in connection with any product or service that the comedians promoted during their lives"; plaintiffs held not protected against production of original play using the Marx Brothers' likenesses and comedic style). *Compare Martin Luther King, supra* above, at page 683, where the court stated that,

> The net result of following [such cases] would be to say that celebrities and public figures have the right of publicity during their lifetimes (as others have the right of publicity), but only those who contract for bubble gum cards, posters and tee shirts have a descendible right of publicity upon their deaths . . . we find no reason to protect after death only those who took commercial advantage of their fame.

See also Hicks v. Casablanca Records, 464 F. Supp. 426, 429 (S.D.N.Y. 1978) ("it would appear that a party claiming the right must establish that the decedent acted in such a way as to evidence his or her own recognition of the extrinsic commercial value of his or her name or likeness, and manifested that recognition in some overt manner, e.g., making *inter vivos* transfer of the rights in the name . . . or posing for bubble gum cards. . . ."); Note, *An Assessment of the Commercial Exploitation Requirement as a Limit on the Right of Publicity*, 96 HARV. L. REV. 1703 (1983).

A celebrity may have a right of publicity in a *former* name. In *Abdul-Jabbar v. General Motors Corp.*, 85 F.3d 407 (9ᵗʰ Cir. 1996) the defendants, General Motors and its advertising agency, unsuccessfully claimed that basketball star Kareem Abdul-Jabbar had abandoned rights to his birth name, Lew Alcindor. The Ninth Circuit held that the defense of abandonment does not apply to proper names because, unlike an ordinary trademark, a person's name is not bestowed for commercial purposes. Thus, the right of publicity in that name is not contingent upon commercial or other use.

10.   ICANN Proceedings

Under the ICANN Uniform Domain Name Dispute Resolution Policy ("UDRP"), discussed in § 8.01, *supra*, a celebrity who has developed trademark significance in his or her name can obtain relief against the bad faith domain name registration of that name by another. In *Madonna Ciccone v. Parisi*, WIPO Case No. D2000-0847 (2000), for example, the performer Madonna had federally registered MADONNA for entertainment services and related goods, and, in a UDRP proceeding, successfully obtained a transfer of rights in the domain name madonna.com from a bad faith registrant. The registrant initially had used it for an "adult entertainment portal website" and later professed a desire to give it to the Madonna Rehabilitation Hospital — on the condition the hospital not transfer it to Madonna. In *Winterson v. Hogarth*, WIPO, Case No. D2000-0235 (2000), the respondent had registered juliaroberts.com, as well as a number of other domain names containing celebrity names, and put them all up for auction. Finding bad faith, the arbitration panel ordered the transfer of the juliaroberts.com domain name to the actress, who was found to have common law trademark rights in her name. *Compare Gordon Summer p/k/a Sting v. Urvan*, WIPO, Case No. 2000-0596 (2000), in which the respondent had made *bona fide* use of the name "Sting" as his nickname prior to registering the domain name sting.com, and there was no indication he was seeking to trade on the goodwill of the complainant singer. In declining to order a transfer, the panel also questioned whether complainant had developed trademark rights in his name.

11.   Copyright Law

An assertion of publicity rights can come into conflict with the copyright law. In *Baltimore Orioles, Inc. v. Major League Baseball Players Ass'n*, 805 F.2d 663 (7ᵗʰ Cir. 1986), *cert. denied*, 480 U.S 941 (1989), the Seventh Circuit held that the right of publicity claims of professional baseball players concerning their televised on-field performances were preempted by the Copyright Act. *See also Laws v. Sony Music Entertainment, Inc.*, 448 F.3d 1134 (9ᵗʰ Cir. 2006) (voice misappropriation claim preempted by Copyright Act where use of previous recording of plaintiff's voice was at issue); Fleet v. CBS Inc., 41 U.S.P.Q.2d 1749 (Cal. Ct. App. 1996) (Copyright Act preempted right of publicity claim based on defendant's alleged unauthorized video reproduction of plaintiff's performance in a film). *Compare Downing v. Abercrombie & Fitch*, 265 F.3d 994 (9ᵗʰ Cir. 2001) (professional surfers' right of publicity claim for use of their images in clothing catalog not preempted simply because images were from a copyrighted photograph); *Brown v. Ames*, 201 F.3d 654 (5ᵗʰ Cir. 2000) (no preemption for blues musicians, songwriters and music producers whose names and likenesses were used on compact discs, posters and videotapes); *Landham v. Lewis Galoob Toys, Inc.*, 227 F.3d 619 (6ᵗʰ Cir. 2000) (no preemption for actor whose character at issue was from a copyrighted movie); *Wendt v. Host International Inc.*, 125 F.3d 806 (9th Cir. 1997) (distinguishing *Fleet* as finding copyright preemption "when the only claimed exploitation came through the distribution of the actor's performance in a copyrighted movie", and allowing actors' right of publicity action to go forward where characters they created in television series *Cheers* were allegedly animatronically imitated in defendant's airport bars); *Midler v. Ford Motor Co.*, 849 F.2d 460 (th Cir. 1988), *cert. denied*, 503 U.S. 951 (1992), in which the Ninth Circuit rejected a copyright preemption argument and granted relief under the common law of misappropriation to a professional singer whose distinctive and widely known voice was imitated in a television commercial.

CHAPTER 9

FREEDOM OF SPEECH AND THE LAW OF TRADEMARKS AND UNFAIR COMPETITION

CONTENTS

9.01 Introduction

Trademarks are normally classified as commercial speech, which has much less First Amendment protection, than, for example, political or artistic speech. However, trademark owners make concerted efforts to, as Justice Frankfurter memorably puts it in *Mishawaka Rubber & Woolen Mfg. Co. v. S.S. Kresge Co.*, 316 U.S. 203, 205 (1943), "impregnate the atmosphere of the market with the drawing power of a congenial symbol." As a consequence, many trademarks may begin to transcend their status as pure source identifiers and take on characteristics of cultural icons. This means they also become either the target or the means of parody, social commentary, and other like uses that go beyond exploiting the consumer goodwill commanded by the marks. In other words, marks can become the subject or the raw material for speech that may fall under the full protection of the First Amendment. It thus becomes necessary to accommodate trademark law's goals of safeguarding owners' trademark rights and preventing public confusion on the one hand, and the First Amendment's goals of protecting speakers' legitimate constitutional interests in freely expressing themselves and fostering robust public debate on the other hand. There are many pathbreaking scholarly contributions to these issues, including Robert C. Denicola, *Trademarks As Speech: Constitutional Implications Of The Emerging Rationales For The Protection Of The Trade Symbols*, 1982 WIS. L. REV. 159 (1982), Rochelle Cooper Dreyfuss, *Expressive Genericity: Trademarks As Language In The Pepsi Generation*, 65 NOTRE DAME L. REV. 397 (1990), and Rebecca Tushnet, *Trademark Law As Commercial Speech Regulation*, 58 S.C. L. REV. 737 (2007), among a host of others. Federal judges also have taken a lively interest. Excerpted below is an article by Pierre Leval, who sits on the Court of Appeals for the Second Circuit. Another influential article is Alex Kozinski's *Trademarks Unplugged*, 68 N.Y.U. L. REV. 960 (1993). Judge Kozinski sits on the Court of Appeals for the Ninth Circuit. Like Judge Leval, he is the author of many influential trademark decisions and dissents (the decisions in *Mattel v. MCA* and *United We Stand*, excerpted below, were authored by Judge Kozinski and Judge Leval, respectively). This chapter provides materials on the encounter between trademark and unfair competition law and the First Amendment. Before entering into this rich and often contentious debate, we start out with a few basic First Amendment principles.

9.02 General First Amendment Principles

The First Amendment to the U.S. Constitution reads in full: "Congress shall make no law respecting an establishment of religion, or prohibiting the free exercise thereof; or abridging the freedom of speech, or of the press; or the right of the people peaceably to assemble, and to petition the government for a redress of grievances." The materials in this Chapter focus on the prohibition against abridgment of the freedom of speech or the press. Though the First Amendment's prohibitions, including those concerning free speech and press, were originally directed only against Congress, the Supreme Court has long applied them against any and all governmental actors, including state and local government. *See, e.g., New York Times v. Sullivan*, 376 U.S. 254, 276-77 (1964) and cases cited therein.

"The First Amendment generally prevents government from proscribing speech . . . or even expressive conduct . . . because of disapproval of the ideas expressed. Content-based regulations are presumptively invalid." *R.A.V. v. City of St. Paul, Minnesota*, 505 U.S. 377, 382 (1992) (citations omitted). The Government bears the burden of showing the constitutionality of any content-based regulations. *Ashcroft v. ACLU*, 542 U.S. 656, 661 (2004). It is a foundational principle of U.S. law that "debate on public issues should be uninhibited, robust, and wide-open, and . . . it may well include vehement, caustic, and sometimes unpleasantly sharp attacks on government and public officials." *New York Times v. Sullivan*, 376 U.S. at 270. Thus, the First Amendment prohibits a public official "from recovering damages for a defamatory falsehood relating to his official conduct unless he proves that the statement was made with 'actual malice'—that is, with knowledge that it was false or with reckless disregard of whether it was false or not." *Id.* at 279-80. The practical effect of this rule is to insulate from liability virtually all forms of criticism, including even the most strident and offensive parody or satire, of public officials and other public figures or entities. For example, the sex magazine *Hustler* published a fictitious interview with the nationally known minister and "televangelist" Jerry Falwell, "in which [Falwell] states that [he had sex for the first time] during a drunken incestuous rendezvous with his mother in an outhouse." *Hustler Magazine v. Falwell*, 485 U.S. 46, 48 (1988). Falwell sued Hustler in state court for libel and intentional infliction of emotional distress. He lost on the libel claim but succeeded in obtaining damages on the emotional distress claim. The Supreme Court reversed, holding that "the First Amendment prohibits [imposing liability for outrageous speech] in the area of public debate about public figures." *Id.* at 53.

The First Amendment protects forms of expressive conduct that do not involve traditional verbal discourse. *See Texas v. Johnson*, 491 U.S. 397, 404 (1989). For example, burning the American flag to express one's "dissatisfaction with the policies of this country [is] expression situated at the core of our First Amendment values" and hence enjoys the full protection of the U.S. Constitution. *Id*. at 411. *See also id*. at 399, 410. The Supreme Court has "recognized the expressive nature of students' wearing of black armbands to protest American military involvement in Vietnam . . .; of a sit-in by blacks in a 'whites only' area to protest segregation . . .; of the wearing of American military uniforms in a dramatic presentation criticizing American involvement in Vietnam . . .; and of picketing about a wide variety of causes . . . ." *Id*. at 404 (citations omitted). All of these are examples of conduct protected under the First Amendment from Government interference. It is a direct consequence of the Supreme Court's commitment to the "robust public debate" principle, first set forth in *New York Times v. Sullivan, supra*, that even subversive advocacy directed against the U.S. Government enjoys First Amendment protection. In his book, *Perilous Times—Free Speech in Wartime* (2004), Professor Geoffrey Stone of the University of Chicago Law School, a leading First Amendment scholar, states that the Supreme Court's modern approach "would seem to permit the punishment of subversive advocacy *only* if three conditions are satisfied: there must be *express* advocacy of law violation; the advocacy must call for *immediate* law violation; and the immediate law violation must be *likely* to occur." *Id*. at 523 (emphasis in original; footnotes omitted; citing numerous cases in support).

9.03   Commercial Speech

Commercial speech, which includes trademarks and commercial advertising, is protected under the First Amendment, but its level of protection is lower than that for noncommercial speech. "Commercial messages . . . do not receive the same level of constitutional protection as other types of protected expression." *Hoffman v. Capital Cities/ABC, Inc.*, 255 F.3d 1180, 1184 (9th Cir. 2001), citing *44 Liquormart, Inc., v. Rhode Island*, 517 U.S. 484 (1996). "[F]alse or misleading commercial speech is not protected [and] may freely be regulated if it is misleading." *Hoffman*, 255 F.3d at 1184-85, citing *Florida Bar v. Went For It, Inc.*, 515 U.S. 618 (1995).

Prior to 1975, "purely commercial advertising received no First Amendment protection." *Bolger v. Youngs Drug Products Co.*, 463 U.S. 60, 64 n.6 (1983). But beginning with *Bigelow v. Virginia*, 421 U.S. 809 (1975), and *Virginia Bd. of Pharmacy v. Virginia Citizens Consumer Council, Inc.*, 425 U.S. 748 (1976), the Supreme Court changed its approach, citing the rationale that "it is a matter of public interest that economic decisions, in the aggregate, be intelligent and well-informed [, to which end] the free flow of commercial information is indispensable," *Virginia Bd. of Pharmacy*, 425 U.S. at 366. Because commercial transactions occur "in an area traditionally subject to government regulation," *Ohralnik v. Ohio State Bar Assn.*, 436 U.S. 447, 455-56 (1978), "we have held that the Constitution accords less protection to commercial speech than to other constitutionally safeguarded forms of expression," *Bolger*, 463 U.S. at 64-65. In accordance with these principles, the Supreme Court has developed the following test "for determining whether a particular commercial speech regulation is constitutionally permissible," *Thompson v. Western States Medical Center*, 535 U.S. 357, 367 (2002):

> [W]e ask as a threshold matter whether the commercial speech concerns unlawful activity or is misleading. If so, then the speech is not protected by the First Amendment. If the speech concerns lawful activity and is not misleading, however, we next ask whether the asserted governmental interest is substantial. . . . If it is, then we determine whether the regulation directly advances the governmental interest asserted, and, finally, whether it is not more extensive than is necessary to serve that interest. . . . Each of these latter three inquiries must be answered in the affirmative for the regulation to be found constitutional.

In studying the materials below, consider how the courts have applied these general principles in trademark and unfair competition cases. To what degree, if ever, should the First Amendment immunize otherwise actionable conduct from trademark and unfair competition law? Should certain kinds of speech messages categorically be beyond the reach of trademark and unfair competition law, or, conversely, be beyond the protections of the First Amendment? How should courts draw the line between constitutionally protected speech and speech that is subject to the normal operation of the trademark and unfair competition laws? How do the courts in the opinions excerpted below draw those lines? Do you see any changes over time in how the lines are drawn?

Judge Leval proposes to resolve apparent First Amendment conflicts by relying on ordinary principles and doctrines of trademark and unfair competition law, rather than by applying the First Amendment directly. Think about his proposal. What features of trademark law is it based on? Does it require any balancing of First Amendment interests and trademark interests? Keep the Leval proposal in your mind as you read the cases excerpted below.

TRADEMARK: CHAMPION OF FREE SPEECH
Columbia Journal of Law & the Arts, WINTER 2004
Pierre N. Leval[1]

In the last quarter century, we have witnessed a new aggressiveness on the part of advertisers, social commentators and wisecrackers in the use of other people's trademarks.

- A tractor maker's television ad suggests its tractors are more rugged than the John Deere product, portraying the Deere Company's famous, mighty leaping deer as frail, weak and quivering. [2]

- Piggybacking on Budweiser's well-known slogan, "Where there's life, there's Bud," a maker of insecticide proclaims, "Where there's life, there's BUGS."[3]

- Jim Henson is sued by Hormel, the maker of Spam, for naming a new porcine Muppet "Spa'am."[4]

- A maker of extra-large size jeans is sued by Jordache when it takes the name "Lardasche."[5]

- Coca-Cola sues over a poster that uses Coke's famous trademark script inviting us to "Enjoy Cocaine."[6]

- The Girl Scouts of America are provoked to sue by a poster showing a wistful, pregnant Girl Scout, who ponders the Girl Scout motto, "Be Prepared."[7]

- Federico Fellini gives the title Ginger and Fred to a film about a pair of Italian dancers who take the glamorous Hollywood duo as their muses.[8]

- The satirical Spy Magazine creates a parody of the famous college cheat series,

---

[1] Reprinted with author's permission. The author has served since 1993 as a judge of the United States Court of Appeals for the Second Circuit. Previously, he served for sixteen years as a judge of the United States District Court for the Southern District of New York. This Article was first delivered as the 16th Annual Horace S. Manges Lecture, given at Columbia Law School on April 1, 2003.

[2] Deere & Co. v. MTD Prods., Inc., 41 F.3d 39 (2d Cir. 1994).

[3] Chem. Corp. of Am. v. Anheuser-Busch, Inc., 306 F.2d 433 (5th Cir. 1962).

[4] Hormel Foods Corp. v. Jim Henson Prods., Inc., 73 F.3d 497 (2d Cir. 1996).

[5] Jordache Enters., Inc. v. Hogg Wyld, Ltd., 828 F.2d 1482 (10th Cir. 1987).

[6] Coca-Cola Co. v. Gemini Rising, Inc., 346 F. Supp. 1183 (E.D.N.Y. 1972).

[7] Girl Scouts of Am. v. Personality Posters Mfg. Co., 304 F. Supp. 1228 (S.D.N.Y. 1969).

[8] Rogers v. Grimaldi, 875 F.2d 994 (2d Cir. 1989).

Cliffs Notes, using Cliffs Notes' traditional cover design.[9]

- An erotic magazine publishes the "L.L. Beam Back-to-School Sex Catalogue," sending up L.L. Bean's earnest, wholesome Maine-woods catalogue.[10]

- A rock band records a song entitled "Barbie Girl," describing the world through the eyes of the ubiquitous Barbie Doll, who proclaims, "Life in plastic, it's fantastic."[11]

In dealing with such cases, courts often treat them as instances of conflict between trademark rights and the First Amendment, envisioning the trademark laws as establishing a continuous one-way highway of exclusivity that runs on until it is blocked by the barrier of the First Amendment. The question I explore is whether this is a correct perception or whether the trademark laws rather represent an integrally complete, multifaceted body of rules, designed to balance a trademark owner's interest in exclusive use of the mark in commerce against society's interest in free expression.

A case in point. Ten years ago, when I was a district judge, I heard a case involving New York magazine.[12] The magazine made a practice of publishing a "Christmas Gifts" issue, featuring expensive, frivolous gift ideas. 1990 was a year of economic downturn; people had lost money. The magazine decided for its "Christmas Gifts" issue to lampoon a new fashion of frugality, with penny-pinching quotes from celebrated misers like Ben Franklin. As part of the joke, it dressed up its front cover in the traditional cover design of an icon of frugality—the Old Farmer's Almanac. The somewhat obscure joke was to imply, "Unlike our usual insouciant, free-spending attitude toward the Christmas season, this time we are giving you suggestions you might expect from a miserly old farm codger."

The Almanac sued for trademark infringement. I ruled in favor of New York. Consumers easily saw that the defendant New York was making a joke. Observing that jokes are protected speech, I ruled that the First Amendment protected New York from liability under the trademark law. As I saw it, the trademark highway of exclusivity was blocked by the First Amendment.

I have no regrets about the ultimate decision but now believe my analysis was flawed. We lawyers learn in kindergarten how important it is to avoid unnecessary constitutional adjudications. Did I need to rely on, even create, constitutional doctrine? Clearly not—for at least two reasons.

First, before making my First Amendment ruling, I had determined that New York's joking reference to the Almanac's cover design was instantly recognizable as a joke. Consumers would not have believed the magazine was sponsored or endorsed by the Farmer's Almanac. It is an essential element of an action for trademark infringement that the defendant have caused a likelihood of confusion—a likelihood that consumers will be confused as to whether the plaintiff is associated with the defendant's product or message. Without likelihood of consumer confusion, the Almanac could not win under the trademark laws. So why make a Constitutional ruling?

The problem goes still deeper. It is a mistake to see the trademark law as a unidirectional rule—a one-way highway of exclusivity eventually blocked off by the First Amendment. To the contrary, the trademark law is a complex, integrated body of rules, which is deeply concerned with the protection of free expression. Trademark, like copyright, does indeed place limitations on speech. But, as in the case of copyright, it has always had as a central concern distinguishing between speech that should be suppressed and speech that should not. Merchants need a source-identifying mark; society requires freedom for certain kinds of messages. Trademark law developed as an

---

[9] Cliffs Notes, Inc. v. Bantam Doubleday Dell Publ'g Group, Inc., 886 F.2d 490 (2d Cir. 1989).

[10] L.L. Bean, Inc. v. Drake Publishers, Inc., 811 F.2d 26 (1st Cir. 1987).

[11] Mattel, Inc. v. MCA Records, Inc., 296 F.3d 894 (9th Cir. 2002).

[12] Yankee Publ'g Inc. v. News Am. Publ'g Inc., 809 F. Supp. 267 (S.D.N.Y. 1992).

integrated body of rules to balance the potential conflict. The trademark law itself is fashioned to protect free-speech interests that may justify uses of a trademark by persons other than its owner. Thus, the essential structure of the trademark law itself protected New York's freedom to make a joking comparison between its own customary prodigality and the famous miserliness of the Almanac. Where the trademark law, by its own terms, protects the unauthorized use of another's trademark, there is no need to turn to the Constitution to justify a judgment in the alleged infringer's favor.

* * *

. . . [T]he law of trademark contains ingredients designed to protect free speech values. In the new controversies, recognition of those ingredients can provide the answers. If the free speech interests that are integral to the law of trademark dictate that the plaintiff cannot prevent the defendant's use of a mark over which the plaintiff claims exclusivity, then the judgment must be in the defendant's favor, and there is no need for the court to consider whether the First Amendment would also command the same result. . . .

It may be surprising, notwithstanding the law's broad protection for the holder of a distinctive mark and, conversely, the insecure protection given the holder of a descriptive mark, that merchants often do not prefer the strong, arbitrary marks. Notwithstanding their legal weakness, merchants in consumer markets commonly seek to secure the exclusive right to marks that inherently carry an advertising message. . . . Such advertising ambitions are in conflict with the long-established objectives of the trademark law. It is the policy of the law to provide for source identification, while protecting free communication. The law thus does not allow a merchant to preempt the exclusive right to an advertising message, to the public's detriment. It is the duty of courts to accord marks that seek such exclusivity as to an advertising message only a narrow scope of exclusivity, if any, so as not to undermine the public's interest in free communication in the marketplace.

Moreover, the exclusive right granted by the law pertains only to use of the mark as a trademark identifying the goods or services of the alleged infringer. Many uses of a trademark simply fall outside the realm of trademark protection because the user is not using the mark as the identifier of its own goods or services, but rather, for instance, to refer to those of the owner of the mark. . . . The secondary user is commenting on the mark and its place in society, not employing that mark as the identifier of its own goods or claiming association with the owner. The free speech-protecting concerns of the trademark law bar the trademark owner from asserting a right to exclude such uses.

The free speech concern thus pervades the common law of trademark. When a person accused of infringing another's trademark asserts that free speech interests protect his conduct from liability, placing it outside the area of trademark's exclusive rights, this claim invokes a long tradition of well-established trademark law. A court which rules in the defendant's favor may have no need to refer to the First Amendment to explain its decision, if the free speech-protecting terms of the trademark law itself compel a resolution in the defendant's favor. . . .

* * *

When lawsuits pit claims of exclusive trademark right against interests of free expression, courts should not run unnecessarily to the Constitution. The governing statutes charge the courts with a delegated duty to seek the answers first in the complex, intelligently balanced terms of the trademark laws themselves. Those terms are designed to balance the needs of merchants for identification as the provider of goods with the needs of society for free communication and discussion. Where the terms of the trademark law adequately protect an accused infringer's use as falling outside the scope of the trademark owner's exclusive right, the court has no need to seek answers in the First Amendment.

DALLAS COWBOYS CHEERLEADERS, INC., v. PUSSYCAT CINEMA, LTD.,
604 F.2d 200 (2ᵈ Cir. 1979)

VAN GRAAFEILAND, CIRCUIT JUDGE:

This is an appeal from orders of the United States District Court for the Southern District of New York granting plaintiff's motions for a preliminary injunction prohibiting Pussycat Cinema, Ltd., and Michael Zaffarano from distributing or exhibiting the motion picture "Debbie Does Dallas." On March 14 this Court granted defendants' motion to stay the injunction and ordered an expedited appeal. The case was argued before us on April 6, following which we dissolved the stay and reinstated the preliminary injunction. We now affirm the orders of the district court.

Plaintiff in this trademark infringement action is Dallas Cowboys Cheerleaders, Inc., a wholly owned subsidiary of the Dallas Cowboys Football Club, Inc. Plaintiff employs thirty-six women who perform dance and cheerleading routines at Dallas Cowboys football games. The cheerleaders have appeared frequently on television programs and make commercial appearances at such public events as sporting goods shows and shopping center openings. In addition, plaintiff licenses others to manufacture and distribute posters, calendars, T-shirts, and the like depicting Dallas Cowboys Cheerleaders in their uniforms. These products have enjoyed nationwide commercial success, due largely to the national exposure the Dallas Cowboys Cheerleaders have received through the news and entertainment media. . . .

Pussycat Cinema, Ltd., is a New York corporation which owns a movie theatre in New York City; Zaffarano is the corporation's sole stockholder. In November 1978 the Pussycat Cinema began to show "Debbie Does Dallas," a gross and revolting sex film whose plot, to the extent that there is one, involves a cheerleader at a fictional high school, Debbie, who has been selected to become a "Texas Cowgirl." . . . In order to raise enough money to send Debbie, and eventually the entire squad, to Dallas, the cheerleaders perform sexual services for a fee. The movie consists largely of a series of scenes graphically depicting the sexual escapades of the "actors". In the movie's final scene Debbie dons a uniform strikingly similar to that worn by the Dallas Cowboys Cheerleaders and for approximately twelve minutes of film footage engages in various sex acts while clad or partially clad in the uniform. Defendants advertised the movie with marquee posters depicting Debbie in the allegedly infringing uniform and containing such captions as "Starring Ex Dallas Cowgirl Cheerleader Bambi Woods" and "You'll do more than cheer for this X Dallas Cheerleader." . . . Similar advertisements appeared in the newspapers.

Plaintiff brought this action alleging trademark infringement under section 43(a) of the Lanham Act (15 U.S.C. s 1125(a)), unfair competition, and dilution of trademark in violation of section 368-d of the New York General Business Law. The district court, in its oral opinion of February 13, 1979, found that "plaintiff ha(d) succeeded in proving by overwhelming evidence the merits of each one of its contentions." Defendants challenge the validity of all three claims.

*　　*　　*

Defendants assert that the Lanham Act requires confusion as to the origin of the film, and they contend that no reasonable person would believe that the film originated with plaintiff. Appellants read the confusion requirement too narrowly. In order to be confused, a consumer need not believe that the owner of the mark actually produced the item and placed it on the market. *See Syntex Laboratories, Inc. v. Norwich Pharmacal Co.*, 437 F.2d 566, 568 (2ᵈCir. 1971); *Boston Professional Hockey Association v. Dallas Cap & Emblem Mfg., Inc.*, 510 F.2d 1004, 1012 (5ᵗʰ Cir.), *cert. denied*, 423 U.S. 868, 96

S.Ct. 132, 46 L.Ed.2d 98 (1975). The public's belief that the mark's owner sponsored or otherwise approved the use of the trademark satisfies the confusion requirement. In the instant case, the uniform depicted in "Debbie Does Dallas" unquestionably brings to mind the Dallas Cowboys Cheerleaders. Indeed, it is hard to believe that anyone who had seen defendants' sexually depraved film could ever thereafter disassociate it from plaintiff's cheerleaders. This association results in confusion which has "a tendency to impugn (plaintiff's services) and injure plaintiff's business reputation . . . ." *See Coca-Cola Co. v. Gemini Rising, Inc.*, 346 F.Supp. 1183, 1189 (E.D.N.Y.1972). . . .

* * *

[D]efendants' use of plaintiff's uniform hardly qualifies as parody or any other form of fair use. . . . Nor does any other first amendment doctrine protect defendants' infringement of plaintiff's trademark. That defendants' movie may convey a barely discernible message . . . does not entitle them to appropriate plaintiff's trademark in the process of conveying that message. *See Interbank Card Association v. Simms*, 431 F.Supp. 131 (M.D.N.C.1977); *Edgar Rice Burroughs, Inc. v. Manns Theatres*, 195 U.S.P.Q. 159 (C.D.Cal.1976); *Coca-Cola Co. v. Gemini Rising, Inc., supra*, 346 F. Supp. at 1191. Plaintiff's trademark is in the nature of a property right, *See Hanover Milling Co. v. Metcalf*, 240 U.S. 403, 413, 36 S.Ct. 357, 60 L.Ed. 713 (1915); *Alfred Dunhill of London, Inc. v. Dunhill Tailored Clothes, Inc.*, 293 F.2d 685, 692, 49 C.C.P.A. 730 (1961), *cert. denied*, 369 U.S. 864, 82 S.Ct. 1030, 8 L.Ed.2d 84 (1962), and as such it need not "yield to the exercise of First Amendment rights under circumstances where adequate alternative avenues of communication exist." *Lloyd Corp. v. Tanner*, 407 U.S. 551, 567, 92 S.Ct. 2219, 2228, 33 L.Ed.2d 31 (1972). Because there are numerous ways in which defendants may comment on "sexuality in athletics" without infringing plaintiff's trademark, the district court did not encroach upon their first amendment rights in granting a preliminary injunction. *See Walt Disney Productions v. Air Pirates*, 581 F.2d 751, 758-59 (9th Cir. 1978); *Reddy Communications, Inc. v. Environmental Action Foundation*, 199 U.S.P.Q. 630, 634 (D.D.C.1977).

* * *

Affirmed.

Notes on *Dallas Cowboys*

This is a trademark infringement case, not a dilution case. At the time it was decided, there was no federal dilution law. What is driving this decision? Note the court's observation that "the public's belief that the mark's owner sponsored or otherwise approved the use of the trademark satisfies the confusion requirement." Does this legal basis for the decision square with the court's factual assessment that there is confusion because defendants' use of plaintiff's mark "has a tendency to impugn plaintiff's services"? Is this an infringement principle or a tarnishment principle? Can, or should, evidence of tarnishment serve as evidence of confusion?

The court rejects defendants' parody defense because plaintiff's trademark, a "property right," should not have to "yield to the exercise of First Amendment rights under circumstances where adequate alternative avenues of communication exist." How adequate is this analysis in the trademark context? To what degree does it square with Judge Leval's preferred approach? Note also that the "alternative avenues" test, which is important in First Amendment law, stems from the Supreme Court case of *Lloyd v. Tanner*, 407 U.S. 551 (1972), which involved the distribution of handbills in a privately owned shopping center.

The shopping center in *Lloyd* was "open generally to the public, with a considerable effort being made to attract shoppers and prospective shoppers, and to create 'customer motivation' as well as customer goodwill in the community. . . . Groups and organizations are permitted, by invitation and advance arrangement, to use the auditorium and other facilities." Respondents in the case were, however, not among those invited groups and organizations. as the Court explained, "On November 14, 1968, the respondents in this case distributed within the Center handbill invitations to a meeting of the "Resistance Community" to protest the draft and the Vietnam war. The distribution, made in several different places on the mall walkways by five young people, was quiet and orderly, and there was no littering. There was a complaint from one customer. Security guards informed the respondents that they were trespassing and would be arrested unless they stopped distributing the handbills within the Center. . . . The guards suggested that respondents distribute their literature on the public streets and sidewalks adjacent to but outside of the Center complex."

The District Court found that the shopping center was the "functional equivalent of a public business district." The Supreme Court disagreed, finding as follows: "The central building complex was surrounded by public sidewalks, totaling 66 linear blocks. All persons who enter or leave the private areas within the complex must cross public streets and sidewalks, either on foot or in automobiles. When moving to and from the privately owned parking lots, automobiles are required by law to come to a complete stop. Handbills may be distributed conveniently to pedestrians, and also to occupants of automobiles, from these public sidewalks and streets. Indeed, respondents moved to these public areas and continued distribution of their handbills after being requested to leave the interior malls. *It would be an unwarranted infringement of property rights to require them to yield to the exercise of First Amendment rights under circumstances where adequate alternative avenues of communication exist.* Such an accommodation would diminish property rights without significantly enhancing the asserted right of free speech" (emphasis added). In short, the "alternative avenues" test arose in the context of real property.

After the *Dallas Cowboys* court adopted the "alternative avenues" test, it became quite influential in the context of trademark law. How strong an analogy is this shopping center case in the area of intellectual property?

The question posed in *Dallas Cowboys* (and answered in the affirmative) is whether parodies can be prohibited on the basis that plaintiff's right in its mark is a property right that defendant has no First Amendment right to use if alternative avenues are available to defendant to make his point. The *Dallas Cowboys* method of handling First Amendment claims in trademark matters by reference to property rights may no longer be good law. For one, the statement that trademarks are in the nature of simple property rights was incorrect when the court made it: "There is no such thing as property in a trade-mark except as a right appurtenant to an established business or trade in connection with which the mark is employed." *United Drug Co. v. Theodore Rectanus Co.*, 248 U.S. 90, 100 (1918). Moreover, the Second Circuit itself repudiated the trademarks-as-property theory a few years later: "[T]rademark is not property in the ordinary sense but only a word or symbol indicating the origin of a commercial product." *Power Test Petroleum Distributors v. Calcu Gas*, 754 F.2d 91, 97 (2ᵈ Cir. 1985). *See also* discussion in Chapter 7. For another thing, the "alternative avenues" test has been criticized by many courts in recent years. The analysis of the test in *Parks v. LaFace Records*, excerpted below, is representative of this more modern approach. Other cases critical of the *Dallas Cowboys* court's application of the "alternative avenues" test include *L.L.Bean, Inc., v. Drake Publishers, Inc.*, 811 F.2d 26, 28–29 (1ˢᵗ Cir. 1987), *Cardtoons, L.C., v. Major League Baseball Players Ass'n*, 95 F.3d 959, 971 (10ᵗʰ Cir. 1996), *Lyons Partnership v. Giannoulas*, 179 F.3d 384 (5ᵗʰ Cir. 1999), and *American Family Life Insurance Co. v. Hagan*, 266 F. Supp. 2d 682 (N.D. Ohio 2002). These cases are discussed in the Notes below.

CLIFFS NOTES, INC., v. BANTAM DOUBLEDAY DELL PUBLISHING GROUP, INC.
886 F.2d 490 (2[d] Cir. 1989)

FEINBERG, CIRCUIT JUDGE:

Defendant Bantam Doubleday Dell Publishing Group, Inc. appeals from an order, dated August 2, 1989, of the United States District Court for the Southern District of New York, Shirley Wohl Kram, J., enjoining defendant-appellant from distributing Spy Notes, a parody of the Cliffs Notes series of paperback books published by plaintiff-appellee Cliffs Notes, Inc. . . . This appeal raises basic questions over application of trademark law to an allegedly infringing literary parody. For reasons given below, we vacate the injunction.

* * *

We start with the proposition that parody is a form of artistic expression, protected by the First Amendment. For example, the Supreme Court has held that the First Amendment bars recovery "for the tort of intentional infliction of emotional distress by reason of" publication of satire "without showing in addition that the publication contains a false statement of fact which was made with 'actual malice.'" *Hustler Magazine v. Falwell*, 485 U.S. 46, 108 S.Ct. 876, 882, 99 L.Ed.2d 41 (1988). Similarly, our decisions have recognized "the broad scope permitted parody in First Amendment law." *Groucho Marx Prod., Inc. v. Day and Night Co.*, 689 F.2d 317, 319 n. 2 (2d Cir.1982); *see Elsmere Music, Inc. v. National Broadcasting Co.*, 623 F.2d 252, 253 (2[d] Cir. 1980) (per curiam) ("in today's world of often unrelieved solemnity, copyright law should be hospitable to the humor of parody . . ."). We have stated the "general proposition" that "parody and satire *are* deserving of substantial freedom—both as entertainment and as a form of social and literary criticism." *Berlin v. E.C. Publications, Inc.*, 329 F.2d 541, 545 (2[d] Cir.) (emphasis in original), cert. denied, 379 U.S. 822, 85 S.Ct. 46, 13 L.Ed.2d 33 (1964). *See generally* Note, Trademark Parody: A Fair Use and First Amendment Analysis, 72 VA.L.REV. 1079 (1986).

At the same time, "[t]rademark protection is not lost simply because the allegedly infringing use is in connection with a work of artistic expression." *Silverman v. CBS Inc.*, 870 F.2d 40, 49 (2d Cir.), *cert. denied*, 492 U.S. 907, 109 S.Ct. 3219, 106 L.Ed.2d 569 (1989). Books are "sold in the commercial marketplace like other more utilitarian products, making the danger of consumer deception a legitimate concern that warrants some government regulation." *Rogers v. Grimaldi*, 875 F.2d 994, 997 (2d Cir.1989).

Conflict between these two policies is inevitable in the context of parody, because the keystone of parody is imitation. It is hard to imagine, for example, a successful parody of Time magazine that did not reproduce Time's trademarked red border. A parody must convey two simultaneous—and contradictory—messages: that it is the original, but also that it is *not* the original and is instead a parody. To the extent that it does only the former but not the latter, it is not only a poor parody but also vulnerable under trademark law, since the customer will be confused.

Thus, the principal issue before the district court was how to strike the balance between the two competing considerations of allowing artistic expression and preventing consumer confusion. We believe that the correct approach in this case was foreshadowed by our decision in *Rogers v. Grimaldi*, upon which appellant relies heavily. In that case, we considered a Lanham Act challenge by the actress Ginger Rogers against the producers and distributors of the film "Ginger and Fred." The movie was not about Ginger Rogers but rather about two Italian cabaret performers who imitated Ginger Rogers and Fred Astaire in their performances. Ginger Rogers contended that the title of the film created the false impression that she was the subject of the film or had endorsed it. *See Rogers*, 875 F.2d at 997. The district court held that the title was absolutely protected against Lanham Act claims by the First Amendment. Although this court's analysis in *Rogers* differed in major respects from that of the district court, we affirmed. We noted that "[b]ecause overextension of Lanham Act restrictions in the area of titles might intrude on First Amendment values, we must construe the Act narrowly to avoid such a conflict," *id.* at 998, and went on to hold that "the Act should be construed to apply to artistic works only where the public interest in avoiding consumer confusion outweighs the public interest in free expression." *Id.* at 999.

It is true that *Rogers*, though a Lanham Act case, was concerned with a very different problem from the one we have here. As indicated, the claim there was that a title was false or at least misleading because it could be (mis)understood to mean that Ginger Rogers was the subject of the work or that she had endorsed it. This case is not about whether a title is false advertising but whether the appearance of a work's cover is confusingly similar to the trademark elements of an earlier cover. Furthermore, the present case contains the added element of parody.

Appellee argues that the *Rogers* approach is not relevant to this case and that we should simply apply the *Polaroid* factors, as the district judge did. Appellee points out that the *Rogers* rule—that the Lanham Act's false advertising prohibition does not apply to titles with some artistic relevance to the underlying work unless they are explicitly misleading, *id.* at 999— does not protect "misleading titles that are confusingly similar to other titles." *Id.* at 999 n. 5. Since appellee claims that the cover of Spy Notes is highly misleading, and points out that the judge so found, appellee seizes upon the quoted language in *Rogers* as support for its position that the case has no application here. However, that language says only that where a title is complained about because it is confusingly similar to another title, the *Rogers* rule that titles are subject to the Lanham Act's false advertising prohibition only if explicitly misleading is inapplicable. But that does not mean, as appellee appears to claim, that nothing in the *Rogers* opinion is relevant to this case.

We believe that the overall balancing approach of *Rogers* and its emphasis on construing the Lanham Act "narrowly" when First Amendment values are involved are both relevant in this case. That is to say, in deciding the reach of the Lanham Act in any case where an expressive work is alleged to infringe a trademark, it is appropriate to weigh the public interest in free expression against the public interest in avoiding consumer confusion. *Id.* at 998-99. *See also Silverman*, 870 F.2d at 48 ("In the area of artistic speech . . . enforcement of trademark rights carries a risk of inhibiting free expression . . . ."). And just as in *Rogers*, where we said that the expressive element of titles requires more protection than the labeling of ordinary commercial products, *Rogers*, 875 F.2d at 998, so here the expressive element of parodies requires more protection than the labeling of ordinary commercial products. Indeed, we have said, in the context of alleged copyright infringement, that a parody is entitled "at least" to conjure up the original and can do more. *Elsmere Music, Inc.*, 623 F.2d at 253 n. 1.

Thus, we hold that the *Rogers* balancing approach is generally applicable to Lanham Act claims against works of artistic expression, a category that includes parody. This approach takes into account the ultimate test in trademark law, namely, the likelihood of confusion " 'as to the source of the goods in question.' " *Universal City Studios, Inc. v. Nintendo Co.*, 746 F.2d 112, 115 (2d Cir.1984) (quoting *Mushroom Makers, Inc. v. R.G. Barry Corp.*, 580 F.2d 44, 47 (2d Cir.1978) (per curiam) (citation omitted), cert. denied, 439 U.S. 1116, 99 S.Ct. 1022, 59 L.Ed.2d 75 (1979)). At the same time, a balancing approach allows greater latitude for works such as parodies, in which expression, and not commercial exploitation of another's trademark, is the primary intent, and in which there is a need to evoke the original work being parodied. Cf. *Dallas Cowboys Cheerleaders, Inc. v. Pussycat Cinema, Ltd.*, 604 F.2d 200, 206-07 (2d Cir.1979) (upholding an injunction, despite First Amendment claims, in a case concerning a pornographic movie with blatantly false and explicitly misleading advertisements).

To apply the *Rogers* approach in this case, we begin by noting the strong public interest in avoiding consumer confusion over Spy Notes. As we put it in *Rogers*, the purchaser of a book, "like the purchaser of a can of peas, has a right not to be misled as to the source of the product." *Rogers,* 875 F.2d at 997-98. But, taking into account that somewhat more risk of confusion is to be tolerated when a trademark holder seeks to enjoin artistic expression such as a parody, the degree of risk of confusion between Spy Notes and Cliffs Notes does not outweigh the well-established public interest in parody. In other words, we do not believe that there is a likelihood that an ordinarily prudent purchaser would think that Spy Notes is actually a study guide produced by appellee, as opposed to a parody of Cliffs Notes. And although the district court found a strong likelihood of confusion between the cover of Spy Notes and that of Cliffs Notes, based on its review of the eight *Polaroid* factors, . . . that determination is a legal conclusion which is reviewable by this court as a matter of law. *Centaur Communications, Ltd. v. A/S/M Communications, Inc.,* 830 F.2d 1217, 1225 (2d Cir.1987); *Plus Products v. Plus Discount Foods, Inc.,* 722 F.2d 999, 1004-05 (2d Cir.1983).

As indicated, we believe that the district court erred. This conclusion is based upon a number of factors. First, the district court apparently thought that the parody here had to make an obvious joke out of the cover of the original in order to be regarded as a parody. We do not see why this is so. It is true that some of the covers of the parodies brought to our attention, unlike that of Spy Notes, contain obvious visual gags. . . . But parody may be sophisticated as well as slapstick; a literary work is a parody if, taken as a whole, it pokes fun at its subject. Spy Notes surely does that, and there are sufficient reasons to conclude that most consumers will realize it is a parody. For example, a substantial portion of the potential audience for Spy Notes—i.e., college students or college-educated adults—overlaps with that for Cliffs Notes. Spy magazine, like Cliffs Notes, is widely read on some college campuses, although presumably for different reasons. As a result, the name "Spy" in the title, the notation "A Spy Book" emblazoned on the cover of Spy Notes and the use of a prepack marketing device prominently displaying the "Spy" name should alert the buyer that Spy Notes is a parody of some sort, or, at least, that it is not the same product as Cliffs Notes.

Furthermore, while the cover of Spy Notes certainly conjures up the cover of Cliffs Notes, the two differ in many respects. In addition to the differences listed in the following paragraphs, which indicate that Spy Notes is a parody of Cliffs Notes, the cover of Spy Notes contains red, blue and white, colors that do not appear on the cover of Cliffs Notes. Also, the Spy Notes cover shows a clay sculpture of New York City rather than a clay sculpture of a bare cliff. In addition, the price quoted on the cover of Spy Notes is about twice the price at which Cliffs Notes is sold, and appellant plans to market Spy Notes in large part through prepacks of 10 copies, which prominently present the Spy name.

In addition, a Cliffs Notes book is not likely to be bought as an impulse purchase. A prospective reader of Cliffs Notes probably has a specific book in mind when going to the bookstore for a study guide. And, even if a consumer did go to a store looking for a Cliffs Notes summary of any of the three books condensed in Spy Notes, that purchaser would not find one. Appellee does not produce Cliffs Notes for these novels, and has no plans to do so. There may be a few purchasers who have been assigned to read the novels who would buy the parody thinking it is a serious work and is produced by Cliffs Notes. In view of the public interest in free expression, that slight risk should be taken in order to allow the parody to be sold. Similarly, it is conceivable, though hardly likely, that some purchaser may mistakenly think that Cliffs Notes itself produced the parody, but that small chance does not justify the injunction here. There is no requirement that the cover of a parody carry a disclaimer that it is not produced by the subject of the parody, and we ought not to find such a requirement in the Lanham Act.

The label "A Satire" is also prominently used five times on the cover (and four on the back) of Spy Notes. Appellee conceded at oral argument that "satire," for this purpose, is the same as "parody." In addition, the prepack, a major promotional tool in which the books will appear in most, although not all, bookstores, bears the legend "The Outrageous Parody from the Creators of Separated at Birth" (the latter was a very popular book authored by Spy magazine editors). These measures should alert most consumers that Spy Notes is, in fact, a parody. Moreover, even for those few readers who might be slightly confused by the cover, the most likely reaction would be to open the book. Both the title page and the copyright notice page indicate that the book is written by the editors of Spy magazine and published by appellant. The copyright notice page states, "Spy Notes is a parody of Cliffs Notes." Furthermore, the reader would encounter the Spy Novel-O-Matic Fiction-Writing Device, which is an immediate tip-off that something non-serious is afoot. . . .

Finally, with few exceptions, most Cliffs Notes are summaries of the traditional "great books," rather than contemporary works or those somewhat outside the mainstream. As indicated above, the Spy editors certainly thought that the three novels were obviously not in the former category and that the purchaser would be aware of the humor of having Cliffs Notes summarize them. Moreover, the books that Spy Notes summarizes are characterized by their spare, stripped-down prose, and uncomplicated plots. The idea of condensing them at all is something of a parody. Thus, the consumer would likely be put on notice from the first that Spy Notes was not Cliffs Notes.

In short, we believe that the district court erred as a matter of law in concluding on the record before it that there was a strong likelihood of confusion. . . . Accordingly, it was error for the district court to enter a preliminary injunction, since there was not a likelihood of success on the merits on this Lanham Act claim. *See Jackson Dairy, Inc. v. H.P. Hood & Sons, Inc.,* 596 F.2d 70, 72 (2d Cir.1979) (per curiam). We are aware that this court recognizes an alternative test for a preliminary injunction—i.e., "sufficiently serious questions going to the merits . . . and a balance of hardships tipping decidedly toward the party requesting the preliminary relief." *Id.* But we have no doubt that appellee's case also does not succeed under this standard, because the balance of hardships does not tip "decidedly toward" appellee.

Conclusion

We conclude that the parody cover of Spy Notes, although it surely conjures up the original and goes to great lengths to use some of the identical colors and aspects of the cover design of Cliffs Notes, raises only a slight risk of consumer confusion that is outweighed by the public interest in free expression, especially in a form of expression that must to some extent resemble the original. The district court's ruling unjustifiably imposes the drastic remedy of a pre-publication injunction upon the cover of a literary parody. Accordingly, for the reasons set forth above, we vacate the injunction against appellant.

*   *   *

Notes on *Cliffs Notes*

The precedential importance of *Cliffs Notes* lies not least in its announcement of the principle that the Lanham Act should be "construed 'narrowly' when First Amendment values are involved . . . ." The court views this as a key element in an approach that seeks to "strike the balance between the two competing considerations of allowing artistic expression and preventing consumer confusion." What are the similarities and differences to Judge Leval's approach? To the First Amendment analysis in *Dallas Cowboys*?

Cliffs Notes is an important and much-cited parody case. What is the court's definition of parody? What is the role of parody in the court's analysis? How outcome-determinative is the concept of parody in the case, either as a First Amendment matter or as a matter of trademark infringement law? Also, to what degree is the decision ultimately based on an actual balance of the trademark interests and the free speech interests? Recall in this regard the court's holding that the district court erred in its conclusion "that there was a strong likelihood of confusion." Since the risk of confusion is only "slight," the court reasoned, the plaintiff's chances of succeeding on the merits was low, and no preliminary injunction should have issued. If plaintiff's claim fails for lack of sufficient likelihood of confusion, what exactly is the function of the court's First Amendment analysis? Does the decision bear out the court's initial prediction that "conflict between these two policies [trademark law and the First Amendment] is inevitable in the context of parody"?

UNITED WE STAND AMERICA, INC., v. UNITED WE STAND AMERICA, NEW YORK, INC.
128 F.3d 86 (2d Cir. 1997)

LEVAL, CIRCUIT JUDGE:

United We Stand America, Inc. ("United") brought this action to enjoin the use of its registered service mark "United We Stand America" by defendants United We Stand, America New York, Inc. ("UWSANY") and Alex Rodriguez. . . .

Background

"United We Stand America" (the "Mark") was a service mark initially used by the principal campaign committee for Ross Perot's 1992 presidential campaign. The Perot committee actively used the Mark in New York and on a national basis from August 1992 onward. Perot's campaign committee established the plaintiff corporation United and, shortly after the 1992 election, assigned its rights in the Mark to the plaintiff. United immediately filed with the Patent and Trademark Office for registration, which became effective in 1994.

Defendant Rodriguez worked with the Perot campaign in New York in 1992 and was aware of its use of the Mark as its slogan. After friction and division among Perot's New York supporters, Rodriguez incorporated UWSANY in October 1992, and became its president. Rodriguez caused UWSANY to use the Mark in connection with its political activities.

In June 1994, United filed a complaint against UWSANY and Rodriguez charging infringement of its Mark. The amended complaint alleges claims of infringement and unfair competition under the Lanham Act, 15 U.S.C. § 1051 *et seq.*, common law infringement and unfair competition under New York law, and violations of N.Y. Business Law §§ 133 and 368-d.

*   *   *

UWSANY's political activities are "services" within the meaning of the Lanham Act.

Appellants contend that UWSANY's political activities, in connection with which it used the Mark, were not "services" within the meaning of the Lanham Act, and that their conduct was, therefore, not within the Act's prohibition. Section 1114(1)(a) bars unauthorized use of a mark in commerce . . . in connection with the sale, offering for sale, distribution, or advertising of any goods or *services* [if] . . . such use is likely to cause confusion. . . .15 U.S.C. § 1114(1)(a) (emphasis added).

The term "services" has been interpreted broadly. As the court explained in *N.A.A.C.P. v. N.A.A.C.P. Legal Defense and Educ. Fund,* the right to enjoin infringement of a trade or service mark "is as available to public service organizations as to merchants and manufacturers." 559 F.Supp. 1337, 1342 (D.D.C.1983) (citation omitted), *rev'd on other grounds,* 753 F.2d 131 (D.C.Cir.), *cert. denied,* 472 U.S. 1021 (1985). In support of this view, McCarthy comments that "retention of a distinct identity [by a non-profit organization that sells no goods] is just as important as it is to a commercial company." 1 , J. THOMAS MCCARTHY, MCCARTHY ON TRADEMARKS AND UNFAIR COMPETITION § 9:5 (4th ed.1996). The protection of the trademark or service mark of non-profit and public service organizations requires that use of the mark by competing organizations be prohibited.

The Lanham Act has thus been applied to defendants furnishing a wide variety of non-commercial public and civic benefits. *See, e.g., Kappa Sigma Fraternity v. Kappa Sigma Gamma Fraternity,* 654 F.Supp. 1095, 1101 (D.N.H.1987) (membership in collegiate Greek-letter fraternity and solicitation of alumni contributions); *American Diabetes Ass'n, Inc. v. Nat'l Diabetes Ass'n,* 533 F.Supp. 16, 20 (E.D.Pa.1981) (solicitation of donations), *aff'd,* 681 F.2d 804 (3ᵈ Cir.1982); *United States Jaycees v. Philadelphia Jaycees,* 490 F.Supp. 688, 691 (E.D.Pa.1980) (public service projects including Special Olympics, Christmas shopping for orphans, and half-way houses), *rev'd on other grounds,* 639 F.2d 134 (3ᵈ Cir.1981); *United States Jaycees v. San Francisco Junior Chamber of Commerce,* 354 F.Supp. 61, 64, 65 (N.D.Cal.1972) (meetings, competitions, and other special events for young men interested in community affairs; community betterment programs), *aff'd,* 513 F.2d 1226 (9ᵗʰ Cir.1975).

Indeed, the Lanham Act has been applied to political organizations engaged in activities virtually identical to UWSANY's, over assertions of the same argument advanced here. . . .

UWSANY was incorporated "to solicit, collect and otherwise raise money" in support of the presidential candidacy of Ross Perot. Since its incorporation, it has engaged in political organizing; established and equipped an office; solicited politicians to run on the UWSANY slate; issued press releases intended to support particular candidates and causes; endorsed candidates; and distributed partisan political literature. These are the services characteristically rendered by a political party to and for its members, adherents, and candidates. Although not undertaken for profit, they unquestionably render a service. We have no doubt that they satisfy § 1114(1)(a)'s requirement that the mark be used in connection with goods or services.

A political organization that adopts a platform and endorses candidates under a trade name performs the valuable service of communicating to voters that it has determined that the election of those candidates would be beneficial to the objectives of the organization. Thus voters who support those objectives can support the endorsed candidates with some confidence that doing so will advance the voters' objectives. If different organizations were permitted to employ the same trade name in endorsing candidates, voters would be unable to derive any significance from an endorsement, as they would not know whether the endorsement came from the organization whose objectives they shared or from another organization using the same name. Any group trading in political ideas would be free to distribute publicity statements, endorsements, and position papers in the name of the "Republican Party," the "Democratic Party," or any other. The resulting confusion would be catastrophic; voters would have no way of understanding the significance of an endorsement or position taken by parties of recognized major names. . . The suggestion that the performance of such functions is not within the scope of "services in commerce" seem to us to be not only wrong but extraordinarily impractical for the functioning of our political system. *See Tomei v. Finley,* 512 F.Supp. 695, 698 (N.D.Ill.1981) (preliminary injunction issued because of strong likelihood of confusion resulting from political party's use of acronym designed to deceive voters into thinking the candidate was of the opposing political party). . . .

. . . UWSANY . . . is using the Mark not as a commentary on its owner, but instead as a source identifier. UWSANY's use of the Mark seeks to identify UWSANY as part of the same political organization or party as United—the party that championed the Perot candidacy. That is a use of the Mark in connection with "services," 15 U.S.C. § 1114(1)(a), and is covered by the Lanham Act.

* * *

UWSANY's use of the Mark is not protected by the First Amendment.

We reject UWSANY's further contention that its use of United's Mark is protected by the First Amendment. UWSANY is not using the phrase "United We Stand America"

reason

for an expressive purpose such as commentary, comedy, parody, news reporting or criticism, *see* [*L.L. Bean, Inc. v. Drake Publishers, Inc.*, 811 F.2d 26 (1st Cir. 1987),] at 32; *Yankee Publishing*, 809 F.Supp. at 276, but instead as a means to associate itself with the political movement that sponsored the Ross Perot campaign. In other words, it is using the slogan as a mark, and using it to suggest the same source identification as plaintiffs. This is precisely the use that is reserved by the Lanham Act to the owner of the mark. Even assuming that UWSANY might communicate its political message more effectively by appropriating United's Mark, such appropriation would cause significant consumer confusion. . . . It is not protected by the First Amendment. *See San Francisco Arts & Athletics, Inc. v. United States Olympic Committee*, 483 U.S. 522, 541 (1987). To allow UWSANY to use United's Mark would not only cause confusion, but would permit it to " 'appropriat[e] to itself the harvest of those who have sown.' " *Id.* at 541, 1 (quoting *International News Service v. Associated Press*, 248 U.S. 215, 239-40, (1918)).

* * *

The judgment of the district court is affirmed.

Notes on *United We Stand America*

UWSANY is unquestionably engaged in political speech. Political speech is at the very core of the First Amendment. No type of speech is more stringently protected. So how can UWSANY lose this case? Consider that UWSANY's political services are held to be "services" under the Lanham Act, no different in principle from any commercial services. Also, UWSANY's use of the mark is held not to be protected by the First Amendment. What precisely is the justification given by the court for each of these holdings? Note that the decision is authored by Judge Pierre Leval, the author of the article excerpted at the beginning of this chapter. Does this decision adhere to the proposal at the heart of that article? Does it involve any balancing of trademark rights and First Amendment values? If not, why not?

MATTEL, INC., v. MCA RECORDS, INC.
296 F.3d 894 (9th Cir. 2002)

KOZINSKI, CIRCUIT JUDGE:

If this were a sci-fi melodrama, it might be called Speech-Zilla meets Trademark Kong.

Barbie was born in Germany in the 1950s as an adult collector's item. Over the years, Mattel transformed her from a doll that resembled a "German street walker," . . . as she originally appeared, into a glamorous, long-legged blonde. Barbie has been labeled both the ideal American woman and a bimbo. She has survived attacks both psychic (from feminists critical of her fictitious figure) and physical (more than 500 professional makeovers). She remains a symbol of American girlhood, a public figure who graces the aisles of toy stores throughout the country and beyond. With Barbie, Mattel created not just a toy but a cultural icon.

With fame often comes unwanted attention. Aqua is a Danish band that has, as yet, only dreamed of attaining Barbie-like status. In 1997, Aqua produced the song Barbie Girl on the album *Aquarium*. In the song, one bandmember impersonates Barbie, singing in a high-pitched, doll-like voice; another bandmember, calling himself Ken, entices Barbie to "go party." (The lyrics are in the Appendix.) Barbie Girl singles sold well and, to Mattel's dismay, the song made it onto Top 40 music charts.

* * *

A. A trademark is a word, phrase or symbol that is used to identify a manufacturer or sponsor of a good or the provider of a service. *See New Kids on the Block v. News Am. Publ'g, Inc.*, 971 F.2d 302, 305 (9th Cir.1992). It's the owner's way of preventing others from duping consumers into buying a product they mistakenly believe is sponsored by the trademark owner. A trademark "inform[s] people that trademarked products come from the same source." *Id.* at 305 n. 2. Limited to this core purpose—avoiding confusion in the marketplace—a trademark owner's property rights play well with the First Amendment. "Whatever first amendment rights you may have in calling the brew you make in your bathtub 'Pepsi' are easily outweighed by the buyer's interest in not being fooled into buying it." *Trademarks Unplugged*, 68 N.Y.U. L.Rev. 960, 973 (1993).

The problem arises when trademarks transcend their identifying purpose. Some trademarks enter our public discourse and become an integral part of our vocabulary. How else do you say that something's "the Rolls Royce of its class"? What else is a quick fix, but a Band-Aid? Does the average consumer know to ask for aspirin as "acetyl salicylic acid"? *See Bayer Co. v. United Drug Co.*, 272 F. 505, 510 (S.D.N.Y.1921). Trademarks often fill in gaps in our vocabulary and add a contemporary flavor to our expressions. Once imbued with such expressive value, the trademark becomes a word in our language and assumes a role outside the bounds of trademark law.

Our likelihood-of-confusion test, *see AMF Inc. v. Sleekcraft Boats*, 599 F.2d 341, 348-49 (9th Cir.1979), generally strikes a comfortable balance between the trademark owner's property rights and the public's expressive interests. But when a trademark owner asserts a right to control how we express ourselves—when we'd find it difficult to describe the product any other way (as in the case of aspirin), or when the mark (like Rolls Royce) has taken on an expressive meaning apart from its source-identifying function— applying the traditional test fails to account for the full weight of the public's interest in free expression.

The First Amendment may offer little protection for a competitor who labels its commercial good with a confusingly similar mark, but "[t]rademark rights do not entitle the owner to quash an unauthorized use of the mark by another who is communicating ideas or expressing points of view." *L.L. Bean, Inc. v. Drake Publishers, Inc.*, 811 F.2d 26, 29 (1st Cir.1987). Were we to ignore the expressive value that some marks assume, trademark rights would grow to encroach upon the zone protected by the First Amendment. *See Yankee Publ'g, Inc. v. News Am. Publ'g, Inc.*, 809 F.Supp. 267, 276 (S.D.N.Y.1992) ("[W]hen unauthorized use of another's mark is part of a communicative message and not a source identifier, the First Amendment is implicated in opposition to the trademark right."). Simply put, the trademark owner does not have the right to control public discourse whenever the public imbues his mark with a meaning beyond its source-identifying function. *See Anti-Monopoly, Inc. v. Gen. Mills Fun Group*, 611 F.2d 296, 301 (9th Cir.1979) ("It is the source-denoting function which trademark laws protect, and nothing more.").

B. There is no doubt that MCA uses Mattel's mark: Barbie is one half of Barbie Girl. But Barbie Girl is the title of a song about Barbie and Ken, a reference that—at least today—can only be to Mattel's famous couple. We expect a title to describe the underlying work, not to identify the producer, and Barbie Girl does just that.

The Barbie Girl title presages a song about Barbie, or at least a girl like Barbie. The title conveys a message to consumers about what they can expect to discover in the song itself; it's a quick glimpse of Aqua's take on their own song. The lyrics confirm this: The female singer, who calls herself Barbie, is "a Barbie girl, in [her] Barbie world." She tells her male counterpart (named Ken), "Life in plastic, it's fantastic. You can brush my hair, undress me everywhere/Imagination, life is your creation." And off they go to "party." The song pokes fun at Barbie and the values that Aqua contends she represents. *See Cliffs Notes, Inc. v. Bantam Doubleday Dell Publ'g Group*, 886 F.2d 490, 495-96 (2[d] Cir.1989). The female singer explains, "I'm a blond bimbo girl, in a fantasy world/Dress me up, make it tight, I'm your dolly."

The song does not rely on the Barbie mark to poke fun at another subject but targets

Barbie herself. . . . The Second Circuit has held that "in general the [Lanham] Act should be construed to apply to artistic works only where the public interest in avoiding consumer confusion outweighs the public interest in free expression." *Rogers v. Grimaldi*, 875 F.2d 994, 999 (2[d] Cir.1989); *see also Cliffs Notes*, 886 F.2d at 494 (quoting *Rogers*, 875 F.2d at 999). . . .

Rogers concluded that literary titles do not violate the Lanham Act "unless the title has no artistic relevance to the underlying work whatsoever, or, if it has some artistic relevance, unless the title explicitly misleads as to the source or the content of the work." *Id.* at 999 (footnote omitted). We agree with the Second Circuit's analysis and adopt the *Rogers* standard as our own.

Applying *Rogers* to our case, we conclude that MCA's use of Barbie is not an infringement of Mattel's trademark. Under the first prong of *Rogers*, the use of Barbie in the song title clearly is relevant to the underlying work, namely, the song itself. As noted, the song is about Barbie and the values Aqua claims she represents. The song title does not explicitly mislead as to the source of the work; it does not, explicitly or otherwise, suggest that it was produced by Mattel. The *only* indication that Mattel might be associated with the song is the use of Barbie in the title; if this were enough to satisfy this prong of the *Rogers* test, it would render *Rogers* a nullity. We therefore agree with the district court that MCA was entitled to summary judgment on this ground. We need not consider whether the district court was correct in holding that MCA was also entitled to summary judgment because its use of Barbie was a nominative fair use. . . .

Mattel separately argues that, under the Federal Trademark Dilution Act ("FTDA"), MCA's song dilutes the Barbie mark in two ways: It diminishes the mark's capacity to identify and distinguish Mattel products, and tarnishes the mark because the song is inappropriate for young girls. *See* 15 U.S.C. § 1125(c); *see also Panavision*, 141 F.3d at 1324.

*   *   *

Barbie easily qualifies under the FTDA as a famous and distinctive mark, and reached this status long before MCA began to market the Barbie Girl song. The commercial success of Barbie Girl establishes beyond dispute that the Barbie mark satisfies each of these elements.

We are also satisfied that the song amounts to a "commercial use in commerce." Although this statutory language is ungainly, its meaning seems clear: It refers to a use of a famous and distinctive mark to sell goods other than those produced or authorized by the mark's owner. *Panavision*, 141 F.3d at 1324-25. That is precisely what MCA did with the Barbie mark: It created and sold to consumers in the marketplace commercial products (the Barbie Girl single and the *Aquarium* album) that bear the Barbie mark.

MCA's use of the mark is dilutive. MCA does not dispute that, while a reference to Barbie would previously have brought to mind only Mattel's doll, after the song's popular success, some consumers hearing Barbie's name will think of both the doll and the song, or perhaps of the song only. . . . This is a classic blurring injury and is in no way diminished by the fact that the song itself refers back to Barbie the doll. To be dilutive, use of the mark need not bring to mind the junior user alone. The distinctiveness of the mark is diminished if the mark no longer brings to mind the senior user alone. . . .

We consider next the applicability of the FTDA's three statutory exemptions. These are uses that, though potentially dilutive, are nevertheless permitted: comparative advertising; news reporting and commentary; and noncommercial use. 15 U.S.C. § 1125(c)(4)(B). The first two exemptions clearly do not apply; only the exemption for noncommercial use need detain us.

A "noncommercial use" exemption, on its face, presents a bit of a conundrum because it seems at odds with the earlier requirement that the junior use be a "commercial use in commerce." [13] If a use has to be commercial in order to be dilutive, how then can it also be noncommercial so as to satisfy the exception of section 1125(c)(4)(B)? If the term "commercial use" had the same meaning in both provisions, this would eliminate one of the three statutory exemptions defined by this subsection, because any use found to be dilutive would, of necessity, not be noncommercial.

Such a reading of the statute would also create a constitutional problem, because it would leave the FTDA with no First Amendment protection for dilutive speech other than comparative advertising and news reporting. This would be a serious problem because the primary (usually exclusive) remedy for dilution is an injunction. . . . As noted above, tension with the First Amendment also exists in the trademark context, especially where the mark has assumed an expressive function beyond mere identification of a product or service. *See* pp. 900-901 *supra; New Kids on the Block*, 971 F.2d at 306-08. These concerns apply with greater force in the dilution context because dilution lacks two very significant limitations that reduce the tension between trademark law and the First Amendment.

First, depending on the strength and distinctiveness of the mark, trademark law grants relief only against uses that are likely to confuse. *See* 5 *McCarthy* § 30:3, at 30-8 to 30-11; *Restatement* § 35 cmt. c at 370. A trademark injunction is usually limited to uses within one industry or several related industries. Dilution law is the antithesis of trademark law in this respect, because it seeks to protect the mark from association in the public's mind with wholly unrelated goods and services. The more remote the good or service associated with the junior use, the more likely it is to cause dilution rather than trademark infringement. A dilution injunction, by contrast to a trademark injunction, will generally sweep across broad vistas of the economy.

Second, a trademark injunction, even a very broad one, is premised on the need to prevent consumer confusion. This consumer protection rationale—averting what is essentially a fraud on the consuming public—is wholly consistent with the theory of the First Amendment, which does not protect commercial fraud. *Cent. Hudson Gas & Elec. v. Pub. Serv. Comm'n*, 447 U.S. 557, 566, 100 S.Ct. 2343, 65 L.Ed.2d 341 (1980); *see Thompson v. W. States Med. Ctr.*, 535 U.S. 357, 122 S.Ct. 1497, 152 L.Ed.2d 563 (2002) (applying *Central Hudson*). Moreover, avoiding harm to consumers is an important interest that is independent of the senior user's interest in protecting its business.

Dilution, by contrast, does not require a showing of consumer confusion, 15 U.S.C. § 1127, and dilution injunctions therefore lack the built-in First Amendment compass of trademark injunctions. In addition, dilution law protects only the distinctiveness of the mark, which is inherently less weighty than the dual interest of protecting trademark owners and avoiding harm to consumers that is at the heart of every trademark claim.

Fortunately, the legislative history of the FTDA suggests an interpretation of the "noncommercial use" exemption that both solves our interpretive dilemma and diminishes some First Amendment concerns: "Noncommercial use" refers to a use that consists entirely of noncommercial, or fully constitutionally protected, speech. *See* 2 Jerome Gilson et al., *Trademark Protection and Practice* § 5.12[1][c][vi], at 5-240 (this exemption "is intended to prevent the courts from enjoining speech that has been recognized to be [fully] constitutionally protected," "such as parodies"). Where, as here, a statute's plain meaning "produces an absurd, and perhaps unconstitutional, result[, it is] entirely appropriate to consult all public materials, including the background of [the statute] and the legislative history of its adoption." *Green v. Bock Laundry Mach. Co.*, 490 U.S. 504, 527 (1989) (Scalia, J., concurring).

* * *

---

[13] [Note that the TDRA contains a "noncommercial use" exemption that is virtually identical to the analogous exemption contained in the FTDA, under which *Mattel* was decided. *See also* discussion in Chapter 8.]

To determine whether Barbie Girl falls within this exemption, we look to our definition of commercial speech under our First Amendment caselaw. *See* H.R.Rep. No. 104-374, at 8, *reprinted in* 1995 U.S.C.C.A.N. 1029, 1035 (the exemption "expressly incorporates the concept of 'commercial' speech from the 'commercial speech' doctrine"); 141 Cong. Rec. S19306-10, S19311 (daily ed. Dec. 29, 1995) (the exemption "is consistent with existing [First Amendment] case law"). "Although the boundary between commercial and noncommercial speech has yet to be clearly delineated, the 'core notion of commercial speech' is that it 'does no more than propose a commercial transaction.' " *Hoffman v. Capital Cities/ABC, Inc.*, 255 F.3d 1180, 1184 (9th Cir.2001) (quoting *Bolger v. Youngs Drug Prod's Corp.*, 463 U.S. 60, 66 (1983)). If speech is not "purely commercial"—that is, if it does more than propose a commercial transaction— then it is entitled to full First Amendment protection. *Id.* at 1185-86 (internal quotation marks omitted).

* * *

Hoffman controls: Barbie Girl is not purely commercial speech, and is therefore fully protected. To be sure, MCA used Barbie's name to sell copies of the song. However, as we've already observed, *see* pp. 901-02 *supra*, the song also lampoons the Barbie image and comments humorously on the cultural values Aqua claims she represents. Use of the Barbie mark in the song Barbie Girl therefore falls within the noncommercial use exemption to the FTDA. For precisely the same reasons, use of the mark in the song's title is also exempted.

* * *

After Mattel filed suit, Mattel and MCA employees traded barbs in the press. When an MCA spokeswoman noted that each album included a disclaimer saying that Barbie Girl was a "social commentary [that was] not created or approved by the makers of the doll," a Mattel representative responded by saying, "That's unacceptable. . . . It's akin to a bank robber handing a note of apology to a teller during a heist. [It n]either diminishes the severity of the crime, nor does it make it legal." He later characterized the song as a "theft" of "another company's property."

MCA filed a counterclaim for defamation based on the Mattel representative's use of the words "bank robber," "heist," "crime" and "theft." But all of these are variants of the invective most often hurled at accused infringers, namely "piracy." No one hearing this accusation understands intellectual property owners to be saying that infringers are nautical cutthroats with eyepatches and peg legs who board galleons to plunder cargo. In context, all these terms are nonactionable "rhetorical hyperbole," *Gilbrook v. City of Westminster*, 177 F.3d 839, 863 (9th Cir.1999). The parties are advised to chill.

AFFIRMED.

APPENDIX

"Barbie Girl" by Aqua

-Hiya Barbie!

-Hi Ken!

You wanna go for a ride?

-Sure, Ken!

-Jump in!

-Ha ha ha ha!

(CHORUS:)

I'm a Barbie girl, in my Barbie world

Life in plastic, it's fantastic

You can brush my hair, undress me everywhere

Imagination, life is your creation

Come on Barbie, let's go party!

(CHORUS)

I'm a blonde bimbo girl, in a fantasy world

Dress me up, make it tight, I'm your dolly

You're my doll, rock and roll, feel the glamour in pink

Kiss me here, touch me there, hanky-panky

You can touch, you can play

If you say "I'm always yours," ooh ooh

(CHORUS)

(BRIDGE:)

Come on, Barbie, let's go party, ah ah ah yeah

Come on, Barbie, let's go party, ooh ooh, ooh ooh

Come on, Barbie, let's go party, ah ah ah yeah

Come on, Barbie, let's go party, ooh ooh, ooh ooh

Make me walk, make me talk, do whatever you please

I can act like a star, I can beg on my knees

Come jump in, be my friend, let us do it again

Hit the town, fool around, let's go party

You can touch, you can play

You can say "I'm always yours"

You can touch, you can play

You can say "I'm always yours"

(BRIDGE)

(CHORUS x2)

(BRIDGE)

-Oh, I'm having so much fun!

-Well, Barbie, we're just getting started!

-Oh, I love you Ken!

* * *

Notes on *Mattel v. MCA*

"What else is a quick fix, but a Band-Aid?," the court asks rhetorically. Such uses that "transcend [the mark's] identifying purpose," the court states, may well enjoy First Amendment protection. What effect might these principles have on some companies' struggles to keep their famous marks from sliding into genericness? *See also* discussion in Chapter 4. Should the law take sides in those struggle, either by accelerating the slide or by aiding trademark owners in stopping it?

The court evinces a notable skepticism toward dilution principles. "Dilution injunctions . . . lack the built-in First Amendment compass of trademark [infringement] injunctions." Is that an accurate assessment? Is dilution law inherently less hospitable to First Amendment considerations that infringement law? Note that this case was decided under the FTDA. Is there anything in the TDRA addressing the court's concerns about the FTDA's relationship to the First Amendment?

The court's core holding on dilution is this: "If speech is not 'purely commercial' — that is, if it does more than propose a commercial transaction— then it is entitled to full

First Amendment protection." Does that mean that even the smallest admixture of a noncommercial dimension will permit otherwise commercial speech to avail itself of the "noncommercial use" safe harbor? What effect might such a principle have on the actions of would-be diluters? Does this principle still apply, given that the FTDA has been replaced by the TDRA?

PARKS v. LaFACE RECORDS
329 F.3d 437 (6th Cir. 2003).

HOLSCHUH, DISTRICT JUDGE:

This is a dispute over the name of a song. Rosa Parks is a civil rights icon who first gained prominence during the Montgomery, Alabama bus boycott in 1955. She brings suit against LaFace Records, a record producer, and OutKast, a "rap" (or "hip-hop") music duo, as well as several other named affiliates, for using her name as the title of their song, *Rosa Parks*. Parks contends that Defendants' use of her name constitutes false advertising under § 43(a) of the Lanham Act, 15 U.S.C. § 1125(a) . . . . Defendants . . . argue that . . . their First Amendment freedom of artistic expression should be a defense as a matter of law to each of these claims. . . .

Parks brought this action in a Michigan state court. Defendants subsequently removed the case to the District Court for the Eastern District of Michigan. Following cross-motions for summary judgment, the district court denied Parks' motion for summary judgment and granted summary judgment for Defendants. Parks now appeals the grant of summary judgment for Defendants. . . .

Rosa Parks is an historical figure who first gained prominence as a symbol of the civil rights movement in the United States during the 1950s and 1960s. In 1955, while riding in the front of a segregated bus in Montgomery, Alabama, she refused to yield her seat to a white passenger and move to the back of the bus as blacks were required to do by the then-existing laws requiring segregation of the races. A 381-day bus boycott in Montgomery flowed from that one event, which eventually became a catalyst for organized boycotts, sit-ins, and demonstrations all across the South. Her single act of defiance has garnered her numerous public accolades and awards, and she has used that celebrity status to promote various civil and human rights causes as well as television programs and books inspired by her life story. She has also approved a collection of gospel recordings by various artists entitled *Verity Records Presents: A Tribute to Mrs. Rosa Parks* (the "*Tribute*" album), released in 1995.

Defendants are OutKast, comprised of recording artists André "Dré" Benjamin and Antwan "Big Boi" Patton; their record producers, LaFace, founded by and named after Antonio "L.A." Reid and Kenny "Babyface" Edmonds; . . . and LaFace's record distributors, Arista Records and BMG Entertainment (collectively "Defendants"). In September 1998, Defendants released the album *Aquemini*. The album's first single release was a song titled *Rosa Parks*, described as a "hit single" by a sticker on the album. The same sticker that contained the name *Rosa Parks* also contained a Parental Advisory warning of "explicit content." J.A. at 60. Because, as later discussed, the critical issue in this case is a determination of the artistic relevance of the title, *Rosa Parks*, to the content of the song, the lyrics obviously must be considered in their entirety. They are as follows:

(Hook)

Ah ha, hush that fuss

Everybody move to the back of the bus

Do you wanna bump and slump with us

We the type of people make the club get crunk

Verse 1: (Big Boi)

Many a day has passed, the night has gone by

But still I find the time to put that bump off in your eye
Total chaos, for these playas, thought we was absent
We takin another route to represent the Dungeon Family
Like Great Day, me and my nigga decide to take the back way
We stabbing every city then we headed to that bat cave
A-T-L, Georgia, what we do for ya
Bull doggin hoes like them Georgetown Hoyas
Boy you sounding silly, thank my Brougham aint sittin pretty
Doing doughnuts round you suckas like then circles around titties
Damn we the committee gone burn it down
But us gone bust you in the mouth with the chorus now
(Hook)
Verse 2: (André)
I met a gypsy and she hipped me to some life game
To stimulate then activate the left and right brain
Said baby boy you only funky as your last cut
You focus on the past your ass'll be a has what
Thats one to live by or either that one to die to
I try to just throw it at you determine your own adventure
Andre, got to her station here's my destination
She got off the bus, the conversation lingered in my head for hours
Took a shower kinda sour cause my favorite group ain't comin with it
But I'm witcha you cause you probably goin through it anyway
But anyhow when in doubt went on out and bought it
Cause I thought it would be jammin but examine all the flawsky-wawsky
Awfully, it's sad and it's costly, but that's all she wrote
And I hope I never have to float in that boat
Up shit creek it's weak is the last quote
That I want to hear when I'm goin down when all's said and done
And we got a new joe in town
When the record player get to skippin and slowin down
All yawl can say is them niggas earned that crown but until then . . .
(Hook)
(Harmonica Solo)
(Hook til fade)
J.A. at 521.

*　*　*

We turn then to Defendants' second argument, that even if Parks could establish some likelihood of confusion, the First Amendment protects Defendants' choice of title.

The First Amendment Defense—Three Approaches

Defendants allege that even if Parks' evidence demonstrates some likelihood of consumer confusion regarding their song and album, their First Amendment right of artistic expression trumps that concern. Defendants make an arguable point. From ancient times, music has been a means by which people express ideas. As such, music is firmly ensconced within the protections of the First Amendment. *See Hurley v. Irish-American Gay, Lesbian & Bisexual Group of Boston,* 515 U.S. 557, 569, 115 S.Ct. 2338, 132 L.Ed.2d 487 (1995) (stating that paintings, music and poetry are "unquestionably shielded" by the First Amendment); *Ward v. Rock Against Racism,* 491 U.S. 781, 790, 109 S.Ct. 2746, 105 L.Ed.2d 661 (1989) ("Music, as a form of expression and communication, is protected under the First Amendment."). However, the First Amendment cannot permit anyone who cries "artist" to have *carte blanche* when it comes to naming and advertising his or her works, art though it may be. As the Second Circuit sagely observed, "[t]he purchaser of a book, like the purchaser of a can of peas, has a right not to be misled as to the source [or endorsement] of the product." *Rogers,* 875 F.2d at 997; *see also Cliffs Notes, Inc. v. Bantam Doubleday Dell Publ'g Group, Inc.,* 886 F.2d 490, 493 (2ᵈCir.1989)("Trademark protection is not lost simply because the allegedly infringing use is in connection with a work of artistic expression." (citation omitted)). Courts have adopted three approaches to balance First Amendment interests with the protections of the Lanham Act: (a) the "likelihood of confusion" test; (b) the "alternative avenues" test; and (c) the *Rogers v. Grimaldi* test. We will examine each one in turn.

a. Likelihood of Confusion Factors Used In Commercial Trademark Cases

One approach is to rely solely on the "likelihood of confusion" factors applied in other, more traditional, trademark cases. . . . Under this approach, we do not pay special solicitude to an asserted First Amendment defense.

* * *

b. Alternative Avenues Test

A second approach is the "alternative avenues" test. This is the test urged upon us by Parks, and endorsed by a panel of the Eighth Circuit. Under the "alternative avenues" test, a title of an expressive work will not be protected from a false advertising claim if there are sufficient alternative means for an artist to convey his or her idea. *See Mutual of Omaha Ins. Co. v. Novak,* 836 F.2d 397, 402 (8th Cir.1987) (creator of parody tee-shirts not protected by First Amendment because he could still produce parody editorials in books, magazines, or film); *Am. Dairy Queen Corp. v. New Line Prods., Inc.,* 35 F.Supp.2d 727, 734 (D.Minn.1998) (no First Amendment protection for an infringing movie title because there were other titles the producers could use); *cf. Anheuser-Busch, Inc. v. Balducci Publ'ns,* 28 F.3d 769, 776 (8th Cir.1994) (First Amendment protection not available to parodist because the confusing trademark use was "wholly unnecessary" to the parodist's stated purpose).

c. Rogers v. Grimaldi Test

Finally, a third approach is the one developed by the Second Circuit in *Rogers v. Grimaldi* and adopted by the district court in this case. Under *Rogers,* a title will be protected unless it has "no artistic relevance" to the underlying work or, if there is artistic relevance, the title "explicitly misleads as to the source or the content of the work." *Rogers,* 875 F.2d at 999. This test was explicitly adopted by the Fifth Circuit in *Westchester Media v. PRL USA Holdings, Inc.,* 214 F.3d 658, 664- 65 (5th Cir.2000), and by a panel of the Ninth Circuit in *Mattel,* 296 F.3d at 902. It was also adopted by a district court in the Third Circuit in *Seale v. Gramercy Pictures,* 949 F.Supp. 331, 339 (1996).

d. Analysis

We conclude that neither the first nor the second approach accords adequate weight to the First Amendment interests in this case. The first approach—unmodified application of the likelihood of confusion factors in trademark cases—gives no weight to First Amendment concerns. Instead, it treats the name of an artistic work as if it were no different from the name of an ordinary commercial product. However, this approach ignores the fact that the artistic work is *not* simply a commercial product but is also a means of communication. . . . The fact that Defendants use the *Rosa Parks* title in advertising does not automatically erase the expressive function of the title and render it mere commercial exploitation; if a song is sold, and the title is protected by the First Amendment, the title naturally will be "inextricably intertwined" with the song's commercial promotion. . . .

The second approach, the "alternative avenues" test, is similarly problematic. The "alternative avenues" test was articulated in *Dallas Cowboys Cheerleaders, Inc. v. Pussycat Cinema, Ltd.,* 604 F.2d 200, 206 (2^d Cir.1979), and is derived from real property law. The test is premised on the notion that, just as a real property owner may exclude a speaker from a shopping mall so long as other locations exist for the speaker to deliver his message, a celebrity may prohibit use of his or her name so long as alternative ways exist for the artist to communicate his or her idea. *See id.* (*citing Lloyd Corp. v. Tanner,* 407 U.S. 551, 567, 92 S.Ct. 2219, 33 L.Ed.2d 131 (1972)). *See also Mutual of Omaha Ins. Co.,* 836 F.2d at 402 (*citing Dallas Cowboys,* 604 F.2d at 206); *Am. Dairy Queen Corp.,* 35 F.Supp.2d at 734.

More than one court has noted the awkwardness of analogizing property rights in land to property rights in words or ideas. . . To suggest that other words can be used as well to express an author's or composer's message is not a proper test for weighing First Amendment rights. . . . Finally, adopting the "alternative avenues" test would needlessly entangle courts in the process of titling works of art; courts would be asked to determine not just whether a title is reasonably "artistic" but whether a title is "necessary" to communicate the idea. We therefore reject the alternative avenues test.

The third approach, the *Rogers* test, was adopted by the district court in this case and has been endorsed by panels in the Second, Fifth, and Ninth Circuits. Although the *Rogers* test has been criticized, *see, e.g.,* 2 J. Thomas McCarthy, McCarthy on Trademarks and Unfair Competition § 10:31 (4th ed.2002), we find it the most appropriate method to balance the public interest in avoiding consumer confusion with the public interest in free expression.

. . . The *Rogers* court, finding that overextension of Lanham Act restrictions in the area of titles might intrude on First Amendment values and that the "alternative avenues" test is insufficient to accommodate the public's interest in free expression, adopted a two-pronged test:

> In the context of allegedly misleading titles using a celebrity's name, that balance [between avoiding consumer confusion and protecting free expression] will normally not support application of the Act unless [1] the title has no artistic relevance to the underlying work whatsoever, or, if it has some artistic relevance, unless [2] the title explicitly misleads as to the source or the content of the work.

Id. at 999.

* * *

[We are persuaded] that *Rogers* is the best test for balancing Defendants' and the public's interest in free expression under the First Amendment against Parks' and the public's interest in enforcement of the Lanham Act. We thus apply the *Rogers* test to the facts before us.

Application of the Rogers *Test*

a. Artistic Relevance Prong

The first prong of *Rogers* requires a determination of whether there is any artistic relationship between the title and the underlying work. *Rogers,* 875 F.2d at 999. Parks contends that a cursory review of the *Rosa Parks* title and the lyrics demonstrates that there is no artistic connection between them. Parks also submits two articles in which members of OutKast are purported to have admitted that the song was not about her. As further evidence, she offers a "translation" of the lyrics of the song *Rosa Parks,* derived from various electronic "dictionaries" of the "rap" vernacular to demonstrate that the song truly has nothing to do with Parks herself. The "translation" of the chorus reads as follows:

> "Be quiet and stop the commotion. OutKast is coming back out [with new music] so all other MCs [mic checkers, rappers, Master of Ceremonies] step aside. Do you want to ride and hang out with us? OutKast is the type of group to make the clubs get hyped-up/excited."

Pl. Br. at 5.

Defendants respond that their use of Parks' name is "metaphorical" or "symbolic." They argue that the historical association between Rosa Parks and the phrase "move to the back of the bus" is beyond dispute and that Parks' argument that the song is not "about" her in a biographical sense is simply irrelevant.

The district court was of the opinion that the artistic relationship between the title and the song was "so obvious that the matter is not open to reasonable debate." *Parks,* 76 F.Supp.2d at 782. The court said:

> Rosa Parks is universally known for and commonly associated with her refusal . . . to . . . "move to the back of the bus." The song at issue makes unmistakable reference to that symbolic act a total of ten times. Admittedly, the song is not about plaintiff in a strictly biographical sense, but it need not be. Rather, defendants' use of plaintiff's name, along with the phrase "move to the back of the bus," is metaphorical and symbolic.

Id. at 780.

Contrary to the opinion of the district court, we believe that the artistic relationship between the title and the content of the song is certainly not obvious and, indeed, is "open to reasonable debate" for the following reasons.

It is true that the phrase "move to the back of the bus" is repeatedly used in the "hook" or chorus of the song. When the phrase is considered *in the context of the lyrics,* however, the phrase has absolutely nothing to do with Rosa Parks. There could be no stronger, no more compelling, evidence of this fact than the admission of "Dré" (André "Dré" Benjamin) that, "We (OutKast) never intended for the song to be about Rosa Parks or the civil rights movement. It was just symbolic, meaning that we comin' back out, so all you other MCs move to the back of the bus." J.A. at 333. . . . The composers did *not* intend it to be about Rosa Parks, and the lyrics are *not* about Rosa Parks. The lyrics' sole message is that OutKast's competitors are of lesser quality and, therefore, must "move to the back of the bus," or in other words, "take a back seat." We believe that reasonable persons could conclude that there is no relationship of any kind between Rosa Parks' name and the content of the song—a song that is nothing more and nothing less than a paean announcing the triumph of superior people in the entertainment business over inferior people in that business. *Back of the Bus,* for example, would be a title that is obviously relevant to the content of the song, but it also would not have the marketing power of an icon of the civil rights movement. . . . Choosing Rosa Parks' name as the title to the song unquestionably enhanced the song's potential sale to the consuming public.

* * *

While Defendants' lyrics contain profanity and a great deal of "explicit" language (together with a parental warning), they contain absolutely nothing that could conceivably, by any stretch of the imagination, be considered, explicitly or implicitly, a reference to courage, to sacrifice, to the civil rights movement or to any other quality with which Rosa Parks is identified. If the requirement of "relevance" is to have any meaning at all, it would not be unreasonable to conclude that the title *Rosa Parks* is *not* relevant to the content of the song in question. The use of this woman's name unquestionably was a good marketing tool—*Rosa Parks* was likely to sell far more recordings than *Back of the Bus*—but its use could be found by a reasonable finder of fact to be a flagrant deception on the public regarding the actual content of this song and the creation of an impression that Rosa Parks, who had approved the use of her name in connection with the *Tribute* album, had also approved or sponsored the use of her name on Defendants' composition.

It is certainly not dispositive that, in response to an interview following the filing of this lawsuit, one of the OutKast members said that using Rosa Parks' name was "symbolic." Where an artist proclaims that a celebrity's name is used merely as a "symbol" for the lyrics of a song, and such use is highly questionable when the lyrics are examined, a legitimate question is presented as to whether the artist's claim is sincere or merely a guise to escape liability. Our task, it seems to us, is not to accept without question whatever purpose Defendants may now claim they had in using Rosa Parks' name. It is, instead, to make a determination as to whether, applying the law of *Rogers,* there is a genuine issue of material fact regarding the question of whether the title is artistically relevant to the content of the song. As noted above, crying "artist" does not confer *carte blanche* authority to appropriate a celebrity's name. Furthermore, crying "symbol" does not change that proposition and confer authority to use a celebrity's name when none, in fact, may exist.

It appears that the district court's rendition of summary judgment for OutKast was based on the court's conclusion that Defendants' use of Plaintiff's name as the song's title was "metaphorical and symbolic." *Id.* at 780. The obvious question, however, is *symbolic of what?* There is no doubt that Rosa Parks is a symbol. As the parties agree, she is "an international symbol of freedom, humanity, dignity and strength." J.A. at 79. There is not even a hint, however, of any of these qualities in the song to which Defendants attached her name. In lyrics that are laced with profanity and in a "hook" or chorus that is pure egomania, many reasonable people could find that this is a song that is clearly *antithetical* to the qualities identified with Rosa Parks. Furthermore, the use of Rosa Parks' name in a metaphorical sense is highly questionable. A metaphor is "a figure of speech in which a word or phrase denoting one kind of object or action is used in place of another to suggest a likeness or analogy between them." *Webster's Third New International Dictionary* 1420 (Phillip Babcock Gove, ed.1976). The use of the phrase "go to the back of the bus" may be metaphorical to the extent that it refers to OutKast's competitors being pushed aside by OutKast's return and being forced to "take a back seat." The song, however, is not titled *Back of the Bus.* It is titled *Rosa Parks,* and it is difficult to equate OutKast's feeling of superiority, metaphorically or in any other manner, to the qualities for which Rosa Parks is known around the world. We believe that reasonable people could find that the use of Rosa Parks' name as the title to this song was not justified as being metaphorical or symbolic of anything for which Rosa Parks is famous. To the contrary, reasonable people could find that the name was appropriated solely because of the vastly increased marketing power of a product bearing the name of a national heroine of the civil rights movement.

We do not mean to imply that Rosa Parks must always be displayed in a flattering manner, or that she should have the ability to prevent any other characterization of her. She is a celebrity and, as such, she cannot prevent being portrayed in a manner that may not be pleasing to her. As the court noted in *Guglielmi v. Spelling-Goldberg Productions*, 25 Cal.3d 860, 160 Cal.Rptr. 352, 603 P.2d 454, 460 (1979) (Bird J., concurring), "[t]he right of publicity derived from public prominence does not confer a shield to ward off caricature, parody and satire." It has been held, for example, that, "[p]arodies of celebrities are an especially valuable means of expression because of the role celebrities play in modern society." *Cardtoons*, 95 F.3d at 972. The present case, however, does not involve any claim of caricature, parody or satire. It involves, instead, the use of a celebrity's name as the title to a song when it reasonably could be found that the celebrity's name has no artistic relevance to the content of the song. It involves, in short, a reasonable dispute whether the use of Rosa Parks' name was a misrepresentation and false advertising or whether it was a legitimate use of a celebrity's name in some recognized form of artistic expression protected by the First Amendment.

*   *   *

There is a genuine issue of material fact whether the use of Rosa Parks' name as a title to the song and on the cover of the album is artistically related to the content of the song or whether the use of the name Rosa Parks is nothing more than a misleading advertisement for the sale of the song.

b. Misleading Prong

In *Rogers*, the court held that if the title of the work is artistically relevant to its content, there is no violation of the Lanham Act *unless* the "title explicitly misleads as to the source or the content of the work." 875 F.2d at 999. . . .

We considered all the facts presented to us and concluded that, with reference to the first prong of the *Rogers* analysis, the issue of artistic relevance of the title *Rosa Parks* to the lyrics of the song is highly questionable and cannot be resolved as a matter of law. However, if, on remand, a trier of fact, after a full evidentiary hearing, concludes that the title *is* used in some symbolic or metaphorical sense, application of the *Rogers* analysis, under the particular facts of this case, would appear to be complete. In the present case, the title *Rosa Parks* "make[s] no explicit statement that the work is about that person in any direct sense." In other words, Defendants did not name the song, for example, *The True Life Story of Rosa Parks* or *Rosa Parks' Favorite Rap*.

*   *   *

III. CONCLUSION

We are not called upon in this case to judge the quality of Defendants' song, and whether we personally regard it as repulsive trash or a work of genius is immaterial to a determination of the legal issues presented to us. Justice Holmes, 100 years ago, correctly observed that, "It would be a dangerous undertaking for persons trained only to the law to constitute themselves final judges of the worth of pictorial illustrations, outside of the narrowest and most obvious limits." *George Bleistein v. Donaldson Lithographing Co.*, 188 U.S. 239, 251, 23 S.Ct. 298, 47 L.Ed. 460 (1903). The same is no less true today and applies with equal force to musical compositions. The point, however, is that while we, as judges, do not presume to determine the artistic quality of the song in question, we have the responsibility, as judges, to apply a legal standard of "artistic relevance" in resolving the rights of Rosa Parks concerning the use of her name and the First Amendment rights of the Defendants in the creation and marketing of a musical composition. . . . Application of that standard involves a recognition that Rosa Parks has no right to control her image by censoring disagreeable portrayals. It also involves a recognition that the First Amendment cannot permit anyone who cries "artist" to have *carte blanche* when it comes to naming and advertising his works.

In this case, for the reasons set forth above, the fact that Defendants cry "artist" and "symbol" as reasons for appropriating Rosa Parks' name for a song title does not absolve them from potential liability for, in the words of Shakespeare, filching Rosa Parks' good name. . . . The question of that liability, however, should be determined by the trier of fact after a full evidentiary hearing and not as a matter of law on a motion for summary judgment.

For the reasons stated, as to Rosa Parks' Lanham Act claim and her common law right of publicity claim, the judgment of the District Court is REVERSED and this case is REMANDED for future proceedings not inconsistent with this Opinion. With respect to Rosa Parks' claims of defamation and tortious interference with a business relationship, the judgment of the District Court is AFFIRMED.

* * *

Notes on *Parks v. LaFace Records*

Note initially the court's trenchant critique of *Dallas Cowboys*, based on its rejection of that court's use of the "alternative avenues" test, analogized into trademark law from the real property (shopping mall) context. Clearly, the court intends to be considerably more respectful of First Amendment principles than *Dallas Cowboys*, bringing a more sophisticated analytic machinery to bear on the question before it. What does the decision hinge on in the end?

Defendants expressly claimed that their use of "Rosa Parks" was metaphorical and symbolic. The court does not appear to doubt that the song's message may well be "that OutKast's competitors are of lesser quality, and, therefore, must 'move to the back of the bus,' or, in other words, 'take a back seat.' " That, however, is not sufficient in the court's eyes. The song "is titled *Rosa Parks*, and it is difficult to equate OutKast's feeling of superiority, metaphorically or in any other manner, to the qualities for which Rosa Parks is known around the world." What is the rule applied by the court here? Is any kind of symbolism enough to activate the *Rogers* safe harbor, or does it have to be of some special quality? What default rule does the court apply? Should summary judgment be granted because a certain metaphoric use *might* underlie defendant's use, or should summary judgment be denied because a certain metaphoric use might not *in fact* have underlied defendant's use? How important, if at all, was the court's respect and admiration for the plaintiff in reaching its decision? Also, note that this decision contains extended discussions of First Amendment issues. How, if at all, would the outcome have differed under the approach advocated in Judge Leval's article, excerpted at the beginning of this chapter?

COCA-COLA CO. v. PURDY
382 F.3d 774 (8th Cir. 2004)

Murphy, Circuit Judge:

This case was brought under the Anticybersquatting Consumer Protection Act by the Washington Post Company and its wholly owned subsidiary Washingtonpost. Newsweek Interactive Company, LLC (the Post entities), the Coca-Cola Company, McDonald's Corporation, and PepsiCo, Inc. to stop William S. Purdy . . . from appropriating Internet domain names . . . that incorporate and are confusingly similar to their trademarks and servicemarks. The district court . . . granted preliminary injunctive relief enjoining defendants from registering or using certain domain names and ordering them transferred to their proper owners. Purdy was later found in contempt and fined for violating the injunctions. He appeals from the preliminary injunctions and the contempt orders.

* * *

In early July 2002 Purdy began registering Internet domain names which incorporated distinctive, famous, and protected marks owned by the plaintiffs. The domain names he registered included drinkcoke.org, mycoca-cola.com, mymcdonalds.com, mypepsi.org, and my-washingtonpost.com. The latter name was almost exactly identical to one which the Washington Post had used to operate an interactive online news service (mywashingtonpost.com), the only distinguishing detail being Purdy's addition of a hyphen.

Purdy typically linked the domain names to the website abortionismurder.com which contains antiabortion commentary and graphic images of aborted and dismembered fetuses. It also contains multiple "What Can I Do?" links to a website where a visitor can purchase hats, shirts, neckties, and license plates with antiabortion themes and make donations using a credit card or bank account number. The content available at abortionismurder.com contained no references to plaintiffs, their products, or their alleged positions on abortion.

For several days in early July 2002 Purdy linked the domain names my-washingtonpost.com and drinkcoke.org to a website displaying what appeared to be a front page originating from washingtonpost.com. The page with this format featured the headline "The Washington Post proclaims 'Abortion is Murder' " and contained graphic images of aborted fetuses next to Coca-Cola's trademark and the words "Things Don't Always Go Better With Coke. Abortion is Murder—*The Real Thing.*' " ("It's the Real Thing" is a registered trademark of the Coca-Cola Company.) Sometime after this litigation began, Purdy also linked many of the domain names to his own websites which contained references to a claim that plaintiffs supported abortion, graphic photos of aborted fetuses, and links to abortionismurder.com.

*   *   *

Purdy argues that the First Amendment entitles him to use the domain names at issue to attract Internet users to websites containing political expression and criticism of the plaintiffs. There is no dispute here about whether the First Amendment protects Purdy's right to use the Internet to protest abortion and criticize the plaintiffs or to use expressive domain names that are unlikely to cause confusion. *Cf. Taubman Co. v. Webfeats,* 319 F.3d 770, 778 (6th Cir.2003) (taubmansucks.com permissible because it removes any confusion as to source); *Name.Space. Inc. v. Network Solutions, Inc.,* 202 F.3d 573, 585-86 (2[d] Cir.2000) (domain names which themselves express a message might be protected). The question raised in this case is whether the First Amendment protects a misleading use of plaintiffs' marks in domain names to attract an unwitting and possibly unwilling audience to Purdy's message. Use of a famous mark in this way could be seen as the information superhighway equivalent of posting a large sign bearing a McDonald's logo before a freeway exit for the purpose of diverting unwitting travelers to the site of an antiabortion rally.

The use of trademarks has not been protected where it is likely to create confusion as to the source or sponsorship of the speech or goods in question. In *San Francisco Arts & Athletics, Inc. v. U.S. Olympic Comm.,* 483 U.S. 522, 541, 107 S.Ct. 2971, 97 L.Ed.2d 427 (1987), for example, the Supreme Court held that organizers of the Gay Olympic Games had no First Amendment right to use and appropriate the value of the Olympics mark in spite of their having an expressive purpose. *See also Anheuser-Busch, Inc. v. Balducci Publ'ns,* 28 F.3d 769, 776 (8th Cir.1994) ("A parody creating a likelihood of confusion may be subject to a trademark infringement action."); *Mutual of Omaha Ins. Co. v. Novak,* 836 F.2d 397, 402 (8th Cir.1987) (upholding injunction against sale of antiwar merchandise bearing words and symbols likely to cause confusion with plaintiff's marks). The First Amendment has also been held not to protect the use of a trademark in a domain name that creates a likelihood of confusion as to the source or sponsorship of the attached website. *See Planned Parenthood Fed'n of Am., Inc. v. Bucci,* 1997 WL 133313, at *10-11 (S.D.N.Y. March 24, 1997) (First Amendment does not prevent injunctive relief against use of plannedparenthood.com, a nonexpressive source identifier), *summarily aff'd,* 152 F.3d 920 (2[d] Cir.1998) (unpublished). Just because an opponent of the war in Iraq might assert an expressive purpose in creating a website with the name lockheedmartincorp.com, for example, the First Amendment would not grant him the right to use a domain name confusingly similar to Lockheed's mark. While Purdy has the right to express his message over the Internet, he has not shown that the First Amendment protects his appropriation of plaintiffs' marks in order to spread his protest message by confusing Internet users into thinking that they are entering one of the plaintiffs' websites. *See* 4 McCarthy § 25:76.

*   *   *

Purdy raises several arguments about the scope and language of the first preliminary injunction as amended on September 5, 2002 and the second preliminary injunction issued on October 1, 2002 (dealing with wpni.org). He argues that the orders amount to an unconstitutional prior restraint on his speech and that they are vague and overbroad. . . .

Purdy's prior restraint argument warrants little discussion. As discussed above, the First Amendment does not protect the deceptive use of domain names that are identical or confusingly similar to another's trademarks, and Purdy's conduct was shown to have likely violated the ACPA. There are many examples where courts have enjoined the use of names that are confusingly similar to protected trademarks. *See, e.g., Novak*, 775 F.2d at 249 (enjoining sale of "Mutants of Omaha" antiwar merchandise that was likely to be confused with Mutual of Omaha insurance). Injunctions of unlawful conduct that is not constitutionally protected are not unconstitutional prior restraints. *Cf. A & M Records, Inc. v. Napster, Inc.*, 239 F.3d 1004, 1028 (9 Cir.2001) (First Amendment does not prevent injunction against unlawful use of copyrighted material); *Dr. Seuss Enters., L.P. v. Penguin Books USA, Inc.*, 109 F.3d 1394, 1403 n. 11 (9 Cir.1997) (rejecting claim that injunction would constitute a prior restraint in violation of the First Amendment).

The district court enjoined Purdy's registration and use of domain names that both (1) incorporate and are identical or confusingly similar to plaintiffs' marks, and (2) do not alert the unwary Internet user to the protest or critical commentary nature of the attached website within the language of the domain name itself. A domain name would violate the district court orders only if were confusing *and* if it failed to put Internet users on notice of the protest or critical commentary nature of the attached website. Thus, Purdy could register and use domain names incorporating plaintiffs' marks, such as PurdySupportsPepsi.com or PurdysCokeSite.com, to publish complimentary or critical commentary because neither name is identical or confusingly similar to any of plaintiffs' marks. *See Taubman*, 319 F.3d at 778 (6 Cir.2003) (taubmansucks.com permissible because it removes any confusion as to source). Because the district court's orders restrict only Purdy's ability to attract visitors with domain names that infringe plaintiffs' rights in their marks, they do not impermissibly regulate the expressive content of his domain names or websites in a way that would violate the First Amendment.

*   *   *

Accordingly, we affirm the orders of the district court granting preliminary injunctive relief, dismiss the appeals of the contempt order and sanctions for lack of jurisdiction, and remand for further proceedings.

*   *   *

Notes on *Coca-Cola v. Purdy*

This case is another example (the first one being *United We Stand*, excerpted above) of a defendant who is unquestionably engaging in core protected speech, but is using the plaintiff's trademark to reach a wider audience. The court is emphatic that the defendant has every right to engage in such speech. However, the court holds, the defendant may not use plaintiffs' trademarks to attract unwitting consumers to his message by misleading them. As long as there is no likelihood of confusion, the court holds, the defendant may even incorporate plaintiffs' marks in domain names containing the defendant's message. Thus, this case centers entirely on likelihood of confusion. Defendant has every right to engage in his chosen speech as long as no likelihood of confusion is created, but his right ends as soon as such a likelihood arises. In short, the *Purdy* court applies the simple likelihood of confusion analysis that the court in *Rosa Parks* rejected. How would the defendants in that case have fared under the test applied in *Purdy*? Conversely, how would the defendant in *Purdy* have fared under a balancing test? Does taking the First Amendment expressly into account lead necessarily to a more speech-protective outcome?

LOUIS VUITTON MALLETIER S.A., v. HAUTE DIGGITY DOG, LLC
507 F.3d 252 (4th Cir. 2007)

NIEMEYER, CIRCUIT JUDGE:

Louis Vuitton Malletier S.A., a French corporation located in Paris, that manufactures luxury luggage, handbags, and accessories, commenced this action against Haute Diggity Dog, LLC, a Nevada corporation that manufactures and sells pet products nationally, alleging trademark infringement under 15 U.S.C. § 1114(1)(a), trademark dilution under 15 U.S.C. § 1125(c), copyright infringement under 17 U.S.C. § 501, and related statutory and common law violations. Haute Diggity Dog manufactures, among other things, plush toys on which dogs can chew, which, it claims, parody famous trademarks on luxury products, including those of Louis Vuitton Malletier. The particular Haute Diggity Dog chew toys in question here are small imitations of handbags that are labeled "Chewy Vuiton" and that mimic Louis Vuitton Malletier's LOUIS VUITTON handbags.

On cross-motions for summary judgment, the district court concluded that Haute Diggity Dog's "Chewy Vuiton" dog toys were successful parodies of Louis Vuitton Malletier's trademarks, designs, and products, and on that basis, entered judgment in favor of Haute Diggity Dog on all of Louis Vuitton Malletier's claims.

On appeal, we agree with the district court that Haute Diggity Dog's products are not likely to cause confusion with those of Louis Vuitton Malletier and that Louis Vuitton Malletier's copyright was not infringed. On the trademark dilution claim, however, we reject the district court's reasoning but reach the same conclusion through a different analysis. Accordingly, we affirm.

Louis Vuitton Malletier S.A. ("LVM") is a well known manufacturer of luxury luggage, leather goods, handbags, and accessories, which it markets and sells worldwide. In connection with the sale of its products, LVM has adopted trademarks and trade dress that are well recognized and have become famous and distinct. Indeed, in 2006, *BusinessWeek* ranked LOUIS VUITTON as the 17th "best brand" of all corporations in the world and the first "best brand" for any fashion business.

*   *   *

Haute Diggity Dog, LLC, which is a relatively small and relatively new business located in Nevada, manufactures and sells nationally-primarily through pet stores-a line of pet chew toys and beds whose names parody elegant high-end brands of products such as perfume, cars, shoes, sparkling wine, and handbags. These include-in addition to Chewy Vuiton (LOUIS VUITTON)-Chewnel No. 5 (Chanel No. 5), Furcedes (Mercedes), Jimmy Chew (Jimmy Choo), Dog Perignonn (Dom Perignon), Sniffany & Co. (Tiffany & Co.), and Dogior (Dior). The chew toys and pet beds are plush, made of polyester, and have a shape and design that loosely imitate the signature product of the targeted brand. They are mostly distributed and sold through pet stores, although one or two Macy's stores carries Haute Diggity Dog's products. The dog toys are generally sold for less than $20, although larger versions of some of Haute Diggity Dog's plush dog beds sell for more than $100.

Haute Diggity Dog's "Chewy Vuiton" dog toys, in particular, loosely resemble miniature handbags and undisputedly evoke LVM handbags of similar shape, design, and color. In lieu of the LOUIS VUITTON mark, the dog toy uses "Chewy Vuiton"; in lieu of the LV mark, it uses "CV"; and the other symbols and colors employed are imitations, but not exact ones, of those used in the LVM Multicolor and Cherry designs.

* * *

For trademark purposes, "[a] 'parody' is defined as a simple form of entertainment conveyed by juxtaposing the irreverent representation of the trademark with the idealized image created by the mark's owner."*People for the Ethical Treatment of Animals v. Doughney ("PETA")*, 263 F.3d 359, 366 (4th Cir.2001) (internal quotation marks omitted). "A parody must convey two simultaneous-and contradictory-messages: that it is the original, but also that it is *not* the original and is instead a parody." *Id.* (internal quotation marks and citation omitted). This second message must not only differentiate the alleged parody from the original but must also communicate some articulable element of satire, ridicule, joking, or amusement. Thus, "[a] parody relies upon a difference from the original mark, presumably a humorous difference, in order to produce its desired effect." *Jordache Enterprises, Inc. v. Hogg Wyld, Ltd.*, 828 F.2d 1482, 1486 (10th Cir.1987) (finding the use of "Lardashe" jeans for larger women to be a successful and permissible parody of "Jordache" jeans).

When applying the *PETA* criteria to the facts of this case, we agree with the district court that the "Chewy Vuiton" dog toys are successful parodies of LVM handbags and the LVM marks and trade dress used in connection with the marketing and sale of those handbags. First, the pet chew toy is obviously an irreverent, and indeed intentional, representation of an LVM handbag, albeit much smaller and coarser. The dog toy is shaped roughly like a handbag; its name "Chewy Vuiton" sounds like and rhymes with LOUIS VUITTON; its monogram CV mimics LVM's LV mark; the repetitious design clearly imitates the design on the LVM handbag; and the coloring is similar. In short, the dog toy is a small, plush imitation of an LVM handbag carried by women, which invokes the marks and design of the handbag, albeit irreverently and incompletely. No one can doubt that LVM handbags are the target of the imitation by Haute Diggity Dog's "Chewy Vuiton" dog toys.

At the same time, no one can doubt also that the "Chewy Vuiton" dog toy is not the "idealized image" of the mark created by LVM. The differences are immediate, beginning with the fact that the "Chewy Vuiton" product is a dog toy, not an expensive, luxury LOUIS VUITTON handbag. The toy is smaller, it is plush, and virtually all of its designs differ. Thus, "Chewy Vuiton" is not LOUIS VUITTON ("Chewy" is not "LOUIS" and "Vuiton" is not "VUITTON," with its two Ts); CV is not LV; the designs on the dog toy are simplified and crude, not detailed and distinguished. The toys are inexpensive; the handbags are expensive and marketed to be expensive. And, of course, as a dog toy, one must buy it with pet supplies and cannot buy it at an exclusive LVM store or boutique within a department store. In short, the Haute Diggity Dog "Chewy Vuiton" dog toy undoubtedly and deliberately conjures up the famous LVM marks and trade dress, but at the same time, it communicates that it is not the LVM product.

Finally, the juxtaposition of the similar and dissimilar-the irreverent representation and the idealized image of an LVM handbag-immediately conveys a joking and amusing parody. The furry little "Chewy Vuiton" imitation, as something to be *chewed by a dog*, pokes fun at the elegance and expensiveness of a LOUIS VUITTON handbag, which must *not* be chewed by a dog. The LVM handbag is provided for the most elegant and well-to-do celebrity, to proudly display to the public and the press, whereas the imitation "Chewy Vuiton" "handbag" is designed to mock the celebrity and be used by a dog. The dog toy irreverently presents haute couture as an object for casual canine destruction. The satire is unmistakable. The dog toy is a comment on the rich and famous, on the LOUIS VUITTON name and related marks, and on conspicuous consumption in general. This parody is enhanced by the fact that "Chewy Vuiton" dog toys are sold with similar parodies of other famous and expensive brands-"Chewnel No. 5" targeting

"Chanel No. 5"; "Dog Perignonn" target-ing "Dom Perignon"; and "Sniffany & Co." targeting "Tiffany & Co."

We conclude that the *PETA* criteria are amply satisfied in this case and that the "Chewy Vuiton" dog toys convey "just enough of the original design to allow the consumer to appreciate the point of parody," but stop well short of appropriating the entire marks that LVM claims. *PETA*, 263 F.3d at 366 (quoting *Jordache*, 828 F.2d at 1486).

Finding that Haute Diggity Dog's parody is successful, however, does not end the inquiry into whether Haute Diggity Dog's "Chewy Vuiton" products create a likelihood of confusion. *See* 6 J. Thomas McCarthy, *Trademarks and Unfair Competition* § 31:153, at 262 (4th ed. 2007) ("There are confusing parodies and non-confusing parodies. All they have in common is an attempt at humor through the use of someone else's trademark"). The finding of a successful parody only influences the way in which the [confusion factors set forth in *Pizzeria Uno Corp. v. Temple*, 747 F.2d 1522, 1527 (4th Cir.1984)] are applied. *See, e.g., Anheuser-Busch, Inc. v. L & L Wings, Inc.*, 962 F.2d 316, 321 (4th Cir.1992) (observing that parody alters the likelihood-of-confusion analysis). Indeed, it becomes apparent that an effective parody will actually diminish the likelihood of confusion, while an ineffective parody does not. We now turn to the *Pizzeria Uno* factors.

A

As to the first *Pizzeria Uno* factor, the parties agree that LVM's marks are strong and widely recognized. They do not agree, however, as to the consequences of this fact. LVM maintains that a strong, famous mark is entitled, as a matter of law, to broad protection. While it is true that finding a mark to be strong and famous usually favors the plaintiff in a trademark infringement case, the opposite may be true when a legitimate claim of parody is involved. As the district court observed, "In cases of parody, a strong mark's fame and popularity is precisely the mechanism by which likelihood of confusion is avoided."*Louis Vuitton Malletier*, 464 F.Supp.2d at 499 (citing *Hormel Foods Corp. v. Jim Henson Prods., Inc.*, 73 F.3d 497, 503-04 (2d Cir.1996); *Schieffelin & Co. v. Jack Co. of Boca, Inc.*, 850 F.Supp. 232, 248 (S.D.N.Y.1994))."An intent to parody is not an intent to confuse the public."*Jordache*, 828 F.2d at 1486.

We agree with the district court. It is a matter of common sense that the strength of a famous mark allows consumers immediately to perceive the target of the parody, while simultaneously allowing them to recognize the changes to the mark that make the parody funny or biting. *See Tommy Hilfiger Licensing, Inc. v. Nature Labs, LLC*, 221 F.Supp.2d 410, 416 (S.D.N.Y.2002) (noting that the strength of the "TOMMY HILFIGER" fashion mark did not favor the mark's owner in an infringement case against "TIMMY HOLEDIGGER" novelty pet perfume). In this case, precisely because LOUIS VUITTON is so strong a mark and so well recognized as a luxury handbag brand from LVM, consumers readily recognize that when they see a "Chewy Vuiton" pet toy, they see a parody. Thus, the strength of LVM's marks in this case does not help LVM establish a likelihood of confusion.

*   *   *

LVM also contends that Haute Diggity Dog's advertising, sale, and distribution of the "Chewy Vuiton" dog toys dilutes its LOUIS VUITTON, LV, and Monogram Canvas marks, which are famous and distinctive, in violation of the Trademark Dilution Revision Act of 2006 ("TDRA"), 15 U.S.C.A. § 1125(c) (West Supp.2007). It argues, "Before the district court's decision, Vuitton's famous marks were unblurred by any third party trademark use." "Allowing defendants to become the first to use similar marks will obviously blur and dilute the Vuitton Marks." It also contends that "Chewy Vuiton" dog toys are likely to tarnish LVM's marks because they "pose a choking hazard for some dogs."

* * *

The TDRA creates three defenses based on the defendant's (1) "fair use" (with exceptions); (2) "news reporting and news commentary"; and (3) "noncommercial use." *Id.* § 1125(c)(3).

We address first LVM's claim for dilution by blurring.

The first three elements of a trademark dilution claim are not at issue in this case. LVM owns famous marks that are distinctive; Haute Diggity Dog has commenced using "Chewy Vuiton," "CV," and designs and colors that are allegedly diluting LVM's marks; and the similarity between Haute Diggity Dog's marks and LVM's marks gives rise to an association between the marks, albeit a parody. The issue for resolution is whether the association between Haute Diggity Dog's marks and LVM's marks is likely to impair the distinctiveness of LVM's famous marks.

In deciding this issue, the district court correctly outlined the six factors to be considered in determining whether dilution by blurring has been shown. *See* 15 U.S.C.A. § 1125(c)(2)(B). But in evaluating the facts of the case, the court did not directly apply those factors it enumerated. It held simply:

[The famous mark's] strength is not likely to be blurred by a parody dog toy product. Instead of blurring Plaintiff's mark, the success of the parodic use depends upon the continued association with LOUIS VUITTON.

Louis Vuitton Malletier, 464 F.Supp.2d at 505. The amicus supporting LVM's position in this case contends that the district court, by not applying the statutory factors, misapplied the TDRA to conclude that simply because Haute Diggity Dog's product was a parody meant that "there can be no *association* with the famous mark as a matter of law." Moreover, the amicus points out correctly that to rule in favor of Haute Diggity Dog, the district court was required to find that the "association" did not impair the distinctiveness of LVM's famous mark.

LVM goes further in its own brief, however, and contends:

When a defendant uses an imitation of a famous mark in connection with related goods, a claim of parody cannot preclude liability for dilution. . . . The district court's opinion utterly ignores the substantial goodwill VUITTON has established in its famous marks through more than a century of *exclusive* use. Disregarding the clear Congressional mandate to protect such famous marks against dilution, the district court has granted [Haute Diggity Dog] permission to become the first company other than VUITTON to use imitations of the famous VUITTON Marks.

In short, LVM suggests that any use by a third person of an imitation of its famous marks dilutes the famous marks as a matter of law. This contention misconstrues the TDRA.

* * *

We begin by noting that parody is not automatically a complete *defense* to a claim of dilution by blurring where the defendant uses the parody as its own designation of source, i.e., *as a trademark.* Although the TDRA does provide that fair use is a complete defense and allows that a parody can be considered fair use, it does not extend the fair use defense to parodies used as a trademark. As the statute provides:

The following shall not be actionable as dilution by blurring or dilution by tarnishment under this subsection:

(A) Any fair use . . . *other than as a designation of source for the person's own goods or services,* including use in connection with . . . parodying. . . .

15 U.S.C.A. § 1125(c)(3)(A)(ii) (emphasis added). Under the statute's plain language, parodying a famous mark is protected by the fair use defense only if the parody is *not* "a designation of source for the person's own goods or services."

The TDRA, however, does not require a court to ignore the existence of a parody that is used as a trademark, and it does not preclude a court from considering parody as part of the circumstances to be considered for determining whether the plaintiff has made out a claim for dilution by blurring. Indeed, the statute permits a court to consider "all relevant factors," including the six factors supplied in § 1125(c)(2)(B).

Thus, it would appear that a defendant's use of a mark as a parody is relevant to the overall question of whether the defendant's use is likely to impair the famous mark's distinctiveness. Moreover, the fact that the defendant uses its marks as a parody is specifically relevant to several of the listed factors. For example, factor (v) (whether the defendant intended to create an association with the famous mark) and factor (vi) (whether there exists an actual association between the defendant's mark and the famous mark) directly invite inquiries into the defendant's intent in using the parody, the defendant's actual use of the parody, and the effect that its use has on the famous mark. While a parody intentionally creates an association with the famous mark in order to be a parody, it also intentionally communicates, if it is successful, that it is *not* the famous mark, but rather a satire of the famous mark. *See PETA,* 263 F.3d at 366. That the defendant is using its mark as a parody is therefore relevant in the consideration of these statutory factors.

Similarly, factors (i), (ii), and (iv)-the degree of similarity between the two marks, the degree of distinctiveness of the famous mark, and its recognizability-are directly implicated by consideration of the fact that the defendant's mark is a successful parody. Indeed, by making the famous mark an object of the parody, a successful parody might actually enhance the famous mark's distinctiveness by making it an icon. The brunt of the joke becomes yet more famous. *See Hormel Foods,* 73 F.3d at 506 (observing that a successful parody "tends to increase public identification" of the famous mark with its source); *see also Yankee Publ'g Inc. v. News Am. Publ'g Inc.,* 809 F.Supp. 267, 272-82 (S.D.N.Y.1992) (suggesting that a sufficiently obvious parody is unlikely to blur the targeted famous mark).

In sum, while a defendant's use of a parody as a mark does not support a "fair use" defense, it may be considered in determining whether the plaintiff-owner of a famous mark has proved its claim that the defendant's use of a parody mark is likely to impair the distinctiveness of the famous mark.

In the case before us, when considering factors (ii), (iii), and (iv), it is readily apparent, indeed conceded by Haute Diggity Dog, that LVM's marks are distinctive, famous, and strong. The LOUIS VUITTON mark is well known and is commonly identified as a brand of the great Parisian fashion house, Louis Vuitton Malletier. So too are its other marks and designs, which are invariably used with the LOUIS VUITTON mark. It may not be too strong to refer to these famous marks as icons of high fashion.

While the establishment of these facts satisfies essential elements of LVM's dilution claim, *see* 15 U.S.C.A. § 1125(c)(1), the facts impose on LVM an increased burden to demonstrate that the distinctiveness of its famous marks is likely to be impaired by a successful parody. Even as Haute Diggity Dog's parody mimics the famous mark, it communicates simultaneously that it is not the famous mark, but is only satirizing it. *See PETA,* 263 F.3d at 366. And because the famous mark is particularly strong and distinctive, it becomes more likely that a parody will not impair the distinctiveness of the mark. In short, as Haute Diggity Dog's "Chewy Vuiton" marks are a successful parody, we conclude that they will not blur the distinctiveness of the famous mark as a unique identifier of its source.

It is important to note, however, that this might not be true if the parody is so similar to the famous mark that it likely could be construed as actual use of the famous mark itself. Factor (i) directs an inquiry into the degree of similarity between the junior mark and the famous mark. If Haute Diggity Dog used the actual marks of LVM (as a parody or otherwise), it could dilute LVM's marks by blurring, regardless of whether Haute Diggity Dog's use was confusingly similar, whether it was in competition with LVM, or whether LVM sustained actual injury. *See* 15 U.S.C.A. § 1125(c)(1). Thus, "the use of

DUPONT shoes, BUICK aspirin, and KODAK pianos would be actionable" under the TDRA because the unauthorized use of the famous marks *themselves* on unrelated goods might diminish the capacity of these trademarks to distinctively identify a single source. *Moseley*, 537 U.S. at 431 (quoting H.R.Rep. No. 104-374, at 3 (1995), *as reprinted in* 1995 U.S.C.C.A.N. 1029, 1030). This is true even though a consumer would be unlikely to confuse the manufacturer of KODAK film with the hypothetical producer of KODAK pianos.

But in this case, Haute Diggity Dog mimicked the famous marks; it did not come so close to them as to destroy the success of its parody and, more importantly, to diminish the LVM marks' capacity to identify a single source. Haute Diggity Dog designed a pet chew toy to imitate and suggest, but not *use*, the marks of a high-fashion LOUIS VUITTON handbag. It used "Chewy Vuiton" to mimic "LOUIS VUITTON"; it used "CV" to mimic "LV"; and it adopted *imperfectly* the items of LVM's designs. We conclude that these uses by Haute Diggity Dog were not so similar as to be likely to impair the distinctiveness of LVM's famous marks.

In a similar vein, when considering factors (v) and (vi), it becomes apparent that Haute Diggity Dog intentionally associated its marks, but only partially and certainly imperfectly, so as to convey the simultaneous message that it was not in fact a source of LVM products. Rather, as a parody, it separated itself from the LVM marks in order to make fun of them.

In sum, when considering the relevant factors to determine whether blurring is likely to occur in this case, we readily come to the conclusion, as did the district court, that LVM has failed to make out a case of trademark dilution by blurring by failing to establish that the distinctiveness of its marks was likely to be impaired by Haute Diggity Dog's marketing and sale of its "Chewy Vuiton" products.

B

LVM's claim for dilution by tarnishment does not require an extended discussion. To establish its claim for dilution by tarnishment, LVM must show, in lieu of blurring, that Haute Diggity Dog's use of the "Chewy Vuiton" mark on dog toys harms the reputation of the LOUIS VUITTON mark and LVM's other marks. LVM argues that the possibility that a dog could choke on a "Chewy Vuiton" toy causes this harm. LVM has, however, provided no record support for its assertion. It relies only on speculation about whether a dog could choke on the chew toys and a logical concession that a $10 dog toy made in China was of "inferior quality" to the $1190 LOUIS VUITTON handbag. The speculation begins with LVM's assertion in its brief that "defendant Woofie's admitted that 'Chewy Vuiton' products pose a choking hazard for some dogs. Having prejudged the defendant's mark to be a parody, the district court made light of this admission in its opinion, and utterly failed to give it the weight it deserved," citing to a page in the district court's opinion where the court states:

At oral argument, plaintiff provided only a flimsy theory that a pet may some day choke on a Chewy Vuiton squeak toy and incite the wrath of a confused consumer against LOUIS VUITTON.

Louis Vuitton Malletier, 464 F.Supp.2d at 505. The court was referring to counsel's statement during oral argument that the owner of Woofie's stated that "she would not sell this product to certain types of dogs because there is a danger they would tear it open and choke on it." There is no record support, however, that any dog has choked on a pet chew toy, such as a "Chewy Vuiton" toy, or that there is any basis from which to conclude that a dog would likely choke on such a toy.

We agree with the district court that LVM failed to demonstrate a claim for dilution by tarnishment. *See Hormel Foods*, 73 F.3d at 507.

* * *

The judgment of the district court is

AFFIRMED.

Notes on *Louis Vuitton*

Note the definition of parody given by the court: "A parody must convey two simultaneous — and contradictory — messages: that it is the original, but also that it is *not* the original and is instead a parody." What is the function of this concept of parody in resolving the trademark infringement prong of the case? The dilution prong?

The court holds that defendant's use of plaintiff's mark is indeed a parody. While the court discusses the confusion factors, it does so in light of that determination. Ironically, the strength of plaintiff's mark becomes its Achilles heel under these circumstances. What analogies are there between the court's analysis of the strength-of-mark factor and the *Mattel* court's analysis of marks that transcend their source-signifying function?

Recall the statement in *Mattel* that dilution injunctions "lack the built-in First Amendment compass" of infringement injunctions since they are not based on a finding of likelihood of confusion. The perceived danger to First Amendment interests was the subject of considerable debate during the drafting of the TDRA. First Amendment concerns led to the inclusion of the following statutory safe harbor language in the TDRA, codified at 15 USC 1125(c)(3):

> (3) EXCLUSIONS- The following shall not be actionable as dilution by blurring or dilution by tarnishment under this subsection [i.e. the TDRA]:

> (A) Any fair use, including a nominative or descriptive fair use, or facilitation of such fair use, of a famous mark by another person other than as a designation of source for the person's own goods or services, including use in connection with—

> (i) advertising or promotion that permits consumers to compare goods or services; or

> (ii) identifying and parodying, criticizing, or commenting upon the famous mark owner or the goods or services of the famous mark owner.

> (B) All forms of news reporting and news commentary.

> (C) Any noncommercial use of a mark.

The *Louis Vuitton* court reads the plain statutory language as *not* automatically providing a complete defense to all dilution claims, and consequently performs a full analysis of the effect of the parody on the dilution claim. In other words, it did not, strictly speaking, find the parody safe harbor applicable to defendant's use of the mark. But if the parody exclusion in the TDRA does not in fact provide a safe harbor for conduct such as that at issue in the *Louis Vuitton* case, what does it add that would not have been present anyway by operation of the First Amendment? After all, constitutional rights do not depend on statutory provisions incorporating them into acts of Congress. Should Section 43(c)(3)(A)(ii) be read to provide that a defendant's use of a mark on a product as a designation of source cannot, as a matter of law, be a permissible fair use? What if any constitutional constraints might such a reading bring into play?

9.04 Notes on Trademarks and Free Speech

Trademarks and Artistic Speech

"At the heart of the First Amendment is the recognition of the fundamental importance of the free flow of ideas and opinions on matters of public interest and concern." *Hustler v. Falwell*, 485 U.S., at 50. Artistic speech, like political speech, is therefore broadly protected from content regulation, which is presumptively invalid with regard to any speech, artistic or otherwise. *See, e.g., R.A.V. v. City of St. Paul*, 505

U.S., at 382 and cases cited therein. Artistic speech cannot be restricted simply because either the Government of a private party is offended by that speech or disapproves of it. *Id. See also Hustler v. Falwell*, 485 U.S. at 53-54 (reciting with approval long history of often caustic cartoons in the United States "from the early cartoon portraying George Washington as an ass down to the present day" and holding that "the First Amendment prohibits [imposing liability for outrageous speech] in the area of public debate about public figures").

The First Amendment's protection of artistic speech extends to "other mediums of expression, including music, pictures, films, photographs, paintings, drawings, engravings, prints, and sculptures." *ETW Corp. v. Jireh Publishing, Inc.*, 332 F.3d 915, 924 (6th Cir. 2003) (citing numerous Supreme Court and other precedents).Thus, the Court of Appeals for the Ninth Circuit held that certain works of photographer Thomas Forsythe depicting Mattel, Inc.'s famous Barbie doll in "various absurd and often sexualized positions" contributed to the public debate about (as Mr. Forsythe put it) "the conventional beauty myth and the societal acceptance of women as objects," thus preventing their forming the basis of trademark infringement liability. *Mattel, Inc., v. Walking Mountain Productions*, 353 F.3d 792, 796 (9th Cir. 2003). Mattel had sued Mr. Forsythe's business entity for copyright, trademark, and trade dress infringement. The court rejected all claims and held, with respect to the trademark claim, that "the public interest in free and artistic expression greatly outweighs its interest in potential consumer confusion about Mattel's sponsorship of Forsythe's work." *Id.* at 807. Other important cases at the intersection of artistic speech and trademark rights include *Parks v. LaFace Records* and *Mattel. Inc., v. MCA Records, Inc.* (both excerpted above).

ETW Corp. v. Jireh Publishing, Inc., supra, turned in substantial part on the status of defendant's expression as noncommercial speech, entitling it to full First Amendment protection.

In that case, the licensing agent for the famous golfer Tiger Woods tried to stop the defendant publisher's marketing of limited edition art prints of a painting by the well-known sports artist Rick Rush which depicted Woods' 1997 victory at the Masters Tournament. The licensing agent asserted trademark rights in Woods' name and likeness, and alleged infringement and right of publicity (see Chapter 8) violations. The painting showed three views of Woods in various poses, with other famous golfers, such as Jack Nicklaus and Arnold Palmer, in the background looking down on him. Summary judgment was granted and affirmed against the licensing agent. "A piece of art that portrays a historic sporting event communicates and celebrates the value our culture attaches to such events. It would be ironic indeed if the presence of the image of the victorious athlete would deny the work First Amendment protection." The court also concluded that the prints "do not propose a commercial transaction [and thus] are entitled to the full protection of the First Amendment," and that the "purely descriptive" use of the "Tiger Woods" name on the inside flap of the envelope for each print and in the narrative description was permitted under the *Rogers v. Grimaldi* test for artistic relevance. (*See Mattel* and *Rosa Parks*, both excerpted above, for extended discussions of the *Rogers v. Grimaldi* test.) Accordingly, plaintiff's rights, including Mr. Woods's right of publicity, "must yield to the First Amendment."

Charles Atlas, Ltd., v. DC Comics, Inc., 112 F. Supp. 2d 330 (S.D.N.Y. 2000), offers a helpful analysis and summary of the law of parody and artistic speech vis-à-vis trademark law. To advertise its services, plaintiff, a company selling bodybuilding courses, had developed an ad campaign featuring a comic strip character and a predictable story line. *Id.* at 331. Defendant, creator and publisher of comic books, based a comic strip on plaintiff's character and story line. *Id.* at 332. The resemblance was clear, but defendant had also introduced substantial variations into the story line and changed plaintiff's message. The court granted summary judgment in defendant's favor on plaintiff's infringement and dilution claims. Defendant raised a twofold challenge to plaintiff's claims, asserting, first, that its use of plaintiff's ad did not constitute use in commerce as required by the Lanham Act, and, second, that its use constituted a parody entitled to First Amendment protection. *Id.* at 335. The court, in an instructive restructuring of defendant's position, stated that "both of DC's asserted defenses ultimately lead to the same analysis, the question of whether defendant used the mark for an expressive purpose, or to create an incorrect association in order to confuse the public." *Id.* The court found that "DC used plaintiff's comic ad not to advance a competing product, but rather as part of a comic book storyline, to convey an idea through a literary/artistic work. . . . As such, we find that defendant's use of plaintiff's ad to be a form of expression, protected by the First Amendment. Against this expressive usage of plaintiff's comic ad, we must balance the question of whether [defendant's comic] character is likely to cause confusion on the part of consumers." *Id.* at 338-39. After an analysis of the facts, the court found any likelihood of confusion to be "slim, and [to be] clearly outweighed by the public interest in parodic expression." *Id.* at 341. Defendant's motion for summary judgment was therefore granted. *Id.*

In *Hoffman v. Capital Cities/ABC, Inc.*, 255 F.3d 1180 (9th Cir. 2001), the Court of Appeals established the actual malice test with respect to right of publicity claims against noncommercial speech. Los Angeles Magazine (owned by defendants) had published a substantially altered photograph of actor Dustin Hoffman in the title role in the move *Tootsie*. *Id.* at 1183. Defendants asserted their conduct was protected by the First Amendment. *Id.* After a bench trial, the district court held the photograph was "an exploitative commercial use not entitled to First Amendment protection." *Id.* at 1184. The Court of Appeals reversed. *Id.* at 1189. The court affirmed the rule that "false or misleading commercial speech is not protected [and] may freely be regulated if it is misleading." *Id.* at 1184-85 (citing *Florida Bar v. Went For It, Inc.*, 515 U.S. 618 (1995). Thus, when speech is "properly classified as commercial, a public figure plaintiff does not have to show that the speaker acted with actual malice." *Hoffman*, 255 F.3d at 1185. The court found, however, that the photograph at issue in the case, and the article accompanying it, was not pure commercial speech. *Id.* "Viewed in context, the article as a whole is a combination of fashion photography, humor, and visual and verbal editorial comment on classics films and famous actors. Any commercial aspects are inextricably intertwined with expressive elements, and so they cannot be separated out from the fully protected whole." *Id.* (citations and quotation marks omitted). The speech in question was thus "entitled to the full First Amendment protection accorded noncommercial speech." *Id.* at 1186. Plaintiff having failed to prove actual malice, the Court of Appeals directed that judgment be entered in favor of defendants. *Id.* at 1189. *See generally*, Zimdahl, *A Celebrity Balancing Act: An Analysis of Trademark Protection under the Lanham Act and the First Amendment Artistic Expression Defense*, 99 NW. J. INT'L L. & BUS. 371 (2005); Gulasekaram, *Policing the Border between Trademarks and Free Speech: Protecting Unauthorized Trademark Use in Expressive Works*, 80 WASH. L. REV. 887 (2005); Timbers and Huston, *The "Artistic Relevance Test" Just Became Relevant: The Increasing Strength of the First Amendment as a Defense to Trademark Infringement and Dilution*, 93 TMR 1278 (2003).

Use of Trademarks to Criticize Commercial Practices

Generally, criticism of company's practices is constitutionally protected. "[T]he expression of opinions as well as facts is constitutionally protected so long as a factual basis underlies the opinion." *Texas Beef Group v. Winfrey*, 201 F.3d 680, 688 (5th Cir. 2000). Thus, absent falsehood misleading use of the company's trademarks, criticizing a company does not constitute tarnishment, libel, slander or other common law or statutory offense even though the criticism may damage the company's business and reputation. *See Texas Beef Group* at 684 (describing massive decline of cattle industry as a result of criticism of industry practices by talk show host Oprah Winfrey; criticism held not actionable).

These principles hold true in the trademark context. However, while criticizing companies is constitutionally protected, exploiting consumer confusion to further the criticism is generally not. *Coca-Cola v. Purdy*, excerpted above, discusses some of the pertinent principles. Other relevant cases include *Taubman Co. v. Webfeats*, 319 F.3d 770, 778 (6th Cir.2003), which held that defendant's domain name, taubmansucks.com, incorporating plaintiff's TAUBMAN mark was permissible because the sucks suffix removed any confusion as to source. *See also Name.Space. Inc. v. Network Solutions, Inc.*, 202 F.3d 573, 585-86 (2[d] Cir.2000) (domain names which themselves express a message might be protected). The principle here is the same as that expressed in *United We Stand* (excerpted above), namely, that a defendant is free to engage in constitutionally protected speech, but is not free to do so by using the plaintiff's trademark in a way that causes consumer confusion. In another case, *OBH, Inc., v. Spotlight Magazine, Inc.*, 86 F. Supp. 2d 176 (W.D.N.Y. 2000), defendants registered the name of the plaintiff newspaper as a domain name, linking it to a web site that contained information critical of plaintiffs. Defendants asserted their web site was a parody of plaintiffs and their web site. *Id.* at 191. The court rejected this position. "Only when a user reads through the web site does he or she discover defendants' actual message. Because defendants' web site relies, at least to some extent, on confusion to make its point, defendants' argument that their use of the mark is a parody must fail." *Id.* Defendants also stated a separate First Amendment defense, arguing that their use of plaintiffs' name for their critical web site is constitutionally protected speech. *Id.* at 197. The court rejected the defense, reasoning that while defendants were free to criticize plaintiffs, they were not free "to use plaintiffs' mark as their domain name in order to deceive Internet users into believing that they were accessing plaintiffs' web site." *Id.* The court therefore granted plaintiffs' motion for a preliminary injunction. *Id.* at 198.

A combination of parodic intent and criticism of plaintiff will not shield a defendant from an injunction if defendant exploited consumer confusion to further his goals. In *People for the Ethical Treatment of Animals v. Doughney*, 263 F.3d 359 (4th Cir. 2001), the Court of Appeals for the Fourth Circuit rejected defendant's claim of parody. Defendant had registered the domain name peta.org, linking it to a web site entitled "People Eating Tasty Animals," an obvious subversion of plaintiff's well-known acronym for its animal rights organization. *Id.* at 362-63. Plaintiff sued, alleging defendant's use of the peta.org domain name constituted trademark infringement, unfair competition, dilution, and cybersquatting. *Id.* at 363. Defendant asserted the domain name parodied plaintiff. The court disagreed, reasoning that while defendant's web site might qualify as a parody, the domain name by itself did not. *Id.* at 365. In order for the domain name to also be a parody, it would have to be displayed simultaneously with the web site. *Id.* But "an internet user would not realize that they were not on an official PETA website until after they had used PETA's mark to access the web page 'www.peta.org.'" *Id.* (citation and quotation marks omitted). Hence the assertion of parody was unavailing. *Id.*

A few cases appear not to fit entirely within this well-established paradigm. In *TMI, Inc., v. Maxwell*, 368 F.3d 433 (5th Cir. 2004), the Fifth Circuit acknowledged a broad right to use domain names for criticism web sites, including domain names that contain the plaintiff's mark but do *not* contain obvious disclaimers such as "sucks." The court held that defendant's registration of a domain name that consisted in its entirety of plaintiff's mark, TrendMaker Homes, neither diluted plaintiff's trademark not violated the ACPA. The website at that domain name contained solely criticism of the plaintiff and thus was entirely noncommercial. Two earlier decisions by other courts with identical fact patterns reached the same result—domain names that consist solely of the plaintiff's mark but linked to noncommercial websites containing defendant's criticism of the plaintiff's business practices did not violate the plaintiff's trademark rights. *See Lucas Nursery and Landscaping, Inc., v. Grosse*, 359 F.3d 806 (6th Cr. 2004); and *Bihari v. Gross*, 119 F. Supp. 2d 309 (S.D.N.Y. 2000). The *Bihari* court, however, did expressly invoke the First Amendment in support of its decision, finding that defendant's websites "concern the business practices and alleged fraud of a well-known interior designer. Such speech is arguably within the sphere of legitimate public concern, which imbues the speech with a heavy presumption of constitutional protection." *Bihari*, 119 F. Supp. 3d at 325-26. However, this was mere *dicta*, and the court's holding was based centrally on the determination that defendant's use of plaintiff's mark did neither dilute the mark nor created a likelihood of confusion. Are there factual differences between cases such as *Coca-Cola v. Purdy*, *United We Stand*, and *People for the Ethical Treatment of Animals* on the one hand, and *TMI*, *Lucas Nursery*, and *Bihari* on the other, that explain the different outcomes? Can these cases be harmonized under consistent principles of trademark and First Amendment law?

Trademarks and Classic Parody

Lyons Partnership v. Giannoulas, 179 F.3d 384 (5th Cir. 1999), provides an analysis of the relationship of parody and trademark law that is broadly representative of the courts' approach to this topic. Plaintiff owned the rights to the children's character "Barney"—the ubiquitous and cloyingly happy "six-foot tall purple 'tyrannosaurus rex.'" *Id.* at 385. Defendant played a sports mascot known as The Chicken and frequently appeared at baseball games. *Id.* at 386. As the court put it, "the Chicken's principal means of income could, perhaps loosely, be referred to as 'performance art.'" *Id.* Importantly for this case, "the Chicken is renowned for his hard hitting satire." *Id.* The dispute arose over the Chicken's act involving the Chicken's appearance together with a Barney look-alike, whom the Chicken would then "flip, slap, tackle, trample, and generally assault . . ." to the amusement of grown-ups and the dismay of some children. *Id.* The court held that the Chicken's act was clearly a parody, which the court defined as "an artistic work that imitates the characteristic style of an author or a work for comic effect or ridicule." *Id.* at 388, citing *Campbell v. Acuff-Rose Music*, 510 U.S. 569 (1994). In assessing the likelihood of confusion, the court stated that the strength of plaintiff's mark "may actually make it easier for the consumer to realize that the use is a parody." *Id.* at 389. The court then explained the proper method for analyzing parody claims in the context of trademark infringement allegations:

> Simply put, although the fact that conduct is a parody is not an affirmative defense to trademark infringement, a parody should be treated differently from other uses that infringe on a trademark. While it is only one factor to consider, it is a factor that must be considered in conjunction with all of the other digits of confusion. When, as here, a parody makes a specific, ubiquitous trademark the brunt of its joke, the use of the trademark for satirical purposes affects our analysis of the factors to consider when determining whether the use is likely to result in consumer confusion.

Id. at 390. Based on these principles, the court affirmed the district court's judgment in the Chicken's favor.

In reaching its holding, the *Lyons* court refused to follow a principle endorsed by several earlier courts, namely that "trademarks are property rights and as such, need not yield to the exercise of First Amendment rights under circumstances where alternative avenues of communication exist." *Id.*, citing *Dallas Cowboy Cheerleaders, Inc., v. Pussycat Cinema, Ltd.* (excerpted *supra*). As discussed above in the Notes accompanying *Dallas Cowboy Cheerleaders*, the "alternative avenues of communication" doctrine employed in that case is based on *Lloyd Corp. v. Tanner*, 407 U.S. 551 (1972), a case involving not intellectual property rights but a shopping mall. *Lyons* is by no means the only court to have criticized *Dallas Cowboys* along these lines. In *American Family Life Insurance Co. v. Hagan*, 266 F. Supp. 2d 682 (N.D. Ohio 2002), the court adopted the critique of the *Dallas Cowboys* doctrine set forth in *L.L.Bean, Inc., v. Drake Publishers, Inc.*, 811 F.2d 26, 28-29 (1st Cir. 1987). The *Hagan* court refused to "equat[e] the rights of a trademark owner with the rights of a property owner." *Hagan*, 266 F.

Supp. 2d at 697. This criticism was also set forth in *Cardtoons, L.C., v. Major League Baseball Players Ass'n*, 95 F.3d 959, 971 (10th Cir. 1996), which cited to *Dallas Cowboys* and stated, "[i]ntellectual property, unlike real estate, includes the words, images, and sounds that we use to communicate, and we cannot indulge in the facile assumption that one can forbid particular words without also running a substantial risk of suppressing ideas in the process" (citation and quotation marks omitted). An analogous criticism is contained in the *Rosa Parks*, excerpted above.

CardToons concerned a parody that directly targeted the plaintiff's marks. Defendant was in the business of selling "parody trading cards featuring caricatures of major league baseball players," *id.* at 962, and "ridiculing the players using a variety of themes," *id.* at 963. Plaintiff, as the "exclusive collective bargaining agent for all active major league baseball players," *id.*, filed suit seeking injunctive relief. The court quickly determined that "defendant's cards, plainly lampooning the players, do not create a likelihood of confusion. The court also initially found, however, that defendant's cards violated plaintiff's right of publicity under Oklahoma law. *Id.* at 968. Examining whether defendant had "a countervailing First Amendment right to publish the cards," *id.*, the court found that the cards were "an important form of entertainment and social commentary that deserve First Amendment protection." Defendant therefore was protected from liability for violating plaintiff's right of publicity, despite the provisions of the Oklahoma statute. *Id.* at 976.

Famous marks sometimes become part of the public vocabulary, which increases the permissibility of parodying them. *See* the discussion in the introduction to this Chapter, and the articles cited there. This principle has recently been endorsed in two opinions by the Court of Appeals for the Ninth Circuit. *See Mattel, Inc., v. MCA Records, Inc.* (excerpted above), and *Mattel, Inc., v. Walking Mountain Productions* (discussed above). But earlier courts also subscribed to this principle. In *L.L. Bean, Inc. v. Drake Publishers, Inc.*, 811 F.2d 26 (1st Cir. 1987), plaintiff, purveyor of upscale clothes featured in a well-known catalogue, sued defendant for including a sexually explicit parody of plaintiff's catalogue in defendant's publication *High Society*, a "monthly periodical featuring adult erotic entertainment." *L.L. Bean*, 811 F.2d at 27. The lower court enjoined defendant under the Maine dilution statute. The First Circuit reversed on First Amendment grounds. Foreshadowing the "iconic mark" doctrine brought to fruition in the 2002 and 2003 *Mattel* decisions by the Ninth Circuit, the court stated, "[f]amous trademarks offer a particularly powerful means of conjuring up the image of their owners, and thus become an important, perhaps at times indispensable, part of the public vocabulary" (quoting the Denicola article). The court held: "Denying parodists the opportunity to poke fun at symbols and names which have become woven into the fabric of our daily life would constitute a serious curtailment of a protected form of expression." *Id.* at 34.

An intent to parody plaintiff's mark does not, by itself, permit an inference that defendant's parodic use creates a likelihood of confusion. In *Jordache Enterprises, Inc., v. Hogg Wyld, Ltd.*, 828 F.2d 1482 (10th Cir. 1987), the defendant marketed a line of "blue jeans for larger women," *id.* at 1483, under the mark "Lardashe," an obvious pun on the slang word "lardass" for corpulent people on the one hand and plaintiff's famous JORDASHE brand of clothes on the other. *Id.* Plaintiff asserted that defendant *intended* to trade upon plaintiffs' mark, permitting an inference of likelihood of confusion. *Id.* at 1485. The Court of Appeals disagreed. "Our single concern here, however, is whether an intent to parody an existing trademark supports an inference of a likelihood of confusion under the reasoning that one who chooses a mark similar to an existing mark intends to confuse the public. . . . We hold that it does not. An intent to parody is not an intent to confuse the public." *Id.* at 1486. Ultimately, the court found there was no likelihood of confusion. *Id.* at 1488. The court's resolution of plaintiff's dilution claim under New Mexico law is also instructive. "Our review of the record convinces us that the public will not associate Lardashe jeans with the appellant or, if they do, they will only make the association because of the parody and not because they believe Jordache Enterprises, inc. manufactures Lardashe jeans. Therefore, there is no likelihood of an injury to appellant, and its dilution claim must fail." *Id.* at 1491.

Direct and obviously intentional parody of plaintiff's product and mark was at issue in *Hormel Foods Corp v. Jim Henson Productions*, 73 F.3d 497 (2[d] Cir. 1996). Jim Henson, creator of the famous "Muppets," was planning to release a movie containing a character named Spa'am. *Id.* at 500-501. Spa'am was a boar, and the name was chosen deliberately to evoke plaintiff's famous mark SPAM for pork luncheon meat. *Id.* Plaintiff's trademark infringement claim was not directed against the Spa'am character in the movie itself, but rather against use of the name and character on movie-related merchandise. *Id.* at 501. The court found that "[t]he elements of parody in Henson's Spa'am merchandise distinguish those products from ones manufactured by [plaintiff]," obviating consumer confusion. *Id.* at 505. The court therefore affirmed the lower court's judgment for defendant.

Parody that is merely a pretext for defendant's commercial exploitation of plaintiff's mark is not protected under the First Amendment and can be enjoined under the Lanham Act. In *Harley-Davidson, Inc. v. Grottanelli*, 164 F.3d 806 (2[d] Cir. 1999), the Second Circuit disallowed defendant's claim that its use of plaintiff's famous bar-and-shield logo in connection with motorcycle-related products was a "protectable parody." *Id.* at 812-13. The court explained the principle for distinguishing permissible from impermissible parody. "We have accorded considerable leeway to parodists whose expressive works aim their parodic commentary at a trademark or a trademarked product, . . . but have not hesitated to prevent a manufacturer from using an alleged parody of a competitor's mark to sell a competing product . . . ." *Id.* at 812 (citations omitted). In the context of defendant's use of a parodic version of plaintiff's mark in effect as a trademark for a competing service, "[permissible] parodic use is sharply limited." *Id.* at 813. Give the facts of the case, there was no protected parody. "Grottanelli's mark makes no comment on Harley's mark; it simply uses it somewhat humorously to promote his own products and services, which is not a permitted trademark parody use." *Id.* The court thus affirmed the district court's injunction against defendant. *Id.* at 814.

A defendant's parody that uses plaintiff's mark normally must take aim at plaintiff or plaintiff's mark, rather than merely use plaintiff's mark to make an unrelated point. In other words, if the use of plaintiff's mark is irrelevant to the point of the parody, the parody may enjoy no First Amendment privilege. This principle was applied in *Elvis Presley Enterprises, Inc., v. Capece*, 141 F.3d 188 (5th Cir. 1998). The Fifth Circuit held that defendant's "Velvet Elvis" bar did not constitute a protectable parody of Elvis Presley. Elvis Presley Enterprises appealed the district court's judgment that defendants' service mark, "The Velvet Elvis," for its nightclub, did not infringe or dilute its trademarks and did not violate its right of publicity in Elvis Presley's name. The Fifth Circuit reversed, on the ground that the district court had failed sufficiently to consider the impact of Capece's advertising practices, and that the district court had misapplied the doctrine of parody.

Generally, the court found, "a parody of a mark needs to mimic the original mark and from this necessity arises the justification for the mimicry, but this necessity wanes when the original mark is not the target of the parody." The court also observed that "while not a defense, parody is relevant to a determination of a likelihood of confusion and can even weigh heavily enough to overcome a majority of the digits of confusion weighing in favor of a likelihood of confusion." However, "[w]ithout the necessity to use Elvis's name, parody does not weigh against a likelihood of confusion in relation to [plaintiff's] marks. *It is simply irrelevant.*" *Id.* (emphasis added). Since defendants' "parody of the faddish bars of the sixties does not require the use of [plaintiff's] marks because it does not target Elvis Presley; therefore, the necessity to use the marks significantly decreases and does not justify the use." Therefore, the court proceeded to evaluate the likelihood of confusion without further reference to defendant's asserted parody, ultimately finding that plaintiff was entitled to injunctive relief.

A similar result obtained in *Dr. Seuss Enterprises, L.P., v. Penguin Books USA, Inc.*, 109 F.3d 1394 (9th Cir. 1997). Defendant had published a book recounting the O.J. Simpson murder trial in a style closely mimicking that of Dr. Seuss's famous children's book *The Cat in the Hat. Id.* at 1396. The court rejected defendant's claim that the work was a protectable parody. "Although [defendant's book] does broadly mimic Dr. Seuss' characteristic style, it does not hold *his style* up to ridicule. The stanzas have no critical bearing on the substance or style of *The Cat in the Hat*." *Id.* at 1401 (emphasis in original) (quotation marks omitted). The court affirmed the grant of a preliminary injunction against defendant, holding that "the claim of parody is no defense where the purpose of the similarity is to capitalize on a famous mark's popularity for the defendant's own commercial use." *Id.* at 1405-06 (citation and quotation marks omitted).

Where defendant's parody of plaintiff's mark is insufficiently transformative, *i.e.* so similar to the original mark that consumers may easily be confused because they cannot tell that they are looking at a parody, an injunction may issue. This is true even though defendant's parodic intent is genuine and defendant is not seeking to exploit plaintiff's mark to sell competing goods. In *Anheuser-Busch, Inc., v. Balducci Publications*, 28 F.3d 769 (8th Cir. 1994) the issue was defendant's plain parody of plaintiff's mark, without any admixture of comparative advertising as in *Deere*. Nevertheless, plaintiff prevailed. Plaintiff, one of the world's leading breweries, owned "the Michelob family of beers . . . ." *Id.* at 771. Defendant, publisher or a humor magazine, included a fake ad for the fictitious "Michelob Oily" beer on is back cover. *Id.* at 772. Defendant's intent was clearly to create a parody of plaintiff's ads, *id.*, and claimed an "absolute First Amendment right to use plaintiff's trademark in its parody.," *id.* at 775. But defendant had altered plaintiff's marks too little. "Balducci carefully designed the fictitious ad to appear as authentic as possible. . . . The disclaimer is virtually undetectable." *Id.* at 774. As a result, plaintiff was able to show notable amounts of consumer confusion. *Id.* at 772-73. On the basis of these facts, the court issued a carefully nuanced ruling reversing the lower court's judgment in defendant's favor. "We do not hold that Balducci's extensive borrowing of Anheuser-Busch's trademarks amounts to a *per se* trademark violation. Unlike copyright and patent owners, trademark owners have no right in gross. . . . By taking steps to insure that viewers adequately understood this was an unauthorized editorial, Balducci might have avoided or at least sharply limited any confusion, and thereby escaped from liability. Absent such measures, Balducci's ad was likely to confuse consumers and fall subject to federal trademark law." *Id.* at 777 (citations omitted).

In contrast to *Balducci*, the court in *Black Dog Tavern Co., Inc., v. Hall*, 823 F. Supp. 48 (D. Mass. 1993), found that defendant's parody of plaintiff's mark was sufficiently different from its target to make confusion unlikely. Defendant sold t-shirts emblazoned with one of two parodic versions of the well-known logo for plaintiff's restaurant and bakery. *Id.* at 51-52. Plaintiff's logo prominently feature a black dog. *Id.* Defendant replaced the dog with either a black hog or the skeleton of a dog. *Id.* The court found that defendant's parody conveyed "just enough of plaintiff's Black Dog marks to allow an ordinarily prudent consumer to appreciate the point of the parody, thereby diminishing the risk of confusion." *Id.* at 57. The court therefore entered summary judgment for defendant. *Id.* at 60.

A humorous reference in defendant's ad to plaintiff's mark may be permissible where defendant uses only limited elements of plaintiff's mark and it is perfectly clear that defendant's reference is a spoof, even though defendant's purpose is entirely commercial. In *Eveready Battery Co., Inc., v. Coors*, 765 F. Supp. 440 (N.D. Ill. 1991), excerpted in Chapter 8, plaintiff, creator of the popular "Energizer Bunny" commercials for its battery products sued defendant for running a beer commercial featuring well-known actor Leslie Nielsen, outfitted in "a conservative, dark business suit, fake white rabbit ears, fuzzy white tail and rabbit feet . . ., [carrying] a life-size bass drum imprinted with the COORS LIGHT logo," and engaging in conduct reminiscent of, but not identical to, the conduct displayed by plaintiff's Energizer Bunny in the familiar commercials. *Id.* at 443. The court found confusion unlikely, and defendant's ad to be a protected parody. *Id.* at 450. "[A]lthough the Coors parody contains similarities to the Eveready mark, it contains conspicuous and resounding differences as well. To the extent that the Coors commercial conveys the message 'that it is the original,' it emphatically conveys 'that it is not the original.' Thus, the court construes the Coors commercial as a permissible parody which does not violate the provisions of the Lanham Act." *Id.*

If any likelihood of confusion is dispelled by defendant's parodic reference to plaintiff's marks, trademark infringement liability will not attach. The First Amendment is then simply not needed to resolve the case. This is the central claim of Judge Pierre Leval's article, excerpted at the beginning of this chapter. *New York Stock Exchange, Inc., v. New York, New York Hotel, LLC*, 69 F. Supp. 2d 479 (S.D.N.Y. 1999), *rev'd on other grounds*, 293 F.3d 550 (2^d Cir. 2002), was decided along these lines. The case involved a parody-like use by defendant of plaintiff's well-known brand. *Id.* at 487. Plaintiff, the New York Stock Exchange, owned trademark rights in its name as well as in the famous façade of its building in Manhattan. *Id.* at 481. Defendant was the owner of a hotel and casino in Las Vegas. *Id.* The casino had a Manhattan theme, "with replicas of several famous buildings including the Empire State Building and the Chrysler Building." *Id.* The cashiers in the hotel were located in a "Financial District" kiosk, which bore a large replica of the façade of plaintiff's building, on which the words NEW YORK NEW YORK SLOT EXCHANGE appeared. *Id.* at 482. Based on these facts, plaintiff sued for trademark infringement and dilution. The court held, on the trademark infringement claim, that "[t]he obvious pun in the variation of the marks, together with the difference in the services offered by the Casino and NYSE, dispel the likelihood of confusion." *Id.* at 488.

On the other hand, where defendant's use of plaintiff's mark is predominantly an attention-getting device and the claim of parodic intent is implausible, plaintiff will probably prevail notwithstanding the genuine humorousness of defendant's use of plaintiff's mark. In *Kraft Foods Holdings, Inc., v. Helm*, 205 F. Supp. 2d 942 (N.D. Ill. 2002), the court rejected defendant's First Amendment defense. Plaintiff, owner of the famous VELVEETA brand for cheese products, had sued defendant for marketing his artwork—characterized by the court as being "of an admittedly adult nature, which is geared toward 'mature audiences,'" *id.* at 944 – under the name "King VelVeeda." Defendant asserted before the court that his use of plaintiff's mark was intended as a parody. *Id.* at 952. In a twist the court called "perhaps most fatal" to defendant's parody claim, defendant had previously "stated twice that he never parodied Kraft or Velveeta and that his use of the name 'VelVeeda' is not a parody of the Kraft cheese products." *Id.* at 953. Given this concession, the court rejected defendant's First Amendment arguments and granted a preliminary injunction in plaintiff's favor. *Id.* at 955.

There are important analytical similarities between trademark parody cases and copyright parody cases. In *Campbell v. Acuff-Rose Music, Inc.*, 510 U.S. 569 (1994), for example, the Supreme Court considered whether a rap parody of Roy Orbison's song, "Pretty Woman," was fair use. It remanded for determination of whether defendant's copying was excessive, and whether the parody would harm the market for potential rap versions of the original. *Compare Anheuser-Busch, Inc. v. L & L Wings, Inc.*, 962 F.2d 316 (4th Cir.), *cert. denied*, 506 U.S. 872 (1992) (Powell, L. dissenting), in which defendant sold t-shirts that closely imitated the famous Budweiser label design, but in place of the beer label references, substituted references to a South Carolina beach resort, e.g., "Contains the Choicest Surf, Sun, and Sand," "King of Beaches," and "This Beach is For You." In reversing the district court's directed verdict for plaintiff and reinstating the jury verdict for defendant, the majority stated, "The purpose of the Lanham Act is to eliminate consumer confusion, not to banish all attempts at poking fun or eliciting amusement." *Id.* at 322. In his dissent, retired Supreme Court Justice Powell, sitting by designation, emphasized that defendant had "borrowed a distinctive mark, without making any discernible changes, and placed that mark on identical products marketed through identical commercial channels" in direct competition with plaintiff, who also sold t-shirts bearing the Budweiser label design. He further observed that the alleged parody lacked any element of ridicule or social commentary. *Id.* at 326-27.

Much has been written on trademark law and parody. Articles include *Keller & Tushnet, Even More Parodic Than the Real Thing: Parody Lawsuits Revisited*, 94 TMR 979 (2004); Cantwell, *Confusion, Dilution and Speech: First Amendment Limitations on the Trademark Estate*, 87 TRADEMARK REP. 48 (1997); Partridge, *Trademark Parody and the First Amendment: Humor in the Eye of the Beholder*, 29 J. MARSHALL L. REV. 4 (1996); Welch, *The Impact of Spin-Offs, Put-Ons and Knock-Offs on Trademark Licensing*, 15 THE LICENSING J. 10 (1995); Smith, *Trademarks, Parody and Consumer Confusion: A Workable Lanham Act Infringement Standard*, 12 CARDOZO L. REV. 1525 (1991); Pattishall, *The Constitutional Foundations of American Trademark Law*, 78 TRADEMARK REP. 456, 469–475 (1988).

Trademarks, Parody, and Political Speech

Several cases have involved a defendant's parodic use of plaintiff's mark in the context of defendant's political speech. That speech is, of course, protected under the First Amendment. It depends on the facts of the case, however, whether defendant's parodic use in this context is also protected. If the use gives rise to a substantial likelihood of confusion, it is subject to Lanham Act liability regardless of the political context. In *MasterCard Int'l. Inc. v. Nader 2000 Primary Committee, Inc.*, 2004 WL 434404 (S.D.N.Y. March 8, 2004), the court resolved a case with strong First Amendment implications entirely via trademark doctrine. For several years, MasterCard had aired its well-known "Priceless Advertisements" containing the slogans "THERE ARE SOME THINGS MONEY CAN'T BUY. FOR EVERYTHING ELSE THERE'S MASTERCARD," and "PRICELESS." *Id.* at 1-2. MasterCard claimed service mark rights in these slogans. For his 2000 campaign ads, presidential candidate Ralph Nader appropriated these slogans in this form: "Finding out the truth: priceless. There are some things that money can't buy." *Id.* at 1. MasterCard sued for trademark infringement, federal and state dilution, misappropriation, and copyright infringement. The court found, after carefully examining all confusion factors, that there simply was no likelihood of consumer confusion between the Nader ads and the MasterCard ads. With respect to the dilution claims, the court found the Nader ads to be noncommercial and hence exempt from dilution claims, but went on to say that even had the ads been commercial, they were not dilutive of MasterCard's marks. *Id.* at 9. "[T]here is no evidence on the record that defendants' limited and political use of plaintiff's marks could weaken those marks' ability to serve as a unique identifier of plaintiff's goods or services." *Id.*

Additional cases involving the intersection of trademark law and overtly political speech include *United We Stand America, Inc., v. United We Stand America, New York, Inc.*, 128 F.3d 86 (2d Cir. 1997) (excerpted above); *Brach van Houten Holding, Inc., v. Save Brach's Coalition for Chicago*, 856 F. Supp 472 (N.D. Ill. 1994); and *Lucasfilm Ltd. v. High Frontier*, 622 F. Supp. 931 (D.D.C. 1985). The plaintiff in *Lucasfilm*, marketer of the famous STAR WARS movies, unsuccessfully sued two public interest groups that used the expression "Star Wars" in their political materials "to characterize the Reagan Administration's Strategic Defense Initiative (SDI) . . . ." *Lucasfilm*, 622 F. Supp. at 932. In *Brach*, the defendant was a coalition of public interest groups devoted to "prevent [plaintiff] from closing its candy factory on the West Side of Chicago." *Brach van Houten*, 856 F. Supp. at 473. The defendant was held liable for incorporating plaintiff's logo into its promotional materials.

The cases use rather different methodologies. *Lucasfilm* was decided on the ground that "[purveying points of view is not a service," and therefore "defendants have not affixed any trademark to any goods or services for sale." *Lucasfilm*, 622 F. Supp. at 934.

Therefore, trademark law did not apply at all to defendants' conduct. *Id*. *Brach* reached the opposite conclusion. "We believe that [defendant's political activities] constitute a 'service within the meaning of the Lanham Act." *Brach van Houten*, 856 F. Supp. at 475-76. Since, in the court's view, "the trademark law generally prevails over the First Amendment where the trademark functions to connote the source of the product or message, rather than being used in a communicative message," and since "[b]eing enjoined from using Brach's logo, but not the Brach's name, will not unduly hinder [defendant's] ability to communicate its ideas," defendant was enjoined from using plaintiff's logo. *Id*. at 476. In *United We Stand*, as we have seen, the court chose an approach different from both *Lucasfilm* and *Brach*, putting the likelihood of confusion analysis at the center of the inquiry, and rejecting defendant's First Amendment defense because defendant used plaintiff's slogan "to suggest the same source identification as plaintiffs."

A similar rationale supported the decision in *MGM-Pathe Comm's. Co. v. Pink Panther Patrol*, 774 F. Supp. 869 (S.D.N.Y. 1991), another case with political overtones. Defendant had merely adopted plaintiff's mark as its own to market its goods and services and could not claim First Amendment protection merely on the basis that the services it offered under the mark constituted political speech. Defendant had appropriated plaintiff's famous Pink Panther mark for its gay rights organization. The court, per Judge Leval, quickly disposed of defendant's claim that "because the Patrol is engaged in political speech, it is less subject to the trademark laws." *Id*. at 877. Judge Leval reasoned: "There is no legal support for this position. The seriousness and virtue of a cause do not confer any right to the use of the trademark of another." *Id*. Plaintiff's motion for a preliminary injunction was granted. *Id*.

In *American Family Life Insurance Co. v. Hagan*, 266 F. Supp. 2d 682 (N.D. Ohio 2002), the plaintiff advertised with the "well-known 'AFLAC Duck' commercials, in which a white duck quacks the company's name in a distinctive, nasal tone." *Id*. at 685. Defendant, campaigning for Governor of Ohio, ran commercials including a "crudely animated character made up of Governor Taft's head sitting on the body of a white cartoon duck; the duck quacks 'TaftQuack' several times during each commercial." *Id*. Plaintiff sued for trademark infringement and dilution. The court found for defendant on all claims, resolving the infringement claim solely on a finding that there was no likelihood of confusion, *id*. at 691, but resolving the dilution claim by reference to the First Amendment. The fact that defendant engaged in political speech was decisive for the court's ruling on dilution. "That the consuming public may associate the AFLAC Duck and the TaftQuack character—a proposition the Court accepts—is an insufficient predicate to support injunctive relief of political speech." *Id*. at 701.

A very different approach—one based on *Dallas Cowboys*—was used in *Mutual of Omaha Insurance Co. v. Novak*, 836 F.2d 397 (8th Cir. 1987). In that case, the court flatly refused to take the First Amendment into account when evaluating what defendant asserted was a parody of plaintiff's mark. Plaintiff is the owner of the mark MUTUAL OF OMAHA for insurance services. *Id*. at 398. Defendant "produced a design reminiscent of [plaintiff's] marks. It uses the words 'Mutant of Omaha' and depicts a side view of a feather-bonneted, emaciated human head. Novak initially put the design on T-shirts along with the words 'Nuclear Holocaust Insurance.'" *Id*. Plaintiff introduced survey evidence of consumer confusion. *Id*. at 400. The court responded as follows to defendant's assertion of First Amendment protection: "Mutual's trademarks are a form of property, . . . and Mutual's rights therein need not yield to the exercise of First Amendment rights under circumstances where adequate alternative avenues of communication exist. . . . Given the circumstances of this case, Mutual's property rights should not yield. . . . We . . . conclude that in the circumstances of this case failure to protect Mutual's trademark rights would amount to an unwarranted infringement of property rights, for it would diminish [those] rights without significantly enhancing the asserted right of free speech." *Id*. at 402 (citations and quotation marks omitted). This is, of course, the same "alternative avenues" approach used in *Dallas Cowboys*, and it is subject to the same criticism discussed above. Particularly after the Second Circuit's decision in *Cliffs Notes*, excerpted above, and given the further criticisms of that decision set forth above, the continued viability of this approach to applying the First Amendment in trademark cases is doubtful. That is not to say that a *Cliffs Notes* approach would not have led to the same end result. If substantial confusion is shown, an injunction ought to issue under the *Cliffs Notes* approach. *See* 886 F.2d at 495 (only "somewhat more" risk of consumer confusion is tolerated). The quantum of confusion shown in *Mutual of Omaha* may well have sufficed to overcome that slightly elevated threshold. But the *Mutual of Omaha* court's flat refusal to engage in any First Amendment analysis at all may no longer reflect the state of current trademark and First Amendment law.

Trademarks and Humor

A defendant's humorously imitative use of a plaintiff's mark may be permissible even though it does not specifically constitute a parody. As with parody proper, the courts apply a mixed analysis of likelihood of confusion and First Amendment considerations. Where there is no or little likelihood of confusion and defendant's use contains an expressive message, defendant's nonparodic yet humorous take on plaintiff's mark may not be actionable.

Yankee Publishing, Inc. v. News America Publishing, Inc., 809 F. Supp. 267 (S.D.N.Y. 1992) is the case decided by Judge Leval and discussed in his article that is excerpted at the beginning of this Chapter. The court found that defendant's humorous imitation of plaintiff's well-known *Old Farmer's Almanac* trade dress did not violate plaintiff's trademark rights. "While there is no doubt that [defendant] published on its cover a recognizable imitation or caricature of the Almanac's trade dress, I find this was done in a manner that made it sufficiently clear to consumers that it was a joke and not a trademark source identifier." *Id.* at 273. "I agree with [plaintiff] that the Christmas cover was not a parody, but believe this makes no difference." *Id* at 279. The court rejected the parties' focus on the narrow issue of parody, instead embedding the issue in a wider First Amendment context, stating that the issue "is not merely that *parody* is accorded First Amendment deference, but rather that the use of a trademark in the communication *of an expressive message* is accorded such deference." *Id.* at 279. Accordingly, the court emphasized that defendant would prevail on a First Amendment basis "even if there was some likelihood of confusion." *Id.* at 275.

In *World Wrestling Federation Entertainment, Inc., v. Big Dog Holdings, Inc.*, 280 F. Supp. 2d 413 (W.D.Pa. 2003), the court, applying a mixed trademark and First Amendment analysis, found that defendants' amusing alterations of plaintiff's well-known brands did not violate plaintiffs' trademark rights or right of publicity. Plaintiff produced professional wrestling shows, TV programs, and associated merchandise, and owned the intellectual property rights to the "popular wrestling characters appearing under unique names and portrayed with unique persona, history, relationship, music and visual appearance, and behavior." *Id.* at 417. Defendant marketed a wide variety of clothing goods that "depict certain graphics as parodies of popular culture" in connection with defendant's "Big Dog" character. *Id.* at 418. Defendant offered a wide range of merchandise depicting plaintiff's characters in a deliberately silly "dog-ified" fashion. *Id.* at 420-23. The court, noting defendant's assertion of a First Amendment-based parody defense, stated that parody "is not an affirmative defense, but only another factor to be considered in determining the likelihood of confusion. Whether a customer is confused is the ultimate question." *Id.* at 431 (footnote omitted). However, citing *Harley-Davidson, Inc., v. Grottanelli*, 164 F.3d 806, 813 n.4 (2nd Cir. 1999), the court noted that "where the unauthorized use of a trademark is part of an expressive work, such as a parody, the Lanham Act must be construed narrowly." *Id.* An evaluation of the applicable confusion test taking these principles into account showed "there is no likelihood of confusion." *Id.* at 440. With respect to plaintiff's right of publicity claim, the court used a substantially stronger First Amendment rule. "Big Dog's use of dogs to poke fun at celebrities and societal icons is an important form of entertainment and expressive commentary that deserves First Amendment protection." *Id.* at 445. Accordingly, the court entered judgment in favor of defendant on the right of publicity claim.

Humor matters. A case similar to *Big Dog*, but perhaps fitting the "joke" category even more clearly, is *Tommy Hilfiger Licensing, Inc., v. Nature Labs, LLC*, 221 F. Supp. 2d 410 (S.D.N.Y. 2002). In that case, the silliness and humorousness of defendant's offerings clearly influenced the court in defendant's favor. Defendant "manufactures, markets and sells a line of pet perfumes whose names parody elegant brands for human consumption." *Id.* at 412. Defendant's pet brand spoofing famous designer Tommy Hilfiger was called "Timmy Holedigger" and sold with the by-line, "If You Like Tommy Hilfiger Your Pet Will Love Timmy Holedigger." *Id.* at 412-13. Many of defendant's products were sold with a display stating, "Strong enough for a man, but made for a chihuahua." *Id.* at 413. The court stated that "when a parodist makes trademark use of another's mark, it should be entitled to less indulgence, even if this results in some residual effect on the free speech rights of commercial actors." *Id.* at 416. Thus, the *Tommy Hilfiger* court used a rule that in the abstract appears slightly more favorable to trademark owners than the rule applied in *Big Dog*. But practically the result was the same as in *Big Dog*. "[D]efendant's use of the mark is an obvious parody or pun, readily so perceived, and unlikely to cause confusion among consumers." *Id.* at 420. Plaintiffs' dilution claim fared no better. Citing "the utter lack of evidence that the selling power of Hilfiger's mark has been diminished," *id.* at 422, and finding "[t]here is nothing to suggest that a designer label has anything to lose from mere association with pets, particularly where the entire association is a light-hearted if somewhat heavy-handed parody," *id.* at 423, the court rejected plaintiff's claim of dilution by blurring and tarnishment. The Fourth Circuit encountered a similar fact pattern, and applied a similar analysis, in *Louis Vuitton v. Haute Diggity Dog*, excerpted above.

Just like parody, humorous use of plaintiff's mark is vulnerable to the objection that it does not differentiate defendant's product strongly enough from plaintiff's product, thus creating unacceptable levels of consumer confusion. In *Schieffelin & Co. v. Jack Co. of Boca, Inc.*, 850 F. Supp. 232 (S.D.N.Y. 1994), plaintiff prevailed on similar grounds as in *Balducci*—defendants' parody was too close to the original product to successfully dispel a likelihood of confusion. Plaintiff, distributor of the famous Dom Perignon champagne, sued defendant, purveyor of "Dom Popignon" popcorn sold in a container shaped like a champagne bottle. *Id.* at 236-38. The court agreed with defendants that their product "is plainly a humorous takeoff on DOM PERIGNON." *Id.* at 248. The court then observed: "The fact that defendants' product is a joke, however, does not end the court's inquiry." *Id.* After carefully examining the parties' respective products, the court concluded: "The short of the matter is that defendants' parody is not sufficiently effective to eliminate a likelihood of confusion on the part of consumers." *Id.* at 250. Accordingly, defendant was enjoined from selling the offending product. *Id.* at 253. The same result obtained in *Hard Rock Café Licensing Corp. v. Pacific Graphics, Inc.*, 776 F. Supp. 1454 (W.D. Wash. 1991). The court rejected defendant's claim of parody because defendant's "wholesale copying of [plaintiff's] logo cannot be explained or excused by parody. . . . [T]he graphics are indistinguishable." *Id.* at 1462. Consequently, defendant was enjoined.

CHAPTER 10
JURISDICTION AND REMEDIES

CONTENTS

10.01 Jurisdiction

Introduction

Trademark and unfair competition cases usually can be brought in either the federal or state courts. *Duncan v. Stuetzle*, 76 F.3d 1480, 1485 (9th Cir. 1996); *Duggan Funeral Service, Inc. v. Duggan's Serra Mortuary, Inc.*, 80 Cal. App. 4th 151 (2000) (federal and state court jurisdiction is concurrent; state court had jurisdiction to cancel federal trademark registration in infringement case). Most are brought in the federal courts, and those involving the federal trademark statute or diversity plus jurisdictional amount are removable to the federal courts. *Domain Name Clearing Co. v. F.C.F., Inc.* 16 Fed. App'x. 108 (4th Cir. 2001) (affirming that the value of the domain name at issue exceeded the $75,000 threshold for diversity jurisdiction); *Duncan v. Stuetzle*, 76 F.3d at 1485–1486; *Vitarroz Corp. v. Borden, Inc.*, 644 F.2d 960, 964 (2[d] Cir. 1981). *See also Amazon, Inc. v. Dirt Camp, Inc.*, 273 F.3d 1271 (10th Cir. 2001) (remanding for determination of whether diversity jurisdiction existed over plaintiff's remaining state law claims). *Compare In re Hot-Hed, Inc.*, 81 U.S.P.Q. 2d 1684 (5th Cir. 2007) granting, in part, a writ of mandamus to remand to state court a trademark and unfair competition case that had been removed to federal court. "As multiple courts have clarified, removal of a trademark infringement action is improper 'when a plaintiff does not clearly state he is seeking relief under the Lanham Act.'" (citations omitted). The federal courts also have supplemental jurisdiction over state law claims "joined with a substantial and related claim" under the Lanham Act. *Mars, Inc. v. Kabushiki-Kaisha Nippon Conlux*, 24 F.3d 1368, 1372 (Fed. Cir. 1994). *Cf. Oliveira v. Frito-Lay, Inc.*, 251 F.3d 56, 64 (2[d] Cir. 2001)(no supplemental jurisdiction after dismissal of federal claims, but defendant allowed to replead state law claims in state court). Set forth below are controlling statutory provisions affording federal jurisdiction in trademark and unfair competition cases:

15 U.S.C. § 1121 The Lanham Act

(a) The district and territorial courts of the United States shall have original jurisdiction, and the courts of appeal of the United States (other than the United States Court of Appeals for the Federal Circuit) and the United States Court of Appeals for the District of Columbia shall have appellate jurisdiction, of all actions arising under this Act, without regard to the amount in controversy or to diversity or lack of diversity of the citizenship of the parties.

28 U.S.C. § 1338 Patents, Plant Variety Protection, Copyrights, Mask Works, Designs, Trade-marks And Unfair Competition

(a) The district courts shall have original jurisdiction of any civil action arising under any Act of Congress relating to patents, plant variety protection, copyrights and trade-marks. Such jurisdiction shall be exclusive of the courts of the states in patent, plant variety protection and copyright cases.

(b) The district courts shall have original jurisdiction of any civil action asserting a claim of unfair competition when joined with a substantial and related claim under the copyright, patent, plant variety protection or trade-mark laws.

If diversity of citizenship exists between the parties and the matter in controversy exceeds $75,000 in value, federal jurisdiction also may be had under 28 U.S.C. § 1332.

Federal jurisdiction over litigation involving the infringement of a federal trademark registration, unfair competition, dilution, and deceptive trade practices is often based upon all of these statutes. When foreign commerce is involved, 28 U.S.C. § 1331 may also provide a basis for federal jurisdiction.

COCA-COLA CO. v. STEWART
621 F.2d 287 (8th Cir. 1980)

BRIGHT, CIRCUIT JUDGE

* * *

Coca-Cola Co. brought suit against the Stewart defendants on September 13, 1972, after its investigators had ordered Coca-Cola or Coke on thirty- five occasions at the Stewarts' restaurants in Riverside, Missouri, and on each occasion had received another product. Coca-Cola Co. filed suit against the Morans on March 12, 1973, after its investigation showed that on twenty- six of twenty-seven occasions when investigators ordered Coca-Cola or Coke at the Morans' Mexican restaurants in Kansas City, another cola product was substituted. On November 22, 1972, and May 4, 1973, final judgments of injunction were entered by consent in these cases.

In order to ascertain whether the appellees were honoring the terms of the injunctions, that is, whether they had ceased passing off substitute products as Coke, the appellant conducted further investigations between 1973 and 1975. These investigations revealed that, in the case of the Stewarts, a product other than Coca-Cola was substituted in response to thirty-one out of thirty-seven orders for Coca-Cola or Coke. In the case of the Morans, another product was substituted in twenty-five out of twenty-seven instances.

On October 14, 1975, appellant filed accusations of civil contempt against appellees. Because appellant sought punitive sanctions, the district court denied its motions and directed that it follow the procedures set forth in Fed. R. Crim. P. 42(b). Appellant then applied for an order directing appellees to show cause why contempt proceedings should not be commenced, filing affidavits in support of its application. The district court, in a memorandum and order to show cause filed January 6, 1976, found "that there exists reasonable cause to believe that [its] injunctive orders . . . have been violated."

Shortly thereafter, the district court on its own motion directed the parties to brief the issue of the court's subject-matter jurisdiction. On May 9, 1979, the district court issued a memorandum and order dismissing appellant's suits. The court held first that the alleged infringement had not occurred "in commerce," as required by the Lanham Act. See 15 U.S.C. § 1114(1)(a) (1976). The court found that there was no evidence that the alleged substitution of some product for Coca-Cola by "purely local" restaurants occurred in commerce, or that it could have any effect on appellant's national operation. The court also held that the amount in controversy was less than the $10,000 required for federal diversity jurisdiction. Citing *Seven-Up Co. v. Blue Note, Inc.*, 260 F.2d 584 (7th Cir. 1958), *cert. denied*, 359 U.S. 966 (1959), the court found that Coca-Cola had failed to establish a nexus between the apparent value of its goodwill and any injury to that goodwill resulting from appellees' acts of substitution.

II.   Jurisdiction Under the Lanham Trade-Mark Act

The Lanham Act is a comprehensive statute designed to safeguard both the public and the trademark owner. Among other things, the statute prohibits "passing off" by a tradesman — *i.e.*, selling another's goods as those of the trademark owner, by use of the owner's mark. *Franchised Stores of New York, Inc. v. Winter*, 394 F.2d 664, 668 (2ᵈ Cir. 1968).

The major issue in this case is the effective reach of this prohibition. Under the terms of the statute, the prohibited act must occur "in commerce." 15 U.S.C. § 1114(1)(a) (1976). 15 U.S.C. § 1127 (1976) explains:

> The word "commerce" means all commerce which may lawfully be regulated by Congress.
>
> . . . .
>
> The intent of this chapter is to regulate commerce within the control of Congress by making actionable the deceptive and misleading use of marks in such commerce[.]

The legislative history of the Lanham Act underlines this intention: "[S]ound public policy requires that trade-marks should receive nationally the greatest protection that can be given them." S. Rep. No. 1333, 79th Cong., 2d Sess., *reprinted in* [1946] U.S. Code Cong. Serv., 1274, 1277.

By consistent interpretation, jurisdiction under the Lanham act encompasses intrastate activity that substantially affects interstate commerce. *See, e.g., Iowa Farmers Union v. Farmers' Educational & Coop. Union*, 247 F.2d 809, 816 (8ᵗʰ Cir. 1957); *Drop Dead Co. v. S. C. Johnson & Son, Inc.*, 326 F.2d 87, 94 (9ᵗʰ Cir. 1963), *cert. denied*, 377 U.S. 907 (1964); *Franchised Stores of New York, Inc. v. Winter, supra*, 394 F.2d at 669. Thus, "in commerce" refers to the impact that infringement has on interstate use of a trademark; it does not mean that an infringer is immune from prosecution under the statute so long as he keeps his infringement entirely within the confines of a state. *World Carpets, Inc. v. Dick Littrell's New World Carpets*, 438 F.2d 482, 488 (5ᵗʰ Cir. 1971). "A substantial effect on interstate commerce is present when the trademark owner's reputation and good will, built up by use of the mark in interstate commerce, are adversely affected by an intrastate infringement." *Franchised Stores of New York, Inc. v. Winter, supra*, 394 F.2d at 669 (citations omitted).

This broad focus comports fully with the modern scope of the commerce clause. The Supreme Court has many times upheld the application of national legislation to purely local activities. For example, in *Wickard v. Filburn*, 317 U.S. 111 (1942), a small farmer challenged federal limitations on the amount of wheat that he could grow for consumption on his farm. The Supreme Court observed:

> That appellee's own contribution to the demand for wheat may be trivial by itself is not enough to remove him from the scope of federal regulation where, as here, his contribution, taken together with that of many others similarly situated, is far from trivial. [*Id.* at 127–128 (citations omitted).]

Generally speaking, if a class of activities is within the reach of federal regulation, the courts have no power to excise individual instances as trivial. *See, e.g., Perez v. United States*, 402 U.S. 146, 154 (1971). In this case, however, the district court found that Coca-Cola Co. had failed to show that appellees' passing off "could have had *any* direct and material effect on [its] national operation; not to mention 'a substantially adverse effect.'. . .". Yet, the affidavits submitted to the district court indicated that over one million gallons of fountain syrup a year were sold by Coca-Cola Co. in metropolitan Kansas City between 1969 and 1972. Coke was widely advertised in the area, and appellant sought to maintain its reputation for high quality products. On a national level, appellant spent over $45,000,000 a year in advertising and marketing of its product. The annual budget of the Trade Research Department in these same years exceeded $350,000.

We believe that these allegations, which are not disputed, support an inference that appellees' acts of passing off substantially affected appellant's interstate operations. The appropriate vantage point is that of the trademark holder. So viewed, appellees' actions jeopardized appellant's carefully nurtured reputation and undermined its claim to a distinctive (*i. e.,* nongeneric) trademark. That appellees' acts of infringement, standing alone, may not have cost Coca-Cola Co. a great deal in terms of lost sales does not detract from the fact that they served to misappropriate appellant's valuable goodwill, which rests on the distinctiveness of its federally protected trademark. The acts of these local retailers must be deemed, in the circumstances of this case, to have had substantial effect on interstate commerce. *See Maier Brewing Co. v. Fleischmann Distilling Corp.,* 390 F.2d 117, 120 (9th Cir.), *cert. denied,* 391 U.S. 966 (1968).

Appellees rely chiefly on *Application of Bookbinder's Restaurant,* 240 F.2d 365, 44 C.C.P.A. 731 (1957), and *Peter Pan Restaurants v. Peter Pan Diner,* 150 F. Supp. 534 (D.R.I. 1957), in support of the district court's holding. Both cases determined that activities of purely local restaurants lie outside the Lanham Act. The *Bookbinder's* decision, however, reflects the Patent Office's once- narrow view of federal trademark registrability, a view never adopted by the federal courts with respect to infringement actions and one since rejected by the Patent Office itself. *See* 1 GILSON, TRADEMARK PROTECTION AND PRACTICE §§ 8.03[3] and 3.02[5] (1976). The *Peter Pan* case can be distinguished on its facts; moreover, it and the cases it cites reflect a minority position that has been widely criticized. *See, e.g.,* 1 Gilson, *supra,* at § 8.03[3].

In our view, this case is governed by the holdings in *Franchised Stores of New York, Inc. v. Winter, supra; Maier Brewing Co. v. Fleischmann Distilling Corp., supra;* and *Pure Foods v. Minute Maid Corp.,* 214 F.2d 792 (5th Cir.), *cert. denied,* 348 U.S. 888 (1954). In all three cases the courts found that the potentially adverse effects of infringement on the plaintiff's reputation and goodwill satisfied the "substantial effect" test. Coca-Cola similarly satisfied the jurisdictional test in the present case. Apart from the clear authority supporting this conclusion, we believe that a contrary holding would seriously undermine the congressional intent behind the Lanham Act — namely, to protect the holders of federally registered trademarks. It would imply that local infringers could pirate a national mark with virtual impunity from federal restrictions, inflicting "death by a thousand cuts" upon the trademark holder.

Accordingly, we reverse the judgment of the district court. The cases will be remanded to that court for further proceedings consistent with this opinion.

JOHN WALKER AND SONS, LTD. v. DeMERT & DOUGHERTY, INC.
821 F.2d 399 (7th Cir. 1987)

COFFEY, CIRCUIT JUDGE

*   *   *

John Walker and Sons, Ltd. ("Walker") produces whiskey in Scotland and markets its product on a worldwide basis, selling it to consumers in various nations including the United States, Panama, and Columbia. Walker is incorporated under the laws of the United Kingdom and has its principal place of business in London, England. In its complaint, Walker alleges that it has consistently used distinctive "Black Label" and "Striding Figure" trademarks in conjunction with the advertising of its whiskey. Walker registered both the "Black Label" and "Striding Figure" trademarks with the United States Patent and Trademark Office. In its complaint, Walker further alleges that "as a result of [its] extensive sales, advertising and promotion, [its] trademarks have acquired a secondary meaning, distinctiveness and commercial magnetism . . . and enjoy a substantial prestige and saleability and are considered to be a high quality."

Defendant-appellee DeMert & Dougherty, Inc. ("DeMert"), is a filler of aerosol cans incorporated under the laws of Illinois with its principal place of business in Oakbrook, Illinois. As part of its services, DeMert acts as an intermediary for its customers in locating can manufacturers who agree to use its customers' artwork on their cans. Defendants-appellees Collection 2000, Blasser Brothers, Inc., S.A., Joseph Blasser, and

Eduardo Blasser jointly market cosmetics and other personal care products. Collection 2000 International, Inc. (Collection 2000) is a Florida corporation with its principal place of business located in Opalocka, Florida, and Blasser Brothers, Inc., S.A. is a Panamanian corporation that maintains a mailing address in Opalocka, Florida. Defendant-appellee Joseph Blasser is a resident of Miami, Florida and an officer of Collection 2000. Eduardo Blasser is also a resident of Miami, Florida, and is the president of Blasser Brothers, Inc., S.A. (Blasser Brothers).

In November, 1982, Collection 2000 executed a contract with DeMert to produce approximately 50,000 spray deodorant cans featuring alleged simulations of Walker's "Black Label" and "Striding Figure" trademarks. Collection 2000 provided DeMert with the initial artwork for the cans, and DeMert filled the deodorant cans and shipped them to a warehouse in Miami, Florida. DeMert was paid approximately $23,900 for filling the cans and placing Collection 2000's artwork on them. The cans of deodorant were subsequently sold in Panama and Columbia through Transcontinental Overseas, Inc., not a party to the suit.

Walker filed suit in the United States District Court for the Northern District of Illinois alleging that the placement of artwork on the deodorant cans and their shipment and subsequent sale constituted a trademark infringement in violation of the Lanham Act, 15 U.S.C. §§ 1051–1127. Walker named DeMert, Collection 2000, Blasser Brothers, and Joseph and Eduardo Blasser as defendants in the action. The trial court granted DeMert's motion for summary judgment on Walker's complaint that DeMert had violated the Lanham Act and also granted the remaining defendants' motion to dismiss without explaining the basis of its decision, holding that an Illinois court cannot exercise personal jurisdiction over Collection 2000, Joseph and Eduardo Blasser and Blasser Brothers. The court also without explanation held that venue was not proper in the Northern District of Illinois. Walker appeals.

* * *

[The court first holds that the lower court has personal jurisdiction and venue there is proper.]

Walker . . . argues that the district court erred in granting DeMert's motion for summary judgment on the grounds that DeMert did not place allegedly infringing goods into interstate commerce as required by § 32(1)(b) of the Lanham Act, 15 U.S.C. § 1114(1)(b) . . . .

The word "commerce" as used in the statute is defined as "all commerce which may be regulated by Congress." 15 U.S.C. § 1127 (1982). It is undisputed that DeMert placed artwork which allegedly infringed on Walker's trademark on the cans it filled with deodorant. While the artwork used on the cans was initially supplied by Collection 2000, DeMert reproduced the artwork for the cans in Illinois and shipped them to Collection 2000 and Joseph Blasser in Florida. Collection 2000 and Joseph Blasser sold the cans to a third party, Transcontinental Overseas, Inc., which in turn resold the cans to consumers in Panama and Columbia.

In *Scotch Whiskey Association v. Barton Distilling Company*, 489 F.2d 809 (7th Cir. 1973), we held that the defendant caused an infringing product to enter into commerce when it shipped labels and bottles from the United States to Panama. Although the final product (whiskey) was produced and sold in Panama, this court concluded that "the 'commerce' involved began with the defendants' acts in the United States and continued to the ultimate distribution of the whiskey." *Id* at 812. Similarly, Walker persuasively argues that DeMert caused an allegedly infringing product to enter interstate commerce in Illinois because DeMert shipped the cans to Florida.

In *Steele v. Bulova Watch Co.*, 344 U.S. 280, 73 S. Ct. 252, 97 L.Ed. 319 (1952), the United States Supreme Court construed the word "commerce" as used in 15 U.S.C. § 1114(1) to include the activities of an American citizen assembling in Mexico component parts shipped from the United States and selling an infringing product in

Mexico. In deciding that the district court had jurisdiction under the Lanham Act, 15 U.S.C. § 1114(1), the Supreme Court stated that "a United States district court has jurisdiction to award relief to [a plaintiff] against acts of trademark infringement and unfair competition consummated in a foreign country by a citizen and resident of the United States." *Id.* at 281, 73 S. Ct. at 253. In *American Rice, Inc. v. Arkansas Rice Growers Cooperative Association,* 701 F.2d 408, 413 (5th Cir. 1983), the court relied on *Steele* to support the proposition that "the Lanham Act revealed a congressional intent to exercise its power to the fullest." In *Scotch Whiskey,* this court relied on Steele and stated:

> In *Steele,* the Supreme Court construed another section of the act, 15 U.S.C. § 1114(1), which creates a civil cause of action against one who uses an infringing mark 'in commerce.' The Court upheld a broad concept of "commerce."

489 F.2d at 812.

We hold that, since DeMert shipped cans of deodorant bearing allegedly infringing trademarks to Florida, the commerce requirement of the Lanham Act was met. The district court held that the "in commerce" requirement of the Lanham Act was not satisfied and therefore the Lanham Act was inapplicable to the present case. Since we hold that the "in commerce" requirement of the Lanham Act was satisfied, we remand because an issue of material fact remains as to whether DeMert actually violated the Lanham Act. Therefore, we reverse the district court's grant of summary judgment in favor of DeMert.

The judgment of the district court is reversed in part and affirmed in part and the case against DeMert, Collection 2000, and Joseph Blasser is remanded for trial consistent with this opinion.

* * *

Notes on Jurisdiction

1. Subject Matter Jurisdiction

a) Extraterritorial Jurisdiction

Under what circumstances, if any, should an American plaintiff be able to successfully sue in a U.S. court against a party's infringing activities which occur in another country? What countervailing principles and factors come into play?

In *Fun-Damental Too Ltd. v. Gammy Industries Corp.,* 42 U.S.P.Q.2d 1348 (2d Cir. 1997) the appellate court affirmed an order requiring defendant to acquire infringing products from a warehouse in China and ship them to the United States, where their sale was preliminarily enjoined. It analyzed the Supreme Court's *Bulova* decision as supplying a three-part test for exercising extraterritorial jurisdiction: "(1) does defendant's conduct have a substantial effect on United States commerce; (2) is defendant a United States citizen; and (3) is there an absence of conflict with trademark rights established under foreign law?" *Id.* at 1358–1359. It concluded the district court's order was a reasonable means of controlling the importation of the infringing products, and noted that defendant was a U.S. corporation and had cited no conflict with its trademark rights under foreign laws. *See also Levi-Strauss & Co. v. Sunrise International Trading Inc.,* 34 U.S.P.Q.2d 1712, 1713–1714 (11th Cir. 1995) (affirming preliminary injunction against U.S. defendants' sale of counterfeit LEVI jeans made in China and a freeze of defendants' assets where some jeans were found in Florida and negotiations and arrangements for shipment were made in U.S.); *Babbitt Electronics, Inc. v. Dynascan Corp.,* 38 F.3d 1161, 1179–1180 (11th Cir. 1994) (Lanham Act applied to sales of cordless telephones in South America because the phones were shipped through a U.S. free trade zone and sales-related activities occurred in the U.S.); *Reebok*

Intern., Ltd. v. Marnatech Enterprises, Inc., 970 F.2d 552, 554–555 (9ᵗʰ Cir. 1992) (affirming preliminary injunction against sale of counterfeit REEBOK shoes in Mexico and a freeze of defendants' assets despite apparently related ongoing litigation in Mexico; "the Mexican litigation presented no conflict with the district court's order because the litigation in Mexico had not yet been concluded"); *American Rice, Inc. v. Arkansas Rice Growers*, 701 F.2d 408 (5ᵗʰ Cir. 1983) (injunction granted though defendant's infringing products sold only in Saudi Arabia); *Les Ballets Trockadero De Monte Carlo Inc. v. Trevino*, 945 F. Supp. 563 (S.D.N.Y. 1996) (preliminarily enjoining defendant from using infringing service mark in connection with ballet performances in Japan); *Calvin Klein v. BFK Hong Kong*, 714 F. Supp. 78 (S.D.N.Y. 1989) (defendant enjoined from selling rejected, defective CALVIN KLEIN sportswear anywhere in world where plaintiff had a presence, jurisdiction for the order deriving from the effect defendant's sales would have on U.S. commerce, including the exclusive rights of plaintiff's licensees and plaintiff's goodwill and reputation).

In *Versace v. Alfredo Versace*, 213 Fed. Appx. 34 (2ᵈ Cir. 2007) (unpublished), Alfredo Versace was making infringing use of that famous last name to sell watches, jeans, handbags and the like on the Internet and elsewhere, even after a preliminary injunction against doing so. The Second Circuit affirmed the permanent injunction against his "using the name 'Versace' in connection with any commercial activity anywhere in the world". Alfredo objected that he was not a U.S. citizen, but "Alfredo's forty years of residence and business activity in the United States, and his relationship with a U.S. corporation . . . are sufficient to support the international reach of the permanent injunction [given] the lack of conflict with foreign law and the existence of a substantial effect on commerce."

Compare International Cafe S.A.L. v. Hard Rock Cafe International (U.S.A.), Inc., 252 F.3d 1274, 1278 (11ᵗʰ Cir. 2001)(case dismissed; while defendant was a U.S. corporation, alleged receipt of royalties from foreign subsidiary did not establish the requisite "substantial effects" in the U.S., and pending civil suits against plaintiff in Lebanon created potential interference with Lebanese court rulings); *Atlantic Richfield Co. v. Arco Globus Int'l Co.*, 150 F.3d 189 (2ᵈ Cir. 1998) (plaintiff's Lanham Act infringement claims did not reach defendant's use of ARCO for its gas and oil operations in the former Soviet Union; defendant was a New York company with a New York office and American employees, but never offered products for sale in the U.S. and "none of the alleged infringer's American activities materially support the foreign use of the mark . . . the mere presence of the infringer in the U.S. will not support extraterritorial application of the Lanham Act"); *Totalplan Corp. of America v. Colborne*, 14 F.3d 824, 830–831 (2ᵈ Cir. 1994) (Lanham Act did not reach defendants' Japanese distribution of infringing cameras where defendants were Canadian and effect on U.S. commerce was not substantial, even though cameras were packaged in and shipped from the U.S.); *Sterling Drug, Inc. v. Bayer AG*, 14 F.3d 733 (2ᵈ Cir. 1994) (declining to mechanically apply three-factor test in case involving foreign corporation with potentially superior rights to the mark under foreign law, but remanding for consideration of injunction against only foreign uses "likely to have significant trademark-impairing effects" on U.S. commerce); *Nintendo of America, Inc. v. Aeropower Co., Ltd.*, 34 F.3d 246, 249–250 (4ᵗʰ Cir. 1994) (while agreeing that sales of infringing videogame cartridges in Mexico and Canada had significant effect on U.S. commerce, remanding extraterritorial portion of injunction for consideration of additional factors of defendants' citizenship and potential conflicts with foreign law). *See also* Bradley, *Extraterritorial Application of U.S. Intellectual Property Law: Territorial Intellectual Property Rights in an Age of Globalism*, 37 VA. J. INT'L LAW 505 (1997); Dabney, *On The Territorial Reach of the Lanham Act*, 83 TRADEMARK REP. 465 (1993).

In *Hawes v. Network Solutions, Inc.*, 337 F.3d 377 (4ᵗʰ Cir. 2003), the plaintiff sued both the domain name registrar for allegedly unlawfully transferring plaintiff's "lorealcomplaints.com" domain name to L'Oreal S.A., a French corporation, pursuant to the order of a French court, and the transferee L'Oreal. Plaintiff's cosmetics business competed with L'Oreal, and he claimed to have registered the domain name for "a forum with which to communicate with L'Oreal concerning problems with its products." Plaintiff failed to appear to defend himself in the French court action filed by L'Oreal that resulted in the transfer order.

The registrar was immune to suit under the Anti-Cybersquatting Consumer Protection Act ("ACPA"), 15 U.S.C. § 1114(D)(i), and no statutory exception to that immunity applied, so dismissal of that portion of the suit was affirmed. The claim against L'Oreal for its actions in the French court to obtain transfer of the plaintiff's domain name, however, was reinstated. The Fourth Circuit emphasized that its decision "does not imply any disrespect of any French court that may have taken jurisdiction of a related dispute in France." Nonetheless, "[a]djudication of an action brought under [the ACPA] involves neither appellate-like review of, nor deference to, any simultaneously pending actions in foreign jurisdictions . . ." In the court's view, this "does not leave the foreign trademark owner bereft of protection", because it "remains free to file a counterclaim" in the U.S. action.

In *McBee v. Delica Co.*, 417 F.3d 107 (1st Cir. 2006), the First Circuit held that, in cases involving the "foreign activities of foreign defendants":

> subject matter jurisdiction under the Lanham Act is proper only if the complained-of activities have a substantial effect on United States Commerce, viewed in light of the Lanham Act.

If this substantial effects test is met, then potential conflict with foreign trademark law also must be considered as a basis for declining jurisdiction. *Id.* at 111. In *McBee*, an American jazz musician sued a Japanese company selling girls clothing there under his name as a trademark, CECIL McBEE. Because the Japanese defendant's website selling the clothing was in Japanese, it lacked the necessary "substantial effect" on U.S. Commerce, and there was no other basis for jurisdiction. Were the court to hold otherwise, "we would be forced to find jurisdiction in almost all false endorsement or trademark cases involving an American plaintiff and allegedly infringing sales abroad."

b) Relief for a Foreign Party in the United States

Under what circumstances should a foreign party be able to obtain relief in this country? In *Buti v. Impressa Perosa S.R.L.*, 139 F.3d 98 (2d Cir. 1998), the declaratory judgment defendant's advertising and promotion in the U.S. of its FASHION CAFE restaurant located in Milan, Italy was not sufficient to constitute "use in commerce". It therefore could not obtain protection under the Lanham Act against plaintiff's FASHION CAFE restaurant located in this country. *See also Person's Co. v. Chistman*, 900 F.2d 1565 (Fed. Cir. 1990) (petition to cancel PERSON'S for clothing based on use in Japan dismissed where petitioner's use had no "effect on U.S. commerce"). Note some of the parallels with the *McBee* decision discussed above. *Compare Int'l Bancorp, LLC v. Societe Des Bains De Mer et Du Cercle Des Estrangers a Monaco*, 329 F.3d 359 (4th Cir. 2005), in which the owner of the trademark "Casino de Monte Carlo" in Monaco successfully stopped the U.S. infringer's use of domain names incorporating some portion of that mark for on-line gambling websites, because the trademark owner had used its mark in U.S. commerce via its substantial advertising expenditures and sales success here (drawing U.S. customers to its casino), along with substantial unsolicited media coverage. See also the discussion in Chapter 3 on foreign companies establishing priority in the U.S.

c) Pendent Jurisdiction

28 U.S.C. § 1338(b) was intended to codify the "related action" doctrine of pendent federal jurisdiction enunciated in *Hurn v. Oursler*, 289 U.S. 238 (1933). In *United Mine Workers v. Gibbs*, 383 U.S. 715 (1966), the Supreme Court held that a claim is related if

"the state and federal claims . . . derive from a common nucleus of operative fact." *See also* 28 U.S.C. § 1367(a) ("in any civil action in which the district courts have original jurisdiction, the district courts shall have supplemental jurisdiction over all other claims that are so related to the claims in the action . . . that they form part of the same case or controversy under Article III of the United States Constitution").

Does this test affect the joinder of federal statutory trademark infringement and state common law unfair competition claims? *See Armstrong Paint & Varnish Works v. Nu-Enamel Corp.*, 305 U.S. 315 (1938); *Astor-Honor, Inc. v. Grosset & Dunlap, Inc.*, 441 F.2d 627 (2[d] Cir. 1971) (copyright infringement and unfair competition). Absent diversity, jurisdictional amount, or federal statutory bases, should a federal court continue to hear and decide what were pendent common-law trademark and unfair competition claims after all claims of statutory trademark infringement have been dismissed? *Compare Textile Deliveries Inc. v. Stagno*, 52 F.3d 46, 49 (2[d] Cir. 1995) (district court properly retained pendent jurisdiction over state law contract claim even though Lanham Act claim dismissed), *with Oliveira v. Frito-Lay, Inc.*, 251 F.3d 56, 64 (2[d] Cir. 2001) (defendant's state law claims dismissed without prejudice to permit refiling in state court after Lanham Act claims were dismissed).

The fact that the parties' breach of contract suit involved trademark rights did not create subject matter jurisdiction under the Lanham Act in *Gibraltar P.R., Inc. v. Ottiki Group*, 104 F.3d 616 (4th Cir. 1997). There, defendant had contended an amendment to the parties' Joint Venture Agreement assigning all of defendant's trademarks to the Joint Venture was invalid, and the appellate court ruled that the Lanham Act was enacted to address the "registration and infringement of trademarks, not ownership disputes arising out of contracts." Similarly, in *International Armor & Limousine Co. v. Moloney Coachbuilders, Inc.*, 272 F.3d 912 (7th Cir. 2001), the court held that it had no subject matter jurisdiction where the trademark claims were merely derivative of contract issues.

d) Declaratory Judgment

Under appropriate circumstances, a party whose conduct might provoke a lawsuit can seek a decree from a federal court to declare its rights under the Declaratory Judgment Act, 28 U.S.C. § 2201(a). For a federal court to assert its discretion to exercise jurisdiction over a declaratory judgment action involving trademarks, (1) it must have federal question jurisdiction; and (2) the declaratory judgment plaintiff must (a) have a reasonable apprehension of liability based upon the defendant's conduct; and (b) have engaged in a course of conduct which has brought it into adversarial conflict with the defendant. *See Starter, Corp. v. Converse, Inc.*, 84 F.3d 592, 596–97 (2[d] Cir. 1996). A threat by the declaratory defendant to bring a lawsuit under the Lanham Act satisfies the first prong. *See id.* at 595. *See also PHC, Inc. v. Pioneer Health Care, Inc.*, 75 F.3d 75, 79 (1st Cir. 1996) (finding federal question jurisdiction even though the declaratory judgment defendant threatened suit under only a Massachusetts statute because its cease-and-desist letter made allegations typical of a § 43(a) claim). A declaratory judgment plaintiff's "definite intent and apparent ability to commence use" of the marks at issue — decided on a case-by-case basis by evaluating factors such as investment, design, manufacturing, and marketing of the products at issue — satisfies the second prong. *See Starter Corp., supra*, at 595–96. However, if the basis for the declaratory suit is solely defendant's opposition to the plaintiff's application to register the trademark, the plaintiff may not be found to have a "reasonable apprehension" of an infringement suit. *See Progressive Apparel Group, Inc. v. Anheuser-Busch, Inc.*, 38 U.S.P.Q.2d 1057 (S.D.N.Y. 1996) (defendant's opposition to plaintiff's application to register ARCADIA for clothing not sufficient to create a reasonable apprehension of a future infringement suit).

e)   ITU Applicants and Intrastate Users

Should subject matter jurisdiction exist in the federal courts where the plaintiff is an intent to use applicant for federal registration who has yet to make use of the mark in commerce? *See Fila Sport, S.p.A. v. Diadora America, Inc.*, 21 U.S.P.Q.2d 1063 (N.D. Ill. 1991) (motion to dismiss granted). What if the activities at issue only occur intrastate? *Compare Coca-Cola v. Stewart, supra, with Fitzgerald v. J&R Chicken & Ribs, Inc.*, 11 U.S.P.Q.2d 384 (D.N.J. 1989), in which the case was dismissed because plaintiff failed to allege any connection with interstate commerce: "On the contrary, plaintiff appears to acknowledge that both his take-out chicken business as well as that of the alleged infringer . . . are local in nature."

f)   Sovereign Immunity

The Lanham Act has been held inapplicable to the federal government in the absence of an express waiver of its sovereign immunity, thus depriving courts of subject matter jurisdiction over Lanham Act suits in which the federal government is an unwilling defendant. *See Preferred Risk Mut. Ins. Co. v. United States*, 86 F.3d 789 (8th Cir. 1996), *cert. denied*, 520 U.S. 1116 (1997). An exception occurred in *Federal Express Corp. v. United States Postal Serv.*, 151 F.3d 536 (6th Cir. 1998), in which Federal Express claimed that the United States Postal Service ("USPS") inaccurately and misleadingly advertised its priority mail services as comparable to or better than the services offered by Federal Express. USPS moved to dismiss for lack of subject matter jurisdiction, arguing that it was not a "person" as defined by the Lanham Act. The Sixth Circuit found the Postal Reorganization Act, 39 U.S.C. § 101 *et seq.*, expressly recognized the USPS as a commercial enterprise capable of suing and being sued, and that the USPS therefore was subject to Lanham Act jurisdiction.

In *College Sav. Bank v. Florida Prepaid*, 527 U.S. 666 (1999), the Supreme Court held that the doctrine of sovereign immunity protects a state from liability under § 43(a) of the Lanham Act for false representations by one of its agencies about its own services. The stage was set for *College Savings* by the Trademark Remedy Clarification Act of 1992. The TRCA amended § 43(a) of the Lanham Act to define "any person" to include "any State, instrumentality of a State or employee of a State or instrumentality of a State acting in his or her official capacity." The TRCA also provided that such State entities "shall not be immune, under the Eleventh Amendment. . . . from suit in Federal court by any person. . . .for any violation under this Act."

The Supreme Court reasoned "the Lanham Act may well . . . protect . . . property interests — notably its provisions dealing with infringement of trademarks. . . [but] misrepresentations concerning [Florida Prepaid's] own products intruded upon no [property] interest over which petitioner had exclusive dominion." The court observed that the unfair competition and misappropriation of "hot news" at issue in *International News Service v. Associated Press (see* § 8.04 Misappropriation) was different in that it amounted to theft of proprietary information, in which a property interest could exist. The Court noted in *dicta* that the Lanham Act's false advertising provisions bear no relationship to the right to exclude inherent in property rights. Do false advertising cases sometimes involve property rights similar to those involved in trademark infringement cases? Should states be immune from trademark infringement suits under the same reasoning? The Supreme Court's *College Savings* decision was applied in insulating a state enterprise from trademark-related actions in *Hapco Farms, Inc. v. Idaho Potato Comm'n*, 238 F.3d 468 (2[d] Cir. 2001) (affirming judgment that defendant, an Idaho state agency, was immune from a suit seeking to cancel the agency's federal trademark registrations).

The Supreme Court also held that there could be no "implied" waiver of immunity by state conduct; an express and unequivocal waiver by the state was required. Florida Prepaid's election to go into competition with private companies, even after being put on notice by the clear language of the TRCA that it would be subject to Lanham Act liability for doing so, therefore did not waive its immunity. Should states be afforded immunity when they can enjoy the benefits of the Lanham Act by suing private companies for similar misrepresentations? *See State Contracting and Engineering Corp. v. State of Florida*, 258 F.3d 1329 (Fed. Cir. 2001) (affirming dismissal of Lanham Act misrepresentation claim against the State of Florida; after *College Savings Bank* only an "unequivocal" express waiver by the state would have prevented dismissal). In a companion case, *Florida Prepaid v. College Sav. Bank*, 527 U.S. 627 (1999), the Supreme Court held that the states also have sovereign immunity from claims of patent infringement, which immunity had not been validly abrogated by the Patent Remedy Act. Note that the Supreme Court decision in *College Savings*, if extended to trademark cases, would not abrogate state trademark laws or the right to sue in state court. It has also been suggested that the grant of trademark registrations in the future might be conditioned on the applicant (including state entities) agreeing to be subject to suit in federal court under the Lanham Act.

Foreign countries also have limited immunity from federal subject matter jurisdiction under the Foreign Sovereign Immunity Act ("FSIA"). 28 U.S.C. §§ 1330 (a), 1604. The FSIA "provides the sole basis for obtaining [subject matter] jurisdiction over a foreign sovereign in the United States." *Republic of Argentina v. Weltover, Inc.*, 504 U.S. 607, 611 (1992) (internal quotation marks omitted); *accord Saudi Arabia v. Nelson*, 507 U.S. 349, 355 (1993). That basis comes from exceptions to the general sovereign immunity, most of which are contained in 28 U.S.C. § 1605:

§ 1605.   General exceptions to the jurisdictional immunity of a foreign state

A foreign state shall not be immune from the jurisdiction of courts of the United States or of the States in any case . . . . in which the action is based (1) upon a commercial activity carried on in the United States by the foreign state; or (2) upon any act performed in the United States in connection with the commercial activity of the foreign state elsewhere; or (3) upon an act outside the territory of the United States in connection with a commercial activity of the foreign state elsewhere and that act causes a direct effect in the United States.

In *Virtual Countries Inc. v. Republic of South Africa*, 63 U.S.P.Q.2d 1993 (2ᵈ Cir. 2002), for example, the Seattle-based plaintiff owned a number of domain names based on the names of foreign countries, including "southafrica.com". When the Republic of South Africa issued a press release stating its intention to claim that domain name through means such as a UDRP proceeding (see Chapter 8), the plaintiff sued in New York for a declaration that defendant had no rights in the domain name. The court determined that only the "direct effect" third clause of the § 1605(a) provision could supply the necessary exception to the Republic's sovereign immunity. Because of "the tentative and indefinite nature of the release" which mentioned only a future intention to use an ICANN proceeding, however, the alleged injury to plaintiff was too speculative, and the necessary "direct effect in the United States" was lacking. Dismissal therefore was affirmed.

2.   Personal Jurisdiction

a)   Generally

Establishing personal jurisdiction over a non-resident defendant is a matter of satisfying the long-arm statute of the particular situs state and demonstrating sufficient minimum contacts to satisfy due process. Typically a court looks for the transaction of business by the defendant within the state, with the cause of action relating to that transaction of business. *See, e.g., Schwarzenegger v. Fred Martin Motor Co.*, 71 U.S.P.Q.2d 1321 (9ᵗʰ Cir. 2004) (defendant, who published advertisements in a locally-circulated Ohio newspaper that contained a small picture of actor Arnold

Schwarzenegger in his "Terminator" role, did not have the necessary "continuous and systematic" contacts with California, and did not purposely avail himself of the privilege of doing business in California, as his acts were targeted at Ohio).

The absence of physical entry into the state by the defendant will not preclude personal jurisdiction, as explained by the Supreme Court in *Burger King Corp. v. Rudzewicz*, 471 U.S. 462, 475 (1985):

> Jurisdiction in these circumstances may not be avoided merely because the defendant did not *physically* enter the forum state. — [I]t is an inescapable fact of modern commercial life that a substantial amount of business is transacted solely by mail and wire communications across state lines, thus obviating the need for physical presence within the state in which business is conducted. So long as a commercial actor's efforts are "purposefully directed" toward residents of another state, we have consistently rejected the notion that an absence of physical contacts can defeat personal jurisdiction there. [Citations omitted].
>
> . . . .
>
> [W]here a defendant who purposefully has directed his activities at forum residents seeks to defeat jurisdiction, he must present a compelling case that the presence of some other considerations would render jurisdiction unreasonable. Most such considerations usually may be accommodated through means short of finding jurisdiction unconstitutional.

This reasoning has been followed in trademark and unfair competition cases. See, e.g., *Wellness Publ'g v. Barefoot*, 128 Fed. Appx. 266 (3d Cir. 2005) (unpub'd) (where defendants had "advertised the books to New Jersey customers, answered the phone when those customers called, and then arranged to have the books shipped to New Jersey addresses," they should have expected "to be subject to jurisdiction in that state"); *Dakota Industries, Inc. v. Dakota Sportswear, Inc.*, 946 F.2d 1384 (8th Cir. 1991) (dismissal reversed where, although infringement defendant had no offices in the state, never advertised there and never directly shipped goods there, it knew that the major impact of the injury would be in that state); *J. Walker & Sons, Ltd. v. Demert & Dougherty, Inc.*, 821 F.2d 399, 404 (7th Cir. 1987) (ongoing business contacts with the state sufficient); *Boston Chicken Inc. v. Market Bar-B- Que Inc.*, 922 F. Supp. 96 (N.D. Ill. 1996) (Minnesota-based company's one dozen shipments of MARKET chicken over thirty years to Illinois customers not sufficient to establish minimum contacts with Illinois).

In *Luv'n Care v. Insta-Mix, Inc.*, 438 F.3d 465, 470-474 (5th Cir. 2006), the district court erred in not finding purposeful availment where the defendant could foresee that Wal-Mart would sell its products in Louisiana. The Fifth Circuit noted that a defendant's awareness that its product will end up in a forum state via the stream of commerce satisfies the personal jurisdiction requirements. Furthermore, "[w]here a defendant knowingly benefits from the availability of a particular state's market for its products, it is only fitting that the defendant be amenable to suit in that state." Insta-Mix filled approximately sixty-five purchase orders for Wal-Mart for items bound for sale in Louisiana. Insta-Mix claimed that Wal-Mart controlled the ultimate destination of the items and Insta-Mix employees had no actual knowledge of that destination until consulting an electronic data system in preparation for this case. The Court rejected this claim, finding it "eminently foreseeable that Insta-Mix's products would reach the market indicated on the company's invoices," and noting the substantial revenue that Insta-Mix derived from sales to Louisiana. Because Luv n' care's infringement claims involved the same products that traveled through the stream of commerce to Louisiana, the connection was sufficient to confer personal jurisdiction. Finally, the Court concluded that "where a product allegedly causes economic injury in Louisiana, it is in the interest of that state to have its courts mediate the dispute."

In *Indianapolis Colts v. Metropolitan Baltimore Football Club Ltd. Partnership*, 34 F.3d 410 (7th Cir. 1994) (Posner, J.), "the only activity of [defendant] undertaken or planned so far in Indiana [was] the broadcast of its [professional football] games nationwide on cable television." Plaintiffs, the Indianapolis Colts football team and the National Football League, alleged that defendant's use of the name Baltimore CFL Colts infringed the Indianapolis Colts name, particularly given that the Indianapolis team previously operated in Baltimore under the name Baltimore Colts. In affirming that the district court had personal jurisdiction over defendant, the Seventh Circuit reasoned (*Id.* at 411):

> The Indianapolis Colts use the trademarks they seek to defend in this suit mainly in Indiana. By choosing a name that might be found confusingly similar to that of the Indianapolis Colts, the defendants assumed the risk of injuring valuable properly located in Indiana. Since there can be no tort without an injury, [citation omitted], the state in which the tort occurs, and someone who commits a tort in Indiana should, one might suppose, be amenable to suit there.

Recognizing the far-reaching scope of such a holding, however, the court further observed that in other intellectual property cases courts had found "the defendant had done more than brought about an injury to an interest located in a particular state". Here, the cable broadcasts into Indiana supplied that additional element, "so we needn't decide whether that addition is indispensable." *See also Miller Yacht Sales, Inc. v. Smith*, 384 F.3d 93 (3[d] Cir. 2004), a trade dress and unfair competition case in which personal jurisdiction existed in New Jersey. In addition to other New Jersey business contacts, defendant met with plaintiff there and obtained the various photographs and floor plans at issue, which defendant sent directly to at least one New Jersey resident and also used in advertisements in boating magazines that circulated in New Jersey. *Compare Hot Wax, Inc. v. Stone Soap Co. Inc.*, 1999 U.S. Dist. LEXIS 4091 (N.D. Ill. 1999), in which plaintiff couldn't establish personal jurisdiction over defendant in Illinois, because plaintiff was a Wisconsin corporation ("Hot Wax's injury, if any, occurred in Wisconsin, not Illinois"), and there was no evidence defendant, a Michigan corporation, "ha[d] solicited or targeted business in Illinois." Simply advertising in national publications which entered Illinois (among other states) was insufficient to subject defendant to jurisdiction there.

For an unusual use of a court's discretion in this area, see *Curtis Management Group, Inc. v. Academy of Motion Picture Arts & Sciences*, 717 F. Supp. 1362 (S.D. Ind. 1989), in which the court struck defendant's motion to dismiss and allowed the action to proceed even though there was no personal jurisdiction or venue, because defendant's affidavits supporting its motion contained false statements.

b)   Foreign Defendants

The considerations in determining whether a foreign defendant is subject to personal jurisdiction in a U.S. court are similar to those for a domestic defendant. *See, e.g., Mattel, Inc. v. MCA Records, Inc.*, 296 F.3d 894 (9th Cir. 2002) (exercising personal jurisdiction over Danish defendants who targeted the distribution and promotion of allegedly infringing "Barbie Girl" song at the U.S., including California; "Mattel's trademark claims would not have arisen 'but for' the conduct foreign defendants purposefully directed toward California, and [personal] jurisdiction over the foreign defendants, who are represented by the same counsel and closely associated with the domestic defendants, is reasonable"). However, the burden in proving jurisdiction may be higher. In *Yahoo!, Inc. v. La Legue Contre Le* Racism *Et L'Antisemitisme*, 145 F. Supp.2d 1168 (N.D. Cal. 2001), for example, the court held that "a plaintiff seeking to hale a foreign defendant into court in the United States must meet a higher jurisdictional threshold than is required when a defendant is [a] United States resident". In that case, there was personal jurisdiction over defendants in plaintiff's declaratory judgment action because the defendants sent a cease and desist letter to the plaintiff's California headquarters, requested that plaintiff perform certain acts there to restrict access to plaintiff's website content, and utilized the U.S. Marshals to effect service of process there.

c) On-Line Activities and Personal Jurisdiction

Burgeoning use of online services and the Internet has presented new issues concerning personal jurisdiction over out-of-state defendants whose only connection with the forum state is through an online connection. In *CompuServe, Inc. v. Patterson*, 89 F.3d 1257 (6th Cir. 1996), a trademark infringement suit, the Sixth Circuit held that an Ohio federal district court had personal jurisdiction over a Texas-based individual whose only connection with Ohio was through plaintiff, an Ohio- based online service provider, that the Texan used to market computer software. The Sixth Circuit found (1) that the Texan purposefully availed himself of the privilege of doing business in Ohio by three years of advertising and collecting payment for software through CompuServe; and (2) that CompuServe's action arose from the Texan's activities in Ohio because he sold his software only on CompuServe, so that his common law trademark rights, if any, arose there. *Id.* at 1264–66. The Texan also had transmitted a litigation threat to CompuServe through electronic mail, which contributed to both findings. *Id.* at 1266.

In *Maritz Inc. v. CyberGold Inc.*, 947 F. Supp. 1328 (E.D. Mo. 1996), a Missouri district court in a trademark infringement action asserted personal jurisdiction over a California-based company, CyberGold, because of CyberGold's website. CyberGold purposely availed itself of the Missouri forum and could reasonably expect to be haled there, according to the court, when it posted information about its allegedly infringing forthcoming service on the Internet and solicited users for e-mail addresses to develop an electronic mailing list. *Id.* at 1333. The potential for the more than 12,000 Missouri Internet users to access CyberGold's website established CyberGold's minimum contacts with Missouri even though only 131 "hits" to the site came from Missouri. *Id.* at n.4. *See also The Christian Science Bd. of Directors of the First Church of Christ, Scientist v. Nolan*, 259 F.3d 209, 216 (4th Cir. 2001) (personal jurisdiction existed in North Carolina over Arkansas defendants who had enlisted North Carolina defendant to download their web design onto his domain, which was located and maintained in North Carolina, and who had consistently supplied information to him there for use on the interactive website); *Zippo Mfg. Co. v. Zippo Dot Com Inc.*, 952 F. Supp. 1119 (W.D. Pa. 1997) (asserting personal jurisdiction over an out-of-state defendant based on approximately 3,000 contacts with forum-state residents who received defendant's Internet news service through an allegedly infringing web site); *Playboy Enterprises, Inc. v. Chuckleberry Publishing, Inc.*, 939 F. Supp. 1032 (S.D.N.Y.), *modified*, 939 F. Supp. 1041 (S.D.N.Y. 1996) (holding defendant in contempt of injunction barring the sale or distribution of PLAYMEN magazine in the U.S. for marketing its adult entertainment services on "playmen.it," a web page uploaded in Italy and accessible in the U.S.).

Compare Pebble Beach Co. v. Caddy, 453 F.3d 1151 (9th Cir. 2006) (passive website for U.K. bed and breakfast did not provide basis for personal jurisdiction in U.S.; "[t]he fact that the [plaintiff's] name 'Pebble Beach' is a famous mark known world-wide is of little practical consequence when deciding whether action is directed at particular forum via the world-wide web"); *Quick Techs. v. Sage Group PLC*, 313 F.3d 338, 345 (5th Cir. 2002) (a website that is nothing more than a "passive advertisement." *i.e.*, "a website that provides product information, toll-free telephone numbers, e-mail addresses, mail addresses, and mail-in order forms, does not support the exercise of personal jurisdiction"); *GTE New Media Serv. v. BellSouth Corp.*, 199 F. 3d 1343, 1347-1349 (D.C. Cir. 2000) ("we reject GTE's theory of jurisdiction, which appears to rest on a view that mere accessibility to an Internet site in the District is enough of a foundation upon which to base personal jurisdiction . . . under this view, personal jurisdiction in Internet-related cases would almost always be found in any forum in the country"); *Mink v. AAAA Dev. LLC*, 190 F.3d 333, 336-37 (5th Cir. 1999) (declining to find personal jurisdiction; "there was no evidence that [the defendant] conducted business over the Internet by engaging in business transactions with forum residents or by entering into contracts over the Internet"); *Cybersell, Inc. v. Cybersell, Inc.*, 130 F.3d 414, 419-20 (9th Cir. 1997) (declining to find personal jurisdiction; while state residents could access the website, the court could not "see how from that fact alone it can be inferred that [the defendant] deliberately targeted its merchandising efforts toward Arizona residents"); *Bensusan Restaurant Corp. v. King*, 937 F. Supp. 295, 301 (S.D.N.Y. 1996), *aff'd*, 126 F.3d 25 (2d Cir. 1997) (New York court had no personal jurisdiction over a Missouri-based defendant whose only connection with New York was through a web page that allegedly infringed the service mark of a New York night club; "[c]reating a site . . . may be felt nationwide — or even worldwide — but, without more, it is not an act purposefully directed toward the forum state").

In a dispute over the trademark CAREFIRST, the plaintiff had sued an Illinois corporation in Maryland in *Carefirst of Md., Inc. v. Carefirst Pregnancy Ctrs., Inc.*, 334 F.3d 390 (4th Cir. 2003). In affirming dismissal for lack of personal jurisdiction, the Fourth Circuit found that the defendant's website, while accessible in Maryland, had "a strongly local character, emphasizing that [defendant's] mission is to assist Chicago-area women in pregnancy crises", and that defendant's receipt through the Internet of a miniscule fraction of its donations ($120 in total) from Maryland residents was insufficient to create jurisdiction.

In *Weber v. Jolly Hotels*, 977 F. Supp. 327, 333 (D.N.J. 1997) the court summarized the Internet jurisdiction cases as follows:

> The cases dealing with this issue can be divided into three categories . . . . The first category includes cases where defendants actively do business on the Internet. *See, e.g., Compuserve*, 89 F.3d 1257. In those instances, personal jurisdiction is found because defendants "enter [] into contracts with residents of a foreign jurisdiction that involve the knowing and repeated transmission of computer files over the Internet." *See Zippo*, 962 F. Supp. at 1124 (citing *Compuserve*, 89 F.3d 1257). The second category deals with situations "where a user can exchange information with the host computer. In these cases, the exercise of jurisdiction is determined by examining the level of interactivity and commercial nature of the exchange of information that occurs on the web site." *Zippo*, 962 F. Supp. at 1124 (citing *Maritz, Inc. v. Cybergold, Inc.* 947 F. Supp. 1328 (E.D. Mo. 1996). The third category involves passive web sites; *i.e.*, sites that merely provide information or advertisements to users. *See Bensusan Restaurant Corp v. King*, 937 F. Supp. 295 (S.D.N.Y. 1996) [*aff'd*, 126 F.3d 25 (1997)]. District courts do not exercise jurisdiction in the latter cases because "a finding of jurisdiction . . . based on an Internet web site would mean that there would be nationwide (indeed, worldwide) personal jurisdiction over anyone and everyone who establishes an Internet web site. Such nationwide jurisdiction is not consistent with traditional personal jurisdiction case law . . . ." *Hearst Corp. v. Goldberger*, 1997 U.S. Dist. LEXIS 2065, 1997 WL 97097, at *1 (S.D.N.Y. Feb. 27, 1997).

In that case, the court held it lacked personal jurisdiction because defendant placed information about its hotels on the Internet as an advertisement, not as a means of conducting business. *See also Park Inns Int'l v. Pacific Plaza Hotels*, 5 F. Supp. 2d 762 (D. Ariz. 1998) (defendant hotel had an interactive website on which Arizona residents could, and did "create, amend or cancel reservations", which, in addition to a posting on an computer reservations network used by Arizona travel agents and a hotel profile in two publications distributed in Arizona, established the court's personal jurisdiction over defendant); *Thompson v. Handa-Lopez, Inc.*, 998 F. Supp. 738 (W. D. Tex. 1998) (personal jurisdiction in Texas district court established where defendant's Internet-based casino operations continuously interacted and entered into contracts with casino players, including players in Texas).

In *Rio Properties, Inc. v. Rio Int'l Interlink*, 284 F.3d 1007 (9th Cir. 2002), defendant's passive website did not provide basis for personal jurisdiction, but its print and radio advertisements to promote the website in the forum state did. In *Toys "R" Us v. Step Two S.A.*, 318 F.3d 446, 452-454 (3[d] Cir. 2003), although the Spanish defendant's commercially interactive websites "do not appear to have been designed or intended to reach customers in New Jersey", the court concluded that they might provide a basis for personal jurisdiction there if combined with "something more" in non-Internet contacts, "such as serial business trips to the forum state, telephone and fax communications directed to [it], purchase contracts with forum state residents . . . and advertisements in local newspapers." The case was remanded for jurisdictional discovery.

d) Domain Name *In Rem* Jurisdiction

The Anticybersquatting Consumer Protection Act of 1999 ("ACPA") amended the Lanham Act to provide for *in rem* jurisdiction over an Internet domain name itself, when personal jurisdiction over the name's registrant cannot be established or the alleged violator cannot, through due diligence, be located. 15 U.S.C. § 1125(d). In *Harrods Ltd. v. Sixty Internet Domain Names*, 302 F.3d 214 (4th Cir. 2002), *in rem* jurisdiction was appropriate over many .com, .org and .net domain names because the plaintiff could not establish personal jurisdiction over the Argentine domain name registrant. The court further concluded that a plaintiff bringing an *in rem* action under § 1125(d) "may, in appropriate circumstances, pursue infringement and dilution claims as well as bad faith registration claims," citing Jennings, *Significant Trademark/Domain Name Issues in Cyberspace*, 663 PLI/Pat 649 (2001). *Harrods* was followed in *Cable News Network, LP v. cnnnews.com*, 66 U.S.P.Q. 2d 1057 (4th Cir. 2003), with the Fourth Circuit affirming judgment against defendant on plaintiff's trademark infringement claim, and affirming the transfer of the domain name to plaintiff. *In rem* jurisdiction may be appropriate where the suit was filed even if the defendant eventually consents to personal jurisdiction elsewhere. *Porsche Cars North America, Inc. v. Porsche.net*, 302 F.3d 248, (4th Cir. 2002) (affirming the retention of *in rem* jurisdiction in Virginia despite the domain name registrant's consent, three days before trial, to jurisdiction in California).

The remedies in such *in rem* actions are limited to forfeiture, cancellation or transfer of the domain name. The suit may be filed "in the judicial district in which the domain name registrar, domain name registry, or other domain name authority that registered or assigned the domain name is located" if the other conditions of the statute are met. 15 U.S.C. § 1125(d)(2)(A). The largest registrar, Network Solutions, Inc., is located in the Eastern District of Virginia. *Caesars World, Inc. v. Caesars-Palace.com*, 112 F. Supp.2d 502 (E.D. Va. 2000)(holding ACPA's *in rem* jurisdiction provision is constitutional). *Compare Mattel, Inc. v. Barbie-club*.com, 310 F.3d 293 (2[d] Cir. 2002) (*in rem* action dismissed because it was not filed in the district of the registrar or similar domain name authority); *Fleetwood Financial Corp. v. Fleetbostonfinancial.com*, 138 F. Supp.2d 121 (D. Mass. 2001) (dismissing *in rem* lawsuit as having been filed in the wrong jurisdiction; neither "the registrar, registry or other domain name authority" was located in Massachusetts).

A domain name registrar is immune to suit under the ACPA. 15 U.S.C. § 1114(D)(i); *Hawes v. Network Solutions, Inc.*, 337 F.3d 377 (4th Cir. 2003) (the registrar was immune, but the court reinstated plaintiff's claim against the French company to whom the registrar allegedly had unlawfully transferred plaintiff's domain name pursuant to a French court's order).

3. Venue

Even though a trademark plaintiff establishes personal jurisdiction over the defendant, the suit still may be subject to dismissal on the basis of improper venue. As stated in *Johnson Creative Arts, Inc. v. Wool Masters, Inc.*, 743 F.2d 947, 949 (1st Cir. 1984):

> The minimum contacts test for personal jurisdiction is based on the *minimum* amount of "fairness" required in order to comport with due process. Venue limitations are generally added by Congress to insure a defendant a fair location for trial and to protect him from inconvenient litigation."

In federal question cases, including those brought under the Lanham Act, Congress has authorized suit "only in the judicial district where all defendants reside, or in which the claim arose." 28 U.S.C. § 1391(b). In trademark infringement suits, where the allegedly infringing activities may occur in a number of different forms, venue arguably could exist in each of those forums as a location where "the claim arose." In *Leroy v. Great Western Corp.*, 443 U.S. 173, 185 (1979), the Supreme Court addressed this type of problem, stating:

> In our view . . . the broadest interpretation of the language of § 1391(b) that is even arguably acceptable is that in the unusual case in which it is not clear that the claim arose in only one specific district, a plaintiff may choose between those two (or conceivably even more) districts that with approximately equal plausibility — in terms of the availability of witnesses, the accessibility of other relevant evidence, and the convenience of the defendant (but *not* of the plaintiff) — may be assigned as the locus of the claim.

See J. Walker & Sons v. Demert & Dougherty, Inc., 821 F.2d 399, 406–407 (7th Cir. 1987), in which the *Leroy* factors such as accessibility of evidence and availability of witnesses weighed in favor of plaintiff, and *Noxell Corp. v. Firehouse No. 1 Barbecue Restaurant*, 760 F.2d 312 (D.C. Cir. 1985), in which the court dismissed a trademark case brought in Maryland where defendant made approximately 1.5% of its allegedly infringing sales, saying:

> [I]n terms of accessibility of relevant evidence (including witness testimony) and the convenience of the [California] defendants, the Northern District of California and the District of Columbia plainly are not places [plaintiff] could choose "with approximately equal plausibility. . . ." Defending a trademark infringement action some 3000 miles from where all employees and corporate records are located would exceed inconvenience — it would occasion a hardship for [defendant] and his current business.

A federal court has discretion under 28 U.S.C. § 1404(a) to transfer a civil action for "the convenience of parties and witnesses, in the interest of justice." *ISI Int'l, Inc. v. Borden Ladner Gervais LLP*, 316 F.3d 731 (7th Cir. 2003) (affirming dismissal of a suit against a Canadian law firm on *forum non conveniens* grounds, in favor of a proceeding in Ontario, Canada, after the U.S. federal law claim was dismissed); *US LIFE Corp. v. American Republic Insurance Corp.*, 218 U.S.P.Q. 298, 309 (D.D.C. 1982). However, venue will not be transferred simply because the situs of litigation is inconvenient for the defendant. *See, e.g., The Road Less Traveled v. Roads Less Traveled*, 49 U.S.P.Q.2d 1061 (N.D. Ill. 1998) (denying defendant's motion to transfer; "[t]ransferring the case to Colorado simply would transfer the inconvenience from [defendant] to plaintiff").

Under a 1988 amendment to the venue statute, for a corporation, residency for venue purposes exists where it is subject to personal jurisdiction. 28 U.S.C. § 1391.

4. Standing

To establish standing under the Lanham Act, a plaintiff normally need only show that it has a legitimate commercial interest in the proceeding's outcome. *See, e.g., Jewelers Vigilance Committee, Inc. v. Ullenberg Corp.*, 853 F.2d 888 (Fed. Cir. 1988) (diamond trade association had standing to oppose an application to register FOREVER YOURS/DEBEERS DIA. LTD. since DeBeers Consolidated Mines is the world's major source of diamonds). *Compare Ritchie v. Simpson*, 170 F.3d 1092 (Fed. Cir. 1999) (professor had standing to oppose applications to register various O.J. Simpson marks for sportwear and other merchandise as comprising "immoral, deceptive, or scandalous matter" under § 2(a), where he asserted that he was a family man and the marks disparaged his family values, making him part of a potentially damaged group; as a result he had a "real interest" in the outcome and a "reasonable basis" for his belief of damage, and was more than a "mere intermeddler").

But see Dovenmuehle v. Gilldorn Mortgage Midwest Corp., 871 F.2d 697 (7th Cir. 1989) (members of family surnamed "Dovenmuehle," lacked standing under § 43(a) to challenge defendant's use of the trade name DOVENMUEHLE, where they had failed to show any interest in the trade name after the sale of their family business, and had only an emotional desire to prevent others from using it); *Berni v. International Gourmet Restaurants, Inc.*, 838 F.2d 642 (2d Cir. 1988) (ex-shareholders had no standing to sue under § 43(a) over the alleged improper transferral of rights in a mark because they could not show that they would sustain commercial or competitive injury); *Jackson v. Lynley Designs, Inc.*, 729 F. Supp. 498 (E.D. La. 1990) (suit alleging plaintiff's name LISA JACKSON was fraudulently used in obtaining registration of that name for clothing dismissed for lack of standing where plaintiff had never engaged in business or attempted to exploit her name commercially).

In order to have standing to pursue a false advertising claim under the Lanham Act, a plaintiff must allege "a commercial injury based upon a misrepresentation about a product" and "that the injury is 'competitive,' or harmful to the plaintiff's ability to compete with the defendant." *Jack Russell Terrier Network v. Am. Kennel Club, Inc.*, 407 F.3d 1027, 1037 (9th Cir. 2005) quoting *Barrus v. Sylvania*, 55 F.3d 468, 469 (9th Cir. 1995). In that case, the Jack Russell Terrier Club of America (the "Club") terminated the charter of a regional chapter that allowed members to register dogs with a competing club. The regional chapter and two breeders sued the Club claiming that the Club's actions violated the Lanham Act and state law. The court of appeals, affirming the district court, concluded that the regional chapter and the breeders were not competitors of the Club. Therefore, they did not have standing to pursue their Lanham Act claims. *See also Conte Bros. Auto., Inc. et al. v. Quaker State Slick 50*, 165 F.3d 221 (3d Cir. 1998) (retailers who only made retail sales of engine additives that competed with defendant's products lacked standing to challenge defendant's alleged false advertising of its products; standing held to be limited to direct competitors and surrogates for direct competitors).

Compare also In re Cult Awareness Network, 151 F.3d 605 (7th Cir. 1998), in which the Seventh Circuit refused to grant standing to the debtor in bankruptcy, the former user of the CULT AWARENESS NETWORK trademark, to object to the trustee's sale of that mark to a purchaser affiliated with the Church of Scientology, an organization often in conflict with the debtor. Noting that the debtor lacked the requisite pecuniary interest in the bankruptcy proceeding's outcome to have standing to object to a bankruptcy order, the Seventh Circuit opined that any Lanham Act concerns about deceptive use of the mark after its transfer would have to be addressed "when and if it arises, by aggrieved consumers, by the Cult Awareness Network's board of directors . . . or perhaps by state or federal authorities, but not in this bankruptcy proceeding."

Consumers generally have been held to lack standing under the Lanham Act. *See, e.g., Serbin v. Ziebart International Corp.*, 11 F.3d 1163 (3d Cir. 1992) (consumers lack standing to bring action for false advertising under § 43(a)), and the discussion on consumer standing in the Misrepresentation section notes in Chapter 9, *supra*. It also has been held that the Lanham Act provides no private remedy for consumers who seek to bring false advertising claims. In *Bacon v. Southwest Airlines Co.*, 997 F. Supp. 775 (N.D. Tex. 1998), involving an advertised ski vacation package, finding no express provision for a private cause of action in the false advertising prong of the Lanham Act, the court considered whether one was implicit. Concluding that "the commercial purpose of the Lanham Act and the existence of judicially and statutorily created state law remedies for misrepresentation" indicated that no private remedy for consumers was implicit either, the court dismissed that portion of plaintiff's complaint. Note, however, that consumers do have standing to contest advertising through the National Advertising Division of the Better Business Bureau, discussed in the Notes in § 8.02 on Misrepresentation. However, that entity relies on voluntary compliance with its orders (backed up by potential action by the FTC) and does not issue monetary awards.

10.02   Remedies

Introduction

The traditional remedies in trademark and unfair competition cases are injunctions, damages, profits and attorneys' fees. 15 U.S.C. §§ 1116–1118. Injunctive relief is ordinarily the principal remedy, and its terms are tailored to the facts of each case. Injunctions may include qualified prohibitions or requirements respecting trade dress, explanatory language, geographical and other limitations, and provisions as the court may deem just and equitable in the particular circumstances (*see, e.g.*, the sections on Geographical Terms and Surnames in Chapter 2). Usually, however, an unqualified injunction is needed to abate the wrong. Occasionally, the serious and immediately damaging consequences of the defendant's activities warrant preliminary injunctive relief. *See Meridian Mutual Insurance, infra.*

At common law and under the Lanham Act, monetary relief may also be awarded to compensate for harm to the plaintiff ("damages") and to reallocate any wrongful gains by the defendant ("profits"). Recovery of damages ordinarily encompasses injury to the plaintiff's goodwill, plaintiff's expenses in counteracting confusion, and plaintiff's lost profits caused by defendant's wrongful acts. In actions arising under the Lanham Act the court may, in its discretion, award treble damages. 15 U.S.C. § 1117. In 1975, the Lanham Act was amended to provide that "the court in exceptional cases may award attorney's fees to the prevailing party." *Id.*

Section 35(a), 15 U.S.C. § 1117(a), provides:

> When a violation of any right of the registrant of a mark registered in the Patent and Trademark Office, or a violation under section 1125(a), shall have been established in any civil action arising under this Act, the plaintiff shall be entitled, subject to the provisions of sections 1111 and 1114, and subject to the principles of equity, to recover (1) defendant's profits, (2) any damages sustained by the plaintiff, and (3) the costs of the action. The court shall assess such profits and damages or cause the same to be assessed under its direction. In assessing profits the plaintiff shall be required to prove defendant's sales only; defendant must prove all elements of costs or deduction claimed. In assessing damages the court may enter judgment, according to the circumstances of the case, for any sum above the amount found as actual damages, not exceeding three times such amount. If the court shall find that the amount of the recovery based on profits is either inadequate or excessive, the court may in its discretion enter judgment for such sum as the court shall find to be just, according to the circumstances of the case. Such sum in either of the above circumstances shall constitute compensation and not a penalty. The court in exceptional cases may award reasonable attorney fees to the prevailing party.

An award of an accounting of profits entitles the plaintiff to the defendant's profits from sales resulting from the wrongful use of an infringing mark. The defendant's sales are presumed to result from the wrongful use unless the defendant proves otherwise, and the gross revenue from sales is considered profit except for the actual costs of materials, production, and direct marketing expenses, or other justifiable deductions proved by defendant. *Id.* Profits are often awarded on a theory of unjust enrichment. *See* the *Alpo Petfoods* case, *infra*. Both damages and profits may be awarded, but the courts have usually avoided the potential for double recovery by excluding lost sales from the calculation of damages where profits are recovered. *Harper House, Inc. v. Thomas Nelson Publishers, Inc.*, 4 U.S.P.Q.2d 1897, 1910–1911 (C.D. Cal. 1987); *Polo Fashions, Inc. v. Extra Special Products, Inc.*, 208 U.S.P.Q. 421, 427 (S.D.N.Y. 1980). *See also Aero Products Int'l v. Intex Rec. Corp.*, 466 F.3d 1000 (Fed. Cir. 2006) (jury award of damages for patent and trademark infringement created impermissible double recovery where both "flowed from the same operative facts: sales of the infringing Intex mattresses").

An injunction prohibiting further use of a mark will prevent the damage of future confusion, but it will neither compensate for the damages caused by infringement nor further the worthy end of destroying the incentive to infringe. Compare the relief afforded in FTC cases discussed in Chapter 10, *infra*.

Injunctive Relief

PERFECT FIT INDUSTRIES, INC. v. ACME QUILTING CO., INC.
646 F.2d 800 (2ᵈ Cir. 1981)

KEARSE, CIRCUIT JUDGE

* * *

Plaintiff Perfect Fit Industries, Inc., and defendant Acme Quilting Co., Inc., are manufacturers of mattress pads. In 1976, Perfect Fit introduced a new variety of mattress cover that it called "BedSack"; this new product was highly successful. Shortly thereafter, Acme began to market a comparable cover called "BedMate." In packaging their respective products, both firms employed printed pieces of cardboard, called J-boards, that bend over the end of the packaged product so that part of the board is visible to buyers whether the packages are laid end-to-end on a table or stacked on a shelf. In designing its own J-boards, Acme deliberately copied the design successfully employed by Perfect Fit on its J-board.

In April 1977, Perfect Fit sued Acme, alleging that Acme's J-board infringed Perfect Fit's common law rights in its trade dress and constituted a false designation of origin in violation of § 43(a) of the Lanham Act, 15 U.S.C. § 1125(a) (1976) . . . .

. . . We [previously] reversed the judgment dismissing Perfect Fit's complaint and remanded the action for entry of an injunction [under New York common law] "against further use of the offending J-boards by Acme." *Perfect Fit Industries, Inc. v. Acme Quilting Co.*, 618 F.2d 950, 955 (2ᵈ Cir. 1980).

On remand, Perfect Fit submitted to the district court a proposed order . . . to (1) enjoin Acme's "use of the trade dress exemplified by "Plaintiff's Exhibits 2 and 3, and any trade dress which is substantially similar thereto"; (2) require Acme to deliver to plaintiff's counsel, for destruction, all material in Acme's possession or control "which comprises and/or illustrates the trade dress exemplified [by] Plaintiff's Exhibits 2 and 3, and any trade dress which is substantially similar thereto"; and (3) require Acme, within fifteen days of entry of the order, to send a letter to customers and other persons to whom Acme had within the preceding six months distributed "any package inserts of the type exemplified by Plaintiff's Exhibits 2 and 3, and any trade dress which is substantially similar thereto"; the letter was to state that Acme had "been enjoined from use of package inserts of the type exemplified by Plaintiff's Exhibits 2 and 3, photographs of which" were to be enclosed in the letter, and to request the return of such package inserts to Acme.

*   *   *

On May 19, 1980, the district court entered its injunctive order, in the form requested by Perfect Fit . . . and issued an opinion stating its reasons for granting the injunction. The order thus enjoined Acme from using the offending trade dress immediately and directed Acme to surrender to Perfect Fit's counsel all offending J-boards and other materials in its possession and to send the recall letter to each of Acme's customers by June 3, 1980.

*   *   *

We turn first to the propriety of the recall provision of the district court's May 19 order. The recall provision is an unusual, and perhaps unprecedented, remedy for a violation of New York's law of unfair competition. Nonetheless, we conclude that the imposition of a recall requirement is well within the district court's broad powers as a court of equity, and that the district court properly exercised these powers in the present case.

*   *   *

We conclude that this was an appropriate case for the exercise of the court's power to require a recall. The district court found that Acme had intentionally copied Perfect Fit's trade dress, and on appeal we held that, as a matter of law, Acme's trade dress was likely to cause confusion among customers, *see* 618 F.2d at 954–55. Acme's infringing trade dress was therefore likely to divert customers from Perfect Fit's product to Acme's. Particularly because the first appeal had prolonged the litigation and therefore increased the probable injury to Perfect Fit, the district court was entirely justified in fashioning swift and complete relief for Perfect Fit. The recall procedure would naturally hasten the removal of the offending materials from public view and therefore seek to end quickly the injury to Perfect Fit.

Acme's argument that the recall provision is unduly burdensome is unpersuasive. Of course, a district court should carefully consider the likely burden and expense of a recall before it imposes the remedy. In some circumstances the imposition of a recall may be unduly onerous, as where the defendant's products are widely distributed and particularly expensive to ship. Or the probable benefit to the plaintiff from a recall may not outweigh the burden to the defendant in some cases even if that burden is relatively light. These are matters to be weighed in the first instance by the district court, and we see no abuse here of the district court's discretion. Nothing in the record developed below suggests that appropriate consideration was not given to these questions or indicates that Acme would suffer unduly under the May 19 order. The order did not require Acme to take extensive action to retrieve the J-boards. The company need only have written its customers requesting a return of the boards and paid the cost of the return for those customers who complied . . . . Acme's evidence concerning the cost of this program was wholly speculative and was founded on the unwarranted assumption that every person contacted would return not only the J-boards, as requested, but the mattress covers as well. Given the flimsiness of Acme's showing of burden, we can hardly say that the district judge abused her discretion in granting the remedy.

Finally, although our opinion in the first appeal referred to an injunction "against further use" of the offending J-boards, 618 F.2d at 955, nothing in our opinion or mandate purported to restrict the district court's discretion to fashion an appropriate decree. We find that the May 19 order was a proper exercise of that discretion.

MERIDIAN MUTUAL INSURANCE v. MERIDIAN INSURANCE GROUP, INC.
128 F.3d 1111 (7th Cir. 1997)

BAUER, J.

* * *

The cast of characters in the present case is as follows: Plaintiff/appellant Meridian Mutual Insurance Company ("plaintiff") is an insurance company headquartered in Indianapolis, Indiana, which currently offers both personal and commercial lines of insurance. This includes homeowner's insurance, car insurance, and the like. Defendant/appellee Meridian Insurance Group, Inc. ("defendant") is an Illinois-based insurance broker engaged in the sale of group life and health insurance plans. Defendant David Schwimmer is president and 97% shareholder of Meridian Insurance Group, and defendant Robert Schwimmer owns the remaining three percent of the company. With these opening credits behind us, we jump into the thick of the plot.

Plaintiff has been engaged in the insurance business since 1953 using the name "Meridian." Plaintiff also holds a registration on the term "MERIDIAN," on the Principal Register, for "underwriting life, health, property and casualty insurance" in International Class 36. The mark was registered on January 31, 1978 and has become incontestible under the Lanham Trademark Act, 15 U.S.C. § 1065. Plaintiff markets its insurance in nine Midwestern states (Illinois, Indiana, Iowa, Kentucky, Michigan, Ohio, Pennsylvania, Tennessee, and Wisconsin) through independent insurance agents — that is, through agents who sell policies from a number of different companies.

On July 22, 1996, Robert Schwimmer filed the articles of incorporation for the defendant in Illinois, adopting a corporate name containing the word "Meridian." This name had been conceived by David Schwimmer, who at the time had no knowledge of the plaintiff's existence. Before incorporating, the defendants had run a corporate name search in Illinois and several contiguous states. This search turned up the fact that "Meridian" could not be used by the defendants in Indiana or California because the name was already being used in some manner in the insurance industry. At any rate, defendant was issued its articles of incorporation by the State of Illinois, and began its brokering of group health and life insurance policies in November 1996. Defendant's sales territory is limited to the Chicago metropolitan area, and it targets as clients only businesses employing between 20 and 1,000 persons.

In December, 1996, plaintiff discovered the defendants' use of the name "Meridian" when it was denied a certificate of authority to do business in Illinois. On January 31, 1997, plaintiff filed suit against the defendants, alleging that their use of "Meridian" constituted service mark infringement, unfair competition, and a deceptive trade practice. The plaintiff also sought a preliminary injunction, which was denied by the district court after a hearing on the merits on February 20, 1997 . . . .

In reviewing a district court's grant or denial of a preliminary injunction, we review the court's findings of fact for clear error, its balancing of factors for an abuse of discretion, and its legal conclusions *de novo*. [Citation omitted]. When considering a motion for a preliminary injunction, a district court must weigh a number of factors. First, it must determine whether the moving party has demonstrated 1) some likelihood of prevailing on the merits, and 2) an inadequate remedy at law and irreparable harm if the injunction does not issue. If the party has done so, the court must next consider 3) the irreparable harm the nonmovant will suffer if the injunction is granted balanced against the irreparable harm to the movant if relief is denied, and 4) the effect granting or denying the injunction will have on nonparties (the "public interest."). *Id.* at 1291. An examination of these factors reveals that the district court erroneously found that there was no likelihood of confusion in this case and that its denial of the plaintiff's motion for a preliminary injunction must be reversed.

1. Likelihood of Prevailing on the Merits

In order to prevail on its motion for a preliminary injunction, the plaintiff first needed to demonstrate that it has a likelihood of success on the merits of its case. In the preliminary injunction context, a "likelihood of success" exists if the party seeking injunctive relief shows that it has a "better than negligible" chance of succeeding on the merits . . . . In the trademark/service mark/unfair competition field, the movant shows a likelihood of success by establishing that 1) he has a protectable mark, and 2) that a "likelihood of confusion" exists between the marks or products of the parties. *International Kennel*, 846 F.2d at 1079, citing *A.J. Canfield Co. v. Vess Beverages, Inc.*, 796 F.2d 903, 906 (7th Cir. 1986) (other citations omitted). It is undisputed in this case that the plaintiff has registered the mark "Meridian" with regard to at least some aspects of the insurance field; therefore, we need only turn our attention to the district court's determination that there was no likelihood of confusion by the parties' concurrent use of the mark "Meridian."

* * *

[The court proceeds to analyze the seven factors traditionally considered by the Seventh Circuit in determining likelihood of confusion, including the evidence of actual confusion].

. . . [W]hether a consumer is confused when he calls a company to buy an insurance policy or when he calls to make a claim under an existing policy is immaterial. The importance . . . rests in the fact that confusion leads to an injury to one of the parties, an outcome which is no less present in the service context than in the sales context. A difference certainly exists in the type of injury incurred: in the sales context, actual confusion can lead to lost profits, whereas in the service context, such as the present case, the injury may be to goodwill or reputation . . . . In this case, the testimony shows that at least one of the callers who accidentally reached the defendant was angry, and that three of the callers were never informed by the defendant of their error. This confusion had the potential to injure the plaintiff's goodwill and reputation with its customers, and the district court erred in once again considering only the sales realm and not the service realm . . . .

* * *

In sum, the following factors support a likelihood of confusion in this case: the similarity in appearance and suggestion of the marks; the area and manner of concurrent use; the degree of care likely to be exercised by consumers; and the presence of actual confusion. Weighed against the other factors [similarity of products, strength of plaintiff's mark and defendant's intent], we believe that the plaintiff has been able to establish that a likelihood of confusion exists in this case, and the district court was erroneous in finding otherwise. As such, the plaintiff's motion for a preliminary injunction was erroneously denied, and we must reverse. However, the finding of a likelihood of confusion does not end our inquiry; three factors still necessitate examination before a preliminary injunction can be granted or refused. Because the district court found that no likelihood of confusion existed, it did not reach these remaining requirements. The record, however, contains information from which we can assess these factors, the task to which we now turn.

2. Inadequate Remedy/Irreparable Harm

The plaintiff next needed to establish that it has an inadequate remedy at law and would suffer irreparable harm if a preliminary injunction does not issue. As we discussed above, the plaintiff has suffered injury to its goodwill through the defendant's use of the name "Meridian." Such damage can constitute irreparable harm for which a plaintiff has no adequate remedy at law. *See Gateway Eastern Ry. Co. v. Terminal R.R. Ass'n of St. Louis*, 35 F.3d 1134, 1140 (7th Cir. 1994) ("showing injury to goodwill can constitute irreparable harm that is not compensable by an award of money damages.") (quoting *Reinders Bros., Inc. v. Rain Bird Eastern Sales Corp.*, 627 F.2d 44, 53 & n.7 (7th Cir.

1980)). The record demonstrates that the plaintiff has satisfied this element and an injunction appears proper.

* * *

3.   Balance of Harms

The third factor in assessing the propriety of an injunction is a balancing of the harms; that is, the irreparable harm the nonmovant will suffer if an injunction is granted is weighed against the irreparable damage the movant will suffer if it is not. In its Rule 59(e) motion, the plaintiff noted that "[d]efendants' method of developing a client base does not depend upon advertising in the public forum," since the defendants generate new business from calling prospective clients and not from advertisements directed to the public at large. Rec. Doc. 27 at 6. In its response, the defendants did not refute these assertions, but argued in a conclusory fashion (and without specific support) that "[t]he scope of the requested injunction would adversely impact defendants in a significant manner." . . . Without elaborating any reasons for his decision, the district judge denied the plaintiff's Rule 59 motion . . .

This amounts to an abuse of discretion, and the district judge should have considered the balance of harms in this case. Our examination of the record shows that the plaintiff's contention in its 59(e) motion are correct, and that the defendants would suffer no (or, at the most, very minimal) irreparable injury if they were enjoined from using "Meridian" in the general public forum. David Schwimmer testified that the defendant contacts prospective clients primarily through "cold calls" to companies of a certain size in the Chicago metropolitan area. The defendants even admit in their response to the 59(c) motion that they do not presently use billboard, newspaper, or broadcast advertising, although they do have a listing in the phone book and a site on the internet. A limited injunction . . . . would cause little harm to the defendants. On the other hand, as outlined above, the plaintiff has suffered, and runs the risk of continuing to suffer, irreparable damage to its goodwill by the defendants' use of the name "Meridian." The harm to the plaintiff if no injunction is issued therefore outweighs any harm to the defendants if one is entered, and this factor weighs in support of granting the plaintiff its requested relief. The district court's failure to consider this factor was an abuse of discretion.

* * *

4.   Public Interest

The final factor to be considered in conjunction with a preliminary injunction is the public interest, which is "the effect that granting or denying the injunction will have on nonparties." *Grossbaum*, 100 F.3d at 1291. The record demonstrates that a limited injunction would not adversely affect the public interest in this case, and this factor is not influential in our determination. As the plaintiff states in its 59(e) brief, the issuance of a limited preliminary injunction will, in essence, maintain the status quo in this case and will prevent, rather than cause, harm to the general public through the elimination of potential confusion. However, the record does not demonstrate that non-parties will be greatly affected by an injunction, and this factor is not of great import in the present case.

In sum, therefore, the plaintiff has demonstrated a likelihood of success on the merits, has shown that it has suffered (and may continue to suffer) irreparable injury from the defendant's use of "Meridian" for which there is no adequate remedy at law, and has shown that the harm it will suffer without an injunction outweighs the irreparable harm to the defendants if an injunction is issued. As such, we find that plaintiff has established that a preliminary injunction is appropriate in this case, and that the district court erred in not issuing one. Therefore, we reverse the district court's denial of preliminary injunction relief and remand this case to the district court with instructions to enter a preliminary injunction prohibiting the defendants from using the name "Meridian" in any public forum, including but not limited to telephone directories, internet pages, billboards, broadcast advertisements, and newspaper advertisements. The injunction shall not prohibit the defendants from carrying on their direct telephone solicitation of clients within the defendant's present operating territory.

Conclusion

For the reasons set forth above, the district court's denial of a preliminary injunction is REVERSED, and this case is REMANDED with instructions to the district court to enter a preliminary injunction against the defendants consistent with this opinion . . . .

Notes on Injunctive Relief

1. Types of Injunctions

In *Ebay, Inc. v. MercExchange L.L.C.*, 547 U.S. 388 (2006), a patent decision that may be followed in trademark and unfair competition cases, the Supreme Court clarified that patent holders seeking a permanent injunction must meet the same four factors applied in most non-patent cases, and reconfirmed those factors, *i.e.*, (1) irreparable harm; (2) inadequacy of legal remedies like monetary damages; (3) the balance of hardships between the rights owner and the infringer warrants an injunction; and (4) a permanent injunction would not harm the public interest.

Injunctive relief can take a variety of forms. A defendant simply may be enjoined from any further infringing or deceptive activity, or may be asked to take affirmative steps to prevent further deception. *See, e.g., Perfect Fit Industries, Inc. v. Acme Quilting Co., supra*, in which the lower court's order that defendant recall, at its expense, the offending materials was found to be a proper exercise of that court's discretion, and *Moore Business Forms, Inc. v. Seidenberg*, 229 U.S.P.Q. 821 (W.D. La. 1985), where defendant was ordered to establish a telephone intercept operator to answer defendant's telephone and advise callers of plaintiff's telephone number. *See also Playskool, Inc. v. Product Development Group, Inc.*, 699 F. Supp. 1056, 1063 (E.D.N.Y. 1988) (defendant that falsely advertised its toy construction set "attaches to" plaintiff's set ordered to recall its products because they might make structures unsafe for children); *Tripledge Products, Inc. v. Whitney Resources, Ltd.*, 735 F. Supp. 1154, 1166–1167 (E.D.N.Y. 1988) (defendant ordered to refund money to customers who ordered falsely advertised windshield wipers); Note, *Trademark Law: Equity's Role in Unfair Competition Cases*, 13 U. HAWAII L. REV. 137 (1991). *Compare Attrezzi, LLC v. Maytag Corp.*, 436 F.3d 32, 43 (1st Cir. 2006) (affirming that defendant could have twelve months to sell off its inventory of products bearing the infringing mark; "there is no indication that the risk of harm to Attrezzi LLC's service mark is likely to increase appreciably because of the additional 12 months of Maytag's competing use").

In domain name cases under the Anti-Cybersquatting Consumer Protection Act, 15 U.S.C. § 1125(d), a court may order that the domain name be transferred to the plaintiff. *See, e.g., Virtual Works, Inc. v. Volkswagen of America, Inc.*, 238 F.3d 264 (4th Cir. 2001) (transferring defendant's "vwnet" domain to the owner of trademark rights in "VW" for automobiles). Transfer to a prevailing plaintiff is not mandatory, however. In *Interstellar Starship Servs. v. Epix, Inc.*, 304 F.3d 936 (9th Cir. 2002), the defendant was enjoined from using the domain name epix.com and the associated website in a manner likely to cause confusion with plaintiff's EPIX mark, but the court declined, under the circumstances, to transfer the domain name to plaintiff.

Section 37 of the Lanham Act, 15 U.S.C. § 1119, provides that in any civil action involving a registered trade mark the court may order the cancellation of a registration. This power in the courts to "rectify the register" provides an important additional remedy in a trademark infringement action.

The Lanham Act's § 42 (15 U.S.C. § 1124) provides for deposit of copies of one's trademark registration with the Bureau of Customs and Border Protection which will then take steps to prohibit importation of merchandise bearing copies or simulations of the mark. *See* Chapter 3, *supra*; Kuhn, *Remedies Available at Customs for Infringement of A Registered Trademark*, 70 TRADEMARK REP. 387 (1980).

2. Contempt

If a defendant attempts to evade the effect of an injunction, a contempt proceeding may then be necessary. *See, e.g., John Zink Co. v. Zink*, 241 F.3d 1256 (10th Cir. 2001) (commercial use of defendant's surname in competition with plaintiff's constituted contempt; attorneys' fees awarded to plaintiff); *Wolfard Glassblowing Co. v. Vanbragt*, 118 F.3d 1320 (9th Cir. 1997) (affirming that defendant was in contempt in trade dress case despite product modifications; "[t]he question is no longer trademark infringement; it is whether [Vanbragt's] new lamp is a colorable imitation of Wolfard's lamp" in violation of the judgment, which is "consistent with the rule that an infringer must keep a fair distance from the 'margin line' "). *Howard Johnson Co. v. Khimani*, 892 F.2d 1512, 1515 (11th Cir. 1990) (ex-franchisee who had been enjoined from using HOWARD JOHNSON'S service marks held in contempt for using name H.J. INNS, a name they admittedly chose to "get as close to Howard Johnson as you could without infringing"); *See also Service Ideas Inc. v. Traex Corp.*, 846 F.2d 1118, 1124 (7th Cir. 1988) (defendant's post-injunction design for its beverage server held "too close to the boundary"). *Cf. Jerry's Famous Deli, Inc. v. Papanicolau*, 72 U.S.P.Q.2d 1523 (9th Cir. 2004) (contempt award of defendant's profits remanded for failure to supply a proper rationale for the amount of the award).

The difficulties of bringing recalcitrant defendants within the scope of an effective injunction are discussed in *Scandia Down Corp. v. Euroquilt, Ltd.*, 772 F.2d 1423 (7th Cir. 1985), and *Taylor Wine Co., Inc. v. Bully Hill Vineyards, Inc.*, 590 F.2d 701 (2[d] Cir. 1978). *See also Abbott Labs. v. Unlimited Beverages, Inc.*, 218 F.3d 1238 (11th Cir. 2000) (defendant "cannot simply remove the 'Naturalyte' name from the enjoined bottle and market the same solution in the same bottle through private retailer in order to bypass the consent judgment . . . .. A consent judgment need not recite every possible way in which a violation might occur when the proscribed conduct is readily ascertainable to an ordinary person"). *Compare Unelko Corp. v. Prestone Prod. Corp.*, 116 F.3d 237 (7th Cir. 1997), where the parties previously had settled a case with the defendant agreeing to "market" the accused yellow bottle trade dress for its water repellant only by encasing each bottle in its own box. In this suit for breach of the agreement, defendant unsuccessfully argued that "market" only meant "shipping", and that it still could feature the trade dress in advertising. The appellate court affirmed that "market" was not an ambiguous term and encompassed the breaching advertising.

3. Voluntary Discontinuance

It is within the discretion of the court to decide that voluntary discontinuance renders the need for an injunction moot. *Blau v. YMI Jeanswear, Inc.*, 129 Fed. Appx. 385 (9th Cir. 2005) (unpub'd) (a request for injunctive relief is mooted where "the reform of the defendant [is] irrefutably demonstrated and total", quoting an earlier Ninth Circuit decision); *Camel Hair & Cashmere Institute, Inc. v. Associated Dry Goods Corp.*, 799 F.2d 6 (1st Cir. 1986) (preliminary injunction motion denied); *Schutt Mfg. Co. v. Riddell, Inc.*, 673 F.2d 202, 207 (7th Cir. 1982). This is true whether discontinuance occurred before or after the suit was filed, although the discretion will usually be resolved against the infringer if discontinuance came after filing. *Scotch Whiskey Ass'n v. Barton Distilling Co.*, 489 F.2d 809 (7th Cir. 1973). *See Mendez v. Saks & Co.*, 485 F.2d 1355, 1375 (2[d] Cir. 1973), in which the court ruled: "It is elementary that a court of equity will not enjoin one from doing what he is not attempting and does not intend to do"; and *Johnny Carson Apparel, Inc. v. Zeeman Manufacturing Co.*, 203 U.S.P.Q. 585, 591 (N.D. Ga. 1978), in which the court stated that "[a]s the acts and practices complained of by plaintiff have been stopped, and the defendants have made clear that they do not intend to resume such, it appears to the court that there is not basis upon which an injunction could issue." *See also Seven-Up Co. v. Coca-Cola Co.*, 86 F.3d 1379 (5th Cir. 1996) (denying plaintiff's request to permanently enjoin defendant, Coca-Cola, from using a misleading sales presentation because, among other reasons, "[n]othing in the record suggests that Coca-Cola has used this presentation since 1991"). *Compare John T. Lloyd Laboratories, Inc. v. Lloyd Brothers Pharmacists*, 131 F.2d 703 (6th Cir. 1942), in which the court ruled: "The mere fact . . . use was discontinued by them before the commencement of this action is no guarantee that they may not resume its use should the injunction be dissolved. If appellants have no such wrongful intent, no injury ensues to them from maintenance of the bar." To similar effect is *Polo Fashions, Inc. v. Dick Bruhn, Inc.*, 793 F.2d 1132 (9th Cir. 1986). The decision generally turns on the court's belief as to the likelihood of repeated misconduct in the future. What factors should influence a court in determining whether an injunction should issue after voluntary discontinuance by an infringer? Should a distinction be made between an isolated instance of unfair competition and a case where several acts are established? Is an infringer's good faith adoption significant?

4. Modification

What bases might there be for modifying an injunction after a passage of years? *Compare Humble Oil & Refining Co. v. American Oil Co.*, 405 F.2d 803 (8th Cir. 1969), *cert. denied*, 395 U.S. 905 (1969) (where a claim of substantial and unforeseeable change of circumstances or oppressive hardship was rejected) with *King-Seeley Thermos Co. V. Aladding Industries, Inc.*, 418 F.2d 31, 35 (2[d] Cir. 1969) ("While changes in fact or in law afford the clearest bases for altering an injunction, the power of equity has repeatedly been recognized as extending also to cases where a better appreciation of the facts in light of experience indicates that the decree is not properly adapted to accomplishing its purposes.") Where plaintiff had established superior rights in "Patsy's" for pasta sauce, but the parties' restaurants previously had co-existed under their "Patsy's" names in New York for decades, the court modified the injunction to allow defendant to continue its restaurant use of the name "Patsy's Pizzeria", and to make "some, although very limited" use of that name on pasta sauce. Among other things, the use "must be a minor component of the labeling", and "must use the name only to identify the maker or distributor of the product." *Patsy's Brand, Inc. v. I.O.B. Realty, Inc.*, 317 F.3d 209 (2[d] Cir. 2003). *Cf. Pimentel & Sons Guitar Makers, Inc. v. Pimentel*, 477 F.3d 1151 (10th Cir. 2007) (because lower court only clarified that the original injunction required defendant to use the disclaimer with *any* business name, not just his guitar-making business, this was not a modification and there was no appellate jurisdiction).

5. Disclaimers

a) Generally

Courts sometimes favor the use of disclaimers in close cases. *See R.J. Toomey Co. v. Toomey*, 683 F. Supp. 873 (D. Mass. 1988) (son required to disclaim association with his father's competing business); *Gucci v. Gucci Shops, Inc.*, 699 F.Supp. 916 (S.D.N.Y. 1988) (Paolo Gucci required to disclaim association from the Gucci leather goods empire).

Consumer studies, however, have indicated that disclaimers are often ineffective in reducing the likelihood of confusion. *See* the discussion in *Home Box Office, Inc. v. Showtime/Movie Channel, Inc.*, 832 F.2d 1311, 1315–16 (2[d] Cir. 1987) (placing the burden on the infringer to produce evidence that the proposed disclaimer would significantly reduce the likelihood of confusion) and *Ford Motor Co. v. Ford Financial Solutions*, 103 F. Supp. 2d 1126, 1128 (N.D. Iowa 2000) (rejecting disclaimer as a remedy). *Cf. Weight Watchers Int'l v. Luigino's, Inc.*, 423 F.3d 137 (2ᵈ Cir. 2005) (rejecting disclaimer; "[w]here, as here, an infringer attempts to avoid a substantial likelihood of confusion by adding a disclaimer, it must establish the disclaimer's effectiveness"); *Westchester Media v. PRL USA Holdings, Inc.*, 214 F.3d 658, 673 (5ᵗʰ Cir. 2000)(despite recognition of cases holding disclaimers to be ineffective, this "unique" and "unusual" case in which, among other things, both magazines derived their titles from the sport polo, was remanded to district court for reconsideration of whether disclaimer remedy might be effective); *Soltex Polymer Corp. v. Fortex Industries*, 832 F.2d 1325, 1330 (2ᵈ Cir. 1987) (citing *Home Box Office*, but noting it is within the discretion of the district court to permit use with a disclaimer where likelihood of confusion is "far less than substantial"). In *ProFitness Physical Therapy Ctr. v. Pro-Fit Orthopedic & Sports Physical Therapy*, 314 F.3d 62, 70-71 (2ᵈ Cir. 2002), citing decisions like *Home Box Office*, the court questioned generally the use of disclaimers as remedies, but noted that "disclaimers might be effective to cure a minimal or moderate amount of confusion". It remanded the case to the district court to "determine the specific level of confusion and fashion relief accordingly". In some instances the mandated use of a disclaimer may even benefit the plaintiff. In *Promatek Indus. v. Equitrac Corp.*, 300 F.3d 808 (7ᵗʰ Cir. 2002), the court affirmed a preliminary injunction mandating use of a disclaimer on defendant's website, despite defendant's objection that the disclaimer unfairly informed consumers of its competitor (plaintiff) and encouraged them to access plaintiff's website.

In *International Kennel Club, Inc. v. Mighty Star, Inc.*, 846 F.2d 1079, 1093 (7th Cir. 1988), the court affirmed the lower court's refusal to order a disclaimer remedy, stating "plaintiff's reputation and good will should not be forever dependent on the effectiveness of fine print disclaimers often ignored by consumers." In *Basile S.p.A. v. Basile*, 899 F.2d 35, 37 (D.C. Cir. 1990), the district court had ordered that the following disclaimer be used on defendant's watches:

> BASILE watches emanate exclusively from Diffusione Basile de Francesco Basile & Co., S.A.S. in Venice, Italy. Diffusione Basile is devoted solely to the manufacture and sale of fine watches throughout the world.

In vacating, the Appellate Court found that "common sense" dictated that the watches will still be known as "Basile watches" under the lower court's injunction. *Id.* at 37. "The disclaimer is inadequate because it uses the appellant's protected name: Basile. The inclusion of 'Venezia' in the court's order would not help American consumers disassociate the watch with appellant's watch manufactured in Milan." *Id.* at 38. *Compare Ty, Inc. v. The Jones Group, Inc.*, 237 F.3d 891, 899 (7ᵗʰ Cir. 2001) (the use of "additional marks on the Beanie Racers may not reduce the likelihood of confusion among consumers because they still may believe that [plaintiff] licensed, approved or authorized [their] production"), and the discussion on the use of house marks in Chapter 7. *See also Versace v. Alfredo Versace*, 213 Fed. Appx. 34 (2ᵈ Cir. 2007) (changing injunction to outright ban on defendant's use of his last name in connection with "a commercial activity anywhere in the world" after defendant failed to comply with disclaimer remedy); the *Dobbs* case in Chapter 2, *supra*; *University of Georgia Athletic Ass'n v. Laite*, 756 F.2d 1535, 1547 (11ᵗʰ Cir. 1985) (rejecting disclaimer defense); *Charles of Ritz Group, Ltd. v. Quality King Distributors*, 832 F.2d 1317, 1324 (2ᵈ Cir. 1987) (following *Home Box Office, supra*, in rejecting disclaimer remedy); Palladino, *Disclaimers Before and After HBO v. Showtime*, 82 TRADEMARK REP. 203 (1992); Comment, *Injunctive Relief for Trademark Infringement - The Second Circuit Misses The Mark: Home Box Office v. Showtime/The Movie Channel*, 62 ST. JOHN'S L. REV. 286 (1988).

b) Disclaimers and Initial Interest Confusion

Disclaimers also may be ineffective in initial interest confusion cases. The use of a domain name that is confusingly similar to the plaintiff's mark, or metatags that incorporate that mark, can create a likelihood of initial interest confusion, as discussed in previous chapters. This is sometimes compared to "bait and switch" tactic, and therefore is actionable even though, after reaching defendant's website, the consumer may subsequently learn that the products or services are not those of the plaintiff. As a consequence, any disclaimer of affiliation with plaintiff on defendant's website would be irrelevant in such cases, because it would not dispel the initial interest confusion that unlawfully brought the consumer to defendant's website in the first place. *See, e.g., Australian Gold, Inc. v., Hatfield*, 436 F.3d 1228 (10th Cir. 2006) ("'a defendant's website disclaimer, proclaiming its real source and disavowing any connection with its competitor, cannot prevent the damage of initial interest confusion, which will already have been done by the misdirection of consumers looking for the plaintiff's website'"); *DaimlerChrysler v. Net, Inc.*, 338 F.3d 201 (6th Cir. 2004) (rejecting defendant's argument that a website disclaimer would be sufficient and transferring the domain name to the plaintiff); *Pacaar Inc. v. Telescan Techs., L.L.C.*, 319 F.3d 243, 253 (6th Cir. 2003) ("A disclaimer disavowing affiliation with the trademark owner read by a consumer after reaching the website comes too late"). *Compare, however, Taubman v. Webfeats*, 319 F.3d 770 (6th Cir. 2003). There plaintiff owned the mark "The Shops at Willow Bend" and sued defendant over its registered domain name "shopsatwillowbend.com." Defendant conducted no commercial activities on the website. In that context, the Court denied preliminary relief and approved defendant's use of a disclaimer and a hyperlink to plaintiff's webite to redirect errant customers. "Here, a misplaced customer simply has to click his mouse to be redirected to [plaintiff's] site" and "[defendant's] website and its disclaimer actually serve to redirect customers to [defendant's] site that might otherwise be lost."

6. Preliminary Injunctions

Under what circumstances should a preliminary injunction be granted? *See, e.g., Ty, Inc. v. The Jones Group, Inc.*, 237 F.3d 891 (7th Cir. 2000) ("Beanie Racers" for racing car plush toys preliminarily enjoined based on plaintiff's rights in "Beanie Babies" for plush toys; defendant's claim of great irreparable harm if enjoined "rings hollow" where it voluntarily assumed the risk, knowing "of Ty's product and the possible confusion that could be created"); *Scotts Co. v. United Industries Corp.*, 305 F.3d 264 (4th Cir. 2002) (sales of defendant's anti-crabgrass control products at issue were seasonal, negating any "actual and imminent injury" and making preliminary relief unnecessary); *Federal Express Corp. v. Federal Expresso, Inc.*, 201 F.3d 168 (2[d] Cir. 2000) (while owner of famous FEDERAL EXPRESS mark "may well ultimately prevail on its dilution claim" against owner of FEDERAL ESPRESSO coffee shops, denial of preliminary injunction affirmed, where defendant operated only two shops and "irreparable harm [is] not imminent"). *See also Dialogo, LLC v. Santiago-Bauza*, 425 F.3d 1 (1st Cir. 2005) (preliminary relief denied where one joint venture partner sued another for using a trademark after the business purportedly was closed down; there was no presumption of irreparable injury as the issues were instead business and profit-related). What weight, if any, should the public interest be given? *See Meridian Mutual Insurance, supra; Tom Doherty Assocs. v. Saban Entertainment*, 60 F.3d 27 (2[d] Cir. 1995); *First Brands Corp. v. Fred Meyer, Inc.*, 809 F.2d 1378 (9th Cir. 1987); Kessler, Sterne & Dillon, *Preliminary Injunctions in Patent and Trademark Cases*, 26 Trial 42 (1990).

A court can order an asset freeze as part of preliminary relief. *See FTC v. Harry*, 2004 U.S. Dist. LEXIS 15588 (N.D. Ill. 2004) (in a case involving health claims in Internet spam, among other things, the court entered a temporary restraining order with asset freeze, finding that there was good cause to believe that the defendant was likely to continue engaging in violations of federal anti-spam laws unless he was immediately restrained, and the court's ability to grant effective final relief to consumers required the asset freeze).

Monetary Relief

The types of monetary relief available include: (1) plaintiff's lost profits; (2) actual damages other than plaintiff's lost profits, e.g. injury to goodwill; (3) defendant's profits; (4) money for corrective advertising; (5) a reasonable royalty; (6) punitive damages (under state law); and (7) attorneys' fees. Plaintiffs may be awarded monetary relief under other theories of injury where a sufficient nexus with defendant's conduct is shown.

1. Damages

ALADDIN MFG. CO. v. MANTLE LAMP CO.
116 F.2d 708 (7th Cir. 1941)

LINDLEY, DISTRICT JUDGE.

* * *

Under the act covering trademarks, Title 15 U.S.C.A. Section 99, plaintiff was "entitled to recover, in addition to the profits to be accounted for by the defendant, the damages. . . ." The procedure is analogous to that in patent cases. *Hamilton-Brown Shoe Co. v. Wolf Bros. & Co.*, 240 U.S. 251. Before passage of the act of 1870, 16 Stat. 270, two remedies were open to the owner of a patent whose rights had been infringed, and he had his election between the two. He might proceed in equity and recover the profits which the infringer had made by the unlawful use of his invention, the infringer in such a suit being regarded as trustee of the owner of the patent as respects such gains and profits; or he might sue at law, in which case he would be entitled to recover, as damages, compensation for the pecuniary injury suffered by the infringement; the measure of damages in such case being not what the defendants had gained but what the plaintiff had lost. When the suit is at law, the measure of damages remains unchanged to the present time, the rule still being that the verdict must be for the actual damages sustained by the plaintiff. Damages of a compensatory character may also be allowed in equity where the gains and profits made by the respondent are not sufficient to compensate for the injury sustained. Gains and profits are still the proper measure of damages in equity suits, except in cases where the injury sustained by the infringement is plainly more than the aggregate of what was made by the respondent, in which event the provision is that the complainant shall be entitled to recover, in addition to the profits to be accounted for by the respondent, the damages he has sustained thereby. *Birdsall v. Collidge*, 93 U.S. 64; *Tilghman v. Proctor*, 125 U.S. 136, at pages 144, 145.

In law the infringer "is regarded as a mere wrong-doer compelled to make compensation for the injury he has inflicted." In equity he has a double character, being first treated as a species of agent or trustee practising the invention for the benefit of its true owner and obliged to pay to him the profits of the enterprise, and then, if, in the judgment of the court, the interests of the plaintiff so require, mulcted as a tort-feasor in a sum sufficient to redress the injury which the plaintiff has sustained." 3 Robinson on Patents, § 1050. In *Hamilton-Brown Shoe Co. v. Wolf Bros. & Co.*, 240 U.S. 251, at page 259, the court, dealing with unfair competition and infringement of a trademark, said: "In the courts of England, the rule seems to be that a party aggrieved must elect between damages and profits, and cannot have both. In this country, it is generally held that in a proper case both damages and profits may be awarded." *See also Child v. Boston & Fairhaven Iron Works, C.C.*, 19 F. 258, at page 259.

* * *

A tort feasor is liable for all consequences naturally resulting, all injuries actually flowing from his wrongful act, whether in fact anticipated or contemplated by him when his tortious act was committed. Recoverable damages, therefore, include compensation for all injury to appellant's business arising from wrongful acts committed by appellee, provided such injury was the natural and proximate result of the wrongful acts. *Fidelity & D. Co. v. Bucki & Son Lumber*, 189 U.S. 135. This includes injury to business standing or good will, loss of business, additional expenses incurred because of the tort and all other elements of injury to the business. 15 AMER. J. JUR. §§ 133, 134, 135, 136 and 138. These are the governing principles applying to compensatory damages.

Exemplary damages are allowed against a tort feasor whose acts are intentionally fraudulent, malicious, wilful or wanton. They have always been recoverable at common law. . . . [S]uch damages are allowed, as sometimes said, in the interest of society, not as compensatory damages but rather in addition thereto, or as elsewhere said, as compensation to the injured party for the wrong suffered, though incidentally they may operate by way of punishment. *Cairo & St. L. R. Co. v. Peoples*, 92 Ill. 97, 34 Am. Rep. 112. They are not a favorite in law, however, *Post v. Buck's Stove & Range Co.*, 8 Cir., 200 F. 918, 43 L.R.A.,N.S., 498; and are, therefore, to be allowed only with caution and confined within narrow limits. Whether damages be compensatory or exemplary, if unliquidated, when determined by the trier of facts, their propriety cannot be governed or measured by any precise yardstick. They must bear some reasonable relationship to the injury inflicted and the amount must rest largely in the discretion of the trier of facts, a discretion not to be arbitrarily exercised. Ordinarily this court will interfere only where it appears that an injustice has been done or it is clear that there has been error in law.

In the present case, there was direct proof that because of the fraudulent and wilful infringement and unfair competition of appellee, appellant incurred legal expenses aggregating $18,515.03. Counsel's fees necessitated by the tort have been said in some instances to be recoverable as a part of the compensatory damages and in other cases as a part of exemplary damages. As the master's finding of wilful and fraudulent conduct is sustained by the evidence, this sum was recoverable as compensatory damages had hence properly included in the amount recommended by him.

* * *

. . . Accordingly the master's report should be approved in the allowance of damages in the sum of $18,515.03 for costs and expenses incurred and in the reduced amount of $25,000 for all other damages. The total recovery should be: Gains and profits $56,626.08; Damages $43,515.03, or a total of $100,141.11.

BIG O TIRE DEALERS, INC. v. GOODYEAR TIRE & RUBBER COMPANY
561 F.2d 1365 (10th Cir. 1977)

LEWIS, CHIEF JUDGE

This civil action was brought by Big O Tire Dealers, Inc. ("Big O") asserting claims of unfair competition against The Goodyear Tire & Rubber Co. ("Goodyear") based upon false designation of origin under 15 U.S.C. § 1125(a) and common law trademark infringement. . . .

* * *

In the fall of 1973 Big O decided to identify two of its lines of private brand tires as "Big O Big Foot 60" and "Big O Big Foot 70." These names were placed on the sidewall of the respective tires in raised white letters. The first interstate shipment of these tires occurred in February 1974. Big O dealers began selling these tires to the public in April 1974. Big O did not succeed in registering "Big Foot" as a trademark with the United States Patent and Trademark Office.

In the last three months of 1973 Goodyear began making snowmobile replacement tracks using the trademark "Bigfoot." From October 1973 to August 1975 Goodyear made only 671 "Bigfoot" snowmobile tracks and sold only 411 tracks. In December 1973 Goodyear filed an application to register "Bigfoot" as a trademark for snowmobile tracks with the United States Patent and Trademark Office; the registration was granted on October 15, 1974.

In July 1974 Goodyear decided to use the term "Bigfoot" in a nationwide advertising campaign to promote the sale of its new "Custom Polysteel Radial" tire. The name "Custom Polysteel Radial" was molded into the tire's sidewall. Goodyear employed a trademark search firm to conduct a search for "Bigfoot" in connection with tires and related products. This search did not uncover any conflicting trademarks. After this suit was filed, Goodyear filed an application to register "Bigfoot" as a trademark for tires but withdrew it in 1975. Goodyear planned to launch its massive, nationwide "Bigfoot" advertising campaign on September 16, 1974.

On August 24, 1974, Goodyear first learned of Big O's "Big Foot" tires. Goodyear informed Big O's president, Norman Affleck, on August 26 of Goodyear's impending "Bigfoot" advertising campaign. . . .

. . . On September 10, Affleck and two Big O directors met in New Orleans, with Kelley and Goodyear's manager of consumer market planning to discuss the problem further. At this time the Big O representatives objected to Goodyear using "Bigfoot" in connection with tires because they believed any such use would severely damage Big O. They made it clear they were not interested in money in exchange for granting Goodyear the right to use the "Bigfoot" trademark, and asked Goodyear to wind down the campaign as soon as possible. Goodyear's response to this request was indefinite and uncertain.

During the trial several Goodyear employees conceded it was technically possible for Goodyear to have deleted the term "Bigfoot" from its television advertising as late as early September. However, on September 16, 1974, Goodyear launched its nationwide "Bigfoot" promotion on ABC's Monday Night Football telecast. By August 31, 1975, Goodyear had spent $9,690,029 on its massive, saturation campaign.

On September 17 Affleck wrote Kelley a letter setting forth his understanding of the New Orleans meeting that Goodyear would wind up its "Bigfoot" campaign as soon as possible. Kelley replied on September 20, denying any commitment to discontinue use of "Bigfoot" and declaring Goodyear intended to use "Bigfoot" as long as it continued to be a helpful advertising device.

On October 9 Kelley told Affleck he did not have the authority to make the final decision for Goodyear and suggested that Affleck call Charles Eaves, Goodyear's executive vice-president. On October 10 Affleck called Eaves and Eaves indicated the possibility of paying Big O for the use of the term "Bigfoot." When Affleck stated no interest in the possibility Eaves told him Goodyear wished to avoid litigation but that if Big O did sue, the case would be in litigation long enough that Goodyear might obtain all the benefits it desired from the term "Bigfoot."

* * *

. . . Goodyear challenges the jury's verdict awarding Big O $2.8 million in compensatory damages and $16.8 million in punitive damages. Goodyear contends Big O failed to prove either the fact or the amount of damages. Big O asserts the evidence supporting the fact of damages falls into two categories: (1) Goodyear's enormous effort to adopt, use, and absorb Big O's trademark virtually destroyed Big O's ability to make any effective use of its "Big Foot" trademark and (2) Goodyear's false statements that "Bigfoot" was available only from Goodyear created the appearance of dishonesty and wrongful conduct by Big O, thereby harming its reputation within the trade and with the public. We agree with the district court that there is sufficient evidence to support the jury's finding of the fact of damages.

* * *

The purpose of general compensatory damages is to make the plaintiff whole. Big O concedes it was unable to prove with precision the amount necessary to make itself whole. However, the district court concluded "[t]he damages awarded by the jury would enable Big O to do an equivalent volume of advertising in the states in which there are Big O dealers to inform their customers, potential customers, and the public as a whole about the true facts in this dispute or anything else necessary to eliminate the confusion." 408 F. Supp. 1232. Moreover, the Supreme Court has pointed out that a plaintiff's inability to prove with precision that amount necessary to make itself whole does not preclude recovery since

> [t]he most elementary conceptions of justice and public policy require that the wrongdoer shall bear the risk of the uncertainty which his own wrong has created.

Bigelow v. RKO Radio Pictures, Inc., 327 U.S. 251, 265.

There is precedent for the recovery of corrective advertising expenses incurred by a plaintiff to counteract the public confusion resulting from a defendant's wrongful conduct. . . . Goodyear contends the recovery of advertising expenses should be limited to those actually incurred prior to trial. In this case the effect of such a rule would be to recognize that Big O has a right to the exclusive use of its trademark but has no remedy to be put in the position it was in prior to September 16, 1974, before Goodyear effectively usurped Big O's trademark. The impact of Goodyear's "Big-foot" campaign was devastating. The infringing mark was seen repeatedly by millions of consumers. It is clear from the record that Goodyear deeply penetrated the public consciousness. Thus, Big O is entitled to recover a reasonable amount equivalent to that of a concurrent corrective advertising campaign.

As the district court pointed out, the jury's verdict of $2.8 million corresponds to 28 percent of the approximately $10 million Goodyear spent infringing Big O's mark. Big O has dealers in 14 states which equal 28 percent of the 50 states. Big O also points out the jury's award is close to 25 percent of the amount Goodyear spent infringing on Big O's mark. Big O emphasizes that the Federal Trade Commission often requires businesses who engage in misleading advertising to spend 25 percent of their advertising budget on corrective advertising.

Taking cognizance of these two alternative rationales for the jury's award for compensatory damages we are convinced the award is not capable of support as to any amount in excess of $678,302. As the district court implied in attempting to explain the jury's verdict, Big O is not entitled to the total amount Goodyear spent on its nationwide campaign since Big O only has dealers in 14 states, thus making it unnecessary for Big O to run a nationwide advertising campaign. Furthermore, implicit in the FTC's 25 percent rule in corrective advertising cases is the fact that dispelling confusion and deception in the consuming public's mind does not require a dollar-for-dollar expenditure. In keeping with "[t]he constant tendency of the courts . . . to find some way in which damages can be awarded where a wrong has been done," we hold that the maximum amount which a jury could reasonably find necessary to place Big O in the position it was in before September 16, 1974, vis-a-vis its "Big Foot" trademark, is $678,302. We arrive at this amount by taking 28 percent of the $9,690,029 it was stipulated Goodyear spent on its "Bigfoot" campaign, and then reducing that figure by 75 percent in accordance with the FTC rule, since we agree with that agency's determination that a dollar-for-dollar expenditure for corrective advertising is unnecessary to dispel the effects of confusing and misleading advertising.

Under Colorado law exemplary damages must bear some relation to the compensatory award. *Barnes v. Lehman*, 118 Colo. 161, 163, 193 P.2d 273, 274. The district court in its post-trial opinion upheld the jury's punitive damage award of $16.8 million as not being disproportionate under Colorado law. We find the district court's determination of the reasonableness of a six-to-one exemplary to compensatory ratio to be persuasive, and thus we defer to the district court's interpretation of Colorado law. Therefore, in light of the reduction in compensatory damages proved, the punitive damage award is similarly reduced to $4,069,812, thus maintaining the jury's and district court's six-to-one exemplary to compensatory ratio.

* * *

[*Remanded*]

2. Profits

HAMILTON-BROWN SHOE CO. v. WOLF BROTHERS & CO.
240 U.S. 251 (1961)

PITNEY, JUSTICE.

* * *

Having reached the conclusion that complainant is entitled to the use of the words "The American Girl" as a trade-mark, it results that it is entitled to the profits acquired by defendant from the manifestly infringing sales under the label "American Lady," at least to the extent that such profits are awarded in the decree under review. The right to use a trade- mark is recognized as a kind of property, of which the owner is entitled to the exclusive enjoyment to the extent that it has been actually used. *McLean v. Fleming*, 96 U.S. 245, 252; *Manhattan Medicine Co. v. Wood*, 108 U.S. 218, 224. The infringer is required in equity to account for and yield up his gains to the true owner, upon a principle analogous to that which charges a trustee with the profits acquired by wrongful use of the property of the *cestui que trust*. Not that equity assumes jurisdiction upon the ground that a trust exists. As pointed out in *Root v. Railway*, 105 U.S. 189, 214, and *Tilghman v. Proctor*, 125 U.S. 136, 148 (patent cases), the jurisdiction must be rested upon some other equitable ground — in ordinary cases, as in the present, the right to an injunction — but the court of equity having acquired jurisdiction upon such a ground, retains it for the purpose of administering complete relief, rather than send the inquired party to a court of law for his damages. And profits are then allowed as an equitable measure of compensation, on the theory of a trust *ex maleficio*. In the courts of England, the rule seems to be that a party aggrieved must elect between damages and profits, and cannot have both. In this country, it is generally held that in a proper case both damages and profits may be awarded. . . .

It is, however, insisted by defendant (petitioner) that whether the recovery be based upon the theory of trademark, or upon that of unfair competition, the profits recoverable should be limited to such amount as may be shown by direct and positive evidence to be the increment to defendant's income by reason of the infringement, and that the burden of proof is upon complainant to show what part of defendant's profits were attributable to the use of the infringing mark. . . . But, as pointed out in the *Westinghouse Case* (p. 618), there is a recognized exception where the plaintiff carries the burden of proof to the extent of showing the entire profits, but is unable to apportion them, either because of the action of the wrongdoer in confusing his own gains with those which belong to plaintiff, or because of the inherent impossibility of making an approximate apportionment. There, "on established principles of equity, and on the plainest principles of justice, the guilty trustee cannot take advantage of his own wrong."

. . . [A] sufficient reason for not requiring complainant in the present case to make an apportionment between the profits attributable to defendant's use of the offending mark and those attributable to the intrinsic merit of defendant's shoes is that such an apportionment is inherently impossible. Certainly, no formula is suggested by which it could be accomplished. The result of acceding to defendant's contention, therefore, would be to deny all compensation to complainant. And it is to be remembered that defendant does not stand as an innocent infringer. Not only do the findings of the Court of Appeals, supported by abundant evidence, show that the imitation of complainant's mark was fraudulent, but the profits included in the decree are confined to such as accrued to defendant through its persistence in the unlawful simulation in the face of the very plain notice of complainant's rights that is contained in its bill. As was said by the Supreme Court of California in a similar case, *Graham v. Plate*, 40 Cal. 593, 598; 6 Am. Rep. 639, 640:

> In sales made under a simulated trade mark it is impossible to decide how much of the profit resulted from the intrinsic value of the commodity in the market, and how much from the credit given to it by the trade-mark. In the very nature of the case it would be impossible to ascertain to what extent he could have effected sales and at what prices except for the use of the trade-mark. No one will deny that on every principle of reason and justice the owner of the trade-mark is entitled to so much of the profit as resulted from the use of the trade-mark. The difficulty lies in ascertaining what proportion of the profit is due to the trade-mark, and what to the intrinsic value of the commodity; and as this cannot be ascertained with any reasonably certainty, it is more consonant with reason and justice that the owner of the trade-mark should have the whole profit than that he should be deprived of any part of it by the fraudulent act of the defendant. . . .

*   *   *

Decree affirmed.

ALPO PETFOODS, INC. v. RALSTON PURINA COMPANY
913 F.2d 958 (D.C. Cir. 1990)

CLARENCE THOMAS, CIRCUIT JUDGE

In this case, Ralston Purina Co. and ALPO Petfoods, Inc., two of the leading dog food producers in the United States, have sued each other under § 43(a) of the Lanham Act, 15 U.S.C. § 1125(a) (1982) (amended 1988), alleging false advertising. ALPO asserts that Ralston has violated § 43(a) by claiming that its Puppy Chow can lessen the severity of canine hip dysplasia (CHD), a crippling joint condition. Ralston, for its part, attacks ALPO's claims that ALPO Puppy Food contains "the formula preferred by responding vets two to one over the leading puppy food."

After a sixty-one-day bench trial, the district court decided that Ralston's CHD-related advertising and ALPO's veterinarian preference advertising both violated § 43(a). *ALPO Petfoods, Inc. v. Ralston Purina Co.*, 720 F. Supp. 194, 209–11 (D.D.C. 1989). The court permanently enjoined both companies from making "advertising or other related claims" similar to those held false, and ordered both parties to disseminate corrective statements. *Id.* at 216–17. Applying § 35(a) of the Lanham Act, 15 U.S.C. § 1117(a) (1982 & Supp. V 1987) (amended 1988), the court also awarded ALPO $10.4 million (plus costs and attorneys' fees). The court reached this figure by determining the amount that Ralston spent on its CHD-related advertising, using that amount as a measure of Ralston's benefit from the advertising, and then doubling the amount to capture the full harm that the advertising caused ALPO. *ALPO*, 720 F. Supp. at 215 (citing *U-Haul Int'l, Inc. v. Jartran, Inc.*, 793 F.2d 1034, 1037 (9th Cir. 1986)). Ralston, in contrast, was awarded only its costs and attorneys' fees. *Id.* at 215, 216.

Ralston appeals the district court's judgment, focusing on the court's determination that the CHD-related advertising claims were false, as well as the court's monetary award to ALPO, its refusal to award similar relief to Ralston, and its broad and expansively implemented injunction.

*   *   *

Section 35(a) authorizes courts to award to an aggrieved plaintiff both plaintiff's damages and defendant's profits, but, as this court noted in *Foxtrap*, 671 F.2d at 641, courts' discretion to award these remedies has limits. Just as "any award based on plaintiff's damages requires some showing of actual loss," *id.* at 642; *see also infra* p. 969 (discussing actual damages under § 35(a)), an award based on a defendant's profits requires proof that the defendant acted willfully or in bad faith, *see Foxtrap*, 671 F.2d at 641; *Frisch's Restaurants, Inc. v. Elby's Big Boy*, 849 F.2d 1012, 1015 (6th Cir. 1988). Proof of this sort is lacking. Ralston's decision to run CHD-related advertising that lacked solid empirical support does not, without more, reflect willfulness or bad faith. *See supra* pp. 965–66; *cf. U-Haul, Int'l, Inc. v. Jartran, Inc.*, 601 F. Supp. 1140, 1147–48 (D. Ariz. 1984) (describing *U-Haul* defendant's targeted comparative advertising, which misrepresented plaintiff's and defendant's prices), *aff'd in part and rev'd in part*, 793 F.2d 1034 (9th Cir. 1986).

In *Conservative Digest* we "left open the possibility that a court could properly award damages to a plaintiff when the defendant has been unjustly enriched." 821 F.2d at 807–08 (citing *Foxtrap*, 671 F.2d at 641 & n. 9). The unjust-enrichment theory, which emerged in trademark cases in which the infringer and the infringed were not competitors, holds that courts should divest an infringer of his profits, regardless of whether the infringer's actions have harmed the owner of the infringed trademark. Awards of profits are justified under the theory because they deter infringement in general and thereby vindicate consumers' interests. *See, e.g., Monsanto Chemical Co. v. Perfect Fit Prods. Mfg. Co.*, 349 F.2d 389, 392, 395–97 (2[d] Cir. 1965), *cert. denied*, 383 U.S. 942 (1966); *see also* 2 McCarthy, Trademarks and Unfair Competiton, 2d Ed., 1984], p. 14 § 30:25(B) (citing cases). As we state below, however, we doubt the wisdom of an approach to damages that permits courts to award profits for their sheer deterrent effect.

* * *

[T]his court in *Foxtrap* advised a district court to make an award that would "deter the defendant, *yet not be a windfall to plaintiff nor amount to punitive damages.*" *Id.* at 642 n. 11 (emphasis added). Based on *Foxtrap*, as well as our concern that deterrence is too weak and too easily invoked a justification for the severe and often cumbersome remedy of a profits award, *see* Koelemay, *Monetary Relief for Trademark Infringement Under the Lanham Act*, 72 Trademark Rep. 458, 493–94, 536–37 (1982), we hold that deterrence alone cannot justify such an award.

Since this case lacks the elements required to support the court's award of Ralston's profits, we vacate the $10.4 million judgment in favor of ALPO. We do not mean, however, to deny ALPO all monetary relief for Ralston's false advertising. Because the district court has so far focused on awarding Ralston's profits, it has not yet decided what actual damages ALPO has proved. On remand, the court should award ALPO its actual damages, bearing in mind the requirement that any amount awarded have support in the record, *see Foxtrap*, 671 F.2d at 642; *Gold Seal*, 129 F. Supp. at 940, as well as the following points about the governing law.

In a false-advertising case such as this one, actual damages under § 35(a) can include:

— profits lost by the plaintiff on sales actually diverted to the false advertiser, *see, e.g., Foxtrap*, 671 F.2d at 642 (trademark case);

— profits lost by the plaintiff on sales made at prices reduced as a demonstrated result of the false advertising, *see, e.g., Burndy Corp. v. Teledyne Indus.*, 748 F.2d 767, 773 (2[d] Cir. 1984);

— the costs of any completed advertising that actually and reasonably responds to the defendant's offending ads, *see, e.g., Cuisinarts, Inc. v. Robot-Coupe Int'l Corp.*, 580 F. Supp. 634, 640–41 (S.D.N.Y. 1984); and

— quantifiable harm to the plaintiff's good will, to the extent that completed corrective advertising has not repaired that harm, *see, e.g., Engineered Mech.*

Servs., Inc. v. Applied Mech. Technology, Inc., 591 F. Supp. 962, 966 (M.D. La. 1984); *see also* Comment, 55 U. CHI. L. REV. at 650–57 (discussing how courts might directly measure good will).

See generally Koelemay, [*Monetary Relief for Trademark Infringement Under the Lanham Act,*] 72 TRADEMARK REP. [458] at 505–07.

When assessing these actual damages, the district court may take into account the difficulty of proving an exact amount of damages from false advertising, as well as the maxim that "the wrongdoer shall bear the risk of the uncertainty which his own wrong has created." *Otis Clapp & Son v. Filmore Vitamin Co.*, 754 F.2d 738, 745 (7th Cir. 1985) (quoting *Bigelow v. RKO Radio Pictures, Inc.*, 327 U.S. 251, 265 (1946). At the same time, the court must ensure that the record adequately supports all items of damages claimed and establishes a causal link between the damages and the defendant's conduct, lest the award become speculative or violate § 35(a)'s prohibition against punishment. *See, e.g., Bigelow*, 327 U.S. at 264 (stating, in antitrust case, that "speculation or guesswork" cannot sustain an award of damages); *Burndy Corp.*, 748 F.2d at 773 (asserted causal connection between defendant's conduct and plaintiff's reduced-price sales lacked support in record; denial of reduced- price sales damages affirmed); *Foxtrap*, 671 F.2d at 642 (same problem with respect to lost sales; damages award vacated and case remanded for detailed findings).

Section 35(a) also authorizes the court to "enter judgment, according to the circumstances of the case, for any sum above the amount found as actual damages, not exceeding three times such amount." Lanham Act § 35(a), 15 U.S.C. § 1117(a) (1982 & Supp. V 1987) (amended 1988). This provision gives the court discretion to enhance damages, as long as the ultimate award qualifies as "compensation and not [as] a penalty." *Id.*; *see* Koelemay, 72 TRADEMARK REP. at 516–19, 521–25 (discussing interplay of damages enhancement provision and antipenalty clause); *see also Getty Petroleum Corp. v. Bartco Petroleum Corp.*, 858 F.2d 103, 112–13 (2[d] Cir. 1988) (in trademark infringement case, interpreting § 35(a) to ban any awards of punitive damages), *cert. denied*, 109 S. Ct. 1642 (1989). Given this express statutory restriction, if the district court decides to enhance damages under § 35(a), it should explain why the enhanced award is compensatory and not punitive.

*   *   *

The foregoing comments on actual damages apply as well to the monetary remedy for ALPO's false advertising. As noted above, the district court held that ALPO's veterinarian preference advertising violated § 43(a). *ALPO*, 720 F. Supp. at 209–11. Despite this decision, the court did not award Ralston any damages or profits under § 35(a) because "[t]he magnitude of the wrongdoing by Ralston in comparison to that of ALPO is so much greater than a damage award would not be justified," because ALPO, but not Ralston, had shown remorse, and because the court considered Ralston's counterclaim "an afterthought." *Id.* at 216; *see also id.* at 212 (finding an injunction the most appropriate redress for ALPO's false advertising).

The Lanham Act does not authorize courts to deny monetary relief for these reasons. Once a party establishes a violation of § 43(a), § 35(a) "entitle[s]" that party to monetary relief, subject only to the statutes referred to in the section and to the principles of equity. Lanham Act § 35(a), 15 U.S.C. § 1117(a); *cf. ALPO*, 720 F. Supp. at 214 (rejecting both parties' "unclean hands" defenses, a ruling that neither party appeals). Since § 35(a) expressly provides for compensation, rather than punishment, courts dealing with offsetting meritorious claims must let the degree of injury that each party proves, rather than the degree of opprobrium that the court attaches to each party's conduct, determine the monetary relief.

At more than one point in this case, Ralston came close to admitting that it cannot prove lost profits. *See* Brief of appellee at 47 & app. B (citing Ralston's statement, in a proposed finding of fact, that none of its regression analyses proved diverted sales);

Reply Brief of Appellant at 18–19 ("Ralston's position . . . is that under a *proper* construction of the Lanham Act, *neither* party can quantify lost profits sufficiently to recover damages."). In this appeal, however, Ralston has shown that it still considers its lost profits a live issue. *See id.* at 18 & n. 40 (citing evidence, other than regressions, of lost sales). Since Ralston has some evidence of lost sales, and since, more importantly, § 35(a) entitles Ralston to damages other than lost profits, *see supra* p. 969, the district court should on remand award Ralston whatever actual damages it has proved. In this connection, as with ALPO's damages, the court should decide whether the parties have already had a sufficient opportunity to prove the types of damages outlined above, or whether further hearings are necessary.

* * *

The court awarded each company the attorneys' fees associated with its successful false-advertising claim. *ALPO*, 720 F. Supp. at 216. Only Ralston has appealed.

Section 35(a) entitles prevailing parties to attorneys' fees "in exceptional cases." This court's decision in *Conservative Digest*, 821 F.2d at 808, establishes an abuse-of-discretion standard for review of attorneys' fees awards. That same decision, however, holds that a court can award a plaintiff her attorneys' fees only in cases involving willful or bad-faith conduct by the defendant; applying that standard, the *Conservative Digest* court affirmed a denial of fees to a plaintiff who had proved trade dress infringement, but not willfulness or bad faith on the part of the infringer. *Id.* Seeing no relevant distinction between fee awards in trade dress infringement actions and fee awards in false-advertising actions, we apply *Conservative Digest* here. *See id.* at 803 (§ 43(a) covers trade dress infringement).

In announcing its fee awards, the district court did not expressly find that Ralston had acted willfully or in bad faith. Indeed, it made no finding that this case is "exceptional" in any respect. *See ALPO*, 720 F. Supp. at 216, 216; *supra* p. 963. During a postjudgment hearing, the court explained that since, in its view, federal agencies are not sufficiently enforcing the laws against false advertising, it had awarded fees "to encourage private attorneys general in this case." Transcript of Motions Hearing at 7 (Sept. 18, 1989). Since neither the court's opinion nor its later statements support the award with a finding of willfulness or bad faith, and since we have decided that any such finding would be clearly erroneous, *see supra* pp. 965–66, we reverse the district court's decision to award attorneys' fees to ALPO. [14]

* * *

3. Attorneys' Fees

INTERNATIONAL STAR CLASS YACHT RACING ASSOCIATION v. TOMMY HILFIGER, U.S.A., INC.
80 F.3d 749 (2ᵈ Cir. 1996)

OAKES, CIRCUIT JUDGE

This appeal involves the availability of monetary relief and attorney fees in a trademark infringement action brought under § 43(a) of the Lanham Act, 15 U.S.C. § 1125(a) (1994). The International Star Class Yacht Racing Association ("ISCYRA")

---

[14] Because ALPO has failed to challenge the district court's award of attorneys' fees to Ralston, we do not disturb the award. *See, e.g., Smith v. Nixon*, 807 F.2d 197, 204 n. 4 (D.C. Cir. 1986) (plaintiffs waived potential claims by neglecting to press them on appeal). Although, in some cases, we might forgive a party's waiver and reverse a district court's determination as plain error, we decline to do so here. This court typically reviews a district court's ruling for plain error only when a party has objected to the ruling on appeal. *See, e.g., Anderson v. Group Hosp., Inc.*, 820 F.2d 465, 469 n. 1 (D.C. Cir. 1987); *Hobson v. Wilson*, 737 F.2d 1, 31–31, 32 n. 96 (D.C. Cir. 1984), *cert. denied*, 470 U.S. 1084(1985).

appeals from a portion of the judgment of the United States District Court for the Southern District of New York (Robert P. Patterson, Jr., *Judge*), entered on May 19, 1995. The district court, after a bench trial, granted ISCYRA's application for a permanent injunction against use of its "STAR CLASS" mark by the appellee Tommy Hilfiger U.S.A., Inc. ("Hilfiger") but denied injunctive relief as to ISCYRA's insignia, a solid five-pointed star. The district court also denied ISCYRA an accounting of Hilfiger's profits, actual damages, and attorney fees.

*   *   *

ISCYRA is a non-profit corporation founded in 1922 for the purpose of governing and promoting the sport of Star Class yacht racing. Star Class sailboats are sophisticated one-design racing craft sailed in high-profile regattas and championship series around the world, including the Summer Olympics. ISCYRA owns the rights to the design of Star Class boats and closely monitors the construction, certification, and registration of each boat in the class. One requirement of a genuine Star Class boat is that its main sail bear the solid red five-pointed star which serves as ISCYRA's insignia or a star of green, blue, silver or gold awarded at ISCYRA championship races. The red star is also used, along with the words "STAR CLASS," on the yachting hats, clothing, flags, decals and pins sold by ISCYRA. ISCYRA permits yacht clubs hosting regattas to use the insignia and "STAR CLASS" on promotional items, and has collected royalties for their use in jewelry and posters.

Hilfiger is a successful designer and marketer of men's clothing with sales of over $227 million in 1993. Its 1994 Spring Collection included garments bearing the words "STAR CLASS" with a solid red five-pointed star. These garments were marketed as "classic nautical sportswear" with "authentic details taken from the sport of competitive sailing" and "elements and patterns taken directly from actual racing sails." Hilfiger's name and flag trademarks also appeared prominently on all the garments, which were marketed in the United States and abroad.

While designing the 1994 Spring Collection, Hilfiger requested a trademark screening search for the words "STAR CLASS" from its attorneys. Hilfiger did not specify that it planned to use the words on "nautical" clothing with details from "competitive sailing," and the search was limited to federal trademarks in class 25, a clothing classification. The screening search did not reveal any identical registered or applied-for federal trademarks, but Hilfiger's attorneys advised it to conduct a "full trademark search" before using the words "STAR CLASS." Hilfiger did not conduct such a search until after it was sued by ISCYRA, at which point it learned that "STAR CLASS" was indeed a mark in the yachting context.

*   *   *

The district court's conclusion that Hilfiger did not act in bad faith or willfully infringe in its use of the "STAR CLASS" mark was based on several factual findings which we review for clear error.

Initially, we note a factual error in the district court's opinion which goes directly to the question of the willfulness of Hilfiger's infringement. The district court stated that the trademark search conducted by Hilfiger prior to its use of ISCYRA's "STAR CLASS" mark was of federal and state marks. In fact, the search was limited solely to registered or applied-for *federal* trademarks; despite its attorneys' advice that a wider search be conducted, Hilfiger did not do one until after ISCYRA filed its suit.

The district court relied on Hilfiger's limited first search as proof that Hilfiger did not "engage in a deceptive commercial practice" or otherwise act in bad faith in using ISCYRA's mark. We are not convinced, however, that such a limited search should exonerate Hilfiger, particularly when Hilfiger ignored the specific advice of its attorneys to search more thoroughly.

The district court also found that although Hilfiger intentionally copied ISCYRA's

"STAR CLASS" mark, it did not intend to copy a trademark owned by another. The court recognized that Hilfiger's failure to offer a "credible innocent explanation" for its use of ISCYRA's mark could support an inference of bad faith under *Centaur Communications, Ltd. v. A/S/M Communications*, 830 F.2d 1217, 1228 (2d Cir. 1987). The court nevertheless concluded that Hilfiger had not willfully infringed on ISCYRA's mark, citing as evidence the limited trademark search discussed above.

In light of Hilfiger's minimal efforts to ascertain whether "STAR CLASS" was, in fact, a trademark, we agree with ISCYRA that the district court clearly erred in finding Hilfiger guilty only of simple copying and not of intent to copy a mark. Given Hilfiger's awareness that it was copying "authentic details . . . from the sport of competitive sailing," it should have shown greater concern for the possibility that it was infringing on another's mark. Hilfiger's choice not to perform a full search under these circumstances reminds us of two of the famous trio of monkeys who, by covering their eyes and ears, neither saw nor heard any evil. Such willful ignorance should not provide a means by which Hilfiger can evade its obligations under trademark law.

In addition to the district court's two clearly erroneous findings, we believe that its analysis of Hilfiger's bad faith was incomplete. First, the district court did not address the fact that Hilfiger failed to conduct a full trademark search on "STAR CLASS" before using the mark in direct contravention of the advice of its attorneys. Other courts have found that an infringer who "acts in reasonable reliance on the advice of counsel" generally cannot be said to have acted in bad faith . . . . Conversely, the *failure* to follow the advice of counsel given before the infringement must factor into an assessment of an infringer's bad faith.

Second, the district court gave no consideration to Hilfiger's conduct after ISCYRA brought suit for trademark infringement. The suit gave Hilfiger notice of its potential trademark violation, and the full search that it conducted soon thereafter confirmed the existence of ISCYRA's mark. Hilfiger nonetheless continued to sell its merchandise with the infringing mark, racking up over $3 million in sales, without regard for the rights of ISCYRA. As counsel for Hilfiger admitted during oral argument, Hilfiger was betting on the fact that ISCYRA would not prevail in its suit. Hilfiger lost that bet, and should not escape the consequences of its conduct. *See Stuart v. Collins*, 489 F.Supp. 827, 832 (S.D.N.Y. 1980) (finding willful infringement when defendant continued to use plaintiff's mark after plaintiff's attorney demanded that it cease, thereby giving "short shrift to plaintiff's claim out of arrogance and confidence that he would not mount any significant legal attack"); *see also Polo Fashions, Inc. v. Dick Bruhn, Inc.*, 793 F.2d 1132, 1135 (9th Cir. 1986) (courts should remove economic incentive to engage in infringing activity); *W.E. Bassett Co.*, 435 F.2d at 664 (an accounting of profits serves to deter willful infringers).

As recognized by the Restatement, an accounting of profits should be limited to cases of fraudulent infringement, i.e. "to acts intended to create confusion or deceive prospective purchasers," *Restatement (Third), supra*, § 37 cmt. e, and not be awarded in cases where a defendant "deliberately but in good faith used a mark." *Id.* We note that, under this standard, Hilfiger cannot lay claim to a "good faith" belief that it was not infringing on ISCYRA's mark because it neither fully explored others' rights to "STAR CLASS" nor ceased its infringing behavior when it was sued. *See Nalpac, Ltd. v. Corning Glass Works*, 784 F.2d 752, 755–756 (6th Cir. 1986) (exploitation of another's mark after knowledge of its existence suggests bad faith).

We conclude that the district court, in determining whether Hilfiger acted in bad faith, relied on two clearly erroneous factual findings and did not consider all the evidence pertaining to the willfulness of Hilfiger's infringement. We therefore remand the issue of Hilfiger's bad faith for reconsideration in light of our analysis above. As a result, we cannot review the district court's denial of an accounting of profits and attorney fees, but instead must vacate the denial and remand.

Notes on Monetary Relief

1. Damages

a) Actual Damages

To recover actual damages, plaintiff must show actual injury, proximately arising from the infringement or deception. *Alpo PetFoods, Inc. v. Ralston Purina Co., supra,* (in false advertising case, actual damages may consist of plaintiff's lost profits from diverted sales, lost profits from having to reduce prices in response to defendant's false advertising, the expense of completed corrective advertising, and quantifiable harm to goodwill, to extent corrective advertising has not repaired that goodwill); *Harper House, Inc. v. Thomas Nelson, Inc.,* 889 F.2d 197, 210 (9th Cir. 1989) (reversing $1.8 million jury award; "[i]n a suit for damages under section 43(a), actual evidence of some injury *resulting from the deception* is an essential element" [emphasis in original]).

b) Actual Confusion

Some courts require proof of actual confusion or deception before awarding actual damages. *Resource Developers, Inc. v. Statute of Liberty - Ellis Island Foundation, Inc.,* 926 F.2d 134, 139 (2^{d} Cir. 1991) (proof of defendant's wrongful intent may raise presumption of actual confusion); *Web Printing Controls Co. v. Oxy-Dry Corp.,* 906 F.2d 1202, 1205 (7th Cir. 1990); *Brunswick Corp. v. Spinit Reel Co.,* 832 F.2d 513, 525 (10th Cir. 1987) ("plaintiff must prove it has been damaged by actual consumer confusion or deception resulting from the violation").

Others do not. *Compare Taco Cabana International, Inc. v. Two Pesos, Inc.,* 932 F.2d 1113, 1126 (5th Cir. 1991), *aff'd.,* 505 U.S. 763 (1992) (rejecting argument that evidence of actual confusion is required, and awarding damages for the blocking of plaintiff's market expansion); *PPX Enterprises, Inc. v. Audiofidelity Enterprises,* 818 F.2d 266, 271–272 (2^{d} Cir. 1987) (where defendant's misrepresentations are "patently fraudulent", direct evidence of actual deception unnecessary); *Getty Petroleum Corp. v. Island Transport Corp.* 878 F.2d 650, 656 (2^{d} Cir. 1989) (proof of actual confusion is "normally required", but jury could use common sense to find defendant's sale of non-GETTY gasoline under plaintiff's GETTY mark caused actual deception).

Survey results also may demonstrate actual confusion for damages purposes. *Schutt Mfg. Co. v. Riddell, Inc.,* 673 F.2d 202, 207 (7th Cir. 1982) (customer reliance may be shown by surveys); Restatement (Third) of Unfair Competition § 36, comment h ("Direct proof of actual confusion or deception is often unavailable, however, and the proof may instead consist of circumstantial evidence such as consumer surveys, market analysis, or the nature of defendant's misconduct").

c) Intent

Proof of wrongful intent is not required for an award of actual damages. *General Electric Co. v. Speicher,* 877 F.2d 531, 536 (7th Cir. 1988) ("even the victim of an innocent infringer is entitled to simple damages, as distinct from the infringer's profits".) However, proof that defendant had an intent to infringe or deceive may create a presumption of actual confusion for damage purposes. *Balance Dynamics Corp. v. Schmitt Industries, Inc.,* 204 F.3d 683, 694 (6th Cir. 2000) (literal falsity of claims combined with evidence of deliberate intent or bad faith can raise presumption of monetary damages even if no actual confusion is shown; in this case, however, evidence showed plaintiff suffered no marketplace injury); *Resource Development v. Statue of Liberty - Ellis Island,* 926 F.2d 134, 140 (2^{d} Cir. 1991); *U-Haul International, Inc. v. Jartran, Inc.,* 793 F.2d 1034, 1040–41 (9th Cir. 1986); Pattishall, *The Impact of Intent in Trade Identity Cases,* 65 Nw. U.L. Rev. 421 (1970).

2. Equitable Doctrines

Laches and acquiescence may bar monetary relief, or restrict a plaintiff to recovery of post-filing damages. *McLean v. Fleming*, 96 U.S. 245, 251 (1878); *Skippy, Inc. v. CPC International, Inc.*, 674 F.2d 209, 212 (4th Cir.), *cert. denied*, 459 U.S. 969 (1982) ("laches will bar a claim for damages for bad faith infringement"); *University of Pittsburgh v. Champion Products, Inc.*, 686 F.2d 1040, 1044 (3d Cir.), *cert. denied*, 459 U.S. 1087 (1982); *Brittingham v. Jenkins*, 914 F.2d 447, 456–57 (4th Cir. 1990) (plaintiff's excessive delay limits entitlement to profits and precludes award of prejudgment interest). The court may also determine that an injunction satisfies the equities of the case. *Champion Spark Plug Co. v. Sanders*, 331 U.S. 125, 131 (1947); *Carl Zeiss Stiftung v. V.E.B. Carl Zeiss Jena*, 433 F.2d 686, 706–07 (2d Cir. 1970), *cert. denied*, 403 U.S. 905 (1971). Similarly, the court may decline to award damages because the defendant has "suffered enough." *Faberge, Inc. v. Saxony Products, Inc.*, 605 F.2d 426, 429 (9th Cir. 1979) (injunction sufficient; costs already incurred by defendant would cause deterrence); *American Express Co. v. American Express Limousine Service, Ltd.*, 785 F. Supp. 334, 338 (E.D.N.Y. 1992) ("defendants have suffered enough to deter future infringement").

3. Plaintiff's Lost Profits

A plaintiff may recover its own lost profits by proving it would have received the profits but for defendant's infringement or deception, and that the amount can be determined with a reasonable certainty. In *Dial One of Mid South Inc. v. Bellsouth Telecomm'ns, Inc.*, 269 F.3d 523 (5th Cir. 2001), $150,000 of plaintiff franchisor's lost profits were awarded where defendants, after notice, failed to remove the listing of plaintiff's ex-franchisee from the Yellow and White Pages directories. *See also BASF Corp. v. Old World Trading Co.*, 41 F.3d 1081 (7th Cir. 1994) (affirming award of $4.2 million in lost profits, prejudgment interest and attorneys' fees in false advertising case); *Intel Corp. v. Terabyte Int'l, Inc.*, 6 F.3d 614, 620–21 (9th Cir. 1993) (calculating a $380,000 lost profits award by taking 95% of Intel's profit margin as applied to defendant's sales); *Alpo Petfoods, supra*; *Brunswick Corp. v. Spinit Reel Co.*, 832 F.2d 513 (10th Cir. 1987) (even where each sale by infringing defendant is not necessarily a lost sale to plaintiff, plaintiff may be entitled to some lesser amount of lost profits). *Compare Thompson v. Haynes*, 305 F.3d 1369 (Fed. Cir. 2002), in which the court affirmed the award of the willful infringer's profits, but vacated the award of the trademark owner's lost profits. As to the trademark owner's alleged lost profits, there was no evidence of even a single lost product sale and the district court's speculation as to one hundred lost sales per month was "too thin a reed on which to support an award of almost two million dollars".

The amount of proven profits can be approximate, but not speculative. *Lindy Pen Co. v. Bic Pen Corp.*, 982 F.2d 1400, 1405 (9th Cir.), *cert. denied*, 510 U.S. 815 (1993) (affirming refusal to award lost profits as too speculative where plaintiff failed to segregate data on the type of telephone order sales in which confusion was likely); *McClaran v. Plastic Indus. Inc.*, 97 F.3d 347 (9th Cir. 1996) (jury award of more than $800,000 in lost profits too speculative where plaintiff had not even entered the market for the infringing goods); *Burndy Corp. v. Teledyne Industries, Inc.*, 584 F. Supp. 656, 664 (D. Conn. 1984), *aff'd.*, 748 F.2d 767 (2d Cir. 1984). *Cf. Ford Motor Co. v. B&H Supply, Inc.*, 646 F. Supp. 975 (D. Minn. 1986) (applying Ford's pricing to the number of counterfeit auto parts sold by defendant despite defendant's contention that Ford would not have made all the sales; "courts necessarily engage in some degree of speculation"). *See also Playtex Prods. v. Procter & Gamble*, 126 Fed. App'x. 32 (2d Cir. 2005) (unpub.) (Playtex successfully showed that P&G's false advertising had caused Playtex to lose profits by evidence of Playtex's market share before and after the false advertising campaign, the nature of the market for the parties' goods, strong brand loyalty among its customers, and the stated goals of P&G's advertising; such circumstantial evidence "can be sufficient to prove causation in a false advertising case just as it can be to prove other propositions"); *Porous Media Corp. v. Pall Corp.*, 173 F.3d 1109, 1122 (8th Cir. 1999) (rejecting allegation that damage award was too speculative; $1.6 million jury verdict was adequately supported by testimony showing the importance of reputation in plaintiff's industry; that defendant damaged that reputation in specific ways; that plaintiff lost "between $5 million and $10 million" in going concern value; and that defendant damaged plaintiff's opportunities to "create a reputation for being the industry leader" and "create a reputation to be able to move onto the next level" beyond the medical oxygen-concentrator market).

In appropriate cases, it may be possible for a plaintiff to recover both damages and profits. *Hamilton-Brown Shoe Co., supra*; *but see Polo Fashions, Inc. v. Extra Special Products, Inc.*, 208 U.S.P.Q. 421, 427 (S.D.N.Y. 1980) (court cannot award damages and profits based on same sales). *Compare Alameda v. Authors Rights Restoration Corp.*, 331 F.3d 472 (5th Cir.) *cert denied* 540 U.S. 1048 (2003) (federal Copyright Act does not preempt federal Lanham Act, or vice versa, so separate recovery under both was permissible); *Nintendo of America, Inc. v. Dragon Pacific International*, 40 F.3d 1007 (9th Cir. 1994), *cert. denied*, 515 U.S. 1107 (1995) (affirming award of both statutory copyright damages and trebled Lanham Act damages against defendant who sold illicit copies of Nintendo games, representing them to be authorized).

4. Corrective Advertising

Money for future corrective advertising to remedy confusion or repair damaged goodwill, often based on a percentage of defendant's expenditures, may be awarded in appropriate cases. *Big O Tire Dealers, Inc., supra*; *West Des Moines State Bank v. Hawkeye Bancorporation*, 722 F.2d 411, 414 (8th Cir. 1983); (25% of defendant's advertising expenditures); *Aetna Health Care Systems, Inc. v. Health Care Choice, Inc.*, 231 U.S.P.Q. 614, 626 (N.D. Okla. 1986) (awarding 25% of infringer's $50,000 advertising expenditures and then trebling it). In *Zelinski v. Columbia 300 Inc.*, 335 F.3d 633 (7th Cir. 2003), the court affirmed a $70,000 corrective advertising award relating to plaintiff's PINBREAKER mark for bowling balls. "[I]t wasn't unreasonable for [plaintiff] to recommend a corrective advertising campaign when [defendant] sold slightly over 3,000 balls [under an identical mark] in Korea and Taiwan". The jury "is entitled to use its common sense" to decide that customers were deceived when purchasing defendant's products, especially "when no amount of inspection would have revealed that [defendant] — not [plaintiff] — manufactured the balls." Previously incurred corrective advertising expenditures also may be reimbursed. *Alpo Petfoods v. Ralston Purina Co., supra*, (upholding enhanced award for plaintiff's "responsive" advertising, but remanding for reduction of the $3.6 million amount for such things as amount attributable to plaintiff's own false advertising statements); *Otis Clapp & Son v. Filmore Vitamin Co.*, 754 F.2d 738, 745 (7th Cir. 1985) (cost of "curative advertising campaign"); *U-Haul International, Inc. v. Jartran, Inc.*, 793 F.2d 1034, 1041 (9th Cir. 1986) (awarding plaintiff $13.6 million for its corrective advertising expenditures, more than twice what defendant spent on its false advertising); *Cuisinarts, Inc. v. Robot-Coupe Int'l Corp.*, 580 F.Supp. 634, 640 (S.D.N.Y. 1984) (cost of "reparative advertising").

However, some courts have observed that an award for future corrective advertising may be a windfall. *See, e.g., Zazu Designs v. L'Oreal S.A.*, 979 F.2d 499, 506 (7th Cir. 1992) (reversing corrective advertising award; plaintiff must show "that 'repair' of the old trademark, rather than adoption of a new one, is the least expensive way to proceed"); RESTATEMENT (THIRD) OF UNFAIR COMPETITION § 36, comment f ("recovery for future expenses may be inappropriate unless the plaintiff can demonstrate a lack of resources or other reasonable justification for its failure to take the corrective measures prior to litigation"). In *Thompson v. Haynes*, 305 F.3d 1369 (Fed. Cir. 2002), the court vacated the award of damages for corrective advertising where the infringer's ads "were not a source of marketplace confusion or damage", opining that "Tenth Circuit precedent does not contemplate the award of damages to counteract an advertising campaign that itself caused no confusion."

See generally Comment, *Money Damages and Corrective Advertising: An Economic Analysis,* 55 U. CHICAGO L. REV. 629 (1988); Keating, *Damages Standards for False Advertising Under the Lanham Act: A New Trend Emerges,* 20 RUTGERS L.J. 125 (1988); Comment, *Monetary Relief for False Advertising Claims Arising Under Section 43(a) of the Lanham Act,* 34 UCLA L. REV. 953 (1987).

5. Reasonable Royalty

Some courts have awarded plaintiff a reasonable royalty for defendant's use of the infringing mark, as if defendant's use were licensed by plaintiff. *See Ventura v. Titan Sports, Inc.,* 65 F.3d 725, 731 (8ᵗʰ Cir. 1995), *cert. denied,* 516 U.S. 1174 (1996) (awarding reasonable royalties to professional wrestling commentator Jesse "The Body" Ventura for infringement of his right of publicity); *Sands Taylor & Wood Co. v. Quaker Oats Co.,* 978 F.2d 947, 963 (7ᵗʰ Cir.), *cert. denied,* 507 U.S. 1042 (1993) (rejecting accounting of profits and suggesting reasonable royalty be used on remand); *Boston Professional Hockey Ass'n v. Dallas Cap & Emblem Mfg., Inc.,* 597 F.2d 71, 76 (5ᵗʰ Cir. 1979) ($20,000 royalty-based damages for sale of merchandise bearing unlicensed sports insignia); *Deering, Milliken & Co. v. Gilbert,* 269 F.2d 191, 193–194 (2ᵈ Cir. 1959) (reasonably royalty trebled).

Other courts, however have questioned the use of a reasonable royalty as a measure of damages. *Bandag, Inc. v. Albolser's Tire Stores,* 750 F.2d 903, 920 (Fed. Cir. 1984) (rejecting reasonable royalty measure as "grossly out of proportion" to the rights appropriated); *Playboy Enterprises, Inc. v. Baccarat Clothing Co.,* 692 F.2d 1272, 1275 (9ᵗʰ Cir. 1982) (rejecting such a measure and observing that simply requiring defendant to pay a license royalty does not adequately take the economic incentive out of trademark infringement).

6. Other Damages

Damages have been awarded under a variety of other legal theories, *e.g.*: injury to happiness and professional standing, *Waits v. Frito-Lay, Inc.,* 978 F.2d 1093, 1102–1106 (9ᵗʰ Cir. 1992), *cert. denied,* 506 U.S. 1080 (1993) (in voice misappropriation case, upholding $100,000 award for fair market value of services, $200,000 for injury to peace, happiness and feelings; $75,000 for injury to goodwill, professional standing and future publicity value, and $2 million in punitive damages); thwarted expansion, *Taco Cabana International, Inc. v. Two Pesos, Inc.,* 932 F.2d 1113, 1125–1127 (5ᵗʰ Cir. 1991), *aff'd.,* 505 U.S. 763 (1992) ("headstart theory": jury award of more than $930,000 for lost profits and licensing fees caused by defendant's bad faith entry under infringing trade dress into geographic areas of natural expansion for plaintiff; award doubled by court); and compensation for anticipated mistaken product liability claims, *Broan Mfg. Co. v. Associated Distributors, Inc.,* 923 F.2d 1232, 1239–41 (6ᵗʰ Cir. 1991) (accepting damage theory based on anticipated mistaken product liability claims against plaintiff caused by defendant's dangerous infringing electrical fans, but remanding for retrial on damages because of errors by trial court).

See generally Carter & Remec, *Monetary Awards for Trademark Infringement Under the Lanham Act,* 86 TRADEMARK REP. 464 (1996); Koelemay, *A Practical Guide to Monetary Relief in Trademark Infringement Cases,* 85 TRADEMARK REP. 263 (1995).

7. Enhanced and Punitive Damages

Under Section 35 courts have the discretion to enhance or decrease the amount of the damage award. *Taco Cabana International, Inc. v. Two Pesos, Inc.,* 932 F.2d 1113, 1127 (5th Cir. 1991), *aff'd.,* 505 U.S. 763 (1992) ("enhancement could . . . provide proper redress to an otherwise undercompensated plaintiff where imprecise damage results fail to do justice, particularly where the imprecision results from defendant's conduct"; doubling of jury award affirmed); *U.S. Structures, Inc. v. J.P. Structures, Inc.*, 130 F.3d 1185 (6[th]Cir. 1997) (ex-franchisee's intentional and willful post-termination use of mark ARCHADECK for deck construction business resulted in award of quadruple damages, the court concluding that the ordinary meaning of 15 U.S.C. § 1117(a) allowed an increase beyond the treble damages referenced in the statute); *Gorenstein Enterprises, Inc. v. Quality Care-U.S.A. Inc.*, 874 F.2d 431, 435 (7th Cir. 1989) (where ex-franchisee had deliberately infringed, "it might have been an abuse of discretion *not* to have awarded [the plaintiff] treble damages, attorneys' fees, and prejudgment interest"); *Ramada Inns, Inc. v. Gadsden Motel Co.*, 804 F.2d 1562, 1568 (11th Cir. 1986) (damages trebled to $141,000 against ex-franchisee who willfully continued to use mark); *U-Haul International, Inc. v. Jartran, Inc.*, 601 F. Supp. 1140, 1150 (D. Az. 1984), *aff'd. in part, rev'd in part, modified in part*, 793 F.2d 1034, 1041–42 (9th Cir. 1986) (doubling the $20 million in false advertising damages due to defendant's willful and malicious conduct); *Tools USA & Equip. Co. v. Champ Frame Straightening Equip. Inc.*, 87 F.3d 654, 656, 662 & n.5 (4th Cir. 1996) (affirming treble damages pursuant to parties' stipulation to compute damages for Lanham Act trade dress infringement under state law treble damages provision).

Compare Ramada Franchise Sys. v. Boychuk, 124 Fed. App'x. 28 (2[d] Cir. 2005) (unpub'd) (affirming refusal to award Lanham Act enhanced damages where plaintiff offered no non-punitive basis for doing so); *Thompson v. Haynes*, 305 F.3d 1369 (Fed. Cir. 2002) (treble damages award vacated; the court "may not, as it did here, simply lump profits together with damages and apply the same measure of enhancement to both"); *Caesars World, Inc. v. Venus Lounge, Inc.*, 520 F.2d 269, 273 (3[d] Cir. 1975) (there can be no increased damages awarded unless at least some amount of damage is first proven; "[t]hree times zero is zero").

Prejudgment interest on the amount of damages also may be awarded. *Gorenstein Enterprises, Inc. v. Quality Care-U.S.A., Inc.*, 874 F.2d 431, 436 (7th Cir. 1989) (advocating that "prejudgment interest should be presumptively available . . . [w]ithout it, compensation of the plaintiff is incomplete and the defendant has an incentive to delay"). *But see American Honda Motor Co. v. Two Wheel Corp.*, 918 F.2d 1060, 1064 (2[d] Cir. 1990) (award of prejudgment interest is within discretion of court but is "normally reserved for 'exceptional' cases").

Punitive damages "operate as 'private fines' intended to punish the defendant and to deter wrongdoing. A jury's assessment of the extent of a plaintiff's injury is essentially a factual determination, whereas its imposition of punitive damages is an expression of its moral condemnation." *Cooper Indus., Inc. v. Leatherman Tool Group*, 532 U.S. 424 (2001). In that case Cooper had unlawfully used depictions of Leatherman's multi-purpose pocket tool (with Leatherman's trademark whited out) in Cooper's marketing materials and catalogs for Cooper's similar ToolZall product. The jury awarded $50,000 in compensatory damages for this reverse passing off and $4.5 million in punitive damages, which the district and appellate courts let stand.

Concluding that the Ninth Circuit in *Cooper v. Leatherman* should have reviewed the punitive damages award *de novo*, rather than under an abuse of discretion standard, the Supreme Court remanded the case. In doing so, it explained that the Eighth Amendment's "prohibition against excessive fines and cruel and unusual punishments" applies, and that a reviewing court considering a punitive damages award should evaluate *de novo* the following factors: "(1) the degree of reprehensibility of the defendant's misconduct, (2) the disparity between the harm (or potential harm) suffered by the plaintiff and the punitive damages award, and (3) the difference between the punitive damages awarded by the jury and the civil penalties authorized or imposed in comparable cases".

The Supreme Court also observed that Cooper had used depictions of Leatherman's product because of Cooper's inability to quickly and cheaply obtain a mock-up of Cooper's yet-to-be released product, rather than any intention to mislead customers. On remand, the Ninth Circuit, in *Leatherman Tool Group, Inc. v. Cooper Indus, Inc.*, 285 F.3d 1146 (9th Cir. 2002), determined the maximum award of punitive damages was $500,000. Among other things, it concluded that, "Cooper's conduct was more foolish than reprehensible."

The Supreme Court further clarified the guidelines for awarding punitive damages in *State Farm Mut. Auto. Inc. Co. v. Campbell*, 538 U.S. 408 (2003). There the award to defendants of $145 million in punitive damages after a $1 million compensatory award was held unconstitutionally excessive. "[C]ourts must ensure that the measure of punishment is both reasonable and proportionate to the amount of harm to the plaintiff and to the general damages recovered." While declining "to impose a bright-line ratio", the Court observed that, "in practice, few awards exceeding a single-digit ratio between punitive and compensatory damages, to a significant degree, will satisfy due process."

Subsequently, in *Ford Motor Co. v. Estate of Tommy Smith*, 538 U.S. 1038 (2003), the Supreme Court applied *State Farm v. Campbell* in setting aside a $290 million punitive damages award against Ford stemming from a fatal 1993 California rollover accident involving a Ford Bronco. It vacated that judgment and remanded the case to the Supreme Court of Kentucky for further consideration in view of the *State Farm v. Campbell* decision. In *Philip Morris USA v. Williams*, 127 S.Ct. 1057 (2007), the Supreme Court clarified that, while harm to nonparties can be considered in determining the reprehensibility of defendant's conduct as a basis for whether to award punitive damages, harm to nonparties can *not* be considered in determining the *amount* of any punitive damages award. To punish the defendant for injuries inflicted on nonparties, without an opportunity to defend the charge, would violate due process.

Punitive damages may be available under state law, but are not expressly available under the Lanham Act. *United Phosphorus Ltd. v. Midland Fumigant, Inc.*, 205 F.3d 1219, 1231 (10th Cir. 2000)(affirming more than $650,000 in punitive damages under state law for egregious infringement and misrepresentations); *Waits v. Frito-Lay Inc.*, 978 F.2d 1093, 1104 (9th Cir. 1992), *cert. denied*, 506 U.S. 1080 (1993) (affirming $2 million punitive damage award under California law); *Jurgens v. McKasy*, 927 F.2d 1552, 1564 (Fed. Cir.), *cert. denied*, 502 U.S. 902 (1991) (punitive damages not authorized under Lanham Act); *Getty Petroleum Corp. v. Bartco Petroleum Corp.*, 858 F.2d 103, 106, 113 (2d Cir. 1988) (vacating $2 million punitive damage award under Lanham Act), *cert. denied*, 490 U.S. 1006 (1989); *Getty Petroleum Corp. v. Island Transportation Corp.*, 878 F.2d 650 (2d Cir. 1989) (affirming $250,000 punitive damage award under New York law). Courts nonetheless sometimes appear to use the enhancement of damages to serve a punitive function under the Lanham Act. *Gorenstein Enterprises, Inc. v. Quality Care-USA, Inc.*, 874 F.2d 431, 435–36 (7th Cir. 1989) (implying courts may treble damages with a punitive purpose).

8. Counterfeiting Damages

In civil counterfeiting actions, an award to the prevailing plaintiff of treble damages or profits and attorneys' fees is mandatory "unless the court finds extenuating circumstances." 15 U.S.C. 1117. *Lacoste Alligator, S.A. v. Goberman*, 1990 U.S. Dist. Lexis 17486 (S.D.N.Y. 1990) (trebled profits plus attorneys' fees); *Louis Vuitton S.A. v. Downtown Luggage Center*, 706 F.Supp. 839, 844 (S.D. Fla. 1988) (same). Because it is sometimes difficult for a trademark owner to prove actual damages in counterfeiting cases, the 1996 Trademark Counterfeiting Act amended the Lanham Act to provide statutory damages from $500 to $10,000 for each mark non-willfully infringed, and up to $1 million for each mark willfully infringed. 18 U.S.C. § 1117(c). *See also* the discussion of federal anticounterfeiting provisions in Chapter 6.

In criminal counterfeiting cases, in addition to imprisonment, up to a $250,000 fine may be assessed against an individual first offender, with a repeat offender liable for up to $1 million. Corporations may be fined up to $1 million for the first offense, and up to $5 million for a second offense. 15 U.S.C. § 1116; 18 U.S.C. § 2320. *See United States v. Hon,* 904 F.2d 803, 804 (2ᵈ Cir. 1990), *cert. denied,* 498 U.S. 1069 (1991) ($6,000 fine); *United States v. Song,* 934 F.2d 105, 109 (7th Cir. 1991) (upholding defendant's five criminal convictions for trafficking in counterfeit goods bearing five different trademarks belonging to five different owners; "the correct unit of prosecution under Section 2320 is the counterfeit mark"). *See also Young v. United States,* 481 U.S. 787 (1987) (plaintiff's counsel in counterfeiting civil action cannot be appointed special prosecutor in subsequent related criminal contempt proceeding due to bias concerns).

The 1996 Trademark Counterfeiting Act added trafficking in goods or services bearing counterfeit marks to the list of "predicate acts" proscribed under the federal Racketeer Influenced and Corrupt Organizations Act (RICO), 18 U.S.C. § 1961(1)(B).

In 2006, the Stop Counterfeiting in Manufactured Goods Act (P.L. 109-181, 120 Stat. 285), amended the criminal provisions of Title 18 to, among other things, require convicted offenders to pay restitution to the trademark owner. *See, e.g., U.S. v. Beydoun,* 469 F.3d 102 (5ᵗʰ Cir. 2006) (evaluating proofs for amount of mandatory restitution, and remanding to district court to determine the restitution amount based on the amount of net profits the legitimate sellers lost as a result of defendant's actions).

9. Cybersquatting Damages

Statutory damages also are available in domain name cybersquatting cases brought under 15 U.S.C. § 1125 (d)(1). Those damages, available under 15 U.S.C. § 1117(d), range from $1,000-$100,000 per domain name. *See, e.g., E & J Gallo Winery v. Spider Webs Ltd.,* 286 F.3d 270 (5ᵗʰ Cir. 2002) ($25,000 for defendant's bad faith registration of ernestandjuliogallo.com); *Shields v. Zuccarini,* 254 F.3d 476 (3ᶠ Cir. 2001)(awarding $10,000 for each violative domain name); *Electronics Boutique Holdings Corp. v. Zuccarini,* 59 U.S.P.Q.2d 1705 (E.D. Pa. 2000)($100,000 for each violative domain name).

10. Defendant's Profits

a) Willfulness and Bad Faith

A plaintiff normally need not prove actual damages to obtain an accounting of defendant's profits. Willfulness and bad faith can be a basis for such an award, but other factors may come into play. *Optimum Technologies, Inc. v. Home Depot USA, Inc.,* 217 Fed. Appx. 899 (11ᵗʰ Cir. 2007) ("an accounting of defendant's profits is appropriate where: (1) the defendant's conduct was willful and deliberate; (2) the defendant was unjustly enriched; or (3) it is necessary to deter future conduct"); *Thompson v. Haynes,* 305 F.3d 1369 (Fed. Cir. 2002) (affirming award of willful infringer's profits); *Bishop v. Equinox Int'l Corp.,* 154 F.3d 1220, 1223 (10ᵗʰ Cir. 1998) (a trademark owner whose mark has been infringed may be entitled to an accounting of profits on the theory of unjust enrichment and deterrence of willful infringement, even in the absence of a showing of actual damages); *Wynn Oil Co. v. American Way Service Corp.,* 943 F.2d 595, 606–07 (6th Cir. 1991); *Burger King Corp. v. Mason,* 855 F.2d 779, 781 (11ᵗʰ Cir. 1988). If defendant has acted willfully, an award of defendant's profits is justified, but not required. *Majer Brewing Co. v. Fleischmann Distilling Corp.,* 390 F.2d 117, 124–124 (9ᵗʰ Cir.), *cert. denied,* 391 U.S. 966 (1968).

The difficulty for many courts has been determining what exactly constitutes "willfulness" and whether it requires bad faith conduct, or something less. *George Basch Co. v. Blue Coral, Inc.,* 968 F.2d 1532, 1537 (2ᵈ Cir.), *cert. denied,* 506 U.S. 991 (1992) ("under any theory, a finding of willful deceptiveness is a prerequisite for awarding profits"); *Sands, Taylor & Wood v. Quaker Oats Co.,* 978 F.2d 947, 961–962

(7th Cir. 1992), *cert. denied*, 507 U.S. 1042 (1993) (acknowledging profits may be available in reverse confusion cases without intent to trade on reputation if there is bad faith conduct, but reversing award under circumstances; "A party who acts in reasonable reliance on the advice of counsel regarding a close question of trademark law generally does not act in bad faith"); *ALPO Petfoods, Inc., supra*; *Wynn Oil Co. v. American Way Service Co.*, 943 F.2d 595, 605 (6th Cir. 1991) (reversing refusal to award profits where evidence showed bad intent).

In *Tamko Roofing Products, Inc. v. Ideal Roofing Co.*, 282 F.3d 23 (1st Cir. 2002), an accounting of defendant's profits did not require a showing of bad faith because the parties directly competed. *See also* Stolte, *Remedying Judicial Limitations on Trademark Remedies: An Accounting of Profits Should Not Require A Finding of Bad Faith*, 87 TRADEMARK REP. 271 (1997). *Compare Gucci Am. v. Gold Center Jewelry*, 158 F.3d 631 (2[d] Cir. 1998) (determining bad faith is not necessary to finding of willfulness in the context of a default judgment; $25,000 awarded to each plaintiff from each defendant, where defendants admitted receiving copies of the complaint, were aware of the lawsuit and damages claim, but chose to ignore it; while "more a product of stupidity than malice", this nonetheless constituted willful conduct).

Many courts have cited the importance of factors other than willfulness in determining whether to award defendant's profits. In *Seatrax, Inc. v. Sonbeck Intern., Inc.*, 200 F.3d 358, 369 (5th Cir. 2000), the court identified the following non-exhaustive list of factors relevant to whether an accounting of profits should be awarded: (1) whether the defendant intended to confuse or deceive; (2) whether sales have been diverted; (3) the adequacy of other remedies; (4) any unreasonable delay in asserting rights; (5) the public interest in making the conduct unprofitable; and (6) whether it is a case of palming off. Noting that the jury did not find the infringement was willful, that evidence of actual damages was lacking and that it was not a case of palming off, the court affirmed that injunctive relief satisfied the equities of the case. Similarly, in *Estate of Bishop v. Equinox Int'l Corp.*, 256 F.3d 1050 (10th Cir. 2001), despite the willfulness of defendant, the court affirmed the denial of an accounting of profits where plaintiff only sold an annual average of 98 bottles of his product, did not lose any sales to defendant, defendant did not benefit from any goodwill associated with the mark, and there was no actual confusion. An injunction plus an award of attorneys' fees was deemed sufficient. *See also Balance Dynamics Corp. v. Schmitt Industries, Inc.*, 204 F.3d 683, 695 (6th Cir. 2000)(affirming denial of accounting of profits where there was no proof that plaintiff lost sales or profits or that plaintiff gained either through the unlawful conduct).

Compare Banjo Buddies, Inc. v. Renosky, 399 F.3d 168, 174 (3[d] Cir. 2005), in which the Third Circuit held that willfulness remained an important equitable factor, but was not a prerequisite to an accounting of a trademark infringer's profits. The court concluded that a 1999 amendment to the Lanham Act replaced "or a violation under section 43(a)" with "a violation under section 43(a) or a willful violation under section 43(c)," and that the "plain language of the amendment indicates that Congress intended to condition monetary awards for § 43(c) violations, but not § 43(a) violations, on a showing of willfulness." *See also Blendco, Inc. v. ConAgra Foods, Inc.*, 132 Fed. App'x. 520 (t Cir. 2005) (unpub.) (affirming award of lost profits; while the "willfulness of the infringement" was an "important factor in deciding whether lost profits are appropriately awarded," willfulness "is not a prerequisite to such an award"); *Xoom, Inc. v. Imageline, Inc.*, 323 F.3d 279 (9th Cir. 2003) ("In determining damages under the Lanham Act, the plaintiff bears the burden of proving a causal connection between its harms and the defendant's profits"; because plaintiff had shown neither actual damages nor that causal link, its damages claim could not be sustained); and *Quick Techs. v. Sage Group PLC*, 313 F.3d 338 (5th Cir. 2002), in which the jury did not award defendant's profits because the infringement was not willful. The appellate court observed that willfulness is only one factor to consider in such an award, but the jury instruction to the contrary was harmless error where no other factor favored the award.

As indicated above, if the parties are not competitors, defendant's profits may nonetheless be awarded to plaintiff under a theory of unjust enrichment. *Burger King Corp. v. Mason*, 855 F.2d 779, 781 (11th Cir. 1988); *Maltina Corp. v. Cawy Bottling Co.*, 613 F.2d 582, 585 (5th Cir. 1980); *Maier Brewing Co. v. Fleischmann Distilling Corp.*, 390 F.2d 117, 121 (9th Cir.), *cert. denied*, 391 U.S. 966 (1968); *Monsanto Chemical Co.*, *supra*. *Compare, Alpo Petfoods, supra* (deterrence cannot justify awarding profits under an unjust enrichment theory); *Raxton Corp. v. Anania Associates, Inc.*, 668 F.2d 622, 625 (1st Cir. 1982) (where no actual damages proven in case between non-competitors, accounting of profits impermissible under state or federal law).

b) Actual Confusion

Some courts have required a showing of actual confusion for an accounting of profits. *Perfect Fit Industries, Inc. v. Acme Quilting Co.*, 618 F.2d 950, 955 (2[d] Cir. 1980), *cert. denied*, 459 U.S. 832 (1982); ("In the absence of proof of an actual confusion of consumers, [plaintiff] is not entitled to damages or an accounting"); *D.C. Comics, Inc. v. Filmation Associates*, 486 F. Supp. 1273, 1284 (S.D.N.Y. 1980). Others have not. *See International Star Class Yacht Racing Ass'n v. Tommy Hilfiger U.S.A.*, 146 F.3d 66 (2[d] Cir. 1998) (even if actual injury or actual consumer confusion is not shown, an accounting of profits still may be awarded to deter a willful infringer from infringing again); *Web Printing Controls Co. v. Oxy-Dry Corp.*, 906 F.2d 1202, 1205 (7th Cir. 1990) (no need to show actual confusion for an accounting of profits); *Wynn Oil Co. v. American Way Service Corp.*, 943 F.2d 595, 606–07 (6th Cir. 1991) (same).

c) Deductions

Once plaintiff proves defendant's gross sales, defendant has the burden to prove any offsetting deductions. *Australian Gold, Inc. v. Hatfield*, 436 F.3d 1228 (10th Cir. 2006) (defendants could not rely on their poor record-keeping to claim that damages were too speculative to be awarded); *Wynn Oil Co. v. American Way Service Corp.*, 943 F.2d 595, 607 (6th Cir. 1991) (defendants had burden to prove deductions from gross receipts, with uncertainties resolved in plaintiff's favor); *Sony Corp. v. Elm State Electronics, Inc.*, 800 F.2d 317, 321 (2[d] Cir. 1986) (failure to consider defendant's offsetting expenses was abuse of discretion); *Boston Professional Hockey Assoc. v. Dallas Cap & Emblem*, 597 F.2d 71, 77 (5th Cir. 1979) ("an infringer should not be allowed to limit a trademark owner to injunctive relief by stonewalling' the question of sales"); *W.E. Bassett Co. v. Revlon, Inc.*, 435 F.2d 656, 665 (2[d] Cir. 1970) (defendant allowed to deduct overhead, most of its operating expenses and federal income taxes on the infringing products); *Jones Apparel Group, Inc. v. Steinman*, 466 F. Supp. 560, 563 n.4 (E.D. Pa. 1979) (there is no "hard and fast rule" as to acceptable deductions).

In some cases only the portion of defendant's profits directly attributable to use of the infringing mark has been awarded. *Holiday Inns. v. Airport Holiday Corp.*, 493 F. Supp. 1025, 1028 (N.D. Tex. 1980), *aff'd.*, 683 F.2d 931 (5th Cir. 1982) (30% of defendant's profits awarded). *Compare Truck Equipment Service Co. v. Fruehauf Corp.*, 536 F.2d 1210, 1222 (8th Cir.) *cert. denied*, 429 U.S. 861 (1976) (where infringement is willful, equity requires that all profits be awarded). *Compare International Star Class Racing Ass'n v. Tommy Hilfiger U.S.A.*, 146 F.3d 66, 72-73 (2[d] Cir. 1998) ("where infringement is especially malicious or egregious, allowing a defendant, especially a dominant competitor who has made use of the mark of a weaker entity, to deduct profits due to its own market dominance in some circumstances inadequately serves the goal of deterrence").

See generally Barber, *Recovery of Profits Under the Lanham Act: Are The District Courts Doing Their Job?*, 82 TRADEMARK REP. 141 (1992); Bussert & Davis, *Calculating Profits Under Section 35 of the Lanham Act: A Practitioner's Guide*, 82 TRADEMARK REP. 182 (1992).

11. Attorneys' Fees

a) Exceptional Cases

After the decision in *International Star Class Yacht Racing Ass'n v. Tommy Hilfiger, U.S.A.*, 80 F.3d 749 (2ᵈ Cir. 1996) excerpted above in the main text, the district court determined on remand that defendant had not acted in bad faith, so that awards of profits and attorneys' fees were not warranted. On appeal, the Second Circuit affirmed. It noted the district court's findings that sales of defendant's clothing were "driven by the prominent use of defendant's marks" and that there was no showing that defendant knew of plaintiff's mark. Furthermore, the district court had found that defendant had no obligation to conduct a more extensive trademark search, given "Hilfiger's use of the Star Class mark as a decoration rather than as a trademark was consistent with the advice of Hilfiger's attorney that *use* and *registration* [of the mark] would require a full trademark search", and the attorneys' advice that Star Class "would be a weak trademark because of the common use of the terms 'Star' and 'Class', encourag[ing] Hilfiger to believe that the use of the term was permissible." In affirming, the appellate court stated, "Although there is some evidence that points toward the existence of bad faith, we cannot say, after review of the record, that we are left with [the] definite and firm conviction that a mistake has been committed' [citations omitted]." In *Tamko Roofing Products, Inc. v. Ideal Roofing Co.*, 282 F.3d 23 (1ˢᵗ Cir. 2002), the court stated that a "mere failure to conduct a trademark search before using a mark may evidence nothing more than carelessness, and so may not warrant an award of fees". However, it nonetheless affirmed the award of attorneys' fees in the absence of bad faith, based on the "totality of circumstances." including defendant's continued use of the mark after a preliminary injunction was granted.

Section 35 authorizes courts to award attorneys' fees in exceptional cases. These typically are cases in which defendant has acted in bad faith. *Stephen W. Boney, Inc. v. Boney Serv.*, 127 F.3d 821, 826 (9ᵗʰ Cir. 1997) (exceptional cases under § 35 occur when infringement is "malicious, fraudulent, deliberate or willful"); *Reader's Digest Assoc. v. Conservative Digest, Inc.*, 821 F.2d 800, 808 (D.C. Cir. 1987) ("Under the Lanham Act, a court must find wilful or bad faith infringement by the defendant in order to award attorneys' fees to the plaintiff"). *Compare M Eagles Tool Warehouse, Inc. v. Fisher Tooling Co.*, 439 F.3d 1335 (Fed. Cir. 2006) ("dearth of evidence" of bad faith intent to deceive precluded award of attorneys' fees on summary judgment); *People for the Ethical Treatment of Animals v. Doughney*, 263 F.3d 359 (4ᵗʰ Cir. 2001) (although defendant registered the domain name in bad faith in violation of the Anti-Cybersquatting Consumer Protection Act, "he did not act with the level of malicious, fraudulent, willful or deliberate behavior necessary for an award of attorneys' fees"); *Ferrero U.S.A., Inc. v. Ozak Trading, Inc.*, 952 F.2d 44, 48 (3d Cir. 1991) (reversing fee award in gray market case where no evidence of bad faith); *Roulo v. Russ Berrie & Co.*, 886 F.2d 931, 942-43 (7ᵗʰ Cir. 1989), *cert. denied*, 493 U.S. 1075 (1990) (willfulness not extreme enough). In *Watec Co., Ltd. v. Liu*, 403 F.3d 645 (9ᵗʰ Cir. 2005) the court vacated and remanded a jury award of attorneys' fees, noting that "the jury's finding that Watec America 'intentionally infringed' does not necessarily equate to the malicious, fraudulent, deliberate or willful conduct that [is] usually require[d] before deeming a case exceptional" so as to warrant an award of attorneys' fees.

Even reliance on advice of counsel in using mark may not preclude an award of attorneys' fees to plaintiff. *TakeCare Corp. v. Takecare of Oklahoma, Inc.*, 889 F.2d 955, 957–58 (10ᵗʰ Cir. 1989) (need to show evidence of the advice and reasonableness of the reliance); *Universal Motor Oils Co. v. Amoco Oil Co.*, 809 F.Supp. 816, 823 (D. Kan. 1992) (reasonable reliance on advice of counsel may negate claim of willfulness).

b)   Circumstances Other than Bad Faith

Circumstances other than bad faith also may render a case exceptional. *Stephen W. Boney, Inc. v. Boney Services, Inc.*, 127 F.3d 821, 827 (9th Cir. 1997) ("While a finding that the losing party has acted in bad faith may provide evidence that the case is exceptional . . . other exceptional circumstances may warrant a fee award"). What other circumstances might justify an award of attorneys' fees? *See, e.g., Patsy's Brand, Inc. v. I.O.B. Realty, Inc.*, 317 F.3d 209 (2[d] Cir. 2003) (defendant had submitted false evidence; "fraudulent conduct in the course of conducting trademark litigation permits a finding that a case is 'exceptional' for purposes of an attorneys' fee award under the Lanham Act"); *Securacomm Consulting, Inc. v. Securacom Inc.*, 224 F.3d 273, 282 (3[d] Cir. 2000)(although the infringement was not willful, defendant's vexatious litigation conduct — "it tried to prevail by crushing plaintiff" — warranted an award of attorneys' fees); *Walt Disney Co. v. Great American Corp.*, 28 U.S.P.Q.2d 1130, 1135 (M.D. Tenn. 1993) (awarding attorneys' fees due to concealment of records and other flagrant abuses of discovery). *Compare Procter & Gamble Co. v. Haugen*, 422 F.3d 727 (10th Cir. 2005) (district court erred in dismissing case as a sanction for plaintiff's alleged discovery misconduct; plaintiff's obligations toward third party data were unclear and could not be the basis for dismissal). In a particularly egregious example, attorneys' fees were awarded to plaintiff in *Te-Ta-Ma Truth Foundation-Family of URI v. World Church of The Creator*, 392 F.3d 248 (7th Cir. 2004), where the defendant, among other things, threatened the plaintiff and its attorneys, and defendant's founder solicited the murder of the presiding judge.

c)   Non-Lanham Act Awards

The "exceptional cases" requirement under the Lanham Act has been held to impose a higher standard for collection of attorney's fees than does Section 505 of the Copyright Act, which gives a court discretion to "award a reasonable attorneys' fee to the prevailing party . . . ." 17 U.S.C. § 505. *See FASA Corp. v. Playmates Toys Inc.*, 108 F.3d 140, 144 (7th Cir. 1997) (remanding for separate consideration of attorneys' fees for litigation involving both copyright and trademark issues and explaining that the standard for collecting attorneys' fees under the Copyright Act is "a generous one" compared to the Lanham Act standard). *Compare Door Sys. v. Pro-Line Door Sys.*, 126 F.3d 1028 (7th Cir. 1997) (considering award of attorneys' fees under different Illinois state law standard and denial under Lanham Act standard).

d)   Prevailing Defendants

A prevailing *defendant* may be awarded attorneys' fees in the appropriate case. *See, e.g. Matrix Motor Co. v. Toyota Motor Sales, U.S.A., Inc.*, 120 Fed. App'x. 30 (9th Cir. 2005) (over $1.1 million awarded to defendant where the likelihood of confusion between the marks was "near zero", the plaintiff had "grossly exaggerated its claims and had no competent evidence to support those claims", and the plaintiff had engaged in discovery abuses); In *Cairns v. Franklin Mint Co.*, 292 F.3d 1139 (9th Cir. 2002), a case involving use of Princess Diana's image on collectible merchandise, over $2 million in attorneys' fees was awarded to defendant where plaintiff's false advertising claim was groundless and "absurd". *See also S Industries, Inc. v. Centra 2000, Inc.*, 249 F.3d 625, 627 (7th Cir. 2001) (awarding defendant attorneys' fees where plaintiff's claims were meritless and it engaged in dilatory tactics); *Tire Kingdom, Inc. v. Morgan Tire & Auto, Inc.*, 253 F.3d 1332, 1336 (11th Cir. 2001) (in false advertising case, plaintiffs submitted no evidence on four of the five necessary Lanham Act elements, and filed the suit in bad faith); *Aromatique, Inc. v. Gold Seal, Inc.*, 28 F.3d 863 (8th Cir. 1994) (plaintiff's false representation to defendant that it had a federal registration for its potpourri packaging, and failure to inform PTO of that false representation when subsequently obtaining a registration was "beyond the pale of acceptable behavior"; fees awarded to defendant); *Scotch Whiskey Ass'n v. Majestic Distilling Co.*, 958 F.2d 594, 599–600 (4th

Cir.), *cert. denied,* 506 U.S. 862 (1992) (fee award to defendant despite absence of bad faith by plaintiff where suit was unfounded); *Orient Express Trading Co. v. Federated Dept. Stores, Inc.,* 842 F.2d 650 (2[d] Cir. 1988) (fee award to defendant where plaintiffs fraudulently obtained registrations "to capitalize on [defendant's] profits and to instigate 'vexatious' litigation").

12. Insurance Coverage

Often business insurance policies will cover the costs of defending an infringement or unfair competition suit under what has come to be called "the advertising injury clause." *See, e.g., M. Century 21, Inc. v. Diamond State Ins. Co.,* 442 F.3d 79 (2[d] Cir. 2006) (advertising injury clause encompassed claims that defendant's "marketing" of the products at issue constituted trademark infringement). In *Letro Prod. v. Liberty Mut. Ins. Co.,* 114 F.3d 1194 (9th Cir. 1997), the plaintiff's insurance company had refused coverage after a third party sued plaintiff for trademark infringement. Following the state court's reasoning in *Lebas Fashion Imports of USA v. ITT Hartford Ins. Group,* 50 Cal. App. 4th 548 (1996), the Ninth Circuit held that the comprehensive general liability policy covered claims of trademark infringement when an "advertising injury is caused by an offense committed in the course of advertising your goods, products or services." Advertising injury was defined as arising, among other things, from a misappropriation of advertising ideas or style of doing business, or an infringement of copyright, title or slogan. The causal nexus was established where the policyholder's alleged infringement occurred in promotional materials and trade pieces. The court concluded that the insurance company had a duty to defend and was liable for breach of contract. *See also Western Int'l Syndication Corp. v. Gulf Insurance Co.,* 222 Fed. App'x. 589 (9th Cir. 2007) (while policy excluded coverage of cases involving "infringement of copyright or trademark", insurance company still had duty to defend because of plaintiff's claims that defendant made disparaging statements); *Charter Oak Fire Ins. Co. v. Hedeen & Co.,* 280 F.3d 730 (7th Cir. 2002) (affirming summary judgment that alleged infringing use of trademark in stationery letterhead was encompassed by advertising injury clause); *Hyman v. Nationwide Mutual Fire Ins. Co.,* 304 F.3d 1179 (11th Cir. 2002) ("because trade dress may encompass marketing or packaging designed to draw attention to a product, it can constitute an 'advertising idea' or 'style of doing business' "); *R. C. Bigelow, Inc. v. Liberty Mutual Ins. Co.,* 287 F.3d 242 (2[d] Cir. 2002) (use of allegedly infringing trade dress in advertising fell within the advertising injury clause); *American Simmental Assoc. v. Coregis Ins. Co.,* 282 F.3d 582 (8th Cir. 2002) (alleged misrepresentation that cattle were "fullbloods" was encompassed by advertising injury provision).

Some courts have narrowly interpreted the standard business policy language in denying coverage to the insured. *See, e.g., Sport Supply Group v. Columbia Cas. Co.,* 335 F.3d 453 (5th Cir. 2003), (the court opined that use of the trademark did not constitute "advertising", so the policy's "misappropriation of advertising ideas under an implied contract" clause did not apply); *Callas Ent. v. Travelers Indem. Co. of Am.,* 193 F.3d 952 (8th Cir. 1999) (allegation of trademark infringement did not properly fall under provision for infringement of "copyright, title or slogan"); *Frog, Switch & Mfg. Co. v. Travelers Ins. Co.,* 193 F.3d 742, 748-49 (3[d] Cir. 1999) ("the allegation that Frog engaged in unfair competition by misappropriating trade secrets relating to manufacture of a product line does not allege misappropriation of advertising ideas or styles of doing business as such", but noting in *dicta* that a trademark might be viewed as an "advertising idea" under Pennsylvania law); *ShoLodge, Inc. v. Travelers Indem. Co.,* 168 F.3d 256 (6th Cir. 1999) (allegation of service mark infringement not covered under "copyright, title or slogan" provision); *Hugo Boss Fashions, Inc. v. Federal Insurance Co.,* 252 F.3d 608, 611 (2[d]Cir. 2001) (because plaintiff's BOSS trademark was not a "trademarked slogan," it did not fall under the policy's coverage). *Compare Sentex Sys. v. Hartford Accident & Indem. Co.,* 93 F.3d 578 (9th Cir. 1996) (the phrase "misappropriation of advertising ideas or style of doing business", encompassed defendant's alleged unfair competition by misappropriation of trade secrets such as customer lists, methods of bidding jobs and marketing techniques). *See generally* Graff, *Insurance Coverage of Trademark Infringement Claims: The Contradictions Among the Courts, and the Ramifications for Trademark Attorneys*, 89 TRADEMARK REP. 939 (1999).

CHAPTER 11
OTHER GOVERNMENTAL REGULATION

CONTENTS

11.01 The Federal Trade Commission

Introduction

The Federal Trade Commission is the leading federal administrative agency protecting consumers and competitors against deceptive advertising. As originally conceived in 1914, the FTC was primarily intended to bolster what was widely believed to be ineffective enforcement of the antitrust laws, rather than to be the watchdog of advertising. *See* Liebling, *Judicial Usurpation of the FTC's Authority: A Return to the Rule of Reason,* 30 J. MARSHALL L. REV. 383 (1996) (an overview of the FTC from its congressional creation to contemporary federal court attempts to limit its authority); Note, *Developments in the Law, Deceptive Advertising,* 80 HARV. L. REV. 1005 (1967). In order to arm the FTC for unbridled antitrust enforcement, § 5 of the original Federal Trade Commission Act broadly declared all "unfair methods of competition in commerce" to be unlawful and "empowered and directed" the FTC to prevent such practices. 15 U.S.C. § 45(a) (1914). *See generally* KANWIT, FEDERAL TRADE COMMISSION (2007).

Notwithstanding this original intent of Congress, over 90 percent of the actions initiated by the FTC during its first two decades were directed against deceptive trade practices rather than antitrust violations. *See* Posner, *The Federal Trade Commission,* 37 U. CHI. L. REV. 47 (1969). Moreover, the FTC's power to prevent deceptive advertising was upheld at the very outset in *Sears, Roebuck & Co. v. FTC,* 258 F. 307 (7th Cir. 1919), and later confirmed in *FTC v. Winsted Hosiery Co.,* 258 U.S. 483 (1922).

Until 1938, however, the FTC's latitude in challenging deceptive practices was severely limited. In *FTC v. Gratz,* 253 U.S. 421 (1920), the Supreme Court held that § 5 of the FTC Act prohibited only those unfair trade practices which were proscribed either by other statutes or by the common law as it was in 1914. In *FTC v. Raladam Co.,* 283 U.S. 643 (1931), the Supreme Court held the FTC could proceed only against practices that harmed competitors, regardless of their effect on consumers. It was not until the decision in *FTC v. R. F. Keppel & Bros., Inc.,* 291 U.S. 304 (1934), and the passage of the Wheeler-Lea Act of 1938 (52 Stat. 111 (1938)) that the FTC Act became a potentially effective weapon to protect consumer interests. In *Keppel,* the Court reversed its decision in *Gratz* on the types of practices prohibited by § 5, stating, 291 U.S. at 310:

> Neither the language nor the history of the Act suggests that Congress intended to confine the forbidden methods to fixed and unyielding categories. The common law afforded a definition of unfair competition and, before the

enactment of the Federal Trade Commission Act, the Sherman Act had laid its inhibition upon combinations to restrain or monopolize interstate commerce which the courts had construed to include restraints upon competition in interstate commerce. It would not have been a difficult feat of draftsmanship to have restricted the operation of the Trade Commission Act to those methods of competition in interstate commerce which are forbidden at common law or which are likely to grow into violations of the Sherman Act, if that had been the purpose of the legislation.

The Wheeler-Lea Act, a reaction to the decision in *Raladam*, amended § 5 of the FTC Act by adding a prohibition against "unfair or deceptive acts or practices in commerce." The purpose of the Amendment was expressed by a Senate Committee member as follows:

> Section 5 of the present act declares unlawful unfair methods of competition in commerce, and the pending bill amends that section by also declaring unlawful, unfair or deceptive acts and practices in commerce. Under the present act it has been intimated in court decisions that the Commission may lose jurisdiction of a case of deceptive and similar unfair practices if it should develop in the proceeding that all competitors in the industry practiced the same methods, and the Commission may be ousted of its jurisdiction, no matter how badly the public may be in need of protection from said deceptive and unfair acts. Under the proposed amendment, the Commission would have jurisdiction to stop the exploitation or deception of the public, even though the competition of the respondent are themselves entitled to no protection because of their engaging in similar practices.

S. Rep. No. 221, 75th Cong. 1st Sess. 3 (1937).

The Wheeler-Lea Amendment also assigned to the FTC jurisdiction over the advertising of foods, drugs, cosmetics, and devices (15 U.S.C. § 52), leaving the regulation of their labeling and packaging to the Food and Drug Administration, 21 U.S.C. §§ 301–394. In subsequent years, the FTC has also been given either total or partial responsibility for enforcing a number of other statutes, many of which are designed to protect the consumer. These acts include the Fair Packaging and Labeling Act, 15 U.S.C. § 1451 *et seq.*; the Consumer Credit Protection Act, 15 U.S.C. §§ 1601–1615, 1631–1641, 16, 71–77; the Fair Debt Collection Practices Act, 15 U.S.C. § 1692 *et. seq*; the Children's Online Privacy Protection Act, 15 U.S.C. § 6501 *et. seq.*; the CAN-SPAM Act, 15 U.S.C. § 7701 *et. seq.*; the Federal Cigarette Labeling and Advertising Act, 15 U.S.C. § 1331 *et seq.*; Trademark Act, 15 U.S.C. § 1064; the McCarran-Ferguson Insurance Act, 15 U.S.C. § 1011 *et seq.*; and the Emergency Petroleum Allocation Act, 15 U.S.C. § 751 *et seq. See, e.g., Brown v. Card Service Center*, 464 F.3d 450 (3d Cir. 2006) (debt collection agency's threatening letter to debtor may have been deceptive or misleading in violation of the Fair Debt Collection Practices Act); *Brown v. Brown & Williamson Tobacco Corp.*, 479 F.3d 383 (5th Cir. 2007) (because defendant used FTC-approved descriptors for its cigarettes and otherwise complied with the Federal Cigarette Labeling and Advertising Act, plaintiff's state law deceptive marketing claims were pre-empted).

In 1973, Congress amended the FTC Act to empower it to seek relief pendente lite against unfair or deceptive practices. 15 U.S.C. § 53. Previously, the FTC had such power in some areas, such as the false advertising of foods, drugs, cosmetics or devices (15 U.S.C. § 52); Wool Products Labeling Act (15 U.S.C. §§ 68–68j); Fur Product Labeling and Advertising Act (15 U.S.C. §§ 69–69j); and Textile Fiber Product Identification Act (15 U.S.C. §§ 70–70k). It could not, however, stop most unfair or deceptive acts or practices during the often lengthy pendency of FTC proceedings. The amendment also gave the FTC authority to apply directly to the courts for enforcement of its orders and for subpoenas, avoiding the delay or obstruction formerly caused by the FTC's dependency on the Justice Department to bring such actions. 15 U.S.C. §§ 49, 53.

In 1975, the Magnuson-Moss Warranty-Federal Trade Commission Improvement Act extended the jurisdiction to matters "affecting commerce." Pub. L. No. 93-637 § 201, 15 U.S.C. §§ 45, 52 (1975), see H.R. REP. No. 93-1107, 93 Cong. 2d. Sess. 45 (1974). Section 5, as amended, states:

Unfair methods of competition in or affecting commerce, and unfair or deceptive acts or practices in or affecting commerce, are declared unlawful.

15 U.S.C. § 45(a)(1). In addition, the Act established standards for warranties and conferred upon the FTC the authority to: (1) issue trade regulation rules defining unfair or deceptive acts or practices, (2) seek civil penalties in federal district court for violations of FTC orders prohibiting unfair acts or practices by individuals already subject to an FTC order as well as by any person, partnership, or corporation which knowingly violates an FTC rule or order, and (3) impose civil penalties of up to $10,000 for each such violation. Pub. L. No. 93- 637 §§ 202(a), 204(b), 205(a), 15 U.S.C. §§ 57(a)(1), 45(m) (1975). The Act also permits the FTC to institute civil actions in either federal or state court seeking consumer redress for injuries caused by rule violations or practices resulting in a cease and desist order. Pub. L. No. 93-637, § 206(a), 15 U.S.C. § 57(b) (1975). Remedies available for such injuries include damages, rescission or reformation of contracts, refund of money or return of property. For additional commentary, see *Empirical Study of the Magnuson-Moss Warranty Act*, 31 STAN. L. REV. 1117 (1979); Schroeder, *Private Actions Under the Magnuson-Moss Warranty Act*, 66 CAL. L. REV. 1 (1978).

In response to criticism that the FTC abused its extensive powers, Congress passed the Federal Trade Commission Improvements Act of 1980, Pub. L. No. 96-252, 94 Stat. 374. The Act, as amended, limits FTC powers affecting insurance, children's advertising, agricultural cooperatives, the funeral industry, private standard-setting and certification, and trademarks asserted by the FTC to have become generic. Pub. L. No. 96-252 §§ 5, 7, 11, 18–20, 94 Stat. 374.

In 1994, the FTC was reauthorized for the first time since 1980, with the passage of the Federal Trade Commission Amendments Act. Pub. L. No. 103–312, 108 Stat. 1691. The Act mandated changes in FTC authority in several areas. *See generally* KANWIT, FEDERAL TRADE COMMISSION § 3.12 (2007). Among other things, the 1994 Act amends § 5 of the FTC Act so that an act or practice may be found "unfair" only if it "is likely to cause substantial injury to consumers which is not reasonably avoidable by consumers themselves and not outweighed by countervailing benefits to consumers or to competition." 15 U.S.C. § 45(n) (1997). The Act also expanded the FTC's procedural ability to bring suit by authorizing the FTC to serve process in any suit on any "person, partnership or corporation" engaged in the dissemination of any false advertisement "wherever it may be found." 15 U.S.C. § 53(a)-(b) (1997).

Organization and Procedures

1. Membership and Staff

One of the Congressional purposes in establishing the Federal Trade Commission was to create an administrative agency free from executive and political control. This legislative intent is reflected in the membership requirements of the Commission (15 U.S.C. § 41): (1) the five commissioners are to be appointed by the President with the confirmation by the Senate for staggered seven-year terms; (2) no more than three of the commissioners may belong to the same political party; and (3) the President may remove a commissioner only for "inefficiency, neglect of duty or malfeasance in office." In *Humphrey's Ex'r v. United States*, 295 U.S. 602 (1935), the Supreme Court held that this last provision prevented President Roosevelt from removing a commissioner simply because he and Roosevelt had different views.

The FTC is organized into four primary components: (1) the Bureau of Consumer

Protection, which enforces all consumer laws within the Commission's jurisdiction; (2) the Bureau of Competition, which enforces the Clayton Act and restraints of trade violating Section 5 of the FTC Act; (3) the Bureau of Economics, which furnishes the enforcement bureaus with economic and statistical information; and (4) the regional offices, which conduct investigations and litigation and provide guidance to business in their respective regions.

2. Investigatory Powers

Section 6 of the Federal Trade Commission Act provides the Commission with the power to "gather and compile information concerning and to investigate" the conduct and practices affecting commerce of any person, partnership or corporation, and to require them to file reports or answer specific questions concerning such matters. 15 U.S.C. § 46. The FTC Improvements Act of 1980 added § 20 to the Act, requiring the FTC in its investigations to use "civil investigative demands" which state the nature of the conduct alleged to be unfair or deceptive. 15 U.S.C. § 57b-1. Civil investigative demands are the only form of compulsory process available in investigations of unfair or deceptive acts or practices. *See* 16 C.F.R. § 2.7(b) (1983), amended 48 Fed. Reg. 41,375 (Sept. 15, 1983); and S. Rep. No. 96-500 at 23–24. In *FTC v. Ken Roberts Co.*, 276 F.3d 583 (D.C. Cir. 2001), for example, the Court upheld the FTC's issuance of civil investigative demands concerning defendant's potentially deceptive advertising of its investment-related instructional materials, over defendant's objection that its advertising came under the jurisdiction of the Commodities Futures Trading Commission and the Securities and Exchange Commission. The use of subpoenas (§§ 9 and 10 of the Act empower the Commission to subpoena witnesses and documents) is now limited to investigations of unfair methods of competition and to adjudicative proceedings. FTC Act §§ 9–10, 15 U.S.C. §§ 49–50; FTC Act § 20, 15 U.S.C. § 57b-1. In addition, the 1980 Act requires that all forms of compulsory process must be signed by a Commissioner acting pursuant to a Commission resolution. FTC Act § 20, 15 U.S.C. § 57b-1(i).

Investigatorial powers have long been available to the FTC in assembling information for possible new Rules or legislation. For many years, however, the courts viewed these powers as a grant apart from the FTC's role as an adjudicative body and therefore not available for prelitigation inquiries concerning possible violations of § 5. *FTC v. American Tobacco Co.*, 264 U.S. 298 (1924). More recent decisions have upheld the FTC's authority to use these broad powers prior to issuing a complaint, e.g., *FTC v. Invention Submission Corp.*, 965 F.2d 1086 (D.C. Cir. 1992), *cert. denied*, 507 U.S, 910 (1993); and to determine compliance with § 5 cease and desist orders. *See United States v. Morton Salt Co.*, 338 U.S. 632 (1950).

3. Nonadjudicative Authority and Functions

a) Industry Guides

Soon after its inception, the FTC was faced with the prospect of prosecuting numerous individual complaints against members of the same industry committing the same offense. With the agreement of industry, which strenuously pleaded ignorance of the meaning of the phrase, "unfair methods of competition" in § 5 of the FTC Act, the Trade Practice Conference Program was adopted as an alternative to case-by-case adjudication. At these conferences, proposed Trade Practice Conference Rules (later called Trade Practice Rules) prepared by FTC attorneys were discussed with representatives of the subject industry and sometimes modified. Once the Commission approved and promulgated the Rules, industry members were asked to indicate their acceptance and proposed compliance with them. Acceptance of the Trade Practice Rules usually resulted in the cessation of a proceeding against an industry member based on a practice covered in the Rules, unless the good faith of the member was considered doubtful.

Trade Practice Rules no longer exist as such. The majority of the rules were rescinded by the FTC in 1978, 43 Fed. Reg. 44,483 and the remaining rules were reclassified as Industry Guides. A Guide is essentially the FTC's interpretation of what constitutes a violation of a statute that it enforces and may apply to a practice which is prevalent in more than one industry. 16 C.F.R. §§ 1.5, 1.6. They are promulgated on the FTC's own initiative or at the request of any interested party or group, when it appears to the FTC that they "would be beneficial in the public interest" and "bring about more widespread and equitable observance of laws administered by the Commission." 16 C.F.R. § 1.6. Many industries are addressed by the Guides. They include, for example, advertising, endorsements, and testimonials, 16 C.F.R. § 255, the dog and cat food industry, 16 C.F.R. § 241, the jewelry, precious metals and pewter industries, 16 C.F.R. § 23, the feather and down products industry, 16 C.F.R. § 253, and the decorative wall paneling industry, 16 C.F.R. § 243. These Guides have no substantive legal effect.

b) Trade Regulation Rules

The FTC also promulgates Trade Regulation Rules. Proceedings to issue these Rules may be initiated by the FTC itself or at the request of any interested party and may include investigations, conferences and hearings following notice of the proposed Rule in the Federal Register. 16 C.F.R. §§ 1.9–1.13. After considering all relevant matters including those presented by interested persons, the Rules are published in the Federal Register. 16 C.F.R. § 1.14. The Rules become effective four days after publication. 16 C.F.R. § 1.14(c). Unlike Industry Guides, Trade Regulation Rules constitute substantive rules of law. 16 C.F.R. § 1.8(a). Thus, the FTC may establish a statutory violation merely by proving that the challenged conduct is prohibited by such a Rule. *National Petroleum Refiners Ass'n v. FTC*, 482 F.2d 672 (D.C. Cir. 1973), *cert. denied*, 415 U.S. 951 (1974). As a result, the FTC can foreclose the defenses that the particular practice is not prohibited by § 5 or that prior adjudications are inapposite or should be overruled.

In 1975, the Magnuson-Moss Act codified the FTC's rule-making powers (15 U.S.C. § 57a(a)(1) (1975)) and provided that notice of proposed rule-making must be given and interested persons must be permitted to testify before the FTC. 15 U.S.C. § 57a(c)(2). With respect to unfair or deceptive acts or practices, the 1994 Act has limited the FTC's authority to prescribe Trade Regulation Rules to situations where the FTC has reason to believe that the unfair or deceptive acts are prevalent. 15 U.S.C. § 57a(b)(3) (1997). According to the Act, such acts or practices can be deemed "prevalent" if (1) the FTC had previously issued cease and desist orders regarding such acts or practices, or (2) any other information available to the FTC indicates a "widespread pattern of unfair or deceptive acts or practices." *Id.*

Trade Regulation Rules are subject to judicial review. 15 U.S.C. § 57a(e)(1)(A) (1997). The Magnuson-Moss Act provides that, within 60 days of a Rule's promulgation, an interested person may challenge the Rule in a federal court of appeals (the court of original jurisdiction for such review). 15 U.S.C. § 57a(e)(5)(B) (1997). The court may set aside a Rule if it finds that the agency's factual determinations are unsupported by substantial evidence in the rule-making record taken as a whole, or if the Rule falls under the provisions of subparagraphs (A), (B), (C), or (D) of 5 U.S.C. § 706(2) (1997), the Administrative Procedure Act ("APA"). 15 U.S.C. § 57a(e)(3) (1997). Under those subparagraphs of the APA, the Rule will be overturned if it is:

(A) arbitrary, capricious, an abuse of discretion, or otherwise not in accordance with law;

(B) contrary to constitutional right, power, privilege or immunity;

(C) in excess of statutory jurisdiction, authority, or limitations, or short of statutory right;

(D)   without observance of procedure required by law.

See, e.g., Pennsylvania Funeral Directors Ass'n v. FTC, 41 F.3d 81, 85 (3^d Cir. 1994) (upholding an amendment to the FTC's funeral industry Rule that made it an unfair practice to charge consumers a casket-handling fee when the consumer had purchased a casket from a third-party); *American Home Products Corp. v. FTC*, 695 F.2d 681, 686 (3^d Cir. 1982) (the court may set aside all FTC factual determinations if they are not supported by substantial evidence in the rule-making record taken as a whole); *American Financial Services v. FTC*, 767 F.2d 957, 985 (D.C. Cir. 1985), *cert. denied*, 475 U.S. 1011 (1986) (the court may set aside all FTC conclusions, other than factual determinations which are held to a substantial evidence standard, if the conclusions are arbitrary, capricious, an abuse of discretion, or otherwise not in accordance with law). *Cf. Funeral Consumer Alliance v. FTC*, 481 F.3d 860 (D.C. Cir. 2007), in which members of a consumer group sought review of the Funeral Rule, and in particular an FTC interpretation of the industry term "cash advance item," as to which they were allegedly overcharged without price disclosure. Because the FTC had only clarified its trade regulation rule, rather than making a substantial amendment to it, the court concluded it had no appellate jurisdiction to hear their petition.

If a Rule is challenged *after* expiration of the 60-day period following promulgation, the substantial evidence standard does not apply and only those procedures codified in the APA are followed. 15 U.S.C. § 57a(e)(5)(B)-(C) (1997); Kanwit, Federal Trade Commission § 6.09 (2007).

c)   Advisory Opinions

In 1962, the FTC also began giving Advisory Opinions as to whether proposed conduct is legal or complies with an outstanding Commission order. These Opinions are usually rendered and published after a conference with the FTC staff and their certification to the Commission. 16 C.F.R. § 1.2. The FTC has, however, placed certain limitations upon the availability of such Opinions:

> A request ordinarily will be considered inappropriate for such advice: (a) where the course of action is already being followed by the requesting party; (b) where the same or substantially the same course of action is under investigation or is or has been the subject of a current proceeding, order, or decree initiated or obtained by the Commission or another governmental agency; or (c) where the proposed course of action or its effects may be such that an informed decision thereon cannot be made or could be made only after extensive investigation, clinical study, testing, or collateral inquiry.

16 C.F.R. § 1.1. While an Advisory Opinion is outstanding, a party will not be prosecuted by the FTC for acting in good faith reliance upon it, but an Opinion may be revoked at any time and a proceeding initiated unless the practice is promptly discontinued. 16 C.F.R. § 1.3.

4.   Adjudicative Procedures

FTC adjudicative proceedings are instituted by issuance of an administrative complaint stating the charges and giving notice of a hearing. The FTC institutes proceedings whenever it has "reason to believe" that § 5, or a provision of any other act that it administers, is being violated and that an adjudicative proceeding would be in the "interest of the public." 15 U.S.C. § 45(b). In nearly all cases, however, the FTC has accorded the alleged offender the opportunity to agree to a consent order during the investigational stage. 16 C.F.R. § 2.31(a).

The FTC generally sends the party a proposed complaint and consent order, together with notice of its intention to institute proceedings. 16 C.F.R. § 2.31(a). If a consent order is accepted, it is placed on public record for sixty days for comment, after which the FTC must either withdraw its acceptance of the order or issue a decision in disposition of the proceeding. 16 C.F.R. §§ 2.32, 2.34. Consent orders are entered in the great majority of cases docketed by the FTC and have the same effect as orders entered after an administrative adjudication. 16 C.F.R. § 2.32. *See* Wald, *FTC Settlement Procedures*, 5 LITIG. 8 (1979). If a consent order is not agreed upon or accepted by the FTC, a formal complaint is issued and the availability of the consent procedure usually is foreclosed. 16 C.F.R. § 2.31(b). After the formal complaint issues, pretrial conferences are held and limited discovery is conducted. 16 C.F.R. §§ 3.21, 3.31.

Thereafter, the matter is heard by an administrative law judge who issues an Initial Opinion. 16 C.F.R. § 3.51. The proceedings are conducted according to evidentiary rules similar to, but less rigid than, the rules ordinarily used in court proceedings. The administrative law judge's decision becomes final unless: (1) a party appeals to the Commission, (2) the Commission stays the decision, or (3) the Commission dockets it for review. 16 C.F.R. §§ 3.51–3.52. On review, the Commission accepts briefs, hears oral arguments, and can make findings of fact in deciding whether to modify, accept or set aside the examiner's decision. 16 C.F.R. §§ 3.52, 3.54.

If a cease and desist order is issued, the respondent may then appeal to a Circuit Court of Appeals within sixty days from the date of service of the order. 15 U.S.C. § 45(c). The appellate court's scope of review is limited to determining whether the Commission's findings of fact are supported by substantial evidence and whether the choice of remedy is within the FTC's powers. The reviewing court is also empowered to issue injunctions enforcing the cease and desist orders. 15 U.S.C. § 45(c). Once the order has become final, the respondent must submit one report within sixty days and further reports if requested by the FTC, setting forth the manner of compliance with the order. 16 C.F.R. § 2.41.

Each separate violation of a final cease and desist order is punishable by a fine of up to $10,000, except that for violations occurring "through continuing failure or neglect of a final order" each day constitutes a separate offense. 15 U.S.C. § 45(1). This penalty is recovered through a civil action in federal district court. 15 U.S.C. § 45(m).

Under the 1973 Amendment to the FTC Act, district courts also are expressly authorized to issue injunctions in civil actions to enforce the Commission's orders. 15 U.S.C. § 45(1). In addition, once an order has been affirmed on appeal, the Commission may seek to enforce it through an action for contempt of the court's enforcement order. *FTC v. Kuykendall*, 371 F.3d 745 (10th Cir. 2004).

Constitutionality

1. Introduction: The History of Commercial Speech Protection under the First Amendment

The First Amendment to the U.S. Constitution provides that "Congress shall make no law . . . abridging the freedom of speech, or of the press . . . ." In *Valentine v. Chrestensen*, 316 U.S. 52 (1942), the Supreme Court stated without any explanation that "purely commercial advertising" is not protected by the First Amendment. For years the lower courts almost unquestioningly adhered to that principle despite the lack of explanation for it. This omission was commented on by Mr. Justice Douglas in a concurring opinion in *Cammarano v. United States*, 358 U.S. 498, 514 (1959): "Those who make their living through exercise of First Amendment rights are no less entitled to its protection than those whose advocacy or promotion is not hitched to a profit motive. . . ."

In *New York Times Co. v. Sullivan*, 376 U.S. 254 (1964), the Supreme Court bypassed an opportunity to explain why "purely commercial speech" was undeserving of First Amendment protection. The issue there was whether a paid advertisement by a civil rights group criticizing police actions deserved protection. The Court ignored the commercial motivation of the *Times* and instead examined the content of the speech, stating that "the publication here was not a 'commercial' advertisement [in that] it communicated information, expressed opinion, recited grievances . . . ." This set the stage for the Court's decision in *Bigelow v. Virginia*, 421 U.S. 809, 826 (1975), striking down a Virginia statute prohibiting the advertising of abortions, in which the Court stated that "commercial speech is not stripped of all First Amendment protection. The relationship of speech to the marketplace does not make it valueless in the marketplace of ideas."

In 1976, in *Virginia State Board of Pharmacy v. Virginia Citizens Consumer Council, Inc.*, 425 U.S. 748, 763 (1976), the Court held invalid a Virginia statute that prohibited pharmacists from advertising prices for prescription drugs, stating that "speech which does no more than propose a commercial transaction is not so removed from truth, science, morality and acts in general, in its diffusion of sentiment on the administration of Government that it lacks all protection." *See also Linmark Associates v. Township of Willingboro*, 431 U.S. 85 (1977) (township ordinance prohibiting the display of "For Sale" signs in an attempt to stem "white flight" held to be in violation of First Amendment); *Carey v. Population Services International*, 431 U.S. 678 (1977) (New York law prohibiting the advertising of contraceptives held unconstitutional); *Bates v. State Bar of Arizona*, 433 U.S. 350 (1977) (Arizona prohibition on attorney advertising held unconstitutional).

After the *Bates* decision, the Court seemed to retreat somewhat in its protection of commercial speech. *Ohralik v. Ohio State Bar Association*, 436 U.S. 447 (1978) (commercial speech should be afforded only a limited measure of protection); *Friedman v. Rodgers*, 440 U.S. 1 (1979) (Texas act which prohibited the practice of optometry under an assumed trade name held constitutional). In *Central Hudson Gas & Electric Corp. v. Public Service Commission*, 447 U.S. 557 (1980), the Court set forth a four-part test for commercial speech: (1) the speech must concern lawful activity and not be misleading; if so, a restriction on it will be held valid only if it (2) seeks to implement a substantial governmental interest; (3) directly advances that interest; and (4) reaches no further than necessary to accomplish the given objective. Further, the Court stated that "the Constitution therefore accords a lesser protection to commercial speech than to other constitutionally guaranteed expression." *Id.* at 563. *See Board of Trustees v. Fox*, 492 U.S. 469 (1989), in which the Court affirmed the test for commercial speech set forth in *Central Hudson*, and clarified that the fourth prong does not require that restrictions on commercial speech be the absolutely least restrictive means of achieving the governmental interests asserted, but only requires a reasonable "fit" between the ends and the means. The Court again reaffirmed the *Central Hudson* test for commercial speech in *44 Liquormart, Inc. v. Rhode Island*, 517 U.S. 484 (1996), and struck down a state's legislative ban on price advertising for alcoholic beverages as violating the First Amendment. In a plurality opinion written by Justice Stevens, the Court reasoned that the ban did not significantly advance the asserted governmental interest and reached beyond what was necessary to accomplish the legislature's goal. *See also Thompson v. Western States Medical Center*, 535 U.S. 357, 367 (2002), and the discussion of commercial speech in Chapter 9. The Court has thus shifted — from according commercial speech no First Amendment protection, to according protection almost equal to that of other forms of speech, then moving back again to a middle ground seemingly still in the process of definition. For a provocative and influential account of the commercial speech doctrine co-authored by an influential sitting federal appellate judge, see two artices by Alex Kozinski and Stuart Banner, *Who's Afraid of Commercial Speech*, 76 VA. L. REV. 627 (1990); and *The Anti-History and Pre-History of Commercial Speech*, 71 TEX. L. REV. 747 (1993).

MAINSTREAM MARKETING SERVICES, INC. v. FEDERAL TRADE COMMISSION
358 F. 3d 1228 (10ᵗʰ Cir. 2004)

EBEL, CIRCUIT JUDGE

The four cases consolidated in this appeal involve challenges to the national do-not-call registry, which allows individuals to register their phone numbers on a national "do-not-call list" and prohibits most commercial telemarketers from calling the numbers on that list. The primary issue in this case is whether the First Amendment prevents the government from establishing an opt-in telemarketing regulation that provides a mechanism for consumers to restrict commercial sales calls but does not provide a similar mechanism to limit charitable or political phone calls. We hold that the do-not-call registry is a valid commercial speech regulation because it directly advances the government's important interests in safeguarding personal privacy and reducing the danger of telemarketing abuse without burdening an excessive amount of speech. In other words, there is a reasonable fit between the do-not-call regulations and the government's reasons for enacting them.

As we discuss below in greater detail, four key aspects of the do-not-call registry convince us that it is consistent with First Amendment requirements. First, the list restricts only core commercial speech — i.e., commercial sales calls. Second, the do-not-call registry targets speech that invades the privacy of the home, a personal sanctuary that enjoys a unique status in our constitutional jurisprudence. *See Frisby v. Schultz*, 487 U.S. 474, 484, 108 S. Ct. 2495, 101 L. Ed. 2d 420 (1988). Third, the do-not-call registry is an opt-in program that puts the choice of whether or not to restrict commercial calls entirely in the hands of consumers. Fourth, the do-not-call registry materially furthers the government's interests in combating the danger of abusive telemarketing and preventing the invasion of consumer privacy, blocking a significant number of the calls that cause these problems. Under these circumstances, we conclude that the requirements of the First Amendment are satisfied.

A number of additional features of the national do-not-call registry, although not dispositive, further demonstrate that the list is consistent with the First Amendment rights of commercial speakers. The challenged regulations do not hinder any business' ability to contact consumers by other means, such as through direct mailing or other forms of advertising. Moreover, they give consumers a number of different options to avoid calls they do not want to receive. Namely, consumers who wish to restrict some but not all commercial sales calls can do so by using company-specific do-not-call lists or by granting some businesses express permission to call. In addition, the government chose to offer consumers broader options to restrict commercial sales calls than charitable and political calls after finding that commercial calls were more intrusive and posed a greater danger of consumer abuse. The government also had evidence that the less restrictive company-specific do-not call list did not solve the problems caused by commercial telemarketing, but it had no comparable evidence with respect to charitable and political fundraising.

The national do-not-call registry offers consumers a tool with which they can protect their homes against intrusions that Congress has determined to be particularly invasive. Just as a consumer can avoid door-to-door peddlers by placing a "No Solicitation" sign in his or her front yard, the do-not-call registry lets consumers avoid unwanted sales pitches that invade the home via telephone, if they choose to do so. We are convinced that the First Amendment does not prevent the government from giving consumers this option.

* * *

The national do-not-call registry's restrictions apply only to telemarketing calls made by or on behalf of sellers of goods or services, and not to charitable or political fundraising calls. 16 C.F.R §§ 310.4(b)(1)(iii)(B), 310.6(a); 47 C.F.R. §§ 64.1200(f)(9).

Additionally, a seller may call consumers who have signed up for the national registry if it has an established business relationship with the consumer or if the consumer has given that seller express written permission to call. C.F.R §§ 310.4(b)(1)(iii)(B(i-ii); 47 C.F.R. § 64.1200(f)(9)(i-iii). Telemarketers generally have three months from the date on which a consumer signs up for the registry to remove the consumer's phone number from their call lists. 16 C.F.R. § 310.4(b)(3)(iv); 47 C.F.R. § 64.1200(c)(2)(i)(D). Consumer registrations remain valid for five years, and phone numbers that are disconnected or reassigned will be periodically removed from the registry. 47 C.F.R. § 64.1200(c)(2); *Telemarketing Sales Rule, Statement of Basis and Purpose*, 68 Fed. Reg. 45804640 (Jan. 29, 2003).

* * *

The national do-not-call registry's telemarketing restrictions apply only to commercial speech. Like most commercial speech regulations the do-not-call rules draw a line between commercial and non-commercial speech on the basis of content. *See Metromedia, Inc. v. City of San Diego*, 453 U.S. 490, 504 n. 11, 101 S. Ct. 2882, 69 L. Ed. 2d 800 (1981) ("If commercial speech is to be distinguished, it must be distinguished by its content."); *Bayes v. State Bar of Ariz.*, 433 U.S. 350, 363, 53 L. Ed. 2d 810, 97 S. Ct. 2691 (1977) (same). In reviewing commercial speech regulations, we apply the Central Hudson test. *Central Hudson Gas & Elec. Corp. v. Pub. Serv. Comm'n of N.Y.*, 447 U.S. 557, 566, 100 S. Ct. 2343, 65 L. Ed. 2d 341 (1980); *see also City of Cincinnati v. Discovery Network, Inc.*, 507 U.S. 410, 416, 429-30, 113 S. Ct. 1505, 123 L. Ed. 2d 99, 119 (1993) (noting that the challenged law drew content-based distinctions between commercial and non-commercial speech and applying more lenient scrutiny under *Central Hudson*); *Florida Bar v. Went For It, Inc.*, 515 U.S. 618, 634-35, 132, L. Ed. 2d 541, 115 S. Ct. 2371 (1995) (This case. . . concerns pure commercial advertising, for which we have always reserved a lesser degree of protection under the First Amendment."); *Lanphere & Urbaniak v. Colorado*, 21 F. 3d 1508, 1513 (10th Cir. 1994) (content-based regulations disadvantaging commercial speech are reviewed pursuant to the lesser degree of First Amendment protection provided in Central Hudson).

Central Hudson established a three-part test governing First Amendment challenges to regulations restricting non-misleading commercial speech that relates to lawful activity. First, the government must assert a substantial interest to be achieved by the regulation. *Central Hudson*, 447 U.S. at 564. Second, the regulation must directly advance that governmental interest, meaning that it must do more than provide "only ineffective or remote support for the government's purpose." *Id.* Third, although the regulation need not be the least restrictive measure available, it must be narrowly tailored not to restrict more speech than necessary. *See id.; Board of Trs. of the State Univ. of N.Y. v. Fox*, 492 U.S. 469, 480, 106 L. Ed. 2d 388, 109 S. Ct. 3028 (1989). Together, these final two factors require that there be a reasonable fit between the government's objectives and the means it chooses to accomplish those ends. *United States v. Edge Broad. Co.*, 509 U.S. 418, 427-28, 113 S. Ct. 2696, 125 L. Ed. 2d 345 (1993).

The government bears the burden of asserting one or more substantial governmental interests and demonstrating a reasonable fit between those interests and the challenged regulation. *Utah Licensed Beverage Ass'n v. Leavitt*, 256 F. 3d 1061, 1069 (10th Cir. 2001). The government is not limited in the evidence it may use to meet its burden. For example, a commercial speech regulation may be justified by anecdotes, history, consensus, or simple common sense. *Went For It*, 515 U.S. at 628. Yet we may not take it upon ourselves to supplant the interests put forward by the state with our own ideas of what goals the challenged laws might serve. *Edenfield v. Fane*, 507 U.S. 761, 768, 123, L. Ed. 2d 543, 113 S. Ct. 1792 (1993).

A. Governmental Interests

The government asserts that the do-not-call regulations are justified by its interests in 1) protecting the privacy of individuals in their homes, and 2) protecting consumers against the risk of fraudulent and abusive solicitation. *See* 68 Fed. Reg. 44144; 68 Fed. Reg. at 4635. Both of these justifications are undisputedly substantial governmental interests.

In *Rowan v. United States Post Office Dep't.*, the Supreme Court upheld the right of a homeowner to restrict material that could be mailed to his or her house. 397 U.S. 728, 90 S. Ct. 1484, 25 L. Ed. 2d 736 (1970). The Court emphasized the importance of individual privacy, particularly in the context of the home, stating that "the ancient concept that 'a man's home is his castle' into which 'not even the king may enter' has lost none of its vitality." *Id*. at 737. In *Frisby v. Schultz*, the Court again stressed the unique nature of the home and recognized that "the State's interest in protecting the well-being, tranquility, and privacy of the home is certainly of the highest order in a free and civilized society." 487 U.S. 474, 484, 108 S. Ct. 2495, 101 L. Ed. 2d 420 (1988) (quoting *Carey v. Brown*, 447 U.S. 455, 471, 100 S. Ct. 2286, 65 L. Ed. 2d 263 (1980)). As the Court held in Frisby:

> One important aspect of residential privacy is protection of the unwilling listener. . . .[A] special benefit of the privacy all citizens enjoy within their own walls, which the State may legislate to protect, is an ability to avoid intrusions. Thus, we have repeatedly held that individuals are not required to welcome unwanted speech into their own homes and that the government may protect this freedom.

Id. at 484-85 (citations omitted). Likewise, in *Hill v. Colorado*, the Court called the unwilling listener's interest in avoiding unwanted communication part of the broader right to be let alone the Justice Brandeis described as "the right most valued by civilized men." 530 U.S. 703, 716-17, 120 S. Ct. 2480, 147 L. Ed. 2d 597 (2000) (quoting *Olmstead v. United States*, 277 U.S. 438, 478, 48 S. Ct. 564, 72 L. Ed. 944 (1928) (Brandeis, J. dissenting)). The Court added that the right to avoid unwanted speech has special force in the context of the home. *Id.*; *see also FCC v. Pacifica Found.*, 438 U.S. 726, 748, 98 S. Ct. 3026, 57 L. Ed. 2d 1073 (1978) ("In the privacy of the home. . .the individual's right to be left alone plainly outweighs the First Amendment rights of an intruder.").

Additionally, the Supreme Court has recognized that the government has a substantial interest in preventing abusive and coercive sales practices. *Edenfield v. Fane*, 507 U.S. 761, 768-69, 123, L. ed. 2d 543, 113 S. Ct. 1792(1993) (The First Amendment. . .does not prohibit the State from insuring that the stream of commercial information flows cleanly as well as freely.") (quoting *Virginia State Bd. of Pharmacy v. Virginia Citizens Consumer Council, Inc.*, 425 U.S. 748, 771-72, 96 S. Ct. 1817, 48 L. Ed. 2d 346 (1976)).

B. Reasonable Fit

A reasonable fit exists between the do-not-call rules and the government's privacy and consumer protection interests if the regulation directly advances those interests and is narrowly tailored. *See Central Hudson*, 447 U.S. at 564-65. In this context, the "narrowly tailored" standard does not require that the government's response to protect substantial interests be the least restrictive measure available. All that is required is a proportional response. *Board of Trs. of State Univ. of N.Y. v. Fox*, 492 U.S. 469, 480, 106 L. Ed. 2d 388 (1989).

In other words, the national do-not-call registry is valid if it is designed to provide effective support for the government's purposes and if the government did not suppress an excessive amount of speech when substantially narrower restrictions would have worked just as well. *See Central Hudson*, 447 U.S. at 564-65. These criteria are plainly established in this case. The do-not-call registry directly advances the government's interests by effectively blocking a significant number of the calls that cause the problems the government sought to redress. It is narrowly tailored because its opt-in character ensures that it does not inhibit any speech directed at the home of a willing listener.

1. Effectiveness

The telemarketers assert that the do-not-call registry is unconstitutionally underinclusive because it does not apply to charitable and political callers. First Amendment challenges based on underinclusiveness face an uphill battle in the commercial speech context. As a general rule, the First Amendment does not require that the government regulate all aspects of a problem before it can make progress on any front. *United States v. Edge Broad. Co.*, 509 U.S. 418, 434, 113 S. Ct. 2696, 125 L. Ed. 2d 345 (1993). "Within the bounds of the general protection provided by the Constitution to commercial speech, we allow room for legislative judgments." *Id.* The underinclusiveness of a commercial speech regulation is relevant only if it renders the regulatory framework so irrational that it fails materially to advance the aims that it was purportedly designed to further. *See Rubin v. Coors Brewing Co.*, 514 U.S. 476, 489, 115 S. Ct. 1585, 131 L. Ed. 2d 532 (1995); *see also Central Hudson*, 447 U.S. at 564 ("If a regulation "provides only ineffective or remote support for the government's purpose" it cannot be said to bear a reasonable fit with that purported objective). Cf. *City of Ladue v. Gilleo*, 512 U.S. 43, 51, 129, L. Ed. 2d 36, 114 S. Ct. 2038 1994 (underinclusiveness provides a basis for a First Amendment claim when it constitutes an "attempt to give one side of a debatable public question an advantage in expressing its views to the people").

In *Rubin*, for example, the Supreme Court struck down a law prohibiting brewers from putting the alcohol content of their product on beer labels, purportedly in an effort to discourage "strength wars." 514 U.S. at 478. However, the law allowed advertisements disclosing the alcohol content of beers, allowed sellers of wines and spirits to disclose alcohol content on labels (and even required such disclosure for certain wines), and allowed brewers to signal high alcohol content by using the term "malt liquor." *Id.* at 488-89. Under these circumstances, the Court concluded that there was a little chance that the beer label rule would materially deter strength wars in light of the "irrationality of this unique and puzzling regulatory framework." *Id.* at 489.

Likewise, in *City of Cincinnati v. Discovery Network*, the Court struck down a law prohibiting commercial newsracks on public property, purportedly in order to promote the safety and attractive appearance of its streets and sidewalks. 507 U.S. 410, 412, 123, L. Ed. 2d 99, 113 S. Ct 1505 (1993). However, the ban applied to only 62 of the 1, 500 to 2,000 newsracks in the city, thus addressing only a "minute" and "paltry" share of the problem. *Id.* at 417-18. Moreover, the challenged ordinance was not enacted in an effort to address problems posed by newsracks, but was actually and "outdated prohibition against the distribution of any commercial handbills on public property. . . enacted long before any concern about newsracks developed." *Id.* For these reasons, the Court held in part II of that opinion that "the city did not establish the reasonable fit we require." *Id.* at 417-18.

Yet so long as a commercial speech regulation materially furthers its objectives, underinclusiveness is not fatal under *Central Hudson*. For example, in *Edge Broadcasting* the Supreme Court approved a regulation that prohibited broadcasters in North Carolina (which did not permit lotteries) from broadcasting lottery advertisements on the radio, even as applied to a broadcaster located near the border of Virginia (where lotteries were legal) whose audience consisted of 92.2 percent Virginians. 509 U.S. 418, 423, 24, 431-33 (1993). The Court found it determinative that the regulation prevented lottery ads from reaching about 127, 000 North Carolina residents (7.8 percent of Edge's listeners):

> It could hardly be denied . . . that these facts, standing alone, would clearly show that applying the statutory restriction to Edge would directly serve the statutory purpose of supporting North Carolina's antigambling policy . . . This

result could hardly be called either "ineffective," "remote," or "conditional." Nor could it be called only "limited incremental support" for the Government interest.

Id. at 432 (citations omitted). The Court rejected Edge's argument that the regulations banning lottery advertising by in-state radio failed materially to advance the government's interests because North Carolina residents were already inundated with lottery advertising from other sources, such as Virginia radio and television programs. *Id.* at 434; *see also Metromedia, Inc. v. City of San Diego,* 453, U.S 490, 511, 101 S. Ct. 2882, 69 L. Ed. 2d 800 (1981) ("Prohibition of offsite advertising is directly related to the stated objectives of traffic safety and esthetics. This is not altered by the fact that the ordinance is underinclusive because it permits onsite advertising").

As discussed above, the national do-not-call registry is designed to reduce intrusions into personal privacy and the risk of telemarketing fraud and abuse that accompany unwanted telephone solicitation. The registry directly advances those goals. So far, more than 50 million telephone numbers have been registered on the do-not-call list, and the do-not-call regulations protect these households from receiving most unwanted telemarketing calls. According to the telemarketers' own estimate, 2.64 telemarketing calls per week — or more than 137 calls annually — were directed at an average consumer before the do-not-call list came into effect. Cf. 68 Fed. Reg. at 44152 (discussing the five-fold increase in the total number of telemarketing calls between 1991 and 2003). Accordingly, absent the do-not-call registry, telemarketers would call those consumers who have already signed up for the registry an estimated total of 6.85 billion times each year.

To be sure, the do-not-call list will not block all of these calls. Nevertheless, it will prohibit a substantial number of them, making it difficult to fathom how the registry could be called an "ineffective" means of stopping invasive or abusive calls, or a regulation that "furnishes only speculative or marginal support" for the government's interests. *See also id.* (noting the effectiveness of state do-not-call lists in reducing unwanted telemarketing calls).

Furthermore, the do-not-call list prohibits not only a significant number of commercial sales calls, but also a significant percentage of all calls causing the problems that Congress sought to address (whether commercial, charitable or political). The record demonstrates that a substantial share of all solicitation calls will be governed by the do-not-call rules. *See* H.R. Rep. No. 102-317, at 19 (1991) ("Most unwanted telephone solicitations are commercial in nature."); 68 Fed. Reg. at 44153-54 (the high volume and unexpected nature of commercial calls subject to the national do-not-call registry makes those calls more problematic than nonprofit calls and solicitations based on established business relationships).

The telemarketers asserted before the FTC that they might have to lay off up to 50 percent of their employees if the national do-not-call registry came into effect. *See* 68 Fed. Reg. at 4631. It is reasonable to conclude that the telemarketers' planned reduction in force corresponds to a decrease in the amount of calls they will make. Significantly, the percentage of unwanted calls that will be prohibited will be even higher than the percentage of all unsolicited calls blocked by the list. The individuals on the do-not-call list have declared that they do not wish to receive unsolicited commercial telemarketing calls, whereas those who do want to continue receiving such calls will not register. Cf. 68 Fed. Reg. at 4632 (under the national do-not-call regulations, "telemarketers would reduce time spent calling consumers who do not want to receive telemarketing calls and would be able to focus their calls only on those who do not object").

Finally, the type of unsolicited calls that the do-not-call list does prohibit — commercial sales calls — is the type that Congress, the FTC and the FCC have all determined to be most to blame for the problems the government is seeking to redress. According to the legislative history accompanying the TCPA, "complaint statistics show that unwanted commercial calls are a far bigger problem than unsolicited calls from political or charitable organizations." H.R. Rep. No. 102-317, at 16 (1991) (noting that non-commercial calls were less intrusive to consumers' privacy because they are more expected and because there is a lower volume of such calls); *see also* 68 Fed. Reg. at 44153. Similarly, the FCC determined that calls from solicitors with an established business relationship with the recipient are less problematic than other commercial calls. 68 Fed. Reg. at 44154 ("Consumers are more likely to anticipate contacts from companies with whom they have an existing relationship and the volume of such calls will most likely be lower.").

Additionally, the FTC has found that commercial callers are more likely than non-commercial callers to engage in deceptive and abusive practices. 68 Fed. Reg. at 4637 ("When a pure commercial transaction is at stake, callers have an incentive to engage in all things that telemarketers are hated for. But non-commercial speech is a different matter."). Specifically, the FTC concluded that in charitable and political calls, a significant purpose of the call is to sell a cause, not merely to receive a donation, and that non-commercial callers thus have stronger incentives not to alienate the people they call or to engage in abusive and deceptive practices, *Id.*; cf. *Village of Schaumburg v. Citizens for a Better Env't*, 444 U.S. 620, 632, 100 S. Ct. 826, 63 L. Ed. 2d 73 (1980) ("Because charitable solicitation does more than inform private economic decisions and is not primarily concerned with providing information about the characteristics and costs of goods and services, it is not dealt with as a variety of purely commercial speech."). The speech regulated by the do-not-call list is therefore the speech most likely to cause the problems the government sought to alleviate in enacting that list, further demonstrating that the regulation directly advances the government's interests.

In sum, the do-not-call list directly advances the government's interests — reducing intrusions upon consumer privacy and the risk of fraud or abuse — by restricting a substantial number (and also a substantial percentage) of the calls that cause these problems. Unlike the regulations struck down in *Rubin* and *Discovery Network*, the do-not-call list is not so underinclusive that it fails materially to advance the government's goals.

2. Narrow Tailoring

Although the least restrictive means test is not the test to be used in the commercial speech context, commercial speech regulations do at least have to be "narrowly tailored" and provide a "reasonable fit" between the problem and the solution. Whether or not there are "numerous and obvious less-burdensome alternatives" is a relevant consideration in our narrow tailoring analysis. *Went For It*, 515 U.S. at 632. A law is narrowly tailored if it "promotes a substantial government interest that would be achieved less effectively absent the regulation." *Ward v. Rock Against Racism*, 491, U.S. 781, 799, 109 S. Ct. 2746, 105 L. Ed. 2d 661 (1989). Accordingly, we consider whether there are numerous and obvious alternatives that would restrict less speech and would serve the government's interest as effectively as the challenged law. *See Central Hudson*, 447 U.S. at 565; *Edge Broad.*, 509 U.S. at 430.

We hold that the national do-not-call registry is narrowly tailored because it does not over-regulate protected speech; rather, it restricts only calls that are targeted at unwilling recipients. Cf. *Frisby v. Schultz*, 487 U.S. 474 U.S. 474, 485, 108 S. Ct. 2495, 101 L. Ed. 2d 420 (1988) ("There simply is no right to force speech into the home of an unwilling listener."); *Rowan v. United States Post Office Dep't*, 397 U.S. 728, 738, 25 L. Ed. 2d 736, 902 S. Ct. 1484 (1970) ("We therefore categorically reject the argument that a vendor has a right under the Constitution or otherwise to send unwanted material into the home of another."). The do-not-call registry prohibits only telemarketing calls aimed at consumers who have affirmatively indicated that they do not want to receive such calls and for whom such calls would constitute an invasion of privacy. *See Hill v. Colorado*, 530 U.S. 703, 716-17, 120 S. Ct. 2480, 147 L. Ed. 2d 597 (2000) (the right of privacy includes an unwilling listener's interest in avoiding unwanted communication).

The Supreme Court has repeatedly held that speech restrictions based on private choice (i.e. — an opt-in feature) are less restrictive than laws that prohibit speech directly. In *Rowan*, for example, the Court approved a law under which an individual could require a mailer to stop all future mailings if he or she received advertisements that he or she believed to be erotically arousing or sexually provocative. 397 U.S. at 729-30, 738. Although it was the government that empowered individuals to avoid materials they considered provocative, the Court emphasized that the mailer's right to communicate was circumscribed only by an affirmative act of a householder. *Id.* at 738. "Congress has erected a wall –or more accurately permits a citizen to erect a wall — that no advertiser may penetrate without his acquiescence. . .The asserted right of a mailer, we repeat, stops at the outer boundary of every person's domain." *Id.*

Likewise, in rejecting direct prohibitions of speech (even fully protected speech), the Supreme Court has often reasoned that an opt-in regulation would have been a less restrictive alternative. In *Martin v. City of Struthers*, the Court struck down a city ordinance prohibiting door-to-door canvassing, nothing that the government's interest could have been achieved in a less restrictive manner by giving householders the choice of whether or not to receive visitors. 319 U.S. 141, 147-49, 63 S. Ct. 862, 87 L. Ed. 1313 (1943) ("The decision as to whether distributors of literature may lawfully call at a home. . .belongs. . .with the homeowner himself. A city can punish those who call at a home in defiance of the previously expressed will of the occupant."). More recently, in *Watchtower Bible & Tract Soc'y of N.Y., Inc. v. Village of Stratton*, the Court struck down a permit requirement for door-to-door advocacy, while noting that another section of the ordinance allowing residents to post "No Solicitation" signs provided ample protection for the unwilling listener. 536 U.S. 150, 153, 168, 169, 122 S. Ct. 2080, 153 L. Ed. 2d 205 (2002); *see also City of Schaumburg v. Citizens for a Better Env't*, 444 U.S. 620, 639, 100 S. Ct. 826, 63 L. Ed. 2d 73 (1980) (The provision permitting homeowners to bar solicitors from their property by posting signs reading 'No Solicitors or Peddlers Invited' suggests the availability of less intrusive and more effective measures to protect privacy.") (citations omitted).

The idea that an opt-in regulation is less restrictive than a direct prohibition of speech applies not only to traditional door-to-door solicitation, but also to regulations seeking to protect the privacy of the home from unwanted intrusions via telephone, television, or the Internet. *See United States v. Playboy Entm't Group, Inc.*, 529 U.S. 803, 815, 120 S. Ct. 1878, 146 L. Ed. 2d 865 (2000) (opt-in targeted blocking of offensive television programming "enables the Government to support parental authority without affecting the First Amendment interests of speakers and willing listeners. . .Simply put, targeted blocking is less restrictive than banning. . ."); cf. *Reno v. ACLU*, 521 U.S. 844, 860 879, 117 S. Ct. 2329, 138 L. Ed. 2d 874 (1997) (striking down an absolute prohibition against making certain sexually explicit material available to minors on the Internet on the grounds that it curtailed the speech of adults, contrasting that regulation with the alternative of facilitating parental control of such material).

* * *

We hold that 1) the do-not-call list is a valid commercial speech regulation under Central Hudson because it directly advances substantial governmental interests and is narrowly tailored; 2) the registry fees telemarketers must pay to access the list are a permissible measure designed to defray the cost of legitimate government regulation; 3) it was not arbitrary and capricious for the FCC to adopt the established business relationship exception; and 4) the FTC has statutory authority to establish and implement the national do-not-call registry.

ANDREWS MORTUARY, INC. v. FEDERAL TRADE COMMISSION
726 F.2d 994 (4ᵗʰ Cir. 1984)

K.K. HALL, CIRCUIT JUDGE.

* * *

THE RULEMAKING PROCEEDING

In 1972, the FTC began an investigation of funeral practices across the nation. As a result of this investigation, the Commission initiated a rulemaking proceeding to regulate the funeral industry. The Commission published a notice containing the text of a proposed rule, a statement of the Commission's reasons for issuing it, and an invitation for public comment. Hearings were scheduled to take place in six cities during 1976.

In response to the FTC's notice, more than 9,000 documents, comprising in excess of 20,000 pages, were submitted by interested parties, including consumers and industry representatives. During the fifty-two days of hearings, 315 witnesses testified. The witnesses also presented exhibits and underwent cross-examination by participating parties or the FTC's Presiding Officer. The hearings generated 14,719 pages of transcripts and approximately 4,000 additional pages of exhibits. Thereafter, another comment period was held for rebuttal of any materials previously admitted into evidence. Forty-seven rebuttal submissions were received.

Following these hearings, the Presiding Officer and commission staff concluded that existing funeral practices left the consumer vulnerable to unfair and deceptive practices, and that state regulation against deceptive funeral practices was dominated by industry interests. These conclusions were published in 1978, and the Commission allowed ninety days for public comment.

Over 1,300 separate comments were received. In February, 1979, the staff and the Bureau Director forwarded to the Commission their final recommendations that a rule be promulgated, but with numerous modifications in response to the comments received. In 1980, the Commission voted to publish for public comment a revised version of the Funeral Rule.

A notice containing the revised rule was published in the *Federal Register* on January 22, 1981, and provided for a sixty-day written comment period, followed by a rebuttal period in which parties could respond to the initial round of comments. After expiration of the comment period and following several public hearings in 1981, the Commission made final revisions to the Funeral Rule and submitted it to both Houses of Congress. When Congressional review expired with no resolution of disapproval, the Commission set January 1, 1984, as the effective date of the Funeral Rule. This appeal followed.

* * *

The rule promulgated by the Commission . . . requires that before any discussion of arrangements, funeral providers: (1) give consumers a written list containing prices of funeral goods and services on an itemized basis (although providers may also quote prices on combinations of goods and services); (2) offer price information to consumers who request it over the telephone; (3) obtain permission from a family member before embalming (except under certain designated circumstances); (4) refrain from requiring use of a casket for cremation; (5) refrain from making specified misrepresentations; and (6) include several short disclosures on the price list informing consumers of their legal rights and purchase options.

* * *

V. THE IMPROVEMENTS ACT AND THE FIRST AMENDMENT

[P]etitioners argue that, even if there is substantial evidence supporting the Commission's conclusions regarding pre-purchase disclosures, the remedy of itemized price lists exceeds the Commission's power under the Improvements Act, and violates petitioners' First Amendment rights of commercial free speech. We disagree.

Section 19(c)(1)(B)(i) of the Improvements Act expressly prohibits the FTC from promulgating a regulation except to the extent that it prohibits funeral providers from "engaging in any misrepresentation." The remedy of price itemization is not inconsistent with this limitation. The Commission's conclusion that itemized pricing is necessary to prevent unwanted and unnecessary purchasing is a judgment that is specifically allowed by Section 19(c)(1)(B)(iii). This section stipulates that the Commission may promulgate rules designed to "prevent [funeral] providers from conditioning the furnishing of any such goods or services." Section 19(c)(1)(A) also supports the Commission's authority to require the remedy of itemized pricing by establishing that the Commission may require funeral providers "to disclose the fees or prices for such goods and services *in a manner prescribed by the Commission*." (Emphasis added).

Nor do we agree that the First Amendment prevents the Commission from remedying deception by means of an affirmative disclosure requirement. Assuming that the sales practices in question are commercial "speech," the First Amendment gives that speech no protection when it is misleading, *Central Hudson Gas & Electric Corp. v. Public Serv. Comm'n*, 447 U.S. 557, 566 (1980), and poses no barrier to any remedy formulated by the Commission reasonably necessary to the prevention of future deception. *American Home Products Corp. v. FTC*, 695 F.2d 681, 713 (3ᵈ Cir. 1982). The practices that the Commission sought to remedy by promulgation of the Funeral Rule were unfair and misleading and thus are not "speech" entitled to First Amendment protection.

*   *   *

Rule affirmed.

2.   Notes on Constitutionality

For examples of how the FTC has regulated commercial speech since *Central Hudson*, 447 U.S. 557 (1980), *see American Medical Ass'n v. FTC*, 638 F.2d 443, 452 (2ᵈ Cir. 1980), *aff'd per curiam by an equally divided court*, 455 U.S. 676 (1982), modifying an FTC order requiring the AMA to cease and desist from promulgating, implementing and enforcing restraints on advertising, solicitation and contract practices by physicians; *United States v. Reader's Digest Ass'n*, 662 F.2d 955, 965 (3ᵈ Cir. 1981), *cert. denied*, 455 U.S. 908 (1982), affirming a district court order penalizing Reader's Digest for violating an FTC Consent Order which had required Reader's Digest to cease and desist from using or distributing simulated checks, currency or "new car certificates" in the company's sweepstakes promotions, and enjoining Reader's Digest from further violations of the Consent Order; *Removatron Int'l Corp. v. FTC*, 884 F.2d 1489 (1ˢᵗ Cir. 1989), upholding an FTC order enjoining petitioners from representing that their hair removal system achieved long- term efficacy without possession of and reliance upon a well-controlled, scientific study; *Litton Industries, Inc. v. FTC*, 676 F.2d 364, 373 (9ᵗʰ Cir. 1982), modifying and enforcing an FTC order requiring Litton to cease and desist from making inadequately substantiated claims with respect to its microwave ovens; and *Bristol-Myers Co. v. Federal Trade Commission*, 102 F.T.C. 21 (1983), enforcing an FTC order requiring Bristol-Myers not to make any performance or freedom-from-side-effects claims for its Bufferin or Excedrin products unless it had a "reasonable basis" for making that claim. *See also Board of Trustees of the State University of New York v. Fox*, 492 U.S. 469 (1989), in which a SUNY regulation barred a tupperware party in a student dormitory. The Court, in an opinion by Justice Scalia, held that application of the least- restrictive-means test of *Central Hudson, supra*, need not require "the least restrictive means but . . . a means narrowly tailored to achieve the desired objective," and remanded for a determination of whether some means other than a complete bar would meet the regulatory objective.

In *Jay Norris Inc. v. FTC*, 598 F.2d 1244 (2ᵈ Cir. 1979), the petitioners challenged a similar order requiring a substantiated "reasonable basis" for any claims regarding the safety and performance of petitioner's gift and novelty products. They argued the Order suppressed even truthful speech and amounted to a prior restraint. Petitioners previously had made deceptive claims as to numerous and various products such as flame guns that would "dissolve the heaviest snow drifts, whip right through the thickest ice" and "completely safe" roach powder which "never loses its killing power — even after years." Noting that the First Amendment does not protect deceptive and misleading speech, the court held that the FTC's remedy was reasonable and constitutional and observed that the doctrine of prior restraint may be inapplicable to commercial speech.

In *FTC v. Brown and Williamson Tobacco Corp.*, 778 F.2d 35 (D.C. Cir. 1985), the court scaled back the lower court's order intended to prevent deceptive claims about a cigarette's tar and nicotine content, on the grounds that the injunction as written would have effectively enshrined the FTC's system of measuring tar and nicotine as the only legitimate testing method, thereby potentially suppressing truthful, non-confusing claims about tar and nicotine content as measured by other systems. Cf. *Kraft, Inc. v. FTC*, 970 F.2d 311 (7ᵗʰ Cir. 1992), upholding the FTC's order enjoining certain Kraft advertising claims, emphasizing that "no First Amendment concerns are raised when facially apparent [false] implied claims are found without resort to extrinsic evidence," and *Novartis Corp. v. FTC*, 223 F.3d 783 (D.C. Cir. 2000), in which the court upheld the FTC's order that petitioner run corrective advertising for a year to help dispel a lingering deception that petitioner's product provided superior back pain relief, finding it did not impermissibly restrict petitioner's free speech in violation of the First Amendment. Citing *Central Hudson*, the court in *Novartis* concluded that "[t]he remedy here advances precisely the 'interest involved', namely the avoidance of misleading and deceptive advertising."

Should the FTC be able to prevent the advertising of false statements concerning a product which are also contained in a book? See *Trudeau v. FTC*, 384 F.Supp.2d 281 (D.D.C. 2005), *aff'd* 456 F.3d 178 (D.C. Cir. 2006) (enjoining false claims in infomercials about cures for diseases (largely based on coral calcium), but allowing an exception for any informational publication that "does not reference any product or service that Trudeau is marketing, does not advertise any product or service related to the content of the publication, and is not sold or marketed in conjunction with a product or service related to the content of the publication"); *Koch v. FTC*, 206 F.2d 311 (6ᵗʰ Cir. 1953), in which the court held that the FTC could regulate the advertising but not the book. Would the fact that the advertising was for the book itself affect this decision? See *Witkower Press, Inc.*, 57 FTC 145 (1960); *Rodale Press, Inc.*, 71 F.T.C. 1184, 1247–1253 (1967) (Comm'r Elman, dissenting), *quoted with approval in Rodale Press, Inc. v. FTC*, 407 F.2d 1252, 1258 (D.C. Cir. 1968) (Robinson, J., concurring).

In *Scientific Manufacturing Co. v. FTC*, 124 F.2d 640 (3ᵈ Cir. 1941), the petitioner was publishing and selling pamphlets that claimed that aluminum utensils were poisonous and caused health risks, claims that with "zeal" he "believ[ed] to be the truth." They were sold and distributed nationally to manufacturers, distributors and salespeople of competitive non-aluminum utensils. The FTC issued a cease and desist order, finding that the claims were false and that the petitioner was supplying an "instrumentality by means of which" such persons who were "uninformed or unscrupulous . . . may deceive or mislead [purchasers] and induce them to purchase utensils made from materials other than aluminum".

The Third Circuit reversed, setting aside the order. It concluded that petitioner was not engaged in and had no material interest in the cooking utensil trade. "[T]he publication, sale and distribution of matter concerning an article of trade by a person not engaged or financially interested in commerce in that trade is not an unfair or deceptive practice within the contemplation of the Federal Trade Commission Act, as amended, if the published matter, even though unfounded or untrue, represents the publisher's honest opinion or belief." The FTC also had failed to show that the pamphlets were actually used in the cooking utensil industry as alleged; if such pamphlets were shown to be "utilized in the trade to mislead or deceive the public or to harm a competitor" it would be "enjoinable." Here there was only speculation by the FTC that such use could be made.

Whether a given advertisement constitutes commercial speech may depend on its content as well as the "means, messages and motives" of its sponsor. In *In re R.J. Reynolds, Inc.*, 5 (CCH) Trade Reg. Rep. (CCH) ¶ 22,522 (April 11, 1988), the FTC challenged an editorial/advertisement sponsored by R.J. Reynolds, describing the results of a health study measuring the effects of smoking cigarettes. The FTC explained that the ad could constitute commercial speech, despite the absence of express promotional language, because the ad referred to a specific product, targeted consumers of the product, discussed the health effects of that product, and was published by means of a paid-for advertisement. *See also Bolger v. Youngs Drug Products*, 463 U.S. 60, 66–67 (1983), in which the Court classified a pamphlet analyzing facts about venereal disease as commercial speech because: (1) the pamphlet was a paid-for advertisement, (2) it referred to a specific product, and (3) the advertisement was motivated by economic gain; and *Peel v. Attorney Registration and Disciplinary Commission of Illinois*, 496 U.S. 91 (1990), in which the Court held that a State may not "completely ban statements that are not actually or inherently misleading, such as certification [of a lawyer] as a specialist by bona fide organizations such as the [National Board of Trial Advocacy]."

In 2004, the "Controlling the Assault of Non-Solicited Pornography and Marketing Act of 2003", 15 U.S.C. § 7701, also known as the CAN-SPAM Act, took effect. It addresses the abusive use of commercial electronic mail, often referred to as "spam". It covers "any electronic e-mail message the primary purpose of which is the commercial advertisement or promotion of a commercial product or service (including content on an Internet website operated for a commercial purpose.)" 15 U.S.C. § 7702(2)(A). Among other things, the Act requires that commercial e-mails be "clearly and conspicuously" labeled as advertisements except when sent to consumers who have affirmatively agreed to receive such messages. 15 U.S.C. § 7704(a)(5). Among other things, this enables consumers to more effectively use software filters to block receipt of such e-mails. The Act also imposes criminal penalties for "fraud and related activity in connection with electronic mail" as defined by the Act, including imprisonment, 15 U.S.C. § 7703, prohibits the use of deceptive subject headers, and requires the e-mailer to provide contact information that will allow recipients to opt out of receiving any future e-mails from the e-mailer. 15 U.S.C. § 7704. The Act is enforced by the FTC as if its violation were an unfair or deceptive act or practice in violation of the FTC Act. 15 U.S.C. § 7706.

There are various constitutional limits on relief which may affect governmental regulation of unfair or deceptive acts or practices. In *Lucas v. South Carolina Coastal Council*, 112 S. Ct. 2886, 2894–5 (1992), in holding that a developer had to be compensated where a state regulatory commission barred development of his beachfront property, the Supreme Court, in an opinion by Justice Scalia, ruled that state "regulations that leave the owner of land without economically beneficial or productive options for its use . . . carry with them a heightened risk that private property is being pressed into some form of public service under the guise of mitigating serious public harm." *See* R. EPSTEIN, BARGAINING WITH THE STATE (1993).

See generally , KANWIT, FEDERAL TRADE COMMISSION, Ch. 22:10 (2007); Ludwikowski, *Proposed Government Regulation of Tobacco Advertising Uses Teens to Disguise First Amendment Violations,* 4 COMMLAW CONSPECTUS 105 (1996); Redish, *Tobacco Advertising and the First Amendment,* 81 IOWA L. REV. 589 (1996); Howard, *The Constitutionality of Deceptive Speech Regulations: Replacing the Commercial Speech*

Doctrine with a Tort-Based Relational Framework, 41 Case W. Res. 1093 (1991); McGowan, *A Critical Analysis of Commercial Speech*, 78 CALIF. L. REV. 359 (1990).

Tests of Deceptiveness

1. Introduction

The Supreme Court has held that the FTC cannot take action against deceptive practices unless the public interest involved is specific and substantial. *FTC v. Royal Milling Co.*, 288 U.S. 212 (1933). If the controversy is private in character and any public interest only incidental, a reviewing court may dismiss the suit without inquiry into the merits. *FTC v. Klesner*, 280 U.S. 19 (1929).

The FTC's articulation of the test for measuring deception under § 5 of the FTC Act has evolved over the years. Historically, acts or practices were found deceptive if their net impression had the capacity to deceive the public as to a material factor in its purchasing decisions. *See Charles of the Ritz Distributors Corp. v. FTC*, 143 F.2d 676 (2d Cir. 1944). The application of this test was construed as affording protection to even the gullible or credulous. *See Charles of the Ritz, supra*; *FTC v. Standard Education Soc'y*, 302 U.S. 112 (1937); *Aronberg v. FTC*, 132 F.2d 165 (7th Cir. 1942). *Cf. Standard Oil Co. of California v. FTC*, 577 F.2d 653, 657 (9th Cir. 1978). However, in 1983 the FTC issued a policy statement which indicated that the FTC will only find acts or practices deceptive if there is a representation, omission or practice likely to mislead a consumer acting reasonably under the circumstances, to the consumer's detriment. FTC, *Policy Statement on Deception, reprinted in* Trade Reg. Rep. (CCH) ¶ 50,455 (October 14, 1983).

The absence of evidence of actual deception, intent to deceive or actual injury to the public, consumers, or competitors, continues to be irrelevant in evaluating whether a material misrepresentation violates § 5. *See Beneficial Corp. v. FTC*, 542 F.2d 611, 617 (3d Cir. 1976), *cert. denied*, 430 U.S. 983 (1977); *FTC v. World Travel Vacation Brokers, Inc.*, 861 F.2d 1020, 1029 (7th Cir. 1988). Furthermore, the fact that a representation is literally true, or deceptive only by omission, does not constitute a defense. *See Kraft, infra*; Alexander, *Federal Regulation of False Advertising*, 17 U. KAN. L. REV. 573 (1969); Millstein, *The Federal Trade Commission and False Advertising*, 64 COLUM. L. REV. 439 (1964).

FTC v. COLGATE-PALMOLIVE CO.
380 U.S. 374 (1965)

MR. CHIEF JUSTICE WARREN

The basic question before us is whether it is a deceptive trade practice, prohibited by § 5 of the Federal Trade Commission Act, to represent falsely that a televised test, experiment, or demonstration provides a viewer with visual proof of a product claim, regardless of whether the product claim is itself true.

The case arises out of an attempt by respondent Colgate-Palmolive Company to prove to the television public that its shaving cream, "Rapid Shave," outshaves them all. Respondent Ted Bates & Company, Inc., an advertising agency, prepared for Colgate three one-minute commercials designed to show that Rapid Shave could soften even the toughness of sandpaper. Each of the commercials contained the same "sandpaper test." The announcer informed the audience that, "To prove RAPID SHAVE'S super-moisturizing power, we put it right from the can onto this tough, dry sandpaper. It was apply . . . soak . . . and off in a stroke." While the announcer was speaking, Rapid Shave was applied to a substance that appeared to be sandpaper, and immediately thereafter a razor was shown shaving the substance clean.

The Federal Trade Commission issued a complaint against respondents Colgate and Bates charging that the commercials were false and deceptive. The evidence before the hearing examiner disclosed that sandpaper of the type depicted in the commercials could not be shaved immediately following the application of Rapid Shave, but required a substantial soaking period of approximately 80 minutes. The evidence also showed that the substance resembling sandpaper was in fact a simulated prop, or "mock-up," made of plexiglass to which sand had been applied. However, the examiner found that Rapid Shave could shave sandpaper, even though not in the short time represented by the commercials, and that if real sandpaper had been used in the commercials the inadequacies of television transmission would have made it appear to viewers to be nothing more than plain, colored paper. The examiner dismissed the complaint because neither misrepresentation — concerning the actual moistening time or the identity of the shaved substance — was in his opinion a material one that would mislead the public.

The Commission, in an opinion dated December 29, 1961, reversed the hearing examiner. It found that since Rapid Shave could not shave sandpaper within the time depicted in the commercials, respondents had misrepresented the product's moisturizing power. Moreover, the Commission found that the undisclosed use of a plexiglass substitute for sandpaper was an additional material misrepresentation that was a deceptive act separate and distinct from the misrepresentation concerning Rapid Shave's underlying qualities. Even if the sandpaper could be shaved just as depicted in the commercials, the Commission found that viewers had been misled into believing they had seen it done with their own eyes. As a result of these findings the Commission entered a cease-and-desist order against the respondents.

An appeal was taken to the Court of Appeals for the First Circuit which rendered an opinion on November 20, 1962, 310 F.2d 89. That court sustained the Commission's conclusion that respondents had misrepresented the qualities of Rapid Shave, but it would not accept the Commission's order forbidding the future use of undisclosed simulations in television commercials. It set aside the Commission's order and directed that a new order be entered. On May 7, 1963, the Commission, over the protest of respondents, issued a new order narrowing and clarifying its original order to comply with the court's mandate. The Court of Appeals again found unsatisfactory that portion of the order dealing with simulated props and refused to enforce it, 326 F.2d 517. We granted certiorari, 377 U.S. 942, to consider this aspect of the case and do not have before us any question concerning the misrepresentation that Rapid Shave could shave sandpaper immediately after application, that being conceded.

*   *   *

II.

In reviewing the substantive issues in the case, it is well to remember the respective roles of the Commission and the courts in the administration of the Federal Trade Commission Act. When the Commission was created by Congress in 1914, it was directed by § 5 to prevent "[u]nfair methods of competition in commerce." Congress amended the Act of 1938 to extend the Commission's jurisdiction to include "unfair or deceptive acts or practices in commerce" a significant amendment showing Congress' concern for consumers as well as for competitors. It is important to note the generality of these standards of illegality; the proscriptions in § 5 are flexible, "to be defined with particularity by the myriad of cases from the field of business." *Federal Trade Comm. v. Motion Picture Advertising Service Co.*, 344 U.S. 392, 394.

This statutory scheme necessarily gives the Commission an influential role in interpreting § 5 and in applying it to the facts of particular cases arising out of unprecedented situations. Moreover, as an administrative agency which deals continually with cases in the area, the Commission is often in a better position than are courts to determine when a practice is "deceptive" within the meaning of the Act. This Court has frequently stated that the Commission's judgment is to be given great weight by reviewing courts. This admonition is especially true with respect to allegedly deceptive advertising since the finding of a § 5 violation in this field rests so heavily on inference and pragmatic judgment. Nevertheless, while informed judicial determination is dependent upon enlightenment gained from administrative experience, in the last analysis the words "deceptive practices" set forth a legal standard and they must get their final meaning from judicial construction. *Cf. Federal Trade Comm. v. R.F. Keppel & Bro., Inc.*, 291 U.S. 304, 314.

We are not concerned in this case with the clear misrepresentation in the commercials concerning the speed with which Rapid Shave could shave sandpaper, since the Court of Appeals upheld the Commission's finding on that matter and the respondents have not challenged the finding here. We granted certiorari to consider the Commission's conclusion that even if an advertiser has himself conducted a test, experiment or demonstration which he honestly believes will prove a certain product claim, he may not convey to television viewers the false impression that they are seeing the test, experiment or demonstration for themselves, when they are not because of the undisclosed use of mock-ups.

We accept the Commission's determination that the commercials involved in this case contained three representations to the public: (1) that sandpaper could be shaved by Rapid Shave; (2) that an experiment had been conducted which verified his claim; and (3) that the viewer was seeing this experiment for himself. Respondents admit that the first two representations were made, but deny that the third was. The Commission, however, found to the contrary, and, since this is a matter of fact resting on an inference that could reasonably be drawn from the commercials themselves, the Commission's finding should be sustained. For the purposes of our review, we can assume that the first two representations were true; the focus of our consideration is on the third which was clearly false. The parties agree that § 5 prohibits the intentional misrepresentation of any fact which would constitute a material factor in a purchaser's decision whether to buy. They differ, however, in their conception of what "facts" constitute a "material factor" in a purchaser's decision to buy. Respondents submit, in effect, that the only material facts are those which deal with the substantive qualities of a product. The Commission, on the other hand, submits that the misrepresentations of *any* fact so long as it materially induces a purchaser's decision to buy is a deception prohibited by § 5.

The Commission's interpretation of what is a deceptive practice seems more in line with the decided cases than that of respondents. This Court said in *Federal Trade Comm. v. Algoma Lumber Co.*, 291 U.S. 67, 78: "[T]he public is entitled to get what it chooses, though the choice may be dictated by caprice or by fashion or perhaps by ignorance." It has long been considered a deceptive practice to state falsely that a product ordinarily sells for an inflated price but that it is being offered at a special reduced price, even if the offered price represents the actual value of the product and the purchaser is receiving his money's worth. Applying respondents' arguments to these cases, it would appear that so long as buyers paid no more than the product was actually worth and the product contained the qualities advertised, the misstatement of an inflated original price was immaterial.

It has also been held a violation of § 5 for a seller to misrepresent to the public that he is in a certain line of business, even though the misstatement in no way affects the qualities of the product. As was said in *Federal Trade Comm. v. Royal Milling Co.*, 288 U.S. 212, 216:

> If consumers or dealers prefer to purchase a given article because it was made by a particular manufacturer or class of manufacturers, they have a right to do so, and this right cannot be satisfied by imposing upon them an exactly similar article, or one equally as good, but having a different origin.

The court of appeals has applied this reasoning to the merchandising of reprocessed products that are as good as new, without a disclosure that they are in fact reprocessed. And it has also been held that it is a deceptive practice to misappropriate the trade name of another.

Respondents claim that all these cases are irrelevant to our decision because they involve misrepresentations related to the product itself and not merely to the manner in which an advertising message is communicated. This distinction misses the mark for two reasons. In the first place, the present case is not concerned with a mode of communications, but with a misrepresentation that viewers have objective proof of a seller's product claim over and above the seller's word. Secondly, all of the above cases, like the present case, deal with methods designed to get a consumer to purchase a product, not with whether the product, when purchased, will perform up to expectations. We find an especially strong similarity between the present case and those cases in which a seller induces the public to purchase an arguably good product by misrepresenting his line of business, by concealing the fact that the product is reprocessed, or by misappropriating another's trademark. In each case the seller has used a misrepresentation to break down what he regards to be an annoying or irrational habit of the buying public — the preference for particular manufacturers or known brands regardless of a product's actual qualities, the prejudice against reprocessed goods, and the desire for verification of a product claim. In each case the seller reasons that when the habit is broken the buyer will be satisfied with the performance of the product he receives. Yet, a misrepresentation has been used to break the habit and, as was stated in *Algoma Lumber*, a misrepresentation for such an end is not permitted.

We need not limit ourselves to the cases already mentioned because there are other situations which also illustrate the correctness of the Commission's finding in the present case. It is generally accepted that it is a deceptive practice to state falsely that a product has received a testimonial from a respected source. In addition, the Commission has consistently acted to prevent sellers from falsely stating that their product claims have been "certified." We find these situations to be indistinguishable from the present case. We can assume that in each the underlying product claim is true and in each the seller actually conducted an experiment sufficient to prove to himself the truth of the claim. But in each the seller has told the public that it could rely on something other than his word concerning both the truth of the claim and the validity of his experiment. We find it an immaterial difference that in one case the viewer is told to rely on the word of a celebrity or authority he respects, in another on the word of a testing agency, and in the present case on his own perception of an undisclosed simulation.

Respondents again insist that the present case is not like any of the above, but is more like a case in which a celebrity or independent testing agency has in fact submitted a written verification of an experiment actually observed, but, because of the inability of the camera to transmit accurately an impression of the paper on which the testimonial is written, the seller reproduces it on another substance so that it can be seen by the viewing audience. This analogy ignores the finding of the Commission that in the present case the seller misrepresented to the public that it was being given objective proof of a product claim. In respondents' hypothetical the objective proof of the product claim that is offered, the word of the celebrity or agency that the experiment was actually conducted, does exist; while in the case before us the objective proof offered, the viewer's own perception of an actual experiment, does not exist. Thus, in respondents' hypothetical, unlike the present case, the use of the undisclosed mockup does not conflict with the seller's claim that there is objective proof.

We agree with the Commission, therefore, that the undisclosed use of plexiglass in the present commercials was a material deceptive practice, independent and separate from the other misrepresentation found. We find unpersuasive respondents' other objections to this conclusion. Respondents claim that it will be impractical to inform the viewing public that it is not seeing an actual test, experiment or demonstration, but we think it inconceivable that the ingenious advertising world will be unable, if it so desires, to conform to the Commission's insistence that the public be not misinformed. If, however, it becomes impossible or impractical to show simulated demonstrations on television in a truthful manner, this indicates that television is not a medium that lends itself to this type of commercial, not that the commercial must survive at all costs. Similarly unpersuasive is respondents' objection that the Commission's decision discriminates against sellers whose product claims cannot be "verified" on television without the use of simulations. All methods of advertising do not equally favor every seller. If the inherent limitations of a method do not permit its use in the way a seller desires, the seller cannot by material misrepresentation compensate for those limitations.

* * *

III.

We turn our attention now to the order issued by the Commission. It has been repeatedly held that the Commission has wide discretion in determining the type of order that is necessary to cope with the unfair practices found, *e.g., Jacob Siegel Co. v. Federal Trade Comm.*, 327 U.S. 608, 611, and that Congress has placed the primary responsibility for fashioning orders upon the Commission, *Federal Trade Comm. v. National Lead Co.*, 352 U.S. 419, 429. For these reasons the court should not "lightly modify" the Commission's orders. *Federal Trade Comm. v. Cement Institute*, 333 U.S. 683, 726. However, this Court has also warned that an order's prohibitions "should be clear and precise in order that they may be understood by those against whom they are directed," *Federal Trade Comm. v. Cement Institute, supra*, at 726, and that "[t]he severity of possible penalties prescribed . . . for violations of orders which have become final underlines the necessity for fashioned orders which are, at the outset, sufficiently clear and precise to avoid raising serious questions as to their meaning and application." *Federal Trade Comm. v. Henry Broch & Co.*, 368 U.S. 360, 367–368.

The Court of Appeals has criticized the references in the Commission's order to "test, experiment or demonstration" as not capable of practical interpretation. It could find no difference between the Rapid Shave commercial and a commercial which extolled the goodness of ice cream while giving viewers a picture of a scoop of mashed potatoes appearing to be ice cream. We do not understand this difficulty. In the ice cream case the mashed potato prop is not being used for additional proof of the product claim, while the purpose of the Rapid Shave commercial is to give the viewer objective proof of the claims made. If in the ice cream hypothetical the focus of the commercial becomes the undisclosed potato prop and the viewer is invited, explicitly or by implication, to see for himself about the ice cream's rich texture and full color, and perhaps compare it to a "rival product," then the commercial has become similar to the one now before us. Clearly, however, a commercial which depicts happy actors delightedly eating ice cream that is in fact mashed potatoes or drinking a product appearing to be coffee but which is in fact some other substance is not covered by the present order.

The crucial terms of the present order — "test, experiment or demonstration . . . represented . . . as actual proof of a claim" — are as specific as the circumstances will permit. If respondents in their subsequent commercials attempt to come as close to the line of misrepresentation as the Commission's order permits, they may without specifically intending to do so cross into the area proscribed by this order. However, it does not seem "unfair to require that one who deliberately goes perilously close to an area of proscribed conduct shall take the risk that he may cross the line." *Boyce Motor Lines, Inc. v. United States*, 342 U.S. 337, 340. In commercials where the emphasis is on the seller's word, and not on the viewer's own perception, the respondents need not fear that an undisclosed use of props is prohibited by the present order. On the other hand, when the commercial not only makes a claim, but also invites the viewer to rely on his own perception, for demonstrative proof of the claim, the respondents will be aware that the use of undisclosed props in strategic places might be a material deception. We believe that respondents will have no difficulty applying the Commission's order to the vast majority of their contemplated future commercials. If, however, a situation arises in which respondents are sincerely unable to determine whether a proposed course of action would violate the present order, they can, by complying with the Commission's rules, oblige the Commission to give them definitive advice as to whether their proposed action, if pursued, would constitute compliance with the order.

Finally, we find no defect in the provision of the order which prohibits respondents from engaging in similar practices with respect to "any product" they advertise. The propriety of a broad order depends upon the specific circumstances of the case, but the courts will not interfere except where the remedy selected has no reasonable relation to the unlawful practices found to exist. In this case the respondents produced three different commercials which employed the same deceptive practice. This we believe gave the Commission a sufficient basis for believing that the respondents would be inclined to use similar commercials with respect to the other products they advertise. We think it reasonable for the Commission to frame its order broadly enough to prevent respondents from engaging in similarly illegal practices in future advertisements. As was said in *Federal Trade Comm. v. Ruberoid Co.*, 343 U.S. 470, 473: "[T]he Commission is not limited to prohibiting the illegal practice in the precise form in which it is found to have existed in the past." Having been caught violating the Act, respondents "must expect some fencing in." *Federal Trade Comm. v. National Lead Co.*, 352 U.S. 419, 431.

The judgment of the Court of Appeals is reversed and the case remanded for the entry of a judgment enforcing the Commission's order.

Reversed and remanded.

Mr. Justice Harlan, whom Mr. Justice Stewart joins, dissenting in part.

*   *   *

The faulty prop in the Court's reasoning is that it focuses entirely on what is taking place in the studio rather than on what the viewer is seeing on his screen. That which the viewer sees with his own eyes is not, however, what is taking place in the studio, but an electronic image. If the image he sees on the screen is an accurate reproduction of what he would see with the naked eyes were the experiment performed before him with sandpaper in his home or in the studio, there can hardly be a misrepresentation in any legally significant sense. While the Commission undoubtedly possesses broad authority to give content to the proscriptions of the Act, its discretion, as the Court recognizes, is not unbridled, and "in the last analysis the words 'deceptive practices' set forth a legal standard and they must get their final meaning from judicial construction" (*ante*, p. 1043). In this case, assuming that Rapid Shave could soften sandpaper as quickly as it does sand-covered plexiglass, a viewer who wants to entertain his friends by duplicating the actual experiment could do so by buying a can of Rapid Shave and some sandpaper. If he wished to shave himself, and his beard were really as tough as sandpaper, he could perform this part of his morning ablutions with Rapid Shave in the same way as he saw the plexiglass shaved on television.

I do not see how such a commercial can be said to be "deceptive" in any legally acceptable use of that term. The Court attempts to distinguish the case where a "celebrity" has written a testimonial endorsing some product, but the original testimonial cannot be seen over television and a copy is shown over the air by the manufacturer. The Court states of this "hypothetical": "In respondents' hypothetical the objective proof of the product claim that is offered, the word of the celebrity or agency that the experiment was actually conducted, does exist; while in the case before us the objective proof offered, the viewer's own perception of an actual experiment, does not exist." But in both cases the viewer is told to "see for himself," in the one case that the celebrity has endorsed the product; in the other, that the product can shave sandpaper; in neither case is the viewer actually seeing the proof; and in both cases the objective proof does exist, be it the original testimonial or the sandpaper test actually conducted by the manufacturer. In neither case, however, is there a material misrepresentation, because what the viewer sees *is* an accurate image of the objective proof.

Nor can I readily understand how the accurate portrayal of an experiment by means of a mock-up can be considered more deceptive than the use of mashed potatoes to convey the glamorous qualities of a particular ice cream; indeed, to a potato-lover "the smile on the face of the tiger" might come more naturally than if he were actually being served ice cream.

It is commonly known that television presents certain distortions in transmission for which the broadcasting industry must compensate. Thus, a white towel will look dingy gray over television, but a blue towel will look a sparkling white. On the Court's analysis, an advertiser must achieve accuracy in the studio even though it results in an inaccurate image being projected on the home screen. This led the Court of Appeals to question whether it would be proper for an advertiser to show a product on television that somehow, because of the medium, looks better on the screen than it does in real life. 310 F.2d 89, 94; 326 F.2d 517, 523, n.16.

A perhaps more commonplace example suggests itself: Would it be proper for respondent Colgate, in advertising a laundry detergent, to "demonstrate" the effectiveness of a major competitor's detergent in washing white sheets; and then "before the viewer's eyes," to wash a white (not a blue) sheet with the competitor's detergent? The studio test would accurately show the quality of the product, but the image on the screen would look as though the sheet had been washed with an ineffective detergent. All that has happened here is the converse: a demonstration has been altered in the studio to compensate for the distortions of the television medium, but in this instance in order to present an accurate picture to the television viewer.

In short, it seems to me that the proper legal test in cases of this kind concerns not what goes on in the broadcasting studio, but whether what is shown on the television screen is an accurate representation of the advertised product and of the claims made for it.

KRAFT v. FEDERAL TRADE COMMISSION
970 F.2d 311 (7th Cir. 1992)

FLAUM, CIRCUIT JUDGE.

*   *   *

Kraft Singles are process cheese food slices. In the early 1980s, Kraft began losing market share to an increasing number of imitation slices that were advertised as both less expensive [than] and equally nutritious as dairy slices like Singles. Kraft responded with a series of advertisements, collectively known as the "Five Ounces of Milk" campaign, designed to inform consumers that Kraft Singles cost more than imitation slices because they are made from five ounces of milk rather than less expensive ingredients. The ads also focused on the calcium content of Kraft Singles in an effort to capitalize on growing consumer interest in adequate calcium consumption.

The FTC filed a complaint against Kraft charging that this advertising campaign materially misrepresented the calcium content and relative calcium benefit of Kraft Singles. The FTC Act makes it unlawful to engage in unfair or deceptive commercial practices, 15 U.S.C. § 45, or to induce consumers to purchase certain products through advertising that is misleading in a material respect. *Id.* at §§ 52, 55. Thus, an advertisement is deceptive under the Act if it is likely to mislead consumers, acting reasonably under the circumstances, in a material respect.

*   *   *

In implementing this standard, the Commission examines the overall net impression of an ad and engages in a three-part inquiry: (1) what claims are conveyed in this ad; (2) are those claims false or misleading; and (3) are those claims material to prospective consumers.

Two facts are critical to understanding the allegations against Kraft. First, although

Kraft does use five ounces of milk in making each Kraft Single, roughly 30% of the calcium contained in the milk is lost during processing. Second, the vast majority of imitation slices sold in the United States contain 15% of the U.S. Recommended Daily Allowance (RDA) of calcium per ounce, roughly the same amount contained in Kraft Singles. Specifically then, the FTC complaint alleged that the challenged advertisements made two implied claims, neither of which was true: (1) that a slice of Kraft Singles contains the same amount of calcium as five ounces of milk (the "milk equivalency" claim); and (2) that Kraft Singles contain more calcium than do most imitation cheese slices (the "imitation superiority" claim). [1]

The two sets of ads at issue in this case, referred to as the "Skimp" ads and the "Class Picture" ads, ran nationally in print and broadcast media between 1985 and 1987. The Skimp ads were designed to communicate the nutritional benefit of Kraft Singles by referring expressly to their milk and calcium content. The broadcast version of this ad on which the FTC focused contained the following audio copy:

> *Lady (voice over):* I admit it. I thought of skimping. Could you look into those big blue eyes and skimp on her? So I buy Kraft Singles. Imitation slices use hardly any milk. But Kraft has five ounces per slice. Five ounces. So her little bones get calcium they need to grow. No, she doesn't know what that big Kraft means. Good thing I do.
>
> *Singers:* Kraft Singles. More milk makes'em . . . more milk makes'em good.
>
> *Lady (voice over):* Skimp on her? No way.

* * *

The visual image corresponding to this copy shows, among other things, milk pouring into a glass until it reaches a mark on the glass denoted "five ounces." The commercial also shows milk pouring into a glass which bears the phrase "5 oz. milk slice" and which gradually becomes part of the label on a package of Singles. In January 1986, Kraft revised this ad, changing "Kraft *has* five ounces per slice" to "Kraft is *made from* five ounces per slice," IDF 28; *see* CX 276F, CX 106 (emphasis added), and in March 1987, Kraft added the disclosure, "one 3/4 ounce slice has 70% of the calcium of five ounces of milk" as a subscript in the television commercial and as a footnote in the print ads.

The Class Picture ads also emphasized the milk and calcium content of Kraft Singles but, unlike the Skimp ads, did not make an express comparison to imitation slices. The version of this ad examined by the FTC depicts a group of school children having their class picture taken, and contains the following audio copy:

> *Announcer (voice over):* Can you see what's missing in this picture?
>
> Well, a government study says that half the school kids in America don't get all the calcium recommended for growing kids. That's why Kraft Singles are important. Kraft is made from five ounces of milk per slice. So they're concentrated with calcium. Calcium the government recommends for strong bones and healthy teeth!
>
> *Photographer:* Say Cheese!
>
> *Kids:* Cheese!
>
> *Announcer (voice over):* Say Kraft Singles.'Cause kids love Kraft Singles, right down to their bones.

. . . . The Class Picture ads also included the subscript disclaimer mentioned above.

* * *

As to the Skimp ads, the Commission found that four elements conveyed the milk

---

[1] Because Kraft concedes that these claims, if made, are false, the second step of the aforementioned inquiry — whether the alleged claims are false — is not before us on appeal.

equivalency claim: (1) the use of the word "has" in the phrase "Kraft has five ounces per slice"; (2) repetition of the precise amount of milk in a Kraft Single (five ounces); (3) the use of the word "so" to link the reference to milk with the reference to calcium; and (4) the visual image of milk being poured into a glass up to a five-ounce mark, and the superimposition of that image onto a package of Singles. It also found two additional elements that conveyed the imitation superiority claim: (1) the express reference to imitation slices combined with the use of comparative language ("hardly any," "but") and (2) the image of a glass containing very little milk during the reference to imitation slices, followed by the image of a glass being filled to the five-ounce mark during the reference to Kraft Singles. The Commission based all of these findings on its own impression of the advertisements and found it unnecessary to resort to extrinsic evidence; it did note, however, that the available extrinsic evidence was consistent with its determinations.

The Commission then examined the Class Picture ads — once again, without resorting to extrinsic evidence — and found that they contained copy substantially similar to the copy in the Skimp ads that conveyed the impression of milk equivalency. It rejected, however, the ALJ's finding that the Class Picture ads made an imitation superiority claim, determining that the ads neither expressly compared Singles to imitation slices, nor contained any visual images to prompt such a comparison, and that available extrinsic evidence did not support the ALJ's finding.

The FTC next found that the claims were material to consumers. It concluded that the milk equivalency claim is a health-related claim that reasonable consumers would find important and that Kraft believed that the claim induced consumers to purchase Singles. The FTC presumed that the imitation superiority claim was material because it found that Kraft intended to make that claim. It also found that the materiality of that claim was demonstrated by evidence that the challenged ads led to increased sales despite a substantially higher price for Singles than for imitation slices.

Finally, the FTC modified the ALJ's cease and desist order by extending its coverage from "individually wrapped slices of cheese, imitation cheese, and substitute cheese" to "any product that is a cheese, cheese related product, imitation cheese, or substitute cheese." The Commission found that the serious, deliberate nature of the violation, combined with the transferability of the violations to other cheese products, justified a broader order. Kraft filed this petition to set-aside the Commission's order or, alternatively, to modify its scope.

* * *

We find substantial evidence in the record to support the FTC's finding. Although Kraft downplays the nexus in the ads between milk and calcium, the ads emphasize visually and verbally that five ounces of milk go into a slice of Kraft Singles; this image is linked to calcium content, strongly implying that the consumer gets the calcium found in five ounces of milk. The fact that the Commission listed four elements in finding an implied claim in the Skimp ads does not mean that those same elements must all be present in the Class Picture ad to reach that same conclusion. Furthermore, the Class Picture ads contained one other element reinforcing the milk equivalency claim, the phrase "5 oz. milk slice" inside the image of a glass superimposed on the Singles package, and it was reasonable for the Commission to conclude that there were important similarities between these two ads. Finally, to support its own interpretation of the ads, the Commission examined available extrinsic evidence and this evidence, in the Commission's view, bolstered its findings.

Kraft asserts that the literal truth of the Class Picture ads — they *are* made from five ounces of milk and they *do* have a high concentration of calcium — makes it illogical to render a finding of consumer deception. The difficulty with this argument is that even literally true statements can have misleading implications.

* * *

Here, the average consumer is not likely to know that much of the calcium in five ounces of milk (30%) is lost in processing, which leaves consumers with a misleading impression about calcium content. The critical fact is not that reasonable consumers might believe that a 3/4 ounce slice of cheese actually contains five ounces of *milk*, but that reasonable consumers might believe that a 3/4 ounce slice actually contains the *calcium* in five ounces of milk.

* * *

In determining that the milk equivalency claim was material to consumers, the FTC cited Kraft surveys showing that 71% of respondents rated calcium content an extremely or very important factor in their decision to buy Kraft Singles, and that 52% of female, and 40% of all respondents, reported significant personal concerns about adequate calcium consumption. The FTC further noted that the ads were targeted to female homemakers with children and that the 60 milligram difference between the calcium contained in five ounces of milk and that contained in a Kraft Single would make up for most of the RDA calcium deficiency shown in girls aged 9–11. Finally, the FTC found evidence in the record that Kraft designed the ads with the intent to capitalize on consumer calcium deficiency concerns.

Significantly, the FTC found further evidence of materiality in Kraft's conduct: despite repeated warnings, Kraft persisted in running the challenged ads.

* * *

With regard to the imitation superiority claim, the Commission applied a presumption of materiality after finding evidence that Kraft intended the challenged ads to convey this message. (Recall that intent to convey a claim is one of three categories qualifying for a presumption of materiality. *See, e.g., Thompson Medical*, 104 F.T.C. at 816–17.) It found this presumption buttressed by the fact that the challenged ad copy led to increased sales of Singles, even though they cost 40 percent more than imitation slices. Finally, the FTC determined that Kraft's consumer surveys were insufficient to rebut this inference and in particular criticized Kraft's survey methodology because it offered limited response options to consumers.

* * *

To reiterate, the FTC's order does two things: it prohibits the Skimp ads and the Class Picture ads (as *currently* designed) and it requires Kraft to base future nutrient and calcium claims on reliable scientific evidence. Kraft mischaracterizes the decision as a categorical ban on commercial speech when in fact it identifies with particularity two nutrient claims that the Commission found actually misleading and prohibits only those claims. It further places on Kraft the (minor) burden of supporting future nutrient claims with reliable data. This leaves Kraft free to use any advertisement it chooses, including the Skimp and Class Picture ads, so long as it either eliminates the elements specifically identified by the FTC as contributing to consumer deception or corrects this inaccurate impression by adding prominent, unambiguous disclosures. *See, e.g., Remo-vatron*, 884 F.2d at 1497. We note one additional consideration further alleviating first amendment concerns; Kraft, like any party to an FTC order, may seek an advisory opinion from the Commission as to whether any future advertisements comply with its order, 16 C.F.R. § 2.41(d), and this procedure has been specifically cited by courts as one method of reducing advertiser uncertainty.

* * *

For these reasons, we hold that the specific prohibitions imposed on Kraft in the FTC's cease and desist order are not broader than reasonably necessary to prevent deception and hence not violative of the First Amendment.

* * *

For the foregoing reasons, Kraft's petition to set-aside the order is DENIED and the Commission's order is ENFORCED.

FEDERAL TRADE COMMISSION v. QT, INC., et al.
512 F.3d 858 (7th Cir. 2008)

EASTERBROOK, CHIEF JUDGE

* * *

According to the district court's findings, almost everything that defendants have said about [their Q-Ray Ionized] bracelet is false. Here are some highlights:

- Defendants promoted the bracelet as a miraculous cure for chronic pain, but it has no therapeutic effect.
- Defendants told consumers that claims of "immediate, significant or complete pain relief" had been "test-proven"; they hadn't.
- The bracelet does not emit "Q-Rays" (there are no such things) and is not ionized (the bracelet is an electric conductor, and any net charge dissipates swiftly). The bracelet's chief promoter chose these labels because they are simple and easily remembered — and because Polaroid Corp. blocked him from calling the bangle "polarized".
- The bracelet is touted as "enhancing the flow of bio-energy" or "balancing the flow of positive and negative energies"; these empty phrases have no connection to any medical or scientific effect. Every other claim made about the mechanism of the bracelet's therapeutic effect likewise is techno-babble.
- Defendants represented that the therapeutic effect wears off in a year or two, despite knowing that the bracelet's properties do not change. This assertion is designed to lead customers to buy new bracelets. Likewise the false statement that the bracelet has a ""memory cycle specific to each individual wearer" so that only the bracelet's original wearer can experience pain relief is designed to increase sales by eliminating the second-hand market and "explaining" the otherwise-embarrassing fact that the buyer's friends and neighbors can't perceive any effect.
- Even statements about the bracelet's physical composition are false. It is sold in "gold" and "silver" varieties but is made of brass.

* * *

The [Federal Trade Commission] Act forbids false and misleading statements, and a statement that is plausible but has not been tested in the most reliable way cannot be condemned out of hand. The burden is on the Commission to prove that the statements are false. (This is one way in which the Federal Trade Commission Act differs from the Food and Drug Act.) Think about the seller of an adhesive bandage treated with a disinfectant such as iodine. The seller does not need to conduct tests before asserting that this product reduces the risk of infection from cuts. The bandage keeps foreign materials out of the cuts and kills some bacteria. It may be debatable *how much* the risk of infection falls, but the direction of the effect would be known, and the claim could not be condemned as false. Placebo-controlled, double-blind testing is not a legal requirement for consumer products.

But how could this conclusion assist defendants? In our example the therapeutic claim is based on scientific principles. For the Q-Ray Ionized Bracelet, by contrast, all statements about how the product works — Q-Rays, ionizations, enhancing the flow of bio-energy, and the like — are blather. Defendants might as well have said: "Beneficent creatures from the 17th Dimension use this bracelet as a beacon to locate people who need pain relief, and whisk them off to their homeworld every night to provide help in ways unknown to our science."

Although it is true, as Arthur C. Clarke said, that "[a]ny sufficiently advanced technology is indistinguishable from magic" by those who don't understand its principles ("Profiles of the Future" (1961)), a person who promotes a product that contemporary technology does not understand must establish that this "magic" actually works. Proof is what separates an effect new to science from a swindle. Defendants themselves told customers that the bracelet's efficacy had been "test-proven"; that statement was misleading unless a reliable test had been used and statistically significant results achieved. A placebo-controlled, double-blind study is the best test; something less may do (for there is no point in spending $1 million to verify a claim worth only $10,000 if true); but defendants have no proof of the Q-Ray Ionized Bracelet's efficacy. The "tests" on which they relied were bunk. (We need not repeat the magistrate judge's exhaustive evaluation of this subject.) What remain are testimonials, which are not a form of proof because most testimonials represent a logical fallacy; post hoc ergo propter hoc. (A person who experiences a reduction in pain after donning the bracelet may have enjoyed the same reduction without it. That's why the "testimonial" of someone who keeps elephants off the streets of a large city by snapping his fingers is the basis of a joke rather than proof of cause and effect.)

* * *

Defendants insist that the placebo effect vindicates their claims, even though they are false — indeed, especially because they are false, as the placebo effect depends on deceit. Tell the patient that the pill contains nothing but sugar, and there is no pain relief, tell him (falsely) that it contains a powerful analgesic, and the perceived level of pain falls. A product that confers this benefit cannot be excluded from the market, defendants insist, just because they told the lies necessary to bring the effect about.

Yet the Federal Trade Commission Act condemns material falsehoods in promoting consumer products; the statute lacks an exception for "beneficial deceit." We appreciate the possibility that a vague claim — along the lines of "this bracelet will reduce your pain without the side effects of drugs" — could be rendered true by the placebo effect. To this extent we are skeptical about language in *FTC v. Pantron I Corp.*, 33 F.3d 1088 (9th Cir. 1994), suggesting that placebo effects always are worthless to consumers. But our defendants advanced claims beyond those that could be supported by a placebo effect. They made statements about Q-Rays, ionization, and bio-energy that they knew to be poppycock; they stated that the bracelet remembers its first owner and won't work for anyone else; the list is extensive.

One important reason for requiring truth is so that competition in the market will lead to appropriate prices. Selling brass as gold harms consumers independent of any effect on pain. Since the placebo effect can be obtained from sugar pills, charging $200 for a device that is represented as a miracle cure but works no better than a dummy pill is a form of fraud. That's not all. A placebo is necessary when scientists are searching for the marginal effect of a new drug or device, but once the study is over a reputable professional will recommend whatever works best.

* * *

Physicians know how to treat pain. Why pay $200 for a Q-Ray Ionized Bracelet when you can get relief from an aspirin tablet that costs 1 cent. Some painful conditions do not respond to analgesics (or the stronger drugs in the pharmacopeia) or to surgery, but it does not follow that a placebo at any price is better. Deceit such as the tall tales that defendants told about the Q-Ray Ionized Bracelet will lead some consumers to avoid treatments that cost less and do more; the lies will lead others to pay too much for pain relief or otherwise interfere with the matching of remedies to medical conditions. That's why the placebo effect cannot justify fraud in promoting a product. Doctor Dulcamara was a charlatan who harmed most of his customers even though Nemorino gets the girl at the end of Donizetti's *L'elisir D'Amore*.

Now for the remedy. Defendants do not contest the terms of the injunction. They do, however, say that the financial award was excessive. The magistrate judge set as his goal the disgorgement of the profits that defendants made while the Q-Ray Ionized Bracelet was heavily promoted with infomercials on late-night television. Disgorging profits is an appropriate remedy. *See FTD v. Febre*, 128 F.3d 530, 534 (7th Cir. 1997); *FTC v. Amy Travel Service, Inc.*, 875 F.2d 564, 571-72 (7th Cir. 1989). But defendants say that the record does not contain evidence about their profits. True, the FTC compiled balance sheets showing profits running in the millions every year. These should not be considered, defendants insist, because when Que Te Park (defendants' principal investor and CEO) testified about the subject, he was asked only whether he could "see" the enterprise's net income (he conceded that he could), not whether the figures are correct, and the FTC's lawyer then forgot to offer the balance sheets themselves as evidence.

This is too clever by half. The FTC made estimates of profits from the Q-Ray Ionized Bracelet business and gave defendants an opportunity to respond. They chose not do so. Park's noncommittal answers avoided any risk of prosecution for perjury but did not meet the FTC's prima facie showing. The magistrate judge was entitled to treat the evasion as an admission that the FTC's computation is in the ballpark. A monetary award often depends on estimation, for defendants may not keep (or may conceal) the data required to make an exact calculation. Defendants' business was a profitable one; that much, at least, they concede. (It is so profitable that they continue to carry it on despite the injunction that requires them to stop making most of their old claims for its efficacy. Today it is sold with testimonials and vaporous statements.) A court is entitled to proceed with the best available information; if defendants thought that their profits for these years were below $16 million, they should have produced their own figures — for once the FTC produces a reasonable estimate, the defendants bear the burden of showing that the estimate is inaccurate. *Febre*, 128 F.3d at 536.

* * *

AFFIRMED.

2.　Notes on Deceptiveness

Acts or practices that are likely to mislead violate § 5 of the FTC Act. *See Kraft, supra.* In determining whether an act, omission or representation is likely to mislead, each phrase is not technically interpreted. *Ward Laboratories, Inc. v. FTC*, 276 F.2d 952 (2^d Cir. 1960), *cert. denied*, 364 U.S. 827 (1960). Rather, it is the overall impression created, with ambiguities construed against the advertiser. *Kraft, supra; American Home Products Corp. v. FTC*, 695 F.2d 681, 687, (3^d Cir. 1983); *Murray Space Shoe Corp. v. FTC*, 304 F.2d 270, 272 (2d Cir. 1962). Literal truth is not a defense when a § 5 violation is alleged. *See Kalwajtys v. FTC*, 237 F.2d 654 (7th Cir. 1956), *cert. denied*, 352 U.S. 1025 (1957); *Kraft, supra; L.G. Balfour Co. v. FTC*, 442 F.2d 1, 17 (7th Cir. 1971). *See also* Stolle, *The FTC's Reliance on Extrinsic Evidence in Cases of Deceptive Advertising: A Proposal for Interpretive Rulemaking*, 74 NEB. L. REV. 352 (1995) (discussing the 1992 *Kraft Inc. v. FTC* decision).

The absence of actual deception, intent to deceive or actual injury to the public, consumers, or competitors, continues to be irrelevant in evaluating whether a misrepresentation violates Section 5. *See Beneficial Corp. v. FTC*,542 F.2d 611, 617 (3^d Cir. 1976), *cert. denied*, 430 U.S. 983 (1977); *FTC v. World Travel Vacation Brokers, Inc.*, 861 F.2d 1020, 1029 (7th Cir. 1988). Furthermore, the fact that a representation is literally true, or deceptive only by omission, does not constitute a defense. *See Kraft v. FTC*, 970 F.2d 311 (7th Cir. 1992) (supporting FTC's finding that Kraft misled consumers about calcium content of its "Singles" cheese slices and about the inference of superiority over competitors' cheese slices); Alexander, *Federal Regulation of False Advertising*, 17 U. KAN. L. REV. 573 (1969); Millstein, *The Federal Trade Commission and False Advertising*, 64 COLUM. L. REV. 439 (1964).

a) Reasonable or Gullible Consumer

Should the FTC protect even gullible consumers? In *In re Cliffdale Associates, Inc.*, [1983-1987 Transfer Binder] Trade Reg. Rep. (CCH) ¶ 22,137 (March 23, 1984), Chairman Miller, writing for the majority, endorsed the "consumer acting reasonably" standard. He stated that the standard was not new, and that it only emphasized long standing Commission policy "that the law should not be applied in such a way as to find that honest representations are deceptive simply because they are misunderstood by a few." While concurring with the majority that respondent's value and performance claims for its Gas Save Valve automobile engine attachment were deceptive, Commissioner Pertschuk dissented as to the endorsement of the new standard. He stated:

> The new deception analysis has a more serious effect that is clearly not unintentional. That is to withdraw the protection of Section 5 from consumers who do not act "reasonably."
>
> . . . .
>
> How will the Commission judge the conduct of consumers who succumb to sales pitches for worthless or grossly over-valued investments? Do "reasonable consumers" buy diamonds or real estate, sight unseen, from total strangers? Is a consumer "acting reasonably" when he or she falls for a hard-sell telephone solicitation to buy "valuable" oil or gas leases from an unknown corporation? Can a consumer "reasonably" rely on oral promises that are expressly repudiated in a written sales contract?
>
> The sad fact is that a small segment of our society makes its livelihood preying upon consumers who are very trusting and unsophisticated. Others specialize in weakening the defenses of especially vulnerable, but normally cautious, consumers. Through skillful exploitation of such common desires as the wish to get rich quick or to provide some measure of security for one's old age, professional con men can prompt conduct that many of their victims will readily admit — in hindsight — is patently unreasonable.
>
> Of course, what strikes me as "unreasonable" consumer behavior may not seem so to other commissioners. The very subjective nature of the "reasonable consumer" standard is cause for concern. How can consumer conduct be measured for reasonableness? I know of no test for it, and I am fearful of the *ad hoc* determination that will be made in the future.

Since the enunciation of the "reasonable consumer" standard in *Cliffdale, supra*, at least one court, in reviewing the application of this adjudicative standard, has found that the FTC bears a greater evidentiary burden in showing a § 5 violation than under the previous "tendency and capacity to deceive" standard. *Southwest Sunsites, Inc. v. FTC*, 785 F.2d 1431, 1436 (9th Cir. 1986). However, courts and commentators are undecided as to whether the "new standard" has actually had any practical effect on FTC enforcement activity.

See Schecter, *The Death of the Gullible Consumer: Towards a More Sensible Definition of Deception at the FTC*, 1989 U. ILL. L. REV. 571, 592–593 (1989); PRIDGEN, CONSUMER PROTECTION AND THE LAW, § 10.04 (2007).

b) Materiality

The courts have held that misrepresentations violating Section 5 must be "material" to a decision to make a purchase. *See Colgate- Palmolive, supra; Kraft, supra; Exposition Press, Inc. v. FTC*, 295 F.2d 869 (2[d] Cir. 1961). Does the requirement of materiality insure public interest? *See Pep Boys — Manny, Moe & Jack, Inc. v. FTC*, 122 F.2d 158 (3[d] Cir. 1941). In the *Colgate* case, the court held that "within reasonable bounds" the FTC may infer that a misrepresentation will be a material factor in the purchase decision. Can the FTC make such an inference if there is contradictory evidence?

In *In re Novartis Corporation*, 1999 FTC LEXIS 63 (1999), *aff'd in*, *Novartis Corp. v. FTC*, 223 F.3d 783 (D.C. Cir. 2000), the maker of DOAN'S pills had made unsubstantiated advertising claims that the pills were superior to other products in relieving back pain. The FTC first observed that "[a] material misrepresentation is one that involves information important to consumers and that is therefore likely to affect the consumer's choice of, or conduct regarding, a product." Here a presumption of materiality was raised, both because "an advertiser's intent to make a claim generally implies that the advertiser believes the claim is important to consumers", and because such a claim regarding back pain "goes to health and to a central characteristic of the product." Novartis contested that presumption of materiality. It argued that its predecessor had run "ads that it knew were ineffective in order to appease retailers who demand manufacturer support for niche brands". However, the FTC found that any assertion that "it ran an eight-year multimillion dollar campaign of ineffective ads is contradicted by the evidence," including evidence of "an 80% increase in dollar sales during the relevant period." Nor was the claim puffery, as Novartis alleged. Consumer studies submitted by Novartis and other evidence did cause the FTC "to look beyond a simple presumption of materiality." Nonetheless, in the end the FTC found the advertising claim material, and barred it, and also ordered corrective advertising to cure the lingering deception caused by the campaign. *See also Kerran v. FTC*, 265 F.2d 246 (10th Cir. 1959), *cert. denied*, 361 U.S. 818 (1959).

Should the FTC be required to explain the basis for such an inference? *See* Justice Harlan's dissent in *FTC v. Mary Carter Paint Co.*, 382 U.S. 46, 49 (1965). Why is a failure to disclose that a product demonstration is simulated a material deception? What other types of nondisclosures might constitute deception? *See FTC v. Figgie Int'l, Inc.*, 994 F.2d 595, 599–600 (9th Cir. 1993); *Keele Hair & Scalp Specialists, Inc. v. FTC*, 275 F.2d 18 (5th Cir. 1960). Is a label misrepresentation more likely to deceive than an advertising misrepresentation? *See Korber Hats, Inc. v. FTC*, 311 F.2d 358 (1[st]Cir. 1962).

c) Other Defenses

In addition to immateriality, there are other defenses to a charge of deception that will be sustained if proven. *See FTC v. Winsted Hosiery Co.*, 258 U.S. 483 (1922) (no deception if term achieves secondary meaning such that consumers are not deceived by manufacturer's representation); *Kidder Oil Co. v. FTC*, 117 F.2d 892 (7th Cir. 1941) (representation merely constitutes puffing); *Waltham Precision Instrument Co., Inc.*, FTC Dkt. 6914, *aff'd on other grounds*, *Waltham Precision Instrument Co. v. FTC*, 327 F.2d 427 (7th Cir. 1964), *cert. denied*, 377 U.S. 992 (1964) (all persons receiving advertisement aware of deceptiveness). Should it be a defense to a charge of deception that consumers received products identical or equal to those they ordered? *See FTC v. Royal Milling*, 288 U.S. 212 (1933). In *FTC v. Algoma Lumber Co.*, 291 U.S. 67, 78 (1934) Justice Cardozo stated: "The consumer is prejudiced if upon giving an order for one thing, he is supplied with something else. . . . In such matters, the public is entitled to get what it chooses, though the choice may be dictated by caprice or by fashion or perhaps by ignorance." Other defenses rejected in FTC cases include *FTC v. Kay*, 35 F.2d 160 (7th Cir. 1929), *cert. denied*, 281 U.S. 764 (1930) (registration of deceptive term as a trademark affords no protection against proceedings under FTC Act); *Gimbel Bros., Inc. v. FTC*, 116 F.2d 578 (2[d] Cir. 1941) (acting on customers' instructions); *National Silver Co. v. FTC*, 88 F.2d 425 (2[d] Cir. 1937) (product defect visible to naked eye).

Does the requirement of a "specific and substantial" public interest merely mean that the FTC should not decide private quarrels between competitors? *Cf. Hershey Chocolate Corp. v. FTC*, 121 F.2d 968 (3[d]Cir. 1941). Could the number of competitors affected be a factor in determining whether a proceeding is in the public interest? *See Branch v. FTC*, 141 F.2d 31 (7th Cir. 1944). What standard should courts use in reviewing the FTC's determination that a proceeding is in the public interest? *See Slough v. FTC*, 396 F.2d 870 (5th Cir. 1968), *cert. denied*, 393 U.S. 980 (1968). *Compare* the discussion on § 43(a) of the Lanham Act in the Misrepresentation section of Chapter 8, *supra*.

Should the question whether the FTC has "reason to believe" an illegal practice is occurring also be a jurisdictional issue? *See Miles Laboratories, Inc. v. FTC*, 140 F.2d 683 (D.C. Cir. 1944), *cert. denied*, 322 U.S. 752 (1944). Note that jurisdiction is a threshold question for the court's determination in granting relief pendente lite. 15 U.S.C. §§ 52, 53; *cf. FTC v. Sterling Drug, Inc.*, 317 F.2d 669 (2d Cir. 1963).

d) Deceptive Initial Offers

A number of decisions prohibit use of deceptive initial offers ("first contact") even if they are rectified before any purchase is made in reliance upon them. *See FTC v. Standard Educ. Society*, 302 U.S. 112 (1937); *Exposition Press, Inc. v. FTC*, 295 F.2d 869 (2d Cir. 1961). False promising of leads to prospective salesmen could also constitute a deceptive first contact. *See Goodman v. FTC*, 244 F.2d 584 (9d Cir. 1957). Is the *Colgate- Palmolive* case also a first contact case? *See Developments in the Law — Deceptive Advertising*, 80 Harv. L. Rev. 1005 (1967).

"Bait and switch" selling is initiated by the advertising of a bargain buy which is intended to lure customers into a store. The deception is carried out when the customers who appear are actively discouraged by sales personnel from purchasing the advertised product, or are told it is unavailable, or when the product upon actual inspection proves to be intrinsically undesirable. The perpetrator of such a scheme expects to sell profitable "switched" merchandise in place of the "bait" merchandise advertised. *See Tashof v. FTC*, 437 F.2d 707 (D.C. Cir. 1970), and the FTC position set forth at 16 C.F.R. §§ 238.0 and 238.1 (1977). Would it be any defense to a "bait and switch" charge that advertising gave notice of limited quantity of cheaper articles? *See United States v. George's Radio & Television Co.*, 1962 Trade Cas. ¶ 70,281 (D.C. Cir. 1962). Is the rationale for illegality similar in "bait and switch" and "first contact" cases? *Compare All-State Indus., Inc. v. FTC*, 423 F.2d 423 (4th Cir. 1970), *cert. denied*, 400 U.S. 828 (1970) *with FTC v. Standard Educ. Society*, 302 U.S. 112 (1937). What other types of pricing practices might be deceptive?

e) Other Deceptive Acts and Practices

There are endless varieties of "deceptive" acts and practices within the ambit of § 5 of the FTC Act. Some of the most important of these offenses in terms of FTC enforcement activity are as follows:

(a) Misrepresentations of facts concerning the business, product or service, *i.e.*, its origin, composition or effectiveness. *See FTC v. Bay Area Bus. Council, Inc.*, 423 F.3d 627 (7th Cir. 2005) (defendant "misled consumers into believing they would receive a credit card in exchange for a hefty 'one-time' fee; $12.5 million in consumer redress awarded"); FTC v. Algoma Lumber Co., 291 U.S. 67, 68 (1934) (Justice Cardozo stating that "the public is entitled to get what it chooses, though the choice may be dictated by caprice or by fashion or perhaps by ignorance"); *Carter's Products, Inc. v. FTC*, 268 F.2d 461 (9th Cir. 1959) (holding that "Carter's Little Liver Pills" product name and advertisements deceptively represented that the pills had a therapeutic action on the liver); *FTC v. Thompson Medical Co.*, 791 F.2d 189 (D.C. Cir. 1986), *cert. denied*, 479 U.S. 1085 (1987) (upholding FTC's ruling that "Aspercreme" for arthritis rub falsely implied that the product contained aspirin and its requirement of a disclaimer); *FTC v. Para-Link Int'l*, 2001 U.S. Dist. LEXIS 17372 (M.D. Fla. 2001) (overstating income potential in connection with sale of at-home paralegal training kit and failing to advise customers regarding legal risks of preparing legal documents). *See also In re Campbell Soup*, 56 Antitrust & Trade Reg. Rep. (BNA) 783 (May 25, 1989) (FTC complaint issued charging that soup company's advertisement falsely represented the health benefits of consuming its products).

(b) Misrepresentations respecting guarantees, endorsements, and testimonials. *See Orkin Exterminating Co.*, *supra*; *National Comm'n on Egg Nutrition v. FTC*, 570 F.2d 157 (7th Cir. 1977), *cert. denied*, 439 U.S. 821 (1978) (prohibiting advertisements misrepresenting existence of scientific evidence that eating eggs increases risk of heart disease); *Warner-Lambert Co. v. FTC*, 562 F.2d 749 (D.C. Cir. 1977) (enjoining petitioner's representations that its mouthwash cured cold symptoms); *Montgomery Ward & Co. v. FTC*, 379 F.2d 666 (7th Cir. 1967) (enjoining representations as to an "unconditional" guarantee where the actual written guarantee was limited notwithstanding the company's policy of honoring its guarantee as advertised); *Goodman v. FTC*, 244 F.2d 584 (9th Cir. 1957) (holding that "Weaver's Guild" falsely implied an association for men for mutual aid and protection); *Adolph Kastor & Bros., Inc. v. FTC*, 138 F.2d 824 (2d Cir. 1943) (Judge Learned Hand ruling that "Scout" on a boy's knife implied endorsement by the Boy Scouts of America). What guarantees besides those concerning product characteristics might be deceptive? *See All-State Indus., Inc. v. FTC*, 423 F.2d 423 (4th Cir. 1970), *cert. denied*, 400 U.S. 828 (1970) (manufacturing output 100 percent guaranteed); *cf. Goodman v. FTC*, 244 F.2d 584 (9th Cir. 1957) (full refund if purchaser not able to complete course).

In *FTC v. Garvey*, 383 F.3d 891, 900 (9th Cir. 2004), defendant Garvey, a retired first baseman for the Los Angeles Dodgers, was hired to star in infomercials promoting Enforma Co.'s dietary supplements. Several weeks before the infomercials were filmed, Enforma sent Garvey and his wife a supply of the supplements. Both of the Garveys lost weight. After the infomercials aired, the FTC filed a complaint against Garvey, alleging he violated Sections 5(a) and 12 of the FTCA. Eventually, the Ninth Circuit affirmed judgment in Garvey's favor. The court noted that "an individual may be subject to injunctive relief if the FTC can prove that an individual 'participated directly' in the acts in question or 'had authority to control them,' " quoting a previous decision. In order to hold a party liable for restitution, "the FTC must also show that the individual had actual knowledge of the material representations, was recklessly indifferent to the truth or falsity of a misrepresentation, or had an awareness of a high probability of fraud along with an intentional avoidance of the truth."

The court noted the ways in which Garvey made himself familiar with the product before filming the infomercials, including using the product, reviewing booklets sent by Enforma, meeting people who had used the supplements with favorable results and reading a study on the supplements' active ingredient in the American Journal of Clinical Nutrition. Based on this evidence, the court concluded that the FTC had "failed to show that Garvey was recklessly indifferent to the truth of his statements or was aware that fraud was highly probable and intentionally avoided the truth." *Garvey*, 383 F.3d at 902. "[T]he substantiation he had was sufficient—at least for someone in Garvey's position—to avoid participant liability." *Id.* The court noted that "there is no settled standard for the level of inquiry to which a commercial spokesperson is held when he or she is hired to participate in a television advertisement." *Id.*

(c) False disparagement and comparison. *Compare Carter Products, Inc. v. FTC*, 323 F.2d 523 (5th Cir. 1963), in which the court held that television use of simulated shaving lather did not provide a valid comparison of the qualities of "Rise" shaving cream and tended to disparage competing lathers, *with FTC v. Sterling Drug, Inc.*, 317 F.2d 669 (2d Cir. 1963), in which an advertisement summarizing the results of a scientific investigation of five leading analgesic products was held *not* to be false or misleading.

(d) Deceptive pricing, sales, and credit practices. *See FTC v. Standard Education Society*, 302 U.S. 112 (1937), in which fictitious testimonials and representations that the encyclopedia was free and the customer only paid for a loose-leaf service were held deceptive; *Charnita v. FTC*, 479 F.2d 684 (3ᵈ Cir. 1973) in which a "judgment note" enabling the holder to enter judgment in state court without notice was held to be a "security interest" within scope of the Truth In Lending Act so that purchasers had to be notified of their right to rescind.

(e) Deceptive promises and omissions regarding the nature, risk and anticipated performance of an investment. *See FTC v. Atlantex Assoc.*, 1989-1 Trade Cas. (CCH) ¶ 68,585 (11ᵗʰ Cir. 1989) (defendant misrepresented oil and gas ventures); *FTC v. Kaplan*, 55 Antitrust & Trade Reg. Rep. (BNA) 938 (December 1, 1988) (defendant misrepresented earning capacity of prospective distributors of burglar alarms); *Southwest Sunsites, Inc. v. FTC*, 785 F.2d 1431 (9ᵗʰ Cir. 1986) (petitioners misrepresented financial risk and nature of investment in parcels of land).

(f) Misrepresentation by omission of material information. *See Theodore Kagen Corp. v. FTC*, 283 F.2d 371 (D.C. Cir. 1960) (per curiam), *cert. denied*, 365 U.S. 843 (1961) (base metal simulating gold); *FTC v. World Travel Vacation Brokers, Inc.*, 861 F.2d 1020, 1023 (7ᵗʰ Cir. 1988) (advertisement for $29 airfare certificates failed to disclose that full costs were added to "hotel cost" determination); *Libbey-Owens-Ford Glass Co. v. FTC*, 352 F.2d 415 (6ᵗʰ Cir. 1965) (per curiam) (television advertisement for automotive window glass failed to disclose use of automobile with windows rolled down); *Royal Oil Corp. v. FTC*, 262 F.2d 741 (4ᵗʰ Cir. 1959) (nondisclosure that oil is reprocessed); *Royal Baking Powder Co. v. FTC*, 281 F. 744 (2ᵈ Cir. 1922) (nondisclosure of change of ingredients).

An exhaustive list of unfair and deceptive trade practices is contained in the C.C.H. Trade Regulation Reporter, which includes the FTC's Industry Guides and Trade Regulation Rules. For a generally comprehensive approach to the problem of categorizing these offenses, *see* KANWIT, FEDERAL TRADE COMMISSION (2007); VON KALINOWSKI, BUSINESS ORGANIZATIONS — ANTITRUST LAWS AND TRADE REGULATIONS (2d ed. 2007).

f) Nutrition Claims

The FTC has recognized the importance of the Nutrition Labelling and Education Act of 1990 (see § 10.02, *infra*) and, in May 1994, formally committed to following the Food and Drug Administration in evaluating nutrition-related claims made in advertising:

> The Commission recognizes the importance of consistent treatment of nutrient content and health claims in food advertising and labeling and seeks to harmonize its advertising enforcement program with FDA's food labeling regulations to the fullest extent possible under the statutory authority of the FTC Act. *FTC Enforcement Policy Statement on Food Advertising*, 59 Fed. Reg. 28388.

The FTC's Enforcement Policy Statement specifically requires that:

> When the context of an ad as a whole conveys to consumers the net impression that the food makes only positive contributions to a diet, or does not contain any nutrients at levels that raise the risk of diet-related disease, the failure to disclose the presence of risk- increasing nutrients is likely to be deceptive. *Id.*

Similarly, the FTC places great emphasis on the need to disclose information about other nutrients in the product where the absence of such information would render the ad deceptive:

. . . disclosure of material information that is necessary to prevent deception may be required under section 5 of the FTC Act. For example, it is misleading to fail to disclose qualifying information necessary to prevent an affirmative statement from creating a misleading impression.

In the context of advertising that makes affirmative nutrient content claims, the Commission's analysis of deception by omission will be based on a consideration of whether a nutrient content claim gives rise to a misleading impression about the absent disclosure of other nutrient information. 59 Fed. Reg. 28392.

g) The Internet and E-Commerce

The development of the Internet and e-commerce has provided a new vehicle for deceptive business practices. The FTC has actively enforced the FTC Act and other statutes against entities using high technology to facilitate illegal schemes, including via the Internet. *The Federal Trade Commission on "Internet Fraud" Before the Subcomm. on Investigations of the U.S. Senate Governmental Affairs Committee* (1998) (statement of Robert Pitofsky, Chairman of the Federal Trade Commission) *reprinted at* <http://ftc.gov/os/9802/internet.test.htm> [hereinafter *"Internet Fraud"*]. The FTC also has created its own extensive Internet website at <www.ftc.gov> to provide information to help businesses and consumers better understand their rights and responsibilities.

Much of the Internet fraud has followed traditional patterns, such as phony business prospects or pyramid schemes that use the global capabilities of the Internet to recruit unsuspecting victims. *See, e.g., FTC v. Fortuna Alliance,* Civ. No. C96-799M (W.D. Wash. 1996) (an Internet pyramid scheme operated out of Washington State with victims all over the world); *FTC v. Nia Cano,* No. 97–7947 IH (AJWx) (C.D. Cal., filed Oct. 29, 1997) (a fraudulent credit scheme involving false promises of high-limit credit with low interest rates). *See also* (cited in *Internet Fraud,* above): *Zygon International, Inc.,* 1996 FTC LEXIS 420 (1996) (consent order as to alleged misrepresentations about product characteristics); and three cases involving the failure of on-line service providers to disclose automatic charges: *American Online, Inc.,* 1996 FTC LEXIS 746 (1996) (consent order subject to final approval); *CompuServ, Inc.,* 1997 FTC LEXIS 110 (1997) (consent order subject to final approval); and *Prodigy Service Corp.,* 1997 FTC LEXIS 109 (1997) (consent order subject to final approval).

Some schemes, however, are unique to the Internet. In *FTC v. Audiotex Connection, Inc.,* No. CV-97 0726 (E.D.N.Y. 1997), defendant's on-line advertisements invited consumers to download software to view an "adult entertainment" website. Accessing the website automatically disconnected the computer from a local Internet service provider and switched the connection to a phone number in the Russian Republic of Moldova. The consumer's modem connection consequently was interrupted and immediately reconnected to the high-priced international line, without the consumer's knowledge or permission. Defendant failed to adequately disclose that consumers would be billed for an international long distance call or that they would need to turn off their computers to end the call. The FTC, with the help of the United States Secret Service, successfully stopped this "Trojan Horse" software scheme, obtaining a temporary restraining order and a stipulated permanent injunction. As a result, over 38,000 consumers received restitution worth an estimated $2.74 million. In *FTC v. Zuccarini,* 2002 U.S. Dist. LEXIS (E.D. Pa. 2002), the defendant engaged in on-line "mousetrapping" by redirecting consumers from their intended destinations on the Web to a series of web pages that displayed advertising and obstructing any exit from those web pages. Defendant's activities were enjoined and nearly $2 million in damages awarded to be deposited into a fund for consumer redress and related remedies.

In *FTC v. Seismic Entm't Prods.,* 2004 U.S. Dist. LEXIS 22788 (D.N.H. 2004), Seismic Entertainment Products ("Seismic") surreptitiously installed software code ("spyware") on consumers' computers that gave Seismic access to the computers to display pop-up advertisements. Seismic then would use the ads to market its anti-spyware software and other products. The software Seismic installed caused many consumers' computers to slow down and crash.

The court granted the FTC a temporary restraining order. Seismic argued that its practice was well-accepted in the Internet community, but the court decided "the argument that 'everyone is doing it' is not persuasive." Acknowledging that Seismic's activities "do not necessarily fit easily into the traditional concepts of unfair and deceptive acts and practices under the FTCA," the court nevertheless concluded that since "affected users were not notified of the defendants' activities and did not know what had caused the problems with their computers," Seismic's practices were "both deceptive and unfair." *See also* the subsequent decision at 441 F. Supp.2d 349 (D.N.H. 2006) (considering individual and corporate liability).

In 2002 the FTC reported that identity theft was far and away the most common consumer fraud complaint it received (42 percent), followed by complaints about Internet auctions (10 percent) and about Internet services and computers (7 percent). 82 *Antitrust Trade Reg. Rep.* (BNA) 66 (January 25, 2002). That year the FTC also announced a crackdown on deceptive "spam" being emailed to consumers. 82 *Antitrust Trade Reg. Rep.* (BNA) 133 (February 15, 2002). This eventually led to the CAN SPAM Act discussed below.

3. Privacy

a) Children's Privacy

The collection of personal information through online websites, especially websites geared toward children, has raised privacy concerns. The FTC issued an opinion letter outlining principles that apply in such situations when children are involved. *See* Robert Pitofsky, Chairman, Federal Trade Commission, *Cyberbanking and Electronic Commerce Conference*, Washington, D.C. (1998), *reprinted at www.ftc.gov/speeches/*. First, the FTC determined that "it would be a deceptive practice under Section 5 of the FTC Act to represent that a website was collecting personally identifiable information for one purpose — such as playing a game — when, in fact, the information was used for another purpose — such as marketing." Second, the FTC declared that under Section 5, "it is likely illegal to collect personal information from children — such as name, e-mail or home address, and telephone number — and to sell or disclose such information to third parties, without providing notice to parents and an opportunity to control the use and collection of the information." *Id.* An FTC investigation revealed that eighty-six percent of 126 randomly visited child-oriented sites collected personal information from children, and that most of the website owners failed to seek prior parental permission or to allow parents to control the collection and use of the information. *Id.*

In 2000, the Children's Online Privacy Protection Act ("COPPA") went into effect. 15 U.S.C. § 6501 *et seq.* It regulates the online collection and use of personal information about children under the age of 13 (*e.g.*, name, address, phone number). The operator of a website targeted to children must post notice about what information the operator collects from children, and how the information is used and disclosed, and must obtain parental consent for the collection, use and disclosure of that information. 15 U.S.C. § 6502(b)(1)(a)(i) and (ii). The operator must maintain reasonable procedures to keep the information confidential and secure, and a parent may refuse to permit the operator's further use, collection or storage of a child's personal information at any time. 15 U.S.C. § 6502(b)1(1)(B) and (b) (1)(D). The child's participation in a game, prize offer or other activity cannot be conditioned on the child's disclosure of more personal information than is necessary to participate. 15 U.S.C. § 6502(b)(1)(C). Some exceptions exist to these obligations, including when the information is used only one time to respond to a child's specific request, and is not stored or used to re contact the child.

The implementing regulations are codified at 16 C.F.R. § 312.

b) Telemarketing

In *Nat'l Fed'n of the Blind v. FTC*, 420 F.3d 331 (4th Cir. 2005), the Fourth Circuit held that the FTC's "Telemarketing Sales Rule" ("TSR"), 16 C.F.R. 310 *et seq.*, was constitutional. *See also* 15 U.S.C. §§ 601 *et seq.* (the Telemarketing Act). The TSR implemented rules limiting the times telemarketers could call, instituted a "do not call" list, required telefunders to provide caller identification information and required telefunders who were soliciting for a particular charity to disclose their role. The court noted that the TSR was a "proper compromise between the important speech interests of charities and the equally important need to protect the public from excessive intrusions into the home." 420 F.3d at 351. "Our Constitution does not prevent the democratic process from affording the American family some small respite and sense of surcease." *Id* at 343.

In addition to the national do-not-call list discussed in the *Manstream Marketing Services* case excerpted above, such lists exist under state law. In *National Coalition of Prayer, Inc. v. Carter*, 455 F.3d 783 (7th Cir. 2006), for example, the court upheld an Indiana statewide do-not-call list that required a solicitor on behalf of a charitable organization to either be a volunteer or an employee of the charitable organization –not a telemarketer. The "state's interest in protecting residents' right not to endure unwanted speech in their own homes outweighs any First Amendment interests the Plaintiff's possess."

c) Spam

The CAN SPAM Act (Controlling the Assault of Non-Solicited Pornography and Marketing Act), also discussed above in the section on Constitutionality, went into effect in 2004. *See* 15 U.S.C. § 7701 *et seq.* The Act was Congress' response to the proliferation of junk email ("spam") over the Internet. The Act establishes requirements for those who send commercial email, imposes penalties for spammers and companies whose products are advertised in spam if they violate the law, and gives consumers the right to ask emailers to stop sending them promotional commercial email.

The Act applies to two different types of emails: (1) commercial electronic mail messages, and (2) transactional and relationship messages. "Commercial electronic mail messages" or "CEMM" are any emails the "primary purpose of which is commercial advertisement or promotion of a commercial product or service." "Transactional and relationship messages" are any emails the "primary purpose of which is to facilitate an agreed-upon transaction or update a customer in an existing business relationship." The Act places many more restrictions on senders of CEMM than it does on "transactional and relationship messages.

With respect to both CEMM and "transactional and relationship messages," the Act prohibits the sender from using false or misleading header information in the email. For example, the sender would violate the Act if, in an attempt to increase the likelihood that its email would be read, it used the subject header "YOU ARE THE WINNER OF OUR SWEEPSTAKES", when, in fact, the recipient had not won any sweepstakes offered by the sender. "Sender" is defined broadly by the CAN SPAM Act.

These restrictions apply also to persons who originate, transmit (excluding routine transmissions such as ISPs), or "procure[] the origination or transmission of [CEMM.]" For purposes of CAN SPAM's prohibitions, procuring is defined to include intentionally paying, providing other consideration to, or inducing another to send such a message. Thus, there may be multiple senders for any single email.

With respect to CEMM only, the Act:

(a) Prohibits the use of deceptive or misleading subject headings, if the sender knows, or should know, that the subject heading would be likely to mislead the recipient about a material fact regarding the contents or subject matter of the message;

(b) Requires the use of a functional return email address or other Internet-based mechanism that clearly and conspicuously allows the recipient to submit a request not to receive future CEMMs from that sender and remains capable of receiving and processing such requests for at least thirty (30) days after transmitting the original message;

(c) Allows the sender to comply with the above-described requirement for a return email address or Internet-based receipt mechanism by providing a list from which the recipient may choose the specific types of messages the recipient wants to receive (opt-in) or does not want to receive (opt-out), as long as the list includes an option whereby the recipient may opt-out of receiving any CEMMs from the sender;

(d) Provides that, once the recipient sends a request indicating that it does not want to receive some or any CEMMs, the sender must, within ten (10) business days after receipt of such request, stop sending the recipient any CEMMs that fall within the scope of the request; and

(e) Requires that the sender must clearly identify the message as an advertisement or solicitation, and a valid physical postal address for the sender, unless the recipient has affirmatively consented to receiving such messages.

CAN SPAM also requires the subject line on commercial email containing "sexually oriented material" to begin with the words SEXUALLY EXPLICIT (in all capitals), and the first-viewed email screen to repeat the warning in a clear and conspicuous manner, unless the recipient has affirmatively opted in to receive such material. For purposes of CAN SPAM, sexually oriented emails include electronic messages that contain links to sexually explicit web sites.

Violators may be subject to criminal or civil penalties. Criminal violations may result in both fines and jail terms, subject to increase for aggravating factors including address harvesting, generating email addresses using automated means, identity theft or fraud. There is no private right of action for CAN SPAM violations, and the Act expressly preempts all state and local law "that expressly regulates the use of electronic mail to send commercial messages, except to the extent that any such statute, regulation or rule prohibits falsity or deception in any portion of a commercial electronic mail message or information attached thereto." FTC and state Attorneys General can obtain civil penalties including statutory damages of $250 per email to a maximum of $2 Million, which amounts may be trebled for aggravating factors or willful and knowing violations. Damages may also be reduced when defendant shows it had implemented reasonable compliance measures.

The Act also charges the FTC with considering the establishment of a national "do-not-email" registry similar to the telemarketing registry and empowers the FCC to issue rules protecting consumers from unwanted wireless messages. Following its review, the FTC advised Congress against creating an email registry, opining that the better alternative is the industry developing reliable email authentication or other alternatives that better identify and stop deceptive spam. More recently, the FTC has opposed state proposals to create registries for children and others who do not wish to receive email advertising alcohol, tobacco, pornographic material or other materials not legal for sale to minors — at least until a registry can be better protected from hackers, phishers, and the like.

In *FTC v. Bryant*, 2004 U.S. Dist. LEXIS 23315 (M.D. Fla. 2004), a CAN SPAM case, the court entered a stipulated preliminary injunction prohibiting defendant from sending commercial email messages that contained materially false or misleading header information, including from or reply-to lines that were falsified, registered to an unrelated third party or obtained through false or fraudulent pretenses or representations. The defendants were also prohibited from making any express or implied representation or omission of material fact, and from stating any of the following in connection with the advertising, promotion, offering for sale or sale of goods or services: that consumers were likely to earn substantial amounts of money; that the defendants would supply consumers with envelopes, postage, mailing lists or sales leads; that defendants would pay consumers for each envelope they stuffed and mailed; or that defendants would fully refund fees where appropriate. *See also FTC v. Avatar*, 2 Trade Cas. (CCH) P74507 (N.D. Ill. 2004) (granting preliminary injunction and asset freeze against "diet patch" email spammers under CAN SPAM, and rejecting defendants' argument that the Act was unconstitutional; "requiring disclosure of information does not amount to a content-based restriction").

Tests of Unfairness

1. Introduction

Section 5 of the FTC Act prohibits "unfair" acts or practices, as well as those that are deceptive. Despite the fact that "unfairness" is a broader concept than deceptiveness, most § 5 proceedings, excluding those involving antitrust violations, have been brought on the ground that the challenged conduct is deceptive. Even when the FTC has attacked certain types of practices on the grounds of unfairness alone, it traditionally avoided applying this standard to advertising. It now appears, however, that the FTC will consider unfairness as an additional standard to regulate advertising. At least part of the impetus for this development must be attributed to the *Sperry & Hutchinson* case, 405 U.S. 233 (1972). In that case, the Supreme Court held that § 5 empowers the FTC to proscribe "unfair" acts or practices regardless of whether they violate the spirit or letter of the antitrust laws. Subsequently, the FTC relied heavily upon *Sperry & Hutchinson* in applying unfairness as a standard for regulating advertising in order to protect consumer interests. *See Orkin, below*; *FTC v. Pfizer, Inc.*, 81 F.T.C. 23 (1972).

ORKIN EXTERMINATING CO. v. FEDERAL TRADE COMMISSION
849 F.2d 1354 (11th Cir. 1988)

CLARK, CIRCUIT JUDGE

* * *

According to its officers, Orkin [a wholly owned subsidiary of Rollins, Inc.] is the largest termite and pest control company in the world. Among the services which Orkin offers to its customers is the treatment of houses, buildings and other structures for the destruction of and protection against termites and other wood infesting organisms. Orkin's agreements with its customers to provide these services are typically embodied in standard printed forms which are not subject to modification by Orkin's agents or customers.

Prior to 1966, Orkin's customers could purchase guarantees for continued protection of a treated structure by paying a specified fee. These guarantees lasted for a stated period, typically between five and fifteen years. In 1966, Orkin began to offer similar guarantees that were, by the terms of its contracts, to last the "lifetime" of a treated structure. Between January 1966, when Orkin started to offer these "lifetime" guarantees, and February 1, 1975, Orkin's contracts for termite protection and control ("pre-1975 contracts") provided that a customer could renew the coverage of its "lifetime" guarantee by paying an annual renewal fee, the amount of which was specified in the contract. The contracts state that as long as a customer continues to pay this annual fee, the guarantee remains in effect for the lifetime of the treated structure, unless the structure is structurally modified after the initial treatment date.

* * *

[A]ll of the contracts stated specifically that Orkin could adjust the annual renewal fee in the event of a structural modification to the treated premises. No other provision in the contract indicates that these fees are subject to increases.

* * *

In 1978, Orkin began to consider increasing the annual fees contained in the pre-1975 contracts. Rollins's general counsel concluded initially that there was no contractual basis for an increase. Yet convinced that Orkin could not have intended to lock the company into a perpetually fixed contract, he sought the advice of the company's law firm. A memorandum produced by the law firm considered the question whether "there [are] any grounds for the claim that a contract which may be renewed or extended from year to year, indefinitely, is unenforceable." It concluded that one unidentified Orkin contract appeared "to be of *indefinite* duration" and would therefore be "terminable by Orkin after a reasonable period of time."

* * *

In August 1980, Orkin began notifying customers who were parties to pre-1975 contracts that the company was going to increase its annual renewal fees. Increase notices were sent to approximately 207,000 pre-1975 customers.

* * *

Many of Orkin's customers complained about the increase in their annual renewal fees. In addition, various officials in seventeen states questioned the lawfulness of Orkin's actions. But customers did not have any real alternative to paying the increased renewal fees. Although some of Orkin's competitors were willing to assume Orkin's obligations of the pre- 1975 contracts, they apparently would not have done so "without imposing conditions that would have resulted in additional charges to Orkin's customers or subsequently raising the renewal fees as expressly permitted in their own contracts." 108 F.T.C. at 347 (footnote omitted).

* * *

In May 1984, the FTC issued an administrative complaint charging that Orkin had committed an unfair act or practice in violation of § 5. The complaint alleged that Orkin's pre-1975 contracts provided for a fixed annual renewal fee and that Orkin had violated the terms of these contracts by unilaterally raising the fees specified therein.

After conducting some pretrial discovery, counsel for the FTC supporting the complaint . . . moved for a summary decision.

* * *

Orkin filed a cross-motion for summary decision on the ground that conduct which is not alleged to be deceptive cannot constitute an "unfair act or practice" within the meaning of section 5. The Administrative Law Judge responsible for the case ruled in favor of the Commission. The ALJ found specifically that (1) Orkin's pre-1975 contracts did provide for a fixed renewal fee and that Orkin had breached these contracts by attempting to raise the renewal fees; (2) these breaches of contract could constitute a violation of § 5; (3) there was substantial consumer injury; (4) consumers could not reasonably have avoided this injury; and (5) there were no countervailing benefits to consumers or competition. The ALJ entered an order requiring Orkin to roll back all fees in pre-1975 contracts to the levels specified in those contracts.

Orkin appealed the ALJ's decision to the Commission. The Commission affirmed all aspects of the ALJ's decision.

* * *

Orkin contends that a "mere breach of contract," which does not involve some sort of deceptive or fraudulent behavior, is outside the ambit of § 5. In support of this proposition, Orkin cites cases that have interpreted state statutes similar to the FTCA, commonly referred to as a "little" § 5 laws, to require "something more" than a simple breach of contract before a given course of conduct can be found "unfair or deceptive." *See United Roasters, Inc. v. Colgate-Palmolive Co.*, 649 F.2d 985 (4th Cir.), *cert. denied,* 454 U.S. 1054 (1981).

*   *   *

Orkin's argument is clearly inconsistent with the ways in which the FTC's unfairness authority has developed, as a result of both legislation and judicial interpretation. *See American Financial Services v. F.T.C.*, 767 F.2d 957, 965–72 (D.C. Cir. 1985) ("A.F.S."), *cert. denied,* 475 U.S. 1011, (1986). The Supreme Court, for example, has "put its stamp of approval on the Commission's evolving use of a consumer unfairness doctrine not moored in the traditional rationales of anticompetitiveness or *deception.*" *Id.* at 971 (emphasis added) (citing *FTC v. Sperry & Hutchinson Co.*, 405 U.S. 233 (1972). Moreover, as the Commission noted, there is nothing which constrains it to follow judicial interpretations of state statutes in construing the agency's § 5 authority. *See* 108 F.T.C. at 361. Orkin's suggestion that we should rely on these cases overlooks the fact that it is the Commission itself which is charged, by statute, with the duty of prescribing "interpretative rules and general statements of policy with respect to unfair or deceptive acts or practices (within the meaning of section [5])." 15 U.S.C. § 57(a)(1).

In 1980, the Commission promulgated a policy statement containing an abstract definition of "unfairness" which focuses upon unjustified customer injury. *See A.F.S.*, 767 F.2d at 971. Under the standard enunciated in this policy statement,

> [t]o justify a finding of unfairness the injury must satisfy three tests. It must be substantial; it must not be outweighed by any countervailing benefits to consumers or competition that the practice produces; and it must be an injury that consumers themselves could not reasonably have avoided.

*   *   *

The Commission's finding of "substantial" injury is supported by the undisputed fact that Orkin's breach of its pre-1975 contracts generated, during a four-year period, more than $7,000,000 in revenues from renewal fees to which the Company was not entitled. As the Commission noted, although the actual injury to individual customers may be small on an annual basis, this does not mean that such injury is not "substantial." 108 F.T.C. at 362 (citing *In re International Harvester, Co.*, 104 F.T.C. 949, 1064 n. 55 (1984); *see also A.F.S.*, 767 F.2d at 972 (Commission's Policy Statement makes clear that injury may be sufficiently substantial if it causes small harm to a large class of people); Averitt, 70 GEO. L.J. at 246.

As for the second prong of the unfairness standard, the Commission noted that "conduct can create a mixture of both beneficial and adverse consequences." 108 F.T.C. at 364 (citing *International Harvester* 104 F.T.C. at 1061). But because "[t]he increase in the fee was not accompanied in an increase in the level of service provided or an enhancement of its quality," the Commission concluded that no consumer benefit had resulted from Orkin's conduct. 108 F.T.C. at 364. The Commission also rejected various arguments that an order requiring Orkin to roll back its fee increases "would have adverse effects on its entire customer base and on many of its competitors." 108 F.T.C. at 365.

*   *   *

With regard to the third prong of the unfairness standard, the Commission concluded that consumers could not have reasonably avoided the harm caused by Orkin's conduct. The Commission's focus on a consumer's ability to reasonably avoid injury "stems from the Commission's general reliance on free and informed consumer choice as the best regulator of the market." *A.F.S.*, 767 F.2d at 976.

* * *

As the Commission explained, "Consumers may act to avoid injury before it occurs if they have reason to anticipate the impending harm and the means to avoid it, or they may seek to mitigate the damage afterward if they are aware of potential avenues toward that end." 108 F.T.C. at 366.

The Commission determined that "neither anticipatory avoidance nor subsequent mitigation was reasonably possible for Orkin's pre-1975 customers." *Id.* at 366. Anticipatory avoidance through consumer choice was impossible because these contracts gave no indication that the company would raise the renewal fee as a result of inflation, or for any other reason.

* * *

We think it important to remember . . . that § 5 by its very terms makes deceptive and unfair practices distinct lines of inquiry which the Commission may pursue. As is suggested above, while a practice may be both deceptive and unfair, it may be unfair without being deceptive. *See A.F.S.*, 767 F.2d at 967; *cf.* Averitt, 70 GEO. L.J. at 265 (deception "is really just one specific form of unfair consumer practice"). Furthermore, the Commission has explained in its Policy Statement that it operates under the assumption that the unfairness doctrine "differs from, and supplements, the prohibition against consumer deception." H.R. Rep. 156, Pt. 1, 98th Cong., 1st Sess. 34 (1983); Trade Reg. Rep. (CCH) ¶ 50,421 at 55,946.

An adoption of Orkin's position would mean that the Commission could never proscribe widespread breaches of retail consumer contracts unless there was evidence of deception or fraud. The Supreme Court has, on more than one occasion, recognized that the standard of unfairness is "by necessity, an elusive one," which defies such a limitation. *See Indiana Federation of Dentists*, 106 S. Ct. at 2016 (citing *Sperry & Hutchinson*, 405 U.S. at 244). The statutory scheme at issue here "necessarily gives the Commission an influential role in interpreting section 5 and in applying to it facts of particular cases arising out of *unprecedented situations*." *F.T.C. v. Colgate-Palmolive Co.*, 380 U.S. 374, 385 (1965) (emphasis added).

* * *

This case may be "unprecedented" to the extent it concerns non- deceptive contract breaches. But given the extraordinary level of consumer injury which Orkin has caused and the fact that deceptiveness is often not a component of the unfairness inquiry, we think the limitation of the Commission's § 5 authority urged by Orkin would be inconsistent with the broad mandate conferred upon the Commission by Congress. Thus, because the Commission's decision fully and clearly comports with the standard set forth in its Policy Statement, we conclude that the Commission acted within its § 5 authority.

* * *

2. Notes on Tests of Unfairness

In *FTC v. Keppel*, 291 U.S. 304 (1934), the Supreme Court held that selling candy by lottery was an "unfair" practice prohibited by § 5 of the FTC Act because it was "contrary to public policy" and considered "unscrupulous" in the industry. *See also Carter Carburetor Corp. v. FTC*, 112 F.2d 722 (8th Cir. 1940); *Chamber of Commerce of Minneapolis v. FTC*, 13 F.2d 673 (8th Cir. 1926). Do the following factors, considered by the FTC in determining unfairness, and quoted with apparent approval by the Supreme Court in *Sperry & Hutchinson*, 405 U.S. 233 (1972), constitute a broader test?

(1) whether the practice, without necessarily having been considered unlawful, offends public policy as it has been established by statute, the common law, or otherwise . . .;

(2) whether it was immoral, unethical, oppressive or unscrupulous;

(3) whether it causes substantial injury to consumers (or competitors or other businessmen).

What additional factors might be considered in determining whether advertising is unfair? *See* FTC Chairman Engman's dissent in *ITT Continental Baking Co. and Ted Bates & Co.*, 83 F.T.C. 865, 90 F.T.C. 181 (1973); Hobbs, *Unfairness at the FTC — The Legacy of S&H*, 47 ABA ANTITRUST L.J. 1023 (1978); Averitt, *Meaning of "Unfair Acts or Practices" in Section 5 of the Federal Trade Commission Act*, 70 GEO. L.J. 225 (1981). In *Pfizer*, the Commission ruled a manufacturer must have a "reasonable basis" for all affirmative product claims. Will requiring advertisers to substantiate claims before making them make it easier for the FTC to enforce § 5 of the FTC Act? *See* Harrington, *Up In Smoke: The FTC's Refusal to Apply the "Unfairness Doctrine" to Camel Cigarette Advertising*, 47 FED. COM. L.J. 593 (1995); Note, *Fairness and Unfairness in Television Product Advertising*, 76 MICH. L. REV. 498 (1978).

In 1980, in a letter to the Consumer Subcommittee of the Senate Committee on Commerce, Science and Transportation, the FTC discussed how it interpreted the *Sperry & Hutchinson* test, *supra*. FTC, *Policy Statement on Unfairness*, [1969-1983 Transfer Binder] Trade Reg. Rep. (CCH) ¶ 50,421 (December 17, 1980). The Commission indicated that consumer injury is the "primary focus" of the FTC Act and the most important of the three *Sperry & Hutchinson* criteria. The "public policy" test was viewed by the Commission not as a separate consideration, but as a means of providing additional evidence on the degree of consumer injury caused by a specific practice. "Unethical or unscrupulous" conduct was viewed as largely duplicative of the first two criteria and not a basis for Commission action. The FTC policy, as set forth in *Orkin*, *supra*, was codified in 1994 in an amendment to § 5. The section now provides that an act or practice may be found "unfair" only if it "is likely to cause substantial injury to consumers which is not reasonably avoidable by consumers themselves and not outweighed by countervailing benefits to consumers or to competition." 15 U.S.C. § 45(n) (1997).

Some unfair practices fall under the Consumer Credit Protection Act, 15 U.S.C. § 1601 *et seq.* Its two major parts are known as the Truth in Lending Act, 15 U.S.C. § 1601 *et seq.* and the Fair Credit Reporting Act, 15 U.S.C. § 1681 *et seq.* The purposes of the Act are to: (1) "assure a meaningful disclosure of credit terms so that the consumer will be able to compare more readily the various credit terms available to him and avoid the uninformed use of credit"; (2) discourage the use of unrestricted garnishment as a basis for the making of predatory extensions of credit; and (3) insure that consumer credit reporting agencies exercise their responsibilities "with fairness, impartiality and a respect for the consumers' right of privacy." 15 U.S.C. §§ 1601, 1671, 1681. The Truth in Lending Act, the Fair Credit Reporting Act and their implementing regulations are largely enforced by the FTC. The Act also provides for a private right of action for damages where a creditor fails to make, or inaccurately makes, a required disclosure or where there is willful or negligent noncompliance by a credit reporting agency. *Rossman v. Fleet Bank*, 280 F.3d 384 (3d Cir. 2002) (holding that plaintiff stated a private action claim under the Truth in Lending Act where credit card company advertised "no annual fee" but reserved the right to impose an annual fee at any time). *See generally* CCH Consumer Credit Guide (4 Vols.); Rubin, *Legislative Methodology: Some Lessons from the Truth-in-Lending Act*, 80 GEO. L. J. 233 (1991); Camden, *Fair Credit Reporting Act: What You Don't Know May Hurt You*, 57 U. CINN. L. REV. 267 (1988).

Additional remedies under various other statutes are also available to the FTC but are used relatively infrequently. The Wool Products Labeling Act, 15 U.S.C. §§ 68–68(j);

and Fur Products Labeling Act, 15 U.S.C. §§ 69–69(j), for example, empower the FTC to seek condemnation orders from the courts. Under the Lanham Act, the FTC may apply to the Patent Office for cancellation of trademark registrations. 15 U.S.C. § 1064.

In 1992, the FTC promulgated extensive guidelines regarding so- called "green" marketing claims. The regulations, set forth at 16 C.F.R. § 260.6 *et seq.*, provide a uniform national standard for advertising claims regarding the environmental merits of particular products. The "green" guidelines contain general principles applicable to all environmental marketing claims, as well as specific examples of approved and disapproved usages of particular claims regarding the environmental attributes or benefits of a product, e.g., "biodegradable," "recyclable," "refillable," "ozone friendly." *Part 260–Guides for the Use of Environmental Marketing Claims*, available at www.ftc.gov.

Remedies

1. Introduction

a) Administrative Remedies

The traditional FTC remedy in false advertising cases has been a cease and desist order requiring either the cessation of the conduct or the disclosure of information necessary to prevent the conduct from being unfair or deceptive. 15 U.S.C. § 45. Within this framework, the FTC has been given wide latitude in fashioning remedial orders. *See Jacob Siegel Co. v. FTC*, 327 U.S. 608 (1946).

In order to meet the demand for greater consumer protection, however, the FTC has initiated several innovative remedial programs. A principal remedial technique is corrective advertising. One form of this remedy requires the advertiser to devote a substantial portion of its future advertising directly to rectifying past deceptions. *Novartis Corp. v. FTC*, 223 F.3d 783 (D.C. Cir. 2000) ("Although Doan's is an effective pain reliever, there is no evidence that Doan's is more effective than other pain relievers for back pain"); *ITT Continental Baking Co.*, 79 F.T.C. 248 (1971) ("PROFILE bread is not effective for weight reduction, contrary to possible interpretations of prior advertising"). A more drastic form of this remedy requires a portion of future advertising to include a confession of wrongdoing. *Wasem's Inc.*, 84 F.T.C. 209 (1974) ("This advertisement is run pursuant to an order of the Federal Trade Commission. I have . . . made various claims which are erroneous or misleading. . . ."). While not a remedy as such, the FTC has also inaugurated an advertising substantiation program requiring that advertisers, on demand, furnish the FTC with documentation substantiating advertising claims. These materials are then placed on the public record for examination.

b) Remedies in the Federal Courts

In conjunction with the issuance of a cease and desist order, the FTC may file suit in the federal courts requesting injunctive as well as monetary equitable relief. Section 19 of the FTC Act states, in part, that:

> [i]f the Commission satisfies the court that the act or practice to which [a] cease and desist order relates is one which a reasonable man would have known under the circumstances was dishonest or fraudulent, the court may . . . grant such relief as the court finds necessary to redress injury to consumers or other persons . . . resulting from the rule violation or the unfair or deceptive act or practice . . . .

15 U.S.C. §§ 57b(a)–(b). Accordingly, under § 19, the Commission may seek restitution or other redress for consumers who made purchases during a period in which the violator reasonably should have known the dishonest or fraudulent nature of the

objectionable practice. *See FTC v. Figgie Int'l, Inc., infra; Windsor Distributing Co. v. FTC*, 77 F.T.C. 204, *aff'd*, 437 F.2d 443 (3ᵈ Cir. 1971).

Additionally, Section 13(b) of the FTC Act provides, in part, that:

> [u]pon a proper showing . . . a temporary restraining order or a preliminary injunction may be granted without bond. . . . Provided further, [t]hat in proper cases the Commission may seek, and after proper proof, the court may issue, a permanent injunction.

15 U.S.C. § 53(b). When read in conjunction with the 1975 amendments to the FTC Act, courts have construed § 13(b) as enabling the FTC to seek preliminary and permanent injunctive relief, as well as "any ancillary relief necessary to effectuate the exercise of the granted powers." *FTC v. Amy Travel Service, Inc.*, 875 F.2d 564, 572 (7ᵗʰ Cir.), *cert. denied*, 493 U.S. 954 (1989) (district court had power to order monetary equitable relief, such as rescission and restitution, and to enter temporary restraining order freezing defendant's assets in a § 13(b) proceeding); *FTC v. Elders Grain, Inc.*, 868 F.2d 901 (7ᵈ Cir. 1989) (district court could order rescission in a § 13(b) proceeding); *FTC v. World Travel Vacation Brokers, Inc.*, 861 F.2d 1020 (7ᵗʰ Cir. 1988) (district court had authority under § 13(b) to grant interlocutory relief); *FTC v. Accent Mktg., Inc.*, 2002 U.S. Dist. LEXIS 12545 (S.D. Ala. 2002) (granting preliminary injunction in connection with deceptive vending machine business and freezing defendants' assets for consumer redress and to prevent further consumer injury, even though the freeze would effectively put defendants out of business); *FTC v. Para-Link, Int'l*, 2001 U.S. Dist. LEXIS 17372 (M.D. Fla. 2001) (ordering freeze on defendants' assets and appointing Receiver "on a permanent basis to wind down the affairs of the work-at-home business, marshal the records and assets of the Defendants, preserve the status quo, and address, as is appropriate, the continuing business activity of the Defendants not prohibited by the injunction").

In addition to the FTC's ability to pursue various forms of consumer redress in the federal courts, the 1973 Amendment to the FTC Act and the Magnuson-Moss Act empower the Commission to seek civil penalties of up to $10,000 per day for violations of FTC orders or trade regulation rules. 15 U.S.C. §§ 45(l), (m). In *United States v. Alpine Indus.*, 77 Fed. App'x. 803 (6ᵗʰ Cir. 2003), defendant in a prior false and deceptive advertising case had been prohibited in a consent order from making product claims about its air-cleaning devices without the support of competent and reliable scientific evidence. A jury then found that defendant had violated the consent order by making insufficiently supported advertising claims that its product removed over 60 indoor pollutants, controlled ambient ozone levels, and produced various health benefits. Based on 1490 days of violations at a $1,000 per day penalty, the FTC was awarded $1,490,000 in civil penalties. *See also FTC v. Kuykendall*, 371 F.3d 745 (10ᵗʰ Cir. 2004), which affirmed that the defendant telemarketers had violated a court order by, among other things, misrepresenting the nature of the magazine subscriptions they sold, threatening to report customers to credit bureaus, and not allowing consumers who were misled to cancel their subscriptions. The court nonetheless allowed defendants on remand to present evidence on offsets against the $39 million sanction originally awarded, e.g., based on refunds to customers or customers expressing satisfaction. The final award would be paid into a court registry, with the FTC allowed to access the funds to reimburse injured consumers, and to compensate itself for reasonable expenses incurred in locating those consumers and processing their claims.

WARNER-LAMBERT CO. v. FEDERAL TRADE COMMISSION
562 F.2d 749 (D.C. Cir. 1977)

WRIGHT, CIRCUIT JUDGE

* * *

Listerine has been on the market since 1879. Its formula has never changed. Ever since its introduction it has been represented as being beneficial in certain respects for colds, cold symptoms, and sore throats. Direct advertising to the consumer, including the cold claims as well as others, began in 1921.

Following the 1972 complaint, hearings were held before an administrative law judge (ALJ). . . . In 1974 the ALJ issued an initial decision sustaining the allegations of the complaint. Petitioner appealed this decision to the Commission. On December 9, 1975 the Commission issued its decision essentially affirming the ALJ's findings. It concluded that petitioner had made the challenged representations that Listerine will ameliorate, prevent, and cure colds and sore throats, and that these representations were false. Therefore the Commission ordered petitioner to:

> (1) cease and desist from representing that Listerine will cure colds or sore throats, prevent colds or sore throats, or that users of Listerine will have fewer colds than non-users;

> (2) cease and desist from representing that Listerine is a treatment for, or will lessen the severity of, colds or sore throats; that it will have any significant beneficial effect on the symptoms of sore throats or any beneficial effect on symptoms of colds; or that the ability of Listerine to kill germs is of medical significance in the treatment of colds or sore throats or their symptoms;

> (3) cease and desist from disseminating any advertisement for Listerine unless it is clearly and conspicuously disclosed in each such advertisement, in the exact language below, that: "Contrary to prior advertising, Listerine will not help prevent colds or sore throats or lessen their severity." This requirement extends only to the next ten million dollars of Listerine advertising.

*　　*　　*

Petitioner relies on the legislative history of the 1914 Federal Trade Commission Act and the Wheeler-Lea amendments to it in 1938 for the proposition that corrective advertising was not contemplated. In 1914 and in 1938 Congress chose not to authorize such remedies as criminal penalties, treble damages, or civil penalties, but that fact does not dispose of the question of corrective advertising.

Petitioner's reliance on the legislative history of the 1975 amendment to the Act is also misplaced. The amendments added a new Section 19 to the Act, authorizing the Commission to bring suits in federal District Courts to redress injury to consumers resulting from a deceptive practice. The section authorizes the court to grant such relief as it "finds necessary to redress injury to consumers or other persons, partnerships, and corporations resulting from the rule violation or the unfair or deceptive act or practice," including, but not limited to,

> recission or reformation of contracts, the refund of money or return of property, the payment of damages, and public notification respecting the rule violation of the unfair or deceptive act or practice.

Petitioner and *amici* contend that this congressional grant *to a court* of power to order public notification of a violation establishes that the Commission by itself does not have that power.

We note first that "public notification" is not synonymous with corrective advertising; public notification is a much broader term and may take any one of many forms. Second, the "public notification" contemplated by the amendment is directed at *past* consumers of the product ("to redress injury"), whereas the type of corrective advertising currently before us is directed at *future* consumers. Third, petitioner's construction of the section runs directly contrary to the congressional intent as expressed in a later subsection: "Nothing in this section shall be construed to affect any authority of the Commission under any other provision of law." [15 U.S.C. § 57b(e) (Supp. V 1975)].

*　　*　　*

According to petitioner, "The first reference to corrective advertising in Commission decisions occurred in 1970, nearly fifty years and untold numbers of false advertising cases after passage of the Act." In petitioner's view, the late emergence of this "newly discovered" remedy is itself evidence that it is beyond the Commission's authority. This argument fails on two counts. First the fact that an agency has not asserted a power over a period of years is not proof that the agency lacks such power. Second, and more importantly, we are not convinced that the corrective advertising remedy is really such an innovation. This label may be newly coined, but the concept is well established. It is simply that under certain circumstances an advertiser may be required to make affirmative disclosure of unfavorable facts.

One such circumstance is when an advertisement that did not contain the disclosure would be misleading. For example, the Commission has ordered the sellers of treatments for baldness to disclose that the vast majority of cases of thinning hair and baldness are attributable to heredity, age, and endocrine balance (so-called "male pattern baldness") and that their treatment would have no effect whatever on this type of baldness. It has ordered the promoters of a device for stopping bedwetting to disclose that the device would not be of value in cases caused by organic defects or diseases. And it has ordered the makers of Geritol, an iron supplement, to disclose that Geritol will relieve symptoms of tiredness only in persons who suffer from iron deficiency anemia, and that the vast majority of people who experience such symptoms do not have such a deficiency.

Each of these orders was approved on appeal over objections that it exceeded the Commission's statutory authority. The decisions reflect a recognition that, as the Supreme Court has stated:

> If the Commission is to attain the objectives Congress envisioned, it cannot be required to confine its road block to the narrow lane the transgressor has traveled; it must be allowed effectively to close all roads to the prohibited goal, so that its order may not be by- passed with impunity.

[*FTC v. Ruberoid Co.*, 343 U.S. 470, 473 (1952).]

Affirmative disclosure has also been required when an advertisement, although not misleading if taken alone, becomes misleading considered in light of past advertisements. For example, for 60 years Royal Baking Powder Company had stressed in its advertising that its product was superior because it was made with cream of tartar, not phosphate. But, faced with rising costs of cream of tartar, the time came when it changed its ingredients and became a phosphate baking powder. . . .

The Commission held, and the Second Circuit agreed, . . . that it was proper to require the company to take affirmative steps to advise the public. . . .

In another case the Waltham Watch Company of Massachusetts had become renowned for the manufacture of fine clocks since 1849. Soon after it stopped manufacturing clocks in the 1950's, it transferred its trademarks, good will and the trade name "Waltham" to a successor corporation, which began importing clocks from Europe for resale in the United States. The imported clocks were advertised as "product of Waltham Watch Company since 1850," "a famous 150-year-old company."

The Commission found that the advertisements caused consumers to believe they were buying the same fine Massachusetts clocks of which they had heard for many years. To correct this impression the Commission ordered the company to disclose in all advertisements and on the product that the clock was not made by the old Waltham company and that it was imported. The Seventh Circuit affirmed, relying on "the well-established general principle that the Commission may require affirmative disclosure for the purpose of preventing future deception."

*   *   *

Here, as in *Royal* and *Waltham*, it is the accumulated impact of *past* advertising that necessitates disclosure in *future* advertising. To allow consumers to continue to buy the product on the strength of the impression built up by prior advertising — an impression which is now known to be false — would be unfair and deceptive.

*   *   *

The Commission has adopted the following standard for the imposition of corrective advertising:

> [I]f a deceptive advertisement has played a substantial role in creating or reinforcing in the public's mind a false and material belief which lives on after the false advertising ceases, there is clear and continuing injury to competition and to the consuming public as consumers continue to make purchasing decisions based on the false belief. Since this injury cannot be averted by merely requiring respondent to cease disseminating the advertisement, we may appropriately order respondent to take affirmative action designed to terminate the otherwise continuing ill effects of the advertisement.

We think this standard is entirely reasonable. It dictates two factual inquiries: (1) did Listerine's advertisements play a substantial role in creating or reinforcing in the public's mind a false belief about the product? and (2) would this belief linger on after the false advertising ceases? It strikes us that if the answer to both questions is not yes, companies everywhere may be wasting their massive advertising budgets. Indeed, it is more than a little peculiar to hear petitioner assert that its commercials really have no effect on consumer belief.

For these reasons it might be appropriate in some cases to presume the existence of the two factual predicates for corrective advertising. But we need not decide that question, or rely on presumptions here, because the Commission adduced survey evidence to support both propositions. We find that the "Product Q" survey data and the expert testimony interpreting them constitute substantial evidence in support of the need for corrective advertising in this case.

We turn next to the specific disclosure required: "Contrary to prior advertising, Listerine will not help prevent colds or sore throats or lessen their severity." Petitioner is ordered to include this statement in every future advertisement for Listerine for a defined period. In printed advertisements it must be displayed in type size at least as large as that in which the principal portion of the text of the advertisement appears and it must be separated from the text so that it can be readily noticed. In television commercials the disclosure must be presented simultaneously in both audio and visual portions. During the audio portion of the disclosure in television and radio advertisements, no other sounds, including music, may occur.

These specifications are well calculated to assure that the disclosure will reach the public. It will necessarily attract the notice of readers, viewers, and listeners, and be plainly conveyed. Given these safeguards, we believe the preamble "Contrary to prior advertising" is not necessary. It can serve only two purposes: either to attract attention that a correction follows or to humiliate the advertiser. The Commission claims only the first purpose for it, and this we think is obviated by the other terms of the order. The second purpose, if it were intended, might be called for in an egregious case of deliberate deception, but this is not one. While we do not decide whether petitioner proffered its cold claims in good faith or bad, the record compiled could support a finding of good faith. On these facts, the confessional preamble to the disclosure is not warranted.

Finally, petitioner challenges the duration of the disclosure requirement. By its terms it continues until respondent has expended on Listerine advertising a sum equal to the average annual Listerine advertising budget for the period April 1962 to March 1972. That is approximately ten million dollars. Thus if petitioner continues to advertise normally the corrective advertising will be required for about one year. We cannot say that is an unreasonably long time in which to correct a hundred years of cold claims. But, to petitioner's distress, the requirement will not expire by mere passage of time. If petitioner cuts back its Listerine advertising, or ceases it altogether, it can only postpone the duty to disclose. The Commission concluded that correction was required and that a duration of a fixed period of time might not accomplish that task, since petitioner could evade the order by choosing not to advertise at all. The formula settled upon by the Commission is reasonably related to the violation it found.

Accordingly, the order, as modified, is

Affirmed.

FEDERAL TRADE COMMISSION v. FIGGIE INTERNATIONAL, INC.
994 F.2d 595 (9th Cir. 1993)

PER CURIAM:

* * *

Figgie manufactures and markets heat detectors for home use under the brand name "Vanguard." Unlike smoke detectors, heat detectors are mechanically operated devices requiring no electricity. . . . Until the 1970s heat alarms were considered efficacious. Thereafter fire safety experts modified their views and recommended smoke detectors over heat detectors as the preferred safety device for most locations, recognizing that there were several problems with heat detectors as a household fire alarm system. . . .

These limitations were demonstrated in a series of test fires conducted by fire-prevention experts in the mid 1970s. In almost all test fires, heat detectors sounded their alarms several minutes later than smoke detectors did. Furthermore, heat detectors usually did not sound until after "tenability limits" (levels of smoke, fumes, heat or other hazardous conditions making escape difficult) had been reached. . . .

The Vanguard heat detector first came on the market in 1959. For many years, the National Fire Prevention Association recommended both smoke and heat detectors as part of a household fire warning system. However, following the tests just described, the NFPA changed its standards. The standard adopted in 1978 required at a minimum that smoke detectors be installed on each level of the home and outside each sleeping area. ALJ ¶ 172. . . .

Figgie knew of the results of the Indiana Dunes and Cal Chiefs tests and knew of the changes in the NFPA standards. However, its representations to consumers during the 1980's did not reflect them. The crux of Figgie's message was that heat detectors could be relied on as life-saving fire warning devices, and that the best protection for one's home is a combination of four or five heat detectors to one smoke detector. . . .

Figgie sold its products to the public through at-home sales visits by distributors. This sales technique "heightened the impact of the materials because the captive consumer's attention is focussed for the duration of the sales presentation." ALJ ¶ 84. In addition to the slide-tape shows, a sales presentation would often include a demonstration using a cardboard house with a tissue paper roof. The salesperson would place a lit candle inside the house while holding a heat detector directly over the tissue. The heat detector would alarm before the paper scorched. ALJ ¶ 62. This dramatic and seemingly informative demonstration was in fact misleading. The cardboard house channelled hot air from the candle directly to the fuse, a situation that would be "completely fortuitous" under actual fire conditions. Also, given that the ignition temperature of paper is 450, the demonstration proved only that a heat detector held inches above a flame will activate sometime before the fuse reaches 450. ALJ ¶ 183. Other forms of sales pressure could also be exerted in the home. Customers who bought less than the recommended number of the more expensive heat detectors were asked to sign a release acknowledging that only "partial fire detection protection" had been purchased. ALJ ¶ 65. Figgie's promotional techniques were very successful: its customers bought four or five heat detectors for every smoke detector. ALJ ¶ 18.

The ALJ concluded that Figgie's representations were misleading and deceptive in the absence of an explanation of the limits of heat detectors and the comparative superiority of smoke detectors. ALJ ¶ 187–88. The ALJ issued an order requiring that Figgie make appropriate disclosures to its customers and avoid all misrepresentations. Specifically, all promotional materials for heat detectors were required to carry the following notice: "CAUTION: In most residential fires dangerous levels of smoke, heat and carbon monoxide gas will build up before the heat detector alarm goes off."

On appeal, the Commission upheld most of the ALJ's findings and conclusions. . . .

* * *

The Commission's cease and desist order was upheld on appeal. *Figgie Int'l, Inc. v. FTC*, 817 F.2d 102 (4th Cir. 1987). . . . FTC then brought the current suit for consumer redress under § 19 for the period between May 18, 1980 and July 20, 1987. . . . On February 9, 1990, the district court concluded that:

> A reasonable man under the circumstances would have known that Figgie's representations that a) Vanguard heat detectors provide the necessary warning to allow safe escape in most residential fires, and b) a combined system of heat detectors and smoke detectors provides significantly greater warning than smoke detectors alone because heat detectors give earlier warning of hot, flaming fires were dishonest or fraudulent.

Summary judgment was therefore granted to FTC on the issue of liability.

On January 14, 1991, the district court granted summary judgment on the amount of redress. The court found that Figgie received $7.59 million in gross revenues from sale of Vanguard heat detectors between the relevant dates, and that consumers paid $49.95 million for them (293,824 units @ $170). The court further concluded that "The Vanguard heat detector's value, given the misrepresentations recommended by Figgie and made by distributors to consumers, is de minimis." Therefore, the court ordered that Figgie pay $7.59 million into a fund which would refund the full purchase price of Vanguard heat detectors to customers. If aggrieved customers claim less than that amount, the balance is to be used for "indirect redress" in the form of corrective advertising or donations to non-profit fire safety organizations. If customers claim more, Figgie is to continue to add to the fund as necessary, to a maximum of $49.95 million.

Figgie timely appeals both summary judgment orders.

* * *

The Federal Trade Commission has two powers relevant to this case, to deal with deceptive trade practices. If satisfied that a firm has been or is using a deceptive practice affecting commerce, the FTC may, after satisfying procedural requirements, order it to cease and desist from the violation. 15 U.S.C. § 45(b). In addition, under 15 U.S.C. § 57b(a)(2),

> If any person, partnership, or corporation engages in any unfair or deceptive act or practice (within the meaning of section 45(a)(1) of this title) with respect to which the Commission has issued a final cease and desist order which is applicable to such person, partnership, or corporation, then *the Commission may commence a civil action against such person, partnership, or corporation in a United States district court or in any court of competent jurisdiction of a State*. If the Commission satisfies the court that the act or practice to which the cease and desist order relates is one which a reasonable man would have known under the circumstances was dishonest or fraudulent, the court may grant relief under subsection (b) of this section.

15 U.S.C. § 57b(a)(2).

The case before us involves only the redress remedy, not the cease and desist remedy.

The latter affects only future conduct. The redress remedy relates to past conduct and requires proof of the extra element that a reasonable person would have known under the circumstances that the practice was dishonest or fraudulent. In this case liability for past conduct would be imposed on Figgie if a reasonable person would have known in the circumstances that it was dishonest or fraudulent for Figgie to use the practices it did to sell heat detectors.

Figgie would have us construe "reasonable person would have known" to require actual knowledge. Although Figgie's argument finds some support in *FTC v. AMREP Corp.*, 705 F. Supp. 119, 127 (S.D.N.Y. 1988), that court's construction does not fit the words and grammar of the statute. Congress unambiguously referred the district court to the state of mind of a hypothetical reasonable person, not the knowledge of the defendant. The standard is objective, not subjective. That Figgie's Vice President-Marketing was innocent of any dishonest intentions, as his declarations establish for purposes of summary judgment, may be probative as to whether a reasonable person would also have been innocent of such intentions, but the issue of law is what a reasonable person would have known, not what Figgie's executive knew. The statute is unambiguous.

C. Dishonest or Fraudulent Practices

Figgie correctly argues that the Commission's findings describing an "unfair or deceptive" trade practice under § 5 do not necessarily describe a "dishonest or fraudulent" one under § 19. Section 19 liability must not be a rubber stamp of § 5 liability. Figgie appears to argue, however, that the Commission's findings alone can never be the basis of § 19 liability. We disagree. When the findings of the Commission in respect to the defendant's practices are such that a reasonable person would know that the defendant's practices were dishonest or fraudulent, the district need not engage in further fact finding other than to make the ultimate determination that a reasonable person would know. This is such a case.

Figgie sold its product to the public on the basis of misrepresentations as to its effectiveness as a fire safety device. Specifically, Figgie misled customers about "the single most useful piece of information" they could have used: that smoke detectors provide earlier warnings for almost all residential fires. . . . Further, it failed to warn that in most instances the warning from heat detectors would come too late to save lives. There is ample evidence in the Commission's findings to satisfy a court that a reasonable person with Figgie's access to the scientific data establishing the relative inferiority of heat detectors would have known that Figgie's vigorous misrepresentations on their behalf were dishonest and fraudulent.

*   *   *

Figgie argues that it was reasonable to act on its own interpretation of the test results until the time the Commission's cease and desist order became final. We disagree. *The Commission found that Figgie's marketing practices were deceptive in light of the test fires and the NFPA's rule changes. Once that information became available in the late 1970's, it was unreasonable for Figgie to ignore it.* If Figgie's practices were "dishonest or fraudulent," it is because of their relationship to the known facts of fire safety, not their relationship to the history of this litigation.

*   *   *

. . . It is well established with regard to § 13 of the FTC Act (which gives district courts the power to order equitable relief) that proof of individual reliance by each purchasing customer is not needed. . . . A presumption of actual reliance arises once the Commission has proved that the defendant made material misrepresentations, that they were widely disseminated, and that consumers purchased the defendant's product. . . . Because Figgie has presented no evidence to rebut the presumption of reliance, injury to consumers has been established.

* * *

The district court's order creates no windfall for Figgie's customers. Refunds are available to those buyers "who can make a valid claim for such redress." Those who paid less than the $170 figure challenged by Figgie (and discussed *infra*) will therefore obtain redress based on the lesser figure. Those consumers who decide, after advertising which corrects the deceptions by which Figgie sold them the heat detectors, that nevertheless the heat detectors serve their needs, may then make the informed choice to keep their heat detectors instead of returning them for refunds.

* * *

The district court's order provides that any unrefunded money be distributed by "donation to one or more nonprofit entities, at the discretion of the Commission, for the support of research, fellowships or consumer education in the field of fire safety." This extraordinary provision cannot be characterized as "redress." The word connotes making amends to someone who has been wronged. The nonprofit organizations, recipients of fellowships, researchers, and educators who might receive the money under this portion of the order were not wronged by Figgie's deceptive sales methods. Calling a fine "indirect redress" does not make it redress. An adjective, such as "indirect," cannot be used to exceed the statutory limitation on the remedy. Congress expressly prohibited exemplary or punitive damages under § 57b(b), so we know that its intent was not to punish deceptive trade practices, only to authorize redress to consumers and others for "injury resulting" from the trade practice. This portion of the award was outside the boundaries of the discretion given to the district court by the statute. The FTC cites cases under other statutes in which similar remedies have been upheld, but in none of these does the statute limit recovery to redress and expressly prohibit exemplary or punitive damages. The district court should modify its order to provide for refund to Figgie of any funds not expended for authorized purposes.

* * *

Accordingly, the summary judgment on liability is AFFIRMED, but the summary judgment on damage is MODIFIED and the order VACATED for modification consistent with this opinion.

Notes on Remedies

The FTC is not limited to proscribing illegal conduct in the precise form in which it existed in the past but may also restrain like or related unlawful acts. *FTC v. Mandel Bros., Inc.*, 359 U.S. 385 (1959). Its remedy, however, must bear a reasonable relationship to the adjudicated illegal conduct. *Jacob Siegel Co. v. FTC*, 327 U.S. 608 (1946). Can the FTC prohibit the false advertising of products not previously misrepresented? *Compare American Home Prod. Corp. v. FTC*, 402 F.2d 232 (6th Cir. 1968) *with Niresk Indus., Inc. v. FTC*, 278 F.2d 337 (7th Cir. 1960), *cert. denied*, 364 U.S. 883 (1960). Can the FTC even prohibit conduct in which the respondent has never engaged? *See Slough v. FTC*, 396 F.2d 870 (5th Cir. 1968), *cert. denied*, 393 U.S. 980 (1968).

What factors should be considered in determining whether an order is too broad? *See Beneficial Corp. v. FTC*, 542 F.2d 611 (3[d] Cir. 1976); *Bankers Securities Corp. v. FTC*, 297 F.2d 403 (3[d] Cir. 1961). In *FTC v. National Lead Co.*, 352 U.S. 419 (1957), the Supreme Court affirmed the prohibition of lawful practices to prevent the recurrence of unlawful ones, reasoning that violators must "expect some fencing in." Is this what the FTC did in *Colgate-Palmolive, supra*? *See also Telebrands Corp. v. FTC*, 457 F.3d 354 (4th Cir. 2006) (enforcing fencing-in order that defendant, who had falsely advertised the alleged benefits of an electronic muscle stimulation abdominal belt, could not make any health, exercise, efficacy, etc. representations about *any* product without prior "competent and reliable scientific evidence that substantiates the representation";

Kraft, *supra*, in which the FTC was held to have the discretion to issue a multi-product, "fencing-in" order extending beyond the violation involving one Kraft cheese product to advertising for all of Kraft's cheese-related products so as to prevent similar deceptive practices in the future; *Sears, Roebuck & Co. v. FTC*, 676 F.2d 385 (9th Cir. 1982) (affirming FTC's order preventing performance misrepresentations regarding any major home appliance, where Sears had previously misrepresented the performance of a dishwasher); *American Home Products Corp. v. FTC*, 695 F.2d 681 (3d Cir. 1982) (upholding FTC's order prohibiting deception extending to all of offending company's non-prescription drugs, not merely the drug for which deception had been found); *Jay Norris v. FTC*, 598 F.2d 1244 (2d Cir.), *cert. denied*, 444 U.S. 980 (1979) (upholding FTC's "all- products" order despite having found deception with regard to only six products). *Compare J.B. Williams v. FTC*, 381 F.2d 883 (6th Cir. 1967) (Commission's order forbidding petitioner from representing that iron deficiency anemia can be self-diagnosed and medicated with Geritol was overbroad as Congressional policy encourages self-help where the consumer is fully informed and the product is safe).

1. Who Is Subject to an FTC Order

Who can be made subject to an FTC order? *See Colgate- Palmolive, supra* (advertising agency); *FTC v. Amy Travel Services, Inc.*, 1989-1 Trade Cas. (CCH) ¶ 68,549 (7th Cir. 1989) (principal shareholders and officers of travel agencies who were involved in various levels of direction in regard to operation of the businesses); *FTC v. Austin Galleries of Illinois*, 1988-2 Trade Cas. (CCH) ¶ 68,341 (N.D. Ill. 1988) (corporate officers liable if they occupied positions of control, knew or should have known that company engaged in deceptive practices and failed to stop those practices); *New York Times*, Aug. 22, 1991, Section D, p. 19 (Volvo's advertising agency paid $150,000 to the FTC to settle allegations that Volvo advertisements, highlighting safety features, used cars with reinforced roofs); McLaughlin & White, *Advertising Agencies: Their Legal Liability Under the Federal Trade Commission Act*, 17 U. KAN. L. REV. 587 (1967). *But see Computer Searching Service Corp. v. Ryan*, 439 F.2d 6 (2d Cir. 1971) (subsidiary corporation); *P.F. Collier & Son Corp. v. FTC*, 427 F.2d 261 (6th Cir. 1970), *cert. denied*, 400 U.S. 926 (1970) (parent corporation); *Coro, Inc. v. FTC*, 338 F.2d 149 (1st Cir. 1964), *cert. denied*, 380 U.S. 954 (1965) (unaware chairman of the board who was also president and largest stockholder); *Benrus Watch Co. v. FTC*, 352 F.2d 313 (8th Cir. 1965), *cert. denied*, 384 U.S. 939 (1966) (disaffiliated personnel).

To establish individual, as opposed to corporate, liability for deceptive trade practices, the FTC must demonstrate that the individual defendants either participated directly in the deceptive acts or practices or had authority to control them. *FTC v. World Media Brokers*, 415 F.3d 758 (7th Cir. 2005). However, the FTC need not show subjective intent to defraud. Instead, the FTC may fulfill the knowledge requirement with evidence that the individuals had "actual knowledge of material misrepresentations, reckless indifference to the truth or falsity of such misrepresentations, or an awareness of a high probability of fraud along with an intentional avoidance of the truth."

In *World Media Brokers*, the appellate court affirmed the district court's finding that defendant's officers were individually liable for the corporation's actions. Their positions within their respective corporations meant that they had authority and control over the corporation's actions.

2. Appellate Review of FTC Orders

Appellate courts have the authority to modify or set aside FTC orders. 15 U.S.C. § 5(c). Their scope of review, however, is essentially limited to determining whether substantial evidence supports the FTC's findings of fact and whether an allowable judgment was made in its choice of remedy. *Jacob Siegel Co., supra. See also FTC v. National Lead Co.*, 352 U.S. 419 (1957); *FTC v. Ruberoid Co.*, 343 U.S. 470 (1952).

Moreover, courts will not interfere with a remedy if it has a "reasonable relation" to the proscribed conduct. *Jacob Siegel Co. v. FTC*, 327 U.S. 608 (1946). On occasion FTC orders have not been upheld because a less drastic remedy would be sufficient. *See FTC v. Royal Milling Co.*, 288 U.S. 212 (1933); *Beneficial Corp. v. FTC*, 542 F.2d 611 (3d Cir. 1976), *cert. denied*, 430 U.S. 983 (1977); *Elliot Knitwear, Inc. v. FTC*, 266 F.2d 787 (2d Cir. 1959). Does this limit the FTC's discretion to fashion orders in "reasonable relation" to the proscribed conduct? *See* Millstein, *The Federal Trade Commission on False Advertising*, 64 COLUM. L. REV. 439 (1964). Should the Court refuse to uphold an FTC order if it would have fashioned a different remedy? *See Waltham Watch Co. v. FTC*, 318 F.2d 28 (7th Cir. 1963), *cert. denied*, 375 U.S. 944 (1963); *Encyclopedia Britannica, Inc. v. FTC*, 605 F.2d 964 (7th Cir. 1979).

3. Orders Cannot Be Punitive

The FTC is empowered to stop and prevent future recurrence of unlawful practices, but not to punish past offenses. *FTC v. Figgie Int'l, Inc.*, *supra*; *Coro, Inc. v. FTC*, 338 F.2d 149 (1st Cir. 1964), *cert. denied*, 380 U.S. 954 (1965). *But see Fedders Corp. v. FTC*, 529 F.2d 1398 (2d Cir. 1976) (requiring the disclosure of information to prevent future claims from being deceptive does not exceed this remedial power); *J.B. Williams v. FTC*, 381 F.2d 884 (6th Cir. 1967) (upholding FTC's requirement that Geritol advertisements affirmatively disclose the negative fact that a majority of persons who experience symptoms of "tiredness" do not experience them because of a vitamin or iron deficiency, and that for those people, Geritol will be of no benefit). *See also American Home Products Corp. v. FTC*, 695 F.2d 681 (3d Cir. 1983); *National Commission on Egg Nutrition v. FTC*, 570 F.2d 157 (7th Cir. 1977), *cert. denied*, 439 U.S. 821 (1978). If the FTC acts with an improper purpose, the accused may be entitled to an award of its attorneys' fees. *FTC v. Freecom Connum's, Inc.*, 401 F.3d 1192, 1201 (10th Cir. 2005) (a bad faith exception will justify an attorneys' fee award where "the claim brought is entirely without color *and* [it] has been asserted wantonly, for purposes of harassment or delay, or other improper purposes"; here, that had not been shown).

Do corrective advertising orders exceed these powers and constitute punishment? *See Removatron Int'l v. FTC*, 884 F.2d 1489, 1500–1501 (1st Cir. 1989) (upholding an FTC order requiring petitioners to include in any advertisement regarding their hair removal system a prominent disclaimer stating that such removal is only temporary, and to send a copy of the order and a notice to all past purchasers of their machine); Note, *Warner Lambert Co. v. FTC: Corrective Advertising Gives Listerine A Taste of Its Own Medicine*, 73 NW. U. L. REV. 957 (1978); Note, *Corrective Advertising Orders of the Federal Trade Commission*, 85 HARV. L. REV. 477 (1971); Note, *Corrective Advertising and the FTC: No Virginia, Wonder Bread Doesn't Help Build Bodies Twelve Ways*, 70 MICH. L. REV. 374 (1970).

What is the line between orders that merely deter and those that punish? *See FTC v. Ruberoid*, 343 U.S. 470 (1952). In 1974, the Ninth Circuit Court of Appeals flatly rejected the argument that the cease and desist power of the FTC Act impliedly permitted the Commission to seek monetary consumer redress as an ancillary form of equitable relief. *Heater v. FTC*, 503 F.2d 321 (9th Cir. 1974). With the enactment of § 19 of the FTC Act, Congress effectively overruled the *Heater* decision by expressly authorizing the Commission to seek monetary relief in courts for rule violations or unfair or deceptive trade practices resulting in cease and desist orders. Pub. L. No. 93-637, Title II, § 206(a), 88 Stat. 2201, 15 U.S.C. § 57(b) (1975). Accordingly, following the 1975 amendments, the Commission has successfully pursued consumer monetary redress under § 19, as well as under § 13(b), of the FTC Act. *See, e.g., FTC v. H.N. Singer, Inc.*, 668 F.2d 1107 (9th Cir. 1982).

4. No Private Cause of Action

Courts have consistently rejected an implied private cause of action under the FTC Act. In *Holloway v. Bristol-Myers Corp.*, 485 F.2d 986 (D.C. Cir. 1973), in which consumers alleged that Bristol-Myers had deceptively advertised its pain reliever Excedrin, the court found that private plaintiffs could not sue under the Act, since neither the legislative history nor the statute indicated Congress' intention to grant such a right, and the FTC's ability to develop a cohesive body of law would be compromised, contrary to legislative design. *See also American Airlines v. Christensen*, 967 F.2d 410 (10th Cir. 1992); *but compare Guernsey v. Rich Plan of the Midwest*, 408 F. Supp. 582 (N.D. Ind. 1976) (allowing action by consumers attempting to compel defendant to comply with an FTC order because the private action did not interfere with FTC's function of defining "unfair or deceptive practices," and would permit the FTC Act to make good on its promise to consumers), *criticized in ABA Distributors, Inc. v. Adolph Coors Co.*, 496 F. Supp. 1194 (W.D. Mo. 1980).

11.02 Food, Drug and Cosmetic Act

Generally

The basic purposes of the FDC Act are to prevent the manufacture, distribution and sales of adulterated and misbranded foods, drugs, devices and cosmetics. *See generally* Hawthorne, Inside the FDA: The Business and Politics Behind the Drugs We Take and The Food We Eat (2005); Hilts, Protecting America's Health: The FDA, Business, and One Hundred Years of Regulation (2004).

A "device" means an instrument, apparatus, implement, machine, contrivance, implant, in vitro reagent, or other similar or related article, including any component, part, or accessory, which is:

(1) recognized in the official National Formulary, or the United States Pharmacopeia, or any supplement to them,

(2) intended for use in the diagnosis of disease or other conditions, or in the cure, mitigation, treatment, or prevention of disease, in man or other animals, or

(3) intended to affect the structure or any function of the body of man or other animals, and which does not achieve its primary intended purposes through chemical action within or on the body of man or other animals and which is not dependent upon being metabolized for the achievement of its primary intended purposes. 21 U.S.C. § 321(h).

Products are "adulterated" under the Act if they (1) contain specific categories of harmful or objectionable substances, (2) contain unnecessary substances, (3) lack a specified quantity or quality of specific categories of substances, (4) are packaged in containers consisting in whole or in part of harmful or dangerous substances, or (5) are prepared, packaged or stored under unsanitary or technically inadequate conditions. 21 U.S.C. §§ 342, 351, 361. Physical adulteration is the use of harmful, objectionable or, in the case of drugs, impure substances; economic adulteration of food is the omission of ingredients, the substituting of cheaper ingredients for valuable ones, or the concealing of defects. A product is "misbranded" under the Act if its labeling is "false or misleading in any particular" or violates any of the numerous specific branding requirements of the Act. 15 U.S.C. §§ 343, 352, 362.

The Secretary of Health and Human Services has primary responsibility for achieving the purposes of the FDC Act and delegates enforcement to the Food and Drug Administration (FDA). The FDA interprets and implements the Act through regulations establishing: (1) definitions and standards for foods when needed to "promote honesty and fair dealing in the interest of the consumers," 21 U.S.C. § 341; (2) lists of safe color additives for food, drugs and cosmetics, 21 U.S.C. § 379e; and (3) tolerances for certain pesticide chemicals in raw agricultural commodities and poisonous or deleterious substances in food, §§ 346, 346a. For an explanation of the administrative procedures followed by the FDA in promulgating regulations, *see* CCH, *Food Drug and Cosmetic Law Reporter* ¶ 2617. Failure to comply with these regulations may cause a product to be deemed adulterated, misbranded or both under the provisions of the Act. In addition, the FDA has a large testing and investigative staff for determining when food, drugs, devices and cosmetics are adulterated or misbranded within the meaning of the Act and these regulations.

Additional regulatory controls exercised by the FDA include: (1) requiring emergency permits for shipping food from contaminated areas, 21 U.S.C. § 344; (2) certifying certain drugs before their shipment, 21 U.S.C. §§ 356, 357; and (3) approving new drugs as being safe and effective before being marketed, 21 U.S.C. § 355. The FDA also promulgates regulations for packaging and labeling under The Fair Packaging and Labeling Act. 15 U.S.C. §§ 1451–61. *See* Merrill, *FDA and the Effects of Substantive Rules*, 35 FOOD DRUG COSM. L.J. 270 (1980); Stimson, *FDA's Standards Policy*, 35 FOOD DRUG COSM. L.J. 300 (1980).

Misbranding and Trademark Approval

The FDA has broad discretion in determining whether the general misbranding prohibition of the Act has been violated by labeling which is "false or misleading in particular." In contrast to the FTC's standards, the misbranding need not be "materially" false or misleading. 21 U.S.C. § 321(n). The term "misbranding" applies only to labels, labeling, and supplementary materials, however, with the FTC regulating almost all advertising for these products. Sachs, *Health Claims in the Marketplace: The Future of the FDA and the FTC's Regulatory Split*, 48 FOOD & DRUG L.J. 263 (1993). Labeling is defined by the Act as "all labels and other written, printed or graphic matter (1) upon any article or any of its containers or wrappers, or (2) accompanying such article." 21 U.S.C. § 321(m). "The term 'label' means a display of written, printed or graphic matter upon the immediate container of any article." 15 U.S.C. § 321(k). This definition has been construed to encompass materials which supplement a label, such as a pamphlet or directions, even though they are given to the consumer or shipped in interstate commerce separate from the product. *United States v. Urbuteit*, 335 U.S. 355 (1948); *Kordel v. United States*, 335 U.S. 345 (1948). In addition, the FDA indirectly regulates advertising by enforcing the FDC Act's requirements that directions be stated on the labeling for each use claimed for a drug. In *Alberty Food Products Co. v. United States*, 185 F.2d 321 (9th Cir. 1950), a drug was held to be misbranded because its label did not give directions for a use claimed in a newspaper advertisement.

The FDA's authority to prevent misbranding of drugs provides it with some regulatory power over the use of trademarks. The FDA can prevent use of a proposed drug trademark independently of objections from the United States Patent and Trademark Office or even if the trademark is already federally registered. *See* Bengtsson and McPaul, *FDA Can Nix Marks Pre-PTO*, The National Law Journal, Oct. 19, 1998; Gentin, *You Say Zantac, I Say Xanax: A Critique of Drug Trademark Approval and Proposals for Reform*, 55 FOOD & DRUG L.J. 255, 260 (2000).

To review drug marks, the FDA's Center for Drug Evaluation and Research ("CDER") created the Labeling and Nomenclature Committee ("LNC") in 1990, with that role expanded in 1993. *See* Boring and Doninger, *The Need For Balancing the Regulation of Pharmaceutical Trademarks Between the Food and Drug Administration and the Patent and Trademark Office*, 52 FOOD & DRUG L.J. 109, 110–11 (1997). In 1999, the primary responsibility for reviewing drug names was shifted from the LNC to the Office of Post-Marketing Drug Risk Assessment ("OPDRA"). *See* Phillips, *The Name Game: New Realities at FDA*, 2000 WL 12033585 (2000). The change was brought about, in part, due to a desire to reduce errors linked to look-alike and sound-alike drug names. *See* Starr, *When Drug Names Spell TROUBLE*, 2000 WL 9185143 (2000). There are ramifications in changing a drug name once it is on the market, so the OPDRA assessed the risk during both the pre-marketing and the post-marketing phases of product development and approval. While drug manufacturers are encouraged to submit proposed proprietary names as early as possible, manufacturers are neither rewarded for submitting names early nor penalized for submitting names late. *See* Phillips, *The Name Game: New Realities at FDA*, 2000 WL 12033585 (2000). In 2002, the responsibility for FDA trademark review was transferred from OPDRA to the FDA Division of Medication Errors and Technical Support (DMETS), part of a new Office of Drug Safety.

Like the OPDRA, the DMETS provides a comprehensive review of all proposed proprietary names. The review includes handwriting analysis studies, verbal analysis studies, and computer-aided analyses. It is important to note, however, that the DMETS does not "approve" trademarks, as its role is strictly consultative. The DMETS provides a uniform consultative safety assessment and makes recommendations, but the ultimate decision rests with the reviewing division director or the Office of the Drug Evaluation Director. *Compare* Phillips, *The Name Game: New Realities at FDA*, 2000 WL 12033585 (2000) (discussing OPDRA).

The joint roles of the PTO and the FDA in the trademark approval process for drugs has created some conflicts. For example, would allowing the FDA to disapprove a New Drug Application (NDA) after the PTO had registered the mark unlawfully subject the company submitting the NDA to duplicative and inconsistent standards? *Cf. Brown-Forman Distillers Corp. v. Mathews*, 435 F. Supp. 5 (W.D. Ky. 1976)(holding that the Bureau of Alcohol, Tobacco and Firearms (BATF) had exclusive jurisdiction to regulate the content of alcoholic beverage labeling because conflicting BATF and FDA regulations would impermissibly subject the industry to duplicative and inconsistent standards). While this issue has yet to be addressed by the courts, *see* Rumore, *The Role of Pharmacists in the Pharmaceutical Trademark Evaluation Process*, 6 J. Pharmacy & L. 83, 85 (1997), it may be that the conflict could be minimized by relying on the distinct purposes of the PTO and the FDA with respect to drug names. *Cf. In re Anthony*, 414 F.2d 1383 (C.C.P.A. 1969)(holding that the roles of the PTO and the FDA in relation to patenting of drug products were entirely different). The PTO "likelihood of confusion" analysis differs substantially from the FDA's analysis of how use of the selected name may affect the health and safety of patients. Therefore, the FDA cannot, and does not, base its safety risk assessment on the findings of the PTO regarding confusing similarity, because the PTO and the FDA reviews serve fundamentally different purposes.

Another potential conflict is created by the PTO's "first to file" policy, compared to the FDA's "first to receive approval" policy. The OPDRA will only consider products currently on the market in the United States when reviewing drug names for sound-alike and look-alike conflicts. *See* Phillips, *The Name Game: New Realities at FDA*, 2000 WL 12033585 (2000). The FDA does not consider intent-to-use ("ITU") applications with the PTO in approving drug names. Thus, if a drug manufacturer filed an ITU application at the PTO before a competitor did so for a similar name, but the competitor received FDA approval first, the competitor would be entitled to use the name and the first-filing company would appear to have lost out despite its prior filing.

The issue also has yet to be resolved by the courts. The legislative history of the Trademark Law Revision Act of 1988 (the "Revision Act") provides some support to a company that first filed a trademark application over a subsequent adopter of a similar FDA-approved mark. The Committee Report for the Revision Act noted that "the definition [of 'use in commerce'] should be interpreted with flexibility so as to encompass various genuine, but less traditional uses, such as those made in test markets, infrequent sales of large or expensive items, or *ongoing shipments of a new drug to clinical investigators by a company awaiting FDA approval*." S. Rep. O. 100-

515, 100th Cong., 2d Sess. 45 (1988) (emphasis added). Moreover, the House Judiciary Committee reported a revised version of the Senate Bill, H.R. 5372, which added a requirement that the use be *"bona fide."* On the Senate floor, Senator DeConcini commented on the House's change:

> The House amended these definitions to assure that the commercial sham of "token use" — which becomes unnecessary under the intent-to-use application system we designed — would actually be eliminated. In doing so, however, Congress' intent that the revised definition still encompass genuine, but less traditional, trademark uses must be made clear. For example, such uses as clinical shipments of a new drug awaiting FDA approval, test marketing, or infrequent sales of large or expensive or seasonal products, reflect legitimate trademark uses in the normal course of trade and are not to be excluded by the House language.

Chisum, *Trademark Acquisition, Registration and Maintenance: A Primer*, 19 AIPLA Q.J. 123, 187 n.8 (1991) (emphasis added). Assuming the clinical investigation shipment constituted valid use in commerce, the ITU applicant could use it to support a Statement of Use, which would permit the application to issue to registration. (*See* Chapter 3, *supra*.) That might provide a basis for a court to enjoin a competitor's FDA approved use of the mark.

Nutritional Labeling

Pursuant to the Nutrition Labeling and Education Act of 1990, Pub. L. No. 101-535, 104 Stat. 2353 (1990), the FDA promulgated sweeping new regulations requiring standardized nutrition labeling for almost all processed foods regulated by the FDA and authorizing appropriate health claims on the labels of such products. 21 C.F.R. § 101.1 *et seq.* The regulations, promulgated in 1993, attempt to ensure that: (1) nutrition information will be virtually universal in the marketplace; (2) information will be up-to-date with the dietary needs of Americans; (3) labels will show how each food fits into an overall healthy diet, nutrient by nutrient; and (4) credibility will be restored to the often hyperbolic marketing claims such as "light," "fat-free," "low-calorie," and "high fiber." FDA, *Taking the Guesswork Out of Good Nutrition, FDA Consumer, Special Report: Focus on Food Labeling*, May, 1993. *See also* 21 C.F.R. §§ 101.54, 101.56, covering specific requirements for nutrient content claims for "good source," "high," "more," "light," and "lite." The FDA has been particularly diligent in prohibiting the use of "heart marks" on labels. In *G.F.A. Brands, Inc. v. Canbra Foods, Ltd.*, 16 U.S.P.Q.2d 1734 (N.D. Cal. 1990), the private litigants disputed whether plaintiff's trademark "Heart Beat" for canola oil was confusingly similar to defendant's "Heartlight" mark for the same product. The court found no likelihood of confusion. However, the FDA subsequently barred the use of *both* names as well as the use of a depiction of a heart on the labels, reasoning that such representations suggested that the products had health benefits, without saying that other dietary factors were necessary to achieve a healthy heart. *See* "P&G Drops No-Cholesterol Labels," *Supermarket News*, Vol. 41, No. 20 (May 20, 1991); "December Trends," *New Product News*, (Jan. 7, 1992). *See also* 21 C.F.R. § 101.14, (referring to the use of a brand name including the term "heart," or use of a heart symbol on a label, as constituting an implied health claim subject to regulation); Michaels, *FDA Regulation of Health Claims Under the Nutrition Labeling and Education Act of 1990: A Proposal for a Less Restrictive Scientific Standard*, 44 EMORY L.J. 319 (1995); Levitt, *FDA Enforcement Under the Nutrition Labeling and Education Act*, 48 FOOD & DRUG L.J. 119 (1993).

Enforcement Guidelines

In the past, the FDC Act was interpreted by some courts as protecting even gullible purchasers from deception. *See* Forte, *The Ordinary Purchaser and the Federal Food, Drug and Cosmetic Act*, 52 VA. L. REV. 1467 (1966). The Act was similarly held to prohibit labels and labeling which merely had a tendency to mislead due to their net impression, ambiguity or contradictions. *See generally* TOULMIN, THE LAW OF FOOD, DRUGS AND COSMETICS, §§ 15, 23–26, 31 (1963). *Compare* the FTC "reasonable purchaser" standard discussed in the Tests of Deceptiveness section of this Chapter, *supra*.

The FDA's enforcement of misleading and false claims under these standards was frequently attacked for being "*ad hoc*, arbitrary, and confusing." Levitt, *FDA Enforcement Under the Nutrition Labeling and Education Act*, 48 FOOD & DRUG L.J. 119 (1993). The newer guidelines issued by the FDA are intended to eliminate these criticisms. FDA labeling enforcement is confined to the circumstances and wording expressly set forth in the promulgated regulations, with the intention of rendering moot the questions of what is false or misleading and what is the proper purchaser protection standard. One commentator has noted that compliance under the new standards "could be envisioned as a matter of holding the label next to the law and the regulations — if they match, the labeling is acceptable; if they do not, the product is misbranded." Levitt, 48 FOOD & DRUG L.J. at 119. Any deviation from the FDA's regulations will, by definition, render the product liable to a charge of misbranding under 21 U.S.C. § 343. The meaning of claims such as "light," "fat free," and "reduced" have been expressly defined by the FDA, for example, eliminating the need to demonstrate the misleading or false nature of such claims; nutrient content claims that have yet to be defined by the FDA are simply not permissible labeling claims. 21 U.S.C. § 343(r).

Exported Drugs

The FDA's role in regulating the marketing and labeling of exported drugs and medical products was substantially changed by the FDA Export Reform and Enhancement Act of 1996, Pub. L. No. 104–134, 110 Stat. 1321 (1996). 21 U.S.C. §§ 381–382 (1997). Under that Act, U.S.-based manufacturers may export an unapproved new drug or medical product without having to obtain FDA approval. The FDA in turn has been given expanded power to control post-export labeling and promotion, with new extraterritorial regulatory authority over the marketing and labeling of all exported drugs and medical products. *See* Helmanis, *The FDA Export Reform and Enhancement Act of 1996: The FDA's New Extraterritorial Authority Over Labeling and Promotional Practices*, 51 FOOD DRUG L.J. 495 (1996).

Remedies

Both civil and criminal remedies are available to prevent violations of the FDC Act, but the FDA must rely upon the Justice Department to bring court actions seeking such relief. 21 U.S.C. § 337(a). The FDA also gains compliance with the Act through its powers to publicize (1) judgments under the FDA Act, (2) its own determinations that a product is dangerous to health or grossly deceptive to consumers, and (3) the results of its investigations. 21 U.S.C. § 375. The Justice Department has discretion both as to the bringing of an action and the relief sought, but generally follows the FDA's recommendations. As discussed above, the FTC has formally committed to harmonizing its advertising enforcement program with the FDA's food labeling regulations in evaluating nutrition-related advertising claims. *FTC Enforcement Policy Statement on Food Advertising*, 59 Fed. Reg. 28388. Amendments to the Act permit individual states to bring court actions within their jurisdictions for specified violations regarding misbranded food if the food at issue is located in the state. 21 U.S.C. § 337(b).

The civil remedies available under the Act are seizure, 21 U.S.C. § 334, and injunction, 21 U.S.C. § 332. Seizure is the more commonly employed and is an *in rem* action against the misbranded or adulterated article itself initiated by the seizure of the article pursuant to an administrative writ of attachment. There are two basic statutory limitations upon seizure. First, the article must be introduced into, or shipped in, interstate commerce, or held for sale thereafter. 21 U.S.C. § 334(a)(1). The courts have interpreted this as also allowing the seizure of products purchased for transportation to another state. *National Confectioners Ass'n v. Califano*, 569 F.2d 690, 693 (D.C. Cir. 1978). Second, multiple seizures cannot be instituted for the same misbranding unless (1) a prior judgment was entered against the misbranding, or (2) it is administratively determined, without a hearing, that the article is dangerous to health or that its label is fraudulent or materially misleading to the injury or damage of the consumer. 21 U.S.C. § 334(a)(1). After seizure, the article is held by the government until final disposition of the case, including appeals. If a condemnation decree is entered at the conclusion of the case, the articles may be destroyed or sold for the benefit of the government. If the claimant wishes to obtain the article to correct the violations, a penal bond may be required which will be forfeited if the violations continue. 21 U.S.C. § 334(d)(1).

Restitution also may be ordered in particular cases. In *United States v. Lane Labs-USA, Inc.*, 427 F.3d 219 (3^d Cir. 2005), the U.S., on behalf of the FDA, had sued defendant Lane Labs for violating the FDC Act by improperly promoting products made from shark cartilage and other natural ingredients as treatments for cancer and HIV/AIDS. The district court concluded that there were unapproved and misbranded drugs, and granted a very broad injunction against any future sales of Lane Labs' products until they received FDA new drug approval. It explained that due to Lane Labs' "past pattern of behavior, in which [they] purposefully flouted the FDCA framework throughout the pendency of this lawsuit . . . an injunction of this scope is warranted." 324 F. Supp. 2d 547, 575 (D.N.J. 2004). It further ordered Lane Labs to pay restitution to purchasers of its products. The appellate court affirmed, finding the order to be within the district court's broad equitable powers, and that it furthered the consumer protection purposes of the Act.

Injunctive relief has two major advantages under the FDC Act. It may be obtained (1) prior to the introduction of an article into interstate commerce and (2) where the FDC Act is violated, but the product is not subject to seizure because it is neither misbranded nor adulterated. *See generally* 21 U.S.C. § 332. A defendant violating an injunction also may be held in criminal contempt. 21 U.S.C. § 332(b). For a comparison of these two civil remedies in FDA cases, *see* Note *Developments In The Law — Deceptive Advertising*, 80 HARV. L. REV. 1005, 1111–1112 (1967).

The criminal remedies under the FDC Act provide for fines or imprisonment with varying degrees of severity depending on the substance of the violation, and the existence of any prior violations of the Act by the offender. 21 U.S.C. § 333. Before the FDA can recommend a criminal action, however, it must afford the accused an opportunity to "present his views" on the alleged violation. 21 U.S.C. § 335. Such hearings both avoid unwarranted litigation and offer the accused an opportunity to correct the violation.

Good faith and lack of knowledge of a violation are not defenses to prosecution under the FDC Act except in specific situations. *See* 21 U.S.C. § 333(c). There are conflicting decisions respecting the effect of an acquittal in a criminal prosecution under the FDC Act on a subsequent civil action under the Act. *See* Dickerman, *Res Judicata — An Acquittal in a Criminal Case Does Not Bar Subsequent Seizure Action*, 7 FOOD DRUG COSM. L.J. 293 (1952). It is well settled, however, that a decision under either the FTC Act or the FDC Act will constitute res judicata barring a later action on the same issues under the other Act. *United States v. An Article of Drug Consisting of 4,680 Pails*, 725 F.2d 976, 984 (5th Cir. 1984).

Another remedy available is "recall," which is the removal or correction of consumer products that violate the FDC Act. Recall is a voluntary action. The FDA may request a recall by the manufacturer, but it may not order a recall. 21 C.F.R. § 7.40 *et seq.*; *see National Confectioners Ass'n v. Califano*, 569 F.2d 690, 694 (D.C. 1978); *United States v. Superpharm Corp.*, 530 F. Supp. 408, 410 (E.D.N.Y. 1981). A request by the FDA for recall is reserved for urgent situations where: (1) a product presents a risk of illness or injury or gross consumer deception; (2) a firm has not initiated a recall of the product; (3) agency action is necessary to protect the public health and welfare, 21 C.F.R. § 7.40 *et seq.*, (1984). Recall generally affords the consumer greater protection than seizure in cases where many lots of the product in question have been distributed. A seizure, however, may be initiated by the FDA when a firm refuses to comply with the FDA request for a recall or when the FDA has reason to believe a recall would be ineffective or when it discovers a violation is continuing, 21 C.F.R. § 7.40 *et seq.* (1984). *See* Weeda, *FDA Seizure and Injunction Actions: Judicial Means of Protecting the Public Health*, 35 FOOD DRUG COSM. L.J. 112 (1980); Note, *Mandatory Food and Drug Recalls: An Analysis of a Developing FDC Enforcement Tool*, 36 FOOD DRUG COSM. L.J. 669 (1981); *Recalls: Legal and Corporate Responses to FDA, CPSC, NHTSA and Product Liability Considerations — A Program*, 39 Bus. Law. 757 (1984).

1. Private Actions

Although there is no private cause of action under the FDC Act, private litigants sometimes use FDA rules and regulations to help demonstrate that a particular claim is misleading. In *Kraft General Foods v. Del Monte Corp.*, 28 U.S.P.Q.2d 1457, 1459, 1461 (S.D.N.Y. 1993), for example, the court relied upon the FDA's definition of "gelatin" as an animal by-product in enjoining as misleading Del Monte's use of "Gelatin Snacks" for a product made from seaweed. *Cf. Mylan Labs. Inc. v. Matkari*, 28 U.S.P.Q.2d 1533, 1539–40 (4th Cir. 1993), in which plaintiff's claim that by placing their drugs on the market, defendants falsely represented that their drugs had been "properly approved by the FDA" was held to constitute an improper attempt to use the Lanham Act as a vehicle by which to enforce the FDC Act; and *Sandoz Pharmaceuticals Corp. v. Richardson Vicks, Inc.*, 902 F.2d 222, 232 (3[d] Cir. 1990), in which the court stated, "the issue of whether an ingredient is properly labeled 'active' or 'inactive' under FDA standards is not properly decided as an original matter by a district court in a Lanham Act case." To similar effect are: *IQ Products Co. v. Pennzoil Products Co.*, 305 F. 3d 368 (5th Cir. 2002), in which the court affirmed the summary dismissal of plaintiff's Lanham Act false advertising claims regarding the labeling of defendants' tire inflator products, because plaintiff "essentially [improperly sought] to enforce the labeling requirements of the FHSA [Federal Hazardous Substances Act] - an action which the CPSC [Consumer Product Safety Commission], the enforcing agency, declined to do," and *Cottrell, Ltd. v. Biotrol Int'l, Inc.*, 191 F.3d 1248 (10th Cir. 1999), in which the court affirmed dismissal of the portion of plaintiff's complaint alleging that label claims for defendants' medical cleaner and disinfectant violated EPA clearance regulations by claiming effectiveness for seven days. "[R]esolution of [that count of] the plaintiff's complaint would require the court to interpret and apply regulations that are exclusively within the province of the EPA." However, it reversed the dismissal of plaintiff's two other EPA — related counts. In the first, plaintiff alleged that defendants' advertising deceptively implied that the EPA had approved their claim of effectiveness for seven days when the EPA had not; "[w]e believe courts are capable of resolving such issues". The second count alleged false label claims about efficacy that also could be determined by a court.

The Eighth Circuit distinguished *Sandoz* and *Mylan* in *Alpharma, Inc. v. Pennfield Oil Co.*, 411 F.3d 934 (8th Cir. 2005), a case involving antibiotic animal feed additives. The court concluded that, because plaintiff's claim for compensatory and punitive damages was not cognizable by the FDA, plaintiff had no duty to exhaust its FDA administrative remedies. The court further held that judicial resolution of the case was proper because the "question of whether Pennfield's [additive] has been approved as safe and effective is much different from the question of whether [the additive] should be approved as safe and effective, and it is only the latter that requires the FDA's scientific expertise." 411 F.3d at 439.

2. Related State Actions

A majority of the states have also enacted laws patterned after the FDC Act. These state statutes often provide their administering agencies with significant powers not possessed by the FDA, such as the regulation of advertising and the administrative prevention of intrastate commerce in the accused food product pending a court's determination of legality under the Act. *See generally* 4 Food Drug Cosm. L. Rep. (CCH); Rosden, The Law of Advertising, § 16.01 *et seq.* (2008).

11.03 The Fair Packaging and Labeling Act

The policy of the Fair Packaging and Labeling Act, 15 U.S.C. § 1451 *et seq.*, is set forth in the Act as follows:

> Informed consumers are essential to the fair and efficient functioning of a free market economy. Packages and their labels should enable consumers to obtain accurate information as to the quantity of the contents and should facilitate value comparisons.

15 U.S.C. § 1451. The Act seeks to achieve these goals by requiring that the following information appear on the labels of all consumer commodities: the identity and source of the product; the net quantity of the contents in specified measures and prominence and, if applicable, the net quantity of the servings represented as being contained in the product. 15 U.S.C. § 1453. Detailed regulations for these labelling requirements are set forth at 16 C.F.R. § 500.1 *et seq.* To the extent that any state or local laws provide more lenient standards for labeling as to the net quantity of contents, they are superseded. 15 U.S.C. § 1461. Expressly excluded from the Act's definition of consumer commodities are meats, pesticides, tobacco, poultry, prescription drugs, alcoholic beverages and seeds. 15 U.S.C. §§ 1459(a)(1)–(5).

In addition to these mandatory labeling requirements, the Act's administering agencies, the FTC and the Department of Health and Human Services, are empowered to issue regulations on a product-by-product basis as necessary to prevent consumer confusion and facilitate value comparison. 15 U.S.C. § 1454. The FTC administers the Act and issues regulations under it for all consumer products, except food, drugs, devices and cosmetics which are under the jurisdiction of the Department of Health and Human Services. These regulations may (1) define standards for characterizing package sizes, i.e., "giant," "family size," "jumbo"; (2) control the use of price savings claims, i.e., "cents off"; (3) require label disclosures of the common names of non-food products and their ingredients; and (4) prevent the marketing of packages less than full, i.e., slack-filling. 15 U.S.C. §§ 1454(c)(1)–(4). Foods are covered by this type of requirement under the FTC Act. These agencies also are empowered to issue regulations, exempting consumer commodities from the mandatory labeling requirements of the Act when compliance is impractical or unnecessary to protect consumers. 15 U.S.C. § 1454(b).

The Act applies only to packagers and labelers of consumer commodities distributed in interstate commerce and to distributors of such commodities in interstate commerce. 15 U.S.C. § 1452(a). It excludes retailers and wholesalers unless they are involved in the packaging or labeling of commodities distributed in interstate commerce. 15 U.S.C. § 1452(b).

Violations of the Act respecting foods, drugs, cosmetics and devices are deemed misbrandings and enforced in accordance with the FDC Act. 15 U.S.C. § 1456(a). Violations respecting other consumer commodities constitute unfair or deceptive acts or practices in commerce and are enforced under the FTC Act. 15 U.S.C. § 1456(b). In addition, the Secretary of the Treasury may refuse to admit any import not complying with the Fair Packaging and Labeling Act. 15 U.S.C. § 1456(c).

11.04   The Consumer Product Safety Act

The Consumer Product Safety Act of 1972, 15 U.S.C. § 2051 *et seq.*, constitutes a Congressional effort to fashion a comprehensive consumer protection statute. The Act resulted from the work of the National Commission on Product Safety which summarized the need for consumer protection from dangerous products as described in the Forward to *National Commission on Product Safety, Final Report* (1976):

> When it authorized the Commission, Congress recognized that modern technology poses a threat to the physical security of consumers. We find the threat to be bona fide and menacing. Moreover, we believe that, without effective governmental intervention, the abundance and variety of unreasonable hazards associated with consumer products cannot be reduced to a level befitting a just and civilized society.

> Rhetoric, educational campaigns, piecemeal legislation, and appeals to conscience serve the useful function of mitigating the fallout of injuries induced by our complex technology. But we believe, on the basis of the evidence presented to us, that a concerned government can and should provide a continuing system to assure that our great technological resources are used to protect consumers from unreasonable product risks.

> Perhaps a case can be made for the acceptability of willful personal risk-taking by an occasional well-informed consumer, but there is no justification for exposing an entire populace to risks of injury or death which are not necessary and which are not apparent to all. Such hazards must be controlled and limited not at the option of the producer but as a matter of right to the consumer. Many hazards described in this report are unnecessary and can be eliminated without substantially affecting the price to the consumer.

> Unfortunately, in the absence of external compulsion it is predictable that there will continue to be an indecent time lag between exposure to a hazard and its elimination. Other advanced nations apparently have discovered this flaw in the output of competitive free enterprise and have made safe products an ongoing governmental objective.

The purposes of the Consumer Product Safety Act are to: "(1) protect the public against unreasonable risks of injury associated with consumer products; (2) assist consumers in evaluating the comparative safety of consumer products; (3) develop uniform safety standards for consumer products and minimize conflicting State and local regulations; and (4) promote research and investigation into the causes and prevention of product-related deaths, illnesses, and injuries." 15 U.S.C. § 2051(b). The Act defines consumer products as products and parts thereof produced or distributed for personal rather than work related consumer use and certain specific products, including tobacco products, firearms, motor vehicles, boats, aircraft, food, drugs, devices and cosmetics. 15 U.S.C. § 2052(a)(1).

To implement the Act and centralize the administration of various other safety laws, Congress created a new administrative agency, the Consumer Product Safety Commission (CPSC). 15 U.S.C. § 2053. The CPSC is also responsible for enforcing the Federal Hazardous Substances Act, Poison Prevention Packaging Act, Flammable Fabrics Act and Refrigerator Safety Act and is required to follow the procedures of those statutes to the extent that the risk from a consumer product is without authority to regulate risks from consumer products which "could be eliminated or reduced to a sufficient extent" under the Occupational Safety and Health Act, The Atomic Energy Act and the Clean Air Act. 15 U.S.C. §§ 2079, 2080. The most important functions of this agency are the promulgation of product safety standards reasonably necessary to prevent or reduce unreasonable risks of injuries to consumers and the banning of products for which no feasible standards could be established to prevent such unreasonable risks. 15 U.S.C.

§ 2056. The Act provides that these standards should be stated in terms of performance requirements when feasible but that they may also include requirements (1) as to composition, contents, design, construction, finish, or packaging, (2) that a consumer product be marked with or accompanied by clear and adequate warnings or instructions, and (3) as to the form of warnings or instructions. 15 U.S.C. § 2056(a).

The Commission is also empowered to (1) require manufacturers to furnish consumer product performance and safety information, 15 U.S.C. § 2076(e), (2) inspect consumer product factories, warehouses and transportation, 15 U.S.C. § 2065, (3) prescribe testing programs, which can be conducted by third parties, for products subject to consumer standards, 15 U.S.C. § 2063(b), and (4) require the use of labeling containing information as to the manufacturer and private labeler of the product and the safety standards applicable to the product, 15 U.S.C. § 2063(c).

The major thrust of the CPS Act is to prohibit the manufacture, offering for sale, or distribution in commerce of any consumer product which does not conform to established safety standards or has been banned under the Act. 15 U.S.C. § 2068(a). These prohibitions, however, do not apply to persons without actual knowledge of the violation who (1) have a manufacturer's or private labeler's certificate of conformance with the safety rules which has been issued in accordance with the Act, or (2) relied in good faith on the manufacturer's or distributor's representation that the product was not subject to any safety rule. 15 U.S.C. § 2068(b).

The Act provides for a variety of enforcement methods, including public and private civil actions, criminal prosecutions and administrative actions. 15 U.S.C. §§ 2069–74. The remedies available to the government through civil actions are fines, injunctions and seizures; however, the Commission does not have authority to proceed administratively in assessing civil penalties. 15 U.S.C. §§ 2069, 2071(a).

Fines can be imposed only against persons who have actual knowledge of a violation of the Act or are presumed to have knowledge because a reasonable man exercising due care would have knowledge under the circumstances. 15 U.S.C. § 2069(a)(1),(d). Such persons are subject to fines of up to $5,000 for each offending product or violation with a maximum penalty of $1,250,000 for related violations. 15 U.S.C. § 2069(a)(1). The maximum penalty amounts are adjusted for inflation every five years in accordance with the Consumer Price Index published by the Department of Labor. 15 U.S.C. § 2069(a)(3). A person who is not the manufacturer, private labeler, or distributor of the product must have actual knowledge of the violation to be fined. 15 U.S.C. § 2069(a)(2). As with the FDC Act, seizures can only be made for violations involving the consumer product itself after its entry into interstate commerce. 15 U.S.C. § 2071(b). Similarly, injunctive relief is available against violations not involving a product and to prevent the introduction of an illegal product into interstate commerce. 15 U.S.C. § 2071(a). In addition, persons and corporations and their directors, officers and agents, who willfully and knowingly violate the Act after being notified of their noncompliance by the Commission, may be fined up to $50,000, imprisoned for one year or both. 15 U.S.C. § 2070.

One of the major innovations of the CPS Act is its provision for private civil actions for the enforcement of CPSC safety rules, remedial orders or injunctions. "Any interested person" may bring such an action thirty days after giving notice of the substance of the claim to the Commission, Justice Department and proposed defendant unless a government action is pending against the same alleged violation. 15 U.S.C. § 2073. If such plaintiff also seeks attorney's fees, such fees and costs will be awarded to the prevailing party. 15 U.S.C. § 2073. The Act also creates a private right of action for injuries caused by knowing violations of any rule or order issued by the Commission. 15 U.S.C. § 2072. *See Baas v. Hoye*, 766 F.2d 1190 (8th Cir. 1989), in which the parents of a deceased infant who had ingested prescription drugs succeeded in their action against pharmacists who had dispensed the drugs in a non-childproof container in violation of a consumer product safety rule. Under this provision of the CPS Act, a plaintiff may recover actual damages in addition to any remedies provided under State or common laws. *See Butcher v. Robertshaw Controls Co.*, 550 F. Supp. 692, 706 (D. Md. 1981) ("15 U.S.C. § 2072(b) preserves any additional remedies that may be available under common law or under Federal or State law"). Although § 2072 of the CPS Act clearly permits a private cause of action for injuries caused by knowing violations of rules issued by the CPSC pursuant to explicit legislative authority, there is disagreement as to whether a private right of action also exists for violations of disclosure or reporting rules. *Compare Drake v. Honeywell, Inc.*, 797 F.2d 603 (8ᵗʰ Cir. 1986) (failure to comply with product hazard reporting rules issued by CPSC does not give rise to private cause of action under the CPS Act) *and Klinger v. Yamaha Motor Corp., U.S.A.*, 738 F. Supp. 898 (E.D. Pa. 1990) (no private cause of action to enforce reporting requirements of Consumer Products Safety Act) *with Wilson v. Robertshaw Controls Co.*, 600 F. Supp. 671 (N.D. Ind. 1985) (private right of action exists for the violation of administrative disclosure provisions of the CPS Act) *and Young v. Robertshaw Controls Co.*, 560 F. Supp. 288 (N.D.N.Y. 1983) (manufacturer's failure to disclose information with respect to a product defect in accordance with CPSC reporting regulations entitled a widow to maintain a private action under the Act for injuries to her decedent).

The Commission itself has certain remedial powers to protect consumers against a substantial product hazard. 15 U.S.C. § 2064. Manufacturers, distributors and retailers of consumer products are required by the Act to notify the Commission upon discovering information which reasonably supports the conclusion that a product presents a substantial product hazard. 15 U.S.C. § 2064(b). After conducting a hearing open to interested persons and determining that a product distributed in commerce presents a substantial product hazard, the Commission may order the manufacturer, distributor or retailer of the product to (1) give a specified public notice of the defect or non-compliance, (2) mail such notice to each manufacturer, distributor or retailer of the product, or (3) mail such notice to every person whom the mailer knows received or was sold the product. 15 U.S.C. § 2064(c). In addition, the Commission may, in the public interest, order the party subject to the order to perform one of the following actions in a manner approved by the Commission: (1) to repair or conform the product to applicable safety standards, (2) to replace the product with a conforming non-defective product, or (3) to refund the purchase price less a reasonable allowance for use. 15 U.S.C. § 2064(d). Such orders may also require a party to reimburse other distributors, manufacturers or retailers of the product for their expenses in carrying out the order. 15 U.S.C. § 2064(e).

11.05 State and Municipal Regulation

State Regulation Generally

The first comprehensive legislative effort to curb unfair trade practices at the state level was the "Printer's Ink" model penal statute which made the use of advertisements containing an "untrue, deceptive or misleading statement" a misdemeanor. Although eventually adopted in some form in almost every state, this statute never proved effective, largely because penal statutes are narrowly construed and state amendments often require proof of negligence or scienter. More recent civil legislation in this area has proved effective, including the Uniform Deceptive Trade Practices Act ("UDTPA"), drafted in 1964, and the Unfair Trade Practices and Consumer Protection Law ("UTPCPL"), which was drafted in 1967 by the FTC in collaboration with state officials and has been enacted in various forms by 49 states and the District of Columbia. *See* International Trademark Association, *State Trademark and Unfair Competition Law* (2007), for summaries of state statutes modeled on these two proposed acts. These Consumer Protection Acts are often characterized as "little FTC Acts" because most of them prohibit "deceptive acts or practices," and confer upon State Attorneys General a jurisdiction analogous to that of a regional Federal Trade Commission. The definition of illegal conduct is included in most states' Consumer Protection Acts in one of the following three forms:

Alternative Form No. 1:

Unfair methods of competition and unfair or deceptive acts or practices in the conduct of any trade or commerce are hereby declared unlawful.

See Fla. Stat. ch. 501.201 *et seq.*

Alternative Form No. 2:

False, misleading or deceptive acts or practices in the conduct of any trade or commerce are hereby declared unlawful.

See N.Y. Gen. Bus. L. §§ 349 *et seq.*

Alternative Form No. 3:

The following unfair methods of competition and unfair or deceptive acts or practices in the conduct of any trade or commerce are hereby declared to be unlawful:

(1) passing off goods or services as those of another;

(2) causing likelihood of confusion or of misunderstanding as to the source, sponsorship, approval, or certification of goods or services;

(3) causing likelihood of confusion or of misunderstanding as to affiliation, connection, or association with, or certification by, another;

(4) using deceptive representations or designations of geographic origin in connection with goods or services;

(5) representing that goods or services have sponsorship, approval, characteristics, ingredients, uses, benefits, or quantities that they do not have or that a person has a sponsorship, approval, status, affiliation, or connection that the person does not have;

(6) representing that goods are original or new if they are deteriorated, altered, reconditioned, reclaimed, used, or secondhand;

(7) representing that goods or services are of a particular standard, quality, or grade, or that goods are of a particular style or model, if they are of another;

(8) disparaging the goods, services, or business of another by false or misleading representation of fact;

(9) advertising goods or services with intent not to sell them as advertised;

(10) advertising goods or services with intent not to supply reasonably expectable public demand, unless the advertisement discloses a limitation of quantity;

(11) making false or misleading statements of fact concerning the reasons for, existence of, or amounts of price reductions;

(12) engaging in any other conduct which similarly creates a likelihood of confusion or of misunderstanding; or

(13) engaging in any act or practice which is unfair or deceptive to the consumer.

See Tex. Bus. & Com. Code §§ 17.41 *et seq.*

In addition, the UTPCPL includes a number of modes of enforcement which have been adopted in various forms by many states. Under these provisions, the attorney-general is usually empowered to promulgate rules and regulations to administer and interpret the Act, and to issue precomplaint "civil investigative demands" for the examination of documents, witnesses and other matters.

Unlike the FTC Act which does not expressly provide for the voluntary compliance procedures employed by the FTC, many of these state statutes contain such provisions. Many also provide for innovative and sometimes drastic remedies in addition to the traditional forms of injunctive relief provided for in all of them. Among the types of remedies which enforcement officials may obtain are: (1) civil penalties for initial violations; (2) suspension or forfeiture of state corporate franchises or licenses to do business; and (3) appointment of receivers for distribution of a violator's assets to aggrieved parties.

The "little FTC Acts" commonly are used to stop deceptive activities akin to those attacked by the Federal Trade Commission. *See, e.g., Pelman v. McDonald's Corp.*, 396 F.3d 508 (2[d] Cir. 2005) (reversing dismissal where plaintiff stated a cause of action under New York "deceptive acts or practices" act against McDonald's alleged misrepresentations about the nutritional value of its food which allegedly led to health problems for children such as obesity and diabetes); *Luskin's, Inc. v. Consumer Protection Division*, 726 A.2d 702 (Md. 1999)("free airfare" advertisement was deceptive and violated Maryland Act where information important to consumers was omitted). In *Mother & Unborn Baby Care of North Texas, Inc. v. Texas*, 749 S.W.2d 533 (Tex. App. 1988), the defendants advertised their pro-life-oriented center in the *Yellow Pages* under "Abortion Services," when, in fact, the facility did not perform abortions but instead attempted to persuade the women who arrived at the center against having an abortion. Finding that defendants violated the Texas Deceptive Trade Practices Consumer Protection Act, Tex. Bus. & Com. Code Ann. §§ 17.41–17.50, by "purposefully attract[ing] pregnant women to their facility by disseminating information which could lead women to believe that abortions were available there," the court affirmed an order enjoining the deceptive conduct and mandating disclosure in advertising. *Id.* at 544.

In *Southwest Starving Artists Group, Inc. v. Mississippi*, 364 So. 2d 1128 (Miss. 1978), under a similar statute, advertising for the sale of paintings from Hong Kong (and other non-U.S. countries) under the name "Southwest Starving Artists Group" was held deceptive. The trial court had found that it was "entirely possible" that the advertising would lead a reasonable person to believe that the paintings were being sold by needy local artists willing to sell at low prices. The imposition of a $1,500 civil penalty and the issuance of a broad injunction against the defendants, as modified, were affirmed. *Compare B. Sanfield, Inc. v. Finlay Fine Jewelry Corp.*, 258 F.3d 578 (7th Cir. 2001), in which defendant's ongoing advertising claim of offering a 50% reduction from some higher price for its jewelry was deceptive under Illinois law and the Lanham Act, but injunctive relief was denied because plaintiff failed to show "either financial injury in the past or any likelihood of future business losses." Could it be that consumers simply are inured to this type of sales pitch for this type of product, so that it has no material effect on any appreciable number of purchasers?

In addition, many of these statutes provide for private causes of action and empower enforcement officials to obtain restitution for consumers. *See State v. Andrews*, 533 A.2d 282 (Md. Ct. Spec. App. 1987). Often the state legislature will specifically provide that FTC and federal court decisions interpreting § 5 of the FTC Act should be relied on by the state courts in determining whether an act or practice is deceptive or unfair. *See Luskin's, Inc. v. Consumer Protection Div.*, 726 A.2d 702 (Md. 1999)(lower court erred in rejecting FTC policy); *V.S.H. Realty, Inc. v. Texaco, Inc.*, 757 F.2d 411, 416 (1st Cir. 1985), and Mass. Gen. Laws. Ann. ch. 93A (Massachusetts Consumer Protection Law "provides no definition of an unfair or deceptive act or practice, and instead directs [the court's] attention to interpretations of unfair acts and practices under the Federal Trade Commission Act. . . ."); *State of Washington v. Readers Digest Ass'n*, 81 Wash. 2d 259 (1972) (looking to federal court interpretations of § 5 of the FTC Act for guidance in applying Washington's Consumer Protection Act). *Cf. City of New York v. Toby's Electronics, Inc.*, 110 Misc. 2d 848, 443 N.Y.S.2d 561 (1981) (applying New York City's Consumer Protection Laws, which required consistency with the rules, regulations and decisions of the FTC and the federal courts in interpreting § 5 of the FTC Act). *See generally* Prigen, Consumer Protection and the Law, § 6.02 (2007); Karns, *State Regulation of Deceptive Trade Practices Under "Little FTC Acts": Should Federal Standards Control?*, 94 Dick. L. Rev. 373 (1990); Leaffer & Lipson, *Consumer Actions*

Against Unfair or Deceptive Acts or Practices: The Private Uses of Federal Trade Commission Jurisprudence, 48 GEO. WASH. L. REV. 521 (1980).

The Uniform Deceptive Trade Practices Act, adopted in a number of states (*see, e.g.*, 815 Ill. Comp. Stat. 510) is a state statute which is essentially identical to the Alternative Form No. 3 of the little FTC Acts noted above. Summarized, the UDPTA affords a statutory basis for injunctive relief for: (1) passing off or likelihood of confusion as to source, sponsorship, approval or certification; (2) false or misleading advertising or other representation of fact; (3) commercial disparagement; or (4) "any other conduct which similarly creates a likelihood of confusion or of misunderstanding." Its application can be very similar to that of § 43(a), 15 U.S.C. § 1125(a), of the Lanham Act. *See, e.g., Weinberg v. Sun Co., Inc.*, 740 A.2d 1152, 1156 (Pa. Super. Ct. 1999)(in applying Pennsylvania Act, "we may look to decisions under [the Federal Trade Commission and Lanham] acts for guidance and interpretation"). In *Bonner v. Westbound Records, Inc.*, 364 N.E.2d 570 (Ill. App. Ct. 1977), for example, the defendants had substantially altered unedited unfinished taped musical performances by the plaintiffs and then released the newly edited result as being performed by the plaintiffs. Finding the public would likely be deceived as to the nature of the recording in violation of the Illinois Act, the court affirmed the grant of a preliminary injunction against defendants. *Compare Gilliam v. American Broadcasting Cos., Inc.*, and the discussion on misrepresentation in Chapter 8, *supra*.

In *Group Health Plan, Inc. v. Philip Morris USA, Inc.*, 344 F.3d 753 (8th Cir. 2003), the court concluded that the Minnesota false advertising and unfair competition statutes were intended to mirror Lanham Act requirements for monetary damages. The dismissal of several HMOs' monetary damages claims against various tobacco companies for allegedly deceptive representations was affirmed, but the claim for injunctive relief against them was remanded. While the evidence in the lower court was insufficient to establish "the extent of harm caused" for damages purposes, it was sufficient "to raise an inference" that harm had occurred for purposes of injunctive relief.

For discussions of various state consumer protection laws, *see* INTERNATIONAL TRADEMARK ASSOCIATION, STATE TRADEMARK AND UNFAIR COMPETITION LAW (2007 ed.); PRIDGEN, CONSUMER PROTECTION AND LAW (2007); Klernan, et al., *Developments in Consumer Fraud Class Action Law*, 537 PLI/PAT 237 (1998); Bender, *Oregon Consumer Protection: Outfitting Private Attorneys General for the Lean Years Ahead*, 73 OR. L. REV. 639 (1994); Dunbar; *Consumer Protection: The Practical Effectiveness of State Deceptive Trade Practices Legislation*, 59 TUL. L. REV. 427 (1984); Batt, *Litigation Under the Idaho Consumer Protection Act*, 20 IDAHO L. REV. 63 (1984); Aycock, *North Carolina Law on Antitrust and Consumer Protection: Sleeping Giant or Illusive Panacea?*, 33 S.C.L. L. REV. 479 (1982); Benedetto, *Illinois Consumer Protection Act*, 69 ILL. B.J. 350 (1981); Langer & Ormstedt, *Connecticut Unfair Trade Practices Act*, 54 CONN. B.J. 388 (1980).

1.   State Law Unfair and Deceptive Trade Practices

While the variety of unfair or deceptive trade practices to be encountered in the marketplace is limited only by the imagination of the unscrupulous, some forms of deception have demonstrated an enduring and unfortunate popularity.

Automobile, heating, air conditioning and appliance repairs, home renovation, door-to-door sales, training schools, real estate and mobile home sales, employment agencies and lending services are some of the areas in which consumers frequently claim to be victimized. *See Grabinski v. Blue Springs Ford Sales, Inc.*, 203 F.3d 1024 (8th Cir. 2000) (affirming award of more than $200,000 in compensatory and punitive damages under the Missouri Merchandising Practices Act and remanding for award of attorneys' fees where defendants' represented that the used car sold to plaintiff was a one-owner car in excellent condition and never wrecked, when in fact it had been damaged in a collision and had other hidden defects); *Wallace v. Partore*, 742 A.2d 1090 (Pa. Super. Ct.

1999)(condition of apartment); *Hall v. Walter*, 969 P.2d 224 (Colo. 1998)(real estate); *Maryland v. Cottman Transmission Systems, Inc.*, 587 A.2d 1190 (Md. Ct. Spec. App.), *cert. denied*, 596 A.2d 627 (Md. 1991) (auto repair); *Meshinsky v. Nichols Yacht Sales, Inc.*, 541 A.2d 1063 (N.J. 1988) (boat repair); *Gabriel v. O'Hara*, 534 A.2d 488 (Pa. Super. 1987) (real estate); *Scott v. Assoc. for Childbirth at Home, Int'l*, 430 N.E.2d 1012 (Ill. 1982) (childbirth education and training services); *State v. Grogan*, 628 P.2d 570 (Alaska 1981) (aircraft repair).

The "chain referral" or "pyramid" scheme is a recurring consumer protection problem. Characteristically, victims are lured into such schemes via spirited introductory "opportunity" meetings in which they are bombarded with affirmations of the great wealth attainable through enlistment in the instigator's marketing plan. The product to be marketed, *e.g.*, cosmetics, is actually of secondary significance. The real objective is to make money through the recruitment of new participants in the plan. Each initiate pays in a large sum of money, either as an entry fee or for a substantial amount of non-returnable inventory. The paid-in money is then distributed among those already participating in the plan. A person desiring a larger percentage normally must make an additional payment into the plan or supply some requisite number of new recruits.

The deception is said to lie in the law of diminishing returns that operates against later initiates. As stated in *Kugler v. Koscot Interplanetary, Inc.*, 120 N.J. Super. 216, 232 (1972):

> A pyramid type practice is similar to a chain letter operation. Such a program is inherently deceptive for the seemingly endless chain must come to a halt inasmuch as growth cannot be perpetual and the market becomes saturated by the number of participants. *See, e.g., State by Lefkowitz v. ITM, Inc.*, 275 N.Y.S.2d 303 (N.Y. Sup. Ct. 1966). Thus many participants are mathematically barred from ever recouping their original investments.

These practices have been enjoined in state courts under state statutes which specifically refer to such pyramid schemes, or under the general statutory prohibitions against unfair or deceptive trade practices. *See, e.g., Watkins v. Alvey*, 549 N.E.2d 74 (Ind. Ct. App. 1990); *Webster v. Membership Marketing, Inc.*, 766 S.W.2d 654 (Mo. Ct. App. 1989); *People ex rel. Hartigan v. Unimax, Inc.*, 523 N.E.2d 26 (Ill. App. Ct. 1988); *Bell v. Commonwealth*, 374 S.E.2d 13 (Va. 1988). They have also been the subject of action by the Federal Trade Commission. *See, e.g., In re Koscot Interplanetary, Inc.*, 86 F.T.C. 1106 (1975), *aff'd sub nom. Turner v. FTC*, 580 F.2d 701 (D.C. Cir. 1978); *In re Ger-Ro-Mar*, 84 F.T.C. 95 (1974), *aff'd in part, rev'd in part*, 513 F.2d 33 (2ᵈ Cir. 1975); *In re Holiday Magic, Inc.*, 84 F.T.C. 748 (1974). *Compare In re Amway Corporation*, Trade Reg. Rep. (CCH) ¶ 21,574 (1979). *See generally* Stone and Steiner, *The Federal Trade Commission and Pyramid Sales Schemes*, 15 PAC. L.J. 879 (1984).

Criminal as well as civil remedies against perpetrators of unfair or deceptive trade practices may be available to state law enforcement officials. The common law of larceny by false pretenses may be applicable if the practices do not fall within specific statutory provisions. However, apparently little use is given to this enforcement tool. Various suggestions have been made by commentators as to why this is so, among them the greater burden of proof required in criminal cases and the necessity of proving intent to defraud under the common law. *See* EBERT, ENFORCEMENT OF STATE DECEPTIVE TRADE PRACTICE STATUTES, *supra*, at 745–46; Gold & Cohan, *State Protection of the Consumer: Integration of Civil and Criminal Remedies*, 12 NEW ENG. L. REV. 933 (1977). For additional commentary, see Geis & Edelhertz, *Criminal Law and Consumer Fraud: A Sociological View*, 11 AM. CRIM. L. REV. 989 (1975).

States also may enact regulations, and authorize regulatory bodies, that relate to a particular industry. In *Ross v. Alabama Bd. of Chiropractic Exam'rs*, 724 So.2d 540 (Ala. 1998), for example, a telephone directory advertisement by two chiropractors violated the Alabama Board of Chiropractic Examiners' rules regulating advertising. In the ad, the chiropractors used the phrase, "Consultation at No Charge," without disclosing that additional charges might be incurred for necessary related services, and they also falsely represented themselves to be members of the American Medical Association. The State Code provided that the Board could fine, suspend or revoke the license of chiropractors found guilty of "advertising in any manner which violates the rules and regulations established by the board." This included a prohibition on false or misleading advertising, and advertising offering "gratuitous services or discounts in connection with professional services." The Board was not required to produce evidence of consumer reaction or confusion to support its finding.

The court concluded that, "because the advertisement offered gratuitous services without including the required language [indicating] that additional charges may be incurred for related services which may have been needed," there was "substantial evidence to support the Board's determination that the advertisement is misleading." One of the defendants testified that performing an examination and eliciting the patient's history would be necessary to the consultation, and that there would be charges for those tasks. The two chiropractors, who shared their practice with a medical doctor, also wrongly portrayed all three practitioners in the advertisement as being members of the AMA. In upholding the Board ruling, the court observed that this "presented information that the Board could easily recognize as misleading, even without evidence of consumer reaction to the advertisement."

2. Private Actions

Although many state consumer protection statutes differ from the FTC Act in that they provide for private causes of action, there have been relatively few reported private consumer actions to date. Plaintiffs typically face strong economic disincentives in bringing such suits, as exemplified by the nominal rescissionary relief awarded to the defrauded consumers in *American Buyers Club of Mt. Vernon, Illinois, Inc. v. Honecker*, 361 N.E.2d 1370 (Ill. App. Ct. 1977) (seller of memberships in retail club who misrepresented that $39 fee would permit members to receive 50% discount on selected items was ordered to rescind members' contract and to return the $39 fee). *See also Kentucky ex rel. Beshear v. ABAC Pest Control*, 621 S.W.2d 705, 707 (Ky. Ct. App. 1981), in which the court found that the economic disincentives to private actions and the legislature's intent to provide a strong consumer protection program required the court to recognize the Attorney General's right to seek restitution on behalf of victims of consumer fraud. Yet, state enforcement officials, due to limited personnel and financial resources, cannot adequately handle all the complaints which they receive. *See Slaney v. Westwood Auto, Inc.*, 322 N.E.2d 768, 776 (Mass. 1975). *See also* Sebert, *Enforcement of State Deceptive Trade Practice Statutes*, 42 TENN. L. REV. 689 (1975); Comment, *Consumer Protection: The Practical Effectiveness of State Deceptive Trade Practices Legislation*, 59 TUL. L. REV. 427, 449 (1984). The enactment of statutory provisions for multiple damages recoveries and attorney's fees in private actions is one way state legislators have sought to encourage greater use of consumer protection law by private individuals. *See* PRIDGEN, CONSUMER PROTECTION AND THE LAW, Ch. 6 (2007); Leaffer & Lipson, *Consumer Actions Against Unfair Deceptive Acts or Practices: The Private Uses of Federal Trade Commission Jurisprudence*, 48 GEO. WASH. L. REV. 521 (1980); Roberts, *Consumerism Comes of Age: Treble Damages and Attorneys Fees in Consumer Transactions — The Ohio Consumer Sales Practices Act*, 42 OHIO ST. L.J. 927 (1981). *See generally* Waxman, *Private Enforcement of Consumer Laws in Wisconsin*, 56 Wis. B. Bull. 22 (May, 1983); Note, *New York Creates a Private Right of Action to Combat Consumer Fraud: Caveat Venditor*, 48 BROOKLYN L. REV. 509 (1982).

Common law actions for fraud and deceit normally require proof of such elements as actual reliance by the plaintiff upon the misrepresentation, and defendant's knowledge of the representation's falsity elements a plaintiff typically need not prove in an action brought under a Consumer Protection Act. *See Brode v. Tax Management, Inc.*, 14

U.S.P.Q.2d 1195 (N.D. Ill. 1990) (because it has no intent requirement, Illinois Act "allows for broader protection than available under common law fraud"); *V.S.H. Realty, Inc. v. Texaco, Inc.*, 757 F.2d 411, 414–15 (1st Cir. 1985); *Slaney v. Westwood Auto, Inc.*, 322 N.E.2d 768, 776 (Mass. 1975). Additional remedies such as attorney fee awards also may be available under statutory but not common law. Given the social goal of eradicating fraud and deceptive dealing by encouraging private actions, should the legislated Acts supercede the common law in this area in all instances? Some courts have sought to limit the application of such statutes, imposing a "public interest" requirement on private actions brought under them. In *Hangman Ridge Training Stables, Inc. v. Safeco Title Ins. Co.*, 719 P.2d 531 (Wash. 1986) (en banc), the court changed the test for the public interest element from one involving the potential for repetition to one dependent on context, *i.e.*, consumer transaction or private dispute, and in *Hall v. Walter*, 969 P.2d 224, 234 (Colo. 1998), the court held that the "challenged practice must significantly impact the public as actual or potential purchasers of the defendant's goods, services or property." In *Newman- Green, Inc. v. Alfonzo-Larrain*, 590 F. Supp. 1083, 1088 (N.D. Ill. 1984), the court, applying Illinois law to a contract controversy between businessmen, dismissed the count brought under that state's Act for lack of the requisite public injury element, stating "a scheme to defraud a single entity in a single course of dealing does not amount to a 'pattern' of deceptive activities." Is such a requirement valid or advisable? *See* Comment, *Private Suits Under Washington's Consumer Protection Act: The Public Interest Requirement*, 54 WASH. L. REV. 795 (1979).

For some examples of state private action decisions in this area, *see Hall v. Walter*, 969 P.2d 224 (Colo. 1998) (landowners had standing in private action under Colorado Act against subdivision developer concerning alleged misrepresentations to third parties about access to landowners' property); *Wallace v. Pastore*, 742 A.2d 1090 (Pa. Super. Ct. 1999)(lessor misrepresented condition of apartment; restitution, treble damages and attorney's fees awarded); *Bennett v. Bailey*, 597 S.W.2d 532 (Tex. Ct. Civ. App. 1980)(unconscionable actions by dance instructors; treble damages and attorney's fees awarded); *Sellinger v. Freeway Mobile Home Sales*, 521 P.2d 1119 (Ariz. 1974) (fraud in mobile home sale; damages award held inadequate and case remanded); *Gour v. Daray Motor Co.*, 373 So. 2d 571 (La. Ct. App. 1979) (manufacturer of automobile engine misrepresented; restitution and attorneys fees awarded); *Moore v. Goodyear Tire and Rubber Co.*, 364 So. 2d 630 (La. Ct. App. 1978) (oppressive debt collecting harassment; actual and general damages and attorney's fees awarded); *Neveroski v. Blair*, 358 A.2d 473 (N.J. Super. 1976) (false certification of termite absence by exterminator; actual and punitive damages and attorney's fees awarded); *Allen v. Morgan Drive Away*, 542 P.2d 896 (Or. 1975) (punitive damages award affirmed for calculated misrepresentations by mover); *Bennett v. Bailey*, 597 S.W.2d 532 (Tex. Ct. Civ. App. 1980) (unconscionable actions by dance instructors; treble damages and attorney's fees awarded).

In *Huu Nam Tran v. Metro. Life Ins. Co.*, 408 F.3d 130 (3^d Cir. 2005), the court of appeals reversed summary judgment for MetLife on plaintiff Tran's fraud, negligent misrepresentation and statutory consumer protection claims resulting from Tran's purchase of a life insurance policy. Tran spoke and read little English. The district court held that Tran had a duty under Pennsylvania law to read the policy or to have someone read it to him and that therefore he could not claim justifiable reliance on the agent's representations.

The court of appeals found that the district court erred in concluding that Pennsylvania law required Tran to read his policy or have it read to him before he could allege fraud. Therefore, the district court's grant of summary judgment was inappropriate. The court reasoned that "even if Tran had read his policy or had it read to him, an examination of the policy terms would not necessarily have revealed that [the agent's] alleged statements were false as to when premium payments would cease." 408 F.3d at 139. Furthermore, the court noted that the Pennsylvania Supreme Court had recently held that a plaintiff "must show that he *justifiably relied* on the defendant's wrongful conduct or representation and that he suffered harm as a result of that reliance." 408 F.3d at 140, emphasis in original.

3. Municipal Regulation

Deceptive practices also may be redressed on the municipal level. Among the obvious advantages in such local enforcement are the accessibility of the enforcement agency to consumers and the attention given problems too small in magnitude to warrant state or federal involvement. However, it may be that the resources necessary to redress consumer grievances effectively under such a code are available realistically only in large metropolitan areas. *See, e.g., City of New York v. Toby's Electronics, Inc.*, 110 Misc. 2d 848, 443 N.Y.S.2d 561 (1981), which implements New York City's civil code. That municipal code is reviewed in Note, *New York City's Alternative to the Consumer Class Action: The Government as Robin Hood*, 9 HARV. J. on LEGIS. 301 (1972). One way to avoid potential conflicts with state law and questions of preemption would be to empower local agencies to enforce the state's unfair and deceptive trade practice law. This also might enable municipalities with limited resources to provide aid to local consumers. *See* Sebert, *Enforcement of State Deceptive Trade Practice Statutes*, 42 TENN. L. REV. 689, 754–55 (1975).

State and local governments may, under appropriate circumstances, regulate the display of a registered trademark, although they may not require that the mark itself be altered. Section 39(b) of the Lanham Act, 15 U.S.C. § 1121(b), provides that, "[n]o state . . . or any political subdivision or any agency thereof may require alteration of a registered mark . . . ." In *Blockbuster Videos v. City of Tempe*, 141 F.3d 1295 (9th Cir. 1998), the court held that, while Tempe, Arizona, under its zoning ordinances, may bar a mark from being publicly displayed, § 39(b) precluded it from requiring alteration of the mark. There, the city of Tempe sought to have plaintiffs Blockbuster Videos and Video Update conform to its shopping center signage requirements as to such things as standard colors, size and location. The court held it could not do so because, for example, "[t]he color red is a characteristic of Video Update's mark [and] [b]y requiring Video Update to change the red color on one of its signs to white letters on a turquoise background, Tempe required Video Update to 'alter' its service mark" in violation of the Lanham Act. However, because § 39(b) "speaks only to alteration" of a mark, a municipality "retains the power to prohibit the use of a mark altogether". Therefore, the court held that "Tempe could prevent Blockbuster from installing its awning service mark on the outside of the building it leased in the shopping center. . . . Precluding display of a mark for zoning purposes is permissible; requiring alteration of a mark is not". *Compare Lisa's Party City, Inc. v. Town of Henrietta*, 185 F.3d 12 (2d Cir. 1999), where the court affirmed summary judgment that a local zoning ordinance did not violate § 39(b)'s prohibition against requiring "alterations" of registered marks by "prohibiting [plaintiff's] use of its multi-colored trademark on an exterior sign in a red-only shopping center." The court narrowly defined the Lanham Act reference to "alteration" as referring to state-mandated changes in the mark itself, which necessarily would be reflected in every subsequent display of the mark in the relevant jurisdiction:

> Congress enacted § 1121(b). . . because state regulations compelled trademark holders to change the character and design of their trademarks throughout an entire statewide jurisdiction. [Citations omitted]. In contrast, local aesthetic and historic regulations simply limit color typefaces and decorative elements to certain prescribed styles. There regulations have no effect on the business' trademarks. They limit only the choice of exterior sign at a particular location. As such, though entirely disallowing the use of a trademark in carefully delimited instances, these regulations do not require "alteration" at all.

The court further pointed out that if Congress was willing to permit localities to forbid signs altogether, surely it was willing to permit "narrower measures such as requiring color conformity or consistent design elements."

APPENDIX
The Lanham Act
TITLE 15. UNITED STATES CODE
COMMERCE AND TRADE

TRADEMARKS AND UNFAIR COMPETITION

CHAPTER 22.   TRADEMARKS

THE PRINCIPAL REGISTER

§ 1051.   Registration of Trademarks

(a)

(1)   The owner of a trademark used in commerce may request registration of its trademark on the principal register hereby established by paying the prescribed fee and filing in the Patent and Trademark Office an application and a verified statement, in such form as may be prescribed by the Director, and such number of specimens or facsimiles of the mark as used as may be required by the Director.

(2)   The application shall include specification of the applicant's domicile and citizenship, the date of the applicant's first use of the mark, the date of the applicant's first use of the mark in commerce, the goods in connection with which the mark is used, and a drawing of the mark.

(3)   The statement shall be verified by the applicant and specify that—

(A)   the person making the verification believes that he or she, or the juristic person in whose behalf he or she makes the verification, to be the owner of the mark sought to be registered;

(B)   to the best of the verifier's knowledge and belief, the facts recited in the application are accurate;

(C)   the mark is in use in commerce; and

(D)   to the best of the verifier's knowledge and belief, no other person has the right to use such mark in commerce either in the identical form thereof or in such near resemblance thereto as to be likely, when used on or in connection with the goods of such other person, to cause confusion, or to cause mistake, or to deceive, except that, in the case of every application claiming concurrent use, the applicant shall—

(i)   state exceptions to the claim of exclusive use; and

(ii)   shall specify, to the extent of the verifier's knowledge—

(I)   any concurrent use by others;

(II)   the goods on or in connection with which and the areas in which each concurrent use exists;

(III)   the periods of each use; and

(IV)   the goods and area for which the applicant desires registration.

(4)   The applicant shall comply with such rules or regulations as may be prescribed by the Director. The Director shall promulgate rules prescribing the requirements for the application and for obtaining a filing date herein.

(b)

(1)   A person who has a bona fide intention, under circumstances showing the good faith of such person, to use a trademark in commerce may request registration of its trademark on the principal register hereby established by paying the prescribed fee and filing in the Patent and Trademark Office an application and a verified statement, in such form as may be prescribed by the Director.

(2)   The application shall include specification of the applicant's domicile and citizenship, the goods in connection with which the applicant has a bona fide intention to use the mark, and a drawing of the mark.

(3)   The statement shall be verified by the applicant and specify—

(A)   that the person making the verification believes that he or she, or the juristic person in whose behalf he or she makes the verification, to be entitled to use the mark in commerce;

(B)   the applicant's bona fide intention to use the mark in commerce;

(C)   that, to the best of the verifier's knowledge and belief, the facts recited in the application are accurate; and

(D)   that, to the best of the verifier's knowledge and belief, no other person has the right to use such mark in commerce either in the identical form thereof or in such near resemblance thereto as to be likely, when used on or in connection with the goods of such other person, to cause confusion, or to cause mistake, or to deceive.

Except for applications filed pursuant to section 44 [15 USCS § 1126], no mark shall be registered until the applicant has met the requirements of subsections (c) and (d) of this section.

(4)   The applicant shall comply with such rules or regulations as may be prescribed by the Director. The Director shall promulgate rules prescribing the requirements for the application and for obtaining a filing date herein.

(c)   Amendment of application under subsection (b) to conform to requirements under subsection (a). At any time during examination of an application filed under subsection (b), an applicant who has made use of the mark in commerce may claim the benefits of such use for purposes of this Act, by amending his or her application to bring it into conformity with the requirements of subsection (a).

(d)   Verified statement that trademark is used in commerce.

(1)   Within six months after the date on which the notice of allowance with respect to a mark is issued under section 13(b)(2) [15 USCS § 1063(b)(2)] to an applicant under subsection (b) of this section, the applicant shall file in the Patent and Trademark Office, together with such number of specimens or facsimiles of the mark as used in commerce as may be required by the Director and payment of the prescribed fee, a verified statement that the mark is in use in commerce and specifying the date of the applicant's first use of the mark in commerce and those goods or services specified in the notice of allowance on or in connection with which the mark is used in commerce. Subject to examination and acceptance of the statement of use, the mark shall be registered in the Patent and Trademark Office, a certificate of registration shall be issued for those goods or services recited in the statement of use for which the mark is entitled to registration, and notice of registration shall be published in the Official Gazette of the Patent and Trademark Office. Such examination may include an examination of the factors set forth in subsections (a) through (e) of section 2 [15 USCS § 1052]. The notice of registration shall specify the goods or services for which the mark is registered.

(2)   The Director shall extend, for one additional 6-month period, the time for filing the statement of use under paragraph (1), upon written request of the applicant before the expiration of the 6-month period provided in paragraph (1). In addition to an extension under the preceding sentence, the Director may, upon a showing of good cause by the applicant, further extend the time for filing the statement of use under paragraph (1) for periods aggregating not more than 24 months, pursuant to written request of the applicant made before the expiration of the last extension granted under this paragraph. Any request for an extension under this paragraph shall be accompanied by a verified statement that the applicant has a continued bona fide intention to use the mark in commerce and specifying those goods or services identified in the notice of allowance on or in connection with which the applicant has a continued bona fide intention to use the mark in commerce. Any request for an extension under this paragraph shall be

accompanied by payment of the prescribed fee. The Director shall issue regulations setting forth guidelines for determining what constitutes good cause for purposes of this paragraph.

(3) The Director shall notify any applicant who files a statement of use of the acceptance or refusal thereof and, if the statement of use is refused, the reasons for the refusal. An applicant may amend the statement of use.

(4) The failure to timely file a verified statement of use under paragraph (1) or an extension request under paragraph (2) shall result in abandonment of the application, unless it can be shown to the satisfaction of the Director that the delay in responding was unintentional, in which case the time for filing may be extended, but for a period not to exceed the period specified in paragraphs (1) and (2) for filing a statement of use.

(e) If the applicant is not domiciled in the United States the applicant may designate, by a document filed in the United States Patent and Trademark Office, the name and address of a person resident in the United States on whom may be served notices or process in proceedings affecting the mark. Such notices or process may be served upon the person so designated by leaving with that person or mailing to that person a copy thereof at the address specified in the last designation so filed. If the person so designated cannot be found at the address given in the last designation, or if the registrant does not designate by a document filed in the United States Patent and Trademark Office the name and address of a person resident in the United States on whom may be served notices or process in proceedings affecting the mark, such notices or process may be served on the Director.

§ 1052. Trademarks Registrable on the Principal Register; Concurrent Registration

No trademark by which the goods of the applicant may be distinguished from the goods of others shall be refused registration on the principal register on account of its nature unless it—

(a) Consists of or comprises immoral, deceptive, or scandalous matter; or matter which may disparage or falsely suggest a connection with persons, living or dead, institutions, beliefs, or national symbols, or bring them into contempt, or disrepute; or a geographical indication which, when used on or in connection with wines or spirits, identifies a place other than the origin of the goods and is first used on or in connection with wines or spirits by the applicant on or after one year after the date on which the WTO Agreement (as defined in section 2(9) of the Uruguay Round Agreements Act [19 USCS § 3501(9)]) enters into force with respect to the United States.

(b) Consists of or comprises the flag or coat of arms or other insignia of the United States, or of any State or municipality, or of any foreign nation, or any simulation thereof.

(c) Consists of or comprises a name, portrait, or signature identifying a particular living individual except by his written consent, or the name, signature, or portrait of a deceased President of the United States during the life of his widow, if any, except by the written consent of the widow.

(d) Consists of or comprises a mark which so resembles a mark registered in the Patent and Trademark Office, or a mark or trade name previously used in the United States by another and not abandoned, as to be likely, when used on or in connection with the goods of the applicant, to cause confusion, or to cause mistake, or to deceive: *Provided*, That if the Director determines that confusion, mistake, or deception is not likely to result from the continued use by more than one person of the same or similar marks under conditions and limitations as to the mode or place of use of the marks or the goods on or in connection with which such marks are used, concurrent registrations may be issued to such persons when they have become entitled to use such marks as a result of their concurrent lawful use in commerce prior to (1) the earliest of the filing dates of the applications pending or of any registration issued under this Act; (2) July 5, 1947, in the case of registrations previously issued under the Act of March 3, 1881, or February 20, 1905, and continuing in full force and effect on that date; or (3) July 5, 1947, in the case of applications filed under the Act of February 20, 1905, and registered after July 5, 1947. Use prior to the filing date of any pending application or a registration shall not be required when the owner of such application or registration consents to the grant of a concurrent registration to the applicant. Concurrent registrations may also be issued by the Director when a court of competent jurisdiction has finally determined that more than one person is entitled to use the same or similar marks in commerce. In issuing concurrent registrations, the Director shall prescribe conditions and limitations as to the mode or place of use of the mark or the goods on or in connection with which such mark is registered to the respective persons.

(e) Consists of a mark which (1) when used on or in connection with the goods of the applicant is merely descriptive or deceptively misdescriptive of them, (2) when used on or in connection with the goods of the applicant is primarily geographically descriptive of them, except as indications of regional origin may be registrable under section 4 [15 USCS § 1054], (3) when used on or in connection with the goods of the applicant is primarily geographically deceptively misdescriptive of them, (4) is primarily merely a surname, or (5) comprises any matter that, as a whole, is functional.

(f) Except as expressly excluded in subsections (a), (b), (c), (d), (e)(3), and (e)(5) of this section, nothing herein shall prevent the registration of a mark used by the applicant which has become distinctive of the applicant's goods in commerce. The Director may accept as prima facie evidence that the mark has become distinctive, as used on or in connection with the applicant's goods in commerce, proof of substantially exclusive and continuous use thereof as a mark by the applicant in commerce for the five years before the date on which the claim of distinctiveness is made. Nothing in this section shall prevent the registration of a mark which, when used on or in connection with the goods of the applicant, is primarily geographically deceptively misdescriptive of them, and which became distinctive of the applicant's goods in commerce before the date of the enactment of the North American Free Trade Agreement Implementation Act [enacted Dec. 8, 1993]. A mark which would be likely to cause dilution by blurring or dilution by tarnishment under section 43(c) [15 USCS § 1125(c)], may be refused registration only pursuant to a proceeding brought under section 13 [15 USCS § 1063]. A registration for a mark which would be likely to cause dilution by blurring or dilution by tarnishment under section 43(c) [15 USCS § 1125(c)], may be canceled pursuant to a proceeding brought under either section 14 or section 24 [15 USCS § 1064 or 1092].

§ 1053. Service Marks Registrable

Subject to the provisions relating to the registration of trademarks, so far as they are applicable, service marks shall be registrable, in the same manner and with the same effect as are trademarks, and when registered they shall be entitled to the protection provided herein in the case of trademarks. Applications and procedure under this section shall conform as nearly as practicable to those prescribed for the registration of trademarks.

§ 1054. Collective Marks and Certification Marks Registrable

Subject to the provisions relating to the registration of trademarks, so far as they are applicable, collective and certification marks, including indications of regional origin, shall be registrable under this Act, in the same manner and with the same effect as are trademarks, by persons, and nations, States, municipalities, and the like, exercising legitimate control over the use of the marks sought to be registered, even though not possessing an industrial or commercial establishment, and when registered they shall be entitled to the protection provided herein in the case of trademarks, except in the case of certification marks when used so as to represent falsely that the owner or a user thereof makes or sells the goods or performs the services on or in connection with which such mark is used. Applications and procedure under this section shall conform as nearly as practicable to those prescribed for the registration of trademarks.

§ 1055. Use by Related Companies Affecting Validity and Registration

Where a registered mark or a mark sought to be registered is or may be used legitimately by related companies, such use shall inure to the benefit of the registrant or applicant for registration, and such use shall not affect the validity of such mark or of its registration, provided such mark is not used in such manner as to deceive the public. If first use of a mark by a person is controlled by the registrant or applicant for registration of the mark with respect to the nature and quality of the goods or services, such first use shall inure to the benefit of the registrant or applicant, as the case may be.

§ 1056. Disclaimer of Unregistrable Matter

(a) The Director may require the applicant to disclaim an unregistrable component of a mark otherwise registrable. An applicant may voluntarily disclaim a component of a mark sought to be registered.

(b) No disclaimer, including those made under subsec. (e) of section 7 of this Act [15 USCS § 1057(e)], shall prejudice or affect the applicant's or registrant's rights then existing or thereafter arising in the disclaimed matter, or his right of registration on another application if the disclaimed matter be or shall have become distinctive of his goods or services.

§ 1057. Certificates of Registration

(a) Issuance and form. Certificates of registration of marks registered upon the principal register shall be issued in the name of the United States of America, under the seal of the Patent and Trademark Office, and shall be signed by the Director or have his signature placed thereon, and a record thereof shall be kept in the Patent and Trademark Office. The registration shall reproduce the mark, and state that the mark is registered on the principal register under this Act, the date of the first use of the mark, the date of the first use of the mark in commerce, the particular goods or services for which it is registered, the number and date of the registration, the term thereof, the date on which the application for registration was received in the Patent and Trademark Office, and any conditions and limitations that may be imposed in the registration.

(b) Certificate as prima facie evidence. A certificate of registration of a mark upon the principal register provided by this Act shall be prima facie evidence of the validity of the registered mark and of the registration of the mark, of the registrant's ownership of the mark, and of the registrant's exclusive right to use the registered mark in commerce on or in connection with the goods or services specified in the certificate, subject to any conditions or limitations stated in the certificate.

(c) Application to register mark considered constructive use. Contingent on the registration of a mark on the principal register provided by this Act, the filing of the application to register such mark shall constitute constructive use of the mark, conferring a right of priority, nationwide in effect, on or in connection with the goods or services specified in the registration against any other person except for a person whose mark has not been abandoned and who, prior to such filing—

(1) has used the mark;

(2) has filed an application to register the mark which is pending or has resulted in registration of the mark; or

(3) has filed a foreign application to register the mark on the basis of which he or she has acquired a right of priority, and timely files an application under section 44(d) [15 USCS § 1126(d)] to register the mark which is pending or has resulted in registration of the mark.

(d)   Issuance to assignee. A certificate of registration of a mark may be issued to the assignee or the applicant, but the assignment must first be recorded in the Patent and Trademark Office. In case of change of ownership the Director shall, at the request of the owner and upon a proper showing and the payment of the prescribed fee, issue to such assignee a new certificate of registration of the said mark in the name of such assignee, and for the unexpired part of original period.

(e)   Surrender, cancellation, or amendment by registrant. Upon application of the registrant the Director may permit any registration to be surrendered for cancelation, and upon cancelation appropriate entry shall be made in the records of the Patent and Trademark Office. Upon application of the registrant and payment of the prescribed fee, the Director for good cause may permit any registration to be amended or to be disclaimed in part: *Provided,* That the amendment or disclaimer does not alter materially the character of the mark. Appropriate entry shall be made in the records of the Patent and Trademark Office and upon the certificate of registration or, if said certificate is lost or destroyed, upon a certified copy thereof.

(f)   Copies of Patent and Trademark Office records as evidence. Copies of any records, books, papers, or drawings belonging to the Patent and Trademark Office relating to marks, and copies of registrations, when authenticated by the seal of the Patent and Trademark Office and certified by the Director, or in his name by an employee of the Office duly designated by the Director, shall be evidence in all cases wherein the originals would be evidence; and any person making application therefor and paying the prescribed fee shall have such copies.

(g)   Correction of Patent and Trademark Office mistake. Whenever a material mistake in a registration, incurred through the fault of the Patent and Trademark Office, is clearly disclosed by the records of the Office a certificate stating the fact and nature of such mistake shall be issued without charge and recorded and a printed copy thereof shall be attached to each printed copy of the registration and such corrected registration shall thereafter have the same effect as if the same had been originally issued in such corrected form, or in the discretion of the Director a new certificate of registration may be issued without charge. All certificates of correction heretofore issued in accordance with the rules of the Patent and Trademark Office and the registrations to which they are attached shall have the same force and effect as if such certificates and their issue had been specifically authorized by statute.

(h)   Correction of applicant's mistake. Whenever a mistake has been made in a registration and a showing has been made that such mistake occurred in good faith through the fault of the applicant, the Director is authorized to issue a certificate of correction or, in his discretion, a new certificate upon the payment of the prescribed fee: *Provided,* That the correction does not involve such changes in the registration as to require republication of the mark.

§ 1058.   Duration

(a)   Each registration shall remain in force for 10 years, except that the registration of any mark shall be canceled by the Director for failure to comply with the provisions of subsection (b) of this section, upon the expiration of the following time periods, as applicable:

(1)   For registrations issued pursuant to the provisions of this Act, at the end of 6 years following the date of registration.

(2)   For registrations published under the provisions of section 12(c) [15 USCS § 1062(c)], at the end of 6 years following the date of publication under such section.

(3)   For all registrations, at the end of each successive 10-year period following the date of registration.

(b)   During the 1-year period immediately preceding the end of the applicable time period set forth in subsection (a), the owner of the registration shall pay the prescribed fee and file in the Patent and Trademark Office—

(1)   an affidavit setting forth those goods or services recited in the registration on or in connection with which the mark is in use in commerce and such number of specimens or facsimiles showing current use of the mark as may be required by the Director; or

(2)   an affidavit setting forth those goods or services recited in the registration on or in connection with which the mark is not in use in commerce and showing that any such nonuse is due to special circumstances which excuse such nonuse and is not due to any intention to abandon the mark.

(c)

(1)   The owner of the registration may make the submissions required under this section within a grace period of 6 months after the end of the applicable time period set forth in subsection (a). Such submission is required to be accompanied by a surcharge prescribed by the Director.

(2)   If any submission filed under this section is deficient, the deficiency may be corrected after the statutory time period and within the time prescribed after notification of the deficiency. Such submission is required to be accompanied by a surcharge prescribed by the Director.

(d)   Special notice of the requirement for affidavits under this section shall be attached to each certificate of registration and notice of publication under section 12(c) [15 USCS § 1062(c)].

(e)   The Director shall notify any owner who files 1 of the affidavits required by this section of the Director's acceptance or refusal thereof and, in the case of a refusal, the reasons therefor.

(f)   If the registrant is not domiciled in the United States, the registrant may designate, by a document filed in the United States Patent and Trademark Office, the name and address of a person resident in the United States on whom may be served notices or process in proceedings affecting the mark. Such notices or process may be served upon the person so designated by leaving with that person or mailing to that person a copy thereof at the address specified in the last designation so filed. If the person so designated cannot be found at the address given in the last designation, or if the registrant does not designate by a document filed in the United States Patent and Trademark Office the name and address of a person resident in the United States on whom may be served notices or process in proceedings affecting the mark, such notices or process may be served on the Director.

§ 1059.   Renewal of Registration

(a)   Subject to the provisions of section 8 [15 USCS § 1058], each registration may be renewed for periods of 10 years at the end of each successive 10-year period following the date of registration upon payment of the prescribed fee and the filing of a written application, in such form as may be prescribed by the Director. Such application may be made at any time within 1 year before the end of each successive 10-year period for which the registration was issued or renewed, or it may be made within a grace period of 6 months after the end of each successive 10-year period, upon payment of a fee and surcharge prescribed therefor. If any application filed under this section is deficient, the deficiency may be corrected within the time prescribed after notification of the deficiency, upon payment of a surcharge prescribed therefor.

(b)   If the Director refuses to renew the registration, the Director shall notify the registrant of the Director's refusal and the reasons therefor.

(c)   If the registrant is not domiciled in the United States the registrant may designate, by a document filed in the United States Patent and Trademark Office, the name and address of a person resident in the United States on whom may be served notices or process in proceedings affecting the mark. Such notices or process may be served upon the person so designated by leaving with that person or mailing to that person a copy thereof at the address specified in the last designation so filed. If the person so designated cannot be found at the address given in the last designation, or if the registrant does not designate by a document filed in the United States Patent and Trademark Office the name and address of a person resident in the United States on whom may be served notices or process in proceedings affecting the mark, such notices or process may be served on the Director.

§ 1060. Assignment

(a)

(1)   A registered mark or a mark for which an application to register has been filed shall be assignable with the good will of the business in which the mark is used, or with that part of the good will of the business connected with the use of and symbolized by the mark. Notwithstanding the preceding sentence, no application to register a mark under section 1(b) [15 USCS § 1051(b)] shall be assignable prior to the filing of an amendment under section 1(c) [15 USCS § 1051(c)] to bring the application into conformity with section 1(a) [15 USCS § 1051(a)] or the filing of the verified statement of use under section 1(d) [15 USCS § 1051(d)], except for an assignment to a successor to the business of the applicant, or portion thereof, to which the mark pertains, if that business is ongoing and existing.

(2)   In any assignment authorized by this section, it shall not be necessary to include the good will of the business connected with the use of and symbolized by any other mark used in the business or by the name or style under which the business is conducted.

(3)   Assignments shall be by instruments in writing duly executed. Acknowledgment shall be prima facie evidence of the execution of an assignment, and when the prescribed information reporting the assignment is recorded in the United States Patent and Trademark Office, the record shall be prima facie evidence of execution.

(4)   An assignment shall be void against any subsequent purchaser for valuable consideration without notice, unless the prescribed information reporting the assignment is recorded in the United States Patent and Trademark Office within 3 months after the date of the assignment or prior to the subsequent purchase.

(5)   The United States Patent and Trademark Office shall maintain a record of information on assignments, in such form as may be prescribed by the Director.

(b)   An assignee not domiciled in the United States may designate by a document filed in the United States Patent and Trademark Office the name and address of a person resident in the United States on whom may be served notices or process in proceedings affecting the mark. Such notices or process may be served upon the person so designated by leaving with that person or mailing to that person a copy thereof at the address specified in the last designation so filed. If the person so designated cannot be found at the address given in the last designation, or if the assignee does not designate by a document filed in the United States Patent and Trademark Office the name and address of a person resident in the United States on whom may be served notices or process in proceedings affecting the mark, such notices or process may be served upon the Director.

§ 1061. Execution of Acknowledgments and Verifications

Acknowledgments and verifications required hereunder may be made before any person within the United States authorized by law to administer oaths, or, when made in a foreign country, before any diplomatic or consular officer of the United States or before any official authorized to administer oaths in the foreign country concerned whose authority shall be proved by a certificate of a diplomatic or consular officer of the United States, or apostille of an official designated by a foreign country which, by treaty or convention, accords like effect to apostilles of designated officials in the United States, and is valid if they comply with the laws of the state or country where made.

§ 1062. Publication

(a) Examination and publication. Upon the filing of an application for registration and payment of the prescribed fee, the Director shall refer the application to the examiner in charge of the registration of marks, who shall cause an examination to be made and, if on such examination it shall appear that the applicant is entitled to registration, or would be entitled to registration upon the acceptance of the statement of use required by section 1(d) of this Act [15 USCS § 1051(d)], the Director shall cause the mark to be published in the Official Gazette of the Patent and Trademark Office; Provided, That in the case of an applicant claiming concurrent use, or in the case of an application to be placed in an interference as provided in section 16 of this Act [15 USCS § 1066], the mark if otherwise registrable, may be published subject to the determination of the rights of the parties to such proceedings.

(b) Refusal of registration; amendment of application; abandonment. If the applicant is found not entitled to registration, the examiner shall advise the applicant thereof and of the reasons therefor. The applicant shall have a period of six months in which to reply or amend his application, which shall then be reexamined. This procedure may be repeated until (1) the examiner finally refuses registration of the mark or (2) the applicant fails for a period of six months to reply or amend or appeal, whereupon the application shall be deemed to have been abandoned, unless it can be shown to the satisfaction of the Director that the delay in responding was unintentional, whereupon such time may be extended.

(c) Republication of marks registered under prior acts. A registrant of a mark registered under the provisions of the Act of March 3, 1881, or the Act of February 20, 1905, may, at any time prior to the expiration of the registration thereof, upon the payment of the prescribed fee file with the Director an affidavit setting forth those goods stated in the registration on which said mark is in use in commerce and that the registrant claims the benefits of this Act for said mark. The Director shall publish notice thereof with a reproduction of said mark in the Official Gazette, and notify the registrant of such publication and of the requirement for the affidavit of use or nonuse as provided for in subsection (b) of Section 8 of this Act [15 USCS § 1058(b)]. Marks published under this subsection shall not be subject to the provisions of section 13 of this Act [15 USCS § 1063].

§ 1063. Opposition to Registration

(a) Any person who believes that he would be damaged by the registration of a mark upon the principal register, including the registration of any mark which would be likely to cause dilution by blurring or dilution by tarnishment under section 43(c) [15 USCS § 1125(c)], may, upon payment of the prescribed fee, file an opposition in the Patent and Trademark Office, stating the grounds therefor, within thirty days after the publication under subsection (a) of section 12 of this Act [15 USCS § 1062] of the mark sought to be registered. Upon written request prior to the expiration of the thirty-day period, the time for filing opposition shall be extended for an additional thirty days, and further extensions of time for filing opposition may be granted by the Director for good cause when requested prior to the expiration of an extension. The Director shall notify the applicant of each extension of the time for filing opposition. An opposition may be amended under such conditions as may be prescribed by the Director.

(b) Unless registration is successfully opposed—

(1) a mark entitled to registration on the principal register based on an application filed under section 1(a) [15 USCS § 1051(a)] or pursuant to section 44 [15 USCS § 1126] shall be registered in the Patent and Trademark Office, a certificate of registration shall

be issued, and notice of the registration shall be published in the Official Gazette of the Patent and Trademark Office; or

(2)   a notice of allowance shall be issued to the applicant if the applicant applied for registration under section 1(b) [15 USCS § 1051(b)].

§ 1064.   Cancellation of registration

A petition to cancel a registration of a mark, stating the grounds relied upon, may, upon payment of the prescribed fee, be filed as follows by any person who believes that he is or will be damaged, including as a result of a likelihood of dilution by blurring or dilution by tarnishment under section 43(c) [15 USCS § 1125(c)], by the registration of a mark on the principal register established by this Act, or under the Act of March 3, 1881, or the Act of February 20, 1905:

(1)   Within five years from the date of the registration of the mark under this Act.

(2)   Within five years from the date of publication under section 12(c) hereof [15 USCS § 1062(c)] of a mark registered under the Act of March 3, 1881, or the Act of February 20, 1905.

(3)   At any time if the registered mark becomes the generic name for the goods or services, or a portion thereof, for which it is registered, or is functional, or has been abandoned, or its registration was obtained fraudulently or contrary to the provisions of section 4 [15 USCS § 1054] or of subsection (a), (b), or (c) of section 2 [15 USCS § 1052] for a registration under this Act, or contrary to similar prohibitory provisions of such prior Acts for a registration under such Acts, or if the registered mark is being used by, or with the permission of, the registrant so as to misrepresent the source of the goods or services on or in connection with which the mark is used. If the registered mark becomes the generic name for less than all of the goods or services for which it is registered, a petition to cancel the registration for only those goods or services may be filed. A registered mark shall not be deemed to be the generic name of goods or services solely because such mark is also used as a name of or to identify a unique product or service. The primary significance of the registered mark to the relevant public rather than purchaser motivation shall be the test for determining whether the registered mark has become the generic name of goods or services on or in connection with which it has been used.

(4)   At any time if the mark is registered under the Act of March 3, 1881, or the Act of February 20, 1905, and has not been published under the provisions of subsection (c) of section 12 of this Act [15 USCS § 1062].

(5)   At any time in the case of a certification mark on the ground that the registrant (A) does not control, or is not able legitimately to exercise control over, the use of such mark, or (B) engages in the production or marketing of any goods or services to which the certification mark is applied, or (C) permits the use of the certification mark for purposes other than to certify, or (D) discriminately refuses to certify or to continue to certify the goods or services of any person who maintains the standards or conditions which such mark certifies:

Provided, That the Federal Trade Commission may apply to cancel on the grounds specified in paragraphs (3) and (5) of this section any mark registered on the principal register established by this Act, and the prescribed fee shall not be required. Nothing in paragraph (5) shall be deemed to prohibit the registrant from using its certification mark in advertising or promoting recognition of the certification program or of the goods or services meeting the certification standards of the registrant. Such uses of the certification mark shall not be grounds for cancellation under paragraph (5), so long as the registrant does not itself produce, manufacture, or sell any of the certified goods or services to which its identical certification mark is applied.

§ 1065. Incontestability of Right to Use Mark Under Certain Conditions

Except on a ground for which application to cancel may be filed at any time under paragraphs (3) and (5) of section 14 of this Act [15 USCS § 1064(3), (5)], and except to the extent, if any, to which the use of a mark registered on the principal register infringes a valid right acquired under the law of any State or Territory by use of a mark or trade name continuing from a date prior to the date of registration under this Act of such registered mark, the right of the registrant to use such registered mark in commerce for the goods or services on or in connection with which such registered mark has been in continuous use for five consecutive years subsequent to the date of such registration and is still in use in commerce, shall be incontestable: *Provided,* That—

(1)   there has been no final decision adverse to registrant's claim of ownership of such mark for such goods or services, or to registrant's right to register the same or to keep the same on the register; and

(2)   there is no proceeding involving said rights pending in the Patent and Trademark Office or in a court and not finally disposed of; and

(3)   an affidavit is filed with the Director within one year after the expiration of any such five-year period setting forth those goods or services stated in the registration on or in connection with which such mark has been in continuous use for such five consecutive years and is still in use in commerce, and the other matters specified in paragraphs (1) and (2) of this section; and

(4)   no incontestable right shall be acquired in a mark which is the generic name for the goods or services or a portion thereof, for which it is registered.

Subject to the conditions above specified in this section, the incontestable right with reference to a mark registered under this shall apply to a mark registered under the Act of March 3, 1881, or the Act of February 20, 1905, upon the filing of the required affidavit with the Director within one year after the expiration of any period of five consecutive years after the date of publication of a mark under the provisions of subsection (c) of section 12 of this Act [15 USCS § 1062(c)].

The Director shall notify any registrant who files the above-prescribed affidavit of the filing thereof.

§ 1066. Interference; Declaration by Director

Upon petition showing extraordinary circumstances, the Director may declare that an interference exists when application is made for the registration of a mark which so resembles a mark previously registered by another, or for the registration of which another has previously made application, as to be likely when used on or in connection with the goods or services of the applicant to cause confusion or mistake or to deceive. No interference shall be declared between an application and the registration of a mark the right to the use of which has become incontestable.

§ 1067. Interference, Opposition, and Proceedings for Concurrent Use Registration or for Cancellation; Notice; Trademark Trial and Appeal Board

(a)   In every case of interference, opposition to registration, application to register as a lawful concurrent user, or application to cancel the registration of a mark, the Director shall give notice to all parties and shall direct a Trademark Trial and Appeal Board to determine and decide the respective rights of registration.

(b)   The Trademark Trial and Appeal Board shall include the Director, the Commissioner for Patents, the Commissioner for Trademarks, and administrative trademark judges who are appointed by the Director.

§ 1068. Action of Director in Interference, Opposition, and Proceedings for Concurrent Use Registration or for Cancellation

In such proceedings the Director may refuse to register the opposed mark, may cancel the registration, in whole or in part, may modify the application or registration by limiting the goods or services specified therein, may otherwise restrict or rectify with respect to the register the registration of a registered mark, may refuse to register any or all of several interfering marks, or may register the mark or marks for the person or persons entitled thereto, as the rights of the parties hereunder may be established in the proceedings: *Provided*, That in the case of the registration of any mark based on concurrent use, the Director shall determine and fix the conditions and limitations provided for in subsection (d) of section 2 of this Act [15 USCS § 1052(d)]. However, no final judgment shall be entered in favor of an applicant under section 1(b) [15 USCS § 1051(b)] before the mark is registered, if such applicant cannot prevail without establishing constructive use pursuant to section 7(c) [15 USCS § 1057(c)].

§ 1069. Application of Equitable Principles in Inter Partes Proceedings

In all inter partes proceedings equitable principles of laches, estoppel, and acquiescence, where applicable may be considered and applied.

§ 1070. Appeals to Trademark Trial and Appeal Board from Decisions of Examiners

An appeal may be taken to the Trademark Trial and Appeal Board from any final decision of the examiner in charge of the registration of marks upon the payment of the prescribed fee.

§ 1071. Appeal to Courts

(a) Persons entitled to appeal; United States Court of Appeals for the Federal Circuit; waiver of civil action; election of civil action by adverse party; procedure.

(1) An applicant for registration of a mark, party to an interference proceeding, party to an opposition proceeding, party to an application to register as a lawful concurrent user, party to a cancellation proceeding, a registrant who has filed an affidavit as provided in section 8 [15 USCS § 1058], or an applicant for renewal, who is dissatisfied with the decision of the Director or Trademark Trial and Appeal Board, may appeal to the United States Court of Appeals for the Federal Circuit thereby waiving his right to proceed under subsection (b) of this section: *Provided*, That such appeal shall be dismissed if any adverse party to the proceeding, other than the Director, shall, within twenty days after the appellant has filed notice of appeal according to paragraph (2) of this subsection, files notice with the Director that he elects to have all further proceedings conducted as provided in subsection (b) of this section. Thereupon the appellant shall have thirty days thereafter within which to file a civil action under subsection (b) of this section, in default of which the decision appealed from shall govern the further proceedings in the case.

(2) When an appeal is taken to the United States Court of Appeals for the Federal Circuit, the appellant shall file in the Patent and Trademark Office a written notice of appeal directed to the Director, within such time after the date of the decision from which the appeal is taken as the Director prescribes, but in no case less than 60 days after that date.

(3) The Director shall transmit to the United States Court of Appeals for the Federal Circuit a certified list of the documents comprising the record in the Patent and Trademark Office. The court may request that the Director forward the original or certified copies of such documents during pendency of the appeal. In an ex parte case, the Director shall submit to that court a brief explaining the grounds for the decision of the Patent and Trademark Office, addressing all the issues involved in the appeal. The

court shall, before hearing an appeal, give notice of the time and place of the hearing to the Director and the parties in the appeal.

(4)   The United States Court of Appeals for the Federal Circuit shall review the decision from which the appeal is taken on the record before the Patent and Trademark Office. Upon its determination the court shall issue its mandate and opinion to the Director, which shall be entered of record in the Patent and Trademark Office and shall govern the further proceedings in the case. However, no final judgment shall be entered in favor of an applicant under section 1(b) [15 USCS § 1051(b)] before the mark is registered, if such applicant cannot prevail without establishing constructive use pursuant to section 7(c) [15 USCS § 1057(c)].

(b)   Civil action; persons entitled to; jurisdiction of court; status of Director; procedure.

(1)   Whenever a person authorized by subsection (a) of this section to appeal to the United States Court of Appeals for the Federal Circuit is dissatisfied with the decision of the Director or Trademark Trial and Appeal Board, said person may, unless appeal has been taken to said United States Court of Appeals for the Federal Circuit, have remedy by a civil action if commenced within such time after such decision, not less than sixty days, as the Director appoints or as provided in subsection (a) of this section. The court may adjudge that an applicant is entitled to a registration upon the application involved, that a registration involved should be canceled, or such other matter as the issues in the proceeding require, as the facts in the case may appear. Such adjudication shall authorize the Director to take any necessary action, upon compliance with the requirements of law. However, no final judgment shall be entered in favor of an applicant under section 1(b) [15 USCS § 1051(b)] before the mark is registered, if such applicant cannot prevail without establishing constructive use pursuant to section 7(c) [15 USCS § 1057(c)].

(2)   The Director shall not be made a party to an inter partes proceeding under this subsection, but he shall be notified of the filing of the complaint by the clerk of the court in which it is filed and shall have the right to intervene in the action.

(3)   In any case where there is no adverse party, a copy of the complaint shall be served on the Director, and, unless the court finds the expenses to be unreasonable, all the expenses of the proceeding shall be paid by the party bringing the case, whether the final decision is in favor of such party or not. In suits brought hereunder, the record in the Patent and Trademark Office shall be admitted on motion of any party, upon such terms and conditions as to costs, expenses, and the further cross-examination of the witnesses as the court imposes, without prejudice to the right of any party to take further testimony. The testimony and exhibits of the record in the Patent and Trademark Office, when admitted, shall have the same effect as if originally taken and produced in the suit.

(4)   Where there is an adverse party, such suit may be instituted against the party in interest as shown by the records of the Patent and Trademark Office at the time of the decision complained of, but any party in interest may become a party to the action. If there be adverse parties residing in a plurality of districts not embraced within the same State, or an adverse party residing in a foreign country, the United States District Court for the District of Columbia shall have jurisdiction and may issue summons against the adverse parties directed to the marshal of any district in which any adverse party resides. Summons against adverse parties residing in foreign countries may be served by publication or otherwise as the court directs.

§ 1072.   Registration as Constructive Notice of Claim of Ownership

Registration of a mark on the principal register provided by this Act or under the Act of March 3, 1881, or the Act of February 20, 1905, shall be constructive notice of the registrant's claim of ownership thereof.

THE SUPPLEMENTAL REGISTER

§ 1091. Supplemental Register

(a) Marks registrable. In addition to the principal register, the Director shall keep a continuation of the register provided in paragraph (b) of section 1 of the Act of March 19, 1920, entitled "An Act to give effect to certain provisions of the convention for the protection of trademarks and commercial names, made and signed in the city of Buenos Aires, in the Argentine Republic, August 20, 1910, and for other purposes," to be called the supplemental register. All marks capable of distinguishing applicant's goods or services and not registrable on the principal register herein provided, except those declared to be unregistrable under subsections (a), (b), (c), (d), and (e)(3) of section 2 of this Act [15 USCS § 1052], which are in lawful use in commerce by the owner thereof, on or in connection with any goods or services may be registered on the supplemental register upon the payment of the prescribed fee and compliance with the provisions of subsections (a) and (e) of section 1 [15 USCS § 1051] so far as they are applicable. Nothing in this section shall prevent the registration on the supplemental register of a mark, capable of distinguishing the applicant's goods or services and not registrable on the principal register under this Act, that is declared to be unregistrable under section 2(e)(3) [15 USCS § 1052(e)(3)], if such mark has been in lawful use in commerce by the owner thereof, on or in connection with any goods or services, since before the date of the enactment of the North American Free Trade Agreement Implementation Act [enacted Dec. 8, 1993].

(b) Application and proceedings for registration. Upon the filing of an application for registration on the supplemental register and payment of the prescribed fee the Director shall refer the application to the examiner in charge of the registration of marks, who shall cause an examination to be made and if on such examination it shall appear that the applicant is entitled to registration, the registration shall be granted. If the applicant is found not entitled to registration the provisions of subsection (b) of section 12 of this Act [15 USCS § 1062] shall apply.

(c) Nature of mark. For the purposes of registration on the supplemental register, a mark may consist of any trade-mark [trademark], symbol, label, package, configuration of goods, name, word, slogan, phrase, surname, geographical name, numeral, device, any matter that as a whole is not functional, or any combination of any of the foregoing, but such mark must be capable of distinguishing the applicant's goods or services.

Explanatory note:

The bracketed word "trademark" has been inserted in subsec. (c) on the authority of Act Aug. 5, 1999, P.L. 106–43, § 6(b), 113 Stat. 220, which amended Act July 5, 1946, ch 540, by striking "trade-marks" each place it appeared and inserting "trademarks".

§ 1092. Publication; Not Subject to Opposition; Cancellation

Marks for the supplemental register shall not be published for or be subject to opposition, but shall be published on registration in the Official Gazette of the Patent and Trademark Office. Whenever any person believes that such person is or will be damaged by the registration of a mark on the supplemental register—

(1) for which the effective filing date is after the date on which such person's mark became famous and which would be likely to cause dilution by blurring or dilution by tarnishment under section 43(c) [15 USCS § 1125(c)]; or

(2) on grounds other than dilution by blurring or dilution by tarnishment, such person may at any time, upon payment of the prescribed fee and the filing of a petition stating the ground therefor, apply to the Director to cancel such registration.

The Director shall refer such application to the Trademark Trial and Appeal Board which shall give notice thereof to the registrant. If it is found after a hearing before the Board that the registrant is not entitled to registration, or that the mark has been abandoned, the registration shall be canceled by the Director. However, no final judgment shall be entered in favor of an applicant under section 1(b) [15 USCS § 1051(b)] before the mark is registered, if such applicant cannot prevail without establishing constructive use pursuant to section 7(c) [15 USCS § 1057(c)].

§ 1093. Registration Certificates for Marks on Principal and Supplemental Registers to Be Different

The certificates of registration for marks registered on the supplemental register shall be conspicuously different from certificates issued for marks registered on the principal register.

§ 1094. Provisions of Chapter Applicable to Registrations on Supplemental Register

The provisions of this Act shall govern so far as applicable applications for registration and registrations on the supplemental register as well as those on the principal register, but applications for and registrations on the supplemental register shall not be subject to or receive the advantages of sections 1(b), 2(e), 2(f), 7(b), 7(c), 12(a), 13 to 18, inclusive, 22, 33, and 42 of this Act [15 USCS §§ 1051(b), 1052(e), (f), 1057(b), (c), 1062(a), 1063–1068, 1072, 1115, 1124].

§ 1095. Registration on Principal Register Not Precluded

Registration of a mark on the supplemental register, or under the Act of March 19, 1920, shall not preclude registration by the registrant on the principal register established by this Act. Registration of a mark on the supplemental register shall not constitute an admission that the mark has not acquired distinctiveness.

§ 1096. Registration on Supplemental Register Not Used to Stop Importations

Registration on the supplemental register or under the Act of March 19, 1920, shall not be filed in the Department of the Treasury or be used to stop importations.

GENERAL PROVISIONS

§ 1111. Notice of Registration; Display with Mark; Recovery of Profits and Damages in Infringement Suit

Notwithstanding the provisions of section 22 hereof [15 USCS § 1072], a registrant of a mark registered in the Patent Office, may give notice that his mark is registered by displaying with the mark the words "Registered in U. S. Patent and Trademark Office" or "Reg. U.S. Pat. & Tm. Off." or the letter R enclosed within a circle, thus (R); and in any suit for infringement under this Act by such a registrant failing to give such notice of registration, no profits and no damages shall be recovered under the provisions of this Act unless the defendant had actual notice of the registration.

§ 1112. Classification of Goods and Services; Registration in Plurality of Classes

The Director may establish a classification of goods and services, for convenience of Patent and Trademark Office administration, but not to limit or extend the applicant's or registrant's rights. The applicant may apply to register a mark for any or all of the goods and services upon or in connection with which he or she is using or has a bona fide intention to use the mark in commerce: *Provided,* That if the Director by regulation permits the filing of an application for the registration of a mark for goods or services which fall within a plurality of classes, a fee equaling the sum of the fees for filing an application in each class shall be paid, and the Director may issue a single certificate of registration for such mark.

§ 1113. Fees

(a) Applications; services; materials. The Director shall establish fees for the filing and processing of an application for the registration of a trademark or other mark and for all other services performed by and materials furnished by the Patent and Trademark Office related to trademarks and other marks. Fees established under this subsection may be adjusted by the Director once each year to reflect, in the aggregate, any fluctuations during the preceding 12 months in the Consumer Price Index, as determined by the Secretary of Labor. Changes of less than 1 percent may be ignored. No fee established under this section shall take effect until at least 30 days after notice of the fee has been published in the Federal Register and in the Official Gazette of the Patent and Trademark Office.

(b) Waiver; Indian products. The Director may waive the payment of any fee for any service or material related to trademarks or other marks in connection with an occasional request made by a department or agency of the Government, or any officer thereof. The Indian Arts and Crafts Board will not be charged any fee to register Government trademarks of genuineness and quality for Indian products or for products of particular Indian tribes and groups.

§ 1114. Remedies; Infringement; Innocent Infringement by Printers and Publishers

(1) Any person who shall, without the consent of the registrant—

(a) use in commerce any reproduction, counterfeit, copy, or colorable imitation of a registered mark in connection with the sale, offering for sale, distribution, or advertising of any goods or services on or in connection with which such use is likely to cause confusion, or to cause mistake, or to deceive; or

(b) reproduce, counterfeit, copy, or colorably imitate a registered mark and apply such reproduction, counterfeit, copy, or colorable imitation to labels, signs, prints, packages, wrappers, receptacles or advertisements intended to be used in commerce upon or in connection with the sale, offering for sale, distribution, or advertising of goods or services on or in connection with which such use is likely to cause confusion, or to cause mistake, or to deceive,

shall be liable in a civil action by the registrant for the remedies hereinafter provided. Under subsection (b) hereof, the registrant shall not be entitled to recover profits or damages unless the acts have been committed with knowledge that such imitation is intended to be used to cause confusion, or to cause mistake, or to deceive.

As used in this paragraph, the term "any person" includes the United States, all agencies and instrumentalities thereof, and all individuals, firms, corporations, or other persons acting for the United States and with the authorization and consent of the United States, and any State, any instrumentality of a State, and any officer or employee of a State or instrumentality of a State acting in his or her official capacity. The United States, all agencies and instrumentalities thereof, and all individuals, firms, corporations, other persons acting for the United States and with the authorization and consent of the United States, and any State, and any such instrumentality, officer, or employee, shall be subject to the provisions of this Act in the same manner and to the same extent as any nongovernmental entity.

(2) Notwithstanding any other provision of this Act, the remedies given to the owner of a right infringed under this Act or to a person bringing an action under section 43(a) or (d) [15 USCS § 1125(a) or (d)] shall be limited as follows:

(A) Where an infringer or violator is engaged solely in the business of printing the mark or violating matter for others and establishes that he or she was an innocent infringer or innocent violator, the owner of the right infringed or person bringing the action under section 43(a) [15 USCS § 1125(a)] shall be entitled as against such infringer or violator only to an injunction against future printing.

(B)   Where the infringement or violation complained of is contained in or is part of paid advertising matter in a newspaper, magazine, or other similar periodical or in an electronic communication as defined in section 2510(12) of title 18, United States Code, the remedies of the owner of the right infringed or person bringing the action under section 43(a) [15 USCS § 1125(a)] as against the publisher or distributor of such newspaper, magazine, or other similar periodical or electronic communication shall be limited to an injunction against the presentation of such advertising matter in future issues of such newspapers, magazines, or other similar periodicals or in future transmissions of such electronic communications. The limitations of this subparagraph shall apply only to innocent infringers and innocent violators.

(C)   Injunctive relief shall not be available to the owner of the right infringed or person bringing the action under section 43(a) [15 USCS § 1125(a)] with respect to an issue of a newspaper, magazine, or other similar periodical or an electronic communication containing infringing matter or violating matter where restraining the dissemination of such infringing matter or violating matter in any particular issue of such periodical or in an electronic communication would delay the delivery of such issue or transmission of such electronic communication after the regular time for such delivery or transmission, and such delay would be due to the method by which publication and distribution of such periodical or transmission of such electronic communication is customarily conducted in accordance with sound business practice, and not due to any method or device adopted to evade this section or to prevent or delay the issuance of an injunction or restraining order with respect to such infringing matter or violating matter.

(D)

(i)

(I)   A domain name registrar, a domain name registry, or other domain name registration authority that takes any action described under clause (ii) affecting a domain name shall not be liable for monetary relief or, except as provided in subclause (II), for injunctive relief, to any person for such action, regardless of whether the domain name is finally determined to infringe or dilute the mark.

(II)   A domain name registrar, domain name registry, or other domain name registration authority described in subclause (I) may be subject to injunctive relief only if such registrar, registry, or other registration authority has—

(aa)   not expeditiously deposited with a court, in which an action has been filed regarding the disposition of the domain name, documents sufficient for the court to establish the court's control and authority regarding the disposition of the registration and use of the domain name;

(bb)   transferred, suspended, or otherwise modified the domain name during the pendency of the action, except upon order of the court; or

(cc)   willfully failed to comply with any such court order.

(ii)   An action referred to under clause (i)(I) is any action of refusing to register, removing from registration, transferring, temporarily disabling, or permanently canceling a domain name—

(I)   in compliance with a court order under section 43(d) [15 USCS § 1125(d)]; or

(II)   in the implementation of a reasonable policy by such registrar, registry, or authority prohibiting the registration of a domain name that is identical to, confusingly similar to, or dilutive of another's mark.

(iii)   A domain name registrar, a domain name registry, or other domain name registration authority shall not be liable for damages under this section for the registration or maintenance of a domain name for another absent a showing of bad faith intent to profit from such registration or maintenance of the domain name.

(iv)   If a registrar, registry, or other registration authority takes an action described under clause (ii) based on a knowing and material misrepresentation by any other person that a domain name is identical to, confusingly similar to, or dilutive of a mark, the person making the knowing and material misrepresentation shall be liable for any damages, including costs and attorney's fees, incurred by the domain name registrant as a result of such action. The court may also grant injunctive relief to the domain name registrant, including the reactivation of the domain name or the transfer of the domain name to the domain name registrant.

(v)   A domain name registrant whose domain name has been suspended, disabled, or transferred under a policy described under clause (ii)(II) may, upon notice to the mark owner, file a civil action to establish that the registration or use of the domain name by such registrant is not unlawful under this Act. The court may grant injunctive relief to the domain name registrant, including the reactivation of the domain name or transfer of the domain name to the domain name registrant.

(E)   As used in this paragraph—

(i)   the term "violator" means a person who violates section 43(a) [15 USCS § 1125(a)]; and

(ii)   the term "violating matter" means matter that is the subject of a violation under section 43(a) [15 USCS § 1125(a)].

(3)

(A)   Any person who engages in the conduct described in paragraph (11) of section 110 of title 17, United States Code [17 USCS § 110], and who complies with the requirements set forth in that paragraph is not liable on account of such conduct for a violation of any right under this Act. This subparagraph does not preclude liability, nor shall it be construed to restrict the defenses or limitations on rights granted under this Act, of a person for conduct not described in paragraph (11) of section 110 of title 17, United States Code [17 USCS § 110], even if that person also engages in conduct described in paragraph (11) of section 110 of such title [17 USCS § 110].

(B)   A manufacturer, licensee, or licensor of technology that enables the making of limited portions of audio or video content of a motion picture imperceptible as described in subparagraph (A) is not liable on account of such manufacture or license for a violation of any right under this Act, if such manufacturer, licensee, or licensor ensures that the technology provides a clear and conspicuous notice at the beginning of each performance that the performance of the motion picture is altered from the performance intended by the director or copyright holder of the motion picture. The limitations on liability in subparagraph (A) and this subparagraph shall not apply to a manufacturer, licensee, or licensor of technology that fails to comply with this paragraph.

(C)   The requirement under subparagraph (B) to provide notice shall apply only with respect to technology manufactured after the end of the 180-day period beginning on the date of the enactment of the Family Movie Act of 2005 [enacted April 27, 2005].

(D)   Any failure by a manufacturer, licensee, or licensor of technology to qualify for the exemption under subparagraphs (A) and (B) shall not be construed to create an inference that any such party that engages in conduct described in paragraph (11) of section 110 of title 17, United States Code [17 USCS § 110], is liable for trademark infringement by reason of such conduct.

§ 1115.   Registration on Principal Register as Evidence of Exclusive Right to Use Mark; Defenses

(a)   Evidentiary value; defenses. Any registration issued under the Act of March 3, 1881, or the Act of February 20, 1905, or of a mark registered on the principal register provided by this Act and owned by a party to an action shall be admissible in evidence and shall be prima facie evidence of the validity of the registered mark and of the registration of the mark, of the registrant's ownership of the mark, and of the registrant's exclusive right to use the registered mark in commerce on or in connection with the goods or services specified in the registration subject to any conditions or limitations stated therein, but shall not preclude another person from proving any legal or equitable defense or defect, including those set forth in subsection (b), which might have been asserted if such mark had not been registered.

(b)   Incontestability; defenses. To the extent that the right to use the registered mark has become incontestable under section 15 [15 USCS § 1065], the registration shall be conclusive evidence of the validity of the registered mark and of the registration of the mark, of the registrant's ownership of the mark, and of the registrant's exclusive right to use the registered mark in commerce. Such conclusive evidence shall relate to the exclusive right to use the mark on or in connection with the goods or services specified in the affidavit filed under the provisions of section 15 [15 USCS § 1065], or in the renewal application filed under the provisions of section 9 [15 USCS § 1059] if the goods or services specified in the renewal are fewer in number, subject to any conditions or limitations in the registration or in such affidavit or renewal application. Such conclusive evidence of the right to use the registered mark shall be subject to proof of infringement as defined in section 32 [15 USCS § 1114], and shall be subject to the following defenses or defects:

(1)   That the registration or the incontestable right to use the mark was obtained fraudulently; or

(2)   That the mark has been abandoned by the registrant; or

(3)   That the registered mark is being used, by or with the permission of the registrant or a person in privity with the registrant, so as to misrepresent the source of the goods or services on or in connection with which the mark is used; or

(4)   That the use of the name, term, or device charged to be an infringement is a use, otherwise than as a mark, of the party's individual name in his own business, or of the individual name of anyone in privity with such party, or of a term or device which is descriptive of and used fairly and in good faith only to describe the goods or services of such party, or their geographic origin; or

(5)   That the mark whose use by a party is charged as an infringement was adopted without knowledge of the registrant's prior use and has been continuously used by such party or those in privity with him from a date prior to (A) the date of constructive use of the mark established pursuant to section 7(c) [15 USCS § 1057(c)], (B) the registration of the mark under this Act if the application for registration is filed before the effective date of the Trademark Law Revision Act of 1988, or (C) publication of the registered mark under subsection (c) of section 12 of this Act [15 USCS § 1062(c)]: *Provided,* *however,* That this defense or defect shall apply only for the area in which such continuous prior use is proved; or

(6)   That the mark whose use is charged as an infringement was registered and used prior to the registration under this Act or publication under subsection (c) of section 12 of this Act [15 USCS § 1062(c)] of the registered mark of the registrant, and not abandoned: *Provided, however,* That this defense or defect shall apply only for the area in which the mark was used prior to such registration or such publication of the registrant's mark; or

(7)   That the mark has been or is being used to violate the antitrust laws of the United States; or

(8)   That the mark is functional; or

(9)   That equitable principles, including laches, estoppel, and acquiescence, are applicable.

§ 1116. Injunctive Relief

(a) Jurisdiction; service. The several courts vested with jurisdiction of civil actions arising under this Act shall have power to grant injunctions, according to the principles of equity and upon such terms as the court may deem reasonable, to prevent the violation of any right of the registrant of a mark registered in the Patent and Trademark Office or to prevent a violation under subsection (a), (c), or (d) of section 43 [15 USCS § 1125]. Any such injunction may include a provision directing the defendant to file with the court and serve on the plaintiff within thirty days after the service on the defendant of such injunction, or such extended period as the court may direct, a report in writing under oath setting forth in detail the manner and form in which the defendant has complied with the injunction. Any such injunction granted upon hearing, after notice to the defendant, by any district court of the United States, may be served on the parties against whom such injunction is granted anywhere in the United States where they may be found, and shall be operative and may be enforced by proceedings to punish for contempt, or otherwise, by the court by which such injunction was granted, or by any other United States district court in whose jurisdiction the defendant may be found.

(b) Transfer of certified copies of court papers. The said courts shall have jurisdiction to enforce said injunction, as herein provided, as fully as if the injunction had been granted by the district court in which it is sought to be enforced. The clerk of the court or judge granting the injunction shall, when required to do so by the court before which application to enforce said injunction is made, transfer without delay to said court a certified copy of all papers on file in his office upon which said injunction was granted.

(c) Notice to Director. It shall be the duty of the clerks of such courts within one month after the filing of any action, suit, or proceeding involving a mark registered under the provisions of this Act to give notice thereof in writing to the Director setting forth in order so far as known the names and addresses of the litigants and the designating number or numbers of the registration or registrations upon which the action, suit, or proceeding has been brought, and in the event any other registration be subsequently included in the action, suit, or proceeding by amendment, answer, or other pleading, the clerk shall give like notice thereof to the Director, and within one month after the judgment is entered or an appeal is taken the clerk of the court shall give notice thereof to the Director, and it shall be the duty of the Director on receipt of such notice forthwith to endorse the same upon the file wrapper of the said registration or registrations and to incorporate the same as a part of the contents of said file wrapper.

(d) Civil actions arising out of use of counterfeit marks.

(1)

(A) In the case of a civil action arising under section 32(1)(a) of this Act (15 U.S.C. 1114) [15 USCS § 1114(1)(a)] or section 220506 of title 36, United States Code, with respect to a violation that consists of using a counterfeit mark in connection with the sale, offering for sale, or distribution of goods or services, the court may, upon ex parte application, grant an order under subsection (a) of this section pursuant to this subsection providing for the seizure of goods and counterfeit marks involved in such violation and the means of making such marks, and records documenting the manufacturer, sale, or receipt of things involved in such violation.

(B) As used in this subsection the term "counterfeit mark" means—

(i) a counterfeit of a mark that is registered on the principal register in the United States Patent and Trademark Office for such goods or services sold, offered for sale, or distributed and that is in use, whether or not the person against whom relief is sought knew such mark was so registered; or

(ii) a spurious designation that is identical with, or substantially indistinguishable from, a designation as to which the remedies of this Act are made available by reason of section 220506 of title 36, United States Code;

but such term does not include any mark or designation used on or in connection with goods or services of which the manufacture [manufacturer] or producer was, at the time of the manufacture or production in question authorized to use the mark or designation for the type of goods or services so manufactured or produced, by the holder of the right to use such mark or designation.

(2)   The court shall not receive an application under this subsection unless the applicant has given such notice of the application as is reasonable under the circumstances to the United States attorney for the judicial district in which such order is sought. Such attorney may participate in the proceedings arising under such application if such proceedings may affect evidence of an offense against the United States. The court may deny such application if the court determines that the public interest in a potential prosecution so requires.

(3)   The application for an order under this subsection shall—

(A)   be based on an affidavit or the verified complaint establishing facts sufficient to support the findings of fact and conclusions of law required for such order; and

(B)   contain the additional information required by paragraph (5) of this subsection to be set forth in such order.

(4)   The court shall not grant such an application unless—

(A)   the person obtaining an order under this subsection provides the security determined adequate by the court for the payment of such damages as any person may be entitled to recover as a result of a wrongful seizure or wrongful attempted seizure under this subsection; and

(B)   the court finds that it clearly appears from specific facts that—

(i)   an order other than an ex parte seizure order is not adequate to achieve the purposes of section 32 of this Act (15 U.S.C. 1114);

(ii)   the applicant has not publicized the requested seizure;

(iii)   the applicant is likely to succeed in showing that the person against whom seizure would be ordered used a counterfeit mark in connection with the sale, offering for sale, or distribution of goods or services;

(iv)   an immediate and irreparable injury will occur if such seizure is not ordered;

(v)   the matter to be seized will be located at the place identified in the application;

(vi)   the harm to the applicant of denying the application outweighs the harm to the legitimate interests of the person against whom seizure would be ordered of granting the application; and

(vii)   the person against whom seizure would be ordered, or persons acting in concert with such person, would destroy, move, hide, or otherwise make such matter inaccessible to the court, if the applicant were to proceed on notice to such person.

(5)   An order under this subsection shall set forth—

(A)   the findings of fact and conclusions of law required for the order;

(B)   a particular description of the matter to be seized, and a description of each place at which such matter is to be seized;

(C)   the time period, which shall end not later than seven days after the date on which such order is issued, during which the seizure is to be made;

(D)   the amount of security required to be provided under this subsection; and

(E)   a date for the hearing required under paragraph (10) of this subsection.

(6)   The court shall take appropriate action to protect the person against whom an order under this subsection is directed from publicity, by or at the behest of the plaintiff, about such order and any seizure under such order.

(7)   Any materials seized under this subsection shall be taken into the custody of the court. The court shall enter an appropriate protective order with respect to discovery by

the applicant of any records that have been seized. The protective order shall provide for appropriate procedures to assure that confidential information contained in such records is not improperly disclosed to the applicant.

(8) An order under this subsection, together with the supporting documents, shall be sealed until the person against whom the order is directed has an opportunity to contest such order, except that any person against whom such order is issued shall have access to such order and supporting documents after the seizure has been carried out.

(9) The court shall order that service of a copy of the order under this subsection shall be made by a Federal law enforcement officer (such as a United States marshal or an officer or agent of the United States Customs Service, Secret Service, Federal Bureau of Investigation, or Post Office) or may be made by a State or local law enforcement officer, who, upon making service, shall carry out the seizure under the order. The court shall issue orders, when appropriate, to protect the defendant from undue damage from the disclosure of trade secrets or other confidential information during the course of the seizure, including, when appropriate, orders restricting the access of the applicant (or any agent or employee of the applicant) to such secrets or information.

(10)

(A) The court shall hold a hearing, unless waived by all the parties, on the date set by the court in the order of seizure. That date shall be not sooner than ten days after the order is issued and not later than fifteen days after the order is issued, unless the applicant for the order shows good cause for another date or unless the party against whom such order is directed consents to another date for such hearing. At such hearing the party obtaining the order shall have the burden to prove that the facts supporting findings of fact and conclusions of law necessary to support such order are still in effect. If that party fails to meet that burden, the seizure order shall be dissolved or modified appropriately.

(B) In connection with a hearing under this paragraph, the court may make such orders modifying the time limits for discovery under the Rules of Civil Procedure as may be necessary to prevent the frustration of the purposes of such hearing.

(11) A person who suffers damage by reason of a wrongful seizure under this subsection has a cause of action against the applicant for the order under which such seizure was made, and shall be entitled to recover such relief as may be appropriate, including damages for lost profits, cost of materials, loss of good will, and punitive damages in instances where the seizure was sought in bad faith, and, unless the court finds extenuating circumstances, to recover a reasonable attorney's fee. The court in its discretion may award prejudgment interest on relief recovered under this paragraph, at an annual interest rate established under section 6621(a)(2) of the Internal Revenue Code of 1986 [26 USCS § 6621(a)(2)], commencing on the date of service of the claimant's pleading setting forth the claim under this paragraph and ending on the date such recovery is granted, or for such shorter time as the court deems appropriate.

Explanatory note:

The bracketed word "manufacturer" has been inserted in subsec. (d)(1)(B) to indicate the word probably intended by Congress.

§ 1117. Recovery for Violation of Rights

(a) Profits; damages and costs; attorney fees. When a violation of any right of the registrant of a mark registered in the Patent and Trademark Office, a violation under section 43(a) or (d) [15 USCS § 1125(a) or (d)], or a willful violation under section 43(c) [15 USCS § 1125(c)], shall have been established in any civil action arising under this Act, the plaintiff shall be entitled, subject to the provisions of sections 29 and 32 [15 USCS §§ 1111, 1114], and subject to the principles of equity, to recover (1) defendant's profits, (2) any damages sustained by the plaintiff, and (3) the costs of the action. The court shall assess such profits and damages or cause the same to be assessed under its direction. In assessing profits the plaintiff shall be required to prove defendant's sales only; defendant must prove all elements of cost or deduction claimed. In assessing damages the court may enter judgment, according to the circumstances of the case, for any sum above the amount found as actual damages, not exceeding three times such amount. If the court shall find that the amount of the recovery based on profits is either inadequate or excessive the court may in its discretion enter judgment for such sum as the court shall find to be just, according to the circumstances of the case. Such sum in either of the above circumstances shall constitute compensation and not a penalty. The court in exceptional cases may award reasonable attorney fees to the prevailing party.

(b) Treble damages for use of counterfeit mark. In assessing damages under subsection (a), the court shall, unless the court finds extenuating circumstances, enter judgment for three times such profits or damages, whichever is greater, together with a reasonable attorney's fee, in the case of any violation of section 32(1)(a) of this Act (15 U.S.C. 1114(1)(a)) or section 220506 of title 36, United States Code, that consists of intentionally using a mark or designation, knowing such mark or designation is a counterfeit mark (as defined in section 34(d) of this Act (15 U.S.C. 1116(d)), in connection with the sale, offering for sale, or distribution of goods or services. In such cases, the court may in its discretion award prejudgment interest on such amount at an annual interest rate established under section 6621(a)(2) of the Internal Revenue Code of 1986 [26 USCS § 6621(a)(2)], commencing on the date of the service of the claimant's pleadings setting forth the claim for such entry and ending on the date such entry is made, or for such shorter time as the court deems appropriate.

(c) Statutory damages for use of counterfeit marks. In a case involving the use of a counterfeit mark (as defined in section 34(d) (15 U.S.C. 1116(d)) in connection with the sale, offering for sale, or distribution of goods or services, the plaintiff may elect, at any time before final judgment is rendered by the trial court, to recover, instead of actual damages and profits under subsection (a), an award of statutory damages for any such use in connection with the sale, offering for sale, or distribution of goods or services in the amount of—

(1) not less than $ 500 or more than $ 100,000 per counterfeit mark per type of goods or services sold, offered for sale, or distributed, as the court considers just; or

(2) if the court finds that the use of the counterfeit mark was willful, not more than $ 1,000,000 per counterfeit mark per type of goods or services sold, offered for sale, or distributed, as the court considers just.

(d) Statutory damages for violation of section 1125(d)(1). In a case involving a violation of section 43(d)(1) [15 USCS § 1125(d)(1)], the plaintiff may elect, at any time before final judgment is rendered by the trial court, to recover, instead of actual damages and profits, an award of statutory damages in the amount of not less than $ 1,000 and not more than $ 100,000 per domain name, as the court considers just.

(e) Rebuttable presumption of willful violation. In the case of a violation referred to in this section, it shall be a rebuttable presumption that the violation is willful for purposes of determining relief if the violator, or a person acting in concert with the violator, knowingly provided or knowingly caused to be provided materially false contact information to a domain name registrar, domain name registry, or other domain name registration authority in registering, maintaining, or renewing a domain name used in connection with the violation. Nothing in this subsection limits what may be considered a willful violation under this section.

§ 1118. Destruction of Infringing Articles

In any action arising under this Act, in which a violation of any right of the registrant of a mark registered in the Patent and Trademark Office, a violation under section 43(a) [15 USCS § 1125(a)], or a willful violation under section 43(c) [15 USCS § 1125(c)], shall have been established, the court may order that all labels, signs, prints, packages, wrappers, receptacles, and advertisements in the possession of the defendant, bearing the registered mark or, in the case of a violation of section 43(a) [15 USCS § 1125(a)] or a willful violation under section 43(c) [15 USCS § 1125(c)], the word, term, name, symbol, device, combination thereof, designation, description, or representation that is the subject of the violation, or any reproduction, counterfeit, copy, or colorable imitation thereof, and all plates, molds, matrices, and other means of making the same, shall be delivered up and destroyed. The party seeking an order under this section for destruction of articles seized under section 34(d) (15 U.S.C. 1116(d)) shall give ten days' notice to the United States attorney for the judicial district in which such order is sought (unless good cause is shown for lesser notice) and such United States attorney may, if such destruction may affect evidence of an offense against the United States, seek a hearing on such destruction or participate in any hearing otherwise to be held with respect to such destruction.

§ 1119. Power of Court Over Registration

In any action involving a registered mark the court may determine the right to registration, order the cancelation of registrations, in whole or in part, restore canceled registrations, and otherwise rectify the register with respect to the registrations of any party to the action. Decrees and orders shall be certified by the court to the Director, who shall make appropriate entry upon the records of the Patent and Trademark Office, and shall be controlled thereby.

§ 1120. Civil Liability for False or Fraudulent Registration

Any person who shall procure registration in the Patent and Trademark Office of a mark by a false or fraudulent declaration or representation, oral or in writing, or by any false means, shall be liable in a civil action by any person injured thereby for any damages sustained in consequence thereof.

§ 1121. Jurisdiction of Federal Courts; State and Local Requirements That Registered Trademarks Be Altered or Displayed Differently; Prohibition

(a) The district and territorial courts of the United States shall have original jurisdiction, [and] the courts of appeal of the United States (other than the United States Court of Appeals for the Federal Circuit) [and the United States Court of Appeals for the District of Columbia] shall have appellate jurisdiction, of all actions arising under this Act, without regard to the amount in controversy or to diversity or lack of diversity of the citizenship of the parties.

(b) No State or other jurisdiction of the United States or any political subdivision or any agency thereof may require alteration of a registered mark, or require that additional trademarks, service marks, trade names, or corporate names that may be associated with or incorporated into the registered mark be displayed in the mark in a manner differing from the display of such additional trademarks, service marks, trade names, or corporate names contemplated by the registered mark as exhibited in the certificate of registration issued by the United States Patent and Trademark Office.

Explanatory note:

The bracketed word "and" has been inserted in subsec. (a) in order to effectuate the probable intent of Congress to have included such word.

The words "and the United States Court of Appeals for the District of Columbia" have been enclosed in brackets in subsec. (a) as superfluous in view of 28 USCS § 41, which includes the District of Columbia among the judicial circuits of the United States.

§ 1121a.   [Transferred]

§ 1122.   Liability of United States and States, and Instrumentalities and Officials Thereof

(a)   Waiver of sovereign immunity by the United States. The United States, all agencies and instrumentalities thereof, and all individuals, firms, corporations, other persons acting for the United States and with the authorization and consent of the United States, shall not be immune from suit in Federal or State court by any person, including any governmental or nongovernmental entity, for any violation under this Act.

(b)   Waiver of sovereign immunity by States. Any State, instrumentality of a State or any officer or employee of a State or instrumentality of a State acting in his or her official capacity, shall not be immune, under the eleventh amendment of the Constitution of the United States or under any other doctrine of sovereign immunity, from suit in Federal court by any person, including any governmental or nongovernmental entity for any violation under this Act.

(c)   Remedies. In a suit described in subsection (a) or (b) for a violation described therein, remedies (including remedies both at law and in equity) are available for the violation to the same extent as such remedies are available for such a violation in a suit against any person other than the United States or any agency or instrumentality thereof, or any individual, firm, corporation, or other person acting for the United States and with authorization and consent of the United States, or a State, instrumentality of a State, or officer or employee of a State or instrumentality of a State acting in his or her official capacity. Such remedies include injunctive relief under section 34 [15 USCS § 1116], actual damages, profits, costs and attorney's fees under section 35 [15 USCS § 1117], destruction of infringing articles under section 36 [15 USCS § 1118], the remedies provided for under sections 32, 37, 38, 42 and 43, [15 USCS §§ 1114, 1119, 1120, 1124, and 1125] and for any other remedies provided under this Act.

§ 1123.   Rules and Regulations for Conduct of Proceedings in Patent and Trademark Office

The Director shall make rules and regulations, not inconsistent with law, for the conduct of proceedings in the Patent and Trademark Office under this Act.

§ 1124.   Importation of Goods Bearing Infringing Marks or Names Forbidden

Except as provided in subsection (d) of section 526 of the Tariff Act of 1930 [19 USCS § 1526(d)], no article of imported merchandise which shall copy or simulate the name of any domestic manufacture, or manufacturer, or trader, or of any manufacturer or trader located in any foreign country which, by treaty, convention, or law affords similar privileges to citizens of the United States, or which shall copy or simulate a trademark registered in accordance with the provisions of this Act or shall bear a name or mark calculated to induce the public to believe that the article is manufactured in the United States, or that it is manufactured in any foreign country or locality other than the country or locality in which it is in fact manufactured, shall be admitted to entry at any customhouse of the United States; and, in order to aid the officers of the customs in enforcing this prohibition, any domestic manufacturer or trader, and any foreign manufacturer or trader, who is entitled under the provisions of a treaty, convention, declaration, or agreement between the United States and any foreign country to the advantages afforded by law to citizens of the United States in respect to trademarks and commercial names, may require his name and residence, and the name of the locality in which his goods are manufactured, and a copy of the certificate of registration of his trademark, issued in accordance with the provisions of this Act, to be recorded in books which shall be kept for this purpose in the Department of the Treasury, under such regulations as the Secretary of the Treasury shall prescribe, and may furnish to the

Department facsimiles of his name, the name of the locality in which his goods are manufactured, or of his registered trademark, and thereupon the Secretary of the Treasury shall cause one or more copies of the same to be transmitted to each collector or other proper officer of customs.

§ 1125. False Designations of Origin, False Descriptions, and Dilution Forbidden

(a) Civil action.

(1) Any person who, on or in connection with any goods or services, or any container for goods, uses in commerce any word, term, name, symbol, or device, or any combination thereof, or any false designation of origin, false or misleading description of fact, or false or misleading representation of fact, which—

(A) is likely to cause confusion, or to cause mistake, or to deceive as to the affiliation, connection, or association of such person with another person, or as to the origin, sponsorship, or approval of his or her goods, services, or commercial activities by another person, or

(B) in commercial advertising or promotion, misrepresents the nature, characteristics, qualities, or geographic origin of his or her or another person's goods, services, or commercial activities,

shall be liable in a civil action by any person who believes that he or she is or is likely to be damaged by such act.

(2) As used in this subsection, the term "any person" includes any State, instrumentality of a State or employee of a State or instrumentality of a State acting in his or her official capacity. Any State, and any such instrumentality, officer, or employee, shall be subject to the provisions of this Act in the same manner and to the same extent as any nongovernmental entity.

(3) In a civil action for trade dress infringement under this Act for trade dress not registered on the principal register, the person who asserts trade dress protection has the burden of proving that the matter sought to be protected is not functional.

(b) Importation. Any goods marked or labeled in contravention of the provisions of this section shall not be imported into the United States or admitted to entry at any customhouse of the United States. The owner, importer, or consignee of goods refused entry at any customhouse under this section may have any recourse by protest or appeal that is given under the customs revenue laws or may have the remedy given by this Act in cases involving goods refused entry or seized.

(c) Dilution by blurring; dilution by tarnishment.

(1) Injunctive relief. Subject to the principles of equity, the owner of a famous mark that is distinctive, inherently or through acquired distinctiveness, shall be entitled to an injunction against another person who, at any time after the owner's mark has become famous, commences use of a mark or trade name in commerce that is likely to cause dilution by blurring or dilution by tarnishment of the famous mark, regardless of the presence or absence of actual or likely confusion, of competition, or of actual economic injury.

(2) Definitions.

(A) For purposes of paragraph (1), a mark is famous if it is widely recognized by the general consuming public of the United States as a designation of source of the goods or services of the mark's owner. In determining whether a mark possesses the requisite degree of recognition, the court may consider all relevant factors, including the following:

(i) The duration, extent, and geographic reach of advertising and publicity of the mark, whether advertised or publicized by the owner or third parties.

(ii) The amount, volume, and geographic extent of sales of goods or services offered under the mark.

(iii)   The extent of actual recognition of the mark.

(iv)   Whether the mark was registered under the Act of March 3, 1881, or the Act of February 20, 1905, or on the principal register.

(B)   For purposes of paragraph (1), "dilution by blurring" is association arising from the similarity between a mark or trade name and a famous mark that impairs the distinctiveness of the famous mark. In determining whether a mark or trade name is likely to cause dilution by blurring, the court may consider all relevant factors, including the following:

(i)   The degree of similarity between the mark or trade name and the famous mark.

(ii)   The degree of inherent or acquired distinctiveness of the famous mark.

(iii)   The extent to which the owner of the famous mark is engaging in substantially exclusive use of the mark.

(iv)   The degree of recognition of the famous mark.

(v)   Whether the user of the mark or trade name intended to create an association with the famous mark.

(vi)   Any actual association between the mark or trade name and the famous mark.

(C)   For purposes of paragraph (1), "dilution by tarnishment" is association arising from the similarity between a mark or trade name and a famous mark that harms the reputation of the famous mark.

(3)   Exclusions. The following shall not be actionable as dilution by blurring or dilution by tarnishment under this subsection:

(A)   Any fair use, including a nominative or descriptive fair use, or facilitation of such fair use, of a famous mark by another person other than as a designation of source for the person's own goods or services, including use in connection with—

(i)   advertising or promotion that permits consumers to compare goods or services; or

(ii)   identifying and parodying, criticizing, or commenting upon the famous mark owner or the goods or services of the famous mark owner.

(B)   All forms of news reporting and news commentary.

(C)   Any noncommercial use of a mark.

(4)   Burden of proof. In a civil action for trade dress dilution under this Act for trade dress not registered on the principal register, the person who asserts trade dress protection has the burden of proving that—

(A)   the claimed trade dress, taken as a whole, is not functional and is famous; and

(B)   if the claimed trade dress includes any mark or marks registered on the principal register, the unregistered matter, taken as a whole, is famous separate and apart from any fame of such registered marks.

(5)   Additional remedies. In an action brought under this subsection, the owner of the famous mark shall be entitled to injunctive relief as set forth in section 34. The owner of the famous mark shall also be entitled to the remedies set forth in sections 35(a) and 36 [15 USCS § 1117(a) and 1118], subject to the discretion of the court and the principles of equity if—

(A)   the mark or trade name that is likely to cause dilution by blurring or dilution by tarnishment was first used in commerce by the person against whom the injunction is sought after the date of enactment of the Trademark Dilution Revision Act of 2006 [enacted Oct. 6, 2006]; and

(B)   in a claim arising under this subsection—

(i)   by reason of dilution by blurring, the person against whom the injunction is sought willfully intended to trade on the recognition of the famous mark; or

(ii) by reason of dilution by tarnishment, the person against whom the injunction is sought willfully intended to harm the reputation of the famous mark.

(6) Ownership of valid registration a complete bar to action. The ownership by a person of a valid registration under the Act of March 3, 1881, or the Act of February 20, 1905, or on the principal register under this Act shall be a complete bar to an action against that person, with respect to that mark, that—

(A)

(i) is brought by another person under the common law or a statute of a State; and

(ii) seeks to prevent dilution by blurring or dilution by tarnishment; or

(B) asserts any claim of actual or likely damage or harm to the distinctiveness or reputation of a mark, label, or form of advertisement.

(7) Savings clause. Nothing in this subsection shall be construed to impair, modify, or supersede the applicability of the patent laws of the United States.

(d) Cyberpiracy prevention.

(1)

(A) A person shall be liable in a civil action by the owner of a mark, including a personal name which is protected as a mark under this section, if, without regard to the goods or services of the parties, that person—

(i) has a bad faith intent to profit from that mark, including a personal name which is protected as a mark under this section; and

(ii) registers, traffics in, or uses a domain name that—

(I) in the case of a mark that is distinctive at the time of registration of the domain name, is identical or confusingly similar to that mark;

(II) in the case of a famous mark that is famous at the time of registration of the domain name, is identical or confusingly similar to or dilutive of that mark; or

(III) is a trademark, word, or name protected by reason of section 706 of title 18, United States Code, or section 220506 of title 36, United States Code.

(B)

(i) In determining whether a person has a bad faith intent described under subparagraph (A), a court may consider factors such as, but not limited to—

(I) the trademark or other intellectual property rights of the person, if any, in the domain name;

(II) the extent to which the domain name consists of the legal name of the person or a name that is otherwise commonly used to identify that person;

(III) the person's prior use, if any, of the domain name in connection with the bona fide offering of any goods or services;

(IV) the person's bona fide noncommercial or fair use of the mark in a site accessible under the domain name;

(V) the person's intent to divert consumers from the mark owner's online location to a site accessible under the domain name that could harm the goodwill represented by the mark, either for commercial gain or with the intent to tarnish or disparage the mark, by creating a likelihood of confusion as to the source, sponsorship, affiliation, or endorsement of the site;

(VI) the person's offer to transfer, sell, or otherwise assign the domain name to the mark owner or any third party for financial gain without having used, or having an intent to use, the domain name in the bona fide offering of any goods or services, or the person's prior conduct indicating a pattern of such conduct;

(VII) the person's provision of material and misleading false contact information when applying for the registration of the domain name, the person's intentional failure to maintain accurate contact information, or the person's prior conduct indicating a pattern of such conduct;

(VIII)   the person's registration or acquisition of multiple domain names which the person knows are identical or confusingly similar to marks of others that are distinctive at the time of registration of such domain names, or dilutive of famous marks of others that are famous at the time of registration of such domain names, without regard to the goods or services of the parties; and

(IX)   the extent to which the mark incorporated in the person's domain name registration is or is not distinctive and famous within the meaning of subsection (c).

(ii)   Bad faith intent described under subparagraph (A) shall not be found in any case in which the court determines that the person believed and had reasonable grounds to believe that the use of the domain name was a fair use or otherwise lawful.

(C)   In any civil action involving the registration, trafficking, or use of a domain name under this paragraph, a court may order the forfeiture or cancellation of the domain name or the transfer of the domain name to the owner of the mark.

(D)   A person shall be liable for using a domain name under subparagraph (A) only if that person is the domain name registrant or that registrant's authorized licensee.

(E)   As used in this paragraph, the term "traffics in" refers to transactions that include, but are not limited to, sales, purchases, loans, pledges, licenses, exchanges of currency, and any other transfer for consideration or receipt in exchange for consideration.

(2)

(A)   The owner of a mark may file an in rem civil action against a domain name in the judicial district in which the domain name registrar, domain name registry, or other domain name authority that registered or assigned the domain name is located if—

(i)   the domain name violates any right of the owner of a mark registered in the Patent and Trademark Office, or protected under subsection (a) or (c); and

(ii)   the court finds that the owner—

(I)   is not able to obtain in personam jurisdiction over a person who would have been a defendant in a civil action under paragraph (1); or

(II)   through due diligence was not able to find a person who would have been a defendant in a civil action under paragraph (1) by—

(aa)   sending a notice of the alleged violation and intent to proceed under this paragraph to the registrant of the domain name at the postal and e-mail address provided by the registrant to the registrar; and

(bb)   publishing notice of the action as the court may direct promptly after filing the action.

(B)   The actions under subparagraph (A)(ii) shall constitute service of process.

(C)   In an in rem action under this paragraph, a domain name shall be deemed to have its situs in the judicial district in which—

(i)   the domain name registrar, registry, or other domain name authority that registered or assigned the domain name is located; or

(ii)   documents sufficient to establish control and authority regarding the disposition of the registration and use of the domain name are deposited with the court.

(D)

(i)   The remedies in an in rem action under this paragraph shall be limited to a court order for the forfeiture or cancellation of the domain name or the transfer of the domain name to the owner of the mark. Upon receipt of written notification of a filed, stamped copy of a complaint filed by the owner of a mark in a United States district court under this paragraph, the domain name registrar, domain name registry, or other domain name authority shall—

(I)   expeditiously deposit with the court documents sufficient to establish the court's control and authority regarding the disposition of the registration and use of the domain name to the court; and

(II)   not transfer, suspend, or otherwise modify the domain name during the pendency of the action, except upon order of the court.

(ii)   The domain name registrar or registry or other domain name authority shall not be liable for injunctive or monetary relief under this paragraph except in the case of bad faith or reckless disregard, which includes a willful failure to comply with any such court order.

(3)   The civil action established under paragraph (1) and the in rem action established under paragraph (2), and any remedy available under either such action, shall be in addition to any other civil action or remedy otherwise applicable.

(4)   The in rem jurisdiction established under paragraph (2) shall be in addition to any other jurisdiction that otherwise exists, whether in rem or in personam.

§ 1126.   International Conventions

(a)   Register of marks communicated by international bureaus. The Director shall keep a register of all marks communicated to him by the international bureaus provided for by the conventions for the protection of industrial property, trademarks, trade and commercial names, and the repression of unfair competition to which the United States is or may become a party, and upon the payment of the fees required by such conventions and the fees required in this Act may place the marks so communicated upon such register. This register shall show a facsimile of the mark or trade or commercial name; the name, citizenship, and address of the registrant; the number, date, and place of the first registration of the mark, including the dates on which application for such registration was filed and granted and the term of such registration; a list of goods or services to which the mark is applied as shown by the registration in the country of origin, and such other data as may be useful concerning the mark. This register shall be a continuation of the register provided in section 1(a) of the Act of March 19, 1920.

(b)   Benefits of section to persons whose country of origin is party to convention or treaty. Any person whose country of origin is a party to any convention or treaty relating to trademarks, trade or commercial names, or the repression of unfair competition, to which the United States is also a party, or extends reciprocal rights to nationals of the United States by law, shall be entitled to the benefits of this section under the conditions expressed herein to the extent necessary to give effect to any provision of such convention, treaty or reciprocal law, in addition to the rights to which any owner of a mark is otherwise entitled by this Act.

(c)   Prior registration in country of origin; country of origin defined. No registration of a mark in the United States by a person described in subsection (b) of this section shall be granted until such mark has been registered in the country of origin of the applicant, unless the applicant alleges use in commerce. For the purposes of this section, the country of origin of the applicant is the country in which he has a bona fide and effective industrial or commercial establishment, or if he has not such an establishment the country in which he is domiciled, or if he has not a domicile in any of the countries described in subsection (b) of this section, the country of which he is a national.

(d)   Right of priority. An application for registration of a mark under sections 1, 3, 4, or 23 of this Act [15 USCS §§ 1051, 1053, 1054, or 1091] or under subsection (e) of this section filed by a person described in subsection (b) of this section who has previously duly filed an application for registration of the same mark in one of the countries described in subsection (b) shall be accorded the same force and effect as would be accorded to the same application if filed in the United States on the same date on which the application was first filed in such foreign country: *Provided*, that—

(1) the application in the United States is filed within six months from the date on which the application was first filed in the foreign country;

(2) the application conforms as nearly as practicable to the requirements of this Act, including a statement that the applicant has a bona fide intention to use the mark in commerce;

(3) the rights acquired by third parties before the date of the filing of the first application in the foreign country shall in no way be affected by a registration obtained on an application filed under this subsection;

(4) nothing in this subsection shall entitle the owner of a registration granted under this section to sue for acts committed prior to the date on which his mark was registered in this country unless the registration is based on use in commerce.

In like manner and subject to the same conditions and requirements, the right provided in this section may be based upon a subsequent regularly filed application in the same foreign country, instead of the first filed foreign application: *Provided*, That any foreign application filed prior to such subsequent application has been withdrawn, abandoned, or otherwise disposed of, without having been laid open to public inspection and without leaving any rights outstanding, and has not served, nor thereafter shall serve, as a basis for claiming a right of priority.

(e) Registration on principal or supplemental register; copy of foreign registration. A mark duly registered in the country of origin of the foreign applicant may be registered on the principal register if eligible, otherwise on the supplemental register herein provided. Such applicant shall submit, within such time period as may be prescribed by the Commissioner, a true copy, a photocopy, a certification, or a certified copy of the registration in the country of origin of the applicant. The application must state the applicant's bona fide intention to use the mark in commerce, but use in commerce shall not be required prior to registration.

(f) Domestic registration independent of foreign registration. The registration of a mark under the provisions of subsections (c), (d), and (e) of this section by a person described in subsection (b) shall be independent of the registration in the country of origin and the duration, validity, or transfer in the United States of such registration shall be governed by the provisions of this Act.

(g) Trade or commercial names of foreign nationals protected without registration. Trade names or commercial names of persons described in subsection (b) of this section shall be protected without the obligation of filing or registration whether or not they form parts of marks.

(h) Protection of foreign nationals against unfair competition. Any person designated in subsection (b) of this section as entitled to the benefits and subject to the provisions of this Act shall be entitled to effective protection against unfair competition, and the remedies provided herein for infringement of marks shall be available so far as they may be appropriate in repressing acts of unfair competition.

(i) Citizens or residents of United States entitled to benefits of section. Citizens or residents of the United States shall have the same benefits as are granted by this section to persons described in subsection (b) of this section.

§ 1127. Construction and Definitions; Intent of Chapter

In the construction of this Act, unless the contrary is plainly apparent from the context—

The United States includes and embraces all territory which is under its jurisdiction and control.

The word "commerce" means all commerce which may lawfully be regulated by Congress.

The term "principal register" refers to the register provided for by sections 1 through 22 hereof [15 USCS §§ 1051–1072], and the term "supplemental register" refers to the register provided for by sections 23 through 28 thereof [15 USCS §§ 1091–1096].

The term "person" and any other word or term used to designate the applicant or other entitled to a benefit or privilege or rendered liable under the provisions of this Act includes a juristic person as well as a natural person. The term "juristic person" includes a firm, corporation, union, association, or other organization capable of suing and being sued in a court of law.

The term "person" also includes the United States, any agency or instrumentality thereof, or any individual, firm, or corporation acting for the United States and with the authorization and consent of the United States. The United States, any agency or instrumentality thereof, and any individual, firm, or corporation acting for the United States and with the authorization and consent of the United States, shall be subject to the provisions of this Act in the same manner and to the same extent as any nongovernmental entity.

The term "person" also includes any State, any instrumentality of a State, and any officer or employee of a State or instrumentality of a State acting in his or her official capacity. Any State, and any such instrumentality, officer, or employee, shall be subject to the provisions of this Act in the same manner and to the same extent as any nongovernmental entity.

The terms "applicant" and "registrant" embrace the legal representatives, predecessors, successors and assigns of such applicant or registrant.

The term "Director" means the Under Secretary of Commerce for Intellectual Property and Director of the United States Patent and Trademark Office.

The term "related company" means any person whose use of a mark is controlled by the owner of the mark with respect to the nature and quality of the goods or services on or in connection with which the mark is used.

The terms "trade name" and "commercial name" mean any name used by a person to identify his or her business or vocation.

The term "trademark" includes any word, name, symbol, or device, or any combination thereof—

(1) used by a person, or

(2) which a person has a bona fide intention to use in commerce and applies to register on the principal register established by this Act,

to identify and distinguish his or her goods, including a unique product, from those manufactured or sold by others and to indicate the source of the goods, even if that source is unknown.

The term "service mark" means any word, name, symbol, or device, or any combination thereof—

(1) used by a person, or

(2) which a person has a bona fide intention to use in commerce and applies to register on the principal register established by this Act,

to identify and distinguish the services of one person, including a unique service, from the services of others and to indicate the source of the services, even if that source is unknown. Titles, character names, and other distinctive features of radio or television programs may be registered as service marks notwithstanding that they, or the programs, may advertise the goods of the sponsor.

The term "certification mark" means any word, name, symbol, or device, or any combination thereof—

(1)   used by a person other than its owner, or

2   which its owner has a bona fide intention to permit a person other than the owner to use in commerce and files an application to register on the principal register established by this Act,

to certify regional or other origin, material, mode of manufacture, quality, accuracy, or other characteristics of such person's goods or services or that the work or labor on the goods or services was performed by members of a union or other organization.

The term "collective mark" means a trademark or service mark—

(1)   used by the members of a cooperative, an association, or other collective group or organization, or

(2)   which such cooperative, association, or other collective group or organization has a bona fide intention to use in commerce and applies to register on the principal register established by this Act,

and includes marks indicating membership in a union, an association, or other organization.

The term "mark" includes any trademark, service mark, collective mark, or certification mark.

The term "use in commerce" means the bona fide use of a mark in the ordinary course of trade, and not made merely to reserve a right in a mark. For purposes of this Act, a mark shall be deemed to be in use in commerce—

(1)   on goods when—

(A)   it is placed in any manner on the goods or their containers or the displays associated therewith or on the tags or labels affixed thereto, or if the nature of the goods makes such placement impracticable, then on documents associated with the goods or their sale, and

(B)   the goods are sold or transported in commerce, and

(2)   on services when it is used or displayed in the sale or advertising of services and the services are rendered in commerce, or the services are rendered in more than one State or in the United States and a foreign country and the person rendering the services is engaged in commerce in connection with the services.

A mark shall be deemed to be "abandoned" if either of the following occurs:

(1)   When its use has been discontinued with intent not to resume such use. Intent not to resume may be inferred from circumstances. Nonuse for 3 consecutive years shall be prima facie evidence of abandonment. "Use" of a mark means the bona fide use of such mark made in the ordinary course of trade, and not made merely to reserve a right in a mark.

(2)   When any course of conduct of the owner, including acts of omission as well as commission, causes the mark to become the generic name for the goods or services on or in connection with which it is used or otherwise to lose its significance as a mark. Purchaser motivation shall not be a test for determining abandonment under this paragraph.

The term "colorable imitation" includes any mark which so resembles a registered mark as to be likely to cause confusion or mistake or to deceive.

The term "registered mark" means a mark registered in the United States Patent and Trademark Office under this Act or under the Act of March 3, 1881, or the Act of February 20, 1905, or the Act of March 19, 1920. The phrase "marks registered in the Patent and Trademark Office" means registered marks.

The term "Act of March 3, 1881," "Act of February 20, 1905," or "Act of March 19, 1920," means the respective Act as amended.

A "counterfeit" is a spurious mark which is identical with, or substantially indistinguishable from, a registered mark.

The term "domain name" means any alphanumeric designation which is registered with or assigned by any domain name registrar, domain name registry, or other domain name registration authority as part of an electronic address on the Internet.

The term "Internet" has the meaning given that term in section 230(f)(1) of the Communications Act of 1934 (47 U.S.C. 230(f)(1)).

Words used in the singular include the plural and vice versa.

The intent of this Act is to regulate commerce within the control of Congress by making actionable the deceptive and misleading use of marks in such commerce; to protect registered marks used in such commerce from interference by State, or territorial legislation; to protect persons engaged in such commerce against unfair competition; to prevent fraud and deception in such commerce by the use of reproductions, copies, counterfeits, or colorable imitations of registered marks; and to provide rights and remedies stipulated by treaties and conventions respecting trademarks, trade names, and unfair competition entered into between the United States and foreign nations.

§ 1128.   National Intellectual Property Law Enforcement Coordination Council

(a)   Establishment. There is established the National Intellectual Property Law Enforcement Coordination Council (in this section referred to as the "Council"). The Council shall consist of the following members—

(1)   The Assistant Secretary of Commerce and Commissioner of Patents and Trademarks [Under Secretary of Commerce for Intellectual Property and Director of the United States Patent and Trademark Office], who shall serve as co-chair of the Council.

(2)   The Assistant Attorney General, Criminal Division, who shall serve as co-chair of the Council.

(3)   The Under Secretary of State for Economic and Agricultural Affairs.

(4)   The Ambassador, Deputy United States Trade Representative.

(5)   The Commissioner of Customs.

(6)   The Under Secretary of Commerce for International Trade.

(7)   The Coordinator for International Intellectual Property Enforcement.

(b)   Duties. The Council established in subsection (a) shall coordinate domestic and international intellectual property law enforcement among federal [Federal] and foreign entities.

(c)   Consultation required. The Council shall consult with the Register of Copyrights on law enforcement matters relating to copyright and related rights and matters.

(d)   Non-derogation. Nothing in this section shall derogate from the duties of the Secretary of State or from the duties of the United States Trade Representative as set forth in section 141 of the Trade Act of 1974 (19 U.S.C. 2171), or from the duties and functions of the Register of Copyrights, or otherwise alter current authorities relating to copyright matters.

(e)   Report. The Council shall report annually on its coordination activities to the President, and to the Committees on Appropriations and on the Judiciary of the Senate and the House of Representatives.

(f)   Funding. Notwithstanding section 1346 of title 31, United States Code, or section 610 of this Act [unclassified], funds made available for fiscal year 2000 and hereafter by this or any other Act shall be available for interagency funding of the National Intellectual Property Law Enforcement Coordination Council.

Explanatory note:

The bracketed words "Under Secretary of Commerce for Intellectual Property and Director of the United States Patent and Trademark Office" have been inserted in subsec. (a)(1) on the authority of § 4741(b)(1) of S. 1948 (113 Stat. 1501A-586), as introduced on Nov. 17, 1999, which was enacted into law by § 1000(a)(9) of Act Nov. 29, 1999, P.L. 106–113.

The bracketed word "Federal" has been inserted in subsec. (b) to indicate the capitalization probably intended by Congress.

§ 1129. Cyberpiracy Protections for Individuals

(1) In general.

(A) Civil liability. Any person who registers a domain name that consists of the name of another living person, or a name substantially and confusingly similar thereto, without that person's consent, with the specific intent to profit from such name by selling the domain name for financial gain to that person or any third party, shall be liable in a civil action by such person.

(B) Exception. A person who in good faith registers a domain name consisting of the name of another living person, or a name substantially and confusingly similar thereto, shall not be liable under this paragraph if such name is used in, affiliated with, or related to a work of authorship protected under title 17, United States Code, including a work made for hire as defined in section 101 of title 17, United States Code, and if the person registering the domain name is the copyright owner or licensee of the work, the person intends to sell the domain name in conjunction with the lawful exploitation of the work, and such registration is not prohibited by a contract between the registrant and the named person. The exception under this subparagraph shall apply only to a civil action brought under paragraph (1) and shall in no manner limit the protections afforded under the Trademark Act of 1946 (15 U.S.C. 1051 et seq.) or other provision of Federal or State law.

(2) Remedies. In any civil action brought under paragraph (1), a court may award injunctive relief, including the forfeiture or cancellation of the domain name or the transfer of the domain name to the plaintiff. The court may also, in its discretion, award costs and attorneys fees to the prevailing party.

(3) Definition. In this subsection, the term "domain name" has the meaning given that term in section 45 of the Trademark Act of 1946 (15 U.S.C. 1127).

(4) Effective date. This subsection shall apply to domain names registered on or after the date of the enactment of this Act [enacted Nov. 29, 1999].

THE MADRID PROTOCOL

§ 1141. Definitions

In this title [15 USCS §§ 1141 et seq.]:

(1) Basic application. The term "basic application" means the application for the registration of a mark that has been filed with an Office of a Contracting Party and that constitutes the basis for an application for the international registration of that mark.

(2) Basic registration. The term "basic registration" means the registration of a mark that has been granted by an Office of a Contracting Party and that constitutes the basis for an application for the international registration of that mark.

(3) Contracting party. The term "Contracting Party" means any country or inter-governmental organization that is a party to the Madrid Protocol.

(4) Date of recordal. The term "date of recordal" means the date on which a request for extension of protection, filed after an international registration is granted, is recorded on the International Register.

(5) Declaration of bona fide intention to use the mark in commerce. The term

"declaration of bona fide intention to use the mark in commerce" means a declaration that is signed by the applicant for, or holder of, an international registration who is seeking extension of protection of a mark to the United States and that contains a statement that—

(A)   the applicant or holder has a bona fide intention to use the mark in commerce;

(B)   the person making the declaration believes himself or herself, or the firm, corporation, or association in whose behalf he or she makes the declaration, to be entitled to use the mark in commerce; and

(C)   no other person, firm, corporation, or association, to the best of his or her knowledge and belief, has the right to use such mark in commerce either in the identical form of the mark or in such near resemblance to the mark as to be likely, when used on or in connection with the goods of such other person, firm, corporation, or association, to cause confusion, mistake, or deception.

(6)   Extension of protection. The term "extension of protection" means the protection resulting from an international registration that extends to the United States at the request of the holder of the international registration, in accordance with the Madrid Protocol.

(7)   Holder of an international registration. A "holder" of an international registration is the natural or juristic person in whose name the international registration is recorded on the International Register.

(8)   International application. The term "international application" means an application for international registration that is filed under the Madrid Protocol.

(9)   International bureau. The term "International Bureau" means the International Bureau of the World Intellectual Property Organization.

(10)   International register. The term "International Register" means the official collection of data concerning international registrations maintained by the International Bureau that the Madrid Protocol or its implementing regulations require or permit to be recorded.

(11)   International registration. The term "international registration" means the registration of a mark granted under the Madrid Protocol.

(12)   International registration date. The term "international registration date" means the date assigned to the international registration by the International Bureau.

(13)   Madrid Protocol. The term "Madrid Protocol" means the Protocol Relating to the Madrid Agreement Concerning the International Registration of Marks, adopted at Madrid, Spain, on June 27, 1989.

(14)   Notification of refusal. The term "notification of refusal" means the notice sent by the United States Patent and Trademark Office to the International Bureau declaring that an extension of protection cannot be granted.

(15)   Office of a Contracting Party. The term "Office of a Contracting Party" means—

(A)   the office, or governmental entity, of a Contracting Party that is responsible for the registration of marks; or

(B)   the common office, or governmental entity, of more than 1 Contracting Party that is responsible for the registration of marks and is so recognized by the International Bureau.

(16)   Office of origin. The term "office of origin" means the Office of a Contracting Party with which a basic application was filed or by which a basic registration was granted.

(17)   Opposition period. The term "opposition period" means the time allowed for filing an opposition in the United States Patent and Trademark Office, including any extension of time granted under section 13 [15 USCS § 1063].

§ 1141a. International Applications Based on United States Applications or Registrations

(a) In general. The owner of a basic application pending before the United States Patent and Trademark Office, or the owner of a basic registration granted by the United States Patent and Trademark Office may file an international application by submitting to the United States Patent and Trademark Office a written application in such form, together with such fees, as may be prescribed by the Director.

(b) Qualified owners. A qualified owner, under subsection (a), shall—

(1) be a national of the United States;

(2) be domiciled in the United States; or

(3) have a real and effective industrial or commercial establishment in the United States.

§ 1141b. Certification of the International Application

(a) Certification procedure. Upon the filing of an application for international registration and payment of the prescribed fees, the Director shall examine the international application for the purpose of certifying that the information contained in the international application corresponds to the information contained in the basic application or basic registration at the time of the certification.

(b) Transmittal. Upon examination and certification of the international application, the Director shall transmit the international application to the International Bureau.

§ 1141c. Restriction, Abandonment, Cancellation, or Expiration of a Basic Application or Basic Registration

With respect to an international application transmitted to the International Bureau under section 62 [15 USCS § 1141b], the Director shall notify the International Bureau whenever the basic application or basic registration which is the basis for the international application has been restricted, abandoned, or canceled, or has expired, with respect to some or all of the goods and services listed in the international registration—

(1) within 5 years after the international registration date; or

(2) more than 5 years after the international registration date if the restriction, abandonment, or cancellation of the basic application or basic registration resulted from an action that began before the end of that 5-year period.

§ 1141d. Request for Extension of Protection Subsequent to International Registration

The holder of an international registration that is based upon a basic application filed with the United States Patent and Trademark Office or a basic registration granted by the Patent and Trademark Office may request an extension of protection of its international registration by filing such a request—

(1) directly with the International Bureau; or

(2) with the United States Patent and Trademark Office for transmittal to the International Bureau, if the request is in such form, and contains such transmittal fee, as may be prescribed by the Director.

§ 1141e. Extension of Protection of an International Registration to the United States Under the Madrid Protocol

(a) In general. Subject to the provisions of section 68 [15 USCS § 1141h], the holder of an international registration shall be entitled to the benefits of extension of protection of that international registration to the United States to the extent necessary to give effect to any provision of the Madrid Protocol.

(b)   If the United States is office of origin. Where the United States Patent and Trademark Office is the office of origin for a trademark application or registration, any international registration based on such application or registration cannot be used to obtain the benefits of the Madrid Protocol in the United States.

§ 1141f.   Effect of Filing a Request for Extension of Protection of an International Registration to the United States

(a)   Requirement for request for extension of protection. A request for extension of protection of an international registration to the United States that the International Bureau transmits to the United States Patent and Trademark Office shall be deemed to be properly filed in the United States if such request, when received by the International Bureau, has attached to it a declaration of bona fide intention to use the mark in commerce that is verified by the applicant for, or holder of, the international registration.

(b)   Effect of proper filing. Unless extension of protection is refused under section 68 [15 USCS § 1141h], the proper filing of the request for extension of protection under subsection (a) shall constitute constructive use of the mark, conferring the same rights as those specified in section 7(c) [15 USCS § 1057(c)], as of the earliest of the following:

(1)   The international registration date, if the request for extension of protection was filed in the international application.

(2)   The date of recordal of the request for extension of protection, if the request for extension of protection was made after the international registration date.

(3)   The date of priority claimed pursuant to section 67 [15 USCS § 1141g].

§ 1141g.   Right of Priority for Request for Extension of Protection to the United States

The holder of an international registration with a request for an extension of protection to the United States shall be entitled to claim a date of priority based on a right of priority within the meaning of Article 4 of the Paris Convention for the Protection of Industrial Property if—

(1)   the request for extension of protection contains a claim of priority; and

(2)   the date of international registration or the date of the recordal of the request for extension of protection to the United States is not later than 6 months after the date of the first regular national filing (within the meaning of Article 4(A)(3) of the Paris Convention for the Protection of Industrial Property) or a subsequent application (within the meaning of Article 4(C)(4) of the Paris Convention for the Protection of Industrial Property).

§ 1141h.   Examination of and Opposition to Request for Extension of Protection; Notification of Refusal

(a)   Examination and opposition.

(1)   A request for extension of protection described in section 66(a) [15 USCS § 1141f(a)] shall be examined as an application for registration on the Principal Register under this Act, and if on such examination it appears that the applicant is entitled to extension of protection under this title [15 USCS §§ 1141 et seq.], the Director shall cause the mark to be published in the Official Gazette of the United States Patent and Trademark Office.

(2)   Subject to the provisions of subsection (c), a request for extension of protection under this title [15 USCS §§ 1141 et seq.] shall be subject to opposition under section 13 [15 USCS § 1063].

(3)   Extension of protection shall not be refused on the ground that the mark has not been used in commerce.

(4)   Extension of protection shall be refused to any mark not registrable on the Principal Register.

(b)   Notification of refusal. If[,] a request for extension of protection is refused under subsection (a), the Director shall declare in a notification of refusal (as provided in subsection (c)) that the extension of protection cannot be granted, together with a statement of all grounds on which the refusal was based.

(c)   Notice to International Bureau.

(1)   Within 18 months after the date on which the International Bureau transmits to the Patent and Trademark Office a notification of a request for extension of protection, the Director shall transmit to the International Bureau any of the following that applies to such request:

(A)   A notification of refusal based on an examination of the request for extension of protection.

(B)   A notification of refusal based on the filing of an opposition to the request.

(C)   A notification of the possibility that an opposition to the request may be filed after the end of that 18-month period.

(2)   If the Director has sent a notification of the possibility of opposition under paragraph (1)(C), the Director shall, if applicable, transmit to the International Bureau a notification of refusal on the basis of the opposition, together with a statement of all the grounds for the opposition, within 7 months after the beginning of the opposition period or within 1 month after the end of the opposition period, whichever is earlier.

(3)   If a notification of refusal of a request for extension of protection is transmitted under paragraph (1) or (2), no grounds for refusal of such request other than those set forth in such notification may be transmitted to the International Bureau by the Director after the expiration of the time periods set forth in paragraph (1) or (2), as the case may be.

(4)   If a notification specified in paragraph (1) or (2) is not sent to the International Bureau within the time period set forth in such paragraph, with respect to a request for extension of protection, the request for extension of protection shall not be refused and the Director shall issue a certificate of extension of protection pursuant to the request.

(d)   Designation of agent for service of process. In responding to a notification of refusal with respect to a mark, the holder of the international registration of the mark may designate, by a document filed in the United States Patent and Trademark Office, the name and address of a person residing in the United States on whom notices or process in proceedings affecting the mark may be served. Such notices or process may be served upon the person designated by leaving with that person, or mailing to that person, a copy thereof at the address specified in the last designation filed. If the person designated cannot be found at the address given in the last designation, or if the holder does not designate by a document filed in the United States Patent and Trademark Office the name and address of a person residing in the United States for service of notices or process in proceedings affecting the mark, the notice or process may be served on the Director.

Explanatory note:

The comma in subsec. (b) has been enclosed in brackets to indicate the probable intent of Congress to delete such punctuation.

§ 1141i.   Effect of Extension of Protection

(a)   Issuance of extension of protection. Unless a request for extension of protection is refused under section 68 [15 USCS § 1141h], the Director shall issue a certificate of extension of protection pursuant to the request and shall cause notice of such certificate of extension of protection to be published in the Official Gazette of the United States Patent and Trademark Office.

(b) Effect of extension of protection. From the date on which a certificate of extension of protection is issued under subsection (a)—

(1) such extension of protection shall have the same effect and validity as a registration on the Principal Register; and

(2) the holder of the international registration shall have the same rights and remedies as the owner of a registration on the Principal Register.

§ 1141j. Dependence of Extension of Protection to the United States on the Underlying International Registration

(a) Effect of cancellation of international registration. If the International Bureau notifies the United States Patent and Trademark Office of the cancellation of an international registration with respect to some or all of the goods and services listed in the international registration, the Director shall cancel any extension of protection to the United States with respect to such goods and services as of the date on which the international registration was canceled.

(b) Effect of failure to renew international registration. If the International Bureau does not renew an international registration, the corresponding extension of protection to the United States shall cease to be valid as of the date of the expiration of the international registration.

(c) Transformation of an extension of protection into a United States application. The holder of an international registration canceled in whole or in part by the International Bureau at the request of the office of origin, under article 6(4) of the Madrid Protocol, may file an application, under section 1 or 44 of this Act [15 USCS § 1051 or 1126], for the registration of the same mark for any of the goods and services to which the cancellation applies that were covered by an extension of protection to the United States based on that international registration. Such an application shall be treated as if it had been filed on the international registration date or the date of recordal of the request for extension of protection with the International Bureau, whichever date applies, and, if the extension of protection enjoyed priority under section 67 of this title [15 USCS § 1141g], shall enjoy the same priority. Such an application shall be entitled to the benefits conferred by this subsection only if the application is filed not later than 3 months after the date on which the international registration was canceled, in whole or in part, and only if the application complies with all the requirements of this Act which apply to any application filed pursuant to section 1 or 44 [15 USCS § 1051 of 1126].

§ 1141k. Affidavits and Fees

(a) Required affidavits and fees. An extension of protection for which a certificate of extension of protection has been issued under section 69 [15 USCS § 1141i] shall remain in force for the term of the international registration upon which it is based, except that the extension of protection of any mark shall be canceled by the Director—

(1) at the end of the 6-year period beginning on the date on which the certificate of extension of protection was issued by the Director, unless within the 1-year period preceding the expiration of that 6-year period the holder of the international registration files in the Patent and Trademark Office an affidavit under subsection (b) together with a fee prescribed by the Director; and

(2) at the end of the 10-year period beginning on the date on which the certificate of extension of protection was issued by the Director, and at the end of each 10-year period thereafter, unless—

(A) within the 6-month period preceding the expiration of such 10-year period the holder of the international registration files in the United States Patent and Trademark

Office an affidavit under subsection (b) together with a fee prescribed by the Director; or

(B)   within 3 months after the expiration of such 10-year period, the holder of the international registration files in the Patent and Trademark Office an affidavit under subsection (b) together with the fee described in subparagraph (A) and the surcharge prescribed by the Director.

(b)   Contents of affidavit. The affidavit referred to in subsection (a) shall set forth those goods or services recited in the extension of protection on or in connection with which the mark is in use in commerce and the holder of the international registration shall attach to the affidavit a specimen or facsimile showing the current use of the mark in commerce, or shall set forth that any nonuse is due to special circumstances which excuse such nonuse and is not due to any intention to abandon the mark. Special notice of the requirement for such affidavit shall be attached to each certificate of extension of protection.

(c)   Notification. The Director shall notify the holder of the international registration who files 1 of the affidavits of the Director's acceptance or refusal thereof and, in case of a refusal, the reasons therefor.

(d)   Service of notice or process. The holder of the international registration of the mark may designate, by a document filed in the United States Patent and Trademark Office, the name and address of a person residing in the United States on whom notices or process in proceedings affecting the mark may be served. Such notices or process may be served upon the person so designated by leaving with that person, or mailing to that person, a copy thereof at the address specified in the last designation so filed. If the person designated cannot be found at the address given in the last designation, or if the holder does not designate by a document filed in the United States Patent and Trademark Office the name and address of a person residing in the United States for service of notices or process in proceedings affecting the mark, the notice or process may be served on the Director.

§ 1141l.   Assignment of an Extension of Protection

An extension of protection may be assigned, together with the goodwill associated with the mark, only to a person who is a national of, is domiciled in, or has a bona fide and effective industrial or commercial establishment either in a country that is a Contracting Party or in a country that is a member of an intergovernmental organization that is a Contracting Party.

§ 1141m.   Incontestability

The period of continuous use prescribed under section 15 [15 USCS § 1065] for a mark covered by an extension of protection issued under this title [15 USCS §§ 1141 et seq.] may begin no earlier than the date on which the Director issues the certificate of the extension of protection under section 69 [15 USCS § 1141i], except as provided in section 74 [15 USCS § 1151n].

§ 1141n.   Rights of Extension of Protection

When a United States registration and a subsequently issued certificate of extension of protection to the United States are owned by the same person, identify the same mark, and list the same goods or services, the extension of protection shall have the same rights that accrued to the registration prior to issuance of the certificate of extension of protection.

TABLE OF CASES

[References are to pages]

1

[References are to pages]

(Rel. 0-0/1960 Pub.725)

[References are to pages]

[References are to pages]

[References are to pages]

I

[References are to pages]

[References are to pages]

(Rel. 0-0/1960 Pub.725)

[References are to pages]

[References are to pages]

[References are to pages]

[References are to pages]

[References are to pages]

[References are to pages]

[References are to pages]

INDEX

[References are to pages.]

[References are to pages.]

FEDERAL TRADE COMMISSION (FTC)—Cont.

Unfairness, tests of
    Generally . . . 649, 652
    Orkin Exterminating Co. v. FTC (1988) . . . 649

FIRST AMENDMENT(See FREEDOM OF SPEECH)

FOOD, DRUG AND COSMETIC ACT

Generally . . . 665
Enforcement guidelines . . . 669
Exported drugs . . . 669
Misbranding and trademark approval . . . 666
Nutritional labeling . . . 668
Remedies . . . 669

FOREIGN REGISTRATION

Generally . . . 95
Multi-national registrations and the Madrid Protocol
    . . . 95

FRANCHISING(See LICENSING AND FRANCHIS-
ING)

FREEDOM OF SPEECH

Generally . . . 503
*Cliffs Notes, Inc. v. Bantam Doubleday Dell Publishing
    Group, Inc. (1989)* . . . 511
Coca-Cola Co. v. Purdy (2004) . . . 531
Commercial speech . . . 505
*Dallas Cowboys Cheerleaders, Inc. v. Pussycat Cin-
    ema, Ltd. (1979)* . . . 509
False and misleading advertising, first amendment con-
    cerns regarding . . . 461
Federal Trade Commission (See FEDERAL TRADE
    COMMISSION (FTC), subhead: Constitutionality)
Humor and trademarks . . . 551
*Louis Vuitton Malletier S.A. v. Haute Diggity Dog, LLC
    (2007)* . . . 534
Mattel, Inc. v. MCA Records, Inc. (2002) . . . 518
Parks v. LaFace Records (2003) . . . 524
Parody and trademarks . . . 544
Political speech and trademarks . . . 549
Publicity rights, first amendment concerns regarding
    . . . 495
Trademarks and
    Generally . . . 540
    Constitutional basis for trademark legislation (See
        TRADEMARK AND UNFAIR COMPETI-
        TION LAW, subhead: Constitutional basis of
        federal trademark legislation)
    Humor . . . 551
    Parody . . . 544
    Political speech . . . 549
*United We Stand America, Inc. v. United We Stand
    America, New York, Inc. (1997)* . . . 516

FTC(See FEDERAL TRADE COMMISSION (FTC))

FUNCTIONALITY

Trade dress (See TRADE DRESS PROTECTION, sub-
    head: Functionality)

G

GENERIC TERMS(See TRADE IDENTITY
RIGHTS, subhead: Loss of rights)

GOVERNMENTAL REGULATION

Generally . . . 607

GOVERNMENTAL REGULATION—Cont.

Bureau of Customs and Border Protection (See GRAY
    MARKET GOODS, subhead: Bureau of Customs
    and Border Protection)
Consumer Product Safety Act . . . 673
Fair Packaging and Labeling Act . . . 672
Federal Trade Commission (See FEDERAL TRADE
    COMMISSION (FTC))
Food, Drug and Cosmetic Act (See FOOD, DRUG
    AND COSMETIC ACT)
Municipal regulation . . . 682
State regulation (See STATE REGULATION)

GRAY MARKET GOODS

Generally . . . 359, 366
A. Bourjois & Co. v. Katzel (1923) . . . 359
Bureau of Customs and Border Protection
    Generally . . . 369
    Federal courts . . . 369
    K Mart decision, Customs' regulations and the
        . . . 369
    Material differences and Customs . . . 371
Copyright Act . . . 372
Free riding and protection of goodwill . . . 367
Goodwill protection . . . 367
Lever Bros. Co. v. U.S. (1993) . . . 364
Material differences . . . 366, 371
Osawa & Co. v. B&H Photo (1984) . . . 362
Prestonettes, Inc. v. Coty (1924) . . . 360
State law provisions . . . 371
Tariff Act . . . 368
Trademark owner involvement . . . 371

I

ICANN

Dispute resolution policy (See INTERNET, subhead:
    ICANN's dispute resolution policy)
Publicity rights . . . 501

INFRINGEMENT

Generally . . . 201
Contributory infringement
    Generally . . . 289, 292
    *Perfect 10, Inc. v. Visa International Service Ass'n
        (2007)* . . . 289
Counterfeiting
    Generally . . . 279, 284
    Criminal counterfeiting . . . 287
    Louis Vuitton S.A. v. Lee (1989) . . . 279
    Post-sale confusion . . . 288
    Seizure orders . . . 285
Defenses (See DEFENSES TO INFRINGEMENT)
Experts (See subhead: Surveys and experts)
Goods and services, similarity of
    Generally . . . 226, 231
    *Dreamwerks Production Group, Inc. v. SKG Stu-
        dio, dba DreamWorks, SKG (1998)* . . . 226
    Goto.com, Inc. v. The Walt Disney Co. (2000)
        . . . 229
Intent
    Generally . . . 268, 273
    Kemp v. Bumble Bee Seafoods, Inc. (2005)
        . . . 270
    My-T-Fine Corp. v. Samuels (1934) . . . 269
    Presumption of infringement . . . 273
    Proof . . . 273

[References are to pages.]

[References are to pages.]

L

LACHES
Generally . . . 312, 318
Bad faith, effect of . . . 324
Black Diamond Sportswear, Inc. v. Black Diamond Equipment, Ltd. (2007) . . . 312
Detrimental reliance or other prejudice . . . 323
Elements of laches
    Generally . . . 319
    Detrimental reliance or other prejudice . . . 323
    Inexcusable delay . . . 320
    Knowledge . . . 320
Inexcusable delay . . . 320
Knowledge . . . 320
Preliminary relief, effect of delay on . . . 325
Sunamerica Corp. v. Sun Life Assurance Co. of Canada (1996) . . . 315

LANHAM ACT
Publicity rights . . . 498
Purpose . . . 83
Text . . . App–1

LICENSING AND FRANCHISING
Generally . . . 144, 153
Antitrust violations (See ANTITRUST VIOLATIONS)
Dawn Donut Co. v. Hart's Food Stores, Inc. (1959) . . . 145
Estoppel, licensee . . . 156
Franchising
    Generally . . . 158
    Liability of franchisor . . . 160
Good faith and fair dealing . . . 159
The Original Great American Chocolate Chip Cookie Co. v. River Valley Cookies, Ltd. (1992) . . . 150
Standing, licensee . . . 157
Stanfield v. Osborne Industries, Inc. (1995) . . . 147
Tax consequences . . . 158

LOST PROFITS(See DAMAGES, subhead: Profits)

M

MADRID PROTOCOL
Multi-national registrations . . . 95

MISAPPROPRIATION
Generally . . . 471, 474
The National Basketball Ass'n v. Motorola, Inc. (1997) . . . 471
Publicity rights (See PUBLICITY RIGHTS)
Voice misappropriation . . . 499

MISREPRESENTATION
Generally . . . 429, 449
Dastar Corp. v. Twentieth Century Fox Film Corp. (2003) . . . 443
False and misleading advertising
    Generally . . . 457
    Comparative use . . . 457
    Disparagement . . . 458
    Dissemination . . . 459
    First Amendment considerations . . . 461
    Proof . . . 462
    Standing . . . 466
Fashion Boutique of Short Hills, Inc. v. Fendi USA, Inc. (2003) . . . 431

MISREPRESENTATION—Cont.
Gilliam v. American Broadcasting Companies, Inc. (1976) . . . 430
Internet misrepresentations . . . 451
Passing off . . . 468
Standing . . . 450, 466
Time Warner Cable, Inc. v. DirectTV, Inc. (2007) . . . 438
Vidal Sassoon, Inc. v. Bristol-Myers Co. (1981) . . . 435

MONETARY RELIEF
Generally (See REMEDIES)
Attorneys' fees (See ATTORNEYS' FEES)
Damages (See DAMAGES)
Profits (See DAMAGES, subhead: Profits)

MUNICIPAL REGULATION
Generally . . . 682

P

PATENTS(See TRADE DRESS PROTECTION)

PERSONAL JURISDICTION(See JURISDICTION, subhead: Personal jurisdiction)

PRINCIPAL REGISTER
Generally . . . 92

PRIVACY
Federal Trade Commission . . . 646

PUBLICITY RIGHTS
Generally . . . 485, 493
Copyright law . . . 501
Descendibility . . . 499
Economic loss . . . 499
First Amendment concerns . . . 495
First sale doctrine . . . 497
ICANN proceedings . . . 501
Incidental commercial use . . . 497
Lanham Act . . . 498
Transfer . . . 499
Voice misappropriation . . . 499
White v. Samsung Electronics America, Inc. (1992) . . . 486
White v. Samsung Electronics America, Inc. (1993) . . . 489
Zacchini case . . . 494

PUNITIVE DAMAGES
Generally . . . 597

R

REGISTRATION
Generally . . . 83
Acquisition and maintenance of
    Generally . . . 90
    Principal register . . . 92
    Supplemental register . . . 94
Benefits of federal registration
    Generally . . . 84, 88
    Incontestability . . . 89
    Park 'n Fly, Inc. v. Dollar Park and Fly, Inc. (1985) . . . 84
Foreign registrations
    Generally . . . 95

[References are to pages.]